T0180502

Lecture Notes in Computer Science　　12250

More information about this series at http://www.springer.com/series/7407

Osvaldo Gervasi · Beniamino Murgante ·
Sanjay Misra · Chiara Garau ·
Ivan Blečić · David Taniar ·
Bernady O. Apduhan · Ana Maria A. C. Rocha ·
Eufemia Tarantino · Carmelo Maria Torre ·
Yeliz Karaca (Eds.)

Computational Science and Its Applications – ICCSA 2020

20th International Conference
Cagliari, Italy, July 1–4, 2020
Proceedings, Part II

 Springer

Editors
Osvaldo Gervasi 🆔
University of Perugia
Perugia, Italy

Sanjay Misra 🆔
Chair- Center of ICT/ICE
Covenant University
Ota, Nigeria

Ivan Blečić 🆔
University of Cagliari
Cagliari, Italy

Bernady O. Apduhan
Department of Information Science
Kyushu Sangyo University
Fukuoka, Japan

Eufemia Tarantino 🆔
Polytechnic University of Bari
Bari, Italy

Yeliz Karaca 🆔
Department of Neurology
University of Massachusetts
Medical School
Worcester, MA, USA

Beniamino Murgante 🆔
University of Basilicata
Potenza, Potenza, Italy

Chiara Garau 🆔
University of Cagliari
Cagliari, Italy

David Taniar 🆔
Clayton School of Information Technology
Monash University
Clayton, VIC, Australia

Ana Maria A. C. Rocha 🆔
University of Minho
Braga, Portugal

Carmelo Maria Torre 🆔
Polytechnic University of Bari
Bari, Italy

ISSN 0302-9743   ISSN 1611-3349 (electronic)
Lecture Notes in Computer Science
ISBN 978-3-030-58801-4   ISBN 978-3-030-58802-1   (eBook)
https://doi.org/10.1007/978-3-030-58802-1

LNCS Sublibrary: SL1 – Theoretical Computer Science and General Issues

This Springer imprint is published by the registered company Springer Nature Switzerland AG
The registered company address is: Gewerbestrasse 11, 6330 Cham, Switzerland

Preface

These seven volumes (LNCS volumes 12249–12255) consist of the peer-reviewed papers from the International Conference on Computational Science and Its Applications (ICCSA 2020) which took place from July 1–4, 2020. Initially the conference was planned to be held in Cagliari, Italy, in collaboration with the University of Cagliari, but due to the COVID-19 pandemic it was organized as an online event.

ICCSA 2020 was a successful event in the conference series, previously held in Saint Petersburg, Russia (2019), Melbourne, Australia (2018), Trieste, Italy (2017), Beijing, China (2016), Banff, Canada (2015), Guimaraes, Portugal (2014), Ho Chi Minh City, Vietnam (2013), Salvador, Brazil (2012), Santander, Spain (2011), Fukuoka, Japan (2010), Suwon, South Korea (2009), Perugia, Italy (2008), Kuala Lumpur, Malaysia (2007), Glasgow, UK (2006), Singapore (2005), Assisi, Italy (2004), Montreal, Canada (2003), and (as ICCS) Amsterdam, The Netherlands (2002) and San Francisco, USA (2001).

Computational science is the main pillar of most of the present research, industrial and commercial applications, and plays a unique role in exploiting ICT innovative technologies. The ICCSA conference series has provided a venue for researchers and industry practitioners to discuss new ideas, to share complex problems and their solutions, and to shape new trends in computational science.

Apart from the general track, ICCSA 2020 also included 52 workshops in various areas of computational science, ranging from computational science technologies to specific areas of computational science, such as software engineering, security, machine learning and artificial intelligence, blockchain technologies, and of applications in many fields. We accepted 498 papers, distributed among 6 conference main tracks, which included 52 in workshops and 32 short papers. We would like to express our appreciation to the workshops chairs and co-chairs for their hard work and dedication.

The success of the ICCSA conference series in general, and of ICCSA 2020 in particular, vitaly depends on the support from many people: authors, presenters, participants, keynote speakers, workshop chairs, session chairs, Organizing Committee members, student volunteers, Program Committee members, Advisory Committee members, international liaison chairs, reviewers, and others in various roles. We take this opportunity to wholeheartedly thank them all.

We also wish to thank our publisher, Springer, for their acceptance to publish the proceedings, for sponsoring part of the Best Papers Awards, and for their kind assistance and cooperation during the editing process.

We cordially invite you to visit the ICCSA website http://www.iccsa.org where you can find all the relevant information about this interesting and exciting event.

July 2020

Osvaldo Gervasi
Beniamino Murgante
Sanjay Misra

Welcome to the Online Conference

The COVID-19 pandemic disrupted our plans for ICCSA 2020, as was the case for the scientific community around the world. Hence, we had to promptly regroup and rush to set in place the organization and the underlying infrastructure of the online event.

We chose to build the technological infrastructure using only open source software. In particular, we used Jitsi (jitsi.org) for the videoconferencing, Riot (riot.im) together with Matrix (matrix.org) for chat and asynchronous communication, and Jibri (github.com/jitsi/jibri) for live streaming sessions on YouTube.

Six Jitsi servers were set up, one for each parallel session. The participants of the sessions were helped and assisted by eight volunteer students (from the Universities of Cagliari, Florence, Perugia, and Bari), who assured technical support and smooth running of the conference proceedings.

The implementation of the software infrastructure and the technical coordination of the volunteers was carried out by Damiano Perri and Marco Simonetti.

Our warmest thanks go to all the volunteering students, to the technical coordinators, and to the development communities of Jitsi, Jibri, Riot, and Matrix, who made their terrific platforms available as open source software.

Our heartfelt thanks go to the keynote speakers: Yaneer Bar-Yam, Cecilia Ceccarelli, and Vincenzo Piuri and to the guests of the closing keynote panel: Mike Batty, Denise Pumain, and Alexis Tsoukiàs.

A big thank you goes to all the 454 speakers, many of whom showed an enormous collaborative spirit, sometimes participating and presenting in almost prohibitive times of the day, given that the participants of this year's conference come from 52 countries scattered over many time zones of the globe.

Finally, we would like to thank Google for letting us livestream all the events via YouTube. In addition to lightening the load of our Jitsi servers, that will allow us to keep memory and to be able to review the most exciting moments of the conference.

We all hope to meet in our beautiful Cagliari next year, safe from COVID-19, and finally free to meet in person and enjoy the beauty of the ICCSA community in the enchanting Sardinia.

July 2020

Ivan Blečić
Chiara Garau

Organization

ICCSA 2020 was organized by the University of Cagliari (Italy), University of Perugia (Italy), University of Basilicata (Italy), Monash University (Australia), Kyushu Sangyo University (Japan), and University of Minho (Portugal).

Honorary General Chairs

Antonio Laganà	Master-UP, Italy
Norio Shiratori	Chuo University, Japan
Kenneth C. J. Tan	Sardina Systems, UK
Corrado Zoppi	University of Cagliari, Italy

General Chairs

Osvaldo Gervasi	University of Perugia, Italy
Ivan Blečić	University of Cagliari, Italy
David Taniar	Monash University, Australia

Program Committee Chairs

Beniamino Murgante	University of Basilicata, Italy
Bernady O. Apduhan	Kyushu Sangyo University, Japan
Chiara Garau	University of Cagliari, Italy
Ana Maria A. C. Rocha	University of Minho, Portugal

International Advisory Committee

Jemal Abawajy	Deakin University, Australia
Dharma P. Agarwal	University of Cincinnati, USA
Rajkumar Buyya	The University of Melbourne, Australia
Claudia Bauzer Medeiros	University of Campinas, Brazil
Manfred M. Fisher	Vienna University of Economics and Business, Austria
Marina L. Gavrilova	University of Calgary, Canada
Yee Leung	Chinese University of Hong Kong, China

International Liaison Chairs

Giuseppe Borruso	University of Trieste, Italy
Elise De Donker	Western Michigan University, USA
Maria Irene Falcão	University of Minho, Portugal
Robert C. H. Hsu	Chung Hua University, Taiwan

Tai-Hoon Kim	Beijing Jaotong University, China
Vladimir Korkhov	Saint Petersburg University, Russia
Sanjay Misra	Covenant University, Nigeria
Takashi Naka	Kyushu Sangyo University, Japan
Rafael D. C. Santos	National Institute for Space Research, Brazil
Maribel Yasmina Santos	University of Minho, Portugal
Elena Stankova	Saint Petersburg University, Russia

Workshop and Session Organizing Chairs

Beniamino Murgante	University of Basilicata, Italy
Sanjay Misra	Covenant University, Nigeria
Jorge Gustavo Rocha	University of Minho, Portugal

Award Chair

Wenny Rahayu	La Trobe University, Australia

Publicity Committee Chairs

Elmer Dadios	De La Salle University, Philippines
Nataliia Kulabukhova	Saint Petersburg University, Russia
Daisuke Takahashi	Tsukuba University, Japan
Shangwang Wang	Beijing University of Posts and Telecommunications, China

Technology Chairs

Damiano Perri	University of Florence, Italy
Marco Simonetti	University of Florence, Italy

Local Arrangement Chairs

Ivan Blečić	University of Cagliari, Italy
Chiara Garau	University of Cagliari, Italy
Ginevra Balletto	University of Cagliari, Italy
Giuseppe Borruso	University of Trieste, Italy
Michele Campagna	University of Cagliari, Italy
Mauro Coni	University of Cagliari, Italy
Anna Maria Colavitti	University of Cagliari, Italy
Giulia Desogus	University of Cagliari, Italy
Sabrina Lai	University of Cagliari, Italy
Francesca Maltinti	University of Cagliari, Italy
Pasquale Mistretta	University of Cagliari, Italy
Augusto Montisci	University of Cagliari, Italy
Francesco Pinna	University of Cagliari, Italy

Davide Spano	University of Cagliari, Italy
Roberto Tonelli	University of Cagliari, Italy
Giuseppe A. Trunfio	University of Sassari, Italy
Corrado Zoppi	University of Cagliari, Italy

Program Committee

Vera Afreixo	University of Aveiro, Portugal
Filipe Alvelos	University of Minho, Portugal
Hartmut Asche	University of Potsdam, Germany
Ginevra Balletto	University of Cagliari, Italy
Michela Bertolotto	University College Dublin, Ireland
Sandro Bimonte	CEMAGREF, TSCF, France
Rod Blais	University of Calgary, Canada
Ivan Blečić	University of Sassari, Italy
Giuseppe Borruso	University of Trieste, Italy
Ana Cristina Braga	University of Minho, Portugal
Massimo Cafaro	University of Salento, Italy
Yves Caniou	Lyon University, France
José A. Cardoso e Cunha	Universidade Nova de Lisboa, Portugal
Rui Cardoso	University of Beira Interior, Portugal
Leocadio G. Casado	University of Almeria, Spain
Carlo Cattani	University of Salerno, Italy
Mete Celik	Erciyes University, Turkey
Hyunseung Choo	Sungkyunkwan University, South Korea
Min Young Chung	Sungkyunkwan University, South Korea
Florbela Maria da Cruz Domingues Correia	Polytechnic Institute of Viana do Castelo, Portugal
Gilberto Corso Pereira	Federal University of Bahia, Brazil
Alessandro Costantini	INFN, Italy
Carla Dal Sasso Freitas	Universidade Federal do Rio Grande do Sul, Brazil
Pradesh Debba	The Council for Scientific and Industrial Research (CSIR), South Africa
Hendrik Decker	Instituto Tecnológico de Informática, Spain
Frank Devai	London South Bank University, UK
Rodolphe Devillers	Memorial University of Newfoundland, Canada
Joana Matos Dias	University of Coimbra, Portugal
Paolino Di Felice	University of L'Aquila, Italy
Prabu Dorairaj	NetApp, India/USA
M. Irene Falcao	University of Minho, Portugal
Cherry Liu Fang	U.S. DOE Ames Laboratory, USA
Florbela P. Fernandes	Polytechnic Institute of Bragança, Portugal
Jose-Jesus Fernandez	National Centre for Biotechnology, CSIS, Spain
Paula Odete Fernandes	Polytechnic Institute of Bragança, Portugal
Adelaide de Fátima Baptista Valente Freitas	University of Aveiro, Portugal

Manuel Carlos Figueiredo	University of Minho, Portugal
Maria Celia Furtado Rocha	PRODEB–PósCultura, UFBA, Brazil
Chiara Garau	University of Cagliari, Italy
Paulino Jose Garcia Nieto	University of Oviedo, Spain
Jerome Gensel	LSR-IMAG, France
Maria Giaoutzi	National Technical University of Athens, Greece
Arminda Manuela Andrade Pereira Gonçalves	University of Minho, Portugal
Andrzej M. Goscinski	Deakin University, Australia
Sevin Gümgüm	Izmir University of Economics, Turkey
Alex Hagen-Zanker	University of Cambridge, UK
Shanmugasundaram Hariharan	B.S. Abdur Rahman University, India
Eligius M. T. Hendrix	University of Malaga, Spain, and Wageningen University, The Netherlands
Hisamoto Hiyoshi	Gunma University, Japan
Mustafa Inceoglu	EGE University, Turkey
Peter Jimack	University of Leeds, UK
Qun Jin	Waseda University, Japan
Farid Karimipour	Vienna University of Technology, Austria
Baris Kazar	Oracle Corp., USA
Maulana Adhinugraha Kiki	Telkom University, Indonesia
DongSeong Kim	University of Canterbury, New Zealand
Taihoon Kim	Hannam University, South Korea
Ivana Kolingerova	University of West Bohemia, Czech Republic
Nataliia Kulabukhova	Saint Petersburg University, Russia
Vladimir Korkhov	Saint Petersburg University, Russia
Rosa Lasaponara	CNR, Italy
Maurizio Lazzari	CNR, Italy
Cheng Siong Lee	Monash University, Australia
Sangyoun Lee	Yonsei University, South Korea
Jongchan Lee	Kunsan National University, South Korea
Chendong Li	University of Connecticut, USA
Gang Li	Deakin University, Australia
Fang Liu	AMES Laboratories, USA
Xin Liu	University of Calgary, Canada
Andrea Lombardi	University of Perugia, Italy
Savino Longo	University of Bari, Italy
Tinghuai Ma	Nanjing University of Information Science and Technology, China
Ernesto Marcheggiani	Katholieke Universiteit Leuven, Belgium
Antonino Marvuglia	Research Centre Henri Tudor, Luxembourg
Nicola Masini	CNR, Italy
Ilaria Matteucci	CNR, Italy
Eric Medvet	University of Trieste, Italy
Nirvana Meratnia	University of Twente, The Netherlands

Noelia Faginas Lago	University of Perugia, Italy
Giuseppe Modica	University of Reggio Calabria, Italy
Josè Luis Montaña	University of Cantabria, Spain
Maria Filipa Mourão	IP from Viana do Castelo, Portugal
Louiza de Macedo Mourelle	State University of Rio de Janeiro, Brazil
Nadia Nedjah	State University of Rio de Janeiro, Brazil
Laszlo Neumann	University of Girona, Spain
Kok-Leong Ong	Deakin University, Australia
Belen Palop	Universidad de Valladolid, Spain
Marcin Paprzycki	Polish Academy of Sciences, Poland
Eric Pardede	La Trobe University, Australia
Kwangjin Park	Wonkwang University, South Korea
Ana Isabel Pereira	Polytechnic Institute of Bragança, Portugal
Massimiliano Petri	University of Pisa, Italy
Maurizio Pollino	Italian National Agency for New Technologies, Energy and Sustainable Economic Development, Italy
Alenka Poplin	University of Hamburg, Germany
Vidyasagar Potdar	Curtin University of Technology, Australia
David C. Prosperi	Florida Atlantic University, USA
Wenny Rahayu	La Trobe University, Australia
Jerzy Respondek	Silesian University of Technology, Poland
Humberto Rocha	INESC-Coimbra, Portugal
Jon Rokne	University of Calgary, Canada
Octavio Roncero	CSIC, Spain
Maytham Safar	Kuwait University, Kuwait
Francesco Santini	University of Perugia, Italy
Chiara Saracino	A.O. Ospedale Niguarda Ca' Granda, Italy
Haiduke Sarafian	Penn State University, USA
Marco Paulo Seabra dos Reis	University of Coimbra, Portugal
Jie Shen	University of Michigan, USA
Qi Shi	Liverpool John Moores University, UK
Dale Shires	U.S. Army Research Laboratory, USA
Inês Soares	University of Coimbra, Portugal
Elena Stankova	Saint Petersburg University, Russia
Takuo Suganuma	Tohoku University, Japan
Eufemia Tarantino	Polytechnic University of Bari, Italy
Sergio Tasso	University of Perugia, Italy
Ana Paula Teixeira	University of Trás-os-Montes and Alto Douro, Portugal
Senhorinha Teixeira	University of Minho, Portugal
M. Filomena Teodoro	Portuguese Naval Academy, University of Lisbon, Portugal
Parimala Thulasiraman	University of Manitoba, Canada
Carmelo Torre	Polytechnic University of Bari, Italy
Javier Martinez Torres	Centro Universitario de la Defensa Zaragoza, Spain
Giuseppe A. Trunfio	University of Sassari, Italy

Pablo Vanegas	University of Cuenca, Ecuador
Marco Vizzari	University of Perugia, Italy
Varun Vohra	Merck Inc., USA
Koichi Wada	University of Tsukuba, Japan
Krzysztof Walkowiak	Wroclaw University of Technology, Poland
Zequn Wang	Intelligent Automation Inc., USA
Robert Weibel	University of Zurich, Switzerland
Frank Westad	Norwegian University of Science and Technology, Norway
Roland Wismüller	Universität Siegen, Germany
Mudasser Wyne	SOET National University, USA
Chung-Huang Yang	National Kaohsiung Normal University, Taiwan
Xin-She Yang	National Physical Laboratory, UK
Salim Zabir	France Telecom Japan Co., Japan
Haifeng Zhao	University of California, Davis, USA
Fabiana Zollo	University of Venice, Italy
Albert Y. Zomaya	The University of Sydney, Australia

Workshop Organizers

Advanced Transport Tools and Methods (A2TM 2020)

| Massimiliano Petri | University of Pisa, Italy |
| Antonio Pratelli | University of Pisa, Italy |

Advances in Artificial Intelligence Learning Technologies: Blended Learning, STEM, Computational Thinking and Coding (AAILT 2020)

Valentina Franzoni	University of Perugia, Italy
Alfredo Milani	University of Perugia, Italy
Sergio Tasso	University of Perugia, Italy

Workshop on Advancements in Applied Machine Learning and Data Analytics (AAMDA 2020)

Alessandro Costantini	INFN, Italy
Daniele Cesini	INFN, Italy
Davide Salomoni	INFN, Italy
Doina Cristina Duma	INFN, Italy

Advanced Computational Approaches in Artificial Intelligence and Complex Systems Applications (ACAC 2020)

Yeliz Karaca	University of Massachusetts Medical School, USA
Dumitru Baleanu	Çankaya University, Turkey, and Institute of Space Sciences, Romania
Majaz Moonis	University of Massachusetts Medical School, USA
Yu-Dong Zhang	University of Leicester, UK

Affective Computing and Emotion Recognition (ACER-EMORE 2020)

Valentina Franzoni	University of Perugia, Italy
Alfredo Milani	University of Perugia, Italy
Giulio Biondi	University of Florence, Italy

AI Factory and Smart Manufacturing (AIFACTORY 2020)

Jongpil Jeong	Sungkyunkwan University, South Korea

Air Quality Monitoring and Citizen Science for Smart Urban Management. State of the Art And Perspectives (AirQ&CScience 2020)

Grazie Fattoruso	ENEA CR Portici, Italy
Maurizio Pollino	ENEA CR Casaccia, Italy
Saverio De Vito	ENEA CR Portici, Italy

Automatic Landform Classification: Spatial Methods and Applications (ALCSMA 2020)

Maria Danese	CNR-ISPC, Italy
Dario Gioia	CNR-ISPC, Italy

Advances of Modelling Micromobility in Urban Spaces (AMMUS 2020)

Tiziana Campisi	University of Enna KORE, Italy
Giovanni Tesoriere	University of Enna KORE, Italy
Ioannis Politis	Aristotle University of Thessaloniki, Greece
Socrates Basbas	Aristotle University of Thessaloniki, Greece
Sanja Surdonja	University of Rijeka, Croatia
Marko Rencelj	University of Maribor, Slovenia

Advances in Information Systems and Technologies for Emergency Management, Risk Assessment and Mitigation Based on the Resilience Concepts (ASTER 2020)

Maurizio Pollino	ENEA, Italy
Marco Vona	University of Basilicata, Italy
Amedeo Flora	University of Basilicata, Italy
Chiara Iacovino	University of Basilicata, Italy
Beniamino Murgante	University of Basilicata, Italy

Advances in Web Based Learning (AWBL 2020)

Birol Ciloglugil	Ege University, Turkey
Mustafa Murat Inceoglu	Ege University, Turkey

**Blockchain and Distributed Ledgers: Technologies
and Applications (BDLTA 2020)**

Vladimir Korkhov	Saint Petersburg University, Russia
Elena Stankova	Saint Petersburg University, Russia
Nataliia Kulabukhova	Saint Petersburg University, Russia

Bio and Neuro Inspired Computing and Applications (BIONCA 2020)

Nadia Nedjah	State University of Rio de Janeiro, Brazil
Luiza De Macedo Mourelle	State University of Rio de Janeiro, Brazil

Computer Aided Modeling, Simulation and Analysis (CAMSA 2020)

Jie Shen	University of Michigan, USA

Computational and Applied Statistics (CAS 2020)

Ana Cristina Braga	University of Minho, Portugal

Computerized Evidence Based Decision Making (CEBDEM 2020)

Clarice Bleil de Souza	Cardiff University, UK
Valerio Cuttini	University of Pisa, Italy
Federico Cerutti	Cardiff University, UK
Camilla Pezzica	Cardiff University, UK

Computational Geometry and Applications (CGA 2020)

Marina Gavrilova	University of Calgary, Canada

**Computational Mathematics, Statistics and Information Management
(CMSIM 2020)**

Maria Filomena Teodoro	Portuguese Naval Academy, University of Lisbon, Portugal

Computational Optimization and Applications (COA 2020)

Ana Rocha	University of Minho, Portugal
Humberto Rocha	University of Coimbra, Portugal

Computational Astrochemistry (CompAstro 2020)

Marzio Rosi	University of Perugia, Italy
Cecilia Ceccarelli	University of Grenoble, France
Stefano Falcinelli	University of Perugia, Italy
Dimitrios Skouteris	Master-UP, Italy

Cities, Technologies and Planning (CTP 2020)

Beniamino Murgante	University of Basilicata, Italy
Ljiljana Zivkovic	Ministry of Construction, Transport and Infrastructure and Institute of Architecture and Urban & Spatial Planning of Serbia, Serbia
Giuseppe Borruso	University of Trieste, Italy
Malgorzata Hanzl	University of Łódź, Poland

Data Stream Processing and Applications (DASPA 2020)

Raja Chiky	ISEP, France
Rosanna VERDE	University of Campania, Italy
Marcilio De Souto	Orleans University, France

Data Science for Cyber Security (DS4Cyber 2020)

Hongmei Chi	Florida A&M University, USA

Econometric and Multidimensional Evaluation in Urban Environment (EMEUE 2020)

Carmelo Maria Torre	Polytechnic University of Bari, Italy
Pierluigi Morano	Polytechnic University of Bari, Italy
Maria Cerreta	University of Naples, Italy
Paola Perchinunno	University of Bari, Italy
Francesco Tajani	University of Rome, Italy
Simona Panaro	University of Portsmouth, UK
Francesco Scorza	University of Basilicata, Italy

Frontiers in Machine Learning (FIML 2020)

Massimo Bilancia	University of Bari, Italy
Paola Perchinunno	University of Bari, Italy
Pasquale Lops	University of Bari, Italy
Danilo Di Bona	University of Bari, Italy

Future Computing System Technologies and Applications (FiSTA 2020)

Bernady Apduhan	Kyushu Sangyo University, Japan
Rafael Santos	Brazilian National Institute for Space Research, Brazil

Geodesign in Decision Making: Meta Planning and Collaborative Design for Sustainable and Inclusive Development (GDM 2020)

Francesco Scorza	University of Basilicata, Italy
Michele Campagna	University of Cagliari, Italy
Ana Clara Mourao Moura	Federal University of Minas Gerais, Brazil

Geomatics in Forestry and Agriculture: New Advances and Perspectives (GeoForAgr 2020)

Maurizio Pollino	ENEA, Italy
Giuseppe Modica	University of Reggio Calabria, Italy
Marco Vizzari	University of Perugia, Italy

Geographical Analysis, Urban Modeling, Spatial Statistics (GEOG-AND-MOD 2020)

Beniamino Murgante	University of Basilicata, Italy
Giuseppe Borruso	University of Trieste, Italy
Hartmut Asche	University of Potsdam, Germany

Geomatics for Resource Monitoring and Management (GRMM 2020)

Eufemia Tarantino	Polytechnic University of Bari, Italy
Enrico Borgogno Mondino	University of Torino, Italy
Marco Scaioni	Polytechnic University of Milan, Italy
Alessandra Capolupo	Polytechnic University of Bari, Italy

Software Quality (ISSQ 2020)

Sanjay Misra	Covenant University, Nigeria

Collective, Massive and Evolutionary Systems (IWCES 2020)

Alfredo Milani	University of Perugia, Italy
Rajdeep Niyogi	Indian Institute of Technology, Roorkee, India
Alina Elena Baia	University of Florence, Italy

Large Scale Computational Science (LSCS 2020)

Elise De Doncker	Western Michigan University, USA
Fukuko Yuasa	High Energy Accelerator Research Organization (KEK), Japan
Hideo Matsufuru	High Energy Accelerator Research Organization (KEK), Japan

Land Use Monitoring for Sustainability (LUMS 2020)

Carmelo Maria Torre	Polytechnic University of Bari, Italy
Alessandro Bonifazi	Polytechnic University of Bari, Italy
Pasquale Balena	Polytechnic University of Bari, Italy
Massimiliano Bencardino	University of Salerno, Italy
Francesco Tajani	University of Rome, Italy
Pierluigi Morano	Polytechnic University of Bari, Italy
Maria Cerreta	University of Naples, Italy
Giuliano Poli	University of Naples, Italy

Machine Learning for Space and Earth Observation Data (MALSEOD 2020)

Rafael Santos	INPE, Brazil
Karine Ferreira	INPE, Brazil

Building Multi-dimensional Models for Assessing Complex Environmental Systems (MES 2020)

Marta Dell'Ovo	Polytechnic University of Milan, Italy
Vanessa Assumma	Polytechnic University of Torino, Italy
Caterina Caprioli	Polytechnic University of Torino, Italy
Giulia Datola	Polytechnic University of Torino, Italy
Federico dell'Anna	Polytechnic University of Torino, Italy

Ecosystem Services: Nature's Contribution to People in Practice. Assessment Frameworks, Models, Mapping, and Implications (NC2P 2020)

Francesco Scorza	University of Basilicata, Italy
David Cabana	International Marine Center, Italy
Sabrina Lai	University of Cagliari, Italy
Ana Clara Mourao Moura	Federal University of Minas Gerais, Brazil
Corrado Zoppi	University of Cagliari, Italy

Open Knowledge for Socio-economic Development (OKSED 2020)

Luigi Mundula	University of Cagliari, Italy
Flavia Marzano	Link Campus University, Italy
Maria Paradiso	University of Milan, Italy

Scientific Computing Infrastructure (SCI 2020)

Elena Stankova	Saint Petersburg State University, Russia
Vladimir Korkhov	Saint Petersburg State University, Russia
Natalia Kulabukhova	Saint Petersburg State University, Russia

Computational Studies for Energy and Comfort in Buildings (SECoB 2020)

Senhorinha Teixeira	University of Minho, Portugal
Luís Martins	University of Minho, Portugal
Ana Maria Rocha	University of Minho, Portugal

Software Engineering Processes and Applications (SEPA 2020)

Sanjay Misra	Covenant University, Nigeria

Smart Ports - Technologies and Challenges (SmartPorts 2020)

Gianfranco Fancello	University of Cagliari, Italy
Patrizia Serra	University of Cagliari, Italy
Marco Mazzarino	University of Venice, Italy
Luigi Mundula	University of Cagliari, Italy

Ginevra Balletto   University of Cagliari, Italy
Giuseppe Borruso   University of Trieste, Italy

Sustainability Performance Assessment: Models, Approaches and Applications Toward Interdisciplinary and Integrated Solutions (SPA 2020)

Francesco Scorza   University of Basilicata, Italy
Valentin Grecu   Lucian Blaga University, Romania
Jolanta Dvarioniene   Kaunas University of Technology, Lithuania
Sabrina Lai   University of Cagliari, Italy
Iole Cerminara   University of Basilicata, Italy
Corrado Zoppi   University of Cagliari, Italy

Smart and Sustainable Island Communities (SSIC 2020)

Chiara Garau   University of Cagliari, Italy
Anastasia Stratigea   National Technical University of Athens, Greece
Paola Zamperlin   University of Pisa, Italy
Francesco Scorza   University of Basilicata, Italy

Science, Technologies and Policies to Innovate Spatial Planning (STP4P 2020)

Chiara Garau   University of Cagliari, Italy
Daniele La Rosa   University of Catania, Italy
Francesco Scorza   University of Basilicata, Italy
Anna Maria Colavitti   University of Cagliari, Italy
Beniamino Murgante   University of Basilicata, Italy
Paolo La Greca   University of Catania, Italy

New Frontiers for Strategic Urban Planning (StrategicUP 2020)

Luigi Mundula   University of Cagliari, Italy
Ginevra Balletto   University of Cagliari, Italy
Giuseppe Borruso   University of Trieste, Italy
Michele Campagna   University of Cagliari, Italy
Beniamino Murgante   University of Basilicata, Italy

Theoretical and Computational Chemistry and its Applications (TCCMA 2020)

Noelia Faginas-Lago   University of Perugia, Italy
Andrea Lombardi   University of Perugia, Italy

Tools and Techniques in Software Development Process (TTSDP 2020)

Sanjay Misra   Covenant University, Nigeria

Urban Form Studies (UForm 2020)

Malgorzata Hanzl   Łódź University of Technology, Poland

Urban Space Extended Accessibility (USEaccessibility 2020)

Chiara Garau   University of Cagliari, Italy
Francesco Pinna   University of Cagliari, Italy
Beniamino Murgante   University of Basilicata, Italy
Mauro Coni   University of Cagliari, Italy
Francesca Maltinti   University of Cagliari, Italy
Vincenza Torrisi   University of Catania, Italy
Matteo Ignaccolo   University of Catania, Italy

Virtual and Augmented Reality and Applications (VRA 2020)

Osvaldo Gervasi   University of Perugia, Italy
Damiano Perri   University of Perugia, Italy
Marco Simonetti   University of Perugia, Italy
Sergio Tasso   University of Perugia, Italy

Workshop on Advanced and Computational Methods for Earth Science Applications (WACM4ES 2020)

Luca Piroddi   University of Cagliari, Italy
Laura Foddis   University of Cagliari, Italy
Gian Piero Deidda   University of Cagliari, Italy
Augusto Montisci   University of Cagliari, Italy
Gabriele Uras   University of Cagliari, Italy
Giulio Vignoli   University of Cagliari, Italy

Sponsoring Organizations

ICCSA 2020 would not have been possible without tremendous support of many organizations and institutions, for which all organizers and participants of ICCSA 2020 express their sincere gratitude:

Springer International Publishing AG, Germany
(https://www.springer.com)

Computers Open Access Journal
(https://www.mdpi.com/journal/computers)

IEEE Italy Section, Italy
(https://italy.ieeer8.org/)

Centre-North Italy Chapter IEEE GRSS, Italy
(https://cispio.diet.uniroma1.it/marzano/ieee-grs/
index.html)

Italy Section of the Computer Society, Italy
(https://site.ieee.org/italy-cs/)

University of Cagliari, Italy
(https://unica.it/)

University of Perugia, Italy
(https://www.unipg.it)

University of Basilicata, Italy
(http://www.unibas.it)

Monash University, Australia
(https://www.monash.edu/)

Kyushu Sangyo University, Japan
(https://www.kyusan-u.ac.jp/)

University of Minho, Portugal
(https://www.uminho.pt/)

Scientific Association Transport Infrastructures, Italy
(https://www.stradeeautostrade.it/associazioni-e-organizzazioni/asit-associazione-scientifica-infrastrutture-trasporto/)

Regione Sardegna, Italy
(https://regione.sardegna.it/)

Comune di Cagliari, Italy
(https://www.comune.cagliari.it/)

Referees

A. P. Andrade Marina	ISCTE, Instituto Universitário de Lisboa, Portugal
Addesso Paolo	University of Salerno, Italy
Adewumi Adewole	Algonquin College, Canada
Afolabi Adedeji	Covenant University, Nigeria
Afreixo Vera	University of Aveiro, Portugal
Agrawal Smirti	Freelancer, USA
Agrawal Akshat	Amity University Haryana, India
Ahmad Waseem	Federal University of Technology Minna, Nigeria
Akgun Nurten	Bursa Technical University, Turkey
Alam Tauhidul	Louisiana State University Shreveport, USA
Aleixo Sandra M.	CEAUL, Portugal
Alfa Abraham	Federal University of Technology Minna, Nigeria
Alvelos Filipe	University of Minho, Portugal
Alves Alexandra	University of Minho, Portugal
Amato Federico	University of Lausanne, Switzerland
Andrade Marina Alexandra Pedro	ISCTE-IUL, Portugal
Andrianov Sergey	Saint Petersburg State University, Russia
Anelli Angelo	CNR-IGAG, Italy
Anelli Debora	University of Rome, Italy
Annunziata Alfonso	University of Cagliari, Italy
Antognelli Sara	Agricolus, Italy
Aoyama Tatsumi	High Energy Accelerator Research Organization, Japan
Apduhan Bernady	Kyushu Sangyo University, Japan
Ascenzi Daniela	University of Trento, Italy
Asche Harmut	Hasso-Plattner-Institut für Digital Engineering GmbH, Germany
Aslan Burak Galip	Izmir Insitute of Technology, Turkey
Assumma Vanessa	Polytechnic University of Torino, Italy
Astoga Gino	UV, Chile
Atman Uslu Nilüfer	Manisa Celal Bayar University, Turkey
Behera Ranjan Kumar	National Institute of Technology, Rourkela, India
Badsha Shahriar	University of Nevada, USA
Bai Peng	University of Cagliari, Italy
Baia Alina-Elena	University of Perugia, Italy
Balacco Gabriella	Polytechnic University of Bari, Italy
Balci Birim	Celal Bayar University, Turkey
Balena Pasquale	Polytechnic University of Bari, Italy
Balletto Ginevra	University of Cagliari, Italy
Balucani Nadia	University of Perugia, Italy
Bansal Megha	Delhi University, India
Barazzetti Luigi	Polytechnic University of Milan, Italy
Barreto Jeniffer	Istituto Superior Técnico, Portugal
Basbas Socrates	Aristotle University of Thessaloniki, Greece

Berger Katja	Ludwig-Maximilians-Universität München, Germany
Beyene Asrat Mulatu	Addis Ababa Science and Technology University, Ethiopia
Bilancia Massimo	University of Bari Aldo Moro, Italy
Biondi Giulio	University of Firenze, Italy
Blanquer Ignacio	Universitat Politècnica de València, Spain
Bleil de Souza Clarice	Cardiff University, UK
Blečić Ivan	University of Cagliari, Italy
Bogdanov Alexander	Saint Petersburg State University, Russia
Bonifazi Alessandro	Polytechnic University of Bari, Italy
Bontchev Boyan	Sofia University, Bulgaria
Borgogno Mondino Enrico	University of Torino, Italy
Borruso Giuseppe	University of Trieste, Italy
Bouaziz Rahma	Taibah University, Saudi Arabia
Bowles Juliana	University of Saint Andrews, UK
Braga Ana Cristina	University of Minho, Portugal
Brambilla Andrea	Polytechnic University of Milan, Italy
Brito Francisco	University of Minho, Portugal
Buele Jorge	Universidad Tecnológica Indoamérica, Ecuador
Buffoni Andrea	TAGES sc, Italy
Cabana David	International Marine Centre, Italy
Calazan Rogerio	IEAPM, Brazil
Calcina Sergio Vincenzo	University of Cagliari, Italy
Camalan Seda	Atilim University, Turkey
Camarero Alberto	Universidad Politécnica de Madrid, Spain
Campisi Tiziana	University of Enna KORE, Italy
Cannatella Daniele	Delft University of Technology, The Netherlands
Capolupo Alessandra	Polytechnic University of Bari, Italy
Cappucci Sergio	ENEA, Italy
Caprioli Caterina	Polytechnic University of Torino, Italy
Carapau Fermando	Universidade de Evora, Portugal
Carcangiu Sara	University of Cagliari, Italy
Carrasqueira Pedro	INESC Coimbra, Portugal
Caselli Nicolás	PUCV Chile, Chile
Castro de Macedo Jose Nuno	Universidade do Minho, Portugal
Cavallo Carla	University of Naples, Italy
Cerminara Iole	University of Basilicata, Italy
Cerreta Maria	University of Naples, Italy
Cesini Daniele	INFN-CNAF, Italy
Chang Shi-Kuo	University of Pittsburgh, USA
Chetty Girija	University of Canberra, Australia
Chiky Raja	ISEP, France
Chowdhury Dhiman	University of South Carolina, USA
Ciloglugil Birol	Ege University, Turkey
Coletti Cecilia	Università di Chieti-Pescara, Italy

Coni Mauro	University of Cagliari, Italy
Corcoran Padraig	Cardiff University, UK
Cornelio Antonella	Università degli Studi di Brescia, Italy
Correia Aldina	ESTG-PPorto, Portugal
Correia Elisete	University of Trás-os-Montes and Alto Douro, Portugal
Correia Florbela	Polytechnic Institute of Viana do Castelo, Portugal
Costa Lino	Universidade do Minho, Portugal
Costa e Silva Eliana	ESTG-P Porto, Portugal
Costantini Alessandro	INFN, Italy
Crespi Mattia	University of Roma, Italy
Cuca Branka	Polytechnic University of Milano, Italy
De Doncker Elise	Western Michigan University, USA
De Macedo Mourelle Luiza	State University of Rio de Janeiro, Brazil
Daisaka Hiroshi	Hitotsubashi University, Japan
Daldanise Gaia	CNR, Italy
Danese Maria	CNR-ISPC, Italy
Daniele Bartoli	University of Perugia, Italy
Datola Giulia	Polytechnic University of Torino, Italy
De Luca Giandomenico	University of Reggio Calabria, Italy
De Lucia Caterina	University of Foggia, Italy
De Morais Barroca Filho Itamir	Federal University of Rio Grande do Norte, Brazil
De Petris Samuele	University of Torino, Italy
De Sá Alan	Marinha do Brasil, Brazil
De Souto Marcilio	LIFO, University of Orléans, France
De Vito Saverio	ENEA, Italy
De Wilde Pieter	University of Plymouth, UK
Degtyarev Alexander	Saint Petersburg State University, Russia
Dell'Anna Federico	Polytechnic University of Torino, Italy
Dell'Ovo Marta	Polytechnic University of Milano, Italy
Della Mura Fernanda	University of Naples, Italy
Deluka T. Aleksandra	University of Rijeka, Croatia
Demartino Cristoforo	Zhejiang University, China
Dereli Dursun Ahu	Istanbul Commerce University, Turkey
Desogus Giulia	University of Cagliari, Italy
Dettori Marco	University of Sassari, Italy
Devai Frank	London South Bank University, UK
Di Francesco Massimo	University of Cagliari, Italy
Di Liddo Felicia	Polytechnic University of Bari, Italy
Di Paola Gianluigi	University of Molise, Italy
Di Pietro Antonio	ENEA, Italy
Di Pinto Valerio	University of Naples, Italy
Dias Joana	University of Coimbra, Portugal
Dimas Isabel	University of Coimbra, Portugal
Dirvanauskas Darius	Kaunas University of Technology, Lithuania
Djordjevic Aleksandra	University of Belgrade, Serbia

Duma Doina Cristina	INFN-CNAF, Italy
Dumlu Demircioğlu Emine	Yıldız Technical University, Turkey
Dursun Aziz	Virginia Tech University, USA
Dvarioniene Jolanta	Kaunas University of Technology, Lithuania
Errico Maurizio Francesco	University of Enna KORE, Italy
Ezugwu Absalom	University of KwaZulu-Natal, South Africa
Fattoruso Grazia	ENEA, Italy
Faginas-Lago Noelia	University of Perugia, Italy
Falanga Bolognesi Salvatore	ARIESPACE, Italy
Falcinelli Stefano	University of Perugia, Italy
Farias Marcos	National Nuclear Energy Commission, Brazil
Farina Alessandro	University of Pisa, Italy
Feltynowski Marcin	Lodz University of Technology, Poland
Fernandes Florbela	Instituto Politecnico de Bragança, Portugal
Fernandes Paula Odete	Instituto Politécnico de Bragança, Portugal
Fernandez-Sanz Luis	University of Alcala, Spain
Ferreira Ana Cristina	University of Minho, Portugal
Ferreira Fernanda	Porto, Portugal
Fiorini Lorena	University of L'Aquila, Italy
Flora Amedeo	University of Basilicata, Italy
Florez Hector	Universidad Distrital Francisco Jose de Caldas, Colombia
Foddis Maria Laura	University of Cagliari, Italy
Fogli Daniela	University of Brescia, Italy
Fortunelli Martina	Pragma Engineering, Italy
Fragiacomo Massimo	University of L'Aquila, Italy
Franzoni Valentina	Perugia University, Italy
Fusco Giovanni	University of Cote d'Azur, France
Fyrogenis Ioannis	Aristotle University of Thessaloniki, Greece
Gorbachev Yuriy	Coddan Technologies LLC, Russia
Gabrielli Laura	Università Iuav di Venezia, Italy
Gallanos Theodore	Austrian Institute of Technology, Austria
Gamallo Belmonte Pablo	Universitat de Barcelona, Spain
Gankevich Ivan	Saint Petersburg State University, Russia
Garau Chiara	University of Cagliari, Italy
Garcia Para Ernesto	Universidad del Pais Vasco, EHU, Spain
Gargano Riccardo	Universidade de Brasilia, Brazil
Gavrilova Marina	University of Calgary, Canada
Georgiadis Georgios	Aristotle University of Thessaloniki, Greece
Gervasi Osvaldo	University of Perugia, Italy
Giano Salvatore Ivo	University of Basilicata, Italy
Gil Jorge	Chalmers University, Sweden
Gioia Andrea	Polytechnic University of Bari, Italy
Gioia Dario	ISPC-CNT, Italy

Giordano Ludovica	ENEA, Italy
Giorgi Giacomo	University of Perugia, Italy
Giovene di Girasole Eleonora	CNR-IRISS, Italy
Giovinazzi Sonia	ENEA, Italy
Giresini Linda	University of Pisa, Italy
Giuffrida Salvatore	University of Catania, Italy
Golubchikov Oleg	Cardiff University, UK
Gonçalves A. Manuela	University of Minho, Portugal
Gorgoglione Angela	Universidad de la República, Uruguay
Goyal Rinkaj	IPU, Delhi, India
Grishkin Valery	Saint Petersburg State University, Russia
Guerra Eduardo	Free University of Bozen-Bolzano, Italy
Guerrero Abel	University of Guanajuato, Mexico
Gulseven Osman	American University of The Middle East, Kuwait
Gupta Brij	National Institute of Technology, Kurukshetra, India
Guveyi Elcin	Yildiz Teknik University, Turkey
Gülen Kemal Güven	Namk Kemal University, Turkey
Haddad Sandra	Arab Academy for Science, Technology and Maritime Transport, Egypt
Hanzl Malgorzata	Lodz University of Technology, Poland
Hegedus Peter	University of Szeged, Hungary
Hendrix Eligius M. T.	Universidad de Málaga, Spain
Higaki Hiroaki	Tokyo Denki University, Japan
Hossain Syeda Sumbul	Daffodil International University, Bangladesh
Iacovino Chiara	University of Basilicata, Italy
Iakushkin Oleg	Saint Petersburg State University, Russia
Iannuzzo Antonino	ETH Zurich, Switzerland
Idri Ali	University Mohammed V, Morocco
Ignaccolo Matteo	University of Catania, Italy
Ilovan Oana-Ramona	Babeş-Bolyai University, Romania
Isola Federica	University of Cagliari, Italy
Jankovic Marija	CERTH, Greece
Jorge Ana Maria	Instituto Politécnico de Lisboa, Portugal
Kanamori Issaku	RIKEN Center for Computational Science, Japan
Kapenga John	Western Michigan University, USA
Karabulut Korhan	Yasar University, Turkey
Karaca Yeliz	University of Massachusetts Medical School, USA
Karami Ali	University of Guilan, Iran
Kienhofer Frank	WITS, South Africa
Kim Tai-hoon	Beijing Jiaotong University, China
Kimura Shuhei	Tottori University, Japan
Kirillov Denis	Saint Petersburg State University, Russia
Korkhov Vladimir	Saint Petersburg University, Russia
Koszewski Krzysztof	Warsaw University of Technology, Poland
Krzysztofik Sylwia	Lodz University of Technology, Poland

Kulabukhova Nataliia	Saint Petersburg State University, Russia
Kulkarni Shrinivas B.	SDM College of Engineering and Technology, Dharwad, India
Kwiecinski Krystian	Warsaw University of Technology, Poland
Kyvelou Stella	Panteion University of Social and Political Sciences, Greece
Körting Thales	INPE, Brazil
Lal Niranjan	Mody University of Science and Technology, India
Lazzari Maurizio	CNR-ISPC, Italy
Leon Marcelo	Asociacion de Becarios del Ecuador, Ecuador
La Rocca Ludovica	University of Naples, Italy
La Rosa Daniele	University of Catania, Italy
Lai Sabrina	University of Cagliari, Italy
Lalenis Konstantinos	University of Thessaly, Greece
Lannon Simon	Cardiff University, UK
Lasaponara Rosa	CNR, Italy
Lee Chien-Sing	Sunway University, Malaysia
Lemus-Romani José	Pontificia Universidad Católica de Valparaiso, Chile
Leone Federica	University of Cagliari, Italy
Li Yuanxi	Hong Kong Baptist University, China
Locurcio Marco	Polytechnic University of Bari, Italy
Lombardi Andrea	University of Perugia, Italy
Lopez Gayarre Fernando	University of Oviedo, Spain
Lops Pasquale	University of Bari, Italy
Lourenço Vanda	Universidade Nova de Lisboa, Portugal
Luviano José Luís	University of Guanajuato, Mexico
Maltese Antonino	University of Palermo, Italy
Magni Riccardo	Pragma Engineering, Italy
Maheshwari Anil	Carleton University, Canada
Maja Roberto	Polytechnic University of Milano, Italy
Malik Shaveta	Terna Engineering College, India
Maltinti Francesca	University of Cagliari, Italy
Mandado Marcos	University of Vigo, Spain
Manganelli Benedetto	University of Basilicata, Italy
Mangiameli Michele	University of Catania, Italy
Maraschin Clarice	Universidade Federal do Rio Grande do Sul, Brazil
Marigorta Ana Maria	Universidad de Las Palmas de Gran Canaria, Spain
Markov Krassimir	Institute of Electrical Engineering and Informatics, Bulgaria
Martellozzo Federico	University of Firenze, Italy
Marucci Alessandro	University of L'Aquila, Italy
Masini Nicola	IBAM-CNR, Italy
Matsufuru Hideo	High Energy Accelerator Research Organization (KEK), Japan
Matteucci Ilaria	CNR, Italy
Mauro D'Apuzzo	University of Cassino and Southern Lazio, Italy

Mazzarella Chiara	University of Naples, Italy
Mazzarino Marco	University of Venice, Italy
Mazzoni Augusto	University of Roma, Italy
Mele Roberta	University of Naples, Italy
Menezes Raquel	University of Minho, Portugal
Menghini Antonio	Aarhus Geofisica, Italy
Mengoni Paolo	University of Florence, Italy
Merlino Angelo	Università degli Studi Mediterranea, Italy
Milani Alfredo	University of Perugia, Italy
Milic Vladimir	University of Zagreb, Croatia
Millham Richard	Durban University of Technology, South Africa
Mishra B.	University of Szeged, Hungary
Misra Sanjay	Covenant University, Nigeria
Modica Giuseppe	University of Reggio Calabria, Italy
Mohagheghi Mohammadsadegh	Vali-e-Asr University of Rafsanjan, Iran
Molaei Qelichi Mohamad	University of Tehran, Iran
Molinara Mario	University of Cassino and Southern Lazio, Italy
Momo Evelyn Joan	University of Torino, Italy
Monteiro Vitor	University of Minho, Portugal
Montisci Augusto	University of Cagliari, Italy
Morano Pierluigi	Polytechnic University of Bari, Italy
Morganti Alessandro	Polytechnic University of Milano, Italy
Mosca Erica Isa	Polytechnic University of Milan, Italy
Moura Ricardo	CMA-FCT, New University of Lisbon, Portugal
Mourao Maria	Polytechnic Institute of Viana do Castelo, Portugal
Mourão Moura Ana Clara	Federal University of Minas Gerais, Brazil
Mrak Iva	University of Rijeka, Croatia
Murgante Beniamino	University of Basilicata, Italy
Muñoz Mirna	Centro de Investigacion en Matematicas, Mexico
Nedjah Nadia	State University of Rio de Janeiro, Brazil
Nakasato Naohito	University of Aizu, Japan
Natário Isabel Cristina	Universidade Nova de Lisboa, Portugal
Nesticò Antonio	Università degli Studi di Salerno, Italy
Neto Ana Maria	Universidade Federal do ABC, Brazil
Nicolosi Vittorio	University of Rome, Italy
Nikiforiadis Andreas	Aristotle University of Thessaloniki, Greece
Nocera Fabrizio	University of Illinois at Urbana-Champaign, USA
Nocera Silvio	IUAV, Italy
Nogueira Marcelo	Paulista University, Brazil
Nolè Gabriele	CNR, Italy
Nuno Beirao Jose	University of Lisbon, Portugal
Okewu Emma	University of Alcala, Spain
Oluwasefunmi Arogundade	Academy of Mathematics and System Science, China
Oppio Alessandra	Polytechnic University of Milan, Italy
P. Costa M. Fernanda	University of Minho, Portugal

Parisot Olivier	Luxembourg Institute of Science and Technology, Luxembourg
Paddeu Daniela	UWE, UK
Paio Alexandra	ISCTE-Instituto Universitário de Lisboa, Portugal
Palme Massimo	Catholic University of the North, Chile
Panaro Simona	University of Portsmouth, UK
Pancham Jay	Durban University of Technology, South Africa
Pantazis Dimos	University of West Attica, Greece
Papa Enrica	University of Westminster, UK
Pardede Eric	La Trobe University, Australia
Perchinunno Paola	Uniersity of Cagliari, Italy
Perdicoulis Teresa	UTAD, Portugal
Pereira Ana	Polytechnic Institute of Bragança, Portugal
Perri Damiano	University of Perugia, Italy
Petrelli Marco	University of Rome, Italy
Pierri Francesca	University of Perugia, Italy
Piersanti Antonio	ENEA, Italy
Pilogallo Angela	University of Basilicata, Italy
Pinna Francesco	University of Cagliari, Italy
Pinto Telmo	University of Coimbra, Portugal
Piroddi Luca	University of Cagliari, Italy
Poli Giuliano	University of Naples, Italy
Polidoro Maria João	Polytecnic Institute of Porto, Portugal
Polignano Marco	University of Bari, Italy
Politis Ioannis	Aristotle University of Thessaloniki, Greece
Pollino Maurizio	ENEA, Italy
Popoola Segun	Covenant University, Nigeria
Pratelli Antonio	University of Pisa, Italy
Praticò Salvatore	University of Reggio Calabria, Italy
Previtali Mattia	Polytechnic University of Milan, Italy
Puppio Mario Lucio	University of Pisa, Italy
Puttini Ricardo	Universidade de Brasilia, Brazil
Que Zeli	Nanjing Forestry University, China
Queiroz Gilberto	INPE, Brazil
Regalbuto Stefania	University of Naples, Italy
Ravanelli Roberta	University of Roma, Italy
Recanatesi Fabio	University of Tuscia, Italy
Reis Ferreira Gomes Karine	INPE, Brazil
Reis Marco	University of Coimbra, Portugal
Reitano Maria	University of Naples, Italy
Rencelj Marko	University of Maribor, Slovenia
Respondek Jerzy	Silesian University of Technology, Poland
Rimola Albert	Universitat Autònoma de Barcelona, Spain
Rocha Ana	University of Minho, Portugal
Rocha Humberto	University of Coimbra, Portugal
Rocha Maria Celia	UFBA Bahia, Brazil

Rocha Maria Clara	ESTES Coimbra, Portugal
Rocha Miguel	University of Minho, Portugal
Rodriguez Guillermo	UNICEN, Argentina
Rodríguez González Alejandro	Universidad Carlos III de Madrid, Spain
Ronchieri Elisabetta	INFN, Italy
Rosi Marzio	University of Perugia, Italy
Rotondo Francesco	Università Politecnica delle Marche, Italy
Rusci Simone	University of Pisa, Italy
Saganeiti Lucia	University of Basilicata, Italy
Saiu Valeria	University of Cagliari, Italy
Salas Agustin	UPCV, Chile
Salvo Giuseppe	University of Palermo, Italy
Sarvia Filippo	University of Torino, Italy
Santaga Francesco	University of Perugia, Italy
Santangelo Michele	CNR-IRPI, Italy
Santini Francesco	University of Perugia, Italy
Santos Rafael	INPE, Brazil
Santucci Valentino	Università per Stranieri di Perugia, Italy
Saponaro Mirko	Polytechnic University of Bari, Italy
Sarker Iqbal	CUET, Bangladesh
Scaioni Marco	Politecnico Milano, Italy
Scorza Francesco	University of Basilicata, Italy
Scotto di Perta Ester	University of Naples, Italy
Sebillo Monica	University of Salerno, Italy
Sharma Meera	Swami Shraddhanand College, India
Shen Jie	University of Michigan, USA
Shou Huahao	Zhejiang University of Technology, China
Siavvas Miltiadis	Centre of Research and Technology Hellas (CERTH), Greece
Silva Carina	ESTeSL-IPL, Portugal
Silva Joao Carlos	Polytechnic Institute of Cavado and Ave, Portugal
Silva Junior Luneque	Universidade Federal do ABC, Brazil
Silva Ângela	Instituto Politécnico de Viana do Castelo, Portugal
Simonetti Marco	University of Florence, Italy
Situm Zeljko	University of Zagreb, Croatia
Skouteris Dimitrios	Master-Up, Italy
Solano Francesco	Università degli Studi della Tuscia, Italy
Somma Maria	University of Naples, Italy
Sonnessa Alberico	Polytechnic University of Bari, Italy
Sousa Lisete	University of Lisbon, Portugal
Sousa Nelson	University of Algarve, Portugal
Spaeth Benjamin	Cardiff University, UK
Srinivsan M.	Navodaya Institute of Technology, India
Stankova Elena	Saint Petersburg State University, Russia
Stratigea Anastasia	National Technical University of Athens, Greece

Šurdonja Sanja	University of Rijeka, Croatia
Sviatov Kirill	Ulyanovsk State Technical University, Russia
Sánchez de Merás Alfredo	Universitat de Valencia, Spain
Takahashi Daisuke	University of Tsukuba, Japan
Tanaka Kazuaki	Kyushu Institute of Technology, Japan
Taniar David	Monash University, Australia
Tapia McClung Rodrigo	Centro de Investigación en Ciencias de Información Geoespacial, Mexico
Tarantino Eufemia	Polytechnic University of Bari, Italy
Tasso Sergio	University of Perugia, Italy
Teixeira Ana Paula	University of Trás-os-Montes and Alto Douro, Portugal
Teixeira Senhorinha	University of Minho, Portugal
Tengku Izhar Tengku Adil	Universiti Teknologi MARA, Malaysia
Teodoro Maria Filomena	University of Lisbon, Portuguese Naval Academy, Portugal
Tesoriere Giovanni	University of Enna KORE, Italy
Thangeda Amarendar Rao	Botho University, Botswana
Tonbul Gokchan	Atilim University, Turkey
Toraldo Emanuele	Polytechnic University of Milan, Italy
Torre Carmelo Maria	Polytechnic University of Bari, Italy
Torrieri Francesca	University of Naples, Italy
Torrisi Vincenza	University of Catania, Italy
Toscano Domenico	University of Naples, Italy
Totaro Vincenzo	Polytechnic University of Bari, Italy
Trigo Antonio	Instituto Politécnico de Coimbra, Portugal
Trunfio Giuseppe A.	University of Sassari, Italy
Trung Pham	HCMUT, Vietnam
Tsoukalas Dimitrios	Centre of Research and Technology Hellas (CERTH), Greece
Tucci Biagio	CNR, Italy
Tucker Simon	Liverpool John Moores University, UK
Tuñon Iñaki	Universidad de Valencia, Spain
Tyagi Amit Kumar	Vellore Institute of Technology, India
Uchibayashi Toshihiro	Kyushu University, Japan
Ueda Takahiro	Seikei University, Japan
Ugliengo Piero	University of Torino, Italy
Valente Ettore	University of Naples, Italy
Vallverdu Jordi	University Autonoma Barcelona, Spain
Vanelslander Thierry	University of Antwerp, Belgium
Vasyunin Dmitry	T-Systems RUS, Russia
Vazart Fanny	University of Grenoble Alpes, France
Vecchiocattivi Franco	University of Perugia, Italy
Vekeman Jelle	Vrije Universiteit Brussel (VUB), Belgium
Verde Rosanna	Università degli Studi della Campania, Italy
Vermaseren Jos	Nikhef, The Netherlands

Vignoli Giulio	University of Cagliari, Italy
Vizzari Marco	University of Perugia, Italy
Vodyaho Alexander	Saint Petersburg State Electrotechnical University, Russia
Vona Marco	University of Basilicata, Italy
Waluyo Agustinus Borgy	Monash University, Australia
Wen Min	Xi'an Jiaotong-Liverpool University, China
Westad Frank	Norwegian University of Science and Technology, Norway
Yuasa Fukuko	KEK, Japan
Yadav Rekha	KL University, India
Yamu Claudia	University of Groningen, The Netherlands
Yao Fenghui	Tennessee State University, USA
Yañez Manuel	Universidad Autónoma de Madrid, Spain
Yoki Karl	Daegu Catholic University, South Korea
Zamperlin Paola	University of Pisa, Italy
Zekeng Ndadji Milliam Maxime	University of Dschang, Cameroon
Žemlička Michal	Charles University, Czech Republic
Zita Sampaio Alcinia	Technical University of Lisbon, Portugal
Živković Ljiljana	Ministry of Construction, Transport and Infrastructure and Institute of Architecture and Urban & Spatial Planning of Serbia, Serbia
Zoppi Corrado	University of Cagliari, Italy
Zucca Marco	Polytechnic University of Milan, Italy
Zullo Francesco	University of L'Aquila, Italy

Contents – Part II

General Track 4: Advanced and Emerging Applications

International Workshop on Advanced Transport Tools and Methods (A2TM 2020)

International Workshop on Advances in Artificial Intelligence Learning Technologies: Blended Learning, STEM, Computational Thinking and Coding (AAILT 2020)

International Workshop on Advancements in Applied Machine Learning and Data Analytics (AAMDA 2020)

International Workshop on Advances in Information Systems and Technologies for Emergency Management, Risk Assessment and Mitigation Based on the Resilience Concepts (ASTER 2020)

International Workshop on Advances in Web Based Learning (AWBL 2020)

General Track 3: Geometric Modeling, Graphics and Visualization

Conditionality of Linear Systems of Equation and Matrices Using Projective Geometric Algebra

Vaclav Skala$^{(\boxtimes)}$ (ID)

University of West Bohemia, Pilsen, Czechia
skala@kiv.zcu.cz
http://www.VaclavSkala.eu

Abstract. Linear systems of equations and their reliable solution is a key part of nearly all computational systems and in a solution of many engineering problems. Mostly, the estimation of the matrix conditionality is used for an assessment of the solvability of linear systems, which are important for interpolation, approximation, and solution of partial differential equations especially for large data sets with large range of values.

In this contribution, a new approach to the matrix conditionality and the solvability of the linear systems of equations is presented. It is based on the application of the *geometric algebra* with the projective space representation using homogeneous coordinates representation. However, the physical floating-point representation, mostly the IEEE 754-219, has to be strictly respected as many algorithms fail due to this.

Keywords: Linear systems of equations · Matrix conditionality · Geometric algebra · Projective space · Duality · Radial basis function · RBF · Partial differential equations · PDE

1 Introduction

Solutions of linear systems of equations are probably one of the most used operations in many applications. Generally, there are two main groups of those:

- non-homogeneous systems of linear equations, i.e. $\mathbf{Ax} = \mathbf{b}$
- homogeneous system of equations, i.e. $\mathbf{Ax} = \mathbf{0}$

Those two groups of linear systems are solved differently, in spite of the fact, that they are dual problems in some sense. Therefore, there should be common methods for solving both groups of such linear systems of equations. The first case is deeply analyzed in the courses of numerical mathematics, while the second one is considered as marginal without advanced solution methods. (In the following, standard properties of the matrices are expected).

Using the *principle of duality* and *projective extension of the Euclidean space* the first type of the linear system, i.e. $\mathbf{Ax} = \mathbf{b}$, can be easily transformed to the second type,

This research was supported by the Czech Science Foundation (GACR) project GA 17-05534S.

O. Gervasi et al. (Eds.): ICCSA 2020, LNCS 12250, pp. 3–17, 2020.
https://doi.org/10.1007/978-3-030-58802-1_1

i.e. $\mathbf{Ax} = \mathbf{0}$. The *geometric algebra* offers more general formalism, which can be used for a better understanding of the linear system of equations properties and behavior.

However, in practical applications, any implementation has to take into consideration the IEEE 754-219 or similar standards of the floating-point physical representation.

1.1   Geometrical Interpretation

Both types of the linear systems of equations, i.e. $\mathbf{Ax} = \mathbf{b}$ and $\mathbf{Ax} = \mathbf{0}$, have a simple geometrical interpretation, which can be easily demonstrated on two simple problems in the E^2 case, see Fig. 1:

– an intersection computation of two lines, i.e. $\mathbf{Ax} = \mathbf{b}$; the matrix $\mathbf{A}$ is $n \times n$
– a line determination given by two points, i.e. $\mathbf{Ax} = \mathbf{0}$; the matrix $\mathbf{A}$ is $n \times (n+1)$

Similarly, in the E^3 case, where three planes intersect in a point or three points define a plane, if no singular cases are considered.

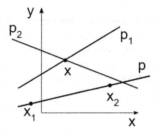

Fig. 1. Examples of "meet" and "union" operations in the E^2 case

Also, the singular or close to the singular case has to be properly solved in both cases. In the first case, if the lines are collinear, in the second one, if two points are the same.

Unfortunately, programmers do not solve such cases correctly in many cases. Usually, a condition like $det(\mathbf{A}) <= eps$ is used for a *"singularity"* detection and *eps* is taken as a "reasonable" small number.

Let us consider the intersection computation of two lines in the E^2 for simplicity. The Cramer's rule can be used and the solution of $\mathbf{Ax} = \mathbf{b}$ is given as $x = Det_x/Det$ and $y = Det_y/Det$. If $Det_x \sim det(\mathbf{A})$ then the x value might be close to 1 regardless of the *eps* value.

As those two problems in Fig. 1 are *dual*, i.e. the *meet* operator in the first case and *union* operator in the second one, the *principle of duality* must be kept [7]. Similarly, in the E^3 case in Fig. 2.

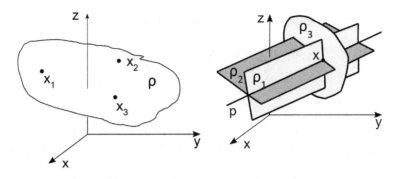

Fig. 2. Examples of "meet" and "union" operations in the E^3 case

1.2 Geometric Algebra

The vector algebra (Gibbs algebra), which is used in engineering practice, uses two basic operations on two vectors $\mathbf{a}, \mathbf{b}$ in E^n:

- the inner product (scalar product or dot product) $c = \mathbf{a} \cdot \mathbf{b}$, where c is a scalar value
- the outer product $\mathbf{c} = \mathbf{a} \wedge \mathbf{b}$ (the cross-product in E^3 $\mathbf{c} = \mathbf{a} \times \mathbf{b}$), where $\mathbf{c}$ is a bivector and has different properties as it represents an oriented area in the n-dimensional space, in general.

The *Geometric Algebra* (GA) uses a "new" product called *geometric product* defined as:

$$\mathbf{ab} = \mathbf{a} \cdot \mathbf{b} + \mathbf{a} \wedge \mathbf{b} \qquad (1)$$

where $\mathbf{ab}$ is the new entity. It should be noted, that it is a "bundle" of objects with different dimensionalities and properties, in general.

In the case of the n-dimensional space, the vectors are defined as $\mathbf{a} = (a_1\mathbf{e}_1 + ... + a_n\mathbf{e}_n)$, $\mathbf{b} = (b_1\mathbf{e}_1 + ... + b_n\mathbf{e}_n)$ and the $\mathbf{e}_i$ vectors form orthonormal vector basis in E^n. In the E^3 case, the following objects can be used if geometric algebra [26]:

1	0-vector (scalar)	$\mathbf{e}_{12}, \mathbf{e}_{23}, \mathbf{e}_{31}$	2-vectors (bivectors)
$\mathbf{e}_1, \mathbf{e}_2, \mathbf{e}_3$,	1-vector (vectors)	$\mathbf{e}_{123}$	3-vector (pseudoscalar)

The significant advantage of the geometric algebra is, that it is more general that than the Gibbs algebra and can handle all objects with dimensionality up to n.

The geometry algebra uses the following operations, including the inverse of a vector.

$$\mathbf{a} \cdot \mathbf{b} = \frac{1}{2}(\mathbf{ab} + \mathbf{ba}) \quad \mathbf{a} \wedge \mathbf{b} = -\mathbf{b} \wedge \mathbf{a} \quad \mathbf{a}^{-1} = \mathbf{a}/||\mathbf{a}||^2 \qquad (2)$$

It should be noted, that geometric algebra is *anti-commutative* and the "pseudoscalar" I in the E^3 case has the basis $\mathbf{e}_1\mathbf{e}_2\mathbf{e}_3$ (briefly as $\mathbf{e}_{123}$), i.e.

$$\mathbf{e}_i\mathbf{e}_j = -\mathbf{e}_j\mathbf{e}_i \quad \mathbf{e}_i\mathbf{e}_i = 1 \quad \mathbf{e}_1\mathbf{e}_2\mathbf{e}_3 = I \quad \mathbf{a} \wedge \mathbf{b} \wedge \mathbf{c} = q \qquad (3)$$

where q is a scalar value (actually a pseudoscalar).

The geometric product of two vectors is represented as:

$$\mathbf{ab} = \sum_{i,j=1}^{n,n} a_i e_i b_j e_j \quad \mathbf{a} \cdot \mathbf{b} = \sum_{i=1}^{n,n} a_i e_i b_i e_i \tag{4}$$

$$\mathbf{a} \wedge \mathbf{b} = \sum_{i,j=1 \& i \neq j}^{n,n} a_i e_i b_j e_j = \sum_{i,j=1, \& i > j}^{n} (a_i b_j - a_j b_i) e_i e_j \tag{5}$$

It is not a "friendly user" notation for a practical application and causes problems in practical implementations, especially due to anti-commutativity of the geometric product.

However, the geometric product can be easily represented by the *tensor product*, which can be easily represented by a matrix. The tensor product for the 4-dimensional case, as the homogeneous coordinates will be used in the following, is represented as:

$$\mathbf{ab} \underset{repr}{\Longleftrightarrow} \mathbf{ab}^T = \mathbf{a} \otimes \mathbf{b} = \mathbf{Q} = \begin{bmatrix} a_1 b_1 & a_1 b_2 & a_1 b_3 & a_1 b_4 \\ a_2 b_1 & a_2 b_2 & a_2 b_3 & a_2 b_4 \\ a_3 b_1 & a_3 b_2 & a_3 b_3 & a_3 b_4 \\ a_4 b_1 & a_4 b_2 & a_4 b_3 & a_4 b_4 \end{bmatrix} = \mathbf{B} + \mathbf{U} + \mathbf{D} \tag{6}$$

where $\mathbf{B} + \mathbf{U} + \mathbf{D}$ are Bottom triangular, Upper triangular, Diagonal matrices, a_4, b_4 will be used for the homogeneous coordinates, i.e. actually w_a, w_b (the projective notation will be explained later), and the operator $\otimes$ means the anti-commutative tensor product.

1.3 Projective Extension of the Euclidean Space

Let us consider the projective extension of the Euclidean space in the E^3 case and use of the homogeneous coordinates. The "hidden" advantage of this is that it enables us to represents points or values close to infinity.

Let us consider a vector $\mathbf{a} = [a_1, a_2, a_3 : a_4]^T, a_4 \neq 0$, which represents actually the vector $(a_1/a_4, a_2/a_4, a_3/a_4)$ in the E^3 space. The ":" symbol within the projective representation is used to distinguish different properties. In the case of a plane, the vector (a_1, a_2, a_3) represents the *"normal vector"* of a plane (actually it is a bivector), while a_4 actually represents a pseudo-distance of a plane from the origin.

Let us consider a second vector $\mathbf{b} = [b_1, b_2, b_3 : b_4]^T, b_4 \neq 0$. It can be seen, that the diagonal of the matrix $\mathbf{Q}$ actually represents the inner product in the projective representation as:

$$[(a_1 b_1 + a_2 b_2 + a_3 b_3) : a_4 b_4]^T \equiv \frac{a_1 b_1 + a_2 b_2 + a_3 b_3}{a_4 b_4} \tag{7}$$

where " $\equiv$ " means projectively equivalent. In the E^3 case, the inner product actually projectively represents the trace $tr(\mathbf{Q})$ of the matrix $\mathbf{Q}$. The outer product (the cross-product in the E^3 case) is then represented respecting the anti-commutativity as:

$$\mathbf{a} \wedge \mathbf{b} \underset{repr}{\Longleftrightarrow} \sum_{i,j=1 \& i > j}^{3,3} (a_i b_j e_i e_j - b_i a_j e_i e_j) = \sum_{i,j \& i > j}^{3,3} (a_i b_j - b_i a_j) e_i e_j \tag{8}$$

It should be noted, that the outer product can be used for a solution of a linear system of equations $\mathbf{Ax} = \mathbf{b}$ or $\mathbf{Ax} = \mathbf{0}$, too.

1.4 Principle of Duality

The principle of duality is an important principle, in general. The duality principle for basic geometric entities and operators is presented by Table 1 and Table 2 [18].

Table 1. Duality of geometric entities

Duality of geometric entities					
Point in E^2	$\underset{\text{DUAL}}{\Longleftrightarrow}$	Line in E^3	Point in E^2	$\underset{\text{DUAL}}{\Longleftrightarrow}$	Plane in E^3

Table 2. Duality of operators

Duality of operators		
Union $\cup$	$\underset{\text{DUAL}}{\Longleftrightarrow}$	Intersection $\cap$

It means, that in the E^2 case a point is dual to a line and vice versa, the intersection of two lines is dual to a union of two points, i.e. line given by two points; similarly for the E^3 case, where a point is dual to a plane [7, 14, 15]. The direct consequence of the principle of duality is that, the intersection point $\mathbf{x}$ of two lines $\mathbf{p}_1, \mathbf{p}_2$, resp. a line $\mathbf{p}$ passing two given points $\mathbf{x}_1, \mathbf{x}_2$, is given as:

$$\mathbf{x} = \mathbf{p}_1 \wedge \mathbf{p}_2 \underset{\text{DUAL}}{\Longleftrightarrow} \mathbf{p} = \mathbf{x}_1 \wedge \mathbf{x}_2 \qquad (9)$$

where $\mathbf{p}_i = [a_i, b_i : c_i]^T$, $\mathbf{x} = [x, y : w]^T$ (w is the homogeneous coordinate), $i = 1, 2$; similarly in the dual case.

In the case of the E^3 space, a point is dual to a plane and vice versa. It means that the intersection point $\mathbf{x}$ of three planes ρ_1, ρ_2, ρ_3, resp. a plane ρ passing three given points $\mathbf{x}_1, \mathbf{x}_2, \mathbf{x}_3$ is given as:

$$\mathbf{x} = \rho_1 \wedge \rho_2 \wedge \rho_3 \underset{\text{DUAL}}{\Longleftrightarrow} \rho = \mathbf{x}_1 \wedge \mathbf{x}_2 \wedge \mathbf{x}_3 \qquad (10)$$

where $\mathbf{x} = [x, y, z : w]^T$, $\rho_i = [a_i, b_i, c_i : d_i]^T$, $i = 1, 2, 3$.

It can be seen that the above formulae is equivalent to the "extended" cross-product, which is natively supported by the GPU architecture. For an intersection computation, we get:

$$\mathbf{x} = \mathbf{p}_1 \wedge \mathbf{p}_2 = \begin{bmatrix} \mathbf{e}_1 & \mathbf{e}_2 & \mathbf{e}_w \\ a_1 & b_1 & c_1 \\ a_2 & b_2 & c_2 \end{bmatrix} \qquad \mathbf{x} = \rho_1 \wedge \rho_2 \wedge \rho_3 = \begin{bmatrix} \mathbf{e}_1 & \mathbf{e}_2 & \mathbf{e}_3 & \mathbf{e}_w \\ a_1 & b_1 & c_1 & d_1 \\ a_2 & b_2 & c_2 & d_2 \\ a_3 & b_3 & c_3 & d_3 \end{bmatrix} \qquad (11)$$

Due to the principle of duality, the dual problem solution is given as:

$$\mathbf{p} = \mathbf{x}_1 \wedge \mathbf{x}_2 = \begin{bmatrix} \mathbf{e}_1 & \mathbf{e}_2 & \mathbf{e}_w \\ x_1 & y_1 & w_1 \\ x_2 & y_2 & w_2 \end{bmatrix} \qquad \rho = \mathbf{x}_1 \wedge \mathbf{x}_2 \wedge \mathbf{x}_3 = \begin{bmatrix} \mathbf{e}_1 & \mathbf{e}_2 & \mathbf{e}_3 & \mathbf{e}_w \\ x_1 & y_1 & z_1 & w_1 \\ x_2 & y_2 & z_2 & w_2 \\ x_3 & y_3 & z_3 & w_3 \end{bmatrix} \qquad (12)$$

The above presented formulae proved the strength of the formal notation of the geometric algebra approach. Therefore, there is a natural question, what is the more convenient computation of the geometric product, as computation with the outer product, i.e. extended cross product, using standard vector algebra approach is not simple.

Fortunately, the geometric product of ρ_1, ρ_2, resp. of $\mathbf{x}_1$ and $\mathbf{x}_2$ vectors using homogeneous coordinates given as the anti-commutative tensor product is given as:

$\rho_1\rho_2$	a_2	b_2	c_2	d_2
a_1	a_1a_2	a_1b_2	a_1c_2	a_1d_2
b_1	b_1a_2	b_1b_2	b_1c_2	b_1d_2
c_1	c_1a_2	c_1b_2	c_1c_2	a_1d_2
d_1	d_1a_2	d_1b_2	d_1c_2	d_1d_2

$\mathbf{x}_1\mathbf{x}_2$	x_2	y_2	z_2	w_2
x_1	x_1x_2	x_1y_2	x_1z_2	x_1w_2
y_1	y_1x_2	y_1y_2	y_1z_2	y_1w_2
z_1	z_1x_2	z_1y_2	z_1z_2	x_1w_2
w_1	w_1x_2	w_1y_2	w_1z_2	w_1w_2

The question is how to compute a line $\mathbf{p} \in E^3$ given as an intersection of two planes ρ_1, ρ_2, which is the dual problem to a line given by two points $\mathbf{x}_1, \mathbf{x}_2$ as those problems are dual. It leads to the Plücker coordinates used especially in robotics [17,21]. Using the geometric algebra, the principle of duality and projective representation, we can directly write:

$$\mathbf{p} = \rho_1 \wedge \rho_2 \quad \underset{\text{DUAL}}{\Longleftrightarrow} \quad \mathbf{p} = \mathbf{x}_1 \wedge \mathbf{x}_2 \qquad (13)$$

It can be seen that the formula given above keeps the duality in the final formulae, too. A more detailed description can be found in [17].

It should be noted that the geometric algebra and the principle of duality offers:

- to solve dual problems by one programming sequence
- it naturally supports parallel programming as it uses vector-vector operations as the SSE instructions or GPU can be used
- the solution can avoid a division operation if the result can be left in the projective representation [24]
- results of operations are in symbolic form, which enables further symbolic processing using vector algebra or geometric algebra rules

2 Solution of Linear Systems of Equations

A solution of a linear system of equations is a part of the linear algebra and used in many computational systems. There are many publications related to methods for a linear system of equations following different criteria:

- memory requirements - linear systems with sparse or tri-diagonal matrices [8], etc.
- algorithm computational complexity [25] using a block decomposition

- parallel processing of large linear systems, especially in connection with GPUs applications [28]
- higher precision of computation and numerical stability [3,24].

It should be noted, that the linear system of equations $\mathbf{Ax} = \mathbf{b}$ can be transformed to the homogeneous system of linear equations, i.e. to the form $\mathbf{D\xi} = \mathbf{0}$, where $\mathbf{D} = [\mathbf{A}|-\mathbf{b}]$, $\xi = [\xi_1, ..., \xi_n : \xi_w]^T$, $x_i = \xi_i / \xi_w$, $i = 1, ..., n$. If $\xi_w \mapsto 0$ then the solution is in infinity and the vector $(\xi_1, ..., \xi_n)$ gives the "direction", only.

As the solution of a linear system of equations is equivalent to the outer product (generalized cross-vector) of vectors formed by rows of the matrix $\mathbf{D}$, the solution of the system $\mathbf{D\xi} = \mathbf{0}$ is defined as:

$$\xi = \mathbf{d}_1 \wedge \mathbf{d}_2 \wedge ... \wedge \mathbf{d}_n \qquad \mathbf{D\xi} = 0, \; i.e. \quad [\mathbf{A}|-\mathbf{b}]\xi = 0 \qquad (14)$$

where: $\mathbf{d}_i$ is the i-th row of the matrix $\mathbf{D}$, i.e. $\mathbf{d}_i = (a_{i1}, ..., a_{in}, -b_i)$, $i = 1, ..., n$

The application of the projective extension of the Euclidean space enables us to transform the non-homogeneous system of linear equations $\mathbf{Ax} = \mathbf{b}$ to the homogeneous linear system $\mathbf{D\xi} = \mathbf{0}$, i.e.:

$$\begin{bmatrix} a_{11} & \cdots & a_{1n} \\ \vdots & \ddots & \vdots \\ a_{n1} & \cdots & a_{nn} \end{bmatrix} \begin{bmatrix} x_1 \\ \vdots \\ x_n \end{bmatrix} = \begin{bmatrix} b_1 \\ \vdots \\ b_n \end{bmatrix} \xleftrightarrow[\text{conversion}]{} \begin{bmatrix} a_{11} & \cdots & a_{1n} & -b_1 \\ \vdots & \ddots & \vdots & \vdots \\ a_{n1} & \cdots & a_{nn} & -b_n \end{bmatrix} \begin{bmatrix} \xi_1 \\ \vdots \\ \xi_n \\ \xi_w \end{bmatrix} = \begin{bmatrix} 0 \\ \vdots \\ 0 \end{bmatrix} \quad (15)$$

It is a very important result as a solution of a linear system of equations is formally the same for both types, i.e. homogeneous linear systems $\mathbf{Ax} = \mathbf{0}$ and non-homogeneous systems $\mathbf{Ax} = \mathbf{b}$. It means, that many problems might be transformed to the outer product application, e.g.. computation of barycentric coordinates [13], length, area, volume og geometric entities [12], etc.

As the solution is formally determined by Eq. 14, formal linear operators can be used for further symbolic processing using standard formula manipulation, as the geometry algebra is multi-linear. Even more, it is capable to handle more complex objects generally in the n-dimensional space, i.e. oriented surfaces, volumes, etc.

Also, it is possible to use the *'functional analysis'* approach: "Let L is a linear operator, then the following operation is valid....". As there are many linear operators like derivation, integration, Laplace transform, etc., there is a huge potential of applications of that to the formal solution of the linear system of equations.

However, it is necessary to respect, that in the case of projective representation specific care is to be taken for deriving the rules for derivation, etc., as actually, a fraction is to be processed.

It should be noted, that a solution is in symbolic representation, too, which can be used for further processing and symbolic manipulation.

3   Matrix and Linear Systems Conditionality

Both types of the linear systems of equations, i.e. $\mathbf{Ax} = \mathbf{b}$ ($\mathbf{A}$ is $n \times n$) and $\mathbf{Ax} = \mathbf{0}$ ($\mathbf{A}$ is $(n+1) \times n$), actually have the same form $\mathbf{Ax} = \mathbf{0}$ ($\mathbf{A}$ is $(n+1) \times n$), now, if the projective representation is used. Therefore, it is possible to show the differences between the matrix conditionality and conditionality (solvability) of a linear system of equations, see Fig. 3.

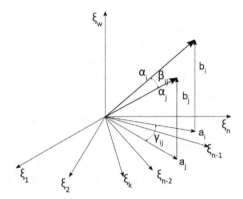

Fig. 3. Difference between matrix and linear system conditionality

For the matrix conditionality, the eigenvalues are usually used [10, 11] and the ratio $rat_\lambda = |\lambda_{max}|/|\lambda_{min}|$ is mostly used as a criterion. It should be noted, that $\lambda \in C$, i.e the eigenvalues are complex, in general. If the ration rat_λ is high, the matrix is said to be ill-conditioned [4,6], especially in the case of large data with a large span of data [22,23]. There are two cases, which are needed to be taken into consideration:

- non-homogeneous systems of linear equations, i.e. $\mathbf{Ax} = \mathbf{b}$. In this case, the matrix conditionality is considered as a criterion for the solvability of the linear system of equations. It depends on the matrix $\mathbf{A}$ properties, i.e. on eigenvalues.

$$\begin{bmatrix} 10^2 & 0 & 0 \\ 0 & 10^0 & 0 \\ 0 & 0 & 10^{-2} \end{bmatrix} \begin{bmatrix} x_1 \\ \vdots \\ x_3 \end{bmatrix} = \begin{bmatrix} b_1 \\ \vdots \\ b_3 \end{bmatrix} \tag{16}$$

A conditionality number $\kappa(\mathbf{A}) = |\lambda_{max}|/|\lambda_{min}|$ is usually used as the solvability criterion. In the case of the Eq. 16, the matrix conditionality is $\kappa(\mathbf{A}) = 10^2/10^{-2} = 10^4$. However, if the 1st row is multiplied by 10^{-2} and the 3rd row is multiplied by 10^2, then the conditionality is $\kappa(\mathbf{A}) = 1$.

Therefore, the estimation of the matrix conditionality using ratio of eigenvalues is not applicable. It should be noted, that the right side vector $\mathbf{b}$ is to be appropriately multiplied.

Classification of possible conditionality evaluation:

- *volumetric* based - as a matrix conditionality the value of $det(\mathbf{A})$ is taken. However, its value is given by a volume of a hyper-polytope (n-dimensional parallelepiped) given by the rows of the matrix $\mathbf{A}$. The "standard" matrix conditionality using eigenvectors is not quite appropriate, as shown above, Eq. 16.
- *area based* - the area of bivectors defined as $||\mathbf{a}_i \wedge \mathbf{a}_j||$. This evaluation was recently used for higher size of the Hilbert matrix is [19, 20]. However, the results were not satisfactory in some cases.
- *angular* - the proposed matrix conditionality, which might be estimated using angles of bivectors formed by the rows i and j of the matrix $\mathbf{A}$. This approach reflects angular relations of all bivectors of the matrix $\mathbf{A}$ or ratios of angles $\gamma_{i,j}$, where $i = 1, ..., n-1, j = k+1, ..., n, i < j$, see Fig. 3. The number of all bivectors is given as $n(n-1)/2$.

It should be noted, that the matrix conditionality does not consider any influence on the values of the vector $\mathbf{b}$ of the system of linear equations $\mathbf{Ax} = \mathbf{b}$. The values of the vector $\mathbf{b}$ might have a significant influence to the solvability of the linear system of equations, see Fig. 3. Also, the values of the vector $\mathbf{b}$ might have a significant influence to the numerical precision.

- a homogeneous system of equations $\mathbf{Ax} = \mathbf{0}$, when the system of linear equations $\mathbf{Ax} = \mathbf{b}$ is expressed in the projective space. In this case, the vector $\mathbf{b}$ is taken into account and bivector area and bivector angles properties can be used for solvability evaluation. The standard *volumetric* evaluation cannot be used, as the matrix $\mathbf{A}$ is not a square matrix.

4   Basic Operations with Matrices

For a solution of a linear system of equations some specific operations are used, e.g.. row multiplication by a non-zero constant, which does not have any influence to the result correctness. Let us have a look at such operations more deeply. The basic operations can be split into two types:

- *row multiplication* by a constant $p \neq 0$. It changes the row values, but does not change the result of the linear system $\mathbf{Ax} = \mathbf{0}$, resp. $\mathbf{Ax} = \mathbf{b}$, if the vector $\mathbf{b}$ is multiplied appropriately.
- *column multiplication* - by a constant $s \neq 0$. This operation is not usually mentioned in numerical methods. It means, that there is a scaling of the relevant element of the vector $\mathbf{x}$ of the system $\mathbf{Ax} = \mathbf{0}$, resp. $\mathbf{Ax} = \mathbf{b}$.

It means, that those two main operations with both linear system of equations $\mathbf{Ax} = \mathbf{0}$, resp. $\mathbf{Ax} = \mathbf{b}$ can be described as

$$\mathbf{PAS\,S}^{-1}\mathbf{x} = \mathbf{0}, \quad \mathbf{Ax} = \mathbf{0}, \quad \mathbf{A} \; n \times (n+1) \tag{17}$$

resp.

$$\mathbf{PAS\,S}^{-1}\mathbf{x} = \mathbf{Pb}, \quad \mathbf{Ax} = \mathbf{b}, \quad \mathbf{A} \; n \times n \tag{18}$$

where: $\mathbf{P}$, resp. $\mathbf{S}$ are diagonal matrices with $p_i \neq 0$, $s_j \neq 0$ multiplicative constants. The matrix $\mathbf{S}$ represents an-isotropic scaling of the size $(n+1) \times (n+1)$ in the first case, resp. $n \times n$ in the second one. It should be noted, that the diagonal matrix $\mathbf{P}$ does not have any influence on the result, due to the projective representation, and because $\mathbf{S}\,\mathbf{S}^{-1}$ is the identity matrix the solution of the linear system of equations is correct in both cases.

It can be easily proved that both operations *do have* an influence on eigenvalues and therefore $\kappa(\mathbf{A}) = |\lambda_{max}|/|\lambda_{min}|$ cannot be used for assessment of the solvability of the linear system of equations. For the same reasons, also the assessment based of the area on bivectors cannot be used.

4.1 Angular Criterion

The only *angular* criterion is invariant to the row multiplications, while only the column multiplication changes angles of the bivectors. There are several significant consequences for the numerical solution of linear systems of equations:

- the solvability of a linear system of equations can be improved by the column multiplications, only, if unlimited precision is considered. Therefore, the matrix-based pre-conditioners might not solve the solvability problems and might introduce additional numerical problems.
- the precision of computation is significantly influenced by addition and subtraction operations, as the exponents must be the same for those operations with mantissa. Also, the multiplication and division operations using exponent change by $2^{\pm k}$ should be preferred.

However, the question is, whether the above presented operations cannot be efficiently used for better numerical stability of numerical solutions. In the matrix operations, it is necessary to respect the floating-point representation [27] as it is a crucial factor in the solution of large or ill-conditioned linear systems of equations.

5 Preconditioning

There are several methods used to improve the ratio $\kappa(\mathbf{A}) = |\lambda_{max}|/|\lambda_{min}|$ of the matrix $\mathbf{A}$ of the linear system, e.g.. matrix eigenvalues shifting or preconditioning [1,2]. The preconditioning is usually based on solving a linear system $\mathbf{A}\mathbf{x} = \mathbf{0}$:

$$\mathbf{M}^{-1}\mathbf{A}\mathbf{x} = \mathbf{M}^{-1}\mathbf{b} \tag{19}$$

where $\mathbf{M}^{-1}$ is a matrix, which can cover complicated computation, including Fourier transform. The inverse operation, i.e. $\mathbf{M}^{-1}$, is computationally very expensive as it is of $O(n^3)$ complexity. Therefore, they are not easily applicable for large systems of linear equations used nowadays. There are some methods based on incomplete factorization, etc., which might be used [11].

5.1 Simplified Preconditioning - A Proposed Approach

The proposed matrix conditionality improvement method requires only determination of the diagonal matrices values $\mathbf{P}$ and $\mathbf{S}$, i.e. multiplicative coefficients $p_i \neq 0$, $s_j \neq 0$, which have to be optimized. This is a significant reduction of computational complexity, as it decreases the cost of finding sub-optimal p_i, s_j values.

The proposed approach was tested on the Hilbert's matrix, which is extremely ill-conditioned. The Hilbert matrix conditionality can be estimated as [5,9].

$$\kappa(\mathbf{H_n}) \simeq e^{3.5n} \tag{20}$$

where n is the size of the Hilbert matrix; for $n = 10$ the conditionality is estimated as $\kappa(\mathbf{H_n}) \simeq 1.568 10^{15}$.

The Hilbert matrix $\mathbf{H}$ defined as:

$$h_{i,j} = \frac{1}{i+j-1} \tag{21}$$

where: $i, j = 1, ...n$.

The experimental results of the original conditionality $\kappa(\mathbf{H}_{orig})$ and conditionality using the proposed method $\kappa(\mathbf{H}_{new})$ are presented in Table 3.

5.2 Preliminary Experimental Results

To prove the proposed approach, the Hilbert matrix was taken, as it is ill-conditioned. The conditionality of the matrix $\mathbf{H}_{orig}$, modified by diagonal matrices $\mathbf{P}$ and $\mathbf{S}$, was evaluated by the $cond(matrix)$ function in the Octave system using the simplified Monte Carlo approach.

Table 3. Conditionality of modified the Hilbert matrix: Experimental results (*with Octave warnings)

N	cond($\mathbf{H}_{orig}$)	cond($\mathbf{H}_{new}$)	N	cond($\mathbf{H}_{orig}$)	cond($\mathbf{H}_{new}$)
3	5.2406e+02	2.5523e+02	7	4.7537e+08	1.4341e+08
4	1.5514e+04	6.0076e+03	8	1.5258e+10	6.0076e+03
5	4.7661e+05	1.6099e+05	9	4.9315e+11	1.3736e+11
6	1.4951e+07	5.0947e+06	10	1.6024e+13	4.1485e+12
			20	1.6024e+13*	4.1485e+12

The experiments proved, that the conditionality cond($\mathbf{H}_{new}$) of the modified matrix using the proposed approach was decreased by more than half of the magnitude for higher values of n, see Table 3. This is consistent with the recently obtained results [16], where the inverse Hilbert matrix computation using the modified Gauss elimination without division operation was analyzed.

The Hilbert matrix conditionality improvement also improved the angular criterion based on maximizing the ratio $\kappa_{rat}(\mathbf{H})$ defined as:

$$\kappa_{rat}(\mathbf{H}) = \frac{\cos \gamma_{min}}{\cos \gamma_{max}} \tag{22}$$

It says, how the angles $\cos \gamma_{ij}$, formed by the vectors $\mathbf{a}_{ij}$ of the bivectors are similar, see Fig. 3. It means, that if the ratio $\kappa_{rat}(\mathbf{A}) \simeq 1$ the angles of all bivectors are nearly equal. In the case of conditionality assessment of the linear system of equations $\mathbf{Ax} = \mathbf{0}$, the angles β_{ij}, formed by the angels α_{ij} have to be taken into account, see Fig. 3. The ratio $\kappa_{rat}(\mathbf{H})$ is then defined as:

$$\kappa_{rat}(\mathbf{H}) = \frac{\cos \beta_{min}}{\cos \beta_{max}} \tag{23}$$

The advantage of the angular criterion is that it is common for the conditionality evaluation in the cases, i.e.:

– the matrix conditionality
– conditionality of the linear system of equations

It should be noted, that this conditionality assessment method gives different values of conditionality of those two different cases, as in the first case only the matrix is evaluated, while in the second one the value of the $\mathbf{b}$ in the $\mathbf{Ax} = \mathbf{b}$ is taken into account.

Table 4. Conditionality of modified the Hilbert matrix: Experimental results (*with Octave warnings)

N	3	4	5	6	7
$\kappa_{rat}(\mathbf{H}_{orig})$	0.54464	0.39282	0.31451	0.26573	0.23195
$\kappa_{rat}(\mathbf{H}_{new})$	0.98348	0.97740	0.98173	0.96283	0.87961

N	8	9	10		20
$\kappa_{rat}(\mathbf{H}_{orig})$	0.20694	0.18755	0.17199	$\cdots$	0.09917*
$\kappa_{rat}(\mathbf{H}_{new})$	0.92500	0.96435	0.96322	$\cdots$	0.74701*

The results presented in Table 4 reflects the improvement of the Hilbert matrix by proposed approach using the diagonal matrices $\mathbf{P}$ and $\mathbf{S}$ used as the multipliers.

6   Conclusion

This contribution briefly presents a new approach to the matrix conditionality and the solvability of linear systems of equations assessment, based on the bivectors angular properties based on geometry algebra. The presented approach enables to make conditionality assessment for both types of linear equations, i.e. $\mathbf{Ax} = \mathbf{b}$ and $\mathbf{Ax} = \mathbf{0}$.

Also, the equivalence of the solution of linear systems of equations with the application of the outer product (extended cross product) has been presented. It offers simple and efficient solutions to many computational problems, if combined with the principle of duality and projective notation. Also, the presented approach supports direct GPU application with a potential of significant speed-up and parallelism. Even more, the approach is applicable to n-dimensional problem solutions, as the geometric algebra is multidimensional.

In the future, the proposed approach will be more deeply analyzed and experimentally verified using numerical operations with values restricted to 2^k as in this case the mantissa value is not changed. The expected application is in the radial basis function interpolation and approximation for large data, when matrices are ill-conditioned, and in the solution of partial differential equations.

Acknowledgment. The author would like to thank their colleagues and students at the University of West Bohemia, Plzen, for their discussions and suggestions and implementations, especially to Michal Smolik and Martin Cervenka for discussions and help with the Octave implementation, to Filip Hacha, Vitek Poor and Jan Kasak for additional verification of some parts in the Octave system. Thanks belong also to anonymous reviewers for their valuable comments and hints provided. This research was supported by the Czech Science Foundation (GACR) No. GA 17-05534S.

Appendix A

Computation of a bivector area in the n-dimensional space can be made as follows:

$$cos(\alpha_{ij}) = \frac{\mathbf{a}_i.\mathbf{a}_j}{||\mathbf{a}_i||\,||\mathbf{a}_j||} \qquad\qquad sin(\alpha_{ij}) = \frac{||\mathbf{a}_i \wedge \mathbf{a}_j||}{||\mathbf{a}_i||\,||\mathbf{a}_j||} \qquad (1)$$

Therefore the square of the bivector area is given as

$$||\mathbf{a}_i \wedge \mathbf{a}_j||^2 = ||\mathbf{a}_i||^2||\mathbf{a}_j||^2 sin^2(\alpha_{ij}) \qquad (2)$$

As the following identity is valid

$$sin^2(\alpha_{ij}) = 1 - cos^2(\alpha_{ij}) \qquad (3)$$

then it can be expressed as

$$||\mathbf{a}_i \wedge \mathbf{a}_j||^2 = ||\mathbf{a}_i||^2||\mathbf{a}_j||^2(1 - cos^2(\alpha_{ij})) \qquad (4)$$

by a substitution of Eq. 1

$$||\mathbf{a}_i \wedge \mathbf{a}_j||^2 = ||\mathbf{a}_i||^2||\mathbf{a}_j||^2(1 - \frac{(\mathbf{a}_i \cdot \mathbf{a}_j)^2}{||\mathbf{a}_i||^2\,||\mathbf{a}_j||^2}) \qquad (5)$$

and algebraic manipulation

$$||\mathbf{a}_i \wedge \mathbf{a}_j||^2 = ||\mathbf{a}_i||^2||\mathbf{a}_j||^2(\frac{||\mathbf{a}_i||^2 \cdot ||\mathbf{a}_j||^2 - (\mathbf{a}_i \cdot \mathbf{a}_j)^2}{||\mathbf{a}_i||^2||\mathbf{a}_j||^2}) \qquad (6)$$

i.e.

$$||\mathbf{a}_i \wedge \mathbf{a}_j||^2 = ||\mathbf{a}_i||^2||\mathbf{a}_j||^2 \frac{||\mathbf{a}_i||^2||\mathbf{a}_j||^2 - (\mathbf{a}_i \cdot \mathbf{a}_j)^2}{||\mathbf{a}_i||^2||\mathbf{a}_j||^2} \qquad (7)$$

Now, reduction can be used

$$||\mathbf{a}_i \wedge \mathbf{a}_j||^2 = ||\mathbf{a}_i||^2 ||\mathbf{a}_j||^2 - (\mathbf{a}_i \cdot \mathbf{a}_j)^2 \tag{8}$$

and finally the square of the area of a bivector is given as:

$$||\mathbf{a}_i \wedge \mathbf{a}_j|| = \sqrt{(||\mathbf{a}_i||^2 ||\mathbf{a}_j||^2 - (\mathbf{a}_i \cdot \mathbf{a}_j)^2)} \tag{9}$$

References

1. Benzi, M.: Preconditioning techniques for large linear systems: a survey. J. Comput. Phys. **182**(2), 418–477 (2002)
2. Chen, K.: Matrix Preconditioning Techniques and Applications. Cambridge Monographs on Applied and Computational Mathematics. Cambridge University Press, New York (2005)
3. Ferronato, M.: Preconditioning for sparse linear systems at the dawn of the 21st century: history, current developments, and future perspectives. ISRN Appl. Math. **4**(ID 127647), 1–49 (2012). An optional note
4. George, A., Ikramov, K.: The conditionally and expected error of two methods of computing the pseudo-eigenvalues of a complex matrix. Comput. Math. Math. Phys. **35**(11), 1403–1408 (1995)
5. Higham, N.J.: Accuracy and Stability of Numerical Algorithms, 3rd edn. SIAM (1961)
6. Ikramov, K., Chugunov, V.: On the conditionality of eigenvalues close to the boundary of the numerical range of a matrix. Doklady Math. **57**(2), 201–202 (1998)
7. Johnson, M.: Proof by duality: or the discovery of "new" theorems. Math. Today **1**(6), 201–213 (1996). An optional note
8. Majdisova, Z., Skala, V.: Big geodata surface approximation using radial basis functions: a comparative study. Comput. Geosci. **109**, 51–58 (2017)
9. Quaerteroni, A., Saleri, F., Gervasio, P.: Scientific Computing with MATLAB and Octave, 3rd edn. Springer, Heidelberg (2010). https://doi.org/10.1007/978-3-642-12430-3
10. Saad, Y.: Iterative Methods for Sparse Linear Systems, 2nd edn. SIAM (2011)
11. Saad, Y.: Numerical problems for Large Eigenvalue Problems, 2nd edn. SIAM (2011)
12. Skala, V.: Length, area and volume computation in homogeneous coordinates. Int. J. Image Graph. **6**(4), 625–639 (2006)
13. Skala, V.: Barycentric coordinates computation in homogeneous coordinates. Comput. Graph. (Pergamon) **32**(1), 120–127 (2008)
14. Skala, V.: Intersection computation in projective space using homogeneous coordinates. Int. J. Image Graph. **8**(4), 615–628 (2008)
15. Skala, V.: Duality, barycentric coordinates and intersection computation in projective space with GPU support. WSEAS Trans. Math. **9**(6), 407–416 (2010)
16. Skala, V.: Modified Gaussian elimination without division operations. In: ICNAAM 2013 Proceedings, AIP Conference Proceedings, vol. 1558, pp. 1936–1939. AIP (2013)
17. Skala, V.: Plücker Coordinates and Extended Cross Product for Robust and Fast Intersection Computation, pp. 57–60 (2016)
18. Skala, V.: "Extended cross-product" and solution of a linear system of equations. Lect. Not. Comput. Sci. **9786**, 18–35 (2016)
19. Skala, V.: High dimensional and large span data least square error: numerical stability and conditionality. Int. J. Appl. Phys. Math. **7**(3), 148–156 (2017)
20. Skala, V.: Least square method robustness of computations: what is not usually considered and taught. FedCSIS **2017**, 537–541 (2017)

21. Skala, V.: Projective Geometry, Duality and Plücker Coordinates for Geometric Computations with Determinants on GPUs, vol. 1863 (2017)
22. Skala, V.: RBF Interpolation with CSRBF of Large Data Sets, vol. 108, pp. 2433–2437 (2017)
23. Skala, V.: RBF Approximation of Big Data Sets with Large Span of Data, vol. 2018-January, pp. 212–218 (2018)
24. Skala, V., Ondracka, V.: A Precision of Computation in the Projective Space, pp. 35–40 (2011)
25. Strassen, V.: Gaussian elimination is not optimal. Numerische Mathematik **13**(4), 354–356 (1969)
26. Vince, J.: Geometric Algebra for Computer Graphics. Springer, London (2008). https://doi.org/10.1007/978-1-84628-997-2
27. |WEB: IEEE 754–2019 - IEEE standard for floating-point arithmetic (2019)
28. Yamazaki, I., Ida, A., Yokota, R., Dongarra, J.: Distributed-memory lattice h-matrix factorization. Int. J. High Perform. Comput. Appl. **33**(5), 1046–1063 (2019)

Research on the Input Methods of Cardboard

Zhiyi Ma[1,2(✉)], Hongjie Chen[1,2], Yanwei Bai[1,2], and Ye Qiu[1,2]

[1] School of Electronics Engineering and Computer Science, Peking University,
Beijing 100871, China
{mazhiyi, chen.hj, byw, qiuye2014}@pku.edu.cn
[2] Key Laboratory of High Confidence Software Technologies, Peking
University, Beijing 100871, China

Abstract. Virtual Reality (VR) is a new technology developed in the 20th century and the demands for VR from all walks of life are increasing, and Cardboard plays an important role in the demands. Facing the current situation that the existing Cardboard input methods cannot meet the actual needs well, aiming at the four typical input methods of Cardboard: buttons, gaze, voice and gestures, the paper conducts an experiment on typical object selection tasks and analyzes the experimental results in the sparse distribution, dense distribution, and sheltered dense distribution. The research results have important practical value for the design and development of the input of Cardboard based applications.

Keywords: Cardboard · Input method · Virtual Reality

1 Introduction

Virtual reality is characterized by immersion, which means that users feel like they are there. In virtual reality applications, output devices and input devices are necessarily. For output devices, displays are the most core parts of virtual reality applications; for input devices, the usual mouses and keyboards have become almost unusable. For this problem, the researchers have proposed many solutions.

Google introduces the concept of Cardboard VR in 2014, and soon afterwards, Cardboard becomes a very cheap head-mounted virtual reality device that can be used with most smartphones. Because of its versatility, this paper chooses it as the support tool for building VR applications. Although Cardboard has the advantages of low price and wide applicability, the disadvantages are also prominent. Because Cardboard's built-in input method uses only one button, the interaction of users with it is very limited. Most Cardboard-based VR applications only provide the viewing function [1], and it is difficult to have further interaction, and therefore the experience of users with it much worse than that of using traditional virtual reality devices.

Although there are currently some studies trying to provide new input methods for Cardboard or compare performance indicators of the existing input methods, these studies all have their own shortcomings. Some studies focus on the design of input methods and lacks research on user feedback [2–4], and others only compare time and accuracy of several input methods in simpler object selection tasks [5, 6].

© Springer Nature Switzerland AG 2020
O. Gervasi et al. (Eds.): ICCSA 2020, LNCS 12250, pp. 18–29, 2020.
https://doi.org/10.1007/978-3-030-58802-1_2

Aiming at the lack of Cardboard input methods and the deficiencies of related researches, the paper conducts an experiment to study the variables related to input methods based on the research [7].

2   Related Work

The researches on Cardboard input methods can be divided into two categories: new interaction of Cardboard, and empirical researches on existing interaction.

2.1   Design of Cardboard Input Methods

Among all the input methods of Cardboard, in addition to the built-in key input, the most popular and successful input method is gaze [2]. Its input process is that a user first uses the focus ray to find an object to be interacted with, then a timer called as a gaze ring appears at this time, and finally the selection operation is triggered when the gaze ring is filled. This method brings convenience for input, but also has some disadvantages. For examples, using the countdown method to let the user choose whether to input or not, it will cause a certain degree of tension, which will reduce the user experience; the user may be mistakenly input due to unfamiliar how to use it or inattention, and it is easy to maintain their concentration so as to fatigue; in virtual reality with high density of objects, frequent appearance of gaze rings will also affect the user's operations; the countdown delays the user's input process, causing unnecessary waits, and it is also difficult to fix the specific delays.

Majed, A.Z. et al. proposed a Cardboard input method, PAWdio [3], which tracks the relative positions of two earbuds for input. Compared with ordinary key input, PAWdio allows users to have a stronger sense of immersion with better accuracy and efficiency. However, this method has only one degree of freedom in operation, and is still affected by the arm span and the length of the headphone cable when in use. In addition, the operation is very different from the ways people operate in the real world.

Based on RGB cameras, Akira, I. et al. proposed an input method [4], which uses the camera in a smart phone for tracking a thumb. When the thumb is raised, the cursor movement in the virtual reality can be controlled by the thumb, and the selection is made when the thumb is pressed. The authors research the method on an object selection task and find that the method has better accuracy and efficiency when the object is larger, but the error rate increases significantly when the object is smaller. The advantage of this method is that gesture input can be completed without using an additional input device, and it works well in some specific scenarios. However, because the control is performed only through a thumb, the input is still limited to the simulation of clicks, and more complex information cannot be input.

Pfeuffer, K. et al. discuss the effect of the object distribution density on user input in gaze mode [8], and the paper takes the object distribution density as a control variable together with more input methods.

2.2 Comparison of Cardboard Input Methods

Tanriverdi,V. et al. study the performance of using focus rays and an arm-extended gripping tool on object selection tasks, and find that using focus rays has an efficiency advantage [5]. Cournia, N. et al. compare the efficiency of using focus rays with the use of handheld controllers in object selection tasks, and find that the use of controllers is more efficient when selecting long-range targets [6]. These efforts focus on the comparison between focus rays and virtual hands, but ignores the comparison between buttons and gaze, which are two most common input methods. In addition, the tasks do not consider the influence of factors such as the distribution density of objects and the shapes of objects on the users' selection of input methods.

Ganapathi, P. et al. first compare buttons and gaze in the different dense distributions of objects, and obtain the following conclusions: the needed time and error rate of gaze input are significantly higher than that of button input in the sheltered dense distribution; in the sparse distributions, users with gaze are more comfortable; in the sheltered dense distributions, button is easier to use. Taken together, they believe that gaze should be used in the sparse distribution and buttons should be used in dense or sheltered dense distributions [7]. Their research is limited to the traditional two input methods, lacking a comparison of other input methods that do not use additional controllers. In addition, their research is limited to square-shaped objects and lacks analysis of other shapes of objects.

3 Experimental Design

3.1 Subjects

There are 20 subjects in this experiment, all of them are undergraduates, and they have no obstacles in using Cardboard's key input and gesture input, etc.

3.2 Experimental Equipment

Two devices used in the experiment are a Cardboard[1] and an Honor 8 smartphone. The main performance parameters of the phone are as follows: the screen size is 5.2 in., the resolution is 1920 * 1080, the operating system is Android 8.0, the processor is Kirin 950, and the storage is 4G RAM and 64G ROM.

3.3 The Experimental Environment

The experimental tool for recording data is developed with Unity 2017.4[2] and Google VR SDK For Unity 1.4[3] [9]. Some changes ARE made based on the work [7].

---

[1] This device uses engineering plastics as the main structure and is functionally no different from a traditional Cardboard.

[2] https://unity3d.com/cn.

[3] https://developers.google.cn/vr/develop/unity/.

The whole experiment consists of two parts, the first part is training and the second part is testing. The training is relatively simple for subjects to familiarize four different input methods.

The test is used to collect experimental data and is complicated. It mainly includes 6 different scenarios, which are composed of squares or ellipsoids in the sparse distribution, dense distribution, or sheltered dense distribution, respectively, see Fig. 1.

The objects in each scenario are divided into two parts, the shape parameters of the two groups of objects on the upper side are the same, and the shape parameters of the group of objects on the lower side are different from those on the upper side. In the sparse distribution and dense distribution, the color of the objects is black and white; in the sheltered dense distribution, the color of the shelters is red, and the other colors are the same. All objects are located on the same plane in a scenario, 47 m from the camera (the default distance unit in Unity, the same below), the two groups of objects on the upper side are 62 m from the ground, and the objects on the lower side are 47 m from the ground. In addition, the relative squares and ellipsoids in the scenarios have the same positions on the three coordinate axes.

3.4   Experimental Task

Focusing on four typical input methods of Cardboard: buttons, gaze, voice and gestures in the sparse distribution, dense distribution, and sheltered dense distribution of objects (balls and cubes), the paper analyzes whether there are significant differences in the following indicators:

- the number of user errors?
- the user time to complete the tasks?
- the user convenience?
- the user satisfaction?

In the above analyses, if there are differences, it is necessary to analyze the impact of the variables.

- What input methods do users prefer?

Among them, user time to complete the tasks and the number of user errors are automatically calculated by our experimental tool [9]; user convenience, user satisfaction, and user preference are obtained by filling in questionnaires after the experiment, and the questions are designed with the 5-point semantic differentiation scale method.

3.5   Design of Experimental Input Methods

The Cardboard input methods involve in the paper include buttons, gaze, voice and gestures. The button input is Cardboard's own function, and is completed by clicking the button on the right of Cardboard to simulate a click on the smartphone screen; gaze input is to fill the gaze ring that appears after the focus ray collides with the target to confirm the user's selection intention, and the system automatically completes the selection when the gaze ring is filled. These two input methods are more common and

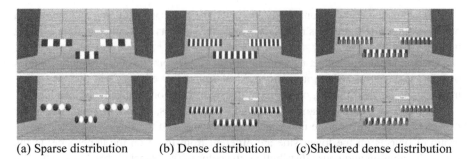

(a) Sparse distribution   (b) Dense distribution   (c)Sheltered dense distribution

Fig. 1. Three distributions of two kinds of objects

will not be described in the paper. The following mainly focuses on voice input and gesture input.

In virtual reality, voice inputs are mainly divided into two categories. One is to simply trigger the corresponding operation by keywords; another is to perform the corresponding operation after semantic analysis of the speech, and the analysis is relatively more complicated. In order to compare with the traditional input methods, the paper uses a combination of focus rays and voice input to select objects. Specifically, the selection process is to find the object to be selected with the focus ray, and then say the command "Pick" to complete the selection. The command word detection uses the voice wake-up function in the voice SDK provided by iFlytek[4].

As far as we know, on the Cardboard platform, there is no related work on analyzing the performance and user feedback of object selection tasks in the different dense distributions of objects, combined gesture input based on RGB cameras with traditional input methods. In order to study this problem, the paper designs and implements an input method combining focus rays with gesture recognition based on RGB cameras. The application process is to first find the object to be interacted with the focus ray, and then make a corresponding gesture to select the object (or execute the instruction bound to the gesture).

Based on typical gesture recognition algorithms and our simple experiment, we design a gesture recognition algorithm and implements it using Opencv For Unity[5]. The algorithm has a good recognition effect in the experiment, and there is no sense of delay at a frame rate of 30 frames/s [9].

4   Experimental Results and Analysis

In the following experiment, in order to further explore the relationship between the indicators in Sect. 3.4 and the effect variables, the paper uses a two-factor analysis of variance with a significance level of 0.05 to compare whether the difference in each

---

[4] https://www.xfyun.cn/.

[5] https://assetstore.unity.com/packages/tools/integration/opencv-for-unity-21088.

indicator is statistically significant when selecting different shapes of objects with different input methods in the different dense distributions of objects.

4.1   Number of Errors

The selection error refers to that the object selected by the user does not match the target. The mean of the number of errors is shown in Fig. 2.

It can be intuitively seen from the Fig. 2 that the average number of errors of gestures and gaze is more, and the average number of errors of buttons and voice is less.

In three distributions,

1) The interaction of input methods and shapes is not significant. Their F and P values, respectively, are (F (3, 152) = 2.586, P > 0.05), (F (3,152) = 0.792, P > 0.05), and (F (3,152) = 0.795, P > 0.05).
2) The main effects of the input methods are significant. Their F and P values, respectively, are (F (3,152) = 9.929, P < 0.05), (F (3, 152) = 15.851, P < 0.05), and (F (3, 152) = 6.575, P < 0.05), and this indicates that there is a significant difference in the number of errors in different input methods in the dense distribution. Turkey's post hoc tests show that the number of gesture input errors is significantly higher than the other three input methods. In addition, there are no significant differences between the other input methods.

When the objects are sparsely distributed, the main effect of the object shapes is also significant (F (1,152) = 9.571, P < 0.05). According to its mean values, it can be seen that the number of errors when selecting ellipsoids is significantly smaller than the number of errors when selecting blocks. The main effect of object shapes is not significant when the objects are densely distributed and sheltered densely distributed ((F (1,152) = 0.090, P > 0.05), (F (1,152) = 0.429, P > 0.05)).

There are two usual reasons of errors. One is that the user may inadvertently move the cursor over a non-target object and the selection is triggered automatically after staying because of the user's inattention, which is often found in gaze input method. Another reason for an error is mainly caused by the "Heisenberg effect". For example, when the user uses gesture input to focus on the gesture, and ignore the cursor has moved to the wrong target, resulting in wrong selection.

4.2   Time to Complete the Tasks

The time to complete the task refers to the time from the start of countdown to the user's correct choice in a scenario. The longer it takes, the less convenient it is for the user to use the input method. The data distribution of the average time to complete the tasks is shown in Fig. 3.

As can be seen from the Fig. 3, the time to complete the tasks gradually rises in the sparse, dense, and sheltered dense distributions. In terms of each denseness, the time required for gesture input is the longest, and the gap between the other three input methods is not large.

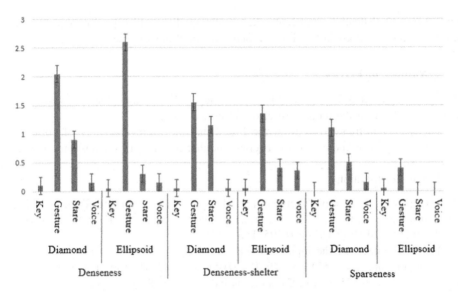

Fig. 2. Average number of errors

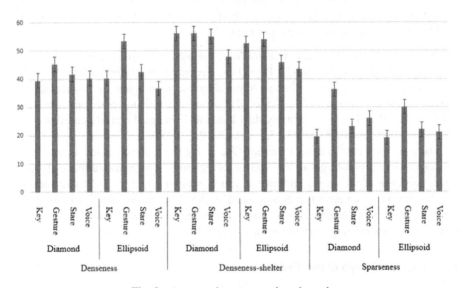

Fig. 3. Average time to complete the tasks

In terms of the interaction between the input methods and the shapes of the objects, the analysis of variance shows that the interactions in the three distributions are not significant, and their F and P values, respectively, are (F (3, 152) = 2.082, P > 0.05), (F (3, 152) = 0.988, P > 0.05), and (F (3, 152) = 0.226, P > 0.05).

For input methods, when the objects are sparsely distributed and the objects are densely distributed, the main effects of the input methods are significant, and their F and P values, respectively, are (F (3,152) = 35.781, P < 0.05), and (F (3,152) = 3.914, P < 0.05). This indicates that the time to complete the task of different input methods are significant differences, and Turkey's post hoc multiple tests also show that gesture input takes significantly longer to complete the task than the other three input methods. The main effect of input methods is not significant in the sheltered dense distribution (F (3,152) = 1.783, P > 0.05).

For object shapes in the sparse distribution, the main effect of them is significant (F (1,152) = 9.836, P < 0.05). According to their means, it can be found that the time for selecting an ellipsoid is significantly less than the time for selecting a block; when the objects are densely distributed and sheltered densely distributed, the main effect of the object shapes is not significant, and their F and P values are (F (1,152) = 0.386, P > 0.05) and (F (1,152) = 2.247, P > 0.05), respectively.

4.3   Comfort

Comfort refers to whether the user will feel uncomfortable when using a specific input method to make a selection, such as feeling tired when using button or gesture input, feeling nervousness when using gaze input, and feeling awkward when using voice input. After the experiment, comfort information was collected by filling in a questionnaire, which related questions are designed using a 5-point semantic differentiation scale (a score of 0 indicates uncomfortable and a score of 5 indicates very comfortable). The average comfort of various input methods is shown in Fig. 4.

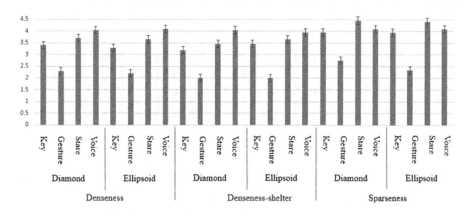

Fig. 4. Average comfort

It can be seen from Fig. 4 that users using gaze input in the sparse distribution have the highest comfort level, and voice input comfort is higher in the other two density distributions. In addition, there is a small difference in comfort when selecting different objects.

In three distributions, the analysis of variance shows that the interaction between the input methods and the shapes of the objects is not significant. Their F and P values, respectively, are (F (3, 152) = 0.431, P > 0.05), (F (3, 152) = 0.069, P > 0.05), and (F (3, 152) = 0.228, P > 0.05).

For input methods, in three distributions, the main effects of them are significant. Their F and P values, respectively, are (F (3,152) = 31.705, P < 0.05), (F (3,152) = 33.943, P < 0.05), and (F (3,152) = 24.746, P < 0.05). This indicates that there are significant differences in the time required to complete the tasks with different input methods. Turkey's post hoc multiple tests also show that the user comfort of gesture input is significantly lower than that of the other three inputs, the comfort of button input is significantly lower than that of voice input, and there is no significant difference between the other input method pairs.

For object shapes, the main effects of object shapes are not significant in three distributions, and their F and P values, respectively, are (F (1,152) = 0.585, P > 0.05), (F (1,152) = 0.138, P > 0.05), and (F (1,152) = 0.256, P > 0.05).

4.4   Convenience

Convenience refers to whether the user is convenient when making a selection using a specific input method. For example, both button input and gesture input require the user to move his hand, gesture input also requires the user to focus on both the hand and the target to be selected, gaze input requires the user to locate quickly when moving on the object, and voice input has certain requirements for the user's command word pronunciation. After the experiment, convenience information was collected by filling in a questionnaire, which related questions are designed using a 5-point semantic differentiation scale (a score of 0 indicates inconvenience and a score of 5 indicates convenience). The average convenience of various input methods is shown in Fig. 5.

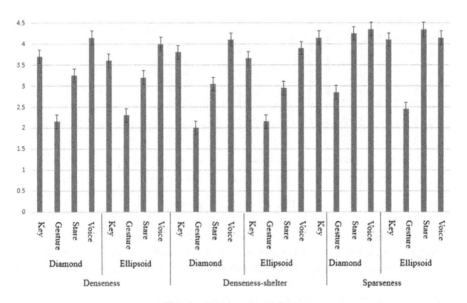

Fig. 5. Average convenience

It can be seen from Fig. 5 that the convenience of gesture input is the lowest, gaze input is the most convenient when the objects are sparsely distributed, and the convenience of voice input is more convenient in other two distributions. In addition, there are small differences in convenience when selecting different objects.

In three distributions, the analysis of variance shows that the interaction between the input methods and the shapes of the objects is not significant. Their F and P values are $(F (3, 152) = 0.447, P > 0.05)$, $(F (3, 152) = 0.207, P > 0.05)$, and $(F (3, 152) = 0.202, P > 0.05)$, respectively.

For input methods, the main effects are significant in three distributions, and their F and P values are $(F (3,152) = 26.186, P < 0.05)$, $(F (3,152) = 30.009, P < 0.05)$, and $(F (3,152) = 24.762, P < 0.05)$, respectively. This indicates that there are significant differences in convenience in different input methods. Turkey's post hoc tests also show that the convenience of gesture input is significantly lower than that of the other three input methods, and there is no significant difference between the other input methods.

For object shapes, the main effects are not significant in three distributions, and their F and P values are $(F (1,152) = 0.791, P > 0.05)$, $(F (1,152) = 0.021, P > 0.05)$, and $(F (1,152) = 0.188, P > 0.05)$, respectively.

4.5   User Preference

User preference refers to that if the user chooses only one input method, which one he will choose. Considering that it is unlikely to design different input methods for objects of different shapes in an application, the questionnaire is designed only for user preferences in three distributions. The statistics are shown in Fig. 6.

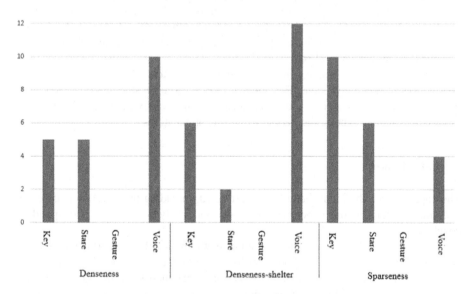

Fig. 6. User preferences in three distributions

It can be seen from Fig. 6 that no subjects choose gesture input, most of the subjects choose key input in the sparse distribution of objects, and most of the subjects choose voice input in the other two distributions.

5   Discussion

From the experimental results in Sect. 4, when the objects are sparsely distributed, the input methods and object shapes have a significant impact on the indicators recorded by the tool [9], such as the number of errors and task completion time, and the shapes of the objects have no significant effect on the comfort and convenience.

When objects are densely distributed, gesture input performs the worst and voice input does best, and there is no significant difference between button input and gaze input. The conclusion is similar in the sheltered dense distribution, and the gesture input performs the worst and the speech input performs best. The reason for the poor performance of gesture input is that users not only focus their attention on the objects to be selected, but also pay attention to the positions and postures of the hands. This affects the users' immersion, and it is also easy for the users to feel fatigue during use; that is, users' convenience and comfort are affected.

In addition, the research results show that there is no significant interaction between object shapes and input methods.

It can also be seen from the experiment that when the objects are sparsely distributed, if users want to perform simple object selection tasks, Cardboard's built-in button input method is enough. When the object is densely distributed or densely distributed with shelters, voice input should be used instead of button input. In addition, if the interactions are complex, voice input is preferred over gesture input.

From the interviews after the experiment, almost no subjects feel that the shapes of the objects have any effect on their choice, but according to the data recorded by our tool [9], the shapes of the objects still have a significant effect. The specific reason for this needs to be further studied.

The subjects in the experiment consisted of 9 boys and 11 girls, and the gender distribution is relatively even. The subjects are all college students and their ages range from 20 to 28 years old, and the age distribution is relatively narrow, but they are more representative among the people using VR applications.

6   Conclusion

The paper studies the input methods of Cardboard, including the experimental design and implementation, the experimental results and analysis, and the corresponding conclusions.

At present, there are other gesture input methods based on smart phone's RGB cameras. For these input methods, further experiments are needed for research. Moreover, the paper only explores the effect of object shapes on the study variables, and does not consider the effect of object size, therefore, it is necessary to further explore whether there is the interaction between object sizes and shapes, and how the interaction affects the tasks of object selections.

Acknowledgments. This work is supported by the National Natural Science Foundation of China (No. 61672046).

References

1. Barbagallo, R.: How to Support Gear and google cardboard in one unity 3D project. http://ralphbarbagallo.com/2015/05/26/how-to-supportgear-vr-and-google-cardboard-in-one-unity3d-project/
2. Anthony, S., Simon, J.: Design and implementation of an immersive virtual reality system based on a smartphone platform. In: IEEE Symposium on 3D User Interfaces on Proceeding, pp. 43 – 46. IEEE (2013)
3. Majed, A.Z., Sam, T., Eelke F.: PAWdio: hand input for mobile VR using acoustic sensing. In: 2016 Annual Symposium on Computer-Human Interaction in Play on Proceedings, pp. 154–158. ACM (2016)
4. Akira, I., Takuya, A., Keigo, S., Shuta, N.: FistPointer: target selection technique using mid-air interaction for mobile VR environment. In: 2017 CHI Conference Extended Abstracts on Human Factors in Computing Systems, pp. 474. ACM (2017)
5. Tanriverdi, V., Robert J.J.: Interacting with eye movements in virtual environments. In: The SIGCHI Conference on Human Factors in Computing Systems on Proceedings, pp. 265–272. ACM (2000)
6. Cournia, N., John. D.S., Andrew T.D.: Gaze- vs. hand-based pointing in virtual environments. In: ACM Conference on Human Factors in Computing Systems on Proceedings, pp. 772–773. ACM (2003)
7. Ganapathi, P., Keyur, S.: Investigating controller less input methods for smartphone based virtual reality platforms. In: 20th International Conference on Human-Computer Interaction with Mobile Devices and Services Adjunct on Proceedings, pp. 166–173. ACM (2018)
8. Pfeuffer, K., Mayer, B., Mardanbegi, D., Gellersen, H.: Gaze + Pinch interaction in virtual reality. In: The 5th Symposium on Spatial User Interaction on Proceedings, pp. 99–108. ACM (2017)
9. Yanwei, B.: Design and implementation of a server cluster monitoring tool based on virtual reality. Master's thesis, Peking University (2018)

Conditionality Analysis of the Radial Basis Function Matrix

Martin Červenka$^{(\boxtimes)}$ and Václav Skala

Faculty of Applied Sciences, University of West Bohemia, Pilsen, Czechia
{cervemar,skala}@kiv.zcu.cz

Abstract. The global Radial Basis Functions (RBFs) may lead to ill-conditioned system of linear equations. This contribution analyzes conditionality of the Gauss and the Thin Plate Spline (TPS) functions. Experiments made proved dependency between the shape parameter and number of RBF center points where the matrix is ill-conditioned. The dependency can be further described as an analytical function.

Keywords: Radial basis function · System of linear equations · Condition number · Matrix conditionality

1 Introduction

Interpolation and approximation of scattered data is a common problem in many engineering and research areas, e.g. Oliver et al. [1] use interpolation (kriging) method on geographical data, Kaymaz [2] finds usage of this technique in structural reliability problem. Sakata et al. [3] model wing structure with an approximation method, Joseph et al. [4] even create metamodels. The RBF methods are also used in the solution of partial differential equations (PDE) especially in connection with engineering problems.

To solve interpolation and approximation problems, we use two main approaches:

- Tesselated approach – it requires tesselation of the data domain (e.g. Delaunay triangulation) to generate associations between pairs of points in the tesselated cloud of points. Some algorithms were developed (Lee et al. [5] show two of them, Smolik et al. [6] show a fast parallel algorithm for triangulation of large datasets, Zeu et al. [7] recently use tesselation for seismic data etc.) for triangulation and tesselation. Even though it seems simple, tesselation is a slow process in general[1].

---

[1] The Delaunay triangulation has time complexity of $O\left(n^{\lceil d/2 \rceil + 1}\right)$, where d is number of tesselated dimensions.

The research was supported by projects Czech Science Foundation (GACR) No. 17-05534S and partially by SGS 2019-016.

© Springer Nature Switzerland AG 2020
O. Gervasi et al. (Eds.): ICCSA 2020, LNCS 12250, pp. 30–43, 2020.
https://doi.org/10.1007/978-3-030-58802-1_3

– Meshless approach – a method based on RBFs can be used, which does not require any from of tesselation. Hardy [8] shown that the complexity of this approach is nearly independent to the problem dimensionality, therefore it is a better alternative to tesselation in higher dimensions. On the other hand, RBF methods require solving a system of linear equations which leads to some problems as well.

There are several meshless approaches e.g. Fasshauer [9] implements some of the meshless algorithms in MATLAB, Franke [10] compares some interpolation methods of the scattered data.

Conditionality of the matrix of a linear system of equation is a key element to determine whether the system is well solvable or not.

RBF research was recently targeted:

– to find out RBF applicability for large geosciences data, see Majdisova [11],
– to interpolate and approximate vector data, see Smolik [12],
– to study robustness of the RBF data for large datasets, see Skala [13,14].
– to find out optimal variable shape parameters, see Skala [15].

This research is aimed to find optimal (or at least suboptimal) shape parameters of the RBF interpolation. This contribution describes briefly analysis of some of the most commonly used RBFs and determines its problematic shape parameters, causing ill-conditionality of the equation system matrix.

2 RBF Approximation and Interpolation

The basic idea behind the RBF approach is the partial unity approach, i.e. summing multiple weighted radial basis functions together to obtain complex interpolating function. The Fig. 1 presents two RBFs (marked by red color) forming an interpolating final function (blue one).

The RBF approach was introduced by Hardy [8] and modified in [16]. Since then, this method has been further developed and modified. Majdisova et al. [17] and Cervenka et al. [18] proposed multiple placement methods. There are also some behavioural studies of the shape parameters, e.g. searching the optimal ones from Wang et al. [19], Afiatdoust et al. [20] or using different local shape parameters from Cohen et al. [21], Sarra et al. [22], Skala et al. [15].

This contribution analyzes the worst cases of the RBF matrix conditionality in order to avoid bad shape parameters, therefore the bad shape parameters can be avoided.

2.1 RBF Method Principle

The RBF interpolation is defined by Eq. 1,

$$h\left(\mathbf{x}_i\right) = \sum_{j=1}^{N} \lambda_j \varphi\left(||\mathbf{x}_i - \mathbf{x}_j||\right) = \sum_{j=1}^{N} \lambda_j \varphi\left(r_{ij}\right) \tag{1}$$

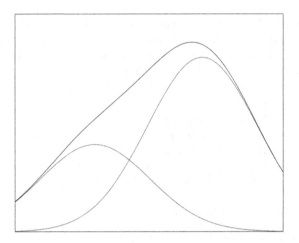

Fig. 1. Two RBFs (in red) and result of the addition (in blue). (Color figure online)

where $h(\mathbf{x}_i)$ is the resulting interpolant, N is the number of RBFs, λ_i is a weight of the i-th RBF, φ is the selected RBF and r_{ij} is a distance between points $\mathbf{x}_i$ and $\mathbf{x}_j$. The points $\mathbf{x}_j$ are all the points on the sampled original function, where the function value is known.

The RBF approximation is slightly different, see Eq. 2. The notation is the same as above, however, $\mathbf{x}_j$ are replaced by reference points $\xi_j, j = 1, \ldots, M$. Some arbitrary (sufficiently small $M \ll N$) number of points from the data domain are taken instead. More details can be found in Skala [23].

$$h(\mathbf{x}_i) = \sum_{j=1}^{M} \lambda_j \varphi\left(||\mathbf{x}_i - \xi_j||\right), \quad i = 1, \ldots, N \tag{2}$$

In both cases, i.e. approximation and interpolation, the equations can be expressed in a matrix form as:

$$\mathbf{A}\boldsymbol{\lambda} = \mathbf{b}, \quad \mathbf{b} = h(\mathbf{x}), \mathbf{A}_{ij} = \varphi_{ij} \tag{3}$$

In the interpolation case, the matrix $\mathbf{A}$ is a square matrix, while in the approximation case, the matrix $\mathbf{A}$ is rectangular and the result is an overdetermined system of linear equations. In this case, we do not obtain exact values for the already calculated reference points ξ_j.

2.2 RBF Classification

There are many RBFs and still new ones are being proposed e.g. Menandro [24]. In general, we can divide the RBFs into two main groups, "global" and "local" ones, see Fig. 3 and Fig. 2.

- **Global** RBFs influence the interpolated values globally. The matrix **A** will be dense and rather ill-conditioned. Typical examples of the global RBF are the Gaussian, the TPS or the inverse multiquadric RBFs.
- **Local** RBFs have limited influence to a limited space near its centre point (hypersphere, in general). The advantage of the local RBFs is that they lead to a sparse matrix **A**. RBFs belonging to this group are called "Compactly Supported" RBFs (CS-RBFs, in short).

Global RBFs are functions, which influence is not limited and its value may be nonzero for each value in its domain. The well-known ones are the Gaussian or the TPS functions. However, there are other functions, see e.g. Table 1 or Lin et al. [25]. Mentioned functions are illustrated in Fig. 2.

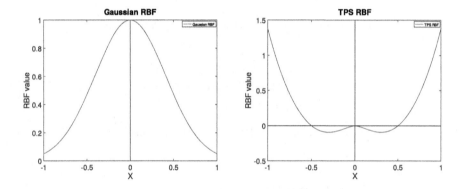

Fig. 2. Some of the global RBF functions.

Table 1. Various global RBF functions.

Name	Expression
Gaussian RBF	$e^{-\alpha r^2}$
TPS RBF	$\frac{1}{2}r^2 \log\left(\beta r^2\right)$
Multiquadratic RBF	$\frac{1}{1+(\epsilon r)^2}$
Inverse Multiquadratic RBF	$\frac{1}{\sqrt{1+(\epsilon r)^2}}$

The **CS-RBF** or compactly supported radial basis function is a function limited to a given interval. Some of CS-RBFs are presented on Fig. 3. Generally, these functions are limited to an interval (usually $r \in \langle 0, 1 \rangle$) otherwise the value equals zero. These functions are defined by Eq. 4, where $P(r)$ is a polynomial function, r is the distance of two points and q is a parameter.

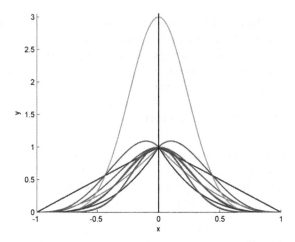

Fig. 3. Some of the CS-RBF functions. [26] (edited)

$$\varphi\left(r\right) = \begin{cases} \left(1-r\right)^{q} P\left(r\right) & 0 \leqslant r < 1, \\ 0 & r \geqslant 1 \end{cases} \tag{4}$$

It should be noted that some new CS-RBFs have been recently defined by Menandro [24].

3   Matrix Conditionality

Assuming a linear system of equations $\mathbf{Ax} = \mathbf{b}$, the condition number of the matrix $\mathbf{A}$ describes how the result (vector $\mathbf{b}$) can change when the input vector $\mathbf{x}$ is slightly modified. This number describes sensitivity to changes in the input vector. We aim for the lowest possible sensitivity, in order to get reasonable results. In terms of linear algebra, we can define conditionality of a normal matrix $\mathbf{A}$ using eigenvalues $\lambda_i \in \mathbb{C}^1$ as:

$$\kappa\left(\mathbf{A}\right) = \frac{\left|\lambda_{max}\left(\mathbf{A}\right)\right|}{\left|\lambda_{min}\left(\mathbf{A}\right)\right|} \tag{5}$$

where $\kappa\left(\mathbf{A}\right)$ is the condition number of the normal matrix $\mathbf{A}$, $\left|\lambda_{max}\left(\mathbf{A}\right)\right|$ is the highest absolute eigenvalue of the matrix $\mathbf{A}$ and $\left|\lambda_{min}\left(\mathbf{A}\right)\right|$ is the lowest absolute eigenvalue of the matrix.

The higher the value $\kappa\left(\mathbf{A}\right)$ is, the more sensitive the matrix $\mathbf{A}$ is, meaning that $\kappa\left(\mathbf{A}\right) = 1$ is the best option, forcing all eigenvalues λ to have the same value.

It is worth noting that the conditionality is closely related to the matrix determinant. In the case when the determinant is zero, we have at least one eigenvalue equaling zero, so the conditionality will be infinite, see Eq. 6.

$$\det(\mathbf{A}) = 0 \rightarrow |\lambda_{min}(\mathbf{A})| = 0 \rightarrow \kappa(\mathbf{A}) = +\infty \Leftrightarrow |\lambda_{max}(\mathbf{A})| \neq 0 \qquad (6)$$

This is only a brief introduction to the matrix conditionality. Details can be found in e.g. Ikramov [27] or Skala [14], some experimental results can be found in Skala [28].

4   Experimental Results of RBF Approximation

In the RBF approximation problem, we normally have two main issues to deal with – selecting number of RBFs and its global shape parameter. To obtain a robust solution, the matrix $\mathbf{A}$ of the linear system of equations should not be ill-conditioned. We did some experiments to show how the condition number of the matrix $\mathbf{A}$ depends on the number of RBFs (N) used and a shape parameter (α or β, see below). To make things easier, all RBFs have been distributed uniformly on $x \in \langle 0, 1 \rangle$ interval and have the same constant shape parameter.

4.1   Gaussian RBF

The Gaussian RBF is defined by Eq. 7. It is the unnormalized probability density function of a Gaussian distribution centred at zero and with a variance of $\frac{1}{2\alpha}$. Variable r denotes the distance from its centre points and α is the shape parameter.

$$\varphi(r, \alpha) = e^{-\alpha r^2} \qquad (7)$$

Figure 4 presents dependence of matrix conditionality on Gaussian RBF shape parameter α and number of uniformly distributed RBF reference points.

A hyperbolic function (Eq. 8) was used to fit extremal points of each curve (Table 2).

Table 2. Analytical form of first 9 hyperboles.

Hyperbole	a	b	c	Hyperbole	a	b	c
1	7.64	38.36	−3.58	6	8.47	1387.35	−30.84
2	13.49	1.93	−7.98	7	17.98	1218.46	−49.14
3	9.17	277.29	−11.95	8	49.16	278.29	−78.53
4	9.44	509.55	−18.37	9	93.81	63.73	16.11
5	12.02	545.66	−31.8				

$$\beta = a + \frac{b}{N + c} \qquad (8)$$

The plot at Fig. 5 describes the situation. These curves describe number of RBFs N and shape parameter α when the matrix is ill-conditioned.

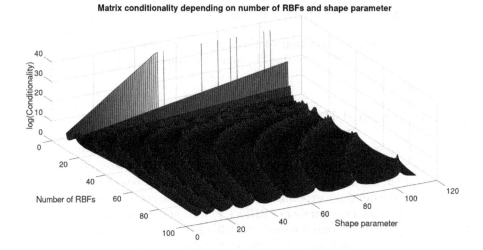

Fig. 4. Matrix conditionality values for Gaussian RBF.

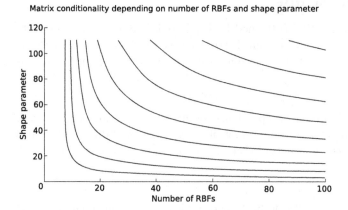

Fig. 5. Worst conditionality shape parameters α for Gauss RBF.

4.2   Thin Plate Spline RBF

The Thin Plate Spline (TPS) radial basis function is defined by the Eq. 9. The TPS was introduced by Duchon [29] and used for RBF approximation afterwards. Variable r is the same as in the Gaussian RBF – the distance from its centre point and parameter β is the shape parameter.

$$\varphi \left(r, \beta \right) = \frac{1}{2} r^2 \log \left(\beta r^2 \right) \tag{9}$$

The Fig. 6 presents a result for a simulated experiment to the recent Gaussian RBF case using the TPS function instead. There is only one curve which has a hyperbolic shape similar to the Gaussian RBF case.

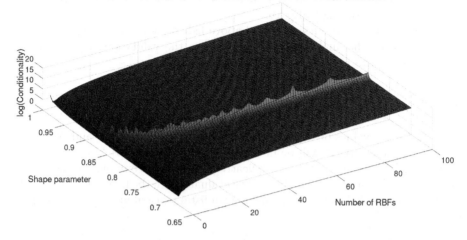

Fig. 6. Matrix conditionality values for TPS RBFs.

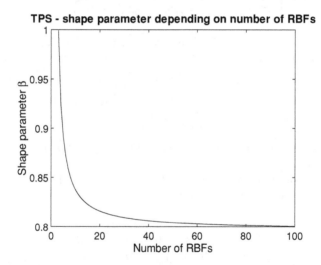

Fig. 7. Worst conditionality shape parameters β for the TPS RBF.

The Fig. 7 also represents the curve, when the matrix $\mathbf{A}$ is close to singular. The Table 3 presents dependency of the β_{exp} shape parameter for different N as an function when the matrix $\mathbf{A}$ is significantly ill-conditioned.

We obtained a hyperbolic function from the graph on Fig. 7 (coefficients are rounded to 2 decimal places).

$$\beta = 0.79 + \frac{0.36}{N - 1.24} \qquad (10)$$

The Table 3 presents the shape parameters β_{calc} evaluated for small numbers of RBF functions according to Eq. 10.

The experimental results presented above led to a question, how the results are related from the analytical side. This led to the validation of experiments with two analytical results described in this section.

5   Theoretical Analysis

Let us calculate values of the TPS shape parameter β for $N = 3$ and $N = 4$ in a way that the matrix $\mathbf{A}$ will be ill-conditioned ($\kappa(\mathbf{A}) = +\infty$).

It should be noted that the multiplicative constant $\frac{1}{2}$ is ommited in the Eq. 11 as it has no influence to the conditionality evaluation. In the first case, i.e. $N = 3$, the RBF matrix $\mathbf{A}$ has the form (using equidistant distribution of RBF center points):

$$\mathbf{A}_3 = \begin{bmatrix} 0 & r^2 \log\left(\beta r^2\right) & (2r)^2 \log\left(\beta 4r^2\right) \\ r^2 \log\left(\beta r^2\right) & 0 & r^2 \log\left(\beta r^2\right) \\ (2r)^2 \log\left(\beta 4r^2\right) & r^2 \log\left(\beta r^2\right) & 0 \end{bmatrix} \tag{11}$$

Let us explore singularity of the matrix $\mathbf{A}_3$, when $\det(\mathbf{A}_3) = 0$, the determinant will have the form:

$$r^6 \begin{vmatrix} 0 & \log\left(\beta r^2\right) & 4\log\left(\beta 4r^2\right) \\ \log\left(\beta r^2\right) & 0 & \log\left(\beta r^2\right) \\ 4\log\left(\beta 4r^2\right) & \log\left(\beta r^2\right) & 0 \end{vmatrix} = 0 \tag{12}$$

As $r \neq 0$ for all pairs of different points, $\lim_{r \to 0} r^2 \log\left(r^2\right) = 0$ and equidistant point distribution.

For the sake of simplicity, we substitute $q = \log\left(\beta r^2\right)$, $a = \log 4$ and use formula $\log(ab) = \log a + \log b$ so we get:

$$\begin{vmatrix} 0 & q & 4(q + a) \\ q & 0 & q \\ 4(q + a) & q & 0 \end{vmatrix} = 0$$

$$8(q + a)q^2 = 0 \rightarrow q = 0 \vee q = -a$$

$$\log\left(\beta r^2\right) = -\log 4 = \log \frac{1}{4}$$

$$\beta r^2 = \frac{1}{4}$$

$$\beta = \frac{1}{4r^2} \tag{13}$$

In the experiments, we used interval $x \in \langle 0, 1 \rangle$ and with three points $(0, 0.5, 1)$. The distance between two consecutive points r is 0.5, which led to $\beta = 1$. This exact value we obtained from experiments as well (see Table 3).

Table 3. β_{exp}-values for TPS RBF for some small N (number of RBFs) obtained by experiment as well as β_{calc} values calculated by Eq. 10

N	β_{exp}	β_{calc}	N	β_{exp}	β_{calc}	N	β_{exp}	β_{calc}
3	1.00000	0.99874	23	0.81338	0.81319	43	0.80535	0.80536
4	0.92206	0.92564	24	0.81264	0.81247	44	0.80515	0.80516
5	0.89118	0.89141	25	0.81197	0.81182	45	0.80496	0.80497
6	0.87182	0.87155	26	0.81135	0.81121	46	0.80477	0.80479
7	0.85909	0.85858	27	0.81078	0.81065	47	0.80459	0.80462
8	0.85002	0.84945	28	0.81025	0.81014	48	0.80442	0.80445
9	0.84324	0.84268	29	0.80976	0.80966	49	0.80426	0.80429
10	0.83799	0.83744	30	0.80930	0.80921	50	0.80410	0.80414
11	0.83379	0.83329	31	0.80888	0.80880	51	0.80395	0.80399
12	0.83037	0.82990	32	0.80848	0.80841	52	0.80380	0.80385
13	0.82753	0.82709	33	0.80811	0.80804	53	0.80366	0.80372
14	0.82512	0.82472	34	0.80776	0.80770	54	0.80353	0.80359
15	0.82306	0.82269	35	0.80743	0.80738	55	0.80340	0.80346
16	0.82128	0.82094	36	0.80711	0.80708	56	0.80328	0.80334
17	0.81973	0.81941	37	0.80682	0.80679	57	0.80316	0.80322
18	0.81835	0.81807	38	0.80654	0.80652	58	0.80304	0.80311
19	0.81713	0.81687	39	0.80628	0.80626	59	0.80293	0.80300
20	0.81605	0.81581	40	0.80603	0.80602	60	0.80282	0.80290
21	0.81507	0.81485	41	0.80579	0.80579	61	0.80272	0.80280
22	0.81418	0.81398	42	0.80557	0.80557	62	0.80262	0.80270

In the second case, i.e. $N = 4$, a similar approach has been taken. In this case the matrix $\mathbf{A}_4$ is defined as:

$$
\mathbf{A}_4 = \begin{bmatrix}
0 & r^2 \log\left(\beta r^2\right) & (2r)^2 \log\left(\beta 4 r^2\right) & (3r)^2 \log\left(\beta 9 r^2\right) \\
r^2 \log\left(\beta r^2\right) & 0 & r^2 \log\left(\beta r^2\right) & (2r)^2 \log\left(\beta 4 r^2\right) \\
(2r)^2 \log\left(\beta 4 r^2\right) & r^2 \log\left(\beta r^2\right) & 0 & r^2 \log\left(\beta r^2\right) \\
(3r)^2 \log\left(\beta 9 r^2\right) & (2r)^2 \log\left(\beta 4 r^2\right) & r^2 \log\left(\beta r^2\right) & 0
\end{bmatrix}
\tag{14}
$$

Similarly as in the case for $N = 3$, we can write the $\det\left(\mathbf{A}_4\right)$ and declare the matrix singular if:

$$
r^8 \begin{vmatrix}
0 & \log\left(\beta r^2\right) & 4\log\left(\beta 4 r^2\right) & 9\log\left(\beta 9 r^2\right) \\
\log\left(\beta r^2\right) & 0 & \log\left(\beta r^2\right) & 4\log\left(\beta 4 r^2\right) \\
4\log\left(\beta 4 r^2\right) & \log\left(\beta r^2\right) & 0 & \log\left(\beta r^2\right) \\
9\log\left(\beta 9 r^2\right) & 4\log\left(\beta 4 r^2\right) & \log\left(\beta r^2\right) & 0
\end{vmatrix} = 0
\tag{15}
$$

Using the substitutions $q = \log\left(\beta r^2\right), a = \log 4$ and $b = \log 9$, we obtain:

$$\begin{vmatrix} 0 & q & 4\,(q+a) & 9\,(q+b) \\ q & 0 & q & 4\,(q+a) \\ 4\,(q+a) & q & 0 & q \\ 9\,(q+b) & 4\,(q+a) & q & 0 \end{vmatrix} \qquad (16)$$

This can be further expressed as:

$$\begin{aligned}
& (4\,(q+a))^4 + q^4 + q^2\,(9\,(q+b))^2 \\
&= -2q^3\,(9\,(q+b)) - 2q\,(4\,(q+a))^2\,(9\,(q+b)) - 2q^2\,(4\,(q+a))^2 \\
&= 256(q+a)^4 + q^4 + 81q^2(q+b)^2 - 18q^3(q+b) \qquad (17) \\
&\quad - 288q(q+a)(q+b)^2 - 32q^2(q+a)^2
\end{aligned}$$

This leads to the cubic equation:

$$\begin{aligned}
(383a - 144b)q^3 + (1216a^2 + 81b^2 - 576ab)q^2 \\
+ (1024a^3 - 288a^2b)q + 256a^4 = 0 \qquad (18)
\end{aligned}$$

Solving this cubic equation (Eq. 18), one real and two complex (complex conjugate) roots are obtained:

$$\begin{aligned}
q_1 &\approx -2.2784 \\
q_2 &\approx -1.1149 + 0.8239i \qquad (19) \\
q_3 &\approx -1.1149 - 0.8239i
\end{aligned}$$

As we have four points distributed uniformly on the interval $x \in \langle 0, 1 \rangle$, the distance between two adjacent nodes is $r = \frac{1}{3}$. Now, using the real root of the Eq. 19, i.e. $q = -2.2784$, we can estimate the shape parameter β as follows:

$$\begin{aligned}
q = \log\left(\beta r^2\right) &\approx -2.2784 \\
\beta r^2 \approx e^{-2.2784} &\approx 0.10245 \qquad (20) \\
\beta \approx \frac{e^{-2.2784}}{r^2} & \\
\beta \approx \frac{e^{-2.2784}}{\left(\frac{1}{3}\right)^2} &= 9e^{-2.2784} \approx 0.92206
\end{aligned}$$

From the experiments, we obtained value $\hat{\beta} = 0.92206$ which is consistent with this theoretical estimation. Both these analytical examples support the argument that the experiments made are correct.

It should be noted, that if irregular point distribution is used, i.e. using Halton points distributions, the ill-conditionality get slightly worse.

6   Conclusion

In this paper, we discussed some properties of the two well-known RBFs. We find out that there are some regularities in the shape parameters, where the RBF matrix is ill-conditioned. Our experiments proved that there are no global optimal shape parameters from the RBF matrix conditionality point of view.

In the future, the RBF conditionality problem is to be explored for higher dimension, especially for $d = 2$, $d = 3$ and in the context of partial differential equations.

Acknowledgement. The authors would like to thank their colleagues and students at the University of West Bohemia for their discussions and suggestions, and especially to Michal Smolik for valuable discussion and notes he provided. The research was supported by projects Czech Science Foundation (GACR) No. 17-05534S and partially by SGS 2019-016.

References

1. Oliver, M.A., Webster, R.: Kriging: a method of interpolation for geographical information systems. Int. J. Geograph. Inf. Syst. **4**(3), 313–332 (1990). https://doi.org/10.1080/02693799008941549
2. Kaymaz, I.: Application of kriging method to structural reliability problems. Struct. Saf. **27**(2), 133–151 (2005). https://doi.org/10.1016/j.strusafe.2004.09.001
3. Sakata, S., Ashida, F., Zako, M.: An efficient algorithm for kriging approximation and optimization with large-scale sampling data. Comput. Meth. Appl. Mech. Eng. **193**(3–5), 385–404 (2004). https://doi.org/10.1016/j.cma.2003.10.006
4. Joseph, V.R., Hung, Y., Sudjianto, A.: Blind kriging: a new method for developing metamodels. J. Mech. Des. **130**(3), 031102 (2008). https://doi.org/10.1115/1.2829873
5. Lee, D.T., Schachter, B.J.: Two algorithms for constructing a Delaunay triangulation. Int. J. Comput. Inf. Sci. **9**(3), 219–242 (1980). https://doi.org/10.1007/BF00977785
6. Smolik, M., Skala, V.: Fast parallel triangulation algorithm of large data sets in E^2 and E^3 for in-core and out-core memory processing. In: Murgante, B., et al. (eds.) ICCSA 2014. LNCS, vol. 8580, pp. 301–314. Springer, Cham (2014). https://doi.org/10.1007/978-3-319-09129-7_23
7. Zeu, Y., Youngseok, S., Joongmoo, B., Soon-Jee, S., Ki-Young, K.: Regularisation of multidimensional sparse seismic data using Delaunay tessellation. J. Appl. Geophys. (2019). https://doi.org/10.1016/j.jappgeo.2019.103877
8. Hardy, R.L.: Multiquadric equations of topography and other irregular surfaces. J. Geophys. Res. **76**, 1905–1915 (1971). https://doi.org/10.1029/JB076i008p01905
9. Fasshauer, G.E.: Meshfree Approximation Methods with MATLAB, vol 6. World Scientific (2007). https://doi.org/10.1142/6437
10. Franke, R.: A critical comparison of some methods for interpolation of scattered data. Technical report, Naval Postgraduate School Monterey CA (1979)
11. Majdisova, Z., Skala, V.: Big geo data surface approximation using radial basis functions: a comparative study. Comput. Geosci. **109**, 51–58 (2017). https://doi.org/j.cageo.2017.08.007

12. Smolik, M., Skala, V., Majdisova, Z.: Vector field radial basis function approximation. Adv. Eng. Softw. **123**, 117–129 (2018). https://doi.org/10.1016/j.advengsoft.2018.06.013
13. Skala, V.: RBF interpolation with CSRBF of large data sets, ICCS. Procedia Comput. Sci. **108**, 2433–2437 (2017). https://doi.org/10.1016/j.procs.2017.05.081
14. Skala, V.: Conditionality of linear systems of equations and matrices using projective geometric algebra. In: Murgante, B., et al. (eds.) ICCSA 2020, LNCS, vol. 12250, pp. 3–17. Springer, Heidelberg (2020)
15. Skala, V., Karim, S.A.A., Zabran, M.: Radial basis function approximation optimal shape parameters estimation. In: Krzhizhanovskaya, V.V., et al. (eds.) ICCS 2020. LNCS, vol. 12142, pp. 309–317. Springer, Cham (2020). https://doi.org/10.1007/978-3-030-50433-5_24
16. Hardy, R.L.: Theory and applications of the multiquadric-biharmonic method 20 years of discovery 1968–1988. Comput. Math. Appl. **19**(8–9), 163–208 (1990). https://doi.org/10.1016/0898-1221(90)90272-L
17. Majdisova, Z., Skala, V.: Radial basis function approximations: comparison and applications. Appl. Math. Model. **51**, 728–743 (2017). https://doi.org/10.1016/j.apm.2017.07.033
18. Cervenka, M., Smolik, M., Skala, V.: A new strategy for scattered data approximation using radial basis functions respecting points of inflection. In: Misra, S., et al. (eds.) ICCSA 2019. LNCS, vol. 11619, pp. 322–336. Springer, Cham (2019). https://doi.org/10.1007/978-3-030-24289-3_24
19. Liu, G., Wang, J.: On the optimal shape parameters of radial basis functions used for 2-d meshless methods. Comput. Meth. Appl. Mech. Eng. **191**(23–24), 2611–2630 (2002). https://doi.org/10.1016/S0045-7825(01)00419-4
20. Afiatdoust, F., Esmaeilbeigi, M.: Optimal variable shape parameters using genetic algorithm for radial basis function approximation. Shams Eng. J. **6**(2), 639–647 (2015). https://doi.org/10.1016/j.asej.2014.10.019
21. Cohen-Steiner, D., Alliez, P., Desbrun, M.: Variational shape approximation. ACM Trans. Graph. (ToG) **23**(3), 905–914 (2004). https://doi.org/10.1145/1015706.1015817
22. Sarra, S.A., Sturgill, D.: A random variable shape parameter strategy for radial basis function approximation methods. Eng. Anal. Boundary Elem. **33**(11), 1239–1245 (2009). https://doi.org/10.1016/j.enganabound.2009.07.003
23. Skala, V.: Fast interpolation and approximation of scattered multidimensional and dynamic data using radial basis functions. WSEAS Trans. Math. **12**(5), 501–511 (2013). E-ISSN 2224-2880
24. Menandro, F.C.M.: Two new classes of compactly supported radial basis functions for approximation of discrete and continuous data. Eng. Rep. (2019). https://doi.org/10.1002/eng2.12028
25. Lin, J., Chen, W., Sze, K.Y.: A new radial basis function for Helmholtz problems. Eng. Anal. Bound. Elem. **36**, 1923–1930 (2012). https://doi.org/10.1016/j.enganabound.2012.07.010
26. Smolik, M., Skala, V.: Large scattered data interpolation with radial basis functions and space subdivision. Integr. Comput. Aided Eng. **25**(1), 49–62 (2018). https://doi.org/10.3233/ICA-170556
27. Ikramov, K.D.: Conditionality of the intermediate matrices of the Gauss, Jordan and optimal elimination methods. USSR Comput. Math. Math. Phys. **18**, 1–16 (1978). https://doi.org/10.1016/0041-5553(78)90159-3

28. Skala, V.: High dimensional and large span data least square error: numerical stability and conditionality. Int. J. Appl. Phys. Math. **7**(3), 148–156 (2017). https://doi.org/10.17706/ijapm.2017.7.3.148-156

29. Duchon, J.: Splines minimizing rotation-invariant semi-norms in Sobolev spaces. In: Schempp, W., Zeller, K. (eds.) Constructive Theory of Functions of Several Variables, vol. 571, pp. 85–100. Springer, Heidelberg (1977). https://doi.org/10.1007/BFb0086566

Information Visualization Applied to Computer Network Security
A Case Study of a Wireless Network of a University

Luiz F. de Camargo[1]([✉]), Alessandro Moraes[1], Diego R. C. Dias[2],
and José R. F. Brega[1]

[1] Universidade Estadual Paulista, São Paulo, Brazil
camargo.luizfelipe@gmail.com, sanfatec@gmail.com, remo@fc.unesp.br
[2] Universidade Federal de São João del-Rei, São João del-Rei, Brazil
diegodias@ufsj.edu.br

Abstract. Computer networks are becoming increasingly vital to the activities of organizations, and their monitoring is necessary to ensure proper functioning. The use of the human cognitive process in decision-making through information visualization (IV) is a viable option for large amounts of data, such as those generated in network monitoring. Considering the need to monitor modern computer networks and the quality gain when using visualization techniques, the objective was to conduct a review study to understand the process of building a monitoring tool using information visualization resources and, from this review, follow with a case study through a tool for visualization application in a university wireless network management. To this end, a systematic literature review was performed, and then a survey of requirements was conducted with the university network managers. With the analysis of the data from the review and the survey, a tool was specified and developed, evaluated in several units of the university. In this way, the results from the review and the requirements survey are observed in time, which allowed the development of a solution using the observed trends, validating them in the use and evaluation of the tool. The main contribution of the work is the resulting tool and its impact on the management of the university wireless network, facilitating the activities of managers.

Keywords: Information visualization · Networks · Security · Management · Network monitoring

1 Introduction

Computer Networks have been increasingly becoming a vital part of the technological structures of any organization. Through them, data is received and transmitted every moment, to the most diverse places. All this flow must be transmitted securely, guaranteeing the availability of the networks for transmission whenever necessary, with the degree of security that the information demands [12].

© Springer Nature Switzerland AG 2020
O. Gervasi et al. (Eds.): ICCSA 2020, LNCS 12250, pp. 44–59, 2020.
https://doi.org/10.1007/978-3-030-58802-1_4

To monitor networks and ensure their security and availability, the computer network administrator should use software that serves as tools for monitoring their network, obtaining real-time and historical information on the status of services and equipment that make up their network. However, effective monitoring to ensure the full operation of a network by recording all incidents that have occurred generates a considerable amount of data, causing problems for the network administrator when analyzing and obtaining new information from this data. To solve this problem, one can make use of the techniques of information visualization, using the human view to help the interpretation of data [7]. As for the project presented in this work, its main objective was to elaborate the architecture and implement a web-based application for information visualization related to the wireless network through dashboards, allowing the visualization of status information of access points and controllers that make up the network in question. As a secondary objective of the proposed project, it aims to carry out a systematic review of content about the use of information visualization applied to computer network security.

Several authors have conducted studies analyzing this area, Guimaraes et al. conducted a review on network management, classifying 285 articles published between 1985 and 2013, according to different taxonomies [6]. Dasgupta et al. sought to understand the human factor in data flow analysis [1]. Very similar to the proposal presented in this paper, using the D3.js library to treat network events through a dashboard one can cite the work done by McKenna et al. [9].

2   Background

Information security is the protection of information from various threats that seek to jeopardize the continuity of a business. Through information security, we seek to minimize the risk arising from these threats, always maximizing the return on business opportunities and investments. Security has three main pillars: confidentiality, integrity, and availability. Information security, even if focused on computer networks, is a vast subject, in a simplified manner, has as it concerns the access of information transmitted over the network by an unauthorized person for reading or modification [12].

Information visualization seeks to represent data sets as images, helping in understanding and making their interpretation more efficient. The use of visualization is appropriate when there is a need to increase human cognitive capabilities instead of replacing them with computational decision-making methods. The creation of a visualization tool should be accomplished by answering three questions: why performs the task, what data is displayed in visualizations, and how to construct the expression language as a design option [10]. Colin Ware [13] justifies the use of visualization through the potentiality of the human brain to process information: "Why should we be interested in visualization? Because the human visual system is a pattern seeker of enormous power and subtlety. The eye and the visual cortex of the brain form a massively parallel processor that provides the highest-bandwidth channel in human cognitive centers".

Stephen Few [4] defines a dashboard as follows: a dashboard is a visual display of the most information needed to achieve one or more objectives that fit entirely on a single computer screen to be monitored at a glance. The term dashboard indicates an indicator panel, such as the indicator panel of a car (speedometer and engine temperature indicator), of an aircraft (flight altitude and wind speed indicator), among other vehicles. Dashboards can be classified into three main groups, according to the target audience to be reached: operational, tactical, and strategic.

3   Systematic Literature Review

This section outlines the systematic literature review undertaken to guide the project.

3.1   Review Objectives and Research Issues

The purpose of this review was to obtain an overview of the use of information visualization techniques in computer network security and, through this, to understand the field of research of information visualization deeply applied to computer network security. After several discussions and previous research, we reached the following main research question: how to build tools that use information visualization techniques applied to the computer network security context? We expanded this central question on the following questions: What programming language is usually used to build this type of tool? What visual techniques are usually used in this type of tool? What data are used in the construction and validation of this type of tool? What is the specific objective of the tool?

3.2   Search Strategy

For the present work, we defined the following search string: (("information" OR "data" OR "analysis") AND ("visualization" OR ("security" OR "defense"))) AND (("network" OR "internet") AND (("security" OR "defense") OR "availability" OR "security visualization")) AND (("security" OR "defense") AND ("visualization" OR "data" OR "data visualization")) AND "visual analytics".

We considered as valid studies only articles published in the English language - journals and conferences. There were no restrictions on the date of publication, considering articles published until the search and identification phase of the studies on 12/12/2018. We applied the search string in the ACM Digital Library (24 studies), IEEE Xplore Digital Library (94 studies), Science Direct (3 studies), Scopus (164 studies), and Engineering Village (205 studies) databases.

3.3   Inclusion and Exclusion Criteria

We defined the following criteria for this review:

- Inclusion - "Affinity of the study with the desired themes"; and "Presents a practical application";
- Exclusion - "Lack of affinity of the study with the desired themes"; "It is not an article"; "Study is not completely available in the English language"; and "It deals with a tool already analyzed".

   In the present work, due to the satisfactory quantity of studies returned, we chose not to perform the quality evaluation.

3.4   Data Extraction

For the present study, the following data composed the extraction form:

- Types of network addressed;
- Visualization techniques used;
- Objectives of visualizations: the motivations were summarized into three categories: "Category 1 - Analysis of abnormal activity in large volumes of historical or long-term data", "Category 2 - Understanding network behavior and detect anomalies", and "Category 3 - Detect, analyze and respond to specific attacks";
- Data source used in visualizations;
- Network layer used; There was development of the tool;
- Name of the tool; Languages used in the construction of the tool; and
- It is a review study (survey and systematic review): It seeks to identify the studies considered as secondary, i.e., previous studies that have already sought to conduct a review work on an area.

3.5   Analysis and Discussion of Results

The number of studies obtained at the end of the review according to the classification can be seen in Table 1.

Types of Computer Networks. Thus, we sought to identify the relationship of the studies with the existing types of networks, with greater focus on the set of protocols "Transmission Control Protocol/Internet Protocol" (TCP/IP) (57 studies) and its specific parts (Border Gateway Protocol (BGP) - 3 studies, Mobile, wireless and cellular - 1 study, Wireless - 3 studies, 4G LTE - 1 study, Voice over Internet Protocol (VoIP) - 1 study).

Table 1. Numbers of studies during the review phases.

Categories	Quantities
Identified studies: these are the studies returned by the selected search system, either manual or electronic	490
Duplicates studies: are those studies that are present in more than one selected database, are counted only once	219
Unique studies: Identified studies - Duplicates studies	271
Unsorted studies: studies that objectively do not meet the inclusion criteria. They are excluded during the selection phase	165
Selected studies: studies that apparently meet the inclusion criteria are included in the selection phase	106
Excluded studies: are those that, after evaluation of the full text, do not meet the inclusion criteria, are excluded during the extraction phase	33
Secondary studies: studies that already proposed, within the theme, a review of content, either through a systematic review, a survey, among other techniques	7
Included studies: studies that, after evaluation of the full text, meet the inclusion criteria, are maintained throughout the process and are used in the extraction phase	66

Network Layer. Within the use of the TCP/IP protocol set, we sought to identify with which network layers the data was related. It is possible to notice the tendency of using data from Layer 2 (51 studies), the network layer, more specifically, data in network flow format (Netflow). The other layers showed little relevance: Layer 1 was present in 7 studies, Layer 3 was present in 3 studies, and Layer 4 was present in 9 studies. However, three studies did not report the network layer used.

Purpose of Visualization. We defined the categories as follows:

- "Category 1 - Analysis of abnormal activity in large volumes of historical or long-term data" - 17 studies;
- "Category 2 - Understanding network behavior and detecting anomalies" - 31 studies; and
- "Category 3 - Detecting, analyzing and responding to specific attacks" - 18 studies.

Data Sources. A total of 56 different data sources were used for data extraction and visualization generation. In Fig. 1, all cited sources are visualized through the word cloud technique. A significant presence of Visual Analytics Science and Technology (VAST) and NetFlow data sources can be verified.

Fig. 1. Data sources used in the studies displayed using the word cloud technique.

Visual Techniques. We applied the most diverse visual techniques in the tools addressed in the participating studies, grouping similar techniques we can cite the presence of 83 different visual techniques used in the constructions of visualizations. Figure 2 shows a visualization using the word cloud technique to demonstrate all the techniques present in the studies.

Development and Language. Among the 66 studies evaluated, the vast majority (62) developed a new tool, and only 4 of them dealt with the implementation of an existing tool. The programming languages used in the development of each tool were analyzed, but 30 studies had no mention of the programming language, and seven studies reported using two combined languages during the development—a tendency of using Java language for server-side applications and Javascript for applications executed in the client-side. We verified the use of several libraries and frameworks for visual development in the analyzed studies. The most used was the D3.js library written in Javascript and cited in 6 studies. D3.js allows the creation of visualizations through the native support of Web browsers to design patterns of Hypertext Markup Language, version 5 (HTML5).

3.6 Review Considerations

From the study carried out, we noticed the possibility of deepening the review, applying a quality assessment of the studies, expanding the number of studies evaluated, and selecting those with greater relevance. It is noticeable that the scenario leads to the development of a tool for monitoring computer networks based on the TCP/IP protocol set, as it is a more widespread network standard in use. A tool to understand the behavior of a network and detect the presence of anomalies (attacks, excessive use of the network, unavailability intervals), also offering the functions of detection of specific attacks and analysis on historical

Fig. 2. Trends being shown through the word cloud technique.

data. The general trend is the development of a tool that uses Layer 2 data, with network flow data; however, the use of another network layer can be considered an opportunity in the research area.

4   Specification

We proposed the development of a tool for network monitoring, presenting an interface in a dashboard format, applicable to the reality of the university and its wireless network structure. We also sought to identify possible limitations in the current monitoring solution through studies on the application of information visualization applied to computer network security. In this way, this paper presents a tool for network monitoring that offers an integrated view of the various aspects that make up the situation of a wireless network, being able to explore them interactively, using techniques of information visualization.

Nowadays, we have been using the Zabbix tool to monitor our university wireless network. However, some limitations are found, mainly regarding the access to the information within the Zabbix interface, since the menus have several levels and are not intuitive, requiring a great effort to locate the desired information. Due to the complexity of the university wireless network, since it is composed of about 32 units distributed in 24 locations, it was decided to initially develop a tool using the context of only one unit and then expand the tool to the other units.

4.1   Requirements Analysis

To obtain a complete dashboard-based monitoring tool, we sought to identify, within the structure of the university, the organizational levels and map the data present on their respective dashboards. A brief presentation of the user profiles obtained with the requirements survey:

Strategic Level. Target audience: Rectory, Computer Networks Group. Objectives: monitor problems, balance loads, and know the service offered.

Data: Controllers: status, associated access points, usage load, associated users, and log. Traffic: total value, the value per unit, and the value per user segment. Users: total connected, total from other institutions, total per segment, and total visitors.

Tactical Level. Target audience: IT directors and network administrators of each unit. Objectives: to know the service offered.

Data: Traffic: total value in the unit, and the value per building or department. Users: total in the unit, total per building or department, total coming from other institutions, and total visitors.

Operational Level. Target audience: Analysts and assistants in the network areas. Objectives: monitor problems, balance loads, and know the service offered.

Data: Access points: status, usage load, associated users, log, and invalid logins. Traffic: total per access point, and total per user.

4.2   Data Collection and Organization

Zabbix Application Programming Interface (API) allows, through POST-type HTML requests with JavaScript Object (JSON) content. Zabbix stores the collected data (JSON format) on its database. However, the data format is not compatible with the format used by the D3.js library. Because of that, the treatment of this data was created through a module developed in PHP language.

4.3   Visual Representations

In this section we detailed the visual techniques selected to build the tool:

Bubble or proportional area graph - used for value comparison and proportion demonstration, allow a quick view of the relative size of objects compared to others, without the need to use scales [8].

Bar graph or column graph - one of the most basic graphs considered, allows easy comparison between different categories that are represented close, with alignment on the axis that represents the value zero and with the representation of the data through its height for the columns and its length for the bars. The use of different colors for highlights or different categories can help according to the desired narrative [8].

A bar graph or stacked columns - using for comparison between data categories; however, these categories can be broken down into segments and compared as part of a whole [8].

A line or time-series graph - displays information such as a series of data points connected by straight line segments. Similar to a scatter plot, except that the measuring points are ordered (usually by their x-axis value) and connected with straight-line segments [8].

4.4 Selected Technology

D3.js is a library written in JavaScript language for generating graphics or visualizations, manipulating and bringing to life data through HTML, Scalable Vector Graphic (SVG), and Cascading Style Sheets (CSS) technologies. It has an emphasis on current Web standards, to use all the capabilities of modern Internet browsers without using proprietary standards.

5   Comparison with Other Tools

In this section, we detailed some tools used to meet the demands of the scenario analyzed, evaluating the advantages and disadvantages compared to our solution. We addressed four tools: Grafana, Kibana, Splunk, and Zabdash. There were performed a simple installation and a brief testing period to obtain more information about each tool.

5.1 Grafana

Grafana is a free tool with a commercial version for creating visualizations in dashboard format obtaining data from several data sources, including Zabbix [5]. The installation of Grafana for testing was performed on the Linux operating system, Ubuntu distribution, version 18.10, through DEB package added to the system after downloading on the page of the manufacturer according to instructions available.

Grafana is a very flexible tool for data visualization, with a plugin for integration with Zabbix, which makes it one of the best options for network monitoring data visualization. However, the graph options and the possibilities of interaction with them represent limitations in comparison with our tool. Grafana supports the following types of graphs: time-series graph with lines, bars, and points, simple status, value table, time heat maps, and alert list.

5.2 Kibana

Kibana is a free data visualization tool that makes up the Elastic Stack or ELK (Elasticsearch, Logstash, and Kibana) software package. It generates visualizations from the data collected by the Logstash tool, treating and manipulating them in the Elasticsearch tool. The projects of the three tools were united in June 2012, giving rise to the current software package [3]. We carried out the tests on the Kibana tool using a virtual machine offered by the Bitnami group with the Elastic Stack (ELK) software package already implemented.

Kibana tool proves to be robust for performing all kinds of data analysis. However, it requires the creation of a scenario prepared using the ELK set. For the need of our university, it is unusual to apply such a complicated solution since there is already a monitoring tool implemented (Zabbix). The proposal of this work is more advantageous because it works as a layer developed on Zabbix. Kibana supports the following types of graphs: area chart, heat map, horizontal bars, line chart, pie chart, vertical bars, value table, pointer, target, and simple metrics.

5.3   Splunk

Splunk is a tool that captures, indexes and correlates various data. Among them from network equipment, in real-time in a searchable repository, from which it can generate graphs, reports, alerts, panels, and views. Splunk version 3.0 was released on August 6, 2007, and that was the first version available to the public [11]. The installation of Splunk Enterprise Trial for testing was performed on the Linux operating system, Ubuntu distribution, version 18.10, through DEB package added to the system after downloading on the page of the manufacturer according to instructions available.

Splunk software proved to be a good option for data analysis, including network data, performing all phases: data collection, treatment, and visualization. However, it has the disadvantage of being a commercial tool, having a free version with certain limitations that may be unfeasible in some specific scenarios. The university should prioritize the use of free software tools, a fact that, together with the limitations presented in the free version, makes it impossible to use Splunk to meet the needs. Splunk supports the following types of graphs: line graph, area graph, column graph, bar graph, pie chart, scatter plot, bubble graph, a single value, radial pointer, fill pointer, marker pointer, grouping chart, and choropleth chart.

5.4   Zabdash

Zabdash is an extension to Zabbix that proposes the addition of a dashboard view generated from the data available in the standard Zabbix interface. It is free and opensource hosted on GitHub and SourceForge. The installation of Zabdash for testing was performed on the Linux operating system, in Ubuntu distribution, version 18.04, through the installation of a folder within the Zabbix structure previously installed through the operating system repository.

Zabdash is a good option for extensive integration with Zabbix and easy installation. However, it has as a limitation the lack of flexibility, because it already has the graphics and panels predefined, without the possibility of customization, showing itself to be an option not very viable for the university scenario. Zabdash supports the following types of graphs: time-series graph, pie chart, and bar graph.

We can conclude that the analyzed tools are options for the application of information visualization in network management and monitoring. Meanwhile,

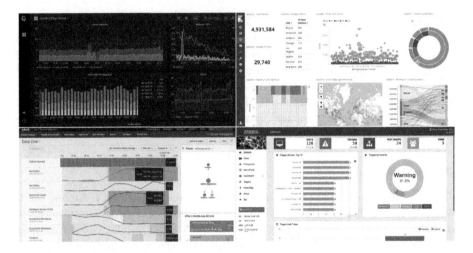

Fig. 3. Grafana, Kibana, Splunk, and Zabdash tools screens.

within the needs raised in the university scenario, the specification presented in this work is more appropriate. Figure 3 shows the screens of the evaluated tools.

Our tool is more advantageous than others since it depends only on Zabbix (a monitoring solution that is already in use, free, easy to deploy, and applies the best visualizations practices). The need for development can be considered a negative point in the comparison, but the use of the D3.js library to speed up the development process and the possible customization options helped to base the decision for development.

6   Development

We defined a modular tool development, adding new functionalities on demand for each module creation. The following modules compose the tool:

- Login: to manage access to the tool;
- Selection of units: to choose the desired unit;
- Data organization: to process data from Zabbix;
- Settings: to customize and storage of settings; and
- Visualization: to create and display graphics.

Figure 4 depicts the modules that make up the application. Figures 5 and 6 depict some of the design decisions made in the development process.

7   Evaluation

We performed tests and simulations using inspection methods such as heuristic evaluation, cognitive walk through, and consistency. The IT university team supported that task.

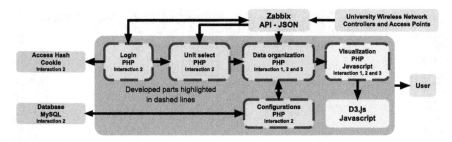

Fig. 4. Diagram showing the modules that make up the application, highlighting them.

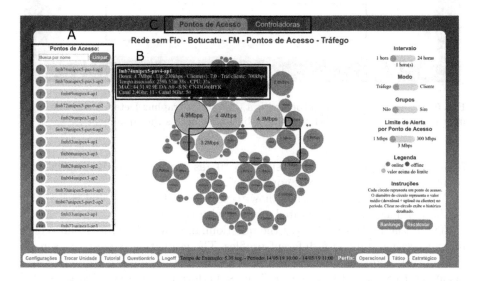

Fig. 5. Design decisions - Detail A shows the side list and the search field; Detail B shows the access point data detail; Detail C shows the top tabs; Detail D shows the elements with the changing colors.

A second IT team unit performed usability tests, mainly evaluating the functioning of the modules that manage usage in multiple units, collecting the opinion of users involved in the tests, to improve the system for the next stage of testing [2]. We considered that test as a target audience sample of the system.

7.1 Questionnaire

We created a questionnaire based on the QUIS questionnaire, created in 1987 by a multidisciplinary group of studies of the University of Maryland Human-Computer Interaction Lab. That is suitable for interface evaluation. The original evaluation model takes into account nine factors. However, we decided to simplify some questions and omit sections that did not apply to the tool context. The questions that made up the QUIS questionnaire had numerical answers ranging

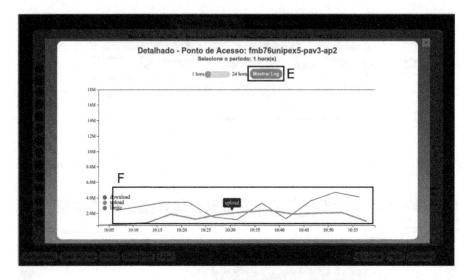

Fig. 6. Design decisions - Lightbox with a time series graphic; Detail E showing highlight time series; and Detail F showing a button to access the equipment log.

from "1" as the most negative aspect to "9" as the most positive aspect, also counting with the option "Not applicable".

We created a tutorial teaching how to use the tool. This tutorial is available on the web pages in an integrated manner with the tool.

The initial audience to apply the questionnaire was defined in 12 university units, selecting units with different profiles. The evaluation request was sent to the network manager in each unit. The feedback was obtained from 10 users, belonging to 8 units distributed in 7 cities, performing the requested tests, and answering the questionnaire. There was difficulty in the adherence of professionals to use and evaluate the tool, even after several contacts, through different means of communication (calls, e-mail messages, and instant messages).

7.2 Questions and Answers

The questionnaire was composed of an identification step, and eight parts focused on different aspects of the interface. The online survey platform Google Forms was used to apply the questionnaire.

We requested the following information to identify the user: e-mail (through login), name, age, and gender. Part 1 of the questionnaire sought to identify how long the user used the tool. Part 2 sought to identify the areas of activity of the users.

Figure 7 depicts an overview of the other parts of the questionnaire.

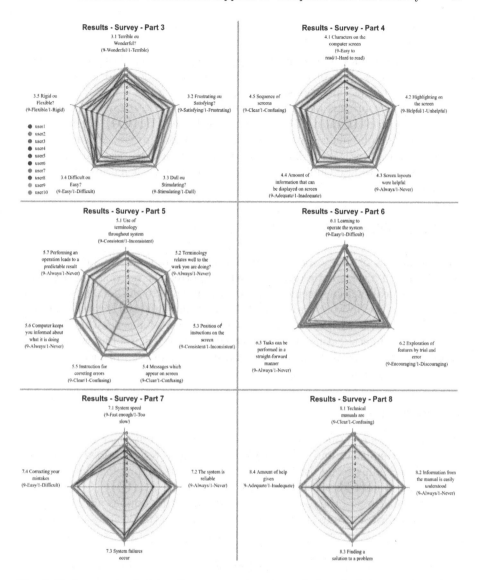

Fig. 7. Radar graphs showing the answers given in parts 3 to 8 of the questionnaire.

7.3   Results

We concluded that the tool pleased in several aspects of the users. The users' sample was of male professionals aged between 30 and 54 years, infrastructure professionals (wireless network, wired network, data centers, and VoIP telephony). They used the tool for one hour per week.

The positive points highlighted by the users were: ease of use, the learning process, the design of the screens, highlights presented, terminology, messages generated by the tool, simplicity in the control options, and absence of failures and errors.

As negative points, we can mention the lack of flexibility of the tool, slowness in some situations, lack of instructions for error correction and feedback from the computer during operations.

Through the process of evaluation of the tool, we can say that the users approved the tool in most of the aspects evaluated. However, there are still improvements to be made. To improve the evaluation process, allowing a more complete and statistically reliable evaluation, it would be necessary for more users to test the tool, including the participation of professionals external to the university.

8   Conclusion

The main result of this work was the tool developed. The secondary objective was to perform a systematic review, which supported the relevance of the work.

Our tool deals with a specific network structure due to the demand presented by the Computer Network Group. It was built using light and flexible programming languages, focused on the web, using its library for generating graphics, facilitating and accelerating the professionals' duties. The tool allows real-time monitoring of the network situation and also an exploration of historical data, to search for anomalies.

8.1   Relevance

This project was relevant mainly because it dealt with the concrete application of several technologies and areas of Computing. The tool obtained at the end of the project aims to be used in all university units, improving the supply of information to network administrators.

The comparison of the tool developed with the other options available in the market added relevance to the work, since that showed the positive and negative points of all the solutions, basing the decision to create a new tool customized according to professionals' needs.

The process of interactive and incremental development combined with the evaluation of the tool by a sample of future users, with positive results, reinforces the relevance to the university, with mostly positive feedback.

8.2   Limitations

We can cite flexibility as a limitation of the tool. That was developed for a specific scenario, not allowing its use in another context (network infrastructure). The problem of flexibility was also noted during the evaluation process carried out by users since the views, and specific parameters that make them up are predefined and do not allow significant customizations.

8.3   Final Considerations

In this work, we presented the whole research process about our tool, its implementation proposal in a university, specification, development process, and the evaluation of users from different university units. The sequence employed in the development of this work allowed the desired results to be achieved, with the final effect of providing the university with a tool for monitoring the wireless network.

References

1. Dasgupta, A., Arendt, D.L., Franklin, L.R., Wong, P.C., Cook, K.A.: Human factors in streaming data analysis: challenges and opportunities for information visualization. In: Computer Graphics Forum, September 2017. https://doi.org/10.1111/cgf.13264
2. Dias, C.C.: Usabilidade na web: criando portais mais acessíveis. Alta Books (2007)
3. Elastic.co: Kibana User Guide [4.6] — Elastic (2018). https://www.elastic.co/guide/en/kibana/current/index.html
4. Few, S.: Information Dashboard Design. O'Reilly, Sebastopol (2006)
5. Grafana Labs: Grafana documentation — Grafana Documentation (2018). http://docs.grafana.org/
6. Guimaraes, V.T., Freitas, C.M.D.S., Sadre, R., Tarouco, L.M.R., Granville, L.Z.: A survey on information visualization for network and service management. IEEE Commun. Surv. Tutor. **18**(1), 285–323 (2016). https://doi.org/10.1109/COMST.2015.2450538
7. Jacobs, K.: Data-Driven Security: Analysis, Visualization and Dashboards, 1st edn. Wiley, Hoboken (2014). https://doi.org/10.1017/CBO9781107415324.004
8. Kirk, A.: Data Visualization: A Successful Design Process: A Structured Design Approach to Equip You With the Knowledge of How to Successfully Accomplish any Data Visualization Challenge Efficiently and Effectively. Packt Publishing, Birmingham (2012)
9. McKenna, S., Staheli, D., Fulcher, C., Meyer, M.: BubbleNet: a cyber security dashboard for visualizing patterns. In: Proceedings of the Eurographics/IEEE VGTC Conference on Visualization, EuroVis 2016, pp. 281–290. Eurographics Association, Goslar (2016). https://doi.org/10.1111/cgf.12904
10. Munzner, T., Maguire, E.: Visualization Analysis & Design. AK Peters, Natick (2015). https://doi.org/10.1002/9781119978176
11. Splunk: Authentication - Splunk Documentation (2018). http://docs.splunk.com/Documentation/CIM/4.11.0/User/Authentication
12. Tanenbaum, A.S., Wetherall, D.J.: Computer Networks, vol. 52. Pearson Prentice Hall, Upper Saddle River (2011). https://doi.org/10.1016/j.comnet.2008.04.002
13. Ware, C.: Information Visualization: Perception for Design (Interactive Technologies). Morgan Kaufmann, Burlington (2004)

Classification of Active Multiple Sclerosis Lesions in MRI Without the Aid of Gadolinium-Based Contrast Using Textural and Enhanced Features from FLAIR Images

Paulo G. L. Freire[1] , Marcos Hideki Idagawa[2] ,
Enedina Maria Lobato de Oliveira[2] , Nitamar Abdala[2] ,
Henrique Carrete Jr.[2] , and Ricardo J. Ferrari[1]($\boxtimes$)

[1] Department of Computing, Federal University of São Carlos,
Rod. Washington Luis, Km 235, São Carlos, SP 13565-905, Brazil
{paulo.freire,rferrari}@ufscar.br
[2] Federal University of São Paulo, Rua Pedro de Toledo, 650,
São Paulo, SP 04039-002, Brazil
https://www.bipgroup.dc.ufscar.br

Abstract. Multiple sclerosis (MS) is an autoimmune demyelinating disease that affects one's central nervous system. The disease has a number lesion states. One of them is known as active, or enhancing, and indicates that a lesion is under an inflammatory condition. This specific case is of interest to radiologists since it is commonly associated with the period of time a patient suffers most from the effects of MS. To identify which lesions are active, a Gadolinium-based contrast is injected in the patient prior to a magnetic resonance imaging procedure. The properties of the contrast medium allow it to enhance active lesions, making them distinguishable from nonactive ones in T1-w images. However, studies from various research groups in recent years indicate that Gadolinium-based contrasts tend to accumulate in the body after a number of injections. Since a comprehensive understanding of this accumulation is not yet available, medical agencies around the world have been restricting its usage to cases only where it is absolutely necessary. In this work we propose a supervised algorithm to distinguish active from nonactive lesions in FLAIR images, thus eliminating the need for contrast injections altogether. The classification task was performed using textural and enhanced features as input to the XGBoost classifier on a voxel level. Our database comprised 54 MS patients (33 with active lesions and 21 with nonactive ones) with a total of 22 textural and enhanced features obtained from Run Length and Gray Level Co-occurrence Matrices. The average precision, recall and F1-score results in a 6-fold cross-validation for active and nonactive classes were 0.892, 0.968, 0.924 and 0.994, 0.987, 0.991, respectively. Moreover, from a lesion perspective, the algorithm misclassified only 3 active lesions out of 157. These results indicate our tool can be used by physicians to get information about active

© Springer Nature Switzerland AG 2020
O. Gervasi et al. (Eds.): ICCSA 2020, LNCS 12250, pp. 60–74, 2020.
https://doi.org/10.1007/978-3-030-58802-1_5

MS lesions in FLAIR images without using any kind of contrast, thus improving one's health and also reducing the cost of MRI procedures for MS patients.

Keywords: Multiple sclerosis · Classification · Supervised learning · Texture · Enhancement

1   Introduction

Multiple sclerosis (MS) is an autoimmune demyelinating disease that attacks one's central nervous system and affects more than 2.3 million people worldwide [21]. The most common form of MS is known as relapsing-remitting and is characterized by episodes of neurological dysfunctions that evolve over a period of time before plateauing and remitting with some degree of recovery [17]. Each MS lesion can be classified into a specific class, namely preactive, active, chronic active and chronic inactive [15]. The active - or enhancing - state indicates that one or more lesions are under an inflammatory condition and it is commonly associated with the period of time a patient suffers most from the effects of MS.

To identify which lesions are active, a Gadolinium-based contrast is injected in the patient prior to the procedure itself. The properties of the contrast enhance active lesions [17], making them distinguishable from other kinds of pathologies in T1-w images. However, recent works [4,14,27] indicate that Gadolinium-based contrasts tend to accumulate in one's brain, bones, skin and other parts of the body after a number of injections.

A comprehensive understanding of this accumulation is not yet available, which has made several agencies, such as the U.S. Food and Drug Administration and the European Medicines Agency, issue statements [10,11,24–26] restricting the usage of Gadolinium-based contrasts only to cases where it is absolutely necessary. There are indications that infrequent contrast administrations pose no threat [16]; however, this is not the case for MS patients, who must undergo a magnetic resonance imaging (MRI) procedure with contrast injections from time to time for the rest of their lives in order to assess how the disease is progressing.

Some works in the literature have used supervised and unsupervised techniques to segment and classify different types of MS lesions [18]. Since it is a challenging task, it is common for techniques to use different features from MR images besides gray level intensity. In [20], the authors used texture analysis to distinguish normal appearing white matter (NAWM) from active MS lesions in T2-w images. They used features extracted from both Gray Level Co-occurrence Matrix (GLCM) and Run Length Matrix (RLM) to help differentiate between the two classes. Using linear discriminant analysis (LDA), partial least squares (PLS) and logistic regression (LR), they were able to get different sets of textural features and results according to each technique. The authors achieved the highest accuracy when using PLS in a 6-texture parameter model with a sensitivity of 0.88 and specificity of 0.81. According to the authors, a limitation of their study concerned the limited number of patients (a total of 21) and active lesions (a total of 58), indicating that further investigations should be conducted in order to confirm their findings in a larger set of data. Another important aspect to consider is that the goal of the authors was to distinguish active MS lesions from NAWM instead of active from nonactive lesions. Though the correct distinction between NAWM and other MS pathologies is crucial, it is not a sufficient condition to withdraw the usage of Gadolinium-based contrast.

In [1], a study was conducted in order to distinguish between three classes of lesions: non-enhancing lesions (NEL), enhancing lesions (EL) and persistent black holes (PBH). The authors used more than 300 textural features from GLCM, RLM, absolute gradient and wavelets extracted from T2-w images. Their dataset comprised 90 patients of which 39 of them had NELs, 32 had PBHs and 19 had ELs. The authors used LDA to classify two classes at a time. In this sense, they verified that 18 features were significant to differentiate NELs from ELs, 14 features to separate NELs and PBHs and other 18 to distinguish ELs from PBHs. Their model yielded perfect classification for NEL vs. EL and EL vs. PBH and a sensitivity and specificity of 0.943 and 0.963, respectively, for NEL vs. PBH. These results are a strong indication that texture analysis can be successfully applied to tell different MS lesion types apart without contrast injection.

Finally, in [8] the authors presented a pipeline for detection and segmentation of MS lesions, including active ones. To this end, they used pre- and post-contrast T1-w images to train their model using a Markov Random Field and textural features. They detected candidate active voxels with a Conditional Random Field classifier. Then, higher order features modeling the texture of the lesion and surrounding tissue were calculated for the patches containing the candidates. They also included an option to use longitudinal information, when available, in order to leverage any differences between time-points. They trained their algorithm with 1760 scans acquired at 180 sites. Applying their model to a test set of 2770 patients led to a sensitivity of 0.91 and average false positive counts of 0.46. A good point made by the authors regarded that active lesions can be as small as 3–10 voxels. This obviously poses a difficulty for segmentation algorithms and must be given special attention in the context of MS. In this sense, textures and patches can mitigate the problem by factoring in the neighborhood information.

Given this scenario, in this work we propose a supervised algorithm to distinguish active from nonactive lesions in Gadolinium-free fluid attenuation inversion recovery (FLAIR) images, thus eliminating the need for contrast injections altogether. The classification task was performed on a voxel level on 54 MS patients - 33 with active lesions and 21 with nonactive ones - using the XGBoost classifier [7]. We used a total of 22 features, including textures extracted from Run Length Matrix and Gray Level Co-occurrence Matrix. The average precision, recall and F1-score results in a 6-fold cross-validation for active and nonactive classes were 0.892, 0.968, 0.924 and 0.994, 0.987, 0.991, respectively. Moreover, from a lesion (instead of voxel) classification perspective, the algorithm misclassified only 3 active lesions out of 157, meaning mistakes on the voxel level are tolerable to some extent when we look at lesions as a whole. These results indicate our tool can be used by physicians to get information about active MS lesions in FLAIR images without using any kind of contrast, thus improving one's health and also reducing the costs of MRI procedures for MS patients.

This paper is divided as follows. In Sect. 2 we present and describe our active and nonactive patient databases, along with explanations of the image features extracted from FLAIR images and the XGBoost classifier; in Sect. 3, we present our results and discuss them; finally, in Sect. 4, we present our conclusions and lay out future works that can be derived from our findings.

2   Materials and Methods

In this section we present the databases used in this work, the preprocessing pipeline applied to the images, the textural features used in the classification step, the classifier itself and the metrics to assess the results.

2.1   Databases

Nonactive Lesions. We used the training data of the Longitudinal MS Lesion Segmentation Challenge of the 2015 International Symposium on Biomedical Imaging [5] as our nonactive lesions database with scans from five patients and a total of 21 time-points (4 patients with 4 time-points and 1 patient with 5 time-points). The imaging sequences were adjusted to produce T1-w, T2-w, PD and FLAIR images, which were all skull-stripped, bias field corrected and registered to the same space. Each time-point included manual lesion annotations by two expert raters. Image dimensions were $181 \times 217 \times 181$ and voxel resolution was $1\,\mathrm{mm}^3$.

Active Lesions. Our active lesions database came from the Demyelinating Diseases Outpatient Clinics - Neurology & Neurosurgery Department - Universidade Federal de São Paulo - (UNIFESP), Brazil. This database comprised scans of 33 patients with FLAIR and post-contrast T1-w images. An expert rater annotated active MS lesions in FLAIR using post-contrast T1-w as a reference for lesion location. Since this database existed prior to this work and the annotations were made on images as they were, 7 patients out of 33 had slightly different acquisition protocols regarding the number of slices per scan. While 26 patients were scanned with image dimensions $384 \times 512 \times 20$, the other 7 were scanned with image dimensions $384 \times 512 \times 25$. However, qualitatively speaking, the extra number of slices in this second group did not interfere with our region of interest (i.e., the brain itself). Voxel resolution was $0.44 \times 0.44 \times 6.5\,\mathrm{mm}^3$ across all images. An example of a patient from this database is shown in Fig. 1.

2.2   Preprocessing

The preprocessing pipeline shown in Fig. 2 was applied to all FLAIR images from both databases.

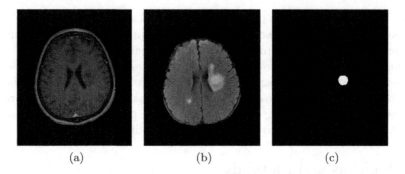

(a)   (b)   (c)

Fig. 1. Patient with active lesions from the UNIFESP database. (a) T1, (b) FLAIR, (c) Active lesion mask annotated by an expert rater.

First, we applied a noise reduction step using the Non-local means technique [3] with $\sigma = 15$. This step is important because it helps mitigate intensity variations, thus creating a smoother brain profile across all images. After that, we applied the N4 algorithm [23] to reduce the bias field effect. Following that, a histogram matching [22] using two matching points was conducted to bring all images to a standard intensity domain. As a reference for this histogram matching we chose the FLAIR scan in the nonactive dataset with the heaviest lesion load (32,3 ml). The rationale behind this choice was to make lesions as representative as possible when matching histograms in both active and nonactive datasets. Finally, all images were rescaled to the $[0, 255]$ interval.

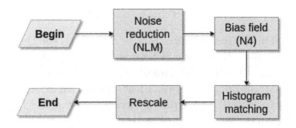

Fig. 2. Preprocessing pipeline.

2.3   Feature Extraction

After completing the preprocessing pipeline explained the previous section, we extracted features to aid in the distinction between active and nonactive lesions. Such features can be divided into two groups, as shown in Fig. 3.

The highlight branch was comprised of Sobel and two other feature images, enhanced and hyperintensity map, generated by the algorithm proposed in [12].

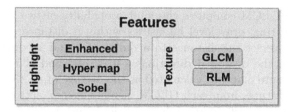

Fig. 3. Classes of extracted features.

In short, these enhanced and hyperintensity map feature images were created by first scattering the histogram in order to attenuate mean intensities and enhance "tail" ones, using it to further highlight hyperintensities through patch comparisons. An example of the images generated from this branch are shown in Fig. 4.

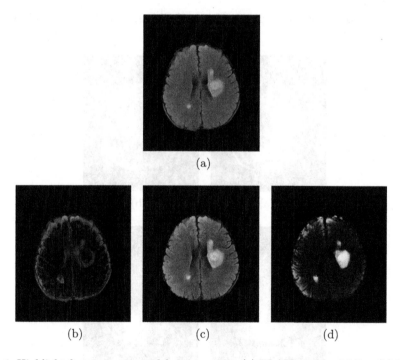

Fig. 4. Highlight features extracted from an active (a) FLAIR image yielding (b) Sobel image, (c) Enhanced image and (d) Hyperintensity map.

The other branch of feature extraction concerned textures and was divided into two techniques: GLCM and RLM. The former was first introduced by [13] and has been widely used in MRI segmentation and classification problems

[1,8,19,20]. The GLCM computes the joint probability of two voxels with the same, or co-occurring, gray level intensities within a distance d and direction θ. In this work, we set the distance to a radius of 2 and 13 directions, scaled analogously from the default 4 directions - 0, 45, 90 and 135° - used in 2D images. Each texture map was calculated as the average of all 13 directions. We extracted eight features from each GLCM, namely energy, entropy, correlation, inverse difference moment, inertia, cluster shade, cluster prominence and Haralick correlation. Similarly, RLM [6] counts the number of times two (or more) voxels with the same gray level intensity occur in a given direction. Features from RLM are mostly related to the fineness and coarseness of a given image represented by long runs and short runs, respectively. We extracted ten features from each RLM, namely short run emphasis (SRE), long run emphasis (LRE), grey level non uniformity (GLN), run length non uniformity (RLN), low grey level run emphasis (LGRE), high grey level run emphasis (HGRE), short run low grey level emphasis (SRLGE), short run high grey level emphasis (SRHGE), long run low grey level emphasis (LRLGE), long run high grey level emphasis (LRHGE).

An example of features extracted from GLCM and RLM are shown in Fig. 5.

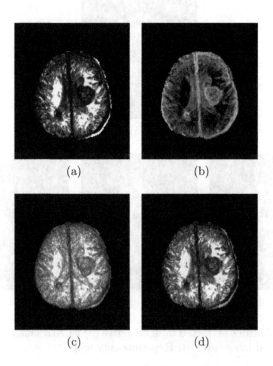

(a)   (b)

(c)   (d)

Fig. 5. Textures extracted from the patient with active lesions depicted in Fig. 4. (a) GLCM Energy, (b) GLCM Entropy, (c) RLM GLN, (d) RLM LRE.

After completing feature extraction, a total of 22 attributes were selected to be used in the classification step.

2.4 Classifier

The classifier used in this paper is the XGBoost [7], a gradient tree boosting algorithm. The main goal of boosting is to improve the accuracy of a given learning algorithm by using an ensemble of weak learners whose joint decision rule has an arbitrarily high accuracy on the training set [9]. We chose XGBoost due to its growing popularity in classification contests [2] and optimized structure that makes it scalable.

Mathematically, given a data set with n samples, indexed by $i = 1 \ldots n$, and m features $D = \{(\mathbf{x}_i, y_i))\}$, where $|D| = n$, $\mathbf{x}_i \in \mathbb{R}^m$ and $y_i \in \mathbb{R}$, a tree ensemble model is comprised of the sum of K functions to predict the output

$$\hat{y}_i = \phi(\mathbf{x}_i) = \sum_{k=1}^{K} f_k(\mathbf{x}_i), \tag{1}$$

where $f_k \in \mathcal{F} = \{f(\mathbf{x}) = w_{q(\mathbf{x})}\}$ with $q : \mathbb{R}^m \to T$ and $w \in \mathbb{R}^T$ is the space of trees. In this context, q is related to the arrangement of each tree that maps a sample to its corresponding leaf index and T is the number of leaves in a tree. Therefore, each f_k is related to one particular tree q and leaf weights w.

In order to learn the functions that will describe the model itself, the following loss function is used as the objective

$$\mathcal{L}(\phi) = \sum_i l(\hat{y}_i, y_i) + \sum_k \Omega(f_k), \tag{2}$$

where

$$\Omega(f_k) = \gamma T + \frac{1}{2}\lambda\|w\|^2, \tag{3}$$

l is a differentiable loss function and Ω is a penalty term to avoid selecting complex trees. The goal is to keep the model simple and highly predictive at the same time. We can think of gradient boosting in the following way:

1. Fit a model to the data, $\mathcal{F}_1(\mathbf{x}) = y$.
2. Fit a model to the residuals (i.e., the loss), $h_1(\mathbf{x}) = y - \mathcal{F}_1(\mathbf{x})$.
3. Create a new model, $\mathcal{F}_2(\mathbf{x}) = \mathcal{F}_1(\mathbf{x}) + h_1(\mathbf{x})$.
4. Repeat steps (1)–(3) until a number M of trees or a sufficiently small difference between loss functions of subsequent steps is reached.

In other words, the algorithm trains successive component classifiers and the output for a test sample $\mathbf{x}$ is based on the outputs of these very same components. The scalability of XGBoost is achieved by analyzing and optimizing cache access patterns, data compression and sharding, which are described in more detail in [7]. Regarding parameters, we set the maximum depth of each tree to one and the number of estimators to 5000 in order to avoid specialization of learners and provide enough of them to get an accurate joint decision rule.

2.5   Metrics

To assess the classification of active and nonactive voxel lesions we used the precision, recall and F1-score metrics defined in Table 1.

Table 1. Metrics used to assess classification of active and nonactive voxel lesion. TP, FP and FN are true positives, false positives and false negatives, respectively.

Metric	Evaluation
Precision	$\frac{TP}{TP+FP}$
Recall	$\frac{TP}{TP+FN}$
F1-score	$2\frac{\text{Precision}\times\text{Recall}}{\text{Precision}+\text{Recall}}$

The ratio of active to nonactive lesions in our databases was roughly 1:4, i.e., the active voxel class had a representativity of approximately 25%. Given this imbalance and the paramount importance of correctly detecting active lesions, the recall and F1-score metrics bear more meaning to the assessment of classification performance. This is due to the fact that the former is related to the actual ground truth and the latter provides a better grasp on the overall performance - which can be distorted by the uneven distribution among both classes of interest.

We also conducted a lesion-level analysis. To do so, the active and nonactive voxels were grouped into connected components, thus indicating how many actual lesions were present in each patient. Given the classification probability of each lesion voxel, we calculated the average probability of any given lesion component being active or nonactive. Let C be a lesion component and p the probability of a given lesion voxel inside C. If the average probability of component C was equal to or greater than 50%, we ranked it as being active; otherwise, we ranked it as nonactive, as indicated in Eq. 4.

$$\text{Class} = \begin{cases} \text{Nonactive,} & \frac{1}{\|C\|}\sum p_{p\in C} < 0.5 \\ \text{Active,} & \text{otherwise.} \end{cases} \tag{4}$$

3   Results and Discussion

In this section we present the voxel-level classification results based on precision, recall and F1-score, as well as the accuracy of our method on a lesion-level basis. Before discussing the results per se, two observations regarding the number of folds are deemed necessary.

First, we set the number of patients per fold to five as a trade-off between the size of the training and test sets in order to make the classifier general enough to avoid overfitting problems. However, since the number of patients with active lesions was 33, the last fold would comprise either 3 or 8 patients. We chose the latter for the sake of generalization. The results using only 3 patients in the training set indicated a strong overfitting, especially for the active lesion class. Hence, we decided to include these 3 patients in the last 5-patient fold. Since this experiment design choice implied in less samples for the training set, thus making the classification task "harder", we decided it was a valid approach. This is the reason why the sixth fold included eight instead of five patients from each class.

Second, as mentioned in Sect. 2.1, the nonactive database was comprised of 5 patients, four of them with four time points and one with five. The rationale to choose which patients with nonactive lesions would go into each fold was to randomly choose one time point per patient when the fold size was five. For the last fold, with eight patients, we simply chose three additional random time points from the first three patients in the nonactive dataset (i.e., the last fold had two time points from the first three patients and one time point from the rest).

The voxel-level classification results are shown in Table 2. The nonactive classification yielded higher results when compared to the active class, especially regarding the precision metric. However, as mentioned in Sect. 2.5, recall and F1-score are more significant when it comes to analyze imbalanced datasets as the one we used in this work. In this sense, we can observe that these two metrics were similar between the active and nonactive classes. Moreover, we verified that most misclassifications occurred when a nonactive voxel was mistaken for an active one. Even though this is not ideal, this result is still better for a physician - who can discard these misclassifications when reviewing the outcome of our approach - than the other way around.

On a lesion-level perspective, 154 out of 157 lesions were correctly classified as active and the classification was perfect for the nonactive class. As mentioned in Sect. 2.5, we averaged the probability of each lesion as a whole and labeled them according to the majority class. We can see that even though the active class did not have precision, recall and F1-score as high as the nonactive class in a voxel-level analysis, the mistakes were compensated by the surrounding voxels comprising the lesion itself. In other words, the voxel-level classification provided a margin of safety for errors, making them less significant when viewed from a coarser granularity. Since the outcome of interest for neurologists and physicians is on the lesion-level, this margin indicates there is room for mistakes on a voxel-level that, to a certain extent, do not interfere on the lesion-level results.

Only one patient, ID 32, did not have their lesions identified as active. Some features from this particular patient are shown in Fig. 6. Visual analysis indicate that not only were the lesions small, they also had an intensity profile too similar to that of nonactive lesions. Moreover, the quality of the FLAIR image itself was rather poor. Even though textural and enhanced features aid in the distinction between both classes, there are cases where the classification step fails to yield the expected output due to conditions that are out our reach but yet have influence on the final outcome.

Table 2. Precision, recall and F1-score metrics for the 6-fold cross-validation.

Patients	Class	Results		
		Precision	Recall	F1-score
1–5	Active	0.945	1	0.972
	Nonactive	1	0.993	0.997
6–10	Active	0.7	0.996	0.823
	Nonactive	1	0.966	0.983
11–15	Active	0.765	1	0.867
	Nonactive	1	0.977	0.988
16–20	Active	0.99	1	0.995
	Nonactive	1	0.998	0.999
21–25	Active	0.887	0.863	0.875
	Nonactive	0.978	0.982	0.98
26–33	Active	0.999	0.958	0.978
	Nonactive	0.991	1	0.995
Weighted avg.	Active	0.892	0.968	0.924
	Nonactive	0.994	0.987	0.991

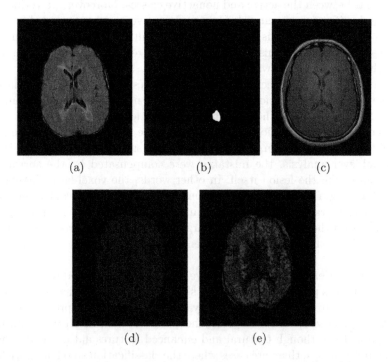

(a)   (b)   (c)

(d)   (e)

Fig. 6. Example of slices from patient ID 32 who had zero lesion hits. (a) FLAIR, (b) active lesion annotation, (c) T1 with Gadolinium enhancement, (d) RLM LRE, (e) RLM GLN.

We can also observe that the standard deviation across all lesions was quite small and the average lesion probability for most patients, both active and nonactive, was close or equal to one. It indicates our classifier was able to accurately distinguish both classes with a high degree of certainty, which is important when dealing with a sensitive healthcare scenario as this one.

To analyze the effect of the features in the classification step, we plotted histograms for all 22 attributes extracted from all images of both active and nonactive datasets. Doing so we observed the RLM features RLE, RLN, GLN showed a significant distinction between both classes, whereas GLCM features, in general, had an overlay between one class and the other. Histograms from RLM and GLCM features are shown in Figs. 7 and 8.

The enhancement effect mentioned in Sect. 2.3 can be seen in histograms shown in Fig. 9. We can see that the enhanced and hyperintensity map features offset and spread the class histograms apart, making them more distinguishable. Extracting good features is of paramount importance for the supervised learning pipeline, since they have a direct effect on the classification step. Therefore, combining dissimilar and relevant textural and enhanced features creates a domain space that is adequate for a proper class separation. However, it is also relevant to note that features with significant overlays cannot be promptly discarded because their combination with other more key/distinct features can be useful for the classification step as a whole, especially when the overlay areas between these features are complementary (i.e., the overlay area between classes in one histogram is the most distinctive area in another).

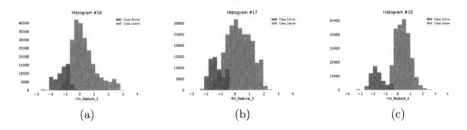

Fig. 7. RLM feature histograms: (a) LRE, (b) RLN and (c) GLN. Class "Lesion" represents the nonactive lesions.

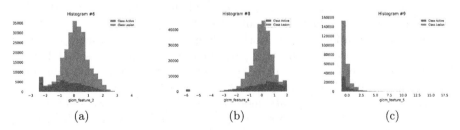

Fig. 8. GLCM feature histograms: (a) Entropy, (b) Inverse Difference Moment and (c) Inertia. Class "Lesion" represents the nonactive lesions.

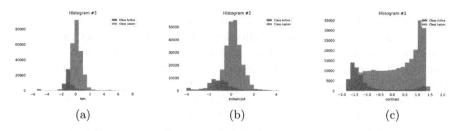

Fig. 9. Enhanced feature histograms: (a) Histogram matched (no enhancement), (b) Enhanced and (c) Hyperintensity Map. Class "Lesion" represents the nonactive lesions.

Overall, the classification accuracy on a lesion-level for the active class was over 98%, indicating that it is possible to identify this particular kind of MS lesion using only FLAIR images and without any kind of contrast agent. In addition, RLM features proved to be the most distinctive ones in this scenario. Performing the classification step on a voxel-level provided us with enough samples to properly train our classifier and also allowed for a margin of safety to take place, "smoothing out" the effects of misclassifications on a lesion-level.

4   Conclusions

This paper presented a supervised classification pipeline to distinguish between active and nonactive MS lesions in FLAIR images without using any contrast agent based on textural and enhanced features to create a feature space where both classes could be easily distinguished using the XGBoost classifier. Our dataset comprised 54 patients, 33 with active lesions and 21 with nonactive ones, with varying lesion loads, shapes, sizes and locations.

Though active lesions represented a small portion of samples when compared to nonactive ones, the results indicate that is possible to tell these two classes apart using information from FLAIR images and without the aid of any sort of contrasts. Out of the 157 active lesions, 154 were correctly identified as so. This is relevant because it unburdens patients from the accumulation of heavy metal based contrasts in their systems, makes it possible for patients with kidney problems to get an assessment of their active lesion progress (since they cannot be injected with contrasts in the first place) and also lowers the cost of the MRI procedure with the elimination of contrast shots.

There are limitations in this work. A larger number of patients would be required to assess the classification performance on a broader set of lesions. Also, lesions were not rated by an independent neuroradiologist, and that could have introduced bias in our study. And finally, we lacked an external validation set, which would make our data more robust. Nonetheless, we were able to show that is very possible to correctly identify active MS lesions without using Gadolinium-based contrasts.

We expect to further investigate these findings by conducting a feature selection and analysis to verify which of them are the most relevant for the classification step and which can be discarded without affecting accuracy. We also intend to create a fully automatic pipeline to segment MS lesions and classify them into active and nonactive without any kind of contrast agent.

Acknowledgements. This work was supported by the São Paulo Research Foundation - FAPESP (grant numbers 2016/15661-0 and 2018/08826-9).

References

1. Ardakani, A.A., Nabavi, S., Farzan, A., Najafabad, B.: Quantitative MRI texture analysis in differentiating enhancing and non-enhancing T1-hypointense lesions without application of contrast agent in multiple sclerosis. Czech and Slovak Neurol. Neurosurg. **113**(6), 700–707 (2017)
2. Bennett, J., Lanning, S.: The Netflix prize. In: KDD Cup and Workshop in Conjunction with KDD (2007)
3. Buades, A., Coll, B., Morel, J.-M.: A non-local algorithm for image denoising. In: IEEE Computer Society Conference on Computer Vision and Pattern Recognition, vol. 2, pp. 60–65 (2005)
4. Burke, L., Ramalho, M., AlObaidy, M., Chang, E., Jay, M., Semelka, R.: Self-reported gadolinium toxicity: a survey of patients with chronic symptoms. Magn. Reson. Imaging **34**, 1078–1080 (2016)
5. Carass, A., et al.: Longitudinal multiple sclerosis lesion segmentation: resource and challenge. NeuroImage **148**, 77–102 (2017)
6. Castellano, G., Bonilha, L., LM, L., Cendes, F.: Texture analysis of medical images. Clin. Radiol. **59**(12), 1061–1069 (2004)
7. Chen, T., Guestrin, C.: XGBoost: a scalable tree boosting system. In: Proceedings of the 22nd ACM SIGKDD International Conference on Knowledge Discovery and Data Mining, KDD 2016, pp. 785–794. ACM, New York (2016)
8. Doyle, A., Elliott, C., Karimaghaloo, Z., Subbanna, N., Arnold, D.L., Arbel, T.: Lesion detection, segmentation and prediction in multiple sclerosis clinical trials. In: Crimi, A., Bakas, S., Kuijf, H., Menze, B., Reyes, M. (eds.) BrainLes 2017. LNCS, vol. 10670, pp. 15–28. Springer, Cham (2018). https://doi.org/10.1007/978-3-319-75238-9_2
9. Duda, O.R., Hart, P.E., Stork, D.G.: Pattern Classification, 2nd edn. Wiley-Interscience, Hoboken (2000)
10. European Medicines Agency: EMA reviewing gadolinium contrast agents used in MRI scans (2016). http://bit.ly/EuropeanMedicinesAgency-2016. Accessed 02 Apr 2017
11. European Medicines Agency: EMA's final opinion confirms restrictions on use of linear gadolinium agents in body scans, July 2017. http://bit.ly/EuropeanMedicinesAgency2017. Accessed 01 July 2019
12. Freire, P.G.L., Ferrari, R.J.: Multiple sclerosis lesion enhancement and white matter region estimation using hyperintensities in FLAIR images. Biomed. Signal Process. Control **49**, 338–348 (2019)
13. Haralick, R., Shanmugam, K., Dinstein, I.: Textural feature for image classification. IEEE Trans. Syst. Man Cybern. **3**(6), 610–621 (1973)
14. Hu, H.H., Pokorney, A., Towbin, R.B., Miller, J.H.: Increased signal intensities in the dentate nucleus and globus pallidus on unenhanced T1-weighted images: evidence in children undergoing multiple gadolinium MRI exams. Pediatr. Radiol. **46**(11), 1590–1598 (2016). https://doi.org/10.1007/s00247-016-3646-3

15. Jonkman, L., et al.: Can MS lesion stages be distinguished with MRI? A port-mortem MRI and histopathology study. J. Neurol. **262**(4), 1074–1080 (2015). https://doi.org/10.1007/s00415-015-7689-4

16. Kromrey, M., et al.: Intravenous injection of gadobutrol in an epidemiological study group did not lead to a difference in relative signal intensities of certain brain structures after 5 years. Eur. Radiol. **27**(2), 772–777 (2016). https://doi.org/10.1007/s00330-016-4418-z

17. Lewis, P.A., Spillane, J.E.: Chapter 7 - Multiple Sclerosis. In: Lewis, P.A., Spillane, J.E. (eds.) The Molecular and Clinical Pathology of Neurodegenerative Disease, pp. 221–251. Academic Press (2019)

18. Litjens, G., et al.: A survey on deep learning in medical image analysis. Med. Image Anal. **42**, 60–88 (2017)

19. Loizou, C.P., Petroudi, S., Seimenis, I., Pantziaris, M., Pattichis, C.S.: Quantitative texture analysis of brain white matter lesions derived from T2-weighted MR images in MS patients with clinically isolated syndrome. J. Neuroradiol. **2015**(42), 99–114 (2014)

20. Michoux, N., Guillet, A., Rommel, D., Mazzamuto, G., Sindic, C., Duprez, T.: Texture analysis of T2-weighted MR images to assess acute inflammation in brain MS lesions. PLoS One **10**(12), e0145497 (2015)

21. Multiple Sclerosis International Federation: 2013 Atlas of MS (2013). http://www.msif.org/about-us/advocacy/atlas/. Accessed 01 Dec 2015

22. Nyul, L.G., Udupa, J., Zhang, X.: New variants of a method of MRI scale standardization. IEEE Trans. Med. Imaging **19**(2), 143–150 (2000)

23. Tustison, N., Gee, J.: N4ITK: Nick's N3 ITK implementation for MRI bias field correction. Penn Image Computing and Science Laboratory (2009)

24. U.S. Food and Drug Administration: FDA Drug Safety Communication: FDA evaluating the risk of brain deposits with repeated use of gadolinium-based contrast agents for magnetic resonance imaging (MRI) (2015). http://www.fda.gov/Drugs/DrugSafety/ucm455386.htm. Accessed 07 May 2018

25. U.S. Food and Drug Administration: FDA warns that gadolinium-based contrast agents (GBCAs) are retained in the body; requires new class warnings, May 2017. https://www.fda.gov/media/109825/download. Accessed 01 July 2019

26. U.S. Food and Drug Administration: Update on FDA approach to safety issue of gadolinium retention after administration of gadolinium-based contrast agents, September 2018. https://www.fda.gov/media/116492/download. Accessed 01 July 2019

27. Beomonte Zobel, B., Quattrocchi, C.C., Errante, Y., Grasso, R.F.: Gadolinium-based contrast agents: did we miss something in the last 25 years? Radiol. Med. **121**(6), 478–481 (2015). https://doi.org/10.1007/s11547-015-0614-1

Automatic Positioning of Hippocampus Deformable Mesh Models in Brain MR Images Using a Weighted 3D-SIFT Technique

Matheus Müller Korb⬤, Ricardo José Ferrari$^{(\boxtimes)}$⬤,
and for the Alzheimer's Disease Neuroimaging

Department of Computing, Federal University of São Carlos,
São Carlos, SP 13565-905, Brazil
rferrari@ufscar.br
https://www.bipgroup.dc.ufscar.br

Abstract. Automatic hippocampus segmentationin Magnetic Resonance (MR) images is an essential step in systems for early diagnostic and monitoring treatment of Alzheimer's disease (AD). It allows quantification of the hippocampi volume and assessment of their progressive shrinkage, considered as the hallmark symptom of AD. Among several methods published in the literature for hippocampus segmentation, those using anatomical atlases and deformable mesh models are the most promising ones. Although these techniques are convenient ways to embed the shape of the models in the segmentation process, their success greatly depend on the initial positioning of the models. In this work, we propose a new keypoint deformable registration technique that uses a modification of the 3D Scale-Invariant Feature Transform (3D-SIFT) and a keypoint weighting strategy for automatic positioning of hippocampus deformable meshes in brain MR images. Using the Mann-Whitney U test to assess the results statistically, our method showed an average improvement of 11% over the exclusive use of Affine transformation, 30% over the original 3D-SIFT and 7% over the non-weighted point procedure.

Keywords: 3D-SIFT · Keypoint registration · Deformable mesh positioning · Hippocampus segmentation · Alzheimer's Disease · MRI

1 Introduction

Alzheimer's disease (AD) is the most common neurodegenerative disease associated with age, affecting approximately 10% of the world population over 60 years old [5]. In Brazil, the average increase in mortality with the underlying cause of AD is 11.7% in men and 13.2% in women [27]. The natural evolution of

---

Alzheimer's Disease Neuroimaging—Disease Neuroimaging Initiative (ADNI) database.

© Springer Nature Switzerland AG 2020
O. Gervasi et al. (Eds.): ICCSA 2020, LNCS 12250, pp. 75–90, 2020.
https://doi.org/10.1007/978-3-030-58802-1_6

this disease manifests cognitive deficiencies that can lead to extreme incapacitation. To date, there is no cure for the AD; however, early diagnosis associated with appropriate treatment helps delay progression of symptoms, improving the patient's quality of life.

In medical centers and research laboratories, the manual hippocampi contouring procedure in magnetic resonance (MR) images used for measuring their volumes is usually conducted by a specialist following some predefined or established protocol [11]. However, the time spent and the visual fatigue of the specialists are limiting factors for many executions of this procedure [2]. As a result, the medical imaging community has become interested in developing fully automatic techniques for hippocampus segmentation in MR images.

In the literature, two automatic approaches have achieved the most promising results for the segmentation of hippocampus in MR images [1]. The first creates and uses multiple atlases, exploring label fusion or aggregation of clinical information [13,15,23], while the second combines atlases and deformable models [14,26,30]. In both cases, image registration techniques play a fundamental role, and an improvement in these algorithms would lead to increase precision of hippocampus segmentation.

In various medical image segmentation scenarios, deformable image registration techniques present the best results because they can successfully deal with anatomical inter-patient brain variation [4]. However, intensity-based registration that rely on optimization of the entire image space are prone to get stuck in local optima, possibly resulting in a large mismatch. By constraining the search space according to anatomical landmarks [6,9], such mismatches are unlikely to occur. Moreover, landmarks-based registration can take advantage of point matches in micro-regions of the brain, which are stable between patients and less susceptible to deformations due to age and neurodegenerative diseases [10].

In this work we present a new technique that uses 3D keypoints to estimate a deformable geometric transformation between a clinical and a template atlas images. The keypoints are automatically detected and matched using a modified version of Scale Invariant Feature Transform (SIFT) algorithm proposed by Rister [24,25], introduced to overcome numerical instabilities presented by the algorithm in the detection of tip-like landmarks. The geometric transformation are used to better positioning deformable hippocampus models in clinical MR images. Besides a modification of the SIFT algorithm, our technique also assigns to each matched pair of points a weighting value, which takes into account its distance to the centroid of hippocampus mesh model positioned via affine registration, to refine the mesh position adaptation.

2   Image Datasets

Two image datasets were used in this study; the first one is composed of synthetic structures and the second contains clinical brain images. In addition, it is presented a description of the topological atlas used for positioning the hippocampus meshes.

2.1 Synthetic Structures

A synthetic image dataset containing 864 tip-like structures was constructed using the parametric model proposed by Wörz et al. [29] with variations of translation, rotation, intensity, tapering, bending, and addition of Gaussian noise and bias field. These structures, which represent small three-dimensional high curvatures, were chosen because their similarity to 3D structures found in specific regions of MR brain images. All images were generated with isotropic resolution of 1 mm, size of $33 \times 33 \times 33$ voxels, and location of the point with maximum curvature mathematically determined.

In addition, a synthetic solid cube of size of $33 \times 33 \times 33$ voxels with constant intensity value 1, and centered in an empty three-dimensional array of size $128 \times 128 \times 128$ voxels, was created and used to investigate the behavior of the 3D-SIFT point detector proposed by Rister et al. [24].

These synthetic images were specifically constructed to evaluate the 3D-SIFT point detector [24] and its modification, making possible to determine the most sensible parameters of the method.

2.2 EADC-ADNI Clinical Dataset

The Alzheimer's Disease Neuroimaging Initiative (ADNI[1]) is part of a project created in 2003 by three research institutions from the United States (the National Institute of Aging, the Institute of Biomedical Imaging and Bioengineering and the Food and Drug Administration), with the aim of promoting the study of AD by making available standardized biomarker data.

The European Alzheimer's Disease Consortium (EADC-ADNI[2]) established a harmonized protocol for the manual segmentation of hippocampus in MR images, allowing more effective comparison between automatic and manual methods. The EADC-ADNI provides 135 T1-weighted (T1-w) RM images with binary masks of manually segmented hippocampi using a standardized protocol. The database contains images of patients between 60 and 90 years old and provides information about the cognitive health condition of each individual: Normal, Mild Cognitive Impairment (MCI), Late MCI (LMCI) and AD.

2.3 Topological Atlas

The topological atlas employed in this study is from the Neuroimage Analysis Center[3] (NAC). The atlas provides manual markings of brain structures of a healthy patient made by specialists in a T1-w MR image, with resolution of $1 \times 1 \times 1$ mm^3 and size of $256 \times 256 \times 256$ voxels. For each demarcated structure, a binary mask was extracted and a triangular mesh was constructed from it. In addition to a T1-w image used as a reference, this atlas also provides 149 meshes of various brain structures, including the left and right hippocampus.

---

[1] http://adni.loni.usc.edu/.

[2] http://www.hippocampal-protocol.net.

[3] http://www.spl.harvard.edu/publications/item/view/2037.

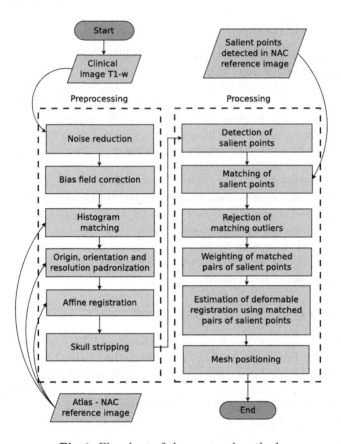

Fig. 1. Flowchart of the proposed method.

3 Methodology

This work proposes a technique for automatic hippocampus mesh positioning in MR images guided by automatically detected 3D salient points. Figure 1 depicts the sequence of steps used in the work.

3.1 Preprocessing

The preprocessing steps include image noise reduction using the Non-Local Means [3], bias field correction using the N4-ITK [17], intensity standardization using the technique of Nyul et al. [21], affine registration using the Nifty-Reg tool [22], skull stripping using the technique of Iglesias et al. [16] and, finally, the transformation of binary masks into three-dimensional meshes using an ITK-Mesh[4] image function.

---

[4] https://itk.org/Doxygen/html/classitk_1_1BinaryMask3DMeshSource.html.

3.2 Keypoint Extraction

Detection. The SIFT algorithm [25] uses a Gaussian scale-space (GSS) representation to detect keypoints. Formally, each level of the GSS representation is defined as a family of derived signals $L(\boldsymbol{x}, \sigma)$ computed as the convolution of the input image $I(\boldsymbol{x})$ with a Gaussian function, $G(\boldsymbol{x}, \sigma)$, as

$$L(\boldsymbol{x}, \sigma) = G(\boldsymbol{x}, \sigma) * I(\boldsymbol{x}), \tag{1}$$

where σ is the standard deviation, $\boldsymbol{x} = (x, y, z)$ corresponding to a spatial position, and $*$ is the convolution operation.

Using the GSS, stable feature point locations can be efficiently detected as extrema out of the convolution of the difference-of-Gaussian (DoG) function with the image, $D(\boldsymbol{x}, \sigma)$, which is computed from the difference of two nearby scales in the GSS separated by a constant multiplicative factor k as

$$\begin{aligned} D(\boldsymbol{x}, \sigma) &= L(\boldsymbol{x}, k\sigma) - L(\boldsymbol{x}, \sigma) \\ &= (G(\boldsymbol{x}, k\sigma) - G(\boldsymbol{x}, \sigma)) * I(\boldsymbol{x}). \end{aligned} \tag{2}$$

The DoG function has a close approximation to the scale-normalized Laplacian-of-Gaussian (LoG) [12], $\sigma^2 \nabla^2 G$, with the advantage of being computationally more efficient. As demonstrated by Lowe [19], this LoG-DoG relation can be expressed as

$$\left((k-1)\sigma^2\right) \nabla^2 G \approx G(\boldsymbol{x}, k\sigma) - G(\boldsymbol{x}, \sigma). \tag{3}$$

Equation 3 incorporates the scaling normalization factor σ^2, and guides the construction of the GSS, i.e, a DoG function pyramid, which is dependent on three factors: the number of Gaussian filter applications (scales) at each downsampling (octave), the number of octaves and, the standard deviation used.

From the DoG pyramid, the minimum and maximum values of the GSS are identified by comparing each point with the six nearest neighbors (up, down, front, back, left, and right) and then with the seven voxels of the next scale and so on. If the point remains as a minimum or a maximum, then it is considered a keypoint candidate. After that, a thresholding based on the relationship between the keypoint magnitude and the highest magnitude found among all keypoint candidates is applied [24], as described by

$$|D(\boldsymbol{x}, \sigma)| < \alpha \max_{\boldsymbol{x}, \sigma} |D(\boldsymbol{x}, \sigma)|, \tag{4}$$

where α is a parameter that is set to a value in the range $[0, 1]$. Equation 4 helps to adjust the threshold according to the contrast of the image, instead of using absolute values.

Before the GSS construction, the image is upsampled by a factor 2 followed by an initial smoothing and downsampling, also by a factor of 2. According to [19] this process assists in the detection of keypoints from information of the high frequencies of the image.

Rotation Invariance. To assign invariance to rotation, each keypoint and its neighborhood in the descriptor vector are rotated until its main orientation aligns with the direction given by the peak in a gradient orientation histogram [19]. In three or more dimensions this repositioning is not so simple, and an applicable alternative involves the analysis of the eigenvectors of a structure tensor (ST) [24], which is computed as

$$ST(\boldsymbol{x}) = \sum_{\boldsymbol{x} \in W} w(\boldsymbol{x}) \nabla I(\boldsymbol{x}) \nabla I^T(\boldsymbol{x}), \tag{5}$$

where $\nabla I(\boldsymbol{x})$ is the gradient of the image I at the spatial position $\boldsymbol{x}$, and $w(\boldsymbol{x})$ is a Gaussian weighted window centered on point $\boldsymbol{x}$. An advantage of this analysis is that it is less sensitive to noise than the partial derivatives [24]. In the matrix form, a structure tensor is represented by

$$ST(\boldsymbol{x}) = \begin{bmatrix} I_x^2(\boldsymbol{x}) & I_x(\boldsymbol{x})I_y(\boldsymbol{x}) & I_x(\boldsymbol{x})I_z(\boldsymbol{x}) \\ I_y(\boldsymbol{x})I_x(\boldsymbol{x}) & I_y^2(\boldsymbol{x}) & I_y(\boldsymbol{x})I_z(\boldsymbol{x}) \\ I_z(\boldsymbol{x})I_x(\boldsymbol{x}) & I_z(\boldsymbol{x})I_y(\boldsymbol{x}) & I_z^2(\boldsymbol{x}) \end{bmatrix}. \tag{6}$$

The analysis of eigenvalues (λ_i) and eigenvectors ($\boldsymbol{q}_i$) of the ST matrix helps to determine the predominant edge orientations and the neighborhood isotropy of a point. Each eigenvector has an associated eigenvalue that implies a direction certainty. The local geometry of a point can thus be assessed by using a function of the eigenvalues of the ST matrix to distinguish edges and corners. This analysis also allows discarding salient points whose eigenvalues magnitudes are close to zero, which is a condition that produces instabilities [20, 24]. Another possibility is to use the relation between the three eigenvalues to discard tubular structures, which do not vary in at least one direction.

To represent the gradient information, the SIFT algorithm [19] uses a vector whose magnitude reflects the maximum change in intensity values and the orientation of the vector corresponds to the direction of the intensity change. In the case of isotropic structures, this representation is problematic because there is no preferred gradient direction. To exemplify this, consider a keypoint located at the tip of a tip-like structure on a less detailed (smoothed) scale. In this case, the side edges are equal and opposite, generating a gradient magnitude value close to zero in this direction. When the relation of the eigenvalues of the tensor structure is used, this type of instability is minimized.

Proposed Modifications to the SIFT Technique. To better assess the performance of the SIFT, in this study we initially tested the algorithm on synthetic images, represented by a cube and tip-like structures, as described in Sect. 2.1. However, to our surprise, the algorithm completely failed to detect both the cube corners and the tips of the tip-like structures. This happened even by testing the algorithm with a large variation of its parameter set. After a thorough investigation, we found that the problem was in the strategy used by Rister et al. [24] to discard unstable keypoints. In their work, unstable keypoints are discarded by thresholding the angle between the image gradient d and eigenvectors q_i of the structure tensor ST, computed as

$$\cos(\theta_i) = \frac{q_i^T d}{\|q_i\| \|d\|}, \tag{7}$$

and analyzing the relation between the eigenvalues as

$$\max_i \left(|\frac{\lambda_i}{\lambda_{i+1}}| \right) > \beta, \tag{8}$$

where the eigenvalues λ_i are organized in ascending order, i.e., $(\lambda_1 < \lambda_2 < \lambda_3)$ and β is set equal to 0.9 in their study.

Because the cube corners and the tip-like structures present approximate isotropy in two of the three dimensions [29], the strategy proposed by Rister et al. (Eqs. 7 and 8) failed to detect them. As a solution, we have eliminated the use Eq. 7 to reduce outliers and focused on the assessment of the local geometry in the neighbor of the point. To this end, we replaced Eq. 8 by

$$T_1 < \left| \frac{\lambda_i}{\lambda_{i+1}} \right| < T_2, \tag{9}$$

where $T_1 = 0.1$ is used to ensure the existence of variance in all 3 directions, even if minimal, and $T_2 = 1.0$ acts as an anisotropic filter for discarding isotropic curvature corners. Therefore, if the absolute eigenvalue ratios of a point are in the interval given by Eq. 9, then it is considered for further analysis, otherwise the point is discarded. Absolute values of the eigenvalue ratios close to 0 indicate a geometric line in at least one of the three dimensions or a numerical instability. By applying the above procedure, points belonging to tubular or plates structures are discarded.

Descriptor. The keypoint descriptor proposed by Rister et al. [25] and used in this research is defined by distinct histograms in a matrix of $4 \times 4 \times 4$ cubic sub-regions, with 12 vertices per histogram, resulting in 768 dimensions that is stored in a one-dimensional vector.

Matching. The matching between two SIFT salient points is performed by comparing the Euclidean distances between the descriptors, represented by uni-dimensional vectors. The analysis of the nearest neighbor was also incorporated to reject a matching if the nearest neighbor is very close to the second nearest neighbor. Such a process has shown to result in the elimination of 90% false positive matches.

Removal of Matching Points Outliers. Because curvatures of the human brain have similar characteristics, during preliminary tests we found matchings between very distant salient points, which turns out to be located in different hemispheres. Such behavior, generated by the rotation invariance of the SIFT [24], occurs because the structural characteristics of the left hemisphere of a brain image may, eventually, be similar to the right hemisphere of another brain image. To circumvent such a problem, Euclidean distance thresholding is used to discard matched points that are more than 50 voxels of distance apart, which are defined in this paper as matching outliers.

3.3   Local Image Transformation

The set of m pairs of 3D salient points, $\{(P_{1,m}, P_{2,m})\}$, is used to estimate a B-spline transformation [18] that maps the spatial locations of the points $P_{1,m}$ to $P_{2,m}$. The resulting transformation, represented by a deformation vector field, is applied to the vertices of the reference mesh, configuring its position and shape to the clinical space of the image.

3.4   Weight Function

In this study, we proposed a weight function based on the Mahalanobis distance [8] between each pair of matched salient points and the centroid of the reference model (NAC hippocampal mask). This function permits a more adequate weight distribution to the cylindrical, elongated and slightly curved shape of the hippocampus, which is the structure of interest in this research.

   To fit the ellipsoid in the hippocampus binary mask, we used the 3D ellipsoid fitting plugin from the ImageJ software[5], which returns the centroid coordinates, $c_{x,y,z}$, and a covariance matrix, Σ, representing the shape and orientation of the ellipsoid. By using these parameters, the Mahalanobis distance from any point $p_{x,y,z}$ in the image to the centroid $c_{x,y,z}$ of the ellipsoid can be calculated as

$$D_{\mathrm{M}}(p) = \sqrt{(p-c)^T \Sigma^{-1}(p-c)}. \tag{10}$$

Considering the B-spline function requires a weight in the $]0,1]$ range for each point, in this study we defined the weight function

$$\rho(p) = e^{-\gamma D_{\mathrm{M}}(p)} \tag{11}$$

to change the influence of each pair of matched salient point in the mesh deformation process. Parameter γ, called herein as Mahalanobis weight, is a constant that controls the exponential decay as the Mahalanobis distance (D_{M}) increases.

3.5   Description of the Model Parameters

In our analysis, we first used the synthetic cube image because of its simplicity and symmetry characteristics. However, to our surprise, the original SIFT algorithm fails badly to detect the its corners, even using a large variation of

---

[5] https://imagejdocu.tudor.lu/tutorial/plugins/3d_ellipsoid.

its parameters. This fact led us to investigate the reasons for the algorithm's failure and to propose the modifications described in Sect. 3.2 to overcome this limitation.

Since the total number of parameters in the method is relatively large (22 in total), we assessed the performance of the SIFT_orig with different variations of its parameters for the detection salient points using synthetic images and selected a subset of the most sensitive ones. These parameters were further optimized to best operate on T1-weighted MR images. A brief description of the selected parameters is given as follows.

The peak threshold parameter (T_{peak}) of the SIFT technique filters small peaks in the DoG scale space and, in this study, it was set to a small value because of the low contrast of the brain tissues in the region of interest (ROI), defined by a hippocampal binary mask. The initial standard deviation (σ_{init}) parameter is related to the image resolution and, in general, a small value should be used to avoid a large discard of high-frequency information. The standard deviation of the DoG pyramid (σ_{DOG}) is a parameter responsible for the construction of the scale-space and consequently the frequency bands of the filters. The number of octaves (N_{oct}), excluding the initial upsampling operation, was fixed to 2 in this work to avoid an excessive number of downsamplings and processing, as images greatly degraded by such operations and, therefore, will not contain relevant information. The number of levels per octave (N_{levels_oct}) is intrinsically linked to the standard deviation of the DoG pyramid; it adjusts the number of scales that will be in each octave. A small number generates few frequency bands for analysis, while a large number generates too many. The matching threshold (T_{match}) controls the importance of the point descriptor. Low values of the matching threshold, for instance, overwhelm the role of the descriptors, making difficult for matchings and assigning a greater relevance to them in discarding possible outliers. High values, on the other hand, reduce the importance of the descriptors, which results in accepting a greater number of matchings. The maximum matching distance (T_{max_dist}) parameter is used to filter the matching points that are too far apart. In this study, this was useful to eliminate matching points located in different hemispheres. The Mahalanobis weight (γ) parameter in Eq. 11 allows us to adjust which points will be the most relevant to the B-spline grid distortions based on the positioning of the meshes in the reference image. With this, greater importance can be attributed to the points close to the hippocampus to estimate the deformable transformation.

3.6   SIFT Parameter Optimization

The Simple Genetic Algorithm (SGA) method, which is available in the PyGMO scientific library[6], was used for fine-tuning the parameters. To this end, only one island, with a population of 50 individuals and five generations, was used. To define the objective function, images from six patients (two from each group Normal, MCI/LMCI, and AD) were selected from the EADC-ADNI dataset using

---

[6] https://esa.github.io/pagmo2/index.html.

random stratified sampling based on the presence of neurodegenerative disease and gender. These images represent approximately 15% of the each stratified population. As for the objective function, we used the mean Dice similarity coefficient of 12 hippocampi, two per patient. This optimization task resulted in the following parameter values: $T_{\text{peak}} = 0.1$, $\sigma_{\text{init}} = 1.0$, $\sigma_{\text{DoG}} = 1.85$, $N_{\text{levels\_oct}} = 2$, $T_{\text{match}} = 0.85$, $T_{\text{max\_dist}} = 50$, and $\gamma = 0.01$.

3.7 Statistical Comparative Analysis

The comparative analysis between different techniques (SIFT [24] and phase congruency (PC) [28] variants, and affine transformation) was conducted using the Mann-Whitney U test [7], which is a non-parametric test of the null hypothesis (H_0) that two samples come from the same population against an alternative hypothesis (H_1), comparing the mean values of the two samples. The test allows us to check whether the difference between the mean Dice values from two different techniques is statistically significant.

4 Results and Discussion

The experiments in this paper are organized into two distinct groups; the first uses synthetic images to evaluate the modifications introduced in the original SIFT technique, and the second uses all clinical MR images from the EADC-ADNI dataset to assess our method. For the following sections, we will refer to the assessed techniques as follows:

- AFFINE: application of the affine transformation only;
- SIFT_orig: original SIFT without the weight function;
- SIFT_orig_w: original SIFT with the weight function;
- SIFT_modif: modified SIFT without the weight function;
- SIFT_modif_w: SIFT modified with the weight function;
- PC: phase congruency without the weight function;
- PC_w: phase congruency with the weight function.

4.1 Evaluation of the Proposed Method on the EADC-ADNI Dataset

In these tests, we assessed the behavior of three methodological variations (AFFINE, SIFT_orig_w, and SIFT_modif_w) for the mesh positioning. The graphs in Fig. 2, which were used to illustrate the stratified results by diagnosis and gender groups, are similar to the population pyramid charts, where two bar graphs, one for each hippocampus, are arranged in a mirrored form with horizontal bars. Each bar represents the mean Dice of a subgroup with the corresponding standard deviation indicated at the bar end by a small horizontal line. In each graph, the two dashed vertical lines represent the mean Dice for the left and right hippocampus of the entire population.

For the assessment of the methods regarding normal and abnormal (neurodegenerative conditions) individuals, the population was divided into four groups, normal cognitive aging (referred herein simply as Nornal) patients, patients with MCI and LMCI, and patients with AD. These corresponding groups contain 42, 27, 16 and 43 individuals, respectively.

As can be observed in Fig. 2(a), the presence of AD worsens the mesh positioning when using the AFFINE method. By analyzing the Normal and AD groups, the mean Dice decreases 16.6% and 24.4% for the male right and left hippocampus, respectively, from Normal to AD. Correspondingly, the results for the female group are 25.5% and 21.4%.

This behavior also occurs when using the SIFT_orig_w, as can be seen in Fig. 2(b). However, the large number of outliers worsen the average positioning of the SIFT_orig_w in relation to the AFFINE method. In this case, the mean Dice results for the male right and left hippocampus decreased 14% and 23.8%, respectively while for the female right and left hippocampus, the corresponding decreases were 13.3% and 36.1%.

The results obtained with the proposed SIFT_modif_w method, shown in Fig. 2(c), indicate an improvement in the mean mesh positioning in relation to age. They also indicate the success obtained by such modifications due to the lower variance of the mean Dice results across the neurodegenerative conditions when compared to the other methods.

Because of the low number of individuals in the MCI (18 males and 11 females) and LMCI (9 males and 8 females) subgroups, the results presented for them precludes any meaningful statistical analysis. These subgroups, together or alone, present themselves as a structural transition between a healthy condition and Alzheimer disease.

Finally, although the resulting Dice values for all experiments seem to be low, it is important to notice that for the best case scenario, i.e., complete overlapping between the ground truth and the positioned meshes, the Dice value will be lower than 1 because the size differences between the meshes. The goal is provide a better mesh positioning to improve the success of mesh adaptation.

4.2 Comparative Analysis Between AFFINE, SIFT Variants, and PC

The results of mesh positioning using the AFFINE, SIFT variants, and PC methods are shown in Table 1. To facilitate the comparison with the other works, results are presented using the Dice metric, Jaccard, Hausdorff distance, and Hausdorff average distances. Although, the preprocessing steps were applied to all 135 images of the EADC-ADNI dataset, the results only refer to 129 individuals, since 6 images were excluded for previous adjustment of the method parameters. The results of the proposed SIFT_modif_w achieved an improvement of approximately 11% in relation to the exclusive use of affine transformation, 30% in relation to the SIFT without modifications, and 7% in relation to the positioning without using the weight function approach.

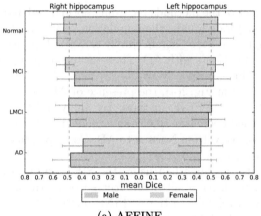

(a) AFFINE

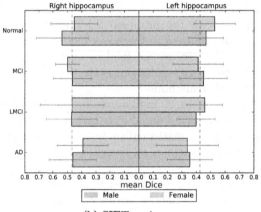

(b) SIFT_orig_w

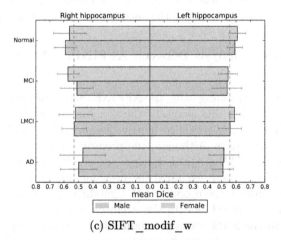

(c) SIFT_modif_w

Fig. 2. Results of hippocampus mesh positioning for the stratified data.

Table 1. Results of the hippocampus mesh positioning for the different methods applied to 129 images of the EADC-ADNI dataset. The p-values were obtained by testing each method against the AFFINE using the mean Dice. A p-value smaller than 0.05 indicates a statistical significance between the mean Dices from a given method and the AFFINE.

Metric		AFFINE	SIFT_orig	SIFT_orig_w	SIFT_modif	SIFT_modif_w	PC	PC_w
Dice	left hip.	0.49 ± 0.12	0.40 ± 0.17 ($U = 12270$) ($p = 0.0000$)	0.42 ± 0.17 ($U = 11286$) ($p = 0.0007$)	0.50 ± 0.10 ($U = 8832$) ($p = 0.6625$)	$\mathbf{0.55 \pm 0.09}$ ($U = 6526$) ($p = 0.0001$)	0.52 ± 0.09 ($U = 8322$) ($p = 0.2182$)	0.52 ± 0.08 ($U = 8194$) ($p = 0.1522$)
	right hip.	0.48 ± 0.12	0.43 ± 0.18 ($U = 10425$) ($p = 0.0408$)	0.46 ± 0.17 ($U = 9418$) ($p = 0.6345$)	0.51 ± 0.13 ($U = 7895$) ($p = 0.0578$)	$\mathbf{0.53 \pm 0.12}$ ($U = 7118$) ($p = 0.0019$)	0.50 ± 0.11 ($U = 8328$) ($p = 0.2214$)	0.51 ± 0.11 ($U = 8241$) ($p = 0.1746$)
Jaccard	left hip.	0.34 ± 0.10	0.26 ± 0.13	0.28 ± 0.14	0.34 ± 0.09	$\mathbf{0.38 \pm 0.08}$	0.35 ± 0.08	0.36 ± 0.09
	right hip.	0.33 ± 0.10	0.29 ± 0.14	0.32 ± 0.14	0.35 ± 0.12	$\mathbf{0.37 \pm 0.11}$	0.34 ± 0.09	0.35 ± 0.10
Hausdorff dist.	left hip.	7.29 ± 1.38	9.09 ± 2.96	8.45 ± 3.08	7.72 ± 2.41	$\mathbf{6.68 \pm 1.38}$	6.79 ± 1.27	6.73 ± 1.22
	right hip.	7.33 ± 1.55	8.72 ± 2.99	8.38 ± 3.01	7.36 ± 1.85	$\mathbf{6.84 \pm 1.51}$	7.16 ± 1.45	7.12 ± 1.44
Hausdorff avg. dist.	left hip.	1.02 ± 0.49	1.75 ± 1.34	1.66 ± 1.45	1.03 ± 0.51	$\mathbf{0.79 \pm 0.28}$	0.91 ± 0.31	0.91 ± 0.32
	right hip.	1.12 ± 0.53	1.64 ± 1.45	1.05 ± 1.83	1.07 ± 0.57	$\mathbf{0.95 \pm 0.50}$	1.04 ± 0.43	1.03 ± 0.43

5   Conclusions and Future Works

In this study we presented an automatic approach for hippocampus deformable mesh positioning using a modified version of the 3D-SIFT salient point detector. The proposed detector was assessed using synthetic volumetric and real MR images. By using the synthetic images, we could identify some limitations of the original 3D-SIFT algorithm and also determine its most sensitive parameters. These parameters were further optimized by a genetic algorithm to best perform on brain MR images.

A weight function was introduced to deliberately change the influence of the detected salient points in the hippocampus mesh positioning. Points closer to the hippocampus received a higher weight and, as a consequence, acted more effectively on the mesh positioning. The weight function has shown to produce better results for the mesh positioning.

Our method was evaluated using clinical MR images stratified on gender and diagnosis conditions. Results showed that the modifications made in the original SIFT significantly decrease the sensitivity of the method to the presence of the Alzheimer's disease.

As future work we intend to explore a more elaborate technique to reject matching outliers and use the result of our mesh initialization technique as input to a deformable simplex mesh model. External energy based on image gradient and texture information will be considered for the model adaptation.

Acknowledgments. Data collection and sharing for this project was funded by the Alzheimer's Disease Neuroimaging Initiative (ADNI) (National Institutes of Health Grant U01 AG024904) and DOD ADNI (Department of Defense award number W81XWH-12-2-0012). ADNI is funded by the National Institute on Aging, the National Institute of Biomedical Imaging and Bioengineering, and through generous contributions from the following: AbbVie, Alzheimer's Association; Alzheimer's Drug Discovery Foundation; Araclon Biotech; BioClinica, Inc.; Biogen; Bristol-Myers Squibb Company; CereSpir, Inc.; Cogstate; Eisai Inc.; Elan Pharmaceuticals, Inc.; Eli Lilly and Company; EuroImmun; F. Hoffmann-La Roche Ltd and its affiliated company Genentech, Inc.; Fujirebio; GE Healthcare; IXICO Ltd.; Janssen Alzheimer Immunotherapy Research & Development, LLC.; Johnson & Johnson Pharmaceutical Research & Development LLC.; Lumosity; Lundbeck; Merck & Co., Inc.; Meso Scale Diagnostics, LLC.; NeuroRx Research; Neurotrack Technologies; Novartis Pharmaceuticals Corporation; Pfizer Inc.; Piramal Imaging; Servier; Takeda Pharmaceutical Company; and Transition Therapeutics. The Canadian Institutes of Health Research is providing funds to support ADNI clinical sites in Canada. Private sector contributions are facilitated by the Foundation for the National Institutes of Health (www.fnih.org). The grantee organization is the Northern California Institute for Research and Education, and the study is coordinated by the Alzheimer's Therapeutic Research Institute at the University of Southern California. ADNI data are disseminated by the Laboratory for Neuro Imaging at the University of Southern California.

Funding Statement. This study was financed in part by the Fundação de Amparo à Pesquisa do Estado de São Paulo (FAPESP) (grant number 2018/08826-9) and the

Coordenação de Aperfeiçoamento de Pessoal de Nível Superior (CAPES) - Finance Code 001.

References

1. Achuthan, A., Rajeswari, M.: Prior integrated segmentation for brain structures: a review. Malays. J. Med. Health Sci. **14**(SUPP1), 190–200 (2018)
2. Bartel, F., Vrenken, H., Herk, M.V., Ruiter, M., Belderbos, J., Hulshof, J., Munck, J.C.: FAst Segmentation Through SURface Fairing (FASTSURF): a novel semi-automatic hippocampus segmentation method. PLoS ONE **14**(1), e0210641 (2019)
3. Buades, A., Coll, B., Morel, J.: A non-local algorithm for image denoising. In: IEEE Conference on Computer Vision and Pattern Recognition, San Diego, CA, USA, vol. 2, pp. 60–65, 20–25 June 2005
4. Carmichael, O.T., Aizenstein, H.A., Davis, S.W., Becker, J.T., Thompson, P.M., Meltzer, C.C., Liu, Y.: Atlas-based hippocampus segmentation in Alzheimer's disease and mild cognitive impairment. Neuroimage **27**(4), 979–990 (2005)
5. Chan, M.: Dementia: a public health priority. Technical report, World Health Organization and Alzheimer's Disease International, Geneva, Switzerland (2017)
6. Cheung, W., Hamarneh, G.: N-SIFT: N-dimensional scale invariant feature transform for matching medical images. In: 4th IEEE International Symposium on Biomedical Imaging: From Nano to Macro, pp. 720–723. Arlington, VA, USA, 12–15 June 2007
7. Corder, G.W., Foreman, D.: Nonparametric Statistics: A Step-by-Step Approach, 2nd edn. Wiley, New York (2014)
8. Duda, R., Hart, P., Stork, D.: Pattern Classification, 2nd edn. Wiley, New York (2001)
9. Ferrari, R.J., Allaire, S., Hope, A., Kim, J., Jaffray, D., Pekar, V.: Detection of point landmarks in 3D medical images via phase congruency model. J. Braz. Comput. Soc. **17**(2), 117–132 (2011). https://doi.org/10.1007/s13173-011-0032-8
10. Fjell, A.M., et al.: Volumetric and microstructural regional changes of the hippocampus underlying development of extended delay long-term memory. bioRxiv - (2019). https://doi.org/10.1101/595827
11. Frisoni, G.B., et al.: The EADC-ADNI harmonized protocol for manual hippocampal segmentation on magnetic resonance: evidence of validity. Alzheimers Dementia **11**(2), 111–125 (2015)
12. Gonzalez, R.C., Woods, R.E.: Digital Image Processing, 3rd edn. Prentice-Hall Inc, Upper Saddle River (2006)
13. Hao, Y., et al.: Local label learning (LLL) for subcortical structure segmentation: application to hippocampus segmentation. Hum. Brain Mapp. **35**(6), 2674–2697 (2014)
14. Hu, S., Coupé, P., Pruessner, J.C., Collins, D.L.: Appearance-based modeling for segmentation of hippocampus and amygdala using multi-contrast MR imaging. Neuroimage **58**(2), 549–559 (2011)
15. Iglesias, J.E., Leemput, K.V., Augustinack, J., Insausti, R., Fischl, B., Reuter, M.: Bayesian longitudinal segmentation of hippocampal substructures in brain MRI using subject-specific atlases. NeuroImage **141**, 542–555 (2016)
16. Iglesias, J.E., Liu, C., Thompson, P.M., Tu, Z.: Robust brain extraction across datasets and comparison with publicly available methods. IEEE Trans. Med. Imaging **30**(9), 1617–1634 (2011)

17. Juntu, J., Sijbers, J., Van Dyck, D., Gielen, J.: Bias Field Correction for MRI Images, vol. 30, 1st edn. Springer, Heidelberg (2005). https://doi.org/10.1007/3-540-32390-2_64

18. Lee, S., Wolberg, G., Shin, S.Y.: Scattered data interpolation with multilevel B-splines. IEEE Trans. Vis. Comput. Graph. **3**(3), 228–244 (1997)

19. Lowe, D.: Distinctive image features from scale invariant keypoints. Int. J. Comput. Vis. **60**(2), 91–110 (2004)

20. Ni, D., et al.: Volumetric ultrasound panorama based on 3D SIFT. In: Metaxas, D., Axel, L., Fichtinger, G., Székely, G. (eds.) MICCAI 2008. LNCS, vol. 5242, pp. 52–60. Springer, Heidelberg (2008). https://doi.org/10.1007/978-3-540-85990-1_7

21. Nyul, L.G., Udupa, J.K., Zhang, X.: New variants of a method of MRI scale standardization. IEEE Trans. Med. Imaging **19**(2), 143–150 (2000)

22. Ourselin, S., Stefanescu, R., Pennec, X.: Robust registration of multi-modal images: towards real-time clinical applications. In: Dohi, T., Kikinis, R. (eds.) MICCAI 2002. LNCS, vol. 2489, pp. 140–147. Springer, Heidelberg (2002). https://doi.org/10.1007/3-540-45787-9_18

23. Pipitone, J., et al.: Multi-atlas segmentation of the whole hippocampus and subfields using multiple automatically generated templates. Neuroimage **101**, 494–512 (2014)

24. Rister, B., Horowitz, M.A., Rubin, D.L.: Volumetric image registration from invariant keypoints. IEEE Trans. Image Process. **26**(10), 4900–4910 (2017)

25. Rister, B., et al.: Scale-and orientation-invariant keypoints in higher-dimensional data. In: IEEE International Conference in Image Processing, Quebec City, QC, Canada, pp. 3490–3494, 27–30 September 2015

26. Shao, Y., Kim, J., Gao, Y., Wang, Q., Lin, W., Shen, D.: Hippocampal segmentation from longitudinal infant brain MR images via classification-guided boundary regression. IEEE Access **7**, 33728–33740 (2019)

27. Teixeira, J.B., Junior, P.R.B.S., Higa, J., Filha, M.M.T.: Mortality from Alzheimer's disease in Brazil, 2000–2009. Cad. Saúde Pública **31**(4), 850–860 (2015)

28. Villa-Pinto, C.H., Ferrari, R.J.: Initialization of deformable models in 3D magnetic resonance images guided by automatically detected phase congruency point landmarks. Pattern Recogn. Lett. **79**, 1–7 (2016)

29. Wörz, S., Rohr, K.: Localization of anatomical point landmarks in 3D medical images by fitting 3D parametric intensity models. Med. Image Anal. **10**(1), 41–58 (2006)

30. Zarpalas, D., Gkontra, P., Daras, P., Maglaveras, N.: Hippocampus segmentation through gradient based reliability maps for local blending of ACM energy terms. In: 10th IEEE International Symposium on Biomedical Imaging, San Francisco, CA, USA, 7–11 April 2013, vol. 10, pp. 53–56 (2013)

Exploring Deep Convolutional Neural Networks as Feature Extractors for Cell Detection

Bruno C. Gregório da Silva[ID] and Ricardo J. Ferrari$^{(\boxtimes)}$[ID]

Department of Computing, Federal University of São Carlos,
São Carlos, SP 13565-905, Brazil
{bruno.gregorio,rferrari}@ufscar.br
https://www.bipgroup.dc.ufscar.br

Abstract. Among different biological studies, the analysis of leukocyte recruitment is fundamental for the comprehension of immunological diseases. The task of detecting and counting cells in these studies is, however, commonly performed by visual analysis. Although many machine learning techniques have been successfully applied to cell detection, they still rely on domain knowledge, demanding high expertise to create handcrafted features capable of describing the object of interest. In this study, we explored the idea of transfer learning by using pre-trained deep convolutional neural networks (DCNN) as feature extractors for leukocytes detection. We tested several DCNN models trained on the ImageNet dataset in six different videos of mice organs from intravital video microscopy. To evaluate our extracted image features, we used the multiple template matching technique in various scenarios. Our results showed an average increase of 5.5% in the F_1-score values when compared with the traditional application of template matching using only the original image information. Code is available at: https://github.com/brunoggregorio/DCNN-feature-extraction.

Keywords: Transfer learning · Cell detection · Feature extraction · Convolutional neural network · Leukocyte recruitment · Intravital video microscopy

1 Introduction

One of the countless applications of automated image analysis involves cell detection in biological experiments. The automatic detection and counting of leukocytes in the microcirculation of living small animals, for instance, can help in the comprehension of immunological mechanisms from inflammatory processes. As a consequence, researchers can develop new drugs and therapeutic strategies to fight several diseases such as multiple sclerosis, atherosclerosis, ischemia-reperfusion injury, rheumatoid arthritis, and cancer [12]. However, this kind of analysis, which is typically done using intravital video microscopy (IVM),

© Springer Nature Switzerland AG 2020
O. Gervasi et al. (Eds.): ICCSA 2020, LNCS 12250, pp. 91–103, 2020.
https://doi.org/10.1007/978-3-030-58802-1_7

becomes an arduous and error-prone task since it is performed by visual observation of the cellular traffic.

Different machine learning methods have been proposed in the last few years to overcome this problem. They are often designed for a particular set of images and tested on private datasets using different evaluation metrics [2]. One common approach is the use of shape information in active contours and gradient vector flow for both leukocytes detection and tracking [5,22–24,26,34,35]. Other works use adaptive template matching [1,14], image-level sets [21], and Monte Carlo [4] technique.

In our previous works, we proposed two different methods for the leukocytes detection based on the local analysis of eigenvalues obtained from Hessian matrices [28,29], and second-order momentum matrices of the phase congruency technique [10,11]. Despite promising results (most above 0.75 for F_1-score measure), these approaches were developed to enhance and detect blob-like structures in IVM images from the central nervous system (CNS) of mice. Therefore, these methods mostly fail when either the cells have distinct appearances or different image acquisition protocols.

Although the works mentioned above have presented significant results, they still rely on domain/business knowledge, demanding high expertise to create handcrafted features capable of describing the object of interest.

In the last decades, the use of artificial neural networks (ANN) or, more specifically, the convolutional neural networks (CNN) have attracted considerable attention because of its ability to learn data representations automatically while dealing with raw data.

Egmont-Petersen et al. [9], for instance, applied an ANN in IVM studies of the mesentery of mice and rats. In their work, they compared the application of an ANN using two training datasets collected from real and synthetic images of cells. Eden et al. [8] also resorted to the use of ANNs for the detection and tracking of leukocytes in IVM. The proposed cell detection approach started using a motion detection algorithm based on the image background subtraction. After this rough detection, they selected only the cells inside the vessel region and used an ANN for the classification of a sub-region as a target (cell) or a non-target, which have afterward their points analyzed by a clustering strategy. The use of these shallow ANN models, however, may not represent complex features, resulting in a low level of generalization and a weak learning of data representations.

In order to have a CNN model with a high level of generalization and without overfitting, a high number of images with labeled objects is required for training it properly. As this condition is not always satisfied, other options should be considered.

It is well-known that the first layers of deep CNNs (DCNN) trained on natural images learn more general features that can be similar to Gabor filters and color blobs [36]. This important statement suggests we can use the output of these layers as feature extractors in a process called transfer learning. Transfer learning is a popular approach in deep learning where a network developed for a specific task may have its weights from early layers used as a feature extractor or as a starting point for training a new model and adapted in response to a new problem. This procedure can exploit the generalization of a previously well-trained architecture in another model setting.

In this study, we explore the transfer learning approach by using different models trained on the ImageNet dataset [25] as feature extractors. The resulting feature maps are then selected and used as input for a multiple template matching (MTM) method. Our results show that features extracted from kernels trained in a different task can increase the performance of the well know template matching technique.

The rest of this paper is organized as follows: in Sect. 2, we describe our methodology and the database used in this work. Results and discussions are presented in Sect. 3, while in the last section, we make our final considerations.

2   Materials and Methods

In this section, we first describe the IVM dataset used in this work and then elaborate on the techniques applied for leukocytes detection and the metrics used to evaluate them.

2.1   IVM Dataset

To evaluate our approach, we used six videos from IVM studies with 705 frames in total that were obtained from distinct image acquisition protocols and four different animal organs: brain, spinal cord, cremaster muscle, and mesentery of mice. Figure 1 shows examples of frames from each one of the videos.

In all videos, the leukocytes were frame-by-frame manually annotated by an expert. All information necessary to describe our dataset are presented in Table 1.

Although some of these videos have a relatively small number of analyzed frames, the total number of manually annotated leukocytes is quite large (see values in Table 1), providing enough data for a proper quantitative evaluation. For more information about the experimental procedures, please refer to our previous works [28,30] and the works of our collaborators Prof. Juliana Carvalho Tavares, Ph.D.[1] [6,7] and Prof. Mônica Lopes-Ferreira, Ph.D.[2] [27].

All the images in our dataset went through the following ordered sequence of processes to 1) remove the extremely blurred images, 2) noise reduction, 3) contrast standardization, 4) video stabilization, and 5) extraction of the region of interest (ROI). The application of these preprocessing techniques is better described in our previous work [28] and is out off the scope of this paper.

---

[1] Department of Physiology and Biophysics, Federal University of Minas Gerais, Belo Horizonte, MG, Brazil.

[2] Special Laboratory of Applied Toxinology (Center of Toxins Immune-Response and Cell Signaling), Butantan Institute, São Paulo, Brazil.

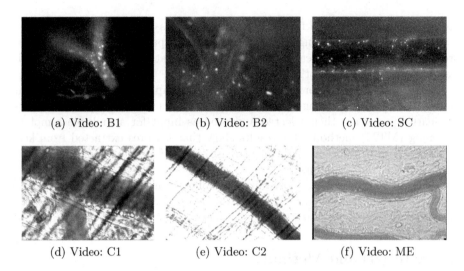

| (a) Video: B1 | (b) Video: B2 | (c) Video: SC |
| (d) Video: C1 | (e) Video: C2 | (f) Video: ME |

Fig. 1. Examples of video frames from different mice organs.

Table 1. Description of the IVM dataset used in this work. B1 and B2: videos from the mice brain; SC: video from the mice spinal cord; C1 and C2: videos from cremaster muscle; ME: video from the mesentery.

Category	ID	Matrix size (px)	Color	# frames analyzed	# annotated leukocytes
CNS	B1	692 × 520	No	220	5827
	B2	460 × 344	No	401	8048
	SC	692 × 520	No	21	1570
			Subtotal:	*642*	*15445*
Cremaster	C1	1392 × 1040	Yes	21	390
Muscle	C2	1392 × 1040	Yes	21	1603
			Subtotal:	*42*	*1993*
Mesentery	ME	720 × 480	Yes	21	291
			Subtotal:	*21*	*291*
				705	**17729**

2.2 Pipeline Overview

Figure 2 illustrates the pipeline of our proposed method for leukocytes detection. The main goal of our approach is to apply the concept of transfer learning using different pre-trained DCNNs and to test the model's genericity when applied for distinct targets. For that, we chose a broad list of models already trained on the ImageNet dataset [25] and used the output of their first convolutional layers in our problem, i.e., in a task entirely different from the original.

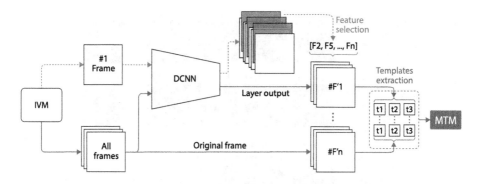

Fig. 2. Pipeline overview of the approach used in this work. (Color figure online)

Conventional DCNN models generally have a small input shape value as default. In this study, however, we decided to rescale our input images into the fixed range of 1400 × 1000 as the massive information contained in this kind of image is composed by small objects that are quite significant for cellular morphology characterization.

With all the images preprocessed and rescaled, we start our detection pipeline by extracting the first frame of each video and passing it forward into the DCNN model until the selected layer. In this work, each selected layer was chosen by visual inspection of its output feature images. Since our image frames present relevant information in small regions, we decided to analyze only the first convolutional layers (shallow layers) of each DCNN.

As a consequence of transfer learning, not all output images present relevant characteristics that could help in a detection process. For this reason, we performed a feature image selection capable of separating only the best set of features to be used next. To accomplish that, we extracted a small ROI previously selected and used it as a template for the template matching technique. We then get the corresponding output maps for each feature image and applied a thresholding technique on each one of then. In this case, the threshold value was set to 0.9, which results in a map of detection candidates with a high probability of being indeed cells. The accuracy of each resulting map was evaluated following the metrics described in Sect. 2.4, but to chose the best set of features, we sorted and normalized the evaluation results in order to selected only those top features whose accumulated value (or retained score) was higher than 0.1. Fig. 3 illustrates the process of feature selection.

After the first passage through our pipeline, illustrated by the green dashed arrows in Fig. 2, we have our best set of image features from the DCNN layer and can now apply our approach to all the video frames. The blue arrows in Fig. 2 show the remaining steps in our pipeline. They are similar to the previous steps, except that we now know what the best feature set is and can finally apply the MTM algorithm to identify the cell candidates. At this step, we also include the original frame image into the vector of selected features. Next in our approach,

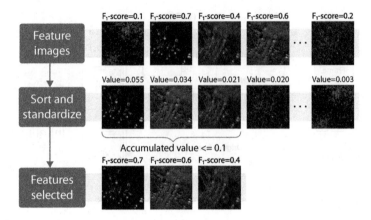

Fig. 3. Steps for feature selection.

we extracted three pre-selected ROIs from the first frames of each video to be used as template images in the entire processing.

2.3 Multiple Template Matching – MTM

As stated before, to perform our cell detection step and consequently test our proposed approach, we used the template matching (TM) technique [13,19,20] with multiple templates. The normalized cross-correlation (NCC) based TM is an algorithm of pattern recognition field that performs the detection of similar objects in an image $I(x,y)$, holding as input the image itself and a template (sub-image) $T(x,y)$ to be detected. The TM algorithm used in this work has as similarity measure the NCC coefficient, computed as:

$$\rho(x,y) = \frac{\sum_r \sum_s \left[T(r,s) - \overline{T}\right] \cdot \left[I\left(x+r, y+s\right) - \overline{I}_T\right]}{\sqrt{\sum_r \sum_s \left[T(r,s) - \overline{T}\right]^2 \cdot \sum_r \sum_s \left[I\left(x+r, y+s\right) - \overline{I}_T\right]^2}}, \tag{1}$$

where $\overline{T}$ is the average value of pixel intensities in $T(x,y)$, $\overline{I}_T$ is the average value of I in the coincident region with the current position of T, and the sums are only realized over the common coordinates of $I(x,y)$ and $T(x,y)$, delimited by the variables r and s of the summations.

The coefficient of correlation ρ indicates the level of similarity between the template T and the current image region. Its scale varies in the range of $[-1,1]$ and is, therefore, normalized by the amplitudes of T and I, wherein $\rho = 1$ means the total correlation between T and the sub-region of I, $\rho = 0$ means that there is no correlation, and $\rho = -1$ means inverse correlation.

As already stated at the beginning of this section, our approach used a set o leukocyte-templates as input for the MTM algorithm. As a result, we have intensity maps with the highest coefficient values indicating the spatial locations in the video frames with high similarity with our selected templates. In the cases where the number of templates is higher than one, a fusion step is employed by summing and normalizing all the MTM output maps. Finally, the resulting maps were thresholded by using different values. These values were defined in the range of [0.7, 0.95], with step of 0.5.

2.4   Metrics of Evaluation

For the evaluation of our approach, the resulting thresholded maps were assessed by comparing the spatial coordinates of the leukocytes' centroids that were manually identified and annotated by an expert (ground truth) with those automatically detected. In this sense, we defined the detection as true when the distance between a manually annotated centroid and an automatically detect one is less or equal than k pixels. This distance value k was estimated according to the average radius of the selected templates for each video.

Accordingly, in this study we defined the number of true positives (TPs) as the accumulated amount of leukocyte positions that were correctly detected by the algorithm, the false positives (FPs) as the accumulated amount of leukocytes automatically detected without correspondence to those manually annotated, and the false negatives (FNs) as the accumulated amount of leukocytes that the algorithm could not identify.

The measures of precision (P), recall (R), and F_1-score [15] were then used to evaluate the overall performance of our proposed approach. These measures are based on the accumulated TPs, FPs, and FNs over the sequence of video frames. They are defined as follows:

$$P = \frac{TPs}{(TPs + FPs)}, \tag{2}$$

$$R = \frac{TPs}{(TPs + FNs)}, \tag{3}$$

$$F_1\text{-}score = 2 \times \frac{P \times R}{P + R}. \tag{4}$$

3   Experimental Results and Discussions

The proposed approach for leukocytes detection was quantitatively evaluated using all the videos detailed in Sect. 2.1 for different pre-trained DCNN models. For the sake of comparison, we also applied the MTM directly to the video frames at gray level intensities, i.e., not passing through any DCNN model.

In Fig. 4, we can see the resulting F_1-score values for all the videos and models processed. For each one of them, we plotted the best values found in our experiments, considering the set of threshold values tested. Each model exhibits three different bars, colored according to the number of templates used in our experiments with the MTM algorithm.

98   B. C. G. da Silva and R. J. Ferrari

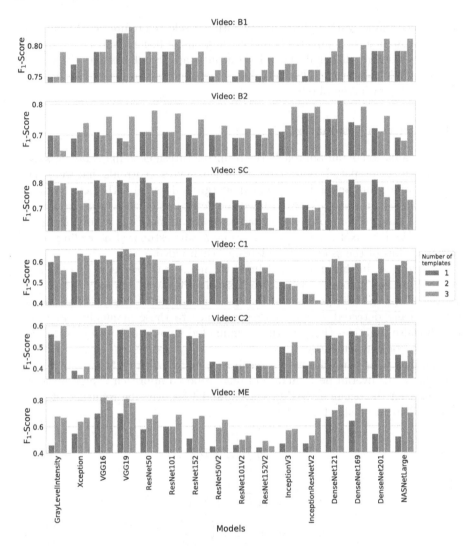

Fig. 4. Output values for each video and DCNN model tested. The colored bar indicates the number of templates used in MTM algorithm.

The plots in Fig. 4 clearly show the use of selected convolutional layers in CNNs positively contribute as generic feature extractors, even coming from models trained for a completely different task. It is also worth noticing that the use of multiple templates can help to recognize targets that are slightly different, like those present in videos B1 and B2.

Although some models did not contribute to the MTM technique in most cases, such as the ResNet50V2, ResNet101V2, ResNet152V2, InceptionV3, and InceptionResNetV2, the majority of them achieved values similar or higher than the application of the MTM using only the gray level intensity information, which also shows the potential of this approach.

Table 2 shows the best set of values found in Fig. 4 for a better quantitative comparison of the methods. Indeed, we can observe that only in the C2 video, our strategy presented the same value as in the gray level image application, while in the remaining results, we had a considerable improvement (up to 14%). Videos C1 and C2, however, still exhibited low F_1-score values (0.66 and 0.60, respectively), which is justifiable since they have the most challenging visual aspects, with a cluttered background and cell sizes in the order of 5 pixels.

Table 2. Best F_1-score values found for each video and DCNN model.

Model	B1	B2	SC	C1	C2	ME
GrayLevelIntensity	0.79	0.70	0.81	0.63	**0.60**	0.68
Xception [3]	0.78	0.74	0.78	0.64	0.41	0.67
VGG16 [31]	0.81	0.76	0.81	0.63	**0.60**	**0.82**
VGG19 [31]	**0.83**	0.76	0.81	**0.66**	0.59	0.81
ResNet50 [16]	0.79	0.78	**0.82**	0.63	0.58	0.69
ResNet101 [16]	0.81	0.77	0.80	0.59	0.58	0.69
ResNet152 [16]	0.79	0.75	0.82	0.59	0.56	0.68
ResNet50V2 [17]	0.78	0.73	0.76	0.60	0.43	0.65
ResNet101V2 [17]	0.78	0.72	0.73	0.62	0.42	0.53
ResNet152V2 [17]	0.78	0.72	0.73	0.57	0.41	0.49
InceptionV3 [33]	0.77	0.79	0.74	0.50	0.52	0.58
InceptionResNetV2 [32]	0.76	0.79	0.71	0.44	0.49	0.66
DenseNet121 [18]	0.81	**0.81**	0.81	0.61	0.55	0.76
DenseNet169 [18]	0.80	0.79	0.81	0.59	0.57	0.77
DenseNet201 [18]	0.81	0.76	0.81	0.61	0.60	0.73
NASNetLarge [37]	0.81	0.73	0.79	0.60	0.48	0.74

Examples of output frames for each processed video are shown in Fig. 5. Each TP point found is illustrated by the green circles in the images, with its respective manual centroid annotation indicated as a cross. The blue circles represent the FP points, while the red squares are the FN ones.

From the images in Fig. 5, we observe that FN points are often the cells very close to each other or the ones whose appearance is quite different from the rest of them. The FP points, however, mostly correspond to bright regions in the images or to the erythrocytes, which are smaller cells that appear as bright blurred points in non-consecutive frames and are not part of the manual annotations. Even so, the final results were quite promising and indicated that pre-trained DCNN models could be a good option for generic feature extraction in IVM.

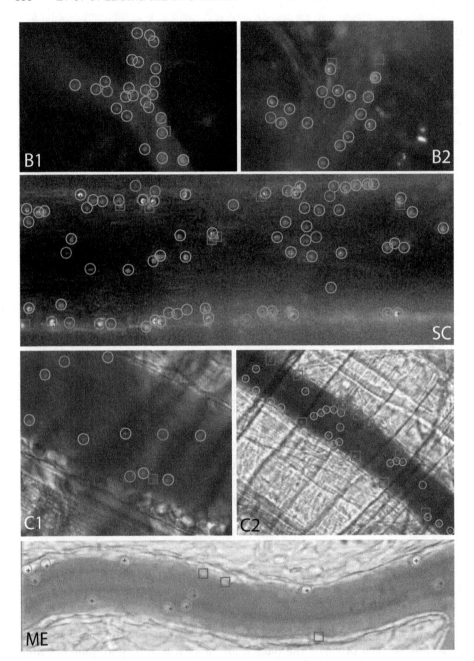

Fig. 5. Examples of MTM outputs for each video in the dataset. Green circles represent the TP points, blue circles the FP points, and red squares the FN points. (Color figure online)

4 Conclusions

Manual detection and counting of leukocytes are still fundamental tasks in IVM studies. However, visual analysis is error-prone and can generate false statistics and wrong interpretations, depending on the professional experience and expertise in the field. In this paper, we explored the transfer learning idea by using pre-trained DCNNs for image feature extraction in the application of cell detection in IVM. In order to create reliable image features, we selected the first convolutional layers of DCNNs pre-trained on ImageNet and tested them as the input for the multiple template matching algorithm.

We conducted several experiments using six different videos from IVM with one, two, and three template images. Our results showed a considerable improvement in the template matching performance, even using generic image features extracted by DCNN models trained for distinct tasks and targets. Despite the great results, in the cases where small cells are predominant, we observed some models do not produce relevant information to perform a robust detection process. However, we proved that pre-trained DCNN models could, indeed, provide generic feature images to be used in different applications.

Our future works include tests with models trained in different datasets and a detection process using different strategies for feature selection and fusion in an adaptive multiple threshold technique.

Code is available at GitHub[3].

Acknowledgments. We would like to thank our collaborators Prof. Juliana Carvalho-Tavares, Ph.D. and Prof. Mônica Lopes-Ferreira, Ph.D. for conducting the biological experiments.

Funding Statement. This study was financed in part by the Coordenação de Aperfeiçoamento de Pessoal de Nível Superior – Brasil (CAPES) – Finance Code 001 and by the Fundação de Amparo à Pesquisa do Estado de São Paulo (FAPESP) (grant numbers 2013/26171-6 and 2018/08826-9).

References

1. Acton, S.T., Wethmar, K., Ley, K.: Automatic tracking of rolling leukocytes in vivo. Microvasc. Res. **63**(1), 139–148 (2002)
2. Akram, S.U., Kannala, J., Eklund, L., Heikkilä, J.: Cell tracking via proposal generation and selection. CoRR abs/1705.03386 (2017). http://arxiv.org/abs/1705.03386
3. Chollet, F.: Xception: Deep learning with depthwise separable convolutions. In: IEEE Conference on Computer Vision and Pattern Recognition (CVPR), pp. 1800–1807. IEEE, Honolulu (2017). https://doi.org/10.1109/CVPR.2017.195
4. Cui, J., Acton, S.T., Lin, Z.: A Monte Carlo approach to rolling leukocyte tracking in vivo. Med. Image Anal. **10**(4), 598–610 (2006)

---

[3] https://github.com/brunoggregorio/DCNN-feature-extraction.

5. Dong, G., Ray, N., Acton, S.T.: Intravital leukocyte detection using the gradient inverse coefficient of variation. IEEE Trans. Med. Imaging **24**(7), 910–924 (2005)
6. Dos Santos, A.C., Barsante, M.M., Arantes, R.M.E., Bernard, C., Teixeira, M.M., Carvalho-Tavares, J.: CCL2 and CCL5 mediate leukocyte adhesion in experimental autoimmune encephalomyelitis an intravital microscopy study. J. Neuroimmunol. **162**(1–2), 122–129 (2005)
7. Dos Santos, A.C., et al.: Kinin B2 receptor regulates chemokines CCL2 and CCL5 expression and modulates leukocyte recruitment and pathology in experimental autoimmune encephalomyelitis (EAE) in mice. J. Neuroinflammation **5**, 49–58 (2008)
8. Eden, E., Waisman, D., Rudzsky, M., Bitterman, H., Brod, V., Rivlin, E.: An automated method for analysis of flow characteristics of circulating particles from in vivo video microscopy. IEEE Trans. Med. Imaging **12**(8), 1011–1024 (2005)
9. Egmont-Petersen, M., Schreiner, U., Tromp, S.C., Lehmann, T.M., Slaaf, D.W., Arts, T.: Detection of leukocytes in contact with the vessel wall from in vivo microscope recordings using a neural network. IEEE Trans. Biomed. Eng. **47**(7), 941–951 (2000)
10. Elisa de Souza, K., Gregório da Silva, B.C., Carvalho-Tavares, J., Ferrari, R.J.: Automatic detection of leukocytes from intravital video microscopy using the phase congruency technique. In: Proceedigns of XI Workshop de Visão Computacional (WVC), pp. 387–391. BDBComp, São Carlos (2015)
11. Elisa de Souza, K., Gregório da Silva, B.C., Carvalho-Tavares, J., Ferrari, R.J.: Detection of leukocytes in intravital microscopy video images using the phase congruency technique. Revista de Informática Teórica e Aplicada **23**(2), 33–55 (2016)
12. Gavins, F.N.E.: Intravital microscopy: new insights into cellular interactions. Curr. Opinion Pharmacol. **12**(5), 601–607 (2012)
13. Gonzalez, R.C., Woods, R.E.: Digital Image Processing. Addison-Wesley, Boston (1992)
14. Goobic, A.P., Welser, M.E., Acton, S.T., Ley, K.: Biomedical application of target tracking in clutter. In: Conference on Signals, Systems and Computers, vol. 1, pp. 88–92. IEEE, Pacific Grove (2001)
15. Goutte, C., Gaussier, E.: A probabilistic interpretation of precision, recall and F-score, with implication for evaluation. In: Losada, D.E., Fernández-Luna, J.M. (eds.) ECIR 2005. LNCS, vol. 3408, pp. 345–359. Springer, Heidelberg (2005). https://doi.org/10.1007/978-3-540-31865-1_25
16. He, K., Zhang, X., Ren, S., Sun, J.: Deep residual learning for image recognition. In: IEEE Conference on Computer Vision and Pattern Recognition (CVPR), pp. 770–778. IEEE, Las Vegas (2016). https://doi.org/10.1109/CVPR.2016.90
17. He, K., Zhang, X., Ren, S., Sun, J.: Identity mappings in deep residual networks. In: Leibe, B., Matas, J., Sebe, N., Welling, M. (eds.) ECCV 2016. LNCS, vol. 9908, pp. 630–645. Springer, Cham (2016). https://doi.org/10.1007/978-3-319-46493-0_38
18. Huang, G., Liu, Z., Van Der Maaten, L., Weinberger, K.Q.: Densely connected convolutional networks. In: IEEE Conference on Computer Vision and Pattern Recognition (CVPR), pp. 4700–4708. IEEE (2017)
19. Khosravi, M., Schafer, R.W.: Template matching based on a grayscale hit-or-miss transform. IEEE Trans. Image Process. **5**(6), 1060–1066 (1996)
20. Lewis, J.P.: Fast template matching. In: Vision Interface, vol. 95. pp. 120–123. Canadian Image Processing and Pattern Recognition Society, Quebec City, Canada (1995)
21. Mukherjee, D.P., Ray, N., Acton, S.T.: Level set analysis for leukocyte detection and tracking. IEEE Trans. Image Process. **13**(4), 562–572 (2004)

22. Ray, N.: A concave cost formulation for parametric curve fitting: detection of leuko-cytes from intravital microscopy images. In: Proceedings of the International Conference on Image Processing, pp. 53–56. IEEE, Hong Kong (2010)
23. Ray, N., Acton, S.T.: Motion gradient vector flow: an external force for tracking rolling leukocytes with shape and size constrained active contours. IEEE Trans. Med. Imaging **23**(12), 1466–1478 (2004)
24. Ray, N., Acton, S.T., Ley, K.: Tracking leukocytes in vivo with shape and size constrained active contours. IEEE Trans. Med. Imaging **21**(10), 1222–1235 (2002)
25. Russakovsky, O., et al.: ImageNet large scale visual recognition challenge. Int. J. Comput. Vis. **115**(3), 211–252 (2015). https://doi.org/10.1007/s11263-015-0816-y
26. Sahoo, S., Ray, N., Acton, S.T.: Rolling leukocyte detection based on teardrop shape and the gradient inverse coefficient of variation. In: International Conference on Medical Information Visualisation, pp. 29–33. IEEE Computer Society, London (2006)
27. dos Santos, J.C., et al.: Stingray venom activates IL-33 producing cardiomyocytes, but not mast cell, to promote acute neutrophil-mediated injury. Sci. Rep. **7**(7912), 2045–2322 (2017). https://doi.org/10.1038/s41598-017-08395-y
28. Gregório da Silva, B.C., Carvalho-Tavares, J., Ferrari, R.J.: Detection of leukocytes in intravital video microscopy based on the analysis of Hessian matrix eigenvalues. In: 28th Conference on Graphics, Patterns and Images, pp. 345–352. IEEE, Salvador (2015). https://doi.org/10.1109/SIBGRAPI.2015.48
29. Gregório da Silva, B.C., Carvalho-Tavares, J., Ferrari, R.J.: Detecting and tracking leukocytes in intravital video microscopy using a Hessian-based spatiotemporal approach. Multidimens. Syst. Sig. Process. **30**(2), 815–839 (2018). https://doi.org/10.1007/s11045-018-0581-5
30. Gregório da Silva, B.C., Freire, P.G.L., Mello, R.F., Bernardes, D., Carvalho-Tavares, J., Ferrari, R.J.: Técnica de estabilização de movimento em microscopia intravital utilizando métodos de co-registro de imagens. In: XXIV Congresso Brasileiro de Engenharia Biomédica (CBEB), pp. 193–196. CBEB, Uberlândia, MG, Brazil (2014)
31. Simonyan, K., Zisserman, A.: Very deep convolutional networks for large-scale image recognitions. In: International Conference on Learning Representations (ICLR) (2015)
32. Szegedy, C., Ioffe, S., Vanhoucke, V., Alemi, A.A.: Inception-v4, inception-resnet and the impact of residual connections on learning. In: Thirty-first AAAI Conference on Artificial Intelligence (2017)
33. Szegedy, C., Vanhoucke, V., Ioffe, S., Shlens, J., Wojna, Z.: Rethinking the inception architecture for computer vision. In: IEEE Conference on Computer Vision and Pattern Recognition (CVPR), pp. 2818–2826. IEEE, Las Vegas (2016). https://doi.org/10.1109/CVPR.2016.308
34. Xu, C., Prince, J.L.: Generalized gradient vector flow external forces for active contours. Sig. Process. **71**(2), 131–139 (1998)
35. Xu, C., Prince, J.L.: Snakes, shapes, and gradient vector flow. IEEE Trans. Image Process. **7**(3), 359–369 (1998)
36. Yosinski, J., Clune, J., Bengio, Y., Lipson, H.: How transferable are features in deep neural networks? In: Advances in Neural Information Processing Systems 27, vol. 2, pp. 3320–3328. Curran Associates Inc, Montreal (2014)
37. Zoph, B., Vasudevan, V., Shlens, J., Le, Q.V.: Learning transferable architectures for scalable image recognition. In: IEEE Conference on Computer Vision and Pattern Recognition (CVPR), pp. 8697–8710. IEEE (2018)

A Smartphone Application for Car Horn Detection to Assist Hearing-Impaired People in Driving

Cleyton Aparecido Dim$^{(\boxtimes)}$ (ID), Rafael Martins Feitosa (ID),
Marcelle Pereira Mota (ID), and Jefferson Magalhães de Morais (ID)

Universidade Federal do Pará, Belém, Brazil
{cleytondim,rafaelmf,mpmota,jeffersonmorais}@ufpa.br

Abstract. This paper presents a smartphone application that displays an onscreen alert and emits a vibration if a car horn is triggered in the traffic, aiming to assist hearing impaired people in driving vehicles. The stages of the construction process are detailed and ways of obtaining the sound frequency of a real-time noise with algorithms using Fast Fourier Transform are discussed, as well as the crossing of these with usual frequency ranges in car horns. The paper also discusses the problems faced in the detection of frequency bands in real traffic, related to the Doppler effect. The testing methodology includes simulations and uses the application in a real traffic environment. As a result of this work we obtained a functional application, customizable by the user, capable of detecting automotive horns.

Keywords: Horn detection · Smartphone · Fast Fourier Transform

1 Introduction

In a society that aims to promote the social and digital inclusion of people with special needs, inclusive actions must extend to the transit system. People must have freedom and ease of movement, enjoying their right to come and go. A breakthrough in this regard is automobiles adapted for people with specific physical needs for mobility or motor coordination.

Several technological advances facilitate drivers' maneuvers through different types of sensors, such as parking sensors, reverse camera or 360° camera. These advances serve as a complement for people without special needs and as an aid for people who have some visual deficit that compromises a good view of the environment around the car in various maneuvers. In Brazil, for instance, the Brazilian Traffic Code [1] admits the inclusion of people with special needs in driving motor vehicles, when the specifics of each case are analyzed by commissions established by state and district transit councils.

However, when we think of hearing impairment, we do not have as many technological advances to assist a person driving a vehicle. Some researches [2]

© Springer Nature Switzerland AG 2020
O. Gervasi et al. (Eds.): ICCSA 2020, LNCS 12250, pp. 104–116, 2020.
https://doi.org/10.1007/978-3-030-58802-1_8

show the difficulties for the hearing impaired from the process of obtaining a
driver's license in Brazil, passing the legal exams, until the act of driving itself,
where it is reported that they can drive vehicles normally, but need a lot of
attention around them during driving since they rely a lot on visual signals and
little or nothing on ambient sounds.

Therefore, the hearing impaired person needs a sound-sensory complement
that allows him to know if a horn was triggered in the surroundings and that,
therefore, he must be more alert to his surroundings to avoid any accident. By
analyzing the horn pattern it may also be possible to inform the driver of the
direction of the sound source or even indicate what information the driver who
triggered the horn is trying to pass to others, in traffic, as a green light alert,
feelings of anger and thanks.

Thus, a person with hearing impairment can be assisted by a system that
reports whether a horn has been blown, the direction of its origin, and, possibly,
what is the intention of the emitting driver, making it possible to take the most
appropriate measures in the direction. Some examples of initiatives to help the
hearing impaired are works that are dedicated to alerting the driver about the
occurrence of a siren in traffic [5], or that try to identify and classify sounds
in the alarm category [3] (bell, horn, siren, among others). But none of them
tries to specifically identify horns in the traffic environment using a common
smartphone.

The purpose of this article is to present the development of a smartphone
application that captures the sounds of the environment and identifies whether
a horn has been triggered, informing the driver by displaying an alert on the
screen and emitting a vibration.

The article is organized as follows. Section 2 deals with related works.
Section 3 describes the methods developed for horn identification. Section 4
presents the developed application. Section 5 presents the test results of using
the application and discusses open problems. Finally, Sect. 6 presents the final
considerations and future work.

2   Related Works

Given the social relevance of the topic, efforts are being made to include people
with hearing impairments in traffic. In the literature we found a proposal for a
traffic sound detection of sirens [5] through the analysis of frequencies extracted
with Fast Fourier Transform (FFT), embedding the system in a device of the
MyRIO platform and counting on accuracy of around 90%. However, this work
is limited to the detection of sirens for emergency vehicles such as ambulances
and police cars and is not dedicated to the detection of specific horns

Also with the motivation to assist the hearing impaired, although not necessarily in an approach of driving vehicles in traffic, there is a work where two
ways of detecting different sounds in the category of alarms are verified [3],
such as horns, sirens, fire alarms, bells, and ringtones, among others. The first
way is through a Neural Network trained with Backpropagation, and the second

with sinusoidal wave analysis in spectrograms. Both proposals resulted in high error rates of around 50%, with the neural network having more false positives and sinusoidal modeling more false negatives. Besides, there is no differentiation between the detected sounds, being categorized only as alarm or non-alarm, and there was no incorporation of the solution in mobile devices for effective use.

Still in the line of neural networks, one research [4] presents a classifier of ambient sounds using the Convolutional Neural Network. This classifier distinguishes sounds between 10 specific classes in an urban environment, including music, dog barking, car horns, and sirens. The data used for the creation of the model and validation was a dataset of sounds related to each sound class. Despite having accuracy rates above 70%, it is not specifically applied for the detection of horns in a traffic environment to aid the hearing impaired, as it is also not proposed to use on smartphones.

Considering the direct analysis of audio in the frequency domain, a work [6] found in the literature that aims to monitor traffic conditions through a smartphone has the detection of horns as one of its components. Using the Discrete Fourier Transform (DFT), an efficient analysis is made to locate peaks at specific frequencies. However, as pointed out in the article itself, there is a great variation in accuracy depending on the environment, and the smartphones themselves, which can have considerable differences in microphone sensitivity. Thus, it was clear that an approach of direct analysis of frequencies, as is the case of our proposal, must be accompanied by the possibility of personalization of the application by the user, which may change the sound sensitivity, specific frequencies or even the algorithm variations which can produce different results in different situations.

In another work [7], the Short Time Fourier Transform (STFT) algorithm is used for better analysis of frequency oscillation, characteristic of sirens. A differential in this research was the application on smart cars, with central processing performed on smartphones. The results of the system evaluation were promising, with the detection being more accurate than the human hearing itself.

Despite having a good accuracy, these works do not include the set proposed in this research: a smartphone application for detecting automotive horns, which in a survey with different manufacturers in Brazil was found to be generally between 400 Hz and 500 Hz. Due to this gap, the system was developed and is detailed in the next sections.

3   Horn Identification

One way to identify automotive horns is to directly analyze the intensity of each frequency range in a beep interval. Since the sound signals are considered temporal functions in the temporal domain, they need to be converted into another domain: frequency, spectral. This conversion is performed through the Discrete Fourier Transform (DFT), which is obtained through the application of the FFT algorithm [8]. The difference between the two domains is shown in the Fig. 1, with the X-axis growing in time in the temporal domain and growing in frequency in the spectral domain.

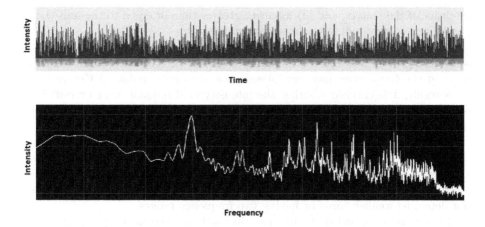

Fig. 1. Sound signal in time and frequency domain

An audio signal is represented computationally by an intensity vector. Applied in an FFT function, a vector is returned whose indexes correspond to a certain frequency range, and their values corresponding to the intensity of the sound in that frequency range. In this work, the JTransforms library of the Java programming language was used to apply the FFT function.

With the new vector, now in the frequency domain, a calculation must be applied to know which frequency range each index in the vector represents. For this, it is necessary to have the sampling rate at which the audio was captured and the vector size obtained by the FFT function, applying the following calculation to obtain a Frequency X Intensity matrix: For every element of the FFT Vector, there is a linked sound intensity with a frequency, such that

$$Frequency = (SampleRate * ElementIndex)/VectorSize. \qquad (1)$$

The Frequency X Intensity matrix obtained is the object of analysis to verify if a horn was triggered in the environment. Two different approaches were used to perform the verification: analysis of average frequency intensity and analysis of maximum frequencies. For each approach, a frequency cancellation vector can be used to calibrate the system, removing the fixed noise that will occur throughout the driver's journey, for example, the noise of the car engine.

3.1 Average Frequency Intensity

In this approach, the general average intensity is obtained, considering each frequency range. The maximum available intensity in the matrix is also obtained. With these two values, it is verified if any frequency of the frequency range of Brazilian horns, 400 Hz to 500 Hz, with a tolerance of 30 Hz to more or less, then considering 370 Hz to 530 Hz, has: i) intensity greater than or equal to the general average; ii) intensity greater than or equal to half the maximum intensity of the matrix; and iii) intensity greater than or equal to the sensitivity parameter, corresponding to the minimum intensity.

If it is verified only if the intensity in the target frequency range is equal or above the general average, a large number of false positives are obtained, since most of the frequencies have an intensity close to zero, reducing the average. As a result, it is checked whether the intensity is also equal to or exceeds half of the fundamental frequency of the sample, which is the frequency of greatest intensity.

Half of the intensity is considered because, in addition to the fact that horns operate in two different frequency ranges, there may also be background noise that exceeds the perceived intensity of the horn, especially when the source is more distant, which would increase the number of false-negative, with the system not detecting weaker horns or having two frequency ranges.

Finally, it is verified if the intensity in the target frequency range is higher than the sensitivity parameter (minimum intensity) so that very low noises, which may not be horns, are not considered since there are background noises in the target range, emitted by the car itself, which could be perceived as horns. The Fig. 2 illustrates the identification of horns by average frequency intensity, showing respectively a case in which a horn does not occur and is not detected by the system, and a case in which the horn occurs and is detected. Algorithm 1 shows the pseudocode of horn detection by average frequency intensity is shown.

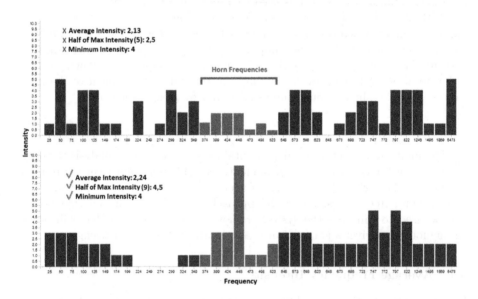

Fig. 2. Identification of horns by average intensity

Algorithm 1. Average Intensity Algorithm

Get Parameters (fmi, fma, i)
md = findAverageIntensity(Matrix)
mo = findHalfMaxIntensity(Matrix)
repeat
  Get next matrix element(fq, in)
  if $fq \geq fmi$ **And** $fq \leq fma$ **And** $in \geq md$ **And** $in \geq mo$ **And** $in \geq i$ **then**
    Return "Horn Detected"
  end if
until reading whole matrix
Return "Horn not Detected"

In the algorithm, the acronyms fq, fmi, fma, in, md, mo, i, are respectively the frequency under analysis, the minimum and maximum frequencies considered as horns, the intensity in the frequency, the average intensity, the medium of the maximum intensity and the minimum intensity to be considered.

3.2   Maximum Frequencies

In the detection by maximum frequencies, the 3 frequency bands of greater intensity are searched in the matrix, verifying next if one of these 3 frequencies is in the horn frequency range, 370 Hz to 530 Hz, including the tolerance. It is also checked whether the frequency considered reaches or exceeds the minimum intensity parameter.

It is not only analyzed the maximum frequency due to the possibility of some background noise reaching a higher intensity than the horn, as well as because of the operation in two frequency ranges in some horns. Thus, the three most intense frequencies are considered to reduce the occurrence of false negatives. Although reduced, false negatives can occur if the environment is loud with high-intensity noise at different frequencies when a horn is triggered. The Fig. 3 illustrates the identification of horns by maximum frequencies, showing, respectively, a case in which a horn does not occur and is not detected by the system, and a case in which the horn occurs and is detected. In Algorithm 2, the pseudocode for horn detection by maximum frequencies is displayed.

3.3   Frequency Cancellation Vector

Situations were found during tests in which the number of false positives was high, such as the operation of the vehicle's engine, affecting both detection modes: by the medium intensity and by the maximum frequencies, as the background noise activates many frequency bands.

To avoid false positives, it was necessary to decrease the sensitivity of the system, informing a higher parameter of minimum intensity. However, this solution can prevent the system from detecting more distant horns, which reach the smartphone with low loudness.

One solution found was to use a vector of initial frequencies to cancel, until its limit of intensities, the readings of the later frequencies. It is a system calibration

---
Algorithm 2. Maximum Frequencies Algorithm

Get Parameters (fmi, fma, i)

mxFqs = findMaxFrequencies(Matrix)

repeat

   Get next matrix element(fq, in)

   if $fq \geq fmi$ **And** $fq \leq fma$ **And** fq **In** $mxFqs$ **And** $in \geq i$ **then**

      Return "Horn Detected"

   end if

until reading whole matrix

Return "Horn not Detected"

---

that when starting the sound verification, firstly the intensity of each frequency is captured. In the sound analysis phase, for each captured audio segment, the corresponding intensity that was captured at the beginning is subtracted from each frequency range. Thus, it is better to start the verification with the vehicle's engine running, so that the intensities of the frequencies emitted by the vehicle will be captured, being subtracted later in each verification.

With the use of the frequency cancellation vector, there is also the subtraction of intensities in the frequency range corresponding to the horns. Thus, the minimum intensity parameter must be reduced so that the most distant horns are detected.

4   Application Development

A smartphone application was developed to detect automotive horns, with adjustable parameters of minimum frequency, maximum frequency, minimum intensity and choice of algorithm to be used in the detection. This application emits a red visual alert and a vibration when a horn is detected. The .apk file to install on Android smartphones is initially available for testing at this address: http://www.filedropper.com/horncheck, to be later made available for free on GooglePlay Store.

The platform chosen for the development of the application was the Android operating system, due to the high participation in the smartphone market, reaching 86.6% in 2019 [9], with a growth trend in the coming years. For coding, this application, the Android Studio development environment with Java programming language was used. JTransforms were used as auxiliary libraries to apply FFT and Musicg functions for manipulating audio data in wave format. The other features such as audio capture and vibration activation were programmed with native Android libraries.

The application has three main screens: the home screen, the settings screen, and the detection screen. The home screen points to the others. In the settings, parameters allow the user to personalize the horn detection by changing, for example, the minimum intensity of the sound to be considered. The detection screen activates the system and emits red visual and vibration alerts if a horn is detected. Figure 4 shows the application screens.

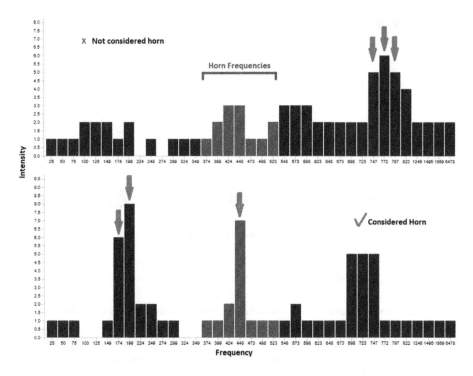

Fig. 3. Horn identification by maximum frequencies

Customizing the application with parameters on the settings screen allows the user to change the frequency range and the minimum intensity, and select the type of calculation to be performed in the detection of the horns. He can choose the calculation based on the average intensity by checking the corresponding option, otherwise, the algorithm used will be the one that considers the maximum frequencies. Also, he can select the option of using the vector of canceling initial frequencies, which will be used in the chosen algorithm.

During the testing phase, a results evaluation module was temporarily incorporated into the application. This module consisted of a screen where the horn detection operated in the background without triggering alerts, with the occurrence of a horn being recorded in an internal file with the time of the event and the configuration parameters used. At the same time, the tester pressed a button on this screen when a horn was heard, and this event was recorded in a second internal file with the time it occurred. There was a third button to record anomalous occurrences in this last file, such as an unusual noise inside the vehicle. Thus, for later evaluation, two files were obtained: one with the occurrences of horns detected by the application, and another with the occurrences of horns heard by the tester, in addition to the anomalies recorded by him. Figure 5 shows this evaluation screen, later removed from the application.

Fig. 4. Application screens

5   Results Obtained

Three simulated scenarios and a real traffic scenario were tested. Each scenario was tested for all the combinations of algorithms available in the application: average intensity without frequency cancellation vector, the average intensity with cancellation vector, maximum frequencies without cancellation vector and maximum frequencies with cancellation vector, adding up to a total of eight different tests performed. Each scenario had several events analyzed ranging from 80 to 100.

The first simulated scenario refers to the verification in real audios of horns of different vehicles on a computer. The second scenario was to check the horns emitted by the vehicle parked with the engine running, with the tester inside this vehicle. The third scenario involved checking horns emitted by a collaborator's vehicle parked at different distances from the tester's vehicle also parked, with a range of distances between vehicles varying from 10 to 80 m. The last scenario was real traffic, with the tester being in the passenger seat while an assistant was driving the vehicle. Table 1 lists the percentage of the accuracy of the horn detector in each scenario, considering the horns heard by the tester.

It is observed in the results table that the accuracy of the simulated scenarios is significant. In the identification of horns emitted by a computer, 95% was achieved with the medium intensity algorithm, reaching 98% when the frequency cancellation vector was used. The algorithm that deals with the identification of maximum frequencies obtained 76% of correct answers with and without the use of the null vector.

In the scenario of own horns, being emitted by the vehicle where the tester is located, both algorithms reach a 95% or more hit rate, reaching 100% in both when using the frequency cancellation vector.

The third scenario, of two cars parked at variable distances in each horn event, has a drop in the hit rate, but maintaining a level above 70%, reaching 80% or more when using the cancellation vector, in both algorithms.

Fig. 5. Evaluation module screen

In the real traffic scenario, accuracy has dropped considerably across all algorithms available in the app, ranging from 35% to 45%. After a temporal analysis of the frequencies in the occurrences of horns, it was found that in real traffic the frequency ranges of the horns oscillated in a proportional displacement pattern when reading their intensities.

From the oscillation pattern, it was realized that it was the Doppler effect [10], which occurs when the source of the sound waves is in motion to an observer. In the Doppler effect when a sound-emitting object is moving, the sound that propagates in the direction of its movement is more bass than the sound that propagates in the direction opposite to its movement. This effect is verified in several works, with one [11], in particular, having presented an experiment on this frequency variation.

Since in real traffic the vehicles are in motion, the sound frequencies perceived by the detector will not always correspond to the frequency originally emitted by the horn. This occurs, for example, when a vehicle is honking behind the tester's car as it approaches. The perceived frequency of this horn will be more treble,

Table 1. Accuracy in each scenario for each algorithm

Scenario	Avr.	Avr. vector	Max.	Max. vector
Computer	95%	98%	76%	76%
Own horn	97%	100%	95%	100%
Parkeds	72%	80%	75%	82%
Real traffic	35%	42%	41%	45%

higher than the original frequency and likely to be outside the range established in the application.

It also occurs in the opposite situation, in which the vehicle is honking its horn in front of the tester's car while moving away from it. In this case, the perceived frequency of the horn will be more severe, lower than the original frequency, also likely to be outside the established range. Figure 6 shows this decrease in the frequency of the sound of a vehicle's horn in front of the tester as it moves further away, showing the shift of frequencies to the left.

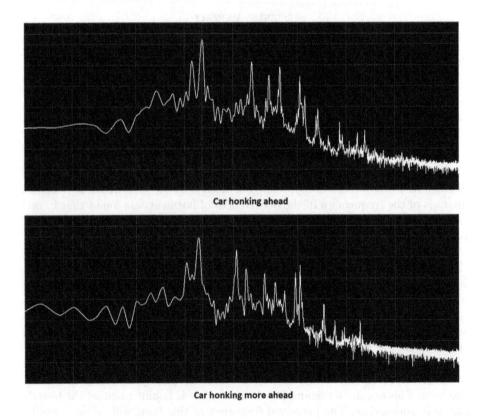

Car honking ahead

Car honking more ahead

Fig. 6. Doppler effect on a moving vehicle's horn

A solution to improve the accuracy of the detector to face the problem of the Doppler effect could be to expand the frequency range considered as a horn. However, this expansion could result in a high number of false positives, with the system interpreting as background horns that might not be horns. Therefore, the Doppler effect must be analyzed and treated in future works to enable the effective use of the application in real transit, with the least possible number of false positives and false negatives.

6   Final Considerations and Future Work

An application for Android smartphones was developed, capable of detecting whether a horn was blown in traffic, to assist people with hearing impairments when driving a car. This application is parameterized by the user, who can choose the frequency bands, the minimum intensity and the algorithm that will perform the verification.

The application uses the Fast Fourier Transform to obtain the frequencies of the sounds and different algorithms to detect the occurrence of automotive horns.

The horn detection system was evaluated with a temporary internal application module, for recording and later analysis of the detected and heard horns. In the evaluation it was found that in real transit, due to the Doppler effect, the accuracy of detection drops considerably, being considered low. The immediate possibility of circumventing the problem that arose due to the Doppler effect would be to increase the frequency range considered as a horn, which could have the negative effect of increasing false horn detection.

For this reason, it is proposed as a future work the improvement of the horn detection system through the treatment of the Doppler effect. A possible way to solve this problem is to analyze sound frequencies temporarily, looking for the proportional and linear increase and decrease patterns of frequencies to detect vehicle horns approaching or moving away from the user.

Another possibility for improving the detection system is the incorporation of machine learning algorithms to analyze the characteristics of sound stretches. Among the possible classifiers can be investigated: decision trees, k-Nearest Neighbors, support vector machine, neural networks, among others.

As a complement to a horn detection approach with the aid of machine learning, the separation of sound sources can be investigated for the analysis of the events separately, as proposed in a paper [12], which presents a method of distinguishing sound sources and performs individual detection through statistical models. This separation of sound events can contribute to the reduction of false positives and deserves to be investigated for incorporation in the horn detection system developed.

Acknowledgments. This study was financed by the Coordenação de Aperfeiçoamento de Pessoal de Nível Superior – Brasil (CAPES), under the Program PROCAD-AMAZÔNIA, process n° 88881.357580/2019-01.

References

1. Brasil: Código de trânsito brasileiro. Lei N° 9.503, de 23 de Setembro de 1997, Presidência da República (2020)
2. Souza, V.M., Mascarenhas, V.D., Soares, J.F.R., et al.: The inclusion of deaf in the traffic. Rev. CEFAC **16**(3), 677–687 (2016)
3. Ellis, D.P.W.: Detecting alarm sounds. In: Proceedings of Consistent and Reliable Acoustic Cues for Sound Analysis, pp. 59–62 (2001)
4. Salamon, J., Bello, J.P.: Deep convolutional neural networks and data augmentation for environmental sound classification. IEEE Signal Process. Lett. **24**(3), 279–283 (2017)
5. Palecek, J., Cerny, M.: Emergency horn detection using embedded systems. In: IEEE 14th International Symposium on Applied Machine Intelligence and Informatics (2016)
6. Mohan, P., Padmanabhan, V., Ramjee, V.: Nericell: RICH monitoring of road and traffic conditions using mobile smartphones. In: Proceedings of the 6th ACM Conference on Embedded Network Sensor Systems, pp. 323–336 (2008)
7. Dabran, I., Elmakias, O., Shmelkin, R., Zusman, Y.: An intelligent sound alarm recognition system for smart cars and smart homes. In: IEEE/IFIP Network Operations and Management Symposium (2018)
8. Cochran, W.T., et al.: What is the fast Fourier transform? Proc. IEEE **55**(10), 1664–1674 (1967)
9. IDC Homepage. https://www.idc.com/promo/smartphone-market-share/os. Accessed 17 Jan 2020
10. Halliday, D., Walker, J., Resnick, R.: Fundamentals of Physics: Extended, 11th edn. Wiley, New York (2018)
11. Saba, M.M.F., Rosa, R.A.S.: The Doppler effect of a sound source moving in a circle. Phys. Teach. **41**(2), 89–91 (2003)
12. Heittola, T., Mesaros, A., Virtanen, T., Eronen, A.: Sound event detection in multisource environments using source separation. In: Proceedings of International Workshop on Machine Listening in Multisource Environments (CHiME), pp. 36–40 (2011)

A Mathematica Package for Plotting Implicitly Defined Hypersurfaces in $\mathbb{R}^4$

Luis A. Anto🆔, Amelia M. Fiestas🆔, Edgar J. Ojeda🆔, Ricardo Velezmoro🆔, and Robert Ipanaqué$^{(\boxtimes)}$🆔

Universidad Nacional de Piura, Urb. Miraflores s/n, Castilla, Piura, Peru
la86926@gmail.com, ame_18_27@hotmail.com,
{eojedam,rvelezmorol,ripanaquec}@unp.edu.pe

Abstract. Plotting implicitly defined geometric objects is a very important topic on computer graphics, computer aided design and geometry processing. In fact, the most important computer algebra systems include sophisticated tools for plotting implicitly defined curves and surfaces. This paper describes a new Mathematica package, `4DPlots`, for plotting implicitly defined hypersurfaces (solids) in $\mathbb{R}^4$ using a generalization of the bisection method that is applied to continuous functions of four variables by recursive bisection of segments contained in their domain. The output obtained is consistent with Mathematica's notation and results. The performance of the package is discussed by means of several illustrative and interesting examples.

Keywords: Implicitly defined hypersurfaces in $\mathbb{R}^4$ · Plotting implicitly defined hypersurfaces in $\mathbb{R}^4$ · Approximation of zeros of functions of four variables · The bisection method over segments in $\mathbb{R}^4$

1 Introduction

Plotting implicitly defined geometric mathematical objects is a very important topic on computer graphics, computer aided design and geometry processing [2, 4–7, 15, 24, 26, 27]. There are several powerful algorithms to obtain points that satisfy the equations that express the curves and surfaces given implicitly [8, 9, 14, 24, 25, 28]. In fact, the most important computer algebra systems include sophisticated tools for plotting implicitly defined curves and surfaces [13, 17, 23, 30, 31]. Currently, there are even online applications to plot these objects [11, 16].

The approximation of zeros of continuous functions of various variables and real value has application to reality, specifically in nonlinear minimization problems [21]. Several works have been carried out to solve the problem of the approximation of zeros of continuous functions of various variables and real value, based on the bisection method [18, 20]. In [3, 22] it has been used to approximate zeros of functions of various variables and real value, thus obtaining the graph of curves and surfaces defined implicitly. Even, there is a previous result to this paper in which the wireframe plots of implicitly defined hypersurfaces is obtained [1].

© Springer Nature Switzerland AG 2020
O. Gervasi et al. (Eds.): ICCSA 2020, LNCS 12250, pp. 117–129, 2020.
https://doi.org/10.1007/978-3-030-58802-1_9

This paper presents a new Mathematica package, 4DPlots, which incorporates a command for visualizing hypersurfaces (solids) inmersed in $\mathbb{R}^4$. The encoding of the command is based on the multivariable bisection method. The command provide the user with a highly intuitive, mathematical-looking output consistent with Mathematica's notation and syntax [19].

The structure of this paper is as follows: Sect. 2 introduce the mathematical definition of the multivariate bisection method and its algorithm. For the sake of illustration, some surface plots are also briefly described in this section. Then, Sect. 3 introduces the new Mathematica package, 4DPlots, and describes the command implemented within. The performance of the package is also discussed in this section by using some illustrative examples to plot implicit hypersurfaces. Finally, Sect. 5 closes with the main conclusions of this paper.

2   Mathematical Preliminaries

2.1   Bisection Method

Theorem 1 (Conservation of the sign). *Let* $f : \mathbb{R} \to \mathbb{R}$ *be continuous on* c *and suppose that* $f(c) \neq 0$. *Then there is an interval* $(c - \delta, c + \delta)$ *in which* f *has the same sign as* $f(c)$.

Theorem 2 (Bolzano). *Let* $f : \mathbb{R} \to \mathbb{R}$ *be continuous at each point of the closed interval* $[a, b]$ *and suppose that* $f(a)$ *and* $f(b)$ *have opposite signs. Then there is at least one* c *in the open interval* (a, b) *such that* $f(c) = 0$.

Theorem 3 (Intermediate value for continuous functions). *Let* $f : \mathbb{R} \to \mathbb{R}$ *be continuous at each point of an interval* $[a, b]$. *If* $x_1 < x_2$ *are any two points of* $[a, b]$ *such that* $f(x_1) \neq f(x_2)$, *the function* f *takes all the values between* $f(x_1)$ *and* $f(x_2)$ *at least once in the interval* (x_1, x_2).

Definition 1 (Zeros of a function from $\mathbb{R}$ **to** $\mathbb{R}$**).** *Let* $f : \mathbb{R} \to \mathbb{R}$ *be continuous on* $[a, b]$, *the zeros of* f *are the elements of the set*

$$\theta_f = \{\, x \in [a, b] \mid f(x) = 0 \,\}.$$

Definition 2 (Bisection method). *Let* $f : \mathbb{R} \to \mathbb{R}$ *be continuous at each point of an interval* $[a, b]$, *with* $f(a) \cdot f(b) < 0$. *The sequence* $\{x_n\}_{n \in \mathbb{N}}$, *such that*

$$x_n(a, b) = \begin{cases} \frac{a+b}{2} & n = 1 \vee f(x_1(a,b)) = 0, \\ \begin{cases} x_{n-1}(x_1(a,b), b) & f(a) \cdot f(x_1(a,b)) > 0, \\ x_{n-1}(a, x_1(a,b)) & \textit{otherwise}. \end{cases} & n > 1. \end{cases}$$

converges to p *when* $n \to \infty$, *with* $f(p) = 0$, *as fast as* $\left\{\left(\frac{1}{2}\right)^n\right\}_{n \in \mathbb{N}}$ *converges to zero.*

The previous definition can be coded without any problem but it is not practical when operating with tolerance, for this reason it will be necessary to resort to an algorithm associated with this method.

Program 1 (Bisection method from definition). *Mathematica code for bisection method, based on previous definition:*

```
x[n_][a_,b_]:=
  If[ n==1 || f[x[1][a,b]]==0, (a+b)/2.,
    If[ f[a] f[x[1][a,b]]>0,
        x[n-1][x[1][a,b],b], x[n-1][a,x[1][a,b]]
    ]
  ]
```

For example, consider finding the zero of $f(x) = e^{-x}(3.2\sin(x) - 0.5\cos(x))$ on the interval $[3, 4]$. An approximation of function's zero using the command implemented in the previous definition ($n = 20$) is:

```
f[x_] := Exp[-x] (3.2 Sin[x] - 0.5 Cos[x])
x[20][3,4]
```

3.29659

It is briefly verified that:

```
f[%]
```

$-5.464291272381732 \times 10^{-8}$

The algorithm of the bisection method used in this paper is based on the algorithm proposed by Burden et al. [10]. The modification is that the maximum number of iterations is not considered.

Algorithm 1 (Bisection method). *To find a solution to $f(x) = 0$ given the continuous function f on the interval $[a, b]$, where $f(a)$ and $f(b)$ have opposite signs:*
INPUT *function f; endpoints a, b; tolerance TOL.*
OUTPUT *approximate solution p.*
Step 1 *Set $i = 1$;*
           $FA = f(a)$.
Step 2 *While $0.5 \cdot (b - a) \geq TOL$ do Steps 3–5.*
       Step 3 *Set $p = 0.5 \cdot (a + b)$;*
               $FP = f(p)$.
       Step 4 *If $FP = 0$ or $|FP| < TOL$ then*
                                    OUTPUT (p);
                                    STOP.
       Step 5 *If $FA \cdot FP > 0$ then set $a = p$;*
                       $FA = FP$
                   else set $b = p$.
Step 6 OUTPUT (p).

Program 2 (Bisection method from algorithm). *Mathematica code for bisection method, based on previous algorithm:*

```
Bisection[fun_,var_,a_,b_,TOL_]:=
 Module[{f=Function[var,fun],A=a,B=b,FA,p,FP},
  FA=f[a];
  While[0.5 (B-A)>=TOL,p=0.5 (A+B);
  FP=f[p];
  If[FP==0||Abs[FP]<TOL,Return[p];Break];
  If[FA FP>0,A=p;FA=FP,B=p];];
  p]
```

If in the previous example it is required that $TOL = 0.001$, then we obtain the next value of p:

```
Bisection[f[x],x,3,4,0.001]
```

3.29688

It is easily verified that the required precision is met, that is, $|f(p)| < 0.001$:

```
Abs[f[%]]
```

0.0000342246

2.2   Multidimensional Bisection Method

According to Gomes [14] the bisection method can be applied to functions of various variables and real value. Based on this, the definition and algorithm for the multivariate bisection method are stated as follows.

Definition 3 (Closed segment). *Let $\bar{a}, \bar{b}$ be in $\mathbb{R}^d$. The line segment with extremes $\bar{a}, \bar{b}$ is the set*

$$\left[\bar{a}, \bar{b}\right] = \left\{ (1 - t)\,\bar{a} + t\bar{b} \mid 0 \leqq t \leqq 1 \right\}.$$

Definition 4 (Multidimensional bisection method). *Let $f : \mathbb{R}^d \to \mathbb{R}$ be continuous at each point of an closed set D. Let $\left[\bar{a}, \bar{b}\right] \subset D$ be with $f(\bar{a}) \cdot f(\bar{b}) < 0$. The sequence $\{x_n\}_{n \in \mathbb{N}}$, such that*

$$x_n\left(\bar{a}, \bar{b}\right) = \begin{cases} \frac{\bar{a}+\bar{b}}{2} & n = 1 \vee f\left(x_1\left(\bar{a}, \bar{b}\right)\right) = 0, \\ \begin{cases} x_{n-1}\left(x_1\left(\bar{a}, \bar{b}\right), \bar{b}\right) & f(\bar{a}) \cdot f\left(x_1\left(\bar{a}, \bar{b}\right)\right) > 0, \\ x_{n-1}\left(\bar{a}, x_1\left(\bar{a}, \bar{b}\right)\right) & otherwise. \end{cases} & n > 1. \end{cases}$$

converges to $\bar{p}$ when $n \to \infty$, with $f(\bar{p}) = 0$, as fast as $\left\{\left(\frac{1}{2}\right)^n\right\}_{n \in \mathbb{N}}$ converges to zero.

Note that in the previous definition each approximation of $\bar{p}$ is always on the segment $\left[\bar{a}, \bar{b}\right]$.

Program 3 (Multidimensional bisection method from definition).
Mathematica code for multidimensional bisection method, based on previous definition:

```
x[n_][a_?VectorQ,b_?VectorQ]:=
 If[ n==1 || f@@x[1][a,b]==0, (a+b)/2.,
   If[ f@@a f@@x[1][a,b]>0,
       x[n-1][x[1][a,b],b], x[n-1][a,x[1][a,b]]
   ]
 ]
```

For example, consider finding the zero of $f(x,y) = x^2 + y^2 - 1$ on the interval $[(0.5, 0.25), (1.25, 1.5)]$. An approximation of function's zero using the command implemented in the previous definition ($n = 20$) is:

```
f[x_, y_] := x^2 + y^2 - 1
x[20][{0.25,0.5},{1.25,1.5}]
```

$\{0.570971, 0.820971\}$

Here it is also briefly verified that:

```
f@@%
```

$2.6268699002685025 \times 10^{-6}$

For the same reasons explained above, we will enunciate an algorithm associated with this method.

Algorithm 2 (Multivariate bisection method). *To find a solution to* $f(\bar{x}) = 0$ *given the continuous function* f *on the closed segment* $[\bar{a}, \bar{b}]$, *where* $f(\bar{a})$ *and* $f(\bar{b})$ *have opposite signs:*
INPUT *function* f; *endpoints* $\bar{a}, \bar{b}$; *tolerance* TOL.
OUTPUT *approximate solution* $\bar{p}$.
Step 1 *Set* $i = 1$;
$$FA = f(\bar{a}).$$
Step 2 *While* $0.5 \cdot ||b - a|| \geq TOL$ *do Steps 3–5.*
Step 3 *Set* $\bar{p} = 0.5 \cdot (\bar{a} + \bar{b})$;
$$FP = f(\bar{p}).$$
Step 4 *If* $FP = 0$ *or* $|FP| < TOL$ *then*
OUTPUT $(\bar{p})$;
STOP.
Step 5 *If* $FA \cdot FP > 0$ *then set* $\bar{a} = \bar{p}$;
$$FA = FP$$
else set $\bar{b} = \bar{p}$.
Step 6 OUTPUT $(\bar{p})$.

Program 4 (Bisection method from algorithm). *Mathematica code for multivariate bisection method, based on previous algorithm:*

```
Bisection[fun_,var?VectorQ_?VectorQ,a_?VectorQ,b_,TOL_]:=
  Module[{f=Function[var,fun],A=a,B=b,FA,p,FP},
   FA=f@@a;
   While[0.5 Norm[B-A]>=TOL,p=0.5 (A+B);
    FP=f@@p;
    If[FP==0||Abs[FP]<TOL,Return[p];Break];
    If[FA FP>0,A=p;FA=FP,B=p];];
   p]
```

If in the previous example it is required that $TOL = 0.001$, then we obtain the next value of $\bar{p}$:

`Bisection[f[x,y],{x,y},{0.25,0.5},{1.25,1.5},0.001]`

$\{0.571289, 0.821289\}$

It is easily verified that the required precision is met, that is, $|f(\bar{p})| < 0.001$:

`Abs[f@@%]`

0.000886917

Figure 1 shows the geometric interpretation of the bisection method in the univariate (left) and bivariate (right) cases. As can be seen, the zeros of the bivariate function form a curve on the xy plane and the approximation of $\bar{p}$ is made on the closed segment $[\bar{a}, \bar{b}]$.

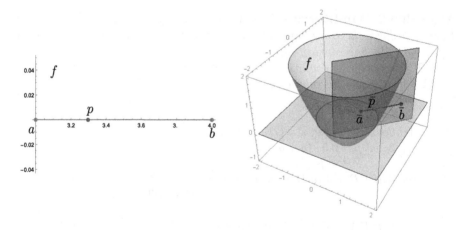

Fig. 1. Geometric interpretation of the bisection method.

If a mesh is constructed over the domain of f (Fig. 2, left), each subinterval that makes up the mesh (both horizontal and vertical) constitutes a closed segment and it is possible to apply the multivariate bisection method on such segments (Fig. 2, right). For example, the roots of a function $f : \mathbb{R}^2 \to \mathbb{R}$ make

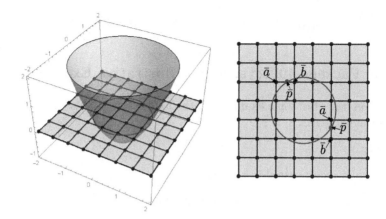

Fig. 2. Construction of a mesh on the domain of f.

up a curve (Fig. 3, left), of a function $f : \mathbb{R}^3 \to \mathbb{R}$ make up a surface (Fig. 3, right), of a function $f : \mathbb{R}^4 \to \mathbb{R}$ make up a solid, and so on.

Extending the ideas presented with the geometric interpretation of the bivariate bisection method, it is possible to have a clear idea of the geometric interpretation of the multivariate bisection method (Fig. 3).

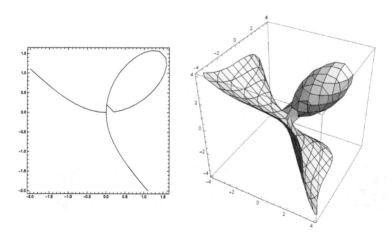

Fig. 3. Zeros of the function $f : \mathbb{R}^2 \to \mathbb{R}$, $f(x, y, z) = x^3 + y^3 - 3xy$ (left) and $f : \mathbb{R}^3 \to \mathbb{R}$, $f(x, y, z) = x^3 + y^3 + z^3 - 3xy - 3xz - 3yz$ (right).

To trace the hypersurfaces, defined implicitly, from the following section a trimetric-trimetric model according to [29] is used. This is,

$$O = \{0, 0, 0\}, \quad \hat{\mathcal{B}} = \left\{ \frac{3}{5\sqrt{3}} (-1, -1, -1), (1, 0, 0), (0, 1, 0), (0, 0, 1) \right\} \quad \text{and}$$

$$\varphi(\mathbf{p}) = \left(p_2 - \frac{3p_1}{5\sqrt{3}}, \ p_3 - \frac{3p_1}{5\sqrt{3}}, \ p_4 - \frac{3p_1}{5\sqrt{3}} \right).$$

3   The Package 4DPlots: Some Illustrative Examples

This section describes some examples of the application of this package. Firstly, we load the package:

```
<<4DPlots.m
```

The command incorporated in this package is:

ImplicitPlot4D

With the ImplicitPlot4D command it is possible to visualize the projections of the graphs of the hyperplanes $H_1 : x = 0$ and $H_2 : y = 0$; and with the built-in Show command, combine both graphics.

```
H1=ImplicitPlot4D[x==0,{x,-1,1},{y,-1,1},{z,-1,1},{w,-1,1}]
```
See Fig. 4 (left)

```
H2=ImplicitPlot4D[y==0,{x,-1,1},{y,-1,1},{z,-1,1},{w,-1,1}]
```
See Fig. 4 (center)

```
Show[H1,H2]
```
See Fig. 4 (right)

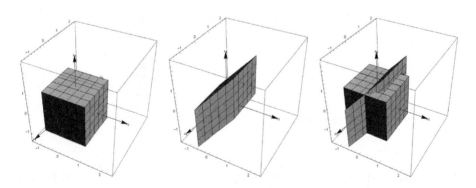

Fig. 4. Two hyperplanes.

The following sentences show the projection of the unit hypersphere H_3 : $x^2 + y^2 + z^2 + w^2 = 1$ and its normal hyperplane $H_4 : w = 1$, at the point $(0,0,0,1)$.

```
H3=ImplicitPlot4D[x^2+y^2+z^2+w^2==1,{x,-1,1},{y,-1,1},{z,-1,1},
    {w,-1,1}]
```

See Fig. 5 (top-left)

```
H4=ImplicitPlot4D[w==1,{x,-1,1},{y,-1,1},{z,-1,1},{w,-1,1}]
```

See Fig. 5 (top-right)

```
Show[H3,H4]
```

See Fig. 5 (bottom-left)

```
Show[H3,H4,ViewPoint->{2.889, -0.756, 1.59}]
```

See Fig. 5 (bottom-right)

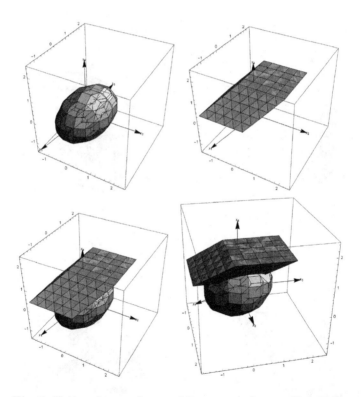

Fig. 5. Unitary hypersphere and its normal plane at $(0,0,0,1)$.

The following sentences allow to obtain the projections of three hyperquadric and one equilateral hyperhyperbola.

```
ImplicitPlot4D[x^2+y^2+z^2==1,{x,-1,1},{y,-1,1},{z,-1,1},{w,-2,2}]
```

See Fig. 6 (top-left)

```
ImplicitPlot4D[x^2+y^2+z^2-w^2==1,{x,-2,2},{y,-2,2},{z,-2,2},
   {w,-2,2}]
```

See Fig. 6 (top-right)

```
ImplicitPlot4D[x^2+y^2-z^2-w^2==1,{x,-2,2},{y,-2,2},{z,-2,2},
   {w,-2,2}]
```

See Fig. 6 (bottom-left)

```
ImplicitPlot4D[x y z w==1,{x,-2,2},{y,-2,3},{z,-2,2},{w,-2,2}]
```

See Fig. 6 (bottom-right)

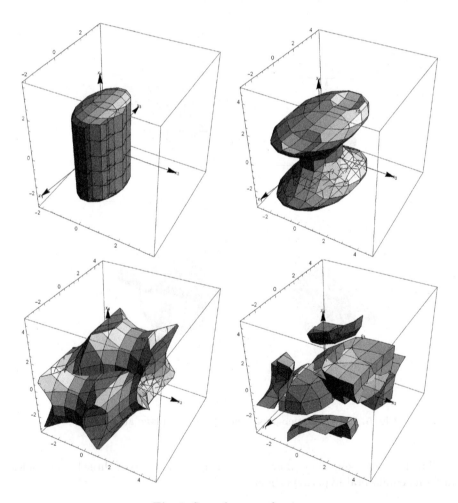

Fig. 6. Some hypersurfaces.

4   Another Possible Command for the Package

The bisection method could extend naturally, from Definition 4, as indicated in the following definition [12].

Definition 5. *Let $F : \mathbb{R}^d \rightarrow \mathbb{R}^h$, $F = (f_1, \ldots, f_h)$, be continuous at each point of an closed set D. Let $[\bar{a}, \bar{b}] \subset D$ be with $\bigwedge_{i=1}^{h} f_i(\bar{a}) \cdot f_i(\bar{b}) < 0$. The sequence $\{\bar{x}_n\}_{n \in \mathbb{N}} = \{x_{1_n}, \ldots, x_{h_n}\}_{n \in \mathbb{N}}$, such that*

$$\bar{x}_n(\bar{a}, \bar{b}) = \begin{cases} \frac{\bar{a} + \bar{b}}{2} & n = 1 \vee F(\bar{x}_1(\bar{a}, \bar{b})) = \bar{0}, \\ \begin{cases} \bar{x}_{n-1}(\bar{x}_1(\bar{a}, \bar{b}), \bar{b}) & \bigwedge_{i=1}^{h} f_i(\bar{a}) \cdot f_i(\bar{x}_1(\bar{a}, \bar{b})) > 0, \\ \bar{x}_{n-1}(\bar{a}, \bar{x}_1(\bar{a}, \bar{b})) & otherwise. \end{cases} \end{cases} \quad n > 1.$$

converges to $\bar{p}$ when $n \rightarrow \infty$, with $F(\bar{p}) = \bar{0}$, as fast as $\{h \left(\frac{1}{2}\right)^n\}_{n \in \mathbb{N}}$ converges to zero.

This definition can be used to approximate zeros of functions such as $F = (x^2 + y^2 + z^2 - 1, x + y + z)$ (Fig. 7, left). Even more bold and based on the isomorphism between $\mathbb{C}$ and $\mathbb{R}^2$, we could approximate the zeros of the function $F = z^2 + w^2 - 1$, where $z = x + iy$ and $w = u + iv$. In fact, some points were obtained which are shown in Fig. 7 (center). Then in Fig. 7 (right), the points are shown along with the graph of the functions $w = \sqrt{1 - z^2}$ and $w = -\sqrt{1 - z^2}$ [12,29].

We emphasize here that by improving the technique or using a more effective method, a new `ImplicitComplexPlot` command can be implemented.

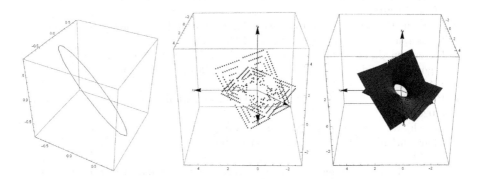

Fig. 7. Zeros of some two-variable functions and a. three real values (left) b. four real values (center and right).

5   Conclusions

In this paper, a new Mathematica package for plotting implicitly defined hypersurfaces (solids) inmersed in $\mathbb{R}^4$ is introduced. The incorporated command in this package will help explore several aspects of various solids immersed in $\mathbb{R}^4$. The algorithm for these commands is based on multivariate bisection method. The performance of the package is discussed by means of some illustrative and interesting examples. Additionally, a compact definition is presented, as well as its respective Mathematica coding, of the bisection method.

All the commands have been implemented in Mathematica version 11.0 and are consistent with Mathematica's notation and results. The powerful Mathematica functional programming [19] features have been extensively used to make the program shorter and more efficient. From our experience, Mathematica provides an excellent framework for this kind of developments.

Acknowledgements. The authors would like to thank to the authorities of the Universidad Nacional de Piura for the acquisition of the Mathematica 11.0 license and the reviewers for their valuable comments and suggestions.

References

1. Anto, L.A.: Aproximación de los ceros de funciones continuas de varias variables reales y valor real mediante el método de bisección con el Mathematica. Universidad Nacional de Piura (2019). http://repositorio.unp.edu.pe/handle/UNP/18923
2. Agoston, M.K.: Computer Graphics and Geometric Modeling, Implementation and Algorithms. Springer, London (2005). https://doi.org/10.1007/b138805
3. Bachrathy, D., Stépán, G.: Bisection method in higher dimensions and the efficiency number. Periodica polytechnica **56**, 81–86 (2012)
4. Barnhill, R.E.: Geometry processing: curvature analysis and surface-surface intersection. In: Mathematical Methods in Computer Aided Geometric Design, pp. 51–60 (1989)
5. Barnhill, R.E.: Geometry Processing for Design and Manufacturing. Society for Industrial and Applied Mathematics (1992)
6. Bærentzen, J., et al.: Guide to Computational Geometry Processing, Foundations, Algorithms, and Methods. Springer, London (2012). https://doi.org/10.1007/978-1-4471-4075-7
7. Bi, Z., Wang, X.: Computer Aided Design and Manufacturing. Wiley, Hoboken (2020)
8. Botsch, M., et al.: Polygon Mesh Processing. A K Peters, Ltd., Natick (2010)
9. Bloomenthal, J., et al.: Introduction to Implicit Surfaces. Elsevier, Amsterdam (1997)
10. Burden, R., et al.: Numerical Analysis, 10th edn. Cengage Learning, Boston (2015)
11. CalcPlot3D   Homepage.   https://www.monroecc.edu/faculty/paulseeburger/calcnsf/CalcPlot3D/. Accessed 18 Apr 2020
12. Fiestas, A.M.: Aproximación de ceros de funciones continuas de dos variables complejas y valor complejo mediante el método de bisección. Universidad Nacional de Piura (2019). http://repositorio.unp.edu.pe/handle/UNP/1963
13. Garvan, F.: The Maple Book. Chapman & Hall/CRC (2002)
14. Gomes, A.J.P.: Implicit Curves and Surfaces: Mathematics, Data Structures and Algorithms. Springer, London (2009)
15. Hartmann, E.: Geometry and Algorithms for Computer Aided Design. Darmstadt University of Technology (2003)

16. Implicit 3D Plot Homepage. http://matkcy.github.io/MA1104-implicitplot.html. Accessed 18 Apr 2020
17. Ipanaqué, R.: Breve manual de Maxima. Eumed.net (2010)
18. López, M.: The multivariate bisection algorithm. ARXIV, 1–19 (2018)
19. Maeder, R.: Programming in Mathematica, 2nd edn. Addison-Wesley, Redwood City (1991)
20. Martin, C., Rayskin, V.: An improved bisection method in two dimensions. Preprint submitted to Elsevier, pp. 1–21 (2016)
21. Morozova, E.: A multidimensional bisection method. In: Proceedings of the Fourteenth Symposium on Computing: The Australasian Theory, pp. 57–62. Australian Computer Society (1989)
22. Multi-Dimensional Bisection Method Homepage. https://www.mm.bme.hu/~bachrathy/research_EN.html#MDBM. Accessed 18 Apr 2020
23. Parekh, R.: Fundamentals of Graphics Using MatLab. CRC Press (2019)
24. Patrikalakis, N., Maekawa, T.: Shape Interrogation for Computer Aided Design and Manufacturing. Springer, Berlin (2010). https://doi.org/10.1007/978-3-642-04074-0
25. Plantinga, S.: Certified Algorithms for Implicit Surfaces (2007)
26. Sarcar, M.M.M., et al.: Computer Aided Design and Manufacturing. PHI Learning Pvt., Ltd. (2008)
27. Shirley, P.: Fundamentals of Computer Graphics, 3rd edn. Taylor & Francis Group (2009)
28. Sultanow, E.: Implizite Flächen. Mathematical Methods in Computer Aided Geometric Design, pp. 1–11
29. Velezmoro, R., Ipanaqué, R., Mechato, J.A.: A mathematica package for visualizing objects inmersed in $\mathbb{R}^4$. In: Misra, S., et al. (eds.) ICCSA 2019. LNCS, vol. 11624, pp. 479–493. Springer, Cham (2019). https://doi.org/10.1007/978-3-030-24311-1_35
30. Wolfram, S.: The Mathematica Book, 5th edn. Wolfram Media Inc. (2003)
31. Zimmermann, P., et al.: Computational Mathematics with SageMath, 1st edn. SIAM- Society for Industrial and Applied Mathematics (2018)

General Track 4: Advanced and Emerging Applications

Strategic Capital Investment Analytics: An Agent Based Approach to California High-Speed Rail Ridership Model

Mark Abdollahian[✉], Yi Ling Chang, and Yuan-Yuan Lee

School of Social Science, Policy and Evaluation, Claremont Graduate University,
Claremont, CA, USA
{mark.abdollahian, yi-ling.chang,
yuan-yuan.lee}@cgu.edu

Abstract. In this paper, we present an agent-based model (ABM) of multi-dimensional transportation choices for individuals and firms given anticipated aggregate traveler demand patterns. Conventional finance, economic and policy evaluation techniques have already been widely adopted to more evidenced based decision-making process with the aim to understand the financial, economic and social impacts on transportation choices. Prior scholars have examined common practices used to measure profitability for investment appraisal including internal rate of return (IRR), net present value (NPV) and risk analysis approaches, incorporating the concepts of time value of money and uncertainty to assess potential financial gains with different transportation projects. However, using conventional capital budget planning or static scenario analysis alone cannot capture significant, interactive and nonlinear project, demand and market uncertainties. Here we build an agent-based model on the current California High-Speed Rail (HSR) to provide insights into firm investment decisions from a computational finance perspective, given the coupling of individual choices, aggregate social demand, and government policy and tax incentives. Given individual level choice and behavioral aspects, we combine financial accounting and economic theory to identify more precise marginal revenue streams and project profitability over time to help mitigate both project and potential, system market risk.

Keywords: Computational finance · Complex adaptive systems · Transportation projects · Agent based modeling · Risk mitigation · Social learning

1 Introduction

Aggregated demand models for public transportation projects are often lacking due to the inability in accounting individual decisions, changing project scope, firm interests and government receptivity. Hence, assumption-based planning approaches [1] can amplify errors across static or dynamic models when using average consumer demand as the indicator to overestimate rates of return or other financial, economic or government scenarios considered during planning. Fluctuation in consumer demand in the

© Springer Nature Switzerland AG 2020
O. Gervasi et al. (Eds.): ICCSA 2020, LNCS 12250, pp. 133–147, 2020.
https://doi.org/10.1007/978-3-030-58802-1_10

transportation industry increases due to the variety of options available, whether by emergent shared-platforms, travelers' socio-demographic preferences, individual specific scenarios, where are they traveling from and to as well as unexpected time related traffic patterns. In fact, prior scholars [2] have suggested that travelers by developing heuristics, may only be able to 'satisfice' and identify feasible, but not always optimal solutions to the choice problem subject to their particular set of constraints. This bottoms up demand estimation challenge significantly contributes to the level of difficulty in deciphering demand and consider all other relevant financial, economic and regulatory factors into a single spreadsheet approach. Other researchers [3] often use statistical modeling techniques in creating a form of integrated model with strict assumptions, compliant with similar to microeconomics principles. Though statistical methods can provide reliable results, their validity can be called into question since the approach inevitably is due to the significant assumptions and scenarios across the range of financial, economic, project and government uncertainty.

Modern techniques of an agent-based structure incorporate flexibility to observe emergent behaviors, creating computational advantages in modeling complex adaptive systems [4]. Our approach advocates an integrated computational finance simulation of understanding the interactive effects of individual choices, firm investment decisions and market outcomes across all scales of human behavior. Obviously, individual micro level choices are constrained and incentivized by the context of their operating environments. Given that individuals act, react and interact socially, networks of behavior can emerge at the meso level. The patterns of these social interactions can produce norms, rules and guide individual behavior. The aggregate results of these create the macro economic, financial and political outcomes surrounding this behavior. Of course, there are dynamic, nonlinear feedback loops across the micro, meso and macro scales which necessitates a complex adaptive systems approach [5].

In general, an agent-based model consists of three elements: agents, an environment, and rules. Agents are assigned characteristics and following behavioral rules define how agents act in the environment and interact with each other. In this specified environment we monitor agents' activities, and interactions to reveal patterns in helping us identify transportation ridership forecast. Our public transportation ridership model is a creation of an integrated model incorporating individual, economic, and financial human behavior with information diffusion theories in network analysis, in which individual agents are categorized into types of travelers, i.e. businessmen and tourists. Simple behavior rules are based on learning and knowledge transfer, shown to prove agents' capability of acting within their tolerance and constraints towards time and cost. Hence, maximizing their benefit from choosing a specific type of transportation to fit their needs. Quantifying the causal effect of human interactions in decision making process requires not only identifying influencers and information receivers, but also of whether individuals are then willing to change their decisions based on the information received.

Our research develops a dynamic agent based modeling framework (Fig. 1) adopting conventional financial accounting calculation as foundation to help predict the outlook of California High-speed Rail project, offering an alternative travel solution from San Francisco to San Diego. We are especially focused in tackling the existing challenges in identifying cost recovery time frame for this capital-intensive project

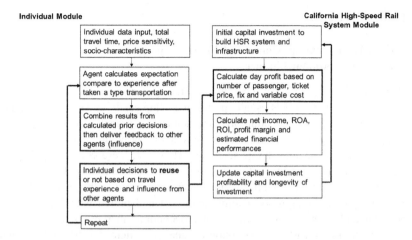

Fig. 1. Proposed California high-speed rail ridership model framework with ABM.

using rider adoption rate extracted from simulating individual travelers' decision making process with available transportation options including plane, bus, train and the upcoming high-speed rail. To increase model fidelity, we incorporate and examine the spread of information based on closeness centrality[1] in addition to choices made from personal travel experience to estimate adoption rate since peer influence plays a critical role in behavior phenomena, from the dissemination of information, to the adoption of new experiences or technologies.

In Sect. 2, we summarize prior related work on travel demand simulation, theoretical approaches, and dynamic interactions between travelers. Section 3 describes our methods, including a description of behavioral choice model and our modification of the theory into behavioral rules agents follow in choosing transportation methods, an additional layer of information spread over dynamic social networks via closeness. The experiment model we design uses data extracted from existing transportation options available in the market matching case study distance between San Francisco to San Diego, along with comparable financial accounting information from Taiwan High Speed Rail Company as a baseline in hopes to mimic closer to reality environment and constraints. The simulation experiment we conduct, the results, and scenario analysis are presented in Sect. 4. An experiment validation process is exemplified through sensitivity analysis described in Sect. 5. Finally, we conclude and discuss valuable implication for capital investment analysis specifically for transportation industry with future direction in Sect. 6.

---

[1] Closeness centrality: In network analysis, closeness centrality measures each individual's position in the network via a different perspective from the other network metrics, capturing the average distance between each vertex and every other vertex in the network.

2 Related Work

2.1 Towards Integrating Macro and Micro Economics with Computational Finance

Capital budget planning is a key determinant driving corporate direction and opportunity for future growth. This is usually performed using easily understood assumption based planning techniques, including average demand, aggregate demand and project finance approaches given various assumptions about how the markets will react, government subsidies or other know scenarios. However, these conventional approaches are often criticized for ineffectiveness in the face of uncertainty. Individual ratio numbers do not provide direct information unless compared with industry averages, and even then, there are significant information left uncaptured with shifts in micro consumer demand coupled with changing macroeconomic market conditions.

For example, many early macroeconomics analyses attempt to understand aggregate relationships, as one of the foundational principle Keynesian consumption function demonstrates the relationship between total consumption and gross national income. The implication of the theory is that consumption is determined by the change in income, therefore under the assumed stable equilibria, there is a relationship between disposable income, aggregated savings, and GDP overtime. Subsequently, many economists have criticized the original model due to behavioral factors, unemployment uncertainty, overall lack of micro factors that can create drastic changes in distribution of income and wealth, thus creating versions of consumption functions. On the other hand, microeconomic theories focus on the study of individual consumer behavior where supply and demand theories have produced rich information on market structure, but with strict assumption based on rationality and utility maximization. Many recent relevant projects we see discuss the benefits of developing multi-model transportation management system to integrate passenger demand uncertainty and unpredictability of traffic, focuses on the impact on travel time, delay, fuel consumption [6].

Here we see an interesting modeling arbitrage opportunity to integrate both macro market theories and data with the microeconomic theories of individual level consumer behavior, much like Schelling's seminal work [7]. Our computational finance model explicitly simulates individual choice sets and social learning with financial accounting operating in dynamic, macro behavioral environments surrounding a project. This helps firms to better identify marginal revenue streams and profitability overtime and hopefully a more reliable and valid assessment of systematic project demand forecasting. We apply our model to the current California High-speed Rail (HSR) project to explore how firms, investors, government and individuals can help mitigate unanticipated risks, such as through changes in individual demand, social learning or macroeconomic shocks.

2.2 Agent-Based Computational Practices with Interactive Agents

As discussed previously, ABMs can provide distinct added value as compared to conventional approaches. First, descriptively for increased model fidelity as agents can interact locally, transfer knowledge and learn in imperfect market conditions which most microeconomic models have difficulty with. Second, adaptability as modeling allows researcher explore potential emergent behavior in a designed environment that is not achievable using traditional methodologies. These advanced techniques have increasingly captured global attention, especially after 2008 financial crisis, with "an agent-based model exploring the systemic consequences of massive borrowing by hedge funds to finance their investments. In their (Economist John Geanakoplo and physicists Doyne Farmers) simulations, the funds frequently get locked into a self-amplifying spiral of losses—much as real-world hedge funds did after August 2007." [8] There is a definite need for a responsive systematic model that can incorporate diverse principles across economics, socio-science and finance practices using individual level information to generate situational macro-solutions.

Recent publications have marked milestones in activity-based approach in traffic simulation and travel analysis, though success is often limited to clear, pre-defined conditions, the results shed light on high dimensional human decisions [9–11]. Lee et al. [12] classified these models theoretically into three major categories: an economics-based approach, a psychology-based approach, and a synthetic engineering-based approach. However, each approach exhibits strengths and limitations. In economics-based models, assumptions are a necessary component in allowing the models to accurately reflect the simplified process dissect from the complex system. "Models of the economics-based approach have a solid theoretical foundation, based mainly on the fundamental assumption that the decision makers are rational, one major limitation, however, is the lack of capability to capture the nature of the human cognition process [13–15]." In an attempt to overcome these limitations, researchers then propose and discuss psychology-based and engineering-based models, exploring ways to replicate human decision-making process and learning mechanism. Although these models account for human cognition, they generally examine human behaviors under simplified and well-controlled laboratory conditions, let alone integrated scale behavior in a complex adaptive system.

Travel behavior is a relevant research topic due to the nature of complexity, travelers' preferences, needs and available resources, combined with available choices and dynamic environmental factors that all of which interacting and contributing to emergent dynamics. "The traditional top-down approach studies what is the performance of a complex transportation system, whereas the bottom-up ABMS approach tries to understand why travelers make those decisions and how does transportation system perform in such a circumstance." [16] In our work here, we build a cognitive roadmap to understand agent's travel decisions, identifying four important stages and intuitively dividing the process of choosing types of transportation into three parts: before-trip, within route and post-trip. In general, travelers' route choice behavior involves learning from previous experiences, heterogeneity of travelers, incomplete network information, and communications among travelers. Those behaviors, which are difficult to model through the conventional equilibrium methods or discrete choice models, are perfect for agent-based modeling techniques. Moreover, using experimental techniques, well-defined decision scenarios can be reproduced, and strategies that humans actually use in dealing with complex situations may be revealed. An ABM approach offers a way to capture the heuristics of decision making in a model which is grounded in empirical data [17]. Our framework combines various theories to combat challenges seen with High Speed Rail projects, including overestimation in ridership, appropriate ticket price based on consumer's sensitivity to cost, and the unknown cost recovery time period for investors.

3   Operational Prototype

Our research relies on two critical theories as the logical foundation to our integrated HSR model.

3.1   Route Choice Behavior Model Theory

In the original Route Choice Behavior Model, the travelers are modeled as agents, who choose a route based on their knowledge of the network prior to each trip (en route choice is not considered in this example). In the route choice model, a traveler agent first decides which route to travel when their trip starts. The traveler could decide to stay on the same route as the previous trip or could decide to change to an alternative route. Behavior rules described as following:

Rule 1 Set Initial Decision then the traveler agent does not change route on n + 1th day.

$$If\left(TT_j^n = TT_{min}^n\right) \tag{1}$$

Rule 2 Threshold, then the traveler agent does not change route on n + 1th day, where ε is a threshold related to the perception error.

$$If\left(TT_j^n - TT_{min}^n\right) \leq \varepsilon \tag{2}$$

Rule 3 Learned From Experience agent changes route with probability (4) and the choice probability is based on the posterior probability given the route choice and previously experienced travel time

$$If\left(TT_j^n - TT_{min}^n\right) > \varepsilon \tag{3}$$

$$\frac{\left(TT_j^n - TT_{min}^n\right)}{TT_j^n} \tag{4}$$

3.2   Modified Behavior Rule for HSR

In our framework (Fig. 2), we are interested in capturing the process of choosing a specific type of transportation tool based prior trip experience or memory. To align with our computational finance goals, we redesign an existing behavioral model to replicate the described decision-making process with an additional element on agents' sensitivity to time and cost. Moreover, to create more realistic scenarios, we are curious how delay plays a role with people's choices and experience. This modification intensifies and speeds up the decision-making process, allowing agents to make frequent dynamic changes according to their memory and constantly updating their learning outcomes.

Rule 1 Set Initial Decision

$$If \left(TT_k^n - TT_{k\,min}^n\right) = time\ threshold, \text{ then agent chooses k as} \tag{5}$$
transportation with an expected total travel time (TT = Total Travel Time)

$$If \left(TC_k^n - TC_{k\,min}^n\right) = cost\ threshold, \text{ then agent chooses k as} \tag{6}$$
transportation with the expected total travel cost (TC = Total Cost)

Rule 2 Dynamic Behaviors From Experience

$$If \left(TT_k^n - TT_{k\,min}^n\right) > time\ threshold, \text{ the agent will change other types of} \tag{7}$$
$transportation\ option\ available \neq k$

$$If \left(TC_k^n - TC_{k\,min}^n\right) > cost\ threshold,\ the\ agent\ will\ change\ other\ types\ of \tag{8}$$
$transportation\ option\ available \neq k$

Rule 3 Impact of Delay on Travel Experience

$$If\ \frac{\left(Tc_k^n - Tc_{k\,min}^n\right)}{\left(TT_k^n - TT_{k\,min}^n\right)*probabilty\ of\ delay_k} > \frac{\left(Tc_k^n - Tc_{k\,min}^n\right)}{\left(TT_k^n - TT_{k\,min}^n\right)},the\ agent\ will\ change \tag{9}$$
$other\ types\ of\ transportation\ option\ available \neq k$

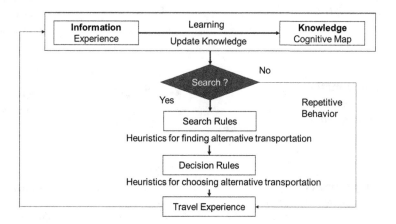

Fig. 2. Flowchart diagram of our micro-level behavior choice model

3.3   Information Diffusion and Social Learning

Agent-based modeling and network analysis have been used as complementary approaches; the former is a method of computationally representing micro-level interactions from which social patterns emerge; the latter is a technique that involves the characterization and structural analysis of socio-demographical patterns which yield inferences on degree of connectivity and how information propagate through the network over time and space. Figure 3 is a representation of our proposed network structure, includes three diffusion processes and three external factors [18].

We apply this approach to the context of transportation ridership. The network in our case is a social network of travelers; i.e. business people as well as tourists (nodes) and the information being diffused is their traveling experience using a specific type of transportation, options include train, bus, plane and high-speed rail system. First, the contacts amongst travelers form a network structure as a basis for diffusion and interaction. Here individuals form expectations around sensitivity to travel length and cost. Second, experiences are shared through direct contacts among individuals (the middle layer). The reach of information spread is based on degree of connectivity using closeness centrality as linkage. Third, the travelers process the information received which become influential to their decision-making process to switch or reuse their current type of transportation (bottom layer), thus accelerating the diffusion by repeating step one to three.

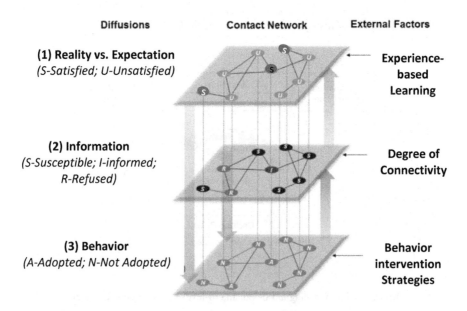

Fig. 3. Conceptual framework of our diffusion model through network structure.

4   Experiment Design

4.1   Descriptive Information

In order to populate our model, we use the current to California High-speed Rail project to *prima facie* provide insights towards validity with individual demand, using real cost and travel time comparable to traveling between San Francisco and San Diego, empowering agents i.e. businessmen and tourists the flexibility to choose among current population alternative transportation options in addition to the hypothetical high-speed rail. By monitoring the emergent phenomena our computational finance ABM generates from the bottom up, we offer alternative insights to project financing and risk mitigation.

The individual behavioral choice rules that are described in the previous section are the only sets of pre-defined calculation embedded in the system. The two types of agents, business people and tourists, are placed in the system to represent the different types of people; businessmen who need to travel may place their focus on efficiency, while tourists who are traveling on a budget constraint would prefer to save cost on transportation. Individual behavior exhibits memory, path-dependence, and hysteresis, non-stochastic behavior, or temporal correlations, including learning and adaptation, hence why we have chosen to use ABMs to understand the non-linear human behavior in transportation ridership problem. Another implied benefit is that the technique is best used when the appropriate level of description or complexity is not known ahead of time and finding the circumstances requires some calibration. "Aggregate differential equations tend to smooth out fluctuations, not ABM, which is important because under certain conditions, fluctuations can be amplified: the system is linearly stable but unstable to larger perturbations" [19]. Knowing consumer preferences for transportation system makes it possible to create virtual agents with similar characteristics mirroring human decision-making process to simulate close-to-reality scenarios.

4.2   Scenario Analysis – Consumer Level

1. Baseline

In Table 1, we include a list of our initial conditions for baseline scenario, representing when high-speed rail first enters the transportation market. Overtime, we observe the fluctuations in demand and a steady increase for each type of transportation that each transportation demand with consumer's first choice as plane, followed by High-speed rail, bus then train (Fig. 4). In Fig. 5, we provide a detailed breakdown among total passengers, 11 businessmen and 5 tourists have changed their preferred type of transportation due to differences incurred in cost and travel time between actual experience and expectation – following our designed behavioral rules. The dynamic movement we have monitored through the bar-chart shows closeness in the two groups of passengers.

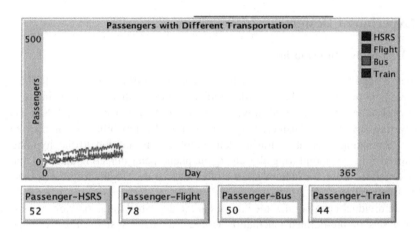

Fig. 4. The number of passengers for each transportation method under initial condition

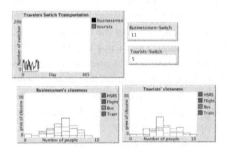

Fig. 5. Number of travelers switch transportations

Table 1. Initial condition

Number of passengers	
Businessmen	50
Tourists	50
Percentage of usage	
Plane	34%
Train	33%
Bus	33%
Arrival time by transportation type	
No delay	

2. Variety of Options

Changing only one parameter from the baseline, in Table 2, we present the HSR system as one of the initial transportation options to observe potential changes in travelers' behavior. Figure 6 captures the exact time length as the baseline, with 78 flight takers and 63 High-speed rail system users and an equal amount of customers choosing between bus and train. From Fig. 6, we can see that the High-speed rail system is a direct competitor to flight, suitable for consumers who are seeking lower price transportation choices and still allow them to arrive at their destination faster than taking the bus or/and train. In addition, we see relatively more consumers are switching (Fig. 7), 20 businessmen and 11 tourists, which further indicate that High-speed rail system has raised an interest among tourists who are price sensitive.

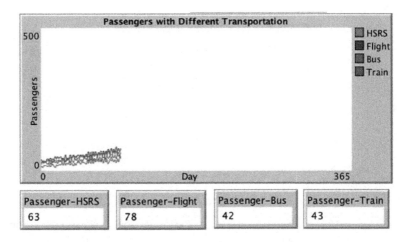

Passenger-HSRS	Passenger-Flight	Passenger-Bus	Passenger-Train
63	78	42	43

Fig. 6. The number of passengers per transportation type when presented with HSR system.

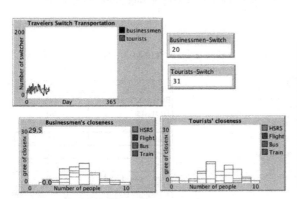

Fig. 7. Number of travelers switch transportation in scenario with variety of options.

Table 2. Variety of options

Number of passengers	
Businessmen	50
Tourists	50
Percentage of usage	
Plane	25%
Train	25%
Bus	25%
High-speed Rail	25%
Arrival time by transportation type	
No delay	

3. The Effect of Delay

In this scenario, we are interested to investigate consequences of transportation delay, and understand the overall effect towards consumer's decision making process. According to data collected by Bureau of Transportation Statistics, we incorporate the average percentage of delay into our model design (Table 3). The pattern emerged from simulation result reveal an interesting fact that with aircrafts having an average of 20% change of delay, there are more traveler demand switching over to High-speed rail system with a total number of 105 passengers surpassing the 81 flight passengers (Fig. 8). As shown in Fig. 9, the probability of delay can cause an increase in frequent switching between the two types of travelers.

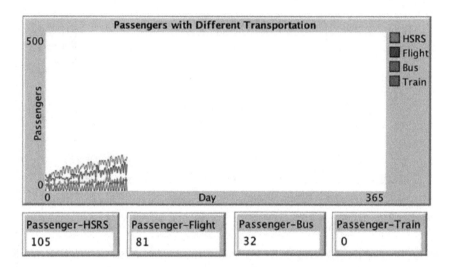

Fig. 8. The number of passengers per transportation incorporating probability of delay

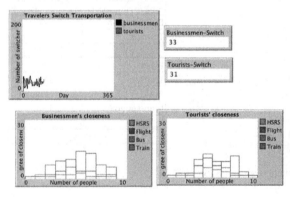

Fig. 9. Number of travelers switch transportation with the probability of delay.

Table 3. The effect of delay

Number of passengers	
Businessmen	50
Tourists	50
Percentage of usage	
Plane	25%
Train	25%
Bus	25%
High-speed Rail	25%
Percentage of Delay by transportation type	
Plane	20%
Train	25%
Bus	20%
High-speed Rail	5%

Overall, the three designed experiments open the possibility to analyze environmental factors, incorporate human network with information spread and better predict aggregated travelers' demand with changes in preferences.

5 Sensitivity Analysis

Next, we conduct a sensitivity analysis using data generated from model simulation results with the goal to understand how do HSR ticket price and corporate tax effect the overall profitability of the project. The result in Table 4 provides sensitivity assessment for investors to plan whether the long-term investment indeed can generate the estimated profit and the cost associated in making these decisions.

Table 4. Two-factor sensitivity analysis heat map from proposed ABM simulation result.

(Net income in thousands)		Ticket Price				
	$604,123.13	433	438	442	450	458
Tax	28.00%	$582,556	$589,312	$594,717	$605,526	$616,336
	28.50%	$593,004	$599,880	$605,382	$616,384	$627,387
	29.00%	$603,451	$610,449	$616,046	$627,242	$638,437
	29.50%	$613,899	$621,017	$626,711	$638,100	$649,488
	30.00%	$624,347	$631,585	$637,376	$648,957	$660,539

6 Concluding Remarks

In our model, travelers are modeled as virtual agents, who choose a type of transportation based on their knowledge and satisfaction from prior experience, which is defined by if their expected cost and travel time match with their actual experience. At first, travelers may have little or no information on the transportation and purely form their expectation at random. Then from experience, travelers can accumulate knowledge to help find a best transportation to fit within their constraints. In our designed behavioral rules, best choices are evaluated by travel cost and total travel time. Travelers form a scale-free network, allowing them to exchange information of their experience of using a specific type of transportation. The two interactive mechanism realistically model human behavior in decision making process.

Traveler demand varies in each designed scenario and displays three distinctive patterns illustrating the complexity behind interaction on individual level and process of choice-making. In this research, we input actual financial data, allowing individual to have different levels of price and travel-time sensitivity based on market available transportation type including airplane, train, and bus, setting a comparable travel distance between San Francisco to San Diego with the current proposed HSR system. The three designed experiments represent possible scenarios that travelers may adopt to a newly introduced transportation option, providing the HSR investing partners a closer-to-reality estimation on project profitability and length of investment return. The benefit of agent-based modeling simulation is the ability to incorporate variation among demand, incorporating agents' interaction on information diffusion by utilizing network analysis to accurately capture the true consumer demand and adoption rate. The promise of our proposed modeling approach allows for better corporate risk mitigation by reducing errors from assumption-based planning approaches. The challenge with traditional capital valuable methods in making large financial decisions rests without complete knowledge of the unknown future consumer preference and industry trends, with a majority of companies going through trial and error costly processes.

7 Future Research Directions

1. Individual agent's socioeconomic attributes

Socio-economic attributes reveals key information on the micro level. In future research, we plan to include income status, education level, age and gender to help us better calibrate our simulation result to reflect a larger population within a specific region. In addition, combining socio-economic status and attributes, we would be able to generate deeper insights allowing companies to target specific consumer preferences and market behaviors. In turn, investing companies can better forecast demand, formulate strategies against risky capital intensive projects.

2. Public-private partnership (PPP) financial accounting to complete build–operate–transfer (BOT)

Many public transportation projects have been successfully deployed and constructed by BOT, including the Taiwan High-speed Rail and the Channel Tunnel between UK and France. These projects have taken multiple trials and extensive investment from multiple parties. Traditional capital budgeting methods often evaluate large investment for public transportation risky, thus decreasing forecasting accuracy on turnover, capital recovery and adoption rate. Traditionally, contracting companies often overestimate the number of passengers in order to present a promising outlook to stay competitive against other companies bidding in the same government contracted projects. This suggest significant room for growth and innovate computational finance approaches that capture individual level choice behavior and the interactive market effects.

References

1. Berner, C.L., Flage, R.: Creating risk management strategies based on uncertain assumptions and aspects from assumption-based planning. Reliab. Eng. Syst. Saf. **167**, 10–19 (2017)
2. Zheng, H., et al.: A primer for agent-based simulation and modeling in transportation applications (No. FHWA-HRT-13-054). Federal Highway Administration, United States (2013)
3. Ben-Akiva, M.E., Lerman, S.R., Lerman, S.R.: Discrete Choice Analysis: Theory and Application to Travel Demand, vol. 9. MIT Press, Cambridge (1985)
4. Tesfatsion, L.: Agent-based computational economics: modeling economies as complex adaptive systems. Inf. Sci. **149**(4), 262–268 (2003)
5. Abdollahian, M., Yang, Z., Coan, T., Yesilada, B.: Human development dynamics: an agent based simulation of macro social systems and individual heterogeneous evolutionary games. Complex Adapt. Syst. Model. **1**(1), 1–17 (2013). https://doi.org/10.1186/2194-3206-1-18
6. Kurzhanskiy, A.A., Varaiya, P.: Traffic management: an outlook. Econ. Transp. **4**(3), 135–146 (2015)
7. Schelling, T.C.: Dynamic models of segregation. J. Math. Sociol. **1**(2), 143–186 (1971)
8. Buchanan, M.: Economics: meltdown modelling. Nature **460**, 680–682 (2009). https://doi.org/10.1038/460680a

9. Kitamura, R.: An evaluation of activity-based travel analysis. Transportation **15**, 9–34 (1988)
10. Ettema, D., Timmermans, H. (eds.): Activity-Based Approaches to Travel Analysis. Pergamon Press, Oxford (1997)
11. Gibson, F.P., Fichman, M., Plaut, D.C.: Learning in dynamic decision tasks: computational model and empirical evidence. Organ. Behav. Hum. Decis. Process. **71**, 1–35 (1997)
12. Lee, S., Son, Y., Jin, J.: An integrated human decision making model for evacuation scenarios under a BDI framework. ACM Trans. Model. Comput. Simul. (TOMACS) **20**(4), Article 23 (2010)
13. Mosteller, F., Nogee, P.: An experimental measurement of utility. J. Polit. Econ. **59**, 371–404 (1951)
14. Opaluch, J.J., Segerson, K.: Rational roots of irrational behavior: new theories of economic decision-making. Northeast. J. Agric. Resour. Econ. **18**(2), 81–95 (1989)
15. Simon, H.A.: A behavioral model of rational choice. Q. J. Econ. **69**, 99–118 (1955)
16. U.S. Department of Transportation, Federal Highway Administration. A Primer for Agent-Based Simulation and Modeling in Transportation Applications. The Exploratory Advanced Research Program
17. Giulia, L., James, P.: Agent-based modeling for financial markets. In: The Oxford Handbook of Computational Economics and Finance (2018)
18. Hammoud, Z., Kramer, F.: Multilayer networks: aspects, implementations, and application in biomedicine. Big Data Analytics **5**(1), 1–18 (2020)
19. Bonabeau, E.: Agent-based modeling: Methods and techniques for simulating human systems. Proc. Natl. Acad. Sci. **99**(Suppl. 3), 7280–7287 (2002)

The Value of Investing in Domestic Energy Storage Systems

Chiara D'Alpaos[✉] and Francesca Andreolli

Department of Civil, Architectural and Environmental Engineering,
University of Padova, Padova, Italy
chiara.dalpaos@unipd.it,
francesca.andreolli@phd.unipd.it

Abstract. In this paper, we investigate whether investments in battery storage systems, coupled with existing PV plants, are profitable in the phasing out of incentives. In detail, we analyze the investment decision of a household, who has already invested in a PV plant and has to decide whether and when to invest in the adoption of battery storage systems (BSS). We provide a Real Option Model to determine the value of the opportunity to invest and its optimal timing. The existing PV plant gives the household the opportunity to invest in BSS adoption, and this opportunity is analogous to a call option. Our findings show that negative NPV investments may turn to be profitable if the household optimally exercises the option to defer. The greater the volatility of energy prices, the greater the option value to defer, and the greater the opportunity cost of waiting (i.e., the greater the energy prices drift), the smaller the option value to defer.

Keywords: Energy storage system · Photovoltaic power plant · Real options

1 Introduction

In the last decade, the European Union set priority targets to mitigate climate change effects and promote energy transition from fossil fuels to renewable energy sources (RES). European Directives 2009/28/EC [1] and 2009/29/EC [2] classified the power sector as one of the most relevant sectors in accelerating the achievement of both the 20-20-20 targets and those set in the 2030 Climate and Energy Framework. Key targets for 2030, as revised upwards in 2018, are a 40% cut in greenhouse gas emissions compared to 1990 levels, at least a 32% share of renewables and at least 32.5% improvement in energy efficiency [3]. RES are therefore expected to play a key role in achieving these challenging goals and in the near-future global energy portfolio [4–7].

Compared to other RES, solar photovoltaic (PV) power plants have a large potential for electricity generation and represent a milestone in the pathway from a fossil-based to a carbon-neutral power sector [8]. In recent years, a large market penetration of PV plants occurred due to price reductions by over 80% from 2008 to 2016 in most competitive markets [9] and to policy incentives [10, 11]. PV already reached cost competitiveness in 2012 in several EU regions (e.g. Southern Germany, Southern Italy, Crete, etc.) and, according to the International Renewable Energy

© Springer Nature Switzerland AG 2020
O. Gervasi et al. (Eds.): ICCSA 2020, LNCS 12250, pp. 148–161, 2020.
https://doi.org/10.1007/978-3-030-58802-1_11

Agency (IRENA), cheaper modules are accelerating the achievement of grid parity in the global solar industry by 2020. Consequently, solar PV may become the competitive backbone of energy transition [12]. Nonetheless, there still exist several barriers to a widespread penetration of PV power generation. PV electricity generation is intermittent and energy storage is required to favor its large-scale deployment [13, 14]. Battery storage systems (BSS) can in fact increase the profitability of residential PV plants and in turn counterbalance the progressive reduction of policy supports, which are expected to be completely abolished in the next years [9, 15–17]. Storage represents a valuable solution to increase electricity self-consumption and reduce households' energy costs [18–21]. Storage units can store excess electricity generated when PV production exceeds demand and reduce the need for grid-purchased electricity when the PV plant is inactive (e.g., when solar irradiation is low or at nighttime). By reducing electricity bills, which represent a hidden housing ownership cost, BSS can contribute reducing households' operating expenses and increase property market value [22, 23][1]. In this context, lithium-ion and lead-acid batteries are the mostly investigated storage systems in literature. Compared to other batteries (e.g., sodium-Sulphur, vanadium redox flow), they proved to be the most cost-effective technologies in increasing self-consumption shares, especially in residential projects [4, 15, 26, 27]. Nonetheless, according to a recent literature review by D'Alpaos et al. [28], there is an ongoing debate in literature on the profitability of investments in small-scale PV plants paired with BSS. Naumann et al. [29], Cucchiella et al. [4], Cuchiella et al. [5], Hassan et al. [30] and Uddin et al. [31] argued that BSS investment costs represent still a barrier to investments. According to Naumann et al. [29], Hassan et al. [30] and Schopfer et al. [9], a cost-effective scenario may arise conditional to their costs reducing by at least 50%. In contrast with the above findings, Arik et al. [26], Olaszi and Ladanyi [32], Abbas et al. [33] and Koskela et al. [8] found that investments in domestic BSS are already profitable, although incentives or real-time pricing schemes are fundamental factors in their widespread adoption. Whereas, Hoppmann et al. [15] proved the need for incentive schemes in the short run as long as investment costs are high.

This paper contributes to this debate. Investments in PV power plants coupled with storage are characterized by high irreversibility and significant uncertainty over energy prices, which affect the trade-off between investment costs and the present value of expected benefits arising from increases in self-consumption. Traditional capital budgeting techniques and, specifically the Net Present Value (NPV) rule, fail to capture the strategic impact of investment projects and the additional value deriving from the opportunity to delay an investment decision. The NPV rule informs investment decisions according to a now-or-never proposition, that is if the investor does not make the investment now, the opportunity is lost forever. By contrast the Real Option approach, firstly proposed by Myers [34], Kester [35] and McDonald and Siegel [36, 37], provides a theoretical framework to account for the value of flexibility of deferring investments, by drawing valuation procedures from the body of knowledge developed for financial options [38].

---

[1] Real estate assets, which are powered by RES and generate smaller carbon footprints, are in fact more attractive for prospective homebuyers [24, 25].

In this paper, we analyze the investment decision of a grid-connected household, who had already invested in a PV power plant and has the opportunity to decide whether and when it is optimal to invest in a storage system, namely a rechargeable lithium-ion battery. In detail, we develop and implement a Real Option model to determine BSS investment value and optimal investment timing. Due to the growth option embedded in the existing PV plant, the opportunity to invest in the storage system is analogous to a call option, which can increase the PV plant value if optimally exercised.

The remainder of the paper is organized as follows. In Sect. 2 the stochastic optimization model is provided; Sect. 3 illustrates model calibration and parameters estimates; in Sect. 4 results are illustrated and discussed; Sect. 5 concludes.

2 Model

Starting from the seminal works by Bertolini et al. [17] and D'Alpaos et al. [28], we investigate the investment decision of a grid-connected household, who has already invested in a domestic PV plant and has to decide the optimal investment strategy in BSS, in order to increase self-consumption (i.e., the share of total PV production directly consumed by the plant owner).

The opportunity to install BSS and store PV energy production permits to reduce energy quotas grid-purchased to satisfy demand during time intervals of plant inactivity.

We introduce the following simplifying assumptions.

Assumption 1
Household's energy demand d per time unit is normalized to $d = 1$ and specifically:

$$d = \xi a + \gamma \tag{1}$$

where a is total PV power generation per unit of time, ξa is the self-consumption quota per unit of time, and γ is the grid-purchased energy quota per unit of time.

Stored energy quota is:

$$s(a) = \eta(a - \xi a) \tag{2}$$

where $\eta \in [0,1]$ is the rate of battery efficiency losses. As in Schopfer et al. [9] and D'Alpaos et al. [28], we assume that battery capacity fades out linearly over time and, due to this capacity degradation [31, 39, 40], the effective usable capacity (i.e., η) can be approximately set in between 100% and 80% of nominal battery capacity, namely 90%.

Assumption 2
In order to increase self-consumption and consequently reduce grid-purchased energy quotas, the household can decide to install a battery. According to literature, it is in fact

possible to increase self-consumption by 13–30% points with a battery storage capacity of 0.5–1.5 kWh per installed kW PV power [4, 5, 18, 41] compared to initial self-consumption rate. Whereas by installing a battery storage capacity of more than 1.5 kWh per installed kW PV power, self-consumption does not significantly increase, and the investment is not cost-effective [41][2].

For the sake of simplification, we assume that the increase in self-consumption quota due to BSS adoption is equal to stored energy quota:

$$s(a) = \eta(a - \xi a) = \Delta(\xi a) \tag{3}$$

where $\Delta(\xi a)$ is the increase in self-consumption.

Assumption 3

BSS investment costs I are irreversible and related to the Levelized Cost of Storage [17, 28]. The Levelized Cost of Storage (LCOS) is a metric, which reflects the unit cost of storing energy. It relates to the "minimum price that investors would require on average per kWh of electricity stored and subsequently dispatched in order to break even on their investments" [46, p.1].

Operation and maintenance costs are negligible [17, 41, 47–49] and consequently set equal to zero. The battery salvage value S is set equal to zero as well.

Assumption 4

Energy produced by the PV plant is not sold in the electricity market, nor energy stored in the battery. Battery adoption is meant to store excess energy quotas produced by the PV plant (i.e., not instantaneously self-consumed) for future self-consumption (e.g., when solar irradiation is low or at nighttime). The above assumption is non-restrictive and it reasonably mimics real world situations, in which BSS are usually installed to increase self-consumption and reduce grid-supplied energy quotas [15, 18, 30, 31, 50–55].

Assumption 5

The buying price of energy is stochastic and evolves over time according to a Geometric Brownian Motion (GBM). This assumption is line with many contributions in literature which adopt a GMB to describe price dynamics [17, 28, 56–59]:

$$dp_t = \mu p_t dt + \sigma p_t dz_t \quad p_0 = p \tag{4}$$

where dz_t is the increment of a Wiener process, μ is the drift term (lower than the market risk-adjusted rate of return $\hat{\mu}$, i.e. $\mu < \hat{\mu}$) and σ is instantaneous volatility.

---

[2] For larger capacities, BSS can only partially discharge during night and the next-day excess PV power will limit battery charge. Since nowadays energy consumption is particularly high in the evening, when there is not PV power generation, BSS are mostly used to satisfy night-time energy demand [17, 42–45]. By storing surpluses in PV production during daytime activity, BSS discharge in late afternoon, night, and early morning, when PV generation is insufficient [18].

According to assumptions 1–5, the household's net benefit Π generated by BSS adoption is:

$$\Pi_t = p_t \Delta(\xi a) + S_t \tag{5}$$

and the battery system present value V^3 in a risk-neutral world [60–62] is:

$$V(\Pi_0) = E\left\{ \int_0^{T_r-\tau} (e^{-rt}\Pi_t^A)dt \right\} \equiv \frac{\Pi}{\delta}\left(1 - e^{-\delta(T_r-\tau)}\right) \quad \Pi_0 = \Pi \tag{6}$$

where E is the expectation operator under a risk-neutral probability measure, r is the risk-free discount rate, T_r is the PV plant residual life, τ is the investment exercise time and δ (i.e., $\delta \equiv \hat{\mu} - \mu > 0$) is the opportunity cost of investing at time $t = 0$ in the battery instead of in a same-riskiness financial security [36][4].

The value of BSS is strongly related to the increase in self-consumption and the reduction in grid-purchased energy, which in turn generates cost savings.

The opportunity to invest in BSS is analogous to a European call option on a constant dividend-paying asset (i.e., the BSS):

$$F(\Pi_t, t) = E_t\left\{ e^{-r(\tau-t)}\max\left[(V(\Pi_t) - I)^+, 0\right] \right\} \tag{7}$$

The solution of (7) is given by the well-known formula derived by Black and Scholes [63]:

$$F(\Pi_t, t) = e^{-\delta(\tau-t)}\Phi(d_1)V_t - e^{-r(\tau-t)}\Phi(d_2)I \tag{8}$$

subject to the terminal condition [62]:

$$\lim_{\tau \to T_r} F(\Pi_t, \tau) = \lim_{\tau \to T_r} \max\left\{(V(\Pi_t) - I)^+, 0\right\} = 0 \tag{9}$$

where

$$d_1(V_t) = \frac{\ln(V_t/I) + (r - \delta + \sigma^2/2)(\tau-t)}{\sigma\sqrt{\tau-t}}, \quad d_2(V_t) = d_1(V_t) - \sigma\sqrt{\tau-t} \tag{10}$$

and $\Phi(x)$ is the cumulative standard normal distribution function.

---

[3] Under the hypothesis that markets are complete, the investment present value coincides with the expected value of discounted cash flows it generates.

[4] It can be easily demonstrated that $\delta \equiv \hat{\mu} - \mu > 0$ [36, 62]. In addition, $\hat{\mu} = r + MRP$, where MRP is market risk premium and $r - \delta$ is the certainty equivalent rate of return.

3 Model Calibration

As in D'Alpaos et al. [28], we consider a household connected to a national grid under a variable rate contract[5], whose expected energy demand on a yearly basis is constantly equal to 1 MWh/y. The household has already invested in a 3 kW PV plant, which represents the average nominal power installed in domestic PV plants in Italy[6].

To calibrate the model we use data driven from the Italian electricity market, recorded in the period April 2004-September 2019.

- The PV plant production a for a 3 kW PV plant is equal to 1500 kWh/year[7].
- The PV plant lifetime T_u is 25 years [10] and its residual life is $T_r = 20 < T_u$.
- The battery lifetime is $T_b = 13$ years [53, 64].
- The price p_t paid by household consumers for grid-purchased energy is indexed to the National Single Price (PUN). It can be demonstrated that p_t evolves over time following a GBM [17, 56–59, 65]. According to recent estimates by D'Alpaos et al. [28], we set $\mu = 1\%$, $\sigma = 34.87\%$ and $p_0(t = 0) = 54$ €/MWh[8].
- Based on Ciabattoni et al. [66], Kastel and Gilroy-Scott [10] and Cucchiella et al. [5], we set $\xi = 0.4$. In addition, according to literature we assume that self-consumption increases by 15%, 20% and 30% points respectively with a battery storage capacity of 0.5, 1.0 and 1.5 kWh per installed kW PV power, respectively [4, 18, 41]. In other words, $\Delta(\xi a) = 15\%$, 20% and 30% respectively.
- Investments costs I accounts for construction and installation costs, plus maintenance and operating costs, integration costs, and indirect costs related to efficiency losses in storage capacity. Following Bertolini et al. [17] and D'Alpaos et al. [28], we assume, as reference value for LCOS, LCOS = 220 €/MWh [9, 67]. Battery investment costs are reported in Table 1.
- The risk free rate of return is equal to the interest rate on Italian Treasury Bonds (BTPs) maturing at 20 years. According to the Italian Department of the Treasury (Dipartimento del Tesoro)[9] $r = 2\%$.
- The opportunity cost $\delta = \hat{\mu} - \mu$, is equal to $\delta = 3.5\%$ and it is estimated by calculating the risk-adjusted rate of return according to the Capital Asset Pricing

---

[5] In Italy, variable rate contracts are based on the National Single Price (PUN), i.e., the average of Zonal Prices in the Day-Ahead Market, weighted for total purchases and net of purchases for Pumped-Storage Units and of purchases by Neighboring Countries' Zones (http://www.mercatoelettrico.org/en/). Under these contracts, prosumers are price-takers.

[6] This installed power can satisfy the average demand of a household of four people. (http://www.fotovoltaiconorditalia.it/idee/impianto-fotovoltaico-3-kwdimensioni-rendimenti).

[7] On average, in Northern Italy, a 1-KW plant produces about 1100 1500 KWh/year, whereas in the South, due to more favorable weather conditions, the average is 1500–1800 KWh/year (www.fotovoltaicoenergia.com; http://re.jrc.ec.europa.eu/pvgis/).

[8] p_0 at time t = 0 is calculated as the average of PUN yearly prices in the period January 2016-September 2019 provided by Gestore Mercati Energetici (GME), a company owned by the Ministry of Economy and Finance, which operates power, gas and environmental markets, vested with the organisation and economic management of the wholesale Power Market.

[9] http://www.dt.tesoro.it/export/sites/sitodt/modules/documenti_it/debito_pubblico/dati_statistici/Principali_tassi_di_interesse_2015.pdf.

Model, i.e. $\hat{\mu} = r + \beta RP$, where βRP is the market risk premium and β measures systematic risk. In line with Bertolini et al. [17], we set $\beta = 0.5$ and $RP = 5\%$.

Table 1 summarizes parameters estimate.

Table 1. Parameters estimates.

Parameter	Value		
a	1500 kWh/kWp		
T	25		
T_r	20		
T_b	13		
μ	1%		
σ	34.87%		
p_0	54 €/MWh		
ξ	40%		
$\Delta(\xi a)$	Increase in self-consumption due to BSS adoption	0.5 kWh/kWp	15%
		1 kWh/kWp	20%
		1.5 kWh/kWp	30%
I	Battery storage capacity (kWh/kWp)	0.5 kWh/kWp	2967 €
		1 kWh/kWp	5934 €
		1.5 kWh/kWp	8901 €
r	2%		
$\hat{\mu}$	4.5%		
δ	3.5%		

4   Results and Discussion

According to our results, when $\mu = 1\%$ and $\sigma = 34.87\%$, the investment NPV is negative and it is equal to −2443 Euros, −5235 Euros and −7853 Euros for battery storage capacity kWh per PV kWp of 0.5, 1.0 and 1.5 kWh per installed kW PV power, respectively. Nonetheless, as shown in Fig. 1, by postponing the decision to invest, BSS adoption becomes profitable although the value of the opportunity to invest is negligible. When $\tau = 1$ year, the value of F is non-negative but approximately zero, for any increase in self-consumption rate. F is concave in τ and when $\tau = T_r = 20$ years F is null, for any self-consumption rate. The optimal investment timing when $\Delta(\xi a) = 15\%$ is equal to $\tau = 11$ years and the opportunity to invest is $F = 5.20$ Euros. For increasing self-consumption rates, F decreases, due to significant increases in BSS investment costs.

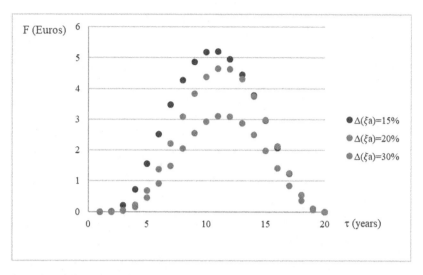

Fig. 1. Value of the opportunity to invest F for $\mu = 1\%$, $\sigma = 34.87\%$, $\Delta(\xi a) = 15\%$, 20%, 30%.

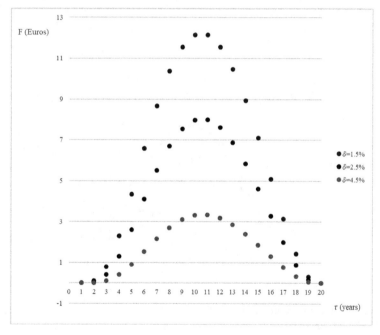

Fig. 2. Value of the opportunity to invest F for $\sigma = 34.87\%$, $\Delta(\xi a) = 15\%$, $\delta = 1.5\%$, 2.5%, 4.5%.

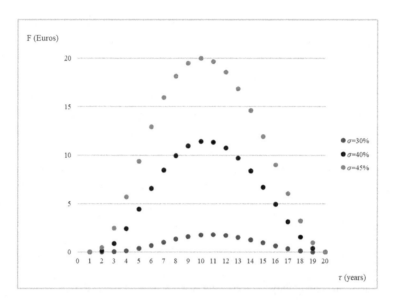

Fig. 3. Value of the opportunity to invest F, for $\Delta(\xi a) = 15\%$, $\mu = 1\%$ and $\sigma = 30\%$, 40%, 50%.

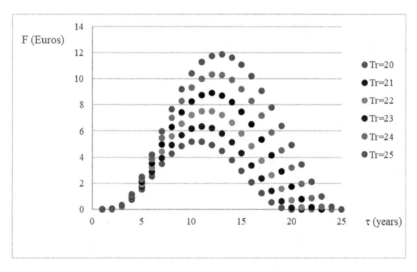

Fig. 4. Value of the opportunity to invest F for $\mu = 1\%$, $\sigma = 34.87\%$, $\Delta(\xi a) = 15\%$, and $T_r = 20, 21, 22, 23, 24, 25$ years.

To test the model results, we performed comparative statics by considering Δ $(\xi a) = 15\%$. Ceteris paribus, for increasing values of the opportunity cost of waiting δ (i.e., when μ increases), the value of the opportunity to invest decreases and, in turn, the option value to defer decreases (Fig. 2). By contrast, in line with usual Real Options theory results, for increasing volatility of energy prices σ, the option value to defer increases and, in turn, the value of the opportunity to invest F increases (Fig. 3). As volatility increases, the value of new information to come, which allows to avoid costly errors and reduce potential losses, increases.

It is worth noting that for increasing values of PV plant residual life T_r, the value of the opportunity to invest and the optimal investment timing increase.

Results illustrated in Fig. 4 clearly show the trade-off between the option value to postpone and the opportunity cost of waiting to invest. The longer the household waits to invest in BSS adoption, the lower the benefits arising from costs saving throughout the PV plant residual life.

In our simulations, battery salvage value is set equal to zero. Nevertheless, by introducing a positive salvage value, results would not substantially change and F would be still concave in τ. A positive salvage value might affect the optimal investment timing and the value of the opportunity to invest. Under the hypothesis of a null salvage value, we obtain a cautious estimate of the option value.

Our results show that, in line with literature [4, 5, 29–31], at current investment costs, batteries are not profitable and their costs represent a significant barrier to BSS adoption. As long as the value of the opportunity to defer is positive, households prefer to postpone BSS adoption, regardless BSS guarantee high self-consumption rates (i.e., 30%) and thus ensure high cost savings.

By considering the value of investment timing flexibility, the set of households' investment strategies enlarge: a negative (static) NPV project, rejected a priori, might be a positive NPV project according to the Real Option approach.

5 Conclusions

In this paper, we investigated whether households may be willing to invest in BSS adoption at current energy market prices, regardless incentive schemes. In detail, we proposed a theoretical and methodological framework, based on the Real Options approach, to determine the value of investing in BSS and its optimal timing. We modeled the opportunity to invest as a call option and investigated whether and to which extent investment value is affected by energy price volatility and investment timing flexibility. The Real Options theory suggests that investment timing flexibility, and specifically the option to defer, has a monetary value and guarantees to limit potential losses by reducing the cone of uncertainty and hedging investment risks.

Our results show that negative NPV investments may turn to be profitable in the future, whenever households exercise the option to defer optimally. At current energy prices, the optimal investment strategy is to defer investment, as the investment NPV is negative. By waiting to investment one year, the investment turns out to be a non-negative NPV investment. The value of the opportunity to invest is concave in exercise time and the investment value is maximum if undertaken at its optimal investment timing. Our findings provide households the optimal investment strategy: i.e., to postpone investment until the optimal investment timing is reached. The higher the volatility of energy prices, the higher the option value to defer; whereas the higher the energy prices drift, the higher the opportunity cost of waiting and, in turn, the smaller the option value to defer.

Future research opportunities will focus on modeling potential decreases in battery costs in order to identify BSS price that triggers investment and investigating whether incentive policy designed to promote self-consumption, rather than PV power generation, can effectively accelerate investments in storage systems.

References

1. European Parliament: Directive 2009/28/EC on the promotion of the use of energy from renewable sources and amending and subsequently repealing Directives 2001/77/EC and 2003/30/EC. Official Journal of the European Union, Brussels, Belgium (2009)
2. European Parliament: Directive 2009/29/EC amending Directive 2003/87/EC so as to improve and extend the greenhouse gas emission allowance trading scheme of the Community. Official Journal of the European Union, Brussels, Belgium (2009)
3. European Commission: Climate Action: Building a World We Like, With Climate We Like. EU Publications (2014)
4. Cucchiella, F., D'Adamo, I., Gastaldi, M.: Photovoltaic energy systems with battery storage for residential areas: an economic analysis. J. Clean. Prod. **131**, 460–474 (2016)
5. Cucchiella, F., D'Adamo, I., Gastaldi, M.: The economic feasibility of residential energy storage combined with PV panels: the role of subsidies in Italy. Energies **10**, 1434 (2017)
6. Noor, S., Yang, W., Guo, M., van Dam, K.H., Wang, X.: Energy Demand Side Management within micro-grid networks enhanced by blockchain. Appl. Energy **228**, 1358–1398 (2018)
7. D'Alpaos, C., Andreolli, F.: The economics of solar home systems: state of art and future challenges in local energy markets. Valori e Valutazioni **24**, 77–96 (2020)
8. Koskela, J., Rautiainen, A., Järventausta, P.: Using electrical energy storage in residential buildings – sizing of battery and photovoltaic panels based on electricity cost optimization. Appl. Energy **239**, 1175–1189 (2019)
9. Schopfer, S., Tiefenbeck, V., Staake, T.: Economic assessment of photovoltaic battery systems based on household load profiles. Appl. Energy **223**, 229–248 (2018)
10. Kastel, P., Gilroy-Scott, B.: Economics of pooling small local electricity prosumers: LCOE & self-consumption. Renew. Sustain. Energy Rev. **51**, 718–729 (2015)
11. Lüth, A., Zepter, J.M., Del Granado, P.C., Egging, R.: Local electricity market designs for peer-to-peer trading: The role of battery flexibility. Appl. Energy **229**, 1233–1243 (2018)
12. International Renewable Energy Agency – IRENA: Renewable Power Generation Costs in 2019, Abu Dhabi (2019). https://www.irena.org/publications/2019/May/Renewable-power-generation-costs-in-2018. Accessed 27 Nov 2019
13. Saboori, H., Hemmati, R., Ghiasi, S.M.S., Dehghan, S.: Energy storage planning in electric power distribution networks – a state-of-the-art review. Renew. Sustain. Energy Rev. **79**, 1108–1121 (2017)
14. Raugei, M., Leccisi, E., Fthenakis, V.M.: What are the energy and environmental impacts of adding battery storage to photovoltaics? A generalized life cycle assessment. Energy Tech. 1901146 (2020) https://doi.org/10.1002/ente.201901146
15. Hoppmann, J., Volland, J., Schmidt, T.S., Hoffmann., V.H.: The economic viability of battery storage for residential solar photovoltaic systems – a review and a simulation model. Renew. Sustain. Energy Rev. **39**, 1101–1118 (2014)
16. Nguyen, S., Peng, W., Sokolowski, P., Alahakoon, D., Yu. X.: Optimizing rooftop photovoltaic distributed generation with battery storage for peer-to-peer energy trading. Appl. Energy **228**, 2567–2580 (2018)

17. Bertolini, M., D'Alpaos, C., Moretto, M.: Do smart grids boost investments in domestic PV plants? Evidence from the Italian electricity market. Energy **149**, 890–902 (2018)
18. Luthander, R., Widén, J., Nilsson, D., Palm, J.: Photovoltaic self-consumption in buildings: a review. Appl. Energy **142**, 80–94 (2015)
19. Schill, W.P., Zerrahn, A.: Long-run power storage requirements for high shares of renewables: results and sensitivities. Renew. Sustain. Energy Rev. **83**, 156–171 (2018)
20. Madlener, R., Specht, J.M.: Business opportunities and the regulatory framework. Environ. Sci. Tech. **46**, 296–326 (2019)
21. Rossi, A., Stabile, M., Puglisi, C., Falabretti, D., Merlo, M.: Evaluation of the energy storage systems impact on the Italian ancillary market. Sustain. Energy Grids Netw. **17**, 100–178 (2019)
22. Black, A.J.: Financial payback on California residential solar electric systems. Sol. Energy **77**, 381–388 (2004)
23. Vimpari, J., Junnila, S.: Estimating the diffusion of rooftop PVs: a real estate economics perspective. Energy **172**, 1087–1097 (2019)
24. D'Alpaos, C., Bragolusi, P.: The market price premium for residential PV plants. In: Bevilacqua, C., Calabrò, F., Della Spina, L. (eds.). New Metropolitan Perspectives, NMP 2020. Smart Innovation, Systems and Technologies, vol. 178, pp. 1208–1216. Springer, Cham (2021). https://doi.org/10.1007/978-3-030-48279-4_112
25. D'Alpaos, C., Moretto, M.: Do Smart grid innovations affect real estate market values? AIMS Energy **7**(2), 141–150 (2019)
26. Arik, A.D.: Residential Battery Systems and the Best Time to Invest: A case study of Hawaii. UHERO Working Paper (2017)
27. Lai, L.S., McCulloch, M.D.: Levelized cost of electricity for solar photovoltaic and electrical energy storage. Appl. Energy **190**, 191–203 (2017)
28. D'Alpaos, C., Andreolli, F., Moretto, M.: Investments in domestic PV plants paired with energy storage: a stochastic dynamic optimization model. In: 30th European Conference on Operational Research, Conference Paper, Dublin, 23–26 June 2019 (2019)
29. Naumann, M., Karl, R.C., Truong, C.N., Jossen, A., Hesse, H.C.: Lithium-ion battery cost analysis in PV-household application. Energy Procedia **73**, 37–47 (2015)
30. Hassan, A.S., Cipcigan, L., Jenkins, N.: Optimal battery storage operation for PV systems with tariff incentives. Appl. Energy **203**, 422–441 (2017)
31. Uddin, K., Gough, R., Radcliffe, J., Marco, J., Jennings, P.: Techno-economic analysis of the viability of residential photovoltaic systems using lithium-ion batteries for energy storage in the United Kingdom. Appl. Energy **206**, 12–21 (2017)
32. Olaszi, B.D., Ladanyi, J.: Comparison of different discharge strategies of grid-connected residential PV systems with energy storage in perspective of optimal battery energy storage system sizing. Renew. Sustain. Energy Rev. **75**, 710–718 (2017)
33. Abbas, F., Habib, S., Feng, D., Yan, Z.: Optimizing generation capacities incorporating renewable energy with storage systems using genetic algorithms. Electronics **7**(7), 100 (2018)
34. Myers, S.C.: Determinants of corporate borrowing. J. Financ. Econ. **5**(2), 147–176 (1977)
35. Kester, W.C.: Today's option for tomorrow's growth. Harvard Bus. Rev. **62**(2), 153–160 (1984)
36. McDonald, R., Siegel, D.R.: Option pricing when the underlying asset earns a below-equilibrium rate of return: a note. J. Financ. **39**(1), 261–265 (1984)
37. McDonald, R., Siegel, D.R.: The value of waiting to invest. Q. J. Econ. **101**, 707–728 (1986)
38. D'Alpaos, C.: The value of flexibility to switch between water supply sources. Appl. Math. Sci. **6**(125–128), 6381–6401 (2012)

39. Braun, M., Büdenbender, K., Magnor, D., Jossen, A.: Photovoltaic self-consumption in Germany using Lithium-ion storage to increase self-consumed photovoltaic energy. In: Proceedings of the International Conference held in Hamburg, München, 21–25 September, pp. 3121–3127 (2009)
40. Dulout, J., Anvari-Moghaddam, A., Luna, A., Jammes, B., Alonso, C., Guerrero, J.: Optimal sizing of a lithium battery energy storage system for grid-connected photovoltaic systems. In: International Conference on DC Microgrids (ICDCM 2017), Nuremberg, Germany, June 2017 (2017)
41. Weniger, J., Tjaden, T., Quaschning, V.: Sizing of residential PV battery systems. Energy Procedia **46**, 78–87 (2014)
42. Lee, S., Whaley, D., Sman, W.: Electricity demand profile of Australian low energy houses. Energy Procedia **62**, 91–100 (2014)
43. Yang, J., Zhang, G., Ma, K.: Real-time pricing-based scheduling strategy in smart grids: a hierarchical game approach. J. Appl. Math. 329656 (2014)
44. Pimm, A.J., Cockerill, T.T., Taylor, P.G.: The potential for peak shaving on low voltage distribution networks using electricity storage. J. Energy Storage **16**, 231–242 (2018)
45. Satre-Meloy, A., Diakonova, M., Grünewald, P.: Daily life and demand: an analysis of intra-day variations in residential electricity consumption with time-use data. Energ. Effi. **13**(3), 433–458 (2019). https://doi.org/10.1007/s12053-019-09791-1
46. Comello, S., Reichelstein, S.: The emergence of cost effective battery storage. Nat. Commun. **10**, 2038 (2019). https://doi.org/10.1038/s41467-019-09988-z
47. Mercure, J.F., Salas, P.: An assessment of global energy resource economic potentials. Energy **46**, 322–336 (2012)
48. Tveten, A.G., Bolkesjø, T.F., Martinsen, T., Hvarnes, H.: Solar feed-in tariffs and the merit order effect: a study of the German electricity market. Energy Policy **61**, 761–770 (2013)
49. Barbose, G., Darghouth, N.: Tracking the Sun: Pricing and Design Trends for Distributed Photovoltaic Systems in the United States, Lawrence Berkeley National Laboratory (2019)
50. Colmenar-Santos, A., Campınez-Romero, S., Perez-Molina, C., Castro-Gil, M.: Profitability analysis of grid-connected photovoltaic facilities for household electricity self-sufficiency. Energy Policy **51**, 749–764 (2012)
51. Moshövel, J., et al.: Analysis of the maximal possible grid relief from PV-peak-power impacts by using storage systems for increased self-consumption. Appl. Energy **137**, 567–575 (2015)
52. Khalilpour, R., Vassallo, A.: Planning and operation scheduling of PV-battery systems: a novel methodology. Renew. Sustain. Energy Rev. **53**, 194–208 (2016)
53. Linssen, J., Stenzel, P., Fleer, J.: Techno-economic analysis of photovoltaic battery systems and the influence of different consumer load profiles. Appl. Energy **185**, 2019–2025 (2017)
54. Kaschub, T., Jochem, P., Fichtner, W.: Solar energy storage in German households: profitability, load changes and flexibility. Energy Policy **98**, 520–532 (2016)
55. Kappner, K., Letmathe, P., Weidinger, P.: Optimisation of photovoltaic and battery systems from the prosumer-oriented total cost of ownership perspective. Energy Sustain. Soc. **9**(1), 1–24 (2019). https://doi.org/10.1186/s13705-019-0231-2
56. Gianfreda, A., Grossi, L.: Forecasting Italian electricity zonal prices with exogenous variables. Energy Econ. **34**(6), 2228–2239 (2012)
57. Fanone, E., Gamba, A., Prokopczuk, M.: The case of negative day-ahead electricity prices. Energy Econ. **35**, 22–34 (2013)
58. Biondi, T., Moretto, M.: Solar grid parity dynamics in Italy: a real option approach. Energy **80**, 293–302 (2015)
59. Bertolini, M., D'Alpaos, C., Moretto, M.: Electricity prices in Italy: data registered during photovoltaic activity interval. Data in Brief **19**, 1428–1431 (2018)

60. Cox, J.C., Ross, S.A.: The valuation of options for alternative stochastic processes. J. Financ. Econ. **3**, 45–166 (1976)

61. Harrison, J.M., Kreps, D.M.: Martingales and arbitrage in multiperiod securities markets. J. Econ. Theory **2**, 381–420 (1979)

62. D'Alpaos, C., Dosi, C., Moretto, M.: Concession length and investment timing flexibility. Water Resour. Res. **42**(2), W02404 (2006)

63. Black, F., Scholes, M.: The pricing of option and corporate liabilities. J. Polit. Econ. **81**, 637–659 (1973)

64. Zucker, A., Hinchliffe, T.: Optimum sizing of PV-attached electricity storage according to power market signals – a case study for Germany and Italy. Appl. Energy **127**, 141–155 (2014)

65. Chen, P.: The investment strategies for a dynamic supply chain under stochastic demands. Int. J. Prod. Econ. **139**, 80–89 (2012)

66. Ciabattoni, L., Grisostomi, M., Ippoliti, G., Longhi, S.: Fuzzy logic home energy consumption modeling for residential photovoltaic plant sizing in the new Italian scenario. Energy **74**(1), 359–367 (2014)

67. Lazard: Levelized cost of storage analysis (2019). https://www.lazard.com/media/450774/lazards-levelized-cost-of-storage-version-40-vfinal.pdf

Human Health Impact of E-Waste in Mexico

J. Leonardo Soto-Sumuano[1,5]([✉]) [ID], José Luis Cendejas-Valdez[2],
Heberto Ferreira-Medina[3,4], J. Alberto Tlacuilo-Parra[5],
Gustavo Abraham Vanegas-Contreras[2], and Juan J. Ocampo-Hidalgo[6]

[1] Departamento de TI, CUCEA-Universidad de Guadalajara, Cuerpo académico
de TI-PRODEP, 45130 Zapopan Jalisco, Mexico
leonardo.lsoto@gmail.com
[2] Departamento de TICS, Universidad Tecnológica de Morelia,
Cuerpo academico TRATEC-PRODEP, 58200 Morelia Michoacán, Mexico
[3] Instituto de Investigaciones en Ecosistemas y Sustentabilidad-UNAM,
58190 Morelia Michoacán, Mexico
[4] Departamento de Sistemas y Computación, Tecnológico Nacional de México,
58117 Morelia Michoacán, Mexico
[5] División de investigación médica,
Instituto Mexicano del Seguro Social, 44340 Guadalajara Jalisco, Mexico
[6] Departamento de Electrónica, Universidad Autónoma Metroplitana Azc.,
02200 Ciudad de México, Mexico

Abstract. Mexico is the third electronic waste generator in America, only
under the U.S. and Brazil. The main contribution of this study is a proposal of a
sustainability model based on the generic cycle (Reduce, Recycle, Reuse) that
allows extending the useful life of electronic waste through the reuse of components. It is known that the elements that contribute to this are: 1) the excessive
technological consumerism, 2) the average short life cycle use of computers, and
3) the huge amount of mobile devices, batteries, and other gadgets left away due
to obsolescence. These phenomena bring every day to increase the generation of
electronic garbage, contributing environmental pollution and the poisoning of
soil, water, and air. This work shows a methodology with the following elements; i) interviews, ii) survey, iii) data analysis, iv) correlations, and v) results
over the impact of human health. In addition, the role they play in the context of
problematic cities is discussed, with the companies that develop software that
require greater hardware re-sources so that their applications work in the best
way, which generates a limited lifetime in the devices and that the software that
is built requires more resources for its optimal operation; thus, advancing the
useful life and becoming technological waste. The new proposed model is based
on; 1) awareness (reduce and reuse), 2) recycling (techniques and ways to reuse
components so that it does not become garbage) and 3) the solution-prevention
that helps minimize the impact on human health (reuse).

Keywords: E-Waste · Survey · Sustainability model · Health impact

O. Gervasi et al. (Eds.): ICCSA 2020, LNCS 12250, pp. 162–173, 2020.
https://doi.org/10.1007/978-3-030-58802-1_12

1   Introduction

In recent years, the human being has been the cause of the deterioration of the environment, it is a topic of interest for nations, governments, and organizations; this is because there has been no culture of caring for the planet. Many are the factors can be mentioned as the cause, but among the most important are: 1) the generation of pesticides and chemical products, 2) deforestation, 3) industrial and domestic waste, 4) fossil fuels and 5) high rates of garbage production, among many others.

Technological development has been very useful for humanity; it has allowed many human activities to be carried out in an easier, faster, and higher quality manner. However, in the last two decades, it has caused great problems with the generation of electronic waste (E-waste). It is currently a serious problem, due to its increase and its inadequate treatment and disposal in many countries. E-waste is burned in open spaces and is disposed of in spaces that pose risks to the environment and human health. This represents a challenge for sustainable development that is one of the goals of the global agenda for the year 2030 towards a sustainable world [1].

E-waste is the result of several trends, such as the global information society that is growing at high speed, a growing number of users of new technologies and the Internet of Things (IoT), rapid technological advances that are driving innovation, efficiency and social and economic development.

In 2017, half of the world's population was already using the internet, networks, and mobile services, which resulted in many people using more than one electronic device, thereby promoting shorter replacement cycles, that's because people are attracted to the newest technology. Specifically, middle-class society worldwide that is able to spend more on electronic devices and consequently generate more garbage.

Although there are several proposals to develop a sustainable model for the management of E-Waste in large cities, many of these have put aside the issue of the impact on human health, in addition to evaluating the population's perception of the problem. In this work, a methodology was used to define a model that allows us to understand the sustainable management of WEEE. The investigation includes the following steps; 1) stakeholder survey, 2) interview with experts, 3) analysis of the perception of the problem among the respondents, 4) proposal of a model that includes the results of the survey.

2   Literature Review

2.1   E-Waste Context

According to [2], all the countries in the world generate a total of 44.7 million metric tonnes (Mt.) per year, which is equivalent to 6.1 kilograms per inhabitant year (kg/inh) on average worldwide. According to this trend, it is expected that by the year 2021 there will be an increase to 52.2 Mt., which is equivalent to 6.8 kg/inh. Of these 47.7 Mt. it is documented that only 20% is collected and properly recycled (this is equivalent to 8.9 Mt.), the most problematic aspect of this is that the remaining 80% is not documented where it is taken, it is thought to be thrown in garbage dumps or in conditions impossible to recycle.

In this context, Asia produces 40.7% of electronic waste worldwide, followed by Europe with 27.5%, Americas with 25.3%, Africa with 5%, and Oceania with 1.6%, as shown in Fig. 1.

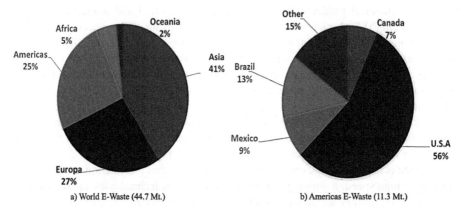

a) World E-Waste (44.7 Mt.)   b) Americas E-Waste (11.3 Mt.)

Fig. 1. Percentage of electronic waste generated in 2016 a) by continent and b) in America [2].

Of the 11.3 Mt that America generated, it is calculated on Latin America that Brazil contributed 1.5 Mt and Mexico 1 Mt, thus becoming the largest generators of electronic waste in America only below the U.S. who contributed 6.3 Mt, which is equivalent to the sum of all the countries in Latin America.

2.2   E-Waste in Cities of Mexico

It is recognized that in Mexico (with a population of 125 million inhabitants in 2019) there are 52 cities with a population ranging from 1 million inhabitants (Minh) to about 9 Minh on Mexico City. Many of these together with other cities conform to large urban areas [3]. In [4] describes that these agglomerations together with human activities generate a strong impact on the environment, increasing the ecological footprint per capita. The generation of garbage and its adequate disposal is a challenge for these large urban areas that bring together several cities. In Mexico, the largest areas per Km^2 are the metropolitan areas; from Mexico Valley (21 Minh), Guadalajara (5 Minh), Monterrey (4 Minh), Puebla-Tlaxcala (3 Minh) and Toluca Valley (2 Minh). The city of Morelia is considered one of the fastest-growing areas in the central-western part of the country with a population of 1 Minh.

On [5] describes the introduction of the new legal waste norm NADF-024-AMBT-2013 in Mexico City in July 2017; this mandates the new segregation of residual waste into five fractions: 1) organic, 2) recyclables, 3) non-recyclables, 4) hazardous and 5) bulky waste. Based on this standard there are three alternatives proposed: a baseline scenario with composting of organics, a scenario that involves anaerobic digestion of organics, and a mechanical–biological treatment scenario with no source separation.

Despite this norm in the cities of Mexico, there are still no clear policies for the separation, recycling and prevention of e-waste. It has also been observed that this norm is not used in the states' capital cities in the interior of the country with more than 1 million inhabitants, this leads to not having regulations that help to solve the problem of contamination by different types of garbage.

2.3   Human Health

In [6] describes that in Mexico City, garbage collection comprises a combination of formal and informal sectors. The study of the electronic waste recovery chain becomes a very important topic to avoid the impact on human health. Regulations and public policies should be part of a sustainable model for handling E-waste. The model proposed in Cruz-Sotelo comprises the phases: 1) source of the garbage, 2) collection and disposal, 3) sales of components that can be recycled, 4) recovery and 5) responsibility of actors.

To measure the impact on human health, the kilograms per ton recycled is used (1000 kg/tr), metals and plastics that can be recycled and are components of refrigerating equipment, large and small electronics, televisions (TVs), and monitors, for equipment of electrical and electronic lighting.

The plastics used are polystyrene (15.9 kg/tr), acrylonitrile butadiene styrene (9.8 kg/tr) and methyl polymethacrylate (3.29 kg/tr) that may contain polycyclic aromatic hydrocarbons (PAHs) [7], polychlorinated biphenyls (PCBs) [8], brominated flame retardants (BFRs) [9] and diphenyl ethers (PBDEs) [10] in concentrations less than 1 kg/tr.

The metals and rare-earth metals that have been detected are aluminum (16 kg/tr), cobalt (0.008 kg/tr), commercial refrigerant (with some metals), copper (10.8 kg/tr), and gold (0.045 kg/tr). Gravel with metals (9.6 kg/tr), lead (2.68 kg/tr), manganese dioxide (0.009 kg/tr), nickel (6.95 kg/tr), palladium (0.070 kg/tr), silver (1.37 kg/tr) and others (5.5 kg/tr) [6, 11].

These components in the open air and in garbage conditions can be harmful to human health when they are exposed to rain and sun, which in contact with humidity form leachates [12] can become toxic and contaminate aquifers, rivers, and lakes.

3   Methodology

Once the problem related to electronic waste in Mexico has been identified and the impact on human health is known, the scope of this work is described, this being a study that combines different types of investigation, such as: 1) exploratory, 2) transversal, 3) descriptive and 4) correlational. As indicated in [13], The steps to follow to achieve this research are shown in Fig. 2.

3.1   Survey

To establish the population to be surveyed, two metropolitan areas in the central-western region of Mexico were delimited. For the metropolitan area of Guadalajara, the

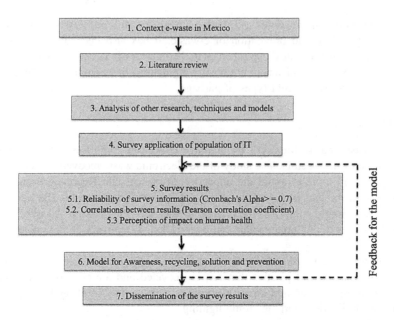

Fig. 2. Proposal methodology used for the construction of a model based on the results of the survey among university students about information and communications technology.

sample of the Universities of Guadalajara and ITESO was selected. For the Morelia metropolitan area, it was carried out at the universities of UNAM, TecNM, and UTM. The survey was carried out among the students, professors, and researchers of said institutions.

The survey was designed with 19 items of which 9 of these are based on the Likert scale, which allows obtaining the perception of the respondents about the most important variables described in the 3 axes as shown in Table 1.

The population was calculated at 1000 people, who are users of information technologies in different universities. With a 95% trust level and a standard error of 5%, the number of people to be surveyed was obtained, as shown in Table 2.

The reliability study was generated using Cronbach's Alpha, applying it to the information of the 285 people surveyed, resulting in .676; demonstrating the reliability of the information obtained. Next, the study of correlations was generated using the Pearson bivariate, considering only the medium-high correlations, the result is shown in Table 3.

3.2   Survey Results

The results of the items selected from the survey are shown below, as shown in Fig. 3.

Respondents were questioned about the impact of WEEE on human health and their knowledge about the diseases that these generate when they become electronic waste. As shown in Table 4.

Table 1. Thematic axes of the questions, survey on WEEE.

Thematic axes	Item	Type
General Information	e-mail	Open
	I. Occupancy	Option
1. Awareness of WEEE	II. Tell us about the perception you have about electrical and electronic equipment waste (WEEE) which becomes "poison" for human health	Likert
	III. You consider the risk of contracting diseases such as anxiety, hypersensitivity, neurosis, depression, stress, among others. It is through contact with waste electrical and electronic equipment (WEEE):	Likert
	IV. Are you aware of the components of electrical and electronic waste (WEEE) such as; batteries, electronic circuits, monitors and bulbs, solar cells and cables, and semiconductors?	Options: yes, no
2. Recycle of WEEE	V. Describe the handling you give to the electronic waste you dispose of:	Options
	VI. Tell us about ways of recycling electronic waste that exist in your region, community or population	Options
	VII. From the following elements, indicate the level of responsibility (0 to 100%) for each element, about the solution and prevention of electronic waste; a) government b) technology providers, c) consumers (garbage generators), d) scheduled obsolescence, e) software that is not updated, f) fashion (influence of the media)	Level 0 to 100%
3. Solution and prevention on human health	VIII. To prevent health problems due to contamination by electronic waste, indicate the level of importance in percentage (0 to 100%) for each subsection independently	Options
	IX. Teaching your family about the risks of contracting diseases because there are no adequate places to recycle electronic waste generated in the cities of Mexico	Likert

In item V, people were questioned about the habits they have when disposing of WEEE, they were questioned about the management they give to the electronic waste when disposing of it. Giving, as a result, 45% say they keep it in a box or place of confinement, 25% throw it away, 20% give it away, 12% sell it, 27% take it to recycle and 4% do something else with WEEE.

Similarly, in item VI it was observed about ways of recycling that exist in their urban area, 37% say they use recycling events, 20% government programs, 13% through recycling plants, 13% with companies of technology, 12% make use of Non-Governmental Organizations (NGOs) and 5% other forms.

Table 2. Data to determine the sample

Reference values	Results
n (sample) =	278
Trust level	95.00%
Z value	1.96
p =	50.00%
q =	50.00%
e =	5.00%
N (population) =	1,000.00

Table 3. Correlation for nine items

Pearson correlation >= 0.4	V. where WEE end	VII. Responsibility				VIII. Prevention of health risks
		VII b) Business	VII c) Users	VII e) Software	VII f) Trend	
II. Poisonous components	0.42					
VII. a) Government		0.51	0.49			
VII. b) Supplier companies			0.66	0.46		
VII. c) Generating users				0.49	0.43	
VII. d) Scheduled obsolescence				0.44	0.55	
VII. e) Non updating software						0.42

In Fig. 4 shows the importance of the actors involved in the generation, recycling, and reuse of WEEE components in urban areas, item VII.

For item VIII regarding human health, questions were raised about the importance of preventing family members from the risks of contracting diseases, since there are no adequate places to deposit electronic waste. 74% of respondents considered it very important, 23% important and 3% indifferent. Finally, for item IX it was observed that of the total of respondents:

- 68% of them consider the implementation of public health programs very important
- 58% think that the solution should be emphasized among the population
- 41% advocate including the topic in educational programs
- 46% agree about promoting certifications for public and private companies

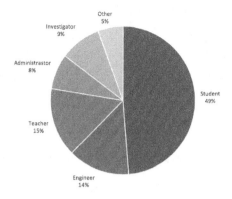

a)   Types of occupation of the respondents

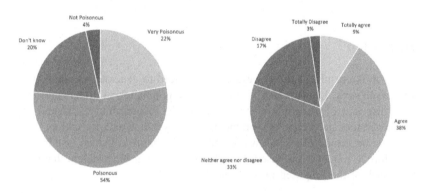

b)   WEEE as poison   c) Human health risks

Fig. 3. For Items I, II and III, a) Occupation and perception of WEEE, b) as poison and c) as a health risk 285 people surveyed.

Table 4. Item IV, perception of WEEE components that affect human health.

Components	Yes	No
a) Batteries and/or accumulators contain elements such as lead and lithium that affect the kidneys, the brain, and the nervous system	89%	11%
b) Electronic circuits contain elements such as silicon that affect the bones, liver and cause psychological disorders	55%	45%
c) Monitors and fluorescent tubes (bulbs) contain elements such as mercury and toxic gases that affect the nervous system, eyes, and skin	76%	24%
d) Solar cells and semiconductors contain toxic plastics such as silicone that cause lung cancer	37%	63%
e) Cables and semiconductors contain arsenic that causes cancer in the respiratory tract	43%	57%

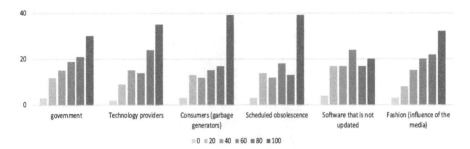

Fig. 4. Item VII, importance of the participation of the different actors in the recycling and disposal of WEEE.

- 51% agree in promoting the adequate disposal of WEEE
- 56% agree with having a greater number of recycling companies in urban cities

4   Discussion

According to the results of the survey, there is a need to generate activities that cover the three main axes: 1) awareness of WEEE in the population of urban cities and their adequate disposal; 2) recycling of WEEE where the responsibility is shared between the user generators and technology providers and 3) solution and prevention, to prevent WEEE from becoming electronic waste and causing harm to human health.

Therefore, a model is proposed that allows addressing the problem that meets the needs of each of the proposed axes. As shown in Fig. 5.

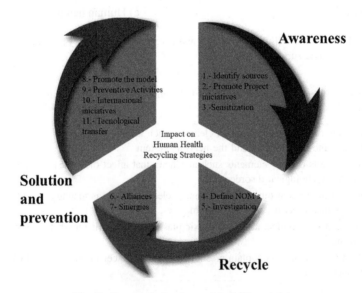

Fig. 5. Proposed circular sustainability model.

The strategies described in the model presented in Fig. 5 are based on the circular model proposed in [14], which are described in eleven items to solve the problem of electronic waste. The proposed model contemplates the same strategies classified in consciousness, recycling, and prevention/solution. Emphasis is placed on the impact on human health, which is described below.

Awareness:

1) Permanently identify the sources of WEEE generation and account for the volumes generated, trying to recycle the kg/t for plastics, metals, and other elements.
2) Promote investment initiatives and projects to develop the necessary infrastructure for the management of WEEE, using information technologies.
3) Develop greater efforts to raise consumer awareness of WEEE with the support of companies and decision-makers.

Recycle:

1) Define more precise NOMs that promote recycling, repairing, and reuse of WEEE. In addition, promote their eco-design to extend their useful life.
2) Promote research in Mexico through projects that consider aspects such as key actors, social framework, urban areas, and regulations.
3) Develop initiatives to strengthen academic, business, government, and society alliances for sustainable WEEE management.
4) Develop synergies between existing initiatives to avoid duplication of efforts and maximize existing resources for managing WEEE.

Solution y Prevention:

1) Publicize the impact of e-waste considering the three axes of the model for human health care.
2) Work on preventive activities such as certifications, dissemination, among the actors and thus avoid contamination by WEEE.
3) Respect international initiatives (ITU-T Study Group 5, PACE [14], and Step [15]).
4) Promote innovation and technology transfer for the sustainable management of WEEE.

The application of the model requires outreach and dissemination activities in urban cities that help raise awareness among citizens and e-waste recyclers about the impact this has on human health. It is observed that the surveyed population is aware of the problem caused by WEEE when it becomes electronic waste, but there are no clear ways to properly dispose of it and there are no known places to take it to recycle.

5 Conclusion

Based on the correlation study, respondents think that the highest correlations demonstrate the level of responsibility they have: 1) users and technology providers, 2) continuing with users and the government, 3) responsibility of users who generate garbage due to the obsolescence of the software, 4) the obsolescence of the electronic equipment because it is not fashionable anymore. However, respondents also think that technology companies would not be responsible of management of WEEE without government regulations.

The survey revealed the response of students, teachers and engineers who are related to information technology, 54% consider e-waste to be a poison for human health and 38% consider it a risk to human health.

It was observed that the perception about the elements that most affect human health in order of importance are: 1) batteries, 2) electronic circuits 3) monitors and fluorescent lights. It was also observed that there is heavy impact related of solar cells and cables; when these elements are disposed cause cancer and damage to the respiratory system.

It was also found that 37% of respondents are aware of recycling events, 20% of government programs and initiatives, and 13% knew about events made by recycling plants and technology companies. However, they think that programs and initiatives will help the government, recycling plants and technology companies to improve the process of handling electronic waste.

It is necessary to take advantage of technology to generate a strategy that enables electronic waste generators to be closer to recycling companies.

Education is an important issue in the solution because there is a need to be included in the study plans and programs, from basic education to higher education; through mandatory workshops, school subjects, and/or courses in the areas related to IT and sustainability. This way the model can be a framework for reducing the ecological footprint in technological areas.

This new model considers the impact on human health, through strategies defined are aimed at reducing the E-waste. Building methodologies attached to the model would help implement public initiatives in cities that do not have regulatory frameworks. Therefore, it is necessary for the government to participate in promoting new norms that regulate the disposal of WEEE in Mexican cities.

Acknowledgments. We are grateful for the support of the Ecosystem Research Institute and Sustainability (IIES), Technological University of Morelia (UTM) and the Guadalajara University (UdeG). Especially to MGTI. Atzimba G. López M. and MTI. Alberto Valencia G. for his comments and support in the figures. To students from the UTM, Marco Rojas F. and Daniel Saucedo P. for his help in the documentation of the model.

References

1. United Nations: About the Sustainable Development Goals. United Nations, 1 January 2017. https://www.un.org/sustainabledevelopment/sustainable-development-goals/. Accessed Nov 2019
2. Baldé, C.P., Forti, V., Gray, V., Kuehr, R., Stegmann, P.: The Global E-waste Monitor 2017. UNU and ITU, Bonn/Geneva/Vienna (2017)
3. INEGI: Encuesta Nacional de Seguridad Pública Urbana. Comunicado de prensa núm. 187/19. México, 17 de Abril de 2019. https://www.inegi.org.mx/contenidos/saladeprensa/bolnes/2019/ensu/ensu2019_04.pdf

4. González-Abraham, C., Ezcurra, E., Garcillán, P.P., Ortega-Rubio, A., Kolb, M., Bezaury Creel, J.E.: The Human Footprint in Mexico: Physical Geography and Historical Legacies (2015)
5. Tsydenova, N., Vázquez Morillas, A., Cruz Salas, A.A.: Sustainability assessment of waste management system for Mexico City (Mexico)—based on analytic hierarchy process. Recycling **3**, 45 (2018)
6. Cruz-Sotelo, S.E., et al.: E-waste supply chain in Mexico: challenges and opportunities for sustainable management. Sustainability **9**, 503 (2017)
7. Tongo, I., Ogbeide, O., Ezemonye, L.: Human health risk assessment of polycyclic aromatic hydrocarbons (PAHs) in smoked fish species from markets in Southern Nigeria. Toxicol. Rep. **4**, 55–61 (2017). ISSN 2214-7500
8. ATSDR: Case Studies in Environmental Medicine Polychlorinated Biphenyls (PCBs), Agency for toxic substances and disease registry, Toxicity, p. 90 (2016)
9. Lyche, J.L., Rosseland, C., Berge, G., Polder, A.: Human health risk associated with brominated flame-retardants (BFRs). Environ. Int. **74**, 170–180 (2015)
10. Linares, V., Bellés, M., Domingo, J.L.: Human exposure to PBDE and critical evaluation of health hazards. Arch. Toxicol. **89**(3), 335–356 (2015). https://doi.org/10.1007/s00204-015-1457-1
11. Rim, K.-T.: Effects of rare earth elements on the environment and human health: a literature review. Toxicol. Environ. Health Sci. **8**(3), 189–200 (2016). https://doi.org/10.1007/s13530-016-0276-y
12. Rivera-Laguna, E., Barba-Ho, L., Torres-Lozada, P.: Determi-nación de la toxicidad de lixiviados provenientes de residuos sólidos urbanos mediante indicadores biológicos. Afinidad, vol. 70(563) (2013)
13. Hernández Sampieri, R., Fernández-Collado, C., Baptista Lu-cio, P.: Metodología de la investigación. McGraw-Hill, México (2010)
14. ITU - United Nations: A New Circular Vision for Electronics, United Nations 1 January 2019. http://www3.weforum.org/docs/WEF_A_New_Circular_Vision_for_Electronics.pdf. Accessed Jan 2020
15. StEP Initiative: Guiding Principles to Develop E-waste Management Systems and Legislation, Solving the E-waste problem, Step White Paper (2016). ISSN 2071-3576. Accessed Jan 2019

A General Model
for Electroencephalography-Controlled
Brain-Computer Interface Games

Gabriel Alves Mendes Vasiljevic$^{(\boxtimes)}$ and Leonardo Cunha de Miranda

Department of Informatics and Applied Mathematics,
Federal University of Rio Grande do Norte (UFRN), Natal, Brazil
`gabrielvasiljevic@ppgsc.ufrn.br, leonardo@dimap.ufrn.br`

Abstract. The rapid expansion of Brain-Computer Interface (BCI) technology allowed for the recent development of applications outside of clinical environments, such as education, arts and games. Games controlled by electroencephalography (EEG), a specific case of BCI technology, benefit from both areas, since they can be played by virtually any person regardless of physical condition, can be applied in numerous serious and entertainment contexts, and are ludic by nature. However, they also share the same challenges of design and development from both fields, especially since they demand numerous specific and specialized knowledge for their development. In this sense, this work presents a model for games using EEG-based BCI controls. The proposed model is intended to help researchers describe, compare and develop new EEG-controlled games by instantiating its abstract and functional components using concepts from the fields of BCI and games. A group of EEG-controlled games from the literature was selected to demonstrate the usefulness and representativeness of the model. The demonstration showed that an overview classification and the details of the selected games were able to be described using the model and its components.

Keywords: BCI · EEG · Game · Model · HCI

1 Introduction

The recent evolution of Brain-Computer Interface (BCI) technologies allowed the development of novel applications both for clinical and domestic environments [4]. Games based on electroencephalography (EEG)—a specific case of non-invasive BCI—are being increasingly developed and applied in both contexts, especially because they can be played potentially by any person regardless of physical impairments, as the EEG signals are read and translated by the application directly from the brain [30,31].

In this context, EEG-based BCI are usually employed in serious games, which are developed and used for any purpose other than (or in addition to) entertainment [12]. These games have potential to be employed in many different fields

© Springer Nature Switzerland AG 2020
O. Gervasi et al. (Eds.): ICCSA 2020, LNCS 12250, pp. 174–189, 2020.
https://doi.org/10.1007/978-3-030-58802-1_13

and applications, such as being a treatment option to help patients in rehabilitation [15] and training cognitive functions through neurofeedback [6,28,29]. However, given the evolution of BCI algorithms and the emergence of consumergrade EEG devices, these games are also starting to be developed to be used solely for entertainment purposes [27], benefiting both healthy and impaired players.

The development of BCI games raises challenges that are related to both fields [9,24]. From the perspective of BCI, the developer must ensure that the system is precise enough to capture, process and identify the target neural mechanism (and thus, the player's intention) accurately in real time. From the perspective of games, the developer must also ensure the game flow, so that the player is immersed into the game, have fun playing it and desire to play it again, even if its purpose is not solely entertainment. Thus, it is required domain over knowledge from many different areas that are related to both games and BCI, including Neurophysiology, Psychology and Human-Computer Interaction (HCI).

Existing models and representative schemes from the literature can describe specific aspects of BCI-based systems or games, in both general and specialized contexts. However, these models can only represent EEG-controlled games as a BCI system or as a game—not as a whole, single entity. To our knowledge, there are currently no model for representing EEG-controlled games and the specific components, attributes and features that constitute them. In this sense, the main objective of this work is to describe a general model for EEG-controlled games, and to demonstrate the usefulness and representativeness of this model with BCI-based games from the literature. The proposed model intends to unite concepts and vocabulary from both fields into a single theoretical framework.

This work is organized as follows: Sect. 2 presents the related work, including other models and how they are related to our study; Sect. 3 describes the proposed model and its development process; Sect. 4 presents a demonstration of the model using games from the literature; Sect. 5 discusses the results of the demonstration and the implications of the model for the literature; and Sect. 6 concludes the paper.

2   Related Work

The related works present models, frameworks and/or conceptual schemes regarding games, BCI systems and BCI-based games. For both fields, there are examples of abstract models and frameworks for representing those systems in a general or specific manner, given that they can be applied in a number of different contexts depending on their purpose. It is reasonable to assume that there is a higher number of models for representing games, given that the field of games is relatively older than the field of BCI. We will focus on describing those that are closely related or pertinent to the scope of this work.

For the field of BCI, the studies from Mason and Birch [19] and Mason et al. [20] are closely related to the scope of our work. In the model presented by

Mason and Birch [19], which was derived using concepts from related fields such as HCI, the BCI system was described based on its functional components, and was employed as a base for constructing a framework and a taxonomy for BCI design. This model and taxonomy were later updated and expanded by Mason et al. [20], using the Human Activity Assistive Technology model as base for its construction. Thus, this model considers BCI systems as an assistive technology, focusing on people with functional limitations that uses these systems to overcome an ability gap and perform an action in the environment.

More recently, Kosmyna and Lécuyer [11] presented a conceptual space for EEG-based BCI systems. The authors described key concepts of BCI systems and their possible values, divided into four axes with nine sub-axes. These axes represent information about *when* the BCI system is used (i.e., the temporal features of the BCI system, such as whether its commands are employed actively or passively by the user); for *what* it is used (its application and employed neural mechanism); *how* it is used (multi-modal aspects of the system); and *where* it is used (virtual, physical or mixed environments). The authors demonstrate their conceptual space by instantiating a set of BCI-based systems from the literature, and found that most systems are based on virtual environments, using event-related (de)synchronization as neural paradigm, and are synchronous (the user must wait for a trigger to use a BCI command).

As stated in Sect. 1, BCIs are usually (but not exclusively) employed in serious games, given the intersection of contexts and applications for both fields. Models and classification schemes for serious games are presented, for example, in the works of Djaouti et al. [2] and De Lope and Medina-Medina [17], which present taxonomic schemes for representing and classifying serious games, while McCallum and Boletsis [21] present a classification scheme for the specific case of serious games for dementia. Considering both fields, there are also studies that focus on representing BCI-based serious games. Sung et al. [24], for example, present a methodology and development architecture for creating new EEG-based serious games, which define roles for experts, game developers and designers in the development process and unify methodologies from both fields.

Although these models can represent a wide variety of BCI-based systems and their related concepts, to our knowledge there are currently no models for representing the case of EEG-controlled games. The BCI models presented in the literature can represent systems in a general manner and as a special case of assistive devices. However, specific components related to the game part of the system may be lost in this context. In the same sense, models for representing games, both general and specific, are not able to represent the components related to the capturing, processing and application of EEG signals from the user to the game. In this context, the model proposed in this work draws inspiration from related works of both fields, and was developed to close the gap between BCI and game systems by representing both as only one entity.

3   Model for EEG-Controlled Games

In this section the proposed general model for EEG-controlled games is presented, including its development process and how its final version was derived.

3.1   Development Process

The model was constructed for representing virtually any kind of game that is controlled in any aspect using EEG. The main principles (px) that guided the construction of the model were that:

p1. The BCI system and the game system should be as less dissociated as possible;
p2. The model should be general enough to represent as best as possible any EEG-controlled game currently available in the literature; and
p3. The model should be expandable and adaptable for specific situations and contexts.

As the model is intended to represent EEG-controlled games, theoretical knowledge from classic BCI works [19,20,31] and the analysis of various BCI games from the literature [3,4,27], in addition to previous experience on both the development and evaluation of such games [26,28–30], served as the foundation for constructing and refining the model. After the derivation of its initial version based on related models as described in Sect. 2, the model was refined in an iterative, incremental process of fitting games obtained from the literature in its components, and thus identifying missing, important components that could help describing those games more accurately. This general development process is illustrated in Fig. 1, and the logic that guided its derivation is described next.

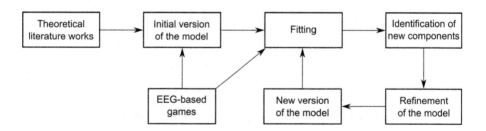

Fig. 1. Development process of the model.

3.2   Model Derivation and Construction

The model itself is based on the classical closed-loop neurofeedback scheme for BCI-based systems (Fig. 2). In this scheme, the BCI system is de-composed into six main steps representing its function: data acquisition, pre-processing, feature

extraction, feature classification/translation, application, and (neuro)feedback
[31]. This scheme is largely seen in a number of primary works, in which the
BCI system architecture is based or adapted from it (e.g., Hasan and Gan [7],
Koo et al. [10], Lalor et al. [14], and Tangermann et al. [25]), and resembles other
BCI-based models, such as the functional model of Mason and Birch [19].

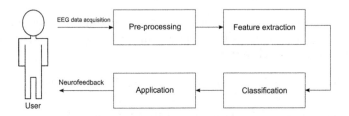

Fig. 2. Classic closed-loop neurofeedback architecture.

In a general sense, the classic BCI system can be seen as a filter (or transducer), receiving and transforming an input signal (the EEG data from the user)
into an output control signal (for the application to consume). The target application then feeds the results of this control signal back to the user, which in
turn consciously or unconsciously alters his/her brain electro-chemical dynamics in response, and this change is then captured by the EEG acquisition device,
composing the closed-loop architecture. Thus, the classic BCI closed-loop architecture scheme from Fig. 2 can be simplified into the following model:

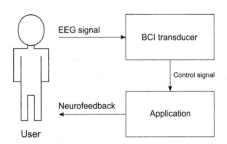

Fig. 3. Simplified closed-loop neurofeedback model.

In the proposed model, based on the model presented in Fig. 3 and in the
context of games, the target application is the game itself, being directly or
indirectly controlled by the control signal provided by the BCI transducer. The
model is derived by an even more simplified scheme (Fig. 4), in which the game
and the BCI transducer are seen as only one entity (based on principle p1 of the
model): the EEG-controlled game, which receives an input from the player, and
provides a feedback based on its current internal state.

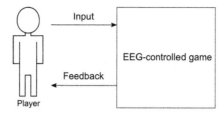

Fig. 4. Simplified EEG-controlled game model.

It is important to notice that, in this simplified scheme, the input is not restricted to an EEG signal, nor is the feedback restricted to a neurofeedback itself. The reason is that, in the context of games, the application can be controlled not only by the EEG signals, but by other forms of controls as well, such as physical ones (e.g., mouse, keyboard, joysticks and gamepads) or other physiological ones (e.g., heart rate, breathing rate and electrodermal activity)[1]. In the same context, the feedback provided by the game can not only represent the response to the EEG-based control, but it can also represent the changes in the game world (and in the objects contained in this world) that were caused both internally by game itself, and externally by the physical and/or physiological controls from the player(s).

These details are fundamental for the detailing of the model. Every component of the simplified model can be further decomposed into several parts: The input is composed of the EEG input and other physical/physiological inputs; the feedback is composed of both the feedback from the game's virtual interface and/or the neurofeedback; and the EEG-controlled game is an implementation that contains the game logic, including the control mechanics and the game world, and an interface to receive the input(s) and to provide feedback to the player. This more detailed model is represented in Fig. 5.

In this model, the optional components are marked with non-continuous lines. The presence of optional components contributes for a more adaptive scheme (based on principle p3 of the model). Here, the other physical and physiological inputs are optional, as the model represents and focus on EEG-controlled games. The control interface receives the input and translates it into control signals, which are employed as control mechanics in the game logic to alter the game world. This change in the game world reflects on the virtual interface, which presents its state to the player in the form of a feedback. This feedback can be visual, auditory or somatosensory (haptic/vibrotactile or thermal). Although the virtual feedback is always present, as it represents the game environment and the status of the game to the player (assuming that a player cannot play a game without knowing at least its status in a finite amount of time), the

---

[1] This is also the reason that the game component is referred as "EEG-controlled" rather than "EEG-based" in this work, as the first term is a generalization of the latter, i.e., it can represent any game that is controlled by EEG, including those that are based solely on this kind of control.

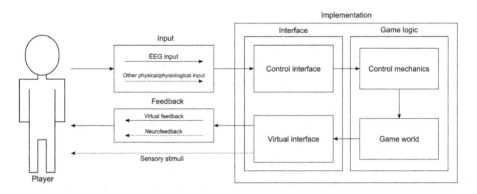

Fig. 5. Detailed EEG-controlled game model.

neurofeedback is optional, as the game can be played using a passive BCI (e.g., passively adjusting the game difficulty using the player's emotions), and thus no neurofeedback is explicitly provided. The sensory stimuli is another optional element which was introduced based on both principles p2 and p3 of the model, as specific control signals (e.g., SSVEP and P300) require an external stimulus to be generated and captured by the EEG acquisition device.

Finally, the detailed model presented in Fig. 5 can be further detailed to represent all components of an EEG-controlled game. This allow for the instantiation of each of these components in a very specific sense, as opposed to a more abstract model. This complete general model can be seen in Fig. 6.

In the complete model, the EEG input is captured in the data collection step by **sensors** connected to an **EEG device**, which transfers the acquired EEG data to the BCI module in the **control interface** for the processing of this data. This include the classic steps in a BCI system, i.e., pre-processing, feature extraction, classification, and sending the classified control signal to the application, i.e., the game. In cases where there is no need for a classifier, in which the system translates the signal's extracted features directly to a continuous variable to be employed by the game (e.g., applying the theta/beta ratio to calculate the players' level of attention), the module transmits the processed feature translation directly to the game after the feature extraction step. There can also be an intermediate, optional step for feature selection before the actual classification, usually employed to increase the classifier's accuracy.

The received **control signals** are then employed as **control mechanics** in the game logic, altering the **game world** and its components, i.e., the **game environment**, and eventual player characters, game objects and Non-Playable Characters (NPCs). Every component in the game world, with exception of the game environment, are optional, as a game can be designed with or without objects and characters, but not without an environment in which the game logic occurs and that the player can interact with it in any manner. If exists, the **player character** can interact with both the environment and its objects and with other non-playable, computer-controlled characters, or even with other

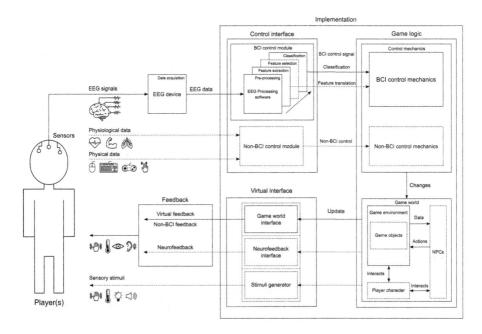

Fig. 6. Complete general EEG-controlled BCI game model.

player characters, in the case of multiplayer games. The **NPCs**, while being agents, can perceive the environment and perform actions in this environment in response to this data.

In the same sense, the other **physical and physiological** data, labelled as "Non-BCI" for a more general term, are handled by their own modules and control their own mechanics within the game logic. They are also optional components, given that the game can be designed to be controlled solely with EEG controls. All these changes, performed by the player or by the game itself, are then updated in the game's **virtual interface**, which is composed by the game world interface, the neurofeedback interface and the stimuli generator.

The **game world interface** is used to represent all components of the game world, including the player character and the NPCs. This interface can contain the neurofeedback interface and the stimuli generator, or these components can be separated, having their own interfaces (e.g., the stimuli generator or the neurofeedback can be contained in a separate screen or a device connected to the subject's body). While the game world interface and the **neurofeedback interface** provide feedback for the subject, the **stimuli generator** provides a sensory stimulus, in accordance with the model in Fig. 5. All the components and their description are summarized in Table 1.

4 Model Demonstration

The method to demonstrate the model is similar to the approach employed by Mason and Birch [19] and Kosmyna and Lécuyer [11], by means of demonstrating its usefulness through the representation of a set of works that describes EEG-based systems/games using the model, and instantiating each of its components. Tables 2 and 3 present the result of this demonstration, with games presented in alphabetical order.

Games were selected from studies using different game genres, control styles and EEG-based control signals to provide more diversity in the data. All positions in the Sensors subcomponent are based on the 10–20 international system [27] and its extended versions. Optional values that were not present in the game were marked as "N/A" (not applied).

5 Discussion

The demonstration of the model wielded some interesting results about its ability to represent and compare games from the literature. The individual representation of each game gives an overview of its contents and allow for the extraction of its concept and design from this description. The open aspect of the description of each component, as opposed to more closed and pre-defined classification values, also gives the researcher or developer more freedom to emphasize on specific aspects that s/he finds pertinent. Thus, although a brief summary of each component was provided for each game for the purpose of demonstrating its representativeness, a more detailed description is also possible.

In comparison to other models from the literature, the proposed model represents the BCI aspect of the game in a similar fashion to most representative schemes of EEG-based systems, as it is based on the classic neurofeedback loop and presents the same EEG signal processing steps. It has the advantage, however, of also representing the details about the game itself, as both aspects are seen as only one entity, in contrast with other BCI models and representations in which the BCI implementation is taken as a separate software or hardware, or in which the game (or any other application) is abstracted and only receives the control signal to consume. The downside of this generalist approach for the representation of games is that some details about its implementation (including the implementation of the BCI module) may be lost, e.g., in which platform the game is intended to run, its genre, the details of the feature extraction and translation steps and so on.

However, although not exhaustively shown in the demonstration, some specific details about the signal processing algorithm could also be represented in the *BCI Control* component depending on the goals of the researcher. Information about the pre-processing steps (e.g., filters and de-noising techniques) or the feature extraction/classification algorithms could help in the comparison of different implementations for the detection and employment of the same neural mechanism. The same could be applied to game-related components, such as

Table 1. All model's components and their description.

Component		Description
EEG data collection	Sensors	The type and amount of sensors that were employed to capture the player's EEG data. In the case of EEG, active or passive electrodes are usually employed. These electrodes can be wet (i.e., they require a saline or conductive substance to help lowering the impedance) or dry, and are generally placed strategically on the scalp depending on the neural mechanism that the researcher intends to identify.
	EEG device	The biosignal amplifier and/or head-mounted device that was employed to receive the EEG data from the sensors. The captured data is usually amplified and pre-processed before being used by the feature extraction and/or classification algorithm. Depending on the device (e.g., consumer-grade EEG devices), the device can also perform the pre-processing and feature extraction/classification steps.
Control interface	BCI control signal	The EEG-based control signal or underlying neural mechanism that was employed as a control command to the game. Examples of these control signals are the SSVEP, P300, motor imagery, and cognitive states, such as attention, relaxation and emotions.
	Non-BCI control	Any other non-BCI control, such as physical/analogical/digital controls (e.g., mouse, keyboard, joystick) and other biophysical signals (e.g., EMG, EOG, ECG).
Control mechanics	BCI	How the EEG-based control is employed to change or to interact with the game world. This include moving or acting with a game character, interacting with objects and/or non-playable characters from the game world or altering the game environment.
	Non-BCI	Similar to the BCI control mechanics, but applied to other, non-BCI controls, if they exist.
Game world		The game world is composed of its **environment**, and eventual **player characters**, non-playable characters (**NPCs**) and **game objects**. Depending on the game rules, the player can act through a player character or directly to the game and its objects.
	Player(s) character(s)	The players' controllable characters in the game world (if it exists), including its amount (single player, multiplayer), and how the player interacts or controls it.
	Environment	The environment that the game takes place. This environment can be virtual (i.e., in a virtual, simulated world) or physical (i.e., in the real world, using physical objects or machines).
Virtual interface		The virtual interface is responsible for providing the player(s) with feedback from the game, as well as external stimuli and neurofeedback. This include the **game world interface**, responsible for the **virtual feedback** that updates the player about the status of the game world; the neurofeedback interface; and the stimuli generator. Note that the latter two can both be included in the game world interface, or be separated (e.g., an external device used to generate visual or auditory stimuli that is separated from the game screen).
	NF interface	Provides the specific feedback that updates the player about his/her internal mental state and/or regarding the result of the signal processing algorithm. This can be, for example, a numerical value, a change in the virtual interface (e.g., an interface element that visually changes according to the classification result, or the movement of an object/character in the game world), a sound, a vibration etc. Note that this feedback may also be embedded in the virtual feedback.
	Stimuli generator	Generates external stimuli to evoke specific brain responses, which are required for exogenous control signals (e.g., P300 and SSVEP). These stimuli can be visual, auditive or somatosensory (e.g., thermal and vibrotactile).

Table 2. Demonstration of the model and its components.

αWoW [13]		
EEG data collection	**Sensors:**	Four wet electrodes, placed at positions P1, P2, CP7, and CP8.
	EEG device:	An Emotiv Epoc.
Control interface	**BCI control:**	Relaxation level, calculated using a FFT of the α frequency band.
	N/BCI control:	Mouse and keyboard.
Control mechanics	**BCI:**	Activates a specific ability that the player can cast to change the shape and powers of its avatar.
	Non-BCI:	Controls the movement of the character and the casting of abilities.
Game world	**Player character:**	A humanoid avatar that can shape-shift into a bear.
	Environment:	Virtual, three-dimensional, multiplayer open world.
Virtual interface	**World interface:**	PC monitor display, with a three-dimensional view of the world and third-person view of the player character.
	NF interface:	Embedded in the game's graphical interface. A bar with a numerical threshold value that indicates whether the player reached the required cognitive state to activate the related ability.
	Stimuli generator:	N/A.
Aiming Game [8]		
EEG data collection	**Sensors:**	Not informed (up to 14 saline electrodes, given the employed device).
	EEG device:	An Emotiv Epoc.
Control interface	**BCI control:**	Emotion (arousal), represented with a value ranging from 1 to 5.
	N/BCI control:	Mouse.
Control mechanics	**BCI:**	Dynamically adjusts the game difficulty, distorting the aim and blurring targets.
	Non-BCI:	Used to point and click the target airplanes in the screen.
Game world	**Player character:**	N/A.
	Environment:	A virtual, 2-dimensional picture of the sky, with moving targets.
Virtual interface	**World interface:**	A PC monitor screen, showing the virtual environment and the player's aim.
	NF interface:	A bar, divided into five segments, shows the player's current level of arousal.
	Stimuli generator:	N/A.
BrainArena [1]		
EEG data collection	**Sensors:**	Two GAMMACaps with eight active electrodes positioned over the parietal region.
	EEG device:	Two g.USBAmp amplifiers.
Control interface	**BCI control:**	Motor imagery, classified using a LDA classifier with band power features extracted using CSP filters.
	N/BCI control:	N/A.
Control mechanics	**BCI:**	The player must perform the indicated imagined movement to move a ball into the target goal.
	Non-BCI:	N/A.
Game world	**Player character:**	N/A.
	Environment:	A black scenario with three feedback gauges, two goals, a ball and instructions for the current imagined movement to be performed by each player.
Virtual interface	**World interface:**	A PC monitor screen, showing all elements of the game world for both players.
	NF interface:	Three feedback gauges in the game screen indicating the intensity of the recognized motor imagery command (left, right), one for each player and one for the cumulative result of the identified imagined movements.
	Stimuli generator:	N/A.
Connect Four [18]		
EEG data collection	**Sensors:**	Nine silver chloride electrodes.
	EEG device:	A 32-channel ActiCap system with a BrainAmp amplifier.
Control interface	**BCI control:**	P300, calculated with a bayesian classifier after spatial and temporal filtering.
	N/BCI control:	N/A.
Control mechanics	**BCI:**	Used to select a target column in a game of Connect Four with two players.
	Non-BCI:	N/A.
Game world	**Player character:**	N/A.
	Environment:	A virtual, two-dimensional Connect Four game board.
Virtual interface	**World interface:**	PC monitor display showing the board and the time left to make a move.
	NF interface:	A rectangle appear over the selected column to indicate the classification result.
	Stimuli generator:	Each column of the game board flashes in sequence to evoke the P300 potential.
Hangman BCI [7]		
EEG data collection	**Sensors:**	Nine electrodes, positioned over the sensorimotor cortex.
	EEG device:	A 64+2 channel Biosemi cap.
Control interface	**BCI control:**	Motor imagery, using a LDA classifier as a initial state for a GMM algorithm.
	N/BCI control:	N/A.
Control mechanics	**BCI:**	Used to move the cursor (left/right) and select a letter in a Hangman game.
	Non-BCI:	N/A.
Game world	**Player character:**	N/A (the hangman is not considered a player character).
	Environment:	A 2-dimensional graphical scenario with the hangman and the possible letters.
Virtual interface	**World interface:**	PC display, showing a two-dimensional view of the virtual environment.
	NF interface:	The chosen letter and the confidence in the classification result appear in the UI.
	Stimuli generator:	N/A.
Mental War [26]		
EEG data collection	**Sensors:**	A single dry electrode, positioned at site Fp1.
	EEG device:	A NeuroSky MindWave.
Control interface	**BCI control:**	Attention level, directly measured using the MindWave's eSense metric.
	N/BCI control:	N/A.
Control mechanics	**BCI:**	The intensity of the attention metric is directly proportional to the force that the character uses to push a rope in a tug-of-war match.
	Non-BCI:	N/A.
Game world	**Player character:**	A human cartoon avatar.
	Environment:	A 2-dimensional graphical scenario that changes according to the game's difficulty.
Virtual interface	**World interface:**	A PC monitor display, showing a two-dimensional view of the world and a third-person view of the player character.
	NF interface:	A vertical bar embedded in the game UI, showing the player's current attention level.
	Stimuli generator:	N/A.

Table 3. Demonstration of the model and its components (continuation).

	MindBalance [14]	
EEG data collection	Sensors:	Two silver chloride scalp electrodes, placed at positions O1 and O2.
	EEG device:	Biopac biopotential amplifiers.
Control interface	BCI control:	SSVEP, using two PSD estimation methods: squared 4-second FFT, and FFT of autocorrelation.
	N/BCI control:	N/A.
Control mechanics	BCI:	The SSVEP command is used to choose the direction of the character movement (left or right) to regain balance in a tightrope.
	Non-BCI:	N/A.
Game world	Player character:	A three-dimensional humanoid-like creature.
	Environment:	A virtual, three-dimensional scenario with a platform and a tightrope.
Virtual interface	World Interface:	PC monitor display, with a 3D view of the environment and a third-person view of the character facing the camera.
	NF interface:	The character animation serves as feedback of the selected movement direction. Auditive feedback is also provided.
	Stimuli generator:	Embedded in the game screen. Two squares with checkerboard patterns flashing at two different frequencies (17Hz and 20Hz) to elicit SSVEP responses.
	MindGame [5]	
EEG data collection	Sensors:	10 electrodes placed over the parietal and occipital regions.
	EEG device:	A Mindset24 EEG amplifier.
Control interface	BCI control:	P300, using PCA as method for feature extraction and FLDA as classifier.
	N/BCI control:	N/A.
Control mechanics	BCI:	Used to select a target tree in the game world. The player must reach all trees to win the game.
	Non-BCI:	N/A.
Game world	Player character:	A two-dimensional cat avatar.
	Environment:	A virtual, 3D room with a checkerboard-styled floor and 2-dimensional trees.
Virtual interface	World Interface:	A display, showing the whole scenario and a third-person view of the character.
	NF interface:	The direction and number of steps of the character's movement serves as feedback for the selected target.
	Stimuli generator:	Each target tree in the game world also serves as stimulus, flashing consecutively.
	Mind the Sheep! [23]	
EEG data collection	Sensors:	Five electrodes, positioned at sites PO3, O1, Oz, O2 and PO4.
	EEG device:	A Biosemi ActiveTwo system.
Control interface	BCI control:	SSVEP, using a canonical correlation analysis algorithm.
	N/BCI control:	Mouse.
Control mechanics	BCI:	Used to select a target dog in the game world.
	Non-BCI:	Used to point to the location to which the selected dog must move.
Game world	Player character:	Several dogs from the game world serve as player-controllable characters.
	Environment:	A virtual playground representing a meadow, with obstacles and fences.
Virtual interface	World Interface:	A PC LCD monitor screen, with a top-view of the game world.
	NF interface:	A circle around the selected dog serves as feedback for the classification result.
	Stimuli generator:	Each of the three possible target dog flashes simultaneously at 7.5, 10 and 12 Hz.
	Pinball [25]	
EEG data collection	Sensors:	64 sensors (implied by the number of channels).
	EEG device:	Not informed.
Control interface	BCI control:	Motor imagery, with CSP filters to extract power features to a LDA classifier.
	N/BCI control:	A lever.
Control mechanics	BCI:	A low-level command is used to control the left and right paddles of a pinball machine, using the respective imagined movement (left hand, right hand).
	Non-BCI:	The player must pull the lever to launch a new ball.
Game world	Player character:	N/A.
	Environment:	A physical pinball machine.
Virtual interface	World Interface:	The machine itself serves as a physical, auditory and visual interface.
	NF interface:	The movement of the paddles serve as feedback for the classified command.
	Stimuli generator:	N/A.
	Space Connection [22]	
EEG data collection	Sensors:	A single dry electrode, positioned at site Fp1.
	EEG device:	A NeuroSky MindWave.
Control interface	BCI control:	The player's level of attention, measured using the NeuroSky's eSense metric.
	N/BCI control:	Mouse, keyboard and relaxation level (measured through respiration rate).
Control mechanics	BCI:	With the attention level above a certain threshold, the player can move objects.
	Non-BCI:	Targeting and movement (Mouse and keyboard); and an ability to freeze time (relaxation level).
Game world	Player character:	Two virtual, 3-dimensional human characters.
	Environment:	A virtual, 3-dimensional spaceship, containing multiple levels with puzzles.
Virtual interface	World Interface:	A PC monitor display, showing a first-person view of the player's character.
	NF interface:	Power bars in the game UI indicate the attention (and relaxation) levels.
	Stimuli generator:	N/A.
	Thinking Penguin [16]	
EEG data collection	Sensors:	A cap with five electrodes, placed at position Cz and four orthogonal sites.
	EEG device:	A 16-channel g.Tec biosignal amplifier.
Control interface	BCI control:	Motor imagery, detected using a LDA classifier for ERS and ERD frequency bands.
	N/BCI control:	A joystick (and a push-button in non-BCI gameplay).
Control mechanics	BCI:	Used to make the character jump to catch fish.
	Non-BCI:	Controls the left-right movement of the character.
Game world	Player character:	A three-dimensional penguin avatar.
	Environment:	A virtual, three-dimensional snowy mountain.
Virtual interface	World Interface:	A 3D virtual reality environment, projected in the walls of a four-sided room.
	NF interface:	The jumping of the penguin serves as feedback for the detection of the desired motor imagery.
	Stimuli generator:	N/A.
	VR Maze [10]	
EEG data collection	Sensors:	Eight electrodes, positioned at the occipital-parietal region.
	EEG device:	A g.Tec g.MOBIlab+ device.
Control interface	BCI control:	SSVEP, detected using a canonical correlation analysis algorithm.
	N/BCI control:	N/A.
Control mechanics	BCI:	Used to select a target tile destination for the player to move.
	Non-BCI:	N/A.
Game world	Player character:	A sphere.
	Environment:	A virtual, three-dimensional grid, with objects or empty spaces in each tile.
Virtual interface	World Interface:	A monitor or an Oculus Rift head-mounted virtual reality device.
	NF interface:	The movement of the sphere in the grid serves as feedback for the selected tile.
	Stimuli generator:	Each tile perpendicular to the sphere flashes at a different frequency as stimulus.

details about the game architecture (e.g., local or networked) or the game genre, which can be described implicitly through the appropriate components.

In the same sense, the values obtained from the demonstration show that it is possible to group common classified values, e.g., the employed EEG device or the virtual interface, which seem to have a limited number of possible values—at least for atomic information, such as whether the interface is virtual or physical; auditive, somatosensory or graphical; and its dimensions. This could allow not only for a pre-defined list of classification values for such specific components, but also to a classification scheme based on these values, i.e., possibly a new taxonomy constructed upon the proposed model. This new taxonomy could separate these classification values in a more direct fashion, as opposed to the descriptive nature of the model's components, allowing for a more direct comparison of games from the literature. However, as games are fundamentally different from one another, open descriptions are still required to fully describe the concept of the game.

Lastly, it is also important to notice that the proposed model, although is not directly a system architecture framework, can be used as a base for the development of new EEG-controlled games and the construction of their software architecture, as its components and their connections are an abstraction and can be instantiated in numerous ways, using any supported and available technology. A similar approach has been employed, for example, by Sung et al. [24], in which the authors built a framework for EEG-based serious games based on their proposed model.

5.1 Limitations

The demonstration of the model also showed some of its limitations. As aforementioned, the first limitation is related to the extension of the described data, which allows for a general overview of the game and how it is played with the BCI controls, but may lack some details about the employed signal processing algorithm and the game, such as its platform and number of players, which have no specific component to represent them and must be implied through the description of related components. The player(s) from Fig. 6, for example, could be a component itself, representing the number of players and the target audience for the game. Although interesting, this approach was not employed in the current model as it is intended to represent EEG-controlled games, and the player is technically not a part of the game itself. However, although the model could be expanded to represent such details more precisely, it remains an open discussion whether the player should be considered a component of the model or an element that participates in its function.

Another limitation is related to the independence of each component in relation to each other. Some components appear to provide less contribution to the general understanding of the game without the complement of other components; for example, the *Player Character* component provides a very specific information that, although generally necessary for the context of the *Control Mechanics* and the *Virtual Interface*, could be implicitly represented through other components. Merging these information into other general components could, however, increase the difficulty in extracting specific data from each game in order to compare them (or to describe the concept of a new game), as too much information would be gathered into a single component.

6 Conclusion

This work presents a generalized model for EEG-based BCI-controlled games. The model is intended to represent such games by describing their functional and abstract components and how they are connected to each other. To demonstrate its usefulness and representativeness, a set of EEG-based BCI games from the literature was described using the components from the model. The demonstration showed that the model is capable of representing aspects both from the classic EEG signal processing steps based on neurofeedback applications, and from the game itself, providing an overview of the game, how the player interacts with it and how it is played using both the BCI and non-BCI controls.

The principles that guided the construction of the model allow for its adaptation to different contexts and applications, and for it to evolve and expand with new components depending on the needs of the researcher. It is expected that, as the model evolves, it will be able to represent not only EEG-controlled games, but also studies involving those games and the contexts in which they are being applied, facilitating its employment in the comparison of different BCI-based studies—e.g., in meta-analyses for comparing the performance of different signal processing algorithms for the classification of EEG signals, or the effects of playing EEG-based serious games in subjects for clinical trials.

The proposed model can also help researchers in the design and development of new EEG-controlled games, and guide future studies that employ those games. Future works, in this sense, involve using the model as a base for the design and development of new EEG-controlled games, as well as conducting and comparing primary studies involving those games. In addition, a model-based taxonomy that groups the possible instantiations of each component hierarchically could also be developed based on the presented demonstration.

Acknowledgements. This work was supported by the Physical Artifacts of Interaction Research Group (PAIRG) at the Federal University of Rio Grande do Norte (UFRN), and partially funded by the Brazilian Federal Agency for Support and Evaluation of Graduate Education (CAPES). We also thank the resources of the PAIRG's Laboratory of Physical and Physiological Computing (PAIRG L2PC) at UFRN.

References

1. Bonnet, L., Lotte, F., Lecuyer, A.: Two brains, one game: design and evaluation of a multiuser BCI video game based on motor imagery. IEEE Trans. Comput. Intell. AI Games 5(2), 185–198 (2013). https://doi.org/10.1109/tciaig.2012.2237173

2. Djaouti, D., Alvarez, J., Jessel, J.P.: Classifying serious games: the G/P/S model. In: Handbook of Research on Improving Learning and Motivation through Educational Games: Multidisciplinary Approaches (2011). https://doi.org/10.4018/978-1-60960-495-0.ch006
3. Ferreira, A.L.S., Marciano, J.N., de Miranda, L.C., de Miranda, E.E.C.: Understanding and proposing a design rationale of digital games based on brain-computer interface: results of the Admiralmind Battleship study. SBC J. Interact. Syst. **5**(1), 3–15 (2014)
4. Ferreira, A.L.S., de Miranda, L.C., de Miranda, E.E.C., Sakamoto, S.G.: A survey of interactive systems based on brain-computer interfaces. SBC J. 3D Interact. Syst. **4**(1), 3–13 (2013)
5. Finke, A., Lenhardt, A., Ritter, H.: The MindGame: a P300-based brain-computer interface game. Neural Netw. **22**(9), 1329–1333 (2009). https://doi.org/10.1016/j.neunet.2009.07.003
6. Friedrich, E.V.C., Suttie, N., Sivanathan, A., Lim, T., Louchart, S., Pineda, J.A.: Brain-computer interface game applications for combined neurofeedback and biofeedback treatment for children on the autism spectrum. Front. Neuroeng. **7**, 21 (2014). https://doi.org/10.3389/fneng.2014.00021
7. Hasan, B.A.S., Gan, J.Q.: Hangman BCI: an unsupervised adaptive self-paced brain-computer interface for playing games. Comput. Biol. Med. **42**(5), 598–606 (2012). https://doi.org/10.1016/j.compbiomed.2012.02.004
8. Henrik, C., Olle, H., Craig, L., Charlotte, S., Jeanette, E.: The aiming game: using a game with biofeedback for training in emotion regulation. In: Proceedings of the DiGRA International Conference: Think Design Play (DiGRA 2011), p. 18 (2011)
9. Kerous, B., Skola, F., Liarokapis, F.: EEG-based BCI and video games: a progress report. Virtual Reality **22**(2), 119–135 (2017). https://doi.org/10.1007/s10055-017-0328-x
10. Koo, B., Lee, H.G., Nam, Y., Choi, S.: Immersive BCI with SSVEP in VR head-mounted display. In: 37th Annual International Conference of the IEEE Engineering in Medicine and Biology Society (EMBC). IEEE (2015). https://doi.org/10.1109/embc.2015.7318558
11. Kosmyna, N., Lécuyer, A.: A conceptual space for EEG-based brain-computer interfaces. PLoS ONE **14**(1), 1–30 (2019). https://doi.org/10.1371/journal.pone.0210145
12. Laamarti, F., Eid, M., Saddik, A.E.: An overview of serious games. Int. J. Comput. Games Technol. **2014**(1), 15 (2014). https://doi.org/10.1155/2014/358152
13. van de Laar, B., Gürkök, H., Bos, D.P.O., Poel, M., Nijholt, A.: Experiencing BCI control in a popular computer game. IEEE Trans. Comput. Intell. AI Games **5**(2), 176–184 (2013). https://doi.org/10.1109/TCIAIG.2013.2253778
14. Lalor, E.C., et al.: Steady-state VEP-based brain-computer interface control in an immersive 3D gaming environment. EURASIP J. Adv. Signal Process. **2005**(19) (2005). https://doi.org/10.1155/asp.2005.3156
15. Lazarou, I., Nikolopoulos, S., Petrantonakis, P.C., Kompatsiaris, I., Tsolaki, M.: EEG-based brain-computer interfaces for communication and rehabilitation of people with motor impairment: a novel approach of the 21st century. Front. Hum. Neurosci. **12**, 14 (2018). https://doi.org/10.3389/fnhum.2018.00014
16. Leeb, R., Lancelle, M., Kaiser, V., Fellner, D.W., Pfurtscheller, G.: Thinking Penguin: multimodal brain-computer interface control of a VR game. IEEE Trans. Comput. Intell. AI Games **5**(2), 117–128 (2013). https://doi.org/10.1109/TCIAIG.2013.2242072

17. Lope, R.P.D., Medina-Medina, N.: A comprehensive taxonomy for serious games. J. Educ. Comput. Res. **55**(5), 629–672 (2017). https://doi.org/10.1177/0735633116681301

18. Maby, E., Perrin, M., Bertrand, O., Sanchez, G., Mattout, J.: BCI could make old two-player games even more fun: a proof of concept with "Connect Four". In: Advances in Human-Computer Interaction, vol. 2012, pp. 1–8 (2012). https://doi.org/10.1155/2012/124728

19. Mason, S.G., Birch, G.E.: A general framework for brain-computer interface design. IEEE Trans. Neural Syst. Rehabil. Eng. **11**(1), 70–85 (2003). https://doi.org/10.1109/TNSRE.2003.810426

20. Mason, S.G., Jackson, M.M.M., Birch, G.E.: A general framework for characterizing studies of brain interface technology. Ann. Biomed. Eng. **33**(11), 1653–1670 (2005). https://doi.org/10.1007/s10439-005-7706-3

21. McCallum, S., Boletsis, C.: A taxonomy of serious games for dementia. In: Games for Health, pp. 219–232 (2013). https://doi.org/10.1007/978-3-658-02897-8_17

22. Muñoz, J.E., Gonçalves, A., Vieira, T., Cró, D., Chisik, Y., Bermúdez i Badia, S.: Space Connection - a multiplayer collaborative biofeedback game to promote empathy in teenagers: a feasibility study. In: Proceedings of the 3rd International Conference on Physiological Computing Systems, pp. 88–97 (2016). https://doi.org/10.5220/0005948400880097

23. Obbink, M., Gürkök, H., Plass-Oude Bos, D., Hakvoort, G., Poel, M., Nijholt, A.: Social interaction in a cooperative brain-computer interface game. In: Camurri, A., Costa, C. (eds.) INTETAIN 2011. LNICST, vol. 78, pp. 183–192. Springer, Heidelberg (2012). https://doi.org/10.1007/978-3-642-30214-5_20

24. Sung, Y., Cho, K., Um, K.: A development architecture for serious games using BCI (brain computer interface) sensors. Sensors **12**(11), 15671–15688 (2012). https://doi.org/10.3390/s121115671

25. Tangermann, M., et al.: Playing pinball with non-invasive BCI. In: Advances in Neural Information Processing Systems 21, pp. 1641–1648 (2008)

26. Vasiljevic, G.A.M., de Miranda, L.C., de Menezes, B.C.: Mental war: an attention-based single/multiplayer brain-computer interface game. In: Gervasi, O., et al. (eds.) ICCSA 2018. LNCS, vol. 10960, pp. 450–465. Springer, Cham (2018). https://doi.org/10.1007/978-3-319-95162-1_31

27. Vasiljevic, G.A.M., de Miranda, L.C.: Brain-computer interface games based on consumer-grade EEG devices: a systematic literature review. Int. J. Hum.-Comput. Interact. 1–38 (2019). https://doi.org/10.1080/10447318.2019.1612213

28. Vasiljevic, G.A.M., de Miranda, L.C.: The effect of auditory stimuli on user's meditation and workload in a brain–computer interface game. Interact. Comput. **31**(3), 250–262 (2019). https://doi.org/10.1093/iwc/iwz014

29. Vasiljevic, G.A.M., de Miranda, L.C.: The influence of graphical elements on user's attention and control on a neurofeedback-based game. Entertain. Comput. **29**, 10–19 (2019). https://doi.org/10.1016/j.entcom.2018.10.003

30. Vasiljevic, G.A.M., de Miranda, L.C., de Menezes, B.C.: Zen cat: a meditation-based brain-computer interface game. In: Gervasi, O., et al. (eds.) ICCSA 2018. LNCS, vol. 10960, pp. 294–309. Springer, Cham (2018). https://doi.org/10.1007/978-3-319-95162-1_20

31. Wolpaw, J.R., Birbaumer, N., McFarland, D.J., Pfurtscheller, G., Vaughan, T.M.: Brain-computer interfaces for communication and control. Clin. Neurophysiol. **113**(6), 767–791 (2002). https://doi.org/10.1016/s1388-2457(02)00057-3

International Workshop on Advanced Transport Tools and Methods (A2TM 2020)

Introducing the Concept of Interaction Model for Interactive Dimensionality Reduction and Data Visualization

M. C. Ortega-Bustamante[1,2], W. Hasperué[2], D. H. Peluffo-Ordóñez[4,5,6(✉)],
M. Paéz-Jaime[5], I. Marrufo-Rodríguez[5], P. Rosero-Montalvo[1,3],
A. C. Umaquinga-Criollo[1], and M. Vélez-Falconi[4,5]

[1] Universidad Técnica del Norte, Ibarra, Ecuador
[2] III-LIDI, Facultad de Informática, Universidad Nacional de La Plata,
La Plata, Argentina
cosme.ortegab@info.unlp.edu.ar
[3] Instituto Superior Tecnológico 17 de Julio, San Miguel de Urcuquí, Ecuador
[4] Yachay Tech University, San Miguel de Urcuquí, Ecuador
[5] SDAS Research Group, Ibarra, Ecuador
diego.peluffo@sdas-group.com
https://www.sdas-group.com
[6] Corporación Univeristaria Autónoma de Nariño, Pasto, Colombia

Abstract. This letter formally introduces the concept of interaction model (IM), which has been used either directly or tangentially in previous works but never defined. Broadly speaking, an IM consists of the use of a mixture of dimensionality reduction (DR) techniques within an interactive data visualization framework. The rationale of creating an IM is the need for simultaneously harnessing the benefit of several DR approaches to reach a data representation being intelligible and/or fitted to any user's criterion. As a remarkable advantage, an IM naturally provides a generalized framework for designing both interactive DR approaches as well as readily-to-use data visualization interfaces. In addition to a comprehensive overview on basics of data representation and dimensionality reduction, the main contribution of this manuscript is the elegant definition of the concept of IM in mathematical terms.

Keywords: Dimensionality reduction · Interaction model · Kernel functions · Data visualization

1 Introduction

Very often, dimensionality reduction (DR) is an essential building block to design both machine learning systems, and information visualization interfaces [1,2]. In simple terms, DR consists of finding a low-dimensional representation of the

---

This work is supported by Yachay Tech and SDAS Research Group (http://www.sdas-group.com).

O. Gervasi et al. (Eds.): ICCSA 2020, LNCS 12250, pp. 193–203, 2020.
https://doi.org/10.1007/978-3-030-58802-1_14

original data (said to be high-dimensional) by keeping a criterion of either data structure preservation, or class-separability ensuring. Recent analysis has shown that DR should attempt to reach two goals: First, to ensure that data points that are neighbors in the original space should remain neighbors in the embedded space. Second, to guarantee that two data points should be shown as neighbors in the embedded space only if they are neighbors in the original space. In the context of information retrieval, these two goals can be seen as precision and recall measures, respectively. In spite of being clearly conflicting, the compromise between precision and recall denes the DR method performance. Furthermore, since DR methods are often developed under determined design parameters and pre-established optimization criterion, they still lack of properties such as user interaction and controllability. These properties are characteristic of information visualization procedures. The eld of data visualization (DataVis) is aimed at developing graphical ways of representing data so that information can be more usable and intelligible for the user [3]. Then, one can intuit that DR can be improved by importing some properties of the DataVis methods. This is in fact the premise on which this research is based.

This emergent research area can be referred as interactive dimensionality reduction for visualization. Its main goal is to link the field of DR with that of DataVis, in order to harness the special properties of the latter within DR frameworks. In particular, the properties of controllability and interactivity are of great interest, which should make the DR outcomes significantly more understandable and tractable for the (no-necessarily-expert) user. These two properties allow the user to have freedom to select the best way for representing data. Then, in other words, it can be said that the goal of this project is to develop a DR framework that facilitates an interactive and quick visualization of data representation to make more intelligible the DR outcomes, as well as to allow users modifying the views of data according to their needs in an affordable fashion.

In this connection, this letter formally introduces the concept of interaction model (IM) as a key tool for both interactive DR and DataVis. Even though the term interaction model has been referred directly or tangentially in previous works [4–8], it has not been formally defined. This paper aims to fill that void. In general terms, the concept of IM refers to a mixture of dimensionality reduction (DR) techniques within an interactive data visualization framework. The rationale of creating an IM is the need for simultaneously harnessing the benefit of several DR approaches to reach a data representation being intelligible and/or fitted to any user's criterion. As a remarkable advantage, an IM naturally provides a generalized framework for designing both interactive DR approaches as well as readily-to-use data visualization interfaces. That said, the main contribution of this manuscript is the elegant definition of the concept of IM in mathematical terms. Also, it overviews some basics of data representation and dimensionality reduction from matrix algebra point of view. A special interest is given to spectral and kernel-based DR methods, which can be generalized by kernel principal component analysis (KPCA) and readily incorporated into a linear IM.

The remaining of this manuscript is organized as follows: Sect. 2 states the mathematical notation for main variables and operators. Section 3 presents a short overview on basic concepts and introductory formulations for DR, with a special interest in KPCA. In Sect. 4, we formally define the concept of IM as well as its particular linear version. Also, the use of DR-based DataVis is outlined. Finally, some concluding remarks are gathered in Sect. 5.

2 Mathematical Notation

For introducing further concepts and describing some mathematical developments, let us consider the following notation: Let $\boldsymbol{X} \in \mathbb{R}^{N \times D}$ be the input data matrix (also called observed space) holding N data points or samples described by a D-dimensional feature set, such that:

$$
\boldsymbol{X} = \begin{pmatrix} x_{11} & \cdots & x_{1l} & \cdots & x_{1D} \\ \vdots & \ddots & \vdots & & \vdots \\ x_{i1} & & x_{il} & & x_{iD} \\ \vdots & & \vdots & \ddots & \vdots \\ x_{N1} & \cdots & x_{Nl} & \cdots & x_{ND} \end{pmatrix} = \begin{pmatrix} \boldsymbol{x}_1^\top \\ \vdots \\ \boldsymbol{x}_i^\top \\ \vdots \\ \boldsymbol{x}_N^\top \end{pmatrix}, \tag{1}
$$

where $\boldsymbol{x}_i \in \mathbb{R}^D$ denotes the i-th data point, $i \in \{1, \dots, N\}$ and $l \in \{1, \dots, D\}$. Likewise, let us consider a lower-dimensional matrix, so-named embedded space, as

$$
\boldsymbol{Y} = \begin{pmatrix} y_{11} & \cdots & y_{1\ell} & \cdots & y_{1d} \\ \vdots & \ddots & \vdots & & \vdots \\ y_{i1} & & y_{i\ell} & & y_{id} \\ \vdots & & \vdots & \ddots & \vdots \\ y_{N1} & \cdots & y_{N\ell} & \cdots & y_{Nd} \end{pmatrix} = \begin{pmatrix} \boldsymbol{y}_1^\top \\ \vdots \\ \boldsymbol{y}_i^\top \\ \vdots \\ \boldsymbol{y}_N^\top \end{pmatrix}, \tag{2}
$$

with $\boldsymbol{y}_i \in \mathbb{R}^d$, such that $d < D$ and $\ell \in \{1, \dots, d\}$. Also, let us suppose that there exists an unknown high dimensional representation space $\boldsymbol{\Phi} \in \mathbb{R}^{D_h \times N}$ such that $D_h \ggg D$, in which calculating the inner product should improve the representation and visualization of resultant embedded data in contrast to that obtained directly from the observed data. Hence, the need for a kernel representation arises to calculate the dot product in the unknown high dimensional space. Let $\phi(\cdot)$ be a function that maps data from the original dimension to a higher one, such that:

$$
\phi(\cdot): \quad \mathbb{R}^D \to \mathbb{R}^{D_h} \tag{3}
$$
$$
\boldsymbol{x}_i \mapsto \phi(\boldsymbol{x}_i).
$$

Therefore, the matrix $\boldsymbol{\Phi}$ can be expressed as:

$$
\boldsymbol{\Phi} = \begin{pmatrix} \boldsymbol{\Phi}_1^\top \\ \vdots \\ \boldsymbol{\Phi}_N^\top \end{pmatrix} \tag{4}
$$

being $\boldsymbol{\Phi}_i = \phi(\boldsymbol{x}_i)$ its i-th column vector.

3 Overview on Dimensionality Reduction and Data Visualization

3.1 Data Representation

Data representation is a wide-meaning term coined by some authors to refer by-and-large to either data transformation or feature extraction. The former consists of transforming data into a new version intended to fulfill a specific goal [9]. The latter, meanwhile, is somewhat as a data remaking in such a manner that input data undergo a morphological deformation, or projection (also called rotation) by following a certain transformation criterion [10]. Also, data representation may be referred to yielding a new data representation -just as a new data matrix being an alternative to the original given one. For instance, a dissimilarity-based representation of input data [11]. An exhaustive review on data representation is presented in [12].

3.2 Dimensionality Reduction

Dimensionality reduction (DR) [13] is the most widely-used data representation approach. Broadly, DR is intended to embed a high-dimensional space $\boldsymbol{X}$ into a lower-dimensional space $\boldsymbol{X}$. More technically, DR can be seen as a data transformation through a certain operator $\mathcal{T}\{\cdot\}$ in the form:

$$\mathcal{T}(\cdot): \quad \mathbb{R}^{N\times D} \to \mathbb{R}^{N\times d} \qquad (5)$$
$$\boldsymbol{X} \quad \mapsto \mathcal{T}\{\boldsymbol{X}\},$$

such that $\boldsymbol{Y} = \mathcal{T}\{\boldsymbol{X}\}$. Such a transformation operator can be ruled by different criteria. Figure 1 depicts the effect of a toy dataset, so-called `Swiss Roll` ($N = 3000$ data points, and $D = 3$ dimensions).

DR Approaches: For instance, pioneer approaches such as principal component analysis (PCA) or classical multidimensional scaling (CMDS) optimize the reduction in terms of variance and distance preservation criterion, respectively [14]. More sophisticated methods attempt to capture the data topology through a non-directed and weighted data-driven graph, which is formed by nodes located at the geometrical coordinates pointed out by the data points represent the nodes, and a non-negative similarity (also called affinity, or Gram) matrix holding the pairwise edge weights. Such data-topology-based criteria has been addressed by both spectral [15] and divergence-based methods [16]. Similarity matrix can represent either the weighting factor for pairwise distances as happens in Laplacian eigenmaps and locally linear embedding [17,18], or a probability distribution as is the case of methods based on divergences such as stochastic neighbour embedding [19]. In this letter, we give especial interest to the spectral approaches -more specifically, to the so-named kernel PCA.

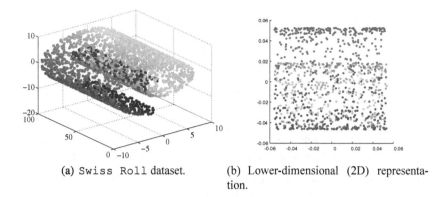

(a) `Swiss Roll` dataset.   **(b)** Lower-dimensional (2D) representation.

Fig. 1. Effect of unfolding a 3D `Swiss Roll`–like toy dataset into a two-dimensional representation through a DR approach based on kernel principal component analysis (KPCA).

Kernel PCA (KPCA): Now, let us recall the high-dimensional space $\boldsymbol{\Phi}$ defined in Sect. 2, let us also consider a lower-rank reconstructed matrix $\widehat{\boldsymbol{\Phi}}$, and a dissimilarity function $\delta(\cdot, \cdot)$. Matrix $\widehat{\boldsymbol{\Phi}}$ is obtained from a lower-rank base whose full-rank version spans $\boldsymbol{\Phi}$, and minimizes $\delta(\boldsymbol{\Phi}, \widehat{\boldsymbol{\Phi}})$. To keep all the KPCA conditions, following developments are done under the assumption that $\boldsymbol{\Phi}$ is centered. Let us define a d-dimensional base $\boldsymbol{W} \in \mathbb{R}^{D_h \times d}$, such that $\boldsymbol{W} = (\boldsymbol{w}^{(1)}, \ldots, \boldsymbol{w}^{(d)})$ and $\boldsymbol{W}^\top \boldsymbol{W} = \boldsymbol{I}_d$, where $\boldsymbol{w}^{(\ell)} \in \mathbb{R}^{D_h}$, $\ell \in \{1, \ldots, d\}$, and $\boldsymbol{I}_d$ is a d-dimensional identity matrix. Since $d < D$, we can say that the base $\boldsymbol{W}$ is lower-rank. Given this, the low-dimensional space can be calculated by means of a linear projection, as follows:

$$\boldsymbol{Y} = \boldsymbol{\Phi}\boldsymbol{W}. \tag{6}$$

Thus, from Eq. 6, we can write that:

$$\widehat{\boldsymbol{\Phi}} = \boldsymbol{Y}\boldsymbol{W}^\top. \tag{7}$$

If we define $\delta(\boldsymbol{\Phi}, \widehat{\boldsymbol{\Phi}}) = ||\boldsymbol{\Phi} - \widehat{\boldsymbol{\Phi}}||_F^2$, where $|| \cdot ||_F$ denotes Frobenius norm. By design, a squared distance is used so that the problem has a dual version that can be readily expressed as a quadratic form. Accordingly, we can pose the following primal optimization problem:

$$\begin{aligned} \min_{\boldsymbol{W}} \quad & ||\boldsymbol{\Phi} - \widehat{\boldsymbol{\Phi}}||_F^2 \\ \text{s. t.} \quad & \boldsymbol{W}^\top \boldsymbol{W} = \boldsymbol{I}_d, d < D, \\ & \boldsymbol{Y} = \boldsymbol{W}^\top \boldsymbol{\Phi}, \end{aligned} \tag{8}$$

which can be expressed as a dual problem in the form:

$$\max_{\boldsymbol{W}} \quad \mathrm{tr}(\boldsymbol{W}^\top \boldsymbol{\Phi}^\top \boldsymbol{\Phi} \boldsymbol{W})$$

$$\text{s. t.} \quad \boldsymbol{W}^\top \boldsymbol{W} = \boldsymbol{I}_d, d < D,$$

$$\boldsymbol{Y} = \boldsymbol{W}^\top \boldsymbol{\Phi},$$

having as a feasible solution for $\boldsymbol{W}$ and $\boldsymbol{Y}$ the eigenvectors associated to the d largest eigenvalues of $\boldsymbol{\Phi}\boldsymbol{\Phi}^\top$ and $\boldsymbol{\Phi}^\top\boldsymbol{\Phi}$, respectively. This theorem is known as optimal low-rank representation widely discussed and demonstrated in [15].

Kernel Trick: Furthermore, by following the Mercer's condition or the so-called kernel trick, we can introduce a kernel function $k(\cdot, \cdot)$, which estimates the inner product $\phi(\boldsymbol{x}_i)^\top \phi(\boldsymbol{x}_j) = k(\boldsymbol{x}_i, \boldsymbol{x}_i)$. By gathering all the pairwise kernel values, we can write a kernel matrix $\boldsymbol{K} = [k_{ij}]$ as:

$$\boldsymbol{K} = \boldsymbol{\Phi}^\top \boldsymbol{\Phi}, \tag{9}$$

where $k_{ij} = k(\boldsymbol{x}_i, \boldsymbol{x}_j)$, and $i, j \in \{1, \ldots, N\}$. As mentioned above, such a kernel matrix captures the data topology and may be considered as a similarity matrix.

3.3 DataVis via Interactive DR

Quite intuitively, one can infer that the premise underlying the use of DR for DataVis purposes is to making directly intelligible the information of a high-dimensional dataset by displaying it into a representation in 3 or less dimensions.

Besides, the incorporation of interactivity into the DR technique itself or DR-based DataVis interfaces enables the users (even non-expert ones) to select a method or tune parameters thereof in an intuitive fashion.

4   Concept of Interaction Model (IM) for DR

4.1   Definition of IM

Herein, the interaction is considered as the ability to incorporate in a readily manner the user's criterion into the stages of the data exploration process. In this case, the DR is the stage of interest. Particularly, we refer to interactivity to the possibility of tuning parameters or selecting methods within an interactive interface. As traditionally done in previous works [8], the interactivity consists of a mixture of functions or elements representing DR techniques. In the following, we formally define the concept of IM:

Definition 1 (Interaction model (IM)). *Under a certain topological space $\mathcal{V}$ and given a set of M functions or elements ($f_m \in \mathcal{V}$) representing M different dimensionality reduction techniques ($\boldsymbol{f} = \{f_1, \ldots, f_M\}$) and a set of weighting* *factors* $\boldsymbol{\alpha} = \{\alpha_1, \ldots, \alpha_M\}$, *an IM is defined as any possible mixture* $\tilde{f} \in \mathcal{V}$ *of such a set, in the form:*

$$\mathrm{IM}\{\cdot\}: \quad \mathcal{V}^M \times \mathbb{R}^M \to \mathcal{V}$$
$$\boldsymbol{f}, \boldsymbol{\alpha} \quad \mapsto \mathrm{IM}_{\boldsymbol{\alpha}}\{\boldsymbol{f}\}, \qquad (10)$$

such that $\tilde{f} = \mathrm{IM}_{\boldsymbol{\alpha}}\{\boldsymbol{f}\}$.

Then, IM can be itself understood as a suitable building block for powering data analysis systems with interactive dimensionality-reduction-driven visualization stages, as depicted in 2.

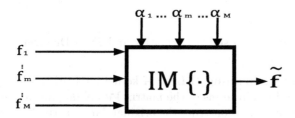

Fig. 2. Graphical explanation of the interaction model (IM) concept aimed at producing a final data representation $\tilde{f}$ in terms of a set of functions $\{f_1, \ldots, f_M\}$ and their corresponding weighting factors $\{\alpha_1, \ldots, \alpha_M\}$.

4.2   Linear IM

As a particular case of the Definition 1, we can define the linear IM as follows:

Definition 2 (Linear IM (LIM)). *Under a certain vector space* $\mathbb{E}$ *and given a set of M functions or elements* $(f_m \in \mathcal{V})$ *representing M different dimensionality reduction techniques* $(\boldsymbol{f} = \{f_1, \ldots, f_M\})$ *and a set of weighting factors* $\boldsymbol{\alpha} = \{\alpha_1, \ldots, \alpha_M\}$, *a LIM is defined as the weighted sum* $\tilde{f} \in \mathcal{V}$ *in the form:*

$$\mathrm{LIM}\{\cdot\}: \quad \mathbb{E}^M \times \mathbb{R}^M \to \mathbb{E}$$
$$\boldsymbol{f}, \boldsymbol{\alpha} \quad \mapsto \mathrm{LIM}_{\boldsymbol{\alpha}}\{\boldsymbol{f}\}, \qquad (11)$$

such that $\tilde{f} = \mathrm{LIM}_{\boldsymbol{\alpha}}\{\boldsymbol{f}\} = \sum_{m=1}^{M} \alpha_m f_m$.

4.3   DR-techniques Representation

As explained [20], spectral DR methods are susceptible to be represented as kernel matrices. Also, in [15] is demonstrated that, when incorporated into a KCPA algorithm, such kernel matrices reach the same low-dimensional spaces as those obtained by the original DR methods. Let us consider the following kernel representations for three well-known spectral DR approaches:

Classical Multi-dimensional Scaling (CMDS): CMDS kernel can be expressed as the double centered, squared Euclidean distance matrix $D \in \mathbb{R}^{N \times N}$ so

$$K_{CMDS} = -\frac{1}{2}(I_N - 1_N 1_N^\top) D (I_N - 1_N 1_N^\top), \tag{12}$$

where the ij entry of D is given by $d_{ij} = ||x_i - x_j||_2^2$.

Laplacian Eigenmaps (LE). Since KPCA is a maximization of the high-dimensional covariance represented by a kernel, LE can be represented as the pseudo-inverse of the graph Laplacian L:

$$K_{LE} = L^\dagger, \tag{13}$$

where $L = D - S$, S is a similarity matrix and $D = \text{Diag}(S 1_N)$ is the degree matrix.

Locally Linear Embedding (LLE): A kernel for LLE can be approximated from a quadratic form in terms of the matrix W holding linear coefficients that sum to 1 and optimally reconstruct the original data matrix X. Define a matrix $M \in \mathbb{R}^{N \times N}$ as $M = (I_N - W)(I_N - W^\top)$ and λ_{max} as the largest eigenvalue of M. Kernel matrix for LLE is in the form

$$K_{LLE} = \lambda_{max} I_N - M. \tag{14}$$

4.4   Use of IM in Interactive DR

To explain how to use the IM for DR purposes, consider the kernel matrices from Sect. 4.3, by setting $M = 3$, as well as $f_1 = K^{(1)} = K_{CMDS}$, $f_2 = K^{(2)} = K_{LE}$ and $f_3 = K^{(3)} = K_{LLE}$. Then, the linear IM applied to spectral DR methods using kernel representations can be expressed as follows:

$$\widetilde{K} = \widetilde{f} = \text{LIM}_\alpha\{f\} = \text{LIM}_\alpha\{K^{(1)}, \ldots, K^{(3)}\} = \sum_{m=1}^{M} \alpha_m K^{(m)}. \tag{15}$$

To add the effect of interactivity, the values of weighting factors α can be provided through a user-friendly and intuitive-to-use interface[1], as those reviewed in [8]. Finally, the low-dimensional space Y is calculated by applying KPCA on $\widetilde{K}$, so:

$$Y = \text{KPCA}(\widetilde{K}), \tag{16}$$

where $\text{KPCA}(\cdot)$ means that the KPCA problem stated in Sect. 3 is solved with the kernel matrix in its argument. The first notion of this approach (even though with no formal definition) is presented in [4]. Figure 3 graphically explains the use of LIM for DR techniques (DRT) following a KPCA approach.

---

[1] Some IM-based interfaces are available at https://sdas-group.com/gallery/.

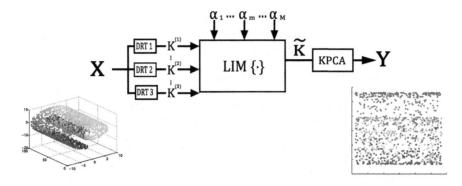

Fig. 3. Graphical explanation of the use of the linear interaction model (LIM) for a KPCA-based DR framework. Specifically, a linear combination of kernel matrices representing DR techniques (DRTs) is considered.

5   Final Remarks

In this work, we have elegantly defined the concept of the so-named interaction model (IM). Such a definition open the possibility of developing more formally new interactive data visualization based on a mixture of dimensionality reduction techniques.

In future works, we will explore and/or develop novel kernel representations arising from other dimensionality reduction methods as well as IM approaches enabling users to readily incorporate their knowledge and expertise into data exploration and visualization.

Acknowledgment. The authors acknowledge to the research project "Desarrollo de una metodología de visualización interactiva y eficaz de información en Big Data" supported by Agreement No. 180 November 1st, 2016 by VIPRI from Universidad de Nariño.

As well, authors thank the valuable support given by the SDAS Research Group (www.sdas-group.com).

References

1. Gou, J., Yang, Y., Yi, Z., Lv, J., Mao, Q., Zhan, Y.: Discriminative globality and locality preserving graph embedding for dimensionality reduction. Expert Syst. Appl. **144**, 113079 (2020)
2. Lee, J.A., Peluffo-Ordóñez, D.H., Verleysen, M.: Multi-scale similarities in stochastic neighbour embedding: reducing dimensionality while preserving both local and global structure. Neurocomputing **169**, 246–261 (2015)
3. Ward, M.O., Grinstein, G., Keim, D.: Interactive Data Visualization: Foundations, Techniques, and Applications. CRC Press (2010)
4. Peluffo-Ordónez, D.H., Alvarado-Pérez, J.C., Lee, J.A., Verleysen, M., et al.: Geometrical homotopy for data visualization. In: European Symposium on Artificial Neural Networks (ESANN 2015). Computational Intelligence and Machine Learning (2015)

5. Salazar-Castro, J., Rosas-Narváez, Y., Pantoja, A., Alvarado-Pérez, J.C., Peluffo-Ordóñez, D.H.: Interactive interface for efficient data visualization via a geometric approach. In: 2015 20th Symposium on Signal Processing, Images and Computer Vision (STSIVA), pp. 1–6. IEEE (2015)
6. Rosero-Montalvo, P., et al.: Interactive data visualization using dimensionality reduction and similarity-based representations. In: Beltrán-Castañón, C., Nyström, I., Famili, F. (eds.) CIARP 2016. LNCS, vol. 10125, pp. 334–342. Springer, Cham (2017). https://doi.org/10.1007/978-3-319-52277-7_41
7. Rosero-Montalvo, P.D., Peña-Unigarro, D.F., Peluffo, D.H., Castro-Silva, J.A., Umaquinga, A., Rosero-Rosero, E.A.: Data visualization using interactive dimensionality reduction and improved color-based interaction model. In: Ferrández Vicente, J.M., Álvarez-Sánchez, J.R., de la Paz López, F., Toledo Moreo, J., Adeli, H. (eds.) IWINAC 2017. LNCS, vol. 10338, pp. 289–298. Springer, Cham (2017). https://doi.org/10.1007/978-3-319-59773-7_30. (Cited by 8)
8. Umaquinga-Criollo, A.C., Peluffo-Ordóñez, D.H., Rosero-Montalvo, P.D., Godoy-Trujillo, P.E., Benítez-Pereira, H.: Interactive visualization interfaces for big data analysis using combination of dimensionality reduction methods: a brief review. In: Basantes-Andrade, A., Naranjo-Toro, M., Zambrano Vizuete, M., Botto-Tobar, M. (eds.) TSIE 2019. AISC, vol. 1110, pp. 193–203. Springer, Cham (2020). https://doi.org/10.1007/978-3-030-37221-7_17
9. Amin, A., et al.: Cross-company customer churn prediction in telecommunication: a comparison of data transformation methods. Int. J. Inf. Manag. **46**, 304–319 (2019)
10. Peluffo, D., Lee, J., Verleysen, M., Rodríguez-Sotelo, J., Castellanos-Domínguez, G.: Unsupervised relevance analysis for feature extraction and selection: a distance-based approach for feature relevance. In: International Conference on Pattern Recognition, Applications and Methods-ICPRAM (2014)
11. Cao, H., Bernard, S., Heutte, L., Sabourin, R.: Dissimilarity-based representation for radiomics applications. CoRR abs/1803.04460 (2018)
12. Zhong, G., Wang, L.N., Ling, X., Dong, J.: An overview on data representation learning: from traditional feature learning to recent deep learning. J. Finance Data Sci. **2**(4), 265–278 (2016)
13. Lee, J.A., Verleysen, M.: Nonlinear Dimensionality Reduction. Springer, Heidelberg (2007). https://doi.org/10.1007/978-0-387-39351-3
14. Borg, I., Groenen, P.J.: Modern Multidimensional Scaling: Theory and Applications. Springer, Heidelberg (2005). https://doi.org/10.1007/0-387-28981-X
15. Peluffo-Ordóñez, D.H., Lee, J.A., Verleysen, M.: Generalized kernel framework for unsupervised spectral methods of dimensionality reduction. In: 2014 IEEE Symposium on Computational Intelligence and Data Mining (CIDM), pp. 171–177. IEEE (2014)
16. Peluffo-Ordóñez, D.H., Lee, J.A., Verleysen, M.: Short review of dimensionality reduction methods based on stochastic neighbour embedding. In: Villmann, T., Schleif, F.-M., Kaden, M., Lange, M. (eds.) Advances in Self-Organizing Maps and Learning Vector Quantization. AISC, vol. 295, pp. 65–74. Springer, Cham (2014). https://doi.org/10.1007/978-3-319-07695-9_6
17. Belkin, M., Niyogi, P.: Laplacian eigenmaps for dimensionality reduction and data representation. Neural Comput. **15**(6), 1373–1396 (2003)
18. Zhang, Z., Wang, J.: MLLE: modified locally linear embedding using multiple weights. In: Advances in Neural Information Processing Systems, pp. 1593–1600 (2007)

19. Hinton, G.E., Roweis, S.T.: Stochastic neighbor embedding. In: Advances in Neural Information Processing Systems, pp. 857–864 (2003)
20. Ham, J., Lee, D.D., Mika, S., Schölkopf, B.: A kernel view of the dimensionality reduction of manifolds. In: Proceedings of the Twenty-First International Conference on Machine Learning, p. 47. ACM (2004)

Some Considerations on the Role of Universities and Research Centers in EU-Funded Sustainable Mobility Projects

Francesco Bruzzone and Silvio Nocera[✉]

IUAV University of Venice, Santa Croce 191 Tolentini, 30135 Venice, Italy
nocera@iuav.it

Abstract. Stakeholder involvement is now part of formal requirements of almost any transportation decision-making process in Europe, increasing the complexity while allowing for better, shared decisions. European institutions strongly promote participatory processes and have developed a regulatory framework as well as guidelines and tools for successful and effective public engagement in transport planning. In this context, a variety of EU funded projects have been set up where territorial partners cooperate with universities and research centers in developing a sustainable mobility project and related public engagement strategies. This paper digs into the history and the current state of stakeholder involvement in transport projects, discussing through a broad literature analysis the theoretical evolution of the concept, controversies, drivers for phases and tools for effective engagement practices. Through the examples of the experience within European projects SMILE and SMART COMMUTING, this paper explores the role that academic institutions can play in engagement processes and possible contributions in terms of technical expertise and know-how transfer. Intermediate results from the projects' engagement efforts seem to validate the European Commission's belief that planned, continuous, open and interactive involvement of Universities may bring to better, shared and desirable decisions, consistently with findings from recent literature.

Keywords: Stakeholder involvement · Public engagement · Transport planning

1 Introduction

Stakeholder involvement or engagement has become common practice in the field of transport planning. Normative pushes and a growing conviction that participative planning brings to better, quicker processes have stimulated the diffusion of a number of involvement tools, each developed and adopted in response to specific needs and objectives within transport planning. In 1969, Arnstein [1] stated that participation is concerned with the redistribution of power, where those normally excluded from decision-making processes had the opportunity to be involved. Nowadays, this concept is incorporated within public participation, widely interpreted as involvement in decision-making with the specific purpose of influencing the choices being made, as

© Springer Nature Switzerland AG 2020
O. Gervasi et al. (Eds.): ICCSA 2020, LNCS 12250, pp. 204–217, 2020.
https://doi.org/10.1007/978-3-030-58802-1_15

opposite to consultation where local authorities receive suggestions and criticism but can simply reject contents considered irrelevant [2]. The overarching goal of engagement is to increase transparency of the decision-making process, with greater input from stakeholders and with their support upon taken decisions [3]. The participative approach is opposed to the DAD (Decide, Announce, Defend) syndrome, a term that in literature identifies planning processes where administrations pay little attention to stakeholder engagement, in the belief that professionals can choose for the best or because politicians feel fully entitled to represent the multitude of interests [4, 5]. Involving stakeholders and aligning their perceptions and views with the judgement of experts and decision-makers can be a challenging task as well as a rewarding experience, resulting in a more effective planning process and enhancing the value of the product [6–8]. According to Bickerstaff et al. [9], effective participation can be achieved by making it open, interactive, continuous, aided with effective feedback from participants. In the opinion of Glass [10] as cited in Lindenau and Boehler-Baedeker [11], public participation has the five key objectives of information exchange, education, support building, supplemental decision-making and representational input. The main targets and benefits of participation in planning processes are effectively synthetized by Krause [12] as follows: making processes more transparent, raising mutual understanding between involved parties, considering ideas, concerns, and everyday knowledge, improving the knowledge basis, increasing acceptability of planning processes. Controversies are still existing, however, on whether participatory processes generally prove effective or – instead - complicate the planning process, resulting in avoidable slowness and bad decision-making, or are grounded in political expediency [13].

The scope of this paper is to describe some successful cases of stakeholder engagement within the frame of EU-funded transport-related programs, validating the European institutions' belief that thoughtful participatory processes bring to better decision-making and highlighting the coordinative and formative role that universities and research institutions in general play within such programs. This is achieved by first presenting a discussion on three major topics:

1) The concept of stakeholders (who should be involved in the transport planning process?);
2) Public engagement in Europe, including a short history of involvement practices, hints to legislation and directives calling for engagement, phases, tools and characteristics of engagement during the transport planning process (why, when and how should stakeholders be involved in the transport planning process?);
3) Open controversies (what needs to be done to make sure the engagement process is effective?).

Moreover, this paper will discuss through the example of EU-funded projects SMILE and SMART COMMUTING the role(s) that the academic world can play within the stakeholder involvement process in transport planning, presenting activities and results of a twofold relation with project partners, seen as both stakeholders within the EU projects (university as administrative entity) and as authorities seeking for the best territorial participatory processes while developing plans and programs object of both SMILE and SMART COMMUTING projects (university as counsellor of administrations).

2 Stakeholder Involvement in Mobility Planning

2.1 A Momentum for Participation

Transport planning that incorporates public participation as an integral element is now a reality across Europe, both from an empirical perspective (registering numerous controversial discussions within urban communities) and from a regulatory perspective [9]. In particular, the European Commission has created a common framework for sustainable and participated mobility planning by promoting SUMPs (strategic Sustainable Urban Mobility Plans) and establishing as a strong principle the need to involve the public throughout the transport planning process, from the very beginning. Despite most countries introduced participation as part of their national planning procedures even before European efforts (prototypal are the cases of France, the UK and the United States), major differences in the levels of stakeholder engagement in different countries can still be registered and public involvement often interacts very little with more traditional transportation planning approaches [6]. The European Commission, by first integrating participation within the framework of environmental planning (since 2004) and by later developing the SUMP concept, has recognized transport planning as a multi-agent, multi-sector and multi-modal process which balances and engages with a wide range of interests, issues and policy areas, favoring a movement towards the development of more inclusive and participatory decision-making processes [14]. The first arguments towards participatory transport planning processes at European level have been encapsulated in a Decision-Makers' Guidebook on developing sustainable urban land use and transport strategies, dated 2004 [15]. Later significant documents are the Commission's Action Plan on Urban Mobility [16] which "encourages the development of incentives, such as expert assistance and information exchange" [17], and the subsequent 2011 White Paper [18] which proposed SUMPs to be a mandatory requirement for cities with a population over 100,000. The promoted concept places particular emphasis on the involvement of citizens and stakeholders, the coordination of policy between sectors (transport, land use, environment, economic development, social policy, health, safety, energy, etc.), between authority levels and between neighboring authorities [19]. In support and within this strong policy indication, a number of European projects have been carried out to provide guidance during the various phases of mobility planning, to identify stakeholders, actions, solutions, and to advice on essential and desirable elements of the planning process [20, 21]. A review of some of such projects can be found in May [16], while the following paragraphs contain some considerations addressing the primary questions of stakeholder engagement: who, why, when and how to involve?

2.2 Stakeholder Involvement: Opportunity or Hindrance for the Transport Planning Process?

Despite political and cultural difference between countries remain present, the way transport decisions are made is changing, and a tendency for more groups to become involved in the decision-making process is clearly visible [22]. A wide range of people and organizations have interests in transport projects and become involved, to varying degrees, in decision-making. These are collectively known as "stakeholders" and may or may not have a professional interest in the project; their opposition can make its process very difficult. Stakeholders are commonly classified into "primary" and "secondary" where primary stakeholders are defined as those with a direct interest, depending from the project or being directly involved in its exploitation in some way, and secondary stakeholders would be those with a more indirect interest [6]. Following similar criteria, the distinction between "stakeholders" and "actors" [23], or "stakeholders" and "citizens" [24] can be found in literature. Interestingly, scholars seem to not fully agree terms: according to Ballantyne et al. [23] "stakeholders are all that have an interest in the system of urban freight transport; whereas actors are those that have a direct influence on the system. Therefore, all actors are, but not all stakeholders are actors." For Le Pira et al. [24], instead, actors can be categorized in three classes: experts (key informants), stakeholders (e.g. institutions, transport companies, environmental associations), and citizens. According to them, experts have high competence but low stake, stakeholders have competence and high stake, and citizens have low competence but act in the public interest, coherently with the public engagement pyramid (Fig. 1, left). A diffused stakeholder classification is that proposed by Gardner et al. [25], based on two levels of interests and two levels of power (Fig. 1, right). Table 1 shows a comprehensive list of typical stakeholder groups involved in transport project, based on outcomes of GUIDEMAPS project [26] and published by Wefering et al. [19] within the European Platform on Sustainable Urban Mobility Plans guidelines for plans development and implementation.

A number of authors recall the importance and the relevance of stakeholder engagement practices, from both a regulatory perspective and from an empirical and academic perspective. A consistent body of literature, however, stresses potential controversies rising from participation processes, particularly claiming that while involvement is now a fundamental requirement of mobility planning, it can lead to counterproductive results, such as slowness and inconclusiveness of the processes, or it can be treated as a sterile, inconvenient step and flattened to political expediency [13]. Lindenau and Boehler-Baedeker [11] synthetize some principle questions concerning the paradigm of participatory planning. In particular, they identify a question of

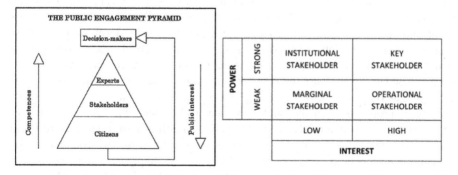

Fig. 1. Diffused types of actor/stakeholder classification. Sources: Le Pira et al. [24] and Gardner et al. [25]

Table 1. Typical stakeholder groups involved in transport projects. Source: GUIDEMAPS project [26]

Typical stakeholder groups involved in transport projects (based on GUIDEMAPS)			
Government / Authorities	**Businesses / Operators**	**Communities / Local Neighbourhoods**	**Others**
Local authorities	Transport operators/ providers	National environmental NGOs	Research institutions
Neighbouring cities	Transport consultants	Motorist associations	Universities
Local transport authority	Car sharing companies	Trade unions	Training institutions
Traffic police	Bicycle rental operators	Media	Experts from other cities
Other local transport bodies	Other mobility providers	Local authority Forums	Foundations
Other local authority bodies	National business associations	Local community organisations	
Politicians	Major employers	Local interest groups	
Other decision-makers	Private financiers	Cycle/walking groups	
Partnering organisations	International/national business	Public transport user groups	
Project managers	Regional/local business	Transport users	
Professional staff	Local business associations	Citizens	
Emergency services	Small businesses	Visitors	
Health & safety executives	Retailers	Citizens in neighbouring cities	
European Union	Utility services (e.g. electric, telecoms)	Disabled people	
Ministry of transport	Engineers/contractors	Landowners	
Other national ministries		Transport staff	
Regional government		Parents/children	
		Older people	

democracy (does participation actually fulfill democratic requirements since it is based on a representative decision-making process, only involving small sections of the public?); a question of acceptance (does participation actually ensure acceptance of transport policy and measures?); a question of quality (some scholars – see Dietz and Stern [27] - argue that the consultation of low-expertise public with a wide range of less significant interests might compromise the expected quality level of participated decisions). Together with principle questions, some practical aspects still pose a challenge to local authorities when carrying out participatory processes, despite EU and local guidelines. A relevant issue is in particular how to take involvement results into account in an ongoing transport planning process and how to come to a joint, accepted decision if proposals from the public are unrealistic, unfeasible and – a matter of particular concern – financially not viable [11]. Authorities have often tried to avoid participatory processes leading to unsatisfactory situations for involved parties by flattening the process to minimum required efforts, thus emptying it from its concep-tualized meaning and grounding them in instrumental political motivations [13]. Ward [28] argues that diverse stakeholder participation in transport planning is potentially beneficial but difficult to achieve. He supports a hypothesis that an increase in stakeholder diversity improves problem definition and innovation diversity, and falsifies the hypothesis that stakeholder inclusion makes planning expensive and inconclusive. However, he also finds that stakeholder involvement is often obstructed by centralized power structures, consistently with other literature reported above. In the long term, a greater dispersal of power in society may be required for ensuring meaningful participation processes, states Ward, but meanwhile forum obstruction by powerful actors can be prevented by enhanced legitimization and guidance from existing authorities, among which universities and research centers. In this regard, the next paragraphs will discuss phases of involvement and tools which have been identified by literature and by authorities as keys towards successful participatory transport planning. The SUMP concept has indeed been developed recently and provides guidance and tools for stakeholders participation; its effectiveness has not yet been proved by a substantial body of literature but results from carried out and ongoing projects are promising [17].

2.3   The Stakeholder Involvement Process

A specific type of involvement and precise targets should be sought in any moment of the planning process. Stakeholder and citizen involvement should be carefully planned, answering four main questions that most EU guidance documents report as backbones of engagement strategies [19, 26]:

– Why (is the engagement process being undertaken)? How will it influence the strategy/scheme?
– Who (should be involved in the decision-making process)?

This first two issues have been discussed in Sect. 2.2, where the scope and critical issues of engagement processes, a definition of stakeholders and key characteristics of the groups to be included in the process have been explored.

– When (should different activities take place/is it (not) appropriate to engage)?
– How (will engagement be undertaken)? What tools and techniques should be used?

These two last questions will be the topic of the following paragraphs, starting from a discussion of possible engagement phases as recognizable in literature.

The transportation decision-making process is normally considered to be composed of six phases [26]: problem definition, option generation, option assessment, formal decision taking, implementation, monitoring and evaluation. At each phase, different levels of public engagement can be identified and adopted, accordingly to the contextually chosen participation tools and to the specific decision-making process [6]. Kelly et al. [3] proposed five levels of stakeholders involvement: the first one deals with stakeholder identification; the second one with a systematic listening activity of requests from stakeholders as well of the social, cultural and economic climate; the third one concerns sharing information with stakeholder, differently from consultation (fourth level) where each stakeholders' perspective is taken into account with the aim of improving the project and its social acceptability. Finally, participation is the level in which interested groups become joint decision makers during the project design and implementation. Buhrmann et al. [29] provided a six-step engagement process, later adopted by CIVITAS project [30] in their "Toolkit on organizing successful consul-tation". The steps are: issue(s) specification, stakeholder identification, actor constel-lation analysis, involvement strategy setup, stakeholder consultation, evaluation and follow-up. According to GUIDELINES project [26] public engagement is a parallel and contextual phase to project management and both are affected by the same con-straints, either contextual barriers (institutional, legal or financial restrictions) or pro-cess barriers (which arise during the various stages of the transport project). Figure 2 shows the "involvement spectrum" as reported in [30].

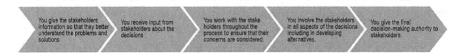

Fig. 2. Possible levels of stakeholder involvement. Source: CIVITAS project [30]

A generalized but at the same time well-received answer to the question of when to engage for achieving successful decision making can be "as early as possible in the course of the process". Recent literature and EU guidelines indeed indicate two major mistakes in former unsuccessful engagement efforts: on the one side, the public has often been informed rather than involved; on the other side involvement practices have been undertaken too late in the process and/or with inappropriate tools and techniques, not considering its dynamic nature [6, 19, 26].

2.4   Participation Tools

Engagement or participation tools are designed to help engaging stakeholder in the decision-making process, in order to achieve broadly accepted solutions to transport problems, addressing controversies and special interests. Selecting the most appropriate tool of engagement is crucial to the process's success, as the choice of unsuitable techniques might not only bring to poorer results, but it can create avoidable barriers to the process as a whole, in case it appears that decision-makers are in some ways being selective in who and how they engage [26]. Using a combination of participation tools likely increases the possibility to gather a more representative response, but the appropriate choice must be related to the purpose of engagement, to the target stake-holders, to the level of expertise of the authority and to available resources [6]. As highlighted in Table 2, originally presented by GUIDEMAPS project [26] and cited or reported by a number of following projects [30] and recent papers on the topic [6, 11], three major tools groups can be identified (information giving and gathering, interactive engagement, hard engagement to reach groups), for a total of eight tools and twenty-seven ore specific techniques or activities.

The first 12 techniques in the GUIDEMAPS's [26] table are examples of infor-mation giving and input collecting. For information-giving purposes, different media can be considered (TV, radio, letters, posters, and anything uploadable on the Internet). An effort to increase the variety and mixture of chosen communicative channels should

Table 2. GUIDEMAPS project tool matrix [26]

Classifications ● generally applicable ○ partially applicable	1. Letters	2. Posters, notices and signs	3. Leaflets and brochures	4. Fact sheets	5. Newsletters	6. Technical reports	7. Telephone techniques	8. Radio shows & TV shows	9. Internet techniques	10. Web-based forums	11. Questionnaire surveys	12. Key person interviews	13. Exhibitions	14. Information centres	15. Information sessions/briefings	16. Public meetings	17. Topical events	18. Community visits	19. Focus groups	20. Workshops	21. Citizen juries	22. Technical working parties	23. Stakeholder conferences	24. Transport visioning events	25. Weekend events	26. Planning for Real®	27. Open-space events
Who to engage																											
Wider audience	○	●	●	○	●		●	●	●	○	●		●	●		●	○			○			○			●	○
Targeted audience	●	○	●	●	○	●	●	●	○		●	●	●	●		●	○	●	●	●	●	●	●	●	●	○	●
When to engage																											
Problem definition	●	●	●	●	●	●	●	●	●	●	●	●	●	●	○	●	○	○	●	●	●	●	●	○	●	●	●
Option generation				○				○		●	○	●		○	○	○	○	●	●	●	●	●	●	●	●	●	●
Option assessment	○	●	●	●	●	●	●	●	●	●	●	●	●	●	●	○	●	●	○	●	●	●	●	○	○	●	○
Formal decision making	○			○		●				○		●		○					○	●							
Implementation plan	○	●	●	●	●	●	●		○	●		●	●	●	○	○	○		○		○		○				
Monitoring and evaluation						●	●			○	●	●						○			○			○			
Type of project																											
Strategy	○	○	●	○	●	●	●	●	●	●	●	●	●	●	●	●	○		●	●	●	●	●	●	●		●
Scheme	●	●	●	●	●	●	●	●	●	●	●	●	●	●	●	●	●	●	●	●	○	●	●	○	●	●	●
Duration of engagement																											
Restricted	●	●	●	●	●	●	●	●	●	●	●	●	●	○	●	●	●	●	●	●	●	●	●	●	●	●	●
Continuous		○		○		●		●	●		●										○						

be made, especially if the target group is not very specific. An synergistic way to combine information giving and input collecting is to open information stands or centers, or to set up information events (techniques 13 to 17). Such activities can be both addressed to a formal public, for instance with hearings, and to a more general audience, for instance through games and playful activities. Techniques 18 to 22 are designed to reach selected stakeholders in small groups. These techniques can result in a more open and productive debate with active participation and ownership of the project, especially when the project length and complexity require slowly digging towards common ground and shared views. Conversation with selected stakeholders can be useful, but should not replace engagement with wider communities.

Techniques 23 to 27 are designed for consultation with large groups of stakeholders and are ideal to test wide range of options or to receive opinions and feedback on the project as a whole. Techniques include holding conferences, workshops and lectures and workshops, or events at which target groups propose solutions through the analysis of the existing situation.

To ensure that the most appropriate tools are adopted at each stage, the participation process should be planned well in advance, possibly by developing community involvement plans [30] if a similar instrument is not framed within the planning process in itself, as it is in the case of SUMPs [15]. In any case, well managed interaction among stakeholders has demonstrated to foster the emergence of coalitions, facilitating the convergence to a well-accepted solution, often changing stakeholders' mind about the policy under discussion [31].

3 Stakeholder Involvement in EU Projects SMART COMMUTING and SMILE

Interreg Adrion project SMILE (FirSt and last Mile Inter-modal mobiLity in congested urban arEas of Adrion Region) aims at enhancing capacity for integrated transport and mobility services and at multimodality; Interreg Central Europe project SMART COMMUTING pursues cooperation in preparing Sustainable Urban Mobility Plans (SUMPs) among partner Functional Urban Areas (FUAs). In both projects, the authors' research unit at IUAV University of Venice is involved as technical partner, with the specific role of coordinating the common transnational strategies and to guide and support project partners - thanks to the specific expertise - in every phase of the process, from the analysis of the status-quo and of possible scenarios to planning and implementation of the chosen strategies, measures and actions. The scope of this section is to highlight the role that academic institutions, thanks to their technical expertise, play in mobility-related EU project, acting as both activators of the project itself (through partner involvement) and as proper technical experts, supporting partners in identifying and engaging stakeholders, local groups, and special interests.

From an engagement perspective, IUAV's role in the projects is twofold. On the one side, the University, as technical partner, is the authority that interacts with the various stakeholders (territorial partners), collecting their needs and suggestions and amalgamating stances to reach a common, shared, project-wide transnational strategy, then devised into local peculiar characteristics at a later stage.

On the other side, IUAV's role is that to provide support in conducting an effective and successful public and stakeholder involvement strategy at each partner's local level.

Being SMILE and SMART COMMUTING projects part of EU programs, the timing schedule for stakeholder engagement had been detailed within the application procedure, in compliance with current recommendations [15, 19, 26]. This has provided a basis for successful involvement, shifting the focus to appropriate tools identification from the very first stage of the projects. IUAV's contribution as technical partner is provided both via telematic means (emails, Skype, digital tools), mostly establishing direct communication channels with single project partners, and at project meetings, when the possibilities to engage project partners and transmit expertise for local involvement strategies are noticeable. This complex situation requires that a wide spectrum of engagement tools is directly used by the University or is explained to project partners for local empirical application.

More in detail, during project meetings (taking place every three to six months) IUAV aims at involving a targeted audience (project partners) through direct engagement in daily activities, promoting group work and discussion to reach a shared solution to the specific objective at hand. In this case, engagement tools such as focus groups, workshops, briefings, technical tables, surveys and questionnaires, field visits and other interactive options are most commonly chosen. In both projects SMILE and

SMART COMMUTING, the interaction among partners with IUAV's guidance has successfully led to the definition of transnational SUMP schemes (or strategies), common cognitive umbrellas under which to elaborate (or reinforce, if already initiated) local SUMPs mirroring local peculiarities [32, 33]. The in-project participatory approach is particularly useful as partners, while experiencing in first person, acquire know-how and capacity to correctly replicate at local level engagement techniques. To ensure that gained skills are effectively used at local level, IUAV prepares templates, reports and documents (to be followed, used as guidelines and/or filled) and constantly checks partner progress. Despite the focus of project meetings clearly being that of establishing a fruitful dialogue between project partners as to reach shared views and outputs and carry the project forwards, the side aspect of expertise transfer to partners is fundamental, and should express not only the potential of the possible results that can be achieved, but also their importance in terms of concrete applications [34–39]. In between project meetings and for the course of the whole project, IUAV is in charge of checking partners' progress. Due to European sustainable mobility guidelines requirements, authorities (in this case, territorial partners of SMILE and SMART COMMUTING projects) are required to constantly involve local stakeholders (target groups) and actively and to continuously report the outputs of the process. The University as technical partner provides materials and suggests options for successful involvement at the various stages, accordingly with

Table 3. SMART COMMUTING targets and values. Source: SMART COMMUTING project application form

D.2 Target groups

Target groups	Please further specify the target groups (e.g., ministry, university, chamber of commerce etc.) - see examples in annex IV of the application manual (classification of target groups)	Target value Please indicate the size of the target group the project aims to actively involve.
Local public authority	It is expected that SMART COMMUTING will involve 40 municipalities belonging to the 7 FUAs in which the project activities will be developed.	40,00
Infrastructure and (public) service provider	It is expected that SMART COMMUTING will involve 21 public transport service companies (on average, 3 per each FUA).	21,00
Education/training centre and school	Schools are big generators of daily commuting, so the main 3 schools in each FUA will be involved in project activities.	21,00
Large enterprises	Large enterprises are, together with schools, big generators of daily commuting. The larger 4 companies in each FUA will be involved in project activities.	28,00
General public	Through the communication strategy channelled through socal media, it will be searched a contact with thousands of commuters (indicatively 5.000 in each FUA), to influence their attitude and change their behaviours.	35.000,00
Interest groups including NGOs	Trade unions and trade associations will be involved in each FUA (5 per area) to disseminate to entrepreneurs and workers the SMART COMMUTING's outputs and results, with the aim of changing the current commuting models.	35,00
Business support organisation	The chambers of commerce in each FUA will be involved in promoting at territorial levels the new approaches and tools set up by SMART COMMUTING, in particular towards the economic stakeholders.	7,00
Regional public authority	As far as possible representatives of regional governments will take part in the works of the institutional coordination structures set up at FUA level and in the annual conferences.	7,00

the project's application forms, with EU guidance, and with emerging local peculiarities. Besides constantly monitoring, checking and correcting project partners' performances, IUAV is available to participate and/or co-organize local engagement events, workshops, and seminars at partners locations, thus actively coordinating public engagement processes. Given the broad approach, according to the different phases of the projects most engagement tools among those discussed in Sect. 2.4 are presented to partners and used. Printed information materials and questionnaires, online information and surveys, digital materials, all with options for interested parties to provide their opinion, are among the most commonly used tools.

Under IUAV's supervision, public engagement activities are being successful. Tables 3 and 4 show predetermined target groups and values which, with IUAV's collaboration, had been identified in a preliminary phase as satisfactory to be reached in the course of the projects.

In both SMILE and SMART COMMUTING projects SUMPs drafts have not yet been finalized, but the numbers of reached "targets" are already positive. According to SMILE communication management, as of January 2020 107 specific target groups had

Table 4. SMILE project targets and values. Source: SMILE project application form

C.2.2 Target groups

Target group/s	Please further specify the target group/s (e.g., bilingual elementary schools, environmental experts, etc.)	Target value Please indicate the size of the target group you will reach. The budget cannot be higher than that of WP Communication
local public authority	The local public authorities will be involved in the depiction of mobility scenarios, elaboration of the SUMP transnational scheme, testing of IT solutions, and hence in using the ouputs generated by the related activities.	10.00
regional public authority	The regional public authorities will share project's activities, outputs and results, and will support local authorities in achieving the expected changes.	10.00
national public authority	The national ministries of infrastructure and transport (starting from Italy, which Ministry is an associated partner in SMILE) will be contacted and involved in order to spread out the use of project's ouputs and results.	7.00
sectoral agency	Regional/local development agencies will use SMILE's outputs (methodology for depicting the mobility scenarios, transnational scheme for SUMPs elaboration, IT solutions) to assist the local authorities in order to make more sustainable the urban mobility	10.00
infrastructure and (public) service provider	IT solutions will be used by bodies in charge of parking management, tourism buses companies, freight delivery companies to make more efficient and intermodal the urban mobility.	30.00
interest groups including NGOs	Civil society organization active in the field of environment and sustainable mobility will be enabled by SMILE's outputs to reinforce their activity aimed at making more liveable the urban areas.	10.00
higher education and research	Mobility scenarios and elaboration of a transnational scheme for SUMPs elaboration will allow higher education & research centres, settled in areas concerned, to refine their knowledge of hosting territory and hence their provision of competent support.	20.00
General public	All the users of motorized vehicles (cars drivers, drivers of tourist buses, freight delivery couriers) could use the APP of SMILE.	20 000.00

been actively involved through communication strategy and website, promotional materials, academic/scientific publications, public events, digital activities, evaluation of dissemination actions. Additionally, more than 20,000 people part of "general public" had been consulted and invited to participate. Up to date data from SMART COMMUTING project are at the time of writing not available to the authors, but similar numbers to those reported for SMILE had been reached halfway through the SUMPs drafting process already.

4 Conclusions

European legislation and guidelines, as well as recent literature on the topic, all recognize that despite some evidences exist that stakeholder involvement processes don't always lead to better transportation decision making, if those processes are carried out correctly and effectively outcomes are strongly positive. In particular, public and stakeholder engagement allows for better, shared decision making, quicker processes, higher stake and public acceptance, higher reliability. Ever since the EU has introduced the SUMP concept for sustainable, participated urban mobility in the early 2000s, a number of authors and projects have published evidence of the positive impacts of public engagement in transport decision making processes. SMILE and SMART COMMUTING are among the EU projects that capitalize on SUMPs theory and develop a transnational SUMP scheme for addressing transport-related problems in urban areas throughout central and Adriatic Europe. This paper has proposed a literature review on public engagement in transport planning, discussing its history and evolution towards its current compulsoriness, past and present controversies, phases and tools for successful stakeholder involvement processes, in accordance with European guidelines. The authors have then introduced an overview of the role that academic institutions play within European mobility-related projects, highlighting their contribution in both engaging and informing project partners and in providing assistance when identifying, engaging and discussing local stakeholders (or group). Details of the role of the authors' research unit within European projects SMILE and SMART COMMUTING have been reported in Sect. 3, showing how within well planned processes and with constant technical support the public engagement process proves effective at reaching and involving a wide public. While for the two mentioned undergoing projects SUMPs drafting has not yet been completed, this paper has brought evidence that continuous, first-stage, well-organized academic inclusion – carried out in compliance with EU indications – leads to successful decision-making, by incorporating multiple perspectives and competences and by facilitating convergence towards shared solutions. It is therefore expectable that SMILE and SMART COMMUTING partners' SUMPs will reflect public perceptions and will encounter easier implementation compared to unilaterally promoted plans and projects or to processes only benefitting from partial, superficial public information activities.

Acknowledgment. This research has been funded through the Interreg Central Europe Programme (2014–2020) under Project SMART-COMMUTING and through the Interreg Adrion Programme (2014–2020) under Project SMILE.

References

1. Arnstein, S.R.: A ladder of citizen participation. J. Am. Plann. Assoc. **35**, 216–224 (1969)
2. Gil, A., Calado, H., Bentz, J.: Public participation in municipal transport planning processes–the case of the sustainable mobility plan of Ponta Delgada, Azores Portugal. J. Trans. Geogr. **19**, 1309–1319 (2011)
3. Kelly, J., Jones, P., Barta, F., Hossinger, R., Witte, A., Christian, A.: Successful transport decision-making – A project management and stakeholder engagement handbook. Guide-maps consortium (2004)
4. Elliott, A.: Social Theory: An Introduction. Routledge, New York (2009)
5. Marincioni, F., Appiotti, F.: The Lyon-Turin high-speed rail: the public debate and perception of environmental risk in susa valley, Italy. Environ. Manage. **43**, 863–875 (2009). https://doi.org/10.1007/s00267-009-9271-2
6. Cascetta, E., Pagliara, F.: Public engagement for planning and designing transportation systems. Procedia Soc. Behav. Sci. **87**, 103–116 (2013)
7. Cappelli, A., Nocera, S.: Freight modal split models: data base, calibration problem and urban application. WIT Trans. Built Environ. **89**, 369–375 (2006)
8. Nocera, S., Tonin, S., Cavallaro, F.: Carbon estimation and urban mobility plans: opportunities in a context of austerity. Res. Transp. Econ. **51**, 71–82 (2015)
9. Bickerstaff, K., Tolley, R., Walzer, G.: Transport planning and participation: the rhetoric and realities of public involvement. J. Transp. Geogr. **10**, 61–73 (2002)
10. Glass, J.: Citizen participation in planning: the relationship between objectives and techniques. J. Am. Plann. Assoc. **45**(2), 180–189 (1979)
11. Lindenau, M., Böhler-Baedeker, S.: Citizen and stakeholder involvement: a precondition for sustainable urban mobility. Transp. Res. Procedia **4**, 347–360 (2014)
12. Krause, J.: Partizipation und Beteiligung bei kommunalen Verkehrsprojekten. In: Gies, J., Hertel, M. (eds.) Beteiligungsprozesse – unterschätztes Potenzial in der Verkehrsplanung. Dokumentation der Fachtagung "kommunal mobil" am 26./27. September 2013 in DessauRoßlau. Deutsches Institut für Urbanistik gGmbh, Berlin, pp. 33–48 (2014)
13. Bickerstaff, K., Walker, G.: Participatory local governance and transport planning. Environ. Plann. A **33**, 431–451 (2001)
14. Booth, C., Richardson, T.: Placing the public in integrated transport planning. Transp. Policy **8**, 141–149 (2001)
15. May, A.D.: Developing Sustainable Urban Land Use and Transport Strategies: A Decision-makers' Guidebook, 2nd edn. European Commission DGRTD, Brussels (2005)
16. European Commission DG Energy and Transport: Action Plan on Urban Mobility. DGTREN, Brussels (2009)
17. May, A.D.: Encouraging good practice in the development of sustainable urban mobility plans. Case Stud. Trans. Policy **3**, 3–11 (2015)
18. European Commission DG Move.: Road Map to a Single European Transport Area: Towards a Competitive and Resource Efficient Transport System (2011)
19. Wefering, F., Rupprecht, S., Bührmann, S., Böhler-Baedeker, S.: Guidelines. developing and implementing a sustainable urban mobility plan. In: Workshop, p. 117, March 2013
20. ELTISplus: The State of the Art of Sustainable Urban Mobility Plans in Europe (2012)
21. ELTISplus: Guidelines: Developing and Implementing a Sustainable Urban Mobility Plan (2014)
22. Aparicio, A.: Assessing public involvement effectiveness in long-term planning. In: Paper Submitted for Presentation and Publication the 86th Annual Meeting of the Transportation Research Board, January (2007)

23. Ballantyne, E.E.F., Lindholm, M., Whiteing, A.: A comparative study of urban freight transport planning: addressing stakeholder needs. J. Transp. Geogr. **32**, 93–101 (2013). https://doi.org/10.1016/j.jtrangeo.2013.08.013

24. Le Pira, M., Ignaccolo, M., Inturri, G., Pluchino, A., Rapisarda, A.: Modelling stakeholder participation in transport planning. Case Stud. Transp. Policy **4**, 230–238 (2016)

25. Gardener, J., Rachlin, R., Sweeny, A.: Handbook of Strategic Planning. Wiley, New York (2008)

26. GUIDEMAPS: Successful transport decision-making - a project management and stakeholder engagement handbook (2004). https://civitas.eu/content/guidemaps-successful-transport-decision-making-project-management-and-stakeholder-engagement. Accessed 14 Feb 2020

27. Dietz, T., Stern, P.C.: Public Participation in Environmental Assessment and Decision-Making. The National Academies Press, Washington, DC (2008)

28. Ward, D.: Stakeholder involvement in transport planning: participation and power. Impact Assess. Project Appraisal **19**, 119–130 (2001)

29. Buhrmann, S., et al.: Users and implementers of innovative concepts. Stakeholder analysis and recommendations for uptake (2009)

30. CIVITAS: Involving stakeholders: toolkit on organizing successful consultations (2009)

31. Quick, K.S., Narváez, G.E., Saunoi-Sandgren, E.: Changing minds through deliberation: citizens' accounts of their changing local transportation policy. TRB 94th Annual Meeting Compendium of Papers, Washington, DC 20001, United States (2015)

32. SMILE. https://smile.adrioninterreg.eu/. Accessed 14 Feb 2020

33. SMART COMMUTING. https://www.interreg-central.eu/Cotent.Node/SMART-COMMUTING.html. Accessed 14 Feb 2020

34. Cavallaro, F., Danielis, R., Nocera, S., Rotaris, L.: Should BEVs be subsidized or taxed? A European perspective based on the economic value of CO2 emissions. Transp. Res. Part D Transp. Environ. **64**, 70–89 (2018)

35. Nocera, S., Ruiz-Alarcón, Q.C., Cavallaro, F.: Assessing carbon emissions from road transport through traffic flow estimators. Transp. Res. Part C Emerg. Technol. **95**, 125–148 (2018)

36. Cavallaro, F., Giaretta, F., Nocera, S.: The potential of road pricing schemes to reduce carbon emissions. Transp. Policy **67**, 85–92 (2018)

37. Nocera, S., Cavallaro, F.: Economic evaluation of future carbon impacts on the Italian highways. Procedia Soc. Behav. Sci. **54**, 1360–1369 (2012)

38. Nocera, S., Tonin, S.: A joint probability density function for reducing the uncertainty of marginal social cost of carbon evaluation in transport planning. In: de Sousa, J.F., Rossi, R. (eds.) Computer-based Modelling and Optimization in Transportation. AISC, vol. 262, pp. 113–126. Springer, Cham (2014). https://doi.org/10.1007/978-3-319-04630-3_9

39. Nocera, S., Irranca Galati, O., Cavallaro, F.: On the uncertainty in the economic evaluation of carbon emissions from transport. J. Transp. Econ. Policy **52–1**, 68–94 (2018)

A Preliminary Investigation of Machine Learning Approaches for Mobility Monitoring from Smartphone Data

Claudio Gallicchio[1] [ID], Alessio Micheli[1] [ID],
Massimiliano Petri[2([⊠])] [ID], and Antonio Pratelli[2]

[1] Department of Computer Science, University of Pisa, Pisa, Italy
{gallicch, micheli}@di.unipi.it
[2] Department of Industrial and Civil Engineering, University of Pisa, Pisa, Italy
{m.petri, a.pratelli}@ing.unipi.it

Abstract. In this work we investigate the use of machine learning models for the management and monitoring of sustainable mobility, with particular reference to the transport mode recognition. The specific aim is to automatize the detection of the user's means of transport among those considered in the data collected with an App installed on the users smartphones, i.e. bicycle, bus, train, car, motorbike, pedestrian locomotion. Preliminary results show the potentiality of the analysis for the introduction of reliable advanced, machine learning based, monitoring systems for sustainable mobility.

Keywords: Sustainable mobility · Machine Learning · Transport mode recognition

1 Introduction

The results of the GOOD_GO platform testing application made in Leghorn Municipality show how the union of its disincentive system for bike theft with the sustainable mobility rewarding system are able of attracting citizens to the use of the APP, providing an important flywheel to encourage sustainable mobility and for bottom-up and low-cost monitoring of daily movements and the impacts of mobility actions implemented by city administrations.

Results also indicated some critical points of the platform, in particular the following elements:

- many users forget to start the movement monitoring and to indicate the mode of transport used inside the GOOD_GO App for smartphone;
- the stolen bicycles detection system is excessively expensive and requires more automation;
- despite the advantage of the very low cost, RFid passive tags are affected by the metal noise of nearby bicycles, significantly disturbing radio frequency messages.

In this paper we describe a way to address the first critical point by investigating the use of Artificial Intelligence, and in particular of Machine Learning, approaches to the

O. Gervasi et al. (Eds.): ICCSA 2020, LNCS 12250, pp. 218–227, 2020.
https://doi.org/10.1007/978-3-030-58802-1_16

management and monitoring of sustainable mobility. The aim is to automatize the recognition of the user's means of transport among those considered in the data collected with the current application (GOOD_GO smartphone App), namely: bicycle (bike), bus, train, car, motorbike, and pedestrian locomotion (foot). In order to develop an automatic detection system, a series of activities have been pursued, in relation to: data acquisition and pre-processing for mobility purposes, formulation of the computational task in the Machine Learning context, selection of input features and of learning models, analysis of the results.

The rest of this paper is structured as follows. In Sect. 2 we introduce the innovative features of the GOOD_GO system and its links to rewards and anti-theft systems. In Sect. 3 we describe the adopted methodologies for estimation of the transport mode from smartphone gathered streams of data, focusing on the required pre-processing steps and on the phases of data and learning models selection. The results of our experimental analysis are given in Sect. 4. Finally, in Sect. 5 we delineate conclusions and future perspectives of our work.

2   The GOOD_GO System

Briefly, here, the whole GOOD_GO sustainable mobility platform and its related SaveMyBike system is presented, remanding readers to other papers where its framework is described in more detail [1–4]. Moreover, we present some data relative to the prototypical test already done involving about one thousand inhabitants of Leghorn Municipality in the end of 2018.

The Good_Go Platform is a 'space of services' for sustainable mobility users linked to ITS sensors and an ICT social platform capable of:

- monitoring bicycle trips and all the other transport modes by using an APP for smartphone;
- creating secure areas for private bike parking;
- finding stolen bicycles;
- rewarding people who perform sustainable trips in the city;
- organizing sustainable mobility competition at different scale level (whole city, institutional system like hospital, university or single company/school).

The platform, by means of the previous presented services, tries to develop features able to attract the interest of citizen in the use of the App and so able to build a significative population sample (at low-cost respect to other data acquisition method like the use of ITS) with the relative trips data. The open source nature of the platform follows the same criteria of low-cost monitoring system, with the possibility to use the code and the App without any license and, then, enabling the mobility monitoring also for little-medium municipalities where financial resources for expensive ITS system are not available.

The testing application done for 4 months in the end of 2018 has showed a great appeal for citizen because in only one week we reached the maximum number of participants (for the prototypical application) of one thousands subscribers to the

GOOD_GO app. In the application more than 1.500 trips were collected along with all information regarding transport modes, emissions, cost and health indices (see Fig. 1).

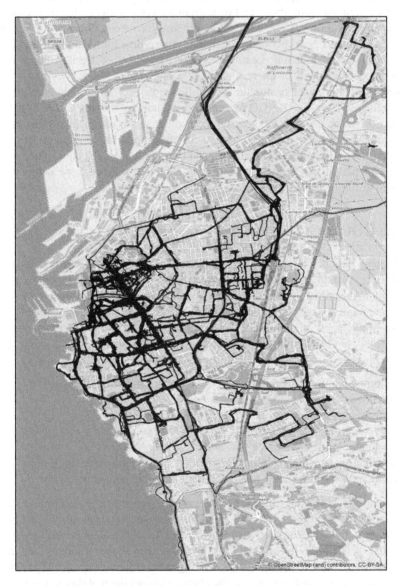

Fig. 1. Monitored trips in the Leghorn testing case.

The App, at the moment, has a section where users need to indicate manually the transport mode (see Fig. 2). In this way, the manual insertion of the transport modes with the tracking by a non-automatic start and end becomes an element of weakness of the system as it introduces possible errors due to following facts:

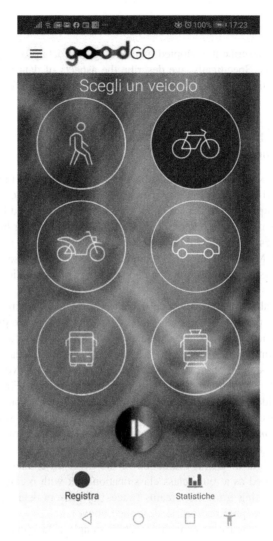

Fig. 2. The form of the smartphone App where to start and stop tracking, selecting the transport mode used.

- the user can forget to start or stop the tracking;
- the user can forget to change transport mode in intermodal trips;
- the user can insert wrong transport mode trying to collect a greater number of points for the reward system (even if there are, however, empirical rules useful to identify these erroneous data entries).

3 Methods

In this section, we describe the adopted methodology for data processing and setup of the learning models. Specifically, we describe the aspects of data pre-processing and learning task definition in Sect. 3.1, while in Sect. 3.2 we focus on feature and learning models selection.

3.1 Data Acquisition, Pre-processing and Formulation of the Computational Learning Task

A careful analysis of the data collected from the users registered to the system through the App developed in the project was necessary. The data were critical in terms of uniformity of sampling, number of available samples for the different means of transport, missing data, significance of the available features (attributes), as well as noise of the samples. While the last two characteristics are common to applications that require the use of Machine Learning methods, and motivate its use, the former have required pre-processing operations that include filtering and imputation (replacement of values).

The input variables include 3D accelerometers, pressure, proximity, speed, longitude, latitude, roll, pitch, bearing, and lumen. In particular, the pre-processing operations applied to each input variable were the following: (a) uniform resampling at constant 1 s resolution, i.e., 1 Hz; (b) filling of NaN (not available) values using padding with the last valid observation; (c) filtering using moving average over periods of 1 min; and (d) uniform resampling at constant 1 min resolution. Finally, to create the inputs to be provided to the Machine Learning models, for each input sequence we extracted 3 features for each input variable, namely *average* (avg), *standard deviation* (std), and *maximum value* (max). The feature extraction in the considered form has allowed the analysis through a set of Machine Learning approaches for vector data (see Sect. 3.2), in the light of a first evaluation of the involved challenges. The learning problem is configured as a multi-class classification task with 6 classes, one for each transport mode, starting from the streams (traces) of sensors data extracted from the smartphone App (and preprocessed as described above).

Overall, the extracted dataset includes 2636 samples, 33 input variables, plus 1 target class variable that encodes the transport medium.

A significant and critical aspect in the present dataset is the strong unbalance of the classes present, i.e. the sequences recorded for each type of transport mode. As shown in Fig. 3, the vast majority of the data pertains to the bike transport mode ($\approx$82%), followed by foot ($\approx$8%) and bus ($\approx$7%), while train and car modes of transportation both represents $\approx$1% of the available data. Only 12 samples for motorbike transportation are available (less than 1% of the data). To counteract the effects of this imbalance in the available data, resampling policies (oversampling) have been considered. Also in consideration of these aspects, the assessment of the learning models' performance was conducted by using both multi-class accuracy (on the 6 classes), and macro F1 score, as follows:

$$accuracy = \frac{\sum_{i=1,\ldots,6} tp_i}{\sum_{i=1,\ldots,6} N_i},$$

$$F1 = 2\frac{precision_{av}\ recall_{av}}{precision_{av} + recall_{av}},$$

where tp_i indicates the number of true positives for the i-th class, N_i is the total number of samples pertaining to the i-th class, $precision_{av}$ and $recall_{av}$ respectively denote the precision and the recall measures, macro-averaged among the classes.

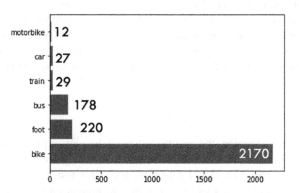

Fig. 3. Available samples for each transport mode.

3.2   Selection of Models and Features

In consideration of the peculiarity of the available data, and to favor the simplicity of the system, the considered approach has been based on the use of features extracted on whole sequences (recorded temporal traces), as described above in Sect. 3.1. Data was divided into a training (or development) set and an external test set (unseen during model calibration phase), according to a stratified 80%–20% split.

We explored different version of the learning tasks, originated from different feature selection policies on the available data. Specifically, we analyzed the following three configurations: (a) *full features*, in which all the input features (processed as described in Sect. 3.1) were considered; (b) *selected features*, comprising the 10 features that were found to be maximally correlated (in absolute value) with the target variable (i.e., max, avg and std of device bearing, max, avg and std of speed, max lumen, std pressure, avg X-accelerometer, and std Z-accelerometer); (c) *ad-hoc features*, where a minimal set of features were selected based on an a-priori presumable significance (i.e., max speed and std on the 3D accelerometers).

In our preliminary experimental analysis, we considered a set of classification models comprising different methodologies, including feed-forward Neural Networks, instantiated as Multi-layer Perceptrons (MLPs) with 1 or 2 hidden layers [5], Random Forest (RF) [6], and K-Nearest Neighbors (K-NN) [7]. All of these learning models were evaluated on all the data configuration described above, i.e. full features, selected features, and ad-hoc features. The software library (scikit-learn) is publicly available [8].

The hyper-parameters of each learning model were optimized (individually for each model) on a nested level of stratified 5-fold cross validation on the training (development) split, using grid search. In particular, for MLP with 1 hidden layer, i.e. MLP-1, we explored values of the hidden layer's size (number of units) in $\{10, 50, 100, 500\}$. For MLPs with 2 hidden layers, i.e. MLP-2, we explored cases the 2 hidden layers had the same size, varying in $\{10, 50, 100, 500\}$. For RF, we explored configurations with a number of estimators (decision trees) in $\{10, 20, 50, 100, 200, 500\}$. For K-NN, we explored the size K of the neighborhood in $\{3, 5, 10, 50, 100\}$. All other hyper-parameters were set to the default values, using the scikit-learn library [8].

4   Results

In this section, we describe the results achieved by our experimental analysis. In consideration of the fact that the available dataset is heavily imbalanced, the macro F1 score was used at phase of model selection, while for test assessment we used the accuracy, on order to have a score that is closer to human understanding.

The achieved results are reported in Table 1, which shows the validation and test performance achieved by MLP-1, MLP-2, RF and K-NN on the three dataset configurations considered (i.e., full features, selected features, ad-hoc features).

Within the limits of the preliminary investigation targeted in this work, the results appear to be very good, with the best models having F1 values and accuracy greater than 0.9 on both validation and external test data. Overall, the best result is achieved by RF in the case of full features configuration, reaching 0.904 of F1 score on validation, 1.00 accuracy on training, and 0.919 accuracy on test. We can also observe that, in general, the higher performance is obtained in the full features configuration, with a gentle reduction in correspondence of the cases of selected features and ad-hoc features configurations. This indicates that the quality of the estimation does not degrade dramatically when a smaller set of input sources is available to the system.

The performance of the best overall model (RF with full features) is further analyzed in Fig. 4, which shows the corresponding confusion matrix on the test set. It is evident to see that the model achieves high accuracy especially on the 3 classes that are sufficiently sampled, i.e. foot, bike and bus. The performance is lower in correspondence of the under-sampled classes, i.e. motorbike, car and train which have 1% of the data compared to the bike class alone, and on which therefore also the test estimation is much less statistically significant.

Table 1. Results achieved on all the dataset configurations by the considered learning models. Best results are highlighted in bold font.

Model	Features	Validation F1-score	Test accuracy
MLP-1	*full*	0.600	0.748
MLP-1	*selected*	0.426	0.608
MLP-1	*ad-hoc*	0.455	0.689
MLP-2	*full*	0.688	0.828
MLP-2	*selected*	0.549	0.773
MLP-2	*ad-hoc*	0.578	0.710
RF	*full*	**0.904**	**0.919**
RF	*selected*	0.902	0.903
RF	*ad-hoc*	0.858	0.814
K-NN	*full*	0.542	0.813
K-NN	*selected*	0.545	0.777
K-NN	*ad-hoc*	0.521	0.754

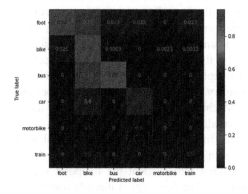

Fig. 4. Confusion matrix for RF, computed on the test set.

Having covered with significantly high values the accuracy for the three main transportation modes where sampling was sufficient for calibration and testing (i.e. bike, bus and foot), the system has shown its potentiality and its flexibility in this context. In addition, confusion matrices of other learning models, such as those based on neural networks, showed a better behavior than RF in some cases confined to specific classes. For example, in Fig. 5 we show the confusion matrix for MLP-1 with full features, from which we can see a gain, in comparison to RF in Fig. 4, on the transportation modes of foot, bus and motorbike. This consideration puts forward further enhancing potentialities in relation to investigations of the interplay between different learning models.

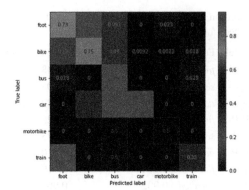

Fig. 5. Confusion matrix for MLP-1, computed on the test set.

5   Conclusions and Perspectives

In this paper we have presented a preliminary experimental analysis of the application of Machine Learning methodologies to the problem of estimating human transportation mode from smartphone sensors. The achieved results were significant. In view of the peculiarities of the data, the overall external test accuracy over 90% represents a positive aspect. The performance scales with the number of samples in the classes, independently of the learning models used. This indicates as a possible line of broadening of the study, the continuation of a data collection, with a focus on the classes that were less sampled so far (i.e., non-cycling vehicles).

Finally, the preliminary research presented in this paper opens the way to further studies also from a Machine Learning perspective. In this regard, an interesting direction consists in conducting a more in-depth cross-validation of the learning models. Another relevant line would be to extend the analysis to learning models for time series, e.g. Recurrent Neural Networks [9] (or hybrid neural architectures), enabling to naturally taking into account the temporal nature of the mobility data involved in the predictions. The final aim is that of contributing to the creation of an advanced and reliable human monitoring system for sustainable mobility. Moreover, monitored data, in the future, will be geoprocessed with data coming from other sources (health or metereologicaldata, land use data [10], data coming from ITS located in the city [11] or data regarding urban and building/activities field) so to extract further important knowledge elements useful for decision support system.

References

1. Petri, M., Frosolini, M., Lupi, M., Pratelli, A.: ITS to change behaviour: a focus about bike mobility monitoring and incentive—the SaveMyBike system. In: 2016 IEEE 16th International Conference on Environment and Electrical Engineering (EEEIC), pp. 1–6. IEEE, June 2016
2. Pratelli, A., Petri, M., Farina, A., Lupi, M.: Improving bicycle mobility in urban areas through ITS technologies: the SaveMyBike project. In: Sierpiński, G. (ed.) TSTP 2017. AISC, vol. 631, pp. 219–227. Springer, Cham (2018). https://doi.org/10.1007/978-3-319-62316-0_18

3. Petri, M., Pratelli, A.: SaveMyBike – a complete platform to promote sustainable mobility. In: Misra, S., et al. (eds.) ICCSA 2019. LNCS, vol. 11620, pp. 177–190. Springer, Cham (2019). https://doi.org/10.1007/978-3-030-24296-1_16
4. Pratelli, A., Petri, M., Farina, A., Souleyrette, R.R.: Improving sustainable mobility through Modal rewarding: the GOOD_GO smart platform. In: Proceeding of the 6th International Conference on Mechanical and Transportation Engineering (ICMTE 2020) (2020, in publication)
5. Haykin, S.: Neural Networks and Learning Machines, 3rd edn. Prentice Hall, Upper Saddle River (2009)
6. Breiman, L.: Random forests. Mach. Learn. **45**(1), 5–32 (2001)
7. Cover, T., Hart, P.: Nearest neighbor pattern classification. IEEE Trans. Inf. Theory **13**(1), 21–27 (1967)
8. Pedregosa, F., et al.: Scikit-learn: machine learning in python. J. Mach. Learn. Res. **12**(Oct), 2825–2830 (2011)
9. Kolen, J.F., Kremer, S.C. (eds.): A Field Guide to Dynamical Recurrent Networks. Wiley, Hoboken (2001)
10. Petri, M., Pratelli, A., Barè, G., Piccini, L.: A land use and transport interaction model for the greater florence metropolitan area. In: Misra, S., et al. (eds.) ICCSA 2019. LNCS, vol. 11620, pp. 231–246. Springer, Cham (2019). https://doi.org/10.1007/978-3-030-24296-1_20
11. Pratelli, A., Petri, M., Ierpi, M., Di Matteo, M.: Integration of bluetooth, vehicle count data and trasport model results by means of datamining techniques. In: 2018 IEEE International Conference on Environment and Electrical Engineering and 2018 IEEE Industrial and Commercial Power Systems Europe (EEEIC/I&CPS Europe), pp. 1–6. IEEE, June 2018

GOOD_GO: An Open-Source Platform to Incentive Urban Sustainable Mobility

Simone Giannecchini[1], Paolo Nepa[2], Alessio Rofi[3],
Massimiliano Petri[4(✉)] [iD], and Antonio Pratelli[4]

[1] Geosolutions s.a.s., Montramito, Italy
[2] Department of Information Engineering, University of Pisa, Pisa, Italy
[3] IDNova s.r.l., Treviso, Italy
[4] Department of Civil and Industrial Engineering, University of Pisa, Pisa, Italy
m.petri@ing.unipi.it

Abstract. Good_Go is the first complete platform to incentive urban sustainable mobility. It contains different modules to incentive use of sustainable mobility like foot, bike, bus or innovative sharing solutions (car-pooling, car-sharing, bike-sharing and others). A first module of the platform is linked to a bike-theft disincentive system with the innovative Bluetooth OBU (On-Board-Unit) called BlueBI able to send an acoustic alarm in case of theft and allowing a participative finding of stolen bikes. A second module is linked to a rewarding platform while a third module allow to organize Mobility Management measures or sustainable mobility competition at different scale level (whole city, institutional system like hospital, university or single company/school).

Keywords: Sustainable mobility · Bluetooth sensors · Mobility management · Rewards · Incentives

1 Introduction

Private car mobility registers a high accident rate: in 2014 it was responsible for over 25,000 fatalities in the EU-28. In addition, in 2014 in the EU-28, around 70% of the overall CO_2 emissions from transport were generated by road mode% [1]. Moreover, in urban areas they occur 38% of the overall fatalities from road transport, and 23% of the overall CO_2 emissions [2]. As a result, a modal shift of at least a part of passenger transport in urban areas, from private car to sustainable transport systems is desirable. Several policies have been adopted in the EU in this direction [3]. Moreover, bike-sharing solutions has a high maintenance costs and, especially in medium size cities, this limits its application.

The Good_Go Platform is the development of the initially called SaveMyBike project, the project that has been developed in order to improve, at first, the private bike mobility [4, 5]. In fact, now, the whole project regards the development of a 'space of services' for sustainable mobility users linked to a second stage of ITS sensors and an ICT social platform called GOOD_GO capable of:

O. Gervasi et al. (Eds.): ICCSA 2020, LNCS 12250, pp. 228–238, 2020.
https://doi.org/10.1007/978-3-030-58802-1_17

- monitoring systematically bicycle trips and all the other transport modes by using an APP for smartphone (inherited from SaveMybike project);
- creating secure areas for private bike parking (developed effectively in Good_Go platform);
- finding stolen bicycles (developed in the final version in Good_Go platform);
- rewarding people who perform sustainable trips in the city (developed in the final version in Good_Go platform);
- organizing sustainable mobility competition at different scale level (whole city, institutional system like hospital, university or single company/school) (developed exclusively in Good_Go platform).

In the following paragraph, leaving an in-depth analysis and description of reward strategies and their state of the art at [6], we present the general Good_Go platform framework and its last developments. Finally, some future developments are described.

2 The General Good_Go Framework

The general idea is to join service for private bikes (and in the future other modes) with a social rewarding platform, called GOOD_GO, to increase sustainable mobility in the city. Then, it integrates hardware and software development with innovative measures regarding transport demand management and, mainly, with rewarding measures.

Firstly, the platform takes data mainly from an app for smartphone that integrates a service for private bikes, based on two types of low-cost equipment, installed on private bikes or on sharing-mobility solutions:

- A first solutions based on RFid/NFC passive tag installed both inside the bike than outside of it. It allows the identification of the bike legitimate owner and its registration in the national bike registry. This system tries to avoid the cycle of used bikes thefts and resale, allowing police-men to check the rightful owner of the bike, during the resale phase.
- A second solutions regards the introduction of a Bluetooth sensor containing an accelerometer allowing bikes theft discouraging and the development of "secure areas" where bicycles could be parked safely: if a bike is stolen, an alarm signal, directed to the bike owner, to all other platform clients and to the police, is activated with a local acoustic alarm; moreover, in case of theft, it is possible the 'participative' bicycle recovery.

Moreover, in order to increase the sustainable mobility 'incentive power', the platform develops a social space where people can: denounce the theft of their bike, post any information about events or any other news related to sustainable mobility and participate to a competition based on points collected from their daily trips monitoring.

In the following sections, after analysis of necessary requirements for a rewarding platform, the two new main parts of the system are described that's to say the new Bluetooth sensors and the rewarding and mobility management platform.

2.1   The Reasons for a Choice

Summarizing the results of the state of art analysis of the aforementioned existing projects [6], one can infer that:

- the mobile app is a fundamental tool for any sort of initiative in this field, whereas the web app should consist in the portal mainly aimed to manage the content provided by the service provider to the engaged community;
- the ICT system has to be able to ingest and process a relatively limited sort of data, related mainly to GPS tracks, but predisposed to provide a very wide range of feedbacks, based on relatively simple processing;
- the most appreciated products include decision support systems, at least for pro-visional services in deferred time.

Those previous experiences also taught that to attract more users and to be effective in changing mobility behavior with citizen categories different by age, interests and social classes, at least 3 elements are fundamental:

- to promote a multi-modal approach for daily mobility,
- to engage different type of "contributors", i.e. enterprises and service providers able to manage different sort of economic advantages, including discounts on goods, services and even local taxes,
- to propose the services using a gamification approach, and dominant link to social networking, environmental awareness, safety, health and wellbeing in general.

It is worthwhile to remind that, for an effective involvement of a contributor, either public or private entity, it is important first to analyze the real scope to satisfy by the ICT solution, in a win-win perspective for both the citizens user and the provider, as the platform success depends at the first by the resources the latter spent in its initial stages.

Good_Go mobility platform takes into account all previous features integrating both external systems by means of an API libraries, ensuring also a Single Sign-On (SSO) access control property. A diagrammatic representation of main components constituting the Good_Go platform is represented in Fig. 1.

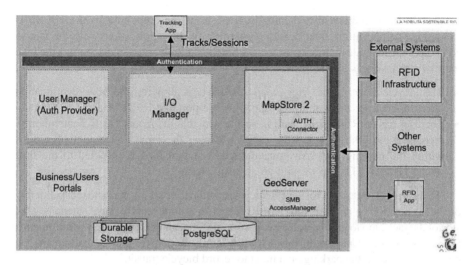

Fig. 1. Good_Go platform general framework

The main differences among Good_Go and the other Smart Mobility platforms, are:

- the platform is entirely developed and based on Open Source software;
- it will offer community based functions to help individuals to find back their bicycle in case of theft and, optionally, to register and integrate the RFID based anti-theft system specifically developed within the project;
- it allows to organize multiple competitions (see forward in the paper).

Citizen, after the registration to the web portal, will have access to the mobile app for the track record and monitoring. He will also be chance to save a personal profile including description and pictures of his own bicycles. On the base of mobility behavior, the user will gain badges allowing discount for public transport tickets or commercial goods. Once the user will reach an adequate badge amount will have chance to request an offered discount, or to accumulate more badges to access at a superior discount level.

2.2   RFID Final Solution

In case of bike theft, the user can immediately send a geocoded notice with all description and pictures of his bike he previously registered. The members of Good_Go community will have the possibility to reply it in case of retrieval, giving the position and a short note. In case the user is using also the RFID anti-theft system, the RFID code is marked in a "blacklist" and notified also to local authorities which are provided with a RFID reader able to detect and recognize the stolen bike during their routine activities. Also in this case, the bicycle owner will be automatically notified in case of retrieval. According to the level of publication chosen by the user, his history can be shared with friends and public, for a community contest regarding km run wealthy and contribution to air pollution reduction.

The RFid solution analyzed initially consists of the employment of UHF-RFID technology to realize an identification system in cycling applications with the aim to contemporary manage multiple bicycles within the parking area. To discourage the bike theft two shrewdness are adopted:

- The bicycle is equipped with passive RFID tags allowing the bike identification after a theft from an operator equipped with a portable RFID reader.
- The user has an RFID smart card in such a way that the reader has to contemporary recognize the bike tags and the user tag during the input and output operations within the parking area. Any unauthorized removal may be notified to the bike owner GOOD_GO App or with an acoustic alarm.

To ensure tags detection for several bicycles within the parking area and independently on the tag position on the bike, the UHF-RFID reader is connected to panel antennas at the side of the rack, and to ground antennas (also named mat antennas), namely a thin antenna placed on the ground underneath the rack with a sturdy random (Fig. 2). A mat antenna can be also installed on the parking area input to record bicycle transit.

A preliminary experimental setup has been realized at the Department of Information Engineering of the University of Pisa where a five-seater bike parking area is available. Five bicycles have been tagged with multiple on-metal tags. In details, five Intermec IT65 tags have been employed. For the measurement campaign, the CAEN ION 4300P reader operating in UHF RFID (865–868 MHz) band has been employed [7] together with the CAEN WANTENNAX019 circularly polarized antenna. Such an antenna has been placed downward and 3.6 m apart from the ground (Fig. 3).

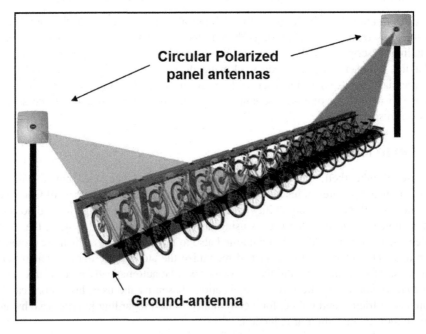

Fig. 2. UHF-RFID system with multiple panel antennas at the side of the rack and ground antenna underneath the rack

An input power of 28 dBm has been used. The bicycles have been placed 30 cm apart each other by occupying an area of about 4 m. The closer bike to the reader antenna is at a distance of about 4 m, while the farer bicycle is at about 6 m. The reader has been able to detect tags fixed on the first three bikes namely up to a distance less than 5 m. It has been noticed that the central section of the bicycle frame is a good installation position to ensure tag detection. Additional measurements have been carried out by using the CAEN R1240IE portable reader connected to a smartphone via Bluetooth, with the aim to verify the possibility of an operator to detect bikes during its daily working activity. The portable reader has been able to detect the bicycle tag at a distance of around

Fig. 3. Measurement setup illustration

1 m by employing an input power of 27 dBm. It is worth noting that the material of bicycle frames influenced measurements scenario (multipath phenomena).

For these last reasons, we decided to use only short range HF RFid solutions installed inside the bike and readable by policemen with an 'ad-hoc developed' telescopic antenna. This system tries to avoid the cycle of used bikes thefts and resale, allowing policemen to check the rightful owner of the bike, during the resale phase.

2.3   Bluetooth Solution

The prototypical application done in 2018 in Leghorn shows the difficulty to involve stakeholders in the recovery of stolen bikes using a RFid reader that is expensive and require too much attention to people (difficult to remember to bring it and to recharge practically every day).

Then, next solutions developed is a Bluetooth active sensor merged with an accelerometer and with an acoustic, bright alarm and talking with a smartphone becoming a real OBU-On Board Unit for bikes (see Fig. 4). Using the Good_Go app people can leave its bike in a parking phase during which, if someone moves it from the starting position, it emits a luminous and acoustic alarm. Moreover, the Bluetooth send a message of alarm readable from all other users with the Good_Go App installed. In this way, every user is a 'city floating reader' and allows to a participatory bike recovery.

One time a user read a stolen bike message, it sends the correct position by means of the Smartphone GPS to the system and, subsequently, to the original bike owner.

Fig. 4. The Bluetooth sensor and an example of its installation on a bike

The sensors has been tested in different positions so to verify the possibility to mount it in different place on the bike and to understand how far from the smartphone it is readable. Figure 5 shows that the signal measured with the RSSI - Received Signal Strength Indicator (dBm) value is good up to 80 m (minimum sensibility is 100 DBm). Moreover, the sensors has been tested with different Smartphone types (Android, IoS) and the value in the graph are the mean relieved for each distance. Results shows that with at least some thousands of users it is possible to cover all urban areas. Figure 6 show the area covered from the 300 Good_Go users Bluetooth in the city of Leghorn during the testing application.

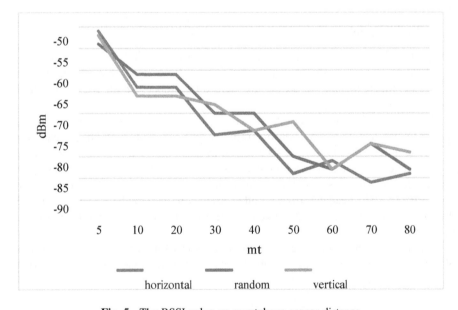

Fig. 5. The RSSI value vs smartphone-sensor distance

Fig. 6. The Bluetooth area covered from 300 users in Leghorn testing application

2.4 Rewarding and Mobility Management Platform

At the level of rewarding policies, the goal of the platform is to develop a real multi-modal reward management system [8, 9], ables to introduce several incentive systems for sustainable mobility, based on the following:

- punctual measures (e.g. reward for crossing given road sections);
- linear measures (e.g. reward for travelling along given roads);
- areal-based measures (e.g. rewards for parking or travelling in a specific area).

All these incentive systems can differ in the level of rewards/credits provided, and can vary according to the time of day, the travel direction (in-out), the journey performed, the type of vehicle, etc. [10].

The general idea is to develop an open system, where each public administration can set up their own rewarding strategies, with the help of stakeholders they consider important for the outcome of their measures/actions.

In addition, the choice of the prototypal application carried out in the city of Leghorn (Italy), arises from the need to simplify and study a prototype easily replicable in other urban realities, even in the search for potential users. Actually, it is not always possible: to obtain a collection of user license plates, from which a list of commuters can be extracted or to have the resources to make interviews at a population sample.

In our case, we have set up a multimodal connection, using the API library, between the platform, the local public transport system and also new sharing mobility systems (like car-pooling, car-sharing, bike-sharing and others). So, every type of sustainable mobility can be joined with the rewarding policies. Moreover, Good_Go implements a multiple-scale competition level with the possibility to organize competition at whole city level (like the one for general citizen sustainable mobility), at institutional system level like a competition for the whole hospital or university system or single competition at individual company/school level. Figure 7 shows the four actual on-going sustainable mobility competition in the Good_Go app with the following form allowing the subscription for one of them. The competitions regard:

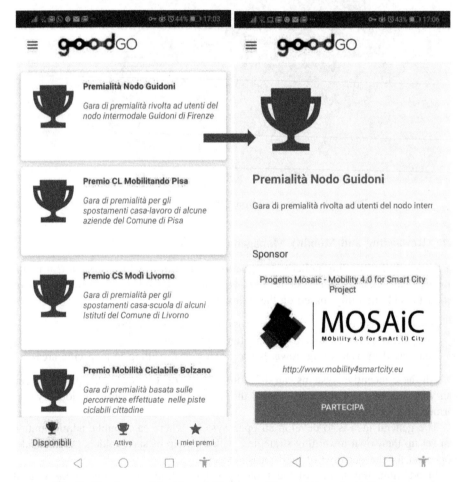

Fig. 7. The four sustainable mobility competition and the subscription form

- a multimodal node of Florence (Italy) transport network (Guidoni is a node where arrive Tram, Bus and there is a big parking area to leave cars);
- an Home-to-Work competition for the city of Pisa (Italy);
- an Home-to-School competition in Leghorn (Italy)
- a bike use only competition for Bolzano (Italy).

Moreover, it has been developed a dashboard to manage the withdrawal of awards for each competition, allowing the subscription of many types of urban shops and companies. These activities can offer discount and free products taking advantage of the advertising provided by the platform itself. In this way, an interesting reward is offered to everyone, with a high level of reward personalization leaving the award system simplified as much as possible and making it easier its broadcasting to citizens and companies.

3   Future Developments

The future development of the project consists of the completion of the multimodal platform with the possibility of setting up rewarding strategies by the administrations, reconstructing a real visual language/wizard to set and customize the rewarding policies. This multimodal system will be linked to a MarketPlace with an increase in the economic viability of the project as the companies subscribed will pay an annual fee (similar to the Nuride system).

In addition, a real and proper wizard will be implemented, for the guided upload of the data about the urban reality under consideration: a very important step for the sustainability of the project. In fact, all existing and tested systems are, currently, valid only for single realities and do not contain automatic setup elements for their application to other cities. Within this development, they will be integrated a system able: to monitor transport modes chosen to perform the displacements, and to analyze their possible replacements with more sustainable transport modes, in order to activate the related rule like a Travel FeedBack Program.

The reward provider, i.e. the local transportation service enterprise, will have access to a specific section of Good_Go portal, in order to manage and publish their discount campaign. This specific content management web tool will allow to easily manage the value for money of the discount and the categories of user that will have access to each offer, according to their profile and mobility habits, other than the offer expiration. Moreover, they will chance to monitor in a dashboard basic result of track data processing and aggregation, useful to improve their service offer and timetable, as such as follow the evolution of habits changes within the community engaged in the initiative. For this last point we will integrate Machine Learning tools able to extract mobility patterns and useful to support Public Administrations decisions [11] also integrating mobility data with data becoming from local urban environment [12].

References

1. European Commission, Statistical pocketbook 2016. https://ec.eu-ropa.eu/transport/facts-fundings/statistics/pocketbook-2016_en
2. European Commission, 2013. Communication from the Commission to the European Parliament, the Council, the European economic and social committee and the committee of the regions, COM(2013)913, Bruxelles (2013)
3. Petri, M., Frosolini, M., Pratelli, A., Lupi, M.: ITS to change behaviour: a focus about bike mobility monitoring and incentive - the SaveMyBike system. In: EEEIC 2016 - International Conference on Environment and Electrical Engineering (2016)
4. Pratelli, A., Petri, M., Farina, A., Lupi, M.: Improving bicycle mobility in urban areas through ITS technologies: the SaveMyBike project. In: Sierpiński, G. (ed.) TSTP 2017. AISC, vol. 631, pp. 219–227. Springer, Cham (2018). https://doi.org/10.1007/978-3-319-62316-0_18
5. Petri, M., Pratelli, A.: SaveMyBike – a complete platform to promote sustainable mobility. In: Misra, S., et al. (eds.) ICCSA 2019. LNCS, vol. 11620, pp. 177–190. Springer, Cham (2019). https://doi.org/10.1007/978-3-030-24296-1_16
6. Pratelli, A., Petri, M., Farina, A., Souleyrette, R.R.: Improving sustainable mobility through modal rewarding: the GOOD_GO smart platform. In: Proceeding of the 6th International Conference on Mechanical and Transportation Engineering (ICMTE 2020) (in publication, 2020)
7. Michel, A., Caso, R., Buffi, A., Nepa, P., Isola, G.: Meandered TWAs array for near-field UHF RFID applications. IET Electron. Lett. **50**(1), 17–18 (2014)
8. Ettema, D., Verhoef, E.: Using rewards as a traffic management tool: behavioural effects of reward strategies. In: Proceedings of the 11th International Conference on Travel Behavior Research, Kyoto, 16–20 August 2006 (2006)
9. Bresciani, C., Colorni, A., Lia, F., Luè, A., Nocerino, R.: Behavioural change and social innovation through reward: an integrated engagement system for personal mobility, urban logistics and housing efficiency. In: Proceedings of the 6th Transportation Research Arena, 18–21 April 2016 (2016)
10. Tertoolen, G., van Kreveld, D., Verstraten, B.: Psychological resistance against attempts to reduce private car use. Transp. Res. Part A: Policy Pract. **32**(3), 171–181 (1998)
11. Petri, M., Pratelli, A., Barè, G., Piccini, L.: A land use and transport interaction model for the greater florence metropolitan area. In: Misra, S., et al. (eds.) ICCSA 2019. LNCS, vol. 11620, pp. 231–246. Springer, Cham (2019). https://doi.org/10.1007/978-3-030-24296-1_20
12. Pratelli, A., Petri, M., Ierpi, M.: Integration of bluetooth, vehicle count data and trasport model results by means of datamining techniques. In: The Application to the Regional Highway S.G.C. Fi-Pi-Li linking Florence to Leghorn and Pisa, 1 Proceedings - 2018 IEEE International Conference on Environment and Electrical Engineering and 2018 IEEE Industrial and Commercial Power Systems Europe, EEEIC/I and CPS Europe (2018)

Development of a Tool for Control Loop Performance Assessment

Javier Jiménez-Cabas[1], Fabián Manrique-Morelos[2],
Farid Meléndez-Pertuz[1(✉)], Andrés Torres-Carvajal[1],
Jorge Cárdenas-Cabrera[1], Carlos Collazos-Morales[3],
and Ramón E. R. González[1,2,3]

[1] Departamento de Ciencias de la Computación y Electrónica,
Universidad de la Costa, Barranquilla, Colombia
fmelendel@cuc.edu.co
[2] Departamento de Innovación, Indutrónica del Caribe, Barranquilla, Colombia
[3] Vicerrectoría de Investigaciones,
Universidad Manuela Beltrán, Bogotá, Colombia

Abstract. This article describes the primary characteristics of a tool developed to perform a control loop performance assessment, named SELC due to its name in Spanish. With this tool, we expect to increase the reliability and efficiency of productive processes in Colombia's industry. A brief description of SELC's functionality and a literature review about the different techniques integrated is presented. Finally, the results and conclusions of the testing phase were presented, performed with both simulated and real data. The actual data comes from an online industrial repository provided by the South African Council for Automation and Control (SACAC).

Keywords: Control performance monitoring · Software · Control loop assessment · Control performance indices

1 Introduction

The need for reliable and effective control systems in the productive sectors of the industry has guided numerous investigations with a focus on the development of the monitoring and assessment of feedback control loop performance. The main objective in this field of research, also known as CPM, is to provide the operators and engineers of a plant the necessary information for determining whether the performance objectives and the desired characteristic response in the controlled process variables are being achieved [1–5].

Advances in literature and software development have been made in many countries like Japan, Brazil, and the USA [6], but remains a novelty in Colombia. Indutronica Del Caribe S.A.S., in collaboration with Colombia's Department of Science, Technology, and Innovation (COLCIENCIAS), decided to support the creation of a new tool to implement CPM in Colombia. This developed tool was named as Control Loop Assessment Software (SELC). Its primary purpose is to increase the operational robustness in industrial processes of the region and a novelty in Colombia.

© Springer Nature Switzerland AG 2020
O. Gervasi et al. (Eds.): ICCSA 2020, LNCS 12250, pp. 239–254, 2020.
https://doi.org/10.1007/978-3-030-58802-1_18

This paper's main objective is to present the methodologies followed in the development of this project and its results. In Sect. 2, we describe the proceedings followed, as well as the functional structure of the tool. Next, results of the tool's testing phase are presented in Sect. 3. Finally, Conclusions and possible aspects to improve are discussed in the conclusion section.

2   Methodology

To achieve the main objective of this project, four (4) methodological phases were defined. These are:

- Phase 1: Functional Architecture Design
- Phase 2: CPM Techniques Identification
- Phase 3: Algorithm Development
- Phase 4: Validation and Test Phase

2.1   Functional Architecture Design

In phase 1, the stages that, in general, constitute the control loop assessment process were defined, using as reference Jelali's book [2]:

- **Benchmark selection.** This step is concerned with the quantification of current performance and the selection of the benchmark against which the current control will be evaluated.
- **Assessment.** In this step, we search for classifying the controller according to its performance, determining whether the controller can be considered healthy or, on the contrary, whether there are corrections needed to be made.
- **Diagnosis.** When the analysis from the previous step indicates that the controller deviates from its desired performance, the causes for this must be identified, and the potential of improvement must be determined without disrupting the running system.
- **Improvement.** After isolating the causes of poor performance, corrective actions, and possible solutions should be suggested to improve system performance. Whether it is sufficient to re-tune, the controller must be determined and re-design or maintained the necessary loop components.

Each of these steps can be worked with different approaches and then properly integrated for a consistent performance monitoring strategy. The Control Loop Performance Software (SELC) developed to focus mainly on the implementation of the first three steps and provide the bases for the optimal implementation of the improvement step.

Figure 1 shows the different functional blocks and several techniques that the tool must possess, using as a base the stages previously identified. Besides the assessment and diagnosis step, a pre-processing step has been added to remove any unwanted trend or noise, or to adjust the data scaling [2], necessary for the validity of the results.

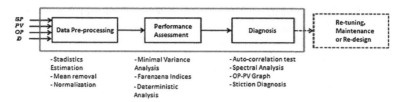

Fig. 1. Functional block for the developed tool.

Besides, performance assessment algorithms contain many options and parameters that the user has to specify. Due to this, the developed tool must provide each user with intuitive and simple access to the available functions and a way to input the necessary parameters. Also, results must be understandable and easy to read.

2.2 CPM Techniques Identification

As PID controllers are the most common type of controller in the local and national industry, chosen control loop assessment techniques for this type of loops were prioritized. To determine the methods to be implemented in the tool, the different criteria to be met by said techniques were established as followed [2]:

- **Non-Invasive:** The process must not interfere with the normal functioning of the plant nor require special tests for obtaining the necessary data.
- **Objective metrics:** The metric or standard must give an idea of the quality of the controller concerning a global standard.
- **Diagnosis Capacity:** Ideally, the results must provide clues about the possible causes of bad performance, as well as the required actions to be taken.
- **Independent of Set-Point changes and disturbances:** Given the number of set-points and perturbations present in each loop, it is desired to ensure the tools' independence on these variables for comparison purposes.
- **Easy Estimation:** preferably, the technique should not need extremely complex calculations or specific process knowledge, to avoid limitations in the application of the method in a real industrial case.

A literature review was performed to search for techniques for performance assessment and valve diagnosis that fulfill these requirements.

Performance Assessment. It was found that performance assessment methods are subdivided in two big families: Stochastic and Deterministic [7]. In general, stochastic methods can be applied with standard operation data and minimal process knowledge, but the information obtained may not be very conclusive. On the other hand, deterministic methods produce definitive metrics, with the disadvantage that the required data needs intrusive ways to get it.

In the stochastic category, we implemented the modification Harris index [8] proposed by Farenzena [9]. The signal is decomposed in three independent components: the time delay component, the control performance component, and the white noise component of the output. With this, we can define three new indices: The NOSI index, the DELI index, and the TUNI index, defined as shown in Eqs. (1–3). Notice that Harris index will be equal to 1 minus the TUNI index.

$$NOSI = \frac{\sigma^2(w_t)}{TSV} \tag{1}$$

$$DELI = \frac{\sigma^2(e_t)}{TSV} \tag{2}$$

$$TUNI = \frac{\sigma^2(g_t)}{TSV} \tag{3}$$

With these indices, it is possible to find which component is contributing the most to the total variance of the process, which facilitates the diagnosis process.

In addition, functionality was added to assess the response of a system against changes in the Set-Point. For this, the indices developed by Swanda and Seborg [10, 11] based on settling time were used.

Valve Diagnosis. To allow preliminary diagnosis, the following methods for valve stiction detection were integrated to the developed tool:

- **Spectral Analysis:** spectrograms can be a useful tool for the analysis of a signal in the frequency domain [12]. Spectral analysis can be useful for oscillation cycle identification in the output of a close system. These cycles can have different causes like wrong tuning, oscillatory disturbances, and actuators' problem.
- **PV vs. OP Graph:** PV vs. OP graph can be used for the diagnosis of valve problems, using pattern recognition [13] or ellipse fitting [14].
- **Kano-Maruta Method for stiction detection:** Kano et al. [15] presented a data-driven model for stiction detection. It is based on the observation that stiction causes the appearance of sections where the valve position does not change even though the controller output changes.
- **Curve fitting method:** He et al. [16] designed a method for stiction detection based on the shape that the signal takes after its first integrating component I a loop with stiction. The more triangular the signal's shape, the worst is the stiction degree.

2.3   SELC: Description of the Tool and Its Functions

After selecting the techniques to be implemented, the algorithm development phase started. In this phase, a programming platform was selected, and the code necessary for the tool operation was written. The chosen programming platform was Matlab due to the following reasons.

- A variety of functions and toolboxes.
- Simulink environment, a product for which there is no reasonable alternative yet.
- It is a compact platform: there is no need to install additional packages or IDLES.
- It is widely used in the scientific community

The tool was named: *"Control Loop Assessment Software"* or SELC because of its acronym in Spanish. Per the functional architecture, an accessible and intuitive graphic user interface was designed. Functions can be easily accessed from a menu found at the top of the tool. Besides, some features use an auxiliary window for improving visual performance.

The Control Loops Assessment Software (SELC) allows its users to evaluate a control system by using both stochastic and deterministic methods. It also provides the option to perform a simple system characterization by fitting either a FOPDT or SOPDT transfer function. This characterization is especially useful for obtaining the time delay necessary for both stochastic and deterministic analysis. Other functionalities include:

- **Data Pre-processing techniques,** such as scaling, mean removal, filtering, data sectioning, and sample time modification.
- **Signal Analysis Techniques,** such as spectral analysis, autocorrelation, and cross-correlation analysis, PV vs. OP graph, and stochastic and deterministic methods for loop performance.
- **Stiction Detection Techniques,** such as curve fitting, ellipse fitting, and Kano-Maruta Method.
- **Others:** Like the possibility to save the obtained results, report generation, graph and figure saving, parameter modification, among others.

For its correct functioning, the data must be introduced in a *comma-separated value* format, organized in 4 columns, where the values for time, process variable, controller output, and set-point must be introduced. A typical view of SELC's user interface with data loaded can be seen in Fig. 2.

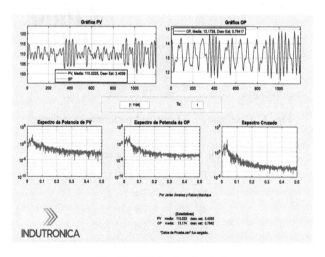

Fig. 2. SELC: data loaded.

3 Test Phase Results

In this section, we present the results of the different test cases used to evaluate the performance of the tool.

CASE STUDY I: Assessment indices estimation with step Setpoint change.
In the first scenario, we modeled a chemical reactor's temperature control loop using the one provided by Smith and Corripio [17, Ch. 9] as a reference. White Noise with power 10^{-B} was introduced to the system to determine the influence of noise in the system performance. The Set-point value for the process was initially set at 87.5 °C, with changes of 10 °C, −30 °C and 24 °C at the instant 100, 300, and 800-time units after the beginning of the simulation.

Once concluded the simulation, the error, defined as the difference between the set-point and the process variable, was calculated using the tool, as shown in Fig. 3. Using the error, the performance indices were calculated, which showed a significant impact of the time delay over the total variance of the process.

After this, a more focalized analysis was made by characterizing the system using the methods provided by the tool. A FOPDT transfer function was fitted to the process, with a goodness of fit of 90%. The parameters are shown in Table 1.

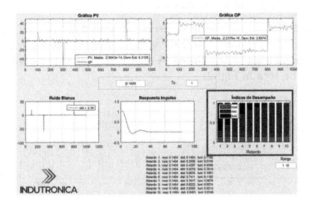

Fig. 3. Case study I – Error and performance indices.

Table 1. FOPDT parameters.

Parameters	Value
K_P	7.4
τ_P	7.5
t_0	3.6

With the estimated time delay, the performance indices are calculated again with the results shown in Table 2. It is, then, confirmed that the time delay is the main contributor over the total variance of the process. This result goes matches with Smith and Corripio's [17, Ch. 9] analysis of this process, where they suggest the need for a cascade controller in this system because of the slowness of a simple feedback control system.

Table 2. Case of study I: Performance indices for the estimated time delay.

Index	Value
NOSI	0.1404
DELI	0.6635
TUNI	0.1961

CASE STUDY II: Performance indices and relation with controller gain, time delay, and white noise.

Using Farenzena's experiments as a guideline [9], a test for the quantification of the influence of the controller gain, time delay, and white noise over the total variance of the process was designed. In the first test, the controller gain K_C was changed over a predefined range of values. The generated data were extracted, and the performance indices were calculated using the developed tool. In Fig. 4, it can be seen the plots of some of the datasets generated. A graph with the overall results is shown in Fig. 5. As can be seen, the TUNI index reports a high value when the controller is not able to respond adequately to changes in the process because of a small controller gain. The TUNI index reaches its minimum for a controller gain around 0.4%CO/%TO and then increases again because the system acquires an aggressive/oscillatory behavior. It can be concluded, then, that the TUNI index successfully captures the impact that the controller gain has over the whole process and that the developed tool is successful in estimating its value.

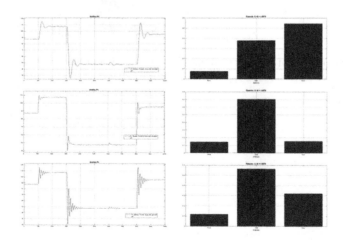

Fig. 4. Plots for some of the tests performed for quantification of the influence of Kc over performance indices. From Top to Bottom: Kc = 0.009, Kc = 0.42 and Kc = 0.72.

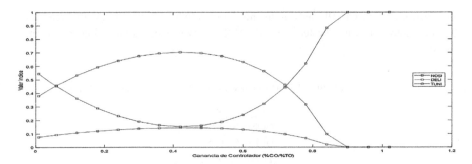

Fig. 5. Controller gains vs Performance indices.

Next, the white noise influence over the performance of the loop was estimated by repeatedly calculating Farenzena's indices for different values of the noise power B. Results show how the NOSI index quantifies the increment successfully in white noise in the system. However, the DELI index maintains its importance over all the tests because of the nature of the process. Plots for some of the tests performed are shown in Fig. 6, with its respective performance indices. A graph with the overall results is shown in Fig. 7.

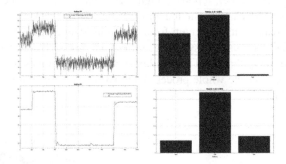

Fig. 6. Plots for some of the tests performed for quantification of the influence of white noise over performance indices. From Top to Bottom: B = −1, B = 2.

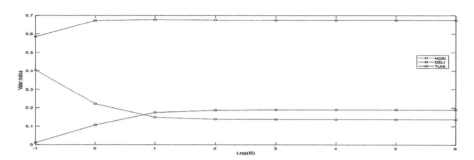

Fig. 7. B logarithm vs. performance indices.

Finally, a test was performed to quantify the influence of time delay on the total variance of the process. The FOPDT model fitted previously was used to generate the data for this test by repeatedly changing the time delay value t_0. Overall, it was shown that the DELI index successfully captures this variation, until the point where the controller is unable to respond adequately to the process, therefore causing instability captured by the TUNI index. The plots for some of the tests performed can be seen in Fig. 8. A graph with the overall results is shown Fig. 9.

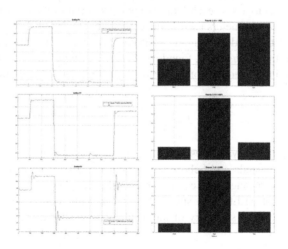

Fig. 8. Plots for some of the tests performed for quantification of the influence of time delay over performance indices. From Top to Bottom: t0 = 1, t0 = 3.75 and t0 = 6.

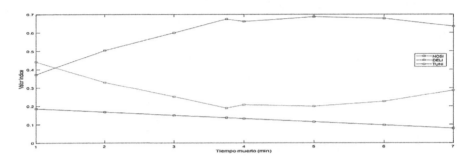

Fig. 9. Time delay vs. performance indices.

CASE STUDY III: Using the tool for Deterministic Controller Assessment based on Set-Point Response Data.

Tests were made for demonstrating the tool's ability to assess control loops systems using the performance indices developed by Swanda and Seborg [10, 11]. A stirred reactor was modeled in Simulink, using as a base the one found in Smith and Corripio's book [17, Ch. 13].

For this system, a set-point step change was programmed to occur at 15-time units, with two different sets of control parameters. The simulated output data was extracted, and SELC was used to assess each loop by the calculation of the deterministic indices. The different sets of parameters used in the case study are shown in Table 3. Set one is a modification of the model's original controller. Set two was obtained by using the optimization function *fminsearch*, found in *MATLAB's optimization toolbox*, using as a cost function the integrated absolute error of the output data concerning the Set-Point, shown in Eq. (4):

$$J = \int |SP - PV| dt \tag{4}$$

As expected, the analysis's results show that controller 2 has a better performance than controller 1. Swanda and Seborg's performance classes place controller 1 in the Excessively Sluggish range and controller 2 in the Fair Performance range. We can conclude, then, that SELC was successful in assessing both controllers using the deterministic analysis. A summary of the results can be shown in Fig. 10.

Table 3. Parameters for tests 1 and 2.

Controller 1	Controller 2
Kc = 1	Kc = 2
τi = 2.3	τi = 1.3
τd = 0.58	τd = 1.5

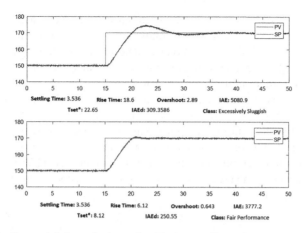

Fig. 10. Deterministic analysis results. Top: controller 1, bottom: controller 2.

CASE STUDY IV: Valve diagnosis for stiction using repository data.

South African Council for Automation and Control (SACAC) provides access to an industrial PID data repository from different sectors of the industry [18]. The repository recollects information belonging to some faulty control loops, which includes categorization of the fault, a basic summary about the loop's nature, and the recorded data for the fault detection tests.

For this case study, we tested the tool's ability to detect stiction by using the datasets found in the repository's stiction section.

Dataset 1 belongs to a pulp and paper plant's flow control loop with valve stiction detected [18]. The provided data was organized in the required format and charged to SELC's workspace. Plots for process variable and controller output against time are shown in Fig. 11.

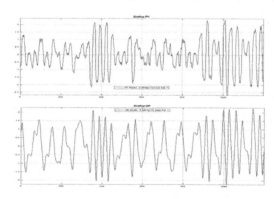

Fig. 11. Dataset 1's plots for process variable and controller output in case study IV.

Data pre-processing by normalization was made, and Kano-Maruta's method A [15] for valve stiction was used due to its high effectiveness in detecting stiction in flow control loops. As expected, valve stiction was detected successfully with a 0.28 stiction index. The curve fitting method is not recommended in this case, due to the irregularity of oscillations. For more information, refer to [16].

Dataset 2 belongs to a chemical plant's faulty level control loop with valve stiction detected [18]. More detailed information can be found in Thornhill's work [19]. Plots for process variable and controller output against time are shown in Fig. 12. As this is a level control loop, and there is no information available about valve position, the Kano-Maruta method is not recommended for valve stiction analysis [15]. Instead, we used curve fitting analysis on the process variables, as the level control loop tends to have an integrating nature [16].

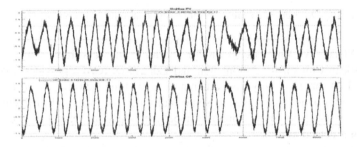

Fig. 12. Dataset 2's plots for process variables and controller output in case study IV.

The data was loaded to the tool's workspace, normalized, and filtered with a 2-time unit filter constant value. As there is a disturbance that may disrupt the results at time 5582, we sectioned the data till time 5500. The result confirmed the presence of valve stiction with a 0.73 stiction index, as seen in Fig. 13.

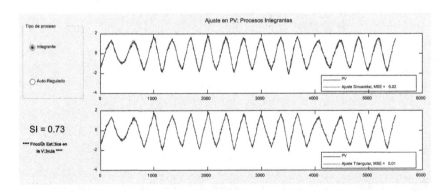

Fig. 13. Valve stiction test for dataset 2. Curve fitting method used.

CASE STUDY V: Tuning assessment using repository data.

For this case study, we tested the tool's ability to detect lousy tuning performance by using the datasets found in the repository's tuning section [18].

Dataset 1 belongs to a pulp and paper plant's quality control loop with indications of tight tuning [18]. The data was organized, loaded in the SELC's workspace, and normalized. Plots for PV vs. time and OP vs. time are seen in Fig. 14. Characterization made using SELC gave a 13.5-time unit delay. Discretized, this would be a delay of 15 discrete inputs. Performance assessment over a delay range from 10 to 20 discrete inputs was made, and it was discovered that the loop presented a TUNI index value close to 1 for every case, as seen in Fig. 15.

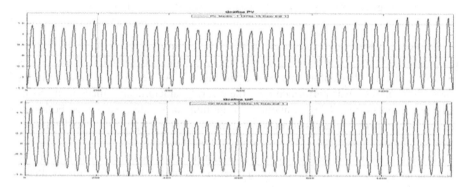

Fig. 14. Plots for process variable and controller output versus time, respectively.

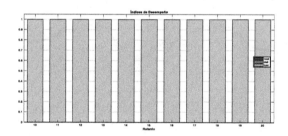

Fig. 15. Performance assessment for dataset 1. Results show an indication of lousy tuning with TUNI values close to 1.

Besides, stiction tests were performed to discard it as the cause of a high TUNI index. Horch's correlation method [20], Kano-Maruta's method A [15], and the curve fitting method [16] were all used for the valve stiction detection, all of them with negative results, as seen in Fig. 16. Although not guaranteed, we can conclude a wrong tuning as the possible cause of bad performance in this loop, keeping in mind the need for testing for another type of faults (faulty sensors, an external disturbance, etc.).

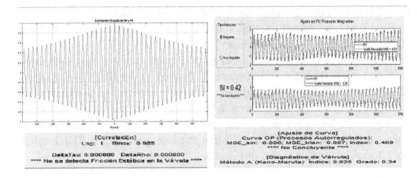

Fig. 16. Stiction Tests FOR dataset 1, case study V. All negative.

Dataset 2 belongs to a chemical plant's flow control loop with traits of sluggish tuning [18]. As proceeded before, data was organized and normalized. Plots for process variable and controller output can be seen in Fig. 17. As Set-Point is variable in this dataset, the analysis was performed over the error. Characterization made using SELC gave us a process time delay of about 4.5-time units or six discrete inputs. Following this result, performance assessment was estimated over a range from 1 to 10 discrete inputs, showing an average TUNI value of around 0.87.

Tests for stiction detection using Kano-Maruta gave positive results, so further analysis is required. The curve fitting method is not reliable due to oscillation irregularity.

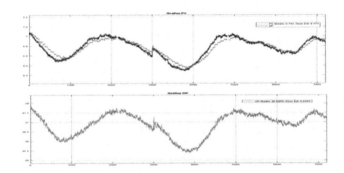

Fig. 17. Dataset 2's plots for process variable and controller output in case study V.

4 Conclusions

This work presents the development process of the Control Loops Assessment Software (SELC), which started because of INDUTRONICA DEL CARIBE's desire for innovation and new product development. This tool rises as an excellent opportunity for the improvement of the efficiency and economic profitability of industrial processes in a country like Colombia, while also helping INDUTRONICA DEL CARIBE to increase its portfolio. The tool's functional architecture includes the options for data pre-processing, signal analysis, and fault diagnosis, and a literature review of each step was presented. Finally, we showed the results of the tool's testing phase, where it was proved SELC's ability for performance assessment and diagnosis. Nevertheless, it is still necessary to test the software with technical data of the region but, at the time of this paper's creation, we are still in the process of contacting industrial plants for the necessary data. Besides, improvement in SELC's functionality should also be considered, like making the software work in real-time.

References

1. Bauer, M., Horch, A., Xie, L., Jelali, M., Thornhill, N.: The current state of control loop performance monitoring–a survey of application in industry. J. Process Control **38**, 1–10 (2016)
2. Jelali, M.: Control Performance Management in Industrial Automation: Assessment. Diagnosis and Improvement of Control Loop Performance. Springer, London (2012). https://doi.org/10.1007/978-1-4471-4546-2
3. Thornhill, N.F., Horch, A.: Advances and new directions in plant-wide disturbance detection and diagnosis. Control Eng. Pract. **15**(10), 1196–1206 (2007)
4. Cardenas-Cabrera, J., et al.: Model predictive control strategies performance evaluation over a pipeline transportation system. J. Control Sci. Eng. **2019**, 1–11 (2019)
5. Borrero-Salazar, A.A., Cardenas-Cabrera, J.M., Barros-Gutierrez, D.A., Jiménez-Cabas, J.A.: A comparison study of MPC strategies based on minimum variance control index performance. Espacios **40**(20) (2019)
6. Longhi, L.G.S., et al.: Control loop performance assessment and improvement of an industrial hydrotreating unit and its economical benefits. Sba Control. Automação Soc. Bras. Autom. **23**(1), 60–77 (2012)
7. Farenzena, M.: Novel methodologies for assessment and diagnostics in control loop management. Universidade Federal do Rio Grande do Sul (2008)
8. Harris, T.J.: Assessment of control loop performance. Can. J. Chem. Eng. **67**(5), 856–861 (1989)
9. Farenzena, M., Trierweiler, J.O.: Quantifying the impact of control loop performance, time delay and white-noise over the final product variability. In: Cancun, Mexico: International Symposium on Dynamics and Control of Process Systems (2007)
10. Swanda, A.P., Seborg, D.E.: Evaluating the performance of PID-type feedback control loops using normalized settling time. IFAC Proc. **30**(9), 301–306 (1997)
11. Swanda, A.P., Seborg, D.E.: Controller performance assessment based on setpoint response data. In: Proceedings of the 1999 American Control Conference, vol. 6, pp. 3863–3867 (1999)
12. Hägglund, T.: Automatic detection of sluggish control loops. Control Eng. Pract. **7**(12), 1505–1511 (1999)
13. Vishnubhotla, A.: Frequency and time-domain techniques for control loop performance assessment (1997)
14. Srinivasan, R., Rengaswamy, R., Miller, R.: Control loop performance assessment. 1. A qualitative approach for stiction diagnosis. Ind. Eng. Chem. Res. **44**(17), 6708–6718 (2005)
15. Choudhury, M.A.A.S., Shah, S.L., Thornhill, N.F., Shook, D.S.: Automatic detection and quantification of stiction in control valves. Control Eng. Pract. **14**(12), 1395–1412 (2006)

16. Maruta, H., Kano, M., Kugemoto, H., Shimizu, K.: Modeling and detection of stiction in pneumatic control valve. Trans. Soc. Instrum. Control Eng. **40**(8), 825–833 (2004)
17. He, Q.P., Wang, J., Pottmann, M., Qin, S.J.: A curve fitting method for detecting valve stiction in oscillating control loops. Ind. Eng. Chem. Res. **46**(13), 4549–4560 (2007)
18. Smith, C.A., Corripio, A.B.: Principles and Practice of Automatic Process Control. Editorial F{é}lix Varela (2012)
19. Bauer, M., Auret, L., le Roux, D., Aharonson, V.: An industrial PID data repository for control loop performance monitoring (CPM). IFAC-PapersOnLine **51**(4), 823–828 (2018)
20. Thornhill, N.F., Cox, J.W., Paulonis, M.A.: Diagnosis of plant-wide oscillation through data-driven analysis and process understanding. Control Eng. Pract. **11**(12), 1481–1490 (2003)
21. Horch, A.: A simple method for detection of stiction in control valves. Control Eng. Pract. **7** (10), 1221–1231 (1999)

Mobility Impacts of the Second Phase of Covid-19: General Considerations and Regulation from Tuscany (Italy) and Kentucky (USA)

Irene Nicotra[1], Massimiliano Petri[2($\boxtimes$)] (iD), Antonio Pratelli[2],
Reginald R. Souleyrette[3], and Teng (Alex) Wang[4]

[1] Department of Transport Planning and Public Transport Services,
Province of Livorno, Livorno, Italy
i.nicotra@provincia.livorno.it

[2] Department of Industrial and Civil Engineering, University of Pisa, Pisa, Italy
{m.petri,a.pratelli}@ing.unipi.it

[3] Department of Civil Engineering, University of Kentucky, Lexington, KY,
USA
souleyrette@uky.edu

[4] Kentucky Transportation Center, University of Kentucky, Lexington, KY,
USA
teng-wang@uky.edu

Abstract. The second phase of the virus Covid-19 is about to start a new configuration of accessibility to activities and cities. This phase, which will be able to see different restriction levels both between different countries and between successive periods, is the great challenge that the whole world is facing and which, if not managed in a planned and strategic way, risks turning into a further catastrophe. The social distancing rules imposed will necessarily lead to an escape from public transport in the cities, which could turn into total congestion of city traffic, leading the cities themselves to paralysis. We need a series of countermeasures that define new mobility capable of mitigating the effects of the mobility offer imbalance by intervening quickly, economically, and, in the short term, emergency on the whole transport chain. This article presents some possible actions to be put in place, and some mobility measures actually applied in Tuscany coastal area.

Keywords: Sustainable mobility · Vehicle routing · Covid-19 · Mobility management

1 Introduction

The second phase of the virus Covid-19 will introduce new mobility concepts and behaviors with increased importance to individually based-transport mode. The European Commission's response to the virus prioritizes keeping citizens healthy. This includes keeping essential transport moving, for example, to transport medical supplies and other essential goods and, in the second phase, to maintain precautions through Personal

© Springer Nature Switzerland AG 2020
O. Gervasi et al. (Eds.): ICCSA 2020, LNCS 12250, pp. 255–268, 2020.
https://doi.org/10.1007/978-3-030-58802-1_19

Protective Equipment-PPE and individual distancing [2]. The effect of the social distancing rules, with all difference between their narrowness among the different European and Extra-European Countries will be a general decrease of Public Transport passengers both from the rail and road system (see Fig. 1 for the Wuhan region). These will due to citizen behaviors and from social distancing rules itself; if for the same number of passengers, when the social distancing within public transport is introduced, the capacity needs to increase. Therefore, the number of operating buses, trains, and trams will increase [3].

This measure will be difficult to implement, especially in cities with a significant portion of transit trips, both because increasing trams and buses take time to change the operating program and, above all, because it would lead to an unsustainable economic balance, with an increase in the supply that would have a decrease in demand. The problem is less pronounced in cities with a high proportion of private automobile trips, as is the case in most American cities. Still, transit is important to many lower income populations, and in larger cities. Impacts on transit have a more profound effect on disadvantaged populations who may already be underserved, and who must go to work outside their home.

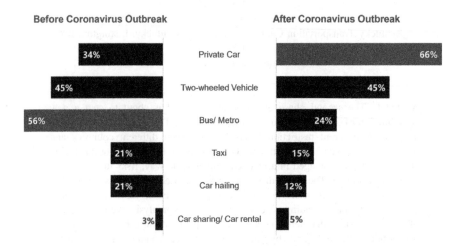

Fig. 1. Modal share in Wuhan Region before and after Coronavirus emergency (Source: [1])

The motorization level (the number of vehicles per 100 inhabitants) will increase with the purchase of cars by even those who did not have this means of travel (Fig. 2 shows the percentage of non-car owners who have indicated that they want to buy a car in a sample survey within the Wuhan region of China). Another effect of Coronavirus second phase will be the practically reset of sharing mobility that needs to find other solutions to remain in the mobility market. Finally, the increase of individual mobility will foster growth in bike use and culture joined together with other sustainable mobility solutions (electric scooter and bike, mini-scooter, etc.).

The rest of this paper is structured as follows. In Sect. 2 we introduce some general considerations and possible measures (including non-actions) to lighten the future private vehicle traffic impact as much as possible while in Sect. 3, we present solutions

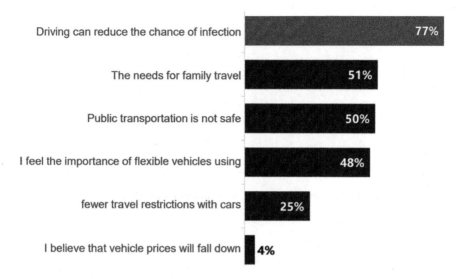

Fig. 2. Reason for new car purchase (Source: [1])

adopted in Tuscany coastal area and considerations for American cities, exemplified by information from the State of Kentucky.

2 Possible Sustainable Mobility Actions

The analysis of possible actions starts in introducing which of these it is good to avoid and not to implement. Administrations, instinctively in reaction to the shock due to the mobility blockage and to the pressure of business owners who want to resume activities quickly, could activate a change in the city's accessibility system, suspending the restrictions on access to controlled traffic areas, to pedestrian areas until the elimination or reduction of parking rates (case applied from 04/05/2020 in a famous Tuscany Municipality). Reducing the restrictions on car traffic would, however, only lead to a congestion acceleration with amplification of the problems indicated in the previous paragraph. It is, therefore, essential to maintain the regulatory regimes for parking and urban access before the onset of CoVID-19.

Moreover, it is key in this phase, to develop an emergency mobility network and to study changes in urban roads to give light-mobility (including pedestrians, cyclists), and micro-mobility users more spaces, especially for pedestrians (see Fig. 3) near commercial activities, and reserved lanes to avoid congestion and encourage sustainable mobility. Such measures on mobility supply, taking into account the reference regulations are often feasible only in large cities like Milan, Berlin, Barcelona, Paris [4], where there are oversized lanes and many connections alternatives for city central nodes that could accommodate the mobility demand changes.

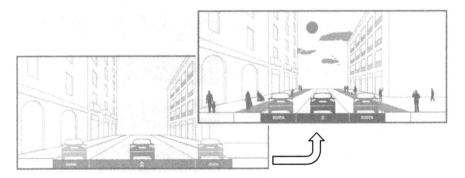

Fig. 3. An example of a pedestrian area extension (Source: [4])

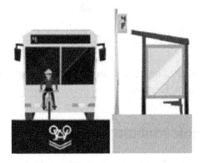

Fig. 4. An example of unsafe solutions for urban cyclists [3]

In this operation, the safety of weak mobility must not be left behind by only focusing on the current emergency needs. For example, a solution presented in a post-Covid manual as shown in Fig. 4, the reductions of lanes width and admixtures of dangerous modes of transport is not safe for cyclists.

It is likely that many of the daily home-to-work or home-to-schools trips, initially made by train or bus, will now take place by car. A possible remediation would be to provide) parking areas at the urban cordon. From these parking areas sustainable mobility networks would then be used, such as bike lines, public transport "'organized' rides, 'or micro-mobility options (e.g., scooters).

It will be important to introduce incentives or restrictions to encourage use of the cordon parking lots andtake the sustainable mobility modes beyond and into the city center. Example incentives include Good_Go and SaveMyBike open-source rewarding platform [5–8] that will be applied soon in some Tuscany Municipalities to incentive bike and foot trips inside the city (see Fig. 5). The reward system requires mobility management tools to achieve specific goals; in detail, it will be possible to:

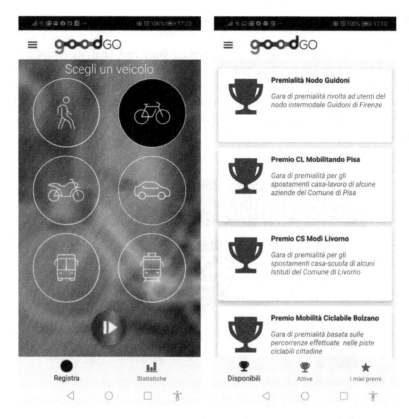

Fig. 5. The sustainable mobility competitions organized inside Good_Go platform and the system to register mobility modes used

- stimulate the use of all sustainable mobility (like the second and third competitions of Fig. 5);
- stimulate to the Park&Ride or Park&Bus at particular intermodal nodes (like the first competition in Fig. 5);
- stimulate the use of smart working hours and trips to avoid the rush hour overlaps and so to use train and bus network capacity at an optimal level;
- stimulate the use of a particular transport mode (like the fourth competition in Fig. 5).

The sharing-mobility, involving Car-Sharing, Bike-Sharing, and Car-Pooling must be rethought at this stage, for example in the following way:

- Car-sharing and Bike-sharing need to become long-period (6–12 months) of rental services, ensuring cleanliness during delivery and providing the vehicle on loan for use to the customer on an individual level;
- Car-Pooling at an peri-urban level (e.g., facilitated by BlaBlaCar) should be rethought as daily commutes with different people could exacerbate the transmission of disease.

3   Measures Applied in Tuscany Center Coastal Area

In this section, we describe the ongoing methodology and analysis regarding some companies located inside the Province of Livorno. In this case, each company had its employees fill out a questionnaire to understand the actual travel behaviors including timetables, work locations, intermediate constraints on home-work trips, and future preferences travel arrangements. Figure 6 shows the start page of the survey/questionnaire.

Fig. 6. The questionnaire for employees

The questionnaire was completed by about 300 employees from the 16 companies involved. A first analysis of the main features of the sample shows (see Fig. 7) that the use of private car goes from 46% in the summer to the 63% in the winter while the mean age of the sample is rather high.

Other important information collected with the questionnaire includes residence and work addresses, work times, and shifts differentiated by day of the week. Based on these data, home-to-work/HW desire lines have been reconstructed. For each employee, a desire line connects the residence with the workplace. Among these, two types of lines are developed, namely:

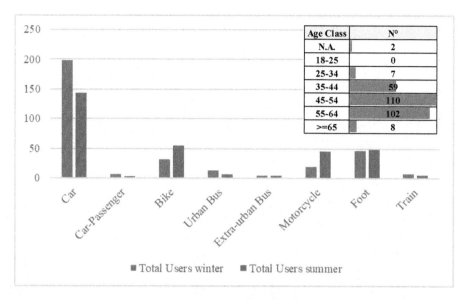

Fig. 7. The main features of the sample of respondents (the actual modal split and the age class)

- the desire lines which concerned access routes to urban areas from neighboring suburban territories;
- the desire lines contained within urban areas.

The analysis was developed separately from the two desire lines clusters. The first group of lines consists of elements often isolated and coming from very distant territories. Groups of users having part of the overlapping home-work journey have been identified. Groups of employees who make up **fixed-composition car-pooling**, with compatible work start and end times have been designed (see the 'employees' pool in Fig. 8). Traditional self-organized car-pooling (like BlaBlaCar or others) cannot be widely used in the second phase of Covid-19, due to the random nature of the ride share match. Composition of fixed users groups facilitates safe travel management.

The second cluster of desire lines (Fig. 8) uses a vehicle routing algorithm to identify groups of employees who can go to work using public transport. The algorithm was also used to identify **public transport journeys with a fixed composition** (maximizing vehicle capacity) and provide the passenger with the security of always finding the same people on the bus. These fixed compositions, both in car-pooling and in urban public transport, also facilitate the identification of individuals to be quarantined in the event of contagion from Covid-19 by one of the passengers (Fig. 9).

The second desire lines group was divided into three urban areas, that is to say the Piombino, Livorno center, and the continuous residential area between Cecina and Rosignano M.mo.

Between the many complex methodologies applied to study and model territorial dynamics [9, 10], we have chosen vehicle routing algorithms. In the following section, we describe the vehicle routing problem used and its features. Lastly, the results are presented.

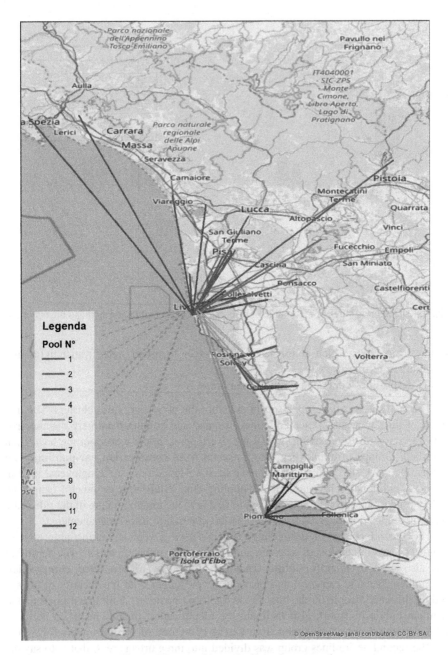

Fig. 8. The set of 'marginal' pools extracted

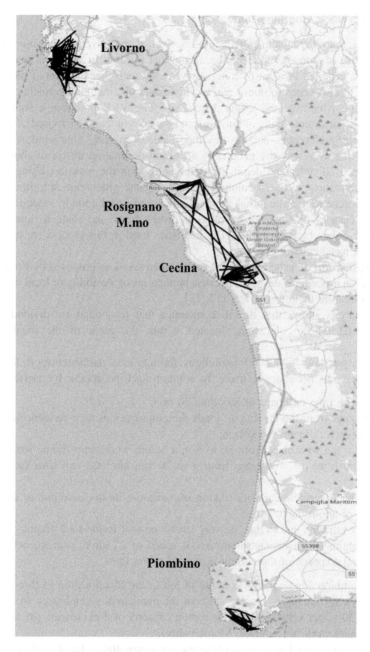

Fig. 9. The three clusters of 'local' travel lines

3.1 The Vehicle Routing Model

The vehicle routing problem (VRP) is a superset of the traveling salesman problem where one set of stops is sequenced in an optimal fashion. In a VRP, a set of orders needs to be assigned to a set of routes or vehicles such that the overall path cost is minimized. It also needs to honor real-world constraints, including vehicle capacities, delivery time windows, and driver specialties. The VRP produces a solution that honors those constraints while minimizing an objective function composed of operating costs and user preferences, such as the importance of meeting time windows.

The VRP solver starts by generating an origin-destination matrix of shortest-path costs between all order and depot locations along with the network. Using this cost matrix, it constructs an initial solution by inserting the orders one at a time onto the most appropriate route. The initial solution is then improved upon by resequencing the orders on each route, as well as moving orders from one route to another, and exchanging orders between routes. The heuristics used in this process are based on a tabu search metaheuristic.

The basic form of Tabu Search (TS) is founded on ideas proposed by Fred Glover [11] based on procedures designed to cross boundaries of feasibility or local optimality, instead of treating them as barriers [12, 13].

The analysis shows that the 16 companies that responded are divided into 40 different total working locations located within the areas of the local clusters themselves.

The analysis saw the search for solutions, through local public transport, linked to a series of elements necessary to make the solution itself acceptable by users:

- Route with time on board of less than 30 min;
- Route starts from the bus depot, loads the employees at their residence and takes them to each different workplace;
- Arrival at the workplace from 30 to 5 min before work entry (home-work trip);
- Departure from the workplace from 5 to 20 min after the exit time (work-home trip);
- Constraint of vehicle capacity (taking into account its decrease due to social distancing of about 65/70%);
- Route constraints due to the one-way streets present in the road graph;
- Assumptions of an average commercial speed of 27 km/h, average between the commercial speeds of the current presented urban lines.

The Piombino Municipality example of led to the identification of three different bus journeys, for the three working shifts of the municipality employees, to be carried out with a 30-seater vehicle with a maximum capacity of 9 passengers per single race (all passengers work in Piombino Municipality).

Starting from a total of 31 possible users, it was possible to build a public transport service with a fixed composition that includes 27 (87% of the total). Figure 10 illustrates the three strokes linking home to work with the various intermediate connections.

In the Cecina Municipality, we analyzed 21 employees of the Collodi Primary School. In this case, the analysis was simpler than before (Piombino case) because the work entry and exit time are the same for all employees. The results individuated a

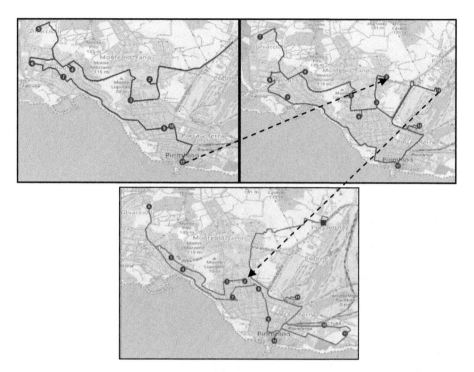

Fig. 10. The three fixed-composition public transport bus strokes with the link between them (dashed lines)

fixed 18 passenger bus ride with a length of about 19 km covered in about 36 min, starting from the busses depot (see Fig. 11).

3.2   Conclusions and Future Developments

The twelve pools/clusters using fixed-composition car-pooling took about 54 users, who would have gone to work independently by driving cars. With only 12 car-pooling groups, a 77% decrease in traffic show both environmental gas emission and congestion reduction benefits in the destination urban areas. This case study showed a practice-ready solution for the short term.

With the second solution based on fixed-component public transport rides, an efficiency of 81% was achieved in the Piombino Municipality. In the Cecina-Rosignano area, a 94% decrease in the equivalent circulating vehicle fleet was achieved. (solution to be implemented in the medium term as it involves a modification of the public transport service scheduling) A summary of all case studies is presented in Table 1, below.

The bicycle use incentive is just getting underway in the Municipality of Livorno and in Rosignano Marittimo, providing rewarding actions differentiated between users type (i.e., long-term participation programs for residents/commuters, with prizes of higher value such as discounts on the purchase of electric bicycles or scooter and more

Fig. 11. The three fixed-composition

Table 1. Results coming from the Case Studies analyzed

Case study	Type	Decrease in circulating cars
Whole Livorno Province	*Fixed car-pooling fleet*	77%
Piombino municipality	*Fixed Public transport fleet*	81%
Cecina-Rosignano area	*Fixed Public transport fleet*	94%
Livorno municipality	*Fixed Public transport fleet*	In progress

immediately rewarding solutions for tourists, such as discounts on products sold by local businesses).

3.3   Considerations for American Cities

The solutions offered in this paper would seem to be applicable and perhaps more helpful to many larger American cities. Still, the sustainability aspects are helpful even to smaller areas independent of immediate public health concerns.

Kentucky is a relatively lower population state, with between 4 and 5 million residents. Its largest city, Louisville, has one of the lowest transit usage rates in the country at 2.7% [14]. Clearly, even a significant reduction in this low of a percentage would do little to cause the auto-centric problems likely to be experienced by more transit dependent regions.

Indeed, the planned response to the crisis in the Kentucky region is focused more on safe usage of public transit as well as lowering demand. However, in most American cities, the problem has been too little demand to support more robust transit services. So, like many other aspects of dealing with the pandemic, there are winners and losers.

The types of specific responses include:

- Transportation Cabinet (DOT) Secretary Jim Gray has issued Emergency Declarations suspending certain regulatory restrictions to support the supply chain [15].
- Transit authorities have implemented various onboard social distancing procedures including limitations on what types of trips can be made, hours of service, stop changes, and hygiene directives [16, 17].
- The University of Kentucky has recommended walking and alternative ways to accomplish the "last mile" to reduce transit demand [18].

3.4   Closure

This paper presented the context and need for a new mobility, at least during and probably after the global pandemic. For this period, several feasible approaches are suggested. Recognizing that each region will need, and be able to implement, these strategies, they were designed to both address the ongoing emergency as well as provide sustainable solutions for years to come. The application of the indicated transport measures will open, in a future monitoring phase, the possibility to evaluate the effective decrease in carbon emissions [19].

References

1. Ipsos, Impact of Coronavirus to new car purchase in China, Game Chargers, 12 March 2020. https://www.ipsos.com/en/impact-coronavirus-new-car-purchase-china
2. European Commission, Coronavirus Response Database. Accessed 28 Apr 2020
3. BikEconomist, Piano d'azione per la mobilità urbana post-Covid published the 16 Apr 2020
4. AMAT-Agenzia Mobilità Ambiente Territorio- Comune di Milano, Strade Aperte Strategie, azioni e strumenti per la ciclabilità e la pedonalità a garanzia delle misure di distanziamento negli spostamenti urbani e per una mobilità sostenibile, Milano 2020, Strategia di adattamento
5. Petri, M., Frosolini, M., Lupi, M., Pratelli, A.: ITS to change behaviour: a focus about bike mobility monitoring and incentive—The SaveMyBike system. In: 2016 IEEE 16th International Conference on Environment and Electrical Engineering (EEEIC), pp. 1–6. IEEE, June 2016
6. Pratelli, A., Petri, M., Farina, A., Lupi, M.: Improving bicycle mobility in urban areas through ITS technologies: the SaveMyBike project. In: Sierpiński, G. (ed.) TSTP 2017.

AISC, vol. 631, pp. 219–227. Springer, Cham (2018). https://doi.org/10.1007/978-3-319-62316-0_18

7. Petri, M., Pratelli, A.: SaveMyBike – a complete platform to promote sustainable mobility. In: Misra, S., et al. (eds.) ICCSA 2019. LNCS, vol. 11620, pp. 177–190. Springer, Cham (2019). https://doi.org/10.1007/978-3-030-24296-1_16

8. Pratelli, A., Petri, M., Farina, A., Souleyrette, R.R.: Improving sustainable mobility through modal rewarding: the GOOD_GO smart platform. In: WSEAS Transactions on Environment and Development, ISSN/E-ISSN: 1790-5079/2224-3496, vol. 16 (2020). Art. #21, pp. 204–218 (2020). https://doi.org/10.37394/232015.2020.16.21

9. Petri, M., Pratelli, A., Barè, G., Piccini, L.: A land use and transport interaction model for the greater florence metropolitan area. In: Misra, S., et al. (eds.) ICCSA 2019. LNCS, vol. 11620, pp. 231–246. Springer, Cham (2019). https://doi.org/10.1007/978-3-030-24296-1_20

10. Pratelli, A., Petri, M., Ierpi, M., Di Matteo, M.: Integration of Bluetooth, vehicle count data and transport model results by means of Datamining techniques. In: 2018 IEEE International Conference on Environment and Electrical Engineering and 2018 IEEE Industrial and Commercial Power Systems Europe (EEEIC/I&CPS Europe), pp. 1–6. IEEE, June 2018

11. Glover, F.: Future paths for integer programming and links to artificial intelligence. Comput. Oper. Res. 13, 533–549 (1986)

12. Glover, F., Laguna, M.: Tabu Search. Kluwer Academic Publishers, Boston (1997)

13. Pratelli, A., Petri, M., Vehicle routing problem and car-pooling to solve home-to-work transport problem in mountain areas. In: Gargiulo, C., Zoppi, C. (eds.) Planning, Nature and Ecosystem Services. FedOAPress, Napoli, pp. 869–880 (2019). (Smart City, Urban Planning for a Sustainable Future. 5), ISBN: 978-88-6887-054-6, https://doi.org/10.6093/978-88-6887-054-6

14. Sivak, M.: Has Motorization in the United States Peaked? Transportation Research Institute, University of Michigan (2014). www.umtri.umich.edu/our-results/publications/has-motorization-us-peaked

15. Kentucky Transportation Cabinet, Office of the Secretary. https://transportation.ky.gov/Pages/Home.aspx. Accessed 07 May 2020

16. Lexington Transit Authority, Additonal COVID-19 Prevention Procedures. https://lextran.com/additionalcovid19procedures/. Accessed 07 May 2020

17. Transit Authority of River City (Louisville Metropolitan Area Transit Authority), Additonal COVID Measures, https://www.ridetarc.org/additional-covid-measures/. Accessed 07 May 2020

18. University of Kentucky, Coronavirus Campus Services. https://www.uky.edu/coronavirus/campus-services. Accessed 07 May 2020

19. Nocera, S., Ruiz-Alarcón, Q.C., Cavallaro, F.: Assessing carbon emissions from road transport through traffic flow estimators. Transp. Res. Part C Emerg. Technol. 95, 125–148 (2018)

International Workshop on Advances in Artificial Intelligence Learning Technologies: Blended Learning, STEM, Computational Thinking and Coding (AAILT 2020)

Model of Intelligent Massive Open Online Course Development

Gulmira Bekmanova[1,2(✉)], Assel Omarbekova[1],
Zulfiya Kaderkeyeva[1], and Altynbek Sharipbay[1,2]

[1] L.N. Gumilyov Eurasian National University, Nur-Sultan, Kazakhstan
gulmira-r@yandex.kz, omarbekova@mail.ru,
zulfiya_83@mail.ru, sharalt@mail.ru
[2] Nuclear University MEPhI, Moscow, Russia

Abstract. **The relevance** of development and extension of massive open online courses (MOOC) got a new wave of development due to the coronavirus pandemic. The importance and necessity of MOOCs will be increasing, however, intelligent systems changed qualitatively since the development of first MOOCs. The intelligent MOOC development with using Kazakh language thesaurus approach is suggested in this paper. The model of intelligent MOOC suggests laying its intellectuality at its designing, using the knowledge base, ontological model of discipline, and their relevant question-answer system and intelligent search. The separate important part of each such MOOC is the intelligent assessment of knowledge and achievement of training's announced results. The suggested MOOC model makes it more effective means for distance, blended and any e-learning. The intelligent MOOC possesses a possibility of its using in e-learning systems without a tutor.

Keywords: Intelligent massive open online course · Intelligent assessment of knowledge · Control over learning results achievement · Ontological model · Kazakh language thesaurus assessment of human language plaintexts

1 Introduction

Since their establishment, the massive open online courses (MOOCs) were meant to revolutionize and democratize higher education [1, 2]. The American publisher, the New York Times called the year of 2012 as a year of massive open online courses. The number of users is consistently and steadily growing since that time. As per 2017 results, the number of online courses participants was over 81 million people. The total number of MOOCs certificates issued for successful learning is also steadily growing [3].

The most popular services are the US platforms Coursera, edX and Udacity, as well as British FutureLearn. Many countries created their national online platforms: France Université Numérique (FUN) – in France, MiriadaX – in the Latin American countries, EduOpen – in Italy, XuetangX – in China, SWAYAM – in India, National platform for open education in Russia (NPOE), Educational platform BilimLand in Kazakhstan.

In 2020, the pandemic and lockdown regime caused a fast growth in number of online courses users. According to the GetCourse platform, hosting distance courses for

© Springer Nature Switzerland AG 2020
O. Gervasi et al. (Eds.): ICCSA 2020, LNCS 12250, pp. 271–281, 2020.
https://doi.org/10.1007/978-3-030-58802-1_20

hundreds of online schools, the sales of courses already increased by 20% in the second half of March compared to the first half of the month. The number of users tried to organize their own courses herein increased by 30% [4].

Over 1 million people completed online additional medical training courses to help coronavirus infected patients [5].

During the quarantine, many online training services, such as Coursera, Khan Academy, GeekBrains, Arzamas made great number of courses free, which also leads to increase of MOOCs users [6].

At the moment the online course should not only provide high-quality content, but comply with current trends and new technologies as well.

Here we list the main trends of online learning which are relevant in 2020:

1) Individual learning path. The modular training courses are becoming increasingly popular where the participant may choose personal learning path, which meets his needs.
2) Mobile training. It is important for participants to have an access not only with a PC, but via mobile device as well.
3) Micro training. With the modern man's limited free time, the educational videos tend to shorten by their duration.
4) Online training with extensive feedback. In order to learn effectively and quickly achieve results, users are willing to pay extra for the feedback function.
5) Community trend and networking. More and more users attend courses not only to obtain knowledge, but also to get acquainted to their like-minded people.
6) Practice-oriented training. Users are more interested in development of practical skills than in obtaining theoretical knowledge.
7) Traineeships and employment as part of an online course. Those educational products that provide traineeships in large companies for students or help the most successful students in finding work by a new, just obtained profession, win the competitive struggle.
8) Blended training. The courses which combine offline and online formats are in demand.
9) Multi-format training. Online courses, where information is presented in various formats, are in demand. Under this approach, information is digested in better way, and the course becomes more replete.
10) Gamification. Perhaps it is the most controversial trend among the mentioned. On the one hand, game mechanics in training work perfectly and help to maintain interest in classes and complete online courses. But - only in case if game mechanics are relevant to educational tasks and help to achieve learning goals [7].

The MOOC development and extension received a new strong impulse for development due to the coronavirus pandemic, and the importance and necessity of MOOCs will be only growing predictably. But the MOOCs existing on the market most often do not use artificial intelligence methods at development of MOOCs. The paper proposes an approach for development of intelligent MOOC from its designing to use artificial intelligence in assessment of student's knowledge that will make it more effective means of distance, blended and any e-learning. These are exactly the modern requirements for MOOCs. There are many various models of MOOCs. The considered variant of MOOC contains the following didactic materials:

- Glossary
- Presentation
- Webinar
- Lecture materials
- Quiz questions
- Practical and/or laboratory tasks
- Individual work tasks
- Final exam materials.

For the MOOCs development, all materials are presented as an ontological model, which is an effective tool for representing knowledge [links]; fuzzy methods for assessing students' knowledge are used to evaluate their knowledge level, which are disclosed in details in the papers [links].

Labor costs for the development of single MOOC are at least 100 h and include the following main stages:

1. Formulation of training results
2. Elaboration of structure and content of MOOC
3. Development of assessment system
4. Creation of MOOC video-content
5. Allocation of MOOC materials on a platform
6. MOOC expertise

Stages of intelligent massive open online course development remain but the content of stages changes.

The formulation of training results is carried out with consideration of the training form, thus the achievement of training results may differ between distant training, blended and traditional one (within the traditional training, MOOC is used as an auxiliary tool, and as the main one in distant training, in blended training, there are high-quality practical and/or laboratory exercises that take place in face to face manner as a rule). The most thoroughly and qualitatively developed assignments, questions, feedback and assessment, which verify the achievement of training results are needed for their guaranteed achievement in distance learning.

2   Related Works

There are articles studying the use of video-supported technology to facilitate learning's latest trend in the e-learning [8], perspectives of e-learning development [9], in which it is pointed out that despite the difference between educational traditions the resulting analysis brings to the surface not only how the values that underpin e-learning development in each region differ but also how specific perspectives influence the respective fields. The researchers acknowledge these differences but also remark on the historic and contemporary symbiosis that has endured even in this relatively new field of e-learning.

E-learning systems actively use artificial intelligence models and methods [10–13]. In the paper [14], authors develop a model to automatically label a post based on the first phase of the interaction analysis model. This allows instructors to automatically identify whether students are stating opinions, clarifying details, or engaging in activities such as providing examples to peers. Manuscript [15] presents a novel approach for developing an affective tutoring system for the MOOCs, which is called ATS-MOOCs. Such system can easily help students to improve their learning performance by recognizing their affective states and then adapting the MOOC content accordingly. Paper [16] shows multidimensional deep learner model combining these features with natural language processing. To illustrate presented method, authors used a benchmark dataset of 29598 posts, from three different academic subject areas. The findings highlight that the combined, multi-dimensional features model is more effective than the text-only (NLP) analysis, showing that future models need to be optimised based on all these dimensions, when classifying urgent posts.

The ontology is successfully applied in modeling systems for various types of knowledge. For instance, ontological models for knowledge presentation are suggested in the paper [17]. Besides, the presentation of ontology models allows converting of a model into an RDF scheme, which will be used for generation of reference reviews [18]. It is disclosed in the paper [19] how semantic hypergraphs are used to create ontological models of morphological rules in the Kazakh language. The ontology of professional competencies and e-CF are considered in the paper [20], it proposes [21] the competence correspondence for training programs to national and international requirements. The modular competencies, ontological approaches and hierarchy analysis are used in the work to compare the competencies of the training program, professional standards and e-CF. There has been built an ontology which comprises competence data and determines their relation.

The elaboration of systems able to make logical conclusions from the knowledge base is rapidly developing all over the world. The extraction of existing and generation of new knowledge and statements from the existing knowledge base is carried out with specialized engines intended to reason and make logical conclusions. In the paper [22], the authors propose to implement RDF to represent knowledge and use a data-query language to extract knowledge. In [23], developers describe methods for a knowledge base processing, extracting triplets, and generating queries.

In the articles [24, 25], we described the developed system for the automatic generation of test questions based on the ontological model. The development of test questions for students' knowledge assessment requires no-nonsense approach. The test tasks of high quality are developed thoroughly in a way that they would not be ambiguous or unclear for the tested students. Various methodologies were investigated under test tasks development as well as deeply studied Bloom's taxonomy. In accordance with taxonomy, the students' skills are divided into six categories, knowledge, comprehension, application, analysis, synthesis and assessment. The most primitive of the skills are knowledge and comprehension, and the most advanced are analysis, synthesis and assessment. It has been decided to generate test tasks to check low level skills of knowledge and comprehension in the process of development in a way that a system able to make full argument would be needed for generating questions for analysis and assessment. Special verbs were determined in accordance with Bloom's taxonomy to develop test tasks. Some of the verbs are for knowledge and definition, to give definition, to enumerate, to name, to explain, etc. Low level skills may be estimated with the mentioned verbs while verbs for classification, finding alternative and description of advantages are used to estimate students' skills of higher level. The developed system generates test questions to assess the skills of low-level students.

The system, according to the taxonomy of B.S. Bloom, automatically generates assignments for assessing knowledge and comprehension of educational material. The development of knowledge bases for intelligent systems is shown in paper [26].

3   Formulation of Training Results

The formulation of training results is carried out with consideration of the training form, thus the achievement of training results may differ between distant training, blended and traditional one (within the traditional training, MOOC is used as an auxiliary tool, and as the main one in distant training, in blended training, there are high-quality practical and/or laboratory exercises that take place in face to face manner as a rule). The most thoroughly and qualitatively developed assignments, questions, feedback and assessment, which verify the achievement of training results are needed for their guaranteed achievement in distance learning.

4   Discipline's Ontological Model

The ontological model of discipline is developed to create the MOOC's structure and content. The ontological model is built in Protégé tool [27]. It was developed at Stanford University in collaboration with the University of Manchester.

The ontology is a powerful and widely used modeling tool for relations between objects belonging to different fields of a subject. The ontology defines a set of representative primitives in the context of computer and information sciences with which we can model a field of knowledge or a discourse. The representative primitives are usually classes (or sets), attributes (or properties), and relationships (or relationships between members within a class). The definitions for representative primitives include information about their meaning and limitations of their logically concerted application.

This formalism determines the "O" ontology as triple (V, R, K), where V – is a set classes for the subject field, R – is a set of relationships between the classes, and K – is a set of attributes within the field [17, 28].

The ontological model consists of the discipline topics and the glossary, each of the discipline topics includes glossary's basic concepts, control questions are developed on the topic linked to the glossary, as well as the assignments to verify the achievement of results by each of the topics, a knowledge base of questions and answers by the ontology is created in human language, the system can self-learn within the framework of a set discipline (see Fig. 1).

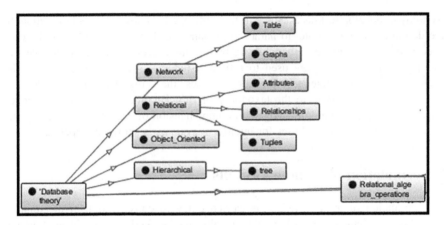

Fig. 1. "Databases theory" discipline's ontological model

The figure (see Fig. 2) shows an ontology fragment by topic of relational algebra operation, "Databases theory" discipline, linked to discipline's competences.

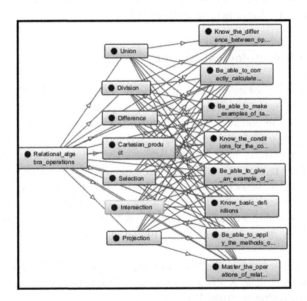

Fig. 2. A fragment of "Databases theory" discipline's one topic ontological model

Such concept allows:

1) To link fragments of video-lecture with glossary's key-words and to rewind the lecture by the key-words.
2) To find answers to the lecture questions automatically in the video-lecture.
3) To carry out the intelligent search in a MOOC within the discipline in the human language [29].

5   Development of the Assessment System

It is suggested to use assessment system based on the open tests for a certain discipline. A student writes his answer which is then compared with a reference etalon answer based on a fuzzy binary relation, set between a student's answer and reference ones synthesized from the knowledge base of a set discipline in accordance with test questions. Then it becomes possible to figure out the competence marks by all modules on assumption of the marks obtained by the disciplines within the modules. As a result we may assess the achievement of training results by the whole educational program, which is calculated as an average from the compulsory results achievement according to the disciplines of the educational program.

Let P – be a finite and nonempty set representing the knowledge base of a given discipline; Q – a finite and nonempty set representing a base of test questions in a given discipline; T – a finite and non-empty set representing a base of standard answers to test questions in a given discipline;

$f: Q \rightarrow T, f(q) = t, q \in Q, t \in T$ (4) – a function to generate answers to asked questions; S – a finite set representing the knowledge base of student answers to test questions in the given discipline.

'Mark' $\rightleftharpoons$

where $\mu_{S \subseteq T}: S \times T \rightarrow]0, 1[$ (12) fuzzy relation function.

In order to calculate the elements of fuzzy relation $S \subseteq T$ it is needed to set members S и T, which are the range of class individuals, range of class properties and the range of semantic arcs incidental to the class.

Intelligent system for evaluating the level of formation of professional competencies of students is described in papers [30–32] in details.

6   Creation of the MOOC Video-Content

Types of video-lectures and video-lessons:

1. Lecturer's video ("talking head"). This is the least productive and didactically ineffective form of distance training.
2. Live video ("for skippers"). It is a video of university lectures recorded directly indoors. For example, the Massachusetts Technology Institute arranged one of the biggest video-lecture collections recorded in lecture hall.
3. Studio video-lectures. Such video records are well edited and directed. All flakes, teacher's "goofs" are deleted. Very often such video-lesson is accompanied with demonstration of images, video clips and very close to a documental film by its level. Currently we are recording video-lectures of math disciplines in such format.
4. Slide films. The footage in this case is in a key place and accompanied by an off-screen comments made by the teacher or speaker. Such film is as close as possible to a documental educational film. Such type of video-lectures is ineffective and may be used as teacher's auxiliary material.

5. Interactive video-lectures and video-lessons. The teacher's monologue is accompanied by slides, video fragments, assignments. It is the most preferable variant of video-lectures (see Fig. 3).

Fig. 3. Database theory MOOC fragment

The figure shows MOOC fragment for Database theory discipline, at the moment the work is being done to implement the open tests based assessment.

7 Allocation of MOOC Materials on a Platform

This stage does not have any difference by MOOC allocation technology. The requirements for a platform itself are changing. It is the platform that carries out the implementation of all functions of intelligent MOOC. Such platform satisfies the following requirements:

1) verification of results achievement by discipline through the connection between content and training results, assignments, open tests based on thesaurus.
2) mechanisms of intelligent assessment of students' knowledge and competences.
3) Ensuring of feedback with students.

8 MOOC Expertise

The expertise includes the standard MOOC expertise for the content and didactic materials quality, technical expertise of video-lectures, and pedagogical expertise of MOOCs. The verification of the MOOC intelligent function operation correctness is engaged additionally for: intelligent search, system's verification of open tests, verification of questions and assignments regarding setting up of competencies and training results.

9   Conclusion

In this work, the model of intelligent massive open online course development has been proposed. The discipline content is presented in a shape of ontological model, which provides possibility to create connections between discipline topics, glossary, assignments and questions. Thus, the intelligent search, questions and answers in human language during learning, verification of achievement of training results through assignments, as well as students' open answers of students become possible. Such approach, despite of being more time consuming at creation of intelligent MOOC, will allow to educate a student with minimal involvement of a teacher in the training process after setting the system. The system has development perspectives as an educational system without teacher's involvement. At the same time, with a huge knowledge base it may be successfully used to guarantee the verification of the training results achievement.

Acknowledgments. The work was supported by the grant financing for scientific and technical programs and projects by the Ministry of Science and Education of the Republic of Kazakhstan (Grant No. AP05132249, 2018–2020).

References

1. Belanger, Y., Thornton, J.: Bioelectricity: A quantitative approach Duke University's first MOOC (2013)
2. Haggard, S.: The maturing of the MOOC. Department for Business Innovation & Skills (2013)
3. Chuang, I., Ho, A.: HarvardX and MITx: Four Years of Open Online Courses – Fall 2012-Summer 2016 (2016)
4. https://www.vedomosti.ru/management/articles/2020/04/08/827543-onlainovie-kursi
5. https://xn–80aesfpebagmfblc0a.xn–p1ai/news/20200413-1847.html
6. https://1prof.by/news/stil-zhizni/attrakcion-shhedrosti-iz-za-koronavirusa-mnogie-servisy-stali-besplatnymi/
7. https://edmarket.ru/blog/top-trends-of-e-learning
8. Chen, Y.: A study of implementing and evaluating an interactive video on demand. New Educ. Rev. **28**(2), 115–125 (2012)
9. Hillen, S., Landis, M.: Two perspectives on e-learning design: a synopsis of a U.S. and a European analysis. Int. Rev. Res. Open Dist. Learn. **15**(4), 199–225 (2014)
10. Sharipbay, A., Barlybayev, A., Sabyrov, T.: Measure the usability of graphical user interface. New Advances in Information Systems and Technologies. AISC, vol. 444, pp. 1037–1045. Springer, Cham (2016). https://doi.org/10.1007/978-3-319-31232-3_98
11. Sharipbay, A., Omarbekova, A., Seifullina, A., Zakirova, A.: Creating intelligent electronic textbooks based on knowledge management. In: The World Congress on Engineering 2014, vol. 1, pp. 224–227 (2014)
12. Sharipbay, A., Omarbekova, A., Nurgazinova, G.: Creating intelligent electronic textbooks in Kazakhstan. In: 6th International Conference on Education and New Learning Technologies. Barcelona/Spain, pp. 2926–2933 (2014)

13. Nurgazinova, G., Golenkov, V., Sharipbay, A., Omarbekova, A., Barlybayev, A.: Designing of intelligent reference system for algebra based on the knowledge database. In: International Conference on Control, Automation and Artificial Intelligence, pp. 230–235 (2015)
14. Pillutla, V.S., Tawfik, A.A., Giabbanelli, P.J.: Detecting the depth and progression of learning in massive open online courses by mining discussion data. Technol. Knowl. Learn. (2020). https://doi.org/10.1007/s10758-020-09434-w
15. Soltani, M., Zarzour, H., Babahenini, M.C., Chemam, C.: An affective tutoring system for massive open online courses. In: Bouhlel, M.S., Rovetta, S. (eds.) SETIT 2018. SIST, vol. 146, pp. 202–211. Springer, Cham (2020). https://doi.org/10.1007/978-3-030-21005-2_20
16. Alrajhi, L., Alharbi, K., Cristea, A.I.: A multidimensional deep learner model of urgent instructor intervention need in MOOC forum posts (2020). https://doi.org/10.1007/978-3-030-49663-0_27
17. Yergesh, B., Mukanova, A., Sharipbay, A., Bekmanova, G., Razakhova, B.: Semantic hyper-graph based representation of nouns in the Kazakh language. Computacion y Sistemas 18(3), 627–635 (2014)
18. Bekmanova, G., Sharipbay, A., Omarbekova, A., Yelibayeva, G., Yergesh, B.: Adequate assessment of the customers actual reviews through comparing them with the fake ones. In: Proceedings of 2017 International Conference on Engineering and Technology, pp. 1–4 (2018)
19. Mukanova, A., Yergesh, B., Bekmanova, G., Razakhova, B., Sharipbay, A.: Formal models of nouns in the Kazakh language. Leonardo Electron. J. Pract. Technol. 13(25), 264–273 (2014)
20. Bazarova, M., Zhomartkyzy, G.: Ontological model of professional competences for ICT-specilaists 6D070300. Vestnik KazNITU. №1 (119), pp. 321–328 (2017)
21. Bazarova, M., Zhomartkyzy, G., Wojcik, W., Krak, Yu.: Construction of individual trajectories of training specialists in the field of information and communication technologies. J. Autom. Inf. Sci. 49(10), 36–46 (2017)
22. Liu, BL., Hu, B., Wang, XY., Zheng, L.: A RDF-based knowledgebase implementation for E-learning. New Horizon in Web-based Learning. In: 3rd International Conference on Web-Based Learning, pp. 45–50 (2004)
23. Wang, L., Zhang, Yu., Liu, T.: A deep learning approach for question answering over knowledge base. In: Lin, C.-Y., Xue, N., Zhao, D., Huang, X., Feng, Y. (eds.) ICCPOL/NLPCC 2016. LNCS (LNAI), vol. 10102, pp. 885–892. Springer, Cham (2016). https://doi.org/10.1007/978-3-319-50496-4_82
24. Omarbekova, A., Sharipbay, A., Barlybaev, B.: Generation of test questions from RDF files using PYTHON and SPARQL. J. Phys. Conf. Ser. 806(1), 012009 (2017)
25. Omarbekova, A., Nurgazinova, G., Sharipbay, A., Barlybayev, A., Bekmanova, G.: Automatic formation of questions and answers on the basis of the knowledge base. Paper presented at the Proceedings of 2017 International Conference on Engineering and Technology (2018)
26. Yelibayeva, G., Mukanova, A., Sharipbay, A., Zulkhazhav, A., Yergesh, B., Bekmanova, G.: Metalanguage and knowledgebase for Kazakh morphology. In: Misra, S., et al. (eds.) ICCSA 2019. LNCS, vol. 11619, pp. 693–706. Springer, Cham (2019). https://doi.org/10.1007/978-3-030-24289-3_51
27. https://protege.stanford.edu/
28. Yergesh, B., Bekmanova, G., Sharipbay, A., Yergesh, M.: Ontology-based sentiment analysis of kazakh sentences. In: Gervasi, O., et al. (eds.) ICCSA 2017. LNCS, vol. 10406, pp. 669–677. Springer, Cham (2017). https://doi.org/10.1007/978-3-319-62398-6_47

29. Sharipbayev, A., Bekmanova, G., Yergesh, B., Mukanova, A., Buribayeva, A.: Semantic retrieval of information in the Kazakh language in elibraries. J. Int. Sci. Pub. Educ. Alter. **10**, part 1, 108–115. (2014)
30. Zulfiya, K., Gulmira, B., Altynbek, S.: Ontological model for student's knowledge assessment. Paper presented at the ACM International Conference Proceeding Series (2019)
31. Zulfiya, K., Gulmira, B., Altynbek, S., Assel, O.: A model and a method for assessing students' competencies in e-learning system. Paper presented at the ACM International Conference Proceeding Series (2019)
32. Barlybayev, A., Kaderkeyeva, Z., Bekmanova, G., Sharipbay, A., Omarbekova, A., Altynbek, S.: Intelligent system for evaluating the level of formation of professional competencies of students (2020)

Flexible Model for Organizing Blended and Distance Learning

Gulmira Bekmanova[✉] and Yerkin Ongarbayev

L.N. Gumilyov Eurasian National University, Nur-Sultan, Kazakhstan
gulmira-r@yandex.kz, ongarbayevy61@mail.ru

Abstract. The proposed flexible model for the organization of mixed and distance learning involves the creation of an individual learning path for student testing before starting training. Based on the learning outcomes, the student is credited to the learning path. The learning path consists of mandatory and optional modules for training, optional modules can be skipped by passing the test successfully. The training model is represented using the ontological model, and the decision-making rules for the model are logical rules.

Keywords: Blended learning · Distance learning · E-learning · Ontological model · Artificial intelligence · Digital literacy · Lifelong learning

1 Introduction

The main goal of this research is to create a flexible model of blended and distance learning, which will allow students and teachers to work more efficiently and effectively organize educational activities. The research also aims to increase interest in intelligent learning systems, blended, distance and e-learning among teachers. The model will be considered on the example of the organization of advanced training courses as lifelong learning for teachers. The course is devoted to the formation of digital skills of university professors, which is supposed to be organized before the start of the new school year. In the context of the COVID-19 pandemic, the universities of the world switched to distance learning, including traditional universities that taught face-to-face. In such circumstances, many teachers felt a lack of digital skills and it was decided to organize long practice-oriented courses for teachers. However, in the context of a large university with a large number of teachers and a wide range of educational programs, which is inherent in classical universities, the level of digital skills of teachers is completely different. However, a survey conducted among teachers showed that teachers of engineering programs want to improve their digital skills, not to mention teachers of humanities. Since the resources of the training Center are limited, and each teacher requires an individual learning path, it became clear there was a need for organization of courses that would help teachers to improve their skills, and it was decided to develop a flexible model for organizing blended and distance learning. This model is applicable both for blended learning and for distance learning and contains online lectures, online tests, as well as practical exercises, which, depending on the type of organization of the lesson, can take place either face-to-face or online. The flexibility

© Springer Nature Switzerland AG 2020
O. Gervasi et al. (Eds.): ICCSA 2020, LNCS 12250, pp. 282–292, 2020.
https://doi.org/10.1007/978-3-030-58802-1_21

of the model is provided with enrollment in this course. Each student passes an entrance test, which determines their level of digital skills. The levels are conditionally divided into four: beginner, elementary, intermediate, advanced. In case of determining the advanced level, digital skills training is not carried out and the applicant can be enrolled in another advanced course. The rest of the tested applicants, depending on the level of skills, are credited to one of three trajectories, which are also quite flexible. If the applicants have any skills at the entrance to the module inside the trajectory, they can skip it by passing the test and immediately get to the next module.

Modern researches in the field of blended, distance, e-learning show that students use technology in various ways, adapting communication tools in accordance with their individual needs [1]. Availability and flexibility of digital resources created the prerequisites for the further development of accessibility and flexibility of education [2].

Thus, the 21st century students tend to exhibit the following characteristics [3]:

1) They prefer multimedia environments, are constantly connected with their peers and most of the time via the Internet,
2) They require several consecutive stimuli (to avoid boredom),
3) They are impatient, and need constant feedback during the assignment completion,
4) They are social and pragmatic,
5) They focus on team spirit,
6) They adapt training to individual needs.

In order to develop a high-quality course that meets modern expectations, it was decided to develop a course for teachers with recorded online lectures on the necessary theoretical knowledge. To support the mastery of practical skills, video instructions have been prepared for working with various services. All instructions are written in the form of text documents for students who prefer a text format, packages of case studies, traditional tasks, questions and tests are developed. The instructors of this course have been given great freedom in creating tasks, so the tasks are prepared in a creative and varied way. Thus, criteria 1) and 2) are satisfied. Constant feedback is provided by the instructor conducting the lesson during the lesson, online and offline. As a necessary part of the course a chat and a forum for participants of the same trajectory is organized. Thus, criterion 3) is satisfied. Some tasks involve the fulfillment of team tasks, therefore, for the performance of such tasks, pedagogical scenarios have been developed for organizing the performance of these tasks in a team, both online and in class, in this way criteria 4) and 5) are satisfied. The flexibility of this model is laid down in the name and the moment of enrolling in the course, and until the end, the student can adapt it to the individual needs, thus, criteria 6) is fulfilled. Given all of the above, a flexible model for organizing blended and distance learning meets these requirements.

2   Related Works

E-learning systems actively use models and methods of artificial intelligence [4–7]. The effectiveness of such training are noted in the articles devoted to the study of the use of blended and distance learning using artificial intelligence.

The article [8] describes the implementation and experience of blended learning in the intellectual learning environment @KU-UZEM. The blended learning model is implemented as a combination of face-to-face learning and e-learning. The intellectual learning environment diagnoses the level of students' knowledge, and also gives feedback and tips to help them in understanding the subject of the course, overcome their mistakes and consolidate the concepts studied. ITest provides an assessment environment in which students can take tests that have been prepared according to their level of study. In [9], the blended learning is achieved through a Learning Management System (LMS) using distance learning technology. LMS consists of course materials supported by flash animation, student records, user roles, and grading systems such as surveys and tests that comply with SCORM standards, and the learning process has been supported by an intelligent program. The article [10] identifies system requirements for an intelligent, mobile blended learning environment (m-Learning). Here, the theories of ontology modeling are developed. A context-sensitive adaptation mechanism, using explicit and implicit knowledge of the student profile model, is proposed. It is shown that the context in which the training takes place is represented by a set of functions that contextually depend on the training modeled as an ontology with multiple relations. The implemented prototype is a partially contextual system for representing m-Learning data. It is concluded that the m-learning environment is useful for the results of the program, mainly for students who study according to the gateogical model. Further work is being carried out to cover the m-Learning requirements that are better suited for students using the model of pedagogical education. Representation ontologies describe a conceptual model, which is the basis of the knowledge representation formalism. Ontology is successfully used in modeling systems for various types of knowledge. For example, ontological models for representing knowledge are proposed in articles [11–16]. The use of ontologies for modeling knowledge in specific areas is a key aspect for integrating information from different sources, for supporting collaboration in virtual communities, for improving the search for information, and, more generally, it is important to justify the existing knowledge. In the field of e-learning, ontologies can be used to model educational areas, as well as to create, organize and update specific learning resources. One of the main problems in modeling educational areas is the lack of experience in the field of knowledge engineering by e-learning participants. The paper [17] presents a comprehensive approach to ontology lifecycle management, used to determine personalized e-learning experience. The development of systems capable of drawing logical conclusions from the knowledge base is developing rapidly around the world. The extraction of existing and the generation of new knowledge and statements from the existing knowledge base is carried out using specialized mechanisms designed for reasoning and logical conclusions [18–23]. In the article [24], the authors propose implementing an Intelligent system for assessing the formation of professional competencies of students based on fuzzy models and logical conclusions from the knowledge base for distance learning systems. В [25] предложена модель и метод оценки компетенций студентов e-learning system. In [25], the authors propose a model and method for assessing students' competencies in the e-learning system.

3   Entrance Testing for Students

Entrance testing for students is carried out in order to determine their level of digital skills. Entrance testing is carried out by a multiple choice test with a single correct answer. The test contains 50% of questions of difficulty level A, 30% of difficulty level B and 20% of questions of difficulty C. The test tasks are developed in accordance with the following requirements for difficulty levels.

Test tasks of difficulty level A:

"identification" of some object or verification of "knowledge-familiarity";

choosing one answer from many knowing just one concept;

open type task aimed at revealing knowledge of the definition of a monosyllabic basic term.

Test tasks of difficulty level B:

it is aimed at the application of previously acquired knowledge in typical situations (that is, in those situations with which the subject is familiar) or to check the "knowledge of copy reproduction". Test tasks of this level of difficulty should include test tasks aimed at thinking related to statements of a conjunctive or disjunctive form or test tasks with several concepts for choosing a subset of the correct options from a given set of conclusions. In some cases, test tasks for compliance and order can be assigned to test tasks of this level of difficulty.

Test tasks of difficulty level C:

it is aimed at the application of acquired knowledge and skills in non-standard conditions (that is, in conditions previously unfamiliar to the subject) or to test "knowledge of skills and application". Test tasks of this level of difficulty include tasks that cause conclusions formulated in the form of statements of an implicative type. Such tasks require the use of reasoning in the form of deductive, inductive inference and analogy, and in order to obtain the final answer, some sequence of conclusions (several concepts) is required.

The percentage of test items, points and its difficulty are presented in Table 1.

Table 1. Digital skills levels

Test difficulty level	Percentage of questions in one test	Range of points	Digital Skill levels
A	25%	0–30	Beginner
A	25%	31–60	Elementary
B	30%	61–95	Intermediate
C	20%	96–120	Advanced

A formalization and a method for calculating the assessment of knowledge on the advanced training course are proposed. They have been considered in [24]. Here, the response in a natural language is evaluated compared to the reference answer from the knowledge base, and, in this case, a simple multiple choice test with a single correct answer is evaluated. In the considered case, the assessment model presented in [24] is simplified and looks as follows:

Let P be a finite and non-empty set representing a knowledge base of a given discipline; Q – a finite and non-empty set representing a base of test questions on a given discipline; S – a finite set representing a knowledge base of student answers to the test questions in a given discipline. Then it is possible to define the following rules for decision making:

If the set of student's answers an empty set, i.e. $S = \emptyset$, it is believed that there is not a single answer to test questions;

If the set of student's answers to the test questions is not an empty set, but is not contained in the knowledge base of a given discipline, i.e., $S \neq \emptyset$ & $S \not\subset P$, then it is believed that a student does not know the material for a given discipline;

If the set of student's answers to the test questions is not an empty set, but completely coincides with the set of correct answers, i.e., $S \neq \emptyset$ & $S = T$, then it is believed that a student fully knows the material which is foreseen in the standard answers;

If the set of student's answers to the test questions is not an empty set, but is strictly contained in the set of correct answers, i.e. $S \neq \emptyset$ & $S \subset T$, then it is believed that a student partially knows the material foreseen in the correct answers;

Теперь, с учетом выше определенных правил для принятия решений можно определить оценку ответов студента на тестовые вопросы в виде следующего нечеткого бинарного отношения: Now, taking into account the above specific rules for decision making, it is possible to determine the assessment of student's answers to the test questions in the form of the following fuzzy binary relationship

$$'Assesment' \rightleftharpoons S{\subseteq}T = \{ <s,t> \mid s \in S, t \in T, \ \mu_{S\subseteq T}(<s,t>)\},$$

Where $\mu_{S\subseteq T} : S \times T \to]0, 1[$ – membership function for fuzzy relations.

To calculate the elements of a fuzzy relation $S{\subseteq}T$, it is necessary to specify the elements of sets S and T that represent the set of individuals of the class, the set of properties of the class and the set of semantic arcs incident to the class.

Now we present the method of assessing the level of knowledge proposed in [21].

Let $Q = \{q_1, q_2, \ldots, q_n\}$ be a set of test questions, $S = \{s_1, s_2, \ldots, s_n\}$ – a set of student's answers to test questions, $T = \{t_1, t_2, \ldots, t_n\}$ – a set of correct answers – $q_1, q_2, \ldots, q_n$, respectively. Then the fuzzy binary relation $S{\subseteq}T$ can be represented using Table 2, in which the elements of the set S serve as row names, and the elements of the set T serve as column names. At the intersection of a row S_k and a column t_l, there is a placed element $\mu_{S\subseteq T}(<s_k, t_l)$, $k = 1, 2, \ldots, n$; $l = 1, 2, \ldots, n$.

Table 2. Definition of a fuzzy binary relation $S \subseteq T$.

	t_1	t_2	$\cdots$	t_n
s_1	$\mu_{S \subseteq T}(<s_1,t_1>)$	$\mu_{S \subseteq T}(<s_1,t_2>)$	$\cdots$	$\mu_{S \subseteq T}(<s_1,t_n>)$
s_2	$\mu_{S \subseteq T}(<s_2,t_1>)$	$\mu_{S \subseteq T}(<s_2,t_2>)$	$\cdots$	$\mu_{S \subseteq T}(<s_2,t_n>)$
$\ldots$	$\ldots$	$\ldots$	$\cdots$	$\ldots$
s_n	$\mu_{S \subseteq T}(<s_n,t_1>)$	$\mu_{S \subseteq T}(<s_n,t_2>)$	$\cdots$	$\mu_{S \subseteq T}(<s_n,t_n>)$

The total score corresponding to Table 2 is calculated by the next formula:

$$\mu_{S \subseteq T}(<s,t>) = \frac{\sum_{k}^{n} \sum_{l}^{n} \mu_{S \subseteq T}(<s_k,t_l>)}{n*n} \tag{1}$$

In the general case, Table 2 can be multidimensional, in which the elements can again be tables, i.e. it can have several levels of hierarchy. For each table, regardless of its hierarchy level, the overall score will be calculated using a formula similar to formula (1). In this case, the overall score of the low-level table will be considered the value of the table element of the nearest upper level.

Thus, we have developed a method for assessing knowledge in a given subject area based on a fuzzy relationship between the sets of student's answers to test questions and the sets of correct answers.

Now we will translate the calculated grade into the grade using the value of the grade relationship in determining the level of the testee:

$$'Assesment' = \begin{cases} \text{beginner, if } 0 \leq \mu_{S \subseteq T}(<s,t>) \leq 0.25 \\ \text{elementary, if } 0.26 \leq \mu_{S \subseteq T}(<s,t>) \leq 0.5 \\ \text{intermediate, if } 0.51 \leq \mu_{S \subseteq T}(<s,t>) \leq 0.79 \\ \text{advanced, if } 0.8 \leq \mu_{S \subseteq T}(<s,t>) \leq 1 \end{cases}$$

After determining the initial level of the student as beginner, elementary, intermediate or advanced, within the framework of the considered course, enrollment for the corresponding learning trajectory is made. Test takers with the advanced level fall into the reserve for admission to courses requiring high professional skills.

4 Ontological Model of a Lifelong Learning Course

The term "ontology" (the word "ontology" comes from the Greek "ontos" - existing and "logos" - concept, teaching, reason), proposed by R. Goklenius, appeared in 1613. At present, the methods of knowledge engineering, the young science of the extraction, structuring, presentation and processing of knowledge are becoming more and more popular. One of such conceptual shifts aimed at further intellectualization of user interaction systems was the emergence of ontologies. Since ontologies were the answer of science to the urgent needs of their time, their appearance also occurred in several areas of knowledge at once. Accordingly, in each of them the resources of the onto-logical type were formed according to their own rules specific to the field of knowl-edge. The ontological model is built in Protégé tool [27]. It was developed at Stanford University in collaboration with the University of Manchester. The Protégé tool is a Java program that is freely distributed and designed to develop (design, modify, view) ontological structures of various subject areas. The program allows you to design ontologies, expanding the hierarchical structure of abstract and concrete classes and slots. Having formed the ontological structure, the ontology editor allows you to generate forms for obtaining knowledge for defining instances of classes and sub-classes. The ontology editor Protégé supports the use of the OWL language, and also allows the generation of HTML documents that display the structure of ontologies. The use of a frame model of knowledge representation allows Protégé to be adapted for editing domain models, which are presented not only in the OWL language, but also in other formats. A comparative analysis of ontology editors by eight key criteria showed Protégé's excellence. Ontological structures can be developed and used in solving many diverse problems, also for multi-user sharing.

The ontology defines a set of representative primitives in the context of computer and information sciences with which we can model a field of knowledge or a discourse. The representative primitives are usually classes (or sets), attributes (or properties), and relationships (or relationships between members within a class). The definitions for representative primitives include information about their meaning and limitations of their logically concerted application.

This formalism determines the "O" ontology as triple (V, R, K), where V – is a set of classes for the subject field, R – is a set of relationships between the classes, and K – is a set of attributes within the field [13].

The ontological model consists of modules for advanced training and tests (Fig. 1).

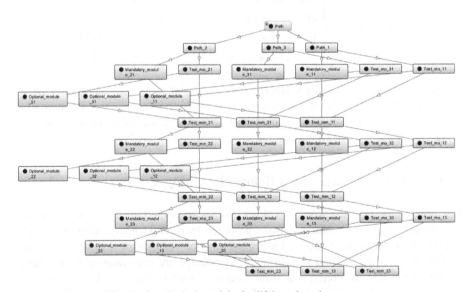

Fig. 1. Ontological model of a lifelong learning course

Each of the modules includes the mandatory modules, completion of which ends with the test and the optional modules, which begin with taking the test and, if the test is passed, it can be skipped. The described ontological model should minimize the inevitable repetitions that arise during the study of the course and provide students and their teachers with the opportunity to create individualized educational trajectories. Both mandatory and optional modules can be implemented both in a blended learning model and in a distance model. In the mixed model, it is assumed that practical classes are held face-to-face, and lectures can be held either online, offline, or face-to-face in a flipped classroom model. In the distance learning model, all classes are held in a remote format.

A possible variant of trajectory 1 in a bracketed formal record, in the case when the student successfully passed the tests for the optional module and does not study them, may look like this:

Path_1:

((((Mandatory_module_11)Test_mm_11) Test_mo_11) Mandatory_module_12) (Test_mm_12) Test_mo_12) (Mandatory_module_13(Test_mm_13) Test_mo_13))

Students are enrolled on Path_1 from among beginner students. The main software products related to computer literacy of teachers are products of Microsoft, therefore, although the teaching is carried out by university employees, the content of the Microsoft course is taken as the basis [27]. The course starts with the required module 11 "Work with Computers" and optional module 11 "Interract with a computer", the mandatory module 12 "Use a computer", optional module 12 "Access information online", the required module 13 "Communicate online", optional module 13 "Participate safely and responsibly online."

The ontological model of the advanced training course allows organizing flexible training in both mixed and distance formats.

An advanced training course should ensure the achievement of the planned learning outcomes. Its development should meet the following principles:

- use of a video lecture or MOOC mechanism;
- the use of didactic materials developed in accordance with the developed university procedure;
- result-centeredness of the course;
- automatic control of the planned results for mastering the competencies (planning and development of assessment tools for the course, providing control of the abilities to apply knowledge in practice at the set deadlines);
- automatic management of the entire educational process based on the selected structured course content (all educational material should be divided into small, easy-to-learn finished fragments, ending with automatic control and assessment of the level of formation of the planned learning outcomes);
- transparency of the criteria for assessing learning outcomes in points established in accordance with the complexity of their formation;
- increasing motivation for learning through the use of various techniques;
- joint training through network technologies of communication and counseling by the students themselves in the process of studying the course;

- the availability of electronic courses for anyone by means of basic Internet technologies, including mobile devices.

Thus, the Flexible model for organizing blended and distance learning based on ontology as the structural basis of the knowledge base allows us to implement the principles of mass variable learning and are able to provide individual educational trajectories.

5 Conclusion

In this paper, a flexible model for organizing blended and distance learning was proposed. The content of the course is presented in the form of an ontological model, which allows creating links between the course modules and test tasks. Based on the entrance testing, the student is enrolled in the learning trajectory. The training path consists of mandatory and additional modules for training, additional modules may be skipped if the test is passed successfully. The training model is represented using the ontological model, and the decision making rules for the model are the logical rules. The advanced training courses based on the ontological model using video lectures increase the efficiency of the learning process due to the growth of students' motivation and the possibility of parallel training of students with significantly different starting capabilities.

6 Further Work

Further work prospects, in our opinion, lie in creating a larger number of courses, based on entrance testing and individualization of the learning path with an improved system for assessing the level of mastering material, which will be based on semantic search, optimal ontology visualization and interactive dialogue.

In the future, it is planned to use the technology of formation and assessment of competencies, which can be used to form the assessment of competence of any EP. The technology is described in article [24]. In developing the technology for assessing competencies, the following points were taken into account: disciplines are the main links in educational activity, and it is the levels of students' mastery of the disciplines that are being evaluated. It is obvious that, evaluating the level of knowledge in the disciplines, in the end, you can correctly establish the level of competencies. In such conditions, it is more convenient to adapt the already accumulated experience and use adapted diagnostic methods within the framework of the competency-based approach. Within the framework of the methodological aspects of the automated competency assessment, a knowledge base will be developed on test questions of various types and difficulty levels. In addition, in technical aspects, researchers will continue to develop software that implements all stages of the semantic analysis of texts based on ontological technologies and natural language processing. The research results can be used to create intelligent distance learning systems and to assess competencies in a natural language.

References

1. Conole, G., de Laat, M., Darby, J.: Disruptive technologies', 'pedagogical innovation': what's new? findings from an in-depth study of students' use and perception of technology. Comput. Educ. **50**(2), 511–524 (2008)
2. Dias, S.B., Diniz, J.A., Hadjileontiadis, L.J.: Towards an Intelligent Learning Management System Under Blended Learning Trends, Profiles and Modeling Perspectives. Springer, Cham (2014). https://doi.org/10.1007/978-3-319-02078-5
3. Redecker, C., Ala-Mutka K., Bacigalupo M., Ferrari A., Punie, Y.: Learning 2.0: The Impact of web 2.0 Innovations on Education and Training in Europe. Joint Research Centre (JRC)-Institute for Prospective Technological Studies (2009). http://is.jrc.ec.europa.eu/pages/Learning-2.0.html
4. Sharipbay, A., Barlybayev, A., Sabyrov, T.: Measure the usability of graphical user interface. In: New Advances in Information Systems and Technologies. AISC, vol. 444, pp. 1037–1045. Springer, Cham (2016). https://doi.org/10.1007/978-3-319-31232-3_98
5. Sharipbay, A., Omarbekova, A., Seifullina, A., Zakirova, A.: Creating intelligent electronic textbooks based on knowledge management. In: The World Congress on Engineering 2014, vol. 1, pp. 224–227 (2014)
6. Sharipbay, A., Omarbekova, A., Nurgazinova, G.: Creating intelligent electronic textbooks in Kazakhstan. In: 6th International Conference on Education and New Learning Technologies. Barcelona/Spain, pp. 2926–2933 (2014)
7. Nurgazinova, G., Golenkov, V., Sharipbay, A., Omarbekova, A., Barlybayev, A.: Designing of intelligent reference system for algebra based on the knowledge database. In: International Conference on Control, Automation and Artificial Intelligence, pp. 230–235 (2015)
8. Köse, U., Deperlioglu, O.: Intelligent learning environments wthin blended learning for ensuring effective C programming course. Int. J. Artif. Intell. Appl. **3** (2012). https://doi.org/10.5121/ijaia.2012.3109
9. Yigit, T., Koyun, A., Yüksel, A., Cankaya, I., Köse, U.: An Example Application of Artificial Intelligence Supported Blended Learning Education Program in Computer Engineering (2014). https://doi.org/10.4018/978-1-4666-6276-6.ch012
10. Newell, D., Davies, P., Austin, R., Moore, P., Sharma, M.: Models for an intelligent context-aware blended m-learning system. In: 2015 IEEE 29th International Conference on Advanced Information Networking and Applications Workshops, Gwangiu, pp. 405–410 (2015). https://doi.org/10.1109/waina.2015.25
11. Yergesh, B., Mukanova, A., Sharipbay, A., Bekmanova, G., Razakhova, B.: Semantic hyper-graph based representation of nouns in the Kazakh language. Computacion y Sistemas **18**(3), 627–635 (2014)
12. Bekmanova, G., Sharipbay, A., Omarbekova, A., Yelibayeva, G., Yergesh, B.: Adequate assessment of the customers actual reviews through comparing them with the fake ones. In: Proceedings of 2017 International Conference on Engineering and Technology, pp. 1–4 (2018)
13. Mukanova, A., Yergesh, B., Bekmanova, G., Razakhova, B., Sharipbay, A.: Formal models of nouns in the Kazakh language. Leonardo Electron. J. Pract. Technol. **13**(25), 264–273 (2014)
14. Bazarova, M., Zhomartkyzy, G.: Ontological model of professional competences for ICT-specilaists 6D070300. Vestnik KazNITU. №1 (119), pp. 321–328 (2017)
15. Zulfiya, K., Gulmira, B., Altynbek, S.: Ontological model for student's knowledge assessment. Paper Presented at the ACM International Conference Proceeding Series (2019)

16. Yergesh, B., Bekmanova, G., Sharipbay, A., Yergesh, B.: Ontology-Based Sentiment Analysis of Kazakh Sentences (2017)
17. Gaeta, M., Orciuoli, F., Ritrovato, P.: Advanced ontology management system for personalised e-Learning. Knowl. Based Syst. **22**(4), 292–301 (2009)
18. Liu, B.L., Hu, B., Wang, X.Y., Zheng, L.: A RDF-based knowledge base implementation for E-learning. New horizon in web-based learning. In: 3rd International Conference on Web-Based Learning, pp. 45–50 (2004)
19. Wang, L., Zhang, Yu., Liu, T.: A deep learning approach for question answering over knowledge base. In: Lin, C.-Y., Xue, N., Zhao, D., Huang, X., Feng, Y. (eds.) ICCPOL/NLPCC -2016. LNCS (LNAI), vol. 10102, pp. 885–892. Springer, Cham (2016). https://doi.org/10.1007/978-3-319-50496-4_82
20. Omarbekova, A., Sharipbay, A., Barlybaev, B.: Generation of test questions from RDF files using PYTHON and SPARQL. J. Phys. Conf. Ser. **806**(1) (2017)
21. Omarbekova, A., Nurgazinova, G., Sharipbay, A., Barlybayev, A., Bekmanova, G.: Automatic formation of questions and answers on the basis of the knowledge base. In: Paper presented at the Proceedings of 2017 International Conference on Engineering and Technology (2018)
22. Yelibayeva, G., Mukanova, A., Sharipbay, A., Zulkhazhav, A., Yergesh, B., Bekmanova, G.: Metalanguage and knowledgebase for Kazakh morphology. In: Misra, S., et al. (eds.) ICCSA 2019. LNCS, vol. 11619, pp. 693–706. Springer, Cham (2019). https://doi.org/10.1007/978-3-030-24289-3_51
23. Sharipbayev, A., Bekmanova, G., Yergesh, B., Mukanova, A., Buribayeva, A.: Semantic retrieval of information in the Kazakh language in elibraries. J. Int. Sci. Publ. Educ. Alternat. **10**(1), 108–115 (2014)
24. Barlybayev, A., Kaderkeyeva, Z., Bekmanova, G., Sharipbay, A., Omarbekova, A., Altynbek, S.: Intelligent System for Evaluating the Level of Formation of Professional Competencies of Students (2020)
25. Zulfiya, K., Gulmira, B., Altynbek, S., Assel, O.: A model and a method for assessing students' competencies in e-learning system. Paper Presented at the ACM International Conference Proceeding Series (2019)
26. https://protege.stanford.edu/
27. https://www.microsoft.com/en-us/digitalliteracy/home

Reshaping Higher Education with e-Studium, a 10-Years Capstone in Academic Computing

Valentina Franzoni$^{(\boxtimes)}$, Simonetta Pallottelli, and Alfredo Milani

Department of Mathematics and Computer Science, University of Perugia, Perugia, Italy
valentina.franzoni@dmi.unipg.it,
{simonetta.pallottelli,milani}@unipg.it

Abstract. E-Studium has been a long-running project of blended e-learning for higher education based on the learning management system Moodle, implemented at University of Perugia, Italy from 2005 to 2015. The capstone culminated in a refined final product, at the basis of the actual academic platform Unistudium. In its ten-years activity, e-Studium has been a learning pathway experience for a variety of applications, included STEM courses, from high school education to high-specialisation academic courses, teacher's qualification, and third mission for technology transfer, with a particular focus on usability and teacher's self-evaluation. The analysis of both objective and subjective evaluations, collected over ten years from activity logs, web analytics, global rankings, and ad hoc questionnaires, together with teachers and students' outcomes, shows how e-Studium contributed to reshaping the educational offer of large-scale learning in University of Perugia and Italy. This paper aims at showing the evolution and the outcomes of e-Studium, under the vision of the contemporary natural evolution of the technological learning economy, assessing and sharing educational experiences based on the evolution of innovative technologies for lifelong e-learning. A particular focus will be given on how such contribution can enhance the actual extraordinary situation, which sees a worldwide unexpected and abrupt need for remote communication due to the COVID-19 emergency.

Keywords: Academic freedom · Institutional diversity · ICT · STEM · Continuous education · Coronavirus

1 Introduction

The learning environment dynamically evolves, both qualitatively and quantitatively, adapting to specific educational situations both for teachers and for students. Real-time events and needs, and online opportunities and paradigms reshape the landscape of learning. Universities no longer have the monopoly of knowledge production but are an active environment where knowledge and learning can more easily meet, in a modern vision of higher education [1]. The actual COVID-19 worldwide emergency stressed the importance of broad and deep experience in e-learning for university and school environments [2]. In this scenario, intending to help who abruptly woke up in a distant learning world from one day to the next, we offered in this paper a case study report of

© Springer Nature Switzerland AG 2020
O. Gervasi et al. (Eds.): ICCSA 2020, LNCS 12250, pp. 293–303, 2020.
https://doi.org/10.1007/978-3-030-58802-1_22

a ten-years-long experience in e-learning and blended learning when it was not mainstream.

E-learning is a well-known application of Internet Computer Technology (ICT) where advanced technologies reduce space and time constraints for learning, giving to education a ubiquitous flavour. Blended learning [3] is a hybrid educational strategy combining e-learning with traditional classroom-based learning to support the educational process and distribute multimedia contents [4]. In such a complex environment, single users, groups, resources and virtual classrooms meet to transfer knowledge and information and to implement online activities [5, 6].

From 2005 to 2015, in the project named e-Studium, cooperation between e-learning technologies and traditional didactics has been implemented and developed, with the adoption of ICT methodologies and systems in the university courses of the faculties of Science and Literature of University of Perugia, Italy. This long experience has included teacher qualification and the so-called third mission, i.e., technology transfer from and to both internal spinoffs and external companies. The main aim of e-Studium, which has been broad anticipation of the STEM (Science, Technology, Engineering and Mathematics) education policy [7], has been a dynamic and versatile didactics evolution, supporting an active learning process with innovative technologies and teaching approaches, to respond to the individual needs of a comprehensive, diverse, and distributed audience. E-Studium goals included:

- integrating traditional didactics with advanced e-learning technologies, through the activation of a Learning Management System (LMS) for the distribution of courses and services, focusing on remote access for off-site students and commutators (notice that in 2005 personal Internet connection was not commonly available, as it can be now in the Covid-19 Italian school situation, where a family may not have the opportunity to connect in real-time several students and workers);
- building a learning management platform, personalised on university-level requirements, with features of usability and accessibility, following standards and establishing guidelines, to ensure equal opportunities independent from gender, culture and language, disabilities, and educational level;
- diffusing computing education with both horizontal (facilitator-students and peer interaction) and vertical (teacher-student) approaches, and increase the usage of ICT for academic teaching;
- providing teachers with both technical information and subjective belief according to their practical opportunities of technology usage in teaching and learning environments, to meet the challenge of facilitating student learning.

Specific tools have been provided for:

- students' automated assessment, where an automated correction of assignments is made by the system, with or without a teacher's proof;
- students' self-assessment;
- teacher's self-evaluation, with a specific focus on inclusion and performance, i.e., detecting and managing diverse needs of underperforming or overperforming students, and detecting which of the provided learning objects were the most or less used, where the less used probably needed a content or presentation review.

2   History of e-Studium

The e-learning an application area of information technology uses the complex ICT environment to distribute multimedia educational content by activating a remote ubiquitous learning environment. In this environment, individuals, groups, resources, natural and virtual classes meet to exchange information and carry out different online activities. The initial environment, when existent, is transformed (quantitatively and qualitatively) to adapt to the specific training situation of both the student and the teacher. Then it becomes a dynamic environment, which changes in real-time; it is reshaped according to the events of the course, the resources available, the activities proposed and how they are carried out.

It is with these prerogatives and scenarios that the idea of creating an e-learning platform that adapts to times, methods, and tools of a more modern didactics was born in the University of Perugia, Italy. Before the Italian law 240/2010 so-called "Gelmini Reform", named after the Italian minister of education of the time, didactics was provided by the Faculties through the Degree Courses. For example, the teaching of "Computer Science Laboratory" of the Degree Course in Biological Sciences, appeared under the Faculty of Science. This was the didactic organisation chart, which in reality, also provided the division into Bachelor and Master degrees. For some time now, we had been witnessing a radical change in the way of understanding and using the teaching-learning dyad, being able to synthesise a scenario that poses precise challenges, highlighting the opportunity, and at the same time the urgency, for university e-learning:

- students progressively demand a higher quality of the learning process;
- students, who for various reasons, because they are workers, or off-site or disabled, or because of regional emergencies such as the coronavirus lockdown, cannot follow lessons in the classroom, require a different way to enjoy learning;
- lecturers and other operators in universities, schools and educational environments face increasing teaching loads and require tools and support to increase teaching quality.

We are talking about the first years of the new millennium, when the need exploited for an organisational model of e-learning in an integrated form, which leads to the so-called blended e-learning, and for course management systems, for support for teaching in presence using online services and materials that allowed a broader use and participation of students (full-time and part-time). Such an approach followed the renewal of university didactics from a quality perspective. Remote participation could become a complete integration on two levels:

- vertical and reserved teacher-student interaction: the student and the teacher communicate remotely, e.g., by email, self-assessment tests, comments on assignments and papers;
- horizontal and public teacher-group interaction: the exchange takes place using both synchronous and asynchronous communication tools such as chat and forums.

In general, the aim was dynamic and versatile didactics, which could effectively support the learning process, using the innovative ICT technologies to respond in a personalised way to the needs of a broad audience of users distributed throughout the territory. With these premises, now more valid than ever, in a national context already ahead in remote communication after the diffusion of online social networks, in 2005 some teachers and researchers of the Department of Mathematics and Computer Science created the e-Studium project. The project, using information and communication technologies, has integrated the traditional teaching of university courses with e-learning services, offering technological and organisational support to all those who wanted to use and experiment with online teaching or simple training interventions. The primary goal of the e-Studium project, right from the choice of the name, was to reshape the teaching approach of the Perugia Studium, i.e., the academic communication approach: Studium was, in fact, the ancient Latin name of the university, officially sanctioned by the Super Specula, issued by Pope Clement V on September 8, 1308. The e-Studium project creation in this new scenario of e-learning technologies aimed at reshaping the university approach without losing the traditional experience obtained through centuries, which however needed to adapt to the pervasive and mass diffusion of networks and communication tools and exploit the new opportunities of the modern world.

3 Project Architecture Outline

See Fig. 1.

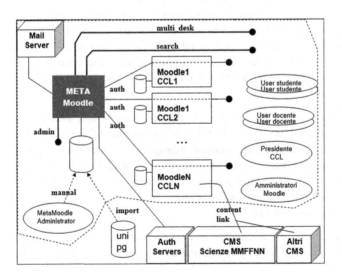

Fig. 1. Project architecture outline

4   Goals of the e-Studium Platform

The e-Studium project [3, 8, 9] redesigns university didactics towards the new scenario of information and communication technologies, with the following objectives:

- providing technological and organisational support to all those who want to use and experiment blended e-learning or remote learning interventions;
- favouring the improvement of the quality of teaching through the adoption of ICT tools.

The e-Studium group researchers have developed through the years specific innovative modules and services that have been tested in different courses, involving thousands of students from the Faculties of Mathematical, Physical, and Natural Sciences, Computer Science, Educational Sciences, Humanities and Philosophy, and others. Under the standards of an international open-source project, they offered to teachers and students various services, e.g., downloading teaching materials, registering for an online exam call, handing in papers and assignments, running tests and exercises, making an appointment, having a virtual reception with the professor, discussing with colleagues, reviewing lesson notes, participating in chats and forums. Such activities could be carried out from home, from the computer lab, as well as from any internet point, or from personal mobile devices, e.g. smartphones and tablets, when they became diffuse. The features of e-Studium have allowed teachers to structure the delivery of information by focusing it on the community of students in their course, with an enhancing interface transparent to the user gradually adapting to the technical advance, e.g., with mobile-style pages first, then responsive design, always following or in some cases preventing the progress of design of graphic users interfaces in a user-centred perspective. The teacher, in the same user-friendly way, could put online notes, exam results, discuss and evaluate projects delivered online, participate in forums with students, carry out automated tests, self-assessment tests, send urgent communications and, finally, monitor in a structured way the participation in activities and the growth path of students learning.

5   Experimental Growth of the Platform

A course in e-Studium is a space that does not replace the traditional lesson, but goes hand in hand with it, amplifying its possibilities of delivery and use, allowing the teacher to keep track of the activities carried out, which are then capitalised and can be revised, reworked and enjoyed without time or place limits. The platform architecture allowed to use it in different ways, for traditional or advanced teaching, from a simple notice board to the most sophisticated use of self-training.

5.1   Preliminary Experimental 1-Year Phase

The e-Studium project, in its first experimental phase, has given service to 13 Study Courses for a total of 301 lessons and a load of 2535 registered and active users. The results of the first year of experimentation of the project, obtained from the monitoring of the system, were considered very positive, fostering to go ahead with the integration and experimentation of innovative functionalities. The evaluation of the results was firstly carried out mainly through surveys and access and usage statistics. The following overview emerged from the processing and comparison of the available data:

- The main activities of the teachers were:
  - Insertion of programs, alerts, events
  - Frequent updates
  - Upload educational material
  - Preparation and download of registration lists
  - Examination quiz
- The main activities of the student were:
  - Exploration and zapping of the courses
  - Reading alerts, news and events
  - Download educational material
  - Registration for events
  - Performing tests and examination quizzes
- Teachers and students have carried out different activities:
  - Mainly in the proximity of events such as course start, exams, project delivery
  - Spreading out almost evenly over the 24 h of the day (there are no preferential time ranges shown by the usage statistics, taking into account the day-night cycle), which shows the use both during lessons both for personal study
  - Less frequently on the weekend, which highlights the integration with the usual weekly participation to the study course
- The duration of the connection, depending on the type of activity and result:
  - For students on average 11 min
  - For teachers on average 5 min

An interesting aspect was highlighted by the extensive use and appreciation shown by students, who pushed and motivated teachers who initially did not participate to the project preliminary experimentation, promoting the over-time expansion to serve an increasing number of users. In all the statistics, carried out subsequently in different periods and years, students are on average, more active than teachers. To be fair, it has to be said that the most considerable boost was given by the students, who insistently and positively requested a more excellent and complete use of this e-learning tool.

Over the years, based on the matured experience and under the push of individual teachers and numerous students, many other teachings courses have been added, up to an entire degree. Among the various applications, there is the management of computing education labs in liberal studies, training and qualification courses for STEM teachers, pre-graduate and post-graduate courses of computer science, the third mission in high schools and external companies.

5.2 Experiment Evolution

To the first activities provided by e-Studium mentioned above, during the following years, essential features have been added to meet the emergent needs of teachers and students:

- Events Registration Form: Enrolment for exam sessions, Reservation for laboratory access queues/shifts, Assignment to classes/shifts, Confirmation to the user via email/SMS, Registration opening/expiration, Digital signatures for examination reports
- Multilingual Keyboard Module: Multilingual content placement, Multilingual online keyboards, with no configuration/installation required
- Mathematical Keyboards Module: Input and visualisation of mathematical symbols in lessons and quizzes
- Online student reception, i.e. one-to-one talks between teacher and student: Slides view, Real-time textual chat, Multi-colored whiteboard, Content Downloading
- Timetable and Attendance Monitoring Module: Online and offline presence, Weighted activities with virtual minutes, Attendance certification and controllability

5.3   Final Advancement Phase

More recently, starting from 2012, a third phase had been launched, called *e-Studium mobile: e-learning on the move*, which aimed to test the advanced approach to provide mobile e-learning services to students and teachers. Through the extension of the functionality of the e-Studium platform, the aim had been to offer:

- advanced support to mobility (e.g., smartphones, tablets);
- dematerialisation of documents (e.g., eBooks and multimedia production);
- social learning (e.g., training social networks, interactive content generation).

In this phase, mobile learning services had been implemented, with the following features:

- display/browse e-Studium contents on widespread mobile devices (e.g., smartphones, PDAs, iPads, Android tablets);
- push/pull communication to mobile devices (e.g., sending communications, results reports, notifications);
- activation/deactivation of services by SMS;
- support for the creation, distribution, and use of eBooks;
- support for the integration of conventional content: whiteboard for content capture and distribution;
- distributed teaching support: interactive lessons, interaction on mobile devices (e.g., video/text chat, whiteboard, low-bandwidth streaming).

The actors involved in this third phase of the project were:

- Department of Mathematics and Informatics, with the role of proposing body, coordination, technological development and integration, and experimenting with mobile learning.
- Faculty of Letters and Philosophy, with the role of experimentation development for mobile learning, development and dissemination of eBook content.
- Bachelor of Science in Primary Education, with the role of experimenting with mobile e-learning, interactive teaching methods, and developing interactive content.

In particular, the different typology of subjects, which included both humanistic and scientific faculties, allowed to experiment a multidisciplinary approach on a wide range of different problems and situations, favouring the reuse and export of the project results to a broader context (other Faculties or schools). Finally, the competences in the field of Information Technology of the Department of Mathematics and Informatics, which complement those of Educational Science Didactics Technologies, offered guarantees of technical and scientific soundness for the objectives of the project.

The implementation and the use of the third-phase functionalities, and the results obtained were strongly encouraging.

The last phase also included the introduction of the teacher self-assessment dashboards [10], and the integration with the G-Lorep platform for cloud services [11, 12].

5.4   Numbers and Facts

E-Studium had been implemented as a Moodle open-source platform [13], which is freely available from the Internet and university labs, and nowadays used by 150090 currently active sites that are officially registered from 242 countries; many of them are universities and high-education centres. Moodle has been benefitting from a broad language translation community effort, to which the e-Studium research group actively contributed. E-Studium has involved 1598 courses taught in blended mode, for a total of 19050 users over ten years. E-Studium served over ten thousand students coming to Perugia University (Italy) from 51 countries.

In ten years, the project served 40 courses, besides doctoral schools, specialisation schools and master, courses for a professional teaching license, and more, for more than 500 topics, more than 300 teachers, more than 8000 registered users.

6   Hardware and Software Resources

In this section, we list the software resources used in e-Studium for ten years.

- Moodle, Open Source Platform for Course Management System
- Multimedia platform software: Flash image compression software, Authoring software, PPT Flash environment conversion, Macromedia Studio, Adobe Suite PDF manager, SMIL.

To the hardware resources listed in this subsection, it has to be added to the network infrastructure, including Internet access and high-speed broadband network connection for the duration of the project. The hardware resources list also includes all the devices used for the project creation but not strictly required to run it:

- Linux server for CMS platform
- Linux server for multimedia distribution support
- Multimedia production station for the preparation of educational material
- Computerised and equipped classroom with at least 20 places for training and use of the platform for teachers/students.

The choice of Moodle can be easily explained through the following features: Open Source software; consolidated development and validation community; thousands of platforms installed; multi-platform and multilingual software; expandable modular approach; research and experimentation possibilities.

There was, therefore, a correct initial choice, due to in-depth research about the available resources, before Moodle gained all the advantages mentioned above, which then proved to be the right one.

7 Evaluation of Learning Outcomes

The learning-pathway and final evaluation of e-Studium came in the form of the descriptive analysis of students and teachers learning outcomes, and of wide-level global rankings and webometrics.

In particular, we had provided:

- objective statistics on learning objects and learning outcomes;
- statistic on usage, via activity logs;
- subjective evaluation from both students and teachers, for the educational project and the platform usability;
- growth in web analytics;
- growth in national university rankings.

Among the most exciting results of the e-Studium project, there is the experimentation of a model of self-evaluation for teachers, based on visual feedback of the frequency of use of their learning objects. The interface provided to the teacher's view two different dashboards, summarising in a visual way using the dimension of the title or a heatmap using colours, to emphasise the frequency of use of the learning object, where a bigger title or a warmer colour means a higher appreciation, i.e. higher number of accesses, and a smaller title or a cooler colour means that students did not use a lot the learning object. Such feedback provided to the teacher a self-evaluation method to adapt or update the learning objects basing on their practical use.

Since the project involved the use of a multimedia platform, it allowed the research group to automatically certify and collect essential data on the use of the platform by users. The evaluation criteria used to measure the achievement of the objective and the impact on the target audience were distinguished into:

- subjective indicators (collection of questionnaires and individual interviews);
- objective indicators (automatic surveys of access and paths, SEO).

In particular, highlighted aspects included the increase in the number of participants by type of user (e.g. a high number of off-site users); the number of activities (e.g., profit test, self-assessment test, distribution of material); the improvement of the teacher-student relationship from an educational and organisational point of view.

Over time, the subjective evaluation showed that the project received unanimous support both from the students who actively animated it and from the teachers who have participated in their way. The system is characterised by extreme ease of use highlighted both by students and teachers, who appreciated being able to reproduce virtually some real entities (e.g., the "course", the "class", the "laboratory") and a whole series of services such as exam registrations, virtual receptions, discussion forums, FAQs, distribution of material, collection of tasks, self-assessment exercises.

Objective data included logs on the origin of the connections, duration of the connections, data on registered and active structures, raw and refined user data such as number, role, active and non-active users, also including the exams and self-assessment results.

8   Conclusion

The e-Studium project has fully achieved its objectives, improving over the years. As an overall result, e-Studium has been considered of particular value stimulating the introduction of technologies for university teaching improvement, and to have effectively achieved this goal with the introduction in the Faculties first, then in the Departments, and later in all the other collateral structures involved. The project now represents a wealth of data, systems and mature technologies that are offered to the University in its new academic teaching service.

It remains that the management of the teaching support of a university structure is a continuous evolutionary process, where new needs and new possibilities emerge continuously, both through interaction with students and teachers, who discover the new opportunities offered by this type of tools and propose new methods and functions and through continuous technological and research innovation in the sector.

It is therefore essential a continuous learning and research activity, for a consolidation of the results, and to reach the goals it is necessary to activate an organic structure that allows continuous innovation, updating and research in support of teaching.

The entire project, with all the information content and experience, gained, represents the core of a valuable service on which the University can develop a complete e-learning service integrated with all other online services already active.

We are convinced that the systematic and organic adoption of this type of technology at University level, and the promotion of their diffusion, can produce a synergy that will bring the provision of educational services to a quality level adequate to the best standards.

Acknowledgements. The e-Studium project had been funded by the Cassa Di Risparmio Foundation of Perugia, Italy and supported from a research group from the Department of Mathematics and Computer Science and the Department of Philosophy, Human and Social Sciences and Education of University of Perugia, Italy. Authors, who have been part of the e-Studium workgroup, thank all the colleagues of the e-Studium team who collaborated to the project over ten years, for their continuous engagement and support in the e-Studium project: Gulianella Coletti, Francesca Conti, Candida Gori, Floriana Falcinelli, Alfredo Milani, Stefano Marcugini, Simonetta Pallottelli, Valentina Poggioni, Gianluca Vinti, Alessandro Costantini, Emanuela Falcinelli, Valentina Franzoni, Judit Jasso, Daniele Manco, Marta Santapolo, Valentino Santucci, Silvia Suriani, Massimo Cimichella, Fabio Rossi. This final work has been partially supported by the PRIN project PHRAME - Phraseological Complexity Measures in learner Italian.

References

1. Isomöttönen, V., Tirronen, V.: Flipping and blending-an action research project on improving a functional programming course. ACM Trans. Comput. Educ. **17**, 1–35 (2016)
2. Vasilevskaya, M., Broman, D., Sandahl, K.: Assessing large-project courses: model, activities, and lessons learned. ACM Trans. Comput. Educ. **15**, 1–30 (2015)
3. Jassó, J., Milani, A., Pallottelli, S.: Blended e-learning: survey of online student assessment. In: Proceedings - International Workshop on Database and Expert Systems Applications, DEXA (2008)
4. Derntl, M., Motschnig-Pitrik, R.: The role of structure, patterns, and people in blended learning. Internet High. Educ. **8**, 111–130 (2005)
5. Alessi, S.M., Trollip, S.: Multimedia for Learning (2001)
6. Ruiperez-Valiente, J.A., Munoz-Merino, P.J., Kloos, C.D., Niemann, K., Scheffel, M., Wolpers, M.: Analysing the impact of using optional activities in self-regulated learning. IEEE Trans. Learn. Technol. **9**, 231–243 (2016)
7. Sanders, M.: STEM, STEM education, STEMmania. Technol. Teach. (2009)
8. Falcinelli, E., Gori, C., Jasso, J., Milani, A., Pallottelli, S.: E-studium: blended e-learning for university education support. Int. J. Learn. Technol. **4**, 110–124 (2009)
9. Falcinelli, E., Gori, C., Jasso, J., Milani, A., Pallottelli, S.: E-studium: an Italian experience of blended e-learning for university education support. In: Proceedings - International Workshop on Database and Expert Systems Applications, DEXA (2007)
10. Franzoni, V., Mengoni, P., Milani, A.: Dimensional morphing interface for dynamic learning evaluation. In: Information Visualisation - Biomedical Visualization, Visualisation on Built and Rural Environments and Geometric Modelling and Imaging, IV 2018 (2018)
11. Franzoni, V., Tasso, S., Pallottelli, S., Perri, D.: Sharing linkable learning objects with the use of metadata and a taxonomy assistant for categorization. In: Misra, S., et al. (eds.) ICCSA 2019. LNCS, vol. 11620, pp. 336–348. Springer, Cham (2019). https://doi.org/10.1007/978-3-030-24296-1_28
12. Tasso, S., Pallottelli, S., Gervasi, O., Sabbatini, F., Franzoni, V., Laganà, A.: Cloud and local servers for a federation of molecular science learning object repositories. In: Misra, S., et al. (eds.) ICCSA 2019. LNCS, vol. 11624, pp. 359–373. Springer, Cham (2019). https://doi.org/10.1007/978-3-030-24311-1_26
13. Brandl, K.: Are you ready to "moodle"? Lang. Learn. Technol. **9**, 16–23 (2005)

International Workshop on Advancements in Applied Machine Learning and Data Analytics (AAMDA 2020)

BodyLock: Human Identity Recogniser App from Walking Activity Data

Karolis Kašys[1], Aurimas Dundulis[1], Mindaugas Vasiljevas[1], Rytis Maskeliūnas[2], and Robertas Damaševičius[1(✉)]

[1] Department of Software Engineering, Kaunas University of Technology, Kaunas, Lithuania
robertas.damasevicius@ktu.lt
[2] Department of Multimedia Engineering, Kaunas University of Technology, Kaunas, Lithuania

Abstract. A person's identity can be recognized based on his/her biometric data such as fingerprints, voice or gait. A person can also be recognized from his/her gait, which requires having sensors capable of detecting changes in speed and direction of movement. Such sensors are readily available on almost every smartphone model. We perform user identity verification using his/her walking activity data captured by smartphone sensors. To support identity verification, we have developed a mobile application for Android-based devices, which has achieved 97% accuracy of identity verification using data from acceleration, gravity and gyroscope sensors of a smartphone and a linear Support Vector Machine (SVM) classifier. The developed unobtrusive human walking analyser provides an additional active layer of protection, which may invoke a stronger authentication measure (mandatory locking) if a threat threshold is exceeded.

Keywords: Biometrics · Gait recognition · Person identification · Mobile app · Smart environment

1 Introduction

In the age of digital information, ubiquitous computing, smart devices and smart environments, the security of a person's data, devices and/or identity is a priority. To protect valuable data and to ensure that only authorized person(s) get access to user device(s) such as smartphones or tablets, a variety of techniques can be used. Password-based identification is, perhaps, the most popular now, but it suffers from eavesdropping and users avoiding the use of complex but secure passwords. As a result, the passwords have a high probability of being cracked or exposed. Moreover, passwords can be forgotten or lost. Furthermore, mobile phones secured with only a password are still vulnerable to data theft when left in an unlocked mode [1]. This is especially important for smartphone users, since smartphones are used to store personal data, emails, photos but also more and more often the commercial data, when smartphones are used in the context of BYOD (bring your own device), when users bring their own devices to workplace and utilize them for any work-related tasks such as to

© Springer Nature Switzerland AG 2020
O. Gervasi et al. (Eds.): ICCSA 2020, LNCS 12250, pp. 307–319, 2020.
https://doi.org/10.1007/978-3-030-58802-1_23

access privileged company information and applications [2]. Therefore, it is important to prevent smartphone intrusion and theft using human biometrics [3]. Using biometrics is becoming a common and popular method of identifying individuals. Examples are fingerprints, iris, voice, face form. Each of these biometrical characteristics has its own advantages, but also disadvantages. Voice recognition requires a microphone, and cameras - to identify the shape and landmarks of the face. A high-resolution sensor is required to read the iris or fingerprints.

Biometrics is a more powerful authentication factor as compared to usual password authentication, but it still has its own disadvantages, such as non-repeatability (the same biometrical features of a user are not identical all the time) and non-revocability (it is a permanent characteristic of the user and can not be changed) [4]. A person can also be recognized from his walking behaviour characteristics (or so-called gait). Such recognition requires sensors capable of detecting changes in speed and direction of movement, i.e. accelerometer and gyroscope. Such sensors can be found on almost every smartphone model currently produced, as well as on several other devices such as smart watches. A person's identity recognition program would allow a person's authentication to allow the use of various security-enhancing systems without additional user intervention (such as passcode entry). Among the various biometric characteristics, gait has been shown to be robust to direct spoofing attacks [5].

Currently, the study of human parameters for a variety of applications, including security but also health diagnostics, is a very relevant topic for research. The examples include iris [6], voice [7], ear biometrics [8], electroencephalography (EEG) biometrics [9]. Gait (walking) is one of the most natural human biometrics. However, gait-based identification has not yet been solved yet. All biometric technologies depend on the quality of the input signal: if the received signal is weak or distorted, the task of identification becomes more difficult. The main challenge for the development of modern biometric algorithms is to overcome these complex conditions and to obtain as much reliable evidence as possible for the high level of personal identification. In addition, human gait differs from other human biometric properties, for example, fingerprints or voice, since its properties change over time due to aging. The human gait also depends on his emotional state, feeling well-being, fatigue, injuries, illnesses, environmental conditions, the type of shoes, etc. Therefore, the creation of a system based on the parameters of a human gait requires that the system continuously trace the characteristics of the human walking characteristics and continually persist in adapting to the present state of the subject.

Biometric security technology depends on the input signal quality: if the received signal is weak or distorted noise, identification task becomes more difficult. The main challenge for modern biometric algorithms to create is to overcome these difficult conditions and to extract the maximum amount of reliable evidence to pinpoint accuracy to make personal status and identity recognition possible. Moreover, human gait is different from other human biometric such as fingerprint or voice, because its properties over time can change significantly. Human gait depends on the emotional state of well-being, fatigue, injuries, diseases, environmental conditions, shoe type, etc. Therefore, developing a reliable security system based on human gait parameters requires following the human gait characteristics in real-time and constantly adapting to the changes in human condition.

Recently, the application of human gait parameters for security applications has been a subject of extensive research. For example, Cola et al. [10] used the acceleration collected at the user's wrist to learn the user's typical gait pattern, and then used anomalies detected in a set of acceleration-based features to identify a possible impostor. The method has been evaluated with 15 subjects, reaching an Equal Error Rate (EER) of 2.9%. De Marsico [11] investigated biometric identification by gait recognition via smartphone accelerometer, and achieved the EER of 7.69%. Derawi and Bours [12] collected data from five users, and constructed three different gait templates, where each template related to varying walking speeds. The phone learned the individual features at the various walk speeds, allowing the phone to recognize the correct user using the proposed Cross Dynamic Time Warping (DTW) Metric. The Correct Recognition Rate (CRR) was 89.3% and the false positive probability was as low as 1.4%. Hoang and Choi [13] proposed a gait based biometric cryptosystem to enhance smartphone user security and privacy. Gait signals were acquired by using an accelerometer sensor in the mobile device and error-correcting codes (ECC) were adopted to deal with intra-class variability of gait measurements. The results using gait samples of 34 volunteers are false acceptance rate (FAR) and false rejection rate (FRR) of 3.92% and 11.76%, respectively, in terms of key length of 50 bits. Watanabe and Sara [14] created a similar gait capture app for Android devices. They collected gait data for 15 subjects in 5 walking states. From the 3-axes accelerometer data, we they extracted 52 features with high accuracy. Nguyen et al. [15] used the signal captured in different positions of mobile phone: in front pocket and on the waist. Using Principal Component Analysis (PCA) and Support Vector Machine (SVM) allowed to achieve an EER of 2.45% and accuracy rate of 99.14% regarding the verification and identification process, respectively. Chetty et al. [16] used smartphone inertial sensor data based on information theory with feature ranking and random forest, ensemble learning and lazy learning classifiers. The best results were achieved by random forests classifier with 96.3% accuracy. Ferrero et al. [17] used the data acquired from the 3-axis accelerometer embedded in a smartphone, and provided the description of walking features in the time (statistical characteristics, moments, root means square of the walking waveform, autocorrelation, cycle rotation metric) and frequency (coefficients of Discrete Fourier Transform (DFT) and Discrete Cosine Transform (DCT)) domains. Fernandez-Lopez et al. [18] implemented accelerometer-based gait recognition (ABGR) using custom gate cycle detection algorithm and achieved and an Equal Error Rate (EER) of 16.38% to 29.07%. Lai et al. [19] extracted frequency features (coefficients of FFT) from gait data obtained using the acceleration sensor and used Weighted SVM to recognize users, reaching 3.5% EER. Yuan and Zhang [20] used periodogram based gait categorization to identify patterns in the walking periodicity, and convolutional neural network (CNN) for based gait-based identification and achieving an accuracy of over 87%. Anusha and Jaidhar [21] used histogram of oriented gradients (HOG), followed by sum variance Haralick texture descriptor calculated from gradient magnitude image to derive low level features which are used for gait recognition. He et al. [22] suggested multi-task generative adversarial networks for learning view-specific gait features. Zhang et al. [23] used Convolutional Neural Network (CNN) for soft biometrics such as age and gender recognition. A review on gait-based identity recognition methods has been presented by Liu et al. [24].

Our aim is to analyse complex human gait characteristics for monitoring the state and identity of a human (smartphone user), to propose methods for selecting reliable gait features, and to develop and approve the passive user state monitoring system, running on a portable mobile device (smartphone) and allows the device to distinguish the changes in the state (condition) of the smartphone user (e.g., change of owner in case of attempted theft) according to his/her gait parameters.

Such system would be most relevant to smart device holders who want to prevent unauthorized access to smartphone data without using too cumbersome methods of security. Our approach follows the multi-layered model of security [25], which calls for different layers of security to address different security challenges. While each layer of security alone does not provide the required defence against attacks, their entirety ensures a higher level of security. Therefore, an unobtrusive human walking analyser could provide an additional active layer of protection, which could invoke a stronger authentication measure (mandatory locking) if a threat threshold is exceeded.

We propose and validate a passive user authentication system that operates on a portable mobile device (smartphone) and allows the device owner to be distinguished from an outsider by its track parameters. Upon detecting a changed owner, the system will take appropriate security measures to ensure the security of the data stored on the device (e.g., blocking access to data, informing the owner about the location of the device, etc.) without waiting for active intruder attempts to connect to the device.

2 Method and Tools

2.1 Overview

In this paper, the following methodology is applied: data acquisition from smartphone sensors; data preprocessing and denoising; feature generation, feature ranking and dimensionality reduction, activity detection and gait model construction. The identification of a subject is performed by comparing the current gait characteristics of a subject with his gait model learned from previous observations during the training stage. The methodology is visualized in Fig. 1.

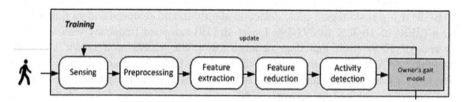

Fig. 1. Overview of the method stages

2.2   Data Acquisition

During data acquisition, the smartphone is kept in a static position - the phone can be located either in the trouser pocket or in the jacket pocket (chest level), which however affects the collected data, even if the same type of activity is performed. In order to avoid this problem, the smartphone needs to be kept in the same constant position with regards to the human body. The raw data provided by the smart phone is accelerometer and gyro data, since these sensors are equipped with most smart devices, but other sensors, for example, will also be taken, if possible, e.g., the magnetic field sensor data, if it helps to more accurately identify identity, but more data does not always mean more accurate results because their information is not relevant.

We have selected gait data in 3 states of walking: State 1 (walking forwards): walking on an even surface and holding the smartphone. State 2 (walking stairs up): going stairs up and holding the smartphone in the pocket. State 3 (walking stairs down): going downstairs and holding the smartphone in the pocket.

The following data set is logged by the developed Android application: Logged time (ms); Raw 3 axes of acceleration data (m/s^2); Raw 3 axes of gravity data (m/s^2); Raw 3 axes of the gyroscope data (rad/s).

2.3   Primary Data Processing

When the data is collected, the primary data processing is carried out - the data is normalized. Removing noise can help increase the accuracy of the results by eliminating unnecessary noisy data, bat also the important information characterising differences between individuals may be smoothed, therefore, the denoising has not been used. A common problem was that the sensor data returned by the device is not acquired at regular time intervals. In that case, a linear time interpolation was used to ensure the equal time interval between two data records.

Another problem was the removal of spikes from the data. The cause for these spikes remained unclear and may be related to phone's hardware behaviour. We have identified the spikes as outliers, which are more than 4 standard deviations (sigmas) away from the signal's mean value, thus guaranteeing that less than 0.1% of data is removed and replaced by the mean of the adjacent values.

2.4   Feature Calculation

In many cases (such as calculation of a mean or a moving average), calculation requires using sliding windows over sensor data. For sliding window, following the suggestion of Primo et al. [26], we use the sliding window of 100 data points with overlap of 50%. As features, we use a set of statistical and other signal features described in [27, 28]. The full list involves 102 different features. Some of the sample features are presented in Table 1.

Table 1. Representative features of smartphone sensor signals

Feature number	Description	Equation (notation)
4–6	Acceleration (x-, y-, and z-axes)	a_x, a_y, a_z
7–9	Gyroscope (x-, y-, and z-axes)	g_x, g_y, g_z
10–15	Moving variance of 100 samples of acceleration and gyroscope data	$\text{var} = \dfrac{1}{N(N-1)}\left(N\sum_{j=1}^{N} x_i^2 - \left(\sum_{i=1}^{N} x_i\right)^2\right),$ here $x = a_x, a_y, a_z, g_x, g_y, g_z$
16–17	Movement intensity of acceleration and gyroscope data	$MI_a = \sqrt{a_x^2 + a_y^2 + a_z^2}$ $MI_g = \sqrt{g_x^2 + g_y^2 + g_z^2}$
18	Movement intensity of difference between acceleration and gyroscope data	$MI_{ga} = \sqrt{(g_x - a_x)^2 + (g_y - a_y)^2 + (g_y - a_y)^2}$
19–21	Moving variance of 100 samples of movement intensity data	$\text{var} = \dfrac{1}{N(N-1)}\left(N\sum_{j=1}^{N} x_i^2 - \left(\sum_{i=1}^{N} x_i\right)^2\right),$ here $x = MI_a, MI_g, MI_{ga}$
22–24	Polar coordinates of acceleration data	$\varphi_a = \arctan\left(a_y, a_x\right),$ $r_a = \sqrt{a_x^2 + a_y^2},$ $z_a = a_z$
25–27	Polar coordinates of gyroscope data	$\varphi_g = \arctan\left(g_y, g_x\right),$ $r_g = \sqrt{g_x^2 + g_y^2},$ $z_g = g_z$
28–30	Polar coordinates of difference between acceleration and gyroscope data	$\varphi_{ag} = \arctan\left(a_y - g_y, a_x - g_x\right),$ $r_{ag} = \sqrt{(a_y - g_y)^2 + (a_x - g_x)^2},$ $z_{ag} = a_z - g_z$

2.5   Classification

For classification we use Support Vector Machine (SVM) [29] with a linear kernel. 80% of data is retained from training and 20% of data is used for testing. The procedure is repeated 20 times using Hold-Out cross-validation, and the results are evaluated using the accuracy, Kappa and F-score metrics. Accuracy is the number of correct guesses made divided by the total number of guesses made. Kappa value compares an observed accuracy with an expected accuracy (random guessing). F-score combines precision and recall, and it characterises the precision (how many samples it classifies correctly) and robustness (it does not miss many positive samples) of the classifier.

3   Implementation and Results

3.1   BodyLock App

The human identity recognizer has been implemented as Android app, called Body-Lock. The app has two parts (see Fig. 2): the device part is responsible for collection of sensor data, generation of features, sending of data to server, and user interface. The server part is responsible for storage of data and classification of walking features. The application itself works silently in the background mode.

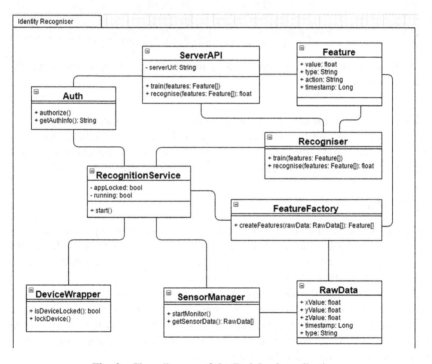

Fig. 2. Class diagram of the BodyLock application

3.2   Data Collection Environment

For our experiments we used walking trajectories of 13 different subjects collected in the office environment (in the SANTAKA valley building of Kaunas University of Technology), which included three different types of trajectories: walking forward, walking upstairs and walking downstairs. All individuals were health without any foot problems. All subjects took the same walking trajectory using a flat-surface corridor about 50 m long, as well as up-stair and down-stairs (see Fig. 3).

Fig. 3. Environment of data collection: walking forward (left), walking upstairs (middle), and walking downstairs (right)

The even floor of the corridor allowed to capture the usual gait characteristics of the subjects without any obstacles or unevenness of the floor. The data capture sessions were organized during the first half of the day to avoid the effect of tiredness, exhaustion at the end of a business day, or office fatigue due to sitting all day.

3.3   Results

The results of feature ranking are presented in Fig. 4. The most important features refer to the 95th and 99th percentiles of acceleration in the X and Z axes of the device, which means that extreme events such as the speed of sudden movements help to recognize people and differentiate one subject from another.

An example of the distribution of sample data is presented in Fig. 5. Here the 2D feature space is formed by only two features (axz_p95, the 95th percentile of acceleration sensor value and in the X-Z axis, and ry_75, the 75th percentile of gyroscope sensor value in the Z axis). Even in this low-dimensional feature space, the gait characteristics of subjects can be clearly separated.

Figure 6 shows the confusion matrix of the classification results.

Finally, Fig. 7 shows the classification results. We have achieved 97% accuracy of correct identification, while the Copen's kappa was 0.944, and F-score was 94%.

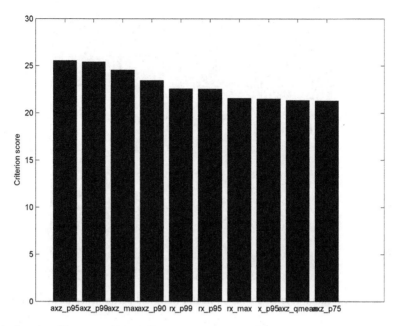

Fig. 4. Results of feature ranking (left) and distribution of data according in feature space of two top ranked features

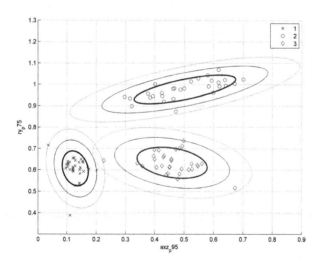

Fig. 5. Results of feature ranking (left) and distribution of data according in feature space of two top ranked features

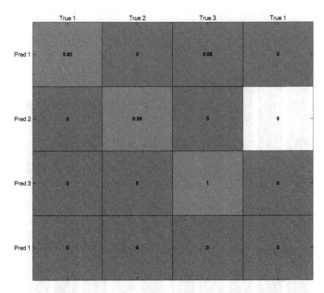

Fig. 6. Classification results: confusion matrix (left) and performance measures (right)

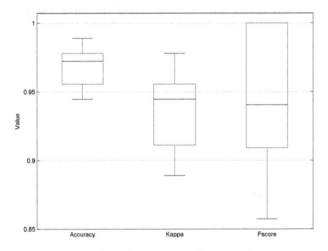

Fig. 7. Classification results: confusion matrix (left) and performance measures (right)

3.4   Evaluation

The limitations of the presented approach towards user identification are as follows:

1) Contamination of data with noise, which may lead to incorrect identification of user. Some lower-end smartphone models have low-quality sensors, which return unreliable data, which can be observed practically by high variability of a sensor signal even if the phone is laying in the static position without any movement.

2) Significant intra-class variability due to changing condition of the subject (e.g., illness, fatigue or stress [30, 31] may influence his/her gait), different shoes and clothes, different environment and flooring conditions (e.g., field environment can vary from solid pavement to grass, sand or snow).
3) Discriminability – the interclass similarities may be large if the sufficiently large number of subjects is explored, thus restricting the discriminability provided by the gait analyser.

One of the key challenges is determining how to achieve required functionality and performance without jeopardizing the user experience and power consumption with the overhead of additional computational burden to the mobile phone. The two-tiered (client-server) approach used in the design of the BodyLock app allowed to move computationally costly operations to the server, thus reducing the performance over-head. However, the data still must be secured during transfer and storage at the cloud server to avoid stealing and impersonation attempts. Gait verification might not reach the same level of reliability as fingerprint or iris recognition. However, it still could be used as a method of continuous (active) authentication for accessing less sensitive content on a smartphone (such as games) or be used in concert with other biometrics (e.g. iris recognition) to provide a more reliable user authentication method.

When combined with other signals such as GPS or WiFi from low energy Bluetooth beacons, it could be used for providing smart localisation [32, 33] services as well.

4   Conclusion

Biometric authentication is a good solution for smartphone users since it relies on the uniqueness of certain physical traits in humans. By continuously and unobtrusively recognizing the phone's owner, the human walking analyser has potential to improve user authentication on the go. Here we described the development of a mobile app for Android-based smartphones, which performs user identity verification using his/her walking activity data. We have achieved 97% accuracy of identity verification using features generated from data acquired from the acceleration, gravity and gyroscope sensors of a smartphone and a linear Support Vector Machine (SVM) classifier. The results achieved are in line with the results achieved by other authors working in the same area of research. As gait-based authentication technologies move towards being deployed as an extra security layer in portable mobile devices, our work represents a step in this direction.

References

1. Crouse, D., Han, H., Chandra, D., Barbello, B., Jain, A.K.: Continuous authentication of mobile user: fusion of face image and inertial measurement unit data. In: International Conference on Biometrics, ICB 2015, pp. 135–142 (2015). https://doi.org/10.1109/ICB.2015.7139043

2. Keith, W.M., Jeffrey, M.V., George, F.H.: BYOD: security and privacy considerations. IT Prof. **14**(5), 53–55 (2012)
3. Ohana, D.J., Phillips, L., Chen, L.: Preventing cell phone intrusion and theft using biometrics. In: IEEE CS Security and Privacy Workshops, SPW 2013, pp. 173–180 (2013). https://doi.org/10.1109/SPW.2013.19
4. Gunasinghe, H., Bertino, E.: PrivBioMTAuth: privacy preserving biometrics-based and user centric protocol for user authentication from mobile phones. IEEE Trans. Inf. Forensics Secur. **13**(4), 1042–1057 (2018). https://doi.org/10.1109/TIFS.2017.2777787
5. Hadid, A., Evans, N., Marcel, S., Fierrez, J.: Biometrics systems under spoofing attack: an evaluation methodology and lessons learned. IEEE Signal Process. Mag. **32**, 20–30 (2015). https://doi.org/10.1109/MSP.2015.2437652
6. Sholokhov, A., Kinnunen, T., Vestman, V., Lee, K. A.: Voice biometrics security: extrapolating false alarm rate via hierarchical bayesian modeling of speaker verification scores. Comput. Speech Lang. **60** (2020). https://doi.org/10.1016/j.csl.2019.101024
7. Wang, K., Kumar, A.: Cross-spectral iris recognition using CNN and supervised discrete hashing. Pattern Recogn. **86**, 85–98 (2019). https://doi.org/10.1016/j.patcog.2018.08.010
8. Olanrewaju, L., Oyebiyi, O., Misra, S., Maskeliunas, R., Damasevicius, R.: Secure ear biometrics using circular kernel principal component analysis, Chebyshev transform hashing and Bose–Chaudhuri–Hocquenghem error-correcting codes. Signal Image Video Process. (2020). https://doi.org/10.1007/s11760-019-01609-y
9. Damaševičius, R., Maskeliunas, R., Kazanavičius, E., Woźniak, M.: Combining cryptography with EEG biometrics. Comput. Intell. Neurosci. **2018** (2018). https://doi.org/10.1155/2018/1867548
10. Cola, G., Avvenuti, M., Musso, F., Vecchio, A.: Gait-based authentication using a wrist-worn device. In: ACM International Conference Proceeding Series, pp. 208–217 (2016). https://doi.org/10.1145/2994374.2994393
11. Marsico, M.D., Mecca, A.: Biometric walk recognizer. Multimed. Tools Appl. **76**(4), 4713–4745 (2016). https://doi.org/10.1007/s11042-016-3654-1
12. Derawi, M., Bours, P.: Gait and activity recognition using commercial phones. Comput. Secur. **39**(PART B), 137–144 (2013). https://doi.org/10.1016/j.cose.2013.07.004
13. Hoang, T., Choi, D.: Secure and privacy enhanced gait authentication on smart phone. Sci. World J. **2014** (2014). https://doi.org/10.1155/2014/438254. Article ID 438254, 8 p.
14. Watanabe, Y., Sara, S.: Toward an immunity-based gait recognition on smart phone: a study of feature selection and walking state classification. Procedia Comput. Sci. **96**, 1790–1800 (2016). https://doi.org/10.1016/j.procs.2016.08.228
15. Nguyen, H., Nguyen, H.H., Hoang, T., Choi, D., Nguyen, T.D.: A generalized authentication scheme for mobile phones using gait signals. In: Obaidat, M.S., Lorenz, P. (eds.) ICETE 2015. CCIS, vol. 585, pp. 386–407. Springer, Cham (2016). https://doi.org/10.1007/978-3-319-30222-5_18
16. Chetty, G., White, M., Akther, F.: Smart phone based data mining for human activity recognition. Procedia Comput. Sci. **46**, 1181–1187 (2015). https://doi.org/10.1016/j.procs.2015.01.031
17. Ferrero, R., Gandino, F., Montrucchio, B., Rebaudengo, M., Velasco, A., Benkhelifa, I.: On gait recognition with smartphone accelerometer. In: 4th Mediterranean Conference on Embedded Computing, MECO 2015, pp. 368–373 (2015). https://doi.org/10.1109/MECO.2015.7181946
18. Fernandez-Lopez, P., Liu-Jimenez, J., Sanchez-Redondo, C., Sanchez-Reillo, R.: Gait recognition using smartphone. In: International Carnahan Conference on Security Technology, pp. 1–7 (2016). https://doi.org/10.1109/CCST.2016.7815698

19. Lai, Q., Chen, B., Xu, C.: Using weighted SVM for identifying user from gait with smart phone. In: 7th International Conference on Cloud Computing and Big Data, CCBD 2016, pp. 41–45 (2017). https://doi.org/10.1109/CCBD.2016.019

20. Yuan, W., Zhang, L.: Gait classification and identity authentication using CNN. In: Li, L., Hasegawa, K., Tanaka, S. (eds.) AsiaSim 2018. CCIS, vol. 946, pp. 119–128. Springer, Singapore (2018). https://doi.org/10.1007/978-981-13-2853-4_10

21. Anusha, R., Jaidhar, C.D.: Human gait recognition based on histogram of oriented gradients and Haralick texture descriptor. Multimed. Tools Appl. (2020). https://doi.org/10.1007/s11042-019-08469-1

22. He, Y., Zhang, J., Shan, H., Wang, L.: Multi-task GANs for view-specific feature learning in gait recognition. IEEE Trans. Inf. Forensics Secur. 14(1), 102–113 (2019). https://doi.org/10.1109/TIFS.2018.2844819

23. Zhang, Y., Huang, Y., Wang, L., Yu, S.: A comprehensive study on gait biometrics using a joint CNN-based method. Pattern Recogn. 93, 228–236 (2019). https://doi.org/10.1016/j.patcog.2019.04.023

24. Liu, C., Zhao, J., Wei, Z.: A review of gait behavior recognition methods based on wearable devices. In: Xie, Y., Zhang, A., Liu, H., Feng, L. (eds.) GSES 2018. CCIS, vol. 980, pp. 134–145. Springer, Singapore (2019). https://doi.org/10.1007/978-981-13-7025-0_14

25. Denman, S.: Why multi-layered security is still the best defence. Network Security, 5–7 (2012)

26. Primo, A., Phoha, V.V., Kumar, R., Serwadda, A.: Context-Aware active authentication using smartphone accelerometer measurements. In: IEEE Conference on Computer Vision and Pattern Recognition (CVPR) Workshops, pp. 98–105 (2014). https://doi.org/10.1109/CVPRW.2014.20

27. Damasevicius, R., Vasiljevas, M., Salkevicius, J., Wozniak, M.: Human activity recognition in AAL environments using random projections. Comput. Math. Methods Med. 2016, 1–17 (2016). https://doi.org/10.1155/2016/4073584

28. Damasevicius, R., Maskeliunas, R., Venckauskas, A., Wozniak, M.: Smartphone user identity verification using gait characteristics. Symmetry 8(10), 100 (2016). https://doi.org/10.3390/sym8100100

29. Cortes, C., Vapnik, V.: Support vector networks. Mach. Learn. 20, 273–297 (1995)

30. Raudonis, V., Maskeliūnas, R., Stankevičius, K., Damaševičius, R.: Gender, age, colour, position and stress: how they influence attention at workplace? In: Gervasi, O., et al. (eds.) ICCSA 2017. LNCS, vol. 10408, pp. 248–264. Springer, Cham (2017). https://doi.org/10.1007/978-3-319-62404-4_19

31. Ulinskas, M., Damaševičius, R., Maskeliunas, R., Woźniak, M.: Recognition of human daytime fatigue using keystroke data. Procedia Comput. Sci. 130, 947–952 (2018). https://doi.org/10.1016/j.procs.2018.04.094

32. Al-Madani, B., Orujov, F., Maskeliūnas, R., Damaševičius, R., Venčkauskas, A.: Fuzzy logic type-2 based wireless indoor localization system for navigation of visually impaired people in buildings. Sensors 19(9) (2019). https://doi.org/10.3390/s19092114

33. Orujov, F., Maskeliūnas, R., Damaševičius, R., Wei, W., Li, Y.: Smartphone based intelligent indoor positioning using fuzzy logic. Future Gener. Comput. Syst. 89, 335–348 (2018). https://doi.org/10.1016/j.future.2018.06.030

An Intelligent Cache Management for Data Analysis at CMS

Mirco Tracolli[1,2,3]($\boxtimes$), Marco Baioletti[1]($\boxtimes$), Diego Ciangottini[3]($\boxtimes$),
Valentina Poggioni[1]($\boxtimes$), and Daniele Spiga[3]($\boxtimes$)

[1] Università degli Studi di Perugia, Perugia, Italy
{marco.baioletti,valentina.poggioni}@unipg.it
[2] Università degli Studi di Firenze, Florence, Italy
[3] INFN Sezione di Perugia, Perugia, Italy
{mirco.tracolli,diego.ciangottini,daniele.spiga}@pg.infn.it

Abstract. In this work, we explore a score-based approach to manage a cache system. With the proposed method, the cache can better discriminate the input requests and improve the overall performances. We created a score based discriminator using the file statistics. The score represents the weight of a file. We tested several functions to compute the file weight used to determine whether a file has to be stored in the cache or not. We developed a solution experimenting on a real cache manager named XCache, that is used within the Compact Muon Solenoid (CMS) data analysis workflow. The aim of this work is optimizing to reduce maintaining costs of the cache system without compromising the user experience.

Keywords: Cache · Optimization · LRU · Intelligent system · Big data · Data science workflow

1 Introduction

The Compact Muon Solenoid (CMS [5]) collaboration is one of the four major experiments at the Large Hadron Collider (LHC) at the European Organization for Nuclear Research (CERN). The experiments that involve the detector and the physics simulations, such as the Monte Carlo simulations, create a considerable amount of data every year. These data are kept on disk (Hard Disk Drives, HDDs) and tape distributed storage systems. HDDs are used for storing analysis data of physicist users because they are much faster than tape, but they are more expensive and hence disk space is limited. The analysis workflow implies that the jobs run on the site (tier) where the requests are made. The current storage system is hierarchical organized (tier levels, Fig. 1) and centrally managed, hence it is not autonomous and it cannot react as a dynamic environment.

The next decades will be characterized by the LHC upgrade to HL-LHC (High Luminosity Large Hadron Collider). As a consequence, an increase of factor 20 is expected for the storage requirements while, on the computing side,

© Springer Nature Switzerland AG 2020
O. Gervasi et al. (Eds.): ICCSA 2020, LNCS 12250, pp. 320–332, 2020.
https://doi.org/10.1007/978-3-030-58802-1_24

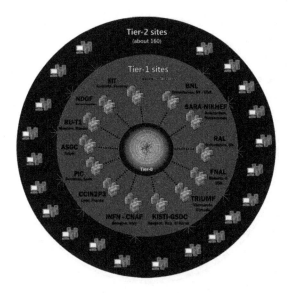

Fig. 1. Current data distribution model [4]

the estimation is about a 30x CPUs necessity. Moreover, we foresee a shift in resources provisioning towards the exploitation of dynamic solutions using private or public clouds and also High-Performance Computing facilities. In this scenario, a key point is an evolution and optimization of the amount of space that is custodial and the CPU efficiency of the jobs that run on "storage-less" resources. In particular, jobs can be instrumented to read data from a geographically distributed cache storage. The cache system will appear as a distributed and shared file system populated with the most requested data; in case of missing information data access will fallback to the remote access. Furthermore, in a possible future scenario based on the data-lake model (Fig. 2), it is reasonable to imagine that many satellite computing centers might appear and disappear dynamically as needed. In this sense, an intermediate and auto-sufficient layer against a centrally managed storage might be a keystone to maintain unaltered the user experience.

A Content Delivery Network (CDN) has many affinities with the cache architecture design, but the cache system has a finer grade infrastructure: the cache layer could be divided into regions (a composition of federated servers) in which each cache not foreseen duplicate files within its federated servers. The cache storage will be, by definition, "non-custodial". Thus, it reduces overall operational costs. To get an idea on the dimensions of the problem we consider, from statistic analysis, that a single cache could manage thousands of requests per day and have a realistic dimension starting from 100 Terabytes of storage.

The main actor in this scenario is XRootD [2,12], a modular, fast, low-latency and scalable file server. This service could be configured in several ways, the main ones are as Redirector and as Data Server. A Redirector can communicate with

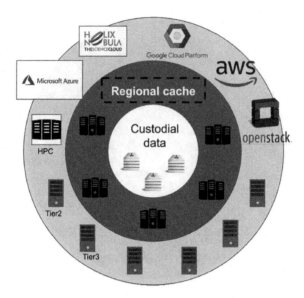

Fig. 2. Data lake model [4]

other Redirectors to resolve a user request. To resolve the request, the Redirector has to find the requested file into one of the available Data Servers and it has to make contact between the user and that server. A Data Server simply serves data from the memory and it implements the data caching part. The Data Server uses the Least Recently Used (LRU) replacement policy as default.

The main reason to choose XRootD is that it has integrated the CMS work-flow in a transparent way for the end-users. In addition, the XRootD service supports a plugin system with which we can interact directly with the cache

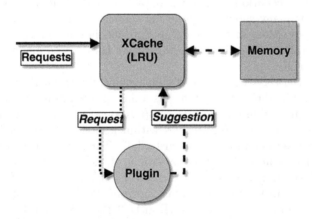

Fig. 3. XRootD plugin schema

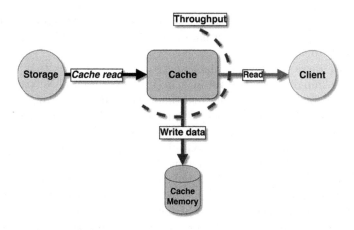

Fig. 4. Schema of the environment

system. The target of this work is to interact with this system finding a method to suggest which files to store or not into the cache (Fig. 3).

With our customized suggestion we target to maximize the throughput of the cache. As you can see in the schema in Fig. 4, we want to minimize the data written by the cache and maximize the amount of data read from the clients.

2 Related Works

As we said in the previous chapter, the introduced data science workflow has many affinities with the CDN networks and also with the web content caching. The purpose of this intermediate layer is to decreases user-perceived latency, to reduces network bandwidth usage, and to reduces loads on the origin servers. Thus, the cache plays a very important role in the whole picture and we need to design an efficient cache replacement algorithms to achieve better performances.

The LRU algorithm is a simple queue where the items are ordered with respect to the times of the last access. Thus the most recently accessed item is placed on top. When a file is requested and it is already in the queue, it is moved to the top. If we need to remove a file, we start from the tail of the queue and we remove the files that are not too much accessed in recent history. Such a policy is known to under-perform in the big data environment as it was initially designed for evicting fixed-size pages from buffer caches[1].

Anyhow, the main characteristics that influence the replacement process are still the same [3,7,11] and they are related only to the file (or object) requested F:

- recency: time of (since) the last reference to F
- frequency: number of requests to F
- size: the size of F

We can add also two more features such as the cost, that represents the price to pay to store F, and some information relative to the access to F, such as the latency or the distance.

Recently, there are several Machine Learning techniques that are used to improve this kind of cache. For instance, in [11] a Deep Neural Network is trained in advance to better manage the real-time scheduling of cache content into a heterogeneous network. In [9] a Deep Recurrent Neural Network is used to predict the cache accesses and make a better caching decision.

Also, other techniques, like the Gradient Boosting Tree, are used in [6] to automate cache management of distributed data.

There are also Deep Reinforcement Learning approaches like [10].

In this article, we will not use a specific Machine Learning technique, but the problem size that we tackle is much higher than the articles mentioned before, both in terms of the number of files and domain-specific features (related to physic data analysis).

3   Data Analysis

The source data used in this work are request logs of user analysis. These logs have information about user requests, such as the filename, etc. The information contained in this database refers to the data popularity research made in CMS[8]. The collected data are archived per day and we focused the experiments on a specific time span, the whole year 2018. Also, to have a realistic simulation of a single cache used within the current data analysis workflow, we decided to filter the requests by region, for example, we choose only the requests coming from Italy (Fig. 5).

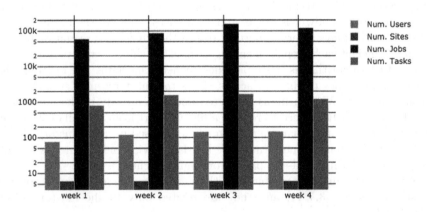

Fig. 5. Data general statistics of Italy requests in January 2018

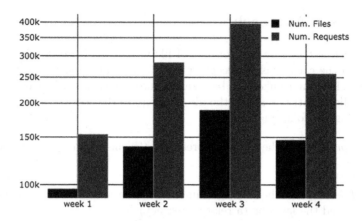

Fig. 6. Number of request statistics of Italy requests in January 2018

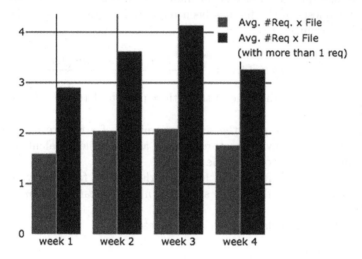

Fig. 7. Average number of request statistics of Italy requests in January 2018

A preliminary analysis of data gives us useful information about the dimension of the problem. In the region IT (Italy), the number of files requested is very high with respect to the number of users and sites where the jobs are run (Fig. 5, 6). The workflow proves that the user can launch tasks having more jobs, and those jobs can request several files. Nevertheless, the number of requests per file is not too high and the average value is small even if we not consider the files requested only 1 time Fig. 7.

However, this trend of the request statistics is confirmed in the other regions and, as a consequence, we expect to have comparable results regardless of the region.

4   Proposed Approach

Our approach is based on the concept of file weight (a score) which is used to determine if the cache has to accept or not the file. The policy is: a file with a smaller weight is more likely to be inserted into the cache. To accomplish this task, we collect statistics about the file to compute the score of a file f at time t, considering the following features:

- $numRequests(f,t)$: the number of requests (frequency) to f until the current time t
- $size(f)$: the file size
- $requestDelta(f,t)$: the average time difference between the previous file requests and the last one (a relative recency)

The average time difference is calculated on the last $k = 32$ requests (or on all the last requests, if the file has been requested $k < 32$ times), according to the following formula:

$$requestDelta(f,t) = \frac{\sum_{i=1}^{k-1} time(f,k) - time(f,i)}{k} \qquad (1)$$

Where $time(f,i)$ is the time of the i–th request to f ($time(f,k)$ is the time of the last request).

The statistics to compute the score (or weight) of a file are maintained in a time window of 14 days. The threshold to accept a file is calculated on the median value of all the collected file weights.

We have selected 3 functional forms of the weight function which aggregate in different ways the three statistics $numRequests(f,t)$, $size(f)$, and $requestDelta(f,t)$.

Each of the 3 forms have α, β, γ as parameters

- Additive form

$$weight_A(f,t) = \alpha \cdot numRequests(f,t) + \beta \cdot size(f) + \gamma \cdot requestDelta(f,t) \qquad (2)$$

- Additive-Exponential form

$$weight_E(f,t) = numRequests(f,t)^\alpha + size(f)^\beta + requestDelta(f,t)^\gamma \qquad (3)$$

- Multiplicative form

$$weight_M(f,t) = numRequests(f,t)^\alpha \cdot size(f)^\beta \cdot requestDelta(f,t)^\gamma \qquad (4)$$

The main measure we focus, as mentioned in the Sect. 1, is the *throughput*, defined in the following way:

$$throughput = \frac{readOnHitData}{writtenData} \qquad (5)$$

where *readOnHitData* is the amount of Megabytes on which the cache had hit and the *writtenData* is the amount of files written (in Megabytes) into cache. However, this measure does not give the whole picture of the effect of our method on the cache system. Moreover, we cannot use only the hit rate measure because we take into account the size of the files. Consequently, we defined the following measures to test the impact of the new strategies:

- Cache disk space: this measure, named **Cost**, quantifies the work done by the cache: the sizes of the files deleted or written on the local storage and the files served in proxy mode. This latest scenario is influenced by the miss data. Hence, this measure can be written as follows:

$$Cost = writtenData + deletedData + readOnMissData \qquad (6)$$

- Network bandwidth: to measure the impact of this constraint we simply take into account the miss data over the bandwidth of the cache. If the network is completely saturated, the cache cannot retrieve files anymore:

$$BandSaturation = \frac{readOnMiss}{cacheBandWidth} \qquad (7)$$

- CPU efficiency: due to the log files we use, we have access to the CPU time and Wall time of each request. This allow us to measure the CPU efficiency as follow:

$$CPUEfficiency = \frac{\sum CPUTime}{\sum WallTime} \qquad (8)$$

We calculate the upper and lower bound of the CPU efficiency using information from the logs. We collect the local CPU efficiency (file served from a tier, indicated in the log features) for the upper bound and the remote CPU efficiency for the lower bound. Then, we consider the difference (19% for the year 2018) to measure the CPU efficiency into the simulation, starting from the log CPU efficiency. We consider a file served by the cache as if it is local, otherwise, it will be a remote file, thus, we subtract the difference in percentage to simulate the loss in performance.

The simulation also takes care about the watermark behavior of the XCache: there are two watermarks, a higher and a lower watermark. When the size of the cache reaches the higher watermark, the cache removes some files until the lower watermark is reached. In our simulations, the cache size was 100 Terabytes and the watermarks was set respectively to 95% and 75% of the cache size.

We used the following algorithm to perform the tests:

To resume the Algorithm 1, we insert a file into the cache only if the file weight is less or equal the average weight of all files we have into the statistic table. We used this algorithm with each functional forms $weight_A, weigth_E, weight_M$ by considering the following values for the parameters α, β and γ: $\{0, \frac{1}{3}, \frac{1}{2}, \frac{2}{3}, 1, 2, 4\}$.

Data: log requests
Result: a cache simulation
Initialization of variables and statistic table
for *each requested file f* **do**
  t ← time of the request
  hit ← *checkFileInCache(f)*
  updateStatistics(f)
  if *hit* **then**
    | *updateLRUQueue(f)*
  else
    if *weight(f, t) ≤ avg(statsTable.weights)* **then**
      | *insertWithLRU(f)*
    end
  end
  checkWatermark()
end

Algorithm 1: Algorithm used to test the functional form of the weight function

5   Experimental Results

Table 1 shows the three measures *Throughput* (Eq. 5), *Cost* (Eq. 6), and *ReadOnHitData* for the LRU cache strategy (used as a baseline in the comparisons) and the best 10 combinations of parameters in each of the 3 functional forms (Eq. 2, 3, 4). The whole results are sorted by throughput, cost and read on hit amount. The main measure we take into account is the throughput because we want to optimize the cache work.

It is possible to see that all the proposed weight functions have a smaller cost with respect to LRU. They have a better throughput, so they write less data into the cache and they still make the clients read a considerable amount of data. They are still outperformed by LRU on *ReadOnHitData* value, but the global work made by the cache is considerably less.

The best functional form was the Additive with Exponential Form, having the best performances in terms of Throughput and Cost. Anyway, it is worth noting that the Additive Form reaches higher *ReadOnHitData* values. Moreover, by observing the parameter values, it is possible to deduce that the number of requests plays a secondary role. Indeed, the value of the α parameter of the best functions is 0.00 and only few of the results have a different value. Two possible explanations are that the range of the number of requests of a file is not comparable with the other two variables (the size of the file is in Megabytes and the delta time in minutes) or that α should take a much higher value to have a significant impact on the score.

During the simulation, we monitored the other measure values using several plots. We define a upper an lower bounds for the measures *BandSaturation* (Eq. 7) and *CPUEfficiency* (Eq. 8) using the data log information. The upper bound for *BandSaturation* is the entire network bandwidth we would like to simulate (10*Gbit*). The upper bound for *CPUEfficiency* is calculated by considering all the files present in the cache, while the lower bound is computed by considering all the files accessed by remote. In the following part we will see a specific view of the year of the top three functions.

Table 1. Test results grouped by function family.

cache				Throughput	Cost	ReadOnHitData
LRU				0.483708	178349611	26327729
Form	α	β	γ	**Throughput**	**Cost**	**ReadOnHitData**
Additive	0.00	0.50	2.00	0.643959	173774548	18793149
Additive	0.00	1.00	4.00	0.643959	173774548	18793149
Additive	0.00	0.50	0.67	0.642360	173757770	18580175
Additive	0.00	0.33	2.00	0.640429	174542198	18623528
Additive	0.00	0.67	4.00	0.640429	174542198	18623528
Additive	0.33	1.00	4.00	0.640004	174010336	18556491
Additive	0.00	0.67	1.00	0.638810	174277036	18672706
Additive	0.00	0.33	0.50	0.638810	174277036	18672706
Additive	0.00	0.33	1.00	0.637943	174116598	18833412
Additive	0.00	0.67	2.00	0.637943	174116598	18833412
AdditiveExp	**0.00**	**0.50**	**0.33**	**0.737599**	**150626930**	**13428482**
AdditiveExp	0.00	0.33	0.33	0.722364	160052405	15912505
AdditiveExp	0.00	0.50	0.50	0.715685	161956500	16153019
AdditiveExp	0.00	0.67	0.67	0.696146	161609673	15457155
AdditiveExp	0.00	0.33	0.00	0.693033	158801312	15735244
AdditiveExp	0.00	0.67	0.50	0.68763	156525555	15012763
AdditiveExp	0.33	0.67	0.67	0.681264	162213056	15011936
AdditiveExp	0.00	0.50	0.00	0.671477	163232309	16836007
AdditiveExp	0.00	0.33	0.50	0.668889	168519018	16758717
AdditiveExp	0.00	0.67	0.33	0.665731	164003690	17574075
Multiplicative	0.00	0.33	0.00	0.693033	158801312	15735244
Multiplicative	0.00	0.50	0.00	0.671477	163232309	16836007
Multiplicative	0.33	0.33	0.33	0.665997	173205320	17519780
Multiplicative	0.00	0.67	0.33	0.664488	172794102	17472908
Multiplicative	0.33	0.00	0.33	0.663508	173055914	17577131
Multiplicative	0.00	1.00	0.33	0.658037	173540416	17428691
Multiplicative	0.00	0.00	0.33	0.657345	172689485	17367026
Multiplicative	0.00	0.33	0.33	0.655531	172804247	17339478
Multiplicative	0.00	0.67	0.00	0.654745	168199648	18575368
Multiplicative	0.33	0.67	0.33	0.652380	173510455	17457726

As a first result, the higher throughput (Fig. 8, Eq. 5) of the functions during the time is maintained in all the simulations. This demonstrates that the constraint to write less and maintain a high output towards the clients is respected.

Besides, we considered during the tests that the available bandwidth was 10*Gbit* and we saw that the miss files have, as consequence, a heavier load on the network. In fact, the bandwidth is always higher than the LRU cache (Fig. 9, Eq. 7). It is possible to understand, from the plot, that the limit of 100% is overcome in several points. Hence, there is not enough bandwidth to satisfy all the traffic requested by the clients. The greater request of the network due to the miss files is not a good point for the weight functions and we need better control over this aspect.

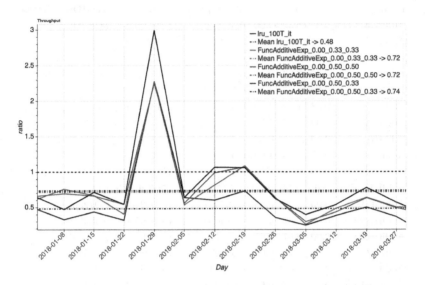

Fig. 8. Throughput detail of the period between January and March with the top 3 functions

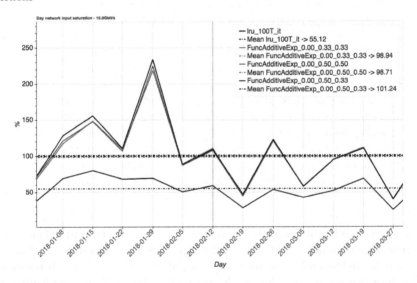

Fig. 9. Bandwidth detail of the period between January and March with the top 3 functions

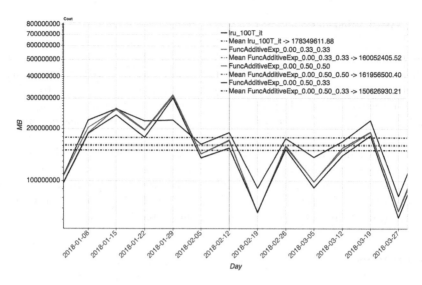

Fig. 10. Cost detail of the period between January and March with the top 10 functions

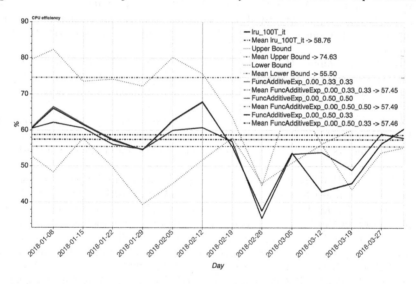

Fig. 11. CPU efficiency detail of the period between January and March with the top 3 functions

Instead, the cost measure (Fig. 10) demonstrates that the target of the function to do less work (from the cache perspective) is fulfilled. The LRU policy cannot compete with the weight functions in terms of the cost measure.

In the end, despite the bandwidth poor results, the CPU efficiency (Fig. 11) seems not to be compromised and still remaining the same. It is around 57% in all the proposed solutions.

6   Conclusions

This work puts a background on how to measure a different behavior of a smarter cache system. Better content management could lead to a more efficient cache, with extra regard to the domain-specific information. The target is to enhance all the measures without losing these improvements in cost and throughput. In particular, we want to decrease the gap between the current caches and the upper bound in the CPU efficiency.

An intelligent cache should have a better CPU efficiency to fulfill the clients expectations. A preliminary study on this aspect found a correlation between the amounts of data read when there is an hit and the CPU efficiency. Hence, the further studies will focus on improve the hit and miss ratio, to optimize the network utilization and, as a consequence, the global CPU efficiency.

References

1. Ali, W., Shamsuddin, S.M., Ismail, A.S., et al.: A survey of web caching and prefetching. Int. J. Adv. Soft Comput. Appl **3**(1), 18–44 (2011)
2. Bauerdick, L., et al.: Xrootd, disk-based, caching proxy for optimization of data access, data placement and data replication. J. Phys.: Conf. Ser. **513**(4), 042044 (2014)
3. Chen, T.: Obtaining the optimal cache document replacement policy for the caching system of an EC website. Eur. J. Oper. Res. **181**(2), 828–841 (2007)
4. Ciangottini, D.: Integrazione di una smart cache italiana federata per CMS. Talk at CCR, Italy (2019)
5. Collaboration, C.M.S., et al.: The CMS experiment at the CERN LHC. Jinst (2008)
6. Herodotou, H.: Autocache: employing machine learning to automate caching in distributed file systems. In: International Conference on Data Engineering Workshops (ICDEW), pp. 133–139 (2019)
7. Koskela, T., Heikkonen, J., Kaski, K.: Web cache optimization with nonlinear model using object features. Comput. Netw. **43**(6), 805–817 (2003)
8. Kuznetsov, V., Li, T., Giommi, L., Bonacorsi, D., Wildish, T.: Predicting dataset popularity for the CMS experiment. arXiv preprint arXiv:1602.07226 (2016)
9. Narayanan, A., Verma, S., Ramadan, E., Babaie, P., Zhang, Z.-L.: Deepcache: a deep learning based framework for content caching. In: Proceedings of the 2018 Workshop on Network Meets AI & ML, pp. 48–53 (2018)
10. Sadeghi, A., Wang, G., Giannakis, G.B.: Deep reinforcement learning for adaptive caching in hierarchical content delivery networks. IEEE Trans. Cogn. Commun. Netw. **5**(4), 1024–1033 (2019)
11. Tian, G., Liebelt, M.: An effectiveness-based adaptive cache replacement policy. Microprocess. Microsyst. **38**(1), 98–111 (2014)
12. XRootD. Xrootd homepage (2020). Accessed 4 Mar 2020

Software Defect Prediction on Unlabelled Datasets: A Comparative Study

Elisabetta Ronchieri[1]($\boxtimes$)(iD), Marco Canaparo[1](iD), and Mauro Belgiovine[2](iD)

[1] INFN-CNAF, Viale Berti Pichat 6/2, Bologna, Italy
elisabetta.ronchieri@cnaf.infn.it
[2] Elettrical and Computer Engineering Department, Northeastern University, Boston, USA

Abstract. Background: Defect prediction on unlabelled datasets is a challenging and widespread problem in software engineering. Machine learning is of great value in this context because it provides techniques - called unsupervised - that are applicable to unlabelled datasets. Objective: This study aims at comparing various approaches employed over the years on unlabelled datasets to predict the defective modules, i.e. the ones which need more attention in the testing phase. Our comparison is based on the measurement of performance metrics and on the real defective information derived from software archives. Our work leverages a new dataset that has been obtained by extracting and preprocessing its metrics from a C++ software. Method: Our empirical study has taken advantage of CLAMI with its improvement CLAMI+ that we have applied on high energy physics software datasets. Furthermore, we have used clustering techniques such as the K-means algorithm to find potentially critical modules. Results: Our experimental analysis have been carried out on 1 open source project with 34 software releases. We have applied 17 ML techniques to the labelled datasets obtained by following the CLAMI and CLAMI+ approaches. The two approaches have been evaluated by using different performance metrics, our results show that CLAMI+ performs better than CLAMI. The predictive average accuracy metric is around 95% for 4 ML techniques (4 out of 17) that show a Kappa statistic greater than 0.80. We applied K-means on the same dataset and obtained 2 clusters labelled according to the output of CLAMI and CLAMI+. Conclusion: Based on the results of the different statistical tests, we conclude that no significant performance differences have been found in the selected classification techniques.

Keywords: Unlabelled dataset · Defect prediction · Unsupervised methods · Machine learning

1 Introduction

A large number of software defect prediction models have been proposed over time to enable developers to determine the most critical software modules to

---

Supported by organization INFN.

O. Gervasi et al. (Eds.): ICCSA 2020, LNCS 12250, pp. 333–353, 2020.
https://doi.org/10.1007/978-3-030-58802-1_25

which they should pay more attention and track carefully [1,2]. Consequently, a prompt recognition of these modules can allow developers to effectively allocate their limited reviewing and testing resources and may suggest architectural improvements. In the last decade, researchers have striven to employ machine learning (ML) techniques in many software engineering (SE) problems, such as defective prediction [3].

In many approaches described in existing literature prediction models learn from historical labelled data within a software project in a supervised way [4]: the model is trained on labelled data (e.g. where defectiveness information is used) and performs prediction on test data. Although supervised approaches are the vast majority, in practice, software projects usually lack classification labels to train a supervised defect prediction model, because it is considered a time and effort consuming activity [5]. Due to the difficulty in collecting label information before building prediction models, unsupervised methods have begun to draw the attention of researchers [6].

Finding the best way to classify unlabelled data is a challenging task. The current approaches use various experiment configurations in terms of software metrics (e.g., belonging to size and complexity category) and performance metrics (e.g., f-measure and accuracy). Li et al. [7] cathegorize them into clustering and non-clustering techniques, some of them are summarized in Table 1.

Table 1. Unsupervised software defect prediction approaches

Category	Approach	Description
Clustering	k-Partition	It is based on the distance data point [8–11]
	Density	It exploits core objects with dense neighborhoods [12]
	Fuzzy	It determines in which a data point can belong to two or more clusters [13,14]
	Spectral clustering	It is based on eigenvalues of the similarity matrix [15,16]
Non-clustering	Expert	In this case expert determine the labels directly [9]
	Threshold	It uses some thresholds to classify instances directly [8,14]

Once clustered the instances of the datasets, the labelling phase is a necessary step in software defect prediction techniques: the expert-based approach labels a cluster by exploiting the decision of an expert [9]; the threshold-based approach decides the cluster label by making use of particular metric threshold values [8,14]; the top half approach labels defective half of the top clusters [17]; the distribution approach is based on the number of nodes of a cluster, the smaller are considered defect prone, the larger non defect-prone [18]; the majority vote uses the most three similar clustering centers [14]; the cross project exploits metrics from user projects [15].

The labelling techniques are characterized by having some limitations, such as relying on experts' information and using suitable metrics' thresholds, and some assumptions like dealing with datasets which include the same features in cross project defect prediction models. Furthermore, it has been shown that their results are uneasy to compare [19].

Previous studies on unlabelled datasets have employed datasets, like the NASA dataset and the clean version of the NASA dataset [20] and the PROMISE dataset [21]. All these datasets are labelled and include different metrics. Therefore, to allow researches to be able to steer their choices when dealing with unlabelled datasets, we have decided to provide a comparative analysis of approaches that are able to overcome the previous limitations by using a new unlabelled dataset built for C++ software.

Our comparative analysis exploits CLAMI [22] that is made up of 4 phases: Clustering, LAbeling, Metrics selection and Instance selection. Its key idea is to label unlabelled datasets by exploiting metrics' magnitude (e.g. median, mean, quantiles), that is metrics' cutoff threshold. In addition to CLAMI, we have explored CLAMI+ [23] an improvement of CLAMI characterized by a different procedure in the metrics' selection phase (see Sect. 3). All the approaches have been applied on a new dataset that has been obtained by extracting and preprocessing its metrics from its software archives. Differently from the majority of previous analysed datasets that are related to C or Java code, ours is the result of a metrics' extraction of a software written in C++ [24]. Finally, we have used the K-means algorithm as another technique to find potentially critical modules.

In this study, we consider a high energy physics (HEP) software project, called Geant4 [25], characterized by a long development history. It represents a valid candidate to systematic comparison approaches applied on unlabelled datasets. For this software we have measured its software characteristics [26] (by using the Imagix 4D framework [27]) to determine its quality evolution over releases and to build a complete set of data on top of which assessing the applicability of software metrics. Considering the amount of data available - i.e., 34 different datasets each for different software modules (such as class, namespace, function, file and variable) - this analysis may help to use these approaches and to concentrate effort only to the most critical software modules of a software project. Our comparison relies on performance metrics, such as accuracy, f-measure and Kappa statistics, and difference tests. Furthermore, we have manually extracted information about defectives of software modules from their software archives to be able to conduct a comparison with real data.

In the remaining parts of this work, we first introduce the terminology Sect. 2. Section 3 introduces the methodology of this comparison, including the research questions, the data used, the frameworks adopted for the analysis, the unsupervised approaches and the ML techniques used. Section 4 further presents the experimental results. Section 5 discusses the results. At last, the work is concluded with future work in Sect. 6.

2 Terminology

Within this section, we introduce a set of definitions we use in the paper, the workflow of unsupervised approaches, the software metrics we have collected and considered in the software datasets, the performance metrics we have used for the discussion and a set of statistical tests we have used to detect differences amongst the various ML techniques.

Definitions - A *software project* contains different releases of the software. Each *software release* is coded by a unique identifier that is composed of one or more numbers. Semantic versioning [28] uses three digits that respectively identify major, minor and patch. Developers increment the major number when they introduce breaking changes; a minor number when they add functionality in a backward compatible way; a patch number when they make all other non-breaking changes. A *module* identifies an element of the software, such as a class, a file, and a function. An *unlabelled* dataset is a set of software metrics for various modules of a given software release. The modules are not labelled with respect to release defects and they are marked with the key term?. A *labelled* dataset is a set of software metrics for various modules of a given software release. The modules are labelled with defective and non defective key terms, such as buggy (B) and clean (C) respectively, according to the unsupervised approaches.

General Workflow - Figure 1 shows the general workflow of software defect prediction on unlabelled datasets.

The *unlabelled dataset* contains for the various modules of a given software releases a set of software metrics. Each software release-specific dataset is split in the training and test datasets respectively to train the model and predict defects: the training dataset starts

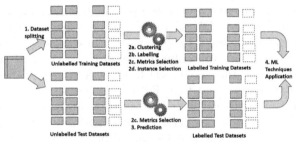

Fig. 1. Workflow.

unlabelled and ends labelled after a set of preprocessing operations related to the adopted unsupervised approaches; the test dataset remains unlabelled. The *training dataset* contains modules labelled as defective (i.e. buggy) or non defective (i.e. clean) according to the unsupervised approaches adopted. Furthermore, each module contains information of some software metrics. Modules with label and software metrics are used to train ML classifiers and to predict new modules as buggy or clean.

Software Metrics - Software metrics provide information on various aspects of software through quantitative measurements [29]. Aspects of software metrics may include: its structure, coupling, maintainability. Metrics can refer to a file, a class, a function or any key software elements that characterize a software.

There are different families of software metrics. In this work we consider size, complexity and object orientation categories. The *size* metrics help to quantify the software size and complexity and suggest the quality of the implementation. Their aim is to identify files, classes or methods that can be hard to understand, reuse, test and modify. For instance, class size metrics can reflect the effort required to build, understand and maintain a class. These metrics go from the comment ratio and size lines of source code up to the size number of statements. The *complexity* metrics help to detect complex code that is difficult to test and maintain. Metrics used to measure this software characteristic are: size metrics (already described), McCabe metrics [30] and Halstead metrics [31]. There are various *object orientation* metrics suites. The most studied one is the Chidamber and Kemerer (CK) metrics suite [32] that aims at measuring design complexity in relation to their impact on external quality attributes, such as maintainability and reusability. The CK metrics are: number of children and depth of inheritance tree related to inheritance and abstraction; weighted methods per class and lack of cohesion in methods pertaining to the internal class structure; coupling between objects and response for a class that are related to relationships among classes.

Performance Metrics - We detail the performance metrics [33] used to assess the considered ML techniques. The metrics are based on the confusion matrix that describes the complete performance of the model by considering the following concepts: a defective instance is defective (i.e. *tp* as true positive); a defective instance is non defective (i.e. *fn* as false negative); a non defective instance is defective (i.e. *tn* as true negative); a non defective instance is non defective (i.e. *fp* as false positive). In this work, we consider the recall metric, the precision metric, the accuracy metric, the f-measure metric, the AUC metric and the Kappa statistic. The *recall* metric $\frac{tp}{tp+fn}$, also called *Probability of Detection* (PD), measures how many of the existing defects are found. The *precision* metric $\frac{tp}{tp+fp}$ measures how many of the found results are actually defects. The *accuracy* metric $\frac{tp+tn}{tp+fn+tn+fp}$ measures the percentage of the correct predictions. The *f-measure* metric $2 \cdot \frac{recall \cdot precision}{recall+precision}$ is the harmonic mean between *recall* and *precision*. The *Probability of False Alarm* (PF) $\frac{fp}{fp+tn}$ is defined as the ratio of false positive to all non-defective modules. Ideally, when used as a performance metric, it is desired to be equal to zero. The *Kappa statistic* $\frac{accuracy-randaccuracy}{1-randaccuracy}$ [34], with the *randaccuracy* equals to $\frac{(tn+fp) \cdot (tn+fn)+(fn+tp) \cdot (fp+tp)}{accuracy \cdot accuracy}$, compares the observed accuracy with the expected accuracy and its value $\in [0, 1]$. If *Kappa statistic* $\in [0.81, 0.99]$, then the value indicates an almost perfect agreement. The *Receiver Operating Characteristics (ROC) curve*, in the field of software prediction, is defined as a tradeoff between the prediction ability to correctly detect defective modules (PD or recall) and non-defective modules (PF) [35]. From a graphical point of view, PD is represented on the Y-axis and PF on the X-axis, while predictor's threshold is varying. The performance of a predictor is better as the curve is closer to coordinates PD = 1 and PF = 0. The *Area Under the Curve (AUC)* metric is the area under the ROC curve and it is commonly used to compare performance of predictors. It measures a model's discriminatory power which represents the area under receiver operating characteristic (ROC) curve [23,36]. Compared to other metrics, AUC has two advantages: it is independent on the definition of a metric threshold and it is robust towards imbalanced datasets. With other performance metrics, a classifier must rely on the determination of a threshold whose value is usually set as the average of all metric' values, this choice may affect the final results of the classifier. Precision and recall are examples of metrics which are highly influenced by imbalanced datasets, making it difficult to conduct a fairly models' comparison.

Performance Differences Tests - We statistically compare the performances achieved by the experimented prediction models. We are going to detect groups of differences between the ML techniques we have considered in this study. These groups are called *blocks* in statistics and are usually linked to the problems met in the experimental study [37]. For example, in a comparative analysis of multiple datasets, each block is related to the results computed on a specific dataset. When dealing with multiple comparison tests, each block is composed of various results each linked to the couple algorithm, datasets. The *Friedman test* [38] is the most common procedure for testing the differences among two o more related samples which represent the performance metrics of the techniques measured across the same datasets. The objective of this test is to determine if we may conclude from a sample of results that there is difference among treatment effects [37]. It is composed of two steps: the first step converts the original results in ranks by calculating a test statistic; the second step ranks the techniques for each problem separately where the best performing techniques is given rank 1. Iman and Davenport [39] showed that Friedman test have a conservative behaviour and proposed a different statistic. Post hoc procedures are employed to obtain what classifier performances better than the one proposed. They usually follows the application of the Friedman test since they take into account the rankings generated by the Friedman procedure. According to [40], Friedman test with Iman and Davemport extension is the most popular omnibus test and is a good choice for comparing more than five techniques. About post hoc tests, comparing all the techniques with one proposed requires the simple but least powerful Bonferroni test, on the contrary, when it is necessary to conduct pairwise comparison, Hommel [41] and Rom are the two most powerful procedures. The *Nemenyi post-hoc test* [42] is used when every classifier is compared to one another. Two classifiers achieve significant different performance if the corresponding average ranks differ by at least the critical difference (CD) $q_\alpha \sqrt{\frac{k(k+1)}{6N}}$ where k is in the number of ML techniques, N is the number of the datasets and q_α is derived from the studentized range statistic divided by $\sqrt{2}$. The Scott-Knott Effect Size Difference (ESD) test [43] is a mean comparison approach based on a hierarchical clustering analysis to partition the set of treatment means into statistically distinct groups. It corrects the non-normal distribution of an input dataset, and merges any two statistically distinct groups that have a negligible effect size into one group.

3   Comparison Methodology

We describe the methodology that we followed to perform our comparison.

Research Questions - We formulate the research questions (RQ) that we answer through this comparison. *RQ1*: which unsupervised approach performs best in terms of our performance metrics? *RQ2*: which supervised technique performs best in terms of our performance metrics in the two unsupervised approaches? *RQ3*: what is the impact of using different cutoff thresholds (i.e. quantiles) on the comparison results? The reason for *RQ1* is that we intend to test the known unsupervised approaches employed both in previous literature and in our work to find which one is performing better than the others. To do so we will compute their results in term of performance metrics. The analysis of *RQ3* provides insights into how the dataset distribution affects the overall performance of our defect prediction experiments. On the one hand, larger datasets entail more generalization and better performance, however, less data for training may have less variance which can cause an improvement in the performance.

Data - Our comparison assesses the CLAMI and CLAMI+ approaches on a multi-release dataset. It is related to the scientific widespread Geant4 software due to its peculiarity: the first 0.0 release was delivered the 15th of December 1998 and it is still under development by an international collaboration that have produced 10 major releases and at least 34 minor releases with various patches. The development time frames sampled in the study ranges 21 years, covering almost a quarter of century of development history.

Figure 2 shows the Geant4 software releases considered for this study over years: for each release number, the + shows the year when the release was delivered, the x shows the year when the related patch was delivered. At the moment, the dataset consists of 34 software releases delivered in almost 20 years of development. There are 66 software metrics for 482 C++ classes, measured for the various releases by using the Imagix 4D tool [27].

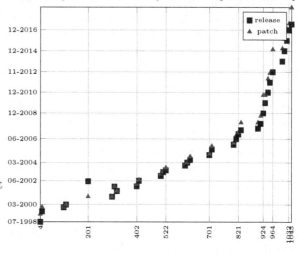

Fig. 2. The Geant4 software releases

The resulting dataset is composed of 34 x 482 classes, 482 are repeated 33 releases. The defect labels are not included in the dataset: we have extracted them by using the release notes that accompany the corresponding software releases.

Framework - In order to conduct this study, we exploit various available frameworks running in Java, Python and R. We have assessed these frameworks leveraging how much effort they required us to be used: Weka [44] is the easiest to use, while Theano [45] requires more expertise.

Unsupervised Approaches - We apply three unsupervised approaches to the examined dataset. The CLAMI approach conducts the prediction on unlabelled dataset by learning from itself. It creates a labelled training sample by using the magnitude of metric values (i.e. the metrics that are greater than of a specific cutoff threshold) and build the model by supervised learning to predict unlabelled modules. This approach consists of clustering, labelling, metrics selection and instance selection phases: clustering groups the modules; labelling estimates the label of groups; metric selection and instance selection select more informative features (i.e., software metrics) and produce training set. In the labeling, CLAMI measures the count of violation (i.e., a metric value is greater than a certain threshold) of a module. The CLAMI+ approach extends the CLAMI one. The main difference concerns the clustering and labelling phases. CLAMI+ uses the violation degree (i.e., transforming the difference between the metric value and the threshold to a probabilistic value) to replace the boolean representation in CLAMI. In this case, how much the instance violated on a metric is considered. The resulting training set is more informative than the one of CLAMI. K-means is a clustering algorithm [46] that depends upon iterative location that partitions dataset into K number of clusters by standard Euclidean distance. There are various variants of the algorithm, we have used the ones implemented in scikit-learn that is based on either Llody's or Elkan's algorithm [47,48]. Since it is simple and flexible these algorithms are very popular in statistical analysis [49]. The defect prediction is performed within-project where the training and test sets are from the same project.

ML Techniques - Aiming at comparing several classification algorithms, we have considered a total of seventeen classifiers, each of which can be categorized according to its statistical approach. We have identified the following categories: statistical classifiers that construct a Bayes optimal classifier; nearest-neighbor methods that classify a module by considering the k most similar samples, where the similarity definition differs among algorithms; neural networks methods that depicts a network structure to define a concatenation of weighting, aggregation and thresholding functions in order to determine a software module probability of being fp; support vector machines classifiers that aim at optimizing a linear decision function to discriminate between fp and non fp modules; tree-based methods that recursively partition the training data; ensembles methods that embody several base classifiers, built independently and put together to obtain a final class prediction. Table 2 provides, for each category, the considered classifiers. A detailed description is available in general textbooks [50].

Evaluation Strategy and Remarks - The focus of our comparison is not an advancement or improvement of existing approaches. We apply them to an unlabelled dataset related to Geant4 software, a stone in the Monte Carlo simulation

Table 2. Classification models

Category	Model	Acronym
Statistical classifiers	Naïve Bayes	NB
	Logistic Regression	LR
	Bayesian Network	BN
Nearest neighbor methods	k-Nearest Neighbor	k NN
Neural networks	Multi-Linear Programming	MLP
	Radial Basis Function Network	RBF net
Support vector machine classifiers	Support Vector Machine	SVM
	Linear Programming	LP
	Least Squares SVM	LS SVM
	Lagrangian SVM	L SVM
Decision tree approaches	C 4.5 Decision Tree	C 4.5
	J48	J48
	Classification and Regression Tree	CART
Ensemble methods	Random Forest	RF
	Logistic Model Tree	LMT
	Adaboost	Adaboost
	Bagging	Bagging

in order to provide an alternative way to control and monitor its development process. The resulting datasets have been checked against the existing documentation in the release note of each new software release. We have been able to trace modules that were changed for bug fixes, minor fixes, warning, and major fixes, finding a correspondence between the documentation and the labelling activity performed by the considered unsupervised approaches.

4   Results

In this section we provide an analysis of the obtained results. To conduct a reasonable comparison among the various releases we have considered the modules that were present in all the releases. This filtering operation has led to a considerable reduction of our training set. More in detail, while the common modules of all the releases were 482, the releases 4, 11 and 1004 for example contain respectively 891, 915 and 2544 modules. In the following, we present the results relative to the various steps of the considered approaches.

Selected Metrics - Table 3 shows the level, the category (i.e. Complexity, Size, Object Orientation), the complete name and the description of all metrics selected either in the CLAMI or the CLAMI+ approach. The file level metrics have been computed both on header (i.e. the .h extension) and source files (i.e. the .cpp extension). Halstead's metrics have been calculated both at file

Table 3. Metrics' description

Level	Category	Acronym	Name	Description
Class (CL)	Complexity	CLhpd	Halstead Program Difficulty (hpd)	Measure of how compactly the class implements its algorithms (Halstead D). This is the inverse of the Halstead Program Level (of abstraction)
Class (CL)	Complexity	CLhpv	Halstead Program Volume (hpv)	Measure of the information content of the class (Halstead V)
Class (CL)	Complexity	CLhme	Halstead Mental Effort (hme)	Measure of the number of elemental mental discriminations necessary to create; or understand; the class (Halstead E)
Class (CL)	Complexity	CLhic	Halstead Intelligent Content	Language-independent measure of the amount of content (complexity) of the class (Halstead I)
Class	Object Orientation	chlvc	Class Hierarchy and Local Vars Coupling	Depth of the hierarchy of derived classes of the class
Class	Object Orientation	ckrfc	CK Response For a Class	Number of methods called by the class's methods; a measure of the class's response (Chidamber and Kemerer RFC)
Class	Object Orientation	ckwmc	CK Weighted Methods per Class	Total cyclomatic complexity for the class's methods (Chidamber and Kemerer WMC)
Class	Object Orientation	mci	Methods Called - Internal	Number of internal methods called by class methods
Class	Object Orientation	mce	Methods Called - External	Number of external methods called by class methods
Class	Object Orientation	emc	External Methods and Coupling	Total number of external classes used and external methods called by class member methods. This is the sum of coupling between classes and external methods called
Class	Size	ntm	Number of Total Members	Total number of members of the class
Class	Object Orientation	cklcm	CK Lack of Cohesion of Methods	Lack of Cohesion of Methods is a measure of the cohesion of the member functions of the class (Chidamber and Kemerer LCOM; 1994 revised definition)
Class	Size	nmm	Number of Member Methods	Number of methods (member functions) of the class
Class	Size	nmpm	Number of Member Private Methods	Number of local methods (private member functions) of the class
Class	Size	nma	Number of Member Attributes	Number of attributes (member variables) of the class
Class	Size	ntm	Number of Total Members	Total number of members of the class
File	Complexity	Hmctcc	McCabe Total Cyclomatic Complexity (mctcc)	Total cyclomatic complexity for all functions defined in the header (H) file or implementation (I) file
File	Complexity	Imcacc	McCabe Average Cyclomatic Complexity	Average cyclomatic complexity for all functions defined in the header (H) file or implementation (I) file
File	Complexity	Hmi, Imi	Maintainability Index (mi)	Measure of the maintainability of the header (H) file or implementation (I) file (Welker MI)
File	Complexity	Ihpd	Halstead Program Difficulty	Measure of how compactly the header (H) file or implementation (I) file implements its algorithms (Halstead D). This is the inverse of the Halstead Program Level (of abstraction)

(continued)

Table 3. (*continued*)

Level	Category	Acronym	Name	Description
File	Complexity	Ihpv	Halstead Program Volume	Measure of the information content of the header (H) file or implementation (I) file (Halstead V)
File	Complexity	Ihic	Halstead Intelligent Content	Language-independent measure of the amount of content (complexity) of the header (H) file or implementation (I) file (Halstead I)
File	Complexity	Ihme	Halstead Mental Effort	Measure of the number of elemental mental discriminations necessary to create; or understand; the header (H) file or implementation (I) file (Halstead E).
File	Complexity	Ihpd	Halstead Program Difficulty	Measure of how compactly the header (H) file or implementation (I) file implements its algorithms (Halstead D). This is the inverse of the Halstead Program Level (of abstraction)
File	Size	Hsb, Isb	Size Bytes (sb)	Size of the header (H) or implementation (I) file in bytes
File	Size	Hidif	Inclusion - Directly Included Files	Number of header files in the project database which are directly included by the header (H) file or implementation (I) file
File	Size	Hitil, Iitil	Inclusion - Transitively Included Lines	Number of lines in header files in the project database which are transitively included by the header (H) file or implementation (I) file.
File	Size	Iitif	Inclusion - Transitively Included Files	Number of header files in the project database which are transitively included by the header (H) file or implementation (I) file
File	Size	Islf	Size - Lines in File	Number of lines in the header (H) file or implementation (I) file.
File	Size	Hslc, Islc	Size - Lines of Comments	Number of lines of comments in the header (H) file or implementation (I) file.
File	Size	Isns	Size - Number of Statements	Number of statements in the header (H) file or implementation (I) file

Table 4. Common metrics between the CLAMI and CLAMI+ approaches over the various quantiles

Acronym	1	2	3	4	5	6	7	8	9	Acronym	1	2	3	4	5	6	7	8	9	Acronym	1	2	3	4	5	6	7	8	9
chlvc	✓		✓		✓		✓	✓		Iitif	✓	✓								Ihic	✓	✓							
ckrfc			✓	✓	✓	✓	✓	✓	✓	Iitil	✓	✓								Ihme	✓	✓							
ckwmc			✓	✓	✓	✓	✓	✓	✓	Ihpd	✓	✓								Isb	✓	✓							
CLhpd	✓		✓		✓	✓	✓	✓	✓	Ihpd	✓									Imi	✓	✓							
CLhpv	✓		✓	✓	✓	✓	✓	✓	✓	Islc	✓									Imctcc									✓
CLhme	✓		✓		✓	✓	✓	✓	✓	ntm				✓			✓	✓		mce									✓
Hmctcc	✓	✓	✓							nma							✓	✓		Isns									✓
Hsb	✓	✓								chlvc										Hslc									✓
Hidif	✓	✓								cklcm										emc									✓
Hmi	✓	✓								CLmcmcc										mce									✓
Hitil	✓	✓								CLhic										Islf	✓	✓							
Imcacc	✓	✓								nmpm										Ihpv	✓	✓							
mci							✓			nmm	✓																		

and class levels: metrics CLhpd, CLhpv, CLhme, CLhic are at class level, while metrics Ihpd, Ihpv, Ihic, Ihme, Ihpd are at file level for the source files. Table 4 indicates the metrics selected both in the CLAMI and CLAMI+ approaches for the different quantiles (cutoff thresholds) among the various releases. Quantiles' numbers from 1 to 9 correspond to 10%, ..., 90% respectively. Quantiles 1 and 2 have focused more on metrics on file level, while quantiles from 3 to 9 have selected object orientation metrics. Metrics CLhpd, CLhpv, CLhme, ckrfc, ckwmc are the ones that share more quantiles from 5 to 9, and they belong to the object orientation or complexity category. Table 5 displays the total number of metrics selected in the CLAMI and CLAMI+ approaches for the different quantiles among the various releases. They go from a minimum of 18 in the 4, 5 and 6 quantiles to a maximum of 52 in the 9 quantile.

Labelled Modules - The percentage of buggy modules on the total modules over the releases for each quantile has been measured. The quantiles are related to the different cut-off values chosen for the metrics. For example, for the release 701 and quantile 5 (which corresponds to the median value of the metrics), CLAMI computes about 60% of buggy modules. The difference between CLAMI and CLAMI+ of the percentage of buggy modules over the various releases for each quantile has been measured. As an example, in release 511 and quantile 5, the values of the difference is about 10. Furthermore, CLAMI predicts 50% of buggy modules, consequently, CLAMI+ predicts about 40% of buggy modules.

It is worth noticing that our manual work has covered just 380 modules, this has reduced the size of our training set. K-means has provided us with two clusters made up of different classes. We checked the different classes of these clusters against the documentation of defectiveness. Afterwards, we collected how CLAMI and CLAMI+ have labelled each class. Both of them have labelled 179 modules as defective in cluster 1, while in cluster 2 CLAMI has labelled 9617 modules as defective and CLAMI+ 9747.

Table 5. Total metrics per approach - CLAMI and CLAMI+ - over the various quantiles

	1	2	3	4	5	6	7	8	9
CLAMI	37	36	35	32	18	18	21	23	47
CLAMI+	36	35	34	18	23	23	47	49	52

ML Techniques - In our study, we have carried out a comparative analysis of all the ML techniques using the average rank calculated on the various performance metrics, such as accuracy, precision, recall, f-measure and AUC. In order to avoid overfitting we have exploited 10 cross-validation [51–53], furthermore, we have excluded all the prediction models whose Kappa statistic scored less than 0.80 in order to have a good agreement. Table 6 presents the different values of average accuracy computed for 4 ML techniques, such as J48, LMT, AdaBoost and Bagging obtained by using ten cross validation in order to avoid overfitting. The best accuracy values are achieved by all the techniques for the first quantile; CLAMI+ approach reaches high scores also in the ninth quantile. The technique that performs the best regardless of the two approaches and quantiles is Adaboost that scores 95.3508 in terms of average accuracy. Regardless of the specific techniques, CLAMI+ performs better than CLAMI in every quantile except the second, third and fourth. Table 7 displays the different values of

average buggy precision computed for 4 ML techniques i.e. J48, LMT, AdaBoost
and Bagging. The technique that performs the best in terms of precision and
regardless of the quantiles and approaches is LMT that scores 0,9385 in terms
of average precision. Except for quantile one, two and nine, CLAMI performs
better than CLAMI+ regardless of the specific technique. Table 8 illustrates the
different values of average buggy recall computed for 4 ML techniques i.e. J48,
LMT, AdaBoost and Bagging. The technique that performs the best in terms
of recall and regardless of the quantiles and approaches is Adaboost that scores
0,9328 in terms of average recall. Except for quantile three and five, CLAMI performs better than CLAMI+ regardless of the specific technique. Table 9 shows
the different values of average buggy f-measure computed for 4 ML techniques
i.e. J48, LMT, AdaBoost and Bagging. The technique that performs the best in
terms of f-measures and regardless of the quantiles and approaches is LMT that
scores 0,9343. Except for quantile one, CLAMI performs better than CLAMI+
in terms of f-measure regardless of the specific technique. Table 10 displays the
different values of average buggy AUC computed for 4 ML techniques i.e. J48,
LMT, AdaBoost and Bagging. The technique that performs the best in terms
of AUC and regardless of the quantiles and approaches is Adaboost that scores
0.9830. CLAMI+ performs better than CLAMI in quantiles 1, 2, 5 and 7 in
terms of AUC regardless of the specific technique.

ML Statistical Comparison - With the aim of comparing the various algorithms
to determine whether and to what extent one outperforms the others, we have
employed some statistical tests on the values of the ML performance metrics.
All the differences obtained have been tested by considering each pair of algorithms and their resulting p-values have been corrected. The differences for the

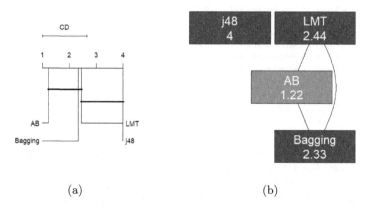

(a)   (b)

Fig. 3. (a): Critical difference plot for the average buggy AUC in the CLAMI approach
(the Nemenyi test at p-value < 0.05): classifiers that are no significantly different are
connected by an horizontal line, (b): Algorithm graph for the average buggy AUC
in the CLAMI approach (the Friedman post-hoc test with Bergmann and Hommel's
correction at p-value < 0.05): classifiers that are not significantly different are connected

Table 6. Average accuracy of the ML techniques

Quantile	Approach	J48	LMT	AdaBoost	Bagging	Quantile	Approach	J48	LMT	AdaBoost	Bagging
1	CLAMI	98.1670	98.1072	98.1381	97.3868	1	CLAMI+	98.8291	98.8101	98.8471	98.5651
2	CLAMI	96.8106	97.1064	96.6285	96.9970	2	CLAMI+	96.9223	96.6182	97.0572	96.3726
3	CLAMI	95.3838	95.1111	95.0132	94.9443	3	CLAMI+	94.6002	94.5518	94.6830	94.5434
4	CLAMI	93.0748	93.2507	93.3463	93.1027	4	CLAMI+	92.7295	92.3045	92.5200	92.7422
5	CLAMI	92.4850	92.4551	91.8897	92.5070	5	CLAMI+	93.2537	93.9593	93.7013	93.6975
6	CLAMI	93.2719	93.5851	93.6380	93.4789	6	CLAMI+	93.7195	93.9813	94.4491	94.0966
7	CLAMI	93.8482	94.4191	94.2796	94.2807	7	CLAMI+	94.9153	95.1850	95.5844	94.9700
8	CLAMI	94.2239	95.5005	95.0125	94.7273	8	CLAMI+	96.6170	96.7744	96.9310	96.2294
9	CLAMI	94.7243	95.0025	95.4197	94.9242	9	CLAMI+	98.7572	99.3769	99.1762	98.8717
	Average rank	3.0000	1.8888	2.3333	2.7777		Average rank	3.0000	2.4444	1.4444	3.1111

Table 7. Average buggy precision of the ML techniques

Quantile	Approach	J48	LMT	AdaBoost	Bagging	Quantile	Approach	J48	LMT	AdaBoost	Bagging
1	CLAMI	0.9884	0.9863	0.9885	0.9849	1	CLAMI+	0.9933	0.9935	0.9926	0.9921
2	CLAMI	0.9804	0.9794	0.9779	0.9760	2	CLAMI+	0.9821	0.9786	0.9816	0.9747
3	CLAMI	0.9720	0.9718	0.9695	0.9657	3	CLAMI+	0.9600	0.9633	0.9609	0.9544
4	CLAMI	0.9495	0.9539	0.9465	0.9419	4	CLAMI+	0.9292	0.9364	0.9327	0.9302
5	CLAMI	0.9274	0.9422	0.9244	0.9275	5	CLAMI+	0.9208	0.9370	0.9269	0.9264
6	CLAMI	0.9204	0.9371	0.9318	0.9228	6	CLAMI+	0.9059	0.9181	0.9135	0.9111
7	CLAMI	0.9125	0.9292	0.9237	0.9244	7	CLAMI+	0.8827	0.8875	0.8886	0.8802
8	CLAMI	0.8779	0.9179	0.9073	0.8944	8	CLAMI+	0.8344	0.8555	0.8697	0.8280
9	CLAMI	0.8662	0.8895	0.9008	0.8914	9	CLAMI+	0.8484	0.9166	0.9116	0.8931
	Average rank	2.7777	1.6666	2.4444	3.1111		Average rank	3.1111	1.4444	1.8888	3.5555

Table 8. Average buggy recall of the ML techniques

Quantile	Approach	J48	LMT	AdaBoost	Bagging	Quantile	Approach	J48	LMT	AdaBoost	Bagging
1	CLAMI	0.9918	0.9931	0.9914	0.9866	1	CLAMI+	0.9944	0.9939	0.9952	0.9926
2	CLAMI	0.9833	0.9878	0.9831	0.9895	2	CLAMI+	0.9829	0.9829	0.9850	0.9838
3	CLAMI	0.9691	0.9662	0.9673	0.9705	3	CLAMI+	0.9682	0.9640	0.9685	0.9738
4	CLAMI	0.9497	0.9467	0.9569	0.9582	4	CLAMI+	0.9481	0.9325	0.9408	0.9478
5	CLAMI	0.9367	0.9194	0.9293	0.9375	5	CLAMI+	0.9297	0.9274	0.9332	0.9330
6	CLAMI	0.9311	0.9191	0.9265	0.9333	6	CLAMI+	0.9060	0.8993	0.9208	0.9113
7	CLAMI	0.9047	0.9047	0.9067	0.9056	7	CLAMI+	0.8760	0.8903	0.9069	0.8840
8	CLAMI	0.8779	0.8908	0.8809	0.8820	8	CLAMI+	0.8802	0.8604	0.8796	0.8877
9	CLAMI	0.8682	0.8539	0.8619	0.8471	9	CLAMI+	0.8018	0.9166	0.8578	0.8367
	Average rank	2.4444	3.0000	2.6666	1.8888		Average rank	2.7777	3.3333	1.6666	2.2222

various performance metrics have been checked with Iman and Davenport (ID)'s omnibus test. For CLAMI we have obtained a p-value < 0.05 just for the AUC metric, while for CLAMI+ we have obtained a p-value < 0.05 for all performance metrics. For these results, there is at least one algorithm that performs differently than the rest and therefore the post-hoc analysis can be performed for further investigation. More precisely, we have applied Nemenyi's test and Friedman's post-hoc test that computes the raw p-value for each pair of algorithms and their correction using Bergmann and Hommel's correction.

Table 9. Average buggy F-measure of the ML techniques

Quantile	Approach	J48	LMT	AdaBoost	Bagging	Quantile	Approach	J48	LMT	AdaBoost	Bagging
1	CLAMI	0.9901	0.9897	0.9899	0.9857	1	CLAMI+	0.9938	0.9937	0.9939	0.9924
2	CLAMI	0.9818	0.9836	0.9805	0.9827	2	CLAMI+	0.9825	0.9807	0.9833	0.9792
3	CLAMI	0.9705	0.9690	0.9684	0.9681	3	CLAMI+	0.9640	0.9636	0.9647	0.9639
4	CLAMI	0.9495	0.9502	0.9516	0.9499	4	CLAMI+	0.9384	0.9342	0.9365	0.9388
5	CLAMI	0.9320	0.9306	0.9266	0.9324	5	CLAMI+	0.9251	0.9321	0.9299	0.9295
6	CLAMI	0.9255	0.9279	0.9290	0.9278	6	CLAMI+	0.9058	0.9085	0.9170	0.9111
7	CLAMI	0.9084	0.9166	0.9149	0.9147	7	CLAMI+	0.8787	0.8886	0.8974	0.8815
8	CLAMI	0.8777	0.9039	0.8937	0.8878	8	CLAMI+	0.8553	0.8569	0.8728	0.8547
9	CLAMI	0.8667	0.8711	0.8801	0.8680	9	CLAMI+	0.8232	0.9166	0.8835	0.8561
	Average rank	3.0000	1.8888	2.2222	2.8888		Average rank	3.0000	2.5555	1.4444	3.0000

Table 10. Average buggy AUC of the ML techniques

Quantile	Approach	J48	LMT	AdaBoost	Bagging	Quantile	Approach	J48	LMT	AdaBoost	Bagging
1	CLAMI	0.9321	0.9820	0.9895	0.9453	1	CLAMI+	0.9117	0.9792	0.9864	0.9757
2	CLAMI	0.9146	0.9729	0.9823	0.9779	2	CLAMI+	0.9297	0.9671	0.9855	0.9668
3	CLAMI	0.9347	0.9678	0.9822	0.9766	3	CLAMI+	0.9254	0.9660	0.9781	0.9737
4	CLAMI	0.9300	0.9682	0.9786	0.9732	4	CLAMI+	0.9291	0.9595	0.9733	0.9740
5	CLAMI	0.9253	0.9639	0.9706	0.9734	5	CLAMI+	0.9385	0.9780	0.9831	0.9804
6	CLAMI	0.9404	0.9789	0.9841	0.9816	6	CLAMI+	0.9295	0.9815	0.9854	0.9821
7	CLAMI	0.9355	0.9800	0.9837	0.9786	7	CLAMI+	0.9246	0.9851	0.9892	0.9836
8	CLAMI	0.9275	0.9868	0.9856	0.9777	8	CLAMI+	0.9144	0.9875	0.9886	0.9778
9	CLAMI	0.9136	0.9791	0.9854	0.9710	9	CLAMI+	0.8868	0.9983	0.9826	0.9314
	Average rank	4.0000	2.4444	1.2222	2.3333		Average rank	4.0000	2.3333	1.2222	2.4444

Considering the CLAMI approach, Fig. 4 shows the results obtained with Nemenyi's test for the AUC metric, according to which there is no significant differences between methods that are grouped together by a horizontal line: the top line represents the axis on which the average ranks of methods (see Table 10) is plotted; the highest (best) ranks are to the right; the critical difference is also shown above the graph. Still for CLAMI, Fig. 3 shows the results obtained with Friedman's post-hoc test with Bergmann and Hommel's correction for the AUC metric, according to which there is no significance differences between methods that have connected nodes: each node reporting the method name with its average rank (see Table 10) is plotted; the highest (best) ranks are not connected. Compared with the critical difference plot, the graph shows more differences between methods. We have performed the same plots for the other performance metrics. According to the ScottKnott ESD test, we have obtained a non negligible effect size for the AUC metric either in the CLAMI and CLAMI+ approaches as shown in Fig. 4 and 5. In both the approaches Bagging is the most influential ML technique.

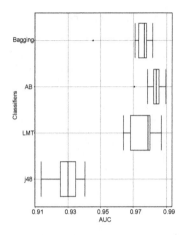

Fig. 4. AUC performance difference for CLAMI

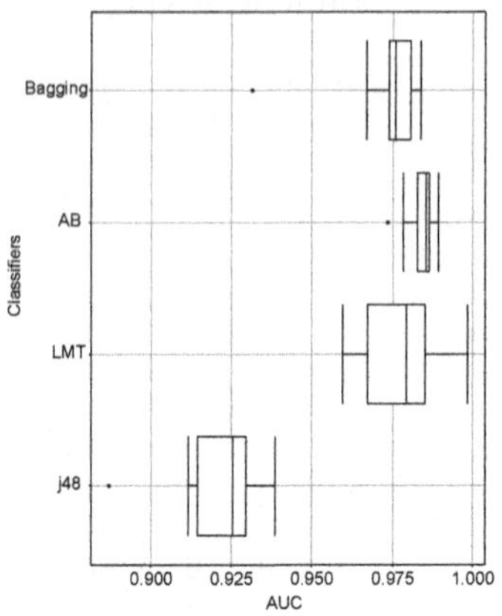

Fig. 5. AUC performance difference for CLAMI+

5 Discussion

In this section we present the answers of our research questions. In regards to RQ1 and RQ2 we employed different performance metrics and statistical tests. In detail, we have used accuracy, precision, recall, f-measure and the area under the receiver operating characteristics (AUC). Accuracy measures the percentage of the correct predictions among all the predictions; precision measures rate of the correctly predicted defective instances among all the instances predicted as defective; recall measures the rate of correctly predicted defective instances among all the actual defective instances. F-measure represents the harmonic mean of precision and recall, AUC measures the area under the ROC curve that is plotted using recall and false positive rate by changing software metrics' cutoff thresholds. All the above metrics have widely used in previous literature in the field of software defect prediction [6, 22, 23, 54, 55]. For statistical tests, we have conducted Iman and Davenport (ID) omnibus test, Nemenyi tests, the Friedman post hoc test with Bergman and Hommel's correction and Scott-KnottESD test. We have followed the guidelines of Demšar [42] for the visual representation of the Nemenyi and Friedman tests.

RQ1: which unsupervised approach performs best in terms of our performance metrics? Two main unsupervised approaches have been involved for the comparison: CLAMI and CLAMI+. They entail varying their metrics' cutoff thresholds and, consequently, the creation of 9 quantiles to conduct the labelling operation, and afterwards, the application of supervised ML techniques - more in detail, we have considered all the ML techniques whose Kappa statistic reached a value superior to 0.80. To find the best approach we have computed the average of all the values of one performance metric over the techniques and then quantiles, giving the same weight to each of them. In regards to accuracy CLAMI+ scores

95.6928 and does better than CLAMI that scores 94.7845. CLAMI achieves a higher result than CLAMI+ in precision (0.9389 vs 0.9253), recall (0.9335 vs 0.9276), f-measure (0.9360 vs 0.9258) and AUC (0.9647 vs 0.9636).

RQ2: which supervised technique performs best in terms of our performance metrics in the two unsupervised approaches? Table 11 introduces the average performance metrics values per techniques over approaches and quantiles. Adaboost achieves the best score in accuracy (95.3508), recall

Table 11. Average performance metrics per techniques over approaches and quantiles

	J48	LMT	Adaboost	Bagging
Accuracy	95.1296	95.3388	95.3508	95.1354
Precision	0.92508	0.9385	0.93602	0.92884
Recall	0.9278	0.9305	0.9329	0.9312
F-measure	0.9260	0.93431	0.9341	0.9291
AUC	0.9246	0.9768	0.9830	0.9722

(0.9329), and AUC (0.9830), whilst LMT performs best in precision (0.9385) and f-measure (0.9343). Concerning the CLAMI and CLAMI+ approaches and the AUC performance metric, J48 has achieved the best average rank. Figure 4 shows that there are no statistical differences within the pairs LMT/Bagging, LMT/Adaboost and Bagging/Adaboost. For CLAMI+ and the accuracy performance metric, J48 and Bagging have achieved the best average rank: there are no statistical differences within the pairs J48/LMT, LMT/Adaboost, LMT/Bagging and J48/Bagging. For CLAMI+ and the precision performance metric, J48 and Bagging have achieved the best average rank: there are no statistical differences within the pairs J48/Bagging and LMT/Adaboost. For CLAMI+ and the recall performance metric, J48 and Bagging have achieved the best average rank: there are no statistical differences within the pairs J48/LMT, J48/Adaboost, LMT/Bagging, Adaboost/Bagging and J48/Bagging. For CLAMI+ and the f-measure performance metric, J48 and Bagging have achieved the best average rank: there are no statistical differences within the pairs J48/LMT, LMT/Adaboost, Adaboost/Baggin, LMT/Bagging and J48/Bagging.

RQ3: what is the impact of using different cutoff thresholds (i.e. quantiles) on the comparison results? Quantiles values affects the resulting performance metrics, as a consequence, metrics' thresholds have to be taken into consideration since the data distribution is not Gaussian.

6   Conclusion

In this paper, we have conducted a comparative analysis of different unsupervised approaches: CLAMI, CLAMI+ and K-means. Once obtained a labelled dataset by exploiting these approaches, we have carried out a second comparison amongst various ML supervised techniques. Starting from an unlabelled software dataset, CLAMI and CLAMI+ allow users to label each instance by exploiting their metrics magnitude. We have applied different supervised ML techniques on the resulting datasets and detected the best ones by using statistical comparisons, such as Iman and Davenport's test, Nemenyi's test, Friedman's post-hoc test with Bergmann and Hommel's correction and Scott-KnottESD test. Among the used 17 ML techniques, we have selected the ones which scored more than 0.80 in the Kappa statistic performance metric: J48, Adaboost, LMT and Bagging. The computed predictive average accuracy metric is around 95% for all the ML techniques. Furthermore, our study has shown that, for CLAMI and CLAMI+, the J48 method performs best according to the average AUC performance metric. In regards to CLAMI+, J48 is followed by: the Bagging method for the average AUC, average accuracy, average precision and average f-measure metrics; and by the LMT method for the average recall metric. Based on the results of our empirical analysis, we conclude that no significant performance differences have been found in the selected classification techniques. Future works based on this study could involve all the datasets for each release of Geant4 (now only 482 modules for each release are considered) and the employment of other clustering unsupervised techniques such as Fuzzy CMeans and Fuzzy SOMs.

Acknowledgment. The authors thank the Imagix Corporation for providing an extended free license of Imagix 4D to perform this work.

References

1. Arar, O.F., Ayan, K.: Software defect prediction using cost-sensitive neural network. Appl. Softw. Comput. **33**, 263–277 (2015)
2. Menzies, T., Greenwald, J., Frank, A.: Data mining static code attributes to learn defect predictors. IEEE Trans. Softw. Eng. **33**, 2–13 (2007)
3. Ronchieri, E., Canaparo, M.: Metrics for software reliability: a systematic mapping study. J. Integr. Des. Process Sci. **22**, 5–25 (2018)
4. Malhotra, R., Bansal, A.J.: Cross project change prediction using open source projects. In: International Conference on Advances in Computing, Communications and Informatics (ICACCI). IEEE (2014). https://doi.org/10.1109/ICACCI.2014.6968347
5. Zhong, S., Khoshgoftaar, T.M., Seliya, N.: Unsupervised learning for expert-based software quality estimation. In: Proceedings of the 8th IEEE International Symposium on High Assurance Systems Engineering. IEEE (2004). https://doi.org/10.1109/HASE.2004.1281739
6. Yang, J., Qian, H.: Defect prediction on unlabeled datasets by using unsupervised clustering. In: Proceedings of the IEEE 18th International Conference on High Performance Computing and Communications; IEEE 14th International Conference on Smart City; IEEE 2nd International Conference on Data Science and Systems (HPCC/SmartCity/DSS) (2016)
7. Li, N., Shepperd, M.J., Guo, Y.: A systematic review of unsupervised learning techniques for software defect prediction. Inf. Softw. Technol. **122**, 106287 (2020)
8. Catal, C., Sevim, U., Diri, B.: Clustering and metrics thresholds based software fault prediction of unlabeled program modules. In: 2009 Sixth International Conference on Information Technology: New Generations, pp. 199–204 (2009)
9. Zhong, S., Khoshgoftaar, T.M., Seliya, N.: Analyzing software measurement data with clustering techniques. IEEE Intell. Syst. **19**(2), 20–27 (2004). https://doi.org/10.1109/MIS.2004.1274907

10. Bishnu, P.S., Bhattacherjee, V.: Software fault prediction using quad tree-based k-means clustering algorithm. IEEE Trans. Knowl. Data Eng. (2012). https://doi.org/10.1109/TKDE.2011.163
11. Aleem, S., Capretz, L.F., Ahmed, F.: Benchmarking machine learning techniques for software defect detection. Int. J. Softw. Eng. Appl. 6(3) (2015). https://doi.org/10.5121/ijsea.2015.6302
12. Alsawalqah, H., Hijazi, N., Eshtay, M., et al.: Software defect prediction using heterogeneous ensemble classification based on segmented patterns. Appl. Sci. 10(1745) (2020). https://doi.org/10.3390/app10051745
13. Yang, B., Zheng, X., Guo, P.: Software metrics data clustering for quality prediction. In: Huang, D.-S., Li, K., Irwin, G.W. (eds.) ICIC 2006. LNCS (LNAI), vol. 4114, pp. 959–964. Springer, Heidelberg (2006). https://doi.org/10.1007/978-3-540-37275-2_121
14. Abaei, G., Selamat, A.: Increasing the accuracy of software fault prediction using majority ranking fuzzy clustering. In: Lee, R. (ed.) Software Engineering, Artificial Intelligence, Networking and Parallel/Distributed Computing. SCI, vol. 569, pp. 179–193. Springer, Cham (2015). https://doi.org/10.1007/978-3-319-10389-1_13
15. Zhang, F., Zheng, Q., Zou, Y., Hassan, A.E.: Cross-project defect prediction using a connectivity-based unsupervised classifier. In: 2016 IEEE/ACM 38th International Conference on Software Engineering (ICSE), pp. 309–320 (2016). https://doi.org/10.1145/2884781.2884839
16. Chang, R., Shen, X., Wang, B., Xu, Q.: A novel method for software defect prediction in the context of big data. In: 2017 IEEE 2nd International Conference on Big Data Analysis (ICBDA), pp. 100–104 (2017). https://doi.org/10.1109/ICBDA.2017.8078785
17. Yan, M., Yang, M., Liu, C., Zhang, X.: Self-learning change-prone class prediction. In: The 28th International Conference on Software Engineering and Knowledge Engineering, SEKE 2016, Redwood City, San Francisco Bay, USA, 1–3 July 2016, pp. 134–140 (2016). https://doi.org/10.18293/SEKE2016-039
18. Park, M., Hong, E.: Software fault prediction model using clustering algorithms determining the number of clusters automatically. Int. J. Softw. Eng. Appl. 8, 199–204 (2014)
19. Herbold, S., Trautsch, A., Grabowski, J.: A comparative study to benchmark cross-project defect prediction approaches. IEEE Trans. Softw. Eng. 44(9), 811–833 (2017)
20. Shepperd, M., Song, Q., Sun, Z., Mair, C.: Data quality: some comments on the NASA software defect datasets. IEEE Trans. Softw. Eng. 39(9), 1208–1215 (2013). https://doi.org/10.1109/TSE.2013.11
21. Peters, F., Menzies, T., Gong, L., Zhang, H.: Balancing privacy and utility in cross-company defect prediction. IEEE Trans. Softw. Eng. 39(8), 1054–1068 (2013). https://doi.org/10.1109/TSE.2013.6
22. Nam, J., Kim, S.: CLAMI: defect prediction on unlabeled datasets (T). In: Proceedings of the 30th IEEE/ACM International Conference on Automated Software Engineering (ASE). IEEE (2015). https://doi.org/10.1109/ASE.2015.56
23. Yan, M., Zhang, X., Liu, C., et al.: Automated change-prone class prediction on unlabeled dataset using unsupervised method. Inf. Softw. Technol. 92, 1–16 (2017)
24. Ghotra, B., McIntosh, S., Hassan, A.E.: Revisiting the impact of classification techniques on the performance of defect prediction models. In: IEEE/ACM 37th International Conference of Software Engineering (2015). https://doi.org/10.1109/ICSE.2015.91

25. Agostinelli, S., Allison, J., Amako, K., et al.: GEANT4 - a simulation toolkit. Nucl. Instrum. Methods Phys. Res. Sect. A **506**(3), 250–303 (2003)
26. Ronchieri, E., Pia, M.G.: Assessing software quality in high energy and nuclear physics: the geant4 and root case studies and beyond. In: Proceedings of the IEEE Nuclear Science Symposium and Medical Imaging Conference (NSS/MIC), Sydney, Australia, Australia (2018)
27. Imagix: Reverse Engineering Tools - C, C++, Java - Imagix. https://www.imagix.com/
28. Preston-Werner, T.: Semantic Versioning 2.0.0 (2013). https://semver.org/spec/v2.0.0.html
29. Fenton, N.E., Neil, M.: A critique of software defect prediction models. IEEE Trans. Softw. Eng. **25**(5), 675–689 (1999)
30. McCabe, T.: A complexity measure. IEEE Trans. Softw. Eng. SE **2**(4), 308–320 (1976)
31. Halstead, M.H.: Elements of Software Science (1975)
32. Chidamber, S.R., Kemerer, C.F.: Metrics suite for object oriented design. IEEE Trans. Softw. Eng. **20**(6), 476–493 (1994)
33. Zhang, H., Zhang, X.: Comments on data mining static code attributes to learn defect prediction. IEEE Trans. Softw. Eng. **33**(9), 635–636 (2007)
34. Landis, J.R., Koch, G.G.: The measurement of observer agreement for categorical data. Biometrics **33**, 159–174 (1977)
35. Yucalar, F., Ozcift, A., Borandag, E., Kilinc, D.: Multiple-classifiers in software quality engineering: combining predictors to improve software fault prediction ability. Eng. Sci. Technol. Int. J. (2019). https://doi.org/10.1016/j.jestch.2019.10.005
36. Yan, M., Xia, X., Shihab, E., et al.: Automating change-level self-admitted technical debt determination. IEEE Trans. Softw. Eng. **45**(12), 1211–1229 (2019). https://doi.org/10.1109/TSE.2018.2831232
37. Garcìa, S., Fernandez, A., Luego, J., Herrera, F.: Advanced nonparametric tests for multiple comparisons in the design of experiments in computational intelligence and data mining: experimental analysis of power. Inf. Sci. **180**, 2044–2064 (2009)
38. Friedman, M.: A comparison of alternative tests of significance for the problem of M rankings. Annal. Math. Stat. **11**(1), 86–92 (1940). https://www.jstor.org/stable/2235971
39. Iman, R.L., Davenport, J.M.: Approximations of the critical region of the friedman statistic. Commun. Stat. **9**, 571–595 (1980)
40. Calvo, B., Santafé, G.: scmamp: statistical comparison of multiple algorithms in multiple problems. R J. **8**(1), 248–256 (2016)
41. Bergmann, B., Hommel, G.: Improvements of general multiple test procedures for redundant systems of hypotheses. Mult. Hypotheses Test. **70**, 100–115 (1988)
42. Demšar, J.: Statistical comparisons of classifiers over multiple data sets. J. Mach. Learn. Res. **7**, 1–30 (2006)
43. Tantithamthavorn, C., McIntosh, S., Hassan, A.E., Matsumoto, K.: An empirical comparison of model validation techniques for defect prediction models. IEEE Trans. Softw. Eng. **43**(1), 1–18 (2017). https://doi.org/10.1109/TSE.2016.2584050
44. Azeem, N., Usmani, S.: Analysis of data mining based software defect prediction techniques. Glob. J. Comput. Sci. Technol. **11** (2011)
45. Wang, J., Ma, Y., Zhang, L., Gao, R., Wu, D.: Deep learning for smart manufacturing: methods and applications. J. Manuf. Syst. **48**, 144–156 (2017)
46. Sculley, D.: Web-scale K-means clustering. In: Proceedings of the 19th International Conference on World Wide Web, WWW 2010, New York, NY, USA, pp. 1177–1178. ACM (2010). https://doi.org/10.1145/1772690.1772862

47. Lloyd, S.: Least squares quantization in PCM. IEEE Trans. Inf. Theor. **28**(2), 129–137 (2006). https://doi.org/10.1109/TIT.1982.1056489

48. Elkan, C.: Using the triangle inequality to accelerate k-means. In: Proceedings of the Twentieth International Conference on International Conference on Machine Learning, ICML 2003, pp. 147–153. AAAI Press (2003), http://dl.acm.org/citation.cfm?id=3041838.3041857

49. Kaur, D., Kaur, A., Gulati, S., Aggarwal, M.: A clustering algorithm for software fault prediction. In: International Conference on Computer and Communication Technology (ICCCT) (2010). https://doi.org/10.1109/ICCCT.2010.5640474

50. Hastie, T., Tibshirani, R., Friedman, J.: The Elements of Statistical Learning: Data Mining, Inference, and Prediction. Springer, Cham (2002)

51. Usama, M., Qadir, J., Raza, A., et al.: Unsupervised machine learning for networking: techniques. applications and research challenges. IEEE Access **7**, 65579–65615 (2019). https://doi.org/10.1109/ACCESS.2019.2916648

52. Domingos, P.: A few useful things to know about machine learning. Commun. ACM **55**(10), 78–87 (2012). https://doi.org/10.1145/2347736.2347755

53. Srivastava, N., Krizhevsky, G.H.A., Sutskever, I., Salakhutdinov, R.: Dropout: a simple way to prevent neural networks from overfitting. J. Mach. Learn. Res. **15**(1), 1929–1958 (2014)

54. Fukushima, T., Kamei, Y., McIntosh, S., Yamashita, K., Ubayashi, N.: An empirical study of just-in-time defect prediction using cross-project models. In: Proceedings of the 11th Working Conference on Mining Software Repositories, MSR 2014, New York, NY, USA, pp. 172–181. ACM (2014). https://doi.org/10.1145/2597073.2597075

55. Jing, X.Y., Ying, S., Zhang, Z.W., Wu, S.S., Liu, J.: Dictionary learning based software defect prediction. In: Proceedings of the 36th International Conference on Software Engineering, pp. 414–423 (2014). https://doi.org/10.1145/2568225.2568320

Artificial Intelligence in Health Care: Predictive Analysis on Diabetes Using Machine Learning Algorithms

Shruti Wadhwa[1] and Karuna Babber[2(✉)]

[1] Nidus Technologies Pvt. Ltd., Chandigarh, India
[2] Post Graduate Government College, Chandigarh, India
karunababber.kb@gmail.com

Abstract. Background: The healthcare organizations are producing heaps of data at alarming rate. This data comprises of medical records, genome-omics data, image scan or wearable medico device data that presents immense advantages and challenges at the same time. These ever growing challenges can be surpassed by applying effective artificial intelligence tools.

Methods: This paper uses the large volume of multimodal patient data to perform correlations between Body Mass Index, Blood Pressure, Glucose levels, Diabetes Pedigree Function and Skin Thickness of people in different age groups with diabetes. Python and data analytic packages are used to predict diabetes among people.

Results: The blood pressure count of diabetic people comes around 75–85 mmHg and sometimes even higher whereas it is in the range of 60–75 mmHg for non-diabetic people. The people with high body mass index and glucose levels of 120–200 mg/dl and more are found to be diabetic as against the lower body mass index with glucose levels of 85–105 mg/dl of normal people. The Diabetes Pedigree Function count of diabetic people has a peak at 0.25 whereas it is 0.125 in case of non-diabetic people. A similar slight difference in values of Age and Skin Thickness has been found for both diabetic and non-diabetic people.

Conclusion: Above results indicate a strong relationship between Blood Pressure, BMI and Glucose levels of people with diabetes whereas a moderate correlation has been found between Age, Skin Thickness and Diabetes Pedigree Function count of people with diabetes. Although present analysis attested many of the previous research findings but getting these inferences matched through analytical tools is a sole purpose of this paper.

Keywords: Blood pressure · Body mass index · Diabetes Pedigree Function · Glucose · Skin thickness · Diabetes · Artificial intelligence

1 Introduction

Intelligent information can be a key for a healthier world. The more data we have, more optimally we can generate health specific information. These days we are surrounded with tons of data from almost every aspect of our lives be it societal, work, science or

© Springer Nature Switzerland AG 2020
O. Gervasi et al. (Eds.): ICCSA 2020, LNCS 12250, pp. 354–366, 2020.
https://doi.org/10.1007/978-3-030-58802-1_26

health. In the technological world the term 'Big data' has been coined to describe such huge volumes of data. Douglas Laney [1] described big data by three V's that is Volume, Velocity and Variety wherein 'Big' part of big data indicates its large volume, velocity represents the rate and speed of data collection and variety stands for different types of organized and unorganized data. Over the time few other authors [2] added two more V's – Veracity and Variability into the big data definition. In the recent years almost every sector of research is analyzing the big data for various purposes. The most challenging task is to manage the heaps of structured and un-structured data [3] and to transform it into subject-oriented information. It is almost impossible to process big data with conventional software; we need technically advanced softwares with high-end computational power to make sense of such huge data. The implementation of Artificial Intelligence tools [4, 5] and algorithms can help us to generate decision-making information.

1.1 Big Data Repository for Healthcare

Healthcare is required at every stage of human life. Professionals come at the first place for primary care consultation, skilled professionals for secondary care, extra or intensive medical treatment comprises tertiary care and highly diagnostic and surgical procedures comes under the ambit of quaternary care [6, 7]. In the recent years multi dimensional model [8] of healthcare for diagnosis, prevention and treatment of health-related issues in human beings has been suggested. At all these levels the health specific accurate information is required at a single stop. So far heaps of health data has been collected from various sources and now it has come to brim where it becomes almost unmanageable with the current available technologies [9, 10]. Big data especially Artificial Intelligence can be viewed as a potential analyzer for improved health services. Figure 1 provides generalized analytic workflow for health care systems.

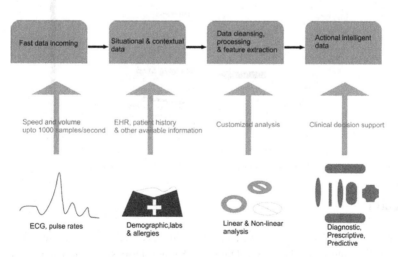

Fig. 1. Generalized analytic workflow for health care systems

1.2   Machine Learning and Healthcare

The machine learning in healthcare has opened plethora of applications [11] to improve patient life but errors in such applications may prove critical at times. A visual approach for 'Case based reasoning' mixed with quantitative and qualitative aspects have been proposed in [12]. The event sequencing of Electronic Health Record (EHR) of the patients [13] using deep learning algorithms are used to detect sepsis. The National Institutes of Health (NIH) of United States has recently started [14, 15] the 'All of Us' initiative (https://allofus.nih.gov) to collect more than one million of patients' data such as EHRs, medical images, environmental and socio-behavioural data. Data mining and machine learning is helping medical professionals make diagnosis easier by bridging the gap between huge data sets and human knowledge [16, 17]. A referential study in artificial intelligence in healthcare and medicine is provided in [18]. Intelligent machines may improve surgical procedures in the times to come [19, 20]. EHRs promise improvement in public health surveillance by timely reporting of disease outbreaks and can facilitate faster data retrieval for health insurance programs [21]. Similar to EHRs, Electronic Medical Records (EMR), Personal Health Records (PHR) and Medical Practice Management (MPM) software [22–24] and other related healthcare components collectively generate heaps of data that can be analyzed to provide real-time clinical care to patients in need. Figure 2 gives the fair idea about the framework for integrating multi-level information in order to provide personalized and cost-effective treatment to patients.

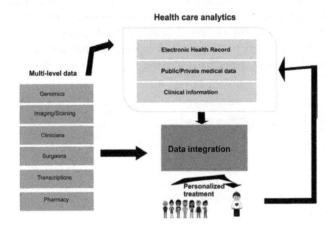

Fig. 2. Framework of healthcare data analytics

2   Data

The observed data has been part of the Pima Indians Diabetes Database collected by National Institute of Diabetes and Digestive Kidney Diseases [25]. The observational data contains different parameters like blood pressure, skin thickness, glucose, Diabetes

Pedigree Function (DPF) and Body Mass Index (BMI) of patients of all ages. Python and its data science related packages are used to carry on the analysis.

Firstly 'Pandas' [26] library file has been imported to read our data from a 'csv' file, then with the help of Extract, Transform, Load (ETL) tools [27] and 'Numpy' library file [28] data is transformed into a usable format to further use it on classification models. Figure 3 shows our dataset with 9 columns and 392 rows. The 'Matplotlib' library functions [29] have been used to draw graphs and other visualizations. The machine learning algorithms available in 'sklearn' library file [30] are used for final predictive analysis.

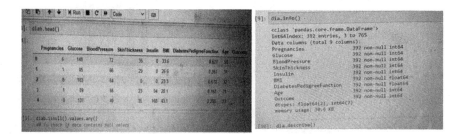

Fig. 3. Dataset with indexed parameters

To start with, we normalize the dataset to split it into two outcomes that is an outcome of zero (0) received for non-diabetic people and an outcome of one (1) received for diabetic people. The following bar graph (Fig. 4) gives us the fair idea.

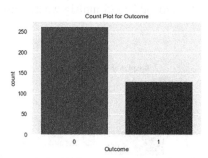

Fig. 4. Bar graph visualization of non-diabetic (0) and diabetic (1) people

From the above figure, it is clear that more than 250 people with '0' outcomes are non-diabetic whereas around 125 people with '1' outcome are diabetic. Now to make inferences of different parameters on diabetes, we have taken number of features into consideration, the details of which are provided in the results section.

3 Results

3.1 Blood Pressure (BP)

The measure of pressure of the blood in the circulatory system is defined as Blood Pressure [31]. In [32] authors explained effect of hypertension on diabetes mellitus. To find a correlation between blood pressure and diabetes, the bar graph (Fig. 5) visualization is provided below:

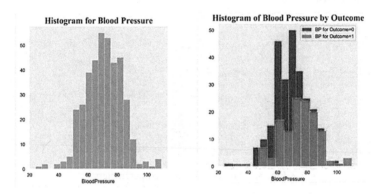

Fig. 5. Bar graph visualization of non-diabetic (0) and diabetic (1) people w.r.t. blood pressure

In graph I, the BP value is about normal with mean around 65–85 mmHg as against the ideal value of 80 mmHg. In graph II, for diabetic patients the BP value plot is little skewed towards right i.e. it is around 75–85 mmHg whereas for non-diabetic people it is around 60–75 mmHg.

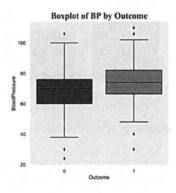

Fig. 6. Box-plots of non-diabetic (0) and diabetic (1) people w.r.t. blood pressure

The box-plot of BP in Fig. 6 shows 'whiskers' that is the maximum value of BP for non-diabetic people at 100 but it is at 110 with few outliers in case of diabetic people. Secondly around 75% diabetic people have BP in the range of 80–85 mmHg whereas in case of non-diabetic people around 75% people have a BP range of 70–75 mmHg. Both the plots indicate strong association between the two parameters.

3.2 Age of People

A person's age may play role for Type 2 Diabetes Mellitus. The risk of type 2 diabetes increases with the rising age [33, 34]. In graph I (Fig. 7), people within the age group of 20 or in their mid 20 s are non-diabetic whereas after the age of 30 and above people are prone to diabetes. In graph II, the median is at 25 years for non-diabetic people but the median for diabetic people is at 32 years. Both the graphs indicate a moderate correlation between the two features.

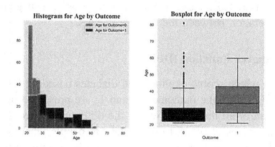

Fig. 7. Bar graph visualization of non-diabetic (0) and diabetic (1) people w.r.t. age

3.3 Body Mass Index (BMI)

The body mass index [35] is a person's weight in kilograms (kg) divided by his/her height in meters (m). The National Institutes of Health (NIH) has adopted BMI as a parameter to define normal weight, overweight and obesity of people rather than the traditional height/weight charts. The graph I (Fig. 8), shows the BMI level of all the people within the different age groups. In graph II, the BMI level peak is from 28–32 for non-diabetic people whereas it is skewed and tilted towards right at 36 for diabetic people.

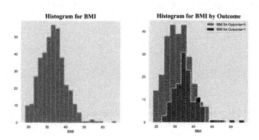

Fig. 8. Bar graph visualization of non-diabetic (0) and diabetic (1) people w.r.t BMI

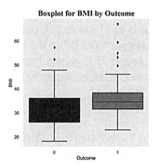

Fig. 9. Bar graph visualization of non-diabetic (0) and diabetic (1) people w.r.t BMI

In the box-plot (Fig. 9) more than 50% diabetic people have high BMI level as against the non-diabetic people. Secondly for diabetic people some outliers are beyond maxima whereas it is not the case in non-diabetic people. The graph visualizations indicate strong correlation between the two parameters.

3.4 Diabetes Pedigree Function (DPF)

It [36] is a function which scores likelihood of diabetes based on family history. Two histograms for DPF of both the outcomes (0 and 1) are presented in Fig. 10. Graph I shows the DPF count of all the people within the different age groups. In graph II the peak of DPF count comes at 0.125 for non-diabetic people whereas it is at 0.25 for diabetic people. The graph indicates nominal relation between two parameters.

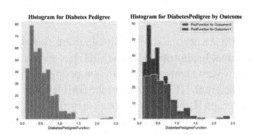

Fig. 10. Bar graph visualization of non-diabetic (0) and diabetic (1) people w.r.t DPF

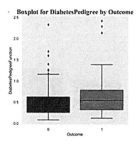

Fig. 11. Bar graph visualization of non-diabetic (0) and diabetic (1) people w.r.t DPF

The box-plot in Fig. 11 shows more than 50% non-diabetic people have a DPF count of 0.4 and it is slightly more with 0.525 DPF count for diabetic people. Secondly both the plots have outliers beyond maxima. Therefore, all the graphs indicate a weak correlation between the two features.

3.5   Skin Thickness

The skin thickness [37] is primarily determined by collagen content and is increased in insulin-dependent diabetes mellitus. The graph I of Fig. 12 provides the skin thickness of both the outcomes (0 and 1). In graph II the peak is at 30 for non-diabetic people whereas it is at 40 for diabetic people. The peak values indicate a moderate relation between the two parameters.

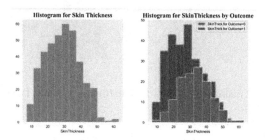

Fig. 12. Bar graph visualization of non-diabetic (0) and diabetic (1) people w.r.t skin thickness

In the box-plot (Fig. 13) more than 50% non-diabetic people have a skin thickness count of 28 whereas the skin thickness count is 34 for more than 50% diabetic people. Secondly very few outliers are beyond the maxima in both the cases and the difference between the maxima value for both diabetic and non-diabetic people is only 3 points. The graphs indicate nominal relation between the two features.

Fig. 13. Bar graph visualization of non-diabetic (0) and diabetic (1) people w.r.t skin thickness

3.6 Glucose Level

The global mean fasting plasma blood glucose level [38] in humans is about 100 mg/dl. The graph I of two histograms in Fig. 14 provides the glucose level of both the outcomes (0 and 1). The graph II shows the glucose level range of non-diabetic people between 85–105 mg/dl with little spike at 100–120 mg/dl whereas the range for diabetic people comes in between 120–200 mg/dl.

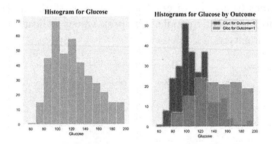

Fig. 14. Bar graph visualization of non-diabetic (0) and diabetic (1) people w.r.t glucose

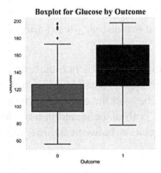

Fig. 15. Bar graph visualization of non-diabetic (0) and diabetic (1) people w.r.t glucose

In the box-plot (Fig. 15) more than 50% of non-diabetic people have glucose level 100–110 mg/dl. But more than 50% diabetic people have a range above 140 mg/dl. Secondly the maxima value for non-diabetic people is 170 mg/dl whereas it is 200 mg/dl in case of diabetic people. All the above graphs indicate a strong correlation between these two parameters.

4 Result Analysis and Discussion

The above provided results were analyzed on few machine learning algorithms and it is found that Logistic Regression, Support Vector Classifier (SVC) and Linear Support Vector Classifiers (LSVC) have performed well with higher mean accuracy rate as compared to Decision Tree, Gaussian Naive Bayes and Random Forest Classifiers [39–41]. The box-plot (Fig. 16) provides the Inter Quartile Range (IQR) of the mean accuracy rate of machine learning algorithms and the Table 1 has detailed readings of the actual mean of accuracy along with standard deviation of machine learning algorithms.

Table 1. Machine learning algorithms with mean of accuracy and standard deviation readings

Machine learning algorithm	Mean of accuracy	Standard deviation
Logistic Regression (LR)	0.789415	0.060090
K Neighbors Classifier (KNN)	0.766935	0.058651
Gaussian NB (NB)	0.767238	0.049213
SVC	0.782964	0.077649
Linear SVC (LSVC)	0.783065	0.062417
Random Forest Classifier (RFC)	0.750706	0.065619
Decision Tree Regressor (DTR)	0.706250	0.094293

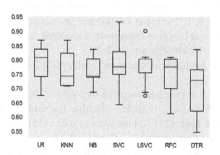

Fig. 16. Performance of machine learning algorithms w.r.t different parameters on outcome variable (1)

By applying the thumb rule of correlation and inferences received by applying machine learning algorithms, we can infer that BP, BMI and Glucose levels of people showed strong correlation with diabetes whereas DPF count, Age and Skin thickness have signalled moderate correlation with diabetes.

5 Conclusion

With the privilege of machine learning algorithms, big data health analytics has opened doors for new predictive systems. On the similar lines, this paper presents a predictive analysis on diabetes. We found strong correlation of diabetes with Blood Pressure, BMI and Glucose levels of people. But Age, Skin Thickness and Diabetes Pedigree Function count have shown moderate relationship with diabetes. Though we may have conventional clinical reports on correlation of these parameters with diabetes but getting these inferences matched through analytical tools is a sole purpose of this paper. Through this paper we successfully predict and visualize the correlations between different parameters on diabetes.

References

1. Laney, D.: 3D Data Management: controlling data volume, velocity and variety, Application delivery strategies. META Group Inc., Stanford (2001)
2. Mauro, A.D., Greco, M., Grimaldi, M.: A formal definition of big data based on its essential features. Libr. Rev. **65**(3), 122–135 (2016)
3. Jacobs, A.: The pathologies of big data. Commun. ACM **52**(8), 36–44 (2009)
4. Dean, J., Ghemawat, S.: Mapreduce: simplified data processing on large clusters. Commun. ACM **51**(1), 107–113 (2008)
5. Belle, A.: Big data analytics in healthcare. Biomed. Res. Int, E **2015**, 370194 (2015)
6. Viceconti, M., Hunter, P., Hose, R.: Big data, big knowledge: big data for personalized healthcare. IEEE J. Biomed. Health Inf. **19**, 1209–1215 (2015)
7. Nasi, G., Cucciniello, M., Guerrazzi, C.: The role of mobile technologies in health care processes: the case of cancer supportive care. J. Med. Internet Res. **17**(2), e26 (2015)
8. Bali, J., Garg, R., Bali, R.T.: Artificial intelligence in healthcare and biomedical research: why a strong computational bioethics framework is required. Indian J. Ophthalmol. **67**(1), 3–6 (2019). https://doi.org/10.4103/ijo.ijo_1292_18
9. Doyle-Lindrud, S.: The evolution of electronic health record. Clin. J. Nurs. **19**(2), 153–154 (2015)
10. Yin, Y.: The internet of things in healthcare an overview. J. Inf. Health Care **1**, 3–13 (2016)
11. Khare, A., Jeon, M., Sethi, I.K., Xu, B.: Machine learning theory and applications for healthcare. J. Healthcare Eng. (2017). https://doi.org/10.1155/2017/5263570
12. Lamy, J.-B., Sekar, B., Guezennec, G., Bouaud, J., Seroussi, B.: Explainable artificial intelligence for breast cancer: a visual case-based reasoning approach. J. Artif. Intell. Med. **94**, 42–53 (2019). https://doi.org/10.1016/j.artmed.2019.01.001
13. Lauritsen, S.M., et al.: Early detection of sepsis utilizing deep learning on electronic health record event sequences. J. Artif. Intell. **104** (2020). https://doi.org/10.1016/j.artmed.2020.101820

14. Shameer, K.: Traditional bioinformatics in the era of real-time biomedical, health care and wellness data streams. Brief. Bioinform. **18**(1), 105–124 (2017)
15. Reform. Thinking on its own: AI in the NHS (2018)
16. Davenport, T., Kalakota, R.: The potential for artificial intelligence in healthcare. Future Healthcare J. **6**(2), 94–98 (2019). https://doi.org/10.7861/futurehosp.6-2-94
17. Jiang, F., et al.: Artificial intelligence in healthcare: past, present and future. Stroke Vasc. Neurol. **0**, e000101 (2017). https://doi.org/10.1136/svn-2017-000101
18. Tran, B.X., et al.: Global evolution of research in artificial intelligence in health and medicine: a bibliometric study. J. Clin. Med. **8**, 360–369 (2019). https://doi.org/10.3390/jcm8030360
19. Moore, S.F.: Harnessing the power of intelligent machines to enhance primary care. J. General Pract. **68**, 6–7 (2018)
20. Nesta. Confronting Dr. Robot creating a people-powered future for AI in health (2018)
21. Reisman, M.: EHRs: the challenge of making electronic data usable and interoperable. J. Pharma Theor. **42**(9), 572–575 (2017)
22. De Moor, G., et al.: Using electronic health records for clinical research: the case of the EHR4CR project. J. Biomed. Inf. **53**, 162–173 (2015). https://doi.org/10.1016/j.jbi.2014.10.006
23. Kaelber, D.C., Jha, A.K., Johnston, D., Middleton, B., Bates, D.W.: A research agenda for Personal Health Records (PHR). J. Am. Med. Inf. Assoc. **15**(6), 729–736 (2008). https://doi.org/10.1197/jamia.m2547
24. Roehrs, A., da Costa, C.A.: Personal health records: a systematic literature review. Med. Internet Res. Nat. Libr. Med. **19**(1), e13 (2017). https://doi.org/10.2196/jmir.5876
25. https://www.kaggle.com/uciml/pima-indians-diabetes-database/
26. https://pandas.pydata.org/
27. Parker, E.: Python & ETL 2020: A list and comparison of the top python ETL tools (2020)
28. https://numpy.org/
29. https://matplotlib.org/
30. https://scikit-learn.org/stable/
31. William, C., Shiel Jr.: Medical definition of blood pressure. J. Medterms Med. Dic. (1998)
32. Tsimihodimos, V., Clicerio, G.-V., Meigs, J.B., Ferrannini, E.: Hypertension and diabetes mellitus. J. Hypertens. **71**, 422–428 (2018). https://doi.org/10.1161/HYPERTENSIONAHA.117.10546
33. Suastika, K., Dwipayana, P., Semandi, M.S., Kuswardhani, R.A.T.: Age is an important risk factor for type 2 Diabetes Mellitus and Cardiovascular Diseases. IntechOpen (2012). https://doi.org/10.5772/52397
34. Kharroubi, A.T., Darwish, H.M.: Diabetes mellitus: the epidemic of the century. World J. Diabetes. **6**(6), 850–867 (2015). https://doi.org/10.4239/wjd.v6.i6.850
35. Nuttall, F.Q.: Body mass index: obesity and health – a critical review. J. Nutr. Today **50**(3), 117–128 (2015)
36. Mercaldo, F., Nardone, V., Santone, A.: Diabetes Mellitus affected patients classification and diagnosis through machine learning techniques. In: International Conference on Knowledge Based and Intelligent Information and Engineering Systems (2017). Procedia Computer Science, vol. 112, pp. 2519–2528
37. Jose Derraik, G.B., Rademaker, M., Cutfield, S.W., Pinto, E.T.: Effects of age, gender and anatomical site on skin thickness in children and adults with diabetes. PLoS One **9**(1) (2014). https://doi.org/10.1371/journal.pone.0086637
38. Frankum, S., Ogden, J.: Estimation of blood glucose levels by people with diabetes: a cross-sectional study. Br. J. Gen. Pract. **55**(521), 944–948 (2005)
39. Biau, G.: Analysis of random forests model. J. Mach. Learn. Res. **13**, 1063–1095 (2012)

40. Marijana, Z.-S., Sarlija, N., Has, A., Bilandzic, A.: Predicting company growth using logistic regression and neural networks, Cortian Oper. Res. Rev. (CRORR), **7**, 229–248 (2016)
41. Wu, D., Jennings, C., Terpenny, J., Gao, R.X., Kumara, S.: A comparative study on machine learning algorithms for smart manufacturing: tool wear prediction using Random Forests. J. Manuf. Sci. Eng. **139**(7) (2017). https://doi.org/10.1115/1.4036350

Learning to Classify Text Complexity for the Italian Language Using Support Vector Machines

Valentino Santucci[1]([✉])(iD), Luciana Forti[1], Filippo Santarelli[2], Stefania Spina[1], and Alfredo Milani[3]

[1] Department of Humanities and Social Sciences,
University for Foreigners of Perugia, Perugia, Italy
{valentino.santucci,luciana.forti,stefania.spina}@unistrapg.it
[2] Istituto per le Applicazioni del Calcolo (CNR), Roma, Italy
f.santarelli@iac.cnr.it
[3] Department of Mathematics and Computer Science, University of Perugia,
Perugia, Italy
alfredo.milani@unipg.it

Abstract. Natural language processing is undoubtedly one of the most active fields of research in the machine learning community. In this work we propose a supervised classification system that, given in input a text written in the Italian language, predicts its linguistic complexity in terms of a level of the Common European Framework of Reference for Languages (better known as CEFR). The system was built by considering: (i) a dataset of texts labeled by linguistic experts was collected, (ii) some vectorisation procedures which transform any text to a numerical representation, and (iii) the training of a support vector machine's model. Experiments were conducted following a statistically sound design and the experimental results show that the system is able to reach a good prediction accuracy.

Keywords: Text classification · Natural Language Processing · Support vector machines

1 Introduction

Natural Language Processing (NLP) is emerging in the recent years as one of the most researched and popular topics in the machine learning community [11,19,23]. NLP based tools allows to develop several real-world applications such as automatic translation, text summarization, speech recognition, chatbots and question answering, etc.

Another interesting application is the classification of a text in different levels of complexity [7] which is key in mood and sentiment analysis, in the detection of hate speech [18], in text simplification, and also in the assessment of text readability in relation to both native and non-native readers.

© Springer Nature Switzerland AG 2020
O. Gervasi et al. (Eds.): ICCSA 2020, LNCS 12250, pp. 367–376, 2020.
https://doi.org/10.1007/978-3-030-58802-1_27

In this work we propose and analyze a supervised learning system for the automatic classification of a text, written in Italian, into different complexity levels according to the Common European Framework of Reference for Languages (CEFR) [8]. The proposed system is freely available online[1] and it can be used in a variety of scenarios like, for instance, to choose texts to be used in a lesson or as part of a language test.

From the computational point-of-view, the supervised system was implemented as a Support Vector Machine (SVM) [20] which learns a numerical model from a *vectorised* representation of the texts. In fact, texts are converted to numeric vectors which correspond to linguistic features computed on top of the tokens, part-of-speech tags and syntactic trees of the given texts.

Therefore, our work focuses both on the computational procedures for calculating the features and on the SVM implementation for learning a classification model.

Regarding the dataset, we have collected 692 texts in Italian language labeled by experts in the field using four levels of the CEFR. Though the dataset is not huge, a thorough tuning of the SVM parameters and features selection procedures allowed to obtain a classification system with good performances.

The rest of the paper is organized as follows. The main design of the system is presented in Sect. 2. The classification model and the numerical features are depicted in, respectively, Sects. 3 and 4. An experimental investigation is provided in Sect. 5, while Sect. 6 concludes the paper by also drawing future lines of research.

2   System Design

The task of learning to classify the complexity of a text has been approached using a supervised classification system whose design is depicted in this section.

Since it is supervised learning, training texts – already classified – are required. For this reason, we collected a dataset of texts labeled by the experts of the CVCL center of the University for Foreigners of Perugia[2]. The texts in the dataset are labeled by means of four increasing levels of difficulty. In order to be compliant with the world of linguistic certifications, the four CEFR proficiency levels B1, B2, C1 and C2 were used[3]. Clearly, this four levels are the target classes of the supervised classification system.

In total, the collected dataset is composed by 692 texts divided among the four classes as depicted in Table 1 which also provides quantitative information about the number of tokens.

---

[1] https://lol.unistrapg.it/malt.

[2] CVCL is the acronym of "Centro Valutazione Certificazioni Linguistiche" which can be translated to "Evaluation Center for Linguistic Certifications". Its website is reachable at https://www.cvcl.it.

[3] CEFR (Common European Framework of Reference for Languages) actually has 6 levels, but the levels A1 and A2 were omitted from our study because linguistic experts do not find them significant for this investigation.

Table 1. Characteristics of the dataset

Class	#Texts	#Tokens
B1	249	45 695
B2	185	90 133
C1	139	95 515
C2	119	104 679
Dataset	692	336 022

Though the four classes have an intrinsic order of difficulty, in this work we ignore such ordering thus to be able to rely on the most used classification models available in the literature. Nevertheless, we must stress that this is not limiting. In fact, in a preliminary investigation, described in [10], we have experimentally proved that considering the intrinsic order of the classes is not relevant for our task.

Figure 1 depicts the main design of the system.

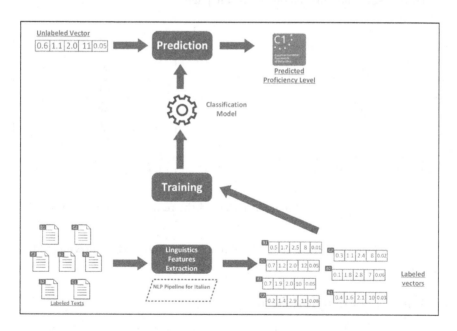

Fig. 1. Main design of the system

The classification model does not directly work with the texts in their pure form. In fact, any text is converted into a vector of numeric features so that learning and classification can employ numerical models. Such numerical vectors are obtained by computing quantitative linguistic features on top of the elaboration performed by NLP pipeline tools for the Italian language.

First, the inner parameters of the classification model are trained using the labeled vectors corresponding to the texts in the considered dataset. Then, any unlabeled text is *vectorised* and fed to the trained model which predicts its proficiency level. Interestingly, not only the predicted class is returned, but the system also provides a normalized distribution of values, one for each class, expressing how likely is the analyzed text to belong to a given class.

This architecture allows, on the one hand, to use the most common classification models available in the machine learning literature [20] and, on the other hand, to build a classification model based only on the linguistic features of the texts that, we believe, are what discriminate texts from the point-of-view of the CEFR levels.

Finally, a user friendly web interface was developed as depicted in Fig. 2: the user types or pastes a text of his/her choice in the provided text area, press the "Analyse" button, then the system transparently executes the prediction procedure of the trained model and shows the predicted CEFR level for the given text, together with a chart showing how the four different levels are represented within the text in terms of percentages. Moreover, additional charts can be recalled by using the buttons on the result page.

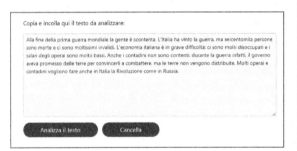 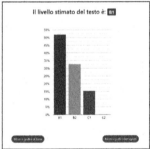

Fig. 2. User interface: the input form and the results of the elaboration

The developed resource is freely available on the web at the following address: https://lol.unistrapg.it/malt.

3   The Classification Model

Regarding the classification model, we made some preliminary experiments using decision trees, random forests, feedforward neural networks and support vector machines. Some of these experiments are described in [10,15]. According to the preliminary results, this work focuses on the Support Vector Machines (SVM) model. Interestingly, given the small size of the dataset, SVM look to work better than the trendy neural network models.

An SVM [20] is a supervised classification model which, given a (training) set of labeled numeric vectors, constructs a set of hyperplanes in a high-dimensional space, which identify the regions of the space corresponding to the different labels, i.e., the CEFR levels in our case.

The SVM implementation of the popular *Sci-Kit Learn* library [17] has been used, while the Gaussian radial basin functions have been considered as kernel functions of the SVM.

4   Numerical Features of a Text

In order to compute the numerical linguistic features for feeding the classifier, we have used a NLP pipeline library which takes into account the Italian language. We found three libraries freely available: Tint [16], UDPipe [21] and Spacy [13]. After some preliminary experiments, we decided to proceed with UDPipe because, from our investigation, it was the most reliable for the Italian language.

The UDPipe library has been used in order to:

- tokenize a text and also split it in sentences,
- annotate any token with its lemma, its part-of-speech tag and other morpho-syntactic properties,
- parse a text in order to build dependency trees for the sentences contained in the text.

Moreover, since constituent trees were not directly computable in UDPipe, we have used the constituent parser for the Italian language of the OpenNLP project [5].

The features considered in this work can be divided in six categories:

1. raw text features,
2. lexical features,
3. morphological features,
4. morpho-syntactic features
5. discursive features,
6. syntactic features.

Some of them are formed by only one number, while others are vectors of several real numbers. Anyway, the vectors of all the numerical features are concatenated in order to form a unique real-valued vector for the given text in input. The length of such a vector is 139. Hence, after the extraction of the numerical features, any text is embedded in the space $\mathbb{R}^{139}$.

In the following, we provide the description of the calculation procedure for the some of the features considered.

4.1   Raw Text Features

The raw text features are computed after the tokenization and include statistics such the average and standard deviation of: the sentence length in tokens, the token length in characters, the text length in sentences and in lemmas.

4.2   Lexical Features

The lexical features are computed basing on the lemmatization of the tokens in the texts. They include statistics such as: the amount of lemmas in the text which are classified in order of availability in a reference vocabulary[4]; the number of nouns considered as Abstract, Semiabstract and Concrete; the lexical diversity, i.e., the ratio between the total number of words and the total number of unique words; etc.

4.3   Morphological Features

Morphological features are reflected by the Morphological Complexity Index (MCI) computed for two word classes: verbs and nouns. The MCI is operationalised by randomly drawing sub-samples of 10 forms of a word class (e.g.. verbs) from a text and computing the average within-sample and across-samples of inflectional exponents. Further details can be found in [6].

4.4   Morpho-Syntactic Features

Based on part-of-speech (POS) tagging and the morphological analysis conducted by UDPipe, statistic values about the following morpho-syntactic features are computed: the subordinate ratio, i.e., the percentage of subordinate clauses over the total number of clauses; the POS tags distribution; the verbal moods distribution; and the dependency tags distribution.

4.5   Discursive Features

Discursive features concerns the cohesive structure among the sentences in a text. In this work we have considered the referential cohesion and the deep causal cohesion.

4.6   Syntactic Features

Based on the dependency and constituent trees of the text in input, some statistics about the syntactic structure of the text are considered as follows: the depth of the parse trees, the non-verbal path lengths, the size of the maximal non-verbal phrase, the percentage of verbal roots, the arity of verbal nodes, etc.

5   Experiments

Experiments were conducted using the SVM classifier model available in the commonly used *SKLearn* module of the Python 3 programming environment [17].

---

[4] "Nuovo Vocabolario di Base De Mauro" that translates to "New Basic Italian Vocabulary".

Every experiment – tuning the SVM hyper-parameters, selecting the features, and assessing the final accuracy of the system – was performed using 5 repetitions of a stratified 10-folds cross-validation executed on the whole dataset of 692 texts.

First, the hyper-parameters C and γ of the SVM model have been tuned by means of a grid search process aimed at optimising the F1 score measure. This measure has been used in order to avoid issues due to the unbalanced nature of the dataset. The whole set of 139 features was considered and the calibrated setting is $C = 2.24$ and $\gamma = 0.02$.

After this tuning, a *features selection* phase was designed by using the well known Recursive Features Elimination (RFE) algorithm [12]. RFE recursively fits the model and removes the weakest feature until a specified number of features is reached. In our work, the well known *permutation feature importance* technique [9] was considered to measure the importance of every feature during the last model fitting. Moreover, to find the optimal number of features, cross-validation was used with RFE to score different feature subsets and select the best scoring collection of features. As depicted in Fig. 3, a subset formed by 54 features – around the 39% of the whole set of features – has obtained the best F1 score in our experiments.

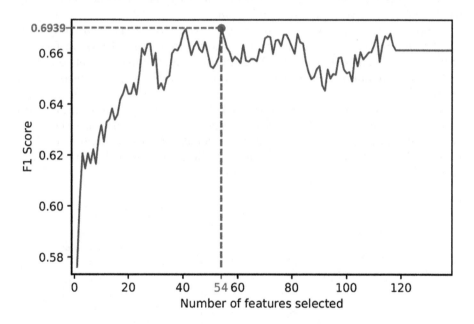

Fig. 3. Features selection graph

Then, the performances of the tuned SVM model trained using the selected features are shown in the confusion matrix provided in Table 2. In this table, each entry X, Y provides the average number – over the 5 repetitions of the

10-folds cross-validation process – of texts which are known to belong to class X, but have been classified by our system to class Y.

Table 2. Confusion matrix

Classes	B1	B2	C1	C2
B1	**214.6**	30.2	4.2	0.0
B2	28.4	**129.8**	23.8	3.0
C1	9.6	28.8	**74.2**	26.4
C2	1.2	9.0	30.0	**78.8**

The correctly classified texts are those in the diagonal of the confusion matrix. They are (in average) 497.4 out of 692, thus the accuracy of our system is about 71.88%.

The confusion matrix also allows to derive the precision and recall measures [20] for all the considered CEFR levels. Our experiments reveal that the B1 level exhibits the highest precision and recall (respectively, 84.55% and 86.18%), while the weakest predictions are those regarding the C1 level (which has 56.13% and 53.38% as, respectively, precision and recall).

Furthermore, it is interesting to observe that most of the incorrectly classified texts are only one level away from their actual CEFR levels. In fact, by aggregating the pairs of levels B1, B2 and C1,C2 into the macro-levels B and C, respectively, we obtain that the average accuracy of the system increases up to 88.50%.

Finally, note that the results discussed in this section are also in line with the 2D visualisations of the dataset provided in Fig. 4 which provides the result of two different executions of the well known dimensionality reduction technique t-SNE [22] executed on the 139-dimensional representation of the dataset. Each point is the two-dimensional representation of a text.

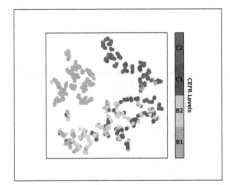 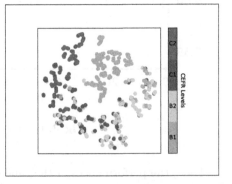

Fig. 4. 2D visualisations of the dataset obtained with two executions of t-SNE.

6 Conclusion and Future Work

In this work we have introduced an NLP tool able to automatically assess the proficiency level of an Italian text used for second language learning purposes.

A dataset of texts labeled by experts was used to learn and evaluate the performance of an SVM classifier model which is trained using linguistic features measured quantitatively and extracted from the texts.

Experiments were held in order to analyze the effectiveness and the reliability of the proposed prototypical classification system. Overall, the classification accuracy obtained is very good and satisfactory for the linguistic experts that use our tool.

Further improvement to our system can be obtained by collecting more data, i.e., more texts labeled by experts, but an interesting future line of research which, in our opinion, deserves to be deeply investigated is the automatic augmentation of the text dataset. Moreover, it can be interesting to include, in the learning procedure, algorithms from the field of evolutionary computation like, for instance, those proposed in [1–4,14].

Acknowledgments. This research was partially supported by: (i) the grant 2018.0424.021 *MALT-IT2. Una risorsa computazionale per Misurare Automaticamente la Leggibilità dei Testi per studenti di Italiano L2*, co-funded by the University for Foreigners of Perugia and by the Fondazione Cassa di Risparmio di Perugia; (ii) Università per Stranieri di Perugia – *Finanziamento per Progetti di Ricerca di Ateneo – PRA 2020*; (iii) Università per Stranieri di Perugia – Progetto di ricerca *Artificial Intelligence for Education, Social and Human Sciences*.

References

1. Baioletti, M., Milani, A., Santucci, V.: A new precedence-based ant colony optimization for permutation problems. In: Shi, Y., et al. (eds.) SEAL 2017. LNCS, vol. 10593, pp. 960–971. Springer, Cham (2017). https://doi.org/10.1007/978-3-319-68759-9_79

2. Baioletti, M., Milani, A., Santucci, V.: Learning Bayesian networks with algebraic differential evolution. In: Auger, A., Fonseca, C.M., Lourenço, N., Machado, P., Paquete, L., Whitley, D. (eds.) PPSN 2018. LNCS, vol. 11102, pp. 436–448. Springer, Cham (2018). https://doi.org/10.1007/978-3-319-99259-4_35

3. Baioletti, M., Milani, A., Santucci, V.: MOEA/DEP: an algebraic decomposition-based evolutionary algorithm for the multiobjective permutation flowshop scheduling problem. In: Liefooghe, A., López-Ibáñez, M. (eds.) EvoCOP 2018. LNCS, vol. 10782, pp. 132–145. Springer, Cham (2018). https://doi.org/10.1007/978-3-319-77449-7_9

4. Baioletti, M., Milani, A., Santucci, V.: Variable neighborhood algebraic differential evolution: an application to the linear ordering problem with cumulative costs. Inf. Sci. **507**, 37–52 (2020). https://doi.org/10.1016/j.ins.2019.08.016

5. Baldridge, J.: The opennlp project, p. 1 (2005). http://opennlp.apache.org/index.html. Accessed 2 Feb 2012

6. Brezina, V., Pallotti, G.: Morphological complexity in written L2 texts. Second Lang. Res. **35**(1), 99–119 (2016). https://doi.org/10.1177/0267658316643125

7. Dell'Orletta, F., Montemagni, S., Venturi, G.: Read-it: assessing readability of Italian texts with a view to text simplification. In: Proceedings of the Second Workshop on Speech and Language Processing for Assistive Technologies, Edinburgh, Scotland, UK, pp. 73–83. Association for Computational Linguistics, July 2011. https://www.aclweb.org/anthology/W11-2308

8. Council of Europe, Modern Languages Division. Council for Cultural Co-operation. Education Committee. Common European Framework of Reference for Languages: learning, teaching, assessment. Cambridge University Press (2001)

9. Fisher, A., Rudin, C., Dominici, F.: Model class reliance: variable importance measures for any machine learning model class, from the "rashomon" perspective. arXiv preprint arXiv:1801.01489 (2018)

10. Forti, L., Milani, A., Piersanti, L., Santarelli, F., Santucci, V., Spina, S.: Measuring text complexity for Italian as a second language learning purposes. In: Proceedings of the Fourteenth Workshop on Innovative Use of NLP for Building Educational Applications, Florence, Italy, pp. 360–368. Association for Computational Linguistics, August 2019. https://www.aclweb.org/anthology/W11-2308

11. Goldberg, Y.: Neural network methods for natural language processing. Synth. Lect. Hum. Lang. Technol. **10**(1), 1–309 (2017)

12. Guyon, I., Weston, J., Barnhill, S., Vapnik, V.: Gene selection for cancer classification using support vector machines. Mach. Learn. **46**(1–3), 389–422 (2002)

13. Honnibal, M., Montani, I.: spaCy 2: natural language understanding with Bloom embeddings, convolutional neural networks and incremental parsing (2017, to appear)

14. Milani, A., Santucci, V.: Asynchronous differential evolution. In: Proceedings of 2010 IEEE Congress on Evolutionary Computation (CEC 2010), pp. 1–7 (2010). https://doi.org/10.1109/CEC.2010.5586107

15. Milani, A., Spina, S., Santucci, V., Piersanti, L., Simonetti, M., Biondi, G.: Text classification for Italian proficiency evaluation. In: Misra, S., et al. (eds.) ICCSA 2019. LNCS, vol. 11619, pp. 830–841. Springer, Cham (2019). https://doi.org/10.1007/978-3-030-24289-3_61

16. Aprosio, A.P., Moretti, G.: Italy goes to Stanford: a collection of CoreNLP modules for Italian. arxiv e-prints, September 2016

17. Pedregosa, F., et al.: Scikit-learn: machine learning in Python. J. Mach. Learn. Res. **12**, 2825–2830 (2011)

18. Santucci, V., Spina, S., Milani, A., Biondi, G., Di Bari, G.: Detecting hate speech for Italian language in social media. In: EVALITA 2018, co-located with the Fifth Italian Conference on Computational Linguistics (CLiC-it 2018), vol. 2263 (2018)

19. Schmidt, A., Wiegand, M.: A survey on hate speech detection using natural language processing. In: Proceedings of the Fifth International Workshop on Natural Language Processing for Social Media, pp. 1–10 (2017)

20. Shalev-Shwartz, S., Ben-David, S.: Understanding Machine Learning: From Theory to Algorithms. Cambridge University Press, Cambridge (2014)

21. Straka, M., Straková, J.: Tokenizing, POS tagging, lemmatizing and parsing UD 2.0 with udpipe. In: Proceedings of the CoNLL 2017 Shared Task: Multilingual Parsing from Raw Text to Universal Dependencies, pp. 88–99 (2017)

22. Van der Maaten, L., Weinberger, K.: Stochastic triplet embedding. In: 2012 IEEE International Workshop on Machine Learning for Signal Processing, pp. 1–6, September 2012. https://doi.org/10.1109/MLSP.2012.6349720

23. Young, T., Hazarika, D., Poria, S., Cambria, E.: Recent trends in deep learning based natural language processing. IEEE Comput. Intell. Mag. **13**(3), 55–75 (2018)

International Workshop on Advanced Computational Approaches in Artificial Intelligence and Complex Systems Applications (ACAC 2020)

Deep Learning for Blood Glucose Prediction: CNN vs LSTM

Touria El Idrissi[1] and Ali Idri[2,3(✉)]

[1] Department of Computer Sciences EMI,
University Mohamed V, Rabat, Morocco
el.idrissit@gmail.com
[2] Software Project Management Research Team, RITC, ENSIAS,
University Mohamed V, Rabat, Morocco
ali.idri@um5.ac.ma
[3] CSEHS-MSDA, University Mohammed VI Polytechnic, Ben Guerir, Morocco

Abstract. To manage their disease, diabetic patients need to control the blood glucose level (BGL) by monitoring it and predicting its future values. This allows to avoid high or low BGL by taking recommended actions in advance. In this study, we propose a Convolutional Neural Network (CNN) for BGL prediction. This CNN is compared with Long-short-term memory (LSTM) model for both one-step and multi-steps prediction. The objectives of this work are: 1) Determining the best configuration of the proposed CNN, 2) Determining the best strategy of multi-steps forecasting (MSF) using the obtained CNN for a prediction horizon of 30 min, and 3) Comparing the CNN and LSTM models for one-step and multi-steps prediction. Toward the first objective, we conducted series of experiments through parameter selection. Then five MSF strategies are developed for the CNN to reach the second objective. Finally, for the third objective, comparisons between CNN and LSTM models are conducted and assessed by the Wilcoxon statistical test. All the experiments were conducted using 10 patients' datasets and the performance is evaluated through the Root Mean Square Error. The results show that the proposed CNN outperformed significantly the LSTM model for both one-step and multi-steps prediction and no MSF strategy outperforms the others for CNN.

Keywords: Convolutional Neural Network · Long-short-term memory network · Multi-step-ahead forecasting · Blood glucose · Prediction · Diabetes

1 Introduction

The diabetes mellitus disease occurs when the glucose metabolism is defected. Type 1 and Type 2 of diabetes mellitus (named respectively T1DM and T2DM) are the main types of diabetes. T1DM is due to a shortage in the insulin produced by the pancreas while T2DM is due to an inappropriate use of the produced insulin [1]. This chronic illness may cause serious health complications such as neuropathy, nephropathy, blindness and others [1]. Diabetic patients can prevent or delay the occurrence of these complications by managing their disease and maintaining their blood glucose level (BGL) within the normal range. This can be achieved by monitoring the BGL manually

© Springer Nature Switzerland AG 2020
O. Gervasi et al. (Eds.): ICCSA 2020, LNCS 12250, pp. 379–393, 2020.
https://doi.org/10.1007/978-3-030-58802-1_28

via sticks or automatically via continuous glucose monitoring (CGM) sensors and then predicting the future values of BGL. If the predicted values tend to be outside the normal range, the diabetic patient can act in advance toward avoiding high or low BGL [1, 2].

Several data mining based prediction techniques were investigated for the BGL prediction problem counting machine learning and statistical techniques [2]. Nevertheless, machine learning and especially deep learning techniques are gaining more interest as they are achieving promising results [3].

The BGL prediction can be considered as a time series (TS) prediction problem where the past values are provided by a CGM device. The TS forecasting can be: 1) a one-step ahead forecasting (OSF) when the prediction concerns the next value or 2) a multi-steps ahead forecasting (MSF) when the prediction concerns the next H values where H is the prediction horizon [4].

In this work, we are interested in the application of deep learning techniques for BGL prediction especially LSTM and CNN in the context of OSF and MSF for 30 min ahead which is good enough to avoid likely increase or decrease of the BGL [5, 6].

In [5], the authors have conducted a comparative study between the five known MSF strategies using the LSTM technique. According to our belief, no similar study was done using the CNN technique and no comparison of the two techniques were performed in the OSF and MSF using the five known MSF strategies. These two points motivate this current study.

The CNN model that we propose in this study is a sequential one using a 1D convolutional layer, followed by a Flatten layer and 2 Dense layers. Regarding the LSTM model, we use the same architecture proposed by [3] as it outperformed significantly a previous LSTM model and an autoregressive model, this LSTM model contains one LSTM Layer tailed by 2 Dense layers.

The objective of the present work is threefold: 1) Getting a performant CNN based on the proposed architecture, 2) Determining the best strategy of MSF using the obtained CNN, and 3) Comparing the CNN and LSTM models for OSF and MSF.

Toward these objectives, we consider the following research questions (RQ):

- (RQ1): what is the best configuration of the proposed CNN?
- (RQ2): Is there an MSF strategy that outperforms the others using the proposed CNN?
- (RQ3): Is the proposed CNN model more accurate than the LSTM model in OSF?
- (RQ4): Is the proposed CNN model more accurate than the LSTM model in MSF?
- (RQ5): Is the performance for OSF maintained for MSF?

This paper is organized into 7 sections. Section 2 states the time series problem and gives an overview of the CNN and LSTM techniques. Section 3 highlights the related work. In Sect. 4, the experimental design is detailed. Section 5 reports and then discusses the results. Threats to validity are presented in Sect. 6 and finally, conclusion along with future works are presented in Sect. 7.

2 Background

In this section, we define the TS problem and identify the strategies used for MSF. Then, we present an overview of the two techniques used in this study: LSTM and CNN. And finally, we present the Wilcoxon test and ranking method.

2.1 Time Series Prediction

Let y_1 to y_N be the N past values of a time series. The TS prediction can be performed for: 1) a single period by determining the next value y_{N+1} which is called one-step ahead forecasting (OSF), or 2) multiple periods by determining y_{N+1} to y_{N+H} which correspond to the H next values, this is called multi-step ahead forecasting (MSF) [4]. The MSF problem is more difficult comparatively to the OSF one. In fact, the former is confronted to the accumulation of errors, the decreasing of accuracy and the increasing of uncertainty [4, 5].

To perform the MSF, five strategies can be used [4, 5]. These strategies are: 1) Recursive, 2) Direct, 3) MIMO (Multi-input Multi-output), 4) DirREC: a combination of Direct and Recursive; and 5) DirMO: a combination of Direct and MIMO. Table 1 presents details about these five MSF strategies.

2.2 LSTM and CNN: An Overview

LSTM and CNN are neural networks (NNs) with special architecture allowing a deep learning. This latter is an emerging technique that have the ability to learn the data characteristics and select relevant features automatically [7]. In this subsection, we start by defining the LSTM then the CNN architecture.

LSTM: Hochreiter and Schmidhuber in [8] came up with a novel architecture of recurrent NNs (RNNs), called LSTM NNs, in order to solve the problem of vanishing or exploding gradient met in the traditional RNNs. The LSTM NNs contains memory cells that have a cell state preserved over time and a gate structure for controlling and regulating the information through the memory cell. With this structure, the LSTM NNs can catch long term dependencies and treat serial data [3, 8].

Table 2 gives details about the memory structure. The following notations are used:

t: The time or sequence number.
X_t: The input vector for t.
Y_t: The output vector for t.
h_t: The hidden vector for t.
C_t: The cell state for t.
W_i, W_f, W_o and W_c: The weight matrices corresponding to each component.
b_i, b_f, b_o and b_c: The bias vectors corresponding to each component.
i_t, f_t, and o_t: The results of the input, forget and output gates respectively.

Note that σ and tanh are respectively the sigmoid and the hyperbolic tangent used as activation functions.

Table 1. MSF strategies.

Strategy	Description	Number of models	Characteristics
Recursive (or iterative)	The prediction is performed iteratively using a OSF model. Each predicted value is used as part of input values to predict the next one	One model with single output	Intuitive and simple. Risk of errors' accumulation
Direct (or independent)	The prediction for each step is performed independently from the others	H models: a model with single output for each step	No errors' accumulation. Dependencies between the estimated values may not be apprehended.
MIMO	The prediction is performed by one model that returns the predicted values in a vector	One model with multiple output	The stochastic dependencies between the predicted values are preserved No prediction flexibility
DirRec	For each step, the prediction is done by a corresponding model based on the past values and the predictions of previous steps	H models with single output	Take advantages from the Recursive and Direct strategies
DirMO	The prediction horizon is divided in B blocks with the same size; each block is predicted based on a MIMO model	B models with multiple output	Take advantages from the Direct and MIMO strategies

Table 2. LSTM memory structure.

Component	Role	Equations
Input gate	Getting the information to be retained	$i_t = \sigma(W_i * [h_{t-1}, X_t] + b_i)$
Forget gate	Getting the information to be ignored	$f_t = \sigma(W_f * [h_{t-1}, X_t] + b_f)$
Output gate	Calculating the output and updating the hidden vector	$o_t = \sigma(W_o * [h_{t-1}, X_t] + b_o)$ $h_t = o_t * tanh(C_t)$
Cell state	Maintaining the information through cells	$C_t = f_t * C_{t-1} + i_t * \hat{C}_t$ Where $\tilde{C}_t = tanh(W_c * [h_{t-1}, X_t] + b_c)$

CNN: The origins of the CNNs go back to the neocognitron model proposed in [9]. They are based on the concept developed in [10] related to the simple and complex cells which were inspired from the animal visual cortex. However, the first successful CNN that was trained by backpropagation was proposed by [11].

A CNN is a feed-forward NN whose main layer is a convolutional one performing a convolution operation. This latter consists of applying and sliding a filter over the input data through an elementwise multiplication [12–14]. The connection weights represent the kernel of the convolution.

The dimension of the filter depends on the type of input data. In fact, 1D is used for sequential data such as text and time series, 2D is used for images and 3D for videos [7]. Multiple filters can be used to be able to extract more useful features [13].

In the case of time series, the convolution is applied based on the following formula:

$$C_t = f(\omega * X_{t:t+l-1} + b) \, \forall t \in [1, T - l + 1] \tag{1}$$

where C_t is the tth element of C which is the vector resulting from the convolution, X is the time series with length T, ω is a 1D filter with length l, b is the bias parameter and f represents the activation function [13].

2.3 Statistical Test and Ranking

The Wilcoxon statistical test is a non-parametric test used to assess if the difference between the performances of two models is significant. This test is performed considering the null hypothesis (NH) that there is no difference between the compared models. The p-value of the considered NH is calculated, if the p-value is less than a certain significance level α, the difference is considered statistically significant [15].

In the case we need to have a ranking of the models, the sum of ranking differences (SRD) is used. It calculates the ranking of the models by summing up the difference of their ranking and an ideal ranking for a certain number of cases. The ideal ranking can be a reference model or the best known model. If such a model does not exist, the ideal ranking can be defined based on the minimum, the maximum or the average of all the models for each case [16].

3 Related Work

Statistical methods and especially autoregressive models were widely used for the BGL prediction. However, a growing trend has been noticed for the use of the machine learning techniques including deep learning [2, 17]. These latter were successfully used in many fields such as image recognition, object detection, sequential data processing, their success is due to their ability to learn automatically the data representation from raw data and extract the relevant features [7].

In the context of BGL prediction, deep learning techniques especially LSTM and CNN were investigated and encouraging results were reached [5]. In fact, the LSTM was used in [3, 17–19] and CNN used in [17, 20]. In [14] CNN and LSTM were combined.

Regarding the strategies of MSF, Direct strategy is the most used one according to [5] and to the best of our knowledge, no study focused on the comparison of LSTM and CNN in the OSF and MSF taking in consideration all the MSF strategies which motivated the current study. However, in [17] LSTM and CNN were compared with other autoregressive models considering only Direct and Recursive strategies, the study did not conclude on the best technique in all the cases and pointed that Direct strategy for LSTM outperformed the Recursive one. In [5], the authors conducted an exhaustive comparison of the five MSF strategies using the LSTM and concluded that there is no significant outperformance of a strategy over the others and noticed that non-recursive strategies tend to be better than recursive ones.

4 Experimental Process

In the first part of this section, the dataset and the performance measurement used for experimentation and evaluation are described. Later, the experimental design adopted for this study is presented.

4.1 Dataset and Performance Measurement

In the experiments, we considered Ten T1DM patients whose data were extracted from the dataset DirecNetInpatientAccuracyStudy available at the site [21]. This dataset was used by [3, 5] and contains the measurements of BGL every 5 min using a CGM device. Note that these patients are taken randomly and a pre-processing of data was required to remove redundant records and outliers between successive records. The dataset of the Ten patients is described in Table 3.

Table 3. Ten patients' data description. The BGL is in mg/dl.

Patients	P1	P2	P3	P4	P5	P6	P7	P8	P9	P10
Number of records	766	278	283	923	562	771	897	546	831	246
Min BGL	40	57	103	40	50	62	42	43	40	72
Max BGL	339	283	322	400	270	400	400	310	400	189
Mean BGL	114.78	120.96	185.89	188.44	179.71	187.45	210.26	152.88	157.50	116.51

In order to assess the performance of the considered models, we consider the frequently used performance measurement RMSE (root-mean-square error) [2] which is calculated as follows:

$$\text{RMSE} = \sqrt{\frac{1}{n}\sum_{i=1}^{n}(\hat{y}_i - y_i)^2} \tag{2}$$

Where y_i and $\hat{y}_i$ represent the measured and the estimated value respectively and n represents the size of the considered sample. The RMSE value ranges in the interval $[0, +\infty[$ and the performance is higher when the RMSE value tends to 0.

4.2 Experimental Design

The empirical evaluation was conducted by considering the following steps: 1) Construction of the best configuration of the CNN model, 2) Development of MSF strategies for the CNN model and 3) Comparison between the CNN model and the LSTM model.

Step 1: Construction of the best configuration of the CNN model. The CNN model that we propose for the BGL prediction is a sequential one starting with a 1D convolutional layer, followed by a Flatten layer and 2 Dense layers. To determine the best configuration using this architecture, we consider a Search Grid (SG) concerning two hyper-parameters which are the kernel size and the number of filters. This SG is inspired from [3, 22] and presented in Table 4. This step is composed of 3 sub-steps which are the following:

Table 4. Search Grid parameters.

Parameter	Signification	Search space
Number of filters	Number of sliding windows	{2, 5, 10, 15, 20, 25}
Kernel size	Dimension of the sliding windows	{2,3,4,5,10}

- Step 1.1: It concerns the data preparation, in fact, the time series is decomposed into couples (X_i, y_i) where X_i is a vector of the input values and y_i is the output value which corresponds the next value following the values of the vector X_i.
- Step 1.2: For each value of the Number of Filters in the SG (Table 4) and each patient, the CNN model is trained and tested. Based on the SRD method, the best value of the Number of Filters is fixed.
- Step 1.3: For each value of the Kernel size in the SG (Table 4) and each patient, the CNN model with the Number of Filters fixed in Step 1.2 is trained and tested. Based on the SRD method, the best value of the Kernel size is fixed.

Step 2: Development of MSF strategies for the CNN model. This step contains 2 sub-steps which are the followings:

- Step 2.1: It concerns the data preparation. Let $X = \{s(t_i)\}$ be a time series where $s(t_i)$ is the BGL recorded at time t_i and d the sampling horizon, the time series X is divided to couples (X_i, y_i) where X_i and y_i are the input and the output data respectively. Table 5 presents the decomposition done for each MSF strategy for 30 min ahead prediction.

Table 5. Data preparation for MSF strategies. HP: Horizon of Prediction; mn: minutes.

MSF strategy	Context	Decomposition
Recursive	HP = 5mn	$X_i = \{s(t_{i-d+1}), ..., s(t_i)\}$ $y_i = s(t_{i+1})$
Direct	HP = 30mn	$X_i = \{s(t_{i-d+1}), ..., s(t_i)\}$ $y_i = s(t_{i+6})$
MIMO	Multiple output for HP = 30mn	$X_i = \{s(t_{i-d+1}), ..., s(t_i)\}$ $y_i = \{s(t_{i+1}), ..., s(t_{i+6})\}$
DirRec	6 models M_j with HP = 5mn, j goes from 1 to 6	For each M_j: $X_i = \{s(t_{i-d-j+2}), ..., s(t_i)\}$ $y_i = s(t_{i+1})$
DirMO	Number of blocks = 2 So, 2 models are trained	For M_1: $X_i = \{s(t_{i-d+1}), ..., s(t_i)\}$ $y_i = \{s(t_{i+1}), ..., s(t_{i+3})\}$ For M_2: $X_i = \{s(t_{i-d+1}), ..., s(t_i)\}$ $y_i = \{s(t_{i+4}), ..., s(t_{i+6})\}$.

- Step 2.2: The performance is evaluated for each patient and each strategy using the RMSE. The models are trained on the training data which represents 66% of the dataset and evaluated on the test data which represents 34% of the dataset. If a difference between the performances is noticed, the statistical tests are applied to assess statistically the observed differences.

Step 3: Comparison between the CNN model and the LSTM model. The comparison is performed between our CNN model and the LSTM model proposed by [3] and used in [5]. The LSTM was developed for OSF and for the five MSF strategies using the same steps as for the CNN model namely data preparation and performance evaluation.

At this step, we compare first the performance of CNN and LSTM for OSF. Then, considering the MSF, we have to make 5 comparisons, in each one, the performances for each strategy with CNN and LSTM are compared. If a difference is noticed, it is assessed statistically by using the statistical tests.

5   Results and Discussion

In this section, we present the results of each step defined in the experimental design. Thereafter, we discuss the empirical results.

For the sake of the experimentations, we developed a tool under Windows 10 using Python-3.6 and the framework Keras 2.2.4 with, as backend, Tensorflow 1.12.0.

5.1 Results

This section presents the empirical results according to each step.

Step1: Construction of the best configuration of the CNN model. After fixing the architecture of our CNN model which is sequence of a convolutional layer (1D), a Flatten layer and 2 Dense layers, we prepared the data to fit the required input and output. Then, we carried out a set of experiments to answer the RQ1 by varying the two hyper-parameter: 1) the Filters' number in sub-step 1.2, and 2) the kernel size in sub-step 1.3.

Figure 1 shows the results of sub-step 1.2 which corresponds to the RMSE obtained for each patient and for each value of Filters' number from the Table 4. We can observe that with 20 Filters, we have the best RMSE. Furthermore, we used the SRD by considering the ideal ranking as the minimum performance. The results of the SRD are presented in Table 6, it shows that 20 Filters achieves the best ranking. At the end of this sub-step, we fixed the number of Filters to 20.

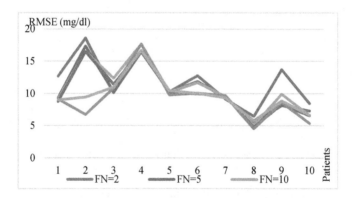

Fig. 1. Performance of CNN with Filters' number (FN) variations.

In sub-step 1.3, the same experiments were conducted by varying the Kernel size with respect to the values determined in Table 4. The results of these experiments are shown in Fig. 2. As there is no clearly dominant value, we use the SRD to rank the obtained models. Table 7 gives the ranking of the models based on SRD method. We can see that a Kernel size equals to 2 had the best ranking.

To summarize and answer the RQ1, 20 Filters and a kernel size equals to 2 give the best configuration of our CNN. This is the configuration of the CNN that will be used in the next steps of our experimental process.

Step 2: Development of MSF strategies for the CNN model. At that step and for each of the five MSF strategies, we started by preparing the data in accordance to the decomposition detailed in Table 5 then we train and validate the corresponding CNN

Table 6. SRD with the variation of Filters' number (FN).

Patients	FN = 2	FN = 5	FN = 10	FN = 15	FN = 20	FN = 25	Min
P1	5	4	3	0	2	1	1
P2	5	4	2	3	0	1	1
P3	0	1	5	4	2	3	1
P4	1	0	4	2	5	3	1
P5	4	3	2	1	0	5	1
P6	5	4	2	0	2	1	1
P7	0	2	3	5	4	1	1
P8	5	3	2	1	0	4	1
P9	5	0	4	1	2	3	1
P10	5	4	2	1	0	3	1
SRD	35	25	29	18	17	25	10

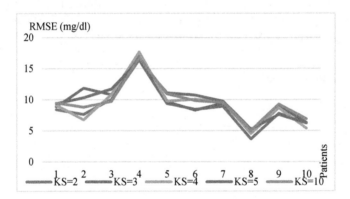

Fig. 2. Performance of CNN with Kernel size (KS) variations.

Table 7. SRD with the variation of Kernel Size (KS).

Patients	KS = 2	KS = 3	KS = 4	KS = 5	KS = 10	Min
P1	0	1	2	3	4	1
P2	1	4	0	3	2	1
P3	1	2	3	4	0	1
P4	1	3	4	0	2	1
P5	0	1	2	4	3	1
P6	1	0	3	4	2	1
P7	0	1	3	4	2	1
P8	0	2	1	4	3	1
P9	1	3	2	0	4	1
P10	2	3	0	1	4	1
SRD	7	20	20	27	26	10

model (s) based on the configuration that we obtained in the previous step. Figure 3 presents the performance in term of RMSE of the considered MSF strategies.

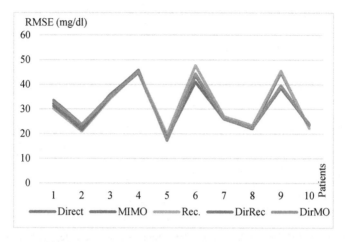

Fig. 3. Performance of CNN using the five strategies.

Figure 3 shows that there is no remarkable difference between the performances of the five strategies. Furthermore, considering the average for RMSE, the values are 31.48, 30.84, 31.60, 30.22 and 31.10 respectively for Direct, MIMO, Recursive, Dir-Rec and DirMO. At that point, there is no need to perform a statistical test.

Thus, the answer for RQ2 is the following: there is no MSF strategy that outperforms the others using the proposed CNN. Besides, the five strategies are giving similar performances.

Step 3: Comparison between the CNN model and the LSTM model. To be able to compare the performances of the CNN and the LSTM models, we performed the experiments on the same datasets. We started by comparing the performance of the two models for OSF, and then the performances of the 30 min' forecasting using each of the MSF strategies are compared. The results are shown in Fig. 4. Figure 4.A represents the results for OSF for both CNN and LSTM, while figures Fig. 4.B, Fig. 4.C, Fig. 4.D, Fig. 4.E and Fig. 4.F represent the results for CNN and LSTM using Direct, MIMO, Recursive, DirRec and DirMO strategies respectively.

Figure 4 shows that CNN outperforms LSTM in OSF and MSF for all the strategies. To assess these findings statistically, we used the Wilcoxon test. Toward this, we formulate 6 NHs which are the followings:

- NH1: The CNN model does not outperform the LSTM model for OSF.
- NH2: The CNN model does not outperform the LSTM model for MSF using Direct strategy.
- NH3: The CNN model does not outperform the LSTM model for MSF using MIMO strategy.

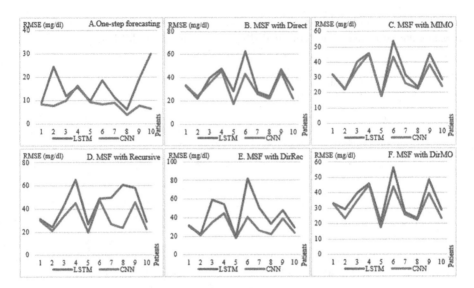

Fig. 4. CNN vs LSTM for one-step ahead forecasting (A) and multi-steps ahead forecasting (B to F).

- NH4: The CNN model does not outperform the LSTM model for MSF using Recursive strategy.
- NH5: The CNN model does not outperform the LSTM model for MSF using DirRec strategy.
- NH6: The CNN model does not outperform the LSTM model for MSF using DirMO strategy.

The statistical tests were Two-tailed with 0.05 as a significance level. The calculated p-values are presented in Table 8. As we can see, all the p-values are under the significance level, thus the CNN outperforms significantly the LSTM for OSF and MSF which answers the RQ3 and RQ4.

Table 8. p-value for the NHs.

NH	NH1	NH2	NH3	NH4	NH5	NH6
p-value	0.00932	0.02202	0.02852	0.00512	0.00512	0.00512

Concerning the RQ5, we remark from Fig. 4, that CNN is maintaining its performance over LSTM for OSF and all the MSF strategies.

5.2   Discussion

In the current study, we propose a CNN model composed of one 1D convolutional layer, one Flatten layer and 2 Dense layers. Our first objective was shaping the best configuration of the suggested CNN model through the tuning of the two hyper-parameters: kernel size and the number of filters. Figures 1 and 2 show that each of these parameters has an influence on the obtained accuracy. Therefore, a careful choice of these parameters is crucial for building a CNN model and other models [5, 14]. Our CNN model performed well relatively to the performances found in literature and reported in [2]. Indeed, the minimum, maximum and mean RMSE for our CNN are respectively 3.66, 16.4 and 8.68. Furthermore, these results show that the CNN can perform well in time series prediction and sequential data in general even though it was traditionally conceived for image processing [7].

Concerning the prediction for the 30 min ahead, five strategies for MSF were developed and compared using the RMSE, the CNN model gives similar performances using these five strategies. These results are not consistent with the finding of the previous work using LSTM [5] where it was noticed that non-recursive strategies tend to be better than recursive ones even though there was no strategy significantly better than the others. Thus, further experiments should be carried out in order to refute or confirm this result for CNN. In the case of confirmation, the MSF strategy to consider should be Direct as it needs to train just one model with no iterations.

The third concern of this study is the comparison between CNN and LSTM. In fact, the performances of the CNN and the LSTM were compared in both the OSF and MSF, the results show that CNN outperforms significantly the LSTM in OSF and MSF using the five MSF strategies. This can be explained by the followings: 1) the CNN are using a small number of parameters since it uses shared weights [7], 2) There is no recurrent connections in the CNN contrarily to the LSTM which makes the process of training faster [14], and 3) The use of multiple filters in CNN helps to extract more useful features [13].

Finally, the performance of the CNN over the LSTM in OSF is maintained for MSF using the five strategies. This persistence is important as it gives some confidence in case we enlarge the prediction horizon.

6   Threats to Validity

We describe in this section the four threats to our study validity. These threats are:

- Internal validity: This threat to validity takes in consideration the evaluation approach. This latter should be appropriate so as the findings of the study are valid. Toward that aim, all the models were trained and tested in different datasets. In fact, 66% of each dataset was used in the training phase while the remaining 34% was used for the evaluation phase.
- External validity: This concerns the perimeter of the study and its ability to be generalized. To ensure this, we took in a random way the datasets of ten patients from a public dataset. These datasets have different sizes. In fact, the records' number varies from 246 to 923. Note that these datasets were previously used by [3, 5].
- Construct validity: The performance is the main criterion to compare the considered models, thus it is essential to use a performance measurement that indicates how far

the models are performant. In our study, we used the RMSE since it is a performance measurement used commonly in the BGL prediction [2].

- Statistical validity: In this study, we aim at determining the best model among the proposed ones through their performance's comparison. When a difference between two models is observed, it is essential to assess statistically this difference. Therefore, we used the Wilcoxon statistical test. Besides, the SRD method is used for ranking.

7   Conclusion and Future Work

This study proposed a CNN model having a 1D convolutional layer, a Flatten layer and two Dense layers. First we had to determine the best configuration by considering the two hyper-parameters: number of filters and kernel size. Then, we developed the MSF strategies using the CNN model to determine the strategy that may outperform the others. And finally, a performance comparison was conducted considering the CNN and LSTM models for one-step ahead forecasting and multi-steps ahead forecasting using the five identified MSF strategies.

The main outcomes of this work were: 1) No MSF strategy outperforms the others for CNN, besides they have similar performances, 2) The proposed CNN outperformed significantly the LSTM model for both one-step and multi-steps prediction.

These propitious results motivate further researches in the use of the CNN model taking in consideration different points such as: tuning other hyper-parameters, considering other input data such as activities and medication and exploring a larger prediction horizon.

References

1. Bilous, R., Donnelly, R.: Handbook of Diabetes. Wiley, Chichester (2010)
2. El Idrissi, T., Idri, A., Bakkoury, Z.: Systematic map and review of predictive techniques in diabetes self-management. Int. J. Inf. Manage. **46**, 263–277 (2019). https://doi.org/10.1016/j.ijinfomgt.2018.09.011
3. El Idrissi, T., Idri, A., Abnane, I., Bakkoury, Z.: Predicting blood glucose using an LSTM neural network. In: Proceedings of the 2019 Federated Conference on Computer Science and Information Systems, FedCSIS, vol. 18, pp. 35–41. IEEE, Leipzig (2019)
4. Taieb, S.B., Bontempi, G., Atiya, A.F., Sorjamaa, A.: A review and comparison of strategies for multi-step ahead time series forecasting based on the NN5 forecasting competition. Expert Syst. Appl. **39**(8), 7067–7083 (2012)
5. El Idrissi, T., Idri, A., Kadi, I., Bakkoury, Z.: Strategies of multi-step-ahead forecasting for blood glucose level using LSTM neural networks: a comparative study. In: Proceedings of the 13th International Joint Conference on Biomedical Engineering Systems and Technologies (BIOSTEC 2020), vol. 5, HEALTHINF, pp. 337–344. SCITEPRESS, Valletta (2020)
6. Fox, I., Ang, L., Jaiswal, M., Pop-Busui, R., Wiens, J.: Deep multi-output forecasting: Learning to accurately predict blood glucose trajectories. In: Proceedings of the 24th ACM SIGKDD International Conference on Knowledge Discovery & Data Mining, pp. 1387–1395. ACM, London (2018)

7. LeCun, Y., Bengio, Y., Hinton, G.: Deep learning. Nature **521**(7553), 436–444 (2015)
8. Hochreiter, S., Schmidhuber, J.: Long short-term memory. Neural Comput. **9**(8), 1735–1780 (1997)
9. Fukushima, K., Miyake, S.: Neocognitron: a new algorithm for pattern recognition tolerant of deformations and shifts in position. Pattern Recogn. **15**(6), 455–469 (1982)
10. Hubel, D.H., Wiesel, T.N.: Receptive fields, binocular interaction and functional architecture in the cat's visual cortex. J. Physiol. **160**(1), 106–154 (1962)
11. LeCun, Y., et al.: Handwritten digit recognition with a back-propagation network. In: Proceedings of Advances in Neural Information Processing Systems, pp. 396–404. MIT Press (1989)
12. LeCun, Y., Bottou, L., Bengio, Y., Haffner, P.: Gradient-based learning applied to document recognition. Proc. IEEE **86**(11), 2278–2324 (1998)
13. Fawaz, H.I., Forestier, G., Weber, J., Idoumghar, L., Muller, P.A.: Deep learning for time series classification: a review. Data Min. Knowl. Discov. **33**(4), 917–963 (2019)
14. Li, K., Liu, C., Zhu, T., Herrero, P., Georgiou, P.: GluNet: a deep learning framework for accurate glucose forecasting. IEEE J. Biomed. Health Inform. **24**(2), 414–423 (2020)
15. Idri, A., Abnane, I., Abran, A.: Missing data techniques in analogy-based software development effort estimation. J. Syst. Softw. **117**, 595–611 (2016)
16. Héberger, K.: Sum of ranking differences compares methods or models fairly. TrAC Trends Anal. Chem. **29**(1), 101–109 (2010)
17. Xie, J., Wang, Q.: Benchmark machine learning approaches with classical time series approaches on the blood glucose level prediction challenge. CEUR Workshop Proc. **2148**, 97–102 (2018)
18. Sun, Q., Jankovic, M.V., Bally, L., Mougiakakou, S.G.: Predicting blood glucose with an LSTM and Bi-LSTM based deep neural network. In: 2018 14th Symposium on Neural Networks and Applications (NEUREL), pp. 1–5. IEEE, Belgrade, Serbia (2018)
19. Mirshekarian, S., Bunescu, R., Marling, C., Schwartz, F.: Using LSTMs to learn physiological models of blood glucose behavior. In: 2017 39th Annual International Conference of the IEEE Engineering in Medicine and Biology Society (EMBC), pp. 2887–2891. IEEE, Seogwipo, South Korea (2017)
20. Zhu, T., Li, K., Herrero, P., Chen, J., Georgiou, P.: A deep learning algorithm for personalized blood glucose prediction. In: KHD@ IJCAI, pp. 64–78 (2018)
21. DirecNet: Diabetes Research in Children Network, http://direcnet.jaeb.org/Studies.aspx. Accessed 01 Apr 2019
22. Hosni, M., Idri, A., Abran, A.: Investigating heterogeneous ensembles with filter feature selection for software effort estimation. In: Proceedings of the 27th International Workshop on Software Measurement and 12th International Conference on Software Process and Product Measurement, pp. 207–220. ACM, Gothenburg, Sweden (2017)

Reconsidering the Risk Society: Its Parameters and Repercussions Evaluated by a Statistical Model with Aspects of Different Social Sciences

Ahu Dereli Dursun[1,2]([mail])

[1] Istanbul Commerce University, Istanbul, Turkey
adereli@ticaret.edu.tr
[2] Institute of Social Sciences, Communication Studies, Istanbul Bilgi University,
Istanbul, Turkey
ahu.dereli.dursun@bilgiedu.net

Abstract. Risk society theory, with its complexity and inclusion of different ideas with respect to the peculiarity of risk in the modern era, the role played by the media in the construction and communication of risk as well as the nature of reflexivity, has had repercussions in various fields. Since multiple elements are to be analysed to reconsider the risk society theory in the current global landscape characterized by emerging threats, an integrated approach has been chosen in this study for a comprehensive evaluation. The majority of the studies conducted on the relevant subject matter lack quantitative analyses; therefore, this study aims at bridging a gap in this regard by elucidating the parameters and implications of the concepts related to the risk society based on the results obtained by quantitative and qualitative analyses. To this end, a survey (including demographic, sociological and psychological items) on risk and economic uncertainty was designed and conducted online. Secondly, content analysis was done on a set of news items focusing on global economy. The results of the survey evaluated with statistical analyses (ANOVA, t-test and correlation analysis) were used to relate the responses to different aspects and thematic qualities of the risk society theory postulated and developed by Ulrich Beck, Anthony Giddens and other social philosophers. The experimental results of the study revealed certain relationships between demographic characteristics and sociological-psychological elements of the risk society theory and its parameters in the individuals' attitudes and perception. Correspondingly, repercussions of the risk society theory have been revealed in the news items handled. The majority of the results obtained support the key postulations of the risk society, which can shed light on understanding the significant transformation of our era along with the social attitudes, fears, insecurity and risk perception among individuals. In addition, the findings can lead to further interpretation of the interplay between economy, media, science and politics, opening up new perspectives toward reconsidering "contemporary" risks.

© Springer Nature Switzerland AG 2020
O. Gervasi et al. (Eds.): ICCSA 2020, LNCS 12250, pp. 394–409, 2020.
https://doi.org/10.1007/978-3-030-58802-1_29

Keywords: Risk society · Uncertainty · Global threats · Demographic difference · ANOVA · Correlation analysis · Statistical analysis · Economy news

1   Introduction

The problematic concerned with defining concepts has become more conspicuous in the global landscape of the current era that is characterized by various threats and uncertainties, including economic downturns, health threats, particularly the uncontrollable spread of coronavirus (COVID-19), wars, refugees' problems, and catastrophes whether they be man-made or natural. Amidst such developments that have both regional and global effects, individuals may not be able to identify the relevant emotion they have been going through. As Fehr and Russell notably remarked [1], "everyone knows what an emotion is, until asked to give a definition". As this apt observation indicates, emotions are hard to define. The same elusiveness regarding definition is in question related to uncertainty and risk. During the decade when Fehr and Russell put forth the elusiveness of an exact definition of emotions in psychology, German sociologist Ulrich Beck put forth the concept of "risk society" which has generated an exhaustive amount of research in various fields such as sociology, economics and political science, to name but three. As well as the concept of "risk society", "risk civilization" of Patrick Lagadec and "risk culture" of Anthony Giddens support the movement that is based on a common principle which regards risk as a characteristic feature of contemporary societies and an essential parameter for their analysis [2]. Whilst the structure of feudal society was dissolved by modernization in the nineteenth century producing the industrial society, industrial society is currently being dissolved by modernization with another modernity coming into being [3]. Beck pronounces this paradigmatic shift from modernity to a "second modernity" in his sociological works, arguing that unwanted and man-made side-effects of modernity generate mounting societal uncertainties. Referred to as "reflexive modernization", this ongoing process conveys a boomerang effect since the majority of unplanned results of processes in modern societies rebound on these societies, forcing them to change in turn [4] and the "second age of modernity" opens new conceptual landscapes [5]. Due to the erosive effects of the conditions in risk society, consensus among competing experts lack regarding the exact definition or probability of a risk object or event. Since the estimates of the probability and extent of risk are intensified by competing powers, confidence in expert decisions are subjected to erosion; and creation of knowledge encounters instability [3,6,7]. Beck's original conceptualization was conceived at a period when people were trying to make sense of the Chernobyl accident while watching the unprepared authorities handle situations that involved risk and environmental destruction [8]. Likewise, the current global landscape is characterized by many threats aforementioned, leading the "risk society" concept to be placed on the global agenda. Risk, in this context, is defined as the prospects of physical harm or loss as a result of a particular process with far-reaching effects, not only related to health but also to property and profit [3]. This state of affairs dominates the social, political and economic discourse with different processes shaping our lives, generating risks and unplanned outcomes for the individuals' well-being as well as the environment, as noted by Giddens [9]. Anyone is vulnerable in the face of risk, and being rich or powerful does not necessarily mean being able to evade risks [3].

With its various parameters in different fields, the risk society concept has been the subject matter of extant research in literature. Reflections on the theory and reviews make up the majority of works [7–13]. The study on the reappraisal of the risk society by [14] places the thesis in view of cultural concerns in contemporary society, while the same author deals with the critique of the world risk society in depth appreciating the explanatory value of the perspective by directing its utility to advance future risk studies [15]. Another work in sociology by [16] puts forth situation of the risks in their social context, as connected to actors' activities. The scope of the theory is not limited to sociology merely, it has had implications in various fields, which underpins its transdisciplinary view. To illustrate, the study of [17] adopts a transdisciplinary view with regard to how risk is induced stating that Beck's risk prevailing future society is likely to be validated. Another paper interprets the government responses to young people and drug use via main concepts based on the risk society theory, revealing that the theory explains some underlying contemporary conflicts [18]. Concerning the requirement of reinvention of politics, the study of [19] points to the fact that nation-state institutions cannot contain global risks like climate change. Cloud computing in the risk society has also been addressed in [20]. As noted above, creation of knowledge encounters instability in the risk society. Thus, additional skills become vital in this context to predict and withstand dangers, according to Beck [3]. Such additional skills to tackle knowledge instability currently can be efficient use of Artificial Intelligence (AI) and other technological innovations. Machine learning technologies have gained significance for accurate risk prediction and management. Among relevant studies, machine learning approach and multiple-discipline datasets were used for the simulation of worldwide terror attack risks [21]; responsible Artificial Intelligence is explored focusing on requirements of fairness, data privacy and accountability concerning real-life applications [22]; the efficiency of data mining methods were demonstrated through a real-world case study from banking for modelling ambiguous occurrences in liquidity risk assessment with Artificial Neural Network (ANN) and Bayesian Network model [23], and a risk management tool using machine learning was assessed for investment purposes in [24]. Some other studies on various risk factors in different fields based on quantitative methods deal with the following topics: effects of cosmopolitanism on environmental psychology [25], comparison of assets with statistical methods in finance [26], risk analysis in the measurement of investment [27], management in construction projects [28], examination of risk mitigation mechanisms in university setting [29], demographic differences in safety proactivity behaviours in small-scale enterprises [30], analysis of the effect of leaders' leadership styles for maritime organization success [31], and exploration of factors of perceived risk concerning people with serious mental illness [32].

Even though the contributions of the risk society theory have been acknowledged in the literature, the criticisms are also in question. One criticism toward Beck and other social theorists is expressed in [33] as this sort of theorising lacks empirical evidence. As an answer to this critical point, young people's lives were used as a context specific example along with quantitative and qualitative data [34]. When compared with earlier works, the current study attempts to provide novel contribution in terms of the methodology chosen, employing quantitative and qualitative approaches, as well as the survey designed. By making use of sociological and psychological aspects that revolve around risk society thesis along with the news element, the study also aims at addressing the issue from a complementary frame with multiple dimensions.

As for the media aspect in the risk society thesis, it can be briefly conveyed that the risks produced in the late modernity bring about usually irremediable harm, and remain invisible. Mass media along with scientific and legal occupations are in the responsible position for the definition of risks [3]. Accordingly, mass media and journalism come into play by rendering risks visible [4] and media are identified as a key arena where the risks and their results are played out, and the emergence of social conflicts plays an informative role [35]. The study of [36] underlines the important role of the media in the construction and communication of risk, presenting the theoretical and methodological issues of risk reporting. One related recent study by [37] examines the way antimicrobial resistance, as a kind of modern risk, is covered in North American newspapers with a focus on reflexive modernization. Regarding visual media, the study of [38] examines the risk society discourses in television reality shows focusing on risk perception and uncertainties. In this study, global news items were selected concerning the elements that undermine modernity on the basis of the risk society thesis. These elements are globalisation, individualisation, gender revolution, underemployment and global risks which are deemed significant when taken collectively, constituting five interrelated processes [9]. The themes of the news reports handled herein also point to these elements, except for gender revolution.

The reason why risk society concept is taken as the theoretical paradigm in this study is derived from the critical and transdisciplinary approach of Beck and Giddens who enrich, merge and critique many prevalent disciplinary perspectives and theoretical approaches related to risk of the time established in the framework of sociology, psychology, geography, anthropology, political science, law and economics [7]. Taking these postulations and different dimensions into consideration, this study sets out to address the following research questions: 1. What is the relationship of demographic characteristics with the sociological and psychological elements of the risk society?, 2. Which parameters of the risk society theory find reflections in the individuals' attitudes and perception?, 3. What are the repercussions of the risk society as covered in a set of news items on global economy?

The organization of the rest of the paper is as follows: Sect. 2 describes the Materials and Methods, Sect. 3 provides the results based on statistical analyses of the survey and the content analysis of the news items. Finally, Sect. 4 is allocated to the discussion and conclusion referring to the research questions.

2 Materials and Method

2.1 Materials

2.2 Respondents

The first approach adopted in this study to reevaluate the risk society conceptualization is the administration of an online survey sent through a link (provided in the data availability part below) to a total of 204 respondents in Turkey in January 2020 based on convenience sampling method. The author designed the survey, with sociological component derived from the concepts and postulations of the risk society concept as conjectured by Ulrich Beck [3] and Anthony Giddens [39,40], and the psychological component including questions based on Financial Threat Scale [41], fearing the unknown: a short version of the Intolerance of Uncertainty Scale [42] and public's initial responses to crisis situations based on the study results by [43].

The general demographic characteristics of the respondents whose survey replies (n = 199) were evaluated are as follows: female and male respondents correspond to 53.5% and 46.5%, respectively, which provides a homogeneous distribution based on gender. University students aged between 17–25 (69.8%) constitute the majority of the respondents, followed by 36–45 and 46–55 age interval, both corresponding to 10.1%. University students and those holding a bachelor's degree make up 67.8%, followed by those holding a Master's degree (15.6%). A bigger portion of the sample (63.3%) stated that they are not currently working while the employed account for 36.7%, students account for 68.8%. 51.4 % have a professional experience of 10 years and more, followed by 1–4 years of experience (31.9%). Most of the respondents reported their economic status as average (56.7%).

News Items. The other approach employed in the study includes the content analysis of 25 global news items (dated from September 2019 to February 2020), the main theme being economy, retrieved from the electronic version of the *Guardian*. News reports with economy content and risk society concepts with the central focus make up the secondary data. Attention was paid to the coverage of different areas across the globe (USA, Turkey, China, Greece, France, Nordic countries, UK, Australia) and the analysis was conducted with respect to the six elements (provided in Sect. 3.3) that address both the sociological and psychological aspects of risk and uncertainty around the theme of economic problems.

2.3 Methods

In this study, a mixed-method approach has been chosen: qualitative analysis (content analysis of the news items and relating the risk society, as the theoretical paradigm, to the results obtained) and quantitative statistical analyses. The survey results were analysed by statistical methods, including the frequency, mean and standard deviation calculation to describe the basic features of the data. The basic analysis used for the reliability analysis is the Cronbach Alpha (α) value measured as 0.736, which indicates an acceptable level (since the rate falls within the range of $.8 > \alpha \geq .7$). For further statistical analyses, Analysis of Variance (ANOVA), t-test and correlation analysis were used. The analyses were performed using IBM SPSS Statistics for Windows, Version 23.0 [44]. Brief information on the tests utilized for statistical analyses is provided below.

ANOVA. ANOVA is used to perform statistical testing on experiments that involve either two or more groups. ANOVA is aptly suited for experimental designs consisting of repeated measures on the same subjects or to reveal different factors in interaction with one another in the experiment [45]. It is a frequently-used statistical procedure for comparing the means of a variable across a number of groups of persons [46]. The formulae used for ANOVA analyses are provided in (1), (2) and (3) [47, 48] as follows:

The variances in the denominator show the application/between group variation, whereas the ones in the numerator denote the error/within group variation.

– Application sum of squares and variance (See (1)) [47, 48]

$$SS_T = \sum_{i=1}^{k} n_i \left(\overline{X_i} - \overline{X_{GM}} \right)^2 \tag{1}$$

$\overline{X_{GM}}$: grand mean; $\overline{X_i}$: group mean
$df_T = k - 1; S_T^2 = \frac{SST}{dF_T}$
– Error sum of squares and variance (See (2)) [47, 48]

$$SS_E = \sum_{j=1}^{n_1} (X_{1j} - \overline{X}_1)^2 + \sum_{j=2}^{n_2} (X_{2j} - \overline{X}_2)^2 + ... + \sum_{j=1}^{n_k} (X_{kj} - \overline{X}k)^2 \tag{2}$$

$dF_E = N - k; S_E^2 = \frac{SS_E}{df_{E}}$
$SS_{TOT} = SS_T + SS_E; df_{TOT} = N - 1$
– Strength of relationship (See (3)) [47, 48]

$$w^2 = \frac{SS_E - (k - 1)S_E^2}{SS_{TOT} + S_E^2} \tag{3}$$

In this study, ANOVA was used for the comparison of three or more groups (i.e. education level, income level and economic status) and to identify whether there is a significant difference between these three groups at a 95% confidence interval.

T-Test. A t-test is a parametric statistical method employed for the comparison of the means of two groups. T- tests are used when the samples fulfil the conditions of normality, independence and equal variance [49].

The formulae for t-test are provided in (4) and (5) [47,48] as follows:

- If the variances are unequal/not homogenous (See (4)), [47,48]:

$$t = \frac{(\overline{X}_1 - \overline{X}_2) - (\mu_1 - \mu_2)}{\sqrt{\frac{s_1^2}{n_1} + \frac{s_2^2}{n_2}}}; \tag{4}$$

df = smaller $n - 1$

- If the variances are equal/homogenous (See (5)), [47,48]:

$$t = \frac{(\overline{X}_1 - \overline{X}_2) - (\mu_1 - \mu_2)}{\sqrt{\frac{(n_1-1)s_1^2+(n_2-1)s_2^2}{(n_1+n_2-2)}} \cdot \sqrt{\frac{1}{n_1} + \frac{1}{n_2}}}; \tag{5}$$

$df = n_1 + n_2 - 2$

T-test was employed in this study to investigate whether there is a difference between the means of two groups (female-male, employed-not employed, etc.).

Correlation Analysis. As a frequently used statistical analysis, correlation analysis enables one to identify whether there is a relationship between two or more variables. If there is a relationship, correlation analysis also demonstrates the intensity and direction of the relationship. Calculated over the correlation coefficient which ranges $-1 < r < +1$, the relationship gets weaker as the correlation coefficient approaches 0 while the opposite holds true when the coefficient is closer to 1. The calculation is made using the formula provided below as indicated in (6), [47,48].

$$r = \frac{\sum xy - \frac{(\sum x)(\sum y)}{n}}{\sqrt{\left(\sum x^2 - \frac{(\sum x)^2}{n}\right)\left(\sum y^2 - \frac{(\sum y)^2}{n}\right)}} \tag{6}$$

The correlation analyses conducted in this study yielded which statements in the survey were correlated.

3   Experimental Results

The relationship based on demographic, sociological and psychological aspects and the risk society concept has been evaluated through the following analyses: the summary results of the questions in the survey (Frequency, Standard Descriptive (SD) and Mean (M)), reliability analysis (Cronbach alpha), ANOVA and t-test, the correlation analysis of some questions in the survey as well as the significance tests of questions in relation to all the questions in the demographic part (see Table 1).

Table 1 presents the breakdown for the selected questions of the survey based on the descriptive statistical analyses mentioned above. Statistical analyses of the results obtained from the survey responses yield certain differences based on different demographic characteristics. The following Subsects. 3.1 and 3.2 address research question 1 and 2 and Subsect. 3.3 provides the results as derived from the content analysis of the news items in answer to research question 3.

Table 1. The descriptive statistical details of the selected questions in the survey.

Descriptive statistics	M	SD	N
11. Individuals have an increasing level of welfare under the current economic circumstances	1.9	1.05	199
12. In recent years, individuals have felt insecure about the future due to economic uncertainty	4.4	0.90	199
13. Today being powerful means having a high level of income	3.7	1.07	199
14. It is mainly the governments' responsibility to manage economic problems	4.1	0.84	199
15. The rapid advancement of technology will lead to a substantial rise in unemployment	3.5	1.05	199
16. Risk is a negative concept	2.4	0.93	199
17. Risk is related to uncertainty and worry	3.1	1.10	199
18. I trust the economy news reported in the mass media (television, radio, newspaper, etc.)	2.1	0.90	198
19. I learn the details related to the threats and risks encountered currently (economic uncertainty, natural disasters, catastrophes, etc.) from mass media	3.6	0.96	199
22. Taking your financial situation into account, how uncertain do you feel?	3.8	1.01	199
23. Considering your financial situation, how much do you feel at risk?	3.7	0.90	199
24. How much do you worry about your current financial situation?	3.4	1.03	199
25. How often do you think about your financial situation?	3.8	0.85	199
26. Uncertainty keeps me from having a full life	3.8	1.12	199
27. Uncertainty stops me from having a firm opinion	3.8	1.02	199
28. When I am uncertain, I can't function very well	3.3	1.18	199
29. Uncertainty makes me vulnerable, unhappy and sad	3.6	1.17	199
30. I think it is unfair that other people seem sure about their future	3.4	1.18	198
31. Being uncertain means that I lack confidence	2.8	1.26	198

3.1   Statistical Analysis Results Based on the Sociological Aspects

Some of the significant findings based on different demographic characteristics obtained by the statistical analyses regarding the sociological aspects in the survey (questions 11–21) are as follows: No significant difference was identified related to the responses provided for the statements (11–19) based on gender. As for the age group, agreement with statement 11 among 17–25 had a higher mean (M = 2.02, SD = 1.046) compared to that of the individuals aged 46 and above (M = 1.54, SD = 0.905). This difference was found to be statistically significant with a relatively higher mean of the younger age group. There was a statistically significant difference across different age groups for statement 12, for which the agreement rates of the middle age and older age group indicated a higher mean score (M = 4.59, SD = 0.657; M = 4.81, SD = 0.402, respectively) compared to that of the younger (M = 4.31, SD = 0.992), revealing the belief in insecurity due to economic uncertainty among older individuals. Likewise, a statistically higher level of agreement was observed among the older age group for statement 13. Younger age group rated higher significantly with respect to the agreement with statement 15 so technology and unemployment correlation is more prevalent among the young age group. Perceiving risk as a negative concept was also relatively higher among the young age group but relating risk to uncertainty and worry was statistically higher in older age group. Having trust in the economy news reported by mass media had a lower mean among the older age group. For the last question in the sociological part (not indicated in the table, numbered 20 in the survey), "Which of the following do you think best describes today's society?", the majority of the respondents (40%) selected the "risk society" option which was followed by "cosmopolitan society" (27.7%). The rates of "modern society", "post-modern society" and "industrial society" were found as 13.3 %, 9.7% and 8.2%, respectively. While 18.7% of the males described today's society as "modern society", this rate was 8.7% among females, demonstrating a significant difference between genders. The rates of the responses for other types of societies were at homogeneous levels. Depending on the age group, respondents in the young age range were more inclined to define today's society as "risk society" compared to the other age groups, which also revealed a statistically significant difference across the age groups. "Cosmopolitan society" was statistically higher among middle and older age groups. Based on the employment status, "risk society" was statistically higher among those who were not working (45.53%) compared to the employed respondents (30.6%). Yet, no significant difference was demonstrated depending on the income level or economic status. As for the correlation analysis of this part, the correlation analyses demonstrated that a moderate positive linear correlation (r = 0.527) existed between statements 16 and 17.

3.2   Statistical Analysis Results Based on the Psychological Aspects

Based on the analyses of the responses in this part, including pyschological components, certain observations that display significance with respect to demegrophic characteristics have been demonstrated. Starting with gender, it was revealed that males (M = 4.05, SD = 0.790) tend to think about their financial situation more frequently than females (M = 3.62, SD = 0.856). It was also observed that the mean scores related to items 22, 23, 24 and 25 of the older age group (those aged 46 and above) (M = 4.35, SD = 0.485; M = 4.12, SD = 0.516; M = 4, SD = 0.632; M = 4.27, SD = 0.452, respectively) were significantly higher than those of the younger group (M = 3.72, SD = 1.050; M = 3.60, SD = 0.906;

$M = 3.26$, $SD = 1.059$; $M = 3.78$, $SD = 0.901$, respectively). Additionally, the middle age group had higher mean scores for items 28 and 30. The mean scores of married individuals were observed to be higher than those who are not married for responses to Items 24, 25, 26 and 31. The mean scores related to items numbered 23, 24 and 25 were higher among employed individuals compared to those who are not employed. In addition, those who are not students had higher mean scores than the students for the items 23, 24, 26, 27 and 31. Another significant finding derived is that when compared with the respondents with a lower level of income, those with a higher income level stated they would feel vulnerable and unhappy due to uncertainty. Item 21 (not indicated in the table) in the survey posed the question: "Which of the following would an economic recession affect most?" The option "other" revealed the highest score (23.6%), followed by governments (23.1%), companies (19.1%), myself (18.6%) and the ones I love (15.6%). Respondents with an income level of TL 3000-7000 perceived the effects of an economic downturn more personally, stating they would themselves be affected most (42.3%) and those who described their economic status as "bad" also took the effects of economic recession more personally (50%) compared to those who described their economic status as "good" (14.8%). Another item not indicated in the table is the last question (numbered 32). "Which of the following condition(s) worry you most?" "Having a lower standard of living" was the option with the highest mean score (65.3%), followed closely by "having a hard time making ends meet" (63.8%). "Being unable to find a job in the future" had a mean score of 51.3% and "being an embarrassment to my family" had 48.7%. The significance tests based on the gender aspect reveal that males (59.8%) are more concerned with being an embarrassment to their families compared to females (39.6%), which is statistically significant. As the most worrying condition, "having a lower standard of living" and "losing my job" were found to be higher among the employed individuals. "Losing my job" was also found to be higher among the ones with a high level of income (50%) compared to individuals with a lower income level (42.3% with income ranging from TL 3000-7000 and 21.4% with income of TL 3000 and less). "Being unable to find a job in the future" was also very high at 83.3% among those who described their economic status as "bad", indicating a prevailing future uncertainty parallel to having a poor economic condition. The correlation analyses for this part showed that a moderate positive linear correlation existed between the following statements: 22 and 24 ($r = 0.530$); 23 and 24 ($r = 0.661$); 26 and 27 ($r = 0.508$); 27 and 28 ($r = 631$) and 28 and 29 ($r = 0.507$). The highest correlation for the data in this study was obtained for the statements 24 and 25, namely worrying and thinking about financial situation.

3.3   Results Obtained from the Content Analysis of Economy News Items

The content analysis of the 25 economy news around the world covered by the *Guardian* focused on the following questions: "1) Is there an element of concern and/or uncertainty?", 2) "Is the tone of the news item optimistic or pessimistic?", 3) "Is there a negative orientation with respect to reducing or eliminating the uncertainty?", 4) "Is there a positive orientation and guidance with respect to reducing or eliminating the uncertainty?", 5) "Are the effects of abruptly emerging global threats on markets included in the economy news item?.," 6) "Are the effects of abruptly emerging global threats on individuals included in the economy news item?" Based on these, the statistical analyses revealed that concern and uncertainty prevailed in the majority of the news items (n = 22, 88%); 16 news items had pessimistic tone while 8 were neutral, and only one was optimistic. Negative orientation was existent in 15 of the news items (60%) while positive orientation in 16, corresponding to 64%. Related to the fifth question, the majority of the news items (60%) covered the effects of abruptly emerging global threats on the markets.

Figure 1 provides the analyses for the aforementioned sixth question with the statistical breakdown of the effects of global threats on individuals as sorted by theme (Fig. 1 (a)) and the frequency of those effects depicted as histogram (Fig. 1 (b)). As Fig. 1 shows, societal problems (45%) have the highest coverage, followed by environmental factors, political unrest, epidemic, wars and technological advances. It should, however, be noted that coronavirus outbreak at the time of the analysis had just emerged in Wuhan, China and COVID-19 was declared a global pandemic by the World Health Organization (WHO) on March 11, 2020, which does not cover the period of the news items' retrieval for the present study. Needless to say, the global and regional landscape as well as the news agenda have changed tremendously after the unprecedented spread of the virus.

4   Discussion and Conclusion

Risk concept has the potential of influencing the perceptions, attitudes, and hopes of individuals as well as responses of the society at emotional, behavioural and cognitive levels. Including the sociological and psychological aspects in the survey items can be considered as one novelty of the study. During the times of economic problems, people naturally are uncertain, fearful and worried about how they will be affected. Based on this premise, one of the principal aims of this study has been to relate the risk concept to economic uncertainty, and thus add further clarity to the subject matter. This section relates the findings of the research results to certain aspects and parameters of risk society theory along with some of its relevant repercussions as per the news items.

The key experimental results based on the survey results assessed by statistical methods demonstrate the predominance of the risk society perception among individuals (n = 78), with the second most common answer being cosmopolitan society (n = 54). Both of these perceptions are also included in the risk society hypothesis so this question yielded parallel results with the postulations of the risk society theory. Post-modern society was also among the choices, yet, only 19 respondents opted for that, which is also parallel with the view of Beck who refused the post-modernist approach because it involves a gap between the past

	Theme	Count	Column N (%)
The effects of abruptly emerging global threats on individuals	Societal problems (discrimination, income gap, decrease in demand, exploitaion of labour, loss of employment)	9	45
	Environmental factors	6	30
	Political unrest (disputes between leaders, commercial problems)	4	20
	Epidemic (virus threat)	4	20
	War (its effects such as flow of refugees, conflict, civil war, terror, etc.)	2	10
	Technologial advances	1	5
	Total	20	100

(a) Statistical breakdown of the effects of global threats on individuals by theme

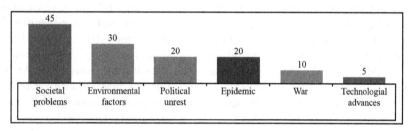

(b) Frequency of the effects of global threats on individuals by theme

Fig. 1. The effects of abruptly emerging global threats on individuals as covered in the news reports analysed (a) Statistical breakdown of the effects of global threats on individuals by theme (b) Frequency of the effects of global threats on individuals by theme.

and today [50]. In the late-modernity, individuals have become more aware of risks, complexity, uncertainty and lack of trust [51]. Parallel to this observation, trust in media was observed to be low as a result of the analyses, which ties well with the risk society hypothesis. No respondent totally agreed with the statement 18. On the contrary, 57 of them totally disagreed and 74 disagreed. Likewise, this concern was mentioned in one news item analysed about Eastern Europe which stated that confidence in the reliability of information provided by mainstream media was low [52]. One finding that did not find resonance with the risk society theory was the relationship between being powerful and having a high level of income. Majority of the respondents agreed with this statement. Yet, as Beck posited, in the second modernity, the way of handling risks is more important than the distribution of power and wealth [4]. Another finding worthy of being discussed is the correlation between having a higher income and feeling unhappy due to uncertainty. This finding is in accordance with the risk society thesis, which is also put forth by Luhmann as "the wealthy have more to lose, the poor starve more often" [7,50]. This analysis is also supported by the question about what worries respondents most. The ones who have the highest income level gave the answer of having a lower standard of living (88.9%). Another worrying situation was "being an embarrassment to my family", which was higher among men (males 55% and female 42%) which could be explained by cultural expectations and the gender role assigned to the male. This also reveals culture and context as two parameters to be considered while theorising on risk society. About the connotation of risk, a higher number of respondents (105) disagreed with the statement "risk is a negative concept". This finding is also in accordance with the risk society arguments put forth by Giddens who made a distinction between positive and negative risks. Risk can be considered an opportunity that can motivate an individual [50]. On the other hand, for Beck, risk is parallel with danger, associated with potential harm [7]. As for the technology and unemployment correlation, it was observed that agreement with this statement was more prevalent among the young age group. This is also in congruence with the risk society theory in which the threats are not only related to environment and health risks but to shifting employment patterns and job insecurity [53]. The repercussion of this situation was covered in the news items analysed which mentioned the advances in AI would affect some sectors negatively [54] and the need to address rapid technological change during faltering growth [55]. Another salient parameter of the risk society, as Beck puts, is that modernization risks emerge in geographically specific areas and universally; moreover, their effects may be unpredictably deleterious [3]. The change in the temporal, spatial and demographic distribution of risk brings about a new category of borderless risks [7]. This consequence is expressed saliently, as analogous to Beck's argument, in one of the news about climate change [56].

As the coronavirus pandemic has conspicuously demonstrated, everyone, regardless of location, race or socioeconomic status, is vulnerable to risk. This situation has also evoked the elusiveness of the risk concept, as noted in the introduction, and succinctly expressed by Beck as: "where everything turns into a hazard, somehow nothing is dangerous anymore [7]". Thus, risk society is not only identified by uncertainty regarding the severity and reality of risk, but also by its elusive nature [7]. The prime feature of the global order is the management of risk [39]. Under such circumstances, global risk may have its hidden emancipatory side effects since modern catastrophes are likely to result in constructive changes in the way of organising lives and societies [57]. Along with this positive note on global risk, it is obvious that risk and uncertainty discourse will remain to be prevalent as the nature of risks is constantly evolving. Accordingly, revisiting the risk society as well as reflecting upon its projective themes in different contexts can provide new insights for future works and open up "new sociological imagination" as humanity is ubiquitously surrounded and tested by complex contemporary risks. Taken together, utilising intelligent systems and AI will enable management and communication of risk more efficient, which will in turn alleviate uncertainty, rendering individuals and societies self-organising.

Acknowledgement. The author would like to express deep gratitude to Assist. Prof. Dr. Yeliz Karaca for her constant encouragement, her academic support and guidance. The author would also like to thank Dr. Aziz Dursun for his heartening support.

Data Availability. The survey questions and responses are available at: https:// docs.google.com/forms/d/17sOFZwH_KcqCSXjqwsD0FjF7ak1EwLSOaES6_a8z_Fg/ edit. The detailed results of the statistical analyses and headlines of the news items analysed are also included within the same link and can be retrieved upon request.

References

1. Fehr, L., Russell, J.A.: Concept of emotion viewed from a prototype perspective. J. Exp. Psychol. Gen. **113**, 464–486 (1984)
2. Boudia, S., Jas, N.: Introduction: risk and risk society in historical perspective. Hist. Technol. **23**(4), 317–331 (2007)
3. Beck, U.: Risk Society: Towards a New Modernity. Sage, Thousand Oaks (1992)
4. Wimmer, J., Quandt, T.: Living in the risk society: an interview with Ulrich Beck. Journal. Stud. **7**(2), 336–347 (2006)
5. Beck, U.: The cosmopolitan perspective: sociology of the second age of modernity. Br. J. Sociol. **51**(1), 79–105 (2000)
6. Adam, B., Allan, S., Carter, C. (eds.): Environmental Risks and the Media. Routledge, London (2013)
7. Ekberg, M.: The parameters of the risk society: a review and exploration. Curr. Sociol. **55**(3), 343–366 (2007)
8. Bosco, E., Di Giulio, G.M.: Ulrich Beck: considerations on his contributions and challenges to the studies in environment and society. Ambiente Soc. **18**(2), 145–156 (2015)
9. Jarvis, D.S.: Risk, globalisation and the state: a critical appraisal of Ulrich Beck and the world risk society thesis. Glob. Soc. **21**(1), 23–46 (2007)
10. Burgess, A., Wardman, J., Mythen, G.: Considering risk: placing the work of Ulrich Beck in context (2018)
11. Kocak, H., Memiş, K.: Ulrich Beck'in Risk Toplum Teorisi Bağlamında Güvenlik ve Özgürlük İkilemi. Afyon Kocatepe Üniversitesi Sosyal Bilimler Dergisi **19**(2), 251–265 (2017)
12. Cuhaci, A.: Ulrich Beck'in Risk Toplumu Kuramı. İstanbul Üniversitesi Sosyoloji Dergisi **3**(14), 129–157 (2007)
13. Esgin, A.: İmal Edilmiş Belirsizlikler Çağının Sosyolojik Yönelimi: Ulrich Beck ve Anthony Giddens Kaynaklı "Risk Toplumu" Tartışmalar. Gaziantep Univ. J. Soc. Sci. **12**(3) (2013)
14. Mythen, G.: Reappraising the risk society thesis: telescopic sight or myopic vision? Curr. Sociol. **55**(6), 793–813 (2007)
15. Mythen, G.: The critical theory of world risk society: a retrospective analysis, risk analysis (2018)
16. Lidskog, R., Sundqvist, G.: Sociology of risk. In: Roeser, S., Hillerbrand, R., Sandin, P., Peterson, M. (eds.) Handbook of Risk Theory, pp. 1001–1027. Springer, Dordrecht (2012). https://doi.org/10.1007/978-94-007-1433-5_40
17. Holford, W.D.: Risk, knowledge and contradiction: an alternative and transdisciplinary view as to how risk is induced. Futures **41**(7), 455–467 (2009)

18. Jones, M.: Anxiety and containment in the risk society: theorising young people and drug prevention policy. Int. J. Drug Policy **15**(5–6), 367–376 (2004)
19. Blok, A., Selchow, S.: Risk society. In: The Wiley-Blackwell Encyclopedia of Social Theory, pp. 1–9 (2017)
20. Bhadra, S.: Cloud computing in the risk society: its issues and hazards. Int. J. Adv. Res. Comput. Eng. Technol. (IJARCET) **8**(11), 446–451 (2019)
21. Ding, F., Ge, Q., Jiang, D., Fu, J., Hao, M.: Understanding the dynamics of terrorism events with multiple-discipline datasets and machine learning approach. PLoS ONE **12**(6), e0179057 (2017)
22. Arrieta, A.B., et al.: Explainable artificial intelligence (XAI): concepts, taxonomies, opportunities and challenges toward responsible AI. Inf. Fusion **58**, 82–115 (2020)
23. Tavana, M., Abtahi, A.R., Di Caprio, D., Poortarigh, M.: An artificial neural network and Bayesian network model for liquidity risk assessment in banking. Neurocomputing **275**, 2525–2554 (2018)
24. Chandrinos, S.K., Sakkas, G., Lagaros, N.D.: AIRMS: a risk management tool using machine learning. Expert Syst. Appl. **105**, 34–48 (2018)
25. Leung, A.K.Y., Koh, K., Tam, K.P.: Being environmentally responsible: cosmopolitan orientation predicts pro-environmental behaviors. J. Environ. Psychol. **43**, 79–94 (2015)
26. Wolski, R.: Risk and return in the real estate, bond and stock markets. Real Estate Manag. Valuat. **25**(3), 15–22 (2017)
27. Merkova, M., Drabek, J.: Use of risk analysis in investment measurement and management. Procedia Econ. Finance **34**, 656–662 (2015)
28. Vidivelli, K.J.D.B., Surjith, E.G.: Risk assessment and management in construction projects. Int. J. Sci. Eng. Res. **5**(8), 387–396 (2014)
29. Bayaga, A., Mtose, X.: Quantitative risk analysis: determining university risk mitigation and control mechanisms. J. Int. Soc. Res. **3**, 55–68 (2010)
30. Wang, Q., Mei, Q., Liu, S., Zhou, Q., Zhang, J.: Demographic differences in safety proactivity behaviors and safety management in Chinese small-scale enterprises. Saf. Sci. **120**, 179–184 (2019)
31. Besikci, E.B.: Strategic leadership styles on maritime safety. Ocean Eng. **185**, 1–11 (2019)
32. Ryan, T.: Perceived risks associated with mental illness: beyond homicide and suicide. Soc. Sci. Med. **46**(2), 287–297 (1998)
33. Austen, L.: The social construction of risk by young people. Health Risk Soc. **11**(5), 451–470 (2009)
34. Zinn, J.O.: Social Contexts and Responses to Risk Network (SCARR) (2004)
35. Cottle, S.: Ulrich beck, risk society and the media: a catastrophic view? Eur. J. Commun. **13**(1), 5–32 (1998)
36. Kitzinger, J.: Researching risk and the media. Health Risk Soc. **1**(1), 55–69 (1999)
37. Capurro, G.: Superbugs in the risk society: assessing the reflexive function of North American newspaper coverage of antimicrobial resistance. SAGE Open **10**(1), 1–13 (2020)
38. Tutar, C.: Risk Toplumu Söylemlerinin Televizyon Reality Programlarında Temsili. Üsküdar Üniversitesi İletişim Fakültesi Akademik Dergisi Etkileşim (4), 88–115 (2019)
39. Giddens, A.: The Consequences of Modernity. Polity Press, Cambridge (1990)
40. Busco, C.: Giddens' structuration theory and its implications for management accounting research. J. Manag. Gov. **13**(3), 249–260 (2009)

41. Marjanovic, Z., Greenglass, E.R., Fiksenbaum, L., Bell, C.M.: Psychometric evaluation of the Financial Threat Scale (FTS) in the context of the great recession. J. Econ. Psychol. **36**, 1–10 (2013)
42. Carleton, R.N., Norton, P.J., Asmundson, G.J.G.: Fearing the unknown: a short version of the intolerance of uncertainty scale. J. Anxiety Disord. **21**, 105–117 (2007)
43. Sperling, W., Bleich, S., Reulbach, U.: Black Monday on stock markets throughout the world-a new phenomenon of collective panic disorder? A psychiatric approach. Med. Hypotheses **71**(6), 972–974 (2008)
44. IBM SPSS Statistics for Windows, Version 23.0, IBM Corp., Armonk, NY, USA (2015)
45. Smalheiser, N.: Data Literacy: How to Make Your Experiments Robust and Reproducible. Academic Press, Amsterdam (2017)
46. Sinharay, S.: An overview of statistics in education (2010)
47. Starnes, D.S., Yates, D., Moore, D.S.: The Practice of Statistics. Macmillan, New York (2010)
48. Wackerly, D., Mendenhall, W., Scheaffer, R.L.: Mathematical Statistics with Applications. Cengage Learning, Boston (2014)
49. Kim, T.K.: T test as a parametric statistic. Korean J. Anesthesiol. **68**(6), 540 (2015)
50. Luhmann, N.: Risk: A Sociological Theory. Aldine de Gruyter, New York (1993)
51. Simonneaux, L., Simonneaux, J.: STEPWISE as a vehicle for scientific and political *Educaction*? In: Bencze, L. (ed.) Science and Technology Education Promoting Wellbeing for Individuals, Societies and Environments. CSSE, vol. 14, pp. 565–587. Springer, Cham (2017). https://doi.org/10.1007/978-3-319-55505-8_27
52. John, H.: Poll reveals majority of eastern Europeans fearful for democracy. The Guardian (2019)
53. Giddens, A, Griffiths, S.: Sociology. Polity Press, Cambridge (2006)
54. Benanav, A.: Automation isn't wiping out jobs, it's that our engine of growth is winding down. The Guardian (2020)
55. Larry, E.: Global economy must be ready for downturn, says new IMF boss. The Guardian (2019)
56. Phillip, I.: IMF: climate crisis threatens global economic recovery. The Guardian (2020)
57. Lombardo, C., Sabetta, L.: Sustainability through unsustainability? Unintended consequences and emancipatory catastrophism. In: Nocenzi, M., Sannella, A. (eds.) Perspectives for a New Social Theory of Sustainability, pp. 103–113. Springer, Cham (2020). https://doi.org/10.1007/978-3-030-33173-3_9

Theory, Analyses and Predictions of Multifractal Formalism and Multifractal Modelling for Stroke Subtypes' Classification

Yeliz Karaca[1(✉)], Dumitru Baleanu[2,3], Majaz Moonis[1], and Yu-Dong Zhang[4]

[1] University of Massachusetts Medical School, Worcester, MA 01655, USA
yeliz.karaca@ieee.org, Majaz.Moonis@umassmemorial.org
[2] Department of Mathematics, Çankaya University, 1406530 Ankara, Turkey
dumitru@cankaya.edu.tr
[3] Institute of Space Sciences, Magurele, Bucharest, Romania
[4] Department of Informatics, University of Leicester, Leicester LE1 7RH, UK
yudongzhang@ieee.org

Abstract. Fractal and multifractal analysis interplay within complementary methodology is of pivotal importance in ubiquitously natural and man-made systems. Since the brain as a complex system operates on multitude of scales, the characterization of its dynamics through detection of self-similarity and regularity presents certain challenges. One framework to dig into complex dynamics and structure is to use intricate properties of multifractals. Morphological and functional points of view guide the analysis of the central nervous system (CNS). The former focuses on the fractal and self-similar geometry at various levels of analysis ranging from one single cell to complicated networks of cells. The latter point of view is defined by a hierarchical organization where self-similar elements are embedded within one another. Stroke is a CNS disorder that occurs via a complex network of vessels and arteries. Considering this profound complexity, the principal aim of this study is to develop a complementary methodology to enable the detection of subtle details concerning stroke which may easily be overlooked during the regular treatment procedures. In the proposed method of our study, multifractal regularization method has been employed for singularity analysis to extract the hidden patterns in stroke dataset with two different approaches. As the first approach, decision tree, Naïve bayes, kNN and MLP algorithms were applied to the stroke dataset. The second approach is made up of two stages: i) multifractal regularization (kulback normalization) method was applied to the stroke dataset and mFr_stroke dataset was generated. ii) the four algorithms stated above were applied to the mFr_stroke dataset. When we compared the experimental results obtained from the stroke dataset and mFr_stroke dataset based on accuracy (specificity, sensitivity, precision, F1-score and Matthews Correlation Coefficient), it was revealed that mFr_stroke dataset achieved higher accuracy rates. Our novel proposed approach can serve for the understanding and taking under control the transient features of stroke.

© Springer Nature Switzerland AG 2020
O. Gervasi et al. (Eds.): ICCSA 2020, LNCS 12250, pp. 410–425, 2020.
https://doi.org/10.1007/978-3-030-58802-1_30

Notably, the study has revealed the reliability, applicability and high accuracy via the methods proposed. Thus, the integrated method has revealed the significance of fractal patterns and accurate prediction of diseases in diagnostic and other critical-decision making processes in related fields.

Keywords: Multifractal Formalism · Fractional brownian motion · Hurst exponent · Fractal pattern · Self-similar process · Stroke · Prediction algorithms · Naïve Bayes algorithm, kNN algorithm, Multilayer Perceptron Algorithm, Multifractal regularization

1   Introduction

Do fractals exhibit ubiquitous patterns? Fractal is the common term for the complex geometric shapes in mathematics that are self-similar with bizarre fragmented patterns. There are key features of fractals, the first is self-similarity, having an iterative nature and level of irregularity and fragmented dimension [1,2]. Fractals are utilized for measuring peculiar phenomena which are challenging to describe objects inclined to repeat themselves on varying scales or which display self-similarity. As fractal analysis is an essential way of measuring various phenomena, it is applied to multiple fields such as economy [3–5], geology [6], space science [7], materials technology [8], epidemiology[9], signal processing (EEG/ECG) [10], diagnostic imaging [11] and brain structure [12–14]. Taking these features into consideration, fractals are ubiquitous in the world, from natural objects to the universal structures, from smallest items to largest scales, including the brain as the most complex organ. For a thorough understanding of the brain and its dynamics, quantification is required since the brain operates on more than one scale and fractal geometry comes to play to address the related challenges.

Stroke is a major CNS disorder leading to death following cancer and cardiovascular disorders, ranking 5th among death causes in the USA. Stroke occurs within a complex network of vessels and arteries [16]. Characterized by a sudden interruption in the blood supply of the brain, strokes are mostly are caused by an immediate blockage of arteries leading to the brain or bleeding into brain tissue. Strokes can display varying symptoms, so they can be difficult to diagnose. In this study, four subtypes of stroke have been handled, which are Large vessel, Small vessel, Cardioenbolic and Cryptogenic (for further details on the subtypes see [12,16]).

When the studies in which fractal and multifractal methods are used for stroke disease are investigated, it is seen many studies yield efficient outcomes exist. The study by [17] is on acute ischemic stroke, revealing an association between decreased fractal dimension of heart rate variability as well as recurrent ischemic stroke following acute ischemic stroke. Their study highlights the importance of the predictive value of fractal dimension. Another study is by [18] and the results yield the importance of fractal parameters of plaque for deter-mining its severity to facilitate diagnostic processes. The comprehensive review study of [19] provides a sketch of related studies on fractals, neurodegeneration and stroke.

Considering the studies on fractal and multifractal analyses, there exists a large body of applications in the literature. To start with medicine, the study by [20] is concerned with retinal vascular fractal dimension in bipolar disorder and schizophrenia by box-counting method utilizing automated algorithm. [21] developed a new methodology for automated differential diagnosis of Alzheimer's using EEG signals with an investigation of three measures of fractality. Besides applications of fractals in medicine, there are studies in other fields. To illustrate, the study by [22] proposed a model for predicting fractal dimensions at differ-ent heights of mining. The authors' model based on the fractal theory achieved appropriate estimation of the position of high-level boreholes. The study by [23] on surface profile reveals that the estimated fractal dimension increased with the sampling length. Another study on reservoirs [24] utilized fractal geometry to develop new models for complex-structured reservoirs by various mathemat-ical dimension types and to develop instantaneous source function via fractal geometry. Additionally, recent works focus on fractal use in different fields, for example, sign language. The study by [25] is on the fractal analysis of a Czech sign language text on three levels of scaling, considering the sign language in terms of fractal dimensions and Hurst exponents.

Precision in forecasting plays a critical role in medicine for patients' survival and life quality. The study by [26] reveals that computer-aided systems with Arti-ficial Intelligence and advanced signal processing techniques can assist physicians with their analyses and interpretation physiological signals and images effec-tively. The study by [27] addresses the timely prediction of stroke by Principal component analysis (PCA). Another study by [28] on pneumonia investigates post-stroke pneumonia prediction models with the utilization of more cutting-edge machine learning algorithms. Their predictive model is found out to be fea-sible for the management of stroke, achieving optimal performance when com-pared with traditional machine learning methods. The study by [29] provides the evaluation of machine learning outcome prediction for stroke. The study results demonstrate that machine learning techniques on extensive datasets were able to predict the functional stroke outcome. Regarding the use of ensem-ble methods, the study by [30] deals with multiple classification algorithms for stroke data prediction. The experimental results revealed that with the classifier Ensemble, higher prediction accuracy was achieved. The study by [14] provides efficient clustering algorithms' application with 2D multifractal denoising tech-niques (Bayesian (mBd), Nonlinear (mNold) as well as Pumping (mPumpD)). The results of the study revealed that 2D mBd technique was the most efficient feature descriptor in terms of accuracy for each subtype of stroke. Concerning the mobile application for stroke dataset, the study of [15] designed a mobile and server application for two stroke subtypes. In their proposed model, they used Multilayer Perceptron Algorithm (MLP), which produced an efficient and informative services framework for stroke determination and management.

Since brain and related diseases present challenges, it is important to generate optimal and reliable methods. Earlier works [17–30] in the literature include classification with machine learning methods; yet, no work exists in the literature in which a multifractal method and comparative analysis methods (decision tree, Naïve bayes, kNN and MLP) have been applied to such an extensive stroke dataset. Both in terms of the dataset studied and the method employed, this study is the first one of its kind for the classification of four stroke subtypes, which are Large vessel, Small vessel, Cardioenbolic and Cryptogenic. Within this framework, the main aim of our study is to develop a balancing methodology for the detection of subtle details of stroke. For this purpose, multifractal regularization was utilized for singularity analysis to extract the hidden patterns in stroke dataset by two different approaches. While the first approach includes the application of decision tree, Naïve bayes, kNN and MLP algorithms to the stroke dataset, the second approach has two stages in itself: firstly, multifractal regularization (kulback normalization) was applied to the stroke dataset and mFr_stroke dataset was generated. Subsequently, the four algorithms stated above were applied to the mFr_stroke dataset.

The rest of the paper is organized as follows. Section 2 deals with the Materials and Methods of the study. Methods of our integrated approach are Multifractal Formalism and Multifractal Analysis, multifractal regularization (Kulback norm) technique in stroke dataset experiments and Prediction Models Using Algorithms: Decision Tree, Naïve Bayes, kNN and MLP. As the subsequent section, experimental results and discussion are provided along with the explanations. As the final section, namely Sect. 4, conclusion is presented.

2   Materials and Methods

2.1   Patient Details

For this study, 1926 individuals were kept under observation by Massachusetts Medical School, University of Worcester, Massachusetts, USA. Compared to the strokes in the nondominant hemisphere, the ischemic strokes in the dominant hemisphere bring about more functional deficits based on the assessment by the National Institutes of Health Stroke Scale (NIHSS).

The total number of ischemic stroke patients, included in our experiments, is 1926 patients (with males [labelled by (1)] and with females [labelled by (0)]). The age of the ischemic stroke patients range from 0 to 104, displaying seven ischemic stroke subtypes (Large vessel (481), Small vessel(228), Cardioenbolic(689), Cryptogenic (528)) as dealt with in this study (see Hindawi for age distribution details of stroke patients). In this study, demographic information, medical history, results of laboratory tests, treatments, and medications data, as can be seen in Table 1, pertaining to 1926 stroke subtypes patients. Table 2 provides the main headings of attributes used for the stroke subtypes.

Table 1. The stroke dataset with the features.

Number of stroke subtypes / TOAST	Main heading of attributes	Data size
Large vessel (481) Small vessel (228) Cardioembolic (689) Cryptogenic (528)	Demographic information (Age, gender) Medical history (HTN, hyperlip, DM, H/O stroke/TIA, AtrialFib, CAD, CHF, PAD/carotid disease, tobacco, ETOH) Results of laboratory test (mRS 90 days, hemorrhagic conversion, NIHSS admission, TPA) Treatment and medication data (Statin, antiHTN, antidiabetic, antiplatelet, anticoagulation, CT perfusion, neurointervantion)	1926×23

TOAST: type/etiology of stroke; TIA; ischemic attack: HTN: hypertension; DM: diabetes mellitus; CAD: coronary artery disease; AtrialFib: atrial fibrillation Stroke; CAD: coronary artery disease; CHF: congestive heart failure; PAD/carotid disease: peripheral arte disease; NIHSS 90 days: National Institutes of Health Stroke Scale 90-day mortality; CT perfusion: computer tomography perfusion, ETOH: alcohol; antiHTN: antihypertensive drugs after acute ischemic stroke; NIHSS discharge: National Institutes of Health Stroke Scale; H/O stroke/TIA: history of transient ischemic attack.

The details on the stroke dataset attributes as used in our study as well as the corresponding descriptions can be seen in [14,15].

2.2 Methods

The key aim of our study is to devise and develop a complementary methodology which could enable the detection of subtle details regarding stroke that may easily be disregarded or overlooked during the regular treatment procedures. Considering the profound complexity of brain, such cases are in question particularly in complex and dynamic structures such as in the case of stroke, which is a disease related to brain. In the proposed method of our study, multifractal regularization method has been employed for singularity analysis to extract the hidden patterns in stroke dataset with two different approaches whose steps are specified below:

(i) The first approach is made up of two stages: a) multifractal regularization (kulback normalization) method was applied to the stroke dataset (X) and mFr_stroke dataset ($\hat{X}$ was generated. b) the four algorithms stated in the first approach were applied to the mFr_stroke dataset.

(ii) As the second approach, decision tree, Naïve bayes, kNN and MLP algorithms were applied to the stroke dataset.

(iii) We compared the results obtained from the first and second approach regarding the stroke dataset and mFr_stroke dataset based on accuracy rate (specificity, sensitivity, precision, F1-score and Matthews Correlation Coefficient).

As a result of all these applications, it has been revealed that mFr_stroke dataset achieved higher accuracy rates for the identification of the subtypes of stroke. Our novel proposed approach can serve for the understanding and taking under control the transient features of stroke while managing the process efficiently.

All the analyses were computed and the figures of the analyses for the study were performed by Matlab [31] and FracLab [32].

Multifractal Formalism and Multifractal Analysis. Common in nature, multifractal systems are a generalisation of a fractal system where a single exponent like the fractal dimension would not prove to be adequate to describe its dynamics. Therefore, continuous spectra of exponents, namely singularity spectrum, would be required [33]. Multifractal analysis, which includes the distortion of datasets extracted from patterns, is employed to analyse datasets. In this way, multifractal spectra will be generated, presenting the way scaling changes over the dataset. Multifractal analysis techniques have various applications, particularly ones regarding prediction of natural phenomena and interpretation of medical images [34,35]. Besides these techniques, multifractal denoising is a regularization technique which places a local restriction on the reconstructed signal. Instead of requiring that the denoised signal pertains to global smoothness class, a regularized signal with prescribed Hölder exponent is to be sought.

Concerning this study, the enhancement or denoising of complex data, namely the stroke dataset, depends on the analysis of the local Hölder regularity. It is herein supposed that data enhancement is analogous to increasing the Hölder regularity at each point [36]. These methods are aligned well to the cases where sort of data is to be recovered are very irregular, for instance, not differentiable with local regularity varying quickly [14].

The most simplified concept of smoothness pertaining to a function is provided via the C^k differentiability. In this context, a bounded function f belonging to $C^1(R^d)$ provided that it has partial derivatives $\partial f/\partial x_i$ everywhere that display continuity and being bounded; while C^k differentiability concerning $k \geq 2$ is defined by the recursion: f belonging to $C^k(R^d)$ [11]. In this case, should it belong to $C^1(R^d)$ and all of its partial derivatives $\partial f/\partial x_i$ belong to $C^{k-1}(R^d)$, the provision of a definition will be for uniform smoothness (in case the regularity exponent k is an integer. Taylor's formula follows the definition of C^k differentiability, conveying that, for any $x_0 \in R^d, C > 0, \delta > 0$ exists and a polynomial P_{x_0} of degree is lower than k (see [37]). This C^k differentiability regarding the consequence is in the accurate form so that a definition of pointwise smoothness could be yielded, which could also be applicable for fractional orders of smoothness. This outcome was converted into a definition ensuing a usual process in mathematics [37].

Definition 2.1. $\alpha \geq 0$, and $x_0 \in R^d$ is a function and $f : R^d \to R$ is $C^\alpha(x_0)$ should there exist $C > 0$, $\delta > 0$ and a polynomial P_{x_0} of degree which is lower than α [37]:

$$if \, |x - x_0| \leq \delta, then \, |f(x) - P_{x_0}(x)| \leq C|x - x_0|^\alpha \tag{1}$$

The Hölder exponent of f at x_0 is $h_f(x_0) = \sup \{\alpha : f is C^\alpha(x_0)\}$ [37].

Among the most broadly employed notions of pointwise regularity, we see the Hölder regularity (see [37] for the step details).

As a last step, $B_r = \{x : |x - x_0| \leq r\}$. It could also be noted that the definition of pointwise Hölder regularity can be weakened, so in this way it is possible to notice that (1) can be reexpressed like this [37]:

$$\|f - P_{x_0}\|_{B_{r,\infty}} \leq Cr^\alpha$$

Through multifractal analysis, the distribution of pointwise regularities (or singularities) of irregular functions f on R^m can be described in a statistical and geometrical manner. The conventional concept of notion of pointwise regularity, as the most frequently employed one is the Hölder [12] (for further details on proceeding equations and theoretical aspects see the references ([13, 37–39]).

Jaffard and Mélot [40, 41] have verified the following: let Ω be a domain of R^m while y is located at the boundary $\partial\Omega$ of Ω, then through taking $P = 0$ or $P = 1$, the condition of $T^p_{\alpha/p}(y)$ pertaining to the characteristic function x_Ω shall concur with the weak α accessibility of Ω bilaterally at y. (assuming $\alpha \geq 0$). Ω is defined to be bilaterally weak accessible at y should there be the existence of two constants C as well as $0 < R < 1$, which is denoted as in (2):

$$\begin{aligned}
&\forall r \leq R \\
&\min\{meas\left(\Omega^c \cap B\left(y, r\right)\right), meas\left(\Omega \cap B\left(y, r\right)\right)\} \\
&\leq Cr^{\alpha+m},
\end{aligned} \tag{2}$$

Here, *meas* refers to the Lebesgue measure, which would enable the applicability of performing of a multifractal analysis regarding the fractal boundaries [42, 43]. Such an analysis also offers numerous applications in different areas including mechanics, physics or chemistry (biology, medicine and so on) in which a lot of occurrences encompass fractal interfaces [39] for further details on proceeding equations and theoretical aspects see the references ([14, 41] and [44–46]).

The multifractal analysis of a particular dataset entails the definition of a function, performing the computation of its multifractal spectrum as well as the classification of every point in line with the corresponding value of $(\beta, f_h(\alpha))$ geometrically. The α value provides local information concerning the pointwise regularity. The value of $f_h(\alpha)$ provides global information. In multifractal denoising, no assumption is made as to the noise structure or how the noise structure interacts with the veri. $s(x, y)$ represents the original signal, and $n(x, y)$ is the noise. $w(x, y)$ denotes the observed signal while $z(x, y)$ is the estimate of the signal, and (x, y) referring to the pixel location [47]. Based on the dataset in our study, a regularized version $z(x, y)$ of $w(x, y)$ fulfilled the following conditions [47].

(1) $z(x, y)$ has proximity with $w(x, y)$ in the multifractal regularization technique sense (Kullback Norm), which comes to mean that $\|z(x, y) - w(x, y)\|_L$, is minimum. Kullback Norm was applied in our study since and distance was minimized by utilising the Kullback norm. One advantage of this is that the calculations become simpler as an analytical minimization replaces the numerical one, which enables further generalizations to be made.

(2) $(\hat{X})$'s local Hölder function is specified.

$\alpha_z = \alpha_w + \delta$, in which $\alpha_z = \alpha_s$ denotes the estimated signal's Hölder regularity, δ refers to a positive function that is user-defined. Thus, the regularity of shall have a larger value than one of the observations everywhere. And, the estimation of the Hölder exponent is done based on a wavelet-based procedure [47]. In the current study, multifractal regularization (Kulback norm) technique was applied to stroke dataset (X). After the application of multifractal regularization to the stroke dataset, mFr_stroke dataset $(\hat{X})$ was generated as a result of regularity-based enhancement $(\hat{X})$ from multifractal regularization (Kullback norm) technique.

2.3 Prediction Models Using Algorithms: Decision Tree, Naïve Bayes, kNN and MLP

Prediction refers to making estimations regarding future relying on previous and current data. Risk and uncertainty are the key elements of prediction and estimation. Estimation refers to the process of finding an estimate in a setting in which the population parameter could be either unstable or uncertain. Accordingly, in our study, four different algorithms [48] (Decision tree algorithm, Naïve bayes algorithm, kNN algorithm and MLP algorithm) were applied for prediction modelling purposes in line with the proposed method for the stroke subtypes' classification. Multilayer perceptron (MLP) Multilayer perceptron (MLP) belongs to a class of feedforward artificial neural network (ANN). An MLP has minimum three layers of nodes, which are an input layer, a hidden layer as well as an output layer. Each node, except for the input, is a neuron which utilises an activation function that is non-linear. Each neuron in the network takes the arithmetic mean of the weight vectors terminated at it. After that, the outcome is transferred to all the neurons in the subsequent layer depending on the activation function used [15,47].

As for the learning technique, MLP employs a supervised learning technique which is referred to as backpropagation for the purposes of training ([47,48] MLP ile ilgili makale). As a superiority compared to a linear perceptron, the non-linear activation and multiple layers of MLP enable the distinguishing the data which are not separable.

The denotations used for the recursion of the weights based on the assumption that sigmoid activation function is used in between the layers are specified in 3. Let for each neuron in the output layer have a neuron output [15,48] and [49].

$$O_k = \frac{1}{1 + e^{-net_K}} \tag{3}$$

Here, O_k signifies the activation value of the output layer (as in 4) [15,48] and [49].

$$net_k = \sum W_{jk} O_j \tag{4}$$

The denotation of the activation values for the hidden layer is specified in 5 and 6.

$$O_j = \frac{1}{1 + e^{-net_j}} \tag{5}$$

$$net_j = \sum_i W_{ij} O_i \tag{6}$$

The recursion of the weights is realized as in 7.

$$W_{jk} = W_{jk} + \Delta W_{jk} \tag{7}$$

Here, ΔW_{jk} refers to the weight recursion value. In the backpropagation algorithm, the error criterion can be used, which is also known as mean square error (see [15,48] and [49] for further details concerning mean square error, dependency of the error on the weights and recursion).

3   Experimental Results and Discussion

The novel approach we proposed in our study serves for the understanding and taking under control the transient features of stroke which is a CNS disorder occurring through a complex network of vessels and arteries. Considering the fact that brain and related diseases pose challenges, generating optimal and reliable methods is of importance. To serve our purpose, have adopted two approaches. The first includes the application of decision tree, Naïve bayes, kNN and MLP algorithms to the stroke dataset. The second approach has two stages: i) multifractal regularization (kulback normalization) was applied to the stroke dataset (X) and mFr_stroke dataset $(\hat{X})$ was generated. ii) the four aforementioned algorithms were applied to the mFr_stroke dataset $(\hat{X})$. The accuracy rates, specificity, sensitivity, precision, F1-score and Matthews Correlation Coefficient were computed. Thus, predictions were performed for the classification of stroke subtypes. Accordingly, Table 2 provides the steps of our proposed integrated approach.

The procedural steps of the proposed approach of our study are specified below in their respective order:

Step 1: Multifractal regularization technique (Kulback normalization) was applied to the stroke dataset (X) and mFr_stroke dataset $(\hat{X})$ was generated: the Display of stroke dataset (X) and mFr_stroke dataset $(\hat{X})$ on Meshplots.

In this study, the stroke dataset has a dimension matrix of (1926×23) (see Table 1 for details) and to the stroke dataset (X), multifractal regularization (kulback normalization) was applied as a result of which mFr_stroke dataset $(\hat{X})$ was generated to detect self-similarity and regularity. Figure 1(a) provides the main attributes regarding the stroke dataset. After the multifractal regularization (Kulback normalization) technique was applied to the stroke dataset (X)

Table 2. The steps of the proposed integrated approach.

Step 1: Multifractal regularization (Kulback normalization) was applied to the stroke dataset (X) and mFr_stroke dataset $(\hat{X})$ was generated: the Display of stroke dataset (X) and mFr_stroke dataset $(\hat{X})$ on Meshplots.

Step 2: The Confusion Matrix Computations of Decision Tree, Naïve Bayes, kNN and MLP algorithms for the classification of stroke subtypes on stroke dataset (X) and mFr_stroke dataset $(\hat{X})$.

Step 3: The accuracy rate results based on decision tree, Naïve bayes, kNN and MLP algorithms for the classification of stroke subtypes on stroke dataset (X) and mFr_stroke dataset $(\hat{X})$

and mFr_stroke dataset $(\hat{X})$ was generated; and Fig. 1(b) presents the multifractal regularity that corresponds to all the attributes in the mFr_stroke dataset through the illustration of meshplots. As Fig. 1(b) depicts, the self-similar and regular patterns have been detected by multifractal regularization, and the theoretical spectrum with increments have been visually illustrated.

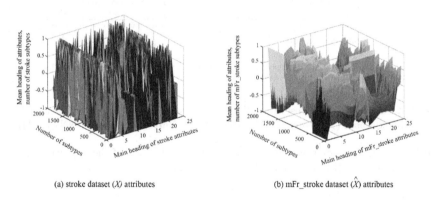

(a) stroke dataset (X) attributes   (b) mFr_stroke dataset $(\hat{X})$ attributes

Fig. 1. Display by Meshplot for (a) stroke dataset (X) attributes (b) mFr_stroke dataset $(\hat{X})$ attributes.

Step 2: The Confusion Matrix Computations of Decision Tree, Naïve Bayes, kNN and MLP algorithms for the classification of stroke subtypes on stroke dataset (X) and mFr_stroke dataset $(\hat{X})$.

In our study, confusion matrices were computed as a result of the application of the four algorithms for prediction purposes regarding the classification of stroke subtypes (see Fig. 2 and Fig. 3). Correspondingly, Fig. 2 provides the confusion matrix results for four algorithms and four stroke subtypes for the stroke dataset. Figure 3 presents the confusion matrix results for four algorithms and four stroke subtypes for the mFr_stroke dataset $(\hat{X})$.

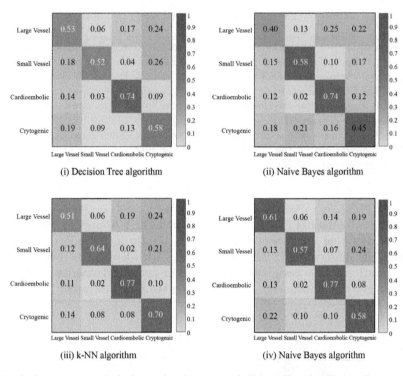

(i) Decision Tree algorithm   (ii) Naive Bayes algorithm

(iii) k-NN algorithm   (iv) Naive Bayes algorithm

(a) Confusion matrix results for four stroke subtypes in stroke dataset (X) with (i) Decision Tree (ii) Naive Bayes (iii) k-NN (iv) MLP

Fig. 2. Confusion matrix results for four stroke subtypes in stroke dataset (X) and mFr_stroke dataset ($\hat{X}$) using (i) Decision tree (ii) Naïve Bayes (iii) k-NN (iv) MLP.

Table 3. The accuracy rate results based on the application of the algorithms for (a) stroke dataset (X) (b) mFr_stroke dataset ($\hat{X}$).

(a) stroke dataset (X)						
Algorithms	Accuracy rate	Sensitivity	Specificity	Precision	False Positive Rate	F1- score	MCC
Decision Tree	0.616	0.561	0.868	0.593	0.131	0.592	0.461
Naïve Bayes	0.554	0.520	0.849	0.540	0.150	0.524	0.378
kNN	0.678	0.660	0.889	0.662	0.110	0.660	0.551
MLP	0.666	0.667	0.885	0.643	0.114	0.637	0.525
(b) mFr_stroke dataset ($\hat{X}$)						
Algorithms	Accuracy rate	Sensitivity	Specificity	Precision	False Positive Rate	F1- score	MCC
Decision Tree	0.860	0.850	0.952	0.846	0.047	0.848	0.801
Naïve Bayes	0.864	0.877	0.955	0.844	0.044	0.855	0.813
kNN	0.513	0.492	0.832	0.466	0.167	0.474	0.310
MLP	**0.886**	0.837	0.961	0.868	0.038	0.871	0.834

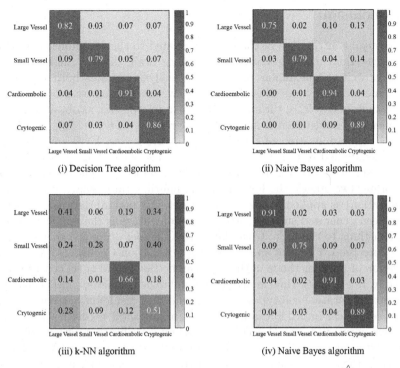

(i) Decision Tree algorithm

(ii) Naïve Bayes algorithm

(iii) k-NN algorithm

(iv) Naïve Bayes algorithm

(b) Confusion matrix results for four stroke subtypes in mFr_stroke dataset $(\hat{X})$ with

(i) Decision Tree (ii) Naïve Bayes (iii) kNN (iv) MLP

Fig. 3. (Figure 2. Cont.) Confusion matrix results for four stroke subtypes in stroke dataset (X) and mFr_stroke dataset $(\hat{X})$ using (i) Decision tree (ii) Naïve Bayes (iii) k-NN (iv) MLP.

Step 3: The accuracy rate results based on decision tree, Naïve bayes, kNN and MLP algorithms for the classification of stroke subtypes on stroke dataset (X) and mFr_stroke dataset $(\hat{X})$.

In this study, Decision tree, Naïve bayes, kNN and MLP algorithms were applied to the stroke dataset (X) and mFr_stroke dataset $(\hat{X})$ for the classification of stroke subtypes. Accordingly, Table 3 shows the accuracy rates (Error, Sensitivity, Specificity, Precision, False Positive Rate, F1-score and Matthews Correlation Coefficient (MCC)) of the aforementioned algorithms for four subtypes of stroke.

As Table 3 shows, the highest accuracy rate (0.886) has been obtained from the mFr_stroke dataset $(\hat{X})$ to which multifractal regularization method (Kullback norm) with the MLP algorithm. In addition, for Naïve Bayes and K-nn, the mFr_stroke dataset $(\hat{X})$ also yielded better results compared to those of stroke dataset (X). The experimental results of our study demonstrate the critical and determining role of multifractal regularization method (Kullback norm) in terms of accuracy based on classification performance.

4   Conclusion

The principal contribution of the study is related to the self-similarity and regularity detection in stroke dataset (X). Since brain displays highly complex, regular as well as self-similar patterns, its analysis requires both morphological and hierarchical views. Based on this view, the method we proposed in this study manifests novelties, through two different approaches, as obtained from the experimental results when compared with previous works [17, 30]. As the first approach, the application of decision tree, Naïve bayes, kNN and MLP algorithms was applied to the stroke dataset, which is one of the novelties in terms of the classification of extensive stroke subtypes dataset. b) The second approach incorporates two stages, the first one being multifractal regularization (kulback normalization) as applied to the stroke dataset (X), and mFr_stroke dataset $(\hat{X})$ having been generated subsequently. The second stage is the application of the four algorithms to the mFr_stroke dataset $(\hat{X})$ as per accuracy, specificity, sensitivity, precision, F1-score and Matthews Correlation Coefficient (MCC). The application of these methods in this way can be the second novel contribution of this study. It is the first time multifractal regularization method has been applied to the stroke dataset's subtypes. The experimental results of our study demonstrate the critical and determining role of multifractal regularization method (Kullback norm) in terms of accuracy based on classification performance since the highest accuracy rate was obtained from mFr_stroke dataset $(\hat{X})$. All things considered, the current study has demonstrated the reliability and applicability with the methods proposed and conducted. Thus, the integrated method utilized has revealed the significance of multifractal patterns and accurate prediction of diseases in diagnostic and other critical-decision making processes in related fields. Accordingly, the integrated approach of this study can serve a facilitating purpose to the physicians regarding the diagnostic and predictive processes for diseases such as stroke and other medical incidents that have to do with the complex dynamics and structures like that of brain.

References

1. Roca, J.L., Rodrıguez-Bermudez, G., Fernandez-Martinez, M.: Fractal-based techniques for physiological time series: an updated approach. Open Phys. **16**(1), 741–750 (2018)
2. Di Ieva, A.: The Fractal Geometry of the Brain, vol. 585. Springer, New York (2016)
3. Li, Z., Liu, Z., Khan, M.A.: Fractional investigation of bank data with fractal-fractional Caputo derivative. Chaos, Solitons Fractals **131**, 109528 (2020)
4. Karaca, Y., Zhang, Y.D., Muhammad, K.: Characterizing complexity and self-similarity based on fractal and entropy analyses for stock market forecast modelling. Expert Syst. Appl. **144**, 113098 (2020)
5. Karaca, Y., Cattani, C.: A comparison of two hölder regularity functions to forecast stock indices by ANN algorithms. In: Misra, S., et al. (eds.) ICCSA 2019. LNCS, vol. 11620, pp. 270–284. Springer, Cham (2019). https://doi.org/10.1007/978-3-030-24296-1_23

6. Dimri, V.P., Ganguli, S.S.: Fractal theory and its implication for acquisition, processing and interpretation (API) of geophysical investigation: a review. J. Geol. Soc. India **93**(2), 142–152 (2019)
7. Nottale, L.: Scale relativity and fractal space-time: theory and applications. Found. Sci. **15**(2), 101–152 (2010)
8. Petrica, V., Maricel, A.: On the transport phenomena in composite materials using the fractal space-time theory. Adv. Compos. Mater. Med. Nanotechnol. **477**, 477–494 (2011)
9. Meltzer, M.I.: The potential use of fractals in epidemiology. Prev. Vet. Med. **11**(3–4), 255–260 (1991)
10. Levy-Vehel, J.: Fractal approaches in signal processing. Fractals **3**(04), 755–775 (1995)
11. Albertovich, T.D., Aleksandrovna, R.I.: The fractal analysis of the images and signals in medical diagnostics. Fract. Anal. Appl. Health Sci. Soc. Sci. **26**, 57 (2017)
12. Karaca, Y., Cattani, C.: Clustering multiple sclerosis subgroups with multifractal methods and self-organizing map algorithm. Fractals **25**(04), 1740001 (2017)
13. Karaca, Y., Moonis, M., Baleanu, D.: Fractal and multifractional-based predictive optimization model for stroke subtypes' classification. Chaos, Solitons Fractals **136**, 109820 (2020)
14. Karaca, Y., Cattani, C., Moonis, M., Bayrak, Ş.: Stroke subtype clustering by multifractal Bayesian denoising with fuzzy C means and K-means algorithms. Complexity **2018**, 15 pages (2018). Article ID 9034647
15. Karaca, Y., Moonis, M., Zhang, Y.D., Gezgez, C.: Mobile cloud computing based stroke healthcare system. Int. J. Inf. Manag. **45**, 250–261 (2019)
16. Norrving, B.: Oxford Textbook of Stroke and Cerebrovascular Disease. Oxford University Press, Oxford (2014)
17. He, L., Wang, J., Zhang, L., Zhang, X., Dong, W., Yang, H.: Decreased fractal dimension of heart rate variability is associated with early neurological deterioration and recurrent ischemic stroke after acute ischemic stroke. J. Neurol. Sci. **396**, 42–47 (2019)
18. Smitha, B.: Fractal and multifractal analysis of atherosclerotic plaque in ultrasound images of the carotid artery. Chaos, Solitons Fractals **123**, 91–100 (2019)
19. Lemmens, S., Devulder, A., Van Keer, K., Bierkens, J., De Boever, P., Stalmans, I.: Systematic review on fractal dimension of the retinal vasculature in neurodegeneration and stroke: assessment of a potential biomarker. Front. Neurosci. **14**, 16 (2020)
20. Appaji, A., et al.: Retinal vascular fractal dimension in bipolar disorder and schizophrenia. J. Affect. Disord. **259**, 98–103 (2019)
21. Amezquita-Sanchez, J.P., Mammone, N., Morabito, F.C., Marino, S., Adeli, H.: A novel methodology for automated differential diagnosis of mild cognitive impairment and the Alzheimer's disease using EEG signals. J. Neurosci. Methods **322**, 88–95 (2019)
22. Zhao, P., Zhuo, R., Li, S., Lin, H., Shu, C.M., Laiwang, B., Suo, L.: Fractal characteristics of gas migration channels at different mining heights. Fuel **271**, 117479 (2020)
23. Zuo, X., Tang, X., Zhou, Y.: Influence of sampling length on estimated fractal dimension of surface profile. Chaos, Solitons Fractals **135**, 109755 (2020)
24. Razminia, K., Razminia, A., Shiryaev, V.I.: Application of fractal geometry to describe reservoirs with complex structures. Commun. Nonlinear Sci. Numer. Simul. **82**, 105068 (2020)

25. Andres, J., Langer, J., Matlach, V.: Fractal-based analysis of sign language. Commun. Nonlinear Sci. Numer. Simul. **84**, 105214 (2020)
26. Raghavendra, U., Acharya, U.R., Adeli, H.: Artificial intelligence techniques for automated diagnosis of neurological disorders. Eur. Neurol. **82**, 41–64 (2019)
27. Cheon, S., Kim, J., Lim, J.: The use of deep learning to predict stroke patient mortality. Int. J. Environ. Res. Public Health **16**(11), 1876 (2019)
28. Ge, Y., et al.: Predicting post-stroke pneumonia using deep neural network approaches. Int. J. Med. Inf. **132**, 103986 (2019)
29. Lin, C.H., et al.: Evaluation of machine learning methods to stroke outcome prediction using a nationwide disease registry. Comput. Methods Programs Biomed. **190**, 105381 (2020)
30. Arai, K., Bhatia, R., Kapoor, S. (eds.): CompCom 2019. AISC, vol. 997. Springer, Cham (2019). https://doi.org/10.1007/978-3-030-22871-2
31. The MathWorks. MATLAB (R2019b) The mathWorks, inc., Natick, MA (2019)
32. Vehel, L., FracLab (2019) project.inria.fr/fraclab/
33. Harte, D.: Multifractals. Chapman and Hall, London (2001)
34. Lopes, R., Betrouni, N.: Fractal and multifractal analysis: a review. Med. Image Anal. **13**(4), 634–649 (2009)
35. Moreno, P.A., et al.: The human genome: a multifractal analysis. BMC Genom. **12**, 506 (2011)
36. Barnsley, M.F.S., Saupe, D., Vrscay, E.R.: Signal enhancement based on hölder regularity analysis. IMA Vol. Math. Appl. **132**, 197–209 (2002)
37. Ben Slimane, M., Ben Omrane, I., Ben Abid, M., Halouani, B., Alshormani, F.: Directional multifractal analysis in the L^p setting. J. Funct. Spaces **2019**, 12 pages (2019). Article ID 1691903
38. Levy Vehel, J.: Signal enhancement based on Hölder regularity analysis. Inria technical report (1999)
39. Heurteaux, Y., Jaffard, S.: Multifractal analysis of images: new connexions between analysis and geometry. In: Byrnes, J. (ed.) Imaging for Detection and Identification, pp. 169–194. Springer, Dordrecht (2007). https://doi.org/10.1007/978-1-4020-5620-8_9
40. Jaffard, S.: Pointwise regularity criteria. C.R. Math. **339**(11), 757–762 (2004)
41. Jaffard, S. and Melot, C.: Wavelet analysis of fractal boundaries. Part 1: local exponents. Commun. Math. Phys. **258**(3), 513–539 (2005)
42. Ben Slimane, M. and Mélot, C.: Analysis of a fractal boundary: the graph of the knopp function. Abstract Appl. Anal. **2015** 14 (2015). Article number 587347
43. Shao, J., Buldyrev, S.V., Cohen, R., Kitsak, M., Havlin, S., Stanley, H.E.: Fractal boundaries of complex networks. EPL (Europhys. Lett.) **84**(4), 48004 (2008)
44. Lutton, E., Grenier, P., Vehel, J.L.: An interactive EA for multifractal Bayesian denoising. In: Rothlauf, F., et al. (eds.) EvoWorkshops 2005. LNCS, vol. 3449, pp. 274–283. Springer, Heidelberg (2005). https://doi.org/10.1007/978-3-540-32003-6_28
45. Donoho, D.L.: De-noising by soft-thresholding. IEEE Trans. Inf. Theory **41**(3), 613–627 (1994)
46. Mandelbrot, B.B., Van Ness, J.W.: Fractional Brownian motions, fractional noises and applications. SIAM Rev. **10**(4), 422–437 (1968)
47. Chen, Y.P., Chen, Y., Tong, L.: Sar Image Denoising Based on Multifractal and Regularity Analysis. In Key Engineering Materials. Trans Tech Publications Ltd. 500, 534–539 (2012)

48. Karaca, Y., Cattani, C.: Computational methods for data analysis. Walter de Gruyter GmbH, Berlin (2018)

49. Zhang, Y., Sun, Y., Phillips, P., Liu, G., Zhou, X., Wang, S.: A multilayer perceptron based smart pathological brain detection system by fractional Fourier entropy. J. Med. Syst. **40**(7), 173 (2016)

Multifractional Gaussian Process Based on Self-similarity Modelling for MS Subgroups' Clustering with Fuzzy C-Means

Yeliz Karaca[1](✉) and Dumitru Baleanu[2,3]

[1] University of Massachusetts Medical School, Worcester, MA 01655, USA
yeliz.karaca@ieee.org
[2] Department of Mathematics, Çankaya University, 1406530 Ankara, Turkey
dumitru@cankaya.edu.tr
[3] Institute of Space Sciences, Magurele, Bucharest, Romania

Abstract. Multifractal analysis is a beneficial way to systematically characterize the heterogeneous nature of both theoretical and experimental patterns of fractal. Multifractal analysis tackles the singularity structure of functions or signals locally and globally. While Hölder exponent at each point provides the local information, the global information is attained by characterization of the statistical or geometrical distribution of Hölder exponents occurring, referred to as multifractal spectrum. This analysis is time-saving while dealing with irregular signals; hence, such analysis is used extensively. Multiple Sclerosis (MS), is an auto-immune disease that is chronic and characterized by the damage to the Central Nervous System (CNS), is a neurological disorder exhibiting dissimilar and irregular attributes varying among patients. In our study, the MS dataset consists of the Expanded Disability Status Scale (EDSS) scores and Magnetic Resonance Imaging (MRI) (taken in different years) of patients diagnosed with MS subgroups (relapsing remitting MS (RRMS), secondary progressive MS (SPMS) and primary progressive MS (PPMS)) while healthy individuals constitute the control group. This study aims to identify similar attributes in homogeneous MS clusters and dissimilar attributes in different MS subgroup clusters. Thus, it has been aimed to demonstrate the applicability and accuracy of the proposed method based on such cluster formation. Within this framework, the approach we propose follows these steps for the classification of the MS dataset. Firstly, Multifractal denoising with Gaussian process is employed for identifying the critical and significant self-similar attributes through the removal of MS dataset noise, by which, mFd_MS dataset is generated. As another step, Fuzzy C-means algorithm is applied to the MS dataset for the classification purposes of both datasets. Based on the experimental results derived within the scheme of the applicable and efficient proposed method, it is shown that mFd_MS dataset yielded a higher accuracy rate since the critical and significant self-similar attributes were identified in the process. This study can provide future direction in different fields such as medicine, natural sciences and engineering as a result

© Springer Nature Switzerland AG 2020
O. Gervasi et al. (Eds.): ICCSA 2020, LNCS 12250, pp. 426–441, 2020.
https://doi.org/10.1007/978-3-030-58802-1_31

of the model proposed and the application of alternative mathematical models. As obtained based on the model, the experimental results of the study confirm the efficiency, reliability and applicability of the proposed method. Thus, it is hoped that the derived results based on the thorough analyses and algorithmic applications will be assisting in terms of guidance for the related studies in the future.

Keywords: Fractional Brownian Motion · Fractional Gaussian process · Hölder regularity · Multifractal analysis · MS · Fuzzy C-means · Classification · Discrete variations · Regularity · Self-similarity

1 Introduction

Multifractional Brownian Motion (mBm) is considered to be one of the stochastic multifractal models employed to analyse and extract dissimilar patterns, images and signals. Fractal Brownian Motion (fBm) provides attention-grabbing models with various related methods for a broad range of phenomena occurring in the natural world. Multifractal analysis tackles the singularity structure of functions or signals both locally and globally. While Hölder exponent at each point provides the local information, the global information is attained by a characterization of the statistical or geometrical distribution of the Hölder exponents occurring, which is referred to as multifractal spectrum. Introduced by Mandelbrot and Van Ness [1], it is a quintessential theoretical model for the Hurst effect [1,2]; and it is regarded as a powerful model in applied mathematics and other related disciplines such as medicine, biology, physics, financial mathematics, and so forth [3–10]. The reason why it is a powerful model for long-range dependent and short-range dependent complex phenomena in practice is due to its capability of detecting and estimating the highly irregular variations of Hölder regularity of generalized multifractional Brownian motion (GMBM) [11]. As a continuous Gaussian process, GMBM extends both the classical mBm and fBm [12]. Additionally, the analyses with these methods are practical and time-saving while dealing with highly irregular signals [13].

Over the last few years, advances in new technologies have provided different methods to characterize and identify the self-similar and complex patterns in natural phenomena and related problems thereof. Accuracy stands out in these processes particularly for critical decision making. Concerning the time-saving aspect and accuracy of the aforementioned methods, Karaca et al. provided a study on Hölder regularity functions (polynomial, periodic (sine), exponential) through the use of Self-Organizing Map (SOM) algorithm for MS clustering [6]. The study by Lahmiri [14] also points out the accuracy aspect of multifractal patterns of electroencephalographic (EEG) signals of patients with epilepsy and healthy individuals. The results of the study demonstrate that the generalized Hurst exponent (GHE) could be employed in an efficient way to make the distinguishing between healthy individuals and epileptic patients. A recent study by

Tafraouti et al. [15] yields an accuracy rate of 96% with their proposed classification approach with the emphasis on fractional Brownian motion (fBm) model that is capable of characterizing natural phenomena, which is crucial for actual clinical practice. The study by David et al. [16] showed the usefulness of the Hurst exponent and fractal dimension for the analysis of EEG signals' dynamics for epileptic patients and healthy individuals. The study of Rohini et al. [17] also found out that Hölder exponent, tangent slope as well as maximum Hölder exponent proved as the most significant methods for differentiating purposes, which is critical concerning the early stage diagnosis of Alzheimer's. Adapted to complex images, signals and other patterns, multifractal denoising methods are significant to extract irregular and hidden elements in complex systems, providing certain enhancements in the noisy data observed. When studies that address such phenomena in the real world are examined, Karaca et al.'s [18] study performed the application of Diffusion Limited Aggregation (DLA), as one of the multifractal denoising methods, on the patients' MRI images for identifying the self-similar and homogenous pixels. The classification for MS subgroups was conducted by ANN algorithms (CFBP and FFBP); and the critical significance of DLA for MS classification was demonstrated through that study [18].

Being an autoimmune neurological disease, Multiple sclerosis (MS) is characterized by a frequently progressive degeneration of the central nervous system (CNS). Inflammatory demyelination occurs in MS cases, which damages the axons and the neurocytes of those axons [19–21]. The onset of the disease is frequently seen in young adults and its prevalence ranges from 2 to 200 in 100,000 depending on the geographical attributes. It was introduced initially by Jean Martin Charcot in 1868 [22, 23]. The present study constitutes three different MS subgroups: RRMS, SPMS and PPMS [9, 24, 25]. Relapsing Remitting MS, the most common course in the disease, is accompanied by recurrent attacks with neurological deficits in various parts of the nervous system. They either resolve completely or nearly completely in a short time while leaving minor deficit. The second subgroup of MS is SPMS which follows an initial course of relapsing-remitting. Most patients in this group experience a progressive deterioration of neurological functions along with the accumulation of disability in time [9, 24, 25]. Finally, PPMS is a subgroup which is characterized by accumulation of disability, with worsening neurological functions, starting from the symptoms' occurrence [9, 24, 25]. There is no early relapse or remission in this subgroup.

Consisting of millions of cells, brain is an inherently complex system itself with its intricate dynamics. Unravelling the complex structure of brain and neural behaviour is critical for diagnostic processes and treatment success. At the same time, it is a challenge to understand how human diseases stem from internal neural irregularities [26]. Advances in artificial intelligence have started to address the challenges in medical settings with the functional computer programs developed which simulate expert human reasoning. Parallel to these developments, algorithms are extensively employed for clustering purposes. Fuzzy C-means (FCM) clustering algorithm is employed accordingly, and modified to do applications on the directional data with a number of advantages. The study by Das and Das [27] proves the advantage of FCM, proposing a fast and accurate segmentation approach for mammographic images with respect to cancer disease, with the use of the kernel based FCM. Their approach yielded the resolution of imprecise and uncertain characteristics in mammograms [27]. William et al.'s study on cervical cancer classification used an enhanced Fuzzy C-means algorithm and their results demonstrate that the method proposed was capable of outperforming many of the other current algorithms [28]. The study of Sheela and Suganthi is concerned with automatic brain tumor segmentation in MRI with the integration of Fuzzy C-means and Greedy Snake Model optimization. The results show that the method used outperformed the conventional segmentation methods concerning brain tumor [29]. Karaca et al. [7] worked on stroke clustering with the application of FCM and K-means algorithms based on multifractal Bayesian denoising and the results demonstrate the higher accuracy level derived by FCM. In the literature, many studies demonstrate accurate classification results for MS and subgroups thereof. Yet, there seems to be a shortage as regards studies that make use of integrated methods.

In this study, we worked on the MS dataset (139×228), based on the MRI and EDSS data belonging to a total of 139 individuals, 120 of whom were diagnosed with MS (76 RRMS, 38 SPMS, 6 PPMS) and 19 people are healthy individuals, constituting the control group. The first contribution of this study is that the dataset is more comprehensive, which is one of the novel aspects of this paper. In addition, even though earlier works [18–25] have been done on various kinds of analyses concerning MS dataset, no study has been reported thus far which relates attributes (MRI images and EDSS scores) by the use of Multifractal denoising method (L2-norm) with Fuzzy C-means algorithm applied for the purpose of clustering. Accordingly, the principal objective of this study is to identify the similar attributes in homogeneous MS clusters and the dissimilar attributes in the different clusters of MS subgroups. Therefore, the purpose has been to demonstrate the accuracy and applicability of the proposed method which is based on such clustering. For this aim, the approach we have proposed is made up of the following steps for the classification of the MS dataset: (i) Multifractal denoising with Gaussian process, one of the Multifractal denoising method, is used in the identification of critical and significant self-similar attributes by removing the noise of the MS dataset (139×228). As a result, mFd_MS dataset (139×228) was generated. (ii) Fuzzy C-means algorithm was applied to the MS dataset and the mFd_MS dataset for the clustering purpose of MS subgroups. The experimental results through the proposed method demonstrate that mFd_MS dataset yielded higher accuracy rates compared to MS dataset since significant, self-similar and regular attributes have been characterized. This shows that characterizing the significant attributes plays a critical role in MS subgroup clustering by multifractal denoising method. Comparing our study with the aforementioned studies [18–25] it is seen that the work has a broad and comparative nature, this is because the mFd_MS dataset as obtained from Multifractal denoising with Gaussian process has been the case in point with the Fuzzy C-means algorithm application for the first time in literature.

The paper is organized as follows: Sect. 2 deals with Materials with the Patient Details subsection; and Methods with the subsections of Fractional Brownian Motion and Extensions, Hölder Regularity Analysis, Multifractal Denoising method (L2-norm) and Fuzzy C-means algorithm. Section 3 presents the Experimental Results, to conclude, Sect. 4 provides the Conclusion and Discussion.

2   Materials and Methods

2.1   The Details of the Patient

In our study, patients (120) diagnosed with a clinical definite MS subgroup (RRMS, SPMS, PPMS) based on McDonald criteria [30] and control group with healthy individuals (19 persons) were followed at Hacettepe University, Faculty of Medicine Neurology and Radiology. The individuals' MRI [6,9,18,25,31] images and their EDSS scores [32] based on the years their MRI images were included in the MS dataset. The individuals are aged 18–65 years (see Table 1). The study has been ethically approved by Hacettepe University, Faculty of Medicine Neurology and Radiology and Hacettepe University Ethics Commission.

Table 1. Number and ages of individuals

Gender/Age	18–25	26–30	31–35	36–40	41–45	46–65
Female	10	22	17	16	9	14
Male	6	11	4	6	4	1

The MS dataset (139×228) is made up of the number of lesion diameters and EDSS scores obtained from the MRI images that belong to 120 MS patients (diagnosed with the subgroups of 76 RRMS, 38 SPMS, 6 PPMS) as well as 19 individuals who are healthy, making up the control group.

2.2   Methods

The MS dataset in our study is made up of the Expanded Disability Status Scale (EDSS) scores and Magnetic Resonance Imaging (MRI) (taken in different years) of patients diagnosed who were diagnosed with one of the MS subgroups, which are RRMS, SPMS and PPMS, while healthy individuals constitute the control group. Through this study, mainly two contributions have been provided. Initially, we proposed the use of Multifractal Denoising method (L2-norm) for identifying the critical and significant self-similar attributes. Another contribution is the application of Fuzzy C-means (FCM) algorithm for the clustering goal. As a result of this process, the similar attributes in homogeneous MS clusters and the dissimilar attributes in the different clusters of MS subgroups were classified. Our method is reliant on the steps stated as follows:

(i) Multifractal denoising with Gaussian process (L2-norm) was employed for identifying the self-similar and significant attributes. Consequently, mFd_MS dataset (139×228) was generated.

(ii) Fuzzy C-means algorithm was applied to the two datasets, which are MS dataset and the mFd_MS dataset for the clustering purpose of the MS subgroups.

(iii) Comparisons of clustering accuracy rates were performed for both datasets (MS dataset and mFd_MS dataset).

The experimental results through the proposed method illustrate that mFd_MS dataset yielded higher accuracy rates compared to MS dataset since significant, self-similar and regular attributes have been characterized. This shows that characterizing the significant attributes plays a critical role in MS subgroup clustering by Multifractal denoising with Gaussian process (L2-norm).

All the computations and related analyses were obtained by the Matlab R2019b [33] and FracLab [34].

Fractional Brownian Motion and Extensions. It is possible to model various phenomena that occur naturally in an effective way through the use of self-similar processes for which observations distant in terms of time or space have strong correlations. This situation indicates that a long-range dependence exists. Therefore, there have been successful uses of self-similar processes to model data that shows long-range dependence emerging in wide-ranging domains, which include but are not limited to medicine ([5–9,18,35]), biology ([36,37]) and economics ([5,38]). Long-memory's empirical presence of in these kinds of series is observed in a given local version of a power spectrum, acting as $|\lambda|^{1-2H}$, as $\lambda \to 0$, in which $H \in]1/2,1[$ refers to the long-memory parameter (see [39]) for a comprehensive monograph of self-similar and long-memory processes with a focus on their statistical and historical sides. There are simple models displaying a long-range dependence, so among them, the fractional Brownian motion (fBm) can be taken into consideration. It was introduced by Mandelbrot et al. in 1968 [1]. The process being null at the origin is defined for real $t \geq 0$ through stochastic integral (1).

$$
\begin{aligned}
&B_{H,C}(t) = CV_H^{1/2} \int_R f_t(s)dB(s) \ with \\
&f_t(s) = \tfrac{1}{\Gamma(H+1/2)}\{|t-s|^{H-\frac{1}{2}}1_{]-\infty,t]}(s) - |s|^{H-1/2}1_{]-\infty,0]}(s)\},
\end{aligned}
\tag{1}
$$

with $B_{H,C}(0) = 0$ and $V_H = \Gamma(2H+1)\sin(\pi H)$; Γ signifies the Gamma function, while B denotes a Brownian motion that is standard. The fractional Brownian motion of index $H(0 < H < 1)$ and scale parameter C, which is Gaussian process $\{B_{H,C}(t), t \geq 0\}$, based on which the mean is 0, along with self-similar and stationary increases as follows (2) [40]:

$$
E\left(\{B_{H,C}(t) - B_{H,C}(s)\}^2\right) = C^2|t-s|^{2H} \quad \forall s,t \in R^+.
\tag{2}
$$

The H index characterizes self-similar aspect of the relevant process [40]. For the estimation of H, variance, maximum likelihood methods (Whittle estimator) as well as covariance based methods (log-periodogram, rescaled range (R/S)) are among the ones that are used mostly [39]. These methods were aimed both at the analysis of fractional Brownian motion and more extensive clusters related to stochastic processes, which is to say those of Gaussian processes which exhibit locally self-similar aspects initially.

It is considered that a zero-mean Gaussian process $\{X(t), t \geq 0\}$, that has stationary increments is self-similar at 0 locally, which is expressed by locally self-similar Gaussian Process. The semi-variance function $v(t)$ is stated by (3) [39, 40]:

$$v(t) = \frac{1}{2} E((X(s+t) - X(s))^2), \tag{3}$$

$t \to 0=$ fulfills the following characteristic (4):

$$v^{2D}(t) = v^{2D}(0) + (-1)^D C|t|^{2H} + o(|t|^{2H}), \tag{4}$$

Based on (2), $0 < H < 1$, D expresses the larger integer in a way that x is 2D-times differentiable. Within the Gaussian framework, the local self-similarity, which is at 0, is equivalent to (4).

Considering $\{V^a(t), t \geq 0\}$ to be the process which is derived by filtering $\{X(t), t \geq 0\}$ with α filter that has the length $l + 1$ and order $p \geq$ Based on this $\sum_{q=0}^{l} a_q q^r = 0$ for $r = 0, ..., p - 1$. Being observed at times $\{0, \frac{1}{N}, ... \frac{N-1}{N}\}$ $\{X(t), t \geq 0\}$ is seen and variations of F of $\{X(t), t \geq 0\}$ and the F variations of X are expressed as follows (5) [39, 40]:

$$V_N(F, a) = \frac{1}{N-l} \sum_{i=l}^{N-1} F\left(V^a\left(\frac{i}{N}\right)\right). \tag{5}$$

Numerous estimation procedures employed recently are based on these kinds of F-variations with a specific choice of (6) [39, 40]:

$$F(t) = H^k(t) \frac{1}{E\left(|V^a(0)|^k\right)} |t|^k - 1. \tag{6}$$

Hölder Regularity Analysis. The Fractional Brownian motion with Gaussian process $B_H(t)$ produces zero mean. The covariance function is seen as in (7) ([7–9, 41]).

$$\text{cov}\{B_H(s), B_H(t)\} = \frac{1}{2}\left\{|s|^{2H} + |t|^{2H} - |s-t|^{2H}\right\} \tag{7}$$

H Hurst exponent, $H = \frac{a}{2}$ and $a \in (0, 1)$ [20]. Fractional Brownian Motion is stated based on (8) with a stochastic integral (see the following references for further details and fomula steps: [3, 8, 42–44]).

For the most critical components of the irregular and singular signals regarding 2-D analysis, it should be noted that the Hölder exponent supplies required information. For this reason, the Hölder base measures the variations in characterizing of the multiple areas that belong to the signal processor. The Hölder exponent, or singularity exponent, characterizes the singularity force at $t = t(0)$ [8,9] to attain a positive measurement which is expressed by a signal $X(t)$ [41–44].

Multifractal Analysis. Multifractals' measurement refers preliminarily to the measuring of a statistic distribution and outcomes based on such measurement provide beneficial information although the essential structure does not display self-affine as well as self-similar behaviours [45,46]. A signal's multifractal analysis comprises the measurement of its regularity at every sample point, the grouping of the points that have the same irregularity as well as the estimating of the fractal dimension, namely the Hausdorff dimension each iso-regularity set subsequently [46].

Multifractal analysis is performed on statistical basis through the analysis of a large deviation, which refers to a stochastic procedure. Here, it is considered that any generality that $T = [0,1]$ remains. $N_n^{\in}(\alpha)\#\{s : \alpha - \varepsilon \leq \alpha_n^s \leq \alpha + \varepsilon\}$ in which α_n^s s the coarse-grained Hölder exponent corresponding to a dyadic interval $I_n^s = [s2^{-n}, (s+1)2^{-n}]$ and this is denoted according to (8) [46]:

$$\alpha_n^s = \frac{\log |Y_n^s|}{-\log n} \tag{8}$$

Y_n^s is observed to be a number which calculates the variation of X in the interval of I_n^s. $Y_n^s := X((s+1)2^{-n}) - X(s2^{-n})$ yields a fundamental level of analytical calculations. It is also possible to derive it in different ways by taking as the wavelet coefficient $x_{n,s}$. For data displaying a large deviation $f_g(\alpha)$ is expressed based on (9) [47,48].

$$f_g(\alpha) = \lim_{\varepsilon \to 0} \lim_{n \to \infty} \sup \frac{\log N_n^\varepsilon(\alpha)}{\log n} \tag{9}$$

It seems obviously evident that no matter what the choice of Y_n^s, f_g shows a range in $\Re^+ \cup \{-\infty\}$ every time [47,48].

Accordingly, multifractal processes have been expanded on by [49,50]. In particular, when the noise characteristics display complex properties, multifractal approach is employed.

Multifractal Denoising Method (L2-norm). Regularization is considered to be an important method in computational processes in order to eliminate the overfitting problem, avoiding the coefficients to fit so that is flawless for overfitting [47,48].

During the application of a relevant computational process, it is possible to experience the unknown option. At that point, L2-norm generates non-sparse coefficients. L2 regularization on least squares is expressed as in (10) [51,52].

$$w^* = \arg \min_w \left(\sum_j \left(t(x_j) - \sum_i w_i h_i(x_j) \right) \right)^2 + \lambda \sum_{i=1}^k w_i^2 \tag{10}$$

The least squares error (LSE) is another term for the L2 norm loss function. While (y_i) refers to the total number of square of the differences belonging to the target value, $f(x_i)$ expresses the estimated values, shown in (12). They are kept to the minimum value [51,52].

$$S = \sum_{i=1}^{n} (y_i - f(x_i))^2 \tag{11}$$

L2 regularization is considered to be efficient in terms of computational processes owing to their analytical solutions. Accordingly, in our study, Multifractal denoising with Gaussian process (L2-norm) is applied to the MS dataset (139×228). As a consequence of regularity-based enhancement, mFd_MS dataset (139×228) has been generated. Subsequently, Fuzzy C-means algorithm was applied to the two datasets, namely MS dataset and mFd_MS dataset to attain an accurate and efficient clustering for the classification of subgroups of MS (RRMS, SPMS and PPMS) and the individuals who are healthy.

Fuzzy C-Means Algorithm. It is a well-known fact that conventional clustering methods work better when homogeneous attributes are handled, while their performance declines when the methods are implemented on inhomogeneous attributes since they are sensitive to noise. At such a stage, Fuzzy C-means, as an unsupervised clustering technique, is employed for medical analyses as well as image processing.

Fuzzy C-means algorithm assigns information to each section by the use of fuzzy memberships [53–56]. If $X = (x_1, x_2, ..., x_n)$, n d-dimensional information shows information needed to divide into c clusters, $\hat{x}_i$ expresses the features data. The indication of the steps of the optimization algorithm are as follows (see Fig. 1) [7,53–56]:

The principal aim of our study is to identify the similar attributes in homogeneous MS clusters and the dissimilar attributes in the different clusters of MS subgroups. Fuzzy C-means algorithm was applied to both the MS dataset $X = (x_1, x_2, ..., x_{139 \times 228})$ and the mFd_MS dataset $\hat{X} = (\hat{x}_1, \hat{x}_2, ..., \hat{x}_{139 \times 228})$ in line with the steps mentioned above for the clustering of the MS subgroups (RRMS, SPMS, and PPMS) and the control group of healthy individuals.

3   Experimental Results

The MS dataset of our study includes Expanded Disability Status Scale (EDSS) scores and Magnetic Resonance Imaging (MRI) (taken in different years) of patients diagnosed with one MS subgroup (RRMS, SPMS and PPMS) and the healthy individuals are involved in the control group. Two contributions have been provided by this study. Firstly, we proposed the use of Multifractal Denoising method (L2-norm) to identify the critical and significant self-similar attributes. Secondly, the application of Fuzzy C-means (FCM) algorithm was

Algorithm 1: FCM algorithm

Input: Dataset with n number of samples
$X = (x_1, x_2, \dots, x_n)$

Method:

1. At the beginning, the construction of the U membership matrix is made
with random values. Afterwards, we determine the fuzzy weight (m), the threshold value on the condition stopping (ε) and the number of clusters (c), which shown in (13).

$$v_j = \frac{\sum_{i=1}^{N} \mu_{ij}^{m} x_i}{\sum_{i=1}^{N} \mu_{ij}^{m}}, 1 \le j \le c \qquad (12)$$

2. The determination of the cluster centres (v_j) is based on Eq. (14),

$$X_{ijG}^2 = \| x_i - v_j \|_G^2 = (x_i - v_j)G(x_i - v_j)^T \qquad (13)$$

3. We calculate the distance between cluster centres based on Eq. (14). In this way, each sample is calculated.

4. The updating of the membership matrix is done based on Eq. (15).

$$\mu_{ij} = \frac{1}{\sum_{k=1}^{c}(D_{ijG}/D_{ikG})^{2/(m-1)}}, 1 \le i \le N, 1 \le j \le c \qquad (14)$$

5. If it is observed that the difference between the membership matrix in the former step and the updated membership matrix is more than the specified threshold value, we repeat the same calculations stated in Step 2
$\| U^{(t+1)} - U^{(t)} \| < \varepsilon$

Output:

Clustering information concerning the n number of samples in the whole dataset is yielded.

Fig. 1. FCM algorithm.

performed for the clustering purpose. As a result, the classification of the similar attributes in homogeneous MS clusters and the dissimilar attributes in the different clusters of MS subgroups was done. To attain the proposed contributions, with the integration of the multifractal approach and Fuzzy C-means application, our method in this study is reliant on the subsequent steps:

(i) Multifractal denoising with Gaussian process (L2-norm) was employed for identifying the critical and significant self-similar attributes. Consequently, mFd_MS dataset (139×228) was generated.

(ii) In order to classify the similar attributes in homogeneous MS clusters and the dissimilar attributes in the different clusters of MS subgroups, FCM algorithm was applied to the MS dataset and the mFd_MS dataset (see Fig. 2).

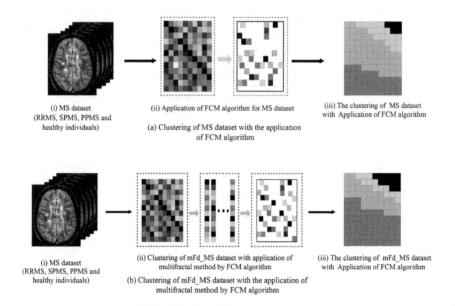

Fig. 2. MS dataset clustering with multifractal method application by FCM algorithm.

As the first step, in order to classify the similar attributes in homogeneous MS clusters and the dissimilar attributes in the different clusters of MS subgroups, Fuzzy C-means algorithm was applied to the MS dataset (Fig. 2(a)). Secondly, Multifractal Denoising with Gaussian process (L2-norm) was applied to the MS dataset for the identification of the critical and significant self-similar attributes; and the mFd_MS dataset (139×228) was generated (Fig. 2(b))). As the next step, Fuzzy C-means was applied to the mFd_MS dataset (139×228).

(iii) Accuracy rates as a consequence of clustering based on the proposed method were compared for both datasets (MS dataset and mFd_MS dataset) (see Table 3 for the results).

The results of characteristic parameters for Fuzzy C-means algorithm are provided in Table 2 below:

Table 2. The characteristic parameters distribution of the FCM algorithm

Parameters	The value of the parameters
Exponent for the partition matrix U	2.0
Maximum number of iterations	1000
Minimum amount of improvement	1e−3

Computation results of FCM clustering algorithm for 1000 iterations are shown in Fig. 3(a) for the MS dataset and Fig. 3(b) for the mFd_MS dataset.

The clustering computation is finalized at the 1000th iteration since there is not any change in the membership matrix according to the previous iteration, which can be seen in Fig. 3(a).

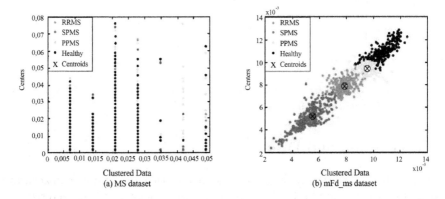

Clustered Data
(a) MS dataset

Clustered Data
(b) mFd_ms dataset

Fig. 3. The results of the clustering analyses of FCM algorithm application for (a) MS dataset (b) mFd_MS dataset.

As can be seen in Fig. 3, the distance between data centres of the MS dataset (139×228) as well as of the mFd_MS dataset (139×228) is calculated (the distance between the data centre and the MS patient within the feature domain). The results which were calculated are stored in matrix μ_{ij} After the 1000th iteration, the MS dataset objective function vector for the MS dataset [1.10, 2.4, 0.4] and for the mFd_MS dataset objective function vector for MS dataset [0.10, 0.14, 0.32] was obtained.

Regarding the calculation of the μ_{ij} for 1000 iterations (see Fig. 3), it has been shown that the clustering performance result for the mFd_MS dataset is higher than that of the MS dataset.

3.1   The Results Based on the Method Proposed

The method we have proposed by multifractal Denoising with Gaussian process (L2-norm) as applied to the MS dataset enabled identifying the critical and significant self-similar attributes; and thus, with Fuzzy C-means, accuracy rate performance was attained high.

The accuracy rate results of classification with Fuzzy-C means algorithm based on our proposed method are presented in Table 3.

As it can be seen from Table 3, the mFd_MS dataset yielded higher accuracy rates compared to MS dataset as a result of the clustering of MS subgroups by Fuzzy C-means. This shows that the analyses done by a Multifractal Denoising method (L2) enables the identifying of the critical and significant self-similar attributes, which contributes to accurate classification that is critical for diagnosis, decision-making and timely management of diseases in medicine. This also

Table 3. The accuracy rate results of classification with Fuzzy-C means algorithm

MS subgroups	MS dataset (%)	mFd_MS dataset (%)
RRMS	71	88.1
SPMS	71.5	88.2
PPMS	81.2	85.4
Healthy	90.1	96.5

ensures and maintains the high quality of life on the patients' side. For physicians, having an early accurate diagnosis certainly assists them.

4   Conclusion and Discussion

Our study has aimed to employ a multifractal approach for obtaining an accurate diagnostic classification for the MS subgroups while tackling the characterization of critical and significant self-similar attributes in the MS dataset. Accordingly, since multifractal analysis proves to be beneficial way to characterize the heterogeneous nature of fractals by dealing with the singularity structure of functions or signals, we have employed it in our study. The use of multifractal analysis is particularly observed concerning wide-ranging phenomena in the natural world. This kind of analysis saves time and is efficient while dealing with highly irregular signals, which is also the case in medicine. As different from previous works ([10–17, 27–29, 52–56]), this study has used Fuzzy C-means for MS dataset for the first time in line with the proposed multifractal approach through which it has been possible to identify the attributes that are critical, regular and self-similar. The experimental results for the MS_dataset and mFd_MS dataset demonstrate that the mFd_MS dataset yielded higher accuracy rates through the multifractal denoising method (L2) with Fuzzy C-means algorithm. Consequently, the approach we have proposed contributes to accurate diagnostic classification which plays a highly decisive role for the diagnostics and timely management of diseases in medicine. This asset also secures and maintains the high quality of life on the patients' side. Regarding future direction, it can be stated that the multifractal approach can be employed in natural sciences as well as engineering apart from medicine.

References

1. Mandelbrot, B.B., Van Ness, J.W.: Fractional Brownian motions, fractional noises and applications. SIAM Rev. **10**(4), 422–437 (1968)
2. Setty, V.A., Sharma, A.S.: Characterizing detrended fluctuation analysis of multifractional Brownian motion. Physica A: Stat. Mech. Appl. **419**, 698–706 (2015)
3. Dumitru, B., Kai, D., Enrico, S.: Fractional Calculus: Models and Numerical Methods, vol. 3. World Scientific (2012)

4. Karaca, Y.: Wavelet-based multifractal spectrum estimation in hepatitis virus classification models by using artificial neural network approach. In: Shapshak, P., et al. (eds.) Global Virology III: Virology in the 21st Century, pp. 73–96. Springer, Cham (2019). https://doi.org/10.1007/978-3-030-29022-1_4

5. Karaca, Y., Zhang, Y.D., Muhammad, K.: Characterizing complexity and self-similarity based on fractal and entropy analyses for stock market forecast modelling. Expert Syst. Appl. **144**, 113098 (2020)

6. Karaca, Y., Cattani, C.: Computational Methods for Data Analysis. Walter de Gruyter GmbH, Berlin (2018). (978–3110496352)

7. Karaca, Y., Cattani, C., Moonis, M., Bayrak, Ş.: Stroke subtype clustering by multifractal Bayesian denoising with Fuzzy C means and K-Means algorithms. Complexity (2018)

8. Karaca, Y., Cattani, C.: A comparison of two Hölder regularity functions to forecast stock indices by ANN algorithms. In: Misra, S., et al. (eds.) ICCSA 2019. LNCS, vol. 11620, pp. 270–284. Springer, Cham (2019). https://doi.org/10.1007/978-3-030-24296-1_23

9. Machado, J.A.T., Baleanu, D., Luo, A.C.: Nonlinear and Complex Dynamics: Applications in Physical, Biological, and Financial Systems. Springer, Berlin (2011). https://doi.org/10.1007/978-1-4614-0231-2

10. Zhang, Y., et al.: Fractal dimension estimation for developing pathological brain detection system based on Minkowski-Bouligand method. IEEE Access **4**, 5937–5947 (2016)

11. Ayache, A., Véhel, J.L.: Generalized multifractional Brownian motion: definition and preliminary results. In: Dekking, M., Véhel, J.L., Lutton, E., Tricot, C. (eds.) Fractals, pp. 17–32. Springer, London (1999). https://doi.org/10.1007/978-1-4471-0873-3_2

12. Ayache, A., Cohen, S., Véhel, J.L.: The covariance structure of multifractional Brownian motion, with application to long range dependence. In: 2000 IEEE International Conference on Acoustics, Speech, and Signal Processing, Proceedings (Cat. No. 00CH37100), vol. 6, pp. 3810–3813. IEEE (2000)

13. Ayache, A., Véhel, J.L.: On the identification of the pointwise Hölder exponent of the generalized multifractional Brownian motion. Stoch. Processes Appl. **111**(1), 119–156 (2004)

14. Magin, R., Ortigueira, M.D., Podlubny, I., Trujillo, J.: On the fractional signals and systems. Sig. Process. **91**(3), 350–371 (2011)

15. Lahmiri, S.: Generalized Hurst exponent estimates differentiate EEG signals of healthy and epileptic patients. Physica A: Stat. Mech. Appl. **490**, 378–385 (2018)

16. El Hassouni, M., Jennane, R., Tafraouti, A.: Evaluation of fractional Brownian motion synthesis methods using the SVM classifier. Biomed. Sig. Process. Control **49**, 48–56 (2019)

17. David, S.A., Machado, J.A.T., Inácio Jr., C.M.C., Valentim Jr., C.A.: A combined measure to differentiate EEG signals using fractal dimension and MFDFA-Hurst, Commun. Nonlinear Sci. Numer. Simul. **84**, 105170 (2020)

18. Rohini, P., Sundar, S., Ramakrishnan, S.: Differentiation of early mild cognitive impairment in brainstem MR images using multifractal detrended moving average singularity spectral features. Biomed. Sig. Process. Control **57**, 101780 (2020)

19. Karaca, Y., Cattani, C., Karabudak, R.: ANN classification of MS subgroups with diffusion limited aggregation. In: Gervasi, O., et al. (eds.) ICCSA 2018. LNCS, vol. 10961, pp. 121–136. Springer, Cham (2018). https://doi.org/10.1007/978-3-319-95165-2_9

20. Compston, A., Coles, A.: Multiple sclerosis. The Lancet **372**, 1502–1517 (2008)
21. Tallantyre, E.C., et al.: Ultra-high-field imaging distinguishes MS lesions from asymptomatic white matter lesions. Neurology **76**(6), 534–539 (2011)
22. Goodwin, S.J.: Multiple sclerosis: integration of modeling with biology, clinical and imaging measures to provide better monitoring of disease progression and prediction of outcome. Neural Regen. Res. **11**(12), 1900 (2016)
23. Multipl Skleroz Tanı ve Tedavi Kılavuzu 2016 Basım Tarihi: Galenos Yayınevi, İstanbul (2016)
24. Sand, I.K.: Classification, diagnosis, and differential diagnosis of multiple sclerosis. Curr. Opin. Neurol. **28**(3), 193–205 (2015)
25. Waxman, S.: Multiple Sclerosis as a Neuronal Disease. Elsevier, Amsterdam (2005)
26. Karaca, Y., Osman, O., Karabudak, R.: Linear modeling of multiple sclerosis and its subgroubs. System **2**, 7 (2015)
27. Siegelmann, H.T.: Complex systems science and brain dynamics. Front. Comput. Neurosci. **4**, 7 (2010)
28. Das, P., Das, A.: A fast and automated segmentation method for detection of masses using folded kernel based fuzzy C-means clustering algorithm. Appl. Soft Comput. **85**, 105775 (2019)
29. William, W., Ware, A., Basaza-Ejiri, A.H., Obungoloch, J.: Cervical cancer classification from Pap-smears using an enhanced Fuzzy C-mean algorithm. Inform. Med. Unlocked **14**, 23–33 (2019)
30. Sheela, C.J.J., Suganthi, G.: Automatic brain tumor segmentation from MRI using greedy snake model and fuzzy C-means optimization. J. King Saud Univ.-Comput. Inf. Sci. (2019)
31. Thompson, A.J., et al.: Diagnosis of multiple sclerosis: 2017 revisions of the McDonald criteria. Lancet Neurol. **17**, 162–173 (2017)
32. Karaca, Y., Zhang Y.D., Cattani, C., Ayan, U.: The differential diagnosis of multiple sclerosis using convex combination of infinite kernels. CNS Neurol. Disord.-Drug Targets (Formerly Curr. Drug Targets-CNS Neurol. Disord.) **16**(1), 36–43 (2017)
33. Bushnik, T.: Expanded disability status scale. In: Kreutzer, J.S., DeLuca, J., Caplan, B. (eds.) Encyclopedia of Clinical Neuropsychology. Springer, New York (2011). https://doi.org/10.1007/978-0-387-79948-3
34. The MathWorks, MATLAB (R2019b). The MathWorks, Inc., Natick (2019)
35. Vehel, J.L.: FracLab (2000). https://project.inria.fr/fraclab/
36. Kuklinski, W.S., Chandra, K., Ruttimann, U.E., Webber, R.L.: Application of fractal texture analysis to segmentation of dental radiographs SPIE. Med. Imaging III: Image Process. **1092**, 111–117 (1989)
37. Collins, J.J., De Luca, C.J.: Upright, correlated random walks: a statistical-biomechanics approach to the human postural control system. Chaos **5**(1), 57–63 (1994)
38. Baleanu, D., Jajarmi, A., Mohammadi, H., Rezapour, S.: A new study on the mathematical modelling of human liver with Caputo-Fabrizio fractional derivative. Chaos Solitons Fractals **134**, 109705 (2020)
39. Granger, C.W.J.: The typical spectral shape of an economic variable. Econometrica **34**, 150–161 (1966)
40. Beran, J.: Statistics for Long Memory Processes. Chapman and Hall, London (1994)
41. Coeurjolly, J.F.: Estimating the parameters of a fractional Brownian motion by discrete variations of its sample paths. Stat. Infer. Stoch. Process. **4**(2), 199–227 (2001)

42. Garcin, M.: Estimation of time-dependent Hurst exponents with variational smoothing and application to forecasting foreign exchange rates. Physica A: Stat. Mech. Appl. **483**, 462–479 (2017)
43. Misawa, M.: Local Hölder regularity of gradients for evolutional p-Laplacian systems. Annali di Matematica **181**(4), 389–405 (2002)
44. Aizenman, M., Burchard, A.: Hölder regularity and dimension bounds for random curves. Duke Math. J. **99**(3), 419–453 (1999)
45. Franchi, B., Lanconelli. E.: Hölder regularity theorem for a class of linear nonuniformly elliptic operators with measurable coefficients. Annali della Scuola Normale Superiore di Pisa-Classe di Scienze **10**(4), 523–541 (1983)
46. Tarquis, A., Giménez, D., Saa, A., Diaz, M.: Scaling and multiscaling of soil pore systems determined by image analysis. Scal. Methods Soil Phys. **19** (2003)
47. Lutton, E., Grenier, P., Vehel, J.L.: An interactive EA for multifractal Bayesian denoising. In: Rothlauf, F., et al. (eds.) EvoWorkshops 2005. LNCS, vol. 3449, pp. 274–283. Springer, Heidelberg (2005). https://doi.org/10.1007/978-3-540-32003-6_28
48. Pu, Y.F., et al.: Fractional partial differential equation denoising models for texture image. Sci. China Inf. Sci. **57**(7), 1–19 (2014). https://doi.org/10.1007/s11432-014-5112-x
49. Yau, A.C., Tai, X., Ng, M.K.: Compression and denoising using l_0-norm. Comput. Optim. Appl. **50**, 425–444 (2011). https://doi.org/10.1007/s10589-010-9352-4
50. Feder, J.: Fractals (Physics of Solids and Liquids). Plenum, New York (1987)
51. Li, L., Chang, L., Ke, S., Huang, D.: Multifractal analysis and lacunarity analysis: a promising method for the automated assessment of muskmelon (Cucumis melo L.) epidermis netting. Comput. Electron. Agric. **88**, 72–84 (2012)
52. Kalavathy, S., Suresh, R.M.: Analysis of image denoising using wavelet coefficient and adaptive subband thresholding technique. Int. J. Comput. Sci. (IJCSI) **8**, 6 (2011)
53. Karaca, Y., Moonis, M., Zhang, Y.-D.: Multifractal analysis with L2 norm denoising technique: modelling of MS subgroups classification. In: Misra, S., et al. (eds.) ICCSA 2019. LNCS, vol. 11620, pp. 257–269. Springer, Cham (2019). https://doi.org/10.1007/978-3-030-24296-1_22
54. Alruwaili, M., Siddiqi, M.H., Javed, M.A.: A robust clustering algorithm using spatial Fuzzy C-mean for brain MR images. Egypt. Inform. J. (2019)
55. Jianzhong, W., Kong, J., Lu, M., Qi, M., Zhang, B.: A modified FCM algorithm for MRI brain image segmentation using both local and non-local spatial constraints. Comput. Med. Imaging Graph. **32**(8), 685–698 (2008)
56. Ahmed, M.N., Yamany, S.M., Mohamed, N., Farag, A.A., Moriarty, T.: A modified Fuzzy C-mean algorithm for bias field estimation and segmentation of MRI data. IEEE Trans. Med. Imaging **21**(3), 193–199 (2002)

Decision Tree-Based Transdisciplinary Systems Modelling for Cognitive Status in Neurological Diseases

Yeliz Karaca[1(✉)] and Elgiz Yılmaz Altuntaş[2]

[1] University of Massachusetts Medical School, Worcester, MA 01655, USA
yeliz.karaca@ieee.org
[2] Galatasaray University, Istanbul, Turkey
elyilmaz@gsu.edu.tr

Abstract. This paper addresses the concept of an up-to-date transdisciplinary system modelling based on decision tree within the framework of systems theory. Systems theory constructs effective models for the analysis of complex systems since this comprehensive theory is capable of providing links between the problems and dynamics of systems. Particularly, for the complex and challenging environments, the solutions to the problems can be managed more effectively based on a systems approach. Neurological diseases concern the brain which has a complex structure and dynamics. Being equipped with the accurate medical knowledge plays a critical role in tackling these neurological problems. The interconnected relationships require a carefully-characterized transdisciplinary approach integrating systems conduct and mathematical modelling. Effective solutions lie in cognitive status, namely awareness and a satisfactory level of health knowledge. Within this framework, this study aims at revealing the lack of required general and medical health knowledge on neurological diseases (Alzheimer's, dementia, Parkinson's, stroke, epilepsy and migraine) among individuals. For this purpose, an online survey was conducted on 381 respondents, through which awareness on medical knowledge and general health knowledge were assessed for each disease. The following approaches (methods) were applied: firstly, rule-based decision tree algorithm was applied since its structure enables the interpretation of the data and works effectively with feature computations. Subsequently, statistical analyses were performed. The decision tree analyses and statistical analyses reveal parallel results with one another, which demonstrate that when compared with the knowledge of elder people, the knowledge of young population is limited in general and medical health knowledge. Compared with previous works, no related work exists in the literature where a transdisciplinary approach with these proposed methods are used. The experimental results demonstrate the significant difference between medical knowledge and general health knowledge among individuals depending on different attributes. The study attempts to reveal a new approach for dealing with diseases, developing positive attitudes besides establishing effective long-term behavioural patterns and strategies based on required knowledge and mindfulness.

© Springer Nature Switzerland AG 2020
O. Gervasi et al. (Eds.): ICCSA 2020, LNCS 12250, pp. 442–457, 2020.
https://doi.org/10.1007/978-3-030-58802-1_32

Keywords: Complex systems · Systems theory · Rule-based Decision Tree analysis · Transdisciplinary systems modelling · Neurological diseases · Data analysis · ANOVA · Health Belief Model · Awareness of medical knowledge

1 Introduction

Every system is characterized by its structure, shaped by time and space while being affected by the factors in its environment. Within this framework, systems theory consists of transdisciplinary study of the systems with a coherent combination of interconnected components. Models constructed accordingly provide advantages for the analysis and depiction of complex systems due to being beneficial for supporting interaction between the system components. Approaches based on the systems theory also help observe the links between problems and the system dynamics, which require a complex analysis for identification and solution of problems [1]. Systems approach has become extensively-employed concept in research and practice in changing environments along with various disciplines such as engineering, natural sciences, social sciences, medicine and so forth [1, 2]. The complexity of neurological diseases requires sophisticated means of analysis. Artificial Intelligence (AI) and related techniques have gained prominence due to their capability of providing applicable solutions to complex problems. Some of the key categories of AI applications include healthcare and medicine, especially for the diagnosis and treatment aspects, patients' medical information, their engagement and observance to the treatment regimen [3]. There is an extensive body of work in the literature regarding AI and its applications concerning neurological diseases. The study of [4] employed the decision tree algorithms for classifying stroke patients' activities and postures. The study revealed that the decision tree algorithms could measure the patients activities accurately.

Neurological diseases concern the disruption of the Central Nervous System (CNS) functions. Neurological diseases are considered to be challenging to identify, diagnose and manage track because of the complexity CNS displays [5]. Consciousness and mindfulness of the individuals afflicted by the disorder and people in their circle also play a critical role for an efficient management efficiently so that life quality can be maintained satisfactorily level. Alzheimer's, dementia, Parkinson's, stroke, epilepsy and migraine addressed in this study, are among the most prevalent ones.

Some information on the neurological diseases included in this study for the model proposed are outlined as follows: Alzheimer's disease is a progressive disorder leading the brain cells to degenerate which is one of the most common reasons for dementia [6–8]. Dementia, with a chronic or a progressive nature, is one of the most frequent forms of Alzheimer's disease, characterized by the disturbance of higher cortical functions Mainly older people are affected [9]. Parkinson's disease is a progressive disorder, affecting movement, with noticeable tremors [10]. Stroke is a medical condition occurring when blood supply to the part of the brain is disrupted. Brain cells die in such a condition. Other symptoms are numbness, vision problems and trouble with walking [11,12]. Epilepsy is a chronic disorder characterized by epileptic seizures, [9,13]. Migraine occurs a result of certain changes in the brain, causing severe head pains [9,14,15].

Being aware of the symptoms may not be adequate, it is also important to have mindfulness, is in medical context defined as self-regulation of attention and adopting an orientation along with transparency, acceptance as well as wanting to learn more about the medical condition [16]. The study [17] indicates the feasibility of computer-based virtual coaching strategies for patient education for helping patients have behavioural changes in the long-term. Another study [18] emphasizes the effectiveness of patient education is based on Internet. Based on the structural equation modelling approach, the study results confirmed empirically the effectiveness and accessibility of the system. These studies show the importance of accessing and having the accurate information effectively while dealing with different health conditions. Health literacy plays a significant role in maintaining good health since it represents the cognitive and social skills that determine the individuals' motivation and ability to understand, gain access to, and use related information [19]. When people's access to health information is improved, capacity of them to use it effectively also increases, and thus health literacy becomes critical for empowerment. The theoretical model related to health communication in this study is based on cognitive theories and communicating health messages. Cognitive theories provide 'continuum accounts of behaviour' (Rutter and Quine) [20], arguing that particular beliefs or perceptions predict a behaviour. In the cognitive theories, Theory of Planned Behaviour [21] and Health Belief Model (HBM) belonging to Becker 1974 [22–24] are two principal approaches applied to the contexts of health communication.

Complex nature of neurologic diseases requires an integrated approach with a transdisciplinary framework and its applications. Mathematical modelling with AI, due to its capability of crafting precision, makes up a transdisciplinary framework including various scientific disciplines. Health communication (HC) is the study and use of communication strategies for informing and influencing individual decisions so that health of the person will be enhanced [25] HC plays an important role in conveying accurate information about healthcare problems to patients, patient acquaintances, public and healthcare practitioners so that efforts are put in to capture the attention and establish awareness among related parties. In order for health communication to achieve effective outcomes, it is important to integrate transdisciplinary approaches [26–30]. Knowledge in the field of health is categorized as general health knowledge, which refers to public medical and healthcare knowledge as well as public medical knowledge, and special health knowledge, which is concerned with individual experiences, medical records as well as personal health status [31].

The approach adopted in this study attempts to be more extensive since it is based on a transdisciplinary framework and its applications while dealing with the data. The dataset of the present study is made up of undergraduate, graduate and PhD Students and employees at Galatasaray University (Istanbul, Turkey). Convenience sampling method was applied to survey the respondents

(381) enrolled online between 27 November 2019 and 27 January 2020. The study was ethically approved by the department administrators at Galatasaray University and the respondents were assured about the confidentiality. The main goal of the paper is to assess the respondents' knowledge and attitudes towards neurological diseases (Alzheimer's, dementia, Parkinson's, stroke, epilepsy and migraine). When it is compared with earlier works [16–19, 26–31], the proposed method in the present study is a novel one conducted for the first time in the literature with the application of the following steps: firstly, decision tree algorithm was applied due to its rule-based structure which enabled the interpretation of the data and feature computations. Next, statistical analyses were performed using ANOVA, Tukey test and t-test. Based on the procedures of the first and subsequent steps, the respondents' medical knowledge scores for each type of disease revealed an average score of (53.98%). Migraine was found out to be the most known disease (83%), while epilepsy indicated the lowest score in terms of general health knowledge (36%). On the other hand, stroke and Alzheimer's diseases are known by people at equal levels (55%) and the knowledge related to dementia follows them (45%). It has also been found that if an individual has or has had a neurological disease, this result is related to only general health knowledge of migraine. People with any kind of neurological disease have greater migraine knowledge score than the people who do not have the disease ($p < 0.05$). From the perspective of the medical knowledge regarding the diseases, epilepsy ($x = 42$, $SD = 26.4$) and migraine scores ($x = 88$, $SD = 16$) of the patients are significantly higher than the scores of healthy individuals ($p < 0.05$). Considering the age characteristic, the highest score for Alzheimer's and dementia was observed among 46–55 age group, for epilepsy and migraine, 36–45 age group had the highest score and finally, for the remaining two diseases, Parkinson's and stroke, individuals aged 55 and above had the highest scores. The last data is significant since Parkinson's and stroke affect elderly population. Overall, these results suggest that young population has a limited level of general and medical health knowledge compared to the knowledge of elder people. The decision tree analyses and statistical analyses performed for the study reveal parallel results with one another. Accordingly, the experimental results demonstrate the significant difference between medical knowledge and general health knowledge among individuals depending on different attributes. These indicate the importance of showing a new approach to tackle diseases, besides developing favourable attitudes and maintaining effective long-term behavioural strategies based on accurate and up-to-date medical knowledge and general health knowledge.

1.1 The Motivation of the Transdisciplinary Proposed Method

The novelty of this paper relies on the concept of transdisciplinary system modelling based on decision tree within the framework of systems theory. When the complex systems are in question, a carefully characterized transdisciplinary approach is required to analyse the interconnected relationships in the system. The principal motivation of this work is derived from providing an integrated approach with the systems approach and mathematical modelling to reveal the knowledge awareness and attitudes towards neurological diseases.

Another contribution concerns revealing the lack of required medical and general health knowledge on neurological diseases among individuals through the decision tree and statistical analyses. Since neurological disorders concern brain which has a complex structure and dynamics, it is important to have access to accurate medical knowledge.

This study is the first of its kind conducted in Turkey. The survey used in this study with its questions is from a novel perspective so that the lack of information concerning the diseases could be revealed. This is important globally because health education programmes and national awareness campaigns should be based on the proof of what individuals know, instead of on what policy educators and experts assume individuals know. Therefore, the relevance of research on public knowledge and understanding of neurological diseases should not be underestimated.

The information flow regarding neurological diseases is also a complex phenomenon since it involves uncertainty or non-linear communication pattern. To deal with the processes effectively, an integrated approach with the support of a transdisciplinary framework and its applications. Health communication plays an important role in transmitting the accurate information about healthcare problems to the patients, patient acquaintances, public and healthcare practitioners so that health communication can achieve effective outcomes.

Based on the transdisciplinary approach and its contribution, the results indicate the significant difference between medical knowledge and general health knowledge in individuals with different attributes. Thus, endeavours come to the foreground to reveal a novel approach for dealing with the diseases, while forming positive attitudes and establishing effective behavioural patterns and strategies in the long term based on mindfulness.

The paper is organized as follows: Sect. 2 includes Materials, with the subheading of Subjects and Design of the Study, and Methods, with the subsections on Decision Tree Structure and Statistical Analyses (ANOVA, Tukey test and t-test). Section 3 handles the Experimental Results and Discussion. Finally, Conclusion is provided in Sect. 4.

2   Materials and Methods

2.1   Materials

Subjects and Design of the Study. The approach followed in this study attempts to be more comprehensive since the study is based on a transdisciplinary framework and its applications while dealing with the data. The dataset of the present study includes undergraduate, graduate and PhD Students and employees at Galatasaray University (Istanbul, Turkey). Convenience sampling method was used to survey the respondents (total of 381) enrolled online. The study was ethically approved by the department administrators at Galatasaray University; and the respondents were made sure about the confidentiality of the data since their identity was not collected. The principal goal of the paper is to assess the respondents' knowledge and attitudes towards neurological diseases (Alzheimer's, dementia, Parkinson's, stroke, epilepsy and migraine). The demographic form included variables to elicit information related to the respondents' gender, age, education level, whether they or their family have any neurological disease, if yes, type of this disease (see Table 1 for demographic characteristics of the respondents).

Table 1. Demographic characteristics of the respondents

Variable	Frequency	Percentage(%)
Gender (n = 381)		
Male	51	13.39%
Female	330	86.61%
Age group (n = 381)		
17–25	43	11.29%
26–35	103	27.03%
36–45	160	41.99%
46–55	61	16.01%
56- +	14	3.67%
Education level (n = 381)		
Bachelor Degree	227	59.58%
M.sc Degree	130	34.12%
Ph.D Degree	24	6.30%
Neurological Disease History in the Family (n = 381)		
Yes	198	52%
No	183	48%
Neurological Disease History in the Individual (n = 381)		
Yes	61	16%
No	320	84%
Types of Diseases seen in the Individual (n = 61)		
Epilepsy	3	5%
Epilepsy, Migraine	2	3%
Stroke, Migraine	2	3%
Migraine	54	89%

The sampling frame consists of the respondents' health knowledge levels as investigated through validated scales. For Alzheimer's, the Alzheimer's Disease Knowledge Scale (ADKS) [32] was used. For Parkinson's, questions were adapted based on the informative presentation of Neurology Association; and for dementia, Dementia Knowledge Assessment Scale (DKAS) [33] was employed.

Finally, National Hospital Seizure Severity Scale [34] was used for epilepsy and
The Migraine Disability Assessment (MIDAS) questionnaire [35] and Headache
Impact Test (HIT) [36] were used for migraine. The knowledge for stroke symptoms was assessed using a portion of the CDC's 2011 Behavioural Risk Factor
Surveillance System Questionnaire [37], including the five signs of stroke, was
used in line with the National Institute of Neurological Disorders and Stroke [38].
These validated tools comprised of 54 items in total; 24 items with true/false
responses and 27 items with a nominal scale including agree, disagree, undecided
options.

2.2 Methods

This paper presents an up-to-date transdisciplinary system modelling based on
rule-based decision tree within the framework of systems theory. The interconnected relationships in a system require a carefully-characterized transdisciplinary approach that integrates systems conduct and mathematical modelling,
which is blended, in this study, in two approaches: the application of decision
tree and statistical analyses along with their comparisons.

Decision Tree Structure. As one of the most common approaches for rule
modelling, a decision tree method represents decisions made in visual form. The
decision tree has a top-down approach to choose the best split. It is used for
labelling the elements correctly on a rule based structure. The labelling presents
a random work performed line with the distributions of the label. The formula
is applied as in (1) below [39–42].

$$I_G(p) = \sum_{i=1}^{J} p_i \sum_{k \neq 1}^{J} p_k = \sum_{i=1}^{J} p_i(1 - p_i)^2 = \sum_{i=1}^{J} p_i - \sum_{i=1}^{J} p_i^2 = 1 - \sum_{i=1}^{J} p_i^2 \quad (1)$$

I_G refers to the measure quantity Gini Impurity for a set of items with J
classes in which i ranges from 1 to J, and p_i denotes the fraction of items which
is labelled with the class i.

Rule based decision tree has mainly two steps, which are generation of rules
and the selection of Interesting Rules [39, 43]. For the application, (2), (3 (4) are
used: The support $S(A)$ of an item set A is defined as follows:

$$S\,(A) = \frac{(number\ of\ transactions\ including\ the\ item\ set\ A)}{(total\ number\ of\ transactions)} \quad (2)$$

The confidence C of a rule $(A \rightarrow B)$ is defined as [42, 43]

$$C(A \rightarrow B) = S(A \cup B)/S(A) \quad (3)$$

$$The\ lift\ L\ of\ a\ rule\ (A \rightarrow B)\ is\ defined\ as\ L(A \rightarrow B) = \frac{S(A \cup B)}{S(B) * S(A)} \quad (4)$$

Statistical Analysis. Original and innovative statistical methodology and complex approaches oriented towards statistical data analysis have recent applications in many fields. Used for the collection, collecting, analysis, organization and interpretation of data, statistical analysis plays a vital role in diverse areas.

The theoretical elements of the statistical analyses applied in this study are explained in the following sections.

ANOVA. The observations that are not reliant on one single factor need variant analysis and their definition is made through the estimation of the parameters given in (5) [43–45]:

$$Y_{ij} = \mu + \alpha_j + \epsilon_{ij} \tag{5}$$

Y_{ij} the score of i participants that are included in j subclass, μ the average of all the scores, α_j the impact of j subclass and ϵ_{ij} is the error term.

$\mu_j = \mu + \alpha_j$,

μ_j is the arithmetic mean of the participants included in the j subclass (for further details on this equation and hypothesis, see [46,47].

TUKEY TEST. Tukey test is a multiple procedure with a single-step, used for finding means which are different from each other significantly. The formula is for the test is given in (6) [48,49]:

$$q_s = \frac{Y_A - Y_B}{SE}, \tag{6}$$

Y_A the larger of the two means that are to be compared, Y_B: the smaller of the two means that are to be compared and SE refers to standard error of the means' sum. (for further details and hypothesis information, see [46,50].

T-TEST. As a parametric test, t-test is used to test the situation when there exists a statistically significant difference between the two independent groups. t-test formula is very similar to Tukey test formula.

Independent-test formula is given in (7)–(9) follows [51–53]:

$$t = \frac{m_A - m_B}{\sqrt{\frac{s^2}{n_A} + \frac{s^2}{n_B}}} \tag{7}$$

$$S^2 = \frac{\sum (x - m_A)^2 + \sum (x - m_B)^2}{n_A + n_B - 2} \tag{8}$$

$$df = n_A + n_B - 2 \tag{9}$$

A and B represent two different groups, where ma refers to the means of Group A and m_B refers to the means of Group B. S^2 is the estimator of the two samples' common variance refers to the Group A size while n_B represents the Group B size. df: n_A degrees of freedom (for further details and assumptions related to the test, see 46).

3   Experimental Results and Discussion

This study, based on the survey results obtained from the respondents, demonstrates a transdisciplinary system modelling which is based on rule-based decision tree within the framework of systems theory, integrating systems approach and mathematical modelling proposed with medical and general health knowledge aspects. Within this complex structure, procedures related to the steps that lead to the experimental results for the proposed method are outlined in Table 2 below:

Table 2. The steps related to the Transdisciplinary Proposed Method

Step 1: Application of rule-based decision tree analysis
Step 2: Application of statistical analysis
Step 3: Comparison of the integrated approach: rule-based
Decision Tree analysis and statistical analysis

All the analyses' results in this study and the depiction of the figure outcomes were performed using the Matlab [54] and SPSS [55]. Explanations for these steps (indicated in Table 2) are elaborated below in their respective order:

Step 1: Application of Rule-based Decision Tree Analysis

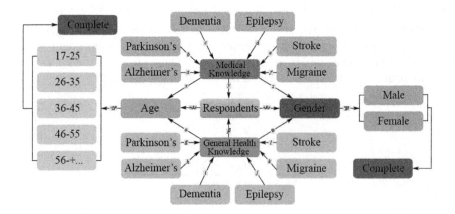

Fig. 1. An example of a decision tree that organizes the flow of questions partly selected from the questionnaire.

Some of the selected results that are significant as obtained from the analyses are provided below:

The decision rule as obtained from dataset in Fig. 1 is presented as Rules 1 and 2:

Rule 1: If General Health Knowledge $\geq$ 76. 416, the class is female.

Rule 2: If General Health Knowledge $\geq$ 85.678, the class is male.

Step 2: Application of Statistical Analysis

First, a pilot study was done among a group of respondents ($N = 30$). based on the survey results obtained from the respondents. It was revealed that the questionnaires were viable to perform the study in Turkish setting. The questionnaires were distributed to the respondents through an online survey program. Discrete variables are presented as count (%) and continuous variables as mean $\pm$ standard deviation (SD). General health knowledge scores and awareness on Medical Knowledge scores were calculated for each type of disease. These scores were subsequently compared for different demographics using ANOVA, Tukey test and t-test.

Table 3 demonstrates the medical knowledge scores of the respondents for each disease type. The Average score was found to be 53.98%. Based on the table, it is obvious that migraine is known well ($M = 81.04$, $SD = 26.51$); on the other hand, epilepsy is not known at a satisfactory level by the respondents included in the sample ($M = 34.69$, $SD = 25.98$).

Table 3. The steps related to the Transdisciplinary Proposed Method

Variable	M	SD
Dementia	43.70	26.00
Stroke	54.27	27.60
Alzheimer's	54.19	23.34
Parkinson's	55.97	29.44
Epilepsy	34.69	25.98
Migraine	81.04	26.69
Average	53.98	26.51

The results of the survey demonstrate the distribution of respondents' general health knowledge related to the neurological diseases addressed in the study. Migraine is the most known disease among other neurological diseases with a score of 83%; however, epilepsy shows the lowest score in terms of awareness and health knowledge, with a score of 36%. Stroke and Alzheimer's are known by people equally (55%) and the knowledge related to dementia follows them (45%). The overall correct answer percentage concerning the general health was found to be 56%.

The survey results indicate the percentage of the correct answers for the items related to each 6 neurological diseases. (F) refers that statement is false and (T) refers that statement is true. For *dementia*, the following statements have been assessed: "Dementia does not often shorten a person's life.": (F) (18%, $M \pm SD = 0.18 \pm 0.25$); "Blood vessel disease (vascular dementia) is the most common form of dementia.": (F) (8%; $M \pm SD = 0.08 \pm 0.27$); "Dementia is a normal part of the ageing process.": (F) (55%, $M \pm SD = 0.55 \pm 0.23$); "Alzheimer's disease is the most common form of dementia.": (T) (54%, $M \pm SD = 0.54 \pm 0.23$); "Difficulty eating and drinking generally occurs in the later stages of dementia.": (T) (63%, $M \pm SD = 0.63 \pm 0.24$). Regarding *stroke*, "Sudden confusion or trouble speaking is one of the symptoms of stroke." (T)(62%, $M \pm SD = 0.62 \pm 0.21$); "Severe headaches with no known cause are seen as symptoms in stroke cases.": (T) (41%; $M \pm SD = 0.41 \pm 0.22$); "Sudden trouble seeing in one or both eyes is one of the symptoms of stroke.": (T) (55%, $M \pm SD = 0.55 \pm 0.21$) and "Sudden chest pain or discomfort is one of the symptoms of stroke". (F) (28%, $M \pm SD = 0.28 \pm 0.24$). The following are statements related to *Alzheimer's*: "Tremor of the hands or arms is a common symptom in people with Alzheimer's disease.": (F) (61%; $M \pm SD = 0.62 \pm 0.27$); "Alzheimer's disease is one type of dementia.": (T) (63%; $M \pm SD = 0.63 \pm 0.28$). For *Parkinson's*, "Parkinson's disease is a brain disease that progresses slowly and is characterized by loss in the brain cells.": (T) (62%, $M \pm SD = 0.62 \pm 0.22$); "Decline or loss of olfactory (smelling) senses is one of the symptoms of Parkinson's disease.": (T) (24%, $M \pm SD = 0.24 \pm 0.26$). For *epilepsy*, the statements are as follows: "Cognition (thinking, reasoning, decision-making, etc.) is affected by epilepsy.": (F) (22%, $M \pm SD = 0.22 \pm 0.28$). Finally, for *migraine*, "Migraine is a series of headache attacks that last a few hours up to a few weeks.": (T) (89%, $M \pm SD = 0.89 \pm 0.06$); "Hereditary and environmental factors play a role in migraine.": (T) (82%, $M \pm SD = 0.82 \pm 0.05$); "Dizziness, numbness, nausea and blurred vision accompany migraine pains.": (T) (88%, $M \pm SD = 0.88 \pm 0.05$).

Based on the statements above, the proposed hypotheses have been tested as follows.

H1: General health knowledge between males and females related to neurological diseases is not equal.

H2: Medical knowledge between males and females related to neurological diseases is not equal.

To test H1 and H2, independent t-test was applied. General health knowledge of Parkinson's and dementia is significantly different between male and female ($p < 0.05$). Females' knowledge score for Parkinson's ($x = 76.52$, $SD = 20.48$) and dementia ($x = 77.05$, $SD = 21.91$) are higher than the score of the males concerning Parkinson's ($x = 68.14$, $SD = 23.49$) and dementia ($x = 66.67.05$, $SD = 31.89$). On the other hand, there is no difference between the genders in terms of general health knowledge score of Alzheimer's, dementia, stroke, epilepsy and migraine ($p > 0.05$). Stroke is the disease which is most commonly known well by both genders ($M_{female} = 85,76$; $M_{male} = 82.84$). Medical knowledge related to neurological diseases varies depending on gender, except for epilepsy ($p < 0.05$). It has been concluded females have more information than males on medical features of Alzheimer's, dementia, Parkinson's, stroke and migraine ($p < 0.05$). The analysis results demonstrate that apart from migraine, medical knowledge scores of all the neurologic diseases are less than the general health knowledge for both genders.

The following hypotheses were presented related to the history in the family and its relationship with the general health knowledge and medical knowledge.

H3: Having a neurological disease history in the family is related to having general health knowledge regarding neurological diseases.
H4: Having a neurological disease history in the family is related to having medical knowledge regarding neurological diseases.

To test H3 and H4, independent t-test was applied in this study. It has been revealed that stroke is well known generally by both groups. Additionally, Alzheimer's ($x = 81.5$, $SD = 14.28$), Parkinson's ($x = 78.40$, $SD = 19.77$) and dementia ($x = 78.40$, $SD = 22.90$) are significantly known better by the group with a neurological disease history in their family ($p < 0.05$). For the medical knowledge scores, there exist no differences between the two groups ($p > 0.05$).

The following hypotheses were presented related to the individual history and its relationship with the general health knowledge and medical knowledge.

H5: Having an individual neurological disease history is related to having general health knowledge of neurological diseases.
H6: Having an individual neurological disease history is related to having medical knowledge of neurological diseases.

Consequently for, Hypotheses 5 and 6: Medical knowledge for dementia [$F(4, 376) = 3.35$, $p = 0.01$], Parkinson's [$F(4, 376) = 3.47$, $p = 0.008$], epilepsy [$F(4, 376) = 3.5$, $p = 0.008$] and migraine [$F(4, 376) = 4.48$, $p = 0.002$] were found greater than the age group of 17–25 for all other age groups. On the other hand, the medical knowledge scores of the respondents concerning stroke and Alzheimer's are significantly equal in each age group ($p > 0,05$).

Post hoc comparisons utilising the Tukey's honestly significant difference (HSD) test showed that in the age group of 18–25, the mean scores for General Health knowledge of Alzheimer's ($M = 71.51$, $SD = 22.87$), Parkinson's ($M = 75.39$, $SD = 21.06$), Alzheimer's ($M = 65.11$, $SD = 26.80$), dementia ($M = 62.20$, $SD = 20.01$), epilepsy ($M = 73.83$, $SD = 27.25$), stroke ($M = 42.13$, $SD = 28.68$) are significantly less than the other age groups. Based on Tukey HSD test results, concerning the medical knowledge, in the age group of 18–25 medical knowledge of dementia ($M = 34.535$, $SD = 27.68$), Parkinson's ($M = 45.93$, $SD = 34.47$), epilepsy ($M = 26.33$, $SD = 23.61$) and migraine ($M = 66.97$, $SD = 38.01$) are significantly less than the other age groups. Overall, these results suggest young population has a more limited general and medical health knowledge compared to the knowledge of elder people.

Step 3: Comparison of the Integrated Approach: Rule-based Decision Tree Analysis and Statistical Analysis
The decision tree analyses and statistical analyses performed reveal parallel

results with one another, which demonstrate that when compared with that of elder people, the knowledge of young population is limited in terms of general and medical health knowledge. In this study where awareness status concerning general health and medical knowledge is the main subject matter. Decision tree analysis and statistical analyses yield significant difference based on gender. While the medical knowledge among males is found at 67.06% and general health knowledge is 82.84%. For females, the medical knowledge is found at 83.21% and general health knowledge is 78.86.

These results indicate that if medical knowledge is conveyed accurately through the viable means, then generable knowledge levels will also consistently rise.

4   Conclusion

In this study, the concept of transdisciplinary system modelling based on decision tree within the framework of systems theory has been addressed. Within the framework of neurological diseases, possessing the accurate medical knowledge through the applicable means and having mindfulness are important in tackling these neurological problems and developing effective strategies in the long term. The main contribution of this paper is to present an integrated approach based on decision tree and statistical analyses (with Independent ANOVA, Tukey test and t-test) through systems approach and mathematical modelling to reveal the knowledge awareness and attitudes towards the six neurological diseases. When compared to earlier works [16–19, 26–31], no study exists in the literature with this approach employed. Secondly, the study has demonstrated a lack of required medical and general health knowledge regarding the neurological diseases among individuals. In the proposed method, first, decision tree algorithm was applied, which enabled the interpretation of the data and feature computations. Further, statistical analyses, ANOVA, Tukey test and t-test, were conducted. The results reveal that young population has a more limited level of general and medical health knowledge compared to elder people's knowledge. Considering that neurological disorders concern the brain which has a complex structure, it is important to have mindfulness and access to accurate medical knowledge for anxiety reduction among patients and being more careful about future strategies regarding the neurological problems and other diseases. In view of these considerations, the following may be supplied for future works as direction:

(1) The proposed model with the combination of the models can open up a new perspective with the application of decision tree concerning transdisciplinary system models,
(2) The transdisciplinary systems model of the study can guide researchers to pay attention to lack of information about diseases and thus take actions accordingly to deal with real world problems effectively,
(3) The approach presented in the study can give a new direction for future works and projects which will integrate mathematical models in transdisciplinary systems.

Consequently, this study attempts to provide a transdisciplinary guidance based on mathematical modelling for future works to be conducted in the relevant and other fields for the effective solution of real world problems.

Data Availability. The link to the survey conducted and some details of the statistical results obtained in this study can be reached if requested at: https://docs.google.com/forms/d/1mBFtl-TLHDWs1ySaHeZdWjFy7pEVB_HkOUQM-pLhYlo/edit?usp=sharing_eip&ts=5e248427&urp=gmail_link.

References

1. Wognum, N., Verhagen, W.J., Stjepandić, J.: Trans-disciplinary systems as complex systems. In: Transdisciplinary Engineering: A Paradigm Shift-Proceedings of the 24th ISPE Inc., International Conference on Transdisciplinary Engineering, vol. 5. IOS Press (2017)
2. Jackson, J., Ware, C., Churchyard, R., Hanseeuw, B.: Interdisciplinary and trans-disciplinary perspectives: on the road to a holistic approach to dementia prevention and care. J. Alzheimer's Dis. Rep., 1–10 (Preprint)
3. Davenport, T., Kalakota, R.: The potential for artificial intelligence in healthcare. Future Healthc. J. **6**(2), 94 (2019)
4. Tan, J.P., et al.: Awareness status of chronic disabling neurological diseases among elderly veterans. Chin. Med. J. **128**(10), 1293 (2015)
5. Siuly, S., Zhang, Y.: Medical big data: neurological diseases diagnosis through medical data analysis. Data Sci. Eng. **1**(2), 54–64 (2016)
6. Pais, M., Martinez, L., Ribeiro, O., Loureiro, J., Fernandez, R., Valiengo, L., Forlenza, O.V.: Early diagnosis and treatment of Alzheimer's disease: new definitions and challenges. Brazilian J. Psychiatry (AHEAD) **42**(4), 431–441 (2020)
7. Nestor, P.J., Scheltens, P., Hodges, J.R.: Advances in the early detection of Alzheimer's disease. Nat. Med. **10**(7), S34–S41 (2004)
8. Karaca, Y., Moonis, M., Siddiqi, A.H., Turan, B.: Gini based learning for the classification of alzheimer's disease and features identification with automatic RGB segmentation algorithm. In: Gervasi, O., et al. (eds.) ICCSA 2018. LNCS, vol. 10961, pp. 92–106. Springer, Cham (2018). https://doi.org/10.1007/978-3-319-95165-2_7
9. Brandt, T., Caplan, L.R., Dichgans, J., Diener, H.C., Kennard, C.: Neurological Disorders: Course and Treatment. Gulf Professional Publishing, Houstan (2003)
10. Weiner, W.J., Shulman, L.M., Lang, A.E.: Parkinson's Disease: A Complete Guide for Patients and Families. JHU Press, Baltimore (2013)
11. Mendelow, A.D., Lo, E.H., Sacco, R.L., Faan, M.M.F., Wong, L.K.: Stroke: Pathophysiology, Diagnosis, and Management. Elsevier Health Sciences, Amsterdam (2015)
12. Karaca, Y., Cattani, C., Moonis, M., Bayrak, Ş.: Stroke subtype clustering by multifractal bayesian denoising with fuzzy C means and K-means algorithms. Complexity **2018**, 15 Pages (2018). Article ID 9034647
13. Shorvon, S., Guerrini, R., Cook, M., Lhatoo, S.: Oxford Textbook of Epilepsy and Epileptic Seizures. OUP, Oxford (2012)
14. Diamond, S., Cady, R.K., Diamond, M.L., Green, M.W., Martin, V.T.: Headache and Migraine Biology and Management. Academic Press, Cambridge (2015)
15. Good, D.C.: Episodic Neurologic Symptoms. In: Clinical Methods: The History, Physical, and Laboratory Examinations, 3rd edn. Butterworths (1990)

16. Bishop, S.R., et al.: Mindfulness: a proposed operational definition. Clin. Psych. **11**, 230–241 (2004)
17. Hudlicka, E.: Virtual training and coaching of health behavior: example from mindfulness meditation training. Patient Educ. Couns. **92**(2), 160–166 (2013)
18. Camerini, L., Camerini, A.L., Schulz, P.J.: Do participation and personalization matter? A model-driven evaluation of an Internet-based patient education intervention for fibromyalgia patients. Patient Educ. Couns. **92**(2), 229–234 (2013)
19. Nutbeam, D.: Health promotion glossary. Health Promotion Int. **13**(4), 357 (1998)
20. Rutter, D., Quine, L.: Social cognition models and changing health behaviours. In: Rutter, D., Quine, L. (eds.) Changing Health Behaviour: Intervention and Research with Social Cognition Models, pp. 1–27. Open University Press, London (2002)
21. Ajzen, I.: The theory of planned behavior. Organ. Behav. Hum. Decis. Process. **50**(2), 179–211 (1991)
22. Becker, M.H.: The health belief model and sick role behavior. Health Educ. Monogr. **2**(4), 409–419 (1974)
23. Becker, M.H., Maiman, L.A., Kirscht, J.P., Haefner, D.P., Drachman, R.H.: The health belief model and prediction of dietary compliance: a field experiment. J. Health Soc. Behav. **18**, 348–366 (1977)
24. Abraham, C., Sheeran, P.: The health belief model. In: Ayers, S., Baum, A., McManus, C., Newman, S., Wallston, K., Weinman, J., et al. (eds.) Cambridge Handbook of Psychology, Health and Medicine Cambridge, pp. 97–102. Cambridge University Press, Cambridge (2007)
25. Bian, J., Guo, Y., He, Z., Hu, X. (eds.): Social Web and Health Research: Benefits, Limitations, and Best Practices. Springer, Cham (2019). https://doi.org/10.1007/978-3-030-14714-3
26. Star, L., Moghadas, S.M.: The role of mathematical modelling in public health planning and decision making. Purple Paper, National Collaborative Center for Infectious Diseases (2010)
27. Cassidy, R., Singh, N.S., Schiratti, P.R., Semwanga, A., Binyaruka, P., Sachingongu, N., Blanchet, K.: Mathematical modelling for health systems research: a systematic review of system dynamics and agent-based models. BMC Health Serv. Res. **19**(1), 845 (2019)
28. Njeuhmeli, E., et al.: Using mathematical modeling to inform health policy: a case study from voluntary medical male circumcision scale-up in eastern and southern Africa and proposed framework for success. PLoS ONE **14**(3), e0213605 (2019)
29. Kreps, G.L., Neuhauser, L.: Artificial intelligence and immediacy: designing health communication to personally engage consumers and providers. Patient Educ. Couns. **92**(2), 205–210 (2013)
30. Brailsford, S.C., Harper, P.R., Patel, B., Pitt, M.: An analysis of the academic literature on simulation and modelling in health care. J. Simul. **3**(3), 130–140 (2009)
31. Fan, H., He, J.: Knowledge base construction based on knowledge fusion process model. In: Chen, H., Zeng, D., Yan, X., Xing, C. (eds.) ICSH 2019. LNCS, vol. 11924, pp. 333–344. Springer, Cham (2019). https://doi.org/10.1007/978-3-030-34482-5_30
32. Brian, D., Carpenter, S.B.: The alzheimer's disease knowledge scale: development and psychometric properties. Gerontologist **49**(2), 236–247 (2009)
33. Annear, M.J., et al.: Dementia knowledge assessment scale: development and preliminary psychometric properties. J. Am. Geriatr. Soc. **63**(11), 2375–81 (2015)

34. O'Donoghue, N.F., Duncan, J.S., Sander, J.W.A.S.: The National Hospital Seizure Severity Scale: a further development of the Chalfont Seizure Severity Scale. Epilepsia **37**, 563–71 (1996)
35. Stewart, W.F.: Reliability of the migraine disability assessment score in a population-based sample of headache sufferers. Cephalalgia **19**(2), 107–114 (1999)
36. Ware, J.E.: Jr practical implications of item response theory and computerized adaptive testing: a brief summary of ongoing studies of widely used headache impact scales. Med. Care **38**(9), 1173–1182 (2000)
37. Centers for Disease Control and Prevention 2011. Behavioral risk factor surveillance system questionnaire (2011)
38. National Institute of Neurological Disorders and Stroke (NINDS). Stroke information page (2013)
39. Meena, K., Tayal, D.K., Gupta, V., Fatima, A.: Using classification techniques for statistical analysis of Anemia. Artif. Intell. Med. **94**, 138–152 (2019)
40. Ghiasi, M.M., Zendehboudi, S., Mohsenipour, A.A.: Decision tree-based diagnosis of coronary artery disease: CART model. Comput. Methods Programs Biomed. **192**, 105400 (2020)
41. Ghiasi, M.M., Zendehboudi, S.: Decision tree-based methodology to select a proper approach for wart treatment. Comput. Biol. Med. **108**, 400–409 (2019)
42. Karaca, Y., Cattani, C.: Computational Methods for Data Analysis. Walter de Gruyter GmbH, Berlin (2018). 978–3110496352
43. González-Rodríguez, G., Colubi, A., Gil, M.Á.: Fuzzy data treated as functional data: a one-way ANOVA test approach. Comput. Stat. Data Anal. **56**(4), 943–955 (2012)
44. Jung, Y., Hu, J.: Reversed low-rank ANOVA model for transforming high dimensional genetic data into low dimension. J. Korean Stat. Soc. **48**(2), 169–178 (2019)
45. De Haan, J.R., et al.: Robust ANOVA for microarray data. Chemometr. Intell. Lab. Syst. **98**(1), 38–44 (2009)
46. Rutherford, A.: ANOVA and ANCOVA: A GLM Approach. Wiley, Hoboken (2011)
47. Girden, E.R.: ANOVA: repeated measures, vol. 84 (1992)
48. Simecek, P., Simecek, M.: Modification of Tukey's additivity test. J. Stat. Plann. Infer. **143**(1), 197–201 (2013)
49. Driscoll, W.C.: Robustness of the ANOVA and Tukey-Kramer statistical tests. Comput. Ind. Eng. **31**(1–2), 265–268 (1996)
50. Mackridge, A., Rowe, P.: A Practical Approach to Using Statistics in Health Research: From Planning to Reporting. Wiley, Hoboken (2018)
51. Feng, Y.C., Huang, Y.C., Ma, X.M.: The application of student's t-test in internal quality control of clinical laboratory. Front. Lab. Med. **1**(3), 125–128 (2017)
52. Wang, D., Zhang, H., Liu, R., Lv, W., Wang, D.: t-test feature selection approach based on term frequency for text categorization. Pattern Recogn. Lett. **45**, 1–10 (2014)
53. Peng, L., Tong, T.: A note on a two-sample T test with one variance unknown. Stat. Method. **8**(6), 528–534 (2011)
54. MathWorks, T.: MATLAB (R2019b). The MathWorks, Inc., Natick (2019)
55. IBM SPSS Statistics for Windows, Version 23.0. IBM Corp., Armonk, NY, USA (2015)

Test Automation with the Gauge Framework: Experience and Best Practices

Vahid Garousi[1,3(✉)], Alper Buğra Keleş[2], Yunus Balaman[2],
and Zeynep Özdemir Güler[2]

[1] Queen's University Belfast, Belfast, Northern Ireland, UK
v.garousi@qub.ac.uk
[2] Testinium A.Ş., Istanbul, Turkey
{alper.keles,yunus.balaman,
zeynep.ozdemir}@testinium.com
[3] Bahar Software Engineering Consulting Limited, Belfast, UK

Abstract. While Behavior-driven development (BDD) tools such as Cucumber are powerful tools for automated testing, they have certain limitations. For example, they often enforce strict syntax for test cases, like the "Given-When-Then" format, which may not always be easy to write for a given test case. A new test automation framework named Gauge (gauge.org) addresses that limitation since it does not prescribe the BDD testing process with a strict syntax. In Gauge, writing a test case is as easy as writing down the flow of test cases in several itemized sentences in a natural language, like English.

In the context of Testinium (testinium.com), a large software testing company which provides software testing services, tools and solutions to a large number of clients, we have actively used the Gauge framework since 2018 to develop large automated front-end test suites for several large web applications.

In this paper/talk, the speakers will share several examples and best practices of developing automated tests in natural-language requirements using the Gauge framework. By learning from the ideas presented in the talk, readers (attendees) will be able to consider applying the Gauge framework in their own test automation projects.

Keywords: Software testing · Test automation · Gauge framework · Industrial experience · Best practices

1 Introduction

If planned and executed properly, test automation can increase efficiency and effectiveness of software testing and thus leading to higher quality software products [1, 2]. On the other hand, just like any other software engineering activity, if not planned and executed properly, test automation can result in failure (google.com/search?q = test +automation+failure).

Test automation technologies are rapidly evolving and new methods and tools constantly appear the in industry. One of the approaches is to the Behavior-Driven Development (BDD) approach [3] which "*describes a cycle of interactions with well-defined outputs, resulting in the delivery of working, tested software that matters*" [4].

© Springer Nature Switzerland AG 2020
O. Gervasi et al. (Eds.): ICCSA 2020, LNCS 12250, pp. 458–470, 2020.
https://doi.org/10.1007/978-3-030-58802-1_33

While the BDD approach and the many tools that support BDD, such as Cucumber, are useful in many contexts for automated testing, they have certain limitations, e.g., [5–8]. For example, they often enforce "strict" syntax for test cases, like the "Given-When-Then" format, which may not always be easy to write for certain test cases [7]. That is one of the main reasons that a recent test automation framework named Gauge (gauge.org) was released by ThoughtWorks in 2018 [5]. Gauge addresses the above limitation since it does not prescribe the BDD testing process with a strict syntax. In Gauge, writing a test case is as easy as writing down the flow of test cases in several itemized sentences in a natural language, like English. Executable test specifications are written in the form of regular natural-language sentences and, using some form of mapping functions, are then directly executed for the purpose of testing.

Development of test suites in such a manner provides various benefits (e.g., enabling testers to write test cases in natural language) and, at the same time, exposes many challenges which have to be addressed, as we will see in the rest of this paper, e.g., flexibility of free text for test scripts can be a demerit as they will not have a defined format.

In the context of Testinium (testinium.com), a large software testing company which provides software testing services, tools and solutions to a large number of clients in several countries, the authors of this paper and their team members have actively used the Gauge framework since 2018 to develop large automated front-end test suites for several large web applications. Our research and development efforts are under the umbrella of a large-scale industry-academia collaboration [9], following the technology transfer guidelines in software engineering [10], and has been conducted in the context and using the funding of a 3-year international European R&D project named the "TESTOMAT – The Next Level of Test Automation" (www.testomatproject.eu), in which 34 industrial/academic partners across six countries are collaborating.

In this paper (talk), the speakers will share several examples and best practices of developing automated tests in natural-language requirements using the Gauge framework. By learning from the ideas presented in the talk, readers (attendees of the talk) will be able to consider applying the Gauge framework in their own test automation projects.

2 Overview of the Industrial Context and Need Analysis

Testinium A.Ş. is a provider of testing services and solutions in Turkey and across Europe. Testinium A.Ş. was founded in year 2010 and has provided automated testing to 50+ clients in several countries so far. In addition to the test service offered to clients, the company has developed and offers two flagship test automation tools: *Testinium* (testinium.com) and *Loadium* (loadium.com). As of Spring 2020, Testinium A.Ş. has about 190 employees. The company works using the agile methodologies in general.

The company has been proactive in adapting novel approaches to increase effectiveness and efficiency of its test activities, and joining the European TESTOMAT project has been one of those initiatives. Almost all of the Systems Under Test (SUTs) tested by test engineers are the clients' web or mobile applications, e.g., the online ticket sales website of several major airlines in Turkey.

A routine ongoing activity in the company is to utilize the latest test automation tools and approaches in the projects. As it has been discussed in the literature, *"Selecting the right tool for the right purpose is a key to success"* [11]. There have been a lot of guidelines and suggestions for choosing the "right" test automation tool in the grey literature (e.g., blogs posts, white papers), and a recent a grey literature review summarized the body of knowledge on the topic [12]. Due to the reasons discussed in the previous section above, i.e., Gauge addressing the shortcomings of the BDD tools/approaches, the team decided to use Gauge as a main tool for UI-based system testing of web applications.

For the purpose of illustration in this paper, as a the running example, we pick one of the Systems Under Test (SUT), a test tool developed in-house, which is one of the company's main offered solutions, *Testinium* (testinium.com). Testinium is a web application which provides various test management features via a web interface to Selenium. Two screenshots from the *Testinium* are shown in Fig. 1, in which the login page and the "all reports" page are visible. To provide more information about features of the tool, we depict its use-case diagram in Fig. 2.

Fig. 1. Two screenshots from the Testinium (testinium.com) test-management system

Fig. 2. Use-case diagram for the Testinium

3 Related Work

Since the Gauge tool is quite recent (released in 2018), except several informal online blog posts and such, there are not any experience reports that we know of, using Gauge.

Various papers have been published on Behavior-driven development (BDD), e.g., [13, 14]. Various books and papers have been published on test automation. One of the books on the topic is entitled "*Experiences of test automation: case studies of software test automation*" [15], which is composed of 29 chapters, all written by industrial test practitioners who reported separate case studies on test automation.

The authors have published a number of experience reports on test automation using different technologies and in different contexts, e.g., [2, 16–21].

4 How the Gauge Tool Works

In Gauge (gauge.org), an automated test case written by writing down the flow of test cases in several itemized sentences in a natural language (like English). Executable test specifications are written in the form of regular natural-language sentences and are then directly executed for the purpose of testing. For illustration, we show in Table 1 the partial test-code listing of a large Gauge test-script that we have developed for the Testinium as the SUT.

To allow test engineers develop test scripts in the varying levels of "abstraction" and to enable highly modular (and higher quality) test scripts [22], Gauge defines five inter-related concepts: test "specification", test "scenarios", test "concepts", test "steps", and step "implementation", the relationship of which are shown in Fig. 3. We also provide an example Gauge test-script for the Testinium in Table 1 in which the above test constructs have been used.

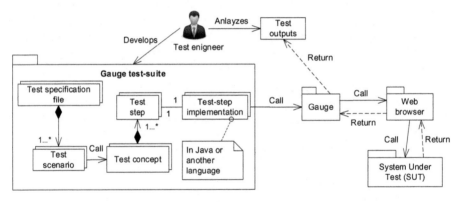

Fig. 3. Architecture of test automation in our approach and building blocks of Gauge test-scripts

Table 1. An example Gauge test-script for the Testinium as the SUT

Level of abstraction: High	1 test "scenarios". Calling 2 test "concepts"	Tags:LoginPage_InputControls * In the Login page, do the controls for the Email field * In the Login page, do the controls for the Password field	Call
	2 test "concepts". 3+4 test "steps"	# In the Login page, do the controls for the Email field * Go to "http://www.testinium.com" address * Check if the "tbEmailOfLogin" element is visible * Login using "testinium" and "passwd**" # Login using \<email> and \<password> * Inside the field "tbEmailOfLogin", write \<email> * Inside the field "tbPasswordOfLogin", write \<password> * Check if the "btnSignInOfLogin" element exists * "btnSignInOfLogin" elementine tikla	Call

Level of abstraction: Low	A step "implementation"	@Step("Inside the field \<key>, write \<text>")
		public void sendKey(String key, String text){
		    ElementInfo elementInfo = Stor
		        Helper.INSTANCE.findElementInfoByKey(key);
		    sendKeyBy(ElementHelper.getElementInfoToBy(elementInfo),
		        elementInfo.getIndex(), text);
		}
			Call the SUT

A test engineer develops a test suite, which could include several (one or more) test *specifications*. Each test *specification* is a ".SPEC" file and includes a set of test *scenarios* (see the test script example in Table 1). We have learnt by experience that a best practice is to correspond each test specification file to each use-case of the system (Fig. 2). For example, we would have one test *specification* file for the "login" use-case, which has several test *scenarios*, one of them being `LoginPage_Input Controls` as shown in Table 1.

Test *concept* is another feature provided by Gauge to enable modularity of test-code, a practice which has been widely encouraged in test automation [22]. For example, in the example of Table 1, there is one test *scenario* (`LoginPage_Input Controls`), which includes calls to two test *concepts*, which are defined in another scope (a .CPT file). In addition to ensuring varying levels of abstraction, such a modularity also support another proven design pattern: *separation of concerns (SoC)*. Each test *concept* can have one or more test *steps* (see the example in Table 1). Test *steps* are the lowest-level entities in terms of abstraction in Gauge. To enable the executability of Gauge test scripts, a test *implementation* (e.g., in Java Selenium) should be developed for each pattern of test *steps*. For example, test *step* "`Inside the field tbEmailOfLogin, write <email>`" will call the corresponding function in Java code in Table 1, which will send the keys, etc. to realize that test steps. In fact, each test *step* is like a function call, and it can include parameters, as seen in the example.

Other parts of the test-automation architecture diagram in Fig. 3 shows how the rest of the process works. A test *implementation* invokes Gauge and Selenium libraries and, via them, calls (exercises) the UI elements in the web application (SUT). Once tests finish executing, test outputs are provided to the test engineer.

5   Developing Gauge Test Suites for Multiple Projects

As mentioned earlier, we have actively used the Gauge framework since 2018 to develop large automated front-end test suites for ten's of large web applications, as SUTs. The SUTs are those developed by our clients and many systems developed in-house, e.g., Testinium (testinium.com). We show in Table 2 the size metrics of three SUTs, as examples, which we have tested using Gauge in the company so far.

For the Testinium as the SUT, we are showing two rows, which we will discuss in more detail in the next section. As part of the company's mission to continuously improve test practices, as our test engineers and we have developed more Gauge test suites, we have found better ways of developing test scripts. Thus, for the Testinium as the SUT, the two rows in Table 2: size metrics "before" systematic test design (pilot phase), and metrics after systematic test design (details are next).

Table 2. Size metrics for several SUTs, tested using Gauge in the company

Systems Under Test (SUT)	Application domain	Number of use-cases (features) tested	# of Gauge test specifications	# of test scenarios	# of test concepts	# of test step calls in test concepts	# of test steps (unique)	Line of Code (LOC) of test implementations	Development effort (engineer-month)
SUT1-Testinium: Before systematic test design	Testinium-: one of the company's test tools	7/13	162	1,667	518	2,658	119	1,123	4
SUT1-Testinium: With systematic test design		13/13	139	518	129	603	44	380	2
SUT2	E-commerce	14	114	539	67	449	41	3,415	4
SUT3	Telecommunications	8	14	181	5,411	508	58	1,348	5

6 Challenges When Developing Large Gauge Test Suites

We synthesize in this section a summary of the challenges that we have faced when developing large Gauge test suites since 2018, and the best practices that we have come up with to address those challenges to be able to develop high-quality maintainable test scripts [22], in Sect. 7.

As it has been widely discussed in the testing community, a test tool alone is not enough to reach successful test automation. Among other important "ingredients" are "a proven [effective] testing process" and "a skilled test team structured to meet the challenges of automation"[1]. Many online articles and blog posts have also highlighted this fact:

- For "successful [test] automation", "only tool is not enough"[2].
- "...while automation may be the answer, a tool is not enough"[1]
- "The selection and usage of an automated testing tool do not guarantee success" [23]

Furthermore, in the context of Gauge, two practitioners have shared the following observations:

- "Gauge follows Markdown Syntax for scripting the tests in an unstructured way - which means more liberty to make the test like a specific document and also more risk of ending up with scripted tests in many different styles. Having some in-team standards will help to prevent any chaos." [8]
- "If you feel that Cucumber is a pain when used in large projects due to its Given-When-Then syntax becoming messy in long run. Gauge can take out that pain to some extent. Even here, the flexibility of free text can be a demerit as they don't have a defined format. But tests may end up looking like a messy text document unless imposed strict restrictions". [6]

For the case of several initial pilot projects that we were developing Gauge test suites, we observed similar challenges as reported by the two quotes above. An example instance of such an issue is shown in Fig. 4. Note that since almost test engineers working in the company are Turkish, the Gauge test scripts have been have developed in Turkish. Even if the scripts text would not be readable to the non-Turkish reader, we can see that, due to different styles of testers writing the scripts, there were many issues, e.g., a lot of variability in length of test cases, duplication in scripts.

---

[1] www.mosaicinc.com/mosaicinc/successful_test.htm.

[2] www.softwaretestinggenius.com/successful-automation-only-tool-is-not-enough/.

```
45  #Login ekranındaki Email alanının kontrollerini yap
46  *"https://accountdev.testinium.com/uaa/login" adresine git
47  *"tbEmailOfLogin" elementinin görünürlüğü "true" mu kontrol et
48  *"testiniumtest1" ve "sifre12345" ile giris yap
49  *"tooltipMessageOfLogin" tooltipi "Please enter a valid email address." textine sahip mi bekleyip kontr
50  *"tbEmailOfLogin" elementinin text alanını sil
51  *"" ve "sifre12345" ile giris yap
52  *"tooltipMessageOfLogin" tooltipi "This field is required." textine sahip mi bekleyip kontrol et
53
54  #Login ekranındaki Password alanının kontrollerini yap
55  *"https://accountdev.testinium.com/uaa/login" adresine git
56  *"tbPasswordOfLogin" elementinin görünürlüğü "true" mu kontrol et
57  *"tbPasswordOfLogin" elementi zorunlu mu kontrol et
58  *"testiniumtest1@mynet.com" ve "" ile giris yap
59  *"tooltipMessageOfLogin" tooltipi "This field is required." textine sahip mi bekleyip kontrol et
60  *Input alanlarini temizle
61  *"tbPasswordOfLogin" elementine "@ƒⒺⒹ₺¥" değerini yaz
62  *Input alanlarini temizle
63  *"tbPasswordOfLogin" elementine "123456" değerini yaz
64  *Input alanlarini temizle
65  *"tbPasswordOfLogin" elementine "qwerty" değerini yaz
66  *Input alanlarini temizle
67  *"testiniumtest1@mynet.com" ve "1234567" ile giris yap
68  *"txtDangerOfLogin" elementi "Email or Password is incorrect!" text değerine sahip mi
69  *Input alanlarini temizle
70  *"testiniumtest1@mynet.com" ve "12345678" ile giris yap
71  *"txtDangerOfLogin" elementi "Email or Password is incorrect!" text değerine sahip mi
72  *Input alanlarini temizle
73  *"testiniumtest2@mynet.com" ve "sifre12345" ile giris yap
74  *şu anki url "https://clouddev.testinium.io" içeriyor mu
75
76  #Login ekranındaki LinkedIn butonunun kontrollerini yap
77  *"https://accountdev.testinium.com/uaa/login" adresine git
78  *"btnLinkedInOfLogin" elementine tıkla
79  *şu anki url "https://www.linkedin.com" içeriyor mu
80
81
82  #Login ekranındaki Forgot butonunun kontrollerini yap
83  *"https://accountdev.testinium.com/uaa/login" adresine git
84  *"btnForgot" elementinin görünürlüğü "true" mu kontrol et
85  *"btnForgot" elementine tıkla ve "https://accountdev.testinium.com/uaa/forgot-password" sayfasina ulas
86  *"btnTestiniumLogoOfLogin" elementine tıkla
```

Fig. 4. Excerpts from Testinium test suites in the pilot phase, in which the test code is of imperfect quality due to ad-hoc test-case design and scripting

While Gauge is a better tool compared to the competitors, and provides a powerful environment to develop test scripts in varying levels of abstraction, the intentional "flexibility" that Gauge provides for developing test steps in natural language can be a disadvantage, as it is easy to end up with a unorganized text document with a lot of issues (such as duplication) which will be hard to inspect and maintain afterwards [22]. Thus, our initial pilot phase showed to be useful in identifying the following two challenges:

- Challenge 1-Need for systematic test-case design: Systematic design of test cases is fundamentally important and crucial for success of any type of testing, either manual or automated testing [24]. However, many surveys and studies are reporting a general weakness in many context in terms of systematic design of test cases [24–26]. If test-cases are not designed systematically, but instead in purely ad-hoc manner, the resulting test suite will generally suffer from low fault detection effectiveness, since there could duplication test logic among test cases, etc. Also, without systematic design of test cases, the team cannot check the progress and also the completion ratio of tests [24].
- Challenge 2-Need for modular/maintainable test-scripts: Test code is a type of source code and just also any source code, it should be developed with high quality [22], e.g., it should be modular, readable and maintainable. This challenge is

slightly related to the previous challenge in that if test cases are not designed systematically, test scripts will be developed in ad-hoc and chaotic manner.

In the next section, we present a best practice that we have found to be effective in addressing the above challenges.

7   Best Practice: Systematic Design of Test Cases

Since the type of SUTs that we have been working on are all web applications, we identified model-based testing (MBT) [27] as the most suitable approach for systematic test-case design. MBT has been shown to be a suitable approach for testing web apps [28, 29], i.e. nodes would be the pages of the web app and edges would be the transitions among the pages (nodes).

Our ultimate goal has been to use automated MBT tools (such as GraphWalker, graphwalker.github.io) also in the process, together with Gauge, but that would be quite counter-intuitive, e.g. since Gauge scripts are supposed to be written by human testers. Thus, as the first phase, we decided to apply a light-weight manual MBT to design our test cases, and have human testers write Gauge test scripts based on them. The rationale was to have an approach which test engineers will easily use without having a heavyweight and sophisticated tooling.

Figure 5 shows the actual first version of the test model that we developed and of course, it was on paper, to highlight the light-weighted nature of our approach. The additions of new nodes and edges to the original paper version were made later on, as we noticed that new parts had to be added. This shows the "incremental" nature of the work. The light-weight nature of our MBT approach is also called "Just barely good enough"[3] modeling in the Agile modeling context.

In our light-weight model-based test design approach, once a test model is designed, we would derive four types of test cases from it:

1. Transition from the current node (page) to its next neighboring nodes (pages)
2. Node to itself (often, error checking, like: Invalid Login)
3. Input UI tests (in single node/page/unit level)
4. End-to-end testing: testing a path of nodes

For example, applying the above approach on the Login use-case of the system, results in deriving six test cases from the first type above (transition from the current node to its next neighboring nodes), as listed below:

- Node-2-node-1: Login to Dashboard: Valid login using regular login
- Node-2-node-2: Login to Forgot Password
- Node-2-node-3: Login to Signup
- Node-2-node-4: Login using LinkedIn
- Node-2-node-5: Login using Google
- Node-2-node-6: Login using GitHub

---

[3] www.agilemodeling.com/essays/barelyGoodEnough.html.

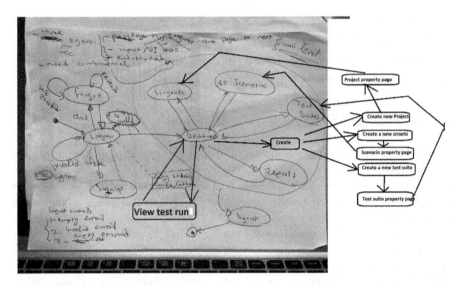

Fig. 5. Systematic design of test cases using light-weight test models

As shown in Table 2, after applying the above systematic approach, we derived 139 Gauge test specifications, and 518 test scenarios for the SUT.

8   Conclusions; Ongoing and Future Works

Now that we have been developing several Gauge test suites using our best practice above, in retrospective, we are able to observe various benefits, compared to our initial phase, in which test-cases were designed in ad-hoc manner.

- **Clarity and road-map for test engineers**: First of all, test engineers have clarity on how to develop Gauge test scripts, since the light-weight model-based test design approach provide a clear road-map for test engineers and makes it easier to know the progress and what additional test cases to derive.
- **Higher quality test script in term of modularity with no/less duplication**: Since the light-weight test design approach breaks the test design problem into smaller parts ("divide and conquer"), test engineers are less likely to develop "spaghetti"-style test scripts with no/less duplication [24].

Our ongoing and future works are in the scope of constantly improving our efforts in developing Gauge test suites, by findings more innovative ways and best practices for these tasks.

Acknowledgements. This work was supported by the European ITEA3 program via the "TESTOMAT (The Next Level of Test Automation)" project with grant number 16032, and by the Scientific and Technological Research Council of Turkey (TÜBİTAK) with grant number 9180076.

References

1. Garousi, V., Mäntylä, M.V.: When and what to automate in software testing? A multivocal literature review. Inf. Softw. Technol. **76**, 92–117 (2016)
2. Garousi, V., Tasli, S., Sertel, O., Tokgöz, M., Herkiloğlu, K., Arkin, H.F.E., Bilir, O.: Automated testing of simulation software in the aviation industry: an experience report. IEEE Softw. **36**(4), 63–75 (2019)
3. Smart, J.F.: BDD in Action: Behavior-Driven Development for the Whole Software Lifecycle. Manning Publications, New York (2014)
4. North, D.: How to sell BDD to the business. https://skillsmatter.com/skillscasts/923-how-to-sell-bdd-to-the-business. Accessed May 2020
5. Maliackal, Z.: Why we built Gauge. https://blog.getgauge.io/why-we-built-gauge-6e31bb4848cd. Accessed May 2019
6. Lakshmi, T.: "Why I chose Gauge over Cucumber. https://medium.com/@divi6.1990/why-i-chose-gauge-over-cucumber-5b3de478d889. Accessed May 2020
7. Matts, C.: The tragedy of Given-When-Then. https://theitriskmanager.com/2019/04/06/the-tragedy-of-given-when-then/. Accessed May 2019
8. Akbari, A.: Cucumber or Gauge? Things to consider when choosing the best Test Automation Framework for your team. https://www.linkedin.com/pulse/things-consider-when-choosing-best-test-automation-framework-akbari/. Accessed May 2020
9. Garousi, V., Shepherd, D.C., Herkiloğlu, K.: Successful engagement of practitioners and software engineering researchers: evidence from 26 international industry-academia collaborative projects. IEEE Software (2019, in press)
10. Gorschek, T., Garre, P., Larsson, S., Wohlin, C.: A model for technology transfer in practice. IEEE Softw. **23**(6), 88–95 (2006)
11. Janicki, M., Katara, M., Pääkkönen, T.: Obstacles and opportunities in deploying model-based GUI testing of mobile software: a survey. Softw. Test. Verif. Reliab. **22**(5), 313–341 (2012)
12. Raulamo, P., Mäntylä, M.V., Garousi, V.: Choosing the right test automation tool: a grey literature review. In: International Conference on Evaluation and Assessment in Software Engineering, pp. 21–30 (2017)
13. Li, N., Escalona, A., Kamal, T.: Skyfire: model-based testing with cucumber. In: IEEE International Conference on Software Testing, Verification and Validation, pp. 393–400 (2016)
14. Sivanandan, S.: Agile development cycle: approach to design an effective Model Based Testing with Behaviour driven automation framework. In: Annual International Conference on Advanced Computing and Communications, pp. 22–25 (2014)
15. Graham, D., Fewster, M.: Experiences of Test Automation: Case Studies of Software Test Automation. Addison-Wesley Professional, Boston (2012)
16. Garousi, V., Keleş, A.B., Güler, Z.Ö., Balaman, Y.: Executable natural-language test specifications: a test-automation experience report. In: Proceedings of the Turkish National Software Engineering Symposium (UYMS) (2019)
17. Shewchuk, Y., Garousi, V.: Experience with maintenance of a functional GUI test suite using IBM rational functional tester. In: Proceedings of the International Conference on Software Engineering and Knowledge Engineering, pp. 489–494 (2010)
18. Garousi, V., Eskandar, M.M., Herkiloğlu, K.: Industry-academia collaborations in software testing: experience and success stories from Canada and Turkey. Software Qual. J. **25**(4), 1091–1143 (2017)

19. Şentürk, Ş., Akın, A., Karagöz, A.B., Garousi, V.: Model-based testing in practice: an experience report from the banking domain. In: Proceedings of the Turkish National Software Engineering Symposium (UYMS) (2019)
20. Urul, G., Garousi, V., Urul, G.: Test automation for embedded real-time software: an approach and experience report in the Turkish industry. In: Proceedings of the Turkish National Software Engineering Symposium (UYMS) (2014)
21. Akin, A., Sentürk, S., Garousi, V.: Transitioning from manual to automated software regression testing: experience from the banking domain. In: Asia-Pacific Software Engineering Conference (APSEC), pp. 591–597 (2018)
22. Garousi, V., Felderer, M.: Developing, verifying and maintaining high-quality automated test scripts. IEEE Softw. **33**(3), 68–75 (2016)
23. Lewis, W.E.: Software Testing and Continuous Quality Improvement. CRC Press, Boca Raton (2017)
24. Eldh, S.: On test design. Ph.D. thesis, Mälardalen University (2011)
25. Garousi, V., Coşkunçay, A., Can, A.B., Demirörs, O.: A survey of software engineering practices in Turkey. J. Syst. Softw. **108**, 148–177 (2015)
26. Garousi, V., Zhi, J.: A survey of software testing practices in Canada. J. Syst. Softw. **86**(5), 1354–1376 (2013)
27. Kramer, A., Legeard, B.: Model-Based Testing Essentials-Guide to the ISTQB Certified Model-Based Tester. Wiley, Hoboken (2016)
28. Koopman, P., Plasmeijer, R., Achten, P.: Model-based testing of thin-client web applications. In: Havelund, K., Núñez, M., Roşu, G., Wolff, B. (eds.) FATES/RV -2006. LNCS, vol. 4262, pp. 115–132. Springer, Heidelberg (2006). https://doi.org/10.1007/11940197_8
29. Monsma, J.R.: Model-based testing of web applications. MSc thesis, Radboud University, The Netherlands (2015)

Coupling an Agent-Based Model with a Mathematical Model of Rift Valley Fever for Studying the Impact of Animal Migrations on the Rift Valley Fever Transmission

Paul Python Ndekou Tandong[1]([⊠]) (ID), Papa Ibrahima Ndiaye[2], Alassane Bah[1],
Dethie Dione[3], and Jacques André Ndione[4]

[1] Department of Mathematics and Computer Science, Cheikh Anta Diop University,
Dakar, Senegal
`pppython@yahoo.fr`, `alassane.bah@gmail.com`
[2] Department of Mathematics, Alioune Diop University, Bambey, Senegal
`papaibra.ndiaye@uadb.edu.sn`
[3] UFR Science de l'Education, de la Formation et du Sport, Gaston Berger
University, Saint Louis, Senegal
`dethiedione79@gmail.com`
[4] Centre de Suivi Ecologique, Dakar, Senegal
`jacques-andre.ndione@cse.sn`

Abstract. Rift valley fever (RVF) is a disease killing principally animals. In this article, we coupled a mathematical model of animal-mosquito interactions with an agent-based model describing the migrations of hosts between cities. The mathematical model describes animal-mosquito interactions in each city and the agent based-model describes the migrations of animals between cities. The coupled model allows to compute at each time the number of infected animals in all cities and to study the impact of host migrations on the dynamics of infections. The obtained results showed that quarantining certain cities can reduce the number of infected hosts. It is also observed that when the density of animal migrations increases, the number of infection cases increases. The developed model brings solutions to both models (mathematical model and agent-based model) limits. This model could help to study and forecasting the Rift Valley Fever transmission and its outbreak in the short and long term.

Keywords: Mathematical modeling · Agent-based modeling · Rift valley fever · Coupling model · Migration · Infectious disease · Artificial intelligence

1 Introduction

Rift Valley fever is an example of emerging arbovirosis [30]. It is widely distributed in Sahelian Africa [1,2]. At present, RVF (Rift Valley Fever) virus is a

© Springer Nature Switzerland AG 2020
O. Gervasi et al. (Eds.): ICCSA 2020, LNCS 12250, pp. 471–485, 2020.
https://doi.org/10.1007/978-3-030-58802-1_34

veterinary health problem in West Africa. During the epidemics period, animal migrations cause new cases of infected animals. Conditions of emergence and re-emergence of RVF motivated the Scientist community to study the impact of animal migrations and animal-mosquito interactions in the spread of RFV. Mathematical models using patches have described the impact of movements of animals and humans on vector-borne disease transmissions [3, 7, 13] B. Adams et al. [4] have studied the impact of human movements on vector-borne disease transmission. M. Alvim et al. [5] have studied the impact of the human mobility on the transmission of vector-borne diseases between cities. Researchers belonging to different disciplines (mathematics, biology, computer science) have worked on the mechanisms of RVF transmission. Holly et al. [6] have proposed a mathematical model describing interactions between two populations of vectors (Aedes and Culex) and one livestock population. Results of their study have shown that in the area where the contact rate between vectors and livestock is near to 1, the number of infected animals tends to multiply. Mpheshet et al. [8] have developed a mathematical model using a nonlinear differential equations to describe RFV infection in the global scale taking into account mosquitoes, livestock and human hosts. Models using vaccination have been used in order to reduce infection rates during epidemics. Ling Xue et al. [10] have developed a mathematical model based on the hierarchcal network taking into account Aedes vexans mosquitoes, Culex poicilipes mosquitoes and the livestock. It is shown that livestock movements, mosquito populations and climate factors play an important role in the spatial propagation of Rift Valley fever viruses. Xue et al. [9] have proposed a new compartmental model for describing RFV transmission microscopic scale and macroscopic scale. Tianchan et al. [11] have developed a mathematical model of RVF integrating a spatial approach [7] in the study of viruses propagation taking into account livestock movements, vertical transmission between mosquitoes and eggs. Gao et al. [7] have shown that the propagation of RFV depends on contacts between livestock and vectors (mosquitoes). Several studies on vector-borne diseases have been carried out using a microscopic scale. Agent-based models have been developed for studying the transmission of vector-borne diseases [12]. Generally, researchers using agent-based models take into account vector behaviors, host behaviors, vector-host interactions in the environment, climate factors impacts in the environment [16]. Hybrid models integrating mathematical [14] and agent-based models have been developed in order to solve limits of each model [15]. For mathematical models using patches in the modeling of infectious diseases, it's not possible to know the dynamics of RVF transmission in all cities at the same time. Mathematical models use the sequential programming that has a great complexity in term of computations. The mathematical model of Rift valley fever transmission doesn't take into account partial migrations of hosts in cities. In this article, we will develop a hybrid model by coupling a mathematical model with an agent-based model in order to show the impact of animal migrations on the growth of the number of infected animals. This model could help to study the dynamics of infected animals at each time in all cities when putting one or several cities in quarantine.

2   Mathematical Model Formulation

Model Description
We propose a mathematical model of RVF transmission between animal hosts
and vectors (Aedes vexans mosquitoes and Culex poicilipes mosquitoes). We take
into account vertical and horizontal transmission. For reducing the complexity of
the model, there exists a recruitment of new species of mosquitoes and animals
at each unit of time. The model of RVF transmission for animals is divided
into four compartments: SEIR. $S_h(t)$ is the compartment of hosts presenting a
risk of infection. $E_h(t)$ is a compartment of infected animals having a virus, not
presenting a sign of infection and not able to infected mosquitoes. $I_h(t)$ is the
compartment of infected animals presenting symptoms of the RVF and able to
transmit the disease. $R_h(t)$ is the compartment of hosts having had an immunity
after an infection with viruses. The size of host populations is N_h and defines
by: $N_h = S_h + E_h + I_h + R_h$.

The model of RVF transmission using Aedes vexans mosquito populations is
divided into three compartments: SEI. $S_a(t)$ is the compartment of Aedes vexans
presenting a risk of infection. $E_a(t)$ is a compartment of infected Aedes vexans
having a virus, not presenting a sign of infection and can not able to infect hosts.
$I_a(t)$ is the compartment of infected Aedes vexans presenting symptoms of RVF
and able to transmit the disease. when infected by the virus of the RVF, each
Aedes vexans Mosquito remains infected during its lifetime. The size of Aedes
mosquito populations is N_a and defines by: $N_a = S_a + E_a + I_a + R_a$.

Q_a is the compartment of infected eggs of Aedes vexans mosquitoes. P_a is
the compartment of Aedes vexans eggs. P_c is the compartment of Culex poicilipes eggs. The model of RVF transmission using Culex poicilipes mosquito
populations is divided into three compartments: SEI. $S_c(t)$ is the compartment
of Culex poicilipes presenting a risk of infection. $E_c(t)$ is a compartment of
infected Culex poicilipes having a virus, not presenting a sign of infection or can
not able to infect hosts. $I_c(t)$ is the compartment of infected Culex poicilipes
presenting symptoms of RVF and able to transmit the disease. Each Culex poicilipes Mosquito remains infected during its lifetime. The size of Culex poicilipes
populations is N_c and defines by: $N_c = S_c + E_c + I_c$.

Mathematical Model of the Transmission
Parameters of the model (Table 1) are defined as follows:
λ_a is the number of eggs laid by each Aedes vexans mosquito, λ_h is the birth
rate of hosts (animals), λ_c is the number of eggs laid by each Culex mosquito,
α_a is the transovarial infection rate of Aedes vexans $1/\gamma_a$ is the development
time of Aedes vexans, $1/\gamma_c$ is the development time of Culex, β_{ha} is the contact
rate:host to Aedes vexans, β_{ah} is the ontact rate: Aedes vexans to host, β_{ch} is the
contact rate: Culex poicilipes to host, β_{hc} is the contact rate: host to Culex, K_h
is the carrying capacity of hosts $\dfrac{1}{d_c}$ is the Lifespan of Culex, $\dfrac{1}{d_h}$ is the Lifespan
of hosts, $\dfrac{1}{d_a}$ is lifespan of Aedes vexans, $\dfrac{1}{i_a}$ is the incubation period in Aedes,

$\dfrac{1}{i_c}$ is incubation period in Culex poicilipes, $\dfrac{1}{i_h}$ is the incubation period in hosts.
The mathematical model is described with the following ordinary differential equations:

$$\begin{cases} \dfrac{dP_a}{dt} = \lambda_a N_a - \lambda_a \alpha_a I_a - \gamma_a P_a \\[2mm] \dfrac{dQ_a}{dt} = \lambda_a \alpha_a I_a - \gamma_a Q_a \\[2mm] \dfrac{dS_a}{dt} = \gamma_a P_a - (d_a + \dfrac{\beta_{ha}.I_h}{N_h}) S_a \\[2mm] \dfrac{dE_a}{dt} = \dfrac{\beta_{ha}.I_h}{N_h} S_a - (d_a + i_a) E_a \\[2mm] \dfrac{dI_a}{dt} = \gamma_a Q_a + i_a E_a - d_a I_a \\[2mm] \dfrac{dN_a}{dt} = \gamma_a (Q_a + P_a) - d_a N_a \end{cases} \tag{1}$$

$$\begin{cases} \dfrac{dP_c}{dt} = \lambda_c N_c - \gamma_c P_c \\[2mm] \dfrac{dS_c}{dt} = \gamma_c P_c - (d_c + \dfrac{\beta_{hc}.I_h}{N_h}) S_c \\[2mm] \dfrac{dE_c}{dt} = \dfrac{\beta_{hc}.I_h}{N_h} S_c - (d_c + i_c) E_c \\[2mm] \dfrac{dI_c}{dt} = i_c E_c - d_c I_c \\[2mm] \dfrac{dN_c}{dt} = \gamma_c (Q_c + P_c) - d_c N_c \end{cases} \tag{2}$$

$$\begin{cases} \dfrac{dS_h}{dt} = \lambda_h.N_h - (\dfrac{d_h N_h}{K_h} + \dfrac{\beta_{ah}.I_a}{N_a} + \dfrac{\beta_{ch}.I_c}{N_c}) S_h \\[2mm] \dfrac{dE_h}{dt} = (\dfrac{\beta_{ah}.I_a}{N_a} + \dfrac{\beta_{ch}.I_c}{N_c}) S_h - (\dfrac{d_h N_h}{K_h} + i_h) E_h \\[2mm] \dfrac{dI_h}{dt} = i_h E_h - (\gamma_h + \mu_h + \dfrac{d_h N_h}{K_h}) I_h \\[2mm] \dfrac{dR_h}{dt} = \gamma_h I_h - \dfrac{d_h N_h}{K_h} R_h \\[2mm] \dfrac{dN_h}{dt} = \lambda_h N_h - \dfrac{d_h N_h}{K_h} N_h - \mu_h I_h \end{cases} \tag{3}$$

3   Disease Free Equilibrium (DFE), P_0

The disease free equilibrium of the models (1), (2), (3) is obtained by setting the right hand side of (1), (2), (3) equals zero and $E_a = I_a = E_c = I_c = E_h = I_h = 0$. If we transform our system in term of proportions in each compartment by posing $x_i = \frac{X_i}{N_i}$, $i \in \{a, c, h\}$, where X_i is a population of compartment i.

Further computation gives: $p_a = \frac{\lambda_a}{\gamma_a}$, $p_c = \frac{\lambda_c}{\gamma_c}$, $s_a = \frac{\lambda_a}{d_a}$, $s_c = \frac{\lambda_c}{d_c}$, $s_h = \frac{\lambda_h K_h}{d_h}$. $P_0 = (p_a, 0, s_a, 0, p_c, s_c, 0, 0, S_h, 0, 0, 0)$, P_0 is a free equilibrium point in term of proportions.

3.1 The Basic Reproduction Number, R_0

The basic reproduction number R_0 is defined as the average number of secondary infection cases generated by an infected animal during its period of infection when it is introduced into a susceptible animal population [26,27,29]. There are many methods for computing the basic reproduction number. In this work, we have used the theorem of Van den Driessche et al. [17]. The DFE (disease free equilibrium) point is P_0. Variables used when occurs an infection are: Q_a, E_a, I_a for the vertical transmission route and E_a, I_a, E_h, I_h, E_c, I_c for the horizontal transmission route. To compute $R_{0,V}$ and $R_{0,H}$, representing respectively the basic reproduction number when there exists a vertical transmission and the basic reproduction number when there exists a horizontal transmission, we used the next generation matrix approach, as described by Diekmann et al. [29] and van den Driessche and Watmough [17]. For the computation of $R_{0,V}$, we expressed the model equations of system (1) concerning the vertical transmission [28] in vector form as the difference between the rate of new infection in compartment i, called $\mathcal{F}_i$ and the rate of transfert between compartment i and all other compartment due to other processes called $\mathcal{V}_i$. For this case, the compartments involved are infected eggs, exposed Aedes vexans female adults and incectious adults of Aedes poicilipes population. The basic reproduction number is calculated as the spectral radius of the next generation matrix, $M = F_v . V_v^{-1}$. Using the same approach, we computed $R_{0,H}$. Finally, we have found the following results.

$$R_{0,V} = \frac{\lambda_a \alpha_a}{d_a}, \; R_{0,H} = \sqrt{\frac{\lambda_h i_h K_h}{d_h(\lambda_h + i_h)(\gamma_h + \mu_h + \lambda_h)}\left(\frac{\beta_{hc}\lambda_c i_c \beta_{ch}}{d_c^2(d_c + i_c)} + \frac{\beta_{ha}\lambda_a i_c \beta_{ah}}{d_a^2(d_a + i_a)}\right)}$$

Description of the Results Concerning the Basic Reproduction Number
Since the model incorporates both vertical and horizontal transmission, R_0 for the systems (1), (2), (3) is the sum of $R_{0,V}$ and $R_{0,H}$ [28], thus, $R_0 = R_{0,V} + R_{0,H}$. We have used the following probability: $\dfrac{i_a}{d_a + i_a}$ is a survival probability of an Aedes vexans mosquito during its incubation period. $\dfrac{i_c}{d_c + i_c}$ is a survival probability of a Culex poicilipes mosquito during its incubation period. $\dfrac{i_h}{d_h + i_h}$ is a survival probability of an animal host during its incubation period.

   Thus $R_0 = \dfrac{\lambda_a \alpha_a}{d_a} + R_{0,H}$. It should be noted that a program to fight against RVF will consist to reduce the value of R_0. The following result comes from the theorem of Van der Driessche et al. [17]. The disease free equilibrium is locally asymptotically stable whenever $R_0 < 1$ and unstable if $R_0 > 1$.

if $R_0 < 1$, In this case, we can expect that the infection could disappear into the host population.

if $R_0 > 1$, each infected host could lead on average more than one new infection. In this case, the disease could persist in each region.

4   The Agent-Based Model of Animal Migrations

In this section, we build an agent-based model describing animal migrations between cities. This agent-based model, coupled with a mathematical model of Rift valley fever help for understanding the impact of migrations on Rift valley fever transmission. We firstly describe the relationships between cities and trucks helping for migrations between cities. Using UML (Fig. 1), we have identified two types of agent: a CityAgent representing a city where exist RVF or not, a TruckAgent representing a truck that allows a certain number of hosts to leave one city to another city.

4.1   Description of the Relationship with the UML Formalism

We suppose that the area of study is divided in cities numbered by $c_1, c_2, .., c_n$. Each city has a local transmission of RVF and uses a mathematical model to describe the propagation of the disease. During the simulation of the mathematical model, the city entity stocks in mathematical variables the number of infected animals at every step. The truck entity help to transport host animals from one city to another city.

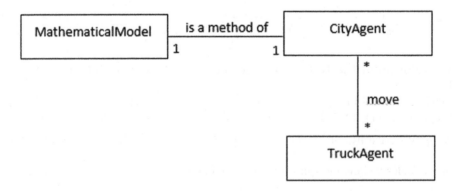

Fig. 1. Architecture of the coupling showing relationships between agent-based model and mathematical model of Rift valley fever in each city.

4.2   Description of Agents

The UML model that we have built allows us to identify two species of agents: The Truck Agent and the City Agent.

City Agent
Each city agent called **CityAgent** uses the mathematical model to compute the number of infected animals at each step of the simulation. The data used by a city agent comes from the mathematical model. Each truck agent is controled by a agent within its environment. One can note that a city agent can refuse or allow to a truck agent the possibility to leave or to enter into a city. Each city agent has the following attributes: each variable of the mathematical model, the total number of animal hosts, the total number of mosquitoes, the total number of truck agent in each city, the number of truck agent that has the authorization to enter in a city, a list of informations about the city border. Every city agent can execute the following methods:controlTruckAgent() allows to control every truck, ComputMathModel() allows for computing the number of infected animals at each step of simulation. detectRfv() allows knowing if there exist RVF infections in the other cities.

Truck Agent
A truck agent allows the transportation of animal hosts from one city to another city. Each truck agent has the following attributes: the number of susceptible animals, the number of susceptible animals, the number of infected animals. Each truck agent has the following methods: MoveCity() allows moving from one city to another city, VerifyMigration() allows verifying if it has the grant to enter into one city, updatData() allows for updating the different values contained within its database.

5   Coupling of EBM Model and ABM Model

The mathematical model describes the dynamics of interactions between animal hosts and mosquitoes causing infections in the city scale. For describing host infections we have used the SEIR model for animal infections and SEI model for mosquito infections. The mathematical model is controled by The agent-based model (ABM) in each city in order to allow the migration of host populations between cities. The main objective of the migration is to study the impact of animal migrations on the prevalence of Rift valley fever in all cities. We have two processes of the transmission RVF, the local transmission and the transmission between cities.

Description of the Coupling
Due to the fact that the simulations will be carried out within the central memory of the computer, we have thought that it's a good thing to model RVF transmission by a mathematical model and the migration of animals between cities by an agent-based model. This collaboration between the two models will help to minimize the storage capacity of the central memory of the computer. At each

time t, using the mathematical model, the city agent computes and stocks the following list values: $L = \{ P_a(t), Q_a(t), S_a(t), E_a(t), I_a(t), P_c(t), S_c(t), E_c(t), I_c(t), S_h(t), E_h(t), I_h(t), R_h(t) \}$. At every arrival in each agent city, each truck agent stocks a certain percentage of the values computed by each city agent and transport them from city to city. Meanwhile, there are a decrease and an increase in each population number due to the arrival and departure of a truck agent. The coupling that exists between the two models is the strong coupling because there exists a transfer of the information (infected populations) from a mathematical model to the agent-based model and from the agent-based model to mathematical model.

6   Numerical Simulation and Results

Experimental Descriptiont

In the platform of the modelling called CORMAS [18] (Fig. 2), each simulation is done in 200 steps corresponding to 200 days of the year. The simulation is organized as follows:

a) in the first part we initialize the virtual learning environment, the parameters that help for creating the different agents.
b) in the second part we use the original data coming from the litterature review.
c) in the last part we analyze the impact of the animal migrations between cities.

Results

To perform the simulation, we have used a grid of 10 square kilometers corresponding to the study of the spread of Rift Valley fever. We also suppose that the area of study is divided into ($n \geq 2$) cities where each city represents a sub-population including Aedes vexans mosquitoes, livestock (hosts) [31] and Culex poicilipes mosquitoes. For exploring migrations of livestock on the space in all cities, we have done the following assumptions:

- every city has epidemiological parameter values.
- initial values of infected populations in cities 2, 3, 4, 5 are initialize to zero.
- Only one city (city number 1) has infected hosts at the beginning of every simulation.

We solved the mathematical model of RVF using a fourth-order Runge-Kutter schema with the time step equal to one day. For studying the transmission of Rift valley fever between cities, a number of simulations were carried out in a virtual platform containing five city agents, five truck agents. Each city agent has a computer program used for the implementation of the mathematical model. We used the following initial values for the mathematical model: for city number 1, 5000 eggs of Aedes vexans mosquitoes, 4999 susceptibles Aedes vexans mosquitoes, 1 infected Aedes vexans mosquito, 5 infected animals, 1000 susceptible hosts, 5000 eggs of Culex poicilipes, 5000 susceptible Culex mosquitoes, others initial values in city 1 are putting to zero. Within city 2, 3, 4, 5 we used 5000 eggs of

Aedes vexans mosquitoes, 5000 susceptibles Aedes vexans mosquitoes, 0 infected Aedes vexans mosquito, 0 infected animal, 1000 susceptible hosts, 5000 eggs of Culex poicilipes, 5000 susceptibles Culex mosquitoes. Several simulations were carried out corresponding to 200 days. For the first simulation, we introduced infected animals only in the city number 1 and not taking into account migrations and obtained results in (Fig. 3) showing the number of infected hosts within all cities. For the second simulation, we take into account truck agent migrations between cities and obtained results in (Fig. 4) showing the number of infected hosts within all cities, in (Fig. 5) and (Fig. 6) showing the number of infected hosts within city number 1 and city number 2. We observed two processes of infected animals. The local evolution of infected animals in each city and the global evolution of infected animals between cities.

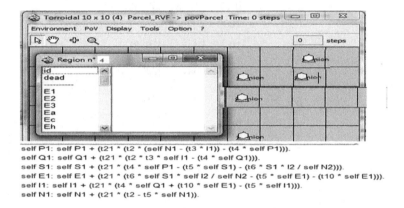

Fig. 2. Screenshot showing the virtual environment, the five vitual cities and the first lines of the source code of the mathematical model managed by city agents.

7 Discussion

Each city agent used a mathematical model for computing the number of infected animals and infected mosquitoes during the spread of Rift valley fever. Due to the fact that, each agent city is autonomous, all city agents carried out their computations at the same time. It's a great advantage because it is possible with this coupled model to know at every time the number of infected cases in all cities at the same time. Several mathematical models used patches for studying migrations between cities, but during the phase of implementation, the sequential programming is used to compute the number of infected animals. Sequential programming has a great cost in term of computations. Comparatively to the mathematical models using patches, the coupled model allows reducing the time of computations because each city agent is in charge of the execution of the mathematical model. The mathematical model using patches

Table 1. Parameters of the mathematical model

Parameter	Value	Units	References
λ_a	0.1	1/day	–
λ_h	0.0027	1/day	–
λ_c	0.1	1/day	–
α_a	0.05	1/day	[25]
$1/\gamma_a$	10	days	[19]
$1/\gamma_c$	10	day	[19]
β_{ah}	0.15	1/day	[32–38]
β_{ha}	0.15	1/day	[32–36]
β_{ch}	0.0176	1/day	[33–36]
β_{hc}	0.15	1/day	[32–36]
K_h	1000	–	–
$\dfrac{1}{d_c}$	10	day	[19–21]
$\dfrac{1}{d_h}$	370	day	[22]
$\dfrac{1}{d_a}$	10	day	[21]
$\dfrac{1}{i_a}$	6	day	[23]
$\dfrac{1}{i_c}$	6	day	[23]
$\dfrac{1}{i_h}$	4	day	[24]

have used the sequential programming and the coupled model used the parallel programming that is known to reduce the time of computations. We note that, if the mathematical model has n patches, if the time of computing in each patch is p, the total time to know the number of infected animals in all patches when executing the mathematical model is p.n comparatively to the coupled model where this number is p. In mathematical models using patches for describing the impact of migrations between cities, authors often used a macroscopic scale comparatively to the coupled model using a microscopic scale between cities. The other advantage of the coupled model is the possibility to take into account environmental factors and behaviors of cities influencing the migration of truck agents. When putting 4 cities agent in quarantine and leave one city with several cases of infected animals (city agent number 1), after the execution of the coupled model in 200 steps of simulation, the total number of infected animals found was approximatively zero (Fig. 3). When allowing migrations of all five truck agents between cities, the total number of infected animals found was 862 (Fig. 4). We can say that animal migrations increase the number of infected animals in each city. Putting some cities in quarantine could help to eradicate RVF disease. On the (Fig. 2) the number of infected animals after 200 steps of simulation in the agent city number 1 is almost zero when there are no migrations, when taking

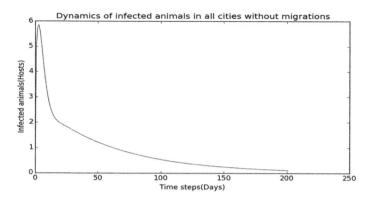

Fig. 3. Dynamics of infected hosts in all cities without migrations. The number of infected hosts is equal to the number of infected hosts within city number 1

account into migrations, on (Fig. 5) the number of infected animals after 200 steps of simulations in agent city number 1 is around 166 and greater than the initial value of infected animals which is 5. We can also say that the number of infected animals in one city that has already been infected could present the new cases of infection (Fig. 5) when migrations were authorized between cities. If the city agent number 2 has zero infected (Fig. 7) and if the migrations of truck agents are allowed, one can observed new infections cases (Fig. 6). The model that we have developed gives the possibilities to control the authorization of animal migrations, to put certain cities in quarantine and observed the dynamics of infections in all cities at the same time whereas the model developed by Buyu et al. [39] have used migrations of animals at each step of simulation and not take into account putting in quarantine certain cities. We can say that avoid migrations of animals in certain cities in the period of epidemics of Rift valley fever could help to eradicate Rift Valley fever. At different geographical locations (in each city), migrations of livestocks (hosts) increase the number of infected animals comparatively to the results obtained by Tianchan et al. [11]. The migration rates from city agent to another city agent have a great impact on the variation in spatial transmission of Rift valley [11], comparatively to our work, we note that the spatial migration of livestock increase the populations of infected and non infected animals (Fig. 4, Fig. 5, Fig. 6).

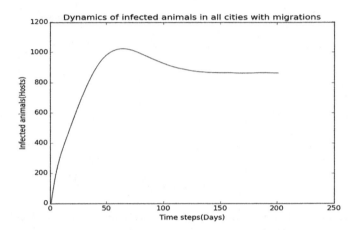

Fig. 4. Dynamics of infected animals with migration in all cities.

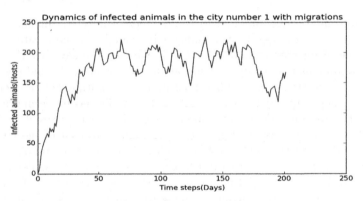

Fig. 5. Dynamics of infected animals with migrations in city number 1

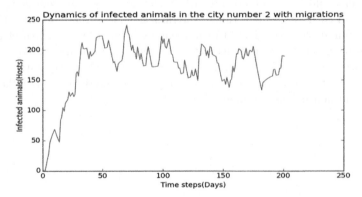

Fig. 6. Dynamics of infected animals with migrations in city number 2

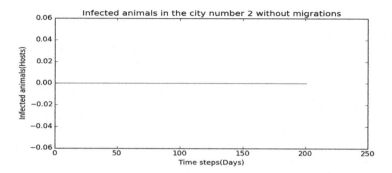

Fig. 7. Dynamics of infected animals without migrations in city number 2

8   Conclusion

In this study, we have built an epidemiological model of the RVF transmission taking into account migrations between cities. Based on previous works, we found that our model confirm the fact that migrations of infected animals increase the total number of infected cases in the environment. This model is a virtual platform helping to simulate the transmission of RVF between cities. This work shows benefices of coupling an agent-based model with a mathematical model in order for studying certain characteristics of the spread of the Rift valley Fever in several cities. The coupled model allows resolving some limits posed by the two models (mathematical model and agent-based model). With the coupled model it is possible to know the average number of infected animal hosts in all cities at every time. We have also shown that the coupled model improves the complexity of the mathematical model using patches in term of the time of computations. We have shown that, when certain cities are in quarantine, it is possible for observing the evolution of the RVF transmission in the other cities. We have shown that, when one city is in quarantine, the new cases of infections could not appear in this city. This coupled model could help in studying the impact of migrations in the transmission of other infectious diseases and their eradication.

References

1. Murgue, B., Zeller, H., Deubel, V.: The ecology and epidemiology of West Nile virus in Africa, Europe and Asia. In: Mackenzie, J.S., Barrett, A.D.T., Deubel, V. (eds.) Japanese Encephalitis and West Nile Viruses. Current Topics in Microbiology and Immunology, vol. 267, pp. 195–221. Springer, Heidelberg (2002). https://doi.org/10.1007/978-3-642-59403-8_10
2. Zeller, H.G., Schuffenecker, I.: West Nile virus: an overview of its spread in Europe and the Mediterranean basin in contrast to its spread in the Americas. Eur. J. Clin. Microbiol. Infect. Dis. **23**(3), 147–156 (2004)
3. Iggidr, A., Sallet, G., Souza, M.O.: Analysis of the dynamics of a class of models for vector-borne diseases with host circulation. Research Report RR-8396, INRIA, p. 20 (2013)

4. Adams, B., Kapan, D.D.: Man bites mosquito: understanding the contribution of human movement to vector-borne disease dynamics. PLoS ONE **4**(8), e6763 (2009)
5. Alvim, M., Iggidr, A., Koiler, J., Sallet, G., Penna, M.L.F., Souza, M.O.: Onset of a vector borne disease due to human circulation-uniform, local and network reproduction ratios. Preprint HAL (2013)
6. Gaff, H.D., Hartley, D.M., Leahy, N.P.: Electron. J. Differ. Equ. **2007**(115), 1–12 (2007). ISSN 1072-669
7. Gao, D., Cosner, C., Cantrell, R.S., Beier, J.C., Ruan, S.: Modeling the spatial spread of rift valley fever in Egypt. Bull. Math. Biol. **75**(3), 523–542 (2013)
8. Mpeshe, S.C., Haario, H., Tchuenche, J.M.: A mathematical model of Rift Valley fever with human host. Acta. Biotheor. **59**, 231–250 (2011)
9. Xue, L., Scott, H.M., Cohnstaedt, L.W., Scoglio, C.: A network-based meta-population approach to model Rift Valley fever epidemics. J. Theor. Biol. **306**, 129–144 (2012)
10. Xue, L., Cohnstaedt, L.W., Scott, H.M., Scoglio, C.: A hierarchical network approach for modeling Rift Valley fever epidemics with applications in North America. PLoS ONE **8**(5), e62049 (2013). https://doi.org/10.1371/journal.pone.0062049
11. Niu, T., Gaff, H.D., Papelis, Y.E., Hartley, D.M.: An epidemiological model of rift valley fever with spatial dynamics. Comput. Math. Methods Med. **2012**(2012), Article ID 138757, 12 p. (2012)
12. Roche, B., Guégan, J.-F., Bousquet, F.: Multi-agent systems in epidemiology: a first step for computational biology in the study of vector-borne disease transmission. BMC Bioinform. **9**, 435 (2008)
13. Paul, P.N.T., Bah, A., Ndiaye, P.I., Ndione, J.A.: An agent-based model for studying the impact of herd mobility on the spread of vector-borne diseases: the case of rift valley fever (Ferlo Senegal). Open J. Model. Simul. **2**, 97–111 (2014). https://doi.org/10.4236/ojmsi.2014.23012
14. Sukumar, S.R., Nutaro, J.J.: Agent-based vs. equation-based epidemiological models: a model selection case study, pp. 74–79. IEEE, December 2012
15. Paul, P.N.T., Bah, A., Ndiaye, P.I., Dione, J.A.: Coupling of an agent-based model with a mathematical model of water pond dynamics for studying the impact of animal herd mobility on the Aedes vexans mosquito populations. J. Mosquitoes Res. **4**(3), 132–141 (2017)
16. Paul, P.N.T., Bah, A., Ndiaye, P.I., Ndione, J.A.: An agent based model to study the impact of intra-annual season's variability on the dynamics of Aedes Vexans and Culex Poicilipes mosquito populations in North Senegal (Ferlo). In: Silhavy, R., Silhavy, P., Prokopova, Z. (eds.) CoMeSySo 2017. AISC, vol. 662, pp. 381–391. Springer, Cham (2018). https://doi.org/10.1007/978-3-319-67621-0_35
17. van den Driessche, P., Watmough, J.: Math. Biosci. **180**, 29–48 (2002)
18. Common-pool Resources and Multi-Agent Simulations. http://cormas.cirad.fr
19. Pratt, H.D., Moore, C.G.: Vector-Borne Disease Control: Mosquitoes, of Public Health Importance and their Control. U.S. Department of Health and Human Services, Atlanta, GA (1993)
20. Bates, M.: The Natural History of Mosquitoes. Peter Smith, Gloucester (1970)
21. Moore, C.G., et al.: Guidelines for Arbovirus Surveillance Programs in the United Sates. Center for Disease Control and Prevention, April 1993
22. Radostits, O.M.: Herd Healthy: Food Animal Production Medicine, 3rd edn. W. B. Saunders Company, Philidelphia (2001)
23. Turell, M.J., Kay, B.H.: Susceptibility of slected strains of Australian mosquitoes (Diptera: Culicidae) to Rift Valley fever virus. J. Med. Entomol. **35**(2), 132–135 (1998)

24. Peters, C.J., Linthicum, K.J.: Rift Valley fever. In: Beran, G.W. (ed.) Handbook of Zoonoses, B: Viral, 2nd edn, pp. 125–138. CRC Press (1994)
25. Freier, J.E., Rosen, L.: Verticle transmission of dengue virus by the mosquitoes of the Aedes scutellaris group. Am. J. Trop. Med. Hyg. **37**(3), 640–647 (1987)
26. Anderson, R.M., May, R.M.: Infectious Diseases of Humans: Dynamics and Control. Oxford University Press, Oxford (1991)
27. Heffernan, J.M., Smith, R.J., Wahl, L.M.: Perspectives on the basic reproductive ratio. J. R. Soc. Interface **2**, 281–293 (2005). EJDE-2007/115 AN EPIDEMIOLOGICAL MODEL 11
28. Lipsitch, M., Nowak, M.A., Ebert, D., May, R.M.: The population dynamics of vertically and horizontally transmitted parasites. Proc. R. Soc. B **260**, 321–327 (1995)
29. Diekmann, O., Heesterbeek, J.A., Metz, J.A.: On the denotion and the computation of the basic reproduction ratio R0 in models for infectious diseases in heterogeneous populations. J. Math. Biol. **28**(4), 365–382 (1990). https://doi.org/10.1007/BF00178324. ISSN 0303-6812
30. Barker, C., Niu, T., Reisen, W., Hartley, D.M.: Data-driven modeling to assess receptivity for rift valley fever virus. PLoS Neglected Trop. Dis. **7**(11), e2515 (2013). https://doi.org/10.1371/journal.pntd.0002515
31. https://www.collinsdictionary.com/dictionary/english/livestock
32. Canyon, D.V., Hii, J.L.K., Muller, R.: The frequency of host biting and its effect on oviposition and survival in Aedes aegypti (Diptera: Culicidae). Bull. Entomol. Res. **89**(1), 35–39 (1999)
33. Hayes, R.O., Tempelis, C.H., Hess, A.D., Reeves, W.C.: Mosquito host preference studies in Hale County, Texas. Am. J. Trop. Med. Hyg. **22**(2), 270–277 (1973)
34. Jones, C.J., Lloyd, J.E.: Mosquitoes feeding on sheep in southeastern Wyoming. J. Am. Mosquito Control Assoc. **1**(4), 530–532 (1985)
35. Magnarelli, L.A.: Host feeding patterns of Connecticut mosquitoes (Diptera: Culicidae). Am. J. Trop. Med. Hyg. **26**(3), 547–552 (1977)
36. Pratt, H.D., Moore, C.G.: Vector-Borne Disease Controls: Mosquitoes, of Public Health Importance and Their Control, U.S. Department of Health and Human Services, Atlanta, Ga, USA (1993)
37. Turell, M.J., Bailey, C.L., Beaman, J.R.: Vector competence of a Houston, Texas strain of Aedes albopictus for Rift Valley fever virus. J. Am. Mosquito Control Assoc. **4**(1), 94–96 (1988)
38. Turell, M.J., Faran, M.E., Cornet, M., Bailey, C.L.: Vector competence of senegalese Aedes fowleri (Diptera: Culicidae) for Rift Valley fever virus. J. Med. Entomol. **25**(4), 262–266 (1988)
39. Wen, B., Teng, Z., Liu, W.: Threshold dynamics in a periodic three-patch rift valley fever virus transmission model. Complexity **2019**, Article ID 7896946, 18 p. (2019). https://doi.org/10.1155/2019/7896946

Deep Learning Algorithms for Diagnosis of Breast Cancer with Maximum Likelihood Estimation

Mehmet Akif Cifci$^{(\boxtimes)}$ ⓘ and Zafer Aslan ⓘ

Faculty of Engineering, Department of Computer Engineering, Istanbul Aydin University, 34295 Istanbul, Turkey
wwwakif@msn.com, zaferaslan@aydin.edu.tr

Abstract. Machine Learning (ML) and particularly Deep Learning (DL) continue to advance rapidly, attracting the attention of the health imaging community to apply these techniques to increase the precision of cancer screening. The most common cancer in women is breast cancer that affects more than 2 million women each year and causes the largest number of deaths from cancer in the female population.

This work provides state-of-the-art research on the contributions and new applications of DL for early diagnosis of breast cancer. Also, it emphasizes on how and which major applications of DL algorithms are going to be benefitted for early diagnosis of breast cancer for which CNNs, one of the DL architectures, will be used. In this study, a DL method to be used for diagnostic and prognostic analysis using the X-ray breast image dataset for breast cancer is studied. Based on the dataset, it is aimed to diagnose breast cancer at an early stage. Thus, it may take place before a clinical diagnosis. For the testing probability of the disease, 21400 X-ray breast images, both normal and cancer, were taken from USF mammography datasets. From these images, 70% is used as the training step, while 30% of images are benefitted for the testing step. After the implementation of the architecture, VGG16 has achieved an overall accuracy of 96.77%, with 97.04% sensitivity and 96.74% as AUC, while Inception-v4 has an overall accuracy of 96.67%, with 96.03% sensitivity and 99.88% as AUC. These results show the high value of using DL for early diagnosis of breast cancer. The results are promising.

Keywords: CNN · Deep learning · Transfer learning · Breast cancer · X-ray

1 Introduction

Breast Cancer is an important public health problem worldwide which is more common among women in the world [1]. Digital mammography is the normal treatment for the diagnosis of breast cancer today; in the field of medical diagnosis, different techniques are used for the classification issue. However, mammography has some limitations, such as difficulty in tumor detection in young patients or in massive cancers [2].

The image extraction function is a significant step in classifying mammograms. Extract these attributes using digital image processing. Breast cancer is a form of

© Springer Nature Switzerland AG 2020
O. Gervasi et al. (Eds.): ICCSA 2020, LNCS 12250, pp. 486–502, 2020.
https://doi.org/10.1007/978-3-030-58802-1_35

cancer that occurs in breast tissues and often occurs on the internal surfaces of the milk ducts [3]. Although the prevalence of human cases is high in women, breast cancer may also occur in men. The properties of cancer determine treatment; surgery, drug therapy radiation, and immunotherapy can be included. Prognosis and survival rates vary widely depending on the type of cancer, its stages, treatment, and the patient's geographic location. If not detected in the early stages, the probability of cure for breast cancer falls significantly [4]. The methodology of Deep Learning (DL) focuses on implementing nonlinear transformations and high-level model abstractions on large datasets. Especially recent developments in DL architectures in myriad fields have already made significant contributions to Artificial Intelligence (AI).

Radiologists nowadays diagnose the breast tumor manually in mammographic or other radiological images, which is a time-consuming and error-prone procedure due to its small size and different lesion shapes, and these manual images are impaired by the existence of low contrast and unclear boundaries between the normal tissues surrounding it [5]. It has been proven that even the most experienced radiologists miss 10–30% of breast cancers during a routine screening in manual diagnosis [6]. When the fatalities are taken into consideration, such as in the USA, breast cancer the leading cause for deaths while it is number one worldwide, and automatic detection becomes a must. In the meantime, the automatic diagnosis is done with Convolutional Neural Networks (CNNs), which attract attention and become popular in image classification. CNNs are multi-layered structures, which is simple when training parameters are less. CNNs are more like biological neural networks, thanks to its weight-sharing network structure in which there are layers called convolution, activation, pooling, and fully connected layers. CNNs have a loss function like softmax in the last layer. Traditional neural networks contain trainable weights; generally, these layers are one-dimensional. The neurons in the layer are completely connected to neighboring neurons [7]. CNNs have been the most prominent developments in the fields of computer vision and AI, which are a sort of mixture of genetics, mathematics, and computer science [8]. Later 2012 was the first year in which CNN rose in popularity when Alex Krizhevsky used an 8-layer CNN to win that year's ImageNet competition (later referred to as AlexNet) [5]. Since then CNN has been the focus of interest. It has been utilized by many companies such as Google, Facebook, etc. CNNs are influenced biologically by the visual cortex which has small cell regions sensitive to different visual field regions. For instance, some neurons fired on vertical edges and some on horizontal or diagonal edges.

Similar tasks for different components in a system are often used by machines and are the basis behind CNNs. A common belief in the profound learning community is that successful profound learning models cannot be produced without a large number of data. Though data is a vital part of networking, the concept of transfer learning reduces data requirements if the data is already processed. Transfer learning is a pre-formed model and a small dataset that can be modified to fine-tune the model [9]. The idea is that the pre-trained model will be an extractor of features.

For many physicians, the precise diagnosis of a cancerous tumor remains a challenging task. The advent of modern medical technology and large volumes of patient data paved the way for the development of new cancer prediction and cancer detection strategies. Although the data evaluation obtained from the admission of patients and physicians contributes significantly to the diagnosis process, additional resources may be applied to promote accurate diagnosis.

Machine Learning (ML) techniques are aimed at removing potential diagnostic errors and providing a fast way to analyze large sections of the data. ML is an artificial information subfield of AI allowing learning without explicit programming, to learn a specific task by displaying it with datasets providing them to learn through experience. In recent decades ML approaches in designing predictive models to promote efficient decision-making have become widespread which make early detection and cancer prognosis possible. In research into cancer, these techniques may be used to classify various patterns in a sample, deciding whether cancer is malignant or benign [10]. The performance of such techniques can be evaluated according to classification, recall, specificity, and accuracy of the area under ROC. In this study, a DL model is projected for the automatic diagnosis of breast cancer. The studied model scenario has an end-to-end architecture without any feature extraction methods and requires raw chest X-ray images to restore the diagnosis [6]. This model is trained with 21400 chest X-ray images, which are not in a regular form taken from USF mammography datasets [11] containing 61% cancerous and 39% percent normal images.

Consequently, the proposed model is therefore intended to be used effectively. Radiologists will not have to wait a long time to determine whether or not a woman has breast cancer. The recovery cycle of patients, which can significantly minimize deaths, will also be a priority.

2   Literature Review

Many ML algorithms are used to get the same solution for breast cancer though most of them have drawbacks and disadvantages because of the CAD system or lack of datasets. It is believed that an algorithm should not only adjust the input instead it should regulate it with the best performance. The input must be given in the best way possible as well. For measurement of tumor analysis data, clinical results are used. The knowledge for this problem solution has been carefully analyzed and studied. It is extremely useful for data classification of patients. In [12], the authors suggested that Wilkins' scale-space techniques would use the original image to create a rougher resolution picture along with a Gaussian center. The method has a major drawback: the locations of the "semantically important" borders on ground scales are difficult to get accurately, and a class of algorithms is introduced that uses a diffusion technique. The algorithm consists of simple local operations on the image, which require parallel hardware applications. While [13], a new two-dimensional method for the medical ultrasound image was developed. Compared to typical images of the basic and second harmonic, the spatial resolution of the devolved image is much higher. Instead of rising harmonic base data, broadband radio frequency image data are decoded. The method was smart rather than the simple harmonic process. The operation has been verified by a fictional vision of captured image data and clinical image data. ML approaches in the past few decades to promote positive decision-making were becoming common in the development of predictive models. In [14], this technique can be used to classify different models in a dataset and thereby determine whether the cancer is malignant or benign. Such techniques can be evaluated based on the particular classification, reminder, accuracy, and the Receiver Operating Characteristics (ROC) region. [15] studied a method based on CNN for the calculation of breast density. The CNN was educated in image features from the picture patches collected from all mammograms and graded as thick, fatty tissues. CNN was trained using local and worldwide statistical tools. The deep neural network (DNN) algorithm for classification of the breast densities in DMs was studied in [16]. The study included 20,000 screening mammograms labeled with a breast density of four levels. The Multiview data was used to discern breast densities by a scratch-based CNN with thick convolutional layers.

According to [17] the precise elimination of boundaries has been an important pre-processing step for the computerized analysis of the chest ultrasound. First, from an ultrasonic image, a rectangular region of interest is selected manually, followed by pre-processing for a reduction in noise and region-based image enhancement. The initial tumor edge is then achieved by using a transform wavelet. In the segmented regions, the authors of [18] suggested a technique of unattended DL for classifying the breast density and risk. The system uses a simple sparse autoencoder to learn the features. Three rating codes have been used for mammographic density scores: pm, fatty breast, and dense breast tissues. Two groups were considered for the mammographic texture score. This ranking was used as a criterion for the section of the breast tissue. The dike mark showed that the divided against the ground truth is fine. Three separate datasets were trained and checked, and the results showed a positive relation to the values that experts manually collected. In order to assist the risk scoring radiologists, the researchers of [19] proposed a CNN based density estimation method. The visual analog ranking of unrevealed images is calculated by CNN. In comparison with 2 independent readers in a clinical environment, the approach showed a good correlation with similar indices. The authors in [20] research a variety of objective methods of assessing image consistency, which was originally proposed for natural images and videos for medical images. Their key approach is to discuss the main questions arising from the acquisition processes of various imagery approaches, for objective quality assessment of still X-ray images. The majority of automated systems, therefore, concentrated on characterizing the epithelial regions of the brain for cancer detection.

3 Materials and Methods

ML models are historically trained in performing useful tasks on the basis of manually designed functions derived from the raw data or from features learned from other models. Through deep learning, computers automatically learn helpful representations and features from the raw data, bypassing this challenging manual. In comparison with traditional ML and AI, DL algorithms have dramatically improved performance [17, 21]. DL has become very common in the medical imaging community in order to detect or diagnose conditions such as lung cancer, brain tumor detections, and segmentation, and is commonly used in various fields, such as image recognition, natural language therapy etc. In ML the most important step is classification in which the decision-making process is done to decide whether an X-ray image is normal or cancerous. I.e. benign, or malignant. On the other hand, DL is an ML-implementation technique that is particularly useful in order to learn patterns from unstructured data-sets. DL enables multi-layered models of data representation to be learned at different levels of abstraction. These techniques have greatly developed emerging technologies in a range of other fields including speech recognition, visual object recognition, object detection, and drug discovery and genomics. It thrives in every area where DL is implemented. CNN's, one of the deepest learning systems, is one of the most related problems for image recognition [22]. Regardless of their ability to interpret images and segmentation, CNNs attract focus. A CNN is a DL-type consisting of many hidden layers, including the overlay, the pooling layer ReLU, and the fully linked layer. CNN shares weights in the convolutional layer, which reduces the memory base and improves network capacity. A modern CNN is usually built by stacking the convolutional layer on top of the input and one or more layers that are completely connected to the classification output in order to link them [23]. Most of the time, maximum pooling layers between convolutional layers are used to improve alternating invariance and reduce map dimensions. In this analysis, the VGG network and Inception-v4 are used as two common CNN structures (see Fig. 1). Furthermore, for each task, we train the model separately. We use the cross-entropic loss function to train the model. Adam's technique is used to obtain optimized model parameters values. Entire implementation was done in Python language.

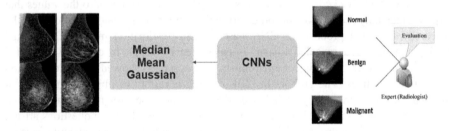

Fig. 1. The proposed method of architecture is presented.

In Fig. 1 as seen, the X-ray images are taken into pre-processed step to cope with the imbalanced data aftermath it is CNNs techniques are applied to process the data, and the output is tuned seamlessly. No area of interest for suspect lesions in the images has been given for the system. In the final step, the data is categorized into three classes as normal, benign, or malignant. Finally, it is ready for radiologists to evaluate.

3.1   Image Dataset

This work is focused on the Digital Database for Mammography Screenings (DDSM) which is a resource for the development of computer algorithms for screen-based use of mammographic image analysis research [11]. Each study contains two images per breast (age at study, ACR abnormality rate of breast density, and image (scanner, spatial resolution)). Moreover, the dataset includes normal, binomial, Poisson exponential Gauss distribution, gamma, inverse Gauss distribution, half binomial, and half

Poisson distributions. Standard functions; in addition to the unit, logit, log, reverse, and force functions, those used by distribution are also included. Precise reference information on pixel-level positions and types of suspect areas applies to photos comprising suspicious areas. Besides, the software is available for viewing mammograms and accurate pictures and for measuring the output of automated image analysis algorithms. The tissue analysis is based on the difference between high and low gray concentrations. Relevant mammographic image parameters related to the tissue allow us to identify them in a normal or abnormal way. Figure 2 shows different types of breast images.

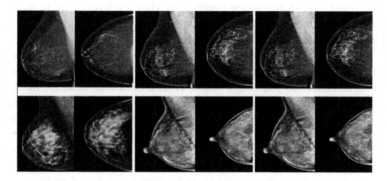

Fig. 2. Different X-ray images of breast dataset

3.2   Maximum Likelihood Estimation

One of the estimating the parameters of a statistical model is Maximum Likelihood Estimation (MLE), which is when applied to the X-ray image dataset provides better estimates for the model's parameters as MLE is benefitted for distinguishing between tumor and non-tumor cells [24]. MLE is the most consistent parameter estimate with sampled data and maximizes likelihood functions. MLE selects the set of values of model parameters that maximize the likelihood function, which has a unified approach; this has been described in the normal distribution and many other problems. Originally established by R.A. Fisher in the 1920s [25], MLE states that the desired possibility distribution is the one that makes the observed data "most likely." In other words, it is to investigate the value of the parameter vector, which maximizes probability functions. If a population has been known to follow a normal distribution, but the mean and variance are unknown, MLE can be used to approximate this with a small population sample by defining common mean and variance values, such that observation is the most likely outcome.

3.3   Pre-processing

Usually, data is inconsistent and also contains incomplete values, irrelevant values, diagrams, etc. Raw data must be parsed, collected, analyzed, and pre-processed before modeling and analysis. This is generally called a munging of data. Data that are often imputed for missing data is a method used to fill or remove the missing values. Pre-processing data is a technique for data collection that converts raw information into a comprehensible format. Real-world data is often inconsistent, incomplete, and is possible to contain various errors.

The main aim of pre-processing is to enhance the image quality by eliminating or reducing unnecessary sections of the background of X-ray images to make it ready for further processing. Mammograms are complex, interpretable medical images. Prepro-cessing is, therefore, essential if the quality is to be improved. The mammogram will be prepared for the next phase. Noise and high-frequency components emitted by filters.

Mean Filtering

Mean filter is used to enhance image quality [26]. Here, each pixel was replaced by the filter with the average density value in the area. It reduces local variance and is easy to accomplish. The typical filter is used to distort an image to eliminate noise, as seen in Fig. 3b. This transforms the mean pixel values into an estimation of the kernel n x n. The center variable pixel intensity is then substituted by the average. It reduces any image noise and smoothes the image edges. What is benefitted from the mean filter is that the filter itself gives the average intensity value of an image used. Especially mammographic images containing microcalcification have a higher mean rather than normal ones. All in all, the mean filter is a simple spatial sliding window filter, which replaces the center in the window with the medium of all pixel values in the window. Typically, the window or kernel is square but can take any shape [27].

I) Averaging operations cause an image to blur and a position of the blur effect [28]. II) When the impulse noise distorted image is applied to an average operation, the impulse noise is decaying and dispersed, but not removed from the noise [29]. III) The mean value of all neighborhood pixels was significantly influenced by a single pixel with a non-representative value [30].

Median Filtering

The median filter is a conventional, nonlinear filter that is especially effective in removing noise from the impulse [31]. The pixel centered in a given window is replaced by the median of this window. As shown in Fig. 3(d), the application of a median filter on a highly polluted image eliminates spikes and thus significantly increases the ratio of signal to noise. The median filter is a nonlinear filter and is effective in removing salt and pepper noise. The median tends to maintain the sharp-ness of the image edges while removing noise. Median filter shall be applied in a moving window fashion to each part of a featured channel. An input image consisting of RGB channels, for example, corresponds to 3 feature channels; a set of features produced after the convolution typically contains several channel numbers. Then, the sequence median formed by all elements is found in that patch. Most of the median filter I) Center-weighted median filter [32]. II) weighted median filter III) Max-median filter increases the effect of window size on the median filtering noise, which is effectively removed [33].

Gaussian Filtering

A Gaussian filter, a linear filter is usually used to blur the image or to reduce noise [34]. Mostly it is used to blur edges and reduce contrast. Gaussian filters are used to correct the weaknesses of X-ray images. That is, the Gaussian filter is applied to every X-ray image to reduce all the noise. Aftermath, X-ray images will have the same feature. When blurring affects X-ray images, it reduces the visualization and visibility of small components in the image [35]. Therefore, it is necessary to apply the Gaussian filter to restore the image from its corrupted version. Here It is used to isolate and quantify the vascular contents of the breast (see Fig. 3c).

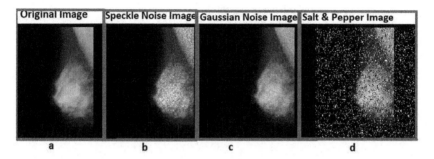

Fig. 3. X-ray images after pre-processing step

4   The Proposed Architecture

In the use of CNN architecture, the proposed DL framework is important. Two DL networks are involved in the system: Inception-v4 and VGG16, the novel suggested for diagnostic and predicational analysis of the breast cancer. DL is a family of hierarchical neural networks that aim to learn how to map the raw data to the desired outcome. The DL model's computer units are specified as layers and built into them to simulate a human brain deduction process. Convolution, bundling, active usage, and batch normalization are the principal machine formulas as described in the supplementary one.

From the 21400 X-ray images, we randomly selected 15000 images as training data and the rest 6400 images as testing data. Among the 15000 images for training data. Then the proposed data labeling method was applied to these 15000 data, and the majority of the unlabeled data were automatically labeled by the algorithm. The initially labeled data and newly labeled data were used to train the architecture.

4.1   Metrics Used in Health Check Systems for Evaluation

Different performance metrics are often used to investigate the performance of different models, such as specificity, accuracy, sensitivity (Table 1).

Table 1. Metrics used for evaluation

Metrics	Description	Formula
Sensitivity: It is the ability of a test to accurately.		$\frac{(TP)}{(TP+FN)}$
Specificity: It refers to how well a test identifies patients who have or do not have the disease.		$\frac{(TN)}{(TN+FP)}$
Accuracy: It is the relationship between the number of samples correctly identified and the number of samples.		$\frac{(TP+TN)}{(TP+FP+FN+TN)}$

4.2   VGG16

Known as its simplicity, VGG16 is one of the best networks; thus, its architecture is simple and deep. It primarily consists of an alternation between convolution layers and dropout layers [36]. VGG16 was the first to use a large number of small 3 × 3 filters in each convolutional layer and combine them in a sequence to emulate the effect of larger receiving areas.

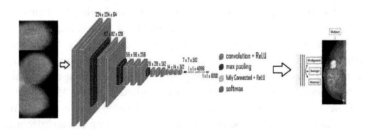

Fig. 4. VGG16 architecture used

However simple in network architecture, exponentially increasing cores lead to higher computation time and a larger size model, which is very expensive in terms of memory and computing costs. The applied VGG16 architecture consists of 13 convolutional layers, five pooling layers.

As seen in Fig. 4. X-ray images are passed through a stack of convolution layers with filters with a receiving area of 3 × 3 [37]. The convolution step is fixed at 1 pixel; The spatial filling of the convolutional layer input is done so that the spatial resolution is maintained after the convolution. Spatial pooling is performed by five max-pooling layers that follow some convoluted layers. Max pooling is performed on a window from step 2 to 2 × 2 pixels.

4.3   Inception-v4

In computer vision, Inception is a striking deep neural network architecture [38]. The startup algorithm performs much better for built-in or mobile computing devices. The way to increase accuracy in deep CNN is to increase the level of work and the number of units in average sizes at each level. Initially, 1 × 1, 3 × 3, 5 × 5 convolution filter and 3 × 3 maximum affinity filter is used. The maximum bonding process in the convolution layer is very effective [30]. The initial is optimal sparse architecture and 3 ∼ 10 × faster than other architecture.

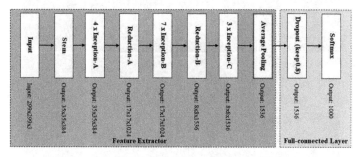

Fig. 5. Inception v4 model of the architecture [39]

From Fig. 5 it can be seen easily that Inception v4 consists of two parts a full layer and an extractor feature that has a lot of convolutional blocks such as 1 stem block, 4 Inception-A blocks, 7 Inception-B blocks, 3 Inception-C blocks, and 1 Average Pooling layer. 1 dropout block and 1 softmax layer are combined with a full-connected layer. Precisely, the stem module is used to exploit the Conv and Max-pool blocks to convert 299 × 299 × 3 image shapes into 35 × 35 × 384 image shapes, which is the Inception-A block input. Alternatively, Inception-A, Inception-B, Inception-C blocks only use Conv and Avg Pooling to convolute higher abstract features of images. Whereas the Inceptions of the same type have the same structure and are directly connected in sequence, concepts of a different type need to be connected by a grid reduction module [40]. For instance, the Reduction-A grid-reduction module, which converts a shape of 35 × 35 to a shape of 17 × 17, is used to connect the Inception-A block and Inception-B block. In addition, the Reduction-B grid-reduction module, which converts 17 × 17 shapes to 8 x 8 shapes, is used to connect the Inception-B block and Inception-C block [41]. The output of the Inception-C block is converted to the 1-Dimension of the 1536 property by the average pool layer [42].

5 Experimental Results and Discussion

This section explains the parameters and presents the results that helped the three classifications explored in this article. We performed experiments with X-ray images to identify and diagnose breast cancer in various separate scenarios. The proposed model was trained to classify X-ray images into three categories: benign, normal, malignant. The efficiency of the proposed model is displayed in Fig. 4 and 5 using VGG16 and Inception v4. The findings show that at the start of the training, there is not a sharp increase in loss values at the beginning of the training. The main reason for this slight increase and decrease is attributed to the number of X-ray data. However, when the proposed model analyzes all X-ray images each cycle of training, the quick ups and downs in the latter part of the training are gradually reduced.

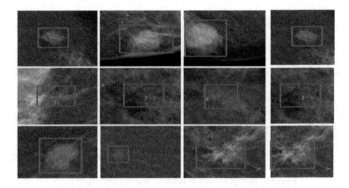

Fig. 6. X-ray images diagnosed as malignant

We fine-tune all the image networks on the training set directly without using ROI annotations and evaluate model performance using per-image validation the area under the curve (AUC) scores. The two best models are used for transfer learning. Figure 6 shows how the images are diagnosed according to their situation based on the model applied.

Table 2. Recall values found after CNN applied.

	VGG16	Inception v4
Benign	97.3	96.8
Malignant	96.34	95.7
Normal	97.5	96.4

5.1   Recall

Recall, known as sensitivity, is the rate of the positive observations accurately predicted to be positive. This measure is especially desirable because of how many observations are correctly diagnosed on the breast images dataset. Accurately identifying a malignant tumor is the main goal of the study. Recall can be thought of as the capacity of a model to identify all of the data points of interest in a dataset that reflects the proportion of real positives that have been correctly identified [43].

The recall values for all two techniques are shown in Table 2. In the model Inception v4 shows a higher result when compared to VGG16

5.2   Accuracy

Accuracy is characterized as a measurement similarity to the norm, or true value, i.e., a highly accurate navigation system may provide measurements that are very close to the norm, true or known values. A strong case for accuracy includes measurements of statistical variation and variance [44]. The accuracy is generally measured by the standard deviation of error. The accuracy of the classifier is a measure of how accurately the classifier can classify cases into their proper categories. It is obtained by dividing the right estimates by a total number of samples in the dataset. It is worth noting that the accuracy is largely dependent on the threshold chosen by the classifier and, therefore, can vary for different testing sets [45]. Therefore, comparing different classifiers is not the best approach, but can provide an overview of the class. As shown in Table 1, the equation can also be used for calculating accuracy where TP and TN reflect one-to-one True Positive and True Negative values [46]. P and N represent the positive and negative population, respectively, of cases of malignant and benign. Accuracy is the number of data points across all properly measured data points. In other words, the number of real positive and true negative is determined by the number of true positive, negative, and false negatives.

Confidence-based accuracy is characterized as a truly positive as well as a true negative ratio. It illustrates how well the architecture handles constructive insights but does not perceive them as negative anticipations. Figure 7 and Table 3 show the accuracy values and VGG16 has the highest performance [47].

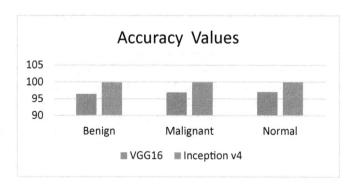

Fig. 7. Accuracy values found after CNN applied

The accuracy values for all two techniques are shown in Table 3. The performance of the different methods is measured by calculating the accuracy.

Table 3. Accuracy values found after CNN applied.

	VGG16	Inception v4
Benign	98.01	97.62
Malignant	95.11	95.8
Normal	97.2	96.6

5.3   ROC Area

ROC is a method commonly used in bioinformatics to test classifier performance [48]. There are four possible results in a dataset; The positive sample is counted as TP when classified correctly, FN when classified incorrectly, TN when classified correctly, and FP when classified incorrectly.

As Fig. 8 shows the efficiency of the classifier, it is a way to display the balance between the cost and the usefulness of a classifier. ROC is one of the most widely used and valuable data mining efficiency indicators. This 2D diagram displays the result of AUC.

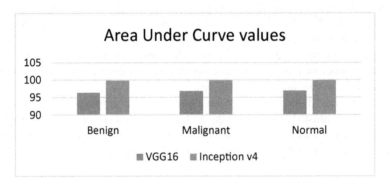

Fig. 8. The area under curve values found after CNN applied

In the upper left quarter of a plot with a high TP ratio and a low FP ratio, a point on the ROC is more preferred. A dot on the crossline y = x reflects a weak predictive classifier based on the random number of TP and FPs [49]. The area under the ROC graph reflects the classifier's performance as displayed in Fig. 8. This is achieved by dividing the area under the graph by the total area of the graph. Values close to 1 indicate the higher performance of the classifier. Percentage values for the ROC area of all two techniques.

6   Result

In this paper, DL architecture for early diagnosis of breast cancer by using a benchmark X-ray images dataset is proposed. Breast cancer is the most dangerous disease as a form of cancer among women. The progress of cancer detection and prediction is, therefore, critical for a healthy life. In this paper, we have discussed two popular ML techniques for Breast Cancer diagnosis. The proposed model shows better results when two methods are taken into consideration. DL is much better than the traditional classification approaches for image classification process and effectively reduced the FN rate with high accuracy, especially when using the VGG16 method. It finishes the test with 96.77% compared to Inception-v4 with and accuracy 96.67%, which is very close to the previous result. The results of the proposed model have a high accuracy of breast cancer images.

DL method to be used to diagnose breast cancer can efficiently and accurately calculate the 21400 collected X-ray images, which soon can be applied to laboratory X-ray images as well. The architecture can be used to screen a large number of suspected people's X-ray data sets to save people's lives and to save limited medical resources and can help the optimization of the diagnosis process. For future work the proposed architecture can constantly learn, adapt, and upgrade.

A more stimulating and a necessary approach for future research would be focusing on differentiating patients who show mild symptoms rather than severe ones, while these symptoms may or may not be displayed correctly on X-ray images.

Conflicts of Interest: The authors declare no conflict of interest.

References

1. Waheed, K.B., et al.: Breast cancers missed during screening in a tertiary-care hospital mammography facility. Ann. Saudi Med. (2019). http://doi.org/10.5144/0256-4947.2019.236
2. Mello-Thoms, C.R., Gandomkar, Z., Brennan, P.C.: A cognitive approach to determine the benefits of pairing radiologists in mammogram reading (2018)
3. Arevalo, J., González, F.A., Ramos-Pollán, R., Oliveira, J.L., Guevara Lopez, M.A.: Representation learning for mammography mass lesion classification with convolutional neural networks. Comput. Methods Programs Biomed. (2016)
4. Litjens, G., et al.: A survey on deep learning in medical image analysis. Med. Image Anal. (2017). http://doi.org/10.1016/j.media.2017.07.005
5. Routray, I., Rath, N.P.: Textural feature based classification of mammogram images using ANN. In: 2018 9th International Conference on Computing, Communication and Networking Technologies (ICCCNT 2018) (2018)
6. Samant, N., Sonar, P.: Mammogram classification in transform domain. In: 2018 5th International Conference on Signal Processing and Integrated Networks (2018)
7. Keren, L., et al.: Paired cycle-GAN-based image correction for quantitative cone-beam computed tomography. Med. Phys. **7**(1), 654–663 (2018)
8. Cifci, M.A.: Deep learning model for diagnosis of corona virus disease from CT images. Int. J. Sci. Eng. Res. **11**(4) (2020)
9. Chougrad, H., Zouaki, H., Alheyane, O.: Deep convolutional neural networks for breast cancer screening. Comput. Methods Programs Biomed. (2018)

10. Campanella, G., et al.: Clinical-grade computational pathology using weakly supervised deep learning on whole slide images. Nat. Med. (2019). http://doi.org/10.1038/s41591-019-0508
11. Cogan, T., Cogan, M., Tamil, L.: RAMS: remote and automatic mammogram screening. Comput. Biol. Med. (2019). http://doi.org/10.1016/j.compbiomed.2019.01.024
12. Robertson, S., Azizpour, H., Smith, K., Hartman, J.: Digital image analysis in breast pathology—from image processing techniques to artificial intelligence. Transl. Res. (2018). http://doi.org/10.1016/j.trsl.2017.10.010
13. Wan, T., Cao, J., Chen, J., Qin, Z.: Automated grading of breast cancer histopathology using cascaded ensemble with combination of multi-level image features. Neurocomputing (2017). http://doi.org/10.1016/j.neucom.2016.05.084
14. Yue, W., Wang, Z., Chen, H., Payne, A., Liu, X.: Machine learning with applications in breast cancer diagnosis and prognosis. Designs 2(2), 13 (2018)
15. Bejnordi, B.E., et al.: Diagnostic assessment of deep learning algorithms for detection of lymph node metastases in women with breast cancer. JAMA - J. Am. Med. 318(22), 2199–2210 (2017)
16. Mambou, S.J., Maresova, P., Krejcar, O., Selamat, A., Kuca, K.: Breast cancer detection using infrared thermal imaging and a deep learning model. Sensors 18(9), 2799 (2018)
17. Al Nahid, A., Mehrabi, M.A., Kong, Y.: Histopathological breast cancer image classification by deep neural network techniques guided by local clustering. Biomed Res. Int. (2018). https://doi.org/10.1155/2018/2362108
18. Tammina, S., et al.: Automated classification of lung diseases in computed tomography images using a wavelet based convolutional neural network. J. Biomed. Sci. Eng. 11(10), 263–274 (2019). https://doi.org/10.4236/jbise.2018.1110022
19. Gao, F., et al.: SD-CNN: a shallow-deep CNN for improved breast cancer diagnosis. Comput. Med. Imaging Graph. (2018). http://doi.org/10.1016/j.compmedimag.2018.09.004
20. Radiological Society of North America: Ultrasound – Breast. Radiology Info (2016)
21. Turkki, R., Linder, N., Kovanen, P.E., Pellinen, T., Lundin, J.: Antibody-supervised deep learning for quantification of tumor-infiltrating immune cells in hematoxylin and eosin stained breast cancer samples. J. Pathol. Inform. (2016)
22. Al Nahid, A., Kong, Y.: Involvement of machine learning for breast cancer image classification: a survey. Comput. Math. Methods Med. (2017)
23. Zhu, C., et al.: Deep learning system to screen coronavirus disease 2019 pneumonia. Appl. Intell. 9(September), 330 (2020)
24. Nandagopal, V., Geeitha, S., Kumar, K.V., Anbarasi, J.: Feasible analysis of gene expression – a computational based classification for breast cancer. Meas. J. Int. Meas. Confed. 140, 120–125 (2019). https://doi.org/10.1016/j.measurement.2019.03.015
25. Zou, S., et al.: Predicting lung nodule malignancies by combining deep convolutional neural network and handcrafted features. Sci. Rep. 2(1), 374–382 (2020). https://doi.org/10.1088/1361-6560/ab326a
26. Becker, A.S., Mueller, M., Stoffel, E., Marcon, M., Ghafoor, S., Boss, A.: Classification of breast cancer in ultrasound imaging using a generic deep learning analysis software: a pilot study. Br. J. Radiol. 91(xxxx), 20170576 (2018)
27. Anderson, R., Li, H., Ji, Y., Liu, P., Giger, M.L.: Evaluating deep learning techniques for dynamic contrast-enhanced MRI in the diagnosis of breast cancer. In: Medical Imaging 2019: Computer-Aided Diagnosis, vol. 10950, p. 1095006. International Society for Optics and Photonics, March 2019
28. Saha, M., Chakraborty, C., Racoceanu, D.: Efficient deep learning model for mitosis detection using breast histopathology images. Comput. Med. Imaging Graph. 64, 29–40 (2018)

29. Mambou, S.J., Maresova, P., Krejcar, O., Selamat, A., Kuca, K.: Breast cancer detection using infrared thermal imaging and a deep learning model. Sensors 18(9), 27 (2018)
30. Golatkar, A., Anand, D., Sethi, A.: Classification of breast cancer histology using deep learning. In: Campilho, A., Karray, F., ter Haar Romeny, B. (eds.) ICIAR 2018. LNCS, vol. 10882, pp. 837–844. Springer, Cham (2018). https://doi.org/10.1007/978-3-319-93000-8_95
31. Delen, D., Walker, G., Kadam, A.: Predicting breast cancer survivability: a comparison of three data mining methods. Artif. Intell. Med. 34(2), 113–127 (2005)
32. Zhang, D., Zou, L., Zhou, X., He, F.: Integrating feature selection and feature extraction methods with deep learning to predict clinical outcome of breast cancer. IEEE Access 6, 28936–28944 (2018)
33. He, K., Zhang, X., Ren, S., Sun, J.: Deep residual learning for image recognition. arXiv: 1512.03385 [cs] (2015)
34. Das, A., Acharya, U.R., Panda, S.S., Sabut, S.: Deep learning based liver cancer detection using watershed transform and Gaussian mixture model techniques. Cogn. Syst. Res. 54, 165–175 (2019)
35. Choukroun, Y., et al.: Mammogram classification and abnormality detection from nonlocal labels using deep multiple instance neural network. In: Eurographics Workshop on Visual Computing for Biology and Medicine (2017)
36. Lee, G.F., Hoogi, A., Rubin, D.: Curated breast imaging subset of DDSM. Cancer Imaging Arch (2016)
37. Torres-Galván, J.C., Guevara, E., González, F.J.: Comparison of deep learning architectures for pre-screening of breast cancer thermograms. In: 2019 Photonics North (PN), pp. 1–2. IEEE, May 2019
38. Broadwater, D.R., Smith, N.E.: A fine-tuned inception v3 constitutional neural network (CNN) architecture accurately distinguishes between benign and malignant breast histology, no. 18133, 59 MDW San Antonio United States (2018)
39. Pham, T.-C., Luong, C.-M., Visani, M., Hoang, V.-D.: Deep CNN and data augmentation for skin lesion classification. In: Nguyen, N.T., Hoang, D.H., Hong, T.-P., Pham, H., Trawiński, B. (eds.) ACIIDS 2018. LNCS (LNAI), vol. 10752, pp. 573–582. Springer, Cham (2018). https://doi.org/10.1007/978-3-319-75420-8_54
40. Deng, J., Ma, Y., Deng-ao, L., Zhao, J., Liu, Y., Zhang, H.: Classification of breast density categories based on SE-attention neural networks. Comput. Methods Programs Biomed., 105489 (2020)
41. Wang, Y., Choi, E.J., Choi, Y., Zhang, H., Jin, G.Y., Ko, S.B.: Breast cancer classification in automated breast ultrasound using multiview convolutional neural network with transfer learning. Ultrasound Med. Biol. (2020)
42. Coccia, M.: Deep learning technology for detection of lung and breast cancer: application in clinical practice (2019)
43. Clancy, K., Zhang, L., Mohamed, A., Aboutalib, S., Berg, W., Wu, S.: Deep learning for identifying breast cancer malignancy and false recalls: a robustness study on training strategy. In: Medical Imaging 2019: Computer-Aided Diagnosis, vol. 10950, p. 1095005. International Society for Optics and Photonics, March 2019
44. Thrall, J.H., et al.: Artificial intelligence and machine learning in radiology: opportunities, challenges, pitfalls, and criteria for success. J. Am. Coll. Radiol. 15(3), 504–508 (2018)
45. Samala, R.K., Chan, H.P., Hadjiiski, L., Helvie, M.A., Richter, C.D., Cha, K.H.: Breast cancer diagnosis in digital breast tomosynthesis: effects of training sample size on multi-stage transfer learning using deep neural nets. IEEE Trans. Med. Imaging 38(3), 686–696 (2018)
46. Abdel-Zaher, A.M., Eldeib, A.M.: Breast cancer classification using deep belief networks. Expert Syst. Appl. 46, 139–144 (2016)

47. Qi, X., et al.: Automated diagnosis of breast ultrasonography images using deep neural networks. Med. Image Anal. **52**, 185–198 (2019)
48. Yuan, X., Xie, L., Abouelenien, M.: A regularized ensemble framework of deep learning for cancer detection from multi-class, imbalanced training data (2018)
49. Wang, J., Yang, Y.: A context-sensitive deep learning approach for microcalcification detection in mammograms. Pattern Recogn. **78**, 12–22 (2018)

Aeroacoustics Investigation of an Uncontrolled and a Controlled Backward-Facing Step with Large Eddy Simulation

Kamil Furkan Taner[1]([✉]), Furkan Cosgun[2], and Baha Zafer[2]

[1] Istanbul University, 34315 Avcilar Istanbul, Turkey
furkantaner96@gmail.com
[2] Istanbul Technical University, 34437 Beyoglu Istanbul, Turkey
cosgun15@itu.edu.tr, zaferba@itu.edu.tr

Abstract. In this study, 3D flow over backward-facing step is solved for low Mach number. Large Eddy Simulation is used to resolve turbulent features into the flow field. Numerical results of turbulent flow field are compared with experimental velocity profiles for different stations and those are validated. Additional to accounting a flow field, sound levels for different located receivers due to backward-facing step flow are determined using Acoustic Analogy (AA) which is firstly proposed by Lighthill. Unsteady flow field variables obtained from computational fluid dynamics commercial code is used as input in Ffowcs Williams-Hawkings (FW-H) Equation, which is an extended version of Lighthill equation. Additionally, some active flow control methodologies are carried out to a flow field to understand better relations between flow controls and acoustic results. These flow control techniques are the suction and blowing with different magnitudes at the bottom of backward-facing step. The controlled cases are also compared with experimental flow field results and validated. Acoustic results are plotted in frequency and time domain. Different active control effects on acoustic results are evaluated and interpreted.

Keywords: Backward-facing step flow · Large eddy simulation · Acoustic analogy · Low mach number · Flow control

1 Introduction

The Backward Facing-Step (BFS) flow is a popular research topic to understand of separated and reattaching flow situations, despite of its simplicity [1]. The Backward-Facing Step (BFS) flows are also called "sudden expansion flow", "diverging channel" or "backward flow" [2]. Due to that the backward-facing step (BFS) is available in many engineering applications and structures, it has been being a significant subject. Gas transport systems, aerospace applications

© Springer Nature Switzerland AG 2020
O. Gervasi et al. (Eds.): ICCSA 2020, LNCS 12250, pp. 503–517, 2020.
https://doi.org/10.1007/978-3-030-58802-1_36

(i.e. aircraft landing systems of aircraft, weapon bays on aircrafts), marine equipment designs, environmental applications (i.e. entrance of harbours, air flow in canyon streets), industrial applications (i.e. wind movements around high-rise buildings), automotive equipments (i.e. automobile's pillars, car sunroofs) are essential engineering problems where the flow of the backward-facing step is investigated [3].

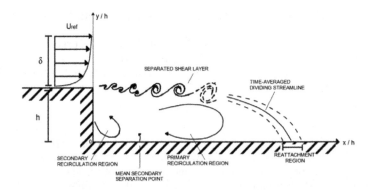

Fig. 1. Nature of backward-facing step flow [4].

Generally, the BFS flow field is divided into four regions: separated shear layer, the primary and secondary recirculation region under the shear layer and the reattachment region. In terms of flow dynamics, the BFS flow occurs with large separation vortices and with some small vortex in the corner (secondary recirculation region) as shown in Fig. 1 [2]. Flow separation from the step edge leads to high speed eddies, large energy losses, vibration and noises [5]. In the last few years, both flow control techniques, the suction and blowing [6,7], not only became interesting research areas in fluid mechanics, but also affected techniques which have a significant role in aeroacoustics. In the literature, the essential part of the experimental and numerical studies has been investigated for high Reynolds and Mach numbers. On the other hand, studies for low Mach number has not been carried out so much. Zheng et al. [5] studied BFS flow with continuous suction and without control by using the turbulence model of LES. The effects of suction control on the flow field were studied for different suction velocities and the results showed that the suction is effective in shortening the reattachment length, reducing the tangential velocity gradients and turbulence fluctuations of reattachment flows. In the study of Uruba et al. [7]. BFS flow was investigated by suction and blowing while using different slot shapes (rectangle or serrated), slot area and flow coefficient which varies from −0.035 up to 0.035. Results indicate that suction and blowing are able to reduce the length of the separation zone whereas slot shapes and slot areas are significant only for blowing. In this case, small cross-section with serrated edge is the most effective. Neumann and Wengle [1] investigated a passive control approach for an unsteady separated flow. The objective of the passive control was to enhance the entrainment rate of the shear layer bounding the separation zone behind the step, thereby reducing the mean reattachment length. DNS and LES at $\mathrm{Re}_h = 3000$ were carried out for all flow cases (uncontrolled and controlled). A certain minimum distance between the step edge (h) and the upstream position of the control fence is required to achieve a maximum reduction of the reattachment length. Choi et al. [8] observed BFS flow numerically. All numerical simulations were investigated with RANS and LES turbulence models using open source CFD package OpenFOAM. The numerical investigation has been implemented for various step angles ($10°$, $15°$, $20°$, $25°$, $30°$, $45°$, and $90°$), different expansion ratios (1.48, 2.00 and 3.27), and Reynolds numbers (5000, 8000, 11000, 15000, 47000 and 64000). As a result, LES shows a better agreement than RANS model. In current study, incompressible flow over backward-facing step for low Mach number has been solved using Large Eddy Simulation. While calculated Reynolds number is 0.0855×10^5 and Mach number is 0.015. Firstly, a mesh independence study has been conducted to determine most efficient mesh size in terms of computational cost and solution's accuracy. Five different mesh sizes have been attempted. After mesh convergence is satisfied, the numerical results for the flow field have been compared and validated with the experimental results. Additional to comparison and validation process, the sound level induced flow over backward-facing step has been determined for different locations using Ffowcs-Williams Hawkings equation. Some active flow control mechanisms have carried out to observe the effects of flow control on aeroacoustics results. These active flow control mechanisms are flow suction-blowing with different magnitudes from a small slot located at the bottom of the step. The controlled flow field results have also compared with the experimental data and validated. In the light of these right flow field results, the sound level comparisons have been computed and which suction or blowing rate is the most effective or the worst in terms of sound levels have been recognized.

2   Numerical Methods and Aeroacoustics Equations

The computational mechanic commercial flow solver is used for numerically discrete temporal conservation equations, which are related to flow field, using the finite volume method. Bounded Central Differencing Scheme is used for spatial discretization. Second Order Implicit Scheme is used for temporal discretization. In addition to these, the pressure-velocity decoupling of discretised equation is carried out by the PISO (pressure implicit with splitting of operators). Non-Iterative Time Advancement solver is used in order to reduce the computational time. Time step size is set as 0.0004 s. and number of time steps is set 5000. Used equations for LES model are obtained by filtering temporal Navier - Stokes equations. The filtered variable is demonstrated below:

$$\overline{\varphi}(x) = \int_D \overline{\varphi}(x^{'})G(x, x^{'})dx^{'} \tag{1}$$

In Eq. (1), "D" represents control volume, "G" is the filter function, which demonstrates resolved eddies scale. Finite volume discretization provides implicitly processing of filtering. Lighthill transformed continuity and momentum equations to a non-homogenous wave equation that has a source term. It considers only aerodynamically generated sounds without solid body interaction. This approach is known as Acoustic Analogy (AA) in aeroacoustics. In Eq. (2) is the Lighthill equation:

$$\frac{\partial^2 \rho}{\partial t^2} - a_{\infty^2} \frac{\partial^2 \rho}{\partial x_{i^2}} = \frac{\partial^2 T_{ij}}{\partial x_i \partial x_j} \tag{2}$$

Lighthill equations were redefined and generalized, using the generalized function theory, by Ffowcs Williams-Hawkings (FW-H). In Eq. (3) is FW-H equation:

$$\frac{1}{a_0} \frac{\partial p^{'}}{\partial t^2} - \nabla p^{'} = \frac{\partial^2}{\partial x_i \partial x_j} \{T_{ij} \ H(f)\} - \frac{\partial}{\partial x_i} \{[P_{ij} n_j + \rho u_i (u_n - v_n)]\} \ \delta \ (f)\}$$
$$+ \frac{\partial}{\partial t} \{[\rho_0 v_i + \rho u_i (u_n - v_n) \delta(f)]\} \tag{3}$$

In the FW-H equations, while the left side is the wave equation form, three source terms are used in the right side. These source terms are loading, thickness and quadrupole respectively. In Eq. (3), the first term on the right side is quadrupole, the second term is loading, and the final term is thickness. In Eq. (3), u_i is component of flow velocity magnitude in x_i direction, u_n is component of flow velocity magnitude in normal of solid surface, v_i is component of solid surface velocity magnitude in x_i direction and v_n is component of solid surface velocity magnitude in normal of solid surface. $\delta(f)$ and H(f) are Dirac delta, Heaviside function respectively. p' represents sound pressure in far field and is defined as (p' = p - p_0). f = 0 also expresses a mathematical surface (f > 0) in external flow problem which is in infinite space. This mathematical surface can be defined as a permeable surface in the flow field. Thus, it facilitates the theoretical investigation and generalization of the definition function. In addition, Green function solutions can be used in free space. T_{ij} is Lighthill stress tensor and it is defined in Eq. (4):

$$T_{ij} = \rho u_i u_j + P_{ij} - a_{0^2}(\rho - \rho_0)\delta_{ij} \tag{4}$$

P_{ij} denotes a compressive stress tensor and is given in Eq. (5) for Stoke Flows:

$$P_{ij} = p\delta_{ij} - \mu \left(\frac{\partial u_i}{\partial x_j} + \frac{\partial u_j}{\partial x_i} - \frac{2}{3} \frac{\partial u_k}{\partial x_k} \delta_{ij} \right) \tag{5}$$

Details about the used receiver locations are shown in Fig. 2. Sum, 35 receivers are set up into BFS's different locations. On the BFS's edge (2 microphones) and bottom walls (8 microphones) have 10 receivers totally. Inside of BFS channel, 7 receivers were placed on R = 2h radius circle with 15° angle and 13 microphones are placed on R = 4h with 15° angle. The radius circles centre point is defined at the step edge. Last 5 receivers are 5h away from the bottom wall and parallel to it.

3   Computational Domain and Boundary Conditions

Examined computational domain is shown in Fig. 3. The domain has a slot where the flow is controlled. The computational domain has the rectangular cross-section. The step height h = 0.025 m, the BFS channel has a length of upstream 16h and the length of downstream is 56h (m). The rectangular cross section has a height 10h and a width of 4h. Velocity at the inlet, the reference velocity, is $U_e = 5$ m/s. The rectangular slot with the size of a = 0.95×10^{-3} m is studied. More information about this geometry can be found in Uruba et al. [7]. In our study, Mach number (Ma) and Reynolds number (Re_h) of computed flow are 0.015 and 0.0855×10^5 respectively. Multi-block structured and non-uniform orthogonal grids are used to divide the computational domain into finite volume cells. Mesh structure is tightly handled in order to analyse the dynamic vortex structure that occurs immediately front step.

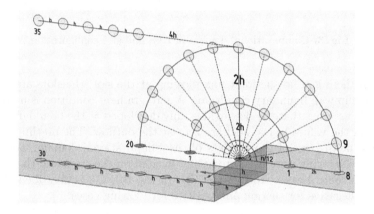

Fig. 2. Location of receivers for BFS geometry.

4   Computational Domain and Boundary Conditions

Examined computational domain is shown in Fig. 3. The domain has a slot where the flow is controlled. The computational domain has the rectangular cross-section. The step height h = 0.025 m, the BFS channel has a length of upstream 16h and the length of downstream is 56h (m).

The rectangular cross section has a height 10h and a width of 4h. Velocity at the inlet, the reference velocity, is $U_e = 5$ m/s. The rectangular slot with the size of a = 0.95×10^{-3} m is studied. More information about this geometry can be found in Uruba et al. [7]. In our study, Mach number (Ma) and Reynolds number (Re_h) of computed flow are 0.015 and 0.0855×10^5 respectively. Multi-block structured and non-uniform orthogonal grids are used to divide the computational domain into finite volume cells. Mesh structure is tightly handled in order to analyse the dynamic vortex structure that occurs immediately front step. The boundary conditions of BFS geometry are expressed precisely. The velocity profile at the channel inlet and at the slot are set as uniform flow. Therefore, a sufficiently long space (16h) is allowed backflow of the step. Moreover, velocity values do not have any stochastic component and their flows are laminar.

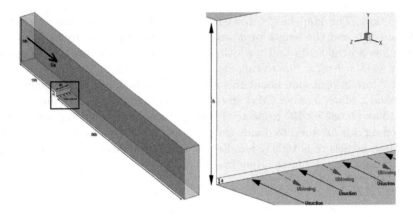

Fig. 3. Computational domain of BFS and slot configuration.

When there is a no suction or no blowing at the slot, the slots are changed to the no-slip wall boundary conditions. A zero gradient condition is used at the outflow. It assumes that the flow field is fully developed at the boundary and the changes in the values in the field are zero at the outflow. The no-slip condition is applied at the rest of the surfaces of the computational domain. Continuous suction and blowing were used at the slot located on the step, and the intensity of the flow control were expressed as C_Q. In Eq. (6), C_Q is described. The C_Q is defined negative for suction and positive for blowing cases.

$$C_Q = \frac{\rho_{s-b} U_{s-b} F_{s-b}}{\rho_e U_e F_e} = \frac{w U_{s-b} a}{w U_e H} = \frac{U_{s-b} a}{U_e H} \tag{6}$$

C_Q is also called the suction and blowing flow coefficient; U_e and F_e are the incoming velocity-flow, which were given from cross-sectional area of channel's inlet; ρ_e is density of incoming air-flow; U_{s-b} and F_{s-b} are the air suction and blowing velocity, which were given from the slot (a); ρ_{s-b} is the density of suction and blowing air. The studied cases with flow control or without control were given in Table 1.

Table 1. Details of studying cases.

Cases	C_Q	$U_{suction}$	$U_{blowing}$
C_0	0	0	0
C_1	−0.01	−13.157	–
C_2	0.01	–	13.157
C_3	−0.035	−46.052	–
C_4	0.035	–	46.052

5   Numerical Results

In the first step, grid independency works are done to investigate optimum mesh size and computational cost. In the numerical studies, ensuring the resolution, accuracy and low computational cost of the solution are crucial. Detailed mesh domain strategy which is used for all mesh sizes is shown in Fig. 4. Therefore, the first step of this section is to include mesh independence tests.

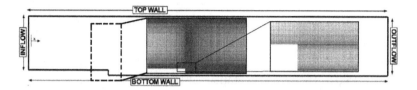

Fig. 4. Meshing strategy of gird-independency work.

Five different cases were generated to obtain the number of mesh size. Total number of elements increase regularly from Case 1 to 5, while the minimum element number is 982 thousand and the maximum number of elements is 4.2 million. When generating mesh structures, we paid attention to maximum aspect ratio of elements. This ratio should not exceed high values. Particularly in the case of turbulent flows, the high aspect ratio value causes divergence.

Table 2. Number of elements of cases used in mesh independency.

Cases	Total number of elements
Mesh 1	*0.982 Million*
Mesh 2	*1.5 Million*
Mesh 3	*2.5 Million*
Mesh 4	*3.3 Million*
Mesh 5	*4.2 Million*

All numerical results, which can be seen in Table 2, for five different cases are compared with the experimental data to define which mesh size is optimum to acquire the best computational cost. The normalised velocity profiles are extracted for different normalised x-direction station after back-step corner, namely $x/h = 2$, 4, 6 and 8. These profiles are shown in Fig. 5. The closing mesh independency study, Case 4 (3.3 million), is chosen as the best nominee for the further computational works.

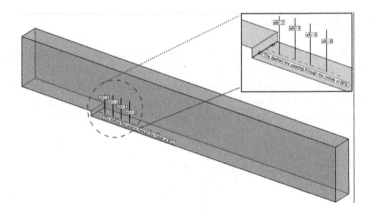

Fig. 5. Four different stations at computational domain.

The results of mesh independency tests are shown in Fig. 6. It is observed that the velocity profiles behave almost the same in all mesh sizes at all four stations. However, it can be said that especially Mesh 4 and 5 give better results at first and second stations ($x/h = 2$, 4). In addition, almost all mesh sizes show exceptionally good results with the experimental data at third and fourth stations ($x/h = 6$, 8). In this respect, Mesh 4 is used in the further studies and flow field results are obtained to calculate acoustic measurements by using this mesh. Furthermore, it is evaluated as a base concept.

Figure 7a, 7b, 8a and 8b show more detailed results with respect to time averaged x direction velocity (u) obtained from four stations and pressure distribution taken from the bottom wall after the step. In Fig. 7a, all stations give significantly good results with experimental study. In Fig. 7b, the mean pressure coefficient, C_P, on the bottom wall of the symmetry plane in the x direction is computed from unsteady flow field results and the numerical simulations are compared with the experimental data. Both results gradually increase to reach maximum point which is observed nearly at the point $x/h = 8.2$. The mean pressure coefficient is defined at the step edge nearly $C_p = -0.18$ for the experimental data and $C_p = -0.16$ for the numerical computation. As it can be seen in Fig. 8, the reattachment point is located at $x = 0.11$. Low pressure territory occurs before the reattachment point, whereas high pressure territory occurring after the reattachment point.

When looking at Fig. 8a, it can be said that shear layer is starting to be formed at the BFS step and it spreads and its thickness increases. The reattachment point shows itself as a point where the sign of pressure value is changed in Fig. 8b. A careful investigation of the velocity profiles in Fig. 7 reveals that the most deviation

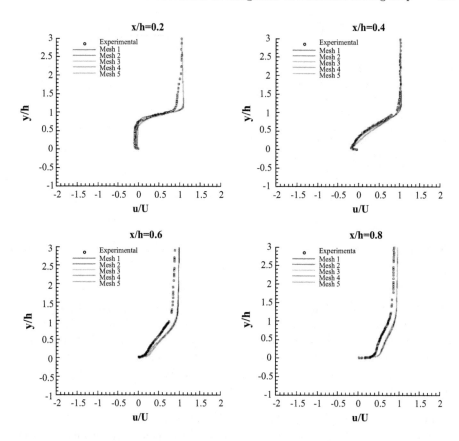

Fig. 6. Mesh independency test results for x direction normalized velocity profile.

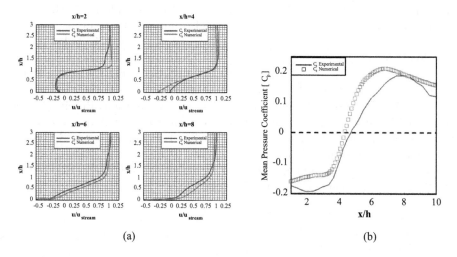

Fig. 7. Comparisons between the experiment and numerical simulation with respect to (a) mean u velocity and (b) mean pressure coefficient.

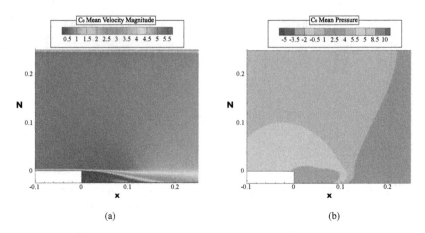

Fig. 8. Time averaged flow field for BFS (a) mean velocity magnitude and (b) mean pressure.

is shown at the reattachment point that is nearly located at $x/h = 4$ region. The acoustic pressures are calculated by using FW-H acoustic analogy. This anology uses flow field pressure values obtained from the acoustic source surface. The source surface is defined at the bottom wall in this study. As mentioned above, 35 receivers were placed but only the results of three specific microphones are given for practical presentation. These are Receiver 9, 20 and 35.

Figure 9 shows the acoustics results of the receivers induced by flow over Backward-Facing Step (BFS) for C_0. The spectrum for Receiver 20 has the highest sound pressure level (SPL) since it is the nearest microphone to the reattachment point region. On the other hand, Receiver 35 has the lowest sound pressure level while Receiver 9 gives 35 dB and 25 dB sound levels 50 Hz 100 Hz respectively. When investigating the flow field results the fact can be seen that main sound source is appeared in front territory of a step which includes upwind and downwind of the reattachment point that those regions have higher pressure changes over time, Fig. 10. In this respect, it can be said that the nearer to the main source region the higher sound level is imposed. This is the main reason why Receiver 20 shows the highest sound levels. In addition, Receiver 9 and Receiver 35 are located at same distance to main source region but Receiver 9 shows higher values compared to Receiver 35. This may be since Receiver 9 is nearer to a boundary layer region compared to Receiver 35. It is estimated that additional to main source surface noise, higher sound levels in Receiver 9's spectrum has also boundary layer noise (Fig. 13).

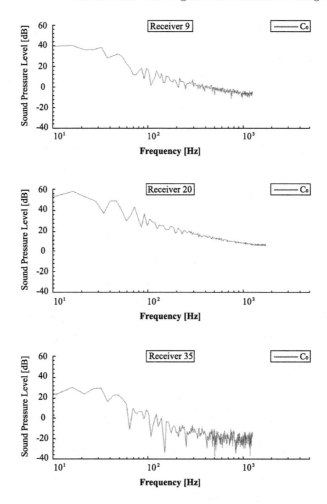

Fig. 9. Acoustics spectrums of bacward facing step for three microphone locations.

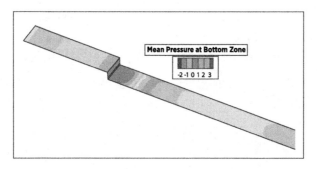

Fig. 10. Pressure distributions on the acoustics source.

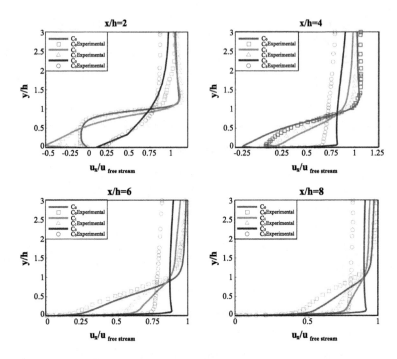

Fig. 11. Velocity profile comparison for C_0, C_1, and C_3 cases.

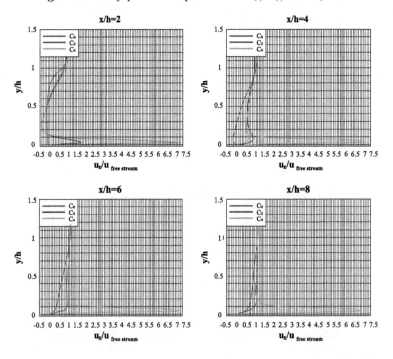

Fig. 12. Velocity profile comparison for C_0, C_2, and C_4 cases.

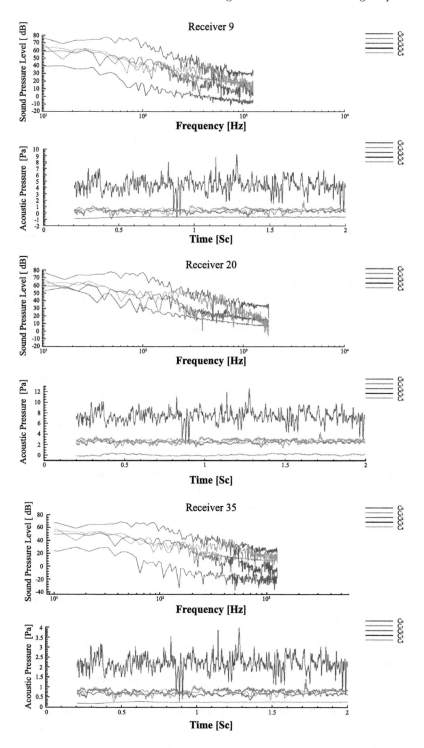

Fig. 13. Aeroacoustics comparisons for different control mechanisms.

6 Conclusion

The geometry of the Backward Facing Step (BFS) causes large energy loses, strong acoustic waves, local pressure, density, and velocity fluctuations. The noise, vibration and undesired acoustic signals due to the structure of BFS geometry can disturb people and decrease ergonomics. Limiting the separation zones, in particular, the recirculation zones, determining to noise levels and reducing them have been crucial so far in fluid mechanics and aeroacoustics researches. Studying a Backward Facing Step (BFS) flow can be applicable to the landing gear cavity problems as well. When the aircraft goes close to the airfield, the landing gear systems swing for landing. At this very moment, Mach number of the aircraft initiates to diminish below 0.2. During this landing operation, landing gear cavity geometry occurs and this cavity geometry is significant for industrial problems and applications. Since the cavity creates huge noises and vibrations. This study can assist to understand this landing gear cavity problem. In the literature, low Mach number studies have not been investigated as much as high Reynold number studies. In this study, the commercial flow solver is used to solve the BFS problem numerically. Large Eddy Simulation approach is applied for better understanding of physics of turbulence, separated/reattached flows and acoustics in the flow field. Ffowcs Williams and Hawkings (FW-H) equation is used as an acoustic model to obtain the noise that is generated by the aerodynamic effects. Totally, 35 receivers set up into the BFS's different locations. These locations are designated with the consideration of the previous studies such as Zafer et al. [9]. The investigated BFS model is taken by Uruba et al. [7]. Flow control techniques (no suction/blowing, suction and blowing situations) are investigated with giving different velocities. First of all, mesh independency works are done to find the best grid system. Thus 5 different mesh structures with a various number of elements are generated. Then, these are compared with each other and the best mesh size is defined. Velocity profiles and mean pressure coefficient (Cp) value are validated between our numerical and experimental results for C_0 case. Cp's experimental value was obtained by Hudy et al. [10]. In addition, the experimental velocity profile values were obtained by Uruba et al. [7]. In the C_0 case, a good agreement is seen between the experimental and numerical results in terms of the velocity profiles, mean pressure coefficient, and reattachment point. After that, different suction velocities were given (Fig. 11) and our numerical results were compared to another numerical study that was done by Zheng et al. [5]. Moreover, the blowing velocities are given (Fig. 12), and their results are added to the study. Finally, for 35 receivers, acoustic results are obtained for all cases (Fig. 13), however; results of receiver 9, 20 and 35 are shared in the study. Receiver 20 is the nearest microphone to the reattachment point region, thus; it is exposed the highest sound pressure. Receiver 9 and 35 are located at same distance to the main source region. Yet, Receiver 9 shows higher values compared to Receiver 35. This result appears since Receiver 9 is nearer to a boundary layer region compared to Receiver 35. It is estimated that additional to main source surface noise, higher sound levels in Receiver 9 spectrum has also boundary layer noise which is radiated from boundary layer distributions of flow which occurs before the step or it can be called as coming flow. The C_1, C_2 and C_4 cases exhibit a similar behaviour between 10 Hz to around 100 Hz. When frequency value hit to around 200 Hz, C_4 case start to display distinctive behaviour until around 600 Hz. It is also noted that when suction velocity increases, SPL value increases. In conclusion, it is commonly expected that the BFS structure should have reduced recirculation zones and the C_0 case (no suction/blowing) has the longest reattachment length compare to the other cases which is investigated.

Giving suction or blowing velocity from the slot creates reduced recirculation zones. However, this leads reverse situations in terms of acoustic result. Although the C_0 has longest reattachment length, it also has the lowest sound pressure level (SPL) than the other cases. In brief, giving suction or blowing from the slot may shorten reattachment, while increasing the sound pressure level.

References

1. Neumann, J., Wengle, H.: DNS and LES of passively controlled turbulent backward-facing step flow. Flow Turbul. Combust. **71**, 297–310 (2003)
2. Chen, L., Asai, K., Nonomura, T., Xi, G., Liu, T.: A review of Backward-Facing Step (BFS) flow mechanisms, heat transfer and control. Thermal Sci. Eng. Prog. **6**, 194–216 (2018)
3. Ozsoy, E.: Numerical simulation of incompressible flow over a three dimensional rectangular cavity. Ph.D. thesis, Istanbul Technical University (2010)
4. Ruisi, R., Zare-Behtash, H., Kontis, K., Erfani, R.: Active flow control over a backward-facing step using plasma actuation. Acta Astronaut. **126**, 354–363 (2016)
5. Zheng, C.R., Zhang, Y.C., Zhang, W.Y.: Large eddy simulation of separation control over a backward-facing step flow by suction. Int. J. Comput. Fluid Dyn. **25**, 59–73 (2011)
6. Abu-Nada, E., Al-Sarkhi, A., Akash, B., Al-Hinti, I.: Heat transfer and fluid flow characteristics of separated flows ecountered in a backward-facing step under the effect of suction and blowing. J. Heat Transfer **129**, 1517–1528 (2007)
7. Uruba, V., Jonas, P., Mazur, O.: Control of channel-flow behind a backward-facing step by suction/blowing. Int. J. Heat Fluid Flow **28**, 665–672 (2007)
8. Choi, H.H., Nguyen, V.T., Nguyen, J.: Numerical invetigation of backward facing step flow over various step angles. Procedia Eng. **154**, 420–425 (2016)
9. Zafer, B., Cosgun, F.: Aeroacoustics investigation of unsteady incompressible cavity flow. J. Faculty Eng. Archit. Gazi Univ. **31**, 665–675 (2016)
10. Hudy, L.M., et al.: Particle image velocimetry measurements of a two/three-dimensional separating/reattaching boundary layer downstream of an axisymmetric backward-facing step. In. AIAA 43rd Aerospace Sciences Meeting and Exhibit, Reno, Nevada, 10–13 January 2005. AIAA Paper 2005-114 (2005)

International Workshop on Affective Computing and Emotion Recognition (ACER-EMORE 2020)

Quantifying the Links Between Personality Sub-traits and the Basic Emotions

Ryan Donovan[(✉)], Aoife Johnson, Aine deRoiste, and Ruairi O'Reilly

Cork Institute of Technology, Cork, Ireland
brendan.donovan@mycit.ie
{aoife.johnson,Aine.DeRoiste,ruari.oreilly}@cit.ie

Abstract. This article describes an exploratory study that aimed to analyse the relationship between personality traits and emotions. In particular, it investigates to what extent the sub-traits of the Five Factor Model has an empirically quantifiable correlation with the Basic Emotions (Anger, Anxiety, Disgust, Fear, Joy, Sadness, Surprise). If links between these personality traits and the basic emotions can be found, then this would enable an emotional-state-to-personality-trait mapping.

In this study, 38 participants answered a Big Five Aspects Scale (BFAS) questionnaire and then watched 12 emotionally provocative film clips along with answering 12 short emotional Likert-scales on their emotional experiences during each film clip. The results showed that (i) four of the seven Basic Emotions outright significantly correlated, while two emotions (Fear and Disgust) approached statistical significance, with at least one of the personality traits and (ii) significant correlations between personality traits and basic emotions could only be identified at the sub-trait level, demonstrating the value in adopting a higher-resolution personality model.

The results supports the long-term goal of this research, which is the enabling of state-to-trait inferences. A method for analysing and visualising such a mapping, that differentiates mappings based on the direction and magnitude of the effect size was also developed. The study contributes a blueprint towards utilising Affective Computing methodology to automatically map these phenomena.

Keywords: Personality · Emotion · Affective computing

1 Introduction

Personality and emotion are two important life components. Personality is the unique and typical way a person feels, perceives, desires, and behaves in the world [42]. Emotion is the brief but potent experience of states like joy, disgust, or sadness. Our personality accurately predicts our academic performances [41], our level of income and occupational success [47], the quantity and quality of

© Springer Nature Switzerland AG 2020
O. Gervasi et al. (Eds.): ICCSA 2020, LNCS 12250, pp. 521–537, 2020.
https://doi.org/10.1007/978-3-030-58802-1_37

our romantic relationships [32], our likelihood of developing mental illnesses [28], the likelihood of being persuaded by certain types of targeted messages, both commercial [23] and political [18,33], amongst many other [48]. Emotions provide important feedback on our goal-progress [14]; they prepare us either to take or avoid certain actions; and they are essential for everyday life decisions [8]. The functioning of both phenomena is necessary for healthy well-being.

A significant body of research exists on the study of personality and emotions as largely distinct phenomena [4,6,29]. In the last two handbook of emotions for psychology researchers, in-depth discussions of modern personality research are limited. In the 2016 version, the discussion of the relationship between emotions and personality largely focuses on the influence of social and individual differences factors, such as social display rules and differences in emotion regulation, rather than personality directly [4]. In the 2010 version, the discussion of personality and emotions focuses primarily on the individual differences in emotion regulation rather than experience [29]. Similarly, in the Cambridge handbook of personality psychology [6], while the relation between emotions and personality is discussed more directly, it is confined to one chapter.

The limited discussion of the relationship between personality and emotions overlooks the fact that they are interwoven with one another and the intersection between the two phenomena is a promising source of scientific inquiry. For example, people tend to describe the personality of another person in terms of that person's typical emotional experiences (e.g. he/she is a happy person, but can be prone to anger; he/she is an fearful person, and is often melancholic)[1,30]. Similarly, neuroscientific research conducted in the last 15 years has repeatedly found substantial correlations between neurological emotion systems and personality traits [9]. Such evidence supports the view that emotions are a springboard for people's personality; how much people feel certain emotions is an indicator of their personality.

Nevertheless, it is unclear what the exact relationship between personality and emotions is. Are people high in certain personality traits more likely to experience certain emotions? The limited evidence collected so far suggests yes. For example, according to a study that monitored the behaviour and emotions of people periodically in their daily lives, extraverted people experienced higher levels of positive emotion (e.g. joy) than introverted people. The study also showed that people high in Neuroticism (who tend to be emotionally unstable) tend to experience higher levels of negative emotion than people low in Neuroticism[1] [36]. However, the emotions that other personality traits are coupled with is yet to be sufficiently quantified.

The intersection of personality and emotions is fertile ground for cross-disciplinary research opportunities. Research in both the fields of personality and emotions have identified key components that are appropriate for rigorous scientific analysis.

---

[1] Positive and negative in this context refers to how pleasant an emotion feels to the person. This is typically referred to as the valence of an emotion.

Personality: The primary components are traits. Traits are typical patterns of emotion, behaviour, cognition, and motivation across situations [35].

Emotion: The primary components are the basic emotions, having been described as the "primary colours" underpinning all our emotional experiences [14].

The identification of such components represents an opportunity to enable a bi-directional emotion-state-to-personality-trait mapping (referred to hereafter as "state-to-trait mapping" or "trait-to-state mapping"). This mapping would correlate the relationship between personality traits and basic emotions, in order to enable inferences of one component based on the other.

Affective computing is in a prime position to enable such state-to-trait mappings. Affective computing researchers have been successful in categorising and automatically detecting the basic emotion states [39,40]. Therefore, if emotive states can be mapped to personality, the ability to automatically assess emotions could provide tools for personality categorisation and automatic detection. Similarly, there is interest in state-to-trait mappings in the area of automated personality synthesis, which is the process of creating technology that can mimic human personalities in their interactions with people [49]. Understanding the emotional make-up of personality configurations would enable artificial intelligence (AI) based systems to appear more human-like (e.g. an extraverted more bubbly personal assistant device, like Siri).

This paper presents an empirical study towards a correlated mapping that can be utilised by researchers for a variety of use cases. The focus of this study is mapping state-to-trait, future work is intended on mapping trait-to-state. An experimental study was conducted in order to assess the relationship between personality traits and the basic emotion. In particular, this study focused on the utility of incorporating a sub-trait level of personality in this assessment. A series of hypothesis will be investigated to quantify the value of sub-traits in assessing the relationship between personality traits and emotions. The results of these hypotheses are evaluated for statistical significance and the state-to-trait mapping is dynamically visualised, enabling analysis of the results.

The remainder of the paper is organised as follows: Sect. 2 discusses the concept of personality traits, their sub-traits, and the basic emotions. Related work on the interconnection between traits and emotions is also discussed. Section 3 details the design, participant pool, materials used, and the procedure for the experimental methodology to quantify the state-trait links. Section 4 presents the descriptive and inferential statistics resulting from the study. Section 5 presents an in-depth discussion of the results. Section 6 presents the overall conclusions with respect to the field at large and recommended future research directions are outlined.

2   Personality Traits and the Basic Emotions

Personality is a multi-levelled psychological phenomenon. The foundational level of personality consists of traits. Traits are defined here as typical patterns of affect, behaviour, cognition, and motivation [11]. Traits represent a person's disposition towards the world [11]. Traits are bi-polar phenomena in that each trait will range from one pole to their opposite pole (e.g. Disagreeable is the opposite pole of Agreeableness). However, people vary on how much they have a trait on a spectrum relative to other people.

The predominant model for identifying and taxonomising important personality traits for analysis is The Five Factor Model (also known as *The Big Five*) [34]. The Five-Factor Model emerged through applying rigorous factor analysis through a large body of trait descriptions [26]. Results across multiple research groups repeatedly found a five-factor solution for taxonomising personality traits. The Five Factor therefore measures people's personality among five broad traits: Openness to Experience, Conscientiousness, Extraversion, Agreeableness, and Neuroticism [37].

The FFM is a hierarchical model of personality traits [26]. The Five Factors are higher-level abstractions of specific aspects of traits, which are called facets. For example, Extraversion is made up of facets such like warmth, excitement-seeking, and gregariousness, all of which correlate significantly with one another. This enables researchers to generalise the influence and effects of these facets under the common factor Extraversion. However, while the FFM provides a reliable predictor for various important outcomes, the broadness of the Five Factors impedes precise predictions.

This impairment has prompted researchers to assess lower-levels of the Five Factor Model hierarchy in order to identify traits that can act as intermediate level between the generalisability offered by the Five-Factors and the precision offered from their facets. Cross-disciplinary research has demonstrated that such an intermediate level exists. Findings in both the areas of behavioural genetics and psychometrics demonstrate that each of The Big Five can be divided into two sub-traits [13]. These 10 sub-traits form an intermediate level in the hierarchy, below the Five Factors and above their facets. This study aims to assess whether the sub-traits can also provide insight to the relationship between emotions and personality. Therefore, the range of the traits considered in this study are listed in Table 1.

Table 1. The Five Factor Model's five broad traits and the associated sub-traits as specified by [13]. The sub-traits are an intermediate level between the broad traits and their associated facets. Each sub-trait correlates highly with its partnered sub-trait ($r \geq .50$)

Personality trait	Sub-trait 1	Sub-trait 2
Openness to experience	Openness	Intellect
Conscientiousness	Industriousness	Orderliness
Extraversion	Enthusiasm	Assertiveness
Agreeableness	Compassion	Politeness
Neuroticism	Withdrawal	Volatility

2.1   The Basic Emotions

This study considers emotions under the basic emotions theory viewpoint. The basic emotions theory (BET) proposes that there exists a limited amount of emotions that are biologically, behaviourally, and psychologically distinct from one another [14,17]. These emotions have distinctive physiological, behavioural, and psychological signals; they are rooted in sub-cortical regions of the brain; they occur quickly and briefly; they motivate consistent forms of context appraisal and consequential actions; they have a distinctive subjective experience; they interact to form more culturally and cognitively mediated emotions, amongst other defining characteristics [14].

The authors do not argue that these emotions and their signals are exactly the same in every culture, but they do consider that there is sufficient similarity across several cultures to justify the inclusion of BET for this study. The authors also do not argue that there exists an exact 1-to-1 mapping between emotions and either their physiological, behavioural, or psychological signals. Research has shown that the origin of emotions emerge from the interaction of a range of physiological, behavioural, and psychological activity [3]. However, at the same time there is strong evidence indicating that there exists a consistent range of behaviour that can be identified and be used to accurately indicate the occurrence of a basic emotion [25]. The article also acknowledges that there are other aspects of emotions that are largely overlooked by this study, such as an emotion's valence and arousal level.

While there is some debate as to which emotions should be considered as "basic" [16], this paper considers the following seven emotions as basic: Anger, Anxiety, Disgust, Fear, Joy, Sadness, Surprise. The inclusion of Anxiety is a modification of the original BET model, which included Contempt instead of Anxiety. Contempt was excluded in this study to align with the consensus view of basic emotion researchers. In a survey that asked 250 emotion researchers which emotions have been empirically established as a basic emotion, the results showed that only 34% of those researchers considered Contempt as an established basic emotion [15]. The same survey did not ask researchers about the status of Anxiety as a basic emotion. Anxiety has been theoretically linked to the personality trait Withdrawal, which is a trait hypothesised to be motivated by a desire to reduce feelings of anxiety [10,11]. Therefore, the status of Anxiety as a basic emotion is investigated here (Table 2).

Table 2. The seven basic emotions considered as part of this work. These emotions are considered to have distinct physiological, behavioural, and psychological signals

Basic Emotions			
Anger	Anxiety	Disgust	Sadness
Fear	Joy	Surprise	

2.2   Links Between Personality Traits and the Basic Emotions

The relationship between Big Five traits and the basic emotions has been, in a limited sense, studied in the past. To date, the strongest correlation identified is in relation to the basic emotions and the personality traits Extraversion and Neuroticism. Extraversion has been found to positively correlate with Joy and Neuroticism has been found to positively correlate with Fear, Anxiety, and Sadness [10].

Extraverted people tend to experience more joy on a daily basis, measured by either self-reports, analysis of behaviour (e.g. how much participants laugh and smile in conversations), or through text [24,31,36]. The sub-traits associated with Extraversion (Assertiveness and Enthusiasm) provide information about the factors that causes Joy for extraverted people. Assertiveness has been positively correlated with the experience of joy with regards to the pursuit of a valued goal. Enthusiasm has been positively correlated with the experience of joy in relation to the attainment of valued goals [11,12].

People high in Neuroticism tend to experience more Fear, Anxiety, and Sadness. Neuroticism is unsurprisingly a key predictor of suffering from mental disorders such as Major Depression Disorder or Generalised Anxiety Disorder [46]. The sub-traits associated with Neuroticism (Withdrawal and Volatility) provide information about the factors that causes these emotions for people high in Neuroticism. Withdrawal has been positive correlated with Anxiety and Sadness in response to the perception of potential threat (e.g. the chance of being criticised). Volatility has been positively correlated with Fear and Sadness in response to a perceived current threat (e.g. the perception that one is being currently criticised).

There are limited empirical findings in the literature detailing the correlation between basic emotions and the traits Openness to Experience, Conscientiousness, and Agreeableness along with their sub-traits. This is a motivating factor for pursuing the current study, to quantitatively assess the relationship between these Big Five Factors and basic emotions.

The following links should be considered as tentative and in the need for further empirical investigation. Openness to Experience has correlated with experiencing all basic emotions more intensely, rather than being underlined by any particular emotion [11]. Conscientiousness has positively correlated with experiencing disgust. A theoretical suggestion for this link has been that disgust motivates conscientiousness people to act [5,11]. Agreeableness has positively with neurological systems that both mimic the emotions of others, or inhibit emotions that might cause conflict [9,10,21]. It is also not clear how the sub-traits of these traits correlate with the basic emotions.

2.3   Experiment Hypotheses

Following from the previous section, the hypotheses used to guide the research were as follows:

1. Each Emotion will correlate significantly and with a substantial effect size with at least one of the Big Five or their sub-traits.
2. Extraversion will positively correlate with the emotion Joy.
3. Neuroticism will positively correlate with at least one of the following emotions, Fear, Anxiety or Sadness.
4. Agreeableness will be negatively correlate with Anger.
5. Conscientiousness will positively correlate with Disgust.
6. Openness to Experience will correlate with a substantial effect size with every emotion, across its two sub-traits.

3   Methodology

The aim of this study is to analyse the relationship between personality and emotions. This necessitates the identification of quantifiable correlations between personality traits, their sub-traits, and the basic emotions. This will provide an empirical basis for a high resolution mapping of state-to-trait analysis.

3.1   Participants

The majority of participants were recruited from Cork Institute of Technology (CIT). These participants were recruited through the main researcher speaking with students about the study, posting informative and recruitment flyers around the campus, and campaigning for participants via the institutes student webpages. The majority of the participants were female (N = 38, Females = 25, Males = 13). Most of the participants were in their twenties or thirties (M = 33.77, SD = 13.93, Range = 19–63).

3.2   Materials

– *Personality Questionnaire.* The Big Five Aspects Scale was used. This is a standardized measure of the FFM traits. The scale is composed of 100 units (e.g. I seldom feel blue). Participants were asked to rate on a Likert-scale how well each statement described themselves. For each of the Big Five traits, there were 10 accompanied statements, which are further split into 5 statements per sub-trait. The Likert-scale ranged from 1 to 5, with 1 representing "strongly disagree" and 5 representing "strongly agree", on how well each statement describes them. The Cronbach Alpha of the sub-scales were: Openness to Experience (.81), Conscientiousness (.85), Extraversion (.85), Agreeableness (.74), Neuroticism (0.85).
– *Emotions Scale.* A short scale was created for the purposes of this study. Whilst there exists several standardised Basic Emotions scales, each of those scales either accounted for other hypothesised basic emotions or did not consider each basic emotion accounted for here (e.g. Anxiety). The question that accompanied each emotion scale was: "While watching the previous film clip, to what extent did you experience these emotions?". Participants answered

each Likert-scale on a range from 1–5, with 1 representing "no degree of such emotion", 3 representing "a moderate degree of such emotion", and 5 representing "a great degree of such emotion". The experiment software required participants to give a response for each of the basic emotions. The overall scale consisted of 84 questions (.95), with Anger (.80), Disgust (83), Fear (.85), Anxiety (.80), Sadness (.76), Joy (.66), and Surprised (.88) all having 12 questions each.

- *Emotional Stimuli.* Film clips were used in order to elicit emotional reactions. Film clips have been shown to reliably elicit emotional expressions by multiple independent research groups. For this study, twelve film clips were selected, the lengths of the film clips varied between 1 to 5 min. Nine of the film clips used in this experiment were selected based on past research indicating they elicited emotional reactions [19,22]. Three new film clips (*Annabelle, Who-Dunnit?*, and *Peep Show*), which have not been used in independent research, were chosen after conducting a pilot study with 8 participants who watched and rated a variety of film clips and self-reported their emotions.

3.3   Procedure

Potential participants were provided with an information sheet explaining the study. Those who were interested in taking part, were invited to fill out a demographic information form, which gathered information about their age, gender, nationality, and previous experience with psychometric tests. Participants who completed this section were invited to take part in the laboratory stage of the experiment. There was two parts to the laboratory stage of the study:

1. Participants completed the Big Five Aspects scale questionnaire in order to attain a baseline reading of their personality. This questionnaire took on average 15 min to complete.
2. Upon completion, a researcher set up film clip recording software on the computer used for the experiment. Given that participants varied in height, there had to be a manual check to ensure that each participant's face occupied the centre of camera's frame[2]. Once this was ensured, the researcher left the room, and the participants watched 12 film clips, always in the same order. After each film clip, participants answered the emotions scale designed for the experiment (see Sect. 3.2) to assess what emotional reactions the participants had whilst watching the film. This stage took on average 45 min to complete. Afterwards participants were debriefed on the study.

4   Results

This section presents the key descriptive and inferential statistics from the study in relation to the hypotheses.

---

[2] The automated analysis of participants video footage captured is not considered here or incorporated into results. It is intended be the subject of a future publication.

4.1   Descriptive Statistics

Emotion Scores: Participants did not experience a dominant emotion through-out the study. The mean and standard deviations of the emotions scores are presented in Table 3.

Table 3. Descriptive statistics for self-reported emotions (M = Mean; SD = Standard Deviation)

Emotion	M	SD	Emotion	M	SD
Fear	2.02	0.66	Anxiety	2.46	0.62
Anger	1.92	0.57	Sadness	2.22	0.49
Joy	1.56	0.37	Surprise	2.83	0.84
Disgust	2.49	0.57			

Personality Scores: Personality scores were around the midway point of 3 and frequency scores were normally distributed. The only exceptions to this were for the traits Agreeableness and Compassion (Table 4).

Table 4. Descriptive statistics for big five aspect scale scores (M = Mean; SD = Standard Deviation)

Trait	M	SD	Trait	M	SD
Openness to Experience	3.55	0.39	Agreeableness	4.02	0.30
>Openness	2.90	0.48	>Compassion	4.22	0.42
>Intellect	3.49	0.51	>Politeness	3.82	0.34
Conscientiousness	3.47	0.57	Neuroticism	2.94	0.45
>Industriousness	3.39	0.59	>Volatility	2.91	0.72
>Orderliness	3.55	0.67	>Withdrawal	2.96	0.42
Extraversion	3.50	0.46			
>Enthusiasm	3.72	0.48			
>Assertiveness	3.27	0.62			

4.2   Inferential Statistics

Inferential statistics in this analysis were interpreted using traditional proto-col. Namely, a correlation was considered statistically significant if $p \leq .05$. However, this analysis also gives values to correlations that approach statistical significance, $p \geq 0.05$ and $p \leq 0.15$. This value is given due to the lack of power of the study, making it apriori likely to make false negatives (see Sect. 5.1), but also to align with the "New Statistics" approach emerging in Psychology [7]. This approach aims to avoid the pitfalls that occur when researchers obsess on whether a p-value is ≤ .05 and has been recommended by multiple independent research groups [2,20]. This obsession has been deemed as one of the primary causes of the replication crisis in psychology [38].

Table 5. Bi-Directional Mappings of Personality Traits and the Basic Emotions

Personality Traits	Fear	Anger	Joy	Anxiety	Sad	Surprise	Disgust
Openness to Experience	0.01	0.06	0.18	0.05	0.15	0.09	0.08
Openness	0.01	0.13	0.18	0.16	0.17	**0.31***	0.24
Intellect	0.00	-0.02	0.11	-0.06	0.07	-0.15	-0.11
Conscientiousness	-0.09	-0.02	-0.16	0.05	-0.03	**-0.30***	-0.19
Industriousness	-0.18	-0.07	-0.24	0.09	-0.11	**-0.36****	**-0.28***
Orderliness	0.01	0.04	-0.05	0.00	0.04	-0.20	-0.08
Extraversion	**-0.28***	-0.13	0.00	-0.19	-0.11	-0.10	-0.15
Assertiveness	-0.22	-0.08	-0.01	-0.10	-0.01	-0.10	-0.17
Enthusiasm	-0.26	-0.14	0.02	-0.22	-0.20	-0.06	-0.07
Agreeableness	-0.18	-0.18	**-0.38****	0.00	-0.04	-0.04	-0.06
Compassion	-0.26	-0.18	**-0.34***	-0.14	-0.07	0.02	-0.08
Politeness	0.01	-0.09	-0.24	0.17	0.01	-0.09	0.00
Neuroticism	0.17	0.27	**0.29***	0.06	**0.35***	0.26	0.26
Withdrawal	0.15	-0.08	**0.33***	0.01	0.01	0.21	0.04
Volatility	0.13	**0.38****	0.17	0.07	**0.43****	0.21	**0.31***

** *Indicates a p-value ≤ .05.*
* *Indicates a p-value ≥ 0.05 and p ≤ 0.15*
*** *Colour of correlation indicates both the strength and direction of the correlation*

Relationship Between Personality Traits and Emotions in Relation to Hypotheses: A Pearson's R correlation was conducted on each personality trait variable with each distinct emotion self-report rating. Given the fact that these phenomena are diverse in nature, personality being a stable trait and emotions being fleeting states, the data needed to be prepared for correlation analysis. For each participant the mean score per emotion was calculated and correlated with the mean score per trait. Table 5 denotes a correlation mapping between each emotion and personality variable. The results are visualised in a manner that indicates their significance in terms of whether they are statistically significant, the magnitude of their effect size, and the direction of the correlation. The results associated with the studies proposed hypothesis, as detailed in Sect. 2.2 are as follows:

1. **Each Emotion will correlate significantly and substantially with at least one of the Big Five or their sub-traits:** Fear and Anxiety were the only emotions not to have a p value less than 0.05. Fear negatively correlated with Extraversion that fit this study's guidelines for approaching significance $r(36) = -0.28$, $p = .13$. While Anxiety also negatively correlated with Extraversion $r(36) = -0.19$, $p = .33$, and a negative correlation with Enthusiasm $r(36) = -0.22$, $p = .24$, neither p-value was statistically significant.

Every other emotion significantly correlated with at least one personality trait.

2. **Extraversion will positively correlate with the emotion Joy:** Extraversion had no linear relationship with reported Joy, $r(36) = .00$, $p = 0.98$. The two sub-traits, Assertiveness ($r(36) = -0.01$, $p = .96$) and Enthusiasm ($r(36) = 0.02$, $p = .91$), insubstantially correlated with Joy.

3. **Neuroticism will positively correlate with at least one of the following emotions, Fear, Anxiety or Sadness:** Neuroticism correlated positively with both Fear ($r(36) = 0.17$, $p = .37$) and Anxiety ($r(36) = 0.06$, $p = .74$), but neither reached statistical significance. Neuroticism did positively correlate with Sadness with a medium effect size, which approached the threshold of statistical significance, ($r(36) = 0.35$, $p = .06$). The sub-trait Volatility had a medium-to-strong positive correlation with Sadness and did reach statistical significance, ($r(36) = 0.43$, $p = .02$). This was the strongest relationship found between personality traits and emotions in the data-set. Volatility also had a medium-to-large positive relationship with Anger, $r(36) = 0.38$, $p = .04$.

4. **Agreeableness will negatively correlate with Anger:** Agreeableness was negatively correlated with Anger with a small effect size ($r(36) = -0.18$, $p = .34$).

5. **Conscientiousness will positively correlate with Disgust:** Conscientiousness was negatively correlated with Disgust, ($r(36) = -0.19$, $p = .96$). This was both true for Orderliness ($r(36) = -0.01$, $p = .69$) and Industriousness ($r(36) = -0.28$, $p = .14$), although Industriousness had a stronger negative relationship with Disgust.

6. **Openness to Experience will correlate with a substantial effect size with every emotion, across its two sub-traits:** Openness to Experience had a substantial effect size with Joy ($r(36) = 0.18$, $p = .33$) and Sadness ($r(36) = 0.15$, $p = .43$). The sub-trait Openness had a substantial relationship with Anger ($r(36) = 0.13$, $p = .49$), Joy ($r(36) = 0.18$, $p = .35$), Anxiety ($r(36) = 0.16$, $p = .41$), Sadness ($r(36) = 0.17$, $p = .38$), Surprise ($r(36) = 0.31$, $p = .10$), and Disgust ($r(36) = 0.24$, $p = .24$). Intellect negatively correlated with a substantial effect size with surprise, but this result was not close to statistical significance.

7. **Relationship Between Personality Traits and Emotions in relation to non-Hypothesised Results:** Agreeableness had a medium-to-strong negative correlation with Joy, $r(36) = -0.38$, $p = .04$. This relationship seemed to be underlined mostly by the sub-trait Compassion, $r(36) = -0.34$, $p = .07$. The sub-trait Industriousness negatively correlated with Surprise, $r(36) = -0.30$, $p = .05$. Disgust positively correlated with disgust with a medium-effect size, $r(36) = 0.31$, $p = .10$.

5   Discussion

In this study, participants answered a personality questionnaire before reporting their emotional experiences with a series of film clips. The immediate goal of this study was to generate a quantitative mapping between the FFM traits and their sub-traits with the basic emotions. The distal goal was to make progress towards automated state-to-trait mappings that can be utilised across academic and industry domains. The results of the study in relation to hypotheses are discussed here.

Hypothesis 1 - Each Emotion will significantly correlate with at least one of the Big Five or their sub-traits. This hypothesis was partially supported. Six of the basic emotions correlated significantly or approached significance with one of the personality traits. Fear correlated with Extraversion; Anger correlated with Volatility: Joy correlated with Agreeableness, Compassion, Neuroticism, and Withdrawal; Sadness correlated with Neuroticism and Volatility; Surprise correlated with Openness, Conscientiousness, and Industriousness; Disgust correlated with Industriousness and Volatility. Only Anxiety failed to significantly correlate or approach statistical significance with a personality trait.

Overall, this result justifies the immediate goal of a state-to-trait quantitative mapping. The fact that the personality traits (and their sub-traits), Openness to Experience (via Openness), Conscientiousness, and Agreeableness, correlated substantially with one of the basic emotions is a significant research contribution. The link between these personality traits and the basic emotions has previously been overlooked, such that their relation to emotions have mostly been inferred rather than empirically quantified. The finding that some of these correlations (e.g. Openness and Surprise) only emerged at the sub-trait level justifies including this level of the trait hierarchy.

Hypothesis 2 - Extraversion will significantly positively correlate with Joy. This hypothesis was not supported. There was no significant correlation found between Extraversion, and its sub-traits Enthusiasm and Assertiveness, with Joy. This result is surprising as Extraversion has consistently positively correlated with positive emotion. Extroverted people on average smile more, laugh more, use more positive emotion language, and report feeling happier than those who score low on Extraversion [50].

The most likely reason for this result is the emotional stimuli used. Joy was the lowest emotion participants experienced while watching the film clips. For one of the targeted Joy-clips, *Peep Show*, half of the participants (n = 18) reported a 1 on the Likert-scale for Joy while watching this film clip, indicating they experienced no degree of Joy. This statistic indicates that our emotional stimuli possibly created a ceiling effect, in that the potential for Joy to be experienced was too low in order to detect the hypothesised relationship.

Hypothesis 3 - Neuroticism will significantly positively correlate with Fear, Anger, Anxiety, and Sadness. This hypothesis was partially supported. Neuroticism positively and close to significance correlated with Sadness and Anger, but surprisingly not with Anxiety or Fear. This partially supports past research that has shown consistent links between Neuroticism and negative emotion states. The sub-trait Volatility significantly and positively correlated with Anger, Sadness, and Disgust. The relationship between Volatility and Sadness was the largest correlation in the data-set. This finding supports the postulation that Volatility represents an emotional unstable and active defence response to negative emotion.

Hypothesis 4 - Agreeableness will significantly negatively correlate with Anger. This hypothesis was not supported. Agreeableness had a negative but non-significant correlation with Anger. Agreeableness and Compassion instead had a significant negative correlation with Joy. Prior research has shown that people high in Compassion are more likely to empathise with the emotion and situation of other people [21]. This result is consistent with that hypothesis. In this study, several film clips targeted negative emotions (e.g. Anger, Sadness, Fear) where the protagonist often experienced something terrible (e.g. The Lion King – the protagonist mourns the death of his father). People high in Agreeableness and in particular Compassion may have strongly empathised with these protagonists. A direction for future research is the use of more balanced film clips to assess whether Agreeableness and Compassion would positive correlate with Joy during positive emotion film clips. If so, this would suggest that Agreeableness is highly sensitive to context in regards to emotional experience.

Hypothesis 5 - Conscientiousness will significantly positively correlate with disgust. This hypothesis was not supported. Conscientiousness, and in particular Industriousness, was negatively associated with Disgust. This result is unlikely to be due to the film clips, as the majority of participants rated both disgust film clips as highly disgusting. This contradicts prior arguments that Conscientiousness people have general disgust sensitivity [44]. Instead in this study people high in Conscientiousness were more likely to be comfortable dealing with disgusting material than people low in Conscientiousness. If one analyses the Disgust emotion, this is not surprising. Disgust is associated with avoidance behaviour (e.g. closing ones mouth and turning ones face away from contaminated food; [45]). Industriousness is a trait characterised by taking action. From this perspective, it is intuitive that Conscientiousness and Industriousness would negatively correlate with Disgust.

Hypothesis 6 - Openness to Experience will substantially correlate with each of the basic emotions, across its two sub-traits. This hypothesis was weakly supported. Openness to Experience positively correlated with Joy and Sadness with an effect size greater than .10, its sub-trait Openness positively correlated with Anger, Anxiety, and Surprise, and Disgust all with $r \geq .10$ and Intellect positively correlated with Joy and negatively correlated with Surprise and Disgust. However, out of these correlations, the only correlation that approached significance was between Openness and Surprise. Also, there was no relationship found between Openness to Experience and Fear and other personality traits had similar patterns of relationships with emotions (e.g. Neuroticism).

5.1 Limitations

The primary limitation of this study was the sample size of 38 participants. Whilst some have argued that 30 participants is the "magic" number for data collection, this is unsupported by hard evidence [27]. An important factor in determining the appropriate number of participants in a study is the usual effect size of the phenomenon being studied. The effect size of relationships between personality traits and other phenomenon tend to be between $r = .20$ and $r = .30$, so based on Cohen's principles, they are small-to-moderate [43]. In order to be statistically confident of reliably finding an effect size between this range, the sample size of a study would need to be between 50 and 83 participants. In order to meet the long-term goal of this research, a larger-scale study with more participants is being planned in order to achieve a robust level of statistical power.

6 Conclusions

Research in the fields of personality and emotion have identified key components suitable for rigorous scientific inquiry. These key components are personality traits and the basic emotions. It has been repeatedly shown that both components are essential for a healthy, successful, and enjoyable life. Given this, it is surprising that these components have been largely treated as distinct. This is despite the fact that there exists a tight interconnection between the two phenomena. There is a need for quantitative research conducted on the correlation of personality traits and the basic emotions. This study aimed to address this need by carrying out a quantitative assessment of the links between personality traits and the basic emotions. Participants in this study answered a personality questionnaire before watching a series of film clips chosen on their ability to elicit emotions. The intermediate goal of this study was to generate a quantitative mapping between the Big Five personality traits and their sub-traits with the basic emotions.

The results of this preliminary study offers a marker for further exploration of this mapping. The statistical analysis found several moderate, by research standards, effect sizes between personality traits and emotions. In particular, the negative relationships found between the sub-trait Compassion with Joy, Industriousness and Disgust, and the powerful positive relationship between Volatility and Sadness demonstrate how the use of a higher-resolution model of personality can identify relationships that lower resolution personality models have been unable to. A future study with a larger population sample should establish a clearer and more fine-grained analysis of the relationship between personality traits and their sub-traits with the basic emotions such that it can form a foundation for Affective computing state-to-trait applications.

References

1. Wilt, J., Revelle, W.: Affect, behavior, cognition, and desire in the big five: an analysis of item content and structure. Eur. J. Pers. **29**, 478–479 (2015)
2. Amrhein, V., Korner-Nievergelt, F., Roth, T.: The earth is flat ($p > 0.05$): significance thresholds and the crisis of unreplicable research. PeerJ **5**, 35445 (2017). https://doi.org/10.7717/peerj.3544
3. Barrett, L.F.: How Emotions are Made: The Secret Life of the Brain. Houghton Mifflin Harcourt, Boston (2017)
4. Barrett, L.F., Lewis, M., Haviland-Jones, J.M.: Handbook of Emotions. Guilford Publications, New York (2016)
5. Bogg, T., Roberts, B.W.: Conscientiousness and health-related behaviors: a meta-analysis of the leading behavioral contributors to mortality. Psychol. Bull. **130**(6), 887 (2004)
6. Corr, P.J., Matthews, G.: The Cambridge Handbook of Personality Psychology. Cambridge University Press, New York (2009)
7. Cumming, G.: The new statistics: why and how. Psychol. Sci. **25**(1), 7–29 (2014)
8. Damasio, A.R.: Descartes' Error. Random House, London (2006)
9. Davis, K.L., Panksepp, J.: The Emotional Foundations of Personality: A Neurobiological and Evolutionary Approach. WW Norton & Company, New York (2018)
10. DeYoung, C.G.: Personality neuroscience and the biology of traits. Soc. Pers. Psychol. Compass **4**(12), 1165–1180 (2010)
11. DeYoung, C.G.: Cybernetic big five theory. J. Res. Pers. **56**, 33–58 (2015)
12. DeYoung, C.G., Hirsh, J.B., Shane, M.S., Papademetris, X., Rajeevan, N., Gray, J.R.: Testing predictions from personality neuroscience: brain structure and the big five. Psychol. Sci. **21**(6), 820–828 (2010)
13. DeYoung, C.G., Quilty, L.C., Peterson, J.B.: Between facets and domains: 10 aspects of the big five. J. Pers. Soc. Psychol. **93**(5), 880 (2007)
14. Ekman, P.: Basic Emotions. Handbook of Cognition and Emotion, pp. 45–60. Wiley, New York (1999)
15. Ekman, P.: What scientists who study emotion agree about. Perspect. Psychol. Sci. **11**(1), 31–34 (2016)
16. Ekman, P., Cordaro, D.: What is meant by calling emotions basic. Emotion Rev. **3**(4), 364–370 (2011)
17. Ekman, P.E., Davidson, R.J.: The Nature of Emotion: Fundamental Questions. Oxford University Press, New York (1994)
18. Gerber, A.S., Huber, G.A., Doherty, D., Dowling, C.M., Panagopoulos, C.: Big five personality traits and responses to persuasive appeals: results from Voter Turnout experiments. Polit. Behav. **35**(4), 687–728 (2012). https://doi.org/10.1007/s11109-012-9216-y
19. Gilman, T.L., et al.: A film set for the elicitation of emotion in research: a comprehensive catalog derived from four decades of investigation. Behav. Res. Methods **49**(6), 2061–2082 (2017). https://doi.org/10.3758/s13428-016-0842-x
20. Giner-Sorolla, R.: Approaching a fair deal for significance and other concerns. J. Exp. Soc. Psychol. **65**, 1–6 (2016)
21. Graziano, W.G., Tobin, R.M.: Agreeableness (2009)
22. Gross, J.J., Levenson, R.W.: Emotion elicitation using films. Cogn. Emot. **9**(1), 87–108 (1995). https://doi.org/10.1080/02699939508408966
23. Hirsh, J.B., Kang, S.K., Bodenhausen, G.V.: Personalized persuasion: tailoring persuasive appeals to recipients' personality traits. Psychol. Sci. **23**(6), 578–581 (2012)

24. Hirsh, J.B., Peterson, J.B.: Personality and language use in self-narratives. J. Res. Pers. **43**(3), 524–527 (2009)
25. Hutto, D.D., Robertson, I., Kirchhoff, M.D.: A new, better BET: rescuing and revising basic emotion theory. Front. Psychol. **9**, 1217 (2018)
26. John, O.P., Naumann, L.P., Soto, C.J.: Paradigm shift to the integrative big five trait taxonomy. In: Handbook of Personality: Theory and Research, vol. 3, no. 2, pp. 114–158 (2008)
27. Kar, S.S., Ramalingam, A.: Is 30 the magic number? Issues in sample size estimation. Nat. J. Community Med. **4**(1), 175–179 (2013)
28. Kotov, R., Gamez, W., Schmidt, F., Watson, D.: Linking "big" personality traits to anxiety, depressive, and substance use disorders: a meta-analysis. Psychol. Bull. **136**(5), 768 (2010)
29. Lewis, M., Haviland-Jones, J.M., Barrett, L.F.: Handbook of Emotions. Guilford Press, New York (2010)
30. Locke, E.A., Latham, G.P.: Further confusion in the study of self-regulation: comments on Cervone, Shadel, Smith, and Fiori. Appl. Psychol. **55**(3), 428–438 (2006)
31. Mairesse, F., Walker, M.A., Mehl, M.R., Moore, R.K.: Using linguistic cues for the automatic recognition of personality in conversation and text. J. Artif. Intell. Res. **30**, 457–500 (2007)
32. Malouff, J.M., Thorsteinsson, E.B., Schutte, N.S., Bhullar, N., Rooke, S.E.: The five-factor model of personality and relationship satisfaction of intimate partners: a meta-analysis. J. Res. Pers. **44**(1), 124–127 (2010)
33. Matz, S.C., Kosinski, M., Nave, G., Stillwell, D.J.: Psychological targeting as an effective approach to digital mass persuasion. Proc. Nat. Acad. Sci. **114**(48), 12714–12719 (2017)
34. McAdams, D.P.: The Art and Science of Personality Development. Guilford Publications, New York (2015)
35. McCrae, R.R., John, O.P.: An introduction to the five-factor model and its applications. J. Pers. **60**(2), 175–215 (1992)
36. Mehl, M.R., Gosling, S.D., Pennebaker, J.W.: Personality in its natural habitat: manifestations and implicit folk theories of personality in daily life. J. Pers. Soc. Psychol. **90**(5), 862 (2006)
37. Nettle, D.: Personality: What Makes You the Way You Are. Oxford University Press, New York (2009)
38. Open Science Collaboration: Estimating the reproducibility of psychological science. Science **349**(6251), aac4716 (2015)
39. Picard, R.W.: Affective Computing. MIT Press, Cambridge (2000)
40. Poria, S., Cambria, E., Bajpai, R., Hussain, A.: A review of affective computing: from unimodal analysis to multimodal fusion. Inf. Fusion **37**, 98–125 (2017)
41. Poropat, A.E.: A meta-analysis of the five-factor model of personality and academic performance. Psychol. Bull. **135**(2), 322 (2009)
42. Revelle, W., Scherer, K.R.: Personality and emotion (2004)
43. Rhea, M.R.: Determining the magnitude of treatment effects in strength training research through the use of the effect size. J. Strength Cond. Res. **18**, 918–920 (2004)
44. Roberts, B.W., Jackson, J.J., Fayard, J.V., Edmonds, G., Meints, J.: Conscientiousness (2009)
45. Rozin, P., Haidt, J., McCauley, C.R.: Disgust. Guilford Press, New York (2008)
46. Saklofske, D., Kelly, I., Janzen, B.: Neuroticism, depression, and depression proneness. Personality Individ. Differ. **18**(1), 27–31 (1995)

47. Seibert, S.E., Kraimer, M.L.: The five-factor model of personality and career success. J. Vocat. Behav. **58**(1), 1–21 (2001)
48. Soto, C.J.: How replicable are links between personality traits and consequential life outcomes? The life outcomes of personality replication project. Psychol. Sci. **30**(5), 711–727 (2019)
49. Vinciarelli, A., Mohammadi, G.: A survey of personality computing. IEEE Trans. Affect. Comput. **5**(3), 273–291 (2014)
50. Watson, D., Clark, L.A.: Extraversion and its positive emotional core. In: Handbook of Personality Psychology, pp. 767–793. Elsevier (1997)

Method of Sentiment Preservation in the Kazakh-Turkish Machine Translation

Lena Zhetkenbay[1], Gulmira Bekmanova[1,2(✉)], Banu Yergesh[1], and Altynbek Sharipbay[1,2]

[1] L.N. Gumilyov, Eurasian National University, Nur-Sultan, Kazakhstan
jetlen_7@mail.ru, sharalt@mail.ru,
gulmira-r@yandex.kz, b.yergesh@gmail.com
[2] Nuclear University MEPhI, Moscow, Russia

Abstract. This paper describes characteristics which affect the sentiment analysis in the Kazakh language texts, models of morphological rules and morphological analysis algorithms, formal models of simple sentence structures in the Kazakh-Turkish combination, models and methods of sentiment analysis of texts in the Kazakh language. The studies carried out to compare the morphological and syntactic rules of the Kazakh and Turkish languages prove their closeness by structure. In this respect, we can assume that taking into account sentiment in machine translation for these combinations of languages will give a good result at preserving the text meaning.

Keywords: Sentiment analysis · Kazakh language · Machine translation · Production rules · Rule-based method · Morphological rules · Ontology

1 Introduction

Kazakh language belongs to the Kipchak group [1], whereas Turkish language belongs to Oguz group of Turkic languages [2]. Both of the languages alike other Turkic languages have an agglutinative property, which is characterized by the ability of forming the word formation and word forms by adding affixes (suffixes) to the each root or stem of a particular word. In this case, suffixes change the semantics (meaning) of words which is part of the semantic category that forms new words, and ending - in the structural category, that can change only the composition of words.

In general, translation from one language to another requires changing of alphabet, vocabulary and semantics of the language. Translation is a type of information service which demand will never disappear, on the contrary, it is growing every year. Problems of translation modeling, their presentation in a computer environment are the main problems of applied linguistics and artificial intelligence. Of course, the automation of translation process will increase its effectiveness, as well as expand human relations.

The machine translation is a computer translation of text from one natural language to another natural language, which is equivalent by content [3].

There are high-quality automatic translation systems from Kazakh to Turkish and vice versa, but experience shows that their quality is not very good. It has been stated that among the systems used, the results of translation systems between language

© Springer Nature Switzerland AG 2020
O. Gervasi et al. (Eds.): ICCSA 2020, LNCS 12250, pp. 538–549, 2020.
https://doi.org/10.1007/978-3-030-58802-1_38

combinations, which do not significantly differ from each other, are much better than translations between language combinations completely different by structure. From such result we can see that a large number of linguistic similarities are very favorable for development of machine translation systems and contribute to successful translation.

Nowadays there are various methods and systems for machine translation of languages [4–6]. The application of any of them depends on the complexity of formalizing the language or the national language entire corpora.

The first research among the Turkic languages was made in an automatic translation from Azerbaijani to Turkish based on a dictionary [7]. The next study on machine translation between Turkic languages was carried out between Crimean Tatars and Turkish [8]. Besides, the problems of machine translation for other Turkic languages, in particular from Turkmen and Uyghur to Turkic languages, are presented in the following papers [9, 10]. The computer analysis of morphology of the Turkmen language and statistical methods were used to eliminate the imprecision between the languages. The architecture of the machine translation system has been developed among the Turkic languages. The most widely used method of two-level morphological analysis was carried out using finite state automatons.

The machine translation works are based on grammar rules in languages other than the Kazakh language, including [10–12]. Bilingual data for the Kazakh-Tatar languages [13], Tatar-Bashkir languages [14], a database developed for Crimean-Tatar-Turkish and Kazakh-Russian and Kazakh-English combinations of languages in the Apertium system and a database of structural rules at the grammatical (morphological, lexical, syntactic) level. An algorithm and a model of lexical analysis for Kazakh-Russian and Kazakh-English language combinations and a technology for automated generation of machine translation grammatical rules based on a parallel corpus has been developed.

Unified tagging system (meta-language), morphological and syntactic models of Kazakh and Turkish languages have been developed for creating a Rule-based machine from Kazakh to Turkish [15–18].

The quality of machine translation depends on the quality of the translation of words expressing emotions from one language to another, and not only words, but emotions as well. For emotions translation, we need to do a sentiment analysis in one language and transfer these emotions to another one. In order to do this, both languages need to have a sentiment knowledge base with marked sentiment level. The sentiment analysis or opinion mining in natural languages is one of the most rapidly growing natural language processing technologies. The sentiment analysis is a field of research which analyzes opinions, moods, ratings, assessments, attitudes and emotions of people related to such objects as products, services, organizations, individuals, problems, events, topics and their features [19]. The sentiment analysis has been applied at various levels, starting with the level of the whole text, and then moving to sentences and/or phrases and aspects levels.

A large number of resources and systems for sentiment analyzing in texts have been developed to date for the English language, a large number of resources and systems for analyzing the polarity of texts have been developed to date [19]. A number of researches are currently being implemented to analyze sentiment for the Russian [20, 21], Turkish [22, 23], Spanish [24], Arabic [25] and other languages. An approach for subjectivity identification in Twitter Microtexts is proposed for the Spanish language [24], which investigates the use of structured information within a social network framework. As for the Arabic language, a semantic approach is proposed for identifying user attitudes and business insights from Arabic social networks by framing ontology. The sentiment text analysis modules, described in the works [26, 27] were implemented for the analysis of Kazakh and Russian texts. In [28] described the sentiment classification approach to measure the machine translation quality and sentiment preservation.

In addition to the above-mentioned main tasks, there are other important tasks, such as creating evaluation dictionaries, emotion recognition, sarcasm detection, etc. Emotion recognition, as is known, is the process of determining human emotions. People differ from each other in terms of their emotions. Emotion recognition technology is a new area of research.

There are interesting researches on emotion recognition from videos based on people's facial expressions, from audio information by intonation, from texts by the writing style [29, 30]. The [31] conducted a survey on the implementation of emotions in robotics and views for the future in the field of Affective computing.

Researches on the emotions recognition from texts in the Kazakh language is just beginning, before that, there were conducted researches in sentiment analysis of texts. However, simple emotions can already be recognized. As the basis of such recognition, we use sentiment analysis of texts. The sentiment analysis of a text is a group of semantic analysis methods designed for automatic identification words that bring a subtle coloring to the text, and an emotional assessment of opinion regarding an object, event, phenomenon, process or its features written in the text.

In the case with the Kazakh-Turkish machine translation, it is necessary to use the previously created semantic base of lexical units [32–34] with a ratings score in the Kazakh language and automatically generate a semantic database of lexical units with a sentiment rating score in Turkish based on the languages similarity. The obtained database is being checked by the experts for its correctness.

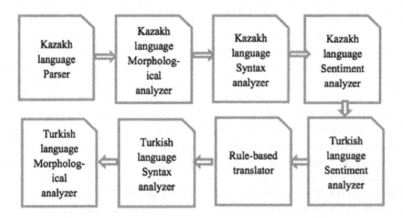

Fig. 1. Kazakh-Turkish machine translation schema

2 Method of Sentiment Analysis in the Kazakh-Turkish Machine Translation

Schema of the Kazakh-Turkish machine translation is shown in Fig. 1.

At the first stage, text processing is done by a special parser, which performs preliminary graphematic processing.

At the second stage the text is processed by morphological analyzer to determine the parts of speech and the features of each part of speech.

The syntax analyzer is engaged at the third stage; the Kazakh sentences structure is being determined.

At the fourth stage the sentiment analyzer is active, which determines the sentiment of the Kazakh text.

The sentiment analyzer for the Turkish language makes a query in the Turkish sentiment knowledge base and compares rating score at the fifth stage, choosing the words closest in terms of ratings and meaning.

The rule-based translator is engaged at the sixth stage. The main idea of such translator is based on the languages similarity. The ontological models for Kazakh and Turkish morphology and syntax are built; the sentiments of the knowledge base are compared.

At the seventh step, the Turkish parser generates the structure of the translated sentence.

The morphological analyzer finally selects the most suitable words in Turkish from the candidates at the eighth stage.

3 Morphological Analyzer

At the stage of morphological analysis, words are processed separately, their basis and changing parts, such as suffix and ending are determined. The grammatical class of words combined with a generalized meaning as grammatical and lexical units, is classified by parts of words.

The morphological analysis ensures definition of normal format of a given form of word and a set of parameters typical for a given type of word.

Up to that time the known morphological analysis methods based on the semantic neuron network [35] and cell automaton, and also algorithm applied jointly with declarative and procedural methods. The morphological analysis algorithm used to solve the tasks set in this work is as follows.

The following algorithm has been used for morphological parsing of words in the Kazakh language:

1. The word is being read.

2 The word root is in the words database.

3 If the word is found then move to the 11th step, otherwise to the 4th one.

4. Every symbol in the cycle, starting from the word's ending is read and searched in the word endings database.

5 If the ending is found, then the search proceeds to the word roots database.

6. Morphological information about word endings is preserved.

7 If the remaining part of the word is in the word roots database, then

8 If it is a verb, the word from the left is then read and the verb tense is determined.

9 If the word is an adjective, its connection is verified with the list of additional words, which may pronounce word before word and lead to its intensifying meaning, if it is within the list then the adjective will be intensifying.

10 Return to the 4th step in case if the word was not found, otherwise return to the 11th step.

11. Complete.

The ontological models, built in the Protégé environment for Kazakh and Turkish morphological rules are compared for every part of speech (see Fig. 2, Fig. 3).

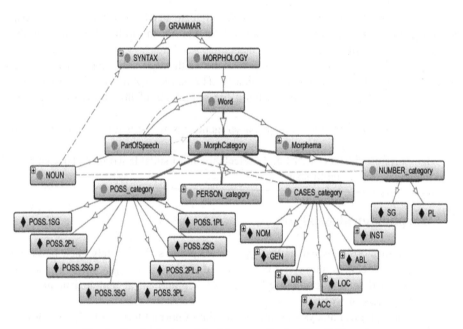

Fig. 2. Ontological model of the noun in the Kazakh language

A comparative analysis of the nouns features showed that out of 54 features 9 of them are present in the Kazakh language, and are absent in the Turkish. Consequently, 83% of nouns features are the same for both languages. Similar results brought comparisons of other parts of speech. This provides possibility to use synchronized knowledge bases, as well as to use rule-based machine translation. The unitary meta-language is used to formulate the rules.

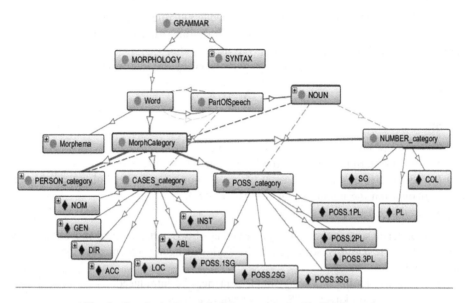

Fig. 3. Ontological model of the noun in the Turkish language

4 Syntax Analyzer

It is known that the formal Context-Free Grammar (CFG) by Chomsky is a math apparatus which allows formal description of syntax in the given language [36, 37]. Currently the CFG is the most widely used formal system for modeling composite structures in human languages.

By using this apparatus, we formalize the syntactic rules of simple narrative sentences in the Turkish language and build their component trees. But for this we need to input special linguistic marks – tags. The parsing model for the Kazakh language is presented in the paper [38]. The tags for sentence elements in the Turkish language will be indicated in the system of the unified meta-language for describing Turkic languages - UniTurk, which are presented in Table 1.

Table 1. Tags for description of the Turkish sentence structure.

Tag	English	Russian	Kazakh	Turkish
S	Simple sentence	Prostoe predlojenie	Jaı sóılem	Yalın cümle
Sub	Subject	Podlejaschee	Bastaýýsh	Özne
Obj	Object	Dopolnenie	Tolyqtaýýsh	Tümleç
Obj 1	Object	Dopolnenie		Nesine
Abr	Abbreviation	Opredelenie	Anyqtaýýsh	
Adl	Adverbial	Obstoyatel'stvo	Pysyqtaýýsh	Zarf tümleci
Pre	Predicate	Skazuemoe	Baıandaýýsh	Yüklem

The CFG consists of a set of rules or deduction rules, each of them expresses methods by which meta-symbols may be grouped and arranged together. The list of abbreviations and their meanings are given in the Table 1.

The CFG of the common G setup is determined by the following parameters [37]:

$$G = \langle N_s, T_s, R, S \rangle \tag{1}$$

where:

N_s – a set of non-terminal symbols (variable);
T_s – a set of terminal symbols (constants): herein $N_s \cap T_s = \emptyset$;
R – set of rules of the form $A \to \alpha$, where A – non-terminal symbol, α – a string of symbols from the infinite set of strings $(N_s \cup T_s)$;
S – initial non-terminal symbol.

The sentence structure may be represented as of two parts: nominal and verbal. The syntax of simple narrative sentences of the Turkish language can be described using a definite CFG.

For instance, let the following simple sentences be introduced:
1. "Samat kitap okuyor" - "Samat is reading a book";
2. "Samat kütüphanede kitap okuyo" - "Samat is reading a book in a library";
3. "Samat annesiyle dün geldi" - "Samat came yesterday with his mother";
4. "En yakın arkadaşım Samat okuyor" - "My best friend Samat is reading";
In order to describe the structures of these sentences for the CFG system parameters, we assign the following values:

$$N_s = \{S, NP, VP, Adj, Adv\}$$

$$T_s = \{S, a, d, e, g, h, \iota, i, k, l, m, n, o, p, r, t, s, \varsigma, u, \ddot{u}, y\}$$

$$R = \{S \to NP|VP,\ NP \to N|N|Adj|Adv,\ VP \to N|V|Adv|NP|VP\}$$

The constituency-based parse trees of the above-mentioned sentences of the Turkish language with using rules of this grammar may be represented as in Fig. 4–7:

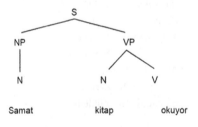

Fig. 4. Parse tree S(NP(N),VP(N,V))

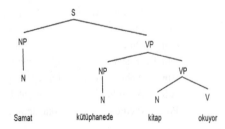

Fig. 5. Parse tree S(NP(N),NP(N,N)),VP(N,V)

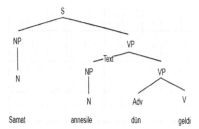

Fig. 6. Parse tree S(NP(N), VP(NP(N)

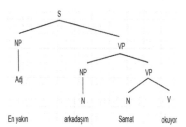

Fig. 7. Parse tree S(NP(Adj), VP(NP (N), VP(N,V)))

In order to formalize the syntactic rules for simple sentences of the Turkish language, we first built trees of components for them using Chomsky's CFG [36, 37], and then, with consideration of their semantics, we developed ontological models in the Protégé environment, which has a free, open ontology editor and framework for building knowledge bases. The Protégé platform supports two main methods for ontology modeling: through the Protégé-Frames editor and through the Protégé-OWL editor. The ontologies built by Protégé are open ones with an easily extensible architecture due to the support of extension modules and can be exported to many formats, including RDF (RDF Schema), OWL and XML Schema.

The result of the parsing is the syntactic structure of the sentence which is presented either in the form of a tree of dependencies, or shaped as a tree of constituency. The syntax defines the rules used to organize words in a sentence based on the following elements: constituency, grammatical relations, subcategories, and dependency relations [35]. The components are word groups that may behave as a whole or a phrase. The components here are described using parts of speech and phrases. The nominal phrase consists of groups of nouns, pronouns, adjectives, numerals (my house, large room). Grammatical relations are the formalization of the sentence structure as relations between subjects, objects, and other concepts. The components are characterized by their role within the sentence, and parts of the sentence are identified. Kazakh language possesses five parts of sentence: Subject, Predicate, Attribute, Adverbial, Object. For example, ol [SUBJECT] kitapty [OBJECT] aldy [Predicate] (he took the book) [35].

5   Features for Sentiment Analysis of Text in the Kazakh Language

The feature here denotes the sentiment character or attribute of a word or phrase. In case of sentiment analysis of the text, parts of speech (noun, adjective, verb, adverb, interjection), the words of negation speech are used as features. For instance in the Kazakh language the following parts of speech bring sentiment to the text: nouns (crime, war), verb (arrest, rejoice, get angry), adjective (beautiful/attractive, good/bad), adverb (really, very, very), interjection (cheers!, excellent!, wow). The words "not", "no" are the words of negation in the Kazakh language. According to the research, the noun is an aspect (object) of discussion, and adjectives mainly determine the semantic orientation (polarity) of the text. The sentiment of emotion word may depend on the context and the object domain.

6   Sentiment Analyzer

The results of morphological and syntactic analysis are used in building a model for sentiment analysis of texts in the Kazakh language. For example, sentiment may be determined with the help of these phrases:

[N] · [V]
[N] · [V] · [Negation]
[ADJ] · [N]
[ADJ] · [Negation] · [N]
 [ADJ] · [V]
[ADJ] · [V] · [Negation]
[ADV] · [ADJ]
[ADV] · [N];
here, ADJ − part of speech, the adjective, N- the noun, Negation − negation words "not/no", V − the verb, ADV − the adverb, · - concatenation .

In order to carry out the sentiment analysis, it is necessary to determine the lexical units of sentiment analysis, which may be words, phrases and sentences in human language. We may calculate the sentiment of the entire text by determining the sentiment features of lexical units.

A production model has been used for modeling the sentiment analysis of texts in the Kazakh language. These models were presented in the papers [32–34].

Dictionary and formal rules based hybrid method has been developed for sentiment analysis of the Kazakh language. The database of lexical units with sentiment ratings in the Kazakh language is used as a dictionary. The database was manually created and tagged by sentiment on a 5-point scale (from −2 to 2). Besides, some words or characters may reverse sentiment rating depending on the context of text. "+ -" symbol is used for such cases. The sentiment of lexical units is measured by the following scores: −2 - very negative; −1 - negative; 0 - neutral; 1 - positive; 2 - very positive. The semantic base comprises not only a list of words and phrases, but also their interpretation and synonyms with sentiment ratings. The database consists of more than 13000 words and phrases built with words related to various parts of speech [33].

The formal rules are used as rules determining the sentiment of texts in the Kazakh language using the production model. Each rule used to determine the sentiment of a text fragment is presented in the form "IF condition, THEN conclusion".

7   Conclusion

In late years, the influence of posts (messages) in social networks, the Internet is observed on changing of business, changing in the population mood regarding various events.

The data obtained from social networks, forums and micro-blogs is of great interest for researches and applications, due to the possibility of publishing real-time reviews and people's moods on any issues with availability of information in huge volumes and in different languages. Now we can track and analyze reviews about a product or company, identify supporters or opponents of a political party or social movement in various fields, predict financial incomes.

In this relation, the preservation of the text sentiment in machine translation from the Kazakh to Turkish language is an interesting and important task.

In this work, we review the method of text sentiment preservation in machine translation between Kazakh and Turkish.

This paper describes the features that affect sentiment determination of texts in the Kazakh language, models of morphological rules and algorithms for morphological analysis, formal models of simple sentence structures of the Kazakh-Turkish combination, models and methods of sentiment analysis of texts in the Kazakh language. The performed studies comparing the morphological and syntactic rules of the Kazakh and Turkish languages prove the similarity of their structure. In this regard we may assume that consideration of sentiment in machine translation for these language combinations will bring a good result while preserving the meaning of the text.

In the future, it is planned to involve experts to evaluate the texts translation results with emotional colors, the works to increase the amount of semantic base with rating score using the machine translator between these languages are also planned.

Acknowledgments.   The work was supported by the grant financing for scientific and technical programs and projects by the Ministry of Science and Education of the Republic of Kazakhstan (Grant No. AP05132249, 2018–2020).

References

1. Kazakh grammar: Phonetics, word formation, morphology, syntax in Kazakh, Astana, Kazakhstan (2002)
2. Lewis, G.: Turkish Grammar, Oxford University Press (2001)
3. Promt, http://www.promt.ru/company/technology/machine_translation/, Accessed 15 Dec 2019
4. Koehn, F.J., Och, M.D.: Statistical phrase-based translation. In: Proceedings of NAACL-HLT, pp. 48–54. Edmonton, Canada (2003)
5. Koehn, H., et al.: Moses: open source toolkit for statistical machine translation. In: Proceedings of the ACL Demo and Poster Sessions, pp. 177–180. Association for Computational Linguistics, Prague (2007)
6. Lagarda, A.L., Alabau, V., Silva, F. R., D'ıaz-de-Lianono, E.: Statistical post-editing of a rule-based machine translation system. In: Proceedings of NAACL HLT. Short Papers, Boulder, pp. 217–220. Association for Computational Linguistics, Colorado (2009)

7. Hamzaoğlu, I.: Machine translation from Turkish to other Turkic languages and an implementation for the Azeri languages. MSc Thesis. İstanbul: Bogazici University (1993)
8. Altıntaş, K.: Turkish to Crimean Tatar Machine Translation System. MSc Thesis, Bilkent University, Ankara (2000)
9. Tantuğ, A.C., Adalı, E., Oflazer, K.: Computer analysis of the turkmen language morphology. In: Salakoski, T., Ginter, F., Pyysalo, S., Pahikkala, T. (eds.) FinTAL 2006. LNCS (LNAI), vol. 4139, pp. 186–193. Springer, Heidelberg (2006). https://doi.org/10.1007/11816508_20
10. Orhun, M., Tantuğ, A. C., Adalı, E.: Rule based analysis of the uyghur nouns. In: Proceedings of the International Conference on Asian Language Processing (IALP), Chiang Mai, Thailand (2008)
11. Abduali, B., Akhmadieva, Z., Zholdybekova, S., Tukeyev, U., Rakhimova, D.: Study of the problem of creating structural transfer rules and lexical selection for the Kazakh-Russian machine translation system on Apertium platform. In: Proceedings of the International Conference Turkic Languages-2015, pp. 5–9. Academy of Sciences of the Republic of Tatarstan Press, Tatarstan (2015)
12. Tukeyev, U., Zhumanov, Z., Rakhimova, D., Kartbayev, A.: Combinational circuits model of kazakh and russian languages morphology. In: Abstracts of International Conference Computational and Informational Technologies in Science, Engineering and Education, pp. 241–242. Al-Farabi KazNU Press, Almaty, Kazakhstan (2015)
13. Salimzyanov, I., Washington, J., Tyers, F.: A free/open-source Kazakh-Tatar machine translation system. Machine Translation Summit XIV (2013)
14. Tyers, F.M., Washington, J.N., Salimzyanov, I., Batalov, R.: A prototype machine translation system for Tatar and Bashkir based on free/open-source components. In: First Workshop on Language Resources and Technologies for Turkic Languages, pp. 11–14 (2012)
15. Bekmanova, G., et al.: A uniform morphological analyzer for the Kazakh and Turkish languages. In: Proceedings of the Sixth International Conference on Analysis of Images, Social Networks and Texts - AIST 2017, pp. 20–30. Moscow, Russia (2017)
16. Yergesh, B., Mukanova, A., Sharipbay, A., Bekmanova, G., Razakhova, B.: Semantic hyper-graph based representation of nouns in the Kazakh language. Computacion y Sistemas 18(3), 627–635 (2014)
17. Yelibayeva, G., Mukanova, A., Sharipbay, A., Zulkhazhav, A., Yergesh, B., Bekmanova, G.: Metalanguage and knowledgebase for kazakh morphology. In: Misra, S., et al. (eds.) ICCSA 2019. LNCS, vol. 11619, pp. 693–706. Springer, Cham (2019). https://doi.org/10.1007/978-3-030-24289-3_51
18. Zetkenbay, L., Sharipbay, A., Bekmanova, G., Kamanur, U.: Ontological modeling of morphological rules for the adjectives in Kazakh and Turkish languages. J. Theor. Appl. Inf. Technol. 91(2), 257–263 (2016)
19. Liu, B.: Sentiment analysis and opinion mining. Synth. Lect. Hum. Lang. Technol. 5(1), 1–167 (2012)
20. Loukachevitch, N.V., Chetviorkin, I.I.: Evaluating Sentiment Analysis Systems in Russian. Artificial intelligence and decision-making, 1, 25–33. Russian (2014)
21. Chetviorkin, I., Loukachevitch, N.: Extraction of russian sentiment lexicon for product meta-domain. In: Proceedings of COLING 2012, pp. 593–610 (2012)
22. Akba, F., Uçan, A., Sezer, E.A., Sever, H.: Assessment of feature selection metrics for sentiment analyses: Turkish movie reviews. In: Proceedings of the 8th European Conference on Data Mining, pp. 180–184 (2014)

23. Eryiğit, G., Çetin, F., Yanık, M., Temel, T., Çiçekli, I.: TURKSENT: A sentiment annotation tool for social media. In: Proceedings of the 7th Linguistic Annotation Workshop & Interoperability with Discourse, ACL 2013, Sofia, Bulgaria (2013)
24. Sixto, J., Almeida, A., López-de-Ipiña, D.: An approach to subjectivity detection on twitter using the structured information. In: International Conference on Computational Collective Intelligence. ICCCI 2016, LNCS, vol. 9875. Springer, Cham (2016)
25. Samir, T., Ibrahim, A.-N.: Semantic sentiment analysis in arabic social media. J. King Saud Univ. Comp. Inf, Sci. **29**(2), 229–233 (2016)
26. Sakenovich, N.S., Zharmagambetov, A.S.: On one approach of solving sentiment analysis task for kazakh and russian languages using deep learning. In: International Conference on Computational Collective Intelligence. ICCCI 2016. LNCS, vol. 9876. Springer, Cham (2016)
27. Abdullin, Y.B., Ivanov, V.V.: Deep learning model for bilingual sentiment classification of short texts. Sci. Tech. J. Inf. Technol. Mech. Optics **17**(1), 129–136 (2017)
28. Lohar, P., Afli, H., Way, A.: Maintaining sentiment polarity in translation of user-generated content. Prague Bull. Math.Linguist. **108**, 73–84 (2017)
29. Gervasi, O., Franzoni, V., Riganelli, M., Tasso, S.: Automating facial emotion recognition. Web. Intelligence. **17**, 17–27 (2019). https://doi.org/10.3233/WEB-190397
30. Majumder, N., et al.: DialogueRNN: an attentive rnn for emotion detection in conversations. In: Proceeding of the AAAI Conference on Artificial Intelligence, 33, pp. 6818–6825. Honolulu (2019)
31. Franzoni, V., Milani, A., Nardi, D., Vallverdu, J.: Emotional machines: The next revolution. Web Intell. **17**, 1–7 (2019). https://doi.org/10.3233/WEB-190395
32. Yergesh, B., Bekmanova, G., Sharipbay, A.: Sentiment analysis of Kazakh text and their polarity. Web Intell. **17**(1), 9–15 (2019)
33. Yergesh, B., Bekmanova, G., Sharipbay, A., Yergesh, M.: Ontology-Based Sentiment Analysis of Kazakh Sentences. In: Gervasi, O., et al. (eds.) ICCSA 2017. LNCS, vol. 10406, pp. 669–677. Springer, Cham (2017). https://doi.org/10.1007/978-3-319-62398-6_47
34. Yergesh, B., Bekmanova, G., Sharipbay, A.: Sentiment analysis of Kazakh phrases based on morphological rules. J. Theor. Appl. Sci. Tech. **2**(38), 39–42 (2016)
35. Sharipbayev, A., Bekmanova, G., Buribayeva, A., Yergesh, B., et al.: Semantic neural network model of morphological rules of the agglutinative languages. Procceding of the SCIS/ISIS 2012, pp. 1094–1099. Kobe, Japan (2012)
36. Jurafsky, D., Martin, J.H.: Speech and Language Processing. An Introduction to Natural Language Processing, Computational Linguistics, and Speech Recognition (2nd ed.). Prentice Hall PTR, Upper Saddle River, NJ, USA (2009)
37. Chomsky, N.: Syntactic Structures. The Hague: Mouton, 1957. (Reissue: Chomsky N. Syntactic Structures. – De Gruyter Mouton) (2002)
38. Sharipbay, A., Razakhova, B., Mukanova, A., Yergesh, B, Yelibayeva, G.: Syntax parsing model of Kazakh simple sentences. In: proceedings of the Second International Conference on Data Science, E-Learning and Information Systems DATA 2019, Article 54, p. 5. Dubai (2019)

Deep Convolutional and Recurrent Neural Networks for Emotion Recognition from Human Behaviors

James J. Deng[1][(✉)] and Clement H. C. Leung[2]

[1] MindSense Technologies, Hong Kong, People's Republic of China
james@mindsense.ai
[2] The Chinese University of Hong Kong, Shenzhen, People's Republic of China
clementleung@cuhk.edu.cn

Abstract. Human behaviors and the emotional states that they convey have been studied by psychologist and sociologists. The tracking of behaviors and emotions is becoming more pervasive with the advent of the Internet of Things (IoT), where small and always connected sensors can continuously capture information about human gestures, movements and postures. The captured information about readable behaviors conveys significant information that can be represented as time series. Few studies in emotion recognition and affective computing have explored the connection between the time series sensors data and the emotional behavior they conveys. In this paper, an innovative approach is proposed to study the emotions and behaviors connected to the time series data. A convolutional network augmented with attention-based bidirectional LSTM is introduced to represent the correlations between behaviors and emotions. The advantage of this model is that it can well recognized emotions by exploiting the data captured by sensors. The experimental results show that the proposed deep learning method outperforms separate schemes and achieves a high degree of accuracy for modelling human behaviors and emotions.

Keywords: Emotion recognition · Convolutional neutral network · Bi-directional LSTM · Attention model · Human behaviors

1 Introduction

Emotion and cognition are the advanced capabilities of artificial intelligence. The theories to model human emotion and cognition are at the base of affective computing [20] and emotion recognition. Many studies [11,13,17] on these areas, conducted by different researchers, brought to different approaches and models.

In psychology and sociology different studies [6,14] elicited the connection between human behaviors like gestures, movement and posture and the emotion they conveyed, for example the frequency of movements, the strength of

© Springer Nature Switzerland AG 2020
O. Gervasi et al. (Eds.): ICCSA 2020, LNCS 12250, pp. 550–561, 2020.
https://doi.org/10.1007/978-3-030-58802-1_39

gestures. The challenge is how to represent the human behaviors and the connected emotions in an accurate and effective way. On the other hand, capturing the human behaviors has become more pervasive and efficient with the advent and development of the Internet of things (IoTs). In fact, smaller and smarter connected mobile devices and sensors, paired with cloud computing for big data storage and analysis, rendered feasible the near real-time behaviors detection and emotions recognition.

The analysis and modeling of human behaviors and emotions using deep learning techniques is motivated by the fact that these human activities are characterized by long and short term sequence features. Recurrent neural network (RNN) and Long Short Term Memory (LSTM) have been widely used in sequence modeling. Furthermore, bidirectional LSTM can use both past and future information with two separate hidden layers, which can represent different states and grades of human behaviors and emotions. An attention-based mechanism [1,3] is then used to focus on the most important information using a separate hidden layer. The deep architecture models can significantly outperform those with shallow architecture, and greatly improves training speed and effectiveness. The convolutioanl neural networks can well extract viiusal information. Therefore, a convolutional neural network augmented with Attention-based deep bi-directional Long Short Term Memory (CNN-ADBLSTM) network architecture is proposed to model human behaviors and emotions, which can well perform prediction tasks such as emotion recognition.

2   Literature Review

Different models have been proposed for emotion representations by different researchers. Usually based on two emotion theories: discrete emotion theory and dimensional emotion theory. Discrete emotion theory employs a finite number of emotional descriptors or adjectives [18] to express basic human emotions (e.g., joy, sadness, anger, contempt, happiness). Ortony et al. [19] proposed an emotion cognition model commonly known as OCC model to hierarchically describe 22 emotion descriptors. More coarser-grained partition (e.g. happy, neutral, and sad) as well as abstraction and similarity of emotions [2,12] have been also been used in various works. The discrete emotion theory main advantage is its ease to explain and to use in practical applications. Dimensional emotion theory states that emotion should be depicted in a psychological dimensional space, which can overcome the disadvantages of discrete theory such as the difficulty to represent continuous changes and to distinguish between similar emotion. Dimensional emotion models such as arousal-valence [22], resonance-arousal-valence [9], and arousal-valence-dominance are widely used in different application domains. Dimensional emotion theory is more likely to be used in computational emotion systems. We shall adopt the discrete emotion theory in this study.

Emotion recognition tasks often adopt human facial expressions, while some studies include body postures [4] and gestures [16,21]. Other studies focus on movements where angry movements tend to be large, fast and relatively jerky, while fearful and sad movements are less energetic, smaller, and slower. Some studies use multiple resources, such as images or sensors, for human behavior recognition [5]. We shall focus on simple human behaviors data captured by accelerometer. The emotions and behaviors analysis and modeling can use traditional machine learning methods for time series analysis [8]. However, deep learning techniques have been successfully applied to the image, video, and audio, with many works carrying out emotion recognition, while fewer studies use sensors data [7,24]. We make some explorations on this area by using sequence models in deep neural network. In our previous work [10], an attention-based bidirectional LSTM model have been applied to recognize emotion from human behaviors. In this paper, we explore the convolutional network augmented attention-based LSTM to evaluate the performance.

3   Human Behavior Representation

Human beings are complex organisms that consist of various subsystems such as neural system, circulatory system, muscular and skeletal systems. All These subsystems work together to activate different physical and physiological changes. Human behaviors are the response of individuals internal and external stimuli, and usually is very strongly influenced by emotions. During the past decades, emotions have been well studied using facial expressions or voice, while there is less research on our bodies and behaviors that also convey rich emotional information or messages, such as a greater amount of muscle tension implying stress, a frequently walk up and down indicating anxiety, and a thumb upward representing an approval and admiring. Considering convolutional and recurrent network have already achieved success in image and time series signals, here we attempt to build time series expressions of behaviors such as gesture, posture and movement, and construct spatial-temporal network to model behaviors and emotions associated with human.

As IoTs and various sensors have been widely used in mobile and wearable devices, human behaviors like gesture, posture or movement can be represented by a set of time series signals obtained from specific sensors. Considering that there are many different sensors like Electrocardiography (ECG), Electromyography (EMG), gyroscope and accelerometers for specific purpose such as health, sports, gesture control and motion in data collection, to simplify, in this paper we only use the accelerometers for human behavior measurement. An accelerometer is a sensor that can measure proper acceleration. Here, we directly use three-dimensional accelerometer data to represent time series human behaviors. For notation, given a recognized human behavior B, for example hitting or shaking, corresponding to a sequence of three-dimensional accelerometer signals, behavior B can be represented by $B = \{x_1, x_2, \cdots, x_N\}$ where x_i denotes for the three-dimensional accelerometer data at timestamp i. Our goal is to predict emotion E conveyed by given behavior B. The following sections will describe the spatial-temporal neural network for modeling behavior and emotion.

4   Modeling Human Behaviors and Emotions

Human behaviors have temporal structure and associated with specific emotions, time sequence provides a natural and intuitive representation. The ultimate goal of this paper is to build a model that can recognize emotion conveyed by human behaviors that may be measured by of multiple temporal physical and physiological signals. As mentioned previously, to simplify, here we only use time series movement to represent human behaviors.

Long Short Term Memory (LSTM) are effective and have shown satisfied results in many sequential information processing tasks (e.g., natural language processing, speech recognition, and human activity recognition). Furthermore, Our previous work has demonstrated that the bidirectional LSTM assisted by attention mechanism achieved the state-of-the-art performance. However, human behaviors like posture or gesture also contains rich spatial information for decoding associated emotion. In order to take account both temporal and spatial information, we shall use the attention-based bidirectional LSTM and convolutional neural network to model human behaviors and emotions in this paper.

4.1   Deep Attention-Based Bidirectional LSTM

There are several methods to construct deep bidirectional LSTM structures. One method is to simply stack bidirectional LSTM in each layer, while another efficient method is that the bidirectional LSTM is located in the bottom layer and the other layers are unidirectional as shown in Fig. 1. The former method works only to a certain number of layers, beyond which the network becomes too slow and difficult to train, likely due to the gradient exploding and vanishing problems, while the latter can resolve these problems. Consequently, in this paper, we apply the latter method to construct a deep structure to modeling human behaviors and emotions in temporal as shown in Fig. 1. The attention model based on the top layer is defined as follows,

$$\alpha_t(s) = \frac{\exp(score(h_t, \bar{h}_{\hat{s}}))}{\sum_{s'} \exp(score(h_t, \bar{h}_{\hat{s}}))} \tag{1}$$

where $socre()$ is an activation function, $f()$ is tahn or relu function, with weight and bias W and b for the network.

$$score(h_t, \bar{h}) = f(h_t^T W \hat{h}_s + b) \tag{2}$$

4.2   Temporal Convolutional Network

The temporal convolutional network plays an important role in processing time series signals. The time series accelerometer signals is feeded to a convolutional network. The 3D filters are used in each convolutional layer, followed by batch normalization and activation steps, where activation function is the Rectified Linear Unit (ReLU). Global average pooling is applied to decrease the dimensionality following the final convolution block. An illustration of the structure of convolutional network is given in Fig. 2.

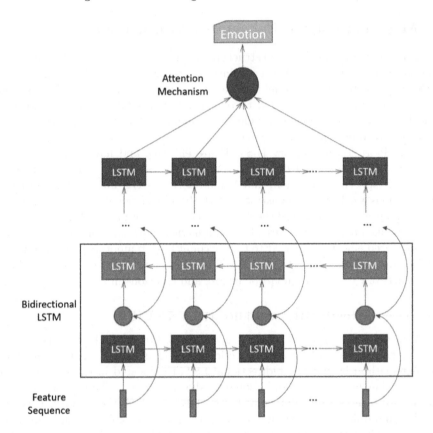

Fig. 1. Deep Attention-based bidirectional LSTM network. Blue rectangles represent forward LSTM units, and green rectangles represent backward LSTM units. Attention mechanism is in place.

4.3   Convolutional and Attention-Based Bidirectional LSTM Network

In order to take advantages of both convolutional and recurrent neural networks, we combine both convolutional and attention-based bidirectional LSTM to construct a hybrid architecture. The convolutional block and LSTM block perceive the same time series input in two different paths. The convolutional block takes 3D accelerometer signals with multiple time steps. Meanwhile, the LSTM block receives 3D accelerometer signals. Through bidirectional and residual connections, the upper LSTM outputs are finally input to attention mechanism.

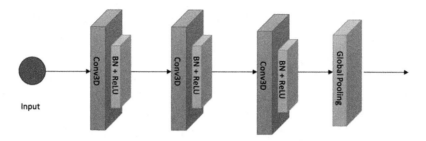

Fig. 2. Convolutional Neural Network. BN denotes for batch normalization.

The residual connections between adjacent layers are given in Eq. 3, and attention layer is calculated following previous Eq. 1.

$$h_t^i = \Lambda(x_t^i, h_{t-1}^i; W^i)$$
$$x_t^{i+1} = h_t^i + x_t^i \tag{3}$$
$$h_t^{i+1} = \Lambda_{i+1}(x_t^{i+1}, h_{t-1}^{i+1}; W^{i+1})$$

The output of global pooling layer and attention layer is concatenated and passed onto a softmax function for emotion recognition. Figure 3 shows the whole network architecture of Convolutional and Attention-based Bidirectional LSTM.

5 Experiments

5.1 Experimental Setup

Ten people (7 males and 3 females) have participated in the experiments. We used wearable brands to collect 3-dimensional accelerometer data. The sampling rate of the accelerometer of given brand is set to 200 HZ. We set five predefined behaviors or movements corresponding to emotions as shown in Table 1. Each participant carried out given behaviors of movement and emotions. Each specific behavior and corresponding emotion is performed by multiple participants. The total amount of dataset we collected is more than 100,000 s. After collecting the original dataset, we normalized each dimensional with zero-mean and unit-variance. Furthermore, we can set more features such as accelerometer shape or contrasts as model input in experiments. Shape features contain curve centroid, flux, flatness and roll-off, and contrast features contain kurtosis, skewness, zero-crossing rate.

5.2 Training and Evaluation Criteria

After preprocessing the dataset, training deep ALSTMmodel with suitable parameters is vitally important for model performance. We divided the dataset into three parts, where 60% of it were used for training, 20% of it were used for

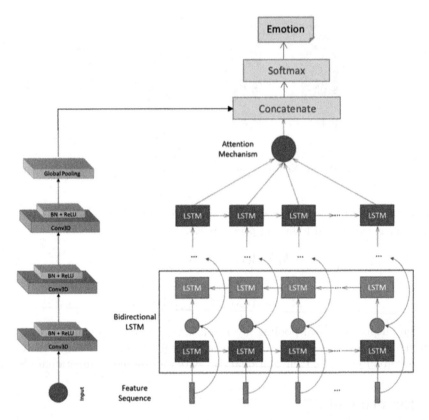

Fig. 3. Hybrid network architecture convolutional neural network augmented with attention-based dep bidirectional LSTM. Blue rectangles represent forward LSTM units, and green rectangles represent backward LSTM units. Attention mechanism is in place. BN denotes for batch normalization. The input and feature space are accelerometer signals.

validation, and the remaining 20% were used for testing. We set the mini-batches with size 128 for training and use Adam optimizer. We attempted different layers with different numbers of hidden states. The length of the training sequence is initially set at 24, which can be larger when more layered are set. As the input sequence dimension is not large, the maximum depth of layers is set as 4 to avoid model overfitting. After the deep convolutional augmented ABLSTM model has been trained, we can apply it to predict the emotion of testing accelerometer data. The emotion recognition is evaluated based on accuracy. The comparison of this hybrid network with separate network is carried out to evaluate its performance.

Table 1. Behavior types and corresponding emotions in data collection

Behaviors ID	Behaviors	Emotions
1	Walk fast and relatively jerky	Angry
2	Walk slowly and smaller	Sad
3	Short movement	Anxiety
4	Up and down	Exciting
5	Arms stretched out to the front	Joy

5.3   Experimental Results

We have trained different deep models using 3D accelerometer data, shape and contrast features. Table 2 shows the comparison of several different layers of Deep LSTM (DLSTM) models and the corresponding bidirectional model (DBLSTM) with and without attention mechanism. Attention-based LSTM (ALSTM) and its bidirectional variant (ABLSTM) models perform better than those without attention mechanism. We can see that the accuracy of ABLSTM (accuracy = 96.1%) is higher than that of DBLSTM (accuracy = 95.2%). This indicates that time series human's behavior data can be well decoded for emotion recognition, that's because different segments of human's time series data can expressing different weights for emotion decoding. Furthermore, as proved in our previous work, deeper models like ADBLSTM-3L, ADBLSTM-4L also exhibit the better performance than ALSTM and ABLSTM. However, it does not mean that the deeper the better for all in practice. Some works [23] have shown that the maximum number of layers is 8 in neural machine translation. Here, we find that when the layers are set to 4, the best performance is achieved, and the average accuracy in validation and testing can be obtained at 97.3%. As the attention is added to the top layer, there are more computation required on model training. However, we find that the loss of mini-batch of training dataset decrease faster yet with higher accuracy than those without attention operation at the same training iterations.

We also evaluated accuracy for five emotion categories using the ADBLSTM-4L, and the results are given in Fig. 4. We can see that the emotion "exciting" shows the highest accuracy, that is because the people's behaviors go up and down repeatedly, which is apparently different from other walking behaviors. Emotion "anxiety" has the lowest accuracy, which means that short movements do not always indicate anxious feelings. In addition, we also divide these five emotions into two large categories of positive and negative. Figure 5 shows the emotion recognition performance in this two coarse categories using the same model. Positive emotions (accuracy = 96.8%) outperform negative emotions (accuracy = 92.6%), suggesting that the two positive emotions such as joy and excitement are easier to recognize from behaviors, while the three negative emotions such as sad, anxiety, and angry are more difficult to recognize. The above results should also depend on the cultural milieu of the person and groups.

Table 2. Comparison of different deep recurrent neural network models

Models	Validation	Testing
LSTM	94.6%	94.9%
BLSTM	95.2%	95.7%
DBLSTM-3L	95.4%	97.0%
DBLSTM-4L	96.7%	97.1%
ALSTM	95.7%	95.2%
ABLSTM	96.1%	96.7%
ADBLSTM-3L	96.8%	97.6%
ADBLSTM-4L	97.2%	97.4%

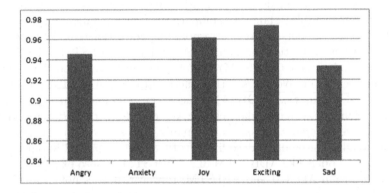

Fig. 4. Comparison of five emotion categories recognition performance

To evaluate the hybrid network performance, we compare it with separate network. Three stacked temporal convolutional blocks was used in the experiment. The convolution kernel was initialized following the initialization proposed by [15]. The learning rate was reduced by a specific factor of every 100 epochs of no improvement in the validation score, until the final learning rate was reached. The comparison results are given in Table 3. We can see that the convolutional network contributes the time series data, and convolutional model augmented with ADBLSTM outperforms the existing state-of-the-art models for emotion recognition. The model CNN-ADBLSTM-4L achived the highest accuracy in validation and testing dataset.

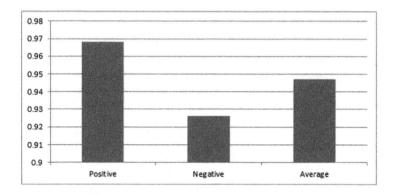

Fig. 5. Two coarse emotion categories recognition performance

Table 3. Comparison of convolutional augmented with attention-based bidirectional LSTM with separate network

Models	Validation	Testing
CNN	95.9%	94.7%
ABLSTM	96.1%	96.7%
CNN-ABLSTM	96.1%	96.4%
ADBLSTM-3L	96.8%	97.6%
CNN-ADBLSTM-3L	97.3%	97.4%
ADBLSTM-4L	97.2%	97.4%
CNN-ADBLSTM-4L	97.3%	97.6%

6   Conclusion

In this paper we introduced an innovative deep learning model for modeling human behaviors and emotions. Using data from IoT devices and recent advances in technology, human posture, gesture, and movement behaviors can be captured by sensors, and be analyzed as well as modeled by deep neural networks. Considering the interaction and correlation of human behaviors and emotions, we introduced a methodology that makes use of the deep convolutional neural network and the attention-based bidirectional LSTM networks to build hybrid network architecture. The bidirectional LSTM is deployed in the bottom layer and an attention-based mechanism is added to focus on important information. This sophisticated design is able to facilitate deep model training. The convoluational blocks can make usage of visual information. Both convoluational and recurrent network outputs are concatenate and used for emotion recognition from time series human behaviors. The experimental results show that the proposed method is able to obtain good emotion recognition performance. Furthermore, this method should scale well for modeling various behaviors and emotions through multiple sensors.

References

1. Bahdanau, D., Cho, K., Bengio, Y.: Neural machine translation by jointly learning to align and translate. CoRR, abs/1409.0473 (2014)
2. Biondi, G., Franzoni, V., Li, Y., Milani, A.: Web-based similarity for emotion recognition in web objects. In: Proceedings of the 9th International Conference on Utility and Cloud Computing, UCC 2016, New York, NY, USA, pp. 327–332. ACM (2016)
3. Cho, K., Courville, A.C., Bengio, Y.: Describing multimedia content using attention-based encoder-decoder networks. IEEE Trans. Multimedia **17**(11), 1875–1886 (2015)
4. Coulson, M.: Attributing emotion to static body postures: recognition accuracy, confusions, and viewpoint dependence. J. Nonverbal Behav. **28**(2), 117–139 (2004). https://doi.org/10.1023/B:JONB.0000023655.25550.be
5. Crane, E., Gross, M.: Motion capture and emotion: affect detection in whole body movement. In: Paiva, A.C.R., Prada, R., Picard, R.W. (eds.) ACII 2007. LNCS, vol. 4738, pp. 95–101. Springer, Heidelberg (2007). https://doi.org/10.1007/978-3-540-74889-2_9
6. De Gelder, B.: Why bodies? Twelve reasons for including bodily expressions in affective neuroscience. Philos. Trans. Roy. Soc. B Biol. Sci. **364**(1535), 3475–3484 (2009)
7. Deng, J., Leung, C., Li, Y.: Beyond big data of human behaviors: Modeling human behaviors and deep emotions. In: 2018 IEEE Conference on Multimedia Information Processing and Retrieval (MIPR), pp. 282–286, April 2018
8. Deng, J.J., Leung, C.H.: Dynamic time warping for music retrieval using time series modeling of musical emotions. IEEE Trans. Affect. Comput. **6**(2), 137–151 (2015)
9. Deng, J.J., Leung, C.H., Milani, A., Chen, L.: Emotional states associated with music: classification, prediction of changes, and consideration in recommendation. ACM Trans. Interact. Intell. Syst. (TiiS) **5**(1), 4 (2015)
10. Deng, J.J., Leung, C.H.C., Mengoni, P., Li, Y.: Emotion recognition from human behaviors using attention model. In: 2018 IEEE First International Conference on Artificial Intelligence and Knowledge Engineering (AIKE), pp. 249–253. IEEE (2018)
11. Dolan, R.J.: Emotion, cognition, and behavior. Science **298**(5596), 1191–1194 (2002)
12. Franzoni, V., Li, Y., Mengoni, P.: A path-based model for emotion abstraction on facebook using sentiment analysis and taxonomy knowledge. In: Proceedings of the International Conference on Web Intelligence - WI 2017, pp. 947–952 (2017)
13. Gratch, J., Marsella, S.: A domain-independent framework for modeling emotion. Cogn. Syst. Res. **5**(4), 269–306 (2004)
14. Harrigan, J.A.: Proxemics, kinesics, and gaze. In: Harrigan, J., Rosenthal, R., Scherer, K.R., Scherer, K. (eds.) The New Handbook of Methods in Nonverbal Behavior Research, pp. 137–198. Oxford University Press, Oxford (2005)
15. He, K., Zhang, X., Ren, S., Sun, J.: Delving deep into rectifiers: surpassing human-level performance on imagenet classification. In: Proceedings of the IEEE International Conference on Computer Vision, pp. 1026–1034 (2015)
16. Hicheur, H., Kadone, H., Grezes, J., Berthoz, A.: The combined role of motion-related cues and upper body posture for the expression of emotions during human walking. In: Mombau, K., Berns, K. (eds). Modeling, Simulation and Optimization of Bipedal Walking. Cognitive Systems Monographs, vol 18. Springer, Heidelberg (2013). https://doi.org/10.1007/978-3-642-36368-9_6

17. Hudlicka, E.: Beyond cognition: Modeling emotion in cognitive architectures. In: ICCM, pp. 118–123 (2004)
18. zard, C.E., Malatesta, C.Z.: Perspectives on emotional development i: differential emotions theory of early emotional development. In: The first draft of this paper was based on an invited address to the Eastern Psychological Association, 1 April 1983. Wiley, Hoboken (1987)
19. Ortony, A., Clore, G.L., Collins, A.: The Cognitive Structure of Emotions. Cambridge University Press, Cambridge (1990)
20. Picard, R.W., et al.: Affective Computing. MIT Press, Cambridge (1995)
21. Roether, C.L., Omlor, L., Christensen, A., Giese, M.A.: Critical features for the perception of emotion from gait. J. Vis. 9(6), 15–15 (2009)
22. Thayer, R.E.: The Biopsychology of Mood and Arousal. Oxford University Press, Oxford (1990)
23. Wu, Y., et al.: Google's neural machine translation system: bridging the gap between human and machine translation. arXiv preprint arXiv:1609.08144 (2016)
24. Zhang, Z., Song, Y., Cui, L., Liu, X., Zhu, T.: Emotion recognition based on customized smart bracelet with built-in accelerometer. PeerJ 4, e2258 (2016)

Exploring Negative Emotions to Preserve Social Distance in a Pandemic Emergency

Valentina Franzoni[1(✉)], Giulio Biondi[2], and Alfredo Milani[1(✉)]

[1] Department of Mathematics and Computer Science,
University of Perugia, Perugia, Italy
valentina.franzoni@dmi.unipg.it, milani@unipg.it
[2] Department of Mathematics and Computer Science,
University of Florence, Florence, Italy
giulio.biondi@unifi.it

Abstract. In this work, we present a multi-agent robotic system which explores the use of unpleasant emotions triggered by visual, sound and behavioural affordances of autonomous agents to interact with humans for preserving social distance in public spaces in a context of a pandemic emergency. The idea was born in the context of the Covid-19 pandemic, where discomfort and fear have been widely used by governments to preserve social distancing. This work does not implicitly endorse the use of fear to keep order but explores controlled and moderate automated exploitations. On the contrary, it deeply analyses the pros and cons of the ethical use of robots with emotion recognition and triggering capabilities. The system employs a swarm of all-terrain hexapods patrolling a public open space and generally having a discrete and seamless presence. The goal is to preserve the social distance among the public with effective but minimal intervention, limited to anomaly detection. The single agents implement critical tasks: context detection strategies, triggering negative emotions at different degrees of arousal using affordances ranging from appearance and simple proximity or movements to disturbing sounds or explicit voice messages. The whole system exhibits an emerging swarm behaviour where the agents cooperate and coordinate in a distributed way, adapting and reacting to the context. An innovative contribution of this work, more than the application, is the use of unpleasant emotions affordances in an ethical way, to attract user attention and induce the desired behaviour in the emergency. This work also introduces a method for assessment of the emotional level of individuals and groups of people in the context of swarm agents. The system extends the experience of the *gAltano hexapod project*, an autonomous agent with image detection and planned object relocation capabilities.

Keywords: Affective computing · Emotion affordance · Autonomous agents · Swarm behaviour · Social distance · COVID

© Springer Nature Switzerland AG 2020
O. Gervasi et al. (Eds.): ICCSA 2020, LNCS 12250, pp. 562–573, 2020.
https://doi.org/10.1007/978-3-030-58802-1_40

1   Introduction

1.1   Background and Ethical Goals

During a pandemic emergency, an exceptional and sometimes surreal situation is present, where the government has to set up and exploit an effective system for social distancing for everyday activities, in a critical equilibrium between lockdown and economical surviving. The perfect environment is not applicable, but strict rules have to be given, especially in a previous phase, where the viral contagion behaviour and epidemiological characteristics of a new disease are still not explicit. Sometimes, preventing a few contacts will lead to avoiding several deaths and a substantial economic loss [1, 2].

In such a situation, during the 2020 Covid-19 spread, for instance, several countries decided to lockdown any non-essential activity [3], and to apply strict rules of social distancing for the remaining [4]. To convince people complying to such rules, sometimes unclear, and often generalised, governments decided to use mass media [5], military forces or even robots heavily to induce in citizens the fear to be caught in illicit activity, thus being fined or threatened to stand trials.

For instance, in Italy several extreme cases can be listed about very expensive or stunning approaches used to frighten people even in less dangerous situations, e.g., flying a police helicopter at low altitude on the shore where a couple had secluded themselves, to splash and frighten them to make them go home [6]; deploying an entire Carabinieri squadron to block a runner on the beach [7]; pushing teenagers or elderly caregivers on the ground, handcuffing them and then taking them to the station to be identified, only for hesitating to provide the required documents and written self-declaration for the activity [8, 9].

Such heavy approach instilled a general fear and tendency to overestimate the rules, in order to avoid as much as possible any case of transgression. As a side effect, it also induced a fear syndrome, often leading to panic, that resulted in trauma in many people [10], with a significant increase in requests for psychotherapeutic assistance during phase two when the lockdown was reduced.

The Italian company Elettronica Cortesi proposed to clients an Artificial Intelligence (AI) tablet with a thermal scanner and facial monitoring to check if the person is correctly wearing a protective mask [11]. Also, the resort city of Cannes on the Côte d'Azur has trialled an AI software for digital surveillance, installed at outdoor markets and on buses, to check people wearing masks, keeping privacy protection [12].

A four-legged robot dog named Spot was set to help social distancing efforts in the Singapore national park of Bishan-Ang Mo Kio, patrolling the area running and looking for people walking together. The yellow and black canine robot with four articulated legs and an injection-moulded hard plastic shell, part of a trial by Boston Dynamics, spawned awe and fear at the same time [13]. Spot runs in the park and gives vocal warnings to visitors to observe the distance measurements, equipped with cameras to assess the correct distance between people and measure their number in the area.

In a pandemic emergency, AI and robots can have a crucial role for some extents, reducing the exposure of law enforcement and healthcare workers to the possible contagion due to physical contacts, given some ethical constraints, e.g., to avoid enabling them to recognise individual citizens or retain personal data. In China, for instance, the decision of the President to use drones to control and identify people breaking the Covid-19 social rules to arrest them raises some ethical concerns for personal privacy and impacts the people's negative perception of the relationship between the State and citizens.

Although robots can be expensive to design, develop and test, such an effort can be done once for many applications, and be more than convenient comparing to the personal risk or the economic loss due to law transgression and thus pandemic spread [14]. Since the fear of the actor triggering the negative emotion can be permanent and tend toward generalised anxiety, an equally relevant point is that it is healthier if the subjects of such action are not human: a robot with an ad-hoc appearance, used only in the specific context, could replace the fear for people with an eerie sensation limited to a specific device, which will not be present in everyday life, thus avoiding a persistent trauma.

1.2   Previous Works

Affective computing is a research area of growing interest, in particular for emotion recognition and triggering. The ability to assess the emotional content of a situation can help to improve the effectiveness of applications in a vast amount of scenarios, e.g., the analysis of trends and information diffusion in social networks [15], recommender systems [16], image recognition [17], semantic context generation [18], social robots [19], and more generally in human-machine interfaces. Sentiment analysis is a widely investigated topic [20]: the aim is to produce semantic annotations focusing on a trivial classification of the stance (i.e. the sentiment) towards an object, only according to its positive, negative or neutral polarity. Emotion recognition works at a deeper level because it is aimed at quantifying the emotional load, concerning various emotions conveyed, e.g., by multimedia objects [21].

Part of the definition of a framework performing semantic analysis is the choice of a proper knowledge source. Web-based similarity measures [22], for instance, evaluate the similarity of terms from the number of occurrences and co-occurrences of such terms in a document corpus, e.g. the documents indexed by a search engine. Such corpora are updated continuously, reflecting the natural evolution of knowledge, and thus constitute an excellent base for real-time applications.

Fundamental studies carried out by psychologists led to the development of various models of emotions, e.g. Ekman, Plutchik, and Lovheim [23]. Such models encompass and reduce the full range of complex human emotions to sets of basic emotions which prove general for all human beings, despite their cultural origin, age or gender. Emotion models induce a numerical representation, often binary, for an object (e.g., user face [24], multimedia document), consisting for instance in a vector of emotions [25] which quantifies, for each emotion of the model, the emotional load associated to the object.

The context of autonomous agents, which could be able to detect and trigger emotions based on a complex multi-source affordance model [26], requires to focus on the individual agent first, and then on the interactive cooperation and reaction of the agents as a swarm, which can be seen as a collective individual or team. The individual autonomous agent in this context is a hexapod robot. This type of robot is particularly suitable for open space outdoors patrolling, because of its capability to move overcoming obstacles and adapting to various terrain types and slopes, thanks to the six-legs design with 18 degrees of freedom. Among others, hexapods usually show a good appearance compared to other insect-looking or animal-appearance robots and their natural and smooth movements allow them to be accepted in human environments where sensible people usually do not accept robots, feeling uncomfortable in their presence. The MSR-H01 model used in the gAItano Hexapod Project [27] on which our model is based, is usually accepted as "cute" or "cool", compared to other "scary" robots. In this project, we aim to add "scary" capabilities, evidenced in an adaptive level, only in case of law transgression, to maintain order and induce eventual trespassers or offenders to restore a legit behaviour in an emergency related to pandemics or other critical situations where social distancing may be a matter of life or death.

2   From GAItano, the Intelligent Hexapod Robot, to the Swarm

The swarm design starts from the *gAItano Hexapod Project* [27], based on the *MSR-H01* robot, created by Mycromagic Systems, measuring a few tens of centimetres (i.e., ~ 1 foot). Our vision cannot base on the original gAItano, because tests show that a small hexapod is considered cute and does not induce the required awe and respect. Thus, considering the average distance considered safe worldwide, we set the hexapods size to a diameter of 1.5 m (i.e., ~ 5 feet). This size is useful as a baseline reference for social distancing.

The hexapod as a type of robot is particularly suitable to move in several directions on any terrain, including stairways and steep or bumpy trails. The material should be light for energy saving: a 3D-printer could be the best tool for a cheap swarm creation, also considering that several free 3-D models for printing hexapods are available on the Web, and the hexapod architecture is suitable to carry much more weight than the robot weight, including micro-controller, servo motors, batteries, sensors.

The original gAItano that we can take as a model is a six-legged hexapod robot, which architecture and software allow smooth movements with 18 grades of freedom for all the legs, and whose goal is to relocate objects in the environment, based on some positioning constraints to match. The robot could patrol an area with a crab walk, look at the environment, identify unordered objects, and push them in the right position. Thus, the underlying software that we previously developed already allows the robot to move in an environment of unknown size, and perform autonomous actions based on AI. If anything changes in the environment during the walk, gAItano can adapt his decisions in real-time. The visual recognition includes coloured blobs recognition. The formal definition of the goal of gAItano is the following: given a real-world (in a desirably limited, but potentially infinite area) where there are objects constituting landmarks, patrol one side of the area with respect to the landmark, keeping it free from objects, thus pushing eventual objects in another side of the area.

gAItano can be defined as a rational computerised agent:

- *autonomous*, or semi-autonomous when remotely controlled through Android or an electromyographic armband;
- *reactive*, since he chooses actions basing on perception;
- *based on a model*, because it keeps the state of visual elements of the environment;

The environment for the hexapod is:

- *partially observable*, with the unique sensor -a camera- providing a partial view, even when the swarm provides additional information;
- *stochastic*, because in the real physical environment unexpected events can happen, e.g., gAItano may accidentally hit an obstacle while pushing an object, a human agent may move unpredictably during the patrol execution;
- *semi-episodic*, since the agent acts mainly on perception and only in few cases on previous ones, except for a few sequential actions such as coming back to the patrol state or following an intervention plan;
- *static*, or *semi-dynamic* in case of human intervention;
- *continuous* both on perceptions and actions;
- *multi-agent*, because of the swarm and of human intervention that can have *collaborative* nature (e.g. when the human emergency team arrives) or *competitive* (e.g. when the human break rules or try to oppose to the robot).

Our swarm of hexapod agents starts from gAItano to design the new hexapods, which have a standard mechanical structure allowing all-terrain movements, including walking on paved roads, lawn or mud. A 360° camera allows to monitor the surrounding area; connectivity can be used to alert other hexapods or law enforcement patrols if a positioning system is available. The hexapod is also provided with lights and sound emitting devices, and it can express some gestures and behaviours, e.g.:

- body shaking/kneeling;
- rising or moving/waving single legs, independently from walking;
- lights turning on/off;
- emitting sounds/voice.

Different gestures can express different intensities using, e.g., the pace and amplitude of shaking/waving, the frequency and intensity of flashing lights and sounds.

3   Negative Emotions Affordances

The most influential models of emotions developed in psychology [28, 31] are the Ekman, Lovheim, and Plutchick models, characterised by the basic idea that any emotion perceived by a human can be expressed by a combination of basic emotions, eventually appearing in different arousal/intensity.

$E_{Ekman.}$ = *[anger, disgust, fear, joy, sadness, surprise]*

$E_{Plutchik}$ = *[anger, anticipation, disgust, fear, joy, sadness, surprise, trust]*

$E_{Lovheim}$ = *[anger, disgust, distress, fear, interest, joy, shame, surprise]*

In our system, some elements are worth to point out:

- the *quantitative aspect* of basic emotions, i.e. emotions can appear in different arousal levels;
- *the polarity of the emotion*, i.e. negative or positive;
- the *(re)action* induced on a human by the emotion, i.e. attraction or repulsion.

In our application context, we can consider the positive/negative *polarity* of emotion as connected with the comfort/pain experienced by a person. According to this point of view, in the Lovheim model *anger, disgust, distress, fear, shame* can be considered negative emotions, while *interest* and *joy* convey positive emotions; in Plutchik *anger, disgust, fear, sadness* are negative, while *joy and trust* are positive; *anger, disgust, fear* and *sadness* are negative in Ekman, in contrast to *joy*. The fact that most emotions have a negative polarity can rely on the evolutionary role of emotions as low-level reactive mechanisms to improve individual survival in situations of danger or risk [29].

Reactions induced by the emotions are, generally speaking, determined by their polarity, i.e. a positive emotion is more likely to be attractive, desirable to follow. In contrast, negative emotions are more likely to generate a repulsive behaviour, a "fight or flight" reaction inducing either contrasting or escaping from the situation which triggered the emotion. Besides the initial physical reaction to the emotion, which includes several well-known variations in parameters, e.g., blood pressure, heartbeat, skin hydration, the reaction at a higher abstraction can be generated by a mixed emotional-cognitive level, e.g., deciding actions which aim to remove the cause of the events triggering the emotions.

The system can be easily adapted to complex models of emotional affordances. Different approaches may include the use of language-based interactions (e.g., text and voice recognition, lip-reading), visual recognition (e.g., face and gestures), and sensors (e.g., skin hydration, heartbeat). Some techniques may be more challenging than others to use in our use case because they require contact, which would need additional hygiene policies. Other sensors are more suitable than others, e.g., sensors of movement, proximity, infrared light to recognise emotions from the natural heating of different parts of the body. In particular cases, ad-hoc devices, e.g., wearables, myoelectric armbands, personal mobile devices such as smartphones, may be an additional support.

4   Swarm Distributed Behaviour

The goal of the hexapod swarm is to maintain a safe situation concerning the people behave in their area of interest or restore safety when it is violated or threatened. In the latter case, the hexapod is firstly attracted by the group of people, then gradually checks the situation and decide if it has to intervene.

Each hexapod is characterised by three primary states:

A) Random Patrolling (RP)
B) Rest Idle (RI)
C) Alert/Intervention (AI)

Transitions between states are shown in Fig. 1.

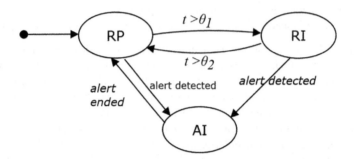

Fig. 1. Transitions between primary states of the hexapods.

4.1 Patrolling State

A hexapod is continuously monitoring the area of interest, detecting eventual violation of safety distance and requirements (e.g., wearing a mask, avoiding contact), and the position, direction and state of other hexapods in view.

The *patrolling action* consists of the hexapod exploring the area with a random walk, driven by the following behavioural rules:

- *Intra-hexapod distance*: maintaining a minimum distance from the other hexapod helps to distribute the walks evenly in the space.
- *Preference for unexplored areas*: choosing unexplored areas in case of parity of evaluation helps to distribute the walks evenly in time.
- *People-hexapod distance*: maintaining a minimal distance from people guarantees discreteness and adds value to the directional action.

The emerging trend of such rules is that hexapods spread uniformly in the surveillance area, maintaining background positions to people. The expected result of patrolling is not only to monitor actual threats proactively but also producing a deterrent effect.

4.2 Idle State

While it is patrolling with no alert after a given time threshold θ_1, the hexapod can stop and rest in an *idle state*, where it continues monitoring the environment from a fixed position without moving (i.e., resting position, energy save). On the other hand, if it remains in the RI state for more than a time interval θ_2, it resumes the RP state.

Threshold θ_1 and θ_2 are determined by a function of time spent in AI states in the previous time units. The decision of moving to RI state is randomised and penalises the presence of other idle agents in the area. If any anomaly is detected while idle or intervention is requested by other hexapods, it moves directly to AI state.

The purpose of RI state is to reflect the fact that after a given time patrolling with no problems detected, the hexapod swarm can move to a more understatement and less energy consumption behaviour; on the other hand, a longer *idle state* could more probably miss detecting violations in other areas, which is the purpose of θ_2. Statistics on the global idles states can help the organisation to optimise the cardinality of the swarm.

4.3 Alert State

When the hexapod detects a potentially critical situation (i.e., potential crowds, violation of social distancing policies) in its area of interest, it checks if the information is sufficient to act. If more information is needed, the hexapod can decide to:

I) ask information to other hexapods in a closer position to the people;
II) approach the position where the people behaviour is potentially dangerous, to collect more evidence.

If intervention is needed, the hexapod should evaluate:

− its possible actions: e.g., move towards the target, use a signal, increase the signal, gently push a person, call the human emergency team;
− the ongoing activity of other hexapods: e.g., if other hexapods are already directing to the same target and their activation level;

then choose if the other hexapods action is already sufficient, or if its intervention is needed. If other hexapods are directed to the same target, the impact of their actions on the situation are evaluated based on the people reaction.

When the hexapod is intervening, various individual actions can be exploited. E.g., indirectly signalling to the people the violation adapting its appearance to trigger negative emotions (e.g., with an alarm sound, with gestures such as waving legs, with flashing lights), at an appropriate level (e.g., increasing volume, gesture extent, lights colour and pace) or directly signalling with a voice message, a gentle push, opposing to a people movement standing in the path. In some cases, the hexapod can intervene as a swarm, coordinating or synchronising actions.

4.4 Critical Situations

Examples of critical situations can be:

• the *low distance within two people* in a queue: intervention of an individual hexapod standing between the two;
• the *low interpersonal distance in a group* (muster or crowd): intervention of more hexapods (swarm) signalling the violation;
• *dangerous people* (individual menace threatening others, e.g. removing the mask when a mask is required, approaching other people in a small place): intervention of a swarm of hexapods, to surround the person and wait for the human emergency team;
• *people needing help*, e.g., panicking inside a crowd, shouting or fainting: intervention of a swarm of hexapods, to surround the person (to contain or protect) and wait for the human emergency team.

To evaluate the situation and to act appropriately, the intelligent hexapod control includes the following variables: emergency level, intervention type, distance to targets, number of hexapods in the area, signal level, signal type, object/people tracking.

The hexapod behaviour in the *alert state* is summarized b the following rules r1-r4:

```
r1) if (Anomaly(target) = uncertain && AgentsCloser(tar-
get) → ask(target, AgentsCloser(target))
r2) if (Anomaly(target) = uncertain && emply(AgentsCloser
(target))
→ approach(target)
r3) if (Anomaly(target) = true && (ExpectedEffects(OtherA-
gents) > AnomalyTarget.level) → Monitor(Area)
r4) if (Anomaly(target) = true && (E = ExpectedEffects
(OtherAgents) < AnomalyTarget.level = A) → DecideActions(-
target,A-E)
```

where *r1* and *r2* characterise the behaviour for an uncertain level of anomaly detection, i.e. request info from other agents or collect evidence autonomously. Rules *r3* and *r4* evaluate expected effects of other agents actions concerning the intervention level required by the detected anomaly. If the expected effects due to the observed actions of other agents is considered a sufficient answer, then the agent does not act, and keeps monitoring the situation; otherwise, it passes the control to *DecideAction(target, level),* where the *target* and the expected *level* of affordance increment by the effect of the action are given.

The kernel of *DecideAction(target, level)* is a series of functions, see Table 1, which, depending on agent and target position, estimate the negative affordance level increment produced by executing that action in the current state. For instance, turning the lights on from a position where lights are not visible, e.g., behind the target, produces a smaller effect than turning on sound emission, provided the sound is loud enough to be heard from target distance.

Table 1. Functions used in DecideAction implementation

FunctionName: *parameters* → + *affordanceLevel_increment*
turnOnLight: target.position → + affordanceLevel$_{turnOnLight}$
flashLight: frequency, pattern, target position → + affordanceLevel$_{flashLight}$
turnOnSound: mode, intensity, target.distance → + affordanceLevel$_{turnOnSound}$
moveToward: target.position → + affordanceLevel$_{moveToward}$
waveLeg: frequency, position → + affordanceLevel$_{waveLeg}$
shakeBody: frequency, position → + affordanceLevel$_{shakeBody}$
combinedActionsAffordance(ownActions, ExpectedEffects(OtherAgents)) → +affordanceLevel$_{totalAffordance}$

Finally, the function *combinedActionsAffordance* evaluates the combined actions affordances concerning actions of the considered agent and actions of other agents observed in the area. The effect of different affordances is not linearly additive. For instance, increasing the sound has a lower effect when the sound is already on, and shaking the body or waving legs when the lights are already flashing with high frequency is not probably producing any significant increment of effects on the target.

Similarly, if the agent is the only one moving toward a target, the affordance of its action is very strong if the agent contributes to surround a target, resulting in a secure threatening effect. On the other hand, a single agent moving toward a target, in whose direction a big swarm is already moving, has a neglectable effect.

4.5   Swarm Reinforcement Learning

The *DecideAction* activity is initially assigned with expected values in term of effects of actions on the observed anomaly situation. Since the real case could be different from the expected one, the level of anomaly could not be reduced if the affordance level is lower than those calculated in the functions of the *DecideAction* activity.

It is straightforward to interpret as an immediate reward the post-action observations about the previously detected anomaly level, i.e. if and how much the affordance level is reduced. Such a reward can be used in Q-learning module [30] to improve the policy for agent behaviour. The *(state, action, reward)* information collected by pre/post action observations is submitted to the Q-learning component, shared by all hexapod agents to learn the optimal policy. The learned policy is periodically updated on the hexapods (see Fig. 2), whose behaviour is thus able to adjust the unavoidable biases introduced by the *DecideAction* functions. Evaluating the effects of actions on the critical situation detected and adapting to people reactions, e.g., when people get used to the hexapods actions, their affordance level reduces, as well as the improvement of a critical situation. We decided to allocate the learning module in a separate shared unit both for computational reasons, i.e. quick reactive decisions required onboard rather than time-consuming online learning and to collect a more extensive set of training data from different hexapods episodes, which avoid learning biases due to a single-agent history.

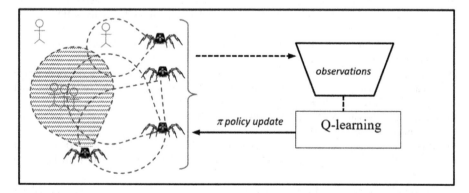

Fig. 2. Anomaly detection, actions and reinforcement learning

References

1. Bostan, S., et al.: The effect of covid-19 pandemic on the turkish society. Electron J. Gen. Med. **17**(6), em237 (2020)
2. Badar Nadeem, A., et al.: Stock markets' reaction to COVID-19: Cases or fatalities? Res. Int. Bus. Finance **54**, 101249 (2020)
3. Gondauri, D., et al.: The study of the effects of mobility trends on the statistical models of the COVID-19 virus spreading. Electron J. Gen. Med. **17**(6), em243 (2020)
4. Wu, J., et al.: Quantifying the role of social distancing, personal protection and case detection in mitigating COVID-19 outbreak in Ontario. Canada. J. Math. Industry **10**, 15 (2020)
5. Mejia, C.R., et al.: The media and their informative role in the face of the coronavirus disease 2019 (COVID-19): validation of fear perception and magnitude of the issue (MED-COVID-19). Electron J. Gen. Med. **17**(6), em239 (2020)
6. https://www.blitzquotidiano.it/video/coronavirus-salerno-elicottero-3164049
7. https://www.liberoquotidiano.it/video/italia/21930179/pescara_runner_carabiniere_quarantena_coronavirus.html
8. https://www.iene.mediaset.it/2020/news/coronavirus-giovane-denuncia-finanzieri-picchiato_759620.shtml
9. https://www.lavocedivenezia.it/scontro-verbale-contro-carabinieri-con-arresto-ai-tempi-del-coronavirus
10. Olff, M., et al.: Screening for consequences of trauma - an update on the global collaboration on traumatic stress. Eur. J. Psychotraumatol. **11**(1), 1752504 (2020)
11. https://www.youtube.com/watch?v=Es2OJpQx_do
12. https://www.bbc.com/news/world-europe-52529981
13. http://www.forbes.com/sites/jonmarkman/2019/10/09/see-spot-run/#7dd5f8f8135f
14. Wells, P., et al.: A socio-technical transitions perspective for assessing future sustainability following the COVID-19 pandemic, Sustainability: Science. Pract. Policy **16**(1), 29–36 (2020)
15. Chiancone, A., Franzoni, V., Niyogi, R., Milani, A.: Improving link ranking quality by quasi-common neighbourhood. In: Proceedings - 15th International Conference on Computational Science and Its Applications, ICCSA 2015, art. no. 7166159, pp. 21–26 (2015)
16. Franzoni, V., Poggioni, V., Zollo, F.: Automated classification of book blurbs according to the emotional tags of the social network Zazie. CEUR Workshop Proceedings **1096**, 83–94 (2013)
17. Gervasi, O., Franzoni, V., Riganelli, M., Tasso, S.: Automating facial emotion recognition. Web Intell. **17**(1), 17–27 (2019)
18. Franzoni, V., Milani, A., Pallottelli, S., Leung, C.H.C., Li, Y.: Context-based image semantic similarity. In: 2015 12th International Conference on Fuzzy Systems and Knowledge Discovery, FSKD 2015, pp. 1280–1284 (2016)
19. Franzoni, V., Milani, A., Nardi, D., Vallverdú, J.: Emotional machines: The next revolution. Web Intell. **17**(1), 1–7 (2019)
20. Milani, A., Rajdeep, N., Mangal, N., Mudgal, R.K., Franzoni, V.: Sentiment extraction and classification for the analysis of users' interest in tweets. Int. J. Web Inf. Syst. **14**(1), 29–40 (2018)
21. Franzoni V., Biondi G., Milani A.: Emotional Sounds of the Crowd, Spectrogram Analysis Using Deep Learning. MTAP-D-20-00101(2020)

22. Franzoni, V., Milani, A.: Heuristic semantic walk for concept chaining in collaborative networks. Int. J. Web Inf. Syst. **10**(1), 85–103 (2014)
23. Vallverdù, J., Franzoni, V., Milani, A.: Errors, biases and overconfidence in artificial emotional modeling. In: Proceedings - 2019 IEEE/WIC/ACM International Conference on Web Intelligence Workshops, WI 2019 Companion, pp. 86–90 (2019)
24. Biondi, G., Franzoni, V., Gervasi, O., Perri, D.: An approach for improving automatic mouth emotion recognition. In: Misra, S., Gervasi, O., Murgante, B., Stankova, E., Korkhov, V., Torre, C., Rocha, A.M.A.C., Taniar, D., Apduhan, B.O., Tarantino, E. (eds.) ICCSA 2019. LNCS, vol. 11619, pp. 649–664. Springer, Cham (2019). https://doi.org/10.1007/978-3-030-24289-3_48
25. Franzoni, V., Biondi, G., Milani, A.: A Web-Based System for Emotion Vector Extraction. In: Gervasi, O., et al. (eds.) ICCSA 2017. LNCS, vol. 10406, pp. 653–668. Springer, Cham (2017). https://doi.org/10.1007/978-3-319-62398-6_46
26. Franzoni, V., Milani, A., Vallverdú, J.: Emotional affordances in human-machine interactive planning and negotiation. In: Proceedings - 2017 IEEE/WIC/ACM International Conference on Web Intelligence, WI 2017, pp. 924–930 (2017)
27. Franzoni, V.: Autonomous hexapod robot with artificial vision and remote control by myo-electric gestures: The innovative implementation tale of gAItano. In: Cyber-Physical Systems for Next-Generation Networks, pp. 143–162 (2018)
28. Franzoni, V., Milani, A., Biondi, G.: SEMO: A semantic model for emotion recognition in web objects. In: Proceedings - 2017 IEEE/WIC/ACM International Conference on Web Intelligence, WI 2017, pp. 953–958 (2017)
29. Darwin, C., Darwin, F.: The expression of the emotions in man and animals. Oxford University Press, USA (2009)
30. Watkins, C.J.C.H., Dayan, P.: Technical note: Q-Learning. Mach. Learn. **8**(3), 279–292 (1992)
31. Ekman, P.: An argument for basic emotions. Cogn. Emot. **6**(3–4), 169–200 (1992)

International Workshop on AI Factory and Smart Manufacturing (AIFACTORY 2020)

A CPS-Based IIoT Architecture Using Level Diagnostics Model for Smart Factory

Byungjun Park and Jongpil Jeong$^{(\boxtimes)}$

Department of Smart Factory Convergence, Sungkyunkwan University, Suwon,
Gyeonggi-do 16419, Republic of Korea
{bjunpark,jpjeong}@skku.edu

Abstract. In this paper, a construction process using a level diagnostic agent was applied to the construction of a smart factory. The current status of the smart factory of the demanding company was measured and the target level was derived, and a cps-based design of the smart factory construction type was proposed. It is suggested that the construction of a CPS simulation based smart factory is more effective in preparation for cloud based smart factory manufacturing in the process of informatization, automation, and intelligence of the smart factory due to the explosive increase of data. In this paper, a Korean-type smart factory adopting an empirical research method that activates the actual construction cases of smart factory level diagnosis according to the basic components of the smart factory, information, automation, and intelligence, and the present examples of each smart factory level as an empirical case.

Keywords: CPS · Industrial Internet of Things (IIoT) · Level diagnostics model · Smart factory

1 Introduction

Smart Factory means a consumer centered intelligent factory that combines next generation digital new technologies and manufacturing technologies that go beyond the existing Factory Automation (FA) level. Various products can be produced in one production line, and it is expected to change from mass customization to individual flexible production system through modularization [1]. The transition to the smart factory is expected to dramatically improve the productivity of the manufacturing industry, and it is also possible to save energy and realize a human centered work environment. It is predicted that it is possible to monitor the manufacturing site in a virtual space and to control it, so that it is easy to manage the plant and to strengthen quality and cost competitiveness [2]. The smart factory, which is a core element of the IIoT(Industrial Internet of Things) trend, aims to realize an intelligent manufacturing factory that finally performs optimization of the smart factory through the informatization and automation of data [3]. Through IIoT, various types of industrial

© Springer Nature Switzerland AG 2020
O. Gervasi et al. (Eds.): ICCSA 2020, LNCS 12250, pp. 577–587, 2020.
https://doi.org/10.1007/978-3-030-58802-1_41

equipment are used as production nodes. Smart factories no longer exist as independent data through the generation, accumulation, and processing of big data generated in the field, and data can be converted and upgraded through connection and convergence. The network manufacturing process can be accelerated. The recently built smart factory aims to continuity of manufacturing process production data and accumulation of key process variable data for each process through cloud computing based on the use of the internet [4]. The composition of the thesis is presented in Chap. 2, the current status and target level of the Smart Factory in Korea and the level diagnosis system. In Chap. 3, the CPS-based IIoT smart factory construction model is introduced, and in Chap. 4, the case study. The case of a smart factory running a CPS-based automated production platform is presented, and in the last Chap. 5, the significance of the paper and the direction of future research are presented.

2   Related Work

The establishment of smart factories in Korean SMEs is more appropriate than the system approach, unlike large corporations, where the factory level diagnosis and the smart factory uptake approach are appropriate. Therefore, in this paper, we will diagnose the smart factory basic level, intermediate level and advanced level according to the field level diagnosis, and propose a plan to build the smart factory at the target level.

2.1   Smart Factory in South Korea

Building a Korean smart factory has achieved the quantitative goal of building 30,000 small and medium-sized SME smart factories in 2022 thanks to the government's support policy, and it is necessary to achieve the goal of establishing an empirical Korean smart factory standard construction process. Accordingly, the direction of building a smart factory in Korea presents an effective construction process that implements the characteristics of data informatization, process automation, and autonomous process enablement, which are necessary to convert from a factory oriented factory level to a smart factory, and has a process to achieve this. Smart Factory means a consumer centered intelligent factory that combines next generation digital new technology and manufacturing technology that goes beyond the existing Factory Automation (FA) level. Various products can be produced in one production line, and it is expected to change from mass customization to individual flexible production system through modularization [5]. The transition to a smart factory is expected to dramatically improve the productivity of the manufacturing industry, and it is also possible to save energy and implement a human centered work environment. It is predicted that it is possible to monitor the manufacturing site in a virtual space and to control it, so that it is easy to manage the plant and to strengthen quality and cost competitiveness.

2.2   Level Diagnosis Model

In the CPS-based smart factory construction, the level diagnosis model consists of a total of 6 stages of the smart factory construction stage, the first stage is the ICT non-application stage, the second stage is the partial standardization and management of performance information, and the third stage is real time monitoring of production information. Possible stages, 4 stages are the steps to analyze and control the collected information, 5 stages are possible for proactive response and decision optimization through simulation, and the last 6 stages are intelligent stages that can be operated autonomously from monitoring to control and optimization. Table 1 defines the conditions and construction stages of the smart factory level verification model.

Table 1. Smart factory level confirmation system

Ranking	Reference model	Characteristic	Conditions (building level)	Score
Level 5	Advancement	Customized & Autonomy	Autonomous operation from monitoring to control and optimization	950 above
Level 4	Medium 2	Optimized & Integrated	Optimization and decision making through simulation	950 above
Level 3	Medium 1	Analyzed & Controlled	Control by analyzing collected information	950 above
Level 2	Basic 2	Measured & Monitored	Real-time monitoring of production information	950 above
Level 1	Basic 1	Identified & Checked	Partial standardization and performance information management	950 above
Level 0	ICT not applied	Unrecognized&unapplied	Unrecognized and ICT not applied	950 above

The smart factory level diagnosis model consists of 44 items in 10 categories and 4 areas including leadership and strategy, product development, information system and automation. Table 2 shows the details of the smart factory level confirmation model.

It is organized in 6 grades from level 0 to level 5 from basic level to advanced level. The evaluation according to the Korean smart factory level diagnosis system leads to the leadership and strategy, product development, process information system up to the smart factory upgrade level requested by the demanding company through on-site diagnosis by process by the consultant visiting the site at the request of the demanding company. This is accomplished by cross-checking 44 items in 10 categories and 4 areas including automation.

Table 2. Smart factory level confirmation system

Division	Evaluation area	Main Content	Number of evaluation items
Management system (100)	1. Leadership & Strategy	Leadership, operational strategy, execution management, performance management and improvement	8
Process (400)	2. Product development	Design and production, development management, process development	12
	3. Production Planning	Standard information management, demand and order response, production plan	5
	4. Process Management	Work allocation, work progress management, abnormal management, work management	5
	5. Quality Management	Prevention, correction, screening and standard management, inspection test	12
	6. Facility Management	Equipment operation, equipment maintenance, electronics, mold and jig management	6
	7. Logistics operation	Purchase outsourcing management, warehouse management, shipment delivery	7
System and Automation (400)	8. Information system	ERP, SCM, MES, PLM, EMS etc.	20
	9. Equipment control	Control model, control flexibility, self diagnosis, network method, support equipment	10
Performance (100)	10. Performance	Productivity, quality, cost, delivery, safety and environment, conservation	12
Sum (1,000)	It consists of 95 evaluation items in 10 modules		95

3   CPS-Based IIOT Architecture for Smart Factory

3.1   A. System Architecture

Currently, most smart factories are based on cloud design [6]. Many of the smart factory architectures involved in manufacturing production are based on these designs, and users of these architectures have access to a shared manufacturing platform. Resources needed anytime, anywhere in a smart factory, fast configuration [7]. This is because resource management is essential. In a cloud-based smart factory, the centralized architecture is very weak [8]. That is, if the central node is compromised, all services are suspended. For that reason, we propose a CPS-based IIoT architecture with the goal of building node supervision and distributed systems to back up all service disruptions, and the architecture of these smart factories is shown in Fig. 1.

The architecture has three tiers. Data detection layer generated in the field of factory, data hub that senses and manages this data through Raspberry Pi, and storage layer that stores it, and firm ware application layer that utilizes various data for processing and purpose through visualization. It consists of 3 layers. The first layer, the data-sensing layer, includes various types of sensors, and one or more microcomputers with specific computing power can obtain various equipment and preprocessing information. The second layer, the data collection and storage layer, stores the collected data, while in conjunction with the management hub layer, analyzes the uploaded data and packages the data

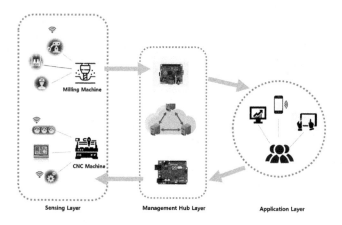

Fig. 1. CPS-based IIoT architecture for a smart factory

to store it in a database. The third layer is a data utilization layer that provides users with various data processing services such as visualization and equipment failure prediction that can be monitored in real time.

3.2 Description of Components

The proposed architecture is divided into two types: intranet and extranet. The intranet aims to collect and store data generated at the manufacturing site, and the extranet aims to use the collected data to provide other data users for visualization data or failure prediction purposes. Intranet consists of data detection layer, data storage and management layer. The data generated by manufacturing equipment at the manufacturing site stored in the intranet is managed by the management hub of each equipment node. Data flow information that is input to the manufacturing line and processed along the line is measured and stored in connection with the sensing node. Figure 2 describes the user friendly data processing analysis road that occurs in intranets and extranets according to data generation, accumulation, and processing in smart factory construction.

The extranet has a major difference between the data management and storage layer and the application layer. Extranets are intended for users who utilize data collected and accumulated, while intranets are intended for data production equipment at the manufacturing site. Therefore, what is required in the extranet is to secure the stability connected to the Internet to always detect the generated data inside the smart factory, and through this, provide services to users such as visualization programs that can utilize data and reasonably access it. It is to provide a variety of ways to provide. Through this, the data user can obtain various processing information related to the production information of the manufacturing site according to the user's demand, and guarantee the high quality of service reflected in real time. Figure 3 displays intra extranet process flowchart.

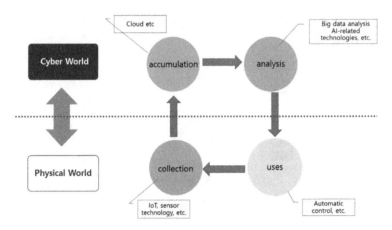

Fig. 2. Intra-extranet data analysis process

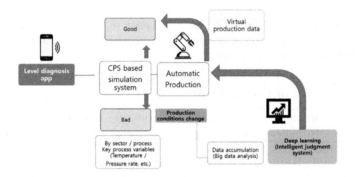

Fig. 3. Process flowchart

In the CPS(Cyber Physical System)-based smart factory building system, a series of processes appearing in the production consistent process line are linked to other smart factories' regional hub factories that perform the same process through data monitoring and real time hub layer data storage and sharing, and the production work is performed in parallel. Twin system technology is attracting attention as a core technology that can solve various social problems and is promoting the growth of related industries [9,10]. Figure 4 explains about CPS relating to Twin System.

The 'digital twin system', a technology that creates the same digital twins as the physical world, is becoming one of the essential technologies for building a smart factory along with AI(Artificial Intelligence), blockchain, and IoT(Internet of Things) [10]. The decline in price is acting as a catalyst to accelerate the convergence of manufacturing and ICT in the 'trillion sensor era' where more than 1 trillion sensors exist by expanding the grafting area of the digital twin. The digital twin is prominent in the 'manufacturing industry' with the trend change of 'personalized production' [11]. The CPS in the manufacturing field is composed

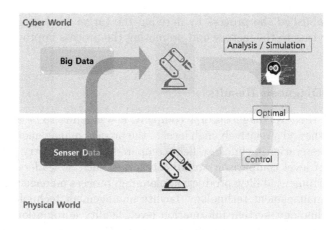

Fig. 4. CPS (Twin System)

of structured digital data such as Operation Technology (OT) systems, namely production information systems (PLM, MES, etc.) and enterprise operating systems (ERP, SCM, CRM, etc.) [12]. By collecting data generated in real time in the production process as a platform, data management system and smart factory self optimization should go beyond the level of managing data by partitions such as each machine, worker, process, and department. The ultimate form of smart factory using cyber physical system technology is digital twin, which is realized by perfectly synchronizing the production activities of the virtual space and the real space [13]. This means that production activities in the real space are accumulated as digital data, and AI analysis technology is applied to it, and intelligent autonomous production activities, that is, defects caused by differences caused by process specific core variables through machine learning, etc. It means that it is possible for factories to learn the patterns themselves and find the optimal solution to defects through accumulated defect data.

4   Case Study: A CPS-Based Automatic Production

4.1   Case Study Overview

T company, which is introduced in Case Study, is a manufacturer of equipment for automobile powertrain (engine/transmission) automatic precision measurement and assembling machines. It is a manufacturing company that manufactures and delivers precision measurement granulators for automobile manufacturing. It is a company that is trying to innovate quality and productivity by converging. In order to build a CPS-based smart factory, we present the process of sensing and storing the data controlled by the line in a digital twin method in the same way as the actual manufacturing process in multiple factories.

First, we diagnosed the current level of T company's smart factory through the smart factory level diagnosis app for manufacturing managers of T company, and then established the process by deriving the target level of smart factory through site visits to the factory and promoting the process improvement direction for this.

4.2   Level Diagnosis Results

As a result of the level diagnosis of T company, it was found to be at a level of 3 levels, which showed a relatively high level in the process management technology and logistics operation technology field compared to the industry. The evaluation factors of level comparison are 10 categories, such as leadership strategy, product development ability, production planning, process management technology, quality management technology, facility management technology, logistics operation technology, system information level, facility automation level, management performance. Figure 5 explains T company smart factory level diagnosis result. The areas that showed the highest position were the process management technology field and the facility management technology field, which are identified as the main reason for T company's CPS-based process construction. The results of the diagnosis were found to be relatively vulnerable in the areas of product development capability and business performance. This is attributed to the fact that the product portfolio of a single type of manufacturing industry is monotonous and the weakness of aggressive sales activities. Accordingly, T company is constructing a smart factory with the goal of level 4 level diagnosis in the direction of expanding the smart factory construction project based on the accumulated technology in the process management technology field, which is a strength.

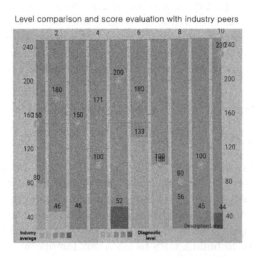

Fig. 5. T company smart factory level diagnosis result

4.3   CPS-Based System Construction

Based on the proposed construction model, the manufacturing production line automation process verified the effectiveness of CPS-based smart factory construction in industrial manufacturing sites. This company has been producing various quality and productivity innovation facilities for a long time in the field, and now has developed the artificial intelligence smart factory platform, which can produce and connect various data by integrating ICT technology with facilities. This platform acts with the goal of quality and productivity innovation by interacting together with products, organizations, companies, technologies, cultures, etc., each with its own value. Figure 6 explains an automatic production platform according to the proposed architecture.

Fig. 6. Automatic Assembly Line

Figure 7 displays architecture of the automatic production platform. Raspberry Pi is attached to a production node that senses data in a field in an automated assembly process line. It can be seen that the data is accumulated in the management hub, and the process is efficiently improved by accumulating temperature and process working time delays or poor process occurrence phenomena such as pressure differential generated in this process and visualizing it through visualization processing.

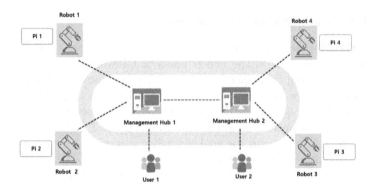

Fig. 7. Example of the automatic production Line platform

5 Conclusion

The CPS-based smart factory construction model using the proposed level diagnostic system shows that it is possible to build a more effective intelligent smart factory compared to the existing cloud based construction. The main contribution of this work is an innovative production oriented approach to CPS-based system. In particular, in the expansion of smart factory construction, the key process variables for each production and manufacturing process through data management which is the process of intelligent smart factory construction, through data informatization and big data analysis through data accumulation and analysis. Through the simulation system, it is shown that the intelligent judgment system enables customized manufacturing processes through virtual production data. Future research tasks include proactive response and decision making through simulation to increase the probability of preliminary preservation. It will be a process identification for the smart factory intelligent process from smart factory monitoring to control and optimization operation, such as scenario optimization.

Acknowledgment. This research was supported by Basic Science Re-search Program through the National Research Foundation of Korea(NRF) funded by the Ministry of Education (NRF-2017R1A6A3A11035613).

References

1. Zawadzki, P., Żywicki, K.: Smart product design and production control for effective mass customization in the industry 4.0 concept. Manage. Prod. Eng. Rev. **7**(3), 105–112 (2016)
2. Wan, J., Yin, B., Li, D., Celesti, A., Tao, F., Hua, Q.: An ontology-based resource reconfiguration method for manufacturing cyber-physical systems. IEEE/ASME Trans. Mechatron. **23**(6), 2537–2546 (2018)
3. Chen, B., Wan, J., Shu, L., Li, P., Mukherjee, M., Yin, B.: Smart factory of industry 4.0: key technologies, application case, and challenges. IEEE Access **6**, 6505–6519 (2017)

4. Wang, S., et al.: Implementing smart factory of industry 4.0: an outlook. Int. J. Distrib. Sens. Netw. **12**(1), 3159805 (2016)
5. Wollschlaeger, M., Sauter, T., Jasperneite, J.: The future of industrial communication: automation networks in the era of the internet of things and industry 4.0. IEEE Ind. Electron. Mag. **11**(1), 17–27 (2017)
6. Wan, J., et al.: Reconfigurable smart factory for drug packing in healthcare industry 4.0. IEEE Trans. Ind. Informat. **15**(1), 507–516 (2019)
7. Wu, D., Rosen, D.W., Wang, L., Schaefer, D.: Cloud-based design and manufacturing: a new paradigm in digital manufacturing and design innovation. Comput. Aided Des. **59**, 1–14 (2015)
8. Cui, A., Stolfo, S.J.: A quantitative analysis of the insecurity of embedded network devices: results of a wide-area scan. In: Proceedings of the 26th Annual Computer Security Applications Conference, Austin, TX, USA, pp. 97–106 (2010)
9. Colombo, A.W., et al. (eds.): Industrial Cloud-Based Cyber-Physical Systems. Springer, Cham (2014). https://doi.org/10.1007/978-3-319-05624-1
10. O'Donovan, P., Leahy, K., Bruton, K., O'Sullivan, D.T.J.: An industrial big data pipeline for data-driven analytics maintenance applications in large-scale smart manufacturing facilities. J. Big Data **2**(1), 1–26 (2015). https://doi.org/10.1186/s40537-015-0034-z
11. Herwan, J., Kano, S., Oleg, R., Sawada, H., Kasashima, N.: Cyber-physical system architecture for machining production line. In: 2018 IEEE Industrial Cyber-Physical Systems (ICPS), St. Petersburg, pp. 387–391 (2018)
12. Felser, M., Rentschler, M., Kleineberg, O.: Coexistence standardization of operation technology and information technology. In: Proceedings of the IEEE Proceedings IEEE Proceedings of the IEEE, vol. 107, no. 6, pp. 962–976, June 2019
13. Lau, J.K.S., Tham, C.K., Luo, T.: Participatory cyber physical system in public transport application. In: IEEE International Conference on Utility and Cloud Computing, Victoria, NSW, pp. 355–360 (2011)

A Hydraulic Condition Monitoring System Based on Convolutional BiLSTM Model

Kyutae Kim and Jongpil Jeong[✉]

Department of Smart Factory Convergence, Sungkyunkwan University, Suwon,
Gyeonggi-do 16419, Republic of Korea
{ryukkt62,jpjeong}@skku.edu

Abstract. In this paper, to monitor the conditions of hydraulic system, a real-time monitoring method based on convergence of convolutional neural networks (CNN) and a bidirectional long short-term memory networks (BiLSTM) is proposed. This method uses CNN and BiLSTM. In the CNN, the feature is extracted from the time-series data entered as an input, and in the BiLSTM, information from the feature is learned. Then, the learned information is sent to the Sigmoid classifier and it classified whether the system is stable or unstable. The experimental results show that compared to other deep learning models, this model can more accurately predict the conditions of the hydraulic system with the data collected by the sensors.

Keywords: Long short term memory · Deep learning · Classification · Convolutional neural networks · Hydraulic system · Bidirectional LSTM

1 Introduction

Mechanical fault diagnosis is an important part of the smart factory and is the key in the 4th industry [1]. Numerous sensors are installed in the hydraulic system to detect failures and the data collected from these sensors can be used to monitor whether the equipment is working properly [2,3].

Recent years has seen a growing popularity of performing fault detection with data collected from these sensors [6]. As data volumes increase and computing power advances, there are increasing attempts to take advantage of deep learning. In particular, convolutional neural networks (CNN) have been widely used in classification problems and it have shown high-performance [4,5]. However, the CNN relies too much on extracting high-dimensional features [7]. Too many convolutional layers cause vanishing gradient, and too few convolutional layers can't find global features [8]. Therefore, this paper proposes a method to monitor the condition of the hydraulic system using a model that combines a CNN and a bidirectional long short-term memory (BiLSTM) networks [9].

© Springer Nature Switzerland AG 2020
O. Gervasi et al. (Eds.): ICCSA 2020, LNCS 12250, pp. 588–603, 2020.
https://doi.org/10.1007/978-3-030-58802-1_42

The data collected from the sensor first enters the CNN for feature extraction, and then into the BiLSTM networks for feature extraction of the long-distance dependence information. Finally, learned features are sent to a sigmoid classifier that identifies the conditions of the hydraulic system [10]. This method can be useful for diagnosing the conditions of a hydraulic system in an actual industrial sites.

The remainder of this paper is organized as follow. Section 2 presents the CBLSTM model proposed in this paper. Section 3 introduces the data used in the experiment, presents the equipment, and the experimental process. Section 4 analyzes the experimental results on the conditions of the hydraulic system. Section 5 concludes with a summary and presents a future study plan.

2   Related Work

In this paper, a model combining a CNN and a recurrent neural networks (RNN) was applied to monitor the condition of a hydraulic system. The fusion model, convolutional bidirectional long short-term memory, reveals the correlation between time-series data that was ignored when using CNN alone, and avoids the gradient vanishing and gradient explosion problems frequently encountered in RNN [11].

2.1   CNN

The CNN is a model inspired by the way the brain's visual cortex works when it recognizes objects [12]. It has received great attention because of its excellent performance in image classification. This has made great strides in machine learning and computer vision applications. One-dimensional CNN can be used to analyze time series data collected from sensors. Several filters in the convolution layer filter the input data and superimpose the obtained results to get feature maps [13]. The feature map of the convolutional layer can be expressed as follows:

$$y_j = F(\sum_{i=0}^{n} x_i \times w_{ij} b_j) \tag{1}$$

y_j is the j-th output data, and x_i is the feature map of the previous layer. w_{ij} is the j-th kernel, b_j is the bias of the j-th kernel.

The pooling layer is usually located immediately after the convolution layer. In the pooling layer, the input data is divided into multiple zones and the maximum values are extracted from the zones to form new data. This is called max pooling. There is another pooling method, which is called average pooling as a method of extracting the average value in a zone. Data that passes through the convolution layer and pooling layer is called a feature map. After the input data is subjected to the convolution calculation, the activation function is applied and then the feature map is created as it passes through the pooling layer [7]. The

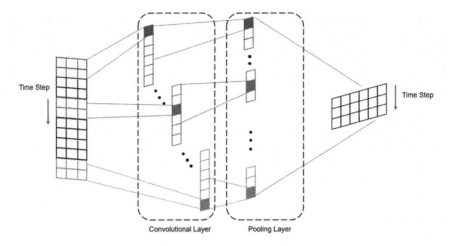

Fig. 1. The structure of the one-dimensional convolutional neural network

set of convolutional layers and pooling layers is a basic structure of CNN (see Fig. 1).

In order for elements in the original data array to participate equally in the operation, virtual elements must be added to both ends of the original array. In this case, using 0 as a virtual element is called zero padding. You can make all elements of the original array participate in the operation equally by adding the appropriate number of zero paddings [14]. The padding method in which all elements of the original array participate in the operation equally is called full padding (see Fig. 2).

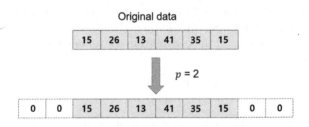

Fig. 2. One-dimensional padding

2.2 LSTM

LSTM was first introduced to overcome the gradient vanishing and gradient exploding problems encountered in RNN. The basic building block of LSTM is a memory cell, which means a hidden layer [15,16]. To solve gradient vanishing and gradient exploding problems, each memory cell has a circular edge that maintains the proper weight $w = 1$. The output of this circular edge is called the cell state. The structure of the LSTM is shown in Fig. 3.

The cell state $C^{(t-1)}$ of the previous time step is changed without being multiplied by any weight directly to obtain the cell state $C^{(t)}$ of the current time step. The flow of information in a memory cell is controlled by several operations described below. In Fig. 2, $\odot$ means element-wise multiplication and $\oplus$ means element-wise addition. Also, $x^{(t)}$ is the input data at time step t, and $h^{(t-1)}$ is the output of the concealed unit at time step $t-1$. The four boxes are represented by a sigmoid function (σ) or tanh activation function and a series of weights. This box is linearly combined after matrix-vector multiplication on the input. The unit calculated by the sigmoid function is called a gate and is output through $\odot$. There are three types of gates in LSTM cells. Forget gate, input gate, output gate.

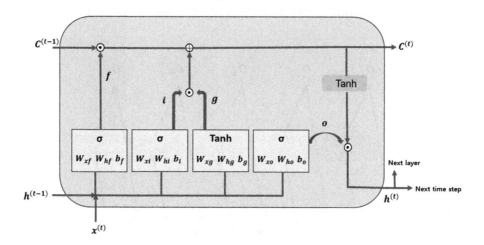

Fig. 3. The structure of the LSTM neurons

The forget gate f_t resets the cell state so that the memory cell does not grow indefinitely. In fact, the forget gate determines what information to pass and what to suppress. It is calculated as:

$$f_t = \sigma(W_{xf}x^{(t)} + W_{hf}h^{(t-1)} + b_f) \tag{2}$$

The input gate (i_t) and input node (g_t) are responsible for updating the cell status, and are calculated as follows.

$$i_t = \sigma(W_{xi}x^{(t)} + W_{hi}h^{(t-1)} + b_i) \tag{3}$$

$$g_t = tanh(W_{xg}x^{(t)} + W_{hg}h^{(t-1)} + b_g) \tag{4}$$

At time step t, the cell state is calculated as follows.

$$C^{(t)} = (C^{(t-1)} \odot f_t) \oplus (i_t \odot g_t) \tag{5}$$

The output gate (o_t) updates the output value of the hidden unit.

$$o_t = \sigma(W_{xo}x^{(t)} + W_{ho}h^{(t-1)} + b_o) \tag{6}$$

Invented in 1997 by Schuster and Faliwal, bidirectional LSTM was introduced to enable networks to utilize larger amounts of information. BiLSTM connects two hidden layers in opposite directions to the same output. With this type of structure, information can be simultaneously obtained from the previous sequences and the subsequent sequences [7]. BiLSTM does not need to modify the input data and their future input information can be reached in the current state [17]. The structure of the BiLSTM network is shown in Fig. 4.

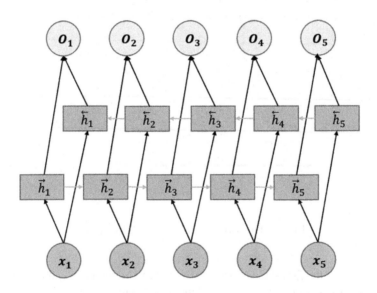

Fig. 4. The structure of the BiLSTM network model

The features of input data are generated as $\overrightarrow{h_t}$ by forward LSTM network, and $\overleftarrow{h_t}$ is generated by inverse LSTM network. And a vector P_t at time step t is generated by the BiLSTM network. The formula is as follows:

$$\overrightarrow{h_t} = \overrightarrow{LSTM}(h_{t-1}, x_t, C_{t-1}) \tag{7}$$

$$\overleftarrow{h_t} = \overleftarrow{LSTM}(h_{t+1}, x_t, C_{t+1}) \tag{8}$$

$$P_t = [\overrightarrow{h_t}, \overleftarrow{h_t}] \tag{9}$$

The model used in this paper was applied with a dropout of 0.2 probability, which can prevent overfitting. In addition, the relu function was used for the activation function, and the sigmoid function was used for the last fully connected layer. Binary-crossentropy was used as a loss function because it is a binary classification model [18]. The formula for sigmoid and cross-entropy error are as follow:

$$f(x) = \frac{1}{1 + e^{-x}} \tag{10}$$

$$E = - \sum_{n=1}^{N} (t_n log(y_n) + (1 - t_n)log(1 - y_n)) \tag{11}$$

In the sigmoid equation, if the value of x moves away from 0 in the negative direction, y is close to 0 because the denominator increases. Also, if the value of x is away from 0 in the positive direction, y is close to 1 because e^{-x} approaches 0.

$t_n \in \{0,1\}$ and $y_n \in [0,1]$, $y_n = \text{Sigmoid(net)}$. The optimization algorithm is a method of finding the point at which the value of the loss function is minimal. Optimization algorithms are very important to efficiently and reliably reach the global optimal solution. In this model, RMSProp was used, which overcomes the drawback of stagnating learning by reducing the amount of correction in Adagrad [19].

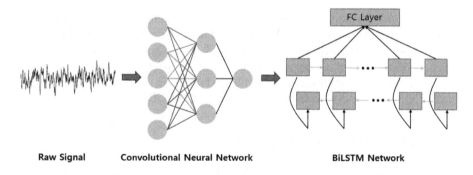

Raw Signal   **Convolutional Neural Network**   **BiLSTM Network**

Fig. 5. Framework of CBLSTM

3   CBLSTM

This paper applies CNN and RNN convergence to monitor the condition of hydraulic system and constructs two networks models: CNN and BiLSTM. CBLSTM effectively resolves the problem that mutual relation between input data is ignored on a single CNN and prevents gradient vanishing and explosion [20,21].

A CBLSTM model is proposed to further improve the accuracy of model predictions [22]. The CBLSTM model consists of three parts: First, the input

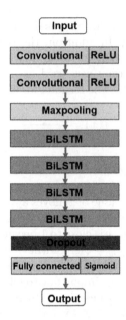

Fig. 6. Diagram of CBLSTM

data is fed into the model and the model extracts local feature from a time series data, primarily using one-dimensional CNN for filtering, In the second part, the BiLSTM network is used for information of long-distance dependence. Finally, the things that learned in the previous layers are transferred to classifier which is used to classify the condition of hydraulic system using sigmoid function. Figure 5 and Fig. 6 show model framework and diagram of CBLSTM.

4   Experiments and Discussion

In this experiment, time series data collected by sensors installed in the hydraulic system test rig were used. This test rig consists of working circuit, cooling circuit, and filtration circuit and the sensors installed in it measure various physical values such as pressure, vibration and temperature. Each sensor has a different sampling rate, which varies 1 Hz 100 Hz. The hardware platform used in this experiment: Intel R CoreTM i7-8700K CPU @ 3.70 GHz, and 32 GB of RAM. The software that was used to test was Python 3.7 and Tensorflow. It was shown in Table 1.

The model used in this paper is CBLSTM, which is a convergence of CNN and BiLSTM. It is consist of 2 one-dimentional convolution layers followed 1 max pooling layer, 2 bidirectional layers and fully connected layer. The parameter settings and diagram for this model are shown in Table 2.

Three models were additionally tested to compare the performance of CBLSTM with other models. The basic LSTM model, bidirectional LSTM, and

Table 1. System specification for experiments

Item	Details
CPU	Intel(R) Core(TM) i7-8700K
CPU Frequency	3.70 GHz
Memory	32 GB
Language	Python 3.7

Table 2. The parameters of CBLSTM network

Layer name	Output feature size	Network
Input layer	(54, 1)	–
Convolution layer1	(52, 62)	Conv1D, kernel size = 3, param = 256
Convolution layer2	(50, 64)	Conv1D, kernel size = 3, param = 12352
Pooling layer	(16, 64)	Maxpooling1D
Bidirectional laer1	(16, 40)	param = 13600
Bidirectional laer2	(16, 40)	param = 9760
Bidirectional laer3	(16, 40)	param = 9760
Bidirectional laer4	40	param = 9760
Dropout	40	–
Fully connected layer	2	Dense, Sigmoid, param = 82
Output layer	2	Binary Crossentropy

CLSTM model combining CNN and LSTM were used. First, in the case of the LSTM model, the loss rapidly decreased as epoch progressed in both training and test. At first, the loss was greater than 0.6, but as learning progressed, it decreased to 0.5. On the other hand, the accuracy did not improve significantly, and it was 0.6 at the beginning of the training and stayed at 0.7 even after the training was completed. Finally, the result of the test was loss of 0.512 and accuracy of 0.680. The test results were not satisfactory and there was a possibility of further development as the learning progressed further (see Fig. 7 and 8).

The second is the result of experiments with bidirectional LSTM. In this case, as with LSTM, the loss was sharply reduced in both training and test. At first it was 0.65, but as learning progressed, it rapidly decreased to 0.45. In the test set, the loss increased sharply when the epoch was 12, but it did not significantly affect the performance. In the case of accuracy, it was about 0.6 at first, and as the epoch increased, the accuracy also increased, finally reaching 0.708 in the test set (see Fig. 9 and 10).

In the case of a combination model of CNN and LSTM, it was very unstable. In the case of loss, the test set showed a significant change, especially when epoch = 3 and 6, the loss increased significantly. Finally, the test results showed that the loss was only reduced to 0.52. Accuracy was seen to improve as learning progressed. There was no significant difference between the training set and the test set, and the accuracy was finally recorded as 0.742, which is better than the LSTM and BiLSTM alone (see Fig. 11 and 12).

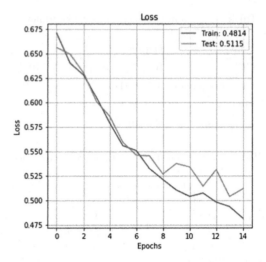

Fig. 7. Loss and accuracy of LSTM in training and test set

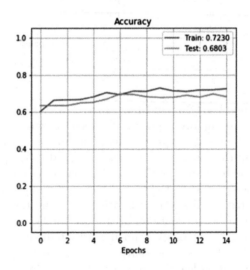

Fig. 8. Loss and accuracy of LSTM in training and test set

For the training parameters, 0.2 for the dropout, 15 for the epoch, and 16 for the batch size, 20% of the total dataset for the training set, and 25% for the validation set. Graphs were shown during the experiment and during the training.

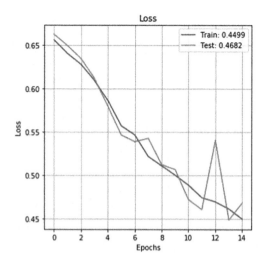

Fig. 9. Loss and accuracy of BiLSTM in training and test set

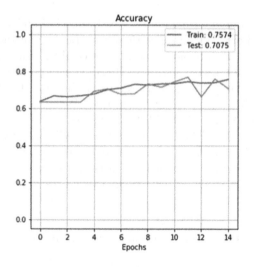

Fig. 10. Loss and accuracy of BiLSTM in training and test set

Looking at the experimental results of CBLSTM, loss decreased stably in the training set, but in the test set, the epcoch increased significantly at 8. The accuracy was lower than that of the training set, but we got decent accuracy (see Fig. 13 and 14). To compare with other models, three more models were tested in addition to CBLSTM. The experimental result of simple LSTM model,

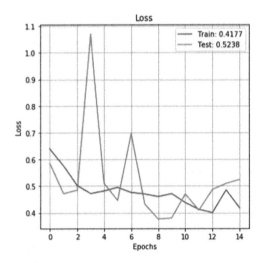

Fig. 11. Loss and accuracy of CLSTM in training and test set

a BiLSTM model, a model combining CNN and LSTM and a model combining CNN and BiLSTM are shown in Fig. 15 and 16. Looking at the loss first, as the learning progressed, all four models were lowered. LSTM and BiLSTM showed similar patterns, and CLSTM and CNNBiLSTM showed similar patterns. The simple LSTM model only reduced the loss to around 0.5, the BiLSTM to 0.45, the CLSTM to 0.43, and the CBLSTM to 0.35. When looking at the accuracy, LSTM was the lowest, and BiLSTM, CLSTM, and CBLSTM were the highest. Finally, the accuracy of CBLSTM increased to 0.83, that of CLSTM increased to 0.8, and BiLSTM and LSTM of 0.75. In particular, CLSTM showed unstable appearance, such as when the epoch was between 12 and 14, the accuracy was greatly reduced (see Fig. 15 and 16). Table 3 shows the loss and accuracy of the train and test sets of the four models.

Table 3. Comparison of accuracy and loss

	Train loss	Train acc	Test loss	Test acc
LSTM	0.481	0.723	0.511	0.680
BiLSTM	0.449	0.757	0.468	0.707
CLSTM	0.417	0.804	0.523	0.742
CBLSTM	0.350	0.833	0.341	0.810

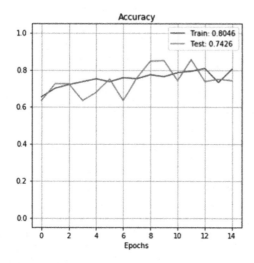

Fig. 12. Loss and accuracy of CLSTM in training and test set

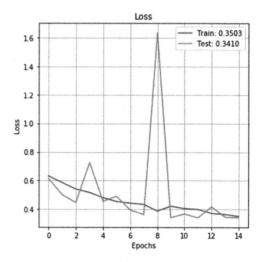

Fig. 13. Loss and accuracy of CBLSTM in training and test set

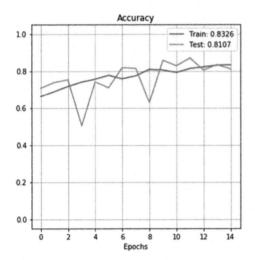

Fig. 14. Loss and accuracy of CBLSTM in training and test set

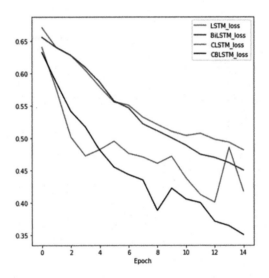

Fig. 15. Loss and accuracy of the training set

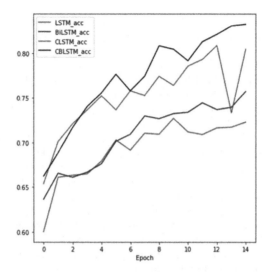

Fig. 16. Loss and accuracy of the training set

5   Conclusion

In this paper, we proposed a method to classify the condition of a system as stable or unstable using data collected from sensors in a hydraulic system using a model combining CNN and BiLSTM. The accuracy of the CBLSTM reached 81%, recording higher accuracy compared to the other three models tested with the same dataset and showing superior performance with lower loss. In a future study, we will add attention modules to the CBLSTM network to develop the model and apply it to other manufacturing domains.

Acknowledgment. This research was supported by the MSIT (Ministry of Science and ICT), Korea, under the ITRC (Information Technology Research Center) support program (IITP-2020-2018-0-01417) supervised by the IITP (Institute for Information & Communications Technology Planning & Evaluation).

This work was supported by the Smart Factory Technological R&D Program S2727186 funded by Ministry of SMEs and Startups (MSS, Korea).

References

1. Mahmood, M.F., Hussin, N.: Information in conversion era: impact and influence from 4th industrial revolution. Int. J. Acad. Res. Bus. Soc. Sci. **8**(9), 320–328 (2018)
2. Helwig, N., Pignanelli, E., Schütze, A.: Condition monitoring of a complex hydraulic system using multivariate statistics. In: 2015 IEEE International Instrumentation and Measurement Technology Conference (I2MTC) Proceedings, pp. 210–215. IEEE (2015)

3. Helwig, N., Pignanelli, E., Schütze, A.: D8. 1-detecting and compensating sensor faults in a hydraulic condition monitoring system. In: Proceedings SENSOR 2015, pp. 641–646 (2015)
4. Lawrence, S., Giles, C.L., Tsoi, A.C., Back, A.D.: Face recognition: a convolutional neural-network approach. IEEE Trans. Neural Netw. **8**(1), 98–113 (1997)
5. Hershey, S., et al.: CNN architectures forlarge-scale audio classification. In: 2017 IEEE International Conference on Acoustics, Speech and Signal Processing (ICASSP), pp. 131–135. IEEE (2017)
6. Mehranbod, N., Soroush, M., Panjapornpon, C.: A method of sensor fault detection and identification. J. Process Control **15**(3), 321–339 (2005)
7. Chen, Q., Xie, Q., Yuan, Q., Huang, H., Li, Y.: Research on a real-time monitoring method for the wear state of a tool based on a convolutional bidirectional LSTM model. Symmetry **11**(10), 1233 (2019)
8. Huang, G., Liu, Z., Van Der Maaten, L., Weinberger, K.Q.: Densely connected convolutional networks. In: Proceedings of the IEEE Conference on Computer Vision and Pattern Recognition, pp. 4700–4708 (2017)
9. Huang, Z., Xu, W., Yu, K.: Bidirectional LSTM-CRF models for sequence tagging. arXiv preprint arXiv:1508.01991 (2015)
10. Han, J., Moraga, C.: The influence of the sigmoid function parameters on the speed of backpropagation learning. In: Mira, J., Sandoval, F. (eds.) IWANN 1995. LNCS, vol. 930, pp. 195–201. Springer, Heidelberg (1995). https://doi.org/10.1007/3-540-59497-3_175
11. Mikolov, T., Karafiát, M., Burget, L., Černockỳ, J., Khudanpur, S.: Recurrent neural network based language model. In: Eleventh Annual Conference of the International Speech Communication Association (2010)
12. Krizhevsky, A., Sutskever, I., Hinton, G.E.: Imagenet classification with deep convolutional neural networks. In: Advances in Neural Information Processing Systems, pp. 1097–1105 (2012)
13. Yang, J., Nguyen, M.N., San, P.P., Li, X.L., Krishnaswamy, S.: Deep convolutional neural networks on multichannel time series for human activity recognition. In: Twenty-Fourth International Joint Conference on Artificial Intelligence, pp. 3995–4001 (2015)
14. Muquet, B., Wang, Z., Giannakis, G.B., De Courville, M., Duhamel, P.: Cyclic pre-fixing or zero padding for wireless multicarrier transmissions? IEEE Trans. Commun. **50**(12), 2136–2148 (2002)
15. Cowan, N.: What are the differences between long-term, short-term, and working memory? Prog. Brain Res. **169**, 323–338 (2008)
16. Cowan, N.: Activation, attention, and short-term memory. Memory Cogn. **21**(2), 162–167 (1993). https://doi.org/10.3758/BF03202728
17. Ullah, A., Ahmad, J., Muhammad, K., Sajjad, M., Baik, S.W.: Action recognition in video sequences using deep bi-directional LSTM with CNN features. IEEE Access **6**, 1155–1166 (2017)
18. Li, C.H., Lee, C.: Minimum cross entropy thresholding. Pattern Recogn. **26**(4), 617–625 (1993)
19. Mukkamala, M.C., Hein, M.: Variants of RMSProp and adagrad with logarithmic regret bounds. In: Proceedings of the 34th International Conference on Machine Learning-Volume 70, pp. 2545–2553. JMLR. org (2017)
20. Huang, Y., Wang, W., Wang, L.: Bidirectional recurrent convolutional networks for multi-frame super-resolution. In: Advances in Neural Information Processing Systems, pp. 235–243 (2015)

21. Cai, R., Zhang, X., Wang, H.: Bidirectional recurrent convolutional neural network for relation classification. In: Proceedings of the 54th Annual Meeting of the Association for Computational Linguistics (Volume 1: Long Papers), pp. 756–765 (2016)
22. Liu, Q., Zhou, F., Hang, R., Yuan, X.: Bidirectional-convolutional LSTM based spectral-spatial feature learning for hyperspectral image classification. Remote Sensing **9**(12), 1330 (2017)

Bearing Fault Detection with a Deep Light Weight CNN

Jin Woo Oh and Jongpil Jeong[✉]

Department of Smart Factory Convergence, Sungkyunkwan University, Jangan-gu,
Suwon, Gyeonggi-do 16419, Republic of Korea
{itdojust,jpjeong}@skku.edu

Abstract. Bearings are vital part of rotary machines. A failure of bearing has a negative impact on schedules, production operation and even human casualties. Therefore, in prior achieving fault detection and diagnosis (FDD) of bearing is ensuring the safety and reliable operation of rotating machinery systems. However, there are some challenges of the industrial FDD problems. Since according to a literature review, more than half of the broken machines are caused by bearing fault. Therefore, one of the important thing is time delay should be reduced for FDD. However, due to many learnable parameters in model and data of long sequence, both lead to time delay for FDD. Therefore, this paper proposes a deep Light Convolutional Neural Network (LCNN) using one dimensional convolution neural network for FDD.

Keywords: Data augmentation · CNN · Light · Fault diagnosis · Bearing

1   1 Introduction

Failures in rotating machinery such as helicopters and wind turbines is the problem of rolling element bearings (REBs). According to a literature review, more than half of the broken machines are caused by bearing faults [1]. Therefore, in prior achieving fault detection and diagnosis (FDD) of bearings is significant tasks as well as it is needed to collect and preprocessing the vibration signals for monitoring bearing condition. Many researchers have studied FDD for collecting, preprocessing and predicting the life of mechanical systems and so these field has become an important research area in industry [2,3]. Machines run almost always reliably, and few defects occur during stable operation of the control process, such as mechanical failures in manufacturing [4,5]. However, the existing traditional data-driven algorithms have a problem in that they are not good at learning the huge number of various and nonlinear data. In addition, due to the nature of the process, if the deformation of the process is slightly different, the data also can be different. This has to be revised each time by experienced experts.

Supported by organization x.

Instead of traditional machine learning algorithms, data-driven deep learning algorithms have ability of automatically learning the discriminative feature representation from input data effectively and accurately. As one of the popular models of deep neural network (DNN) is CNN, it has been applied in many fields, such as recognizing image and speech analysis [6–8]. However, many parameters of the model require a lot of time to process complex data generated in the industry and to detect and diagnose faults. Therefore, as mentioned above, this paper proposes a deep light weight CNN model.

The remainder of this paper is structured as follows. In Sect. 2, Overall description of the CNN is introduced briefly. In Sect. 3, the proposed fault diagnosis method based on deep light weight CNN is explained. In Sect. 4, The effectiveness of the proposed method is described. Finally, the conclusions are drawn in Sect. 5.

2 Convolutional Neural Network

Convolutional neural network (CNN) mainly consist of convolutional layer (CL), pooling layer (PL) and fully-connected layer (FL) as well as activation and loss functions. In the CL, a number of filters are used to perform filtering of input time series data and the obtained feature maps are overlapped to form an output feature map of the CL. Convolution operations in CL have translation invariant that means translation invariant makes the CNN invariant to translation. Invariance to translation means that if we translate the inputs the CNN will still be able to detect the class to which the input belongs.

PL extracts the fixed length feature vector from the feature maps for feature dimension reduction. Consequently, CL can extract important features and simplify the complexity of the network computation. PL provide an approach to down sampling feature maps by summarizing the presence of features in patches of the feature map. Two common pooling methods are average pooling and max pooling that summarize the average presence of a feature and the most activated presence of a feature respectively.

FL in a neural networks are those layers where all the inputs from one layer are connected to every activation unit of the next layer. In most popular machine learning models, the last few layers are full connected layers which compiles the data extracted by previous layers to form the final output. It is the second most time consuming layer second to CL.

As per the published literature [9,10], a neural network is referred to as shallow if it has single FL. Whereas, a deep CNN consists of CL, PL, and FC layers. In this paper, we assume a CNN model N1 as deep/shallow compared to another CNN model N2, if the number of trainable layers in N1 is more/less than N2, respectively.

2.1 One Dimensional and Two Dimensional CNN

One dimensional neural network (1D CNN) can be applied to time series analysis of sensor data [11,12]. Compared to one-dimensional processing, two-dimensional processing has a relatively complex structure and also requires more time and calculation resources. For example, the computational load of 3×1 convolution is only one-third compared to 3×3 convolution.

CNNs share the same characteristics regardless of 1D, 2D or 3D and follow the same approach. The main difference is in the dimensions of the input data and the way the feature detector (or filter) slices across the data. The difference can be seen in Fig. 1, while the 1D CNN filter learns the features of stride 1 all the way down, while the 2D CNN slicing horizontally and vertically filters the data with RGB. It can be seen that the difference remains in terms of the amount of computation brought by the difference in learning operations.

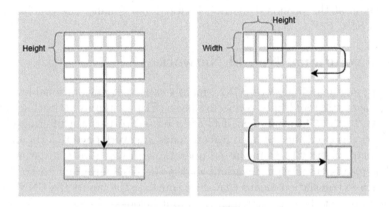

Fig. 1. Difference between 1D CNN and 2D CNN

3 The Proposed Methods

In this paper, a deep Light Convolutional Neural Network (CNN) model for rotating machinery fault detection is designed based on 1D CNN.

3.1 Model Structure

The parameters and computational time in a proposed CNN are affected by the number of channels, filters, data length, stride size. As shown in Fig. 2, the proposed model structure have conv-1 to conv-4 convolution layers of the network include convolution operations, rectified linear unit (ReLU) activation functions. The use of a ReLU activation function increase the rate of convergence and prevent a gradient explosion and vanishing problems. Maximum pooling is used in the pool-1 to pool-4 to make model have translation invariant and reduce the dimensionality of the data.

In FL, in dense layer, we use only use 10 nodes. In general, it is demonstrated in [13] that the FL needs a lot of nodes to get better performance, but a model with a large number of CLs and PLs needs fewer neurons in the FC.

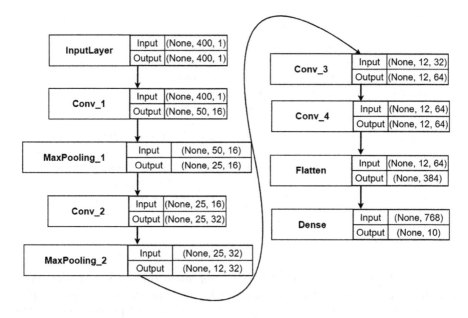

Fig. 2. The propose model overall structure

3.2 Experimental Model and Its Comparison

As mentioned in Sect. 3.1, depend on the number of filters, filter size, data length, data shape and connection mode, the performance of the model and the amount of space occupied can be vary. To demonstrate the effectiveness of proposed deep light CNN using the 1D-CNN as shown in Fig. 2, we use basic model of 1D CNN, 2D CNN and reference [14] for the performance comparison. The layers of the models were set identically and possibly. The name of models and its layers can be seen in Table 1.

The proposed model is designed to have the lightness and high performance of the model as much as possible. Therefore, in order to numerically confirm that the proposed model has achieved its purpose, the computation of the floating numbers and contain parameters of the convolutional layers and fully connected layers can be calculated by the following equations:

$$Parameters_{conv} = K_h \times K_w \times C_{in} \times C_{out} + C_{out} \tag{1}$$

$$Params_{sfc} = I \times O + O \tag{2}$$

$$FLOP_{conv} = 2 \times H \times W \times K_h \times K_w \times C_{in} \times C_{out} \tag{3}$$

$$FLOP_{sfc} = 2 \times I \times O \tag{4}$$

Table 1. Comparison between the proposed model and other models

	Proposed Model	1D-CNN	2D-CNN	Reference [14]
Input length	400 × 1	400 × 1	400 × 1	400 × 1
Layer1	Conv1d-16	Conv1d-32	Conv2d-32	Conv1d-32
Layer2	maxPool-16	maxPool-32	maxPool-32	maxPool-32
Layer3	Conv1d-32	Conv1d-64	Conv2d-64	Conv1d-5, Conv1d-5
				Conv1d-5, maxPool-5
Layer4	maxPool-32	maxPool-64	maxPool-64	maxPool-5, Conv1d-5
				Conv1d-5, Conv1d-5
Layer5	Conv1d-64	Conv1d-128	Conv2d-128	maxPool-5, maxPool-5
Layer6	Conv1d-64	maxPool-128	maxPool-128	Dense-100
Layer7	Dense-10	Dense-64	Dense-64	Dense-10
Layer8		Dense-10	Dense-10	
Layer9				

Where $Parameters_{conv}$ and $FLOP_{conv}$ represent the number of parameters and the computation of floating numbers in the convolutional layers, respectively. $Params_{sfc}$ and $FLOP_{sfc}$ represent the number of parameters and the computation of floating numbers in the fully connected layer respectively. H, W and C_{in} are the height, width and number of channels of the input feature map respectively. K_h and K_w represent the size of the convolution filter and C_{out} is the number of convolution filters. I is the dimensionality of the input and O is the dimensionality of the output.

4   Experiments and Analysis

The hardware and software environments are described in Table 2. To evaluate the calculation time, we used CPU for model training.

Table 2. The hardware and software environment.

Hardware environment	Software environment
CPU Intel Core i7-8700K,	Windows TensorFlow 2.0
3.7 GHz,	framework and Python
Six-core twelve threads	and Python programming
Programming language	language
Six-core twelve threads	
Memory 16 GB	

(1) Normal Signal   (2) Inner Fault Signal

(3) Ball Fault Signal   (4) Outer Fualt Signal

Fig. 3. Vibration signals.

4.1 Data Description

In order to evaluate the performance of the proposed model, data from the Case Western Reserve University Bearing Fault Data is used. Signals of four types can be seen in Fig. 4, including normal, inner race fault, ball fault, outer race fault. After the vibration signals are augmented and then datasets are composed of various signals. The dataset A, B, C and D contain four types of bearing health and the datasets are operated under 0, 1, 2 and 3 hp respectively. For each type of fault, there are three type of diameters, that is, 0.007, 0.014, and 0.021. Segment size of signal for 1D CNN is 400, so each segment contains 400 points. The details of vibration datasets are described in Table 3.

Table 3. Vibration datasets

Data sets	Load condition	Training samples	Validation samples	Test samples	Fault types	Fault diameters	Classification
		1650	192	240	Normal	0	0
		1650	192	240	Ball	0.007	1
		1650	192	240	Ball	0.014	2
A	0 hp	1650	192	240	Ball	0.021	3
B	1 hp	1650	192	240	Inner-race	0.007	4
C	2 hp	1650	192	240	Inner-race	0.014	5
D	3 hp	1650	192	240	Inner-race	0.021	6
		1650	192	240	Outer-race	0.007	7
		1650	192	240	Outer-race	0.014	8
		1650	192	240	Outer-race	0.021	9

4.2 Experimental Result and Analysis

As mentioned in Sect. 3.2, in order to demonstrate the effectiveness of our proposed method, we used the comparison models. There are x training data used in the experiment, x valid data, and x test data. First, the results of models of training results and valid data are shown in Fig. 3. As you can see in Fig. 3, you can see that models are resistant to overfitting and the performance is similar. Since Case Western Reserve University Bearing dataset is simple and well refined, all of models can have good performance. Also it can be seen in Table 4. all models same Precision, Recall, F1-Score but notice that the proposed model have most low Parameters, FLOPs, Training Time(s).

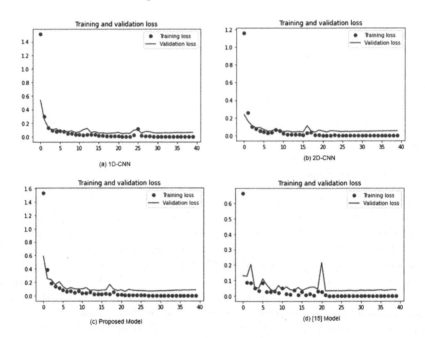

Fig. 4. Comparison training loss and validation loss of models

Table 4. Vibration datasets

Model	Parameters (KB)	FLOPs	Training time (s)	Precision	Recall	F1-score
Proposed model	49	9.08×10^5	124	0.99	0.99	0.99
1D-CNN	190	6.88×10^6	200	0.99	0.99	0.99
2D-CNN	198	1.35×10^7	332	0.99	0.99	0.99
Reference [14]	203	6.81×10^7	433	0.99	0.99	0.99

The classification result of the 10 class of samples is shown in the following confusion matrix in Fig. 5. The identification of each faulty label in each method is represented in the form of a confusion matrix. According to the results from Fig. 5, This represents the accumulated difference between all predictions and actual values in the course of learning. In general, the accuracy of the labels and actual labels predicted by all models has similar performance.

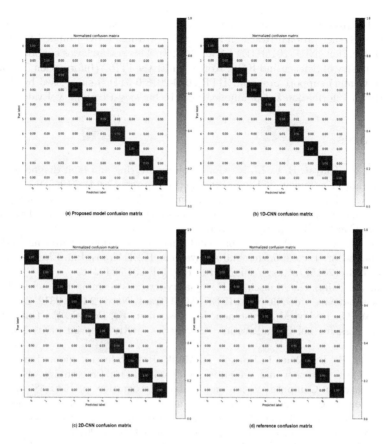

Fig. 5. The comparison results of fault identification using the proposed methods without data augmentation and with augmentation.

5   Conclusion

The proposed model is expected to be able to suggest a direction to solve the delay time problem in the actual process. In particular, the proposed model can significantly reduce the parameters and FLOPs compared to other models. As mentioned 3.1, we can be able to reduce FL nodes and then reduce a lot of parameters in the proposed model.

As a future study, However, there are a few more problems with FDD. Since in industry, process control always run anomaly, the available labels are limited and at the same time there is a challenge to create a model that is resistant to noise in the process. All models were able to achieve good performance in terms of performance, because the data was simple and well-purified, so additional experiments is to prove the performance of the model when complex data and noise-caught data.

Acknowledgments. This research was supported by Basic Science Research Program through the National Research Foundation of Korea (NRF) funded by the Ministry of Education (NRF-2016R1D1A1B03933828). This research was supported by the MSIT (Ministry of Science and ICT), Korea, under the ITRC (Information Technology Research Center) support program (IITP-2020-2018-0-01417) supervised by the IITP (Institute for Information & Communications Technology Planning & Evaluation).

References

1. Nandi, S., Toliyat, H.A., Li, X.: Condition monitoring and fault diagnosis of electrical motors–a review. IEEE Trans. Energy Convers. **20**(4), 719–729 (2005)
2. Liu, X., Choo, K.K.R., Deng, R.H., Lu, R., Weng, J.: Efficient and privacy-preserving outsourced calculation of rational numbers. IEEE Trans. Dependable Secure Comput. **15**(1), 27–39 (2016)
3. Qiao, W., Lu, D.: A survey on wind turbine condition monitoring and fault diagnosis-Part I: components and subsystems. IEEE Trans. Ind. Electron. **62**(10), 6536–6545 (2015). https://doi.org/10.1109/TIE.2015.2422112
4. Kim, J., Caire, G., Molisch, A.F.: Quality-aware streaming and scheduling for device-to-device video delivery. IEEE/ACM Trans. Netw. **24**(4), 2319–2331 (2015)
5. Ranjan, C., Reddy, M., Mustonen, M., Paynabar, K., Pourak, K.: Dataset: rare event classification in multivariate time series. arXiv preprint arXiv:1809.10717 (2018)
6. Girshick, R., Donahue, J., Darrell, T., Malik, J.: Rich feature hierarchies for accurate object detection and semantic segmentation. In: Proceedings of the IEEE Conference on Computer Vision and Pattern Recognition, pp. 580–587 (2014)
7. Tompson, J., Goroshin, R., Jain, A., LeCun, Y., Bregler, C.: Efficient object localization using convolutional networks. In: Proceedings of the IEEE Conference on Computer Vision and Pattern Recognition, pp. 648–656 (2015)
8. Gao, L., Guo, Z., Zhang, H., Xu, X., Shen, H.T.: Video captioning with attention-based LSTM and semantic consistency. IEEE Trans. Multimedia **19**(9), 2045–2055 (2017)
9. Takahashi, N., et al.: Deep convolutional neural networks and data augmentation for acoustic event detection. arXiv preprint arXiv:1604.07160 (2016)
10. Zhang, H., et al.: mixup: Beyond empirical risk minimization. arXiv preprint arXiv:1710.09412 (2017)
11. Zhao, R., Yan, R., Wang, J., Mao, K.: Learning to monitor machine health with convolutional bi-directional LSTM networks. Sensors **17**(2), 273 (2017)
12. Zhang, W., Peng, G., Li, C.: Bearings fault diagnosis based on convolutional neural networks with 2-D representation of vibration signals as input. In MATEC web of conferences, vol. 95, p. 13001. EDP Sciences (2017)
13. Basha, S.H.S., et al.: Impact of fully connected layers on performance of convolutional neural networks for image classification. Neurocomputing **378**, 112–119 (2020)
14. Zilong, Z., Wei, Q.: Intelligent fault diagnosis of rolling bearing using one-dimensional multi-scale deep convolutional neural network based health state classification. In: 2018 IEEE 15th International Conference on Networking, Sensing and Control (ICNSC). IEEE (2018)

Air Pollution Measurement Platform Based on LoRa and Blockchain for Industrial IoT Applications

Yohan Han and Jongpil Jeong$^{(\boxtimes)}$

Department of Smart Factory Convergence, Sungkyunkwan University, Suwon, Gyeonggi-do 16419, Republic of Korea
{coco0416, jpjeong}@skku.edu

Abstract. Air pollution poses risks such as global warming and ecosystem changes. Contaminants such as harmful gas, particulate matter and residual material generated in factories are the main causes of air pollution. Therefore, there is a need for strict control of contaminants occurring in the factory. In this paper, we propose a new platform using the Internet of Things (IoT) and blockchain to monitor the air quality without restriction of space. The proposed platform provides a service that collects data in real-time through the IoT sensor device based on LoRa (Long Range) based on the contaminant generated in the factory and transmits the encrypted data to the cloud through the transaction technology of the blockchain. Using this platform, air pollution generated in factories can be managed in real-time and data integrity can be preserved. Through this study, it is possible to measure and monitor contaminants generated in the air and use them as important data to improve and overcome environmental problems caused by air pollution.

Keywords: Air pollution · IoT · Blockchain · LoRa · Cloud computing

1 Introduction

Technological development and industrialization are leading to risks such as global warming and ecosystem changes. Air pollution is a contaminant exposed to air such as harmful gas, particulate matter, and residual material. In particular, contaminant generated in factories is a major cause of air pollution. Global warming is caused by contaminants such as carbon dioxide (CO_2), methane, ozone (O_3), and nitrogen dioxide (NO_2) reflecting and absorbing solar radiation, which increases the average surface temperature of the earth over a long period of time, which causes temperature rise and sea level rise, ocean acidification, hydrological cycle changes, etc. According to the World Health Organization's (WHO) 2014 report, air pollution is the leading cause of death worldwide. Particulate matter refers to a small substance of less than PM2.5 in air, which penetrates into the human lungs and circulatory system and is very harmful to the human body. Exposure to particulate matter can cause cardiovascular disease, lung disease, respiratory disease and various cancers [1].

© Springer Nature Switzerland AG 2020
O. Gervasi et al. (Eds.): ICCSA 2020, LNCS 12250, pp. 613–622, 2020.
https://doi.org/10.1007/978-3-030-58802-1_44

According to the Organization for Economic Cooperation and Development (OECD), the Republic of Korea's partition matter level is serious, which is three times the average of 38 countries, and the early death rate from air pollution is expected to increase by about three times in 50 years. Looking at the seasonal changes in domestic air pollution, the concentration of sulphur dioxide (SO_2), nitrogen dioxide (NO_2), and carbon monoxide (CO) in winter is high due to the increase in heating fuel consumption in winter. Particularly, particulate matter appears to be high in spring due to eolian dust. In addition, in China, smog occurs frequently in the winter when the amount of coal dependence is increased by about 70%, and this is a phenomenon in which air pollution concentration increases due to flying to the Republic of Korea in the west or northwest wind. The government of the Republic of Korea measures and manages the air pollution level at each industrial site through government agencies considering the seriousness of the contents. One of the methods is a measurement test through an external organ, and because the tester judges the measurement result, it causes side effects such as measurement timing, inaccuracy, deterioration, and manipulation. Due to this, it is difficult to obtain accurate inspection results, which makes it difficult to manage air pollution.

Therefore, in this paper, we propose a new platform using the Internet of Things (IoT) and blockchain to monitor the air quality without restriction of space. The proposed platform provides a service that collects contaminant generated in the factory in real-time through a LoRa (Long Range)-based IoT sensor device and transmits encrypted data to the cloud through the transaction technology of the blockchain. Using this platform, air pollution generated in factories can be managed in real-time and data integrity can be preserved. LoRa IoT network, an IoT-only network, is a low power wide area (LPWA) technology that helps objects communicate with each other and improves data processing efficiency and maintains data integrity through blockchain encryption technology and message distribution transmission protocol. It provides a sharing function, cloud provides various services such as Infrastructure as a Service (IaaS), Platform as a Service (PaaS), and Software as a Service (SaaS). LoRa IoT network provides differentiated network service suitable to meet various requirements in fusibility and expandability of IoT sensor.

The composition of this paper is as follows: Sect. 2 describes the relevant research. Section 3 introduces the designed architecture of the proposed IoT platform, and Sect. 4 conducts experiments on the proposed platform. Finally, Sect. 5 presents conclusions and future research directions.

2   Related Work

Air pollution through technology development and industrialization is causing serious environmental pollution worldwide [2]. Changes in the ecosystem due to global warming cause problems such as climate change, disasters, and various diseases, and the economic loss caused by these increases significantly each year [3]. In particular, particulate matter can penetrate human respiratory organs and circulatory systems and cause various diseases [4]. The contaminant is standardized according to the concentration in air. There are several methods to measure air quality, and IoT is very effective in measuring contaminant and concentration in air. IoT is growing as the most representative technology in industry 4.0 by connecting objects and providing data for interaction [5]. IoT provides a high level of extendability and flexibility by enabling communication between different objects [6]. The study of [7] proposes a system supporting IoT protocol for data collection and analysis. The study of [8] ensured stability by integrating a universal IoT framework for real-time analysis of IoT data in an uncontrolled environment. The study of [9] studied blockchain-based industrial IoT cyber physical system (CPS) to protect data collected from IoT. In addition, the study of [10] proposed four methods to enhance the security of the IoT sensor device, and the study of [11] presented the IoT blockchain platform for data integrity. Air pollution is measured through IoT sensor and collected data is transmitted to local server and cloud. Cloud is being used for network support for IoT technology [12]. IoT-based cloud big-data storage system is studied [13]. The next section introduces the designed architecture of the proposed IoT platform.

3 Air Pollution Measurement Platform

We present an air pollution measurement platform using IoT sensor device, LoRa wireless network, and blockchain. The proposed platform implements an optimized IoT network based on the LoRa wireless network, uses blockchain technology to transmit the integrity of the collected data, and transmits it to the cloud to provide air pollution measurement service and visualization. This section introduces the four components necessary for platform configuration. The architecture of the air pollution measurement platform is shown in Fig. 1.

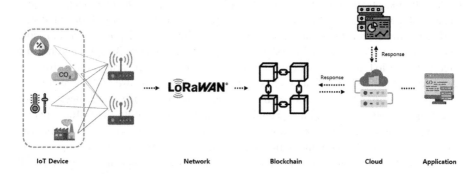

Fig. 1. Architecture of the air pollution measurement platform.

3.1 IoT Architecture

IoT is a device that can sense, store and transmit data over the Internet without human intervention. Data can be collected from the inside or outside of objects, locations and people. IoT realizes the integration of various manufacturing devices with sense, identification, process, and communication functions. First, data is collected through sensors and actuators, and then connected to a network that can be delivered to an IoT gateway. It then consists of an IoT data system that can convert the collected low data into digital signals, filter and pre-process it for analysis. The third layer is a Fog or Edge device responsible for data processing and data analysis, and this layer is where visualization and AI technology can be applied. Finally, it is transmitted to the cloud to store, manage, and analyze data. Figure 2 shows described in detail as four layers of the IoT architecture.

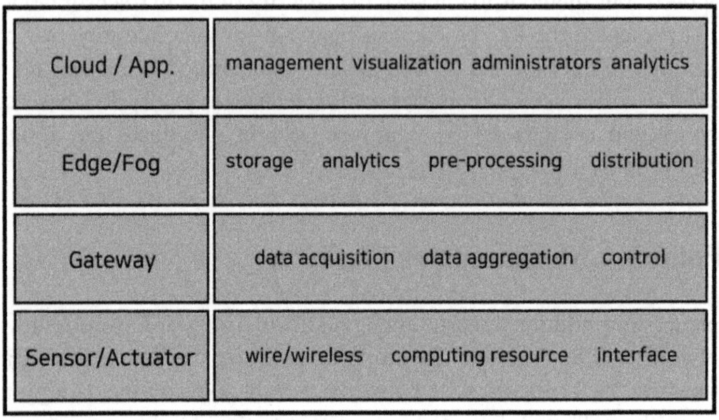

Cloud / App.	management visualization administrators analytics
Edge/Fog	storage analytics pre-processing distribution
Gateway	data acquisition data aggregation control
Sensor/Actuator	wire/wireless computing resource interface

Fig. 2. Four layers of IoT architecture.

3.2   LoRa Network

LoRa network, an IoT-only network, is a LPWA network that helps objects communicate with each other. Unlike a network that requires hypervelocity, broadband network equipment and communicates over 10 km with minimal power consumption, there is no need for a separate base station or repeater equipment. By applying the chip directly to the IoT device, data can be exchanged, and the infrastructure construction cost is lower than LTE or 5G, and it has high extendability. Because of these features, it is used as an IoT-only network and provides network services that meet various requirements such as availability, extendability, and security. With the LoRa network, the power consumption is low, allowing the device battery life to last for years. The LoRa technology standard implements IoT with low data transmission speed and machine-to-machine wireless communication with a battery that lasts more than 10 years in the range of up to 10 miles. Figure 3 is the structure of LoRa network.

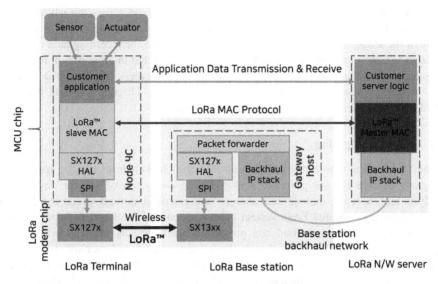

Fig. 3. Architecture of LoRa network

3.3 Blockchain Technology

The blockchain technology securely preserves the data collected through the IoT sensor and transmits it to the manager. Blockchain is a new technology that integrates decentralization, encryption, time stamp, and consensus algorithm, and provides functions of sustainability, compatibility, and extendability. The data collected through the IoT sensor consists of a distributed structure that is recorded in each block and stored as a private blockchain. In addition, it is possible to guarantee the integrity of data by granting authority to access a node to a specific party and directly comparing and verifying the data of distributed stored nodes. Figure 4 is the service function of the blockchain provided by the proposed platform.

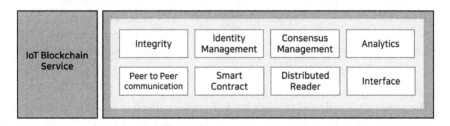

Fig. 4. IoT blockchain service

IoT blockchain service provides various services such as integrity, identity management, consensus management, analytics, peer-to-peer communication, smart contract, distributed leader, and interface. The distributed ledger is a consensus of replicated, shared, and synchronized digital data that spread across the whole block-chain network, where all participants with the network can have their own selfsame copy of the ledger. It also provides a secure storage space for recording data collected through IoT sensors. Any changes to the ledger are reflected in all copies in real-time. The leader is either authorized or not authorized, regardless of whether a specific person can execute the peer to verify the transaction. Through big-data analysis, blockchain provides efficient services for data storage.

3.4 Cloud Computing

Application utilizes the encrypted data through the blockchain to use the application program suitable for the purpose. Application is composed of storage device and analysis tool. Services include data analysis and extended storage. Cloud can process and analyze big-data that Edge system cannot support. If furnished with proper user application solutions, the cloud can provide business intelligence and presentation options that help humans interact with the system, control and monitor it and make informed decisions on the basis of reports, data viewed in real time. These features allow users to control and manage the system through mobile and web applications. Data transmitted through the application layer at the industrial site can be monitored by personnel in remote management and supervisory institutions.

4 Experiments

In this paper, an experiment was conducted to measure and monitor the air pollution condition to verify the proposed platform. In this experiment, Particulate Matter (PM 2.5), Ozone (O_3), Nitrogen Dioxide (NO_2), and Carbon Monoxide (CO) data were collected and the description of each gas is shown in Table 1.

Table 1. Introduction and description of detection gas.

Detection gas	Unit	Standard (avg.)	Measurement method
Particulate matter (PM 2.5)	$\mu g/m^3$	0–35 (24 h)	β-ray absorption method
Ozone (O_3)	ppm	0–0.090 (1 h)	U.V photometric method
Nitrogen dioxide (NO_2)	ppm	0–0.1 (1 h)	Chemiluminescent method
Carbon monoxide (CO)	ppm	0–9 (8 h)	Non-dispersive infrared method

The sensor data collected through the IoT sensor collection board is stored on the blockchain network via the LoRa network, encrypted and transmitted to Application & Cloud. Data sent to the cloud detects air pollution and abnormal data. IoT sensor collection board is easy to collect data in the field and is advantageous for single task execution. The power supply voltage of the IoT sensor collection board used in the experiment is 5 V, the maximum current consumption is 40 mA, and the general purpose input/output (GPIO) is 20. Figure 5 shows the IoT sensor collection board.

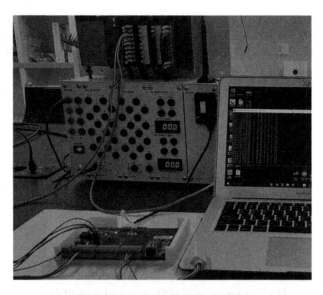

Fig. 5. IoT sensor collection board

Data collected through the sensor board is connected to the network through the LoRa module. When the network is established, data is transmitted to the Luniverse blockchain Platform. Encrypt the data by applying the measured data to the blockchain. Create a DApp and store the measured data in the DApp. Then, apply the created DApp to the side chain and connect it with the main chain. When a transaction occurs, it is compensated with a cryptocurrency created by itself. Lastly, the encrypted data is transmitted to the Amazon Web Services (AWS) cloud, and the data analysis and visualization application is performed. The aforementioned four gases are the result of the measurement in Seoul from March 1 to 10, 2020 and are as follows.

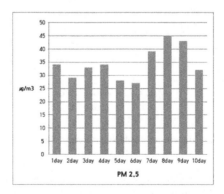

Fig. 6. Concentration of PM 2.5 measured over 10 days

Figure 6 is the result for Particulate Matter (PM 2.5). The normal standard of PM 2.5 is 0–35 μg/m^3 on average for 24 h and 25 μg/m^3 on average for 10 days. However, the values on the 8th and 9th days were measured higher than the normal standard.

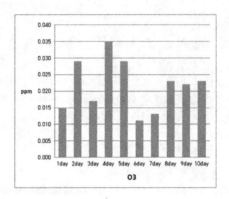

Fig. 7. Concentration of O$_3$ measured over 10 days

Figure 7 is the result for Ozone (O$_3$). The normal standard of O$_3$ is 0–0.090 ppm for 1 h average and 0.025 ppm for 10 days average. However, the values for days 2, 4, and 5 were relatively high, and days 6 and 7 were relatively low.

Figure 8 is the result for Nitrogen Dioxide (NO$_2$). The normal standard for NO$_2$ is 0 to 0.1 ppm for an hour, and 0.029 ppm for 1 h average of 10 days. The values on days 2, 4, and 5 were relatively low. I guess this has to do with the weather.

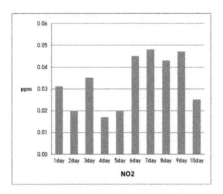

Fig. 8. Concentration of NO$_2$ measured over 10 days

Figure 9 is the result for Carbon Monoxide (CO). The normal standard of CO is 0–9 ppm for 8 h, and 0.518 ppm for 10 days. Most of the gas was in the normal range. The measurement results may differ depending on the season and location, and different results may be obtained depending on the measurement method.

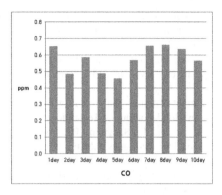

Fig. 9. Concentration of CO measured over 10 days

5 Conclusion

Contaminants such as harmful gas, particulate matter and residual material generated in factories are the main causes of air pollution. We deviated from the traditional measurement methods mentioned above and utilized IoT for strict control and management of data. We proposed a new platform using Internet of Things (IoT) and Blockchain and provides services to collect data in real time through IoT sensor devices based on LoRa (Long Range) and transmit encrypted data to the cloud through the Blockchain's transaction technology. It is expected that this study will contribute slightly to overcoming environmental problems caused by air pollution. Future research will monitor the runoff and concentration of chemical substances in the factory based on the proposed platform, and will study an intelligent air cleaning system that can be ventilated automatically when a failure indication occurs. In the future, we will continue to conduct various research activities in this field to collect, process, and analyze various data through IoT in smart factory.

References

1. Chang, S.: A mobile application for fine dust monitoring system. In: IEEE International Conference on Mobile Data Management, pp. 336–339 (2017)
2. Yohan, H.: A novel architecture of air pollution measurement platform using 5G and blockchain for industrial IoT application. Procedia Comput. Sci. **155**, 728–733 (2019)
3. Seungho, K.: Development of an IoT-based atmospheric environment monitoring system. In: International Conference on Information and Communication Technology Convergence, pp. 861–863 (2017)
4. Fong, A.: An automated solution for disease control and management to combat the health impact of indoor air pollution. In: IEEE Conference on Industrial Electronics and Applications, pp. 472–476 (2012)
5. Kortuem, G.: Smart objects as building blocks for the Internet of things. IEEE Internet Comput. **14**(1), 44–51 (2012)

6. Fazio, M.: Heterogeneous sensors become homogeneous things in smart cities. In: Sixth International Conference on Innovative Mobile and Internet Services in Ubiquitous Computing, pp. 775–780 (2012)
7. Lohokare, J.: An IoT ecosystem for the implementation of scalable wireless home automation systems at smart city level. In: IEEE Region 10 Conference, pp. 1503–1508 (2017)
8. Hong, H.: Supporting internet-of-things analytics in a fog computing platform. In: IEEE International Conference on Cloud Computing Technology and Science, pp. 138–145 (2017)
9. Jang, S.-H., Guejong, J., Jeong, J., Sangmin, B.: Fog computing architecture based blockchain for industrial IoT. In: Rodrigues, J.M.F., et al. (eds.) ICCS 2019. LNCS, vol. 11538, pp. 593–606. Springer, Cham (2019). https://doi.org/10.1007/978-3-030-22744-9_46
10. Singh, M.: Blockchain: a game changer for securing IoT data. In: IEEE 4th World Forum on Internet of Things, pp. 51–55 (2018)
11. Hang, L.: Design and implementation of an integrated IoT blockchain platform for sensing data integrity. Sensors 19(10), 1–26 (2019)
12. Daejun, A.: Big-data search engine based cloud computing network architecture in smart factory environment. In: International Conference on Intelligent Autonomous Systems (2019)
13. Gu, S.: IoT-based big data storage systems in cloud computing: perspectives and challenges. IEEE Internet Things J. 4(1), 75–87 (2017)

Real-Time Inspection of Multi-sided Surface Defects Based on PANet Model

Yohan Han and Jongpil Jeong[✉]

Department of Smart Factory Convergence, Sungkyunkwan University, Suwon,
Gyeonggi-do 16419, Republic of Korea
{coco0416, jpjeong}@skku.edu

Abstract. Quality of products is the most important factor in manufacturing. Machine vision is a technique that mainly performs human cognitive judgment in the industrial field or performs a task that is generally difficult for a human. However the detection of traditional methods of scanning with human eyes has many difficulties due to repetitive tasks. Recently, an artificial intelligence machine vision has been studied to improve these problems. Using the vision inspection system, it is possible to collect information such as the number of products, defect detection, and types without human intervention, which maximizes the operation-al efficiency of a company such as productivity improvement, quality improvement, and cost reduction. Most of the vision inspection systems currently in use are single-sided images, which collect and inspect one image of the product. However, in the actual manufacturing industry, products that are valid for single-sided image inspection are limited to some product groups, and most require multi-sided image inspection. In addition, the inspection system used in the field must meet the production speed required by the actual manufacturing site and inspect the defects of the product. In this paper, we propose a deep neural network-based vision inspection system that satisfies the multi-sided image inspection and fast production speed of products. By implementing seven cameras and optical technology, multi-sided images of the product are collected simultaneously, and a defect in the product can be quickly detected in real time using a PANet (Path Aggregation Network) model. Through the proposed system, it is possible to inspect product defects at the level required at the manufacturing site, and the information obtained in the inspection process will be used as a very important data to evaluate and improve product quality.

Keywords: AI · Deep learning · Machine vision · Defect inspection · PANet

1 Introduction

With the advent of Industry 4.0, the development of IT technology has brought new changes to the manufacturing industry. The smart factory is an intelligent factory that maximizes the operational efficiency of companies such as productivity improvement, quality improvement, and cost reduction by applying Information and Communication Technology (ICT) to all production processes from product planning to sales. The smart factory is pursuing multi-volume, small-scale production method that meets

O. Gervasi et al. (Eds.): ICCSA 2020, LNCS 12250, pp. 623–633, 2020.
https://doi.org/10.1007/978-3-030-58802-1_45

various requirements of customers and rapidly produces, away from the existing mass production method. It is meaningful to improve production efficiency for products by real-time identification.

In particular, quality is a very important factor in manufacturing. Product quality has a significant impact on the company's growth and securing market competitiveness, and is considered as the first priority in implementing a smart factory. As the manufacturing environment changes, the production system to satisfy this needs to change. Accordingly, many studies are being conducted to improve the quality, which is representative of product defect inspection. Traditionally, product defects were visually inspected by the operator. However, it is difficult to detect defects due to reduced productivity and poor accuracy due to repetitive work. Recently, artificial intelligence (AI) testing systems have been studied to improve these problems. The artificial intelligence inspection system refers to the detection of product defects by collecting, processing, and analyzing product images by replacing the role of the operator with a vision camera and artificial intelligence. By using this method, it is possible to improve productivity and increase detection accuracy and reduce the operating cost of the company.

Most machine vision currently in use collects and inspects a single image of a product by single-sided image. However, in the real manufacturing industry, products that are valid for single-sided inspection are limited to some product groups such as printed circuit board (PCB), semiconductor, display and most of them want multi-sided inspection. Multi-sided inspection requires a high level of hardware and software technology and in particular, the product must be inspected while meeting the production speed required by the actual production site.

In this paper, we propose a system that satisfies the product's multi-sided inspection and fast production speed. By implementing 7 cameras and optical technology, multi-sided images of the product are collected at the same time. In addition, defects of products can be accurately inspected in real-time by using a PANet (Path Aggregation Network). Through the data training model, it is possible to inspect multi-sided defects of products with minimum time and improve the quality of multi-sided products. We classified 3,024 defect databases into 4 defect types and trained a total of 16,000 times. As a result, 98.12% mAP, 98.00% Recall and 98.06% F1 Score were achieved. Through this study, information such as product type, defect location and size can be checked and this can be used as a very important data for evaluating and improving the quality of production products.

The composition of this paper is as follows. Section 2 describes related work. Section 3 introduces the components of the proposed inspection system and Sect. 3.2 describes the PANet model used for data analysis. Section 4 conducts experiments on the proposed system. Finally, Sect. 5 presents conclusion and presents future research directions.

2 Related Work

A machine vision system is a system that inspects products produced at a manufacturing site through a camera [1]. The machine vision enables the number of products, product specs and perfect inspection without human intervention, which maximizes the operational efficiency of the enterprise, including productivity improvement, quality improvement and cost reduction [2]. Traditional machine vision uses a rule-based machine learning algorithm. These algorithms require manual design of product feature extraction and take a lot of time [3]. Due to the development of technology, artificial intelligence has been introduced, attracting attention in many fields. Artificial intelligence is limited because it mimics the structure of a human brain's neural network, but thinking and judgment are possible.

In general, artificial neural networks are implemented as Deep Neural Network (DNN) [4]. Convolution Neural Network (CNN) is the most powerful and effective DNN for recognizing image objects [5]. CNN's deep multi-layers architecture can extract more powerful features than manually built functions and all features are automatically extracted from training data using a back-propagation algorithm [6]. The convolution network provides an end-to-end solution ranging from low defect images to predictions, alleviating the requirement to manually extract suitable features [7]. In addition, the convolutional detection network allows the object to be detected in a few milliseconds using the exact location and size information of the object [8]. However, CNN has a disadvantage that processing speed is relatively slow.

With the advent of PANet, which recently improved the CNN, it is possible to perform defect inspection quickly and accurately. The PANet uses the existing pyramid network, Feature Pyramid Networks (FPN), as a backbone to add an additional three-stage model to improve accuracy [9]. The study of [10] conducted real-time steel strip defect inspection through the improved YOLO detection network. With the advent of the improved deep learning model, the machine vision system is continuously evolving as the processing speed increases and the accuracy increases [11]. Thanks to advances in technology that meet the speed of production of real products, machine vision is available in almost all production facilities. The study of [12] suggested a solution that can easily detect various defects of products through one or more cameras and machine vision software. The study of [13] proposed a study that inspects the number of holes in the PCB through the machine vision system. According to this study, accuracy of more than 95% can be guaranteed, and the study of [14] inspected the odd number defects of the PCB through various image processing technologies such as Otsu Thresholding, Canny Edge Detection, Morphological Process and Hough Circle Transform. [15] studied defects in conveyor belt. In addition, [16] studied cracks and defects occurring in railways.

In this paper, we propose a system that satisfies the multi-faceted inspection and fast production speed of products. The next section describes the Inspection System for PANet Model.

3 Inspection System for PANet Model

3.1 Components of the Inspection System

The components and considerations for designing and implementing the AI vision inspection system are as follows [17].

- Camera: Resolution, Frames Per Second (FPS), Interface, Type, Shutter, Mount
- Lens: Image Size, Focal Length, Field of View (FoV), Working Distance (WD)
- Illumination: Light source types, Intensity, Number of light sources and Angles
- Software: Image acquisition, Image pre-processing, Image processing, Analytics

The inspection system consists of product recognition device, image acquisition device, image processing device and product classification device. Product recognition devices mainly consist of sensors, triggers, etc., and image acquisition devices consist of cameras, lenses, lighting and industrial PC (IPC). The collected images are processed and analyzed through the PANet model at the image processing unit stage, and finally, the product classification unit stage classifies the products according to the results.

Figure 1 shows the structural diagram of an image acquisition device that includes 7 cameras, and each camera has an angle of 60°. When the product moves on the conveyor belt, the optical sensor recognizes the product and the camera and illumination are activated through hardware trigger and ethernet to capture the product image. The collected images are processed through the deep learning model and classify products according to the analysis results.

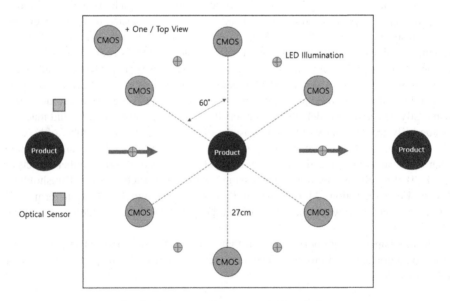

Fig. 1. Structure of image acquisition device.

(a) **Product Recognition Device**

The product recognition device is used to detect a product produced through a conveyor belt and trigger a camera module so that the camera can be photographed at a predetermined time and location. The proposed system uses a radar sensor to detect the product because it is suitable for accuracy and quick response to product detection. The signal detected by the radar sensor triggers the camera and lights for image acquisition. Since the product produced on the conveyor belt is a moving subject, images are collected in a moving state rather than in a stationary state. Therefore, it is a trigger signal that calculates the production speed of a product and gives a signal so that the camera can be photographed at a predetermined time and location.

The trigger is mainly used when a user shoots an image in an aperiodic manner such as a constant frame rate. The trigger mode can operate in two ways: hardware trigger and software trigger. A hardware trigger is an electrical signal input and acts as a trigger, and a software trigger acts as a trigger by instruction. Hardware triggers are ideal for ultra-precise applications that are not suitable for software triggers inherent latency, so it is common to apply hardware triggers to vision inspection systems.

(b) **Image Acquisition Device**

The image acquisition device is a process of collecting an image of an inspection product through an optical system, and is mainly composed of a camera, a lens, lighting, and IPC. A total of seven complementary metal-oxide semiconductor (CMOS) cameras are used, which consist of one Top View and six Around Views. Based on the depth of focus (DoF) of the product, the number of cameras that do not generate image blind spots across the product is 6 and the angle of each camera is 60°. Also, when calculating the distance from the product, a focal length of 27 cm was set.

For accurate and fast inspection, an image-taking camera is very important. Depending on the type of product and production speed, appropriate cameras and lenses are required. Therefore, based on the collected information, the necessary components for selecting cameras and lights are obtained. The components required for camera and lighting selection are as follows.

- Camera: Sensors, Effective Pixels, Frame Rate, Color, Shutter, Interface
- Lens: Imager Size, Focal Length, Aperture Range, Mount

The most important thing in a camera is an image sensor. The image sensor works in conjunction with the lens to receive light data. The lens also accepts light data through a focus ring that focuses and an iris that controls the amount of light. Therefore, it is essential to consider Focal Length (FL), Frames Per Second (FPS), Field of View (FoV), and Working Distance (WD) to select cameras and lenses.

Field of View (FoV) refers to the horizontal *(H)* or vertical *(V)* area that can be obtained with the configured optical system. The formula is as follows.

- $FoV\,(H)\,or\,(V) = \frac{Sensor\,Size\,(H)\,or\,(V)}{Magnification}$
- $Magnification = \frac{Sensor\,Size\,(H)\,or\,(V)}{FoV\,(H)\,or\,(V)}$

The light source is also very important to collect quality images from the product. This is because, in the process of illuminating the product through lighting, if the product has a shadow, the shaded part cannot be inspected for defects. Therefore, when the product to be inspected is selected, the distance and angle between the camera and the light source should be set through experiments. Whether it is to reflect light directly to an object, indirectly, or whether to use coaxial, transmissive, or backlit lighting at a certain angle, and at what angle, and which color of lighting is used, it greatly affects the inspection results. Therefore, when selecting a light source, it is most important to find the optimal condition after sufficiently experimenting with various conditions.

(c) **Image Processing Device**

Through the image processing and analysis process collected through the image acquisition device, it is determined as a normal product or a defective product. Typically, a camera manufacturer provides a library of cameras. This is called software development kit (SDK), and the most commonly used SDK compilers and languages are Visual Studio and C/C#.

(d) **Product classification Device**

The product classification device classifies the product as a normal product or a defective product based on the results obtained through the image processing device. The image detected through inspection sends a signal to the actuator according to the result, and the actuator is located in the result part of the inspection system and operates as a motor at the center point of the conveyor belt. The result value received through inspection is transferred to the actuator, so that the normal product flows as it is, and the defective product is classified as a separate left by the actuator to reach the defective parts.

3.2   Inspection System for PANet Model

Recently, due to the development of artificial intelligence (AI) technology, image processing technology through machine learning has been studied a lot. PANet (Path Aggregation Network) is a model optimized for real-time image recognition. PANet is an algorithm that uses the existing pyramid network, FPN as a backbone and adds an additional three-level model. In general, the more low-level features that are first extracted, the greater the distance to the output, the result is not reflected sufficiently in the result due to the long distance. To compensate for this, a method in which the extracted features are reflected in the result is introduced. Figure 2 shows the structure of a typical PANet [18].

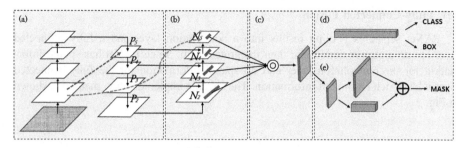

Fig. 2. Architecture of PANet detection network [18]

(a) FPN Backbone

Feature Pyramid Networks (FPN) Backbone is an existing pyramid type network. Because the low-level layer does not contribute much to the final prediction, the prediction result is incorrect, so each black layer of this pyramid is like a layer in the structure diagram, but it is actually composed of ResNet-50. To reach the top level, it passes a very large number of layers, and as a result, the Propagate does not work smoothly.

(b) Bottom-up Path Augmentation

PANet constructs a new Nn pyramid of simple convolution layers. The new pyramid only takes one shortcut and a few convolution layers, like the green dotted line, in order for the low-level layer to reach the high-level layer. This means that smooth information flow is possible compared to the existing Backbone Model. Although all Nn layers have different resolutions, they have the same 256 filters and are implemented by Pn and Concatenate the result of down sampling $Nn-1$ with 3×3 Convolution operation of Stride 2.

(c) Adaptive Feature Pooling

The region of interest is extracted for each Nn through the ROI Align technique. Since the feature map has a difference in resolution of the final output, if you set the ROI with Naive, there may be a problem of inconsistent with the exact pixel corresponding to the output. The technique to correct this is ROI Align. Then, ROI of all Nn layers is pooled element-wise.

(d) Box Branch

If you want to simply classify the instances into boxes, you can connect the multi-sided pooling results to the Fully-connected Layer as shown in the above structure diagram, and apply the following method to perform segmentation.

(e) **Fully-Connected Fusion**

PANet separates pooling results into a convolution layer and a fully-connected layer for accurate prediction and then integrates them. Since PANet has spatial information for the convolution layer and no spatial information for the fully-connected layer it has a rich amount of information. The specific implementation method is shown in Fig. 3.

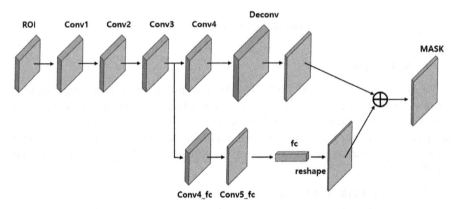

Fig. 3. Mask prediction branch with fully-connected fusion [18]

4   Experiments

In this paper, we conducted an experiment on a cosmetic case produced in a real factory to examine defects in the product. Cosmetic cases of PE, PP and ABS material produce various effects from injection, painting, and assembly processes such as scratches, scars, pollution, unassembled. The defect image is shown in Fig. 4. These defects not only affect the appearance of the product, but also the durability of the product. Therefore, it is very important to improve production quality by inspecting defects in products.

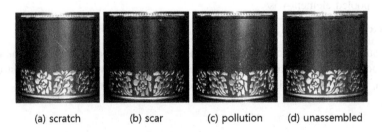

(a) scratch   (b) scar   (c) pollution   (d) unassembled

Fig. 4. Several types of surface defects on cosmetic case

4.1   Defect Database

We collect the defect database of products in the assembly process, which is the final stage of product production. In this paper, a total of four types of defect images were collected. Each image is cropped to 608 * 608 before being transmitted over Ethernet. The defect data base collected for the experiment has 3,024 images of 4 types. Details of the data set are given in Table 1. Bulleted lists may be included and should look like this:

Table 1. Dataset of cosmetic case surface defect images

	Scratch	Scar	Pollution	Unassembled	Total 2
Training	779	642	481	322	2224
Test	200	200	200	200	800
Total 1	979	842	681	522	3024

4.2   Training

The proposed system consists of seven complementary metal oxide semiconductor (CMOS) cameras, shadow-less diffused ring lights, optical sensor, hardware trigger and electric precipitator to acquire multi-sided image of the product. In addition, PANet algorithms were training from Window10 pro equipped with i7-9700F, DDR4-32 GB and GTX 2080 Ti, and four types of defect database were training a total of 16,000 times. During the training process, batch 64, resolution 608 * 608, learning rate 0.00261 and activation function Leaky ReLU. The time taken to detect defects in 800 test images was 8 s, mAP 98.12%, recall 98.00% and F1 score 98.06%.

4.3   Real-Time Analysis

The time to inference the multi-sided image of the product through the proposed system is 0.224 s on average and the time to inspect per image is only 0.032 s on average. The production speed at the actual production site is 0.09 m/s and the distance of the camera is 22–35 cm. In order to meet the production speed required at the production site, the speed of 32–45 FPS must be guaranteed. As a result of analysis using the PANet algorithm proposed in this paper, the inspection speed required at the production site was fully satisfied by achieving a speed of 35 FPS. Finally, normal and defective products were classified through separate classifiers. The detection details are shown in Table 2, and the detection results are shown in Fig. 5.

(a) scratch   (b) scar   (c) pollution   (d) unassembled

Fig. 5. Detection results of 4 types of surface defects on cosmetic cases

Table 2. Detection results (mAP & recall)

	Scratch	Scar	Pollution	Unassembled	Average
mAP	98.47%	97.03%	97.01%	100.00%	98.13%
Recall	97.00%	98.00%	97.51%	99.55%	98.02%

5   Conclusion

We have established a system that meets multi-sided inspection of products and fast
production speed. Defects were inspected for four types that occurred during the
production of cosmetic cases and the results show that the proposed system achieves
98.12% mAP, 98.00% Recall and 98.06% F1 score. Using a PANet defects in products
can be inspected in real time and information such as product type, defect location and
size can be checked, which can be used as a very important data to evaluate and
improve the quality of production products. Through the proposed system, defect
inspection is possible in the environment required by the actual manufacturing site, the
more defect types and sample data are obtained, the better the results will be.

References

1. Nashat, S.: Machine vision for crack inspection of biscuits featuring pyramid detection scheme. J. Food Eng. **120**, 233–247 (2014)
2. Khude, P.: Object detection, tracking and counting using enhanced BMA on static background videos. In: 2013 IEEE International Conference on Computational Intelligence and Computing Research (2013)
3. LeCun, Y.: Deep learning. Nature **521**, 436–444 (2015)
4. Demuth, H.: Neural Network Design. Martin Hagan (2014)
5. Krizhevsky, A.: ImageNet classification with deep convolutional neural networks. In: 2012 Advances in Neural Information Processing Systems (2012)
6. Bengio, Y.: Representation learning: a review and new perspectives. IEEE Trans. Pattern Anal. Mach. Intell. **35**(8), 1798–1828 (2013)
7. Sermanet, P.: Overfeat: integrated recognition, localization and detection using convolutional networks. 2013 arXiv preprint arXiv:1312.6229 (2013)
8. Redmon, J.: You only look once: unified, real-time object detection. In: 2016 IEEE Conference on Computer Vision and Pattern Recognition (CVPR), pp. 779–788 (2016)
9. Liu, S.: Path aggregation network for instance segmentation. In: 2018 IEEE/CVF Conference on Computer Vision and Pattern Recognition, no. 116, pp. 8759–8768 (2018)
10. Li, J.: Real-time detection of steel strip surface defects based on improved YOLO detection network. IFAC-Papers OnLine **51**(21), 76–81 (2018)
11. Baygin, M.: A new image stitching approach for resolution enhancement in camera arrays. In: 2015 9th International Conference on Electrical and Electronics Engineering (ELECO), pp. 1186–1190 (2015)
12. Yaman, O.: A new approach based on image processing for detection of wear of guide-rail surface in elevator systems. Int. J. Appl. Math. Electron. Comput. **4**, 296–300 (2016)
13. Wang, W.: A machine vision based automatic optical inspection system for measuring drilling quality of printed circuit boards. IEEE Access **5**, 10817–10833 (2017)
14. Baygin, M.: Machine vision based defect detection approach using image processing. In: 2017 International Artificial Intelligence and Data Processing Symposium (2017)
15. Yang, Y.: On-line conveyor belts inspection based on machine vision. Optik-Int. J. Light Electron Opt. **125**(19), 5803–5807 (2014)
16. Yaman, O.: PSO based diagnosis approach for surface and components faults in railways. Int. J. Comput. Sci. Softw. Eng. (IJCSSE) **5**(5), 89–96 (2016)
17. Bahaghighat, M.: Designing quality control system based on vision inspection in pharmaceutical product lines. In: 2018 International Conference on Computing, Mathematics and Engineering Technologies (2018)
18. Lie, S.: Path aggregation network for instance segmentation. In: 2018 IEEE/CVF Conference on Computer Vision and Pattern Recognition, no. 116, pp. 8759–8768 (2018)

Estimation of Greenhouse Gas Emissions in Cement Manufacturing Process Through Blockchain and SSL Based IoT Data Analysis

Byeongseop Kim, Myungsoo Kim, and Jongpil Jeong$^{(\boxtimes)}$

Department of Smart Factory Convergence, SungKyunKwan University, Suwon, Gyeonggi-do 16419, Republic of Korea
{for98ever, sioals, jpjeong}@skku.edu

Abstract. Recently, the Internet of Things (IoT) system, which supports human activities based on various types of real data, has attracted attention in various fields. However, the behavior of the system is determined based on the actual data, so if an attacker changes the data, a critical problem can occur on the system. Therefore, to ensure the reliability of real data, many researchers have studied data management platforms that use security management technology. In the proposed platform, the pre-manufacturing phase of the cement manufacturing process attempted to ensure the reliability of the generated data by having data produced using blockchain techniques through the distributed ledger of blockchain. In the manufacturing phase, Secure Socket Layer (SSL), also known as digital certificates, is also used to establish encrypted connections between the browser or user's computer and the server or website. SSL connections protect sensitive data exchanged in each session from interference from unauthorized users. Design a management platform that can verify the integrity of stored data over proposed SSL and block chain. Testers collected in real time from the system provide integrity for the calculation of carbon emissions. You will have the opportunity to drastically reduce the manpower and time funds required for the current first and second stages of verification.

Keywords: Internet of Things (IoT) system · Blockchain · SSL · Greenhouse gas emissions

1 Introduction

Recently, various types of IoT systems have been developed to support human activities in various fields. For example, to support physical distribution systems, existing IoT systems attempt to deploy GPS devices to continuously track the location information of the transport vehicle to avoid production location camouflage [1].

These IoT systems can generate real data and analyze and achieve data in an appropriate manner. However, the behavior of the system is determined based on the actual data, so if the data cannot be reliably stable, the system can have a critical problem. In particular, many devices such as GPS and smartphones that generate real data may not have sufficient functionality for security measures, so the generated data is prone to tamper. In a physical distribution system, location information through

© Springer Nature Switzerland AG 2020
O. Gervasi et al. (Eds.): ICCSA 2020, LNCS 12250, pp. 634–645, 2020.
https://doi.org/10.1007/978-3-030-58802-1_46

manipulation of GPS data in transport vehicles provides inaccurate data to intermediate traders or end consumers, such as distance to the country of origin and to the country destination through modulation or modification of the country of origin invoice.

To ensure the reliability of real data, many researchers have studied data management platforms that utilize block chain technology [2–4]. A block chain is a highly available distributed system consisting only of user terminals and can monitor data update procedures between terminals to ensure the integrity of records. For IoT systems, the block chain is used as a distributed database to ensure the integrity of stored data. Therefore, this study suggests a platform for calculating carbon emissions in cement manufacturing process through real-time data management by establishing encrypted connections using block chains and Secure Socket Layer (SSL) authentication, also known as digital certificates at the manufacturing stage, to provide stable IoT services by ensuring actual data integrity and reliability during the pre-manufacturing stage [5].

The proposed platform verifies the integrity of the titer modulation by applying the distributed ledger function of the block chain at the pre-manufacture stage, standard security technology for building encrypted links at the manufacturing stage, and establishing a secure connection between the web server and the browser. Design a platform for a s. real-time data collection system called 'SSL Handshake' that end users cannot see to assess the validity of the proposed platform. The design platform measures the data collected at each data generation point and calculates carbon emissions based on it. Data with such real-time and integrity can be effectively verified for calculating greenhouse gas emissions.

2   Related Work

2.1   Energy Management System

Energy Management System (EMS) is defined as an integrated energy solution for visualizing and optimizing energy flow and use of energy for commercial buildings, workplaces (factories), housing, social infrastructure (power networks, transportation networks, etc.) using ICT technology and control technology [6, 7]. EMS is classified as HEMS (Home EMS) for residential use, Building EMS for building use, Factory EMS for factory use, and CEMS (City/Community) for regional use, and has monitoring of energy flows such as gas, power, and control of facilities and equipment. In Korea, the FEMS Installation Verification Criteria Guide is provided by the Korea Energy Management Corporation by applying it to factories through the IT-based Energy Service Company (ESCO) pilot project promoted by the Ministry of Industry in 2011 [8]. In particular, FEMS is a factory energy management system that monitors and controls the energy supply and use of energy and operation of power distribution, air conditioning, lighting, etc. as well as production line facilities in the plant [9]. These systems include monitoring functions that collect and show values from facilities, as well as process management, performance management, control, analysis functions and related databases that manage the facilities, existing Enterprise Resource Program (ERP) and linkage with the Manufacturing Execution System (MES). The energy management system should be able to propose production process methods and energy policies that reduce energy by analyzing energy usage using the data collected. In particular, it is starting to introduce an active ICT-based energy management system that provides the ultimate goal of optimal energy patterns by combining IoT technology, big data, and smart factory [10, 11].

2.2 Greenhouse Gas Generation in Cement Manufacturing Process

Direct emission factors related to greenhouse gas generation in the cement manufacturing process include emissions from fixed combustion facilities such as boilers, emissions from the manufacturing process, combustion of transportation means for transportation, use of refrigerant for each facility, and emission of omission due to substation of fire extinguishing facilities. etc. [12]. The indirect emission factors can also be defined as the purchase of electricity, and the distinction between the manufacturing process operating boundaries for direct and indirect emissions of the business site in relation to the calculation can be defined as shown in Fig. 1.

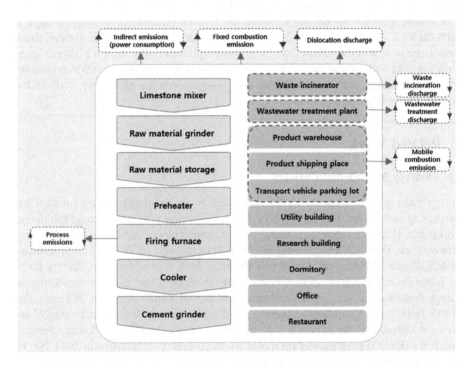

Fig. 1. Boundaries for the calculation of greenhouse gas emissions at cement sites

2.3 Block Chain Technology

A block chain is a distributed data management platform originally proposed for cryptocurrency. When a call is exchanged between users, the history is registered in a "block," a unit of data structure. Blocks are continuously generated to form a one-way list of links that can detect unauthorized data changes. Each block has a hash value calculated by entering the contents of the previous block into a prescribed one-way hash function. When data in a particular block is modulated, the hash value of the block differs from the hash value of the next block, making it easy to detect data modulation and ensure the integrity of the recorded data.

So far, a data management system utilizing block chain technology has been proposed to support various IoT systems [1, 2, 13–15]. Such research has used block chain technology to establish a stable data management system to ensure the integrity of stored data.

However, if the data were modulated before it was stored in a block chain, the accuracy of the data cannot be guaranteed. Data modulation can cause some problems in the IoT service. For example, in a raw material delivery system, the location information of the country of origin and the transport zone can be modulated by malicious users to disguise the production zone, which can cause serious problems in calculating carbon emissions.

3 Data Management Platform for Estimation of Greenhouse Gas Emissions

In this study, we want to establish a data management platform that can store various types of data generated through IoT service delivery procedures. Update records, as well as the latest data, are recorded by SSL and blockchain on the assumed data management platform.

3.1 Pre-manufacturing Process

Figure 2 shows an overview of external data management systems using blockchain. As illustrated in this drawing, various types of IoT data, such as location information, are transmitted from IoT devices such as GPS sensors, and the management function of each data is implemented as an external smart contract on the block chain. Similar to the functional entity supported by the new block chain appearing in external smart contracts and automatically performs the programmed procedure when a request is received from a user or other smart contract [16, 17]. Smart contract execution records are recorded in the block chain, allowing users to access update records as well as the latest values of each data. In smart contracts, templates for data structures are defined and users invoke the ability to update data structures when registering data. As a result, the data is recorded as transactions in the block chain as illustrated in Fig. 2.

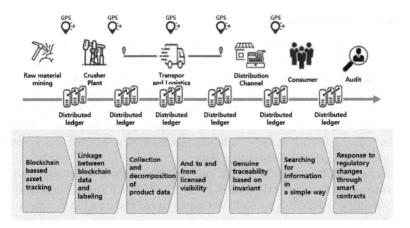

Fig. 2. Tracking raw material information using blockchain

It can minimize problems such as data modulation that can occur during the distribution process of raw materials, save time and cost of identifying causes when problems arise, and raw material mining and processing companies enter key information into the blockchain network along with transaction details. Distributors can check the source and information of raw materials in real time and identify customer evaluations and preferences. In addition, the consumer's headquarters (supervisor) can check compliance with regulations across the supply chain, generate certification and audit records for supply chain management, and in the process, all raw material mining companies, processing companies, logistics warehouses, distributors and regulators will be participants in the distribution process, and consumers can access the blockchain network of mobile application servers to check necessary information.

3.2   Manufacturing Process

The facility energy monitoring system proposed in Fig. 3 is a schematic diagram of the hierarchy with the systems associated with other production facilities. IoT devices will be installed in each of the plant's corresponding facilities and the accumulated instructions that are inspected through the gateway will be transmitted wirelessly to the server. At this time, PLC, monitoring control, and data collection system (SCADA) are operating systems that control sensors. The Energy Management System (EMS) is a system that monitors and controls energy use and operation status, and has a system with monitoring and analysis functions proposed in this paper, such as control functions, process management, and performance management. The energy management system plays an interim role in organically connecting and expanding with the Enterprise Resource Planning (ERP) that manages the production process through the Manufacturing Execution System (MES) and Product Lifecycle Management (PLM) to manage the products such as the top raw materials. For data generated within the manufacturing process, each management system is encrypted with Secure Socket Layer (SSL) in real time to ensure that data received through the integrity network has not been changed as a burden [18].

3.3 Calculation Process

As shown in Fig. 4, when calculating greenhouse gas emissions in the cement man-ufacturing process, a template of IoT data structure is defined during the pre-manufacturing and manufacturing phase, and the user invokes the function of updating the data structure when registering the data. As a result, data generated during the manufacturing process is encrypted and real-time interface with Secure Sockets Layer (SSL) as shown in Figs. 2 and 3, and data generated from outside is recorded as a greenhouse gas emission calculation platform after being collected in the data control system by verifying integrity as a transaction in a block chain.

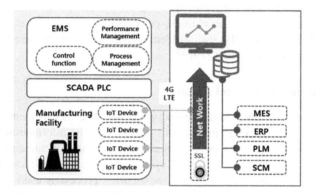

Fig. 3. Manufacturing process IoT data management system using SSL

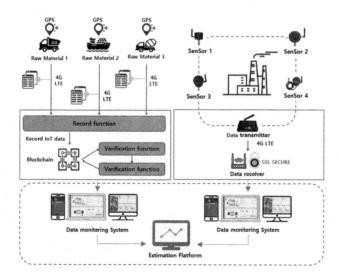

Fig. 4. Manufacturing process IoT data management system using blockchain & SSL

4 Implementation and Use Cases

Reducing greenhouse gas emissions to prevent climate change has now become an irresistible trend. Since the Paris climate agreement was reached in 2015, countries around the world have laid legal grounds to implement the agreement, and South Korea has begun to control local companies' greenhouse gas emissions by introducing a "carbon emission trading system" that prices greenhouse gas emissions.

In line with government policies, local companies are at a considerable cost to reduce greenhouse gas emissions. However, although most of the policies being implemented to achieve the national greenhouse gas reduction target are focused on the industrial sector, they go through the process of identifying sources of greenhouse gas emissions, calculating emissions, and verifying the systematic structure of the results, but lack real-time feasibility. In addition, cement manufacturing sites that are being discussed in the study face the real problem of purchasing carbon credits, which are increasing day by day over time [19].

4.1 Configuring Devices and Features

In the study, the company designs an encrypted IoT data management platform and calculates greenhouse gas emissions. In this system, location information measured by a transport vehicle's GPS device is subject to verification of authenticity, and the measured data is submitted to the Internet's block chain via a 4G/LTE cellular network. In addition, data generated during the manufacturing process is used to create symmetrical session keys, which are encrypted over SSL by encrypting data in transit.

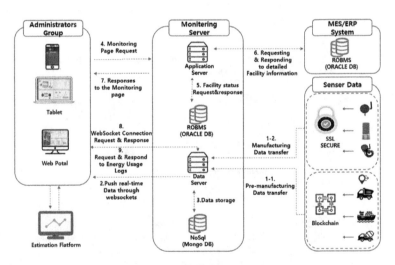

Fig. 5. Greenhouse gas emissions estimation system

Figure 5 shows an implementation environment for calculating carbon emissions by monitoring and retrieving data collected in real time before and during the manufacturing phase. Servers use Tomcat WAS servers and use Mongo databases and Oracle databases for search and analysis to collect data entering IoT devices. It is implemented on a Web-based basis and run in the Web, App environment of computers and mobile tablets so that field workers can conveniently input and search in real time at work sites.

Sensor data transmitted from IoT devices is sent to data service via web network and stored in database in real time. In addition, when an administrator requests monitoring data after setting up a configuration for the set-up period, he or she accesses the MES/ERP system through the application server and receives the information to respond.

4.2 System Implementation and Practices

Mobile devices such as smartphones are equipped with management programs so that process-related teams can monitor greenhouse gas emissions in real time anytime, anywhere. Service support of server data allows smartphones to view real-time update emissions results and visually display construction activities synchronized with virtual models. The system was first implemented to test the viability and applicability of the actual manufacturing process. It is supported by block chain data through various SSL-encrypted IoT devices in the manufacturing stage and GPS systems in the manufacturing shear system. Implementation and direct emissions can be monitored by the computing platform in real time and displayed visually as shown in Fig. 6.

Figure 7 shows the current status of installation and operation of IoT sensors installed at the site.

This is the result of the search screen for the calculation of carbon emissions by quarter or year for the entire facility. The results of pattern analysis from real-time to maximum years can be derived according to the calculation time setting for data retrieval, including direct and indirect carbon emission analysis corresponding to each calculation history. Thus far, it has served as an opportunity to develop the passive calculation process for carbon emission calculations into an active process.

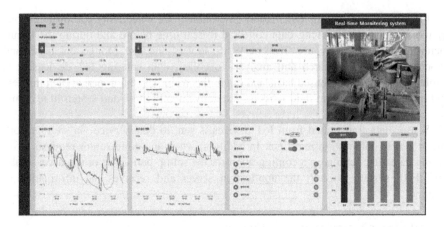

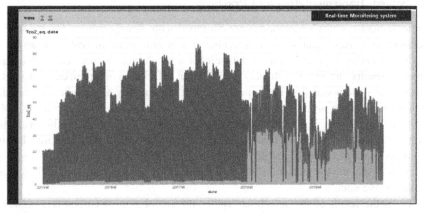

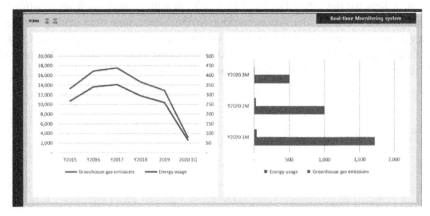

Fig. 6. Greenhouse gas emissions estimation system

Fig. 7. IoT sensor monitoring system

5 Conclusion

In this study, we proposed a platform for calculating carbon emissions through reliable IoT data management that prevents data modulation by using SSH internal network security, block chain and transaction data analysis that can guarantee both the integrity and reliability of IoT data. The proposed platform made clear that the reliability of the measured data for the system can be correctly verified, indicating the efficiency in calculating the corresponding carbon emissions from the proposed platform. In the future, we will study technologies that speed up data extraction through the introduction of distributed access through edge computing to the block chain or the introduction of industrial 5G. In order to enhance the reliability of the verification results, the government will also study ways to incorporate some of the verification functions implemented by the relevant ministries and agencies of the country into the block chain to expand the scope of application of the program to local governments or national levels.

Acknowledgements. This work was supported by the Industrial Cluster Program funded by the Ministry of Trade, Industry and Energy (MOTIE, Korea) and the Korea Industrial Complex Corporation [Project Number: SKN19ED].

This research was supported by the MSIT (Ministry of Science and ICT), Korea, under the ITRC (Information Technology Research Center) support program (IITP-2020-2018-0-01417) supervised by the IITP (Institute for Information and Communications Technology Planning and Evaluation).

References

1. He, W., Tan, E.L., Lee, E.W., Li, T.Y.: A solution for integrated track and trace in supply chain based on RFID & GPS. In: 2009 IEEE Conference on Emerging Technologies & Factory Automation, pp. 1–6. IEEE (2009)
2. Truong, N.B., Sun, K., Lee, G.M., Guo, Y.: GDPR-compliant personal data management: a blockchain-based solution. IEEE Trans. Inf. Forensics Secur. **5**(15), 1746–1761 (2020)
3. Al Omar, A., Rahman, M.S., Basu, A., Kiyomoto, S.: MediBchain: a blockchain based privacy preserving platform for healthcare data. In: Wang, G., Atiquzzaman, M., Yan, Z., Choo, K.-K.R. (eds.) SpaCCS 2017. LNCS, vol. 10658, pp. 534–543. Springer, Cham (2017). https://doi.org/10.1007/978-3-319-72395-2_49
4. Li, H., Zhu, L., Shen, M., Gao, F., Tao, X., Liu, S.: Blockchain-based data preservation system for medical data. J. Med. Syst. **42**(8), 141 (2018)
5. Hasegawa, Y., Yamamoto, H.: Highly reliable IoT data management platform using blockchain and transaction data analysis. In: 2020 IEEE International Conference on Consumer Electronics (ICCE), pp. 1–6. IEEE (2020)
6. Seo, S.-O., Baek, S.-Y., Keum, D., Ryu, S., Cho, C.-H.: A tutorial: information and communications-based intelligent building energy monitoring and efficient systems. KSII Trans. Internet Inf. Syst. **7**(11) (2013)
7. Kim, S.-T.: Fems technology trend and application plan. Technical report, Korean Environmental Industry Technology Institute (KEITI) (2015)
8. Shim, H.-S.: Fems installation standard guide. Technical report, Korea Energy Agency (2015)

9. Kim, C.W., Kim, J., Kim, S.M., Hwang, H.T.: Fems technology embodiment and applied cases to save energy in manufacturing business. Mag. SAREK **44**(1), 22–27 (2015)
10. Lee, H.-B.: The improvement of steam energy-efficiency through fems based on it (2015)
11. Lee, H., Yoo, S., Kim, Y.-W.: An energy management framework for smart factory based on context-awareness. In: 18th International Conference on Advanced Communication Technology (ICACT), Pyeongchang, pp. 685–688. IEEE (2016)
12. Kim, C.-G., et al.: A planning study for the application of new guidelines for the national greenhouse gas IPCC in response to the climate change agreement. Technical report. Korea Energy Economics Institute (2008)
13. Arumugam, S.S., et al.: IoT enabled smart logistics using smart contracts. In: 8th International Conference on Logistics, Informatics and Service Sciences (LISS), Toronto, pp. 1–6. IEEE (2018)
14. Xie, C., Sun, Y., Luo, H.: Secured data storage scheme based on block chain for agricultural products tracking. In: 3rd International Conference on Big Data Computing and Communications (BIGCOM), Chengdu, pp. 45–50. IEEE (2017)
15. Pervez, H., Haq, I.U.: Blockchain and IoT based disruption in logistics. In: 2nd International Conference on Communication, Computing and Digital systems (C-CODE), Islamabad, pp. 276–281. IEEE (2019)
16. Sandor, A.: Security of dynamic authorisation for IoT through blockchain technology (2018)
17. Niya, S.R., et al.: A blockchain-based scientific publishing platform. In: IEEE International Conference on Blockchain and Cryptocurrency (ICBC), Seoul, pp. 329–336. IEEE (2019)
18. Hwang, H., Seo, Y., Kim, T.: The development of a web-based realtime monitoring system for facility energy uses in forging processes. J. Internet Comput. Serv. **19**(1), 87–95 (2018)
19. Greenhouse gas reduction and emission trading system (2020)

Non-intrusive Load Monitoring Based on Regularized ResNet with Multivariate Control Chart

Cheolhwan Oh and Jongpil Jeong[✉]

Department of Smart Factory Convergence, Sungkyunkwan University, Suwon,
Jangan-gu, Gyeonggi-do 16419, Republic of Korea
{dhdldzhkf13,jpjeong}@skku.edu

Abstract. With the development of industry and the spread of the
Smart Home, the need for power monitoring solution technologies
for effective energy management systems is increasing. Of these, non-
intrusive load monitoring (NILM), is an efficient way to solve the electricity consumption monitoring problem. NILM is a technique to measure
the power consumption of individual devices by analyzing the power data
collected through smart meters and commercial devices. In this paper,
we propose a deep neural network (DNN)-based NILM technique that
enables energy disaggregation and power consumption monitoring simultaneously. Energy disaggregation is performed by learning a deep residual network for performing multilabel regression. Real-time monitoring
is performed using a multivariate control chart technique using latent
variables extracted through weights of the trained model. The energy
disaggregation and monitoring performance of the proposed method is
verified using the public NILM Electricity Consumption and Occupancy
(ECO) data set.

Keywords: Non-intrusive load monitoring · Deep neural network ·
Multivariate statistical process control · Regularization

1 Introduction

Recently, the use of electronics in most homes and buildings has become an
indispensable factor for convenience of living, and the introduction of equipment
using power in factories has been increasing due to the automation of factories
following industrial development. $CO2$ emissions increased by 43% as the total
energy use from 1984 to 2004 increased by 49% due to rapid industrial growth.
The analysis of the effect of the method of feedback to consumers on the use
of energy was conducted by the Electric Power Research Institute (EPRI) in
the United States [1]. According to the results of their research, the energy-
saving effect occurs when providing energy consumption patterns to end-users.
Providing detailed power consumption information for each device in real-time
produced an energy-saving effect of approximately 12% on average.

© Springer Nature Switzerland AG 2020
O. Gervasi et al. (Eds.): ICCSA 2020, LNCS 12250, pp. 646–661, 2020.
https://doi.org/10.1007/978-3-030-58802-1_47

Intrusive load monitoring (ILM) monitors energy usage through smart meters connected to each device that requires monitoring. ILM measures the energy consumption directly for each device, so it has the advantage of high accuracy [2], but because each device requires the installation of a smart meter, it is difficult to manage and expensive and, thus, challenging to generalize [3]. Non-intrusive load monitoring (NILM) uses a single smart meter that captures aggregated electrical energy signals. The goal of this technique is to discover devices that contribute to aggregated signals. NILM is preferred over ILM in both academia and industry [4] because it reduces financial costs and the burden on users or homeowners to participate in the energy monitoring process.

NILM is a method of separating the total electrical load of a building measured at a single point into individual device signals using a combination of electrical collection systems and signal processing algorithms [5]. It extracts the features of the data collected by signal processing and performs load identification through the extracted features [6].

In NILM, the feature extraction process significantly influences the load identification to be performed later, so selecting and applying an appropriate feature extraction method from the collected power data is an essential task. Many studies have proposed feature extraction methods to improve the performance of load identification, contributing to the development of NILM technology [7,8].

Deep learning technology that can automatically extract features by learning data continues to develop rapidly and is being applied positively in various industries. In contrast to traditional methods of extracting direct features, deep learning models automatically extract features from raw data [9]. In the field of NILM, a deep learning approach has also been proposed, and its effectiveness has been proven [10].

In this paper, we propose an NILM framework based on deep learning algorithms. The proposed method performs energy disaggregation through multilabel regression by training a deep learning model. Moreover, by extracting the latent variable of electrical signal data as a feature through the trained model, and using this feature to draw a multivariate control chart, it provides an end-user with a monitoring dashboard system that can report real-time energy usage. Our primary contribution is extending and applying the control chart—a monitoring methodology used predominantly in process control—to the NILM field. Furthermore, we use a deep learning model already trained for energy disaggregation, reducing the required effort.

The rest of this paper is organized as follows. Section 2 discusses related work. Section 3 explains the control chart in statistical process control. Section 4 describes the proposed NILM framework. Section 5 presents experiments conducted to evaluate the performance of the proposed approach and describes the experimental results. Section 6 discusses our conclusions.

2 Related Works

2.1 Non-intrusive Load Monitoring

NILM was introduced by Hart in the 1980s [5]. Since its introduction, several NILM algorithms have been proposed to analyze data collected at low and high sampling rates. For directly estimating the power demand of each device from the aggregate power signal, an approach based on a hidden Markov model (HMM) [11] and factorial HMM (FHMM) [12] has been studied. Another powerful option for solving signal processing problems is graph signal processing (GSP) [13,14].

In previous research, both steady-state and transient state analyses were used to separate the energy consumption per device. In steady-state analysis, active power, reactive power, current waveform, and harmonic components were used as features for load disaggregation [15]. Transient energy and transient shapes were used to disaggregate the loads in transient state analysis [16,17]. Features extracted from steady-state and transient states were used in combination to increase accuracy [18,19]. The researchers relied on hand-made feature extractors such as the Fourier transform, wavelet transform, spectral-domain representation, and electrical parameters. However, these extractors are time-consuming and error-prone, creating difficulty in finding the optimal feature for disaggregation [20].

As a solution, researchers have begun using deep neural networks (DNNs) that can automatically extract features by learning the hidden patterns of raw signals. In [10], three types of DNN structures—long short-term memory (LSTM) units, a denoising autoencoder, and a regression model—were used to predict the start time, end time, and average power demand of each device. Lukas et al. [21] proposed a combination of HMM and DNN for energy disaggregation, demonstrating results that surpass FHMM. In [22], the researchers proposed an architecture with a deep recurrent LSTM network for supervised disaggregation of loads that outperformed alternatives for loads representing the periodicity of energy consumption. He et al. [23] used multiple parallel convolution layers with various filter sizes to improve the disaggregation performance of LSTM-based models. Barsim et al. [24] proposed a deep residual network-based disaggregation model and found that deeply-stacked layers could be effective for energy disaggregation. Researchers found that a convolutional neural network (CNN) architecture based on seq2seq or seq2point may be more effective in energy disaggregation [25,26]. Other researchers proposed a supervised learning method in which a 1D CNN-RNN model combining CNN and RNN is applied to NILM [27].

3 Control Chart in Statistical Process Control

Statistical process control (SPC) is a methodology that finds solutions or improvement by identifying and interpreting problems based on data, rather than monitoring the system with a guess. It is mainly used for quality control [28].

3.1 Multivariate Control Charts

A univariate control chart can be easily applied and interpreted by directly using operational data instead of a mathematical model. However, univariate SPC methods can cause erroneous results when applied to multivariate data with a high correlation between variables, and it is not efficient to draw a control chart for each variable [29].

A multivariate control chart capable of simultaneously observing changes in two or more management items is required to efficiently manage two or more related data or to simultaneously monitor a process. Several multivariate control charts have been proposed, such as the Hotelling's T^2 chart, multivariate EWMA chart, and multivariate CUSUM chart [29]. Hotelling's T^2 chart is the most widely used [30]. The T^2 statistic is calculated as follows:

$$T^2 = (x - \bar{x})^T S^{-1}(x - \bar{x}), \tag{1}$$

where $\bar{x}$ and S are the sample mean vectors and sample covariance matrices, respectively, determined from past data $X \in R^{n \times m}$ collected in the control state, in which n and m are the numbers of samples and variables. This is used as a statistic to determine the similarity between the data collected in the control state and the newly measured data. Hotelling's T^2 statistic refers to the Mahalanobis distance between historical data collected in the control state and new measurements. The upper control limit of the T^2 chart is based on the assumption of normality and follows the F distribution [28]. Equation (2) can be used to calculate the upper control limit, which is the critical value.

$$UCL_{T^2} = \frac{m(n+1)(n-1)}{n(n-m)} F_{(m,n-m,\alpha)}, \tag{2}$$

In Eq. (2), the significance level α is the type I error rate. This is the maximum allowable limit for false alarms that misjudge positive as negative. $F_{(m,n-m,\alpha)}$ is the upper α th quantile of the F-distribution with m and $(n - m)$ degrees of freedom.

However, the multivariate process control based on Hotelling's T^2 is not useful for data with many correlated variables. If there are many correlation variables, it is difficult to invert the covariance matrix S because the covariance matrix becomes nearly a singular matrix, which leads to problematic results [31]. Furthermore, including many highly correlated variables in the data may cause multicollinearity, deteriorating the ability to detect progress shifts [32]. Consequently, various latent-variable-based control charts for extracting features from raw data have been proposed.

3.2 Latent Variable Based Multivariate Control Charts

Hotelling's T^2 chart based on principal component analysis (PCA) is a representative case among latent variable-based control chart methodologies. PCA is a technique that finds axes orthogonal to each other while preserving the variance of data as much as possible and transforms the data in the high-dimensional space into low-dimensional space without linear correlation [33]. This is similar to the T^2 chart without PCA described in Eqs. (1) and (2), except that a Q chart for performing residual analysis is added and used together. First, the data matrix X is decomposed into individual elements through PCA, and the individual elements are further divided into principal component subspaces (PCS) and residual subspaces (RS) according to the number of principal components selected, as follows:

$$X = \hat{X} + \tilde{X} = \hat{T}\hat{P}^T + \tilde{T}\tilde{P}^T = \begin{bmatrix} \hat{T} \ \tilde{T} \end{bmatrix} \begin{bmatrix} \hat{P} \ \tilde{P} \end{bmatrix}^T = TP^T, \tag{3}$$

where $T = \begin{bmatrix} \hat{T} \ \tilde{T} \end{bmatrix}$ and $P = \begin{bmatrix} \hat{P} \ \tilde{P} \end{bmatrix}$ are the score and loading matrices, respectively. $\hat{T} \in R^{n \times p}$ and $\tilde{T} \in R^{n \times m - p}$ are score matrices belonging to PCS and RS, respectively, and $\hat{P} \in R^{m \times p}$ and $\tilde{P} \in R^{m \times m - p}$ are loading matrices belonging to PCS and RS, respectively. For the number of principal components p, after drawing the scree plot, select the number of principal components corresponding to the elbow point or the number of principal components that can explain the variance as desired by the user. After determining the number of principal components p, the PCA-based T^2 statistic can be calculated, which is calculated as follows:

$$\hat{t} = x\hat{P}, \tag{4}$$

$$T_{PCA}^2 = \hat{t}\hat{\Lambda}^{-1}\hat{t}^T, \tag{5}$$

Where $\hat{t}$ is the score vector of x in the PCS and $\hat{\Lambda}$ is the diagonal matrix of the largest eigenvalues of the covariance matrix of $\hat{X}$. The upper control limit of PCA-based T^2 is calculated as Eq. (6), which is almost the same as Eq. (2), as follows:

$$UCL_{T_{PCA}^2} = \frac{p(n+1)(n-1)}{n(n-p)} F_{(p,n-p,\alpha)}, \tag{6}$$

However, because the T_{PCA}^2 statistic calculated through Eq. (5) uses only the information in the PCS, variations occurring in the RS may not be detected [34]. Therefore, the Q chart is additionally used to detect shifts that cannot be explained only by the information contained in PCS. The Q chart can be constructed using the residuals obtained from RS. PCA-based Q statistics monitor the squared error between the true vector x and the vector $\hat{x}$ estimated by PCA. The PCA-based Q statistic is calculated as follows:

$$Q_{PCA} = (x - \hat{x})(x - \hat{x})^T = \tilde{x}\tilde{x}^T, \tag{7}$$

Assuming the Q statistic, squared prediction error, follows a normal distribution, we can calculate the upper control limits of the Q chart with the following approximation based on the weighted chi-squared distribution [35]:

$$UCL_{Q_{PCA}} = \frac{v}{2m}\chi^2_{(2m^2/v,\alpha)}, \tag{8}$$

where m and v are the sample mean and variance of Q_{PCA}, respectively, and α is the type I error rate. This functions accurately even when the prediction error does not follow a normal distribution [36].

However, the PCA-based MSPC technique is based on the linearity of data. Therefore, using PCA as-is without removing nonlinearity does not accurately reflect the information in the data and limits the accuracy of detecting anomalies. Consequently, researchers have proposed various methodologies to reflect nonlinearity, the most being the kernel method. Researchers [37] proposed kernel PCA (KPCA), which removes nonlinearity by mapping data to a high level using a kernel function to achieve data linearity. Furthermore, it extracts latent variables considering nonlinearity by applying PCA to linearized data. KPCA is favored because it is simple to use and can adequately consider the nonlinearity of data. In the field of process monitoring, several studies extracted latent variables using KPCA and applied to multivariate control charts, and their effectiveness has been proven [38–40].

PCA- and KPCA-based multivariate control charts are used to monitor the system that generates X data by identifying latent variables representative of the relationship of X and obtaining a control limit. However, in several cases, we prefer to monitor not X but the output Y produced by the system, for which partial least squares (PLS) is the most commonly used alternative to PCA. PLS shares similarities with PCA. Whereas PCA extracts latent variables that maximize the variance of the linear combination of X, PLS extracts latent variables that maximize the covariance between the linear combination of X and Y [41].

Just as PCA uses a matrix X consisting of measurements of process variables to monitor process variables, PLS-based control charts can also monitor quality variables using matrix Y consisting of measurements of quality variables. However, PLS, like PCA, cannot consider the nonlinearity of data. Therefore, KPLS-based methodologies for considering nonlinearity have been proposed. Furthermore, PLS- and KPLS-based multivariate control chart techniques have been proposed to monitor the status of the products produced during the process [42].

Recently, a method of applying the latest deep learning method to extract latent variables for use in a multivariate control chart has been proposed. The authors [43] proposed a method of extracting latent variables and applying them to a multivariate control chart using an unsupervised learning algorithm, one of the deep learning methods. Latent variables were extracted using a variational autoencoder model capable of extracting the feature of the independent variable X, confirming that the performance of the proposed method is superior to that of the existing PCA- and KPCA-based multivariate control charts.

4   Proposed Method

This section explains the proposed method. We propose an NILM methodology based on DNN algorithms. The primary contribution is an energy disaggregation and real-time monitoring dashboard based on the training of a single neural network model.

The proposed method is divided into three keywords. First, sequence-to-point learning corresponds to the form of the input/output data of a neural network model for performing energy disaggregation. Second, the regularized residual network corresponds to the architecture of a DNN performing NILM. Regularization is used to extract latent variables to be used in multivariate control charts. The last keyword, latent-variable-based multivariate control charts, aims to provide real-time monitoring dashboards to end-users. The latent variables needed to implement a multivariate control chart are extracted from the residual network for energy disaggregation and consumption prediction—no additional process is used to extract latent variables for implementing a multivariate control chart.

4.1   Sequence-to-Point Learning

We generalized the energy disaggregation problem of NILM as a prediction problem using a neural network model into a regression model that predicts the energy consumption of individual electronic devices $Y \in R^{n \times k}$ using data $X \in R^{n \times m}$ collected from the main power line. In this model, n is the number of data records collected according to the sampling rate of the smart meter and m is the number of features of the electrical data set collected and stored by the smart meter installed on the main power line. These features typically include voltage and current, phase, power factor, and I-V trajectory [6]. k is the number of electronic devices requiring prediction of energy consumption through a regression model.

For defining the regression problem for energy disaggregation as a sequence-to-point neural network model, the original electrical data matrix X is sliced into a specific sequence length l, which is expressed as a three-dimensional array W through the following procedure:

$$X = \{x_1, x_2, \cdots, x_n\}, \tag{9}$$

$$S_{i:j} = \{x_i, x_{i+1}, \cdots, x_j\}, 1 \leq i \leq j \leq n, \tag{10}$$

$$W = \{S_{1:l}, S_{2:l+1}, \cdots, S_{n-l+1:n}\}, \tag{11}$$

A method of improving the energy disaggregation performance by predicting the energy consumption Y corresponding to the midpoint of an individual sequence was proposed [25], but because this method predicts the midpoint of the sequence, a time delay of $\frac{l}{2}$ occurs. The lower the sampling rate and longer the sequence length l, the more challenging the model becomes for real-time monitoring. Therefore, we designed the input/output structure of the model to predict energy consumption corresponding to the endpoint of each sequence rather than the midpoint.

4.2   Regularized ResNet Based Multivariate Control Charts

The primary feature of the residual network is the residual shortcut connection between consecutive convolutional layers. The difference between a residual network and a typical convolutional network, such as a fully convolutional network (FCN), is that a linear shortcut residual connection is added to connect the input and output of the residual block [44]. Through this connection, the residual network robustly adapts to the degradation problem, which was one of the chronic problems in DNNs, facilitating the neural network training for feature extraction by building the neural network into a deeper structure.

Therefore, we used a deep residual network to sufficiently extract features from the electrical data collected by the smart meter. The structure of the model in this study consists of six residual blocks, each composed of three layers; the end of the model is composed of a global average pooling (GAP) layer and regularized linear activation function to perform multilabel regression.

In general neural network architectures, it is common not to apply regularization to the layer that performs classification and regression using latent variables extracted through the previous layer. However, because we need to monitor the energy consumption Y of individual electronic devices through latent variables extracted from the GAP layer, the GAP layer must contain enough information about Y. Accordingly, we apply strong regularization to the linear activation function layer that performs regression such that the latent variable extracted from the GAP layer does not depend on the weight of the linear activation function layer. In this study, regularization was performed through L2-norm and Max-norm [45].

The overall structure of the model is illustrated in Fig. 1. Researchers demonstrated that a residual network designed with this architecture and parameters is effective in extracting features from time-series data [46] and provided strong guidelines for designing a residual network for feature extraction of time-series data. Algorithm 1 is the pseudocode for a method of monitoring energy consumption using a multivariate control chart.

5   Experiment and Performance Analysis

5.1   Experimental Data

We used the Electricity Consumption and Occupancy (ECO) data set for our experiment, which was collected from six swiss households over eight months [47] at a sampling rate of 1 Hz.

For the main meter, the ECO dataset has 16 metered variables, including total power consumption, three-phase power, neutral current, three-phase current, three-phase voltage, and phase angles of $V12$, $V13$, $I1-V1$, $I2-V2$, and $I3-V3$. The sub-metered data consists of several types of appliances. Because the data collected from the main meter in the ECO dataset is multivariate with 16 variables, it is suitable for use in this study, which proposes a methodology for monitoring energy usage based on a multivariate control chart.

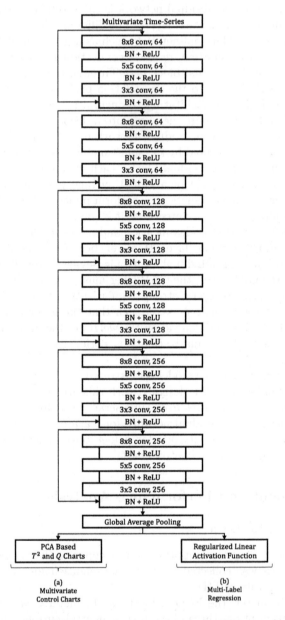

Fig. 1. The architecture of the residual network for energy disaggregation. In (a), latent variables are extracted., and in (b), multi-label regression is performed to predict the energy consumption of each electronic device

---

Algorithm 1: Multivariate Control Charts based on Latent Variable extracted from Regularized ResNet

---

Input: training set $X_{tr} \in R^{n \times m}$ and $Y_{tr} \in R^{n \times k}$
Input: test set $X_{te} \in R^{r \times m}$ and $Y_{te} \in R^{r \times k}$
Input: sequence length l
Input: Explained variance v
Input: Regularization parameter λ and c
Input: Type 1 error rate α

1   $W_{tr} \leftarrow$ Reshaping data X_{tr} by l through equations (11)
    /* Train predictive models   */
2   Let $Residual\,Block_i$, where $i = \{1, 2, \cdots, d\}$
3   $\theta \leftarrow$ Initialize the parameters of the predictive models
4   **while** *Update until θ converges* **do**
5      $Z_{tr_1} = Residual\,Block_1(W_{tr})$
6      $\cdots$
7      $Z_{tr_d} = Residual\,Block_d(Z_{tr_{d-1}})$
8      $Z_{tr_{gap}} = GAP(Z_{tr_d})$ // 3d array to 2d matrix
9      $H = Linear\,Activation\,Function(Z_{tr_{gap}}, L2 = \lambda, Max-norm = c)$
10      $Cost = Mean\,Squared\,Error(H, Y_{tr})$
11      $\theta \leftarrow$ Update the parameters through the gradient of $Cost$
12 **end**
    /* Set threshold for control charts based on α */
13 Train PCA model through $Z_{tr_{gap}}$, The number of PC is selected by v.
14 $UCL_{T^2_{PCA}} \leftarrow$ Calculate the control limit of the T^2 chart through Eq(6)
15 $UCL_{Q_{PCA}} \leftarrow$ Calculate the control limit of the Q chart through Eq(8)
    /* Monitoring for energy consumption alarm   */
16 **for** *$j = 1$ to $r-l+1$* **do**
17      $S_{j:l+j-1} \leftarrow$ Reshaping data X_{te} through equations (10)
18      $z_{te_{gap}} = GAP(S_{j:l+j-1})$ // 2d matrix to 1d vector
19      $t_{te} = PCA(z_{te_{gap}})$ // Calculate score vector
20      $T^2_{PCA} \leftarrow$ Calculate T^2 statistics based on t_{te} through Eq(5)
21      $Q_{PCA} \leftarrow$ Calculate Q statistics based on t_{te} through Eq(7)
22   **if** $T^2_{PCA} \geq UCL_{T^2_{PCA}}$ *and* $Q_{PCA} \geq UCL_{Q_{PCA}}$ **then**
23   energy consumption alarm
24   **end**
25 **end**

In the ECO data set, the number and type of electronic devices that collect data for each household differ, as are the ratios of the total amount of power consumed by each electronic device to the total energy consumption of each household. Of the six houses, house2 collected data from the largest number of household appliances, and electricity consumption covered by the smart plugs was also highest. Therefore, we conducted an experiment using data collected from house 2. House2 collects data from 12 individual electronic devices.

In this paper, we experiment using the data collected in January 2013 from the total data from House 2. The stove corresponding to the data from the tenth electronic device is not continuously collected. Therefore, the experiment is performed only on 11 data points, excluding the stove. The periods used are January 1–21, 2013, for training data, and January 22–28, 2013, for test data. The model was trained using data for three weeks, and the trained model was tested using data collected during the following one week.

5.2 Parameter Configuration

Each residual block is first composed of three convolutions whose output is added to the residual block's input and then fed to the next layer. The number of filters for convolutions is fixed at 64, 128, and 256, with a ReLU activation function preceded by a batch normalization operation. In each residual block, the filter's length is set to 8, 5, and 3, respectively, for the first, second, and third convolution. The stride is fixed at 1. The padding is set so that the input and output of the layer are equivalent. For residual network optimization, we used Adam optimizer with a learning rate of 0.001 as the optimization Algorithm, and the loss was set to the mean square error (MSE). The training was performed for 1000 epochs, and the batch size was set to 4096. The validation data set used as much as 10% of the training data set. λ and c are set to 0.1 and 1, respectively.

The number of principal components of PCA performed to implement T^2 and Q charts using latent variables extracted from the last GAP layer of the residual network was selected based on explained variance, and the threshold was set to 80%. Furthermore, the type I error rate of the control limit α was set to 5%.

The sequence length l for performing sequence-to-point learning was set to 60 in the experiment. We use the data collected from x_{t-59} to x_t to predict the energy consumption y_t.

5.3 Performance Evaluation and Analysis

We use four metrics to evaluate the performance of multi-label regression performed by the residual network from various perspectives. The metrics we used are Root Mean Square Error (RMSE), Signal Aggregate Error (SAE), Normalized Disaggregation Error (NDE), and Accuracy.

First, we evaluate the performance of the residual network using RMSE metrics, which are commonly used to evaluate the predictive performance of regression models. RMSE $= \sqrt{\frac{1}{T} \sum_{t=1}^{T} (\hat{y}_t^i - y_t^i)^2}$. Where, $\hat{y}_t^i$ and y_t^i are prediction and ground truth of the i-th electronic device at the t-th time step, respectively.

The second metric, SAE, is known to evaluate the model in terms of the total error in energy over a period of time. SAE $= \frac{|\sum_{t=1}^{T} \hat{y}_t^i - \sum_{t=1}^{T} y_t^i|}{\sum_{t=1}^{T} y_t^i}$. In contrast to the SAE, which focuses on energy consumption over a period of time, the third metric, NDE, is a measure of whether the predictive model predicts energy consumption well at every time point. NDE $= \frac{\sum_{t=1}^{T} (\hat{y}_t^i - y_t^i)^2}{\sum_{t=1}^{T} (y_t^i)^2}$. The fourth metric, accuracy, evaluates whether the total energy is properly classified regardless of whether each electronic device is a low-power or high-power device [48]. Accuracy $= 1 - \frac{\sum_{t=1}^{T}\sum_{i=1}^{k}|\hat{y}_t{}^i - y_t^i|}{2\sum_{t=1}^{T}\sum_{i=1}^{k} y_t^i}$. We compare our experimental results with those of previously proposed researchers to evaluate the performance of our proposed model.

We conducted a comparative evaluation using the methods suggested by the researchers in [14] and their experimental results. They proposed a method to improve energy disaggregation performance by extracting patterns and features from multivariate data collected from the main meter using a graphical modeling approach, a spatiotemporal pattern network (STPN). Furthermore, they provide the experimental results of FHMM, combinatorial optimization (CO), and probabilistic finite-state automaton (PFSA), which are general methodologies for performing energy disaggregation in NILM, along with the experimental results of their proposed method. They conducted experiments using training and test data sets collected during the same period used in our study. The performance metrics RMSE, AE, NDE, and accuracy for the five energy disaggregation models are listed in Table 1. Based on the experiment, the prediction of the residual network using sequence-to-point learning outperforms other methods (Fig. 2).

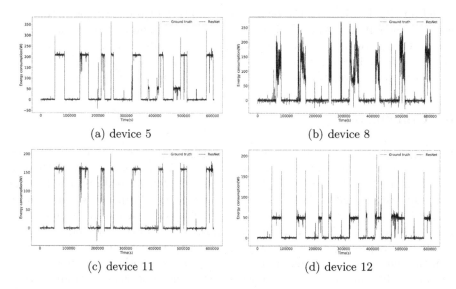

(a) device 5   (b) device 8

(c) device 11   (d) device 12

Fig. 2. Example of the difference between the ground truth and prediction for each electronic device predicted by our proposed residual network.

For evaluating the monitoring performance of a multivariate control chart, we confirm whether energy consumption rapidly increased when statistics exceeded the control limit. By identifying the level at which the multivariate control chart caused a false alarm, we evaluate the performance of the control chart drawn with the latent variable extracted by our proposed method. When the statistics exceed the control limit, if the statistics outside the control limit are higher

Table 1. The device-level RMSE, SAE, NDE and Acc. Best results are shown in bold.

Method	Metrics	Device number											Sum	Acc.
		1	2	3	4	5	6	7	8	9	11	12		
FHMM	RMSE	1.6	203.0	30.8	45.4	87.1	37.4	170.0	59.6	19.2	68.7	27.1	749.9	0.56
	SAE	0.3	0.1	56.1	0.1	0.5	0.1	3.9	0.3	0.3	0.5	0.3	62.5	
	NDE	1.0	0.9	76.1	0.9	0.6	0.7	4.1	0.8	1.2	0.6	0.8	87.7	
CO	RMSE	2.2	197.4	42.1	72.2	94.2	71.4	138.0	60.3	30.3	64.5	29.4	802.0	0.44
	SAE	0.5	0.1	92.4	0.1	0.6	0.3	2.6	0.1	1.5	0.4	0.3	98.9	
	NDE	1.9	0.9	142.5	2.3	0.7	2.7	2.7	0.8	3.0	0.6	1.0	159.1	
PFSA	RMSE	1.1	139.3	4.3	41.5	36.1	35.9	64.9	35.3	15.0	30.4	12.4	416.2	0.70
	SAE	0.026	0.070	1.314	0.018	0.034	**0.006**	0.159	0.046	0.142	0.028	0.052	1.895	
	NDE	0.504	0.443	**1.497**	0.772	0.100	0.676	0.601	0.265	0.732	0.124	0.171	5.885	
STPN	RMSE	1.1	68.6	6.3	38.7	8.4	35.4	57.4	24.2	15.5	5.8	6.1	267.5	0.84
	SAE	0.022	**0.022**	1.708	**0.003**	0.016	0.032	0.596	**0.001**	**0.087**	0.006	0.056	2.549	
	NDE	0.522	0.108	3.218	0.673	0.005	0.655	0.470	0.124	0.781	0.004	0.041	6.601	
ResNet	RMSE	**1.0**	**29.8**	5.2	**29.3**	6.2	**25.1**	**25.6**	**23.7**	12.4	**5.3**	**3.2**	**166.8**	**0.93**
	SAE	**0.005**	0.049	**0.839**	0.008	**0.006**	0.040	**0.048**	0.003	0.159	**0.003**	**0.007**	1.167	
	NDE	**0.489**	**0.020**	2.181	**0.386**	**0.003**	**0.330**	**0.093**	**0.119**	**0.501**	**0.003**	**0.011**	4.136	

based on the T-test than the energy consumption of the previous l, they are classified as outliers. The monitoring performance is evaluated by calculating the false positive rate (FPR) (i.e., one-specificity, false alarm rate) [49]. FPR decreased from 13.8% for the general PCA-based T^2 and Q chart to 9.5% for ResNet without regulation and 4.9% for ResNet with regularization.

6   Conclusion

In this paper, we proposed a framework to simultaneously perform energy disaggregation and multivariate control chart-based monitoring as a method of extracting features through a sequence-to-point learning-based residual network from multivariate data collected from the main meter. Our primary contribution is achieving both tasks simultaneously by training only one model. Moreover, we proposed a framework for applying multivariate control chart techniques, commonly used in process management, to NILM. Experimental results demonstrate that the neural network model trained by our proposed method can extract latent variables sufficient for the monitoring of energy consumption of electronic devices and energy disaggregation. In this study, the performance was evaluated only with FPR because the energy increase event could not be separately extracted from the energy data. Furthermore, because experiments have not been applied through all regulations, it was not possible to identify which regulatory methods and parameters are optimal. Therefore, future research should apply additional regulatory methodologies to data that can accurately specify abnormal events.

Acknowledgments. This research was supported by the MSIT (Ministry of Science and ICT), Korea, under the ITRC (Information Technology Research Center) support program (IITP-2020-2018-0-01417) supervised by the IITP (Institute for Information & Communications Technology Planning & Evaluation).

References

1. Neenan, B., Robinson, J., Boisvert, R.N.: Residential electricity use feedback: a research synthesis and economic framework. Electric Power Research Institute, March 2009
2. Strbac, G.: Demand side management: benefits and challenges. Energy Policy **36**(12), 4419–4426 (2008)
3. Suzuki, K., Inagaki, S., Suzuki, T., Nakamura, H., Ito, K.: Nonintrusive appliance load monitoring based on integer programming. In: 9th 2008 SICE Annual Conference, pp. 2742–2747. IEEE (2008)
4. Hosseini, S.S., Agbossou, K., Kelouwani, S., Cardenas, A.: Non-intrusive load monitoring through home energy management systems: a comprehensive review. Renew. Sustain. Energy Rev. **79**, 1266–1274 (2017)
5. Hart, G.W.: Nonintrusive appliance load monitoring. Proc. IEEE **80**(12), 1870–1891 (1992)
6. Ruano, A., Hernandez, A., Ureña, J., Ruano, M., Garcia, J.F.: NILM techniques for intelligent home energy management and ambient assisted living: a review. Energies **12**(11), 2203 (2019)
7. Sadeghianpourhamami, N., Ruyssinck, J., Deschrijver, D., Dhaene, T., Develder, C.: Comprehensive feature selection for appliance classification in NILM. Energy Build. **151**, 98–106 (2017)
8. Wang, A.L., Chen, B.X., Wang, C.G., Hua, D.: Non-intrusive load monitoring algorithm based on features of V-I trajectory. Electr. Power Syst. Res. **157**, 134–144 (2018)
9. Bengio, Y., Courville, A., Vincent, P.: Representation learning: a review and new perspectives. IEEE Trans. Pattern Anal. Mach. Intell. **35**(8), 1798–1828 (2013)
10. Kelly, J., Knottenbelt, W.: Neural NILM: deep neural networks applied to energy disaggregation. In: Proceedings of the 2nd ACM International Conference on Embedded Systems for Energy-Efficient Built Environments, pp. 55–64. ACM (2015)
11. Makonin, S., Popowich, F., Bajić, I.V., Gill, B., Bartram, L.: Exploiting HMM Sparsity to perform online real-time nonintrusive load monitoring. IEEE Trans. Smart Grid **7**(6), 2575–2585 (2015)
12. Lange, H., Bergés, M.: Efficient inference in dual-emission FHMM for energy disaggregation. In: Workshops at the Thirtieth AAAI Conference on Artificial Intelligence (2016)
13. He, K., Stankovic, L., Liao, J., Stankovic, V.: Non-intrusive load disaggregation using graph signal processing. IEEE Trans. Smart Grid **9**(3), 1739–1747 (2018)
14. Liu, C., Akintayo, A., Jiang, Z., Henze, G.P., Sarkar, S.: Multivariate exploration of non-intrusive load monitoring via spatiotemporal pattern network. Appl. Energy **211**, 1106–1122 (2018)
15. Nakano, Y., Murata, H.: Non-intrusive electric appliances load monitoring system using harmonic pattern recognition-trial application to commercial building. In: International Conference on Electrical Engineering, Hong Kong, China (2007)

16. Chen, K.-L., Chang, H.-H., Chen, N.: A new transient feature extraction method of power signatures for nonintrusive load monitoring systems. In: 2013 IEEE International Workshop on Applied Measurements for Power Systems (AMPS), pp. 79–84. IEEE (2013)

17. Chang, H.-H., Lian, K.-L., Su, Y.-C., Lee, W.-J.: Power-spectrum-based wavelet transform for nonintrusive demand monitoring and load identification. IEEE Trans. Ind. Appl. 3(50), 2081–2089 (2014)

18. Liang, J., Ng, S.K.K., Kendall, G., Cheng, J.W.M.: Load signature study-part I: basic concept, structure, and methodology. IEEE Trans. Power Deliv. 25(2), 551–560 (2009)

19. Liang, J., Ng, S.K.K., Kendall, G., Cheng, J.W.M.: Load signature study-part II: disaggregation framework, simulation, and applications. IEEE Trans. Power Deliv. 25(2), 561–569 (2010)

20. Sirojan, T., Phung, B.T., Ambikairajah, E.: Deep neural network based energy disaggregation. In: 2018 IEEE International Conference on Smart Energy Grid Engineering (SEGE), pp. 73–77. IEEE (2018)

21. Mauch, L., Yang, B.: A novel DNN-HMM-based approach for extracting single loads from aggregate power signals. In: 2016 IEEE International Conference on Acoustics, Speech and Signal Processing (ICASSP), pp. 2384–2388. IEEE (2016)

22. Mauch, L., Yang, B.: A new approach for supervised power disaggregation by using a deep recurrent LSTM network. In: 2015 IEEE Global Conference on Signal and Information Processing (GlobalSIP), pp. 63–67. IEEE (2015)

23. He, W., Chai, Y.: An empirical study on energy disaggregation via deep learning. In: 2nd International Conference on Artificial Intelligence and Industrial Engineering (AIIE 2016). Atlantis Press (2016)

24. Barsim, K.S., Yang, B.: On the feasibility of generic deep disaggregation for single-load extraction. arXiv preprint arXiv:1802.02139 (2018)

25. Zhang, C., Zhong, M., Wang, Z., Goddard, N., Sutton, C.: Sequence-to-point learning with neural networks for non-intrusive load monitoring. In: Thirty-Second AAAI Conference on Artificial Intelligence (2018)

26. Chen, K., Wang, Q., He, Z., Chen, K., Hu, J., He, J.: Convolutional sequence to sequence non-intrusive load monitoring. J. Eng. 2018(17), 1860–1864 (2018)

27. Çavdar, İ.H., Faryad, V.: New design of a supervised energy disaggregation model based on the deep neural network for a smart grid. Energies 12(7), 1217 (2019)

28. Montgomery, D.C.: Introduction to Statistical Quality Control. Wiley, New York (2007)

29. Lowry, C.A., Montgomery, D.C.: A review of multivariate control charts. IIE Trans. 27(6), 800–810 (1995)

30. Hotelling, H.: Multivariate Quality Control. Techniques of Statistical Analysis. McGraw-Hill, New York (1947)

31. Seborg, D.E., Mellichamp, D.A., Edgar, T.F., Doyle III, F.J.: Process Dynamics and Control. Wiley, New York (2010)

32. Ku, W., Storer, R.H., Georgakis, C.: Disturbance detection and isolation by dynamic principal component analysis. Chemom. Intell. Lab. Syst. 30(1), 179–196 (1995)

33. Wold, S., Esbensen, K., Geladi, P.: Principal component analysis. Chemom. Intell. Lab. Syst. 2(1–3), 37–52 (1987)

34. Mastrangelo, C.M., Runger, G.C., Montgomery, D.C.: Statistical process monitoring with principal components. Qual. Reliab. Eng. Int. 12(3), 203–210 (1996)

35. Box, G.E.P., et al.: Some theorems on quadratic forms applied in the study of analysis of variance problems, I. Effect of inequality of variance in the one-way classification. Ann. Math. Stat. **25**(2), 290–302 (1954)

36. van Sprang, E.N.M., Ramaker, H.-J., Westerhuis, J.A., Gurden, S.P., Smilde, A.K.: Critical evaluation of approaches for on-line batch process monitoring. Chem. Eng. Sci. **57**(18), 3979–3991 (2002)

37. Schölkopf, B., Smola, A., Müller, K.-R.: Nonlinear component analysis as a kernel eigenvalue problem. Neural Comput. **10**(5), 1299–1319 (1998)

38. Lee, J.-M., Yoo, C., Choi, S.W., Vanrolleghem, P.A., Lee, I.-B.: Nonlinear process monitoring using kernel principal component analysis. Chem. Eng. Sci. **59**(1), 223–234 (2004)

39. Ge, Z., Yang, C., Song, Z.: Improved kernel PCA-based monitoring approach for nonlinear processes. Chem. Eng. Sci. **64**(9), 2245–2255 (2009)

40. Mansouri, M., Nounou, M., Nounou, H., Karim, N.: Kernel PCA-based GLRT for nonlinear fault detection of chemical processes. J. Loss Prev. Process Ind. **40**, 334–347 (2016)

41. Geladi, P., Kowalski, B.R.: Partial least-squares regression: a tutorial. Anal. Chim. Acta **185**, 1–17 (1986)

42. Yi, J., Huang, D., He, H., Zhou, W., Han, Q., Li, T.: A novel framework for fault diagnosis using kernel partial least squares based on an optimal preference matrix. IEEE Trans. Ind. Electron. **64**(5), 4315–4324 (2017)

43. Lee, S., Kwak, M., Tsui, K., Kim, S.B.: Process monitoring using variational autoencoder for high-dimensional nonlinear processes. Eng. Appl. Artif. Intell. **83**, 13–27 (2019)

44. He, K., Zhang, X., Ren, S., Sun, J.: Deep residual learning for image recognition. In: Proceedings of the IEEE Conference on Computer Vision and Pattern Recognition, pp. 770–778 (2016)

45. Srivastava, N., Hinton, G., Krizhevsky, A., Sutskever, I., Salakhutdinov, R.: Dropout: a simple way to prevent neural networks from overfitting. J. Mach. Learn. Res. **15**(1), 1929–1958 (2014)

46. Wang, Z., Yan, W., Oates, T.: Time series classification from scratch with deep neural networks: a strong baseline. In: International Joint Conference on Neural Networks (IJCNN), pp. 1578–1585. IEEE (2017)

47. Beckel, C., Kleiminger, W., Cicchetti, R., Staake, T., Santini, S.: The ECO data set and the performance of non-intrusive load monitoring algorithms. In: Proceedings of the 1st ACM Conference on Embedded Systems for Energy-Efficient Buildings, pp. 80–89 (2014)

48. Kolter, J.Z., Johnson, M.J.: REDD: a public data set for energy disaggregation research. In: Proceedings of the SustKDD Workshop on Data Mining Applications in Sustainability (2011)

49. Zheng, D., Li, F., Zhao, T.: Self-adaptive statistical process control for anomaly detection in time series. Expert Syst. Appl. **57**, 324–336 (2016)

International Workshop on Air Quality Monitoring and Citizen Science for Smart Urban Management. State of the Art and Perspectives (AirQ&CScience 2020)

Estimating Air Pollution Related Solar Insolation Reduction in the Assessment of the Commercial and Industrial Rooftop Solar PV Potential

G. Fattoruso[1]($\boxtimes$), M. Nocerino[2], G. Sorrentino[2], V. Manna[2],
M. Fabbricino[2], and G. Di Francia[1]

[1] DTE/FSD/SAFS Lab, ENEA RC Portici, P.Le E. Fermi 1, 80055 Portici, Italy
grazia.fattoruso@enea.it
[2] Civil Construction and Environmental Engineering Department, University of
Naples Federico II, Via Claudio, 21, Naples, Italy

Abstract. Air pollution is a serious issue and it has been becoming increasingly urgent over last year, mainly as a result of its effects on human health. Recently, however, a number of scientific papers has appeared reporting on air pollution effects in other fields such as the photovoltaic energy generation and, notably, on the relation between the reduction of the solar insolation reaching the PV systems and $PM_{2.5}$ concentrations in the air. In this study, the rooftop solar PV potential of commercial and industrial (C&I) buildings at regional scale has been estimated tacking into account the spatially distributed solar insolation reduction factor, due to the $PM_{2.5}$ in the air. High resolution LiDAR data and advanced digital surface modeling techniques have been used for determining the available suitable rooftop area and estimating the technical solar PV potential of the C&I rooftops. For the C&I study area of Aversa Nord (South Italy), we find that the suitable rooftops have annually a total electric power potential of 50.75 GWh/$year$. For this area, an annual average $PM_{2.5}$ concentrations of about 13 µg/m^3 results in a nearly 5% annual solar insolation reduction. Thus, if properly located, the large scale rooftop PV systems could significantly decrease primary energy consumption and contribute to reduce the CO2 emissions.

Keywords: $PM_{2.5}$ concentration · Solar PV potential · LiDAR data and DSM

1 Introduction

Air pollution is a serious issue and it has been becoming increasingly urgent over last years, especially in the cities. While we have much learned about the effects of the air pollution on human health, only very recently its effects in other sectors have begun to be considered and investigated.

In this paper, we investigate such the impact of the haze on solar PV energy potential. As a matter of facts, recent major haze events affecting several cities around the world (e.g. Singapore, Delhi, among others) induced some researchers [1] to investigate the impact such haze events might cause on the energy output of solar PV

© Springer Nature Switzerland AG 2020
O. Gervasi et al. (Eds.): ICCSA 2020, LNCS 12250, pp. 665–677, 2020.
https://doi.org/10.1007/978-3-030-58802-1_48

installations. In particular, they investigated and quantified the effects of fine air particulate matter on the effective solar irradiance reaching a PV module, being these particles the main contributor to haze events. Correlating measured particulate concentrations and solar insolation in Delhi, it was estimated that the insolation received by silicon PV panels was reduced by about 12% or 200 kWh/m^2 per year due to air pollution. The analysis was extended to 16 more cities around the world and insolation reductions were estimated ranging from 2.0% (Singapore) to 9.1% (Beijing) [1, 2].

According to the EU's re-cast renewable energy directive [3], by 2030, EU countries have to reach the target of the 32% in the energy production by renewable technologies. To achieve that, they need to increase their use of renewables including the solar PV systems whose contribution is evaluated as significant [4].

Until a few years ago, the major contribution to the renewable energy production came from the ground large scale PV plants [5]. In spite of the environmental benefits and advantages, the diffusion of large scale solar PV farms has caused undesirable impacts on land use, landscape, and biodiversity. In order to mitigate the adverse effects, over recent years, the new country regulations have foreseen specific exceptions for installations of ground large size PV systems and promoted measures addressing towards the use of suitable building surfaces - rooftops and facades, for distributed solar PV systems deployments.

These developments have taken advantage of the EU orientation to promote the decentralized electricity generation with renewable technologies including the rooftop PV systems as well as the continuously decreasing costs of the distributed PV installations. Moreover, several studies (see [4, 6, 7] among others) have shown that the existing buildings' rooftops across the EU countries can provide the room for significantly increasing the PV electricity production and often at lower costs.

However, the roof area covers a wide range of PV installations sizes, from residential rooftops characterized by PV systems of even just a few kWp to large commercial and industrial (C&I) roofs with PV systems reaching even hundreds KWp. While in literature several geospatial methodologies were developed for addressing the question on how to estimate to a high level of accuracy the solar PV potential of urban buildings' rooftops (see [4, 8, 10, 11] among others), there is little understanding on the assessment of the rooftop solar PV potential of the C&I areas.

This study has addressed the use of large scale rooftop PV systems and focused on rooftop solar PV potential assessment of the C&I buildings at regional scale tacking into account the spatially distributed solar insolation reduction factor, due to the PM$_{2.5}$ concentration in the air. High resolution LiDAR data and advanced digital surface modeling techniques have been used to determine the available suitable rooftop area and estimating the technical solar PV potential of the C&I rooftops.

The solar insolation reduction factor has been calculated through the empirical relation between PM$_{2.5}$ concentration and reduction in insolation, developed by the authors in a previous work [9] by using high resolution in field data gathered in the city of Naples (South Italy). The case study is the industrial area of Aversa Nord, one of the greatest regional C&I zones of Campania (South Italy).

2   Background and Previous Works

The photovoltaics potential analysis for a site or area is generally carried out taking into account resource, technical and economic levels. In particular, the resource potential is evaluated through the annual incident solar radiation. It can be affected by environmental parameters to be eventually considered such as ambient temperature, wind speed as well as the fine particulate matter in the air which is the main cause of haze reducing the visibility. The technical potential is given by the available suitable surface area and PV system technical performance while the economic potential depends on technology costs.

This study specifically addresses large scale rooftop PV systems and focuses on resource and technical potential assessment of the C&I building rooftops using a high-resolution light detection and ranging (LiDAR) data and digital surface modeling techniques.

For assessing rooftop solar PV potential, there are different spatial methodologies mainly characterized by the specific scale, ranging from local to regional or continental level. Basically, all these methodologies include two main steps: (1) the estimation of available suitable rooftop area and (2) the estimation of solar energy potential.

The literature methodology reviews (see [4, 8], among others) show that the main difference is the method used to determine the available roof area. These methods are based on spatial analysis and distinguished in low-level, medium-level and high-level depending on detail level of data models and solar radiation algorithms. [4, 8, 10].

At large scale, the first high-level methodology has been developed by Bodis et al. [4] to assess rooftops solar PV potential across the EU building stock as a whole. A previous work on EU-wide assessment had been previously developed by Defaix et al. [12] using a medium-level technique.

It is to be noted that the high-level methodologies addressing large areas are generally demanding in terms of data collection and computing power. To overcome this complexity, in literature, the assessment process is performed for a pilot area at local scale, eventually to be extended at a wider scale. In this regard, Rodriguez et al. (2018) [8] developed a high resolution spatial assessment of the PV potential at urban and regional scale, by using 3D city models and a novel procedure based on the state-of-the-art available roof area reduction coefficients. An extensive literature review, that shows the great variety of reduction coefficients used for calculating the available building rooftop area, is available in [8].

Applying a high resolution approach, the potential roof area is derived by the 3D model of the built area that identifies the geometry of the buildings that shape it. However, many circumstances may lead to the reduction of the initial roof area. For determining the suitable roof area, it occurs to perform an architectural and a solar suitability analysis. At this scope, a set of architectural (such as *construction restriction, shading effects, service area*, among others) and solar reduction factors (such as *orientation losses, slopes of roof, separation of the PV panels*, among others) is applied. On the basis of them, an utilization factor is defined which identifies the available roof area suitable to the PV installations. So, the technical solar PV potential is estimated through the available roof area and the incoming solar energy radiation converted in electrical potential on the basis of the PV modules efficiency as well as the performance ratio.

In this study, the authors intended to estimate the rooftop solar PV potential for C&I built areas at regional scale through a spatial analysis based on high resolution LiDAR data and an insolation reduction factor, ad hoc defined, due to the air pollution. LiDAR data are processed to estimate the available C&I rooftop area and the air pollution related solar radiation reduction and to provide the spatial information needed to apply the architectural and solar suitability criteria.

It is to be noted that the C&I rooftop solar PV potential has been rarely specifically addressed in the literature. In [13], a preliminary study was carried out in Minneapolis, aimed at being extended at the entire Minnesota, analyzing the solar insolation to assess the PV potential capacity of the C&I rooftops for large scale solar PV installations using LiDAR data and GIS methods.

3   The Methodology

The objective of this study has been to assess the solar PV potential of the C&I buildings for large scale rooftop PV installations, taking into account a new reduction factor, due to $PM_{2.5}$ concentrations in the air, in order to support the diffusion of renewable solar electric energy generation.

To do that, a high resolution digital surface model (DSM) of the C&I built area is generated by processing LIDAR data. On the basis of spatial information derived from DSM, the available rooftop area is identified and a spatially distributed solar radiation model, taking into account air pollution, is generated. Combining these spatial layers and defined reduction factors, the technical solar PV potential for the suitable building rooftops of the C&I study area is estimated.

3.1   The Case Study

The final objective of this study is to generate a high resolution solar radiation cadaster of the C&I building stock referred to the Campania, a region located in South Italy. This region counts 137 C&I areas which cover a ground surface varying from 0.26 Km^2 to 8.16 Km^2. These areas consist in middle and large factories which operate in several sectors – textile, gold, tanning, shoe, food ones. The mayor C&I zones (about 27%) are completely integrated within the residential areas. Thus, the solar PV potential of their rooftops can be considered as integral part of the solar PV potential of the regional building stock.

In this paper, as case study, the rooftop technical PV potential is investigated for the industrial area of Aversa Nord, one of the greatest regional C&I zones. It covers a ground area of 5,82 kmq across the municipalities of Teverola, Carinaro and Gricignano di Aversa, including around 1000 factories of which the major part operates in the textile sector (Fig. 1).

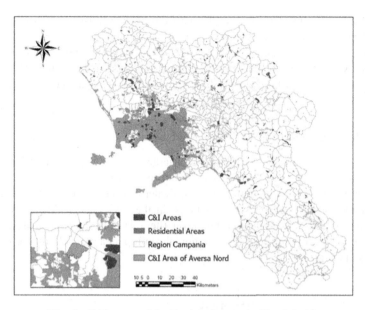

Fig. 1. C&I areas of the Region Campania (South Italy)

3.2 Data

Data sources used as input in the proposed calculation process for estimating the rooftop solar PV potential of the area study are summarized in the Table 1. It includes various GIS databases used to locate the study area (items 1, 2), identify the building footprints (item 3), model the available rooftop area (item 4) and map the air pollution related solar irradiance (items 4, 5).

Table 1. Datasets used in the methodology and their source

Name	Type	Year	Source	Description
The Corine Land Cover	Vector layer (100 m)	2018	Copernicus	Inventory on land cover of EU
Local administrative boundaries	Vector data	2011	ISTAT	National inventory on the regional and local administrative boundaries
LiDAR data	Points cloud - xyz data (2 m)	2013	National PST Project	Point clouds by LiDAR technology covering the national territory
National building stock	Vector layer	2013	National PST Project	National inventory on the building stock including footprint layer with building height attributes
Fine Particulate Matter Measurements	Vector layer	2018	ARPAC database	Annual average $PM_{2.5}$ concentrations dataset by the regional air quality gauge stations network of ARPAC

The GIS software platform used for performing step-by-step the proposed procedure is ESRI-ArcGIS Pro Advanced. Various toolsets have been used including geoprocessing, spatial analysis and 3D analysis tools as well as ad-hoc developed solution tools for extruding the available building rooftops from LiDAR point clouds, processing the elevation surfaces, interpolating air pollution data, and performing solar and shade analysis.

3.3   Determination of the Available Roof Area

For estimating the available rooftop area for large scale PV systems to be installed on C&I buildings, the first step is to derive a rooftops layer

Assuming the building rooftop area equivalent to the related footprints area, the potential rooftops for solar PV installations, in the C&I area of Aversa Nord, were derived through the building footprints layer (item 4) related to this area, identifying 368 potential building rooftops and a potential rooftop area of 1.37 km^2 for PV panels deployments (Fig. 2).

Fig. 2. The C&I built area layer of Aversa Nord

It is known that many factors may lead to the reduction of the potential roof area. These factors, for the present study, were derived from high resolution elevation models of the study area as well as from literature reviews.

At this scope, using a 3D LiDAR point cloud (LAS) dataset (item 3), two elevation models have been derived, one showing elevation of the ground (DTM) and one showing elevation of features and buildings on top of the ground (DSM).

Thus, on the basis of slope and aspect raster layers derived from DSM and the building footprints layer, the suitable rooftops orientation and slopes were derived removing the rooftop areas with a slope steeper than 45° and with an aspect value less than 22.5° or more than 337.5°.

As a matter of facts, the suitable rooftops for large scale PV installations must be flat or have a maximum slope of 45°, as steep slopes tend to receive less sunlight. At the same way, they must be south-facing, as north-facing rooftops in the northern hemisphere receive less sunlight.

For simplicity, in this study, some reduction factors' values were defined after reviewing related publications. In particular, for the factor Construction Restriction (CON), referred to space already occupied by elements located on the roof, we used the value of 0.8 as suggested by [14]. Similarity, for the factor of Separation of PV panels (GCR – Ground Cover Ratio), referred to the distance between the panels to avoid reciprocal shadowing, was chosen the value of 0.42 [15]. Accordingly, being already accounted the available space in GCR, the value of SA, referred as the necessary space for PV maintenance and access, was set to 1 [15].

Applying these reduction factors, the available rooftop area is reduced to 1.07 km^2.

3.4   Determination of Solar Energy Potential

The solar radiation reaching the available rooftops is the main factor for assessing if buildings have technical potential for solar panel installation. The annual insolation $[KWh/m^2year]$ is here calculated on the ground and on the roofs of the buildings, based on DSM of the area, using the Area Solar Radiation tool. This tool calculates the radiation taking into account the position of the sun throughout the year and at different times of the day, taking into account obstacles that may block sunlight such as nearby trees or buildings and the slope and orientation of the surface. In this way, also the shading effects which affect the incoming solar energy are calculated.

Once obtained the solar radiation map, the insolation reduction due to the fine particulate particles in the air has been evaluated using the empirical method developed in [9].

Solar Insolation Reduction. Recent studies have discussed how the fine particulate matter in the air may affect energy yield of PV installations [1, 2].

A similar study has been carried out by the authors with the scope of quantifying the effects of the fine particulate concentrations in the air on the solar insolation in the city of Naples. An empirical relation between the PM$_{2.5}$ concentrations and the reduction in solar insolation has been developed using local high-frequency insolation and pollution data [9]. The functional relation is given by:

$$\frac{I(PM_{2.5})}{I_0} = exp\left(\frac{-PM_{2.5}}{250}\right) \tag{1}$$

where I_0 is the isolation at 0 μg/m^3 and I is the insolation affected by $PM_{2.5}$ concentrations.

For Naples, we found that solar insolation reaching a potential PV installation site was reduced by 5% or 66,20 kWh/m¯, per year between May 2018 and May 2019 due to air pollution.

On the basis of the findings of this research, it is evident that the insolation reduction related to the air pollution is a factor to be considered because in some cases it could result in a substantial difference in the assessment of solar PV potential.

The functional relation (1) enables a way to estimate the solar insolation reduction in the generation of the solar radiation distribution model of the C&I built area.

At this step of the calculation process, a continuous map of $PM_{2.5}$ distribution on the C&I built area (Fig. 3) was generated based on the dataset of the $PM_{2.5}$ measured points (item 5) and averaged over the year, by the regional air quality gauge stations network, using a geo-statistical interpolation technique - Ordinary Kriging.

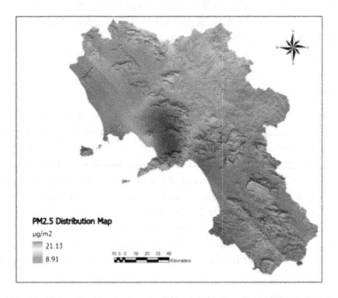

Fig. 3. $PM_{2.5}$ distribution map of the region Campania (South Italy)

Combining the $PM_{2.5}$ distribution and solar radiation raster layers in the map-algebra statement based on the Eq. (1), a high resolution (2 m) solar isolation distribution model affected by the fine particulate was derived for the C&I built area (Fig. 4).

The derived insolation reduction map (value %) in Fig. 5 shows that the solar insolation reaching the C&I rooftops is reduced by about 5%, due to annual average $PM_{2.5}$ concentrations of about 13.38 μg/m3 on the study area.

Finally, only buildings with solar insolation on their roof above a threshold value which indicates a minimum amount of radiation that is required for the installation, were considered. Assuming the threshold value of 800 kWh/m^2 [15], the rooftops with lower solar radiation were removed from available rooftop area on the basis of the derived solar radiation distributed model.

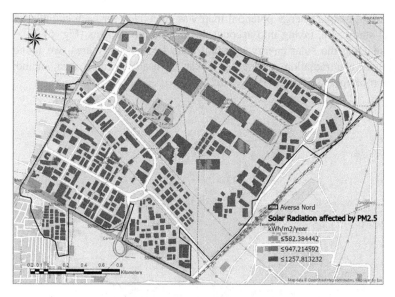

Fig. 4. Map of solar insolation affected by $PM_{2.5}$ in the air

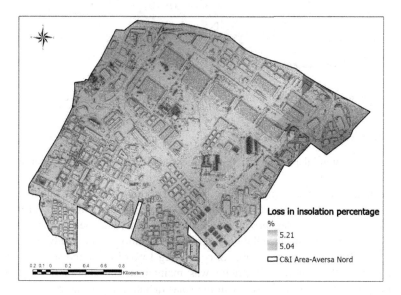

Fig. 5. PM2.5 related solar insolation reduction map

In addition, a minimum roof area was considered, so buildings whose roof areas were below that minimum value were not taken into account. We chose a minimum roof area of 140 m^2 which is that required for the installation of a PV systems with minimum nominal power of 20 kWp, considering a minimum area of 7 m^2 for one kWp [15].

As result, a solar energy potential map was calculated for each suitable rooftop of the C&I study area, taking into account the air pollution effects (Fig. 6)

Aggregating the solar energy potential data, for our study area, we found a total amount of solar radiation received per year by usable rooftop area, including 134 suitable rooftops, of 393.45 GWh/*year*.

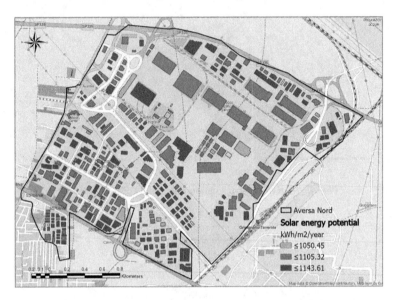

Fig. 6. Solar energy potential map for usable rooftop area of Aversa Nord

3.5   Technical PV Potential

The technical potential is defined by implementing PV panels on all suitable rooftop surface.

To estimate its annual value on the study area, the usable solar radiation values were converted to electric power production potential. The amount of power that solar PV panels can produce depends not only on solar radiation, but also the solar PV panels' efficiency and the installation's performance ratio. In this study, we assumed that the solar PV panels were capable of converting 15% of incoming solar energy into electricity, and 86% of that electricity was maintained throughout the installation. Combining these reduction factors with the solar radiation layer, the rooftop technical PV potential for each suitable rooftop of the our C&I area was calculated as shown in Fig. 7.

Aggregating the technical PV potential, we found that the whole C&I built area generated a total annual electric power amount by rooftop PV systems of 50.75 GWh/*year* which might cover partially or totally the electricity demand of the C&I buildings as well as provide the electricity surplus produced to the electricity grid.

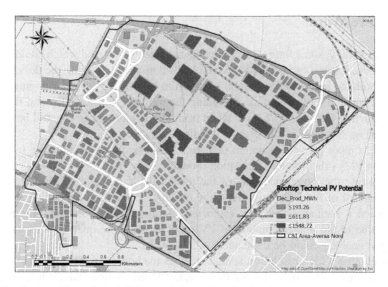

Fig. 7. Rooftop technical PV potential map for the C&I built area of Aversa Nord

4 Conclusions

Locating suitable building surfaces as facades or rooftops for solar PV installations can contribute to increase the use of renewable technologies in the energy production.

To address that, concerning large scale PV systems, through a high resolution spatial analysis, we have identified the suitable rooftops and estimated the rooftop solar PV potential of a C&I built area. The applied methodology is based on available rooftop surface analysis, irradiance simulation and reduction coefficients estimation. Specifying properly the architectural and solar reduction factors is fundamental for determining accurately the rooftop solar PV potential. At this scope, the effects of the air pollution by fine particulate matter on the solar PV energy potential of the C&I rooftops have been investigated, including in the calculation process the related reduction factor, calculated by an empirical relation previously developed. This reduction factor can result in a substantial difference in the assessment of solar PV potential.

A realistic scenario for distributed large scale PV implementations has been developed in the case study of Aversa Nord, to be extended at all regional C&I built areas. From the results obtained, using the entire suitable rooftop space, the pilot C&I area can generate a total electricity power amount of 50.75 GWh/year which might cover partially or totally the electricity demand of the C&I buildings and provide the electricity surplus produced to the electricity grid. Then, for the investigated area, an annual average $PM_{2.5}$ concentration of about 30 $\mu g/m^3$ results in a nearly 5% annual solar insolation reduction.

In conclusion, if properly located, the large scale rooftop PV systems could significantly decrease primary energy consumption and contribute to reduce the CO_2 emissions.

5 Future Work

During this study, some future developments have been identified which could result in more precise rooftop technical PV potential calculations. First of all, the developments of a 3D building model of the C&I built area from LiDAR data that could return a more detailed available rooftop surface, including the rooftops' forms – tiled and flat. Thus, some reduction factors, which have taken from the literature review, could be properly calculated on the basis of the precise buildings geometry.

Then, a more precise insolation reduction factor could be obtained by using high resolution $PM_{2.5}$ distribution simulation models.

Regarding the aggregated data of the technical PV potential, analysing the electricity demand of the C&I built areas, the coverage percentage depending on several PV efficiency scenarios could be estimated. Similarity, the potential CO_2 emission savings due to the implementation of PV modules could be quantified as well as an economic analysis could be developed.

Developing a high resolution spatial analysis methodology for estimating the C&I rooftop energy power potential for large scale PV installations taking into account a comprehensive set of reduction factors is clearly the main challenge in a future research work in order to extend this analysis at regional scale.

Acknowledgements. We thank the Regional Agency for Environmental Protection (ARPAC) operating in Campania (South Italy) in the person of Eng. Paolo D'Auria, for providing solar radiation and $PM_{2.5}$ measurements by the regional air quality monitoring network.

References

1. Peters, I.M., Karthik, S., Liu, H., Buonassisi, T., Nobre, A.: Urban haze and photovoltaics. Energy Environ. Sci. **11**, 3043–3054 (2018)
2. Liu, H., et al.: The impact of haze on performance ratio and short-circuit current of PV systems in Singapore. IEEE J. Photovolt. **4**, 1585–1592 (2014)
3. Council of European Union: Directive (EU) 2018/2001 of the European Parliament and of the Council on the promotion of the use of energy from renewable sources (2018)
4. Bódis, K., Kougias, I., Jäger-Waldau, A., Taylor, N., Szabó, S.: A high-resolution geospatial assessment of the rooftop solar photovoltaic potential in the European Union. Renew. Sustain. Energy Rev. **114**, 109309 (2019)
5. Castillo, C.P., e Silva, F.B., Lavalle, C.: An assessment of the regional potential for solar power generation in EU-28. Energy Policy **88**, 86–99 (2016)
6. Weiss, W., Biermayr, P: Potential of Solar Thermal in Europe, Report of the EU-funded project RESTMAC (2010)
7. Defaix, P., Van Sark, W., Worrell, E., de Visser, E.: Technical potential for photovoltaics on buildings in the EU-27. Sol. Energy **86**, 2644–2653 (2012)
8. Rodríguez, L.R., Duminil, E., Ramos, J.S., Eicker, U.: Assessment of the photovoltaic potential at urban level based on 3D city models: a case study and new methodological approach. Solar Energy **146**, 264–275 (2017)

9. Nocerino M., et al.: Assessing the impact of Haze on solar energy potential using long term of $PM_{2.5}$ concentration and solar insolation field data in Naples, Italy. In: Workshop AISEM 2020, LCNS in Electrical Engineering, Springer, (under review)

10. Freitas, S., Catita, C., Redweik, P., Brito, M.C.: Modelling solar potential in the urban environment: state-of-the-art review. Renew. Sustain. Energy Rev. **41**, 915–931 (2015)

11. Byrne, J., Taminiau, J., Kurdgelashvili, L., Kim, K.N.: A review of the solar city concept and methods to assess rooftop solar electric potential, with an illustrative application to the city of Seoul. Renew. Sustain. Energy Rev. **41**, 830–844 (2015)

12. Borfecchia, F., et al.: Remote sensing and GIS in planning photovoltaic potential of urban areas. Eur. J. Remote Sensing **47**, 195–216 (2014). https://doi.org/10.5721/eujrs20144713

13. Online report: A map showing potential solar energy production of commercial, industrial, and mixed used buildings in Minneapolis (2014). https://www.arcgis.com/home/item.html?id=b5d60dabc48b47828bc1dc4111ad253c

14. Schallenberg-Rodríguez, J.: Photovoltaic techno-economical potential on roofs in regions and islands: the case of the Canary Islands. Methodological review and methodology proposal. Renew. Sustain. Energy Rev. **20**, 219–239 (2013)

15. Moser, D.: Rapporto sull'importanza dell'energia solare su scala regionale e sul potenziale di sviluppo dell'energia solare a livello locale. Technical report (2015). https://doi.org/10.13140/RG2.1.4794.9284

International Workshop on Automatic Landform Classification: Spatial Methods and Applications (ALCSMA 2020)

Computer-Aided Geomorphic Seabed Classification and Habitat Mapping at Punta Licosa MPA, Southern Italy

Crescenzo Violante[(✉)] [ID]

Institute of Heritage Science, CNR, Via G. San Felice, 8, Naples, Italy
Crescenzo.violante@cnr.it

Abstract. Accurate seafloor maps serve as a critical component for under-standing marine ecosystems and are essential for marine spatial planning, management of submerged cultural heritage and hazard risk assessments. In September 2001 the Marine Protected Area (MPA) of Punta Licosa has been mapped using a multibeam echosounder (MBES) and a side scan sonar (SSS) system in support of the Geosed project. Such seabed investigations has allowed for high-resolution bathymetric measurements and acoustic seafloor characterization through backscatter imagery.

Based on visual interpretation of the data, the present study utilized a computer-aided seabed classification approach to map marine landform features and seabed composition of the study area. The results were then translated into a complete coverage geomorphologic map of the area to define benthic habitats. Offshore shelf plain make up more than half of the region (52.2%), with the terraces making up another 10.2% of the total area. Slopes make up a cumulative 30.1% of the study area. Scarp features comprise 4.3% while ridge features reach only 3.2% of the total study area. Benefits of the computer-aided seabed classification approach used in this study consisted in a fairly accurate geo-morphic classification, while the effectiveness of a semi-automated approach for identifying substrate composition from backscatter data mostly relied on the level of acoustic artefacts present within the survey area.

Keywords: Habitat mapping · Geomorphology · Spatial analysis · Multibeam · Backscatter · DEM

1 Introduction

The mapping of seabed habitats is now recognized as an important tool for both marine resource management and scientific study. Many government organizations managing coastal resources are developing standards for seafloor and benthic habitat character-ization and mapping [1–4]. These studies mainly rely on marine geophysical surveys [5–8] that enable to map the spatial distribution and the physical aspects (such as sediment characteristics, water depth and morphology) of benthic habitats (potential benthic habitat), while providing a means of estimating the occurrence of biota that commonly utilize that habitat type [9–11].

© Springer Nature Switzerland AG 2020
O. Gervasi et al. (Eds.): ICCSA 2020, LNCS 12250, pp. 681–695, 2020.
https://doi.org/10.1007/978-3-030-58802-1_49

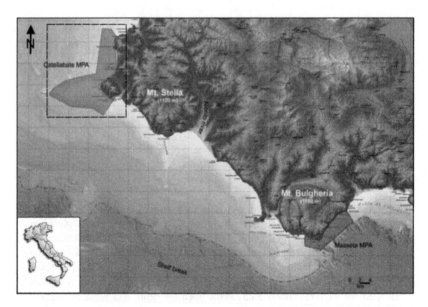

Fig. 1. Location of the study area (dashed box) with the indication of the shelf break (red dashed line) (Color figure online)

Among the physical attributes mapped and measured in detail in recent times using multibeam sonar equipment is the geomorphology of the seafloor. Seafloor geomorphology is a first order descriptor containing information such as relief, geology, geologic history, and formative processes that provides a synthesis of attributes and information relevant for characterizing physical habitats [12–14]. Bathymetry data and seafloor intensity data (backscatter) can be integrated with ground-truthing data to produce categorical maps of geomorphic features and biotopes that predict distributions of biota and substrates across broad spatial scales [15, 16]. Evaluating the usefulness of seafloor geomorphology as a proxy for characterization of complex benthic biological communities is an active area of global marine research effort [13, 17].

The applications of automated techniques to geomorphic seabed classification may provide essential information to benthic habitat mapping [18–20]. As the volume of high-resolution seabed data increases globally, there is a growing interest in automated approaches to seabed terrain analysis based on gridded bathymetric data (DEMs) [21, 22]. These approaches typically involves segmentation of the seafloor into more or less homogeneous classes that exhibit a defined variation in size, scale and shape of geomorphic features such as landforms and their sub-components (landform elements) [23, 24]. While automated approaches offer promising benefits of repeatability, the application of these classification techniques to seabed mapping remains a developing field of study.

In Italy, the Ministry of Environment endorsed the European Directives Natura 2000 and Marine Strategy (2008/56/CE) that establish habitats of priority importance and a framework of necessary measures to achieve or maintain good environmental status in the marine environment. Nevertheless, no action has been taken at national level for developing a methodology that includes geomorphic features. This led to the production of maps that identify the structure of biotic communities on the base substrate features (bionomic maps) without defining other physical components that affect the abundance and distribution of benthic organisms on the seabed [25].

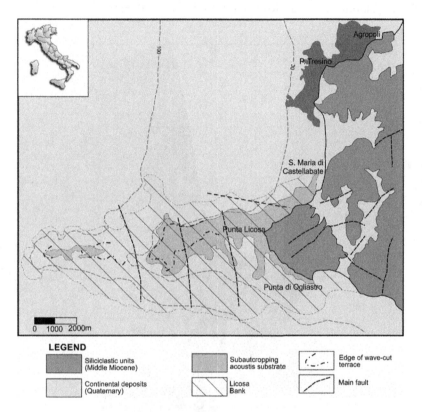

Fig. 2. Geologic sketch map of the study area.

The study area is located within the official boundary of the Cilento, Vallo di Diano, and Alburni Geopark in southern Italy and covers an area of about 140 km^2 down to a depth of − 135 m (Fig. 1). It is characterized by minor embayment with soft sediments, which alternates with rocky shore and cliffed coast and headlands, to which associates a diversity of habitats both along the coast and on the seabed. The marine coastal areas are actively colonized by phanerogams (Posidonia oceanica) and dominated by coarse biogenic sediments and carbonate buildups made by encrusting organisms (bioconstructions). Since 2009 it is part of the "Santa Maria di Castellabate" Marine Protected Area (MPA) which has been established on the bases of marine species and habitats of priority importance for the European Union.

The morphological features of the seabed off the Santa Maria di Castellabate marine coastal area are dominated by the Licosa Bank (LB) which represents the seaward prosecution of the Punta Licosa promontory (Fig. 2). The LB extends in an east-west direction up to 13 km from the coast, with a relief ranging from 40 to 125 m above the seabed. Rocky substrates, past sea level oscillations, and slope instability phenomena affecting the LB resulted in a very complex morphologic pattern fostering benthic environments that are characterized by a very high biological productivity. On the LB, wave-cut platforms occur at two main depth levels: - 20 and - 50 m.

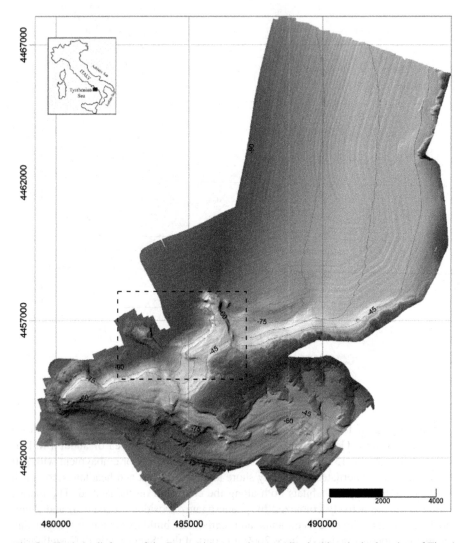

Fig. 3. Shaded relief map of the Punta Licosa marine area. Dashed box is the location of Fig. 4.

The aim of this paper is to characterize and map the seafloor off Punta Licosa promontory in the Cilento coast using a computer-aided geomorphic seabed classification. Automated segmentation of DEM surface obtained from multibeam bathymetry of the study area allowed for the identification of marine landforms and landform elements that were translated into classified geomorphic features by visual interpretation of the data. Following this approach, benthic maps that include seabed geomorphology and composition were obtained from bathymetry and backscatter data aided by seafloor sedimentological data. The results were then compared with previous seabed classifications in the Punta Licosa MPA [26, 27] to examine the relative ability of semi-automated and manual techniques for identifying and mapping sea-floor geomorphic features.

2   Materials and Methods

2.1   MBES and SSS Data Acquisitions and Processing

In July 2001 the seabed off Punta Licosa was mapped by IAMC-CNR_Napoli using the CNR research vessel Tethys. Swath bathymetry and backscatter data were collected using a 100 kHz Reson Seabat 8111 Tx/Rx multibeam (MBES) and 100 kHz Klein Side Scan Sonar (SSS) systems. Surveys were operated at speeds of 3 to 6 knots with distances between adjacent transects run to achieve 20%–50% overlap. Sound velocity data were collected daily as water column profiles to correct for variability in through-water sound speeds associated with changing densities within the water mass. Vessel motion and position were logged using a MAHRS inertial navigation system, produced by Teledyne with DGPS corrections in real-time. Bathymetric soundings were processed edited and cleaned using PDS 2000. Cleaned soundings were then gridded using weighted averaging to produce 5 m cell size digital elevation models (DEM; Fig. 3).

The SSS system was equipped with ultra-short baseline positioning (USBL) to accurately locate the tow-fish position relative to the vessel. The collected backscatter data were corrected for navigation and slant range distortion. Mosaicking of the sidescan sonar records resulted in backscatter maps with sub-meter resolution (Fig. 4).

2.2   Ground-Truthing Data Collection and Processing

Sediment grab samples were collected within the study area to characterize the seabed substrates and ground-truth the SSS backscatter data. Sediment samples were collected from R/V Tethys in September 2008. A total of 20 sediment samples were recovered between 18 m and 77 m water depth, using Van-Veen grab samplers deployed via the rear-A crane. Sediment texture and composition was described onboard to determine the character of the samples. Additionally, towed video inspections by Remote Operated Vehicle (ROV) were carried out in 2014 from aboard the CNR research vessel Urania using a Pollux III equipped with HD color camera [28].

Grain size properties of the sediment samples were determined by sieve separation of the gravel, sand, and mud fractions and by laser granulometry on the combined mud and sand fractions, using a Sympatec analyzer. Sandy biogenic sediments constitute the dominant sediment fraction in the survey area (78.41%), composed mostly of skeletal grains and bioclastic material (87%). Nine of the collected samples were classified as coarse sand with gravels, four as coarse sand, three as muddy sand, one as fine sand,

and two as sandy mud. The overall mud fraction is 22.6%. Gravel-dominated sediment occurs mostly along the coast at the base of rocky cliffs. However, very coarse sand and gravel are very common up to a depth 100 m.

3 Interpretation of Seafloor Landforms

Landforms were classified adapting a free stand-alone application (BRESS) [29, 30]. The BRESS algorithm performs a bathymetry-derived segmentation, that is, a segmentation of the DEM surface, through the identification of its seafloor geomorphological elements, and provides statistical layers that characterize the identified segments. This application implements principles of topographic openness and pattern recognition to identify terrain features from bathymetric DEMs that can be classified into easily recognizable landform types such as valleys, slopes, ridges, and flats ("bathy-morphon" architypes) [31].

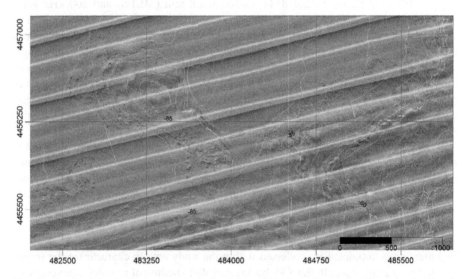

Fig. 4. Detail of the backscatter map obtained from Side Scan Sonar data. Location in Fig. 2.

"Bathymorphon" architypes represent the relative landscape relationships between a single DEM grid node and surrounding grid nodes as assessed in eight directions around the node (the four cardinal directions and the four main inter-cardinal directions). The position of a grid node relative to others in the terrain are determined via a line-of-sight method looking out in each direction by a user defined search annulus specified by an inner and outer search radius. The search annulus units are grid nodes, so the length of this is dependent directly on the resolution of the input raster grid.

The line-of-sight principle is implemented by using a user-defined parametric angular flatness threshold and the difference between the zenith and the nadir angles of a grid node. Based on angular flatness and the above defined angular difference, each node is assigned to a bathymorphon class that expresses the degree of dominance or enclosure of a node location on an irregular surface (i.e., the openness) [32] at the user-identified scale (i.e., the search annulus). Reasonable values for angular flatness and search annulus are obtained by extensive testing aimed to outline landform features that are more comparable to visual interpretation [33].

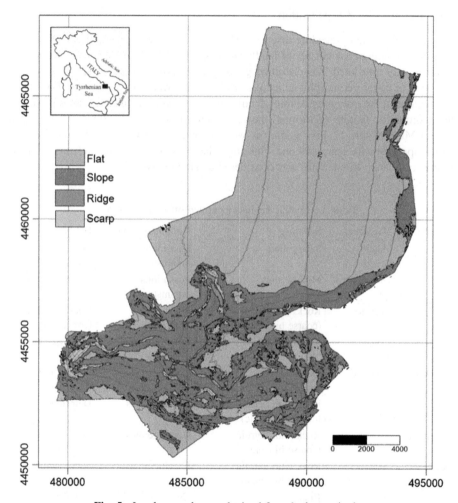

Fig. 5. Landscape classes obtained from bathymetric data

The bathymorphons can be grouped into a relatively small (from ten to four) number of landform classes that capture most of the relevant morphologic relationships related to landform description. In the study area testing of the key parameters (i.e. search annulus and flatness) resulted in landform classes that were systematically evaluated within 3D visualization software to assess if the prominent landform features of interest were correctly identified (Fig. 5). Outcomes for an effective spatial segmentation of the DEM surface off Punta Licosa were found mostly associated with flatness parameter of 1.0°, and inner and outer radius of 5 and 20 grid nodes respectively, which identified flats, ridges and slopes classes. However, flatness parameter of 5.0°, an inner radius of 1grid nodes and an outer radius of 10 was used to characterize steep and narrow seafloor areas (scarp features).

3.1   Geomorphic Classification

The semi-automated procedure discussed above allowed the segmentation of the study area into homogeneous classes of landforms that, based on their size, scale and shape, were directly translated into classified geomorphic features or processed as landform elements of larger geomorphic units (e.g. shelf plain, terrace and shoreface). Following this approach, the polygons defining landform classes were renamed as appropriate for the geomorphic feature (geoforms) they represent throughout the extent of the Punta Licosa MPA (Table 1). Five geoforms were associated with flat landform class, one with slope, one with scarp and one with ridge class. As no valley/channel classes occur in the study area, this feature was considered as slope class.

Table 1.   Benthic habitats identified off Punta Licosa.

Landform	Geoform	Substrate	Dominant biota	Habitat
Flat	Shelf plain	Sandy mud	Fossorious organisms	Shelf muddy plain
	Shoreface	Muddy sand	Fossorious organisms	Sandy shoreface
	Terrace	Rock with detritic (coarse biogenic)	Posidonia oceanica	Rocky detritic terrace
	Terrace	Muddy detritic	Fossorious organisms	Muddy detritic terrace
	Terrace	Detritic (coarse biogenic)	Coralligenous	Detritic terrace
Slope	Slope	Rock with detritic (coarse biogenic)	Coralligenous	Detritic slope
Scarp	Scarp	Rock with detritic (coarse biogenic)	Coralligenous	Scarp with coralligenous
Ridge	Ridge	Rock with detritic (coarse biogenic)	Coralligenous	Ridge with coralligenous
–	Boulder field	Rock	Coralligenous or hydroids	Boulder

The geoform terms used for classifying the investigated seabed area were sourced from several classification schemes including the coastal and marine ecological classification standard [4], hydrographic dictionary [34] and the standardization of undersea feature names [35].

4   Classification of Seabed Composition

The substrate classification was derived from the backscatter data supported by the ground-truthing results from sediment grab sampling. Representative areas of distinct backscatter intensity (classes) were selected as training areas with a Sea floor Classification utility (SeaClass) produced by Triton Elics™. Using these samples, a map of the sea floor depicting the defined classes was created (see Fig. 4).

The user-defined categories recognized 11 acoustic facies in the survey area. Five acoustic facies are associated with sediment grain size, one corresponds to hard substrata, two relate to biological features (carbonate buildups and seafloor vegetation), one is associated with landslide blocks and one correspond to sediment remobilization.

The substrate map shows that the flat areas are variably comprised of muddy, fine and coarse sand facies, which are irregularly distributed between the offshore shelf plain and the Licosa bank.

Sandy muds represent the most dominant soft-substrate class (58% of the mapped area), comprising the majority of the offshore shelf plain and foot slope areas. Coarse sands, identified by consistently high and irregular backscatter intensity, are the second most dominant substrate type (38% of the mapped area) and comprise the majority of slope areas. Fine sands are associated with consistently low backscatter reflectance and occur in shoreface areas, while rocks mostly form bathymetric highs, and locally occur along slopes and terraces.

5   Geomorphic Features and Benthic Habitats

Substrate features aided by benthic community data from video and scuba inspections were combined with geomorphic features by Geographic Information System (GIS) overlay analysis to discriminate benthic habitats of the study area that are described below (Fig. 6 and Table 1).

Plains: These cover 81.6 km² in water depth ranging from 30 to 130 m with average gradients nearly reaching 1°. Plains composed of sandy mud in water depths of more than 30 m (offshore plains) mostly occupy the northern sector of the survey area (70.8 km²). This sector is also occupied by plains that are characterized by muddy sand in water depths of less than 30 m (sandy shoreface).

Slopes: Gentle slopes cover 39.7 km² of the survey area, from the top of the LB up to a depth of ∼120 m. In this area gradients range from 5° near the top of the LB to 3° in the distal areas. Seabed composition is characterized by coarse biogenic sand with a fine gravel fraction locally reaching 25%, with a higher mud fraction in water depths of more than 80 m. In its middle and lower parts, the slope is characterized by several mounds ranging from a few to 65 m in diameter corresponding to coralligenous bioconstructions while sediment remobilization from the top of the LB occur the upper parts of the slope.

Scarps: These are steeply sloping narrow areas ranging from 5 to 15° mostly composed of hard bottoms that cover 4.2 km^2 along slopes in water depth ranging from −25 to −120 m.

Terraces: Two main wave-cut terraces with slightly convex slopes are present at the top of the LB at depth levels of - 20 and - 50 m on average. These structures cover 3.6 km^2 and are characterized by sediment covers of gravel and very coarse organogenic sand colonized by Posidonia oceanica meadows. Nearly flat, slightly concave, terraces also occupy 4.7 km^2 in 44–85 m water depth. Here the seabed is composed of muddy detritic sediments with sparse mound-shaped bioconstructions reaching 30 m in diameter.

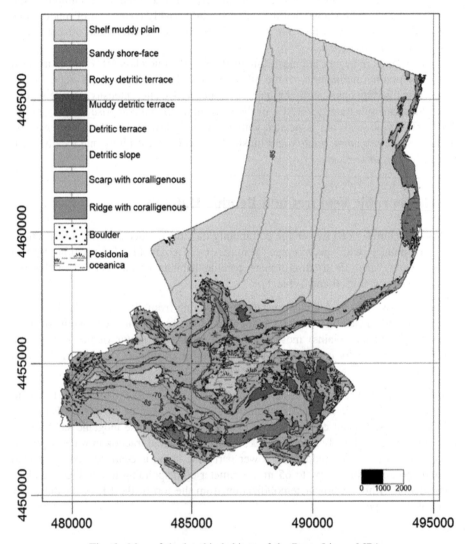

Fig. 6. Map of the benthic habitats of the Punta Licosa MPA

Ridges: These are elongated narrow elevations with steep sides mostly composed of hard bottoms that cover 3.1 km^2 in water depth ranging from 15 to 120 m. They occur on top of shallow seabed reliefs and along slope as well as isolated structures in shelf areas. In these areas seabed composition is characterized by sandy mud with elongated coralligenous bioconstructions.

Boulder fields: Metric and plurimetric rocky boulders resulting from slope recession are scattered on the seabed up to distances of several hundred meters from the base of the LB. They cover 2.4 km^2 in water depth ranging from 80 to 130 m and are mostly colonized by small coralligenous bioconstructions.

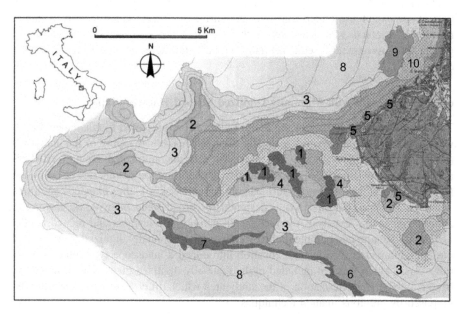

Fig. 7. Punta Licosa habitat map. (1) Spur of coralligenous bioconstruction. (2) Wave-cut terrace with mixed organogenic cover. (3) Slope with mixed organogenic sediments. (4) Depositional terrace. (5) Rock. (6) Deep terrace with bioclastic cover. (7) Ledge with coralligenous. (8) Shelf muddy plain. (9) Sandy fringe with bioclast. (10) Offshore transition. Redrawn from [27]

6   Discussion

The methodological approach presented in this study was mainly aimed to discuss the use of relatively simply and freely available tools for semi-automated seabed classification in the frame of the geophysical methodologies that are currently applied to benthic habitat mapping. The free stand-alone application BRESS has offered the opportunity to test this approach in the Punta Licosa MPA. The automatic seafloor segmentation resulting from BRESS algorithm applied to bathymetry-based DEM surface of the study area allowed identifying terrain features that were classified into easily recognizable landform. Landform classes were then translated into classified geomorphic features on base of their size, scale and shape, using several classification schemes reported in literature [4, 34, 35].

Both stages of seafloor segmentation and geomorphic interpretation required significant user inputs and visual inspections. Expert knowledge of feature identification has resulted to be particularly important in the stage of geomorphic interpretation to include landforms within the context of the surrounding seascape and ensuring the features identified match the geoform definitions. On the other hand, adopting a semi-automated approach for the surface elements classification significantly reduced the time to digitize manually feature boundaries.

Overall, the level of bathymetric artefacts present within a survey area affected only to a lesser extent the effectiveness of the surface elements classification. A higher number of artefacts was associated with Side Scan Sonar survey, which required a greater time investment to edit manually the acoustic facies derived from backscatter data.

6.1   Comparison with Manually Digitized Seabed Habitat Map

The map of benthic habitats of the Punta Licosa MPA presented in this paper (Fig. 6) was compared with a previous manually digitized seafloor mapping of the study area (Fig. 7) [23, 24]. The comparison indicates that the automated method (BRESS) applied in the present study is most effective at capturing the boundaries of prominent features, which subsequently formed the boundaries of the mapped geoforms. Although this method was mostly designed for broad scale bathymetric features, it allowed the spatial extent of the recognized geomorphic features and related benthic habitats to be quite comparable to the extents of those manually digitized. Furthermore, the semi-automated seafloor classification introduced a landscape type referred to the ridge class, which was not included in the manually digitized maps. This resulted in a benthic habitat characterization of the study area which differ to some extent from that proposed by previous manual techniques.

7   Conclusion

The approach developed through this work provides clues on how to consistently classify geomorphic units that are relevant to benthic habitat mapping by using a relatively simple and freely available tools for semi-automated seabed segmentation (BRESS). Habitat mapping of the study area utilized several complementary geophysical technologies including multibeam and Side Scan Sonar systems and Remote Operated Vehicle (ROV). These surveys has allowed for high-resolution bathymetric measurements and acoustic seafloor characterization that resulted in backscatter map of the seabed and production of bathymetric DEMs.

The BRESS terrain analysis algorithm used in this work was effective at generating meaningful landform maps through a segmentation of the DEM surface, which were used to identify geomorphic units. This tool allowed for high speed classification of terrain over complex morphology that characterize the study area and proved to be effective at classifying small scale geomorphic features. Integration of landform and substrate classifications to produce seabed character and geomorphology maps still required significant subjective expert interpretation to generally delineate among the different landscape classes and to quality control of the landform classification output.

Acknowledgments. I am grateful to the Master of R/Vs Urania and Thetis Captains Emanuele Gentile and Aimone Patanè and all the crewmembers for their significant contribution to the geophysical survey operations. Thanks also to the two anonymous reviewers who provided valuable feedback which greatly improved the manuscript. This work was supported by the project PON-IDEHA, Innovation for Data Elaboration in Heritage Areas, financed by the Italian Ministry of the University and Scientific and Technologic Research.

References

1. Pickrill, R.A., Kostylev, V.E.: Habitat mapping and national seafloor mapping strategies in Canada. In: Todd, B.J., Greene, H.G. (eds.) Mapping the Seafloor for Habitat Characterization. Geological Association of Canada, Special Paper, vol. 47, pp. 483–495 (2007)
2. Cogan, C.B., Todd, B.J., Lawton, P., Noji, T.T.: The role of marine habitat mapping in ecosystem-based management. ICES J. Mar. Sci. **66**, 2033–2042 (2009)
3. FGDC (Federal Geographic Data Committee): Coastal and Marine Ecological Classification Standard. Federal Geographic Data Committee, Reston, VA (2012)
4. Andersen, J.H., et al.: European broad-scale seabed habitat maps support implementation of ecosystem-based management. Open J. Ecol. **8**, 86–103 (2018)
5. Roff, J.C., Taylor, M.E.: A geophysical classification system for marine conservation. Aquat. Conserv. Mar. Freshw. Ecosyst. **10**, 209–223 (2000)
6. Kostylev, V.E., Todd, B.J., Fader, G.B.J., Courtney, R.C., Cameron, G.D.M., Pickrill, R.A.: Benthic habitat mapping on the Scotian Shelf based on multibeam bathymetry, surficial geology and sea floor photographs. Mar. Ecol. Progr. Ser. **219**, 121–137 (2001)
7. Ehrhold, A., Hamon, D., Guillaumont, B.: The REBENT monitoring network, a spatially integrated, acoustic approach to surveying nearshore macrobenthic habitats: application to the Bay of Concarneau (South Brittany, France). ICES J. Mar. Sci. **63**, 1604–1615 (2006)
8. Violante, C., Mazzola, S.: Geophysical techniques for protection and management of marine habitat: example from the Campania offshore, Eastern Tyrrhenian Sea. In: Proceedings of the 7th EUREGEO—EUropean congress on REgional GEOscientific Cartography and Information Systems, Bologna, Italy, pp. 395–397 (2012)
9. Post, A.L.: The application of physical surrogates to predict the distribution of marine benthic organisms. Ocean Coast. Manage. **51**, 161–179 (2008)
10. Nichol, S., Huang, Z., Howard, F., Porter-Smith, R., Lucieer, V.L., Barrett, N.: Geomorphological classification of reefs–draft framework for an Australian Standard; Report to the National Environmental Science Program, Marine Biodiversity Hub. Geoscience Australia, Canberra, Australia, p. 27 (2016)
11. Greene, H.G., Bizzarro, J.J., O'Connell, V.M., Brylinsky, C.K.: Construction of digital potential benthic habitat maps using a coded classification scheme and its application. In: Todd, B.J., Greene, H.G. (eds.) Mapping the Seafloor for Habitat Characterisation. Geological Association of Canada Special Paper 47, St. Johns, Newfoundland, pp. 141–156 (2007)

12. Harris, P.T.: From Seafloor Geomorphology to Predictive Habitat Mapping: Progress in Applications of Biophysical Data to Ocean Management. Geoscience Australia, Canberra (2012)
13. Harris, P.T., Baker, E.K. (eds.) Seafloor Geomorphology as Benthic Habitat: GeoHAB Atlas of Seafloor Geomorphic Features and Benthic Habitats, 2nd edn. p. 1045. Elsevier Science, Burlington (2020)
14. Althaus, F., Williams, A., Kloser, R.J., Seiler, J., Bax, N.J.: Evaluating geomorphic features as surrogates for benthic biodiversity on Australia's western continental margin. In: Todd, B. J., Greene, H.G. (eds.) Mapping the Seafloor for Habitat Characterization. Geological Association of Canada, Canada, pp. 665–679 (2012). https://doi.org/10.1016/b978-0-12-385140-6.00048-7
15. Olenin, S., Ducrotoy, J.: The concept of biotope in marine ecology and coastal management. Mar. Pollut. Bull. **53**, 20–29 (2006)
16. Brown, C.J., Sameoto, J.A., Smith, S.J.: Multiple methods, maps, and management applications: Purpose made seafloor maps in support of ocean management. J. Sea Res. **72**, 1–13 (2012)
17. Harris, P.T., Baker, E.K. (eds.): Seafloor Geomorphology as Benthic Habitat: GeoHAB Atlas of Seafloor Geomorphic Features and Benthic Habitats, p. 947. Elsevier Science, Burlington (2012). https://doi.org/10.1016/B978-0-12-385140-6.00071-2
18. Ismaila, K., Huvenneb, V.A., Masson, D.G.: Objective automated classification technique for marine landscape mapping in submarine canyons. Mar. Geol. **362**, 17–32 (2015). http://dx.doi.org/10.1016/j.margeo.2015.01.006
19. Preston, J.: Automated acoustic seabed classification of multibeam images of Stanton Banks. Appl. Acoust. **70**, 1277–1287 (2009). https://doi.org/10.1016/j.apacoust.2008.07.011
20. Olaya, V.: Basic land-surface parameters. In: Hengl, T., Reuter, H. (eds.) Geomorphometry, Concepts, Software, Application, pp. 141–169. Elsevier, Burlington (2009)
21. Diesing, M., Green, S.L., Stephens, D., Lark, R.M., Stewart, H.A., Dove, D.: Mapping seabed sediments: Comparison of manual, geostatistical, object-based image analysis and machine learning approaches. Cont. Shelf Res. **84**, 107–119 (2014)
22. Schmidt, J., Hewitt, A.: Fuzzy land element classification from DTMs based on geometry and terrain position. Geoderma **121**, 243–256 (2004)
23. MacMillan, R., Shary, P.: Landforms and landform elements in geomorphometry. Dev. Soil Sci. **33**, 227–275 (2009). ISSN 0166-2481. https://doi.org/10.1016/s0166-2481(08)00009-3
24. Evans, I.S.: Geomorphometry and landform mapping: What is a landform? Geomorphology **137**, 94–106 (2012)
25. Violante, C., De Lauro, M., Esposito, E.: Fine-scale seabed habitats off Capri Island, southern Italy. In: Harris, P.T., Baker, E.K. (eds.) Seafloor Geomorphology as Benthic Habitat. GeoHAB Atlas of Seafloor Geomorphic Features and Benthic Habitats. 2nd edn. pp. 439–450 (2020). https://doi.org/10.1016/B978-0-12-814960-7.00024-5
26. D'Angelo, S., Di Stefano, F., Fiorentino, A., Lettieri, M., Russo, G., Violante, C.: The map of the marine landscapes and habitats of Cilento, Vallo di Diano and Alburni Geopark. Linking geo- and bio- diversity with a multiscalar approach. In: Proceedings of the 12th European Geoparks Conference, 8 p. (2013)
27. D'Angelo, S., Stefano, F., Fiorentino, A., Lettieri, M.A., Russo, G., Violante, C.: Marine landscapes and habitats of Cilento Geopark (Italy). Linking geo- and bio- diversity with a multiscalar approach. In: Harris, P.T., Baker, E.K. (eds.) Seafloor Geomorphology as Benthic Habitat. GeoHab Atlas of Seafloor Geomorphic Features and Benthic Habitats. 2nd edn. pp. 421–437 (2020). https://doi.org/10.1016/B978-0-12-814960-7.00023-3

28. Violante, C., De Lauro, M.: Oceanographic cruise Seascape_14. Technical report, CNR Solar, 10 p. (2014)
29. Masetti, G., Mayer, L.A., Ward, L.G.: A bathymetry- and reflectivity based approach for seafloor segmentation. Geosciences **8**(14) (2018). https://doi.org/10.3390/geosciences8010014
30. Hydroffice: Bathymetric- and Reflectivity-Based Estimator of Seafloor Segments (BRESS) (2019). https://www.hydroffice.org/bress/main
31. Jasiewicz, J., Stepinski, T.F.: Geomorphons - a pattern recognition approach to classification and mapping of landforms. Geomorphology **182**, 147–156 (2013). https://doi.org/10.1016/j.geomorph.2012.11.005
32. Yokoyama, R., Shirasawa, M., Pike, R.J.: Visualizing topography by openness: a new application of image processing to digital elevation models. Photogramm. Eng. Remote Sens. **68**, 257–266 (2002)
33. Sowers, D.C., Masetti, G., Mayer, L.A., Johnson, P.l., Gardner, J.V., Armstrong, A.A.: Standardized geomorphic classification of seafloor within the United States atlantic canyons and continental margin. Front. Mar. Sci. 28 January 2020 (2020). https://doi.org/10.3389/fmars.2020.00009
34. International Hydrographic Organisation (IHO): Hydrographic Dictionary; International Hydrographic Bureau: Monaco, French, p. 281 (2014)
35. International Hydrographic Organisation (IHO): Standardization of Undersea Feature Names: Guidelines, Proposal Form, Terminology, 4th ed.; Bathymetric Publication No. 6; International Hydrographic Bureau: Monaco, French, p. 38 (2017)

Comparison of Different Methods of Automated Landform Classification at the Drainage Basin Scale: Examples from the Southern Italy

Dario Gioia[1]([⊠]) [iD], Maria Danese[1] [iD], Mario Bentivenga[2] [iD],
Eva Pescatore[2], Vincenzo Siervo[2], and Salvatore Ivo Giano[2] [iD]

[1] ISPC-CNR, Tito, Potenza, Italy
dario.gioia@cnr.it
[2] Facoltà di Scienze, Università della Basilicata, Potenza, Italy

Abstract. In this work, we tested the reliability of two different methods of automated landform classification (ACL) in three geological domains of the southern Italian chain with contrasting morphological features. ACL maps deriving from the TPI-based (topographic position index) algorithm are strictly dependent to the search input parameters and they are not able to fully capture landforms of different size. Geomorphons-based classification has shown a higher potential and can represent a powerful method of ACL, although it should be improved with the introduction of additional DEM-based parameters for the extraction of landform classes.

Keywords: Geomorphometry · Automatic landform classification · Geomorphological mapping · Southern Italy · DEM analysis

1 Introduction

In the last years, several factors such as availability of high-resolution DEMs, advances in computer power and the growing ability of research group to produce GIS-aided tools have promoted the development of many procedures and algorithms of automated classification/extraction of landforms [1]. Many works demonstrated that landform maps based on unsupervised classification represent a key tool in different research fields such as geomorphology, geology, archaeology, soil science and seismology [2–7]. Automatic classification of landform (ACL) provides several advantages than the traditional methods of geomorphological analysis, such as photo-interpretation and field surveys. Firstly, the use of an appropriate algorithm of landform classification overcomes the issue of the subjective interpretation of the user and the low reproducibility of "hand-made" geomorphological maps. Moreover, the full coverage of a study area can be useful in different applications, aimed at the investigation of the relationships between landforms and other parameters [8]. Although these factors should promote a fast growth of the application of ACL methods, the maps deriving by such an approach are frequently not able to fully define the spatial pattern of landforms

© Springer Nature Switzerland AG 2020
O. Gervasi et al. (Eds.): ICCSA 2020, LNCS 12250, pp. 696–708, 2020.
https://doi.org/10.1007/978-3-030-58802-1_50

and are affected by high-level noise. However, a relevant limitation of the method is due to its high scale-dependence. Landforms pertained to different geological landscapes have peculiar dimensions and in a first step the ACL should include the hierarchical definition of type and size of landforms occurring at different scales [1]. Most of the ACL approaches are focused on the characterization of mesoscale landforms (size-scale of hundred meters) and are strictly dependent of the search window size. Finally, this kind of approach does not provide any information about the time and origin of the geomorphic features [2], thus implying additional steps of "experts" in map interpretation.

Due to these limitations, the time-consuming traditional approaches of landform recognition and mapping are still the preferred ones by geomorphologists whereas extensive validation studies on the ACL are lacking.

In this paper, we try to fill this gap through the comparison of ACL maps coming from two of the most promising methods of automatic/semiautomatic landform extraction. The first method is the well-known TPI-based classification [9], and the second one is the geomorphons algorithm, recently proposed by [10]. Results of the ACL obtained by the two methods have been investigated in three different landscapes of southern Italy, featured by contrasting geological and geomorphological characters (Fig. 1). A comparison between two different ACL methods was carried out in the three test areas and the robustness and reliability of the two unsupervised classification methods have been discussed.

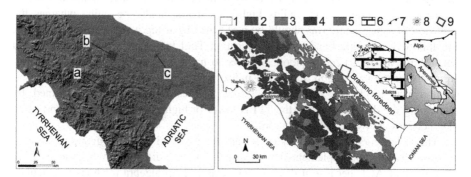

Fig. 1. (A) Geographical location (red boxes indicate study areas: a) axial zone; b) foredeep; c) foreland) and (B) geological sketch map of study areas. Legend: 1) Pliocene-Quaternary clastics and Quaternary volcanics; 2) Miocene syntectonic deposits; 3) Cretaceous to Oligocene ophiolite-bearing internal units (Ligurian units); 4) Mesozoic-Cenozoic shallow-water carbonates of the Apenninic platform; 5) Lower-middle Triassic to Miocene shallow-water and deep-sea succession of the Lagonegro unit; 6) Mesozoic-Cenozoic shallow-water carbonates of the Apulian platform; 7) Thrust front of the chain; 8) Volcanoes; 9) Study areas (Color figure online)

2 Methods

The existing methods of ACL are mainly based on the extraction of first and second orders DEM-derivative attributes (slope and curvature). Local surface shape is frequently combined to the relative slope position of the landform elements thus to group the landscape sectors with similar statistical parameters and within a selected moving windows [1, 11]. Available algorithms are strictly dependent of the moving windows size and clustering can be cell-based or object-based [12, 13].

In this work, we test the accuracy of two different procedures of ACL in three study areas where also an interpretation of the "real" landforms based on an "expert" geomorphological analysis was realized. Application of the two algorithms of automated landform classification has been carried out using high-resolution DEMs (i.e. spatial resolution of 5 m for the axial and foredeep sectors and 8 m for the foreland area) deriving from Airborne LIDAR surveys. The DEMs are freely available.

The first one is a well-known algorithm that classifies landform units through a combination of TPI value and slope thresholds. TPI-based slope classification has been performed using an ArcGIS tool developed by Jenness Enterprises [9]. The algorithm evaluates the elevation difference between a cell and the average elevation around it within a predetermined radius. Positive TPI values indicate that the pixel has an elevation value higher than the average ones of the neighborhood searching window, whereas negative values are representative of a pixel with a lower elevation than the average of the search radius. TPI is strongly influenced by the search radius dimension: in particular, a large search radius highlights major landscape units, whereas the detection of minor landforms should be performed by using a small radius [4, 6, 14]. For this reason, in the Landform Classification Tool two search radii are inserted, a smaller and a larger neighborhood, in order to try to capture different sizes or landforms. After the calculation of the TPI index, a slope position index (i.e. SPI) classification was produced, where ten discrete classes (landforms) are obtained by combining the degree to which the TPI is lower or higher than the average and some slope classes set by default in the tool.

The second method used to realize a landform map and named as geomorphon, was proposed by [10] and implemented in a Grass GIS tool. It differs from the other existing algorithms of ACL because it does not use classic map algebra methods to calculate elevation differences inside the neighborhood. Conversely, it uses a computer vision approach, a pattern-based classification that self-adapts to the local topography. This technique utilizes the line-of-sight principle to evaluate a D quantity in each surrounding; more specifically, such an approach takes in count not only the elevation differences but also the zenith and nadir angles in the profiles and the lookup distance and should ensure identification of a landform at their most appropriate spatial scale [10]. Landform classification is derived from the extraction of Local Ternary Patterns (LTP). LTP are the basic micro-structure that constitute each existing type of landform and are named geomorphons; through the combination of geomorphon, landforms are extracted, in particular the first ten classes given back by the algorithm constitute the most frequent existing landform elements [10]. Also in this method, there are an inner and an outer search radius as input parameters, but the analysis is more independent from them compared to the TPI-based method. In fact, the neighborhood of the geomorphon method is self-adapting. The input radii instead have the aim to simplify the algorithm execution and bound it in the inserted areas, because otherwise, for each pixel, every time it would be achieved for all the raster. Finally, in the geomorphon method, also a flatness threshold (similar to the slope classification used in the TPI-based landform classification, but limited to areas considered flat) should be defined.

3 Study Cases

3.1 Regional Geological Framework

The comparison of the two methods of automatic extraction of landforms was carried out in three study areas belonging to different morphotectonic domains of the southern Italian chain. It is a northeast-verging fold-and-thrust belt deriving from the deformation of Mesozoic–Cenozoic shallow-water and deep-sea sedimentary succession pertained to the western border of the African-Apulian plate, and related Neogene–Pleistocene foredeep and satellite-basin deposits [15]. The foreland area is represented by the Apulian carbonate platform and represents the lower and subducting plate of the orogenic system. Starting from the Late Oligocene, the migration of the thrust front toward the north-east promoted the progressive deformation of pre-orogenic and syntectonic deposits from the inner (i.e. south-western) to the outer sectors of the belt. Pliocene-Pleistocene tectonic evolution of the chain was related to the activity of strike-slip and extensional faulting, which dismembered the contractional structure and promoted both the formation of many continental intermontane basins and the deep vertical incision of the fluvial net [16].

The landscape evolution of the southern Apennine chain was strictly related to its tectonic evolution, which in turn controlled also the distribution of the following NW-SE-trending main geological and geomorphological domains: the inner and axial zone of the chain (south-west sector), the outer zone of the chain (front of the chain/foredeep) and the foreland area (Fig. 1).

The axial zone of the chain is mainly constituted by impressive mountain ridges, bordered by steep slopes, frequently related to the activity of high-angle faults ([16] and references therein). These fault-related mountain blocks are mainly carved by erosional processes in Mesozoic shallow-water carbonate and in deep-sea sedimentary rocks of the same age. Quaternary faulting and base level lowering promoted the creation and evolution of tectonic and morphological depressions, which are crossed by longitudinal V-shaped valleys with thalwegs generally placed between 500 and 700 m of elevation a.s.l. Another peculiar feature of this sector is the presence of several orders of low-angle erosional surfaces and fluvial terraces, which are arranged in a staircase geometry between 500 and 2000 m of elevation a.s.l. ([16] and references therein).

The outer-zone and the front of the chain are featured by a NW-SE-trending thrust sheet system producing the same trend of morphostructural ridges, which are mainly carved by erosional processes affecting Cretaceous-to-Miocene pelagic deposits [15]. These units overlap the Pliocene and Pleistocene clastic deposits of the Bradano Foredeep, represented by a thick regressive succession of marine clay, and marine-to-transitional sands and gravels. The top of the foredeep succession is formed by alluvial units corresponding to large and gently-dipping plain-surfaces deeply dissected by the main rivers. These rivers exhibit a low slope gradient of longitudinal profiles in the middle/lower reaches where flow as wide braided- and meander-type fluvial patterns [17–19]. Widespread badlands also occurred in sectors where marine clay deposits crop out [20, 21].

The Foreland area is formed by an asymmetric NW–SE trending horst and graben system bordered by normal and transtensive faults inherited from late Cretaceous faulting activity. The Adriatic side (i.e.: the north-easternmost sector) of the foreland corresponds to a north-east gently-dipping carbonate landscape, which is also featured by karstic landforms and by the presence of several generations of Middle to Late Pleistocene marine terraces [22]. A well-developed drainage network cut both the karst landscape and the sequence of marine terraces: it is formed by regularly spaced and N-25–30°-trending flat-bottomed valleys with steep scarps [14].

4   Results

4.1   ACL Map of the Study Areas

High-resolution DEMs of the three test areas have been processed in order to automatically extract the main landforms of some of the geological domains of the southern Italian Apennines (Fig. 1). In order to select the most appropriate search radii in the TPI-based classification, we compared TPI values for different search radii with landforms detected through geomorphological analysis. We chose a neighborhood with an annulus shape. The dimensions of the radii chosen are reported in Table 1:

Table 1. Search radius size for the study areas (expressed in meters) in the TPI-based classification.

Areas	Smaller neighbourhood		Larger neighborhood	
	Inner radius	Outer radius	Inner radius	Outer radius
Axial zone	5	15	50	80
Foredeep area	5	15	25	40
Foreland area	8	24	40	100

Similarly, for the geomorphon-based method different input parameters where inserted and chosen after a preliminary analysis of the main landforms of the study areas carried by an "expert" geomorphological analysis. For all the three study areas it was highlighted that the best radius is of 10 cells and the flatness threshold is 1.

TPI-derived maps showed a high level of influence from the search windows and the selection of the most suitable ACL map was done through a visual inspection of "manual" landform mapping and the support of "expert" geomorphological analyses. On the contrary, ACL maps based on geomorphon highlight a low level of dependency to the input parameters and neighborhood sizes, as supposed by the study of the algorithm.

Axial Zone of the Chain

Comparison between the TPI and geomorphon classifications was carried out in a peculiar landscape of the axial zone of the chain (Fig. 1). From a geomorphological viewpoint, the test area shows a heterogeneous landscape featured by an alternation of impressive ridges with steep slopes and flat depressions.

Fluvial net is well developed and V-shaped valleys are prevalent. Moreover, a main braided river flowing into a wide floodplain (i.e. the Basento River) is placed in the north-western sector. Several orders of low-relief erosional land surfaces also occurred at the top and along the main slopes. In Fig. 2 results outcoming from the ACL analysis using the two above mentioned algorithms are shown.

The TPI-based ACL map discriminates 10 landform classes, which are distributed as follow: open slope and upper slope classes were the larger ones with a percentage of about 42% and 21%, respectively; fluvial landforms are mainly classified as U-shaped valleys (i.e. 18.7% of the total area) with a general overestimation of the "real" valleys size. Flat areas such as small intermontane basins and floodplains of main rivers are also well recognized.

The ACL map deriving from the geomorphon classification, using a line of sight of 50 m and a threshold for the flat area of 1° portrays an articulated landscape featured by a well-developed drainage network that dissects a number of ridges and slopes with different orientations. The slope class is the most representative landform whereas the flat areas exhibit a high level of noise. The map is able to delineate the fluvial net of the study area (i.e. "valley" class, Fig. 2) with a higher level of accuracy than the SPI map. Moreover, the mountain tops and ridges and the main watersheds appear well delineated.

Outer Front and Foredeep Area

The test area of this sector (Fig. 3) is a relatively «simple» landscape, since it is featured by a NE-dipping gently terraced surfaces moderately dissected by wide fluvial valleys and by the tributary fluvial net. The two ACL maps showed contrasting results (Fig. 3). In the TPI-based map, the most represented class is represented by flat areas, with a percentage of about 50.0% of the total area. Other relevant landform classes are open and upper slopes, which cover 23% and 12% of the total area, respectively. Fluvial net was largely identified as U-shaped valleys. This map shows a good potential to detect the sub-horizontal flat top terraced surface as well as the main valley flanks and their thalwegs.

The geomorphons-based map was extracted using the same search windows used for the southern Apennines axial zone and the flat threshold has been set to 1°. Slope class is the largest one with a percentage of 53% of the total area whereas the flat areas cover only 11% of the entire territory. This latter class can be associated to the undissected remnants of the terraced surfaces whereas the terrace edges are frequently classified as slope areas.

In this case, the geomorphons-based method is not able to differentiate valley flanks and gently-dipping surfaces, thus it could be useful to introduce a slope threshold, able to discriminate gently-dipping landform and steeper slopes.

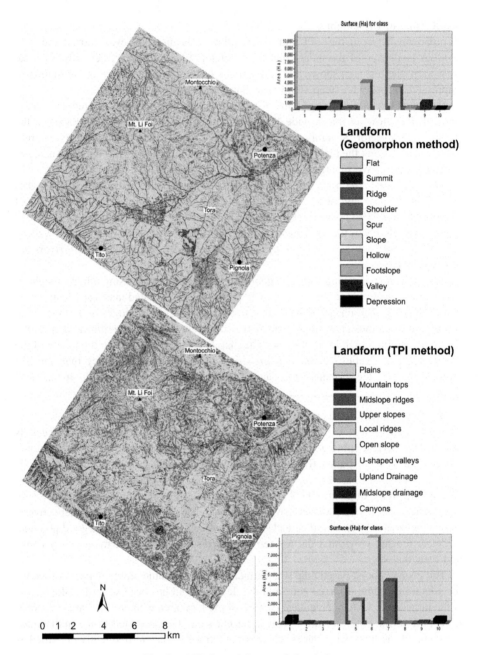

Fig. 2. ACL for axial zone of the chain

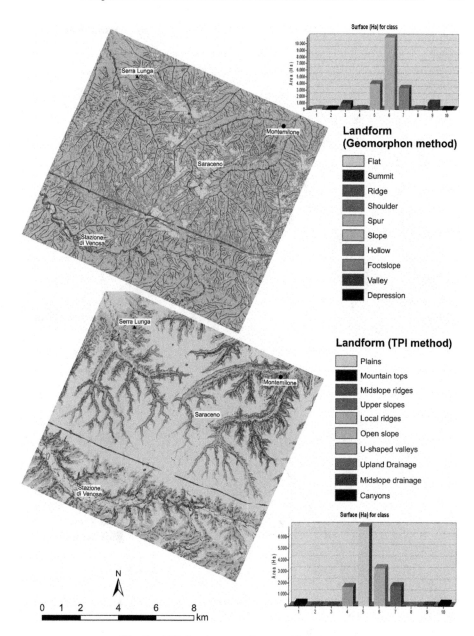

Fig. 3. ACL for the outer front and foredeep area

Foreland Area

The third study area is a small catchment of the central sector of the Apulia foreland and corresponds to a karstic landscape carved in Cretaceous shallow-water limestones (Fig. 4).

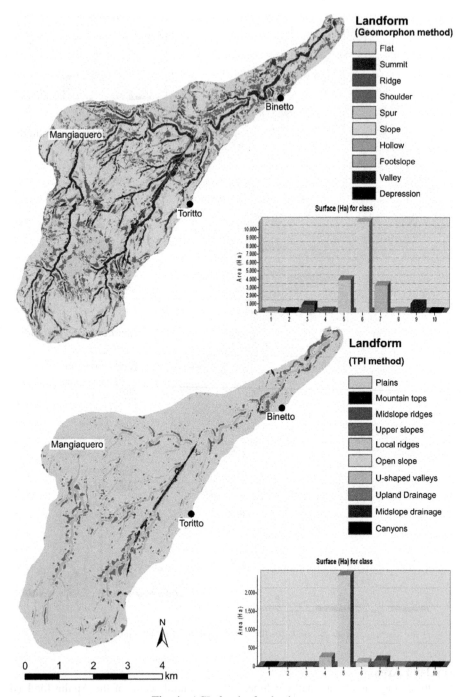

Fig. 4. ACL for the foreland area

The test area is a low-relief carbonate landscape with typical karst features and a well-defined drainage network, known as the Murge. The latter is formed by regularly spaced and N-25–30°-trending flat-bottomed valleys with steep scarps [14].

These landforms have a subtle topographic expression and are hard to recognize by classical geomorphological analyses. Recently, the application of the TPI-based landform classification at a catchment scale has been already tested as a fast and effective approach to delineate the main landforms of the Murge area [14].

TPI-based ACL map (Fig. 4) is dominated by flat areas, which represent about 80% of the total area. Flat-bottomed valleys (U-shaped valley class, see Fig. 4) and their steep flanks are discontinuously delineated.

Geomorphons-based classification was performed using the same parameters adopted for axial and foredeep areas. The map showed a better delineation of the drainage network than the TPI-based classification and related SPI map and portrayed the main fluvio-karstic landforms of the study area. Due to the general low-angle dip of the landscape, slope class is the largest one in the map but local flat areas also occurred. These sectors coincide with NW-SE-elongated sub-horizontal areas where fluvial landforms disappeared (see for example the north-westernmost sector of the map) and can be related to marine terraces related to past ancient base levels.

5   Discussion and Concluding Remarks

Advantages and limitations of two different algorithms of ACL have been investigated in three sectors of southern Italy, characterized by contrasting geological and geo-morphological characters. The first element that emerges from the study is that the comparison between the two ACL methods, in order to identify the best method, is not an easy task. In fact, an extensive field control was required to verify the full suitability of the results of ACL at a large scale. Nevertheless, preliminary geomorphological analysis based on "expert" users suggested that the two algorithms could represent a basic tool to recognize the main geomorphological elements of the study areas.

Visual comparison of the ACL maps in the study areas highlights a strong differ-ence between the two algorithms, which provided different landform classifications mainly in the foredeep and foreland sectors. Although a robust assessment of the accuracy degree of landform extraction from the two algorithms should include a detailed geomorphological mapping and a quantitative comparison from "expert" delineation of landforms and automatic classification, we provide an attempt to quantitatively compare the results coming from the two ACL methods through the grouping of landform classes of the two methods with similar features. In particular, we argued that eight of ten classes extracted by the two algorithms can be reasonably considered as similar landforms whereas two classes (i.e. footslope and hollow in the geomorphons-method; U-shaped valleys and upland drainage in the TPI classification) does not have a direct correspondence. The similarity between each class of the two methods is highlighted using the same colours in Fig. 2, 3 and 4 and allowed us to quantitatively compare the two classification methods. For example, geomorphon class "named" as plain has been interpreted as similar to the class "flat" of the TPI-method, thus we represented both with light grey.

In order to investigate the obtained results from a quantitative viewpoint, we have extracted the total number of pixels showing the similar landform in the two methods. Results highlight that differences are apparently not so high since they vary from the 7 to 17% (diagrams in Fig. 5).

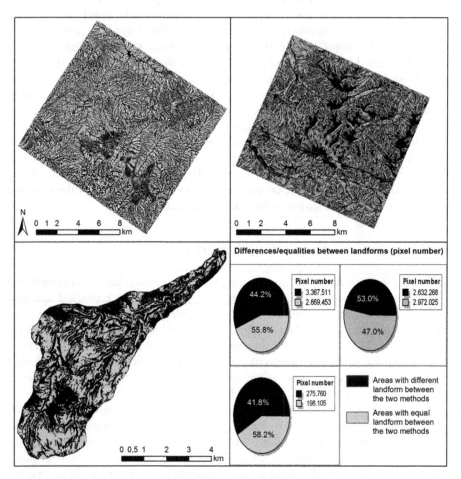

Fig. 5. Visual and quantitative comparison between the areas with similar (and different) landforms obtained from the ACL methods here used. 1) Axial zone of the chain; 2) foredeep area; 3) foreland area.

In particular, inequalities are greater than equalities in the axial zone of the chain and in the foreland area. Instead in the outer front and foredeep areas we have more similar pixel than with different landforms. However, despite to this measure, if we look at the difference/equalities maps (Fig. 5), we can see how much the results of the two methods differ and which are the hot spot of these differences: in the axial zone of the chain, geomorphons-method is able to delineate the fluvial net of the study area (i.e. "valley" class, Fig. 2) with a higher level of accuracy than the TPI map but tend to underestimate several sub-horizontal landforms of the study area such as alluvial plain and top of intermontane basins. ACL maps of the foredeep and foreland areas show more pronounced differences. In the foredeep area, the main geomorphological element (i.e. the gently-dipping terraced surfaces) is classified differently and TPI-based map is not able to detect minor fluvial channels and incisions. The geomorphons-based map portrays the undissected remnants of the terraced surfaces in a more satisfactory manner but it is not able to differentiate between the gently-dipping terrace surfaces and steeper flanks of the main valleys. A similar result can be observed in the foreland area where gemorphons-based provided a more detailed delineation of the main landforms than the TPI-based method. Also in this case, the simple introduction of a slope threshold in the geomorphons-method can help to improve the landform classification and to discriminate between peculiar geomorphological elements such as gently-dipping landsurfaces and steeper slopes related to fluvial deepening.

Our preliminary analyses suggested that geomorphons-based classification is a promising tool for automatic landform classification and can provide better results than more consolidated algorithms such as the TPI-based classification. Of course, the method needs to be deeply tested in other landscapes and/or at a wider scale but the encouraging preliminary results suggest a high potential of the proposed approach although the introduction of a slope threshold to differentiate gently-dipping and steeper slopes is required.

References

1. Hengl, T., Reuter, H.I.: Geomorphometry: Concepts, Software, Applications. Developments in Soil Science, Amsterdam (2008)
2. Wieczorek, M., Migon, P.: Automatic relief classification versus expert and field based landform classification for the medium-altitude mountain range, the Sudetes, SW Poland. Geomorphology **206**, 133–146 (2014)
3. Kramm, T., Hoffmeister, D., Curdt, C., Maleki, S., Khormali, F., Kehl, M.: Accuracy assessment of landform classification approaches on different spatial scales for the Iranian Loess Plateau. ISPRS Int. J. Geo-Inf. **6**, 366 (2017)
4. Gioia, D., Bavusi, M., Di Leo, P., Giammatteo, T., Schiattarella, M.: A geoarchaeological study of the Metaponto coastal belt, Southern Italy, based on geomorphological mapping and GIS-supported classification of landforms. Geografia Fisica e Dinamica Quaternaria **39**, 137–148 (2016)
5. Caruso, A., Clarke, K., Tiddy, C., Delean, S., Lewis, M.: Objective regolith-landform mapping in a regolith dominated terrain to inform mineral exploration. Geosciences **8**, 318 (2018)
6. De Reu, J., et al.: Application of the topographic position index to heterogeneous landscapes. Geomorphology **186**, 39–49 (2013)
7. Di Leo, P., et al.: Ancient settlement dynamics and predictive archaeological models for the Metapontum coastal area in Basilicata, Southern Italy: from geomorphological survey to spatial analysis. J. Coast. Conserv. **22**(5), 865–877 (2017). https://doi.org/10.1007/s11852-017-0548-y

8. Danese, M., Gioia, D., Biscione, M., Masini, N.: Spatial methods for archaeological flood risk: the case study of the Neolithic Sites in the Apulia Region (Southern Italy). In: Murgante, B., et al. (eds.) ICCSA 2014. LNCS, vol. 8579, pp. 423–439. Springer, Cham (2014). https://doi.org/10.1007/978-3-319-09144-0_29

9. Jenness, J., Brost, B., Beier, P.: Land facet corridor designer: extension for ArcGIS. Jenness Enterprises (2011). http://www.jennessent.com/arcgis/land_facets.htm

10. Jasiewicz, J., Stepinski, T.F.: Geomorphons—a pattern recognition approach to classification and mapping of landforms. Geomorphology 182, 147–156 (2013)

11. Dikau, R., Brabb, E.E., Mark, R.K., Pike, R.J.: Morphometric landform analysis of New Mexico. Z. für Geomorphol. Supplementband 101, 109–126 (1995)

12. d'Oleire-Oltmanns, S., Eisank, C., Dragut, L., Blaschke, T.: An object-based workflow to extract landforms at multiple scales from two distinct data types. IEEE Geosci. Remote Sens. Lett. 10, 947–951 (2013)

13. Drăguţ, L., Blaschke, T.: Automated classification of landform elements using object-based image analysis. Geomorphology 81, 330–344 (2006)

14. Teofilo, G., Gioia, D., Spalluto, L.: Integrated geomorphological and geospatial analysis for mapping fluvial landforms in Murge Basse Karst of Apulia (Southern Italy). Geosciences (Switzerland) 9, 418 (2019)

15. Pescatore, T., Renda, P., Schiattarella, M., Tramutoli, M.: Stratigraphic and structural relationships between Meso-Cenozoic Lagonegro basin and coeval carbonate platforms in southern Apennines, Italy. Tectonophysics 315, 269–286 (1999)

16. Schiattarella, M., Giano, S.I., Gioia, D.: Long-term geomorphological evolution of the axial zone of the Campania-Lucania Apennine, Southern Italy: a review. Geol. Carpath. 68, 57–67 (2017)

17. Bentivenga, M., Coltorti, M., Prosser, G., Tavarnelli, E.: A new interpretation of terraces in the Taranto Gulf: the role of extensional faulting. Geomorphology 60, 383–402 (2004)

18. Giano, S.I., Giannandrea, P.: Late Pleistocene differential uplift inferred from the analysis of fluvial terraces (southern Apennines, Italy). Geomorphology 217, 89–105 (2014)

19. Gioia, D., Schiattarella, M., Giano, S.: Right-angle pattern of minor fluvial networks from the ionian terraced belt, Southern Italy: passive structural control or foreland bending? Geosciences 8, 331 (2018)

20. Piccarreta, M., Capolongo, D., Bentivenga, M., Pennetta, L.: Precipitation and dry-wet cycles influence on badland development in a semi-arid area of Basilicata region (Southern Italy). Geografia Fisica e Dinamica Quaternaria 7, 281–289 (2005)

21. Del Prete, M., Bentivenga, M., Amato, M., Basso, F., Tacconi, P.: Badland erosion processes and their interactions with vegetation: a case study from Pisticci, Basilicata, Southern Italy. Geografia Fisica e Dinamica Quaternaria 20, 147–155 (1997)

22. Gioia, D., Sabato, L., Spalluto, L., Tropeano, M.: Fluvial landforms in relation to the geological setting in the "Murge Basse" karst of Apulia (Bari Metropolitan Area, Southern Italy). J. Maps 7, 148–155 (2011)

Tools for Semi-automated Landform Classification: A Comparison in the Basilicata Region (Southern Italy)

Salvatore Ivo Giano[1](✉) (ID), Maria Danese[2] (ID), Dario Gioia[2] (ID),
Eva Pescatore[1], Vincenzo Siervo[1], and Mario Bentivenga[1] (ID)

[1] Dipartimento di Scienze, Università della Basilicata, Potenza, Italy
ivo.giano@unibas.it, vsiervo@gmail.com
[2] ISPC-CNR, Tito (Potenza), Italy

Abstract. Recent advances in spatial methods of digital elevation model (DEMs) analysis have addressed many research topics on the assessment of morphometric parameters of the landscape. Development of computer algorithms for calculating the geomorphometric properties of the Earth's surface has allowed for expanding of some methods in the semi-automatic recognition and classification of landscape features. In such a way, several papers have been produced, documenting the applicability of the landform classification based on map algebra. The Topographic Position Index (TPI) is one of the most widely used parameters for semi-automated landform classification using GIS software. The aim was to apply the TPI classes for landform classification in the Basilicata Region (Southern Italy). The Basilicata Region is characterized by an extremely heterogeneous landscape and geological features. The automated landform extraction, starting from two different resolution DEMs at 20 and 5 m-grids, has been carried out by using three different GIS software: Arcview, Arcmap, and SAGA. Comparison of the landform maps resulting from each software at a different scale has been realized, furnishing at the end the best landform map and consequently a discussion over which is the best software implementation of the TPI method.

Keywords: Geomorphology · Morphometry · Topographic Position Index (TPI) · DEMs · GIS software · Southern Italy

1 Introduction

Landforms are geomorphic features of the Earth's landscape generated by the interaction between erosional and depositional processes. Landforms can range from large-scale features, such as plains and mountain ranges to small-scale features such as single hills and valleys [1]. Starting from the last century, the geomorphometric properties of the Earth, which at first were hand-made measured [2, 3], have had an acceleration in their computation from the introduction of computer technology and GIS-based spatial analysis. The use of Digital Elevation Models (DEMs), the development of powerful GIS software with a user-friendly programming environment, and the increase in computer computing capabilities have allowed for an increase in the development of

O. Gervasi et al. (Eds.): ICCSA 2020, LNCS 12250, pp. 709–722, 2020.
https://doi.org/10.1007/978-3-030-58802-1_51

computer algorithms in different disciplines. Among them, several geomorphological tools of automatic mapping of landforms based on different classification criteria and indexes [2, 4, 5] have been developed. This computer-based approach has permitted users to reduce computational time and to produce statistically-based information on landscape features [6].

The GIS application for semi-automated landform classification known as topographic position index (TPI) is an algorithm used in topographic and DEM analysis; it allows a classification of the landscape in slope position classes and landform categories [7, 8]. The ability of TPI to subdivide the features of a landscape into landform categories is mainly based on topography, this is the method suitable for recognition of morphometric properties of landforms. In fact, the TPI is widely used by many authors in a variety of landscapes throughout the world, in order to classify their characteristic landforms ([7] in the USA; [1] in Turkey; [9] in Belgium; [10] in Iran; [11] in Italy; [12] in Greece).

The goal of the study was designed to check the best landform map extracted by means of the three GIS software using the same landform classification, considering that: 1) TPI index is scale-depending and its values must change with DEM grid resolution, and 2) the algorithms developing the semi-automatic landform extraction are quite the same running in different GIS application as Arcview 3.x, Arcmap 10.x, and SAGA. The study area of the Basilicata Region, located in the southern Italian Apennines chain. This area was selected because here a variety of sedimentary rocks produced a complex landscape that is characterized by many morphological features varying from mountain shapes, reaching over 2000 m of altitude a.s.l., to hills and coastal landscapes [13]. The comparison of different landform maps was made for two different size resolution DEMs at 20 m and 5 m; the results were discussed to assess which map (and consequently which software) produced the best landform extraction with regard to the real morphological features of the landscape.

2 Method: The TPI-Based Classification

Among the many geomorphological methods classifying the landscape features in morphological units or classes, the approach adopted in this paper follows the relief classification which is based on the concept of the topographic position index (TPI). The method was proposed by Weiss (2001) [7] and implemented by Jenness (2006) [8] in different GIS-based software. The topographic position Index (TPI) is calculated as the difference between the elevation value of a cell and the average elevation of the neighbourhood around that cell [7]. This represents a quantitative relief index. The algorithm is implemented with a combination of map algebra functions and returns a classification of the index into slope position and landform types. The TPI index is expressed by the following equation:

$$TPI_i = M_i - \sum_{n-1} \frac{M_n}{n} \qquad (1)$$

where i is the i_{th} cell of the analysed raster, M_i is the elevation in the i cell, M_n is the elevation of the n pixels belonging to the neighbourhood of i, n is the total number of cells belonging to the neighbourhood of i. Positive values of TPI indicate that the elevation in the cell i is higher than the average value in the neighbourhood cells, thus it allows recognizing ridges; whereas negative values suggest that the elevation in the cell i is lower than the average value in its surrounding, thus it allows to recognize valleys. TPI values near zero are representative of both flat areas and constant slopes.

The classification of the TPI values provides a fast and powerful means in the extraction of landscape morphological classes [8]. The index is scale-dependent so it varies both with the variation of the cell size in the input DEM and with the size of the neighbourhood selected for the TPI computation. In fact, the calculation of TPI from DEM at different scales and with different thresholds provide an analysis of relief forms of various sizes [14]. Consequently, the choice of the appropriate DEM resolution and the neighbourhood size are important parameters for satisfactory results of classification and are, also, related to the goal of the project. When utilizing the neighbourhood, it is important to define both its shape and its appropriate size. For the shape there are many options: among them, one can choose a circle or an annulus radii of the search window. In both cases, the classification tool requires two values (or search radii) for the calculation: a smaller neighbourhood is useful to identify small and local hills and valleys, while the larger neighbourhood identifies larger features [8]. A different landform classification was obtained by Weiss (2001) [7] using a combination of two TPI grid values, large and small neighbourhood,. In such a way, a point of the landscape with a negative TPI value in a small neighbourhood and a positive value in a large neighbourhood can identify a small valley in a larger hilltop and will reasonably be classified as upland drainage. Conversely, a point with a positive TPI value in a small neighbourhood and a negative value in a large neighbourhood can reasonably indicate a small hill or a ridge in a larger valley [8]. Of course, in the case of the circle shape, there will be only one search radius for the small neighbourhood and one search radius for the large one, while in the case of the annulus shape, an inner and an out radii are required, both for the small and for the large neighbourhood. So for the annulus search window, four thresholds have to be defined.

Based on both the TPI threshold values and the slope distribution at each point, the landscape can be classified into discrete slope position classes [7]. This means that TPI values above an established threshold are classified as ridgetops or hilltops, whereas TPI values below the threshold are classified as valley bottom or depressions. Moreover, TPI values near zero are classified as a flat plain or mid-slope areas [7, 8]. Considering the variability of the elevation values within a neighbourhood of a cell, it is useful to define the threshold TPI values in terms of standard deviations from the elevation. In this sense, grid cells with the same TPI value may be classified in different areas.

The TPI and slope combination leads the generation of 10 landform classes listed as follow: 1) Deep narrow canyons/V-shaped river valleys, 2) Midslope drainage/Local valley in plains, 3) Upland incised drainages/headwaters, 4) U-shaped valleys, 5) Plains, 6) Open slopes, 7) Upper slopes/Flat ridge tops/Mesas, 8) Local ridge/hilltops in broad valleys, 9) Midslope ridges or lateral drainage divides/Local ridge in plains, 10) Mountain top/High ridges.

3 Case Study: The Basilicata Region Landforms

3.1 Geology and Geomorphology of the Study Area

The Basilicata Region, located in southern Italy, is part of the Miocene-Quaternary fold-and-thrust belt of southern Apennines chain (Fig. 1) formed by east-verging tectonic units ([15] and references therein) overlapping on the Apulian Platform to form a large duplex geometry [16]. The average direction of the chain axis is approximately N150°, corresponding to the strike of both the main thrusts and younger coaxial normal faults. Extensional tectonics is still active along the axis of the chain deforming Pleistocene sediments [17–22]. Such a complex structural setting produced a mountain chain over 2000 m high and a regional divide oriented NW-SE that separates the drainage network towards south-west in the Tyrrhenian Sea, northeast in the Adriatic Sea, and east in the Ionian Sea.

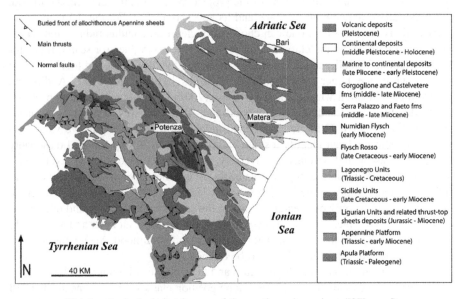

Fig. 1. Geological sketch map of the southern Apennines ([27], mod).

The western and southern sectors of Basilicata are included in the axial zone of the chain, showing high relief with mountains peaks which rise to about 2000 m a.s.l. along the peaks of the Pollino Massif. Faulted-block mountains bounded by high-angle fault scarps are alternated with tectonically-induced basins filled by fluvial to lacustrine deposits that pit the landscape ([19, 23, 24] among others). The uplift rate of the block-faulted mountain front was not constant in time and space because tectonics, in association with climate inputs, generated alluvial fans landforms with different geometry on the side of the basins [24]. The western and southern sectors of the Basilicata represent the geological backbone of the region and are formed by shallow-water carbonate platform units; deep-water siliceous units; siliciclastic arenaceous and clayey units; metamorphic and crystalline units; clastic successions representing the infill of Pliocene and Pleistocene marine to continental syntectonic basins. The central sector of the Basilicata corresponds to the eastern front of the chain and shows hilly reliefs that not exceed 1100 m of altitude. The fluvial valleys are oriented from NE to SW in the northern sector and from E to W in the southeasternmost sector of the study area; here, they transversally cut the Bradano foredeep. The sector is mainly formed by sandstone and clay-rich rocks forming the tectonic units of the embricate frontal thrust unit of the chain. The more external and eastern sector of the Basilicata Region is represented by the Pliocene to Pleistocene Bradano foredeep of the Apennines and is mainly constituted by conglomerates, sands, and clays forming a hilly plan landscape fairly dipping toward the east and transversally incised by the drainage network [13]. It represents the remnant of marine terraced surfaces uplifted in Quaternary times as a consequence of the growth of the Apennines [25, 26].

3.2   Input Parameter Selection for the Case Study

The TPI-based landform classification was implemented in three different tools developed for three different software that computes the same algorithm of landscape classification. The first tool computes the TPI grids in the ArcView 3.x application [8], the second in the ArcGis 10.x [8], and the third, developed by Conrad (2011) [28] employs the calculation of Guisan et al. (1999) [29], in the SAGAgis.

The first step was the parameter choice, corresponding to the cell size of the input DEM. For the purpose of the study, a multiscalar approach was carried out using a 20 m-resolution DEM and a higher resolution (i.e. 5 m) DEM of the Basilicata Region. The DEMs are freely available and downloadable at the following links: http://www.sinanet.isprambiente.it/it/sia-ispra/download-mais/dem20/view, and https://rsdi.regione.basilicata.it for the 5 m DEM. In order to calculate attributes for landform analysis using the 20 m and 5 m DEMs, a slope analysis was realized to generate slope maps using the spatial analysis tools of each application.

The second step of the adopted procedures involved the selection of neighborhood size and shape. An annulus shape was used. Moreover, in order to find the best threshold, an iterative process involving many TPI sizes was used to recognizes complex landscape features. After this process, it was highlighted that the best threshold depended on the input raster resolution and that it is also proportional to a factor f, according to the following expression:

$$\text{Threshold} = \text{Cellsize} * \text{f} \tag{2}$$

where f values can be found as scheduled in Table 1.

The f factor for each neighbourhood element is represented by a range of values because it depends also on the landscape mean slope. Usually, with low values of slopes, best results are obtained by using low f in the range, whereas higher values of the mean slope return best results with high f values in the defined range.

In the Basilicata Region, final values were chosen as follows: the TPI value, in the 20 m resolution DEM, was calibrated ranging two annulus neighbourhoods, the small neighborhood with an inner radius of 40 m and an outer radius of 100 m, and the large

Table 1. f values to find the best thresholds for a TPI-based landform classification.

Neighbourhood element	f
Small neighbourhood:	
Inner Radius	2÷3
Outer Radius	5÷6
Large neighbourhood:	
Inner Radius	10÷30
Outer Radius	25÷30

neighborhood with an inner radius of 200 m and an outer radius of 500 m. The TPI value, for the 5 m resolution DEM, was calibrated using in the small neighborhood the inner radius of 15 m and the outer radius of 30 m, and in the large neighborhood the inner radius of 60 m and the outer radius of 120 m. This combination furnished the best landform maps, according to an expert geomorphological inspection of the maps.

4 Results

With the aim to recognize the main morphological features of the study area, the TPI-based automated landform extraction and classification were elaborated from three GIS applications Arcview, Arcmap, and SAGA. Even if the TPI expression is apparently the same, results furnished three landform maps containing different spatial distribution for the ten landform classes. The TPI was calibrated assuming an annulus neighborhood values of 40–100 m (inner radius and outer radius, respectively) for small neighborhood and of 200–500 m for large neighborhood.

The spatial distribution of the automated landforms listed in Table 1 and their correspondence with the morphological features of the landscape was analyzed using both a 20 m- and a 5 m resolution DEM, respectively. With the aims to better discuss the results of the semi-automatic landform classification, the ten landform classes were grouped into main 4 classes which included homogenous features of the landscape affected by similar sculpturing processes. In this way, we have selected the following four landform categories: A) fluvial valley landforms, including deep narrow canyon/V-shaped river valley (n. 1 in Table 1), midslope drainage/local valley in plain (n. 2 in Table 1), upland incised drainage/headwater (n. 3 in Table 1), and U-shaped valley (n. 4 in Table 1) landform classes; B) plain landforms, including the plains class in the automatic extraction (n. 5 in Table 1); C) slope landforms, including open slope (n. 6 in Table 1) and upper slope/flat ridge top/mesa (n. 7 in Table 1) landform classes; D) summit landforms, which include local ridge/hilltops in broad valley (n. 8 in Table 1), midslope ridge or lateral drainage divide/local ridge in plain (n. 9 in Table 1), and mountain top/high ridge (n. 10 in Table 1) landform classes.

Table 2. List of the automated landform classification.

N.	Landform classes	CAT
1	Deep narrow canyons/V-shaped river valleys	A
2	Midslope drainage/Local valley in plains	A
3	Upland incised drainages/headwaters	A
4	U-shaped valleys	A
5	Plains	B
6	Open slopes	C
7	Upper slopes/Flat ridge tops/Mesas	C
8	Local ridge/hilltops in broad valleys	D
9	Midslope ridges or lateral drainage divides/Local ridge in plains	D
10	Mountain top/High ridges	D

4.1   Landform Maps Extracted from a 20 m-Resolution DEM

The fluvial valley landforms (category A, Table 1), include canyons, shallow valleys, U-shaped valleys, and midslope valleys. The first and second landforms, extracted and classified by the Arcview and SAGA Gis applications, perfectly delimitate the flood-plains areas (Fig. 2a,b). These landforms, located in both the mountainous and hilly landscapes of the Basilicata, are well-bordered and showing a spatial continuity with the middle-lower floodplains of the Bradano, Basento, Agri, and Sinni rivers. Furthermore, they show a good distribution of the drainage network of the Region with a particular definition of those well-detected by the Arcmap application (Fig. 2c). In this latter application, also the low-order streams are well detected thus to define the spatial distribution of low-order drainage basins (Fig. 2c). It is worth noting that these land-forms are detected in the upstream fluvial valleys whereas in the middle to lower reaches they pass to a different landform as a plain.

In the north-eastern side of the Region, the deep-incisions of the fluvial net with steep-slope flanks carved in Cretaceous limestone (i.e. the so-called "Gravine" land-forms, which represent a peculiar fluvial landform of the Matera area [30]) - were recognized by all the three applications (Fig. 2).

The plain surface landforms (category B, Table 1) of the Basilicata landscape can be attributed to different several flat landforms categories that can be listed as: the present-day coastal plain of the Ionian Sea; the marine terraces of the Ionian Arc; the floodplains of the middle and lower reaches of the Bradano, Basento, Agri, Sinni, Cavone, and their tributaries; the plain surfaces of the intermontane basins; the terraced fluvial surfaces of the Bradano foredeep (Fig. 2). Plain landforms automatically extracted by Arcview and SAGA Gis software well-surrounded the flat areas corresponding to the Ionian coastal plain, the floodplains, and the flat surfaces of inter-montane basins. This well-recognition of landforms was not provided by the Arcmap extraction that discriminates the flat surfaces, and particularly floodplains as well as shallow valleys, thus furnishing a too detailed map which is not corresponding to the landform bounds. In this case the representation is probably influenced by the strongly marked valley landforms (Fig. 2c). The non-optimal automatic recognition of plain

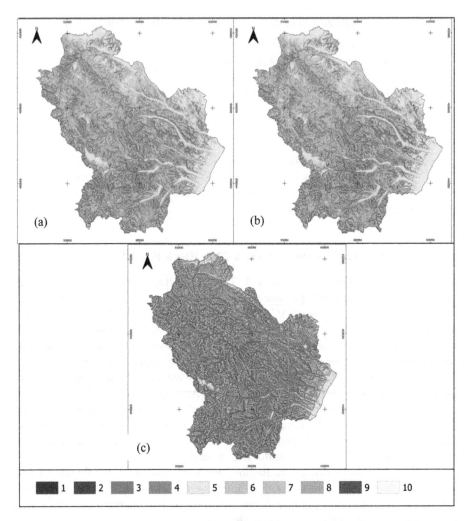

Fig. 2. Maps of semi-automated landform classification extracted from a 20 m resolution DEM and using the tools contained in the Arcview (a), in the SAGA (b), and in the Arcmap (c) GIS applications. Legend: 1) Deep narrow canyons/V-shaped river valleys, 2) Midslope drainage/Local valley in plains, 3) Upland incised drainages/headwaters, 4) U-shaped valleys, 5) Plains, 6) Open slopes, 7) Upper slopes/Flat ridge tops/Mesas, 8) Local ridge/hilltops in broad valleys, 9) Midslope ridges or lateral drainage divides/Local ridge in plains, 10) Mountain top/High ridges.

landforms means that too high TPI values were selected and, therefore, lower values of small and large neighborhoods should provide better results. Among the plain landforms, the high and low terraced surfaces are partially detected by the algorithms of all the three software. They are horizontal surfaces that in geomorphology can be assigned to altiplanes, which in some cases correspond to planation surfaces or mesas. In this sense, the algorithm detected all these high-elevated surfaces as open slopes and mesas.

It is worth noting that only small high-elevated flat surfaces are recognized by the SAGA Gis software that not approaching their real spatial distribution. Finally, a clear recognition of both the flatness surface and the inner edge of Ionian marine terraces was made by the Arcview and SAGAGis tools detecting about 5 surfaces in the area included between the Bradano and Agri rivers (Fig. 2a,b).

In the slope landforms of the category C (Table 1), both open and upper slope or mesas landforms are well-represented thus forming the most landscape of the study area. Slope landforms extracted by Arcview and SAGA Gis represent all the sectors connecting the mountain tops to the fluvial valley features, with a spatial predominance of the open slopes landforms. The upper slopes or mesas are less distributed and are mainly placed under the watersheds or ridges (Fig. 2a,b). In the Arcmap an enlargement of the fluvial valley and mountain top landforms has produced a narrowing of the slope landforms that are few represented in the map of Fig. 2c.

The higher morphostructural features (category D, Table 1) corresponding to several orders of watershed divides/mountain ridges and classified as mountain tops and high ridges by the semi-automatic extraction are quite well represented and reveal a good spatial continuity. It is the case of the ridge alignments oriented NNW-SSE and NW-SE of the central and southern sector of the Basilicata Region (Fig. 2). Conversely, lower ridges and lower watersheds are poorly discriminated because they are included in both open slopes, upper slopes, and mesas.

4.2   Landform Maps Extracted from a 5 m-Resolution DEM

The fluvial valley landforms pertaining to the class (A) extracted from the Arcview and SAGA applications show a similar distribution of the areas (Fig. 3a,b). A small difference is detectable only in the plain view distribution of upland incised drainages and U-shaped valleys landforms that reveal a shifting of the landform boundaries (numbers 3 and 4, Fig. 3, respectively). Conversely, the Arcmap application has emphasized the extraction of U-shaped valley landforms that at the edge of fluvial floodplains and the drainage network is better represented than the previous application (Fig. 3c). The radial drainage network of the Vulture volcano extracted from the Arcview and SAGA applications is clearly reproduced and differ from those of the Arcmap that is too detailed thus to mask the classical radial fluvial pattern of the volcano.

The plain surface landforms included in the class (B) and related to several flat landforms categories as above listed (Table 2) are well recognized by all the applications. The present-day coastal plain of the Ionian Arc and the staircase of marine terrace surfaces are very well extracted; moreover, the inner edge of each marine terrace also appears well outlined. The boundaries of the several hanged marine terraces due to the strong vertical incision produced by the fluvial network are less defined. Both the coastal plain and the marine terrace landforms are transversally cut by the main four eastward rivers of the Basilicata Region, which flow within wide floodplains: in this case, the best extraction is coming from the Arcmap application. The same condition has been observed in the extraction of the larger flat tops of several intermontane basins in which the boundaries of the undissected floodplain and the lower-altitude stair of fluvial terraces are well discriminated. Conversely, local and smaller flat plains of intermontane basins (see for example the fluvial terraces of the

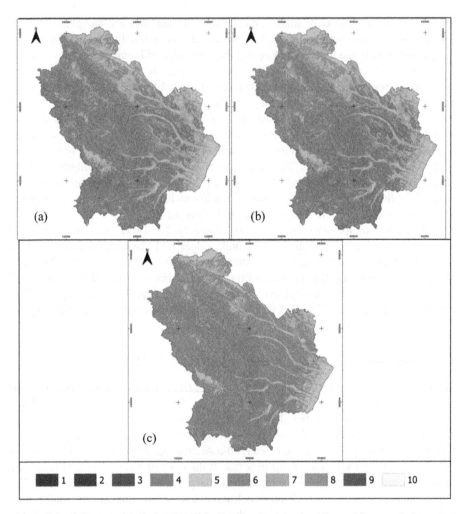

Fig. 3. Maps of semi-automated landform classification extracted from a 5 m resolution DEM and using the tools contained in the Arcview (a), in the SAGA (b), and in the Arcmap (c) GIS applications. Legend: 1) Deep narrow canyons/V-shaped river valleys, 2) Midslope drainage/Local valley in plains, 3) Upland incised drainages/headwaters, 4) U-shaped valleys, 5) Plains, 6) Open slopes, 7) Upper slopes/Flat ridge tops/Mesas, 8) Local ridge/hilltops in broad valleys, 9) Midslope ridges or lateral drainage divides/Local ridge in plains, 10) Mountain top/High ridges.

Pergola-Melandro basin located to north-west of the Agri basin) are classified as flat ridge top or mesas by the Arcmap application.

The slope landforms class (C) formed by open and upper slope or mesas landforms are not well extracted by the Arcview and SAGA applications; in fact, they classified as main landform open slope features (6 in Fig. 3a,b) but did not fully capture flat ridge top or mesas. A completely different extraction has been done by the Arcmap application, that emphasizes the mesas landforms (7 in Fig. 3c) and greatly decreases the representation for open slopes. There is a relevant mistake in the extraction of mesas landforms using the Arcmap application, corresponding to the inner and outer slopes of the terrace edges of fluvial and marine terraces. In this case, the automated extraction has failed the recognition and cannot be applied, in our opinion.

Finally, the higher features of the class (D) are very detailed in the extraction thus to provide a poor identification and delimitation of these landforms. Midslope ridges (9 in Fig. 3) are fragmented and minimized in the Arcview and SAGA extraction while they are a bit more detailed in the Arcmap application. The spatial continuity is very low and there are too many pixels corresponding to different landforms that produced an elevated background noise in the map. Finally, A peculiar feature of the semi-automated extractions is the high noise of the maps and their low degree of readability. This is common to all the three software applications and can be attributed to the high definition of the 5 m DEMs.

The percentages of landform classes obtained by the semi-automated extraction and by using the three applications have provided the differences of landform distribution in the area of Basilicata Region in both the case of 20 m resolution and 5 m resolution DEMs, respectively (Fig. 4). Fluvial valley landform of class (A) shows quite the same percentage of distribution in both the 20 m and 5 m DEMs. A first anomalous high percentage was only obtained by the Arcmap application in both the DEMs that differs from the others applications, as in the case of the deep narrow canyons/V-shaped river valleys (n. 1 in Table 1) that ranging its values from 26.4% to 13% of distribution with regard to the other frequency distributions that are less than 5% of the total values (Fig. 4). The second anomalous high percentage was obtained from the U-shaped valleys (n. 4 in Table 1) values that ranging from 22.9% to 12.7% compared to the values of the other applications that are around 5%.

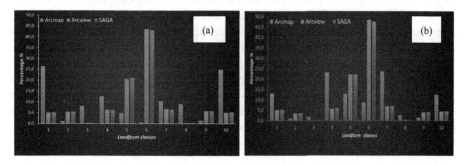

Fig. 4. Percentages of landform classes extracted from the three GIS applications and related to 20 m resolution (a) and 5 m resolution (b) DEMs. Numbers of landform classes are referred to the list of Table 1.

Conversely, in the slope landforms class (C) the percentage values of extracted landform by the Arcmap application is low regarding those obtained from the Arcview and SAGA applications, as reported in the Open slopes (n. 6 in Table 1) reaching a value ranging from 8.7% to 0.8% (Fig. 4). The Upper slopes, flat ridge tops, and mesas landforms (n. 7 in Table 1) show high percentage values in Arcmap suggesting an anomalously high detection and classification of these features by the algorithm. In the final landform class (D) including all the higher-altitude morphological features of the Region the only difference among the three applications and the two DEMs is represented by the Mountain top and High ridges (n. 10 in Table 1). Here, the Arcmap application has detected high percentage values of this landform if compared to other applications, ranging from 24.9% to 12.5% (Fig. 4).

We can conclude that there is a low difference in percentage values between the semi-automated landforms classification obtained by the Arcview and SAGA GIS applications and the only discrepancy is those of the Arcmap. This difference can be observed in both the two 20 m and 5 m resolution DEMs.

4.3   Conclusions

The application of the TPI index, aimed at the semi-automated extraction and classification of landforms in the Basilicata Region, has been carried out. The landform extraction was realized by using three different tools running on the Arcview, Arcmap, and the SAGA GIS software. The study area was selected considering its high variety of outcropping rocks producing a complex landscape and many types of landforms varying from coastal plains to high mountain shapes reaching over 2000 m of altitude. Three landform maps have been extracted from the GIS applications and the same procedure has been applied to 20 m and 5 m resolution DEMs thus to obtain six landform maps. The comparison among the different maps allowed to discuss the best map representation, that is discriminate what map has produced the better and representative landforms. The comparison among the three landform maps classification, extracted from the 20 m grid DEM, showed a general well distribution of fluvial valley (A), plain (B), slope (C), and (D) landforms. These landform categories (see Table 1) are very well extracted by the Arcview and SAGA applications, whilst a less quality representation was furnished by the Arcmap application. The different extraction probably attributed to the radii value will be investigated with more detail in future. The three maps extracted from the 5 m grid DEM showed a better representation of landforms from the Arcmap application, particularly those related to the Ionian coastal plain, with regards to the others. In conclusion, the 20 m DEM furnished the better results using the Arcview and SAGA application, whilst the 5 m DEM shows the good landform extraction by using the Arcmap application.

References

1. Tagil, S., Jenness, J.: GIS-based automated landform classification and topographic, landcover and geologic attributes of landforms around the Yazoren Polje. Turkey. J. Appl. Sci. **8**(6), 910–921 (2008)
2. Horton, R.E.: Erosional development of streams and their drainage basins; hydrophysical approach to quantitative morphology. GSA Bull. **56**(3), 275–370 (1945)

3. Strahler, A.N.: Quantitative analysis of watershed geomorphology. Trans. Am. Geophys. Union **38**, 913–920 (1957)
4. Hammond, E.H.: Analysis of properties in land form geography: an application to broad-scale land form mapping. Ann Assoc. Am. Geograph. **54**(1), 11–19 (1964)
5. Pike, R.J.: A bibliography of geomorphometry, the quantitative representation of topography; supplement 3.0, Report pp. 99–140 (1999)
6. Evans, I.S., D.U.D.o. Geography: General Geomorphometry, Derivatives of Altitude, and Descriptive Statistics. Defense Technical Information Center, Ft. Belvoir (1972)
7. Weiss, A.: Topographic position and landforms analysis. Poster Presentation. In: ESRI User Conference, San Diego, CA, (2001)
8. Jenness, J.: Topographic Position Index (tpi_jen.avx) extension for ArcView 3.x, Jenness Enterprises (2006). http://www.jennessent.com/arcview/tpi.htm
9. De Reu, J., Bourgeois, J., Bats, M., et al.: Application of the topographic position index to heterogeneous landscapes. Geomorphology **186**, 39–49 (2013)
10. Seif, A.: Using topography position index for landform classification (Case study: Grain Mountain). Bull. Environ. Pharmacol. Life Sci. **3**(11), 33–39 (2015)
11. Gioia, D., Bavusi, M., Di Leo, P., et al.: A geoarchaeological study of the Metaponto coastal belt, southern Italy, based on geomorphological mapping and GIS-supported classification of landforms. Geografia Fisica e Dinamica Quaternaria **39**, 137–148 (2016)
12. Athanasios, S., Anagnostopoulou, O.: Landform Analysis Using Terrain Attributes. A GIS Application on the Island of Ikaria (Aegean Sea, Greece). Ann. Valahia Univ. Targoviste Geograph. Ser. **17**(1), 90–97 (2017)
13. Giano, S.I., Giannandrea, P.: Late Pleistocene differential uplift inferred from the analysis of fluvial terraces (southern Apennines, Italy). Geomorphology **217**, 89–105 (2014)
14. Zwoliński, Z., Stefańska, E.: Relevance of moving window size in landform classification by TPI, Geomorphometry for Geosciences. In: Jasiewicz, J., Zwoliński, Zb., Mitasova, H., Hengl, T. (eds.) Adam Mickiewicz University in Poznań - Institute of Geoecology and Geoinformation, International Society for Geomorphometry, Poznań (2015)
15. Pescatore, T., Renda, P., Schiattarella, M., et al.: Stratigraphic and structural relationships between Meso-Cenozoic Lagonegro basin and coeval carbonate platforms in southern Apennines, Italy. Tectonophysics **315**(1–4), 269–286 (1999)
16. Patacca, E., Scandone, P.: Geology of the Southern Apennines. Bollettino della Societa Geologica Italiana, Supplemento **7**, 75–119 (2007)
17. Di Leo, P., Giano, S.I., Gioia, D., Mattei, M., Pescatore, E., Schiattarella, M.: Evoluzione morfotettonica quaternaria del bacino intermontano di Sanza (Appennino meridionale). Alp. Meditarranean Quat. (Il Quaternario) **22**(2), 189–206 (2009)
18. Giano, S.I., Gioia, D., Schiattarella, M.: Morphotectonic evolution of connected intermontane basins from the southern Apennines, Italy: the legacy of the pre-existing structurally controlled landscape. Rendiconti Lincei **25**(2), 241–252 (2014)
19. Giano, S.I., Schiattarella, M.: Age constraints and denudation rate of a multistage fault line scarp: an example from Southern Italy. Geochronometria **41**(3), 245–255 (2014)
20. Giano, S.I., Pescatore, E., Agosta, F., et al.: Geomorphic evidence of quaternary tectonics within an underlap fault zone of southern Apennines, Italy. Geomorphology **303**, 172–190 (2018)
21. Bavusi, M., Chianese, D., Giano, S.I., et al.: Multidisciplinary investigations on the Roman aqueduct of Grumentum (Basilicata, Southern Italy). Ann. Geophys. **47**(6), 1791–1801 (2004)
22. Giano, S.I., Lapenna, V., Piscitelli, S., et al.: New geological and geophysical data on the structural pattern of the quaternary slope deposits in the Agri high valley, southern Apennines. Alpine Mediterranean Quaternary **10**(2), 589–594 (1997)

23. Aucelli, P.P.C., D'Argenio, B., Della Seta, M., et al.: Intermontane basins: quaternary morphoevolution of Central-Southern Italy. Rendiconti Lincei **25**(2), 107–110 (2014)
24. Giano, S.: Quaternary alluvial fan systems of the agri intermontane basin (southern Italy): tectonic and climatic controls. Geol. Carpath. **62**(1), 65–76 (2011)
25. Bentivenga, M., Coltorti, M., Prosser, G., et al.: A new interpretation of terraces in the Taranto Gulf: the role of extensional faulting. Geomorphology **60**(3), 383–402 (2004)
26. Bentivenga, M., Coltorti, M., Prosser, G., et al.: Recent extensional faulting in the Gulf of Taranto area: Implications for nuclear waste storage in the vicinity of Scanzano Ionico (Basilicata). Bollettino della Societa Geologica Italiana **123**(3), 391–404 (2004)
27. Piedilato, S., Prosser, G.: Thrust sequences and evolution of the external sector of a fold and thrust belt: an example from the Southern Apennines (Italy). J. Geodyn. **39**(4), 386–402 (2005)
28. Conrad, O.: SAGA-GIS Tool Library Documentation (v4.0.1), Tool Topographic Position Index (TPI) (2011). http://www.saga-gis.org/saga_tool_doc/4.0.1/ta_morphometry_18.html. LNCS
29. Guisan, A., Weiss, S.B., Weiss, A.D.: GLM versus CCA spatial modeling of plant species distribution. Plant Ecol. **143**(1), 107–122 (1999)
30. Beneduce, P., Festa, V., Francioso, R., et al.: Conflicting drainage patterns in the Matera Horst Area, southern Italy. Phys. Chem. Earth **29**(10), 717–724 (2004)

High-Resolution LiDAR-Derived DEMs in Hydrografic Network Extraction and Short-Time Landscape Changes

Maurizio Lazzari[✉]

CNR ISPC, C/da S. Loja Zona Industriale, 85100 Tito Scalo, PZ, Italy
maurizio.lazzari@cnr.it

Abstract. In this paper an automatic methodology to extract the channel network from high-resolution LiDAR-derived DTMs and a semi-quantitative methodology to assess the short-time landscape evolution of a test-area, located in southern Italy, have been applied. In particular, the technique used is based on a local nonlinear filter together with the global geodesic optimization for channel head and drainage network extraction. Further, the two Lidar acquisition for the year 2012 and 2013 have been used to detect hydrographic network changes and slope evolution in terms of erosion and deposition pattern and then compare them with the slope processes (landslides and linear erosion).

Keywords: LiDAR · Hydrographic network · Fluvial landscape · Calciano · Basilicata

1 Introduction

During last twenty years, new methods of acquisition of high-resolution, high-quality topographic data have provided, in unprecedented manner, the opportunity to investigate landscapes and landforms at the scale of geomorphological process [1]. One of the most significant advances is airborne laser swath mapping (ALSM) or LiDAR that nowadays gives the way to a new generation of high-resolution (0.5 to 2 m) digital terrain models (DTMs) offering new possibilities to use detailed representations of surface features [2, 3].

Thanks to the availability of these non-conventional datasets, researchers have the ability to analyze landforms at a scale ranging from few meters to decimetres which is crucial to investigate slope and fluvial processes.

This gives new insights for the study of the "geomorphological signatures" of surface processes and their significance in terms of landscape evolution.

Recent application of high resolution topography concentrated on identification and extraction of geomorphological features [4–6], landslides morphology and activity detection [7–10], river channel morphology [11], tectonic geomorphology [12], geoarcheology [13], landscape change [14].

High resolution topography also favourites the development of new and advanced methods of terrain analysis in particular for channel network extraction. New methods based on landform curvature have been developed [2, 15–18].

© Springer Nature Switzerland AG 2020
O. Gervasi et al. (Eds.): ICCSA 2020, LNCS 12250, pp. 723–737, 2020.
https://doi.org/10.1007/978-3-030-58802-1_52

The proposed methods detect thresholds in topographic curvature for channel network identification and hillslope channel transition, thus providing an alternative to classical methodologies for channel network extraction such has, for example, a constant threshold contributing area [19–21], a slope dependent threshold contributing area [22, 23], and also a threshold on local curvature [24, 25].

Few studies have explored the potentiality of Lidar application to landform change detection and landscape evolution [14], mainly due to the high costs for data acquisition. Further the recent availability of the technology, such as UAV survey, constrains often a too short timescale to detect changes in the landscape. On other hand multi-temporal acquisition of Lidar data could be very useful to define spatial patterns of erosion and deposition and to estimate sediment flux within the landscape and the consequent landscape evolution. This constitutes a future challenge in geomorphology to develop new geomorphic transport law [26].

In this paper a case study located in Basilicata region (southern Italy), whose peculiarity is to be a rapid evolving landscape, is proposed. The climate regime, the sparse vegetation and the high erodible lithology result in a deep dissected landscape with the presence of badlands and landslides on the steepest slopes [27].

A semi-quantitative methodology to assess landscape evolution in this area on the base of multitemporal Lidar data analyses has been applied. In particular, it has been considered the technique proposed by [16, 17], based on a local nonlinear filter together with the global geodesic optimization for channel head and drainage network extraction. Further two Lidar acquisition for the year 2012 and 2013 have been used to detect landscape changes in term of erosion and deposition pattern and then compare them with the actual hillslope channel configuration.

1.1 Study Area

The study was carried out in a test site located in the central sector of the Basilicata region, southern Italy (Fig. 1), about 2 km east of the Calciano town on the right side of Basento river.

The area is located along the outer thrust-front of the Lucanian Apennine Chain, where the turbiditic arenaceous-marly Miocene formations of Serra Palazzo outcrop. Above the Miocene substratum there is the regressive succession of Bradanic Foredeep, in stratigraphic contact with angular discordance, represented by Argille Supappennine Fm. (lower Pleistocene), characterized by silty-clayey and sandy-clayey deposits [28], laminates and with bioturbation, reportable to a shallow water sea of Sicilian in age (*small Gephyrocapsa* Zone; [29, 30]). Toward the top this formation gradually passes, in continuity of sedimentation, to the regressive sandy-conglomerate, reportable to depositional delta, coastal systems and continental systems (plain alluvial).

The interaction of the regional uplift with other local driving factors, such as the relative changes of the sea level, sinsedimentary and post-depositional tectonics, action of the erosion, has contributed to define the actual geological and geomorphologic setting of the study area.

The dominant clayey lithological nature and the north-east exposure of the study area favour conditions the development of mudflow, shallow landslides triggering and

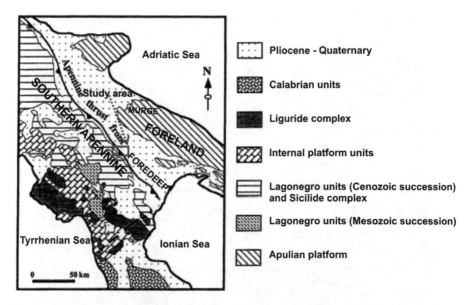

Fig. 1. Geographic location of the study area (red rectangle) and geological framework. (Color figure online)

deep retrogressive channel erosion (gullies), that determinates also high sedimentation rates at the base of the slopes.

2 Materials and Methods

2.1 LiDAR Data Acquisition

The acquisition of laser scanning data was carried out by CNR and Aerosigma srl on May 2012 and May 2013 (Fig. 2), using a full-waveform scanner, RIEGL Q680i on board twin-engine plane P68 victor B - Partenavia to obtain a higher spatial resolution, with a Ground Sampling Distance (GSD) of about 5 cm with overlap of 70% and sidelap of 30% (Table 1).

The processing of laser point cloud was made using the commercial Terrasolid software, one of the most complete and efficient software for laser points processing. In particular, TerraScan, TerraPhoto and TerraModel by Terrasolid package has been used [31].

2.2 DTMs Extraction

The DTMs of different years (2012 and 2013) of the study area were first standardized (precision, accuracy, reference systems) and then analyzed, area by area, to make differences among multitemporal DTMs (Fig. 3).

To determine high-resolution DTM from laser scanning point clouds filtering and classification processing was performed. The extraction of unclassified.las data was

Fig. 2. Flight plan trajectories for LIDAR airborne remote sensing

followed by the post-processing phase of the point cloud, i.e. the processing chain aimed at their classification. Every peculiar feature of the scene, represented by points that satisfy a certain property, is inserted in special classes (ground, vegetation, buildings, electricity lines, roads), which include points with similar characteristics.

In the case study, the classification procedures were carried out with the help of the Terrasolid modules, specifically the Terrascan module, the most common, as well as the most robust and performing commercial classification application.

Initially, an analysis of the entire territory was made to be processed in order to apply the correct "ground" classification parameters.

The cleaning of the point cloud is a fundamental step in the classification phase as it allows you to "move" spurious points (the presence of which is inevitable) in a class that is not taken into consideration in subsequent elaborations. This discrimination was carried out through a terrascan macro carried out in two steps:

- Elimination of low spurious points, or better known as Low Points
- Elimination of high points

The low points have been classified by inserting a reference altitude which is far lower with the minimum altitude of the acquisition scene (>0.5 m).

The ground points were interpolated with a Delaunay triangulation, the most popular TIN interpolation. TIN is generally able to represent abrupt changes in the land surface, because the density of the triangle can be varied easily and so it is able to incorporate discontinuities. TIN-grids have been interpolated to derive the cell-based DEMs. Each raster cell contains a size of height determined before resembling, and

Table 1. Synthesis of the main characteristics of the Lidar multitemporal acquisitions in the test area of Calciano.

Characteristics of the Lidar survey	1st acquisition	2nd acquisition
Time	May 2012	May 2013
Full Waveform ALS	Riegl Q680i inertial platform/GPS Novatel Fsas	Riegl Q680i inertial platform/GPS Novatel Fsas
Size of the acquired area	1000 ha	1000 ha
Flight height	600 m	600 m
Scan speed	62 m/s	62 m/s
Opening angle	20°	20°
Flight lines orientation	NW-SE	NW-SE
Beam divergence	0.65 mrad	0.65 mrad
Pulse repetition	120.000 Hz	120.000 Hz
Average point cloud density	20 points/m^2	20 points/m^2
Digital camera	Phase one Ixa 180R 80MP	Phase one Ixa 180R 80MP
Orthophoto RGB pixel size – Geotiff	5 cm	5 cm
density of points	4 pt/m^2	4 pt/m^2
reference system	UTM 33 - WGS 84	UTM 33 - WGS 84
Vertical precision Horizontal precision	<15 cm <25 cm	<15 cm <25 cm

calculated by the TIN height, in the center of the same cell. In particular, for the aim of this study a DTM (Grid ASCII) with a cell size of 1 m was produced in UTM 33 – WGS 84 – orthometric height (international standard).

2.3   Network Extraction

LiDAR derived DTM permits direct detection of channels. New algorithms have been proposed for the automatic extraction of channel network from high resolution DTM obtained from airborne LiDAR data, such as [15] and [16]. Both of them are based on the local slope and landform curvature concepts, whilst traditional methodologies are based on drainage area and local slope thresholds. Tarolli and Dalla Fontana [2] showed that the curvature derived from high-resolution topography using a Lidar-derived DEM, seems to improve channel network extraction because it permits to recognize in detail concave-convergent terrain associated with fluvial erosion processes.

According to these considerations, in order to extract the channel network from high-resolution LiDAR derived DTM of Calciano test-area, an automatic methodology has been applied. Between the two algorithms proposed by [15] and [16] it has been used the second one, i.e. [15] according the results discussed in detail in [17]. It compares the capability of [15] and [16] to extract the channel network, capturing

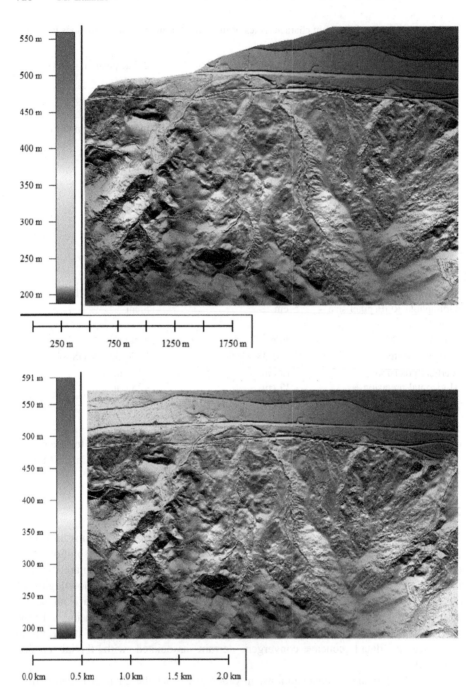

Fig. 3. DEMs extracted by LIDAR data of 2012 (up) and 2013 (below).

channel heads, detecting relevant channel disruptions corresponding to landslides and extracting representative channel cross sections in the Rio Col Dur Basin, in the Dolomites (Alps Italy), a complex mountainous landscape, where both gentle and steep slope areas are present. Lidar-derived DTM with a spatial resolution of 1 m.

Passalacqua et al. [16] script proposed to the community a Matlab toolbox named GeoNet, where the accumulation area was computed outside the code and the curvature threshold was visually determined from quantile-quantile plot. The choice of the parameters is automatic and the accumulation area is computed inside the code.

Before to run DTM image processing GeoNet considers DTM (as a geotiff format): to each option a tiff tag is assigned. These tags are used to store geotiff information of any type.

Passalacqua et al. [16] starts by applying a smoothing filter on the original data-set for removing noise and irregularities which can reduce the detection of the edges of features at the scale of interest and identify features as entities that persist over a range of scale.

GeoNet applies the non linear filter performed by [32]. From a numerical point of view it exactly used the Perona and Malik filter proposed by [33].

The choice of using nonlinear filter as smoothing filter is especially motivated by the space-scale paradigm that the Perona and Malik [32] formulated to address the degradation of spatial localization of natural boundaries, especially at larger scales of smoothing, due to the isotropic criteria which characterize other smoothing filters (see for example Gaussian filtering used by [15] to extract channel network).

The isotropic nature of many smoothing filters does not allow to respect the natural boundaries of the features, which may represent important discontinuities in the landscape.

In particular, the Perona and Malik [32] filter method consider these three criteria:

1) causality: a scale-space representation should have the property that no spurious feature should be generated passing from finer to coarser resolutions, as stated by [34] and [35];
2) immediate localization: the region boundaries should be sharp and meaningful at each resolution;
3) piecewise smoothing: at all resolutions the smoothing should be preferentially intraregion that interregion.

If $h_0(x,y) = h(x,y;t)$ represents the original high resolution digital elevation model the nonlinear filtering operation can be expressed as:

$$\partial_t h(x, y, t) = \nabla \cdot [c(x, y, t)\nabla h] = c(x, y, t)\nabla^2 h + \nabla c \cdot \nabla h \qquad (1)$$

where t indicates that the derivative is taken in time, c is the diffusion coefficient dependent of the space, ∇ is the gradient operator.

The best situation to choose the diffusion coefficient c is in the way that the nonlinear filter achieves noise reduction and emphasizes edges, without smoothing across boundaries, i.e. the situation in which the channel boundaries location is known and so $c = 0$ at the boundary and $c = 1$ everywhere else.

The channel location is not known in advance but only an estimate of it or the knowledge of some geometric characteristics may be computed. According [32] a first estimate of the edges $\vec{E}(x, y, t)$ location within the non linear space-scale paradigm can be given by the gradient of the elevation $h(x,y,t)$ at the location (x,y) and time t:

$$\vec{E}(x, y, t) = \nabla h(x, y, t) \tag{2}$$

being the diffusion coefficient c a function of the magnitude of the gradient $c = p(|\nabla h|)$ where $p(|\nabla h|)$ is the *edge stopping function* able to avoid diffusion across boundaries and computed using the following formula:

$$p(|\nabla h|) = \frac{1}{1 + (|\nabla h|/\lambda)^2} \tag{3}$$

where λ is a constant estimated from the 90% quantile of the probability distribution function of the absolute values of the gradient throughout the digital elevation model image [32]. Such Eq. (1) can be written as:

$$\partial_t h(x, y, t) = \nabla[p(|\nabla h|)\nabla h] \tag{4}$$

which is the nonlinear filter equation used in [16].

GeoNet allows to select as a parameter of the algorithm the N number of nonlinear filtering iterations, the number of steps needed to achieve noise reduction and discontinuities enhancement before proceeding with channel extraction. This value must be defined on the base of the scale of the objects it wants removing from the digital elevation model data. In particular, it has been tested as the skeleton appear for different value of N in the original data and finally the best number filter iterations for our case study is N = 50.

GeoNet by [16] proceeds creating a skeleton of the likely channelized pixels using the quantile-quantile plot of the curvature (as in the work by [15]) and then to further narrow the skeleton by introducing a threshold of the contributing area, the so called area threshold.

Skeleton is a binary matrix where pixels that satisfy the threshold criteria (area threshold and geometric curvature) have a value of 1, while pixels that do not satisfy them have a value of 0.

For the quantile-quantile plot of the curvature [16] used the definition of geometric curvature of the isoheight contours, defined as

$$k = \nabla \cdot \left(\frac{\nabla h}{|\nabla h|} \right) \tag{5}$$

and computed by standard finite differences.

As concerns the quantile-quantile plot of the curvature, it could be possible to use also the Laplacian curvature (as employed in [15]). A discussion about the advantages to obtain the skeleton of the pixels using geometric curvature is in [16]. It is a value which depends on the landscape in analysis; its selection must be small enough to not interfere with channel initiation and large enough to effectively reduce the presence of isolated convergent areas which appear as noise in the skeleton [16, 17].

In this study the value of area threshold is of 4000 m^2 and threshold quantile-quantile curvature = 1.

After the identification of the likely channelized pixels (i.e. the creation of the skeleton using the curvature and the contributing area), GeoNet by [16] performed the extraction of the channels using the geodesic curves. It is defined as curves of minimal cost among all the possible curves C connecting point a (starting point) and point b (ending point):

$$g(a, b) : = \arg \min_{C \in \Omega} \int_a^b \Psi(s)ds \tag{6}$$

where $\Psi(C) : \Omega \rightarrow \mathbb{R}^+$ represents the cost of traveling on a curve $C \in \Omega$.

The cost function Ψ includes surface curvature and flow accumulation because they are the topographic attributes that distinguish channels from the rest of the landscape. In particular, curves with the positive curvature above threshold defined from the quantile-quantile plot and large value of flow accumulation are preferred to all the possible curves connecting two points.

Formally the geodesic curve is computed by gradient descendent on the distance function, backtracking from the downstream point b. So, the geodesic is the integral curve of ∇d starting at point b and the gradient is computed on the surface.

When the Skeleton obtained by the thresholding curvature and contributing area is computed and the channel extracted, the algorithms proceeds with the detection of the end points. They are identified as the points at which the skeleton end.

Because the skeleton is wider than one pixel, the point taken as end point is located at the end of the skeleton and at minimum geodesic distance from the outlet. So to define the end points a cost function is chosen to penalize the paths along which the drainage area does not have large flow accumulation and along which the curvature is not large compared to the surrounding points. The cost function is:

$$\Psi = \frac{1}{(\alpha A + \delta K)} \tag{7}$$

where, A is the contributing area, K is the geometric curvature and α e δ are two constants. The contributing area was computed using the D_{inf} algorithm [36]. The choice of the α e δ constants of the cost function is based on the optimal computation of the geodesic distance.

The purpose of these constants is to take care of the dimensionality of ψ (as A is measured in m^2, while k in 1/m) and of the difference in the order of magnitude between the quantities employed (A varies between 1 and 5×10^5 m^2, while k has been normalized and thus varies between 0 and 1).

Other parameters used are: DEM smoothing quantile = 0.9; Point search box size = 30.

3 Results

Following the previously illustrated methodology a processing of the data of the two DEMs was carried out obtaining the curvature, using Perona-Malik filtered data, and skeleton obtained by thresholding curvature (Fig. 4).

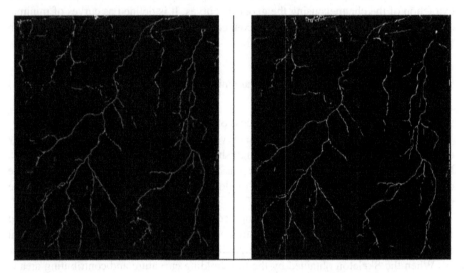

Fig. 4. Skeleton of pixels obtained by thresholding curvature and contributing area for the Calciano test-site, obtained by Dem 2013 on the left and by DEM 2012 on the right.

From the skeleton of Fig. 4, it can detect the river network outlet, as the point with the maximum flow accumulation area, computed, for example, using the Dinf algorithm [36]. After the outlet of the network has been identified, it can proceed with the detection of the end points applying the cost function. These are identified as the points at which the branches end. Since the channels are wider than one pixel, the actual point taken as end point is the one which belongs to the minimum geodesic distance path. The river network has been extracted and the geostructure for channel heads and drainage paths created (Fig. 5).

Among the advantages that the analysis of multidemporal LIDARs by DEMs offers there is certainly the possibility of verifying the evolution of the hydrographic network in a short time-span, through the new positions reached by the channels head points.

The comparison of the two scenarios of 2012 and 2013 (Fig. 6) shows, in fact, that the minor hydrographic network is rapidly evolving with retrogressive channels, which tend to achieve an equilibrium profile. Nevertheless, along this north-facing slope, it is quickly altered and changed by the presence of several shallow landslides.

Among other applications, the subtraction of DEMs (Fig. 7) with spatial analysis using Map algebra functions in ArcGIS or QGIS, allows to identify the fast-changing areas of the slope for the combined action of erosion and deposition, exercised, respectively, by the hydrographic network and landslides [37].

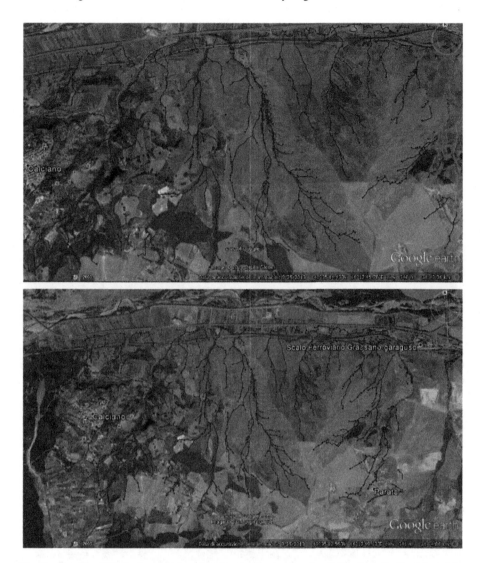

Fig. 5. Results of the hydrographic network extraction and end points automatically detected for the study area (2013 below and 2012 up) with the GeoNet tool by [16] on a Google earth photobase. The black dots indicate the channel heads.

Figure 7 shows, in fact, the extent of the accumulation (riverbeds and some portions of the slopes) and erosional (along the slopes) areas of the study area, expressed in m.

734   M. Lazzari

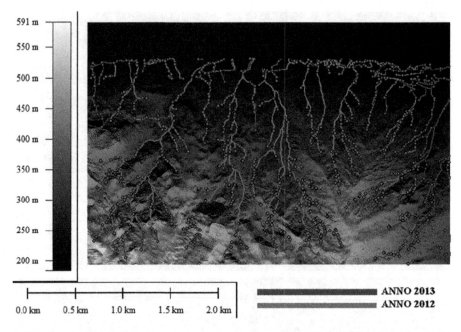

Fig. 6. Comparison between the two hydrographic networks of 2013 and 2012, extracted with GeoNet, projected on the DEM 2013. The red and fuchsia dots indicate the channel heads for each hydrographic networks.

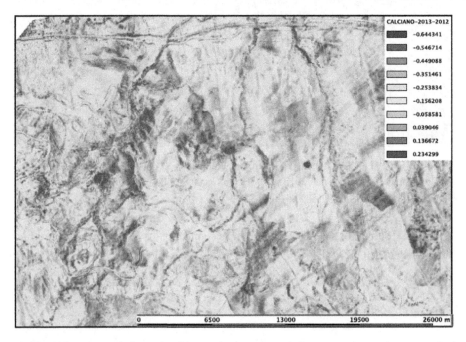

Fig. 7. Altimetric variations (positive values = accumulation; negative values = erosion) calculated between the two LIDAR-derived DEMs of 2012 and 2013.

4   Conclusions

In this paper an automatic methodology, based on Passalacqua et al. script [16], to extract the channel network from high-resolution LiDAR-derived DTMs and a semi-quantitative methodology to assess the short-time landscape evolution of a test-area, located in Basilicata (southern Italy), have been applied.

In particular, the technique used is based on a local nonlinear filter together with the global geodesic optimization for channel head and drainage network extraction. Further, the two Lidar acquisition for the year 2012 and 2013 have been used to detect hydrographic network changes and slope evolution in terms of erosion and deposition pattern.

High-resolution DEMs offer new opportunities for extracting detailed features from landscapes (e.g., channels, erosional/depositional areas, channel heads), but also challenges in hydrographic network developing.

Availability of this data provides new opportunities to study the spatial organization of landscapes and channel network features and the comparison of high-resolution DEMs for the investigation of short-term evolution of complex areas largely affected by widespread fluvial and slope processes, increasing the accuracy of environmental transport models, and inform decisions for targeting conservation practices.

Automatic extraction of detailed and localized geomorphic features of interest, such as channel networks, is very important for accurate estimation of sediment sources and flux transport, especially along slopes, where morphoevolutive mechanisms are complex and difficult to interpret using only the geomorphological field survey.

References

1. Dietrich, W.E., Perron, J.T.: The search for a topographic signature of life. Nature **439**, 411–418 (2006)
2. Tarolli, P., Dalla Fontana, G.: Hillslope to valley transition morphology: new opportunities from high resolution DTMs. Geomorphology **113**, 47–56 (2009)
3. Tarolli, P., Arrowsmith, J.R., Vivoni, E.R.: Understanding earth surface processes from remotely sensed digital terrain models. Geomorphology **113**, 1–3 (2009)
4. Smith, M.J., Rose, J., Booth, S.: Geomorphological mapping of glacial landforms from remotely sensed data: an evaluation of the principal data sources and an assessment of their quality. Geomorphology **76**, 148–165 (2006)
5. Frankel, K.L., Dolan, J.F.: Characterizing arid region alluvial fan surface roughness with airborne laser swath mapping digital topographic data. J. Geophys. Res. **112**, F02025 (2007). https://doi.org/10.1029/2006JF000644
6. Arrowsmith, J.R., Zielke, O.: Tectonic geomorphology of the San Andreas Fault (2009)
7. McKean, J., Roering, J.J.: Objective landslide detection and surface morphology mapping using high-resolution airborne laser altimetry. Geomorphology **57**, 331–351 (2004). https://doi.org/10.1016/S0169-555X(03)00164-8
8. Glenn, N.F., Streutker, D.R., Chadwick, D.J., Tahckray, G.D., Dorsch, S.J.: Analysis of LiDAR-derived topography information for characterizing and differentiating landslide morphology and activity. Geomorphology **73**, 131–148 (2006)

9. Ardizzone, F., Cardinali, M., Galli, M., Guzzetti, F., Reichenbach, P.: Identification and mapping of recent rainfall-induced landslides using elevation data collected by airborne LiDAR. Nat. Hazards Earth Syst. Sci. **7**, 637–650 (2007)

10. Booth, A.M., Roering, J.J., Perron, J.T.: Automated landslide mapping using spectral analysis and high resolution topographic data: Puget Sound lowlands, Washington, and Portland Hills, Oregon. Geomorphology **109**, 132–147 (2009)

11. Cavalli, M., Tarolli, P., Marchi, L., Dalla Fontana, G.: The effectiveness of airborne LiDAR data in the recognition of channel bed morphology. CATENA **73**, 249–260 (2008)

12. Hilley, G.E., Arrowsmith, J.R.: Geomorphic response to uplift along the Dragon's zone from high resolution topography: an example from the Cholame segment, Geomorphology; special issue on high resolution topography (2008). http://doi.org/10.1016/j.geomorph.2009.01.002

13. Ninfo, A., Fontana, A., Mozzi, P., Ferrarese, F.: Remote sensing and LiDAR applications in the alluvial geoarchaeology of NE Italy. Il Quaternario Ital. J. Quat. Sci. **24**, 194–196 (2011)

14. Stock, J.D., Rosener, M.N., Hanshaw, M.N., Tribble, G.W., Field, M.E., Schmidt, K.M., Brooks, B.A.: Conversion of steep Hawaiian hillslope transport from soil creep to overland flow accelerates erosion rates over 100-fold: Eos Trans. AGU, 89(53), Fall Meet. Suppl. Abstract H53G-06 (2008)

15. Lashermes, B., Foufoula-Georgiou, E., Dietrich, W.E.: Channel network extraction from high resolution topography using wavelets. Geophys. Res. Lett. **34**, L23S04 (2007). https://doi.org/10.1029/2007GL031140

16. Passalacqua, P., Do Trung, T., Foufoula-Georgiou, E., Sapiro, G., Dietrich, W.E.: A geometric framework for channel network extraction from LiDAR: nonlinear diffusion and geodesic paths. J. Geophys. Res. **115**, F01002 (2010). https://doi.org/10.1029/2009jf001254

17. Passalacqua, P., Tarolli, P., Foufoula-Georgiou, E.: Testing space-scale methodologies for automatic geomorphic feature extraction from LiDAR in a complex mountainous landscape. Water Resourc. Res. **46**, W11535 (2010). https://doi.org/10.1029/2009WR008812

18. Passalacqua, P., Belmont, P., Foufoula-Georgiou, E.: Automatic geomorphic feature extraction from lidar in flat and engineered landscapes. Water Resour. Res. **48** (2012)

19. O'Callaghan, J., Mark, D.: The extraction of drainage networks from digital elevation models. Comput. Vis. Graph. Image Process. **28**, 328–344 (1984)

20. Tarboton, D.G., Bras R.L., Rodriguez-Iturbe I.: The analysis of river basins and channel networks using digital terrain data, Rep. 326, Ralph M. Parson Lab., Dep. of Civ. Eng., Mass. Inst. of Technol., Cambridge (1989)

21. Tarboton, D.G., Bras, R.L., Rodriguez-Iturbe, I.: On the extraction of channel networks from digital elevation data. Hydrol. Processes **5**, 81–100 (1991)

22. Montgomery, D.R., Dietrich, W.E.: Channel initiation and the problem of landscape scale. Science **255**, 826–830 (1992)

23. Dietrich, W.E., Wilson, C.J., Montgomery, D.R., McKean, J.: Analysis of erosion thresholds, channel networks and landscape morphologyusing a digital terrain model. J. Geol. **3**, 161–180 (1993)

24. Rodriguez-Iturbe, I., Rinaldo, A.: Fractal River Basins. Chance and Self-Organization, 528 p. Cambridge University Press, New York (1997)

25. Heine, R.A., Lant, C.L., Sengupta, R.R.: Development and comparison of approaches for automated mapping of stream channel networks. Ann. Assoc. Am. Geogr. **94**(3), 477–490 (2004)

26. Dietrich, W.E., Bellugi, D., Sklar, L.S., Stock, J.D., Heimsat, A.M., Roering, J.J.: Geomorphic transport laws for predicting landscape form and dynamics. In: Iverson, R.M., Wilcock, P. (eds.) Prediction in Geomorphology, pp. 103–132. American Geophysical Union (2003)

27. Lazzari, M., Gioia, D., Anzidei, B.: Landslide inventory of the Basilicata region (Southern Italy). J. Maps (TJOM) **14**(2), 348–356 (2018)

28. Azzaroli, A., Perno, U., Radina, B.: Note illustrative della Carta Geologica d'Italia: F°188, "Gravina di Puglia". Serv. Geol. It., Roma, p. 57 (1968)

29. Lazzari, M., Pieri, P.: Modello stratigrafico-deposizionale della successione regressiva infrapleistocenica della Fossa Bradanica nell'area compresa tra Lavello, Genzano e Spinazzola. Mem. Soc. Geol. It. **57**(1), 231–237 (2002)

30. Lazzari, M.: Il comportamento tettonico e sedimentario del bacino d'avanfossa Bradanica durante il Pleistocene inferiore. Volume in memoria di ALFREDO JACOBACCI "Evoluzione delle conoscenze geologiche dell'Appennino Apulo-Campano e Tosco-Umbro-Marchigiano. Mem. Descr. Carta Geol. It. **LXXVII**, 61–76 (2008)

31. Soininen, A.: TerraScan User's Guide. Terrasolid, Helsinki (2005)

32. Perona, P., Malik, J.: Scale-space and edge detection using anisotropic diffusion. IEEE Trans. Pattern Anal. Mach. Intell. **12**(7), 629–639 (1990)

33. Catté, F., Lions, P.L., Morel, J.M., Coll, T.: Image selective smoothing and edge detection by non linear diffusion. SIAM J. Numer. Anal. **29**(1), 182–193 (1992)

34. Witkin, A.P.: Scale-space filtering. Paper presented at 10th International Joint Conference on Artificial Intelligence. ACM Inc., New York (1983)

35. Koenderink, J.: The structure of images. Biol. Cybern. **50**(5), 363–370 (1984). https://doi.org/10.1007/BF00336961

36. Tarboton, D.G.: A new method for the determination of flow directions and contributing areas in grid digital elevation models. Water Resour. Res. **33**(2), 309–319 (1997)

37. Dewitte, O., Jasselette, J.-C., Cornet, Y., Van Den Eeckhaut, M., Collignon, A., Poesen, J., Demoulin, A.: Tracking landslide displacements by multi-temporal DTMs: a combined aerial stereophotogrammetric and LIDAR approach in western Belgium. Eng. Geol. **99**, 11–22 (2008)

International Workshop on Advances of Modelling Micromobility in Urban Spaces (AMMUS 2020)

Evaluation of Pedestrians' Behavior and Walking Infrastructure Based on Simulation

Tiziana Campisi[1], Socrates Basbas[2], Giovanni Tesoriere[1],
Antonino Canale[1], Panagiotis Vaitsis[2](✉), Dimitris Zeglis[2],
and Charilaos Andronis[2]

[1] Faculty of Engineering and Architecture, University of Enna Kore, Cittadella
Universitaria, 94100 Enna, Italy
[2] School of Rural and Surveying Engineering, Aristotle University
of Thessaloniki, 54124 Thessaloniki, Greece
pvaitsis@topo.auth.gr

Abstract. Sustainable mobility mainly refers to cycling, walking, e-scooters, public transport etc. The increase of the usage of these means of transport against the use of motorised vehicles can improve the overall quality of the urban environment. Pedestrian streets play a significant role towards the direction of sustainable mobility and the facilitation of environment friendly daily trips. This research concerns one of the most important pedestrian streets in the centre of the city of Thessaloniki, Greece. The evaluation of the existing situation in the pedestrian street together with the evaluation of various scenarios concerning changes in the behaviour and direction of movement of pedestrians due to incidents is examined in the framework of this paper. The evaluation took place by using the pedestrian simulation software PTV Viswalk and four different scenarios were tested. The first scenario is the base scenario referring to the existing situation. The second scenario deals with an increase in the pedestrian flow due to unexpected events. The other two scenarios refer to evacuation phenomenon, thus preventing access to part of the pedestrian street. The examination concerns the pedestrian Level of Service (LOS) and the identification of critical segments of the pedestrian street in terms of pedestrians' flow and composition. The simulation results show that even in the case of doubling of pedestrian flow, this will not cause an overall significant drop in LOS, except for specific sections of the pedestrian street. These results can assist the authorities so to minimize walking difficulties in the pedestrian street and at the same time to take care for waiting areas and the provision of optimum evacuation routes.

Keywords: Pedestrians · Pedestrian street · PTV Viswalk · Evaluation ·
Evacuation · Simulation · Level of service · Incident

© Springer Nature Switzerland AG 2020
O. Gervasi et al. (Eds.): ICCSA 2020, LNCS 12250, pp. 741–753, 2020.
https://doi.org/10.1007/978-3-030-58802-1_53

1   Introduction

Transportation systems can be assessed in a variety of ways. Evaluation methods take into consideration various parameters including users, transport modes, the land use system, transportation problems and solutions, mobility patterns, performance indicators etc. There are many methods to examine the performance of the transport system, each of which reflects particular perspectives regarding "who", "what", "where", "how", "when" and "why". Different methods favor different types of users and transport modes, different land use models and different solutions to transport problems. Motorized traffic is easier to be examined, but this approach only considers a narrow range of transport problems and solutions. Mobility is more difficult to be examined, since it requires monitoring of people's travel behavior [1]. Pedestrian mobility is still not understood by everyone as a possible solution to the problem of traffic congestion and therefore as an effective and efficient mode of transport for short and medium distance travel. Accessibility is more difficult to be examined, since it requires taking the land use system into account, but it reflects the final goal of transport more precisely and allows the widest range of problems and solutions to be considered [2]. Evaluation can take place in existing infrastructures or it can refer to hypothetical scenarios in order to mitigate the critical issues, especially those which are associated to incident management.

This paper focuses on the evaluation of the Level of Service (LOS) of a pedestrian street which is located in the center of the city of Thessaloniki, Greece. There are several studies which investigate the LOS in pedestrian streets using microsimulation techniques in the city of Thessaloniki [3–6]. In other studies the views of the pedestrians in relation to the infrastructure that they use is examined. Such views are examined in the cities of Trikala and Thessaloniki, Greece [7, 8]. The examination of the environmental impacts due to pedestrianization schemes is also an important aspect which must be considered. Similar research was carried out in Greek cities, including the city of Thessaloniki, Greece [9, 10].

The pedestrian street which is examined in the framework of the present paper attracts a large number of visitors on a daily basis since it includes an important archaeological site and a large number of commercial activities.

The LOS was calculated considering four different scenarios in order to identify the potential critical points as far as the movement of pedestrians during an incident is concerned [11]. Collected data include pedestrian flow, pedestrian speed and pedestrians' personal and trip characteristics. The evaluation took place through the use of the pedestrian simulation software PTV Viswalk [12].

2   Methodology

Several studies in the literature discuss various collective phenomena observed in pedestrian crowded situations. This issue has recently attracted the interest of a rapidly increasing number of scientists. In this aspect, the present research focuses on pedestrian dynamics in normal and in the presence of an incident situation.

The acquired data were necessary to construct the Origin-Destination (O-D) matrices which together with the cartographic background are perquisites for the implementation of the pedestrian simulation software PTV Viswalk [12].

The models were calibrated using PTV Viswalk to reflect the "real" movement and behavior of pedestrians by adjusting different possible parameters in an open and at the same time confined area [13]. PTV Viswalk was implemented considering the social force model that governs the interaction between individuals [14]. Vehicles and pedestrians are simulated as single objects within a larger system [15]. The movement of pedestrians cannot be predictable, therefore compared to vehicle movement, it is more complex to simulate these movements. The PTV Viswalk software was developed in addition to PTV Vissim software [16], with the aim of simulating and analyzing pedestrian flows, more realistic than it is possible using only PTV Vissim software. When PTV Viswalk is used separately, it is not possible to simulate vehicular traffic. This paper aims to determine the LOS of walking facilities, considering the perceptions of pedestrians. For this work, an investigation of the pedestrian flows was carried out in the Gounari-Navarinou pedestrian street, Thessaloniki, Greece.

Monitoring was conducted between the 15th and the 30th of May 2019, during the morning and afternoon period when the market and the surrounding activities are in function. In addition, a questionnaire-based survey was conducted in September 2019 in order to identify the preferences and intentions of the pedestrians (Fig. 1).

Fig. 1. Location and views of the Gounari-Navarinou pedestrian street Source of the map: [17]

Following the Helbing model and pedestrians' LOS definition it is possible to obtain the pedestrian densities and the respective LOS for the various subareas of the pedestrian street. Many parameters can be adjusted in PTV Viswalk to calibrate a model to reflect reality as possible as it can be. These parameters include the speed of different users, the composition and the variation of the pedestrian flow. This research shows a comparison of different scenarios where the composition of the flow remains constant while the flow is increased, and the movement conditions changed from normal conditions [18, 19] to evacuation conditions due to an incident, with restriction in the infrastructure imposed by the presence of an obstacle [20]. Through these comparisons it can be investigated what will happen in the event of an incident. More specifically how bottlenecks in the movement of pedestrians can be avoided and how people can move away.

As already mentioned, this work focused on the assessment of the pedestrian level of service (PLOS) relating to a section dedicated to exclusive use by pedestrians. The section runs along some areas characterized by monuments and archaeological excavations; therefore, the section is in use by both tourists and residents.

Four different scenarios were considered in the framework of this research. Scenarios 1 and 2 considered the presence of the two origin and destination nodes (Fig. 2, nodes A and B) together with five secondary nodes (Fig. 2, nodes C, D, E, F, G) that correspond to the accesses of the secondary roads that intersect with the studied stretch. During the evaluation of the current flows (scenario 1) and the hypothesis of doubling the flow (scenario 2), pedestrian composition was considered unchanged. In both cases, the standard travel speeds related to the gender and age groups of pedestrians were considered. Furthermore, a hypothesis has been made to analyze two non-standard conditions and to evaluate the level of service of the infrastructure in the event of an evacuation. This evaluation is important since it allows to mitigate the impacts on people passing through in the event of a hypothetical closure of some parts of the infrastructure in question due to an unexpected incident. Therefore, it was hypothesized to consider access and exit from the under-study section, excluding the possibility of access/exit from node E (3rd scenario) and access/exit from node F (4th scenario). Furthermore, in the 4th scenario, it has been hypothesized that the stretch of the road bordering the archaeological area had suffered a narrowing due to a possible maintenance of the infrastructure. These nodes were respectively closed to the pedestrian flow as their position is strategic with respect to the areas with the highest number of tourists and residents near the archaeological area. In the case of an evacuation (scenarios 3 and 4), a higher travel speed was hypothesized caused by the instinctive response of people to move from the examined area to the exit nodes. Table 1 presents the four scenarios.

Table 1. Description of the four scenarios tested

n°	Descriptions of the four scenarios
1st	Normal condition with daily pedestrian flow along the total length of the pedestrian street Standard pace/rate
2nd	Normal condition with double daily pedestrian flow along the total length of the pedestrian street Standard pace/rate
3rd	Evacuation scenario with access denied in the final part of the pedestrian street (node E on secondary direction) increased pace for evacuation Increased pace/rate for evacuation
4th	Evacuation scenario with restricted area in the final part of the pedestrian street (node F on secondary direction). Increased pace/rate for evacuation

Fruin (1971) has defined different levels of comfort for pedestrian movements based on macroscopic magnitudes [21]. The concept of Level of Service in terms of comfort has been defined as a criterion for public safety in infrastructures. LOS connects different flow qualities with ratios of the maximum capacity of a structure. The capacity of a facility is defined as the maximum sustainable range at which people can reasonably be expected to cross a uniform point or segment of a lane during a specified period, usually in individuals per hour. Each service level represents a range of operating conditions in which level A represents the best operating conditions and level F the worst. Fruin applied his calculations to urban environments like city streets in normal conditions. Table 2 presents a comparison between LOS of Fruin and Highway Capacity Manual 2010 (HCM2010) values [22].

Table 2. Comparison of LOS by Fruin and HCM2010

	LEVEL OF SERVICE LOS OF WALKAY					
	A	B	C	D	E	F
	Free flowing	Minor conflicts	Some restrictions to speed	Restricted movement for most	Restricted movement for all	Shuffing moments for all
Period (1971)	**FRUIN**					
space (m²/ped)	>3.20	2.3-3.2	1.4-2.3	0.9-1.4	0.5-0.9	<0.5
flow rate (ped/min/m)	<23	23-33	33-49	49-66	66-82	variable
average speed (m/s)	>1.321	>1.270	>1.219	>1.143	>0.762	<0.762
Period (2010)	**HCM**					
space (m²/ped)	<5.60	3.7-5.6	2.2-3.7	1.4-2.2	0.75-1.4	<=0.75
flow rate (ped/min/m)	<16	16-23	23-33	33-49	49-75	variable

3   Description of the Undertaken Research

3.1   Study Area

As mentioned above, an investigation of the pedestrian flows was carried out in the Gounari-Navarinou pedestrian street, Thessaloniki, Greece. Thessaloniki is the second biggest city in the country with a population of around one million inhabitants. The specific pedestrian street is considered as on one of the most important pedestrian streets in the city center. The under-study area is characterized by the presence of an important archaeological site and various commercial activities. This area of the pedestrian street extends from Tsimiski street to Egnatia street. These two streets serve large traffic volumes on a daily basis. The main nodes on the investigated pedestrian street are presented in Fig. 2. The total width of the pedestrian street is around 20 m for a representative cross-section. Street furniture, green areas and shy distances are around 14.5 m in total. Therefore, the active width used by the pedestrians is around 5.5 m. There are four cases along the pedestrian street, where there are conflicts between the vehicular traffic and the pedestrians (please see nodes A, C, D and B in Fig. 2). It must be mentioned at this point that there are traffic lights at conflict points (nodes) A, D and B, so pedestrian movement is characterized by acceptable level of safety and comfort. Low traffic volumes together with traffic calming measures characterize conflict point (node) C, thus providing a rather safe environment for the pedestrians. Parking is not allowed along the pedestrian street except for emergency and service vehicles.

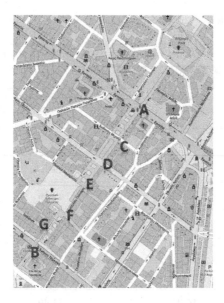

Fig. 2. Under study area: Gounari-Navarinou pdestrian street and respective nodes Source of the map: [17]

3.2   Data Collection

In addition to the evaluation of the functional characteristics of the pedestrian street, an estimate of pedestrian flows was made based on field counts. Estimations were also made concerning the age of the pedestrians. Such monitoring is necessary in order to be able to calibrate, as close as possible to real conditions, the characteristics of the composition of pedestrian flows. Pedestrian actual flows are presented in Table 3 while pedestrian actual flows in terms of pedestrians' estimated age are presented in Table 4 (counts made between 15 and 30 of May 2019).

Table 3. Pedestrian flows in terms of gender

First week			Second week			Average values from both weeks		
Gender								
Male	Female	Total	Male	Female	Total	Male	Female	Total
285	327	612	327	347	674	306	337	643
310	371	681	361	409	770	335	390	725
465	404	869	437	370	807	451	387	838
331	302	633	405	313	718	368	307	675

Table 4. Pedestrian flows in terms of their estimated age

First week			Second week			Average values from both weeks		
Age								
<18	18–64	>64	<18	18–64	>64	<18	18–64	>64
79	425	94	105	497	97	92	461	95
114	484	82	102	570	86	108	527	84
290	542	37	293	486	28	291	514	32
74	505	47	62	562	87	68	533	67

It must be mentioned at this point that data were collected for two weeks and thus it became possible to identify that the peak flow corresponds to 12:00–13:00. The data presented in Tables 3 and 4 as disaggregated by gender and age groups and as totals (as shown in the different columns of Tables 3 and 4). The pedestrian parameters related to each scenario are presented in the following Table 5.

Pedestrian dynamics modeling and their implementation in a computer is a demanding process which requires knowledge of transport and computer simulation. The purpose of this paper is to carry out an evaluation through a microsimulation tool by comparing different scenarios. In particular, the fourth scenario involved a reduction in the walkable area due to a hypothetical neighboring maintenance; this area is also characterized by the presence of an archaeological site that attracts tourists. Therefore, this scenario requires simulating an evacuation condition in a reduced infrastructure condition. The area subject to this hypothesis is shown in Fig. 3 hereinafter.

For the simplicity of calculations, the infrastructure is divided into subareas and in particular the Gounari-Navarinou pedestrian street has been divided into 63 sections or subareas (Fig. 4).

The software for the estimation of the pedestrian LOS requires the acquisition of data related to the composition of pedestrian flows (age, gender and presence of wheelchairs or disabled people) and their respective speeds.

Table 5. Pedestrian parameters related to each scenario

	Scenario			
	1st	2nd	3rd	4th
Length (m)	370			
Width (m)	15–22			1.0 m closed to archeological area
Condition	Normal	Normal	Evacuation with access denied in E node	Evacuation + restricted area in node F
Pedestrian flow (ped/h)	1799	3598	3598	3598
Pedestrian speed (m/s)	Young = 1,35–1,45 Adult = 1,25–1,33 Elderly = 1,1–0.95 Wheelchair = 0,95 Stroller = 0,95		Young = 4,85–4,67 Adult = 4,49–4,31 Elderly = 3,95 Wheelchair = 3,23 Stroller = 3,23	
Pedestrian composition	56% female (28% adult + 28% elderly) 44% male (22% adult + 22% elderly) of which women with children (2%) and people with wheelchairs (2%)			

Fig. 3. Restricted area on Gournari-Navarinou pedestrian street close to the archeological site
Source of the map: [17]

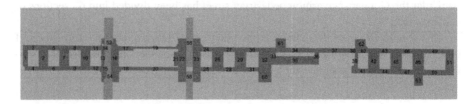

Fig. 4. Sub-areas of the pedestrian street

4   Microsimulation Results

The survey results showed that over 75% of the pedestrians are not accompanied. 12% walk together with other pedestrians (as a group), while the remaining part is constituted by women with children or prams. Almost 60% of the observed pedestrians move in the Gournari-Navarinou pedestrian street for leisure activities, while the rest walks for working purposes or to return home. Over 20% of them visited the under-study pedestrian street at least once a day. These results were concluded by the questionnaire-base survey in the pedestrian streets of the under-study area.

The pedestrian flow has been evaluated during the peak hour period, where the flow was equal to 2166 ped/h (at 12:00–13:00). The LOS evaluation of the under-study pedestrian street was based on the analysis of four different scenarios, considering the current situation (base scenario) and an increasing percentage of flux linked to the study area. The speed of pedestrians is based on a hundred counts and it is equal to 1.35 m/s. A reduced speed has been considered for the elderly as well as for women with children and for people with wheelchairs.

The beginning and the end of the pedestrian area are marked respectively by the letter A and B (please see Fig. 2).

The model was calibrated in the framework of the simulation process by considering the different parameters relating to the presence of different categories of pedestrians and their mutual attraction/disturbance. More specifically, different speeds assumed or presence of area narrowings or movement priorities were considered. It is considered as appropriate step not to use the default values but to calibrate the model considering the counts made and the lifestyles of the pedestrians as recorded during the questionnaire-based survey. Table 6 shows the variability of the LOS in accordance with aforesaid HCM2010 standards, describing with chromatic scale evaluation useful for easier reading of the subsequent results shown on the map.

Minimum and maximum values of LOS used in the microsimulation process are presented in Table 6.

Table 6. Minimum and Maximum values of Level of Service (LOS) used in the microsimulation process

Min(ped/m^2)	max (ped/m^2)	Colour	LOS
Min	0,178		A
0,178	0,270		B
0,270	0,454		C
0,454	0,714		D
0,714	1,330		E
1,330	max		F

The microsimulation has allowed comparing the scenarios assessing pedestrian speed and density. The results concerning LOS are presented in Fig. 5.

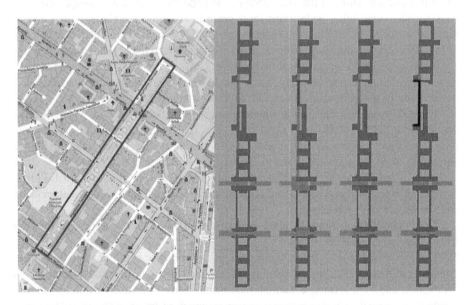

Fig. 5. Comparison of LOS for each scenarios in the study area Source of the map: [17]

The study was conducted considering a series of hypotheses for the calibration of the scenarios to first study the problems connected with both the variation of the flow and a possible geometric variation of the pedestrian area. It is clear that the scenarios do not consider all the combinations of admissible solutions but those most frequently expected, therefore the work presented is by way of example but not exhaustive. In particular it is the variation of service level shown with scenarios 1 and 2 doubling the pedestrian flow, and also through scenarios 3 and 4 proposing a variation, or rather a narrowing, and analyzing the critical issues that have appeared.

The simulation layouts show a reduction in the level of service near sub-areas 14 and 17 in correspondence with the intersection with the street during scenario 2 of doubling the pedestrian flow, corresponding to vehicular traffic in Ioannou Michail street (Node C). The third scenario involves a reduction in the level of service in the smaller areas due to the formation of a bottleneck that slows down pedestrians (sub areas 40–43–46–49). At the same time, there is a reduction in LOS from A to C in correspondence with scenario 4 along the section which is geometrically reduced (brown area) and adjacent to the archaeological area (considering areas 34–37 and 38).

Generally, the work reveals a consistent variation of LOS only near the restricted areas or with reduced geometry and this is strictly connected also to the variation of speed and the variation of flow. The comparison of the scenarios has been included in Table 7 in terms of perceived density, average speed and speed variance. In particular, the results show that in scenario 2 with a doubling of the flow there is an increase that goes beyond the doubling for density but an increase of less than 10% for the speed variation has increased pedestrian outflow (due to the dangerous situation). There are roughly similar variations in scenarios 3 and 4.

Table 7. Comparison of the results for each scenario

Scenarios	Density (pedestrians/m^2)	Average speed (m/s)	Variance of speed (m^2/s^2)
1st scenario	0,1164	1,1167	0,0017
2nd scenario	2,8902	0,9772	0,0021
3rd scenario	0,0366	*4,1286	0,0560
4th scenario	0,1037	*3,9859	0,0958

*speeds are higher for a faster pace during the evacuation phase

5   Discussion

Sustainability and accessibility in the field of transportation can be an incentive to construct pedestrian-type areas, allowing vulnerable road users to use them taking into account comfort and safety criteria. It is well-known that mode choice is strongly related to the subjective well-being [23] and this is the reason why pedestrians' perception of comfort and safety aspects plays an important role.

The study area has been selected for its high historical and cultural value but also for its value as a reconstructed pedestrian street and also for the presence of numerous commercial activities. Through an in-situ investigation which allowed monitoring of pedestrian flows and through the microsimulation it was possible to compare different scenarios by observing the changes in the pedestrian Level of Service.

The selected scenarios aim to highlight the variation in the behavior of pedestrians in terms of speed and the formation of bottlenecks as the infrastructural conditions of the standard type or evacuation or even narrowing of an area to be evacuated vary.

The simulation of several case studies with a variation of the pedestrian composition allows to preventively knowing the areas where critical issues can arise. In addition, the simulation allows preventing this by implementing a series of actions in advance such as infrastructure improvement or reduction in the presence of obstacles or the control and regulation of flows in some areas.

Further research with more extensive data collection is needed in order to examine more complicated scenarios and to assess the behavior of pedestrians under critical situations. The present research was based on counts made by observers in the field. Future research must take advantage of video recording for the pedestrians' trajectories.

References

1. Zegeer, C.V.: Pedestrian Facilities Users Guide: Providing Safety and Mobility. Diane Publishing, Darby (2000)
2. Evans, G.: Accessibility, urban design and the whole journey environment. Built Environ. **35** (3), 366–385 (2009)

3. Campisi, T., Basbas, S., Canale, A., Tesoriere, G., Nikiforiadis, A., Vaitsis, P.: Sensitivity analysis and the alternative optimization of the pedestrian level of service: some considerations applied to a pedestrian street in Greece. In: XXIV International Conference Living and Walking in Cities, Brescia, Italy (2019)

4. Lazou, O., Sakellariou, A., Basbas, S., Paschalidis, E., Politis, I.: Evaluation of LOS at pedestrian streets and qualitative factors. A pedestrians' perception approach. In: 7th International Congress on Transportation Research, Athens, 5–6 November, pp. 1–15 (2015)

5. Basbas, S., Campisi, T., Canale, A., Nikiforiadis, A., Gruden, C.: Pedestrian level of service evaluation in an area close to an under-construction metro line in Thessaloniki, Greece. Transp. Res. Procedia **45**, 95–102 (2020)

6. Amprasi, V., Politis, I., Nikiforiadis, A., Basbas, S.: Comparing the microsimulated pedestrian level of service with the users' perception: the case of Thessaloniki, Greece, coastal front. Transp. Res. Procedia **45**, 572–579 (2020)

7. Basbas, S., Konstantinidou, C., Gogou, N.: Pedestrians' needs in the urban environment: the case of the city of Trikala, Greece. In: Pratelli, A., Brebbia, C.A. (eds.) Proceedings of the 16th International Conference Urban Transport and the Environment in the 21st Century - Urban Transport XV, Wessex Institute of Technology, Limassol. WITpress (2010). WIT Trans. Build Environ. **111**, 15–22

8. Papaioannou, P., Basbas, S., Anastasiadou, A., Vouzoukou, D., Politis, I.: How walking conditions affect pedestrian preferences: the case of Thessaloniki, Greece. In: 17th Conference on Walking and Liveable Communities, Hong Kong, China, 3–7 October 2016 (2016)

9. Pitsiava-Latinopoulou, M., Basbas, S.: The impact of pedestrianization schemes on the environmental quality at central areas. In: Sucharov, L.J., Brebbia, C.A. (eds.) Proceedings of the 6th International Conference Urban Transport and the Environment in the 21st Century - Urban Transport VI, Wessex Institute of Technology, Cambridge. Advances in Transport, vol. 6, pp. 503–512. WITpress (2000)

10. Taxiltaris, C., Basbas, S., Nikolaou, K., Tzevelekis, I.: Environmental impact evaluation of major pedestrianization schemes through the use of modelling techniques. Fresenius Environ. Bull. **11**(10a), 800–805 (2002)

11. Petritsch, T.A., et al.: Pedestrian level-of-service model for urban arterial facilities with sidewalks. Transp. Res. Rec. **1982**(1), 84–89 (2006)

12. PTV Group: PTV Viswalk (2020). https://www.ptvgroup.com/en/solutions/products/ptv-viswalk/

13. Campisi, T., Tesoriere, G., Canale, A.: The pedestrian microsimulation applied to the river Neretva: the case study of the Mostar "old bridge". In: AIP Conference Proceedings, vol. 2040, no. 1, p. 140004. AIP Publishing LLC (2018)

14. Helbing, D., Molnar, P.: Social force model for pedestrian dynamics. Phys. Rev. E **51**(5), 4282 (1995)

15. Laufer, J., Planner, P.T.: Passenger and pedestrian modelling at transport facilities. In 2008 Annual AIPTM Conference, Perth, Australia (2008)

16. PTV Group: PTV Vissim (2020). https://www.ptvgroup.com/en/solutions/products/ptv-vissim/

17. © OpenStreetMap contributors. https://www.openstreetmap.org

18. Beutin, T.: PTV Viswalk realistic simulation of pedestrian flows. In: Materialy Ros.-Germ. konf. po transportnogradostroitel'nomu planirovaniju "Sovershenstvovanie obrazovanija v oblasti gorodskogo i transportnogo planirovanija, pp. 4–8 (2012)

19. Martén, J.B., Henningsson, J.: Verification and validation of Viswalk for building evacuation modelling. Journal **5**, 135–144 (2014)

20. Tesoriere, G., Canale, A., Severino, A., Mrak, I., Campisi, T.: The management of pedestrian emergency through dynamic assignment: some consideration about the "Refugee Hellenism" Square of Kalamaria (Greece). In: AIP Conference Proceedings, vol. 2186, no. 1, p. 160004. AIP Publishing LLC (2019)
21. Fruin, J.J.: Pedestrian planning and design, 206 p. (1971)
22. HCM 2010: Highway Capacity Manual. TRB, Washington, DC (2010)
23. Vaitsis, P., Basbas, S., Nikiforiadis, A.: How eudaimonic aspect of subjective well-being affect transport mode choice? The case of Thessaloniki, Greece. Soc. Sci. **8**(1), 9 (2019)

The Evaluation of Home-School Itineraries to Improve Accessibility of a University Campus Trough Sustainable Transport Modes

Antonino Canale[1] , Tiziana Campisi[1(✉)] , Giovanni Tesoriere[1] ,
Luigi Sanfilippo[2], and Alberto Brignone[2]

[1] Faculty of Engineering and Architecture,
Cittadella Universitaria, University of Enna Kore, 94100 Enna, Italy
tiziana.campisi@unikore.it
[2] V&B Software Services Ltd., Via P. Mascagni 29/4,
20037 Paderno Dugnano, MI, Italy

Abstract. Sustainable mobility is often related to the balance between supply and demand transport, including in its development in terms of connection between the behavioural and economic factors. Furthermore, the investigation of travel reason is useful for the aforementioned selection, also correlating with the different age groups and gender. There is a growing need for young people to access university campuses but the transport supply is often not adapted to student needs. This problem involves compromising not only accessible status but also sustainability and therefore the environmental, economic and social aspect. In this way, it emerges that is necessary to adapt to the growing transport services with student economic availability, travel distance and waiting times. This work explored the accessibility of a university campus (school node), through interviews considering a current transport offer and home–school reason. It was also linked to the availability of parking lots adjacent to the campus and the occupancy rates of the various neighbouring car parks were also calculated, monitoring the aforementioned areas for about a month using video cameras and sensors. The research investigated both travel distances in Euclidean and network terms and both travel times through the use of a micro-simulation tool and a linear equation. The study shows as a first research step that the shared mobility solution saves time but also highlights the critical issues of the service that should be better adapted to the students' needs in terms of rate, type of car and subscription.

Keywords: Sustainable mobility · Shared mobility · Micro-simulation · Travel time

1 Introduction

The evolution of university campuses is often linked to a growing demand for transport which is not homogeneous from an economic and social point of view, as students have different incomes or different transport habits.

© Springer Nature Switzerland AG 2020
O. Gervasi et al. (Eds.): ICCSA 2020, LNCS 12250, pp. 754–769, 2020.
https://doi.org/10.1007/978-3-030-58802-1_54

The growing need to simplify access to these areas and the need to solve the problem of congestion on closed roads has become one of the aspects that most promote the sustainability (environmental, economic and social) of universities.

The accessibility aspect is based on the interactions between transport and land use defined by different variables, such as travel time.

According to [1, 2] the choice of the different types of transport modes may be related to the different expansion of urban contexts.

The accessibility aspect is also an efficient way to assess environmental and social impacts and also the sustainability of transport and land use provisions in accordance with [3].

In terms of transport offer, accessibility can be guaranteed not only through an offer of infrastructures and services but also through a shared and integrated planning and design through I-BIM (Building Information Modeling for Infrastructures) methods that helps to improve accessibility considering aspects such as costs and safety, parameters that also affect travel time [4, 5].

There are several models in the literature that at various scales define and optimize transport processes and thus also improve travel times [6].

In order to define a specific sustainability value, this document aims to compare the different modes of transport for a specific category of demand, considering travel time, Euclidean distance and network distance in accordance with [7] considering the Kore home-to-school travel motivation defined to exemplify as "home-to-school".

The current transport offer is characterized by private cars, university DRT buses and car sharing.

Travel times were studied by monitoring socio-demographic and spatial characteristics in the first phase by interviewing a sample of university students in accordance with [8–11].

The use of micro-simulation tools allows the comparison of scenarios in standard or emergency conditions, mitigating the criticality of transport in a preventive way. The following paragraphs describe the methodology used and the results obtained with reference to the university context considered.

2 Methodology

The objective of this research is to evaluate the travel time covered by university students considering the different forms of mobility that allow them to move daily from their places of residence to the university area examined. This research has been carried out in the following steps:

- the collection of data relating to the monitored campus and surrounding residential areas (no. of students, no. of parking lots, occupancy rate, mode of transport, etc.). In this step of analysis, socio-demographic and travel habits parameters have been acquired considering closed type answers.
- the definition of an interview method and the selection of the sample. In this step of analysis we chose the sample to investigate and the method of face-to-face interview.

- the processing of the data obtained from the interviews for the evaluation of travel time through micro-simulation tools.

In this step the results obtained from the interviews allowed to know the habits of moving from home to the University, the evaluation of parking occupancy rates in the case of moving by car and the perception that each student has of the move in terms of time.

- the evaluation and comparison of scenarios that take into account the values of travel time. In this step we have selected the modes of transport by private car, car sharing or DRT bus dedicated to students, estimating for each one even partial mobility on foot.
- the description of a linear correlation for the average value of the total travel time.
- the analysis of the results in terms of distance and travel speed and comparison for each mode of transport. In this step the distances in Euclidean and network terms have been considered considering the different nodes of origin and the same node of destination.

Moreover the travel times obtained by the micro-simulation and those perceived by the students, acquired during the interview, have been evaluated and compared.

Analysis of Interview Data
The area under investigation was located in a mountain town (Enna) where Kore University is the most recent.

The University is composed of 4 Faculties, but this research has investigated in depth a part of them related to the Faculties of Engineering and Architecture and Human Sciences.

The research started from a real scenario where shared mobility is currently managed by a private company that has not considered the reduction of tuition fees.

The results of the interview highlighted the main habits of university students moving from their place of residence to the area of the university under investigation. Subsequently, using a micro traffic simulator approach, it was possible to compare the different modal choices (private car, car sharing or DRT bus) in terms of travel times. The following paragraphs provide more details on the various stages of analysis.

Interview Description and Sample Selection
The interview was based on 17 questions that could be answered either with a yes/no answer (4 questions) or with a single choice between multiple options (13 questions).

The interview was based on the acquisition of socio-demographic variables and travel habits as described in Table 1 below (Table 2).

Table 1. List of parameters included on interview linked to socio-demographic attributes

	Variable	Possible reply	Variable	Possible reply
Socio-demographic	Gender	M-F	Car ownership	YES-NO
	Age	18–21 22–25 >26	bike ownership	YES-NO
	Residence area	Santa Lucia (O1) Sant'Anna (O2) Ferrante (O3)	National car sharing experience	YES-NO
	Faculty	Engineering and Architecture Human Science	Driver-licence ownership	YES-NO

Table 2. List of parameters included on interview linked to transport habits

	Variable	Possible reply	Variable	Possible reply
Transport habits	H_S transport mode	walking by car by car sharing by DRT bus other	DRT bus use frequency	never rarely (several times a week) often (several times a day)
	Travel distance perception	0-500 m 500-750m 750-1000m >1000m	Travel time perception	5-10min 10-15min 15-20min >20min
	walking frequency	never rarely(several times a week) often (several times a day)	own car use frequency	never rarely (several times a week) often (several times a day)
	Parking frequently used closed to University	P0 P1 P2	Car-sharing Parking closed University and frequently used	CSP3 other
	itinerary frequently used	IT1 =O1/P0/P1/D IT2 =O1/P0/P1/P2/D IT3= O2/P0/P1/D IT4= O2/P0/P1/P2/D IT5= O3/P0/P1/D IT6= O3/P0/P1/P2/D	IT7 =O1/CSP3 IT8= O2/CSP3 IT9= O3/CSP3 IT10=O1/O2/BS/D	
	Free parking occupancy rate experience	OR=100% OR=90% OR=80% OR=70%	OR=60% OR=50% OR<50%	

The units selected for the interview were represented by 442 university students (IS titled) and represent about 20% of the total number of students who attended the selected faculties (titled TS).

The sample was defined on the basis of a fair distribution in terms of age and gender. All students evaluated had a regular lease or property agreement, excluding those living in the university dormitory. The itineraries analysed considered as origin (O) several areas adjacent to the University and a single destination point (D) corresponding to the part of the campus examined. In the evaluation of the itineraries, the positions of the free stalls for private and car sharing vehicles and bus stops in the vicinity of the described area were taken into account.

Micro-simulation Tool Description

The results of the interview were implemented and processed through the Cube Dynasim tool [16].

Cube Dynasim is a dynamic micro traffic simulation software based on stochastic events. It is based on car following and gap acceptance models for the assessment of moving vehicles and their iteration. The modeling of transport systems allows to compare different scenarios through the creation of layers and to use O/D matrices and traffic compositions to simulate realistic flows, to consider public transport (with PT module) by setting the relative frequency and to analyze the outputs of the time loss functions.

The transport network was implemented by defining specific arcs and nodes useful for the implementation of the O/D matrix and identifying the transport requests of university students expressed during the interview phase. The calibration processes have made it possible to make the traffic parameters more realistic on the basis of the travel habits acquired and the related perceived mobility data.

The simulation took place considering a disturbance flow within the considered transport network, recorded in value through a camera system and imported into the tool during the calibration phase. The travel time criterion made it possible to measure the time taken by a vehicle to travel along the network between an input and an output section of a specific data collector.

The model made it possible to enter not only the points of origin and destination but also the location of the stables and stops related to the Demand Responsive Transport bus (title DRT bus).

Example Evaluation of Average Linear Travel Times

The evaluation of the travel time was carried out thanks to the data obtained from the interviews, i.e. through the instrument of micro-simulation and a linear analytical estimation. This work shows a first step of investigation related to the linear value of the average travel time from an origin to the destination defined "ALTTod". It is estimated considering a disturbance flow generated by vehicular traffic during peak hours and acquired through sensors and cameras.

In this document, the evaluation of the travel time was assessed in terms of the overall travel and also taking into account the time related to the distance between the car parks and the destination and between the destination and the bus stops from the destination. For each mode of transport, an ALTTod value given by the linear sum of several values has been defined as Eq. 1 and 2.

$$ALTTod = \sum\nolimits_{i,j \in Pod} tij \; \forall o, d \in W \tag{1}$$

$$ALTTod \geq \sum\nolimits_{i,j \in Pod} tij \; \forall o, d \in W, Pod \in Kod \tag{2}$$

where

   t_{ij} = time rate considering each arc ij
   $ALTT_{od}$ = average liner travel time to reach from origin "or" to destination d
   W = set of arcs traveled
   Kod = set of possible itineraries
   Pod = choice of means of transport from origin or destination d
   i, j = extremes of the arc

For each mode of transport it was possible to define the average linear travel time (minutes) as described in Table 3.

An "OTHER" value has been added to each of these calculated times.

This value considers the following times related to:

- unforeseen events (strikes, accidents)
- time waster due to excessive urban stops
- technical problems (no electricity, blocked level crossings, poor maintenance)
- professionalism of staff and drivers
- service management issues

This step is useful to validate the application of a modal choice model considered as a "random utility" model, within which each choice alternative is associated with a utility function.

Table 3. ALTT description for each evaluated transport mode

Transport mode	Average Linear Travel Time (minutes)	
Own vehicle	$ALTT_{odcar}$	$T_{avg\ vehicle\ recognition} + (T_{avg\ on\ board} + T_{avg\ travel} + T_{avg\ parking\ election}) + T_{avg\ off\ board} + T_{avg\ walking}$
Car-sharing	$ALTT_{od\ carsharing}$	$T_{avg\ vehicle\ recognition} + (T_{avg\ on\ board} + T_{avg\ travel} + T_{avg\ parking\ election}) + T_{avg\ off\ board} + T_{avg\ walking}$
University minibus	$ALTT_{od\ DRTbus}$	$T_{avg\ waiting\ time} + (T_{avg\ on\ board} + T_{avg\ travel}) + T_{avg\ off\ board} + T_{avg\ walking}$

Study Area Description

Enna is a mountain city consisting of 3 large districts (Pergusa, Enna Alta and Enna Bassa). The district of Enna Alta is a residential and touristic area with many offices and shops, the streets that connect Enna Alta with Enna Bassa are very steep and do not have dedicated lanes (bicycle, bus or emergency). The district of lower Enna is residential but also home to hospitals, universities and many schools and supermarkets.

The streets of Enna bassa have a lower slope and are characterized by the presence of sidewalks that make it possible to walk.

The study was conducted considering the different modes of transport commonly used by students for home-university travel (defined with home-school motivation).

It was considered appropriate to consider that travel distance within 500 m are generally made on foot while those with a greater radial distance require the use of different modes of transport as shown in Fig. 1. In the estimation of distances, the centre corresponds to the evaluated campus, defining as the travel destination correlated to the interviewed students.

Fig. 1. Radial distance for mobility related to the monitored area

The University of Enna Kore is located between the neighborhood of Santa Lucia (O1), Sant'Anna (O2) and Ferrante (O3) while a new campus located around 3 km away in not urban area. The investigated faculties are located in the Ferrante area (O3) like described on Fig. 2 below.

Fig. 2. Investigated main nodes of the investigated area

Estimates of travel time took into account the parking areas located near the Campus and the interview with a sample of students showed that the FP0 free parking lot reserved to enrolled students was always occupied, being undersized for the students' transport demand.

The free parking areas generally selected by students are called FP01 and FP02.

On-site surveys and interviews showed that the free parking spaces analyzed have 99% occupancy rates for Campus P0 and 85% and 75% for free parking spaces named P1 and P2 respectively. The OR values were obtained both from the respondents' opinions and from observation through the cameras.

The value of the occupancy rate refers to the time period in the morning between 8:00 and 10:00 a.m. when students generally go from school to university.

This occupancy rate varies during the day due to the movement of people living in the surveyed areas for various reasons. During this period, in fact, there is generally the absence of vehicles of non-university residents and the presence of their cars living or arriving in that area.

All the evaluated residential areas are characterized by a value equal to 90% as they are inhabited by university students and therefore the fact of not having considered the movements of non-university residents did not have much influence on the results.

To date, only two of the three areas have car sharing parking spaces less than 50 m away. In fact, the O3 has no stalls for this service.

During the selection of the parking area, students preferred to first find a place in the reserved parking lot, then aim to find a free parking space and then use paid parking as the last option.

As for the minibus, all students of the University can use this system for free by showing their university card on board.

Tables 4 and 5 show a schematization of the areas of origin/destination of the sample movements as described by the results of the interviews.

Table 4. Origin nodes and relative description

Origin	Definition	Potential transport Demand/supply	Transport mode
O1	Santa Lucia	125	Own car
O2	Sant' Anna	109	Car sharing Minibus
O3	Ferrante	200	Own car
CSP1	Car sharing (3 stalls) Santa Lucia	8	Car sharing
CSP2	Car sharing (5 stalls) Sant'Anna		

Table 5. Destination nodes and relative description

Destination	Definition	Potential transport Demand/supply	Transport mode
D	University Campus	2100 (TS)/442 (IS)	
FP0	Free parking (25 stalls) Campus	25 stalls	Own car
FP1	Free parking (20 stalls)	20 stalls	
FP2	Free parking (15 stalls)	15 stalls	
BS	Bus stop	2 bus stop origin 1 bus stop destination	Minibus
CSP3	Car sharing (3 stalls) Campus	3 stalls	Car-sharing

The selected itineraries are showed on figures below.

The origin and destination nodes of each route have been highlighted in red. The green nodes represent the car sharing stables, while the yellow ones represent free parking. Considering the Origin in O1,

Figure 3 shows the transport network defined by a graph described by arcs and nodes. The different eligible routes were IT1, IT2 and IT7 for the private and shared mobility system.

The origin and destination car parks in car sharing and the free car parks used mainly by students going to the Campus have been identified.

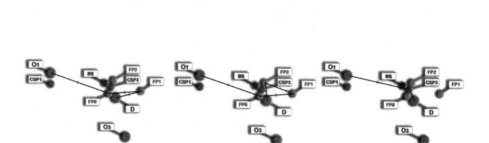

Fig. 3. Itinerary IT1-IT2-IT7 networks with O1 origin for own and car sharing

The same was also done for the O2 and O3 centroids as shown in the two figures below (Fig. 4).

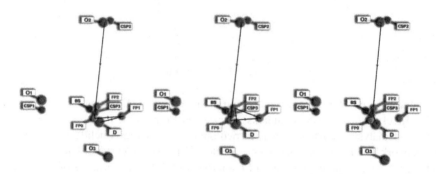

Fig. 4. Itinerary IT3-IT4-IT8 networks with O2 origin for own and car sharing

All the roads used are of a dual lane secondary suburban type with bus stops on the right (Fig. 5).

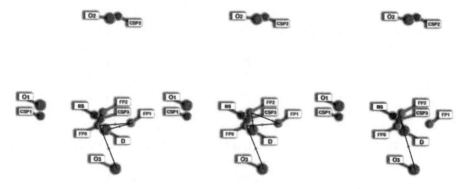

Fig. 5. Itinerary IT5-IT6-IT9 networks with O3 origin

In particular, the DRT bus service and relative presence of stops for the exclusive use of university students was assessed, with stops for getting on and off near the places of origin of the movement and a unique destination stop as shown in the figure below (Fig. 6).

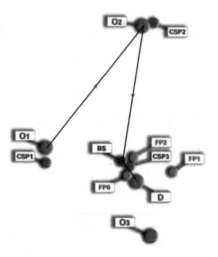

Fig. 6. Itinerary IT10 related to minibus

Table 6 shows the itineraries according to Origins/Destinations, considering the daily travel of the university students interviewed from Home to School (H-S).

A first analysis on distances was carried out considering the Euclidean measure and the network The Euclidean distances evaluated do not consider the differences in slope between the areas and the presence of main road links. All the distances of the network are greater than 500 m. Moreover, it was estimated that more than 70% of the distances exceed 1000 m, thus increasing the need to move with a motorized vehicle.

Table 6. Monitored network and itinerary details

Itinerary	Origin	Destination	Stops destination	Distance (m)	
				Euclidean	Network
IT1	O1	D	P1	481 m	1251 m
IT2	O1		P2	481 m	1974 m
IT3	O2		P1	758 m	1950 m
IT4	O2		P2	758 m	2673 m
IT5	O3		P1	294 m	1382 m
IT6	O3		P2	294 m	2105 m
IT7	O1		CSP3	481 m	620 m
IT8	O2		CSP3	758 m	1319 m
IT9	O3		CSP3	294 m	751 m
IT10	O1/O2		BS	481 m	1890 m

3 Results

Interview Results

The interviews were carried out during the month of October 2019 to 442 students living in Enna, representing about 20% of the student population of the two faculties. The sample was homogeneously composed of 49% of men and 51% of women between the ages of 19 and 25. The sample interviewed is made up of 90% of the people who have a regular lease and live in the areas surveyed, while 10% are owners of the properties where they live in the same areas.

For the medium distances (500–1000 m) it was observed with regard to the investigated sample (IS) that the distribution of transport modes reached a value of 70% for users using private cars instead 27% chose the mini-bus, and similarly 1.5% for both public transport (PT) and shared mobility (MS).

PT was not considered as a mode of transport in this first phase of analysis as it was used by a small percentage. The reason for this value is related to the free ticket and the dedicated service with a higher travel frequency and stops closer to the University. With regard to movement habits for the reason H-S was obtained that:

- considering the distance <500 m, more than 55% of the sample travels on foot, 25% by minibus and 20% by car.
- considering the distance between 500 and 1000 m, about 40% of the sample passes every day by private car while about 38% uses the DRT bus while 22% goes on foot.
- Considering the distance >1000 m about 50% go by private car and 45% by DRT bus while 5% continue on foot.

Only 3% of the sample used the car-sharing service for the H-S move once a week.

The DRT bus service allows the transfer of a maximum of 8 users and stops in every area of origin and in front of the Campus area (BS). Approximately 98.5% of the sample has not yet used H-S in Enna as the rates and the subscription are expensive.

The remaining 1.5% used MS from April 2019 to January 2020 at least once, opting for sharing with other users. In fact, vehicle sharing with other users is viewed positively by more than 85% of the sample as it allows to halve the costs of the service. In addition, about 80% of the sample has a driving licence and finally about 30% have already had experience in Italy with the car sharing service.

Microsimulation Results

The travel time estimate was made by initially considering the average travel time value for each mode of transport analyzed and comparing this value with the value perceived by the individual users expressed during the interview.

Through the use of traffic micro-simulation it was possible to accurately assess this concept of lost or gained time. With reference to the output data of the micro-simulation and the mathematical evaluation defined in the previous paragraphs, it was possible to obtain the following data from the table (Tables 7, 8 and 9).

Table 7. Interval of gain time for each itinerary

	DT $_{\text{gain time}}$ Considering travel time on board (min)		
	P1	P2	BS
O1	62%	82%	81%
O2	71%	84%	59%
O3	66%	83%	/

Table 8. Average Linear Travel Time (ALTT) with own vehicle

	T_{odcar} (sec)	$T_{\text{walking avg}}$ (sec)	T_{avg} (sec)	T_{avg} (min)	$T_{\text{StudentPerceived}}$ (min)
IT1	251,01	450	701,007	12	20
IT2	322,21	380	702,212	12	15
IT3	301,79	450	751,790	13	20
IT4	460,78	380	840,782	14	20
IT5	268,59	450	718,592	12	15
IT6	441,64	380	821,642	14	20

Table 9. Comparison of Average Linear Travel Time (ALTT) without own vehicle

	$T_{\text{odcar-sharing}}$ (sec)	$T_{\text{walking avg}}$ (sec)	T_{avg} (sec)	T_{avg} (min)	$T_{\text{StudentPerceived}}$ (min)
IT7	184,189	300	484,188	8	10
IT8	236,167	300	536,167	9	10
IT9	204,301	300	504,301	8	10
	$T_{\text{od DRTbus}}$ (sec)	$T_{\text{walking avg}}$ (sec)	T_{avg} (sec)	T_{avg} (min)	$T_{\text{StudentPerceived}}$ (min)
IT10	806,768	500	1306,768	22	30

Although a time saving of more than 40% was estimated, students expressed through interviews that they intend to use the car-sharing service longer, only if a revised service is implemented and reshaped to the students' needs.

The results show through a linear combination of fares and travel time that the car-sharing service is the one that allows a transfer with the shortest time. This is due to both the location of the origin and destination car parks and the absence of a time rate used to find a stall. In fact, the car sharing system implemented on the university campus provides for the presence of dedicated stalls instead for transport by private vehicle provides free and paid parking.

The most common approximation of the generalized cost of transport consists in considering two factors, namely time and cost according to

$$C_k = \alpha(ALTT)_k + \beta(AD)_k$$

Where C_k = travel cost

ALTT = average linear travel time
AD = arc distance (m)
α, β = specific parameters

It was found that a function such as the one described above can explain 60–80% of the total value of the travel choices. The unreasonable times are instead related to perceptions, variability of cost information or general errors. Therefore the next research step will be to find the values of a and b in order to assess the overall cost of the defined travel.

4 Conclusion

The sustainable development of an area with a university vocation is closely linked to preventive transport assessments that can mitigate the discrepancies between demand related to students and those working at the university and supply in terms of services and infrastructure. It is desirable to disseminate policies that can guarantee shared or public services, preferably with low environmental impact, to the growing demand for university students and allow the spread of new forms of mobility. The vision of a functional university campus is closely linked to the supply of transport that allows students to reach their destination. It is therefore necessary to extend the conventional notion of accessibility, seen as simply related to the demand for physical mobility, and take it as an indicator of the quality of urban space from the point of view of movement. Accessibility must be understood as the immediate and total usability of the built space, giving the user the management of his or her time. Accessibility is guaranteed with a positive trend through urban planning that presupposes the development of services such as parking lots or new stalls for public mobility. Survey campaigns and periodic interviews can highlight the advantages and critical points of the services provided.

The present work shows a methodology for the choice of mobility based on the concept of travel time acquired with microsimulation tools and recalculated by combining various time rates through a linear combination.

The accessibility of a university campus where car sharing services have recently evolved. The main objective is to understand the actual propensity of each student to use sustainable modes of transport, decreasing the use of private vehicles. The analysis was carried out through different phases: the first one was related to the acquisition of traffic data through sensors and video cameras considering the analysed area. The second phase was related to the acquisition of student data through the administration of questionnaires. The results were used for the calibration of microscopic models that allowed to evaluate the travel time for each mode of transport examined.

The third step was linked to the calculation of average travel times in order to compare the different modes of transport and have a first "vision" of the students' transport habits. In particular, the research considered the possibility of using the private vehicle or alternative forms of mobility such as the DRT bus and car sharing service. The evaluation of travel times with one's own vehicle considered the possibility of free parking as the first choice, considering at peak times the occupancy rates of the three observed parking areas. The synergy of local authorities with universities could lead to a mobility model in line with the sustainable development objectives defined in the United Nations Agenda 2030 and therefore to a more environmentally friendly, economically efficient and more integrated system. The work is preparatory to a subsequent evaluation of the cost of transport according to the previous equation and also to the evaluation of the probability linked to the choice of transport modes with the implementation of the logit model for a random choice of transport.

Acknowledgments. The authors acknowledge financial support from the MIUR (Ministry of Education, Universities and Research [Italy]) through a project entitled WEAKI TRANSIT: WEAK-demand areas Innovative TRANsport Shared services for Italian Towns (Project code: 20174ARRHT/CUP Code: J74I19000320008), financed with the PRIN 2017 (Research Projects of National Relevance) program. We authorize the MIUR to reproduce and distribute reprints for Governmental purposes, notwithstanding any copyright notations thereon. Any opinions, findings, and conclusions or recommendations expressed in this material are those of the authors and do not necessarily reflect the views of the MIUR.

Funding. This research work was partially funded by the MIUR (Ministry of Education, Universities and Research [Italy]) through a project entitled WEAKI TRANSIT.

Conflicts of Interest. The authors declare no conflict of interest.

References

This paper is the result of the joint work of the authors. 'Abstract' 'Introduction' 'Methodology' and 'Results' were written jointly by the authors. TC and AC focused on the state of the art. TC and LS designed the methodological approach and discussion. Supervision and research funding AB, TC and GT.

1. Kawabata, M.: Spatiotemporal dimensions of modal accessibility disparity in Boston and San Francisco. Environ. Plann. A **41**(1), 183–198 (2009). https://doi.org/10.1068/a4068
2. Acampa, G., Ticali, D., Parisi, C.M.: Value of travel time: an economic assessment for transport appraisal decision-makers. In: AIP Conference Proceedings, vol. 2186, no. 1, p. 160009. AIP Publishing LLC, December 2019. https://doi.org/10.1063/1.5138077
3. Salonen, M., Toivonen, T.: Modelling travel time in urban networks: comparable measures for private car and public transport. J. Transp. Geogr. **31**, 143–153 (2013). https://doi.org/10.1016/j.jtrangeo.2013.06.011
4. Acampa, G., Forte, F., De Paola, P.: B.I.M. Models and Evaluations. In: Mondini, G., Oppio, A., Stanghellini, S., Bottero, M., Abastante, F. (eds.) Values and Functions for Future Cities. GET, pp. 351–363. Springer, Cham (2020). https://doi.org/10.1007/978-3-030-23786-8_20

5. Campisi, T., Acampa, G., Marino, G., Tesoriere, G.: Cycling master plans in Italy: the I-BIM feasibility tool for cost and safety assessments. Sustainability **12**(11), 4723 (2020). https://doi.org/10.3390/su12114723

6. Calabrò, G., Torrisi, V., Inturri, G., Ignaccolo, M.: Improving inbound logistic planning for large-scale real-world routing problems: a novel ant-colony simulation-based optimization. Eur. Transp. Res. Rev. **12**, 1–11 (2020). https://doi.org/10.1186/s12544-020-00409-7

7. Buczkowska, S., Coulombel, N., de Lapparent, M.: A comparison of Euclidean distance, travel times, and network distances in location choice mixture models. Netw. Spatial Econ. **19**(4), 1215–1248 (2019). https://doi.org/10.1007/s11067-018-9439-5

8. Daisy, N.S., Hafezi, M.H., Liu, L., Millward, H.: Understanding and modeling the activity-travel behavior of university commuters at a large Canadian university. J. Urban Plann. Dev. **144**(2), 04018006 (2018). https://doi.org/10.1061/(ASCE)UP.1943-5444.0000442

9. Varela, J.M.L., Börjesson, M., Daly, A.: Estimating values of time on national travel survey data. In: 7th Symposium of the European Association for Research in Transportation (hEART 2018) (2018)

10. El-Geneidy, A., Levinson, D., Diab, E., Boisjoly, G., Verbich, D., Loong, C.: The cost of equity: assessing transit accessibility and social disparity using total travel cost. Transp. Res. Part A: Policy Pract. **91**, 302–316 (2016). https://doi.org/10.1016/j.tra.2016.07.003

11. Torrisi, V., Ignaccolo, M., Inturri, G.: Estimating travel time reliability in urban areas through a dynamic simulation model. Transp. Res. Procedia **27**, 857–864 (2017). https://doi.org/10.1016/j.trpro.2017.12.134

12. Campisi, T., Canale, A., Tesoriere, G., Renčelj, M.: The newest public transport system applied to turbo roundabouts. In: Proceedings of the Institution of Civil Engineers-Engineering Sustainability, pp. 1–8. Thomas Telford Ltd., March 2020. https://doi.org/10.1680/jensu.19.00008

13. Danner, D., Chimba, D., Soloka, K.: Invited Student Paper-Microsimulation of University Campus Evacuation Challenges: A Case Study (No. 18-00226) (2018)

14. Campisi, T., Torrisi, V., Ignaccolo, M., Inturri, G., Tesoriere, G.: University propensity assessment to car sharing services using mixed survey data: the Italian case study of Enna city. Transp. Res. Procedia **47**, 433–444 (2020). https://doi.org/10.1016/j.trpro.2020.03.155

15. Sun, C., Cheng, J., Lin, A., Peng, M.: Gated university campus and its implications for socio-spatial inequality: evidence from students' accessibility to local public transport. Habitat Int. **80**, 11–27 (2018). https://doi.org/10.1016/j.habitatint.2018.08.008

16. Bentley Systems: Cube Dynasim reference manual version 6.11 (2020)

Exploring the TTMS's Impact to the Accessibility of a Long Distance Stretch Using Micro-simulation Approach

Tiziana Campisi[1]([✉]) [iD], Giovanni Tesoriere[1] [iD], Luigi Sanfilippo[2],
Alberto Brignone[2], and Antonino Canale[1] [iD]

[1] Faculty of Engineering and Architecture, University of Enna Kore,
Cittadella Universitaria, 94100 Enna, Italy
tiziana.campisi@unikore.it
[2] V&B Software Services LTD.,
Via P. Mascagni 29/4, 20037 Paderno Dugnano (MI), Italy

Abstract. Road maintenance is generally analyzed considering complex types of work which must respect two considerable aspects: the first relating to the safety of workers, road users and those who somehow come into contact with the area on the other; the second instead correlated to the reduction of the impacts due to the shrinkage of the superstructure which entails criticalities to the transit vehicle flow. The evaluated parameters are the type of road, the position but also with the duration, visibility, speed and type of traffic. This work focuses on the evaluation of two different construction site layouts related to the TTMS (Temporary Traffic Management Scheme) which are periodically implemented in a medium-high traffic section of a small mountain town. The monitored area is located in one of the main connecting arteries of the city, adjacent to the main areas of attraction linked to the nearby commercial, residential and university areas. The study was addressed through the use of a micro-simulation tool. The results demonstrate how a different extension of the section to be maintained can drastically reduce the level of service (LOS), keeping equal vehicle flow.

This approach is useful for road managers and local Authorities in order to analyze the impacts produced by the construction site in terms of increased congestion of the vehicle flow, evaluating this as the dimensions of the construction site vary. This preventive assessment aims to consider the best solution to be implemented in order not to interfere with other activities as this could further reduce the accessibility of the adjoining places.

Keywords: Accessibility · TTMS · Micro-simulation · Road maintenance

1 Introduction

The road construction site is generally defined like an element of discontinuity and disturbance that cannot be foreseen by motorists and road users. The signals must be suitable and capable of informing users, guiding them and convincing them to behave appropriately for a situation "not habitual" in order to increase the global safety (road users and workers of the building site) maintaining an adequate fluency of traffic demand.

© Springer Nature Switzerland AG 2020
O. Gervasi et al. (Eds.): ICCSA 2020, LNCS 12250, pp. 770–783, 2020.
https://doi.org/10.1007/978-3-030-58802-1_55

The necessary precautions must be applied in order to maintain a perfect efficiency and optimal visibility during all time.

The national and local regulation also establishes the procedures for delimiting and signaling construction sites, the feasibility of the day and night visibility of the road workers, as well as the necessary measures for traffic regulation, as well as the procedures for carrying out the works on road construction sites.

The area of the construction site (for example for open manholes) closed to in crossroads or on high-speed roads, are generally prohibited only with the "work in progress" signal without any operational means of coverage.

The elements to be taken into account in a building site are:

- the type of road and its geometric characteristics (number of lanes by direction of travel, presence or absence of emergency lanes or quayside, etc.);
- the interval time (short-term sites present difficulties in preliminary planning of the intervention and require speed of execution and movement of the area affected by the works);
- the importance of the construction site, according to the effects on traffic and the footprint on the road;
- visibility at different conditions (rain, snow, fog, etc.);
- geo-location: urban area, level roads or on works of art, singular points such as intersections or junctions, etc.;
- the speed and the traffic composition (their variability during the life of the construction site can cause chain collisions);
- the execution of works in continuously different and new environments, with variable characteristics and positions that affect safety (schools, hospitals, other services);
- high probability of creating unexpected situations, such as the presence of unknown services.

A traffic management plan was often used to keep workers safe from vehicles and equipment both outside and within roadside worksites [1]. Traffic management plan templates can be used to assess workers' compliance with safety precautions to improve traffic controls, the security of the work area, and general protection of all workers.

In literature different research was focused on the problem of road maintenance considering the efficiency of the construction site layout and temporary traffic management (TTMS) such as the use of narrow aisles or the closure of them [2]. According to [3, 4] it was observed that the narrowing of the lanes shows some important behaviour of the drivers and the presence of heavy vehicles has a significant impact on the reduction of the capacity of the road section. In this work, the effect on traffic performance of various parameters (e.g. vehicle flow, percentage of heavy vehicles, lengths of road work areas and speed limits) was tested and compared considering the Level of Service (LOS). In order to select the better scenario to applied, data of previously implemented construction sites were collected and evaluated. Therefore the same data was used for steps of verification, calibration and model validation processes [5].

The preventive assessment of the possible layouts and related critical issues allows the increase in the phenomenon of traffic congestion with consequent potential increase in CO_2 emissions and potential accidents in accordance with [6]. The comparison of maintenance scenarios can also be found in the literature in confined environments or with a narrow pedestrian vocation where they are often compared not only to changing flows but also considering emergency evacuation scenarios [7].

Planning of maintenance and design activities considering IBIM systems can solve some critical issues in terms of costs and safety [8, 9].

This research shows how lengthening a stretch of road construction site on a lane can lead to a reduction in the level of service of a high-flow road axis and therefore generate problems for access to the various neighboring residential and commercial areas.

The comparison of the scenarios was carried out using the micro-simulation tool Cube Dynasim [10] and the process and results were better described in the following paragraphs.

2   Methodology

The study of traffic scenario through the application of microscopic models generally evaluate the action of each single moving vehicle in the traffic network and also allows to investigate the influence between nearby vehicles for each moment and each point in space. After the selection of the parameters, this tool returns a lot of information to the operator, also giving the possibility to observe the movement of vehicles in different circumstances.

In a road section, on average, the speed of the vehicles will be given by a decreasing function of the density of the vehicles: if there is no one, you can go at maximum speed, obviously respecting the limit imposed by the traffic regulation at that point (as in the case study 30 km/h in the city).

The software consider both car following and chance lane model. Through the car following model it is possible to analyse the influence in the presence of other machines and therefore how the speed is affected by them: in fact the closer the vehicles are to each other and the more the scenario will present slowdowns up to the stopping distance. The lane changing model is instead useful to calculate the different parameters that influence possible congestion phenomenon [9]. There are three main factors that were assessed in the decision process are the need, the opportunity and the safety of a lane change respectively. The need or the opportunity to change the lane is determined by calculating, for each driver, a risk factor, which is a function of the relative position of the vehicle with respect to the object that gives rise to the need for a lane change. The study focused on the preventive assessment of maintenance scenarios along the selected stretch of road.

The stretch of road interrupted by two layouts was considered after several observations on the site and monitoring of vehicular flows of the closed intersection through detection systems such as sensors and cameras. Specifically, flow data acquisition campaigns were carried on 2019.

The maximum peak flow generated by the union of the usual traffic component (citizens) with the commuter one (university students) but also the influence made by the closed commercial areas. The composition of the traffic was selected taking into account the data records while the location of the construction site was selected by choosing the lane where major maintenance was recorded and the stretch in which the most critical situations arise due to vehicular currents in the opposite direction and the presence of public transport vehicles that have stops nearby and trucks moving from/to loading/unloading areas and logistics of commercial areas It was hypothesized to study the effect of the lengthening (doubling) of a road construction site located along the same lane in the first instance. The comparison was made through the calculation outputs such as travel speed or the number of stops and the synthetic judgment on the level of service as the TTMS changes was described using the LOS index.

2.1 Microsimulation Tool Description

In the last 10 years, various tools have been developed that allow to study different vehicle and pedestrian scenarios in a preventive way, starting from models that represent vehicular and/or pedestrian actions [11] describing in detail the variations of parameters such as speed, the number of stops and the length of the queues. Over the years, the micro-simulators have proved to be useful tools to mitigate the impacts generated by the increase in flow or to evaluate the critical points (points of conflict) generated by incorrect geometric design [12–14].

This research was carried out implementing 3 scenarios through the use of Cube Dynasim tool [15]. It is a graphical tool that allows you to extract data from a database to create graphs related to vehicle flows and related parameters such as travel time, travel speed, delay, etc.

The software realistically show the interaction among different type of road users (motorised vehicle, bicycles and pedestrians interacting with all the other vehicles and the environment).It is completely interactive 2D and 3D animations. The applied model was stochastic type.

The traffic flow was analysed considering specific matrix O/D and flow composition and the presence of traffic light signs to respect the alternating sense. The comparison can be made between scenarios based on collected data and scenarios based on project hypotheses, thus correlating to future forecasts.

3 Description of the Undertaken Research

3.1 Study Area

The monitored area is located in the district named Enna Bassa. It has undergone several transformations from an urban and infrastructural point of view in the last ten years. In fact, this area has been enhanced as a craft area with the inclusion of various commercial activities such as supermarkets and workshops. The road intersection is also one of the major access points to the city for those coming from the west of Sicily.

Recently the infrastructure has been installed undo a traffic light intersection with a sloping roundabout that connect the commercial areas located in the South and East (that include low-cost MMR and a multi-brand shopping center) with the other areas. This area is also considerable because it is the main connection between the University area with the new Campus and therefore during weekdays it is crossed by a stream also composed of an aliquot of university students as well as commuters and inhabitants.

The hub is characterized by the presence of local bus stops with a frequency of 30–35 min crossing this area facilitating travel from the upstream part of the city with a tourist and tertiary vocation with the downstream one with a residential/commercial vocation (Fig. 1).

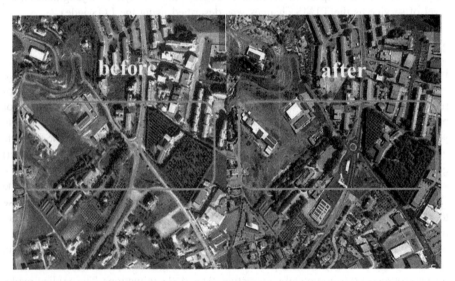

Fig. 1. Monitored area before and after roundabout execution (Image source: Google Earth 2019)

The images also show an enhancement of the neighboring residential areas and the presence of several workshops and a nursing home. The North-South direction allows access to the city from the other neighbors while the East-West direction let the connection between the part a upstream and downstream of the city.

The arms of the roundabout and relative flow directions were respectively named (Table 1):

The traffic flows directed to/from the cities bring the names of Enna Alta (EA) and Enna Bassa (EB) with flows in the North-West direction and vice versa and the city of Caltanissetta (CL) with the flows to and from Enna in the South-North direction and vice versa. The transit flows between the two cities are characterized not only by vehicular traffic but also heavy traffic and suburban buses. The commercial areas have been identified with the MMR code instead the residential one with the letter D. Finally

Table 1. Traffic flow direction of monitored road network

Direction ID	Details	Flow composition
MMR_R	MMR area_Roundabout	LV-HV
EA_R	Enna Alta_Roundabout	LV-HV-LocalBUS
R_EB	Roundabout_Enna Bassa	LV-HV-Locla BUS-ExtraBUS
CL_R	Caltanisetta_Roundabout	LV-HV-ExtraBUS
CL_EB	Caltanissetta_Enna Bassa	LV-HV-ExtraBUS
EB_CL	Enna Bassa_Caltanissetta	LV-HV-ExtraBUS
D_R	Residential area_Roundabout	LV-HV-LocalBUS
EB_R	Enna Bassa_Roundabout	LV-HV-LocalBUS-ExtraBUS

where

LV = light vehicle (car, van, sport utility….)

HV = heavy vehicle (truck, cement mixer, ambulance…)

the traffic flows entering and leaving the roundabout report the node R. The peak flow monitored by cameras and sensors, measured at peak time between 8:30 and 09:30 is equal to 1250 veh/h.

The composition of traffic is equal to: 90% light vehicles, heavy vehicles 5% and bus 5%. In the North South direction, extra-urban buses run with a frequency of 1 bus every 50 min. In the North-West direction, minibuses and city buses pass frequently. In the areas surrounding the roundabout there are stops for the city bus. The stretch of construction site is located in the lane that connects the node EB with the roundabout R and is characterized by the presence of vertical and traffic light signs with an extension of 50 m in the first layout and 100 m in the second as shown in Fig. 2.

Fig. 2. TMMS1 layout and relative route distance (Image source: Google Earth 2019)

This traffic direction is characterized by single lane for motorized vehicle and a sidewalk for pedestrian located to the right of the lane (width about 1.50 m).

In particular, TTMS1 layout (with extension of 50 m) placed on the right lane (direction EB_R) allows alternate transit along the direction indicated in Fig. 3.

The micro simulation layout can help in understanding the alternating flows in the adjacent lanes as shown below.

Fig. 3. Microsimulation results with increasing of traffic queue for TMMMS1

The TTMS2 layout (with extension of 100 m) is placed in the same direction allows alternate transit along the directions considering the route distance indicated on figure below (Fig. 4).

Fig. 4. TMMS2 layout and relative route distances (Image source: Google Earth 2019)

In this case, the construction site interferes with the flows exiting the secondary road located to the EAST, generating greater congestion problems as shown in Fig. 5.

Fig. 5. Microsimulation results with increasing of traffic queue

The comparison between the different scenarios was calculated considering the main parameters that describe the fluidity of vehicular traffic, i.e. the length of the queues and the number of stops and subsequently estimating the level of LOS service.

4   Microsimulation Results

4.1   Comparison of Scenarios

The TTMS layouts were implemented considering a traffic flow setting by a traffic light system with total traffic cycle of 80 s on TTMS1 (with respectively 26 of green and 4 of yellow) and with 110 s on TTMS 2 (with 24 s of green and 4 of yellow).

The tool made it possible to count the vehicles that pass through selected points of the sub-network during a predetermined time interval. The case study focused on the territory of Enna where a 4-arm sloping roundabout was recently built. The vehicular flow saturation hypothesis was studied for each arm by evaluating the variations of 4 distinct variables. From the point of view of the length of the queues, the direction D_R has the highest increasing value, passing from the standard scenario to the maintenance scenario TTMS2, instead the direction CL_R changing to standard to TTMS1 as described in Fig. 6.

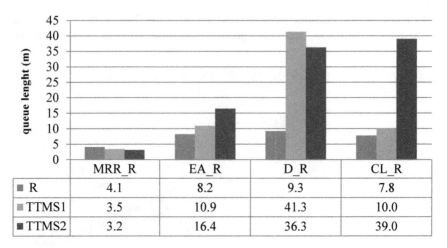

	MRR_R	EA_R	D_R	CL_R
R	4.1	8.2	9.3	7.8
TTMS1	3.5	10.9	41.3	10.0
TTMS2	3.2	16.4	36.3	39.0

Fig. 6. Comparison of queue length(m) considering different scenarios

The STOP number is considered as another evaluation criterion and considers vehicles in a stopped state. The value depends on two threshold speeds (lower and upper) respectively. In fact, a vehicle is in a stopped state if, when it entered the subnet, its speed was lower than the minimum limit and since then it has not reached a speed higher than the maximum limit or if, because it has slowed down or has not reached or exceeded the upper limit. In terms of STOP number, proximity to congestion is further confirmed along EB_R direction (lane where is placed the TTMS) as described in Fig. 7 for both TTMS layouts.

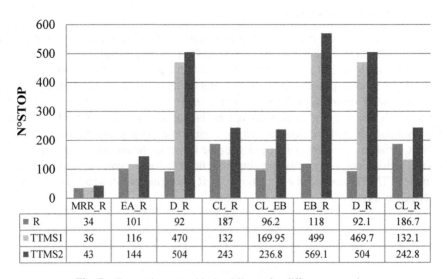

	MRR_R	EA_R	D_R	CL_R	CL_EB	EB_R	D_R	CL_R
R	34	101	92	187	96.2	118	92.1	186.7
TTMS1	36	116	470	132	169.95	499	469.7	132.1
TTMS2	43	144	504	243	236.8	569.1	504	242.8

Fig. 7. Compariosn considering N°stop for different scenarios

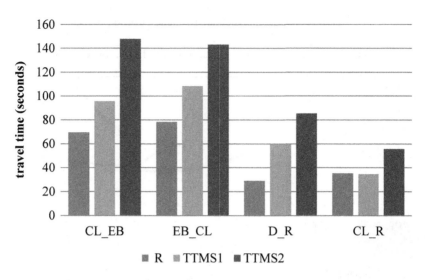

Fig. 8. Compariosn considering Travel time (seconds) for different scenarios

This criterion represents - for each vehicle that leaves the sub network - the time elapsed since it first crossed the entry point. Considering the travel time, on the other hand, direction CL_EB and EB_CL are those with the highest values, especially with the increase in the construction site area as shown in Fig. 8.

Finally, a synthetic judgment of LOS was expressed by evaluating the overall delay of the intersection in the neighboring roundabout as shown in the table below, which shows that the infrastructure under recorded flow conditions and considering the geometry implemented has an optimal level of service while this reduces drastically from level A to level C positioning a construction site of about 100 m along the lane with EB_R direction. The North-South direction is affected by the increase in the size of the construction site by reducing the level of service beyond the intersection in the roundabout as shown in the layout of the TTMS2 scenario, as there is a substantial increase in the length of the queues and the number of stops they produce basically congestion in this direction (Table 2).

Table 2. Level of Service LOS layout and RD values (roundabout delay seconds)

Level of Service (LOS)	Layout with LOS for each arms
A B C D E F	
scenario R	

scenario R

RD	LOS
4,32	A

scenario TTMS1

RD	LOS
12,44	B

scenario TTMS2

RD	LOS
27,16	C

5 Conclusion

Sustainable urban infrastructure development must consider the variability of the scenarios that characterize the road infrastructures.

Different scenarios are generally considered like standard or maintenance or evacuation phenomena. This study highlights how micro-simulation analysis can analyze and mitigate the problems connected to the presence of a road construction located in a high-traffic road which can generate a problem of accessibility to nearby areas.

The scenarios were selected after a period of monitoring (about 1 year) through inspections and photographic reports and having ascertained the most applied construction site layouts.

The comparison between the different functional parameters of the infrastructure and the synthetic judgment expressed through the LOS show that the analyzed area has undergone a general reduction of the points of conflict through the construction of an inclined roundabout. Considering the peak of the traffic flow, the recent infrastructure undergoes a change in the level of the LOS service from A to C caused by the presence of a TTMS that does not allow the use of a lane for a space of 50 and 100 meters respectively. The layouts allow an alternating sense of the use of the unoccupied lane but with particular reference to the TTMS2 layout, there is a reduction in manoeuvres and an increase in critical issues with a greater tendency to road congestion.

The location of local bus stops and private access closed to the residential and commercial areas were also considered. This study lays the foundations for other comparisons relating to the other arms of the roundabout and allows the person responsible for the road to evaluate how the presence of the construction site can generate possible conflicts between vehicular currents and therefore reduce the general safety of the infrastructure. The limitation of this work consists in a partial analysis of possible construction site layout, not considering the possibility to have 2 or 3 maintenance sites in the same time. This study also did not consider different traffic flow composition. These assessments will be the subject of future research. The obtained results can be hypothesized in terms of the possible impact mitigation scenarios and at the same time lay the foundations for a more in-depth assessment of the case studies.

Acknowledgments. The authors acknowledge financial support from the MIUR (Ministry of Education, Universities and Research [Italy]) through a project entitled WEAKI TRANSIT: WEAK-demand areas Innovative TRANsport Shared services for Italian Towns (Project code: 20174ARRHT/CUP Code: J74I19000320008), financed with the PRIN 2017 (Research Projects of National Relevance) program. We authorize the MIUR to reproduce and distribute reprints for Governmental purposes, notwithstanding any copyright notations thereon. Any opinions, findings, and conclusions or recommendations expressed in this material are those of the authors and do not necessarily reflect the views of the MIUR.

Funding. This research work was partially funded by the MIUR (Ministry of Education, Universities and Research [Italy]) through a project entitled WEAKI TRANSIT.

Conflicts of Interest. The authors declare no conflict of interest.

References

This paper is the result of the joint work of the authors. 'Abstract' 'Introduction' 'Methodology' and 'Results' were written jointly by the authors. TC and AC focused on the state of the art. TC and LS designed the methodological approach and discussion. Supervision and research funding AB, TC and GT.

1. Soczówka, P., Żochowska, R.: Work zones and temporary traffic organization at roundabout - review of selected solutions. In: Macioszek, E., Akçelik, R., Sierpiński, G. (eds.) TSTP 2018. LNNS, vol. 52, pp. 13–23. Springer, Cham (2019). https://doi.org/10.1007/978-3-319-98618-0_2

2. Ghosh, L.E., Abdelmohsen, A., El-Rayes, K.A., Ouyang, Y.: Temporary traffic control strategy optimization for urban freeways. Transp. Res. Rec. **2672**(16), 68–78 (2018). https://doi.org/10.1177/0361198118797461

3. Nassrullah, Z., Yousif, S.: Development of a microsimulation model for motor-way roadworks with narrow lanes. IEEE Trans. Intell. Transp. Syst. (2019). https://doi.org/10.1109/TITS.2019.2910159

4. Torrisi, V., Ignaccolo, M., Inturri, G.: Analysis of road urban transport network capacity through a dynamic assignment model: validation of different measurement methods. Transp. Res. Procedia **27**, 1026–1033 (2017). https://doi.org/10.1016/j.trpro.2017.12.135

5. Otković, I.I., Deluka-Tibljaš, A., Šurdonja, S.: Validation of the calibration methodology of the micro-simulation traffic model. Transp. Res. Procedia **45**, 684–691 (2020). https://doi.org/10.1016/j.trpro.2020.02.110

6. Cárdenas, O., Valencia, A., Montt, C.: Congestion minimization through sustain-able traffic management: a micro-simulation approach. LogForum **14** (2018). https://doi.org/10.17270/J.LOG.2018.260

7. Tesoriere, G., Canale, A., Severino, A., Mrak, I., Campisi, T.: The management of pedestrian emergency through dynamic assignment: some consideration about the "Refugee Hellenism" Square of Kalamaria (Greece). In: AIP Conference Proceedings, vol. 2186, no. 1, p. 160004. AIP Publishing LLC, December 2019. https://doi.org/10.1063/1.5138072

8. Campisi, T., Acampa, G., Marino, G., Tesoriere, G.: Cycling master plans in Italy: the I-BIM feasibility tool for cost and safety assessments. Sustainability **12**(11), 4723 (2020). https://doi.org/10.3390/su12114723

9. Acampa, G., Bona, N., Grasso, M., Ticali, D.: BIM: Building information modeling for infrastructures. In: AIP Conference Proceedings, vol. 2040, no. 1, p. 140008. AIP Publishing LLC, November 2018. https://doi.org/10.1063/1.5079197

10. Bentley Systems. Cube Dynasim reference manual version 6.1 (2020)

11. Gipps, P.G.: A model for the structure of lane-changing decisions. Transp. Res. Part B Methodol. **20**(5), 403–414 (1986). https://doi.org/10.1016/0191-2615(86)90012-3

12. Campisi, T., Canale, A., Tesoriere, G., Lovric, I., Čutura, B.: The importance of assessing the level of service in confined infrastructures: some considerations of the old Ottoman pedestrian bridge of Mostar. Appl. Sci. **9**(8), 1630 (2019). https://doi.org/10.3390/app9081630

13. Saha, U., Islam, M.F., Neema, M.N.: A Microsimulation based approach to investigate intersection performance: a case study on Bhulta intersection of Dhaka. In and Practice (iCERP2019) 4th GCSTMR World Congress, p. 129, January 2019

14. Tesoriere, G., Campisi, T., Canale, A., Zgrablić, T.: The surrogate safety appraisal of the unconventional elliptical and turbo roundabouts. J. Adv. Transp (2018). https://doi.org/10.1155/2018/2952074
15. Campisi, T., Mrak, I., Canale, A., Tesoriere, G.: The surrogate safety measures evaluation of a staggered crossing on the delta area of Rijeka. In: AIP Conference Proceedings, vol. 2186, no. 1, p. 160006. AIP Publishing LLC, December 2019 https://doi.org/10.1063/1.5138074
16. https://www.citilabs.com/software/cube/cube-dynasim/

Understanding Willingness to Use Dockless Bike Sharing Systems Through Tree and Forest Analytics

Ioannis Politis[(⊠)] [iD], Ioannis Fyrogenis [iD],
Efthymis Papadopoulos [iD], Anastasia Nikolaidou [iD],
and Eleni Verani [iD]

Laboratory of Transportation Engineering, Department of Civil Engineering,
School of Technology, Aristotle University of Thessaloniki,
541 24 Thessaloniki, Greece
{pol,fyrogeni,efthympg,nikolaid,verani}@civil.auth.gr

Abstract. In this paper we explore factors that affect Bike Sharing System (BSS) usage and how they differentiate between discrete groups of potential users. BSS have known a rampant growth during recent years, through technological advances, re-evaluated business models and reinvention of the mean's utility. Yet, for a realized use of dockless BSS and a successful integration in the urban mobility ecosystem to be achieved, the factors that promote willingness to use them need to be explored. By using a sample of 500 stated preference data, classification trees and random forest models are built for three groups of potential BSS users; car users, bus users and pedestrians. Among the considered factors are BSS cost gains, BSS In Vehicle Time (IVT) and Out of Vehicle Time (OVT) gains, trip frequency, purpose and duration. More specific, it was found that BSS potential, increases for short duration trips of up to 21 min for car users. Bus users and pedestrians were found to be more likely to choose a BSS option for a higher cost up to 0,60 and 0,75 euros respectively. On the other side sociodemographic characteristics such as household income, gender, education level and occupation did not found to be the dominant factors for the mode choice decision. OVT is found only to be relatively important for bus users, while the cost gains are comparatively more significant for bus users and pedestrians.

Keywords: Bike Sharing Systems · Willingness to use · Classification tree · Random forest

1 Introduction

Urbanization has been an increasingly rising trend in recent years. Cities are expected to amass 68% of the world's population by 2050 [1]. This combined with the car-dominant paradigm of recent years, makes adopting socially, environmentally and economically sustainable practices an urgent necessity. The emergence of sharing economies and shared mobility in particularly is widely considered a much promising solution to this predicament. More specifically, increased usage of Bike Sharing Systems (BSS) and cycling in general has been correlated with an abundance of positive

© Springer Nature Switzerland AG 2020
O. Gervasi et al. (Eds.): ICCSA 2020, LNCS 12250, pp. 784–795, 2020.
https://doi.org/10.1007/978-3-030-58802-1_56

externalities, such as health benefits [2], reduced traffic congestion [3] such as environmental benefits [4].

BSSs' evolutionary history can be summed up in four generations of systems. The first generation of BSSs first appeared in 1965 in Amsterdam and they became known as "White Bikes" [5]. The bikes were randomly allocated in the city center and free for public use, something that made them susceptible to wear, vandalism and theft and resulted in the system's cease of operations. The second generation, known as "Coin Deposit Systems" began operations in Denmark in 1991 consisted of bikes with a lock installed, that users could unlock by a refundable deposit [4]. While this attempted to improve on the first generation's failures, it only partially did, as there was no mechanism in place to limit the bike-share usage times and the users often kept the bicycles for extended periods of time. The third generation of BSSs, that started operating in France in 1998 (known as "IT based systems") was better equipped to handle those problems [5]. It included docking stations with smart technology that made it possible to know when a bike was taken to and from a station [6]. It also incorporated electronic means of payment and high deposits that made it possible to identify the users and deter theft. While the fourth generation of BSS was already defined by many field experts before the rise of dockless BSS, as a system that is demand responsive and a fully integrated part of the city's transportation system, during recent years it has come to be identified with the rise of dockless BSSs [6, 7].

Dockless BSS' explosive growth started in China in 2015 and expanded worldwide. The systems' flexibility allows users to choose the starting and ending point of their trips without depending on rigidly placed docking stations. This is made possible by Global Position System (GPS) sensors that are installed on its bike and the widespread use of smart devices by users that allow them to easily locate, unlock and ride the bicycles in the urban environment [8]. Currently, the operational BSSs around the world are a mix of third and fourth generation systems, that often operate complimentary to one another.

Taken aback by this surge in usage and the sudden emergence of bicycles – and later scooters – in city streets, municipalities and governments lagged behind with regulations, something that created difficulties with formulating frameworks that would enable BSSs to become an integrated part of urban transportation [9].

For BSS and micromobility to reach a fully realized and optimized usage that will make it a part of a robust and resilient urban mobility system, the factors and mechanisms that make it an appealing mode of transport and increase its modal share need to be thoroughly understood.

2 Literature Review

A lot of work has already been published that explores both factors and user characteristics that enhance BSS usage. A big amount of the literature focuses on identifying the characteristics of BSS users, comparing them to the non-user population, mainly using revealed preference data, both in form of system-use data and user surveys.

Regarding the sociodemographic characteristics of BSSs users many of the studies found significant difference between bike-sharing users and the general population.

A large number of studies found current BSS users to be younger on average compared to the general population [5, 10, 11]. While the users' income was found to be significantly different by the rest of the population in a number of studies, it was not consistently found to be higher or lower [5, 11–13]. A higher education level was also identified as a contributing factor in some studies [10, 14]. While most studies agree that male users are more likely to prefer BSS, some conclude that females are [10–12, 15].

Other parts of pertinent literature have examined the way environmental factors contribute towards increased BSS usage. Improved infrastructure, such as an extended network of bicycle lanes, mixed land use, docked BSS station placemaking and weather conditions have all been found to significantly affect BSS usage [16–19].

On the contrary, little work has been done to examine users' willingness to switch to BSS usage. Campbell et al. [20] determined that trip characteristics such as trip distance, temperature, precipitation and air quality were factors that mainly effected whether users considered using BSS instead of their currently preferred mode of transport, while sociodemographic characteristics weren't found as important. Li & Kamargianni utilize short-distance, revealed and stated preference data to examine mode choice, with emphasis on bike-sharing. The results showed that choosing BSS heavily depended on air pollution, weather conditions, cost and travel time and less so on socioeconomic characteristics [21].

Based on the existing literature, a question that arises is which factors most heavily incentivize potential BSS users, that currently prefer other modes of transport, to use bike sharing across all urban trip durations:

- Does the proposed population clustering (e.g. car-bus-foot) effectively support different micro-mobility strategies?
- If yes, how and in which manner the various mode and personal characteristics are affecting the mode choice process? What are the threshold values for changing the mode choice behavior towards dockless BSS?
- Is the proposed tools used in the study (classification trees and random forest analytics) appropriate to interpret dockless BSS potential?

3   Survey Design

In order to tackle those questions, a stated preference survey was designed on the Limesurvey platform [22] and deployed on-field by trained interviewers, equipped with tablets. The data collection took place from April 2019 to May 2019 in Thessaloniki, Greece and a sample of 500 answers was collected.

The survey was answered by users of the three currently dominant modes of transport in Thessaloniki; car users, bus users and pedestrians, depending on which of those modes they used for their most frequent trip. The interviewees were asked about the characteristics of their last typical trip, including duration, IVT (In Vehicle Time) and OVT (Out of Vehicle Time), cost etc. Using those answers, competing values of cost, IVT and OVT for the BSS (or total trip time in the case of pedestrians) were calculated by the survey algorithm and presented to the interviewees in the last section of the survey as a set of 9 mode choosing scenarios. In those scenarios the interviewees had to choose between their current mode of preference, with the cost, IVT and OVT they stated, and the dockless BSS with varying competing combinations of cost, OVT and IVT.

The variables that were collected via the survey, along with their types, levels when applied and descriptions can be seen in Table 1.

Table 1. Variables of the factors affecting willingness to use BSSs that were explored

Variable name	Variable abbreviation	Variable type	Levels/Units	Description
Cost.gain	Cs.	Numeric	Euros	The monetary gain by using BSS compared to the currently preferred mode of transport
IVT.gain	IVT	Numeric	Minutes	The IVT gain by using BSS compared to the currently preferred mode of transport
OVT.gain	OVT	Numeric	Minutes	The OVT gain by using BSS compared to the currently preferred mode of transport
T.gain	T.g	Numeric	Minutes	The total trip time gain by using BSS compared to walking (for pedestrian potential users)
Cost.BSS	C.B	Numeric	Euros	The Cost of the BSS (for pedestrian potential users)
Gender	Gnd	Categorical	Male Female	The gender of the potential user
Age group	AgG	Ordinal	18–24 25–34 35–44 45–54 55–64 65+	The age group of the potential user
Education	Edc	Ordinal	Higher Lower	The education level of the potential user (stratified into higher and lower education)
Occupation	Occ	Binary	Stable Not stable	The current occupation of the potential user (stratified into stable and not stable categories, based on the user's daily schedule)

(continued)

Table 1. (*continued*)

Variable name	Variable abbreviation	Variable type	Levels/Units	Description
Household income	HsI	Ordinal	0–400 € 401–800 € 801–1200 € 1201–1600 € 1601–2000 € 2001–2400 € 2400+ €	The potential user's household income
Private bike ownership	PBO	Binary	Yes No	Whether the potential user owns a private bike
Trip frequency	TrF	Ordinal	Once a day 2–3 times a day 3–5 times a week 3–5 times a month	How often the potential user repeats the specific trip
Trip purpose	TrP	Categorical	Work Education Entertainment Other social reasons	The purpose of the potential user's specific trip
Trip duration	TrD	Numerical	Minutes	The duration of the potential user's specific trip

4 Results

For each of the three groups of potential users (car users, bus users and pedestrians) a classification tree and a random forest model were built. The sample was split into a training and a testing set using a 4:1 split ratio and the models' results were validated using the testing set. 10-fold cross validation was used to fit the models and the hyperparameters of both models were tuned using grid search to select the optimal value in order to increase the model's predictivity. To achieve shorter interpretable trees, the tree models were furtherly pruned for the minimum leaf node size to be consisting of 50 or more observations. The analysis was performed in the R language for statistical computing [23]. The package dplyr [24] was used for data manipulation and the packages rpart [25], randomForest [26] and caret [27] for model fitting. The results were visualized with the rpart.plot [28] and ggplot2 [29] packages.

4.1   Car Users

The classification error of the classification tree shown in Fig. 1 was 18.59%. As can be easily interpreted from the tree, variables related to mode specific features such as duration and cost are closer to the root node (upper part of the tree). Reduced trip duration and especially increased IVT gain appear to be critical factors towards preferring the BSS. The thresholds chosen by the model for those factors are relatively low, as the first split of the dataset happens for trips shorter or longer than 21 min, while car users would require significant IVT benefits in order to make the switch to BSS. On the other hand while reduced cost gain does make preferring the BSS more likely, car users can prefer the BSS even at a slightly higher cost per trip. The combination of factors that seems to increase the likelihood of prefering the BSS over the car is a combination of low trip duration, high IVT gains, relatively younger age groups and work as a trip purpose.

The random forest model that was fitted for car users had a classification error of 10.70%. The relative importance of the variables that were used in the model is shown in Fig. 2. Similarly, to the results of the classification tree the variables that contribute most to decision making are cost gain, trip duration and IVT gain, while household income also stands out.

4.2   Bus Users

The classification error of the classification tree shown in Fig. 3 was 25.86%. As can be seen by the tree, variables relative to mode specific factors are closer to the root node of the three and seem more crucial toward splitting the sample in homogenous groups based on mode choice. Increased cost gain appears to have an important role towards choosing the BSS over the bus. Users with higher education were more likely to prefer the BSS, especially with decreased IVT compared to the bus. The combination of factors that increases the likelihood of preferring the BSS the most is users with higher education that perform shorter duration trips, on a daily basis but only if the BSS is not a much more expensive option.

The random forest model that was fitted for bus users has a classification error of 11.64%. The relative importance of the variables that were used in the model is shown in Fig. 4. Similarly to the results of the classification tree the most important factor in terms of contributing to decision making is the cost gain, while IVT gain, trip duration and OVT (Out of Vehicle Time) gain, as well as household income also are also found to be important.

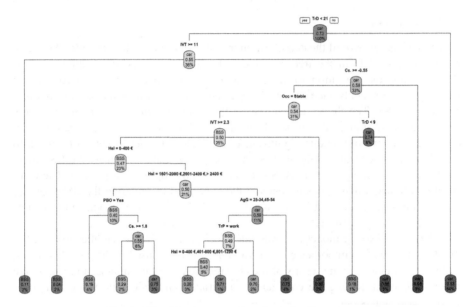

Fig. 1. Classification tree of mode choice for car users

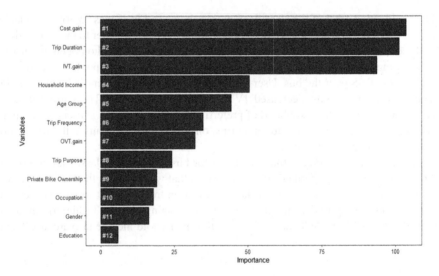

Fig. 2. Variable importance derived from the random forest model for car users

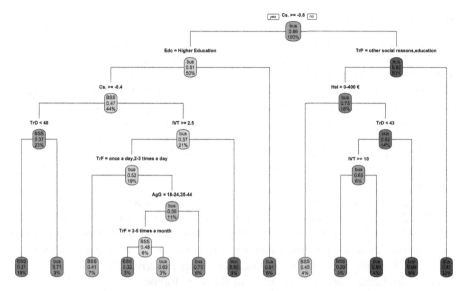

Fig. 3. Classification tree of mode choice for bus users

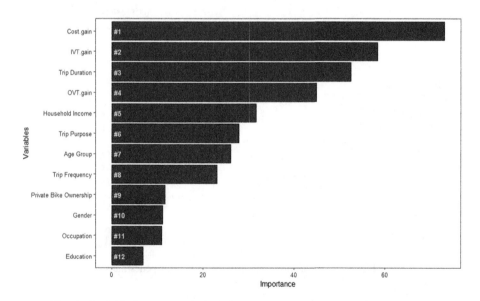

Fig. 4. Variable importance derived from the random forest model for bus users

4.3   Pedestrians

The classification error of the classification tree shown in Fig. 5 was 22.76%. As can be observed by the tree, variables relative to mode specific factors are closer to the tree's root and are more significant towards splitting the data in homogenous groups based on their choices. Decreased BSS cost appears to be crucial towards preferring the BSS, as 90% of the pedestrians preferred walking if the cost was higher than 0.75 Euros. Time gains is not found to be an important factor for decision in case of high BSS cost. Although, time gains from trips with the BSS also increase the chances of preferring the BSS over walking. The combination of factors that increases the likelihood of preferring the BSS the most is low BSS cost and increased time gains compared to walking.

The random forest model that was fitted for pedestrians had a classification error of 10.57%. The relative importance of the variables that were used in the model is shown in Fig. 6. Similarly, to the results of the classification tree the most important factor in terms of contributing to decision making is the cost of the BSS with a significant difference from the second, that is time gain from preferring the BSS. Household income, trip duration and the age group of the users follow.

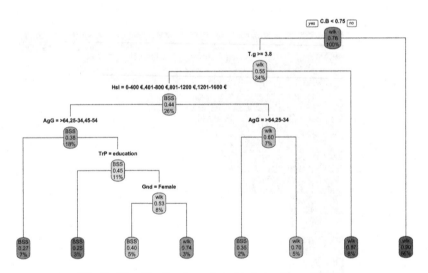

Fig. 5. Classification tree of mode choice for pedestrians

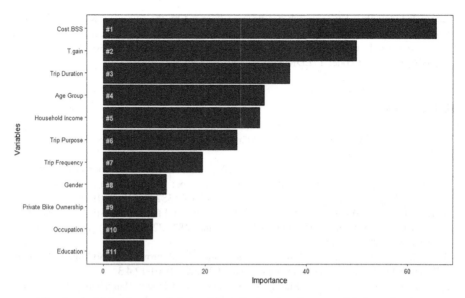

Fig. 6. Variable importance derived from the random forest model for pedestrians

5 Discussion and Conclusions

Taking into consideration all the results that were presented in Sect. 4, re-emerging or common themes, as well as discrete differences can be noticed. Cost gain, trip duration and IVT gain are the three variables with the greatest importance for all three user groups. Both car and bus users would be willing to use the BSS even if its cost is slightly higher compared to their mode of preference but only if using it is accompanied with IVT gains, while pedestrians would consider using BSS if the cost is low and it offers them trip time gains. OVT gains can be a significant factor towards using BSS for bus users, something that is true to a much lesser degree for car users. If the times it takes to locate a shared bike and get to its location is significantly less than the time it takes to walk to the bus stop and wait for the bus, this time gain is more likely to make them consider using the BSS. Furthermore, the relative importance of the possible cost gain that comes with using the BSS is higher for bus users and pedestrians compared to car users, indicating that for those groups of users keeping the BSS costs as low as possible is a more crucial factor.

The above results can have a meaningful impact on shaping the landscape of future urban mobility, in a way that it incorporates a modal share that makes the most out of each mode's strengths. Gaining a deeper understanding of the mechanisms that drive decision making in mode choice can become a powerful tool for policy makers and mobility stakeholders, allowing them to formulate future management policies, operational and business plans in a way that promotes three-pronged sustainability and maximizes each mode's positive externalities. Future research can include further analysis of the willingness to use BSS, by quantifying the effect of the incentives on different user groups and for different trip lengths.

Acknowledgements. This research has been co-financed by the European Regional Development Fund of the European Union and Greek national funds through the Operational Program Competitiveness, Entrepreneurship and Innovation, under the call RESEARCH – CREATE – INNOVATE (project code: T1EDK-04582).

References

1. Departemen of Economic and Social Affairs United Nation: World Urbanization Prospects 2018 (2018)
2. Cavill, N., Foster, C., Oja, P., Martin, B.W.: An evidence-based approach to physical activity promotion and policy development in Europe: contrasting case studies. Promot. Educ. **13**, 104–111 (2006). https://doi.org/10.1177/10253823060130020104
3. Hamilton, T.L., Wichman, C.J.: Bicycle infrastructure and traffic congestion: evidence from DC's Capital Bikeshare. J. Environ. Econ. Manag. **87**, 72–93 (2018). https://doi.org/10.1016/j.jeem.2017.03.007
4. DeMaio, P.: Bike-sharing: history, impacts, models of provision, and future. J. Public Transp. **12**, 41–56 (2009). https://doi.org/10.5038/2375-0901.12.4.3
5. Shaheen, S.A., Zhang, H., Martin, E., Guzman, S.: China's Hangzhou public bicycle: understanding early adoption and behavioral response to bikesharing. Transp. Res. Rec. J. Transp. Res. Board. **2247**, 33–41 (2011). https://doi.org/10.3141/2247-05
6. Shaheen, S.A., Guzman, S., Zhang, H.: Bikesharing in Europe, the Americas, and Asia. Transp. Res. Rec. J. Transp. Res. Board. **2143**, 159–167 (2010). https://doi.org/10.3141/2143-20
7. Gu, T., Kim, I., Currie, G.: To be or not to be dockless: empirical analysis of dockless bikeshare development in China. Transp. Res. Part A Policy Pract. **119**, 122–147 (2019). https://doi.org/10.1016/j.tra.2018.11.007
8. Institute for Transportation & Development Policy: The Bikeshare Planning Guide. Institute for Transportation & Development Policy (2018)
9. Zarif, R., Pankratz, D., Kelman, B.: Small is Beautiful (2019). https://doi.org/10.1049/me:19900212
10. LDA Consulting: Capital Bikeshare 2011 Member Survey Report, Washington, DC (2012)
11. Buck, D., Buehler, R., Happ, P., Rawls, B., Chung, P., Borecki, N.: Are bikeshare users different from regular cyclists? Transp. Res. Rec. J. Transp. Res. Board. **2387**, 112–119 (2013). https://doi.org/10.3141/2387-13
12. Ogilvie, F., Goodman, A.: Inequalities in usage of a public bicycle sharing scheme: socio-demographic predictors of uptake and usage of the London (UK) cycle hire scheme. Prev. Med. **55**, 40–45 (2012). https://doi.org/10.1016/j.ypmed.2012.05.002
13. Rixey, R.A.: Station-level forecasting of bikesharing ridership. Transp. Res. Rec. J. Transp. Res. Board. **2387**, 46–55 (2013). https://doi.org/10.3141/2387-06
14. Fuller, D., et al.: Use of a new public bicycle share program in Montreal. Canada. Am. J. Prev. Med. **41**, 80–83 (2011). https://doi.org/10.1016/j.amepre.2011.03.002
15. Martin, E.W., Shaheen, S.A.: Evaluating public transit modal shift dynamics in response to bikesharing: a tale of two U.S. cities. J. Transp. Geogr. **41**, 315–324 (2014). https://doi.org/10.1016/j.jtrangeo.2014.06.026
16. Bachand-Marleau, J., Lee, B.H.Y., El-Geneidy, A.M.: Better understanding of factors influencing likelihood of using shared bicycle systems and frequency of use. Transp. Res. Rec. J. Transp. Res. Board. **2314**, 66–71 (2012). https://doi.org/10.3141/2314-09

17. Buck, D., Buehler, R.: Bike lanes and other determinants of capital bikeshare trips. In: 91st Transportation Research Board Annual Meeting (2012)
18. Cervero, R., Duncan, M.: Walking, bicycling, and urban landscapes: evidence from the San Francisco bay area. Am. J. Public Health **93**, 1478–1483 (2003). https://doi.org/10.2105/AJPH.93.9.1478
19. Zhao, J., Deng, W., Song, Y.: Ridership and effectiveness of bikesharing: the effects of urban features and system characteristics on daily use and turnover rate of public bikes in China. Transp. Policy **35**, 253–264 (2014). https://doi.org/10.1016/j.tranpol.2014.06.008
20. Campbell, A.A., Cherry, C.R., Ryerson, M.S., Yang, X.: Factors influencing the choice of shared bicycles and shared electric bikes in Beijing. Transp. Res. Part C Emerg. Technol. **67**, 399–414 (2016). https://doi.org/10.1016/j.trc.2016.03.004
21. Li, W., Kamargianni, M.: Providing quantified evidence to policy makers for promoting bike-sharing in heavily air-polluted cities: a mode choice model and policy simulation for Taiyuan-China. Transp. Res. Part A Policy Pract. **111**, 277–291 (2018). https://doi.org/10.1016/j.tra.2018.01.019
22. Limesurvey. https://www.limesurvey.org/. Accessed 20 July 2019
23. R Core Team: R: A language and environment for statistical computing (2020). https://www.r-project.org/
24. Wickham, H., Francois, R., Henry, L., Muller, K.: dplyr: A Grammar of Data Manipulation (2019). https://cran.r-project.org/package=dplyr
25. Therneau, T., Atkinson, B.: rpart: Recursive Partitioning and Regression Trees (2019). https://cran.r-project.org/package=rpart
26. Liaw, A., Wienar, M.: Classification and Regression by randomForest. R News **2**, 18–22 (2002)
27. Kuhn, M.: caret: Classification and Regression Training (2019). https://cran.r-project.org/package=caret
28. Milborrow, S.: rpart.plot: Plot "rpart" Models: An Enhanced Version of "plot.rpart" (2019). https://cran.r-project.org/package=rpart.plot
29. Wickham, H.: ggplot2: Elegant Graphics for Data Analaysis. Springer, New York (2016). https://doi.org/10.1007/978-3-319-24277-4

An Ordered Logit Model for Predicting the Willingness of Renting Micro Mobility in Urban Shared Streets: A Case Study in Palermo, Italy

Tiziana Campisi[1(✉)] , Nurten Akgün[2] ,
and Giovanni Tesoriere[1]

[1] University of Enna Kore, Cittadella Universitaria, Enna, Italy
tiziana.campisi@unikore.it
[2] Faculty of Engineering and Natural Sciences, Bursa Technical University,
16330 Bursa, Turkey

Abstract. Sustainable transport modes, particularly micro-mobility, allows to reduce possible congestion phenomena in urban traffic. In this study, the aim is to make a contribution to increase micro-mobility use by exploring the impacts of socio-demographic, vehicle ownership (car, bicycle and micro mobility), level of infrastructure service and road users' perception in safety, comfort and chaotic environment on renting micro-mobility in a shared urban street. The study area is a historical center called Via Maqueda in Palermo, Italy, which is rich in commercial and cultural activities. A survey with 200 individuals is carried out for the data collection regarding the aim of the study.

The analysis starts with a descriptive statistics in order to illustrate the characteristics of the predictor variables. This is followed by relaxing p-value method for selecting the statistically significant predictor variables with 90% confidence level. These selected predictor variables are applied into an ordinal logit model. The results suggest that one unit increase in car ownership decrease the willingness of renting a micro mobility by log odds of −0.74, given all the other predictors are held constant. One unit increase in age group decrease the willingness of renting micro-mobility in shared urban streets. The outcomes will guide decision makers to understand who the average road users are and what are their needs in terms of further developments of the micro-mobility system in urban shared streets. The originality of this paper consists the perceptions of road users, such as safety and comfort, on micro-mobility that can encourage to use this sustainable urban travel mode in restricted traffic areas.

Keywords: Micro-mobility · New mobility users · Relaxing p-value method · Ordered logit model

1 Introduction

Transport in today's cities have been dominated by private cars, which generally have only one passenger on board. Decision makers have been aware of the environmental and social impacts of high amount of private car on the traffic and constantly have been

© Springer Nature Switzerland AG 2020
O. Gervasi et al. (Eds.): ICCSA 2020, LNCS 12250, pp. 796–808, 2020.
https://doi.org/10.1007/978-3-030-58802-1_57

looking for solutions to eliminate these influences by providing advanced accessibility and livability in urban [1, 2]. Currently there is a growing understanding of the benefits of new sustainable travel modes, particularly micro mobility, in special situations such as pandemic. It is believed that individual non-motorized means of transport with low economic and environmental impact can be an optimal solution [3–7].

Micro mobility vehicles, including electric scooter, hover-board, segway, mono-wheel and electric bike [8] offer a chance to achieve this aim by reducing travel time for short distances and waiting time on congested roads. In heavy traffic congestion, micro-mobility compared to private car provides faster means of travel in urban cities [9]. Micromobility are very light to carry and do not require the use of ad hoc parking. In addition, micro-mobility vehicles have several more advantages such as not requiring any certificate/license, allowing rapid movements from door to door, reducing crowds in public transport, which is essential for disable and elder road users, focusing routes that are in limited traffic areas.

In recent years, there has been a growing tendency to consider sharing, rather than owning vehicles [10, 11]; similarly, sharing micro-mobility has been spreading rapidly, particularly in the western countries. Sharing micro-mobility vehicles is very suitable for large cities where the traffic congestion is a vital issue [12]. Majority of European governments are in favor of spreading shared micro-mobility [13]. Most particularly, shared e-scooter is one of the most promising new micro-mobility solutions in urban. Sharing service offers people an opportunity to rent a micro-mobility vehicle by booking and paying for it through the mobile app.

Despite all these advantages, the studies [14–19] suggested that there have been some barriers to increase the use of micro-mobility in urban. It was showed that travel choices of means of transport were influenced by sociodemographic characteristics. Majority the users of both bicycles and e-scooters have been male. This result may depend on difference in comfort perception of women and men, road users' social and cultural heritage, the perception of the risk that is higher in women. In addition, women may not prefer to use micro-mobility as a means of moving from home to office because office clothing makes handling difficult. Tendency of the use of micro-mobility also was influenced by age of road user, because there was a requirement of elasticity of the spine in posture and good reflexes for sudden braking. Therefore, it was suggested that further relevant studies should consider sociodemographic parameters.

Micro-mobility vehicles compared to other transportation modes occupy the least amount of area on road space and they do not need area for parking. Road users often do not need to move at great speed because they tend to move for short journeys. Therefore, micro-mobility is an outstanding mode in shared urban spaces by its efficient use of the area.

However, it is considered that there should be a banning of the micro-mobility in shared spaces. The studies [20–22] showed that the rapid increase of micro-mobility use at shared spaces without specific rules reduced safety for pedestrians, particularly for elder and young road users. Micro-mobility has been used on shared sidewalks with approximately 17 km/h [23]. The risk for pedestrians to be hit increases while sharing roads with micro-mobility vehicles. Therefore, decision makers have been considering adapting strict regulations for existence of micro-mobility. For instance, Italy and

Germany have been showing an effort to integrate micro-mobility into the shared spaces; however, France and Spain have been considering the banning option [24].

In Italy, which was the case study country in this paper, a limitation of micro-mobility use was established considering some age groups, possession of a license for rental and use of devices in different time of the day. In addition, the places where you can use the micro-mobility vehicles and travel speed are regulated by rules. However, with respect to the suggested [8, 9, 11] barriers for micro-mobility use, an optimum solution still has been a research gap in the literature. Regarding the state-of-the-art review, this paper aimed to understand the relationship between road user perceptions, sociodemographic, infrastructure, vehicle ownership and shared micro-mobility in shared urban spaces. Following section presented the developed methodology considering the relevant state of the art review. Section 3 showed the details of data collection and this was followed by Sect. 4 which illustrated the results. Finally, discussions based on the results and limitations of the study were presented in Sect. 5.

2 Methodology

The overall aim of this study was to gain a fundamental understanding of how the socio-demographic characteristics, vehicle ownership (car, bicycle and micro mobility), level of service and road perception impact the attitude of renting micro mobility in shared urban streets. A series of analytical steps were carried out including descriptive statistics, relaxing p-value and ordered logit model. Regarding the suggestion in the state of art review [25], analysis needs to start with a descriptive statistics in order to illustrate the description of the data. In addition, descriptive statistics also guides to gain a better understanding of the results in the further applied models. With respect to exploring the relationship between considered variables, correlation analysis or Pearson's chi square test should be applied instead of fitting a regression model [26–28]. However, these statistical techniques cannot explain to what extent do the independent predictors has influence on dependent variable. Therefore, regression models should be considered if the aim is to gain a deeper understanding about the interaction between the variables [29]. Regression analysis predicts an outcome variable from one or several independent variables [30]. If only one independent variable is used in the prediction, the model is called simple regression; and if more than one independent variable is applied to the analysis, the model is called multiple regression. There are several types of regression models and the difference comes from the characteristics of the dependent variable [31]. For investigating the impacts of independent predictors on a dependent continuous variable, linear regression should be applied [32]. The formula of linear regression is as follows [33]:

$$Y = \beta_0 + \beta_1 X_1 + \ldots \beta_n X_n$$

where Y is the response variable; β_0 is the coefficient of the unknowns; $X_1, \ldots X_n$ are the predictor variables; and $\beta_1, \ldots, \beta_n$ are the coefficients of the predictor variables.

In some datasets, the dependent variable is a categorical response. Considering the assumption of the linear regression, which states that there is a linear relationship between dependent and independent variables, a categorical dependent variable cannot fit to the calculations. Therefore, logit models should be used for categorical dependent variables. Logit model predicts the increase of probability of occurrence for dependent variable when there is one unit increase in predictor variable. If the number of categories is only two such as yes or no (1, 0), it is suggested that binary logit model should be used [31]. The formula of logit model is as follows [30]:

$$(p) = \log(Odds) = \beta_0 + \beta_1 X_1 + \ldots \beta_n X_n$$

When the ordinal scale presents interval/ratio scale, such as the categories "Very high, High, Medium, Low, Very low)", ordered logit model should be applied [31]. The dependent variable in ordered logit model, which is also known as proportional odds model, is in a meaningful sequential order. In such case, there is a confusion for whether a linear regression should be applied or not. Previous studies suggested that there are several inconveniences when a linear regression was applied for sequential ordered dependent data [32, 33]. The formula of ordered logit model is given as follows:

$$logit(p_1) = log\frac{p_1}{1 - p_1} = \alpha_1 + \beta_1 X_1 + \ldots + \beta_n X_n$$

$$logit(p_1 + p_2) = log\frac{p_1 + p_2}{1 - p_1 - p_2} = \alpha_2 + \beta_1 X_1 + \ldots + \beta_n X_n$$

$$logit(p_1 + p_2 + \ldots + p_n) = log\frac{p_1 + p_2 + \ldots + p_n}{1 - p_1 - p_2 - \ldots - p_n} = \alpha_n + \beta_1 X_1 + \ldots + \beta_n X_n$$

$$p_1 + p_2 + \ldots + p_{n+1} = 1$$

where p_n is the probability of one unit change in dependent variable.

While more predictor variables in a regression model increase the accuracy of the results, adding too many causes inefficiency and overfitting. On the other hand, biased results may occur if fewer variables are added into a regression model. Therefore, the model should be simple but avoid any biased outcomes. The number of predictors needs to be determined carefully [34]. It is suggested that relaxing p-value should be applied in order to carry out a statistically accurate selection method. In relaxing p-value method, both simple ordinal logit model for each individual predictor variables and a full multiple ordinal logit model should be applied [29]. From the outcomes, the predictor variable, which are statistically significant above 90% level of confidence, should be selected and applied in a final model. In this paper, after the descriptive statistics, relaxing p value method was applied to select the predictor variables. This was followed by a final full model of ordered logit. The following section will describe the undertaken research including the study area and data collection survey.

3   Description of the Undertaken Research

Palermo is a metropolitan city, which is in the north-western Sicily. There are 660.00 inhabitants (52% women and 48% men). The investigated area is called via Maqueda which is located 1.5 km from the historic center of the city of Palermo. The area of the historic center is characterized by a low slope which encourages the use of micro-mobility. The traffic limitation (named ZTL) has reduced the number of private cars in the different streets of Palermo; therefore, many inhabitants recently have been using micro-mobility, particularly scooters, vehicles for less than a year. As shown in Table 1, the data used in this paper was recorded by using CCTV cameras in March 2019. The four CCTV cameras were placed at the access points of the Via Maqueda and used by Local Police. This system allowed to estimate the peak value of the micro-mobility flow along the road.

Table 1. Investigated area (blue color) located in the historical city center of Palermo; road geometry and flow details. Source: Map data copyrighted OpenStreetMap contributors and available from https://www.openstreetmap.org

Variables	Measures	Geo-localization
Length [m]	1380	
Effective width [m]	10-11 (sidewalk about 1.5)	
Pedestrian flow [ped/h]	Max flow: 1000peds/h, Average flow: 640peds/h	
Micro-mobility flow [unit/h]	Max flow 490 u/h Average flow 330 u/h	

A questionnaire with 200 individuals was carried out in December 2019. The data was processed statistically using the Likert scales which was adopted to express judgments and/or the individual's answers given to each question. This technique is widely used in psychometrics to measure attitudes and opinions through the administration of questionnaires. In the first part of the questionnaire, five possible alternatives for each item were recorded as follows: completely agree, agree, uncertain, disagree, completely disagree. The second and third parts of the questionnaire data related to the aptitude for using the micro-mobility vehicles and the perception of road users on the level of infrastructure service was collected. In the last part of the dataset, the propensity to rent micro-mobility vehicle and the frequency of movement along the examined area was asked to the individuals (See Table 2).

Table 2. Monitored variables of survey

		Variables	Option provided
A Socio-demographic		A.1 Gender	☐Male ☐ Female
		A.2 Age	☐18-24 ☐25-39 ☐ 40-54 ☐ 55-64 ☐ ≥65
		A.3 Job	☐student ☐worker ☐ retiree ☐ other
		A.4 car ownership	☐YES ☐ NO
		A.5 bike ownership	
		A.6 Micro-mobility ownership	
B Transport attitude		B.1 Rent attitude	**Likert scale** ☐1= disagree ☐2= partially disagree ☐3=I cannot evaluate ☐4=partially agree ☐5= agree
		B.2 walking attitude	**Temporal scale** ☐ Every day ☐ 4 times per week ☐ 2-3 times per week ☐ Once per week ☐ More rarely
		B.3 Road usability	
		B.4 LOS value	☐ A ☐ B ☐ C ☐ D ☐ E ☐ F
C Travel perception		C.1 Safe	**Likert scale** ☐1= disagree ☐2= partially disagree ☐3= I cannot evaluate ☐4=partially agree ☐5= agree
		C.2 Comfort	
		C.3 Chaos	

4 Data Analysis

Results of each analysis step, namely descriptive statistics, relaxing p-value and ordered logit model, are detailed in the following sections

4.1 Descriptive Statistics

A descriptive statistics was carried out in order to explore the details of each considered variable namely, gender, age group, owning a car, owning a bike, having a micro mobility, profession, road use, level of infrastructure service, road user's perception on safety, comfort and chaotic condition in a shared urban street (See Table 3). The investigated sample size consisted of 200 individuals which corresponds to approximately 60% of the average flow recorded at the entrance of Via Maqueda during the daily time slot.

Gender distribution was homogeneous with 53% of men and 47% of women. This numerical balance avoided biased results in further modelling steps. 36% of the participants were ranged in age group 40–54. This was followed by 26.5% for 55–65 and 21.5% for 25–39. Car ownership was 85.5% among the participants, however bike

Table 3. Statistical results related to monitored variables

Variable	Units and frequency
A.1	Female = 106 (47%); Male = 94(54%)
A.2	(18–24) = 21 (10,5%); (25–39) = 43 (21,5%); (40–54) = 72 (36%); (55–65) = 53 (26,5%); (65 ≤) = 11 (5,5%)
A.3	Student = 29 (14,5%); worker = 112 (56,0%); retiree = 51(25,5%); other = 8 (4%)
A.4	Yes = 171 (85,5%); No = 29 (14,5%)
A.5	Yes = 67 (33,5%); No = 133(66,5%)
A.6	Yes = 87(43,5%); No = 113 (56,5%)
B.3	(every day) = 4(2%); (four times per week) = 12(6%); (two-three times per week) = 29(14,5%); (once per week) = 74(37%); (more rarely) = 81 (40,5%)
B.4	A = 1(0,5%); B = 5(5,5%); C = 28(14%); D = 67(33,5%); E = 86(43%); F = 13 (6,5%)
C.1	1 = 7(3,5%); 2 = 68(34%); 3 = 97(48,5%); 4 = 26(13%); 5 = 2(1%)
C.2	1 = 18(9%); 2 = 47(23,5%); 3 = 80(40%); 4 = 49(24,5%); 5 = 6(3%)
C.3	1 = 2(1%); 2 = 19;(9,5%); 3 = 52(26%); 4 = 76(38%); 5 = 51(25,5%)

ownership was far less by 33.5%. Having a micro-mobility was approximately 44% in the explored sample. This showed that at least approximately half of the participants had an experience of using micro-mobility. 59.5% of the sample was familiar to the considered street by using the road at least one per week. 83% of the participants founded the infrastructure less than Level C. This was a significant low percentage and needed a further investigation in the following model.

4.2   Ordered Logit Model with Relaxing P-Value

The relaxing p-value method was carried out in order to select the statistically significant predictors at 90% confidence level. In this method, both simple and multiple ordered logit model were applied (See Table 4). The results showed that the variables, namely age group, car ownership and profession, were statistically significant at 90% of level of confidence.

These three selected variables were applied in a last full model of ordered logit (See Table 5). The results suggested that one unit increase in car ownership decreased the willingness of renting a micro mobility by log odds of −0.74, given all the other predictors were held constant. Regarding to the reference category of age group 18–24, one-unit increase reduced the probability of willingness of renting micro-mobility in shared urban streets for participant aged between 25 and 54 with statistically significance at 95% confidence level. Conversely, the participants aged over 65 were 3.98 times more likely to rent a micro mobility with statistically significance at 95% confidence level. However, with respect to the descriptive statistics, the number of participants aged over 65 were only 5.5% of the sample. Therefore, there was a wide range of 95% confidence interval for odds ratio between 1.00 and 15.95. The results for

Table 4. Relaxing P-value method

Variables[a]	Simple ordered logit				Multiple ordered logit[b]			
	Coefficient	P-Value	Odds Ratio	95% confidence interval for odds ratio	Coefficient	P-Value	Odds Ratio	95% confidence interval for odds ratio
A.1	(reference category = male)							
Female	0.20	0.45	1.22	L 0.73 U 2.03	0.41	0.15	1.51	L0.86 U 2.64
A.2	(reference category = 18-24)							
25–39	−0.74	0.12	0.48	L 0.19 U 1.22	−1.23	**0.03**	0.29	L 0.10 U 0.87
40–54	−0.55	0.21	0.58	L 0.24 U 1.37	−1.00	**0.05**	0.37	L 0.14 U 0.98
55–65	−0.02	0.96	0.98	L 0.40 U 2.40	−0.52	0.32	0.59	L 0.21 U 1.65
65 ≤	0.79	0.23	2.20	L 0.61 U 7.93	1.16	0.11	3.20	L 0.76 U13.57
A.4	−0.53	0.15	0.59	L 0.28 U 1.21	−0.68	**0.10**	0.51	L 0.22 U 1.15
A.5	−0.42	0.14	0.66	L0.38 U1.14	−0.37	0.23	0.69	L0.37 U 1.27
A.6	0.09	0.73	1.09	L0.65 U1.83	0.38	0.18	1.46	L 0.84 U 2.53
A.3	(reference category = worker)							
Student	−0.19	0.62	0.82	L0.39 U1.76	−1.11	**0.02**	0.33	L0.13 U0.85
Retiree	0.11	0.73	1.11	L0.61 U2.01	0.14	0.68	1.15	L0.60 U 2.20
Other	−2.17	**0.00**	0.11	L0.03 U0.46	−2.62	**0.00**	0.07	L 0.12 U 0.30

[a]The reference category for each variable, namely owning a car, owning a bike, having a micro mobility vehicle, road use, infrastructure level, bike safe, bike comfort and bike chaos, is NO
[b]Cut 1 = −5.11; Cut 2 = −3.30; Cut 3 = −1.26; Cut 4 = 1.13

profession showed that compared to workers as taken the reference category students were less likely to rent a micro-mobility (odds ratio 0.31) at 95% confidence level. The same influence was observed for participants who were recorded as others; however, participants with other profession were 4% of the sample regarding to the descriptive statistics.

Table 5. Final ordered logit model

Variables[a]	Coefficient[b]	P-Value	Odds ratio	95% confidence interval for odds ratio Lower Upper
A.2 (reference category = 18–24)				
25–39	−1.01	**0.05**	0.36	L0.13 U0.98
40–54	−0.88	**0.06**	0.42	L0.16 U1.05
55–65	−0.44	0.36	0.64	L0.25 U1.67
65 ≤	1.38	**0.05**	3.98	L1.00 U15.95
A.4	−0.74	**0.05**	0.48	L0.22 U1.04
A.3 (reference category = worker)				
Student	−1.17	**0.01**	0.31	L0.13 U0.75
Retiree	0.11	0.73	1.12	L0.60 U2.07
Other	−2.29	**0.00**	0.10	L0.03 U0.40

[a]The reference category for Owning a Car is NO
[b]Cut 1 = −4.26; Cut 2 = −2.48; Cut 3 = −0.53; Cut 4 = 1.81

5   Discussions and Limitations

Micro-mobility vehicles, including electric scooter, hover-board, segway, monowheel and electric bike [8], have been providing several advantages such as reducing traffic congestion [9], eliminating social and environmental effects [3, 4] and helping to keep social distance in extreme health conditions. Besides these positive influences, there were some barriers to increase the use of micro-mobility in urban streets [15–17]. In addition, a research gap in the state-of-the-art review was explored about the impacts on shared micro-mobility in shared urban streets. Therefore, this paper aimed to find out what were these impacts and to what extend did they influence willingness of renting micro-mobility. A questionnaire analysis with 200 individuals was conducted in the city of Palermo, Italy. The study area was selected based on availability for data collection. It is recommended to carry out a similar analysis in a different area with higher number of observations. This may help to generalize the results in a global perspective.

The results suggested that the willingness for renting micro-mobility statistically significantly was affected by age group. The propensity to rent a micro-mobility decreased when the age of participant increased. This suggested that young people were more likely to rent a micro-mobility in shared urban streets. This outcome was consistent with the literature since there was a requirement of elasticity of the spine in posture and good reflexes for sudden braking.

Regarding gender, there was no difference in propensity for renting between female and male. The studies in the literature given in Sect. 1 suggested that males are more likely to use micro-mobility compared to females because of comfort and safety perception. However, the results in this paper suggested that the similar trend was not observed for renting micro-mobility in shared urban spaces. In addition, safety, comfort and chaotic situation on shared urban streets did not influence individuals' willingness of renting. The results suggested that students compared to working class were more likely to rent micro-mobility in shared streets. This was consistent with the results of age impact. In addition, individuals who owns a car were found to be less likely to rent micro-mobility in shared spaces.

In overall, results showed that renting micro-mobility in shared urban streets was fit with younger student class without owning a private car. Therefore, further studies should focus on figure out how to attract elder working class for willingness in renting micro-mobility in shared spaces or switch their travel mode from private car using to micro-mobility services. The results of this paper will guide decision makes to find out how to increase the use of micro mobility in urban shared spaces.

Regarding the limitations, this study was carried out with 200 participants and the number of individuals in the further studies should be increased for improving the accuracy of the results. In addition, the recent local legislation in the case study area has allowed the use of micro-mobility in shared spaces since few months ago; therefore an investigation over a longer period of time can be necessary in order to gain a better understanding. This also can confirm the results which were obtained in this study. The further step of this study will be enlarged in order to be able to evaluate the flow transiting not only on via Maqueda but also within the major streets that are essential part of the transport network.

Acknowledgments. This study was supported by the MIUR (Ministry of Education, Universities and Research [Italy]) through a project entitled WEAKI TRANSIT: WEAK-demand areas Innovative TRANsport Shared services for Italian Towns (Project code: 20174ARRHT/CUP Code: J74I19000320008), financed with the PRIN 2017 (Research Projects of National Relevance) programme. We authorize the MIUR to reproduce and distribute reprints for Governmental purposes, notwithstanding any copyright notations thereon. Any opinions, findings and conclusions or recommendations expressed in this material are those of the authors, and do not necessarily reflect the views of the MIUR.

References

This paper is the result of the joint work of the authors. 'Abstract' 'Introduction' 'Methodology' and 'Results' were written jointly by the authors. TC and NA focused on the state of the art. TC designed the methodological approach and discussion. Supervision and research funding NA, TC and GT.

1. Zagorskas, J., Burinskienė, M.: Challenges caused by increased use of e-powered personal mobility vehicles in european cities. Sustainability **12**(1), 273 (2020). https://doi.org/10.3390/su12010273
2. Loukopoulos, P., Jakobsson, C., Gärling, T., Meland, S., Fujii, S.: Understanding the process of adaptation to car-use reduction goals. Transp. Res. Part F Traff. Psychol. Behav. **9**(2), 115–127 (2006). https://doi.org/10.1016/j.trf.2005.09.003
3. Olia, A., Abdelgawad, H., Abdulhai, B., Razavi, S.N.: Assessing the potential impacts of connected vehicles: mobility, environmental, and safety perspectives. J. Intell. Transp. Syst. **20**(3), 229–243 (2016). https://doi.org/10.1080/15472450.2015.1062728
4. Lia, F., Nocerino, R., Bresciani, C., Colorni Vitale, A., Luè, A.: Promotion of E-bikes for delivery of goods in European urban areas: an Italian case study. In: Transport Research Arena (TRA) 5th Conference: Transport Solutions from Research to Deployment, pp. 1–10 (2014)
5. Torrisi, V., Ignaccolo, M., Inturri, G.: Toward a sustainable mobility through a dynamic real-time traffic monitoring, estimation and forecasting system: The RE.S.E.T. project. In: Town and Infrastructure Planning for Safety and Urban Quality - Proceedings of the 23rd International Conference on Living and Walking in Cities, LWC 2017, pp. 241–247 (2018). https://doi.org/10.1201/9781351173360-32
6. Torrisi, V., Ignaccolo, M., Inturri, G.: Innovative transport systems to promote sustainable mobility: developing the model architecture of a traffic control and supervisor system. In: Gervasi, O., et al. (eds.) ICCSA 2018. LNCS, vol. 10962, pp. 622–638. Springer, Cham (2018). https://doi.org/10.1007/978-3-319-95168-3_42
7. Ignaccolo, C., Giuffrida, N., Torrisi, V.: The queensway of New York city. A proposal for sustainable mobility in queens. In: Town and Infrastructure Planning for Safety and Urban Quality, pp. 69–76 (2018). https://doi.org/10.1201/9781351173360-12
8. Madapur, B., Madangopal, S., Chandrashekar, M.N.: Micro-mobility infrastructure for redefining urban mobility. Euro. J. Eng. Sci. Tech. **3**(1), 71–85 (2020).https://doi.org/10.33422/ejest.v3i1.163
9. McKenzie, G.: Urban mobility in the sharing economy: A spatiotemporal comparison of shared mobility services. Comput. Environ. Urban Syst. **79**, 101418 (2020). https://doi.org/10.1016/j.compenvurbsys.2019.101418
10. Basbas, S., Campisi, T., Canale, A., Nikiforiadis, A., Gruden, C.: Pedestrian level of service assessment in an area close to an under-construction metro line in Thessaloniki, Greece. Transp. Res. Procedia **45**, 95–102 (2020)
11. Hardt, C., Bogenberger, K.: Usage of e-scooters in urban environments. Transp. Res. Procedia **37**, 155–162 (2019). https://doi.org/10.1016/j.trpro.2018.12.178
12. Shaheen, S., Cohen, A.: Shared Micromobility Policy Toolkit: Docked and Dockless Bike and Scooter Sharing (2019)
13. Campisi, T., Torrisi, V., Ignaccolo, M., Inturri, G., Tesoriere, G.: University propensity assessment to car sharing services using mixed survey data: the Italian case study of Enna city. Transp. Res. Procedia **47**,433–44 (2020). https://doi.org/10.1016/j.trpro.2020.03.155

14. Moreau, H., de Jamblinne de Meux, L., Zeller, V., D'Ans, P., Ruwet, C., Achten, W.M.: Dockless e-scooter: a green solution for mobility? Comparative case study between dockless e-scooters, displaced transport, and personal e-scooters. Sustainability **12**(5), 1803 (2020). https://doi.org/10.3390/su12051803

15. CoMoUK in 2019

16. McKenzie, G.: Shared micro-mobility patterns as measures of city similarity: Position Paper. In Proceedings of the 1st ACM SIGSPATIAL International Workshop on Computing with Multifaceted Movement Data, pp. 1–4 (2019). https://doi.org/10.1145/3356392.3365221

17. Barnes, F.: A Scoot, Skip, and a JUMP Away: Learning from Shared Micromobility Systems in San Francisco (2019)

18. Gössling, S.: Integrating e-scooters in urban transportation: Problems, policies, and the prospect of system change. Transp. Res. Part D Transp. Environ. **79**, 102230 (2020). https://doi.org/10.1016/j.trd.2020.102230

19. Campisi, T., Acampa, G., Marino, G., Tesoriere, G.: Cycling master plans in Italy: the I-BIM feasibility tool for cost and safety assessments. Sustainability **12**(11), 4723. https://doi.org/10.3390/su12114723

20. Warnick, A.: Shareable scooters offer risks, benefits for transportation. Am. J. Public Health **109**(11), 1479 (2019). https://doi.org/10.2105/AJPH.2019.305354

21. Ishmael, C.R., et al.: An early look at operative orthopaedic injuries associated with electric scooter accidents: bringing high-energy trauma to a wider audience. JBJS **102**(5), e18 (2020). https://doi.org/10.2106/JBJS.19.00390

22. Nellamattathil, M., Amber, I.: An evaluation of scooter injury and injury patterns following widespread adoption of E-scooters in a major metropolitan area. Clin. Imaging **60**(2), 200–203 (2020). https://doi.org/10.1016/j.clinimag.2019.12.012

23. Sikka, N., Vila, C., Stratton, M., Ghassemi, M., Pourmand, A.: Sharing the sidewalk: a case of E-scooter related pedestrian injury. Am. J. Emerg. Med. **37**(9), 1807-e5 (2019).https://doi.org/10.1016/j.ajem.2019.06.017

24. James, O., Swiderski, J.I., Hicks, J., Teoman, D., Buehler, R.: Pedestrians and e-scooters: an initial look at e-scooter parking and perceptions by riders and non-riders. Sustainability **11**(20), 5591 (2019). https://doi.org/10.3390/su11205591

25. Akgün, N., Dissanayake, D., Thorpe, N., Bell, M.C.: Cyclist casualty severity at roundabouts - to what extent do the geometric characteristics of roundabouts play a part? J. Saf. Res. **67**, 83–91 (2018). https://doi.org/10.1016/j.jsr.2018.09.004

26. Harrell, F.: Regression Modeling Strategies: With Applications to Linear Models, Logistic Regression, and Survival Analysis. 1 edn. Springer, New York (2001). https://doi.org/10.1007/978-1-4757-3462-1

27. Montgomery, D.C., Peck, E.A., Vining, G.G.: Introduction to Linear Regression Analysis. Fifth Edition. Wiley, New York (2012)

28. Schneider, A., Hommel, G., Blettner, M.: Linear regression analysis part 14 of a series on evaluation of scientific publications. Deutsches Ärzteblatt Int. **107**(44), 776–782 (2010). http://dx.doi.org/10.3238/arztebl.2010.0776

29. Akgün, N.: Investigating the Impacts on Cyclist Casualty Severity at Give Way Roundabouts with Mixed Traffic. Newcastle University (2019)

30. Field, A.: Discovering Statistics Using SPSS. 3 edn. SAGE Publications Ltd, London (2009)

31. Menard, S.: Applied logistic regression analysis. 2 edn. SAGE, London (2002). https://dx.doi.org/10.4135/9781412983433

32. McKelvey, R.D., Zavoina, W.: A statistical model for the analysis of ordinal level dependent variables. J. Math. Sociol. **4**(1), 103–120 (1975). https://doi.org/10.1080/0022250X.1975.9989847

33. Winship, C., Mare, R.D.: Regression models with ordinal variables. Am. Sociol. Rev. 512–525 (1984). https://doi.org/10.2307/2095465
34. Peduzzi, P., Concato, J., Kemper, E., Holford, T.R., Feinstein, A.R.: A simulation study of the number of events per variable in logistic regression analysis. J. Clin. Epidemiol. 49(12), 1373–1379 (1996). https://doi.org/10.1016/S0895-4356(96)00236-3

Quantifying the Negative Impact of Interactions Between Users of Pedestrians-Cyclists Shared Use Space

Andreas Nikiforiadis[1]([✉]) [iD], Socrates Basbas[1] [iD],
Tiziana Campisi[2] [iD], Giovanni Tesoriere[2] [iD],
Marina Iliana Garyfalou[1], Iasonas Meintanis[1], Thomas Papas[1],
and Mirto Trouva[1]

[1] School of Rural and Surveying Engineering, Aristotle University
of Thessaloniki, AUTh Campus, 54124 Thessaloniki, Greece
anikiforiadis@topo.auth.gr
[2] Faculty of Engineering and Architecture, University of Enna Kore,
Cittadella Universitaria, 94100 Enna, Italy

Abstract. In recent years, many efforts are being made for the promotion of active modes of transport. Due to this reason, as well as due to the limited available public space, the co-existence of pedestrians and cyclists is a very common phenomenon, which requires extensive investigation. The design and implementation of pedestrians-cyclists shared use space is a widely used technical choice, when the road infrastructure is unsuitable for hosting cyclists and thus the separation of cyclists from the motorized traffic is considered advisable. However, the co-existence of pedestrians and cyclists is not always harmonious and the interactions between them can have a negative impact in their perceived comfort and safety. The present research aims to quantify this negative impact of the various kinds of interactions, by considering the users' attitudes and by applying the Analytical Hierarchy Process method. The attitudes of users were captured through questionnaire surveys, that were directed to both pedestrians and cyclists in the city of Palermo, Italy. The results of the analysis are being compared with the results of a previous attempt to quantify the impact of interactions. Through this comparison, useful conclusions and notes for further research are deriving.

Keywords: Pedestrians · Cyclists · Shared space · Analytical Hierarchy Process (AHP)

1 Introduction

One of the main transport policy aims in European level is the promotion of walking and cycling for commuting [1, 2]. The prioritization of this aim is attributed to the fact that walking and cycling provide significant benefits in terms of health, well-being, environment and economy [3–8]. However, in order to achieve this goal, appropriate infrastructures within cities should be developed. To facilitate the design and management of transport infrastructures, it is crucial to use methodologies for their

© Springer Nature Switzerland AG 2020
O. Gervasi et al. (Eds.): ICCSA 2020, LNCS 12250, pp. 809–818, 2020.
https://doi.org/10.1007/978-3-030-58802-1_58

evaluation. The most widespread scale for measuring the satisfaction that a transport system or infrastructure provides to the users and therefore to assess them, is the level of service (LOS), which takes values from A to F; LOS A expresses the higher level of satisfaction and LOS F expresses the lowest level of satisfaction [9].

For the assessment of pedestrians' and cyclists' infrastructures various methodologies have been proposed. Some of these methodologies are based on quantitative characteristics of the infrastructure [9–11], other methodologies are based on qualitative characteristics [12–15] and there are also other methodologies that combine quantitative and qualitative characteristics of the infrastructure [16, 17]. Also, many studies apply microsimulation tools for the evaluation of pedestrian infrastructures [18–20].

Concerning the assessment of infrastructures that are being used equally by pedestrians and cyclists, i.e. pedestrians-cyclists shared spaces, a notable methodology is the one that has been proposed by Botma [21], which was later incorporated in the Highway Capacity Manual. Botma's methodology proposes the hindrance concept, where pedestrians' and cyclists' perceived hindrance can be expressed by the "events", that is the interactions between the shared-use infrastructures' users. Botma defined two types of events, the meetings and the passings (or overtakings) and the main assumption of his methodology was that overtakings have twice a negative impact to the users comparing with the meetings. A recent study attempted to investigate this negative impact and to cover this research gap, by conducting questionnaire surveys in both pedestrians and cyclists in the city of Thessaloniki, Greece [22].

The present paper aims to examine the negative impact of the interactions between the pedestrians-cyclists shared-use infrastructures' users, in the city of Palermo, Italy. The examination of the impact of these phenomena can provide an answer in the research question "Can the quantified negative impact of the events that was computed in the city of Thessaloniki be considered as global or the negative impact of the events differs from country to country, or even from city to city?".

2 Methodology

Based on an extension of Botma's definition of events, which was proposed by Hummer et al. [23], there are six possible types of events that a pedestrian can experience in a shared-use infrastructure:

- Face-to-face interaction (meeting) with another pedestrian
- Face-to-face interaction (meeting) with a cyclist
- Interaction while overtaking (passing) another pedestrian
- Interaction while a pedestrian is being passed by another pedestrian
- Interaction while a pedestrian is being passed by a cyclist
- Delayed passing

and six types of events that a cyclist can experience in a shared-use infrastructure:

- Face-to-face interaction (meeting) with a pedestrian
- Face-to-face interaction (meeting) with another cyclist
- Interaction while passing a pedestrian

- Interaction while passing another cyclist
- Interaction while a cyclist is being passed by another cyclist
- Delayed passing.

These event types are presented in Fig. 1; where the upper sketches present the meetings, sketches (d), (e), (f) the overtakings and the last sketch express the delayed passing (this event describes a situation when a user wants to pass another user or a group of users, but he/she is forced to reduce his/her speed and wait behind people due to high users' density in the infrastructure).

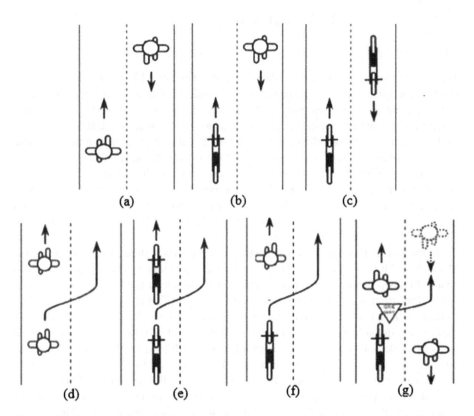

Fig. 1. Graphical presentation of the events between users of pedestrians '-cyclists' shared-use infrastructures (adapted from: [24]).

For the quantification of the negative impact of the abovementioned event types, taking into account the users' attitude, several methods for assigning weights can be used. Examples include the Analytical Hierarchy Process (AHP) [25, 26], the Conjoint Analysis (CA) [27], the Potentially All Pairwise RanKings of all possible Alternatives (PAPRIKA) [28] methods. Based on the selection of the weighting method, the questionnaire is being developed. In the present paper, the AHP method was selected in order to be consistent with the previous attempt of assigning weights to the events [22] and to ensure that possible differences are not a result of the selected method. In addition, for keeping the consistency between the two studies, as well as to keep the questionnaires brief, it was opted to include only eight pairwise comparisons in the questionnaires and to examine the additional seven pairwise comparisons indirectly, through the transitivity rule. In these pairwise comparisons the users had to evaluate the negative impact in terms of comfort and safety, of one event type in comparison with the negative impact of another event type. The responses were then analyzed through descriptive statistics and through AHP techniques for computing the weights.

3 Description of the Undertaken Research

3.1 Study Area

The analysis focuses in the city of Palermo, Italy. The city of Palermo which has over 600,000 inhabitants and a large percentage of tourists has undergone a transformation from the point of view of mobility in the last decade, applying some strategies aiming to reduce noise and environmental pollution, as well as to enhance the attractiveness of the historic center. Among the strategies that the Local Administration applied, notable is the pedestrianization of via Maqueda and the orthogonal area called Cassaro, that goes from the Cathedral to the port area. These strategies have led to greater use of shared mobility and micro-mobility, with the presence of scooters and mono-wheels. Generally, there are about 27 cycle routes scattered throughout the city of Palermo and its province with slopes varying between 5 and 28%. In the historical center there are currently about 17 km of cycle paths.

In the city of Palermo there is a historic and important street, which is called Via Maqueda and it is also known as la Strada Nuova. Via Maqueda has over the years seen a radical transformation from a road completely for vehicular use into a pedestrian-only street. The under-study section is above all a Limited Traffic Zone (Zona a Traffico Limitato – ZTL), where vehicle transit is guaranteed only during specific hours for loading and unloading of goods in favor of commercial activities. Three years ago, a one-way cycle lane was established from Piazza Verdi towards the Quattro Canti. In this section, many conflicts between pedestrians and cyclists are being observed, provoking controversy on several occasions. For years this area had suffered from a slow downturn that has stopped, since a few years ago (around 2015) car traffic was restricted. At the same time, various commercial and restaurant activities have arisen, promoting trade in this area. Also, this street is about 1.5 km long and runs along many historical and architectural sights and has become a significant destination for tourists and many citizens who prefer using it either for work or leisure during all days of the week. At this time, Via Maqueda is a shared space (see Fig. 2), which is regularly being used by micro-mobility vehicles and classic bicycles or bicycles with pedal assistance.

Fig. 2. Snapshots from via Maqueda.

3.2   Data Collection

Researchers utilized a questionnaire from a previous study [22] and they adapted it in order to keep it brief and comprehensive. The main aim of the questionnaire is to capture the attitudes of the shared space users concerning the impact that the various events have on their comfort and safety (as perceived by them). To achieve this several pairwise comparisons between the different events were included. Also, through the questionnaire the demographic characteristics of the users, as well as their opinion about the level of service of the infrastructure and the possibility of sharing the same space without segregating pedestrians and cyclists were captured.

The questionnaire survey was carried out between 16th of January and 28th of February 2020, with the method of face-to-face interviews. This method was considered appropriate, since the clarifications to the users about the pairwise comparisons were necessary. Finally, 275 valid questionnaires were gathered by pedestrians and 210 valid questionnaires were gathered by cyclists, who were using the Via Maqueda street.

4   Survey Results

4.1   Descriptive Statistics

Pedestrians' Questionnaires. The sample of pedestrians is approximately equally distributed regarding gender, since 52.7% of the respondents are male and 47.3% are female. The sample is also well distributed concerning the age of the respondents, since 28.9% of them are aged between 25 and 39 years old, 29.7% are aged between 40 and 54 years old, 27.8% are aged between 55 and 64 years old and 13.6% are older than 64 years old. The 35.4% of the respondents use the via Maqueda every day and an additional 35.4% use the specific infrastructure at least one time per week. Regarding the level of service (LOS) that the pedestrians perceive when using the specific infrastructure, the most popular answer is D (44.4%). Only 1.1% of the sample perceive LOS B or greater, while 40.4% of the sample perceive LOS E or lower.

Cyclists' Questionnaires. The sample of cyclists is unequally distributed between males (71.4%) and females (28.6%). This difference in the percentages may indicate that males are much more likely than females to use bicycle for their daily trips; as this is usually the case in countries where cycling in not a popular mode of transport [29–31]. The age distribution of the cyclists' sample also follows a different pattern comparing with the one of pedestrians' sample. The 12.4% of the respondents are aged between 25 and 39 years old, 25.2% are aged between 40 and 54 years old, 51.4% are aged between 55 and 64 years old and 11% are older than 65 years old. In contrast with pedestrians, only 4.3% of the cyclists' sample use via Maqueda daily with a bicycle, but an additional 32.9% cycles in the specific infrastructure at least one time per week. Regarding the cyclists' perceived satisfaction, extremely low LOS were stated. More specifically, any of the cyclists of the sample stated LOS A or LOS B, while just 1 (0.5%) cyclist stated LOS C. On the other hand, a strong 95.2% of cyclists perceive an unacceptable LOS (45.2% perceive LOS E and 50% perceive LOS F). The negative assessment of via Maqueda is attributed to the fact that pedestrians occupy a large portion of the street and therefore cyclists often have to wait behind people, reduce their speed and make maneuvers through the crowd.

4.2   Assignment of Weights

Weights from Pedestrians' Viewpoint. Through the use of the transitivity rule and the application of the AHP techniques, weights were computed and assigned to the various event types (see Table 1). It can be understood that pedestrians perceive higher annoyance when they are being passed by a cyclist. "Delayed passing" and "meeting a cyclist" were also considered very annoying situations when walking in the shared-use infrastructure. Finally, the event types that concern interaction with another pedestrian (i.e. being overtaken by another pedestrian, meeting another pedestrian, overtaking another pedestrian) were found less annoying.

Weights from Cyclists' Viewpoint. The corresponding procedure for analyzing the responses in the pairwise comparisons was also made for the sample of cyclists. The obtained results for the events' weights from cyclists' viewpoint are presented in Table 2. It can be seen that both "delayed passing" and "passing a pedestrian" create great annoyance to cyclists when using a shared-use infrastructure. "Passing another cyclist" and "meeting a pedestrian" are also two undesired situations for cyclists. On the other hand, the event types "being passed by another cyclist" and "meeting a cyclist" turned out to be less annoying.

Table 1. Assignment of weights from pedestrians' viewpoint.

Event type	Weight
Being passed by a cyclist	0.26
Delayed passing	0.20
Meeting a cyclist	0.18
Being passed by another pedestrian	0.13
Meeting another pedestrian	0.13
Pass another pedestrian	0.10

Table 2. Assignment of weights from cyclists' viewpoint.

Event type	Weight
Delayed passing	0.21
Passing a pedestrian	0.21
Passing another cyclist	0.19
Meeting a pedestrian	0.18
Being passed by another cyclist	0.13
Meeting another cyclist	0.08

5   Discussion and Conclusions

The identification and the quantification of the negative impact of the various types of events on pedestrians' and cyclists' perceptions is essential for the development of reliable methodologies that attempt to capture the LOS of the infrastructures, that are being used by different user types. Before the present paper the only research that attempted to assign weights in the different event types was carried out in the city of Thessaloniki, Greece [22]. Thus, the main objective of the present paper is to investigate if the weights that were computed in the case of Thessaloniki can be generalized or they are different per country, or even per city.

Both similarities and differences can be identified by comparing the events' weights in the city of Palermo with those in the city of Thessaloniki. The most important similarity is that pedestrians tend to be more annoyed by interactions which involve cyclists, and cyclists tend to be more annoyed by interactions which involve pedestrians. The enhancement of this conclusion by the present paper makes clear that the co-existence of different types of users is not always harmonious, due to their different characteristics (e.g. mass, speed, unpredictable change of direction). Thus, when designing shared-use infrastructures, appropriate measures are needed for minimizing the interaction points and more importantly the conflict points between pedestrians and cyclists. In addition, the results from Palermo provide more evidence that Botma's assumption, i.e. overtakings negative impact is twice stronger than that of meetings, cannot be considered valid, at least for some cases. It seems that overtakings have slightly more strong negative impact comparing to meetings, but not as much as Botma assumed.

On the other hand, the main difference in the results from the two cities concern the "delayed passings". In contrast with the results from Thessaloniki, where the "delayed passings" were found to be by far the most annoying event type for both pedestrians and cyclists, the results from Palermo indicate that this event is indeed much undesired by the shared-use infrastructure users, but its' quantified negative impact is close enough to the quantified negative impact of other event types. This difference in the results in the two cities, could possibly indicate a difference in shared space users' perceptions, based on the culture, habits and infrastructure attributes.

For the facilitation of the evaluation of pedestrians-cyclists shared-use infrastructures through the usage of appropriate methodologies, it is essential to identify standard values, which will express the various event types' weights, in terms of the negative impact on the perceived comfort and safety of pedestrians and cyclists. In order to achieve this, the conduction of similar surveys and analyses in other countries is necessary. This process can provide globalized values that are well adapted to the results of the different individual countries, or it can alternatively provide values that are well adapted to clusters of countries if it is considered preferable to group countries on the basis of their mobility and infrastructure characteristics.

Acknowledgement. This study was supported by the MIUR (Ministry of Education, Universities and Research [Italy]) through a project entitled WEAKI TRANSIT: WEAK-demand areas Innovative TRANsport Shared services for Italian Towns (Project code: 20174ARRHT/CUP Code: J74I19000320008), financed with the PRIN 2017 (Research Projects of National Relevance) programme. We authorize the MIUR to reproduce and distribute reprints for Governmental purposes, notwithstanding any copyright notations thereon. Any opinions, findings and conclusions or recommendations expressed in this material are those of the authors, and do not necessarily reflect the views of the MIUR.

References

1. COM (2011) 144: White Paper: Roadmap to a Single European Transport Area – Towards a competitive and resource efficient transport system. European Commission, Brussels (2011)
2. Campisi, T., Acampa, G., Marino, G., Tesoriere, G.: Cycling master plans in Italy: the I-BIM feasibility tool for cost and safety assessment. Sustainability **12**(11), 4723 (2020)
3. Oja, P., et al.: Health benefits of cycling: a systematic review. Scand. J. Med. Sci. Sport. **21**(4), 496–509 (2011)
4. Singleton, P.: Walking (and cycling) to well-being: modal and other determinants of subjective well-being during the commute. Travel Behav. Soc. **16**, 249–261 (2018)
5. Vaitsis, P., Basbas, S., Nikiforiadis, A.: How eudaimonic aspect of subjective well-being affect transport mode choice? The case of Thessaloniki, Greece. Soc. Sci. **8**(1), 9 (2019)
6. Litman, T.A.: 2017. Evaluating active transport benefits and costs. guide to valuing walking and cycling improvements and encouragement programs. Prepared for Victoria Transport Policy Institute (2017)
7. Blondiau, T., van Zeebroeck, B., Haubold, H.: Economic benefits of increased cycling. Trans. Res. Proc. **14**, 2306–2313 (2016)

8. Ignaccolo, C., Giuffrida, N., Torrisi, V.: The queensway of New York city, a proposal for sustainable mobility in queens. In: Pezzagno, M., Tira, M. (eds.) Town and Infrastructure Planning for Safety and Urban Quality: Proceedings of the XXIII International Conference on Living and Walking in Cities (LWC 2017), CRC Press, Boca Raton (2018)

9. HCM 2010: Highway Capacity Manual. Washington, D.C.: Transportation Research Board (2010)

10. Landis, B.W., Vattikuti, V.R., Ottenberg, R.M., McLeod, D.S., Guttenplan, M.: Modelling the roadside walking environment: A pedestrian level of service. Transportation Research Record 1773, TRB. Washington, D.C: National Research Council (2001)

11. Tan, D., Wang, W., Lu, J., Bian, Y.: Research on methods of assessing pedestrian level of service for sidewalk. J. Transp. Syst. Eng. Inf. Technol. 7(5), 74–79 (2007)

12. Dixon, L.: Bicycle and pedestrian level-of-service performance measures and standards for congestion management systems. Transportation Research Record 1538, TRB. Washington, D.C: National Research Council (1996)

13. Jaskiewicz, F.: Pedestrian level of service based on trip quality. transportation research circular, Transportation Research Board. National Research Council, Washington D.C (2000)

14. Asadi-Shekari, Z., Moeinaddini, M., Zaly Shah, M.: A pedestrian level of service method for evaluating and promoting walking facilities on campus streets. Land Use Policy **38**, 175–193 (2014)

15. Frazila, R.B., Zukhruf, F., Ornando Simorangkir, C., Burhani, J.T.: Constructing pedestrian level of service based on the perspective of visual impairment person. In: MATEC Web of Conferences vol. 270, pp. 03009 (2019)

16. Mōri, M., Tsukaguchi, H.: A new method for evaluation of level of service in pedestrian facilities. Transp. Res. Part A Gen. **21**(3), 223–234 (1987)

17. Nikiforiadis, A., Basbas, S.: Can pedestrians and cyclists share the same space? The case of a city with low cycling levels and experience. Sustain. Cities Soc. **46**, 101453 (2019)

18. Campisi, T., Basbas, S., Canale, A., Tesoriere, G., Nikiforiadis, A., Vaitsis, P.: Sensitivity analysis and the alternative optimization of the pedestrian level of service: some considerations applied to a pedestrian street in Greece. In: XXIV International Conference Living and Walking in Cities, Brescia, Italy (2019)

19. Amprasi, V., Politis, I., Nikiforiadis, A., Basbas, S.: Comparing the microsimulated pedestrian level of service with the users' perception: the case of Thessaloniki, Greece, coastal front. In: 2nd International Congress on Transport Infrastructure and Systems in a changing world, Rome, Italy (2019)

20. Basbas, S., Campisi, T., Canale, A., Nikiforiadis, A., Gruden, C.: Pedestrian level of service assessment in an area close to an under-construction metro line in Thessaloniki, Greece. In: 2nd International Congress on Transport Infrastructure and Systems in a changing world, Rome, Italy (2019)

21. Botma, H.: Method to determine level of service for bicycle paths and pedestrian-bicycle paths. Transp. Res. Rec. **1502**, 38–44 (1995)

22. Garyfalou, I.M., Meintanis, I., Papas, T., Trouva, M., Nikiforiadis, A., Basbas, S.: Application of the Analytical Hierarchy Process for the investigation of the impact of different event types on the safety and comfort of pedestrians and cyclists in shared-use infrastructures. In: 9th International Congress on Transportation Research, Athens, Greece (2019). (in Greek)

23. Hummer, J., et al.: User perceptions of the quality of service on shared paths. Transp. Res. Rec. **1939**, 28–36 (2005)

24. Fowler, M., Lloyd, W., Munro, C.: Technical Paper e Shared Path Widths. IPENZ Transportation Group Conference Christchurch (2010)

25. Saaty, T.L.: The Analytic Hierarchy Process. McGraw-Hill, New York (1980)
26. Ignaccolo, M., Inturri, G., García-Melón, M., Giuffrida, N., Le Pira, M., Torrisi, V.: Combining Analytic Hierarchy Process (AHP) with role-playing games for stakeholder engagement in complex transport decisions. Transp. Res. Proc. **27**, 500–507 (2017)
27. Green, P., Srinivasan, V.: Conjoint analysis in consumer research: issues and outlook. J. Consum. Res. **5**, 103–123 (1978)
28. Hansen, P., Ombler, F.: A new method for scoring additive multi-attribute value models using pairwise rankings of alternatives. J. Multi Criteria Decis. Anal. **15**, 87–107 (2009)
29. Heinen, E., van Wee, B., Maat, K.: Commuting by bicycle: an overview of the literature. Transp. Rev. **30**, 59–96 (2010)
30. Pojani, D., Bakija, D., Shkreli, E., Corcoran, J., Mateo-Babiano, I.: Do Northwestern and Southeastern Europe share a common "Cycling Mindset"? Comparative analysis of beliefs toward cycling in the Netherlands and the Balkans. Eur. J. Transp. Infrastruct. Res. **17**, 25–45 (2017)
31. Prati, G.: Gender equality and women's participation in transport cycling. J. Transp. Geogr. **66**, 369–375 (2018)

Shared Mobility and Last-Mile Connectivity to Metro Public Transport: Survey Design Aspects for Determining Willingness for Intermodal Ridesharing in Athens

Alexandros Deloukas[1] ⓘ, Georgios Georgiadis[2] ⓘ,
and Panagiotis Papaioannou[2(✉)] ⓘ

[1] Attiko Metro S.A., 11525 Athens, Greece
adeloukas@ametro.gr
[2] Department of Civil Engineering, School of Engineering,
Aristotle University of Thessaloniki, 54124 Thessaloniki, Greece
papa@civil.auth.gr

Abstract. People living in peri-urban low-density areas may not choose the urban rail because they are hindered by the 'first/last mile' problem. The issue concerns poor bus feeder service to rail stations and/or congested Park&Ride facilities at respective intermodal hubs. Shared mobility in the form of carpooling is a viable alternative in connection to urban rail, especially when appropriate incentives and ridematching tools are effectuated. A multi-modal ride-matching app combining flexible (carpooling) and scheduled (rail and bus public transport) mobility is stipulated by the Horizon 2020 Ride2Rail project. Two intermodal hubs of urban rail along the 20 km-long corridor connecting the Athens basin with the Athens airport in Eastern Attica, Greece, are selected as a case study. The paper envisages the behavioural underpinning of combined rail-rideshare travel companion platform in the first/last mile context through the design of a SP experiment, as mode choice is concerned. All main access and egress modes of intermodal hubs are considered in the mode choice experiment, namely driving alone, using bus feeder, carpool driving and carpool riding. Tested parameters pertain particularly to incentive mechanisms increasing ridesharing to intermodal hubs, contextual preferences related to the trip purpose and perceived barriers of shared mobility.

Keywords: Carpooling · Metro · Shared mobility · Last-mile · Public Transport

1 Introduction

Rail Public Transport (PT) modal shares in peri-urban low density areas are often disappointing due to the 'first/last mile' (FM/LM) problem. This problem pertains to poor bus PT feeder services to/from rail PT stations and/or congested Park and Ride (P&R) facilities at the respective intermodal hubs which hinder access to rail PT stations either by PT or private cars. Shared mobility in the form of carpooling (being a form of ridesharing) is a viable alternative in connection to urban rail, especially when

© Springer Nature Switzerland AG 2020
O. Gervasi et al. (Eds.): ICCSA 2020, LNCS 12250, pp. 819–835, 2020.
https://doi.org/10.1007/978-3-030-58802-1_59

appropriate incentives and ridematching tools are effectuated. Thus, carpooling may complement PT and amplify rail ridership.

A multi-modal ridematching app combining flexible (carpooling) and scheduled (rail, PT) mobility is stipulated by the EU H2020 Ride2Rail project; Ride2Rail consists of 17 partners including ATTIKO METRO of Greece. In the case of Athens, the project aims among others at reducing single-occupant car trips, car-kms travelled as well as GHG emissions. Two intermodal hubs of urban rail along the 20 km-long corridor connecting Athens basin with Athens International Airport (AIA) in Eastern Attica are selected as a case study. Having intermodal hubs as a shared trip end for a part of a journey increases the likelihood of congruent trip ends and successful ridematching.

The paper envisages the behavioural underpinning of combined rail-rideshare travel companion platform in the first/last mile context through the design (and conduct in a later stage) of a Stated Preference (SP) experiment, as mode choice is concerned.

All main access and egress modes at intermodal hubs are considered in the mode choice experiment, namely driving alone, using PT bus feeder, carpool driving and carpool riding. Tested parameters pertain particularly to incentive mechanisms increasing ridesharing to intermodal hubs, contextual preferences related to the trip purpose as well as perceived barriers of shared mobility.

The main objective of the paper is to enhance the understanding of travellers' decision using carpooling as the access or egress mode to/from intermodal hubs of urban rail. Another objective is to draft a suitable design for a SP experiment that will distil information about ridesharing behaviour. Revealed preference (actual) behaviour is influenced by habit, supply limitations or (uncontrolled) system effects, thus is more constrained into explaining factors impacting ridesharing.

Novel features of the paper refer to the design of the SP carpool experiment for a part - first/last mile - of an entire journey, namely the trip to/from an intermodal hub. The experiment being conducted at a region-wide level covers short-distance trips complementing the use of the (line-haul) PT mode. Based on the survey data, realistic (to the respondent) alternative mode usage scenarios are generated during the interview for use in the SP part of the survey. Discrete choice modelling will be used to analyse the data and several specifications are to be developed in a next phase to help explain the forces that impact ridesharing to intermodal hubs.

The paper is structured in 5 sections. Section 2 presents the relevant literature review, aiming to identify potential factors affecting the decision to become carpool driver or rider. Notional issues and the concept of dynamic ridesharing are described. An overview of the study area along with the underlying travel data and information is given in Sect. 3. Section 4 elaborates on the methodological issues concerning the field survey, the questionnaire structure, the sampling technique and the SP experimental design. The final section presents the next steps of this research and attempts an overview of the main points of this effort until now.

2   Literature Review

2.1   General

Ridesharing, and in particular carpooling, is an efficient mobility form which may fill service gaps to rail stations and other PT terminals. PT gaps are evident in low density areas. Affected communities have an interest to enhance low cost accessibility to trunk-haul lines (TCRP 2012).

According to Furuhata et al. (2013), *'Ridesharing'* refers to a mode of transportation in which individual travellers share a vehicle for a trip and split travel costs such as fuel, toll, and parking fees with others that have similar itineraries and time schedules. They consider informal carpools involving family members and related persons (e.g. friends, co-workers) as well as formal carpools involving unrelated persons (unknowns). A slightly different definition from ICARO project final report (ICARO 1999), states that *'Car-pooling* is at least two people riding in a car usually belonging to one of the occupants, whether one person always drives or the carpoolers alternate cars. Each member would have made the trip independently if the carpool had not been there. Driver and passengers know before the trip that they will share the ride and at what time they will be leaving. Professional and/or commercial vehicles are excluded'.

Carpooling is served by private cars for various trip purposes. In a US survey in Texas, 50% of carpool vehicles using High Occupancy Vehicle (HOV) lanes were carrying two or more occupants who were commuters (Li et al. 2007). However, other trip purposes may also be satisfied by the carpool mode such as recreation or shopping.

Ways of filling up mobility needs of people in low density areas are equivalent to solving the 'last-mile' problem in logistics terms. Thus, carpooling is a modal form which complements PT for short-distance rides. In contrast, long-distance carpools fully replace PT rides, thus deteriorating sustainability (Stiglic et al. 2018).

Environmental concerns (e.g. car-kms and GHG emission savings) are further reasons for promoting carpooling and ridesharing in general. Carpools reduce Single-Occupant (SOV) car trips leading both to road and parking decongestion. Less parking-search traffic and need for parking spaces are additional benefits. User concerns (e.g. minimization of car-kms, excess driving time and travel costs) are aligned in this respect with environmental concerns, demonstrating a win-win situation. Car-kms and tons of GHG emission savings as well as increases in car occupancy levels are prevalent KPIs from the *community* perspective. From the *user* perspective, appropriate KPIs pertain to excess driving time (delay), travel costs and comfort levels.

Ridersharing platforms and apps are more appropriate for the formation of formal carpools. Large employers' platforms or large trip generators mobility plans (e.g. universities, shopping malls, etc.), may also serve as carpool enabling mechanisms.

In the rail-rideshare context of peripheral low-density areas we distinguish:

– drivers and riders (passengers) opting to use the rail (carpool multimodality)
– drivers dropping off riders (passengers) at intermodal hubs and continuing by car to their final destination (carpool rider multimodality, 'Kiss&Ride' mode)
– both driver and rider completing their journey by carpool (carpool unimodality).

Only carpool multimodality contributes to the road and parking decongestion in the city centre.

Intermodal hubs are a critical component for promoting carpooling in a region. The rail-rideshare combination of intermodal hubs provides a ridematching advantage. The hubs as shared and fixed trip ends (but transfer points over the entire journey) enable shorter detours and less inconvenience for the carpool drivers, thus allowing more feasible ride matches than complete-journey carpools where both trip ends are variable. In case of long journeys, the proportion of trips with similar O-D pairings is small due to the distance friction. The tolerances for detour delays and walk time measure the spatial flexibility of the ridemates. Narrow departure time windows and schedule rigidity of the carpoolers are further limitations for ridematching. The temporal flexibility of ridemates (e.g. earliest possible departure time, latest possible arrival time) greatly impacts the ridematching success rate.

2.2   Factors Impacting Ridesharing Behaviour

Prominent factors in the literature having an impact on ridesharing behaviour are:

- *In-vehicle travel time*, perceived differently by carpool drivers and by (incidentally more relaxed) riders. According to Hunt and McMillan (1997), the relationship between the value of time of a rider and a driver for commuters is approximately 0.69.
- *Detour time*, i.e. delay of the carpool driver to pickup and drop-off the rider at a meeting point (home or out-of-home); excess driving time represents an inconvenience factor for the driver. The value of detour time to the value of direct travel time amounts about 1.4 for commuters (Hunt and McMillan 1997).
- *Walk time* of the rider to an out-of-home meeting point. The value of walking time to the value of in-vehicle travel time amounts about 1.8 in Athens (Spanos et al. 1997)
- *Travel cost* (normally shared equally among car poolers) includes - apart of fuel cost – toll cost and possibly parking cost. The latter is shared equally through the number of car occupants, if they are unrelated; in case of family members or friends, mostly the driver assumes the burden.
- *Type of relationship* between ridemates (family members, friends/co-workers, unknowns)
- *Availability of and waiting time for a Guaranteed Ride Home (GRH)* referring to riders. The value of GRH availability approximates the PT ticket fare for commuters (Hunt and McMillan 1997). Overall, a return trip outwards, must not be done with the inward driver too.
- Existence of HOVs which stipulate time savings to carpoolers by providing exclusive lanes for them.

Olsson et al. (2019) carried out a meta-analysis of 18 recent studies on carpooling and calculated effect sizes of 20 different factors. Their results indicated a very weak influence of socio-demographics on carpooling. Influential are fuel costs and economic benefits as well as socio-psychological factors and attitudes, such as desire for socializing or lack of trust and loss of privacy. Policy incentives and situational factors (e.g. area density, PT service level) are also drivers of carpooling. Interestingly, issues such as 3ʳᵈ party liability insurance or driving behaviour have not been considered. Buliung et al. (2009) estimated in the Greater Toronto Hamilton Area in Canada that the number of carpool platform users within 1 km of the place of residence increases significantly the odds of starting to carpool through the platform; potential match locations in excess of 3 kms have a little impact on carpooling. This important finding is an advice to embrace suburban municipalities and raise at the neighbourhood level the awareness of the ridesharing platform.

Effective policy incentives for carpooling seem to be preferential parking for car-pooling vehicles as well as discounted parking fees. Another incentive is the granting of free PT tickets or even taxi ride to provide the GRH stimulus (Menczer 2007). A certain factor is the ridematching transaction cost, dependent on the design features of mobile apps. Relevant socioeconomic characteristics pertaining to carpool propensity are home location, age, gender, household size, number of household cars over number of driver licenses, schedule flexibility, activity constraints, mode currently used (inertia) as well as current direct–trip characteristics

2.3 P&R Facilities

It is well known that parking constraints in central urban destinations generally increase the PT share (Morrall and Bolger 1996), which is also true for the Athens case (Polydoropoulou et al. 1998). However, referring to peri-urban areas close to trip origins, Merriman (1998) provided evidence that increases in the capacity of parking-constrained suburban rail stations increase rail ridership. Depending on time period and other variables, the author observes that system-wide between 0.75 and 1.5 additional boarders are associated with an additional parking space. Nevertheless, expansion of parking capacity is cost-intensive and detrimental to a sustainable transit-oriented development around stations. A smarter way to increase rail ridership without expanding parking capacity around suburban stations is to increase ridesharing to P&R hubs. Such an option was studied in Thessaloniki, Greece in 1997, as part of the ICARO project demo case combining carpool use, the implementation of an HOV lane and the provision of a P&R facility (ICARO 1999). The study findings indicated consistently that an increase in carpooling use is achieved when additional measures such as preferential parking for car poolers are taken.

2.4 Dynamic Ridesharing

Dynamic ridesharing is facilitated by ride matching platforms and apps. ICARO project examined, 20 years ago, one of the first real-world carpool matching centres established in co-operation with individual companies in Brussels, Belgium. The ultimate aim was to promote carpooling and to encourage employees to put carpooling into practice. A matching index was devised in a ridematching platform allowing the pairing of carpool drivers with prospective passengers based on trip and person characteristics. Apart from the trip characteristics of the prospective ridemates, other specific requests from both sides were taken into account when calculating the index. According to the project findings, a carpool matching service could be part of a larger transport co-ordination centre. PT operators could also be involved in matching prospective carpoolers ICARO (1999).

Another such initiative is the Carpool Zone app which is part of the Smart Commute programme started in 2005 in Toronto Area (GTHA) in Canada (Buliung et al. 2009). The specific programme encourages commuters to explore various commuter options like carpooling, teleworking, transit, cycling, walking or flexible work hours. Some 50 major employers work with local authorities to offer customized commuter services.

Today, technology with mobile apps and GPS-enabled devices allow easier ride-matching. Dynamic ridesharing apps match ride offers of drivers as Travel Service Providers/TSPs (supply-side) and requests of riders as passengers (demand-side). Such apps reduce the transaction costs of ridematching and facilitate carpool formation (Amey et al. 2011). There is evidence that they increase the willingness to rideshare (Lee et al. 2016). Blockchain technology is a trust-building mechanism envisaged by the RIDE2RAIL project to enhance ridesharing with unknowns.

Dynamic ridesharing is predisposed for single, non-recurring trips, unsteady work time or shift work. However, commuters with recurring trips may also use a platform to establish a more stable carpool and eventually share driving in turn (platform as a networking tool for carpool acquaintanceship). It is noted that social or recreation trips typically exhibit a higher than 2.0 car occupancy rate, whereas commuting trips a lower than 1.2; thus, promoting carpooling among commuters seems to be a more efficient strategy. Rideshare platforms need an initial phase to stabilize. It is common to incentivize early adopters to gain a sufficient driver-to-rider ratio and a critical mass of offers and requests. A minimum success rate for ridematching is a condition for potential participants to continue using the platform.

2.5   SP Experiments and Carpooling

SP experiments with hypothetical trade-off games have been used in a few studies of carpooling choice behaviour. All concern entire journeys from initial trip origins to final destinations. Experiments for the propensity to participate in carpooling schemes as a driver or as a rider have shown the importance of, inter alia, working schedule flexibility, weather conditions and perceived rider vs. driver profile respectively (Tahmasseby et al. 2016). Correia and Viegas (2011) merge together carpool drivers and riders in the form of a single alternative to driving alone/with family. Higher willingness to carpool characterises younger persons and lower income people. A highly positive and significant Alternative Specific Constant (ASC) represents an unexplained preference for carpooling. Trust-building was intended through the formation of car clubs. Focusing on the home to work trip towards city centre, Van der Waerden et al. (2015) asked car drivers in an SP experiment to choose between driving alone and carpooling, in a similar setting of Correia and Viegas (2011). Most influential was the flexibility of working hours, time and cost variables.

In the SP experiment of Ciari and Axhausen (2012), respondents choose among car, PT, carpooling as driver and carpooling as rider. The experiment is conducted at a nation-wide level in Switzerland covering trips longer than 10 kms, thus carpool alternatives antagonize PT mode by design. The in-vehicle Value of Time (VoT) of the carpool passengers is higher than the VoT of the carpool driver and the latter is higher than that of the single driver. Pertaining to the carpool rider, the value of walk time is 16% higher compared to the in-vehicle VoT. A contextual preference for carpooling was associated with work as trip purpose.

With respect to Greece, an SP experiment took place in Thessaloniki, two decades ago, in the framework of the EU ICARO project (ICARO 1999; Papaioannou and Georgiou 2001). Thessaloniki is inhabited by almost one million people and PT services are provided by buses only. The survey goal was to determine the percentage of persons willing to carpool under specific circumstances from home to work during the morning peak. The survey covered a specific area as home origins and the city centre as work destinations. Attributes in the SP games included the total journey time by car with and without the existence and use of an HOV lane by car poolers, the trip cost and the occupancy rate. A fractional factorial design of 9 combinations was employed instead of the full SP design of 27 combinations. Trip time and cost values were taken as % of the respective average figures. Surveyed persons had to make a choice between a hypothetical option and the revealed one (paired choice). VoT figures for carpool drivers and riders were obtained, showing that there is a ratio of 1.56 between these two categories. Survey findings indicated that 5% of those asked are willing to carpool as riders for a 17 min. journey (3.5 km) provided they would save 60% of their initial trip cost and they would also reduce their journey time by 25%. Parking search time savings were not explicitly mentioned but they were taken as part of the overall journey time.

3 Case Study

3.1 Study Area and Background Information

The study area of this research is the catchment zone of the 20-km long air-rail corridor between "Doukissis Plakentias" and Athens Airport rail stations along "Attiki Odos" toll road. This area comprises territories of five (5) municipalities with low population densities compared to the core centre of the Athens municipality (Table 1).

Table 1. Demographic & travel demand features of municipalities represented in the study area

Municipality	Total area (km^2)	Population	Population density (inh/km^2)	24 h travel demand	PT share (%)
Athens	39	664,046	17,026.8	1,491,531	78
Vrilissia	3.9	30,741	7,882.3	64,142	32
Penteli	36.1	34,934	967.7	27,051	27
Pallini	29.4	54,415	1,850.9	66,088	30
Paiania	53.2	26,668	501.3	28,833	27
Koropi	102	30,307	297.1	57,712	26

The spatio-temporal distribution of the inward travel demand refers to morning peak (MP) trip productions of the five municipalities directed to the centre of Athens; the outward demand pertains to afternoon peak trip productions from the centre to them. Metro and suburban rail PT services connect Doukissis Plakentias (DP) station with the airport as well as three (3) intermediate stations, namely: "Pallini", "Kantza" and "Koropi" (KR). Hub selection criteria refer to varying parking characteristics, distance from the CBD, rail service level and suburban vs extra-urban land use. Along this corridor, DP and KR stations were selected as intermodal hubs for accommodating last-mile ridesharing trips (Fig. 1). DP suburban station is regarded as the gate to the main city of Athens while KR extra-urban station is the last stop before the airport, and it is located 13 kms south of DP. Both metro and suburban rail services are offered towards Athens and airport from KR and DP hubs. Inwards service level at DP, with a combined headway of 4 min, is comparatively higher to that at KR featuring a combined headway of 12 min. (Table 2). Thus, it is expected that some travellers living closer to KR may divert to the better serviced DP hub to catch the train.

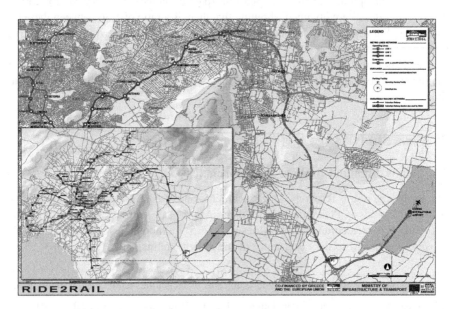

Fig. 1. Athens metro network and intermodal hubs (in yellow) (Source: ATTIKO METRO) (Color figure online)

In the selected corridor setting, using urban rail to reach a central destination is typically faster than using the car, the radial arterials being persistently congested. The PT share of Athens' trip attractions (Table 1) is an evidence in this respect.

The following bus lines (Table 3) comprise the bus feeder routes of the two intermodal hubs. Boarding figures for morning period and 24 h are also provided. Nights and weekends seem to be very suitable periods for dynamic ridesharing as a

Table 2. Rail service level in the selected intermodal hubs

Metro/suburban rail station	Morning peak headway (minutes)			Span of service		Morning peak boardings	
	Met.	Sub	Comb	Metro	Suburban	Initial	Transfer
Doukissis Plakentias	5	20	4	05:30–24:00 (02:00)[a]	06:00–23:00	2,009	692
Koropi	30	20	12	06:30–23:30	06:00–23:00	91	287

[a]Fridays and Saturdays

feeder mode to the (sub)urban rail featuring a high service level. The net effect is a higher rail utilization in low traffic periods through an otherwise suppressed demand.

Table 3. Bus feeder services and boardings recorded in the selected intermodal hubs

Metro/suburban rail station	Bus line	MP headway (min)	Span of service	Destination	Boardings	
					MP	24 h
Doukissis Plakentias (DP)	301	45	05:00–23:00	Pallini-Penteli	109	1,298
	302	35	05:00–23:45	Pallini	364	4,333
	306	35	05:30–22:30	Pallini	372	4,429
	307	40	06:15–23:30	Pallini-Paiania	287	3,417
	405	35	05:30–23:30	Vrilissia-Penteli	260	3,095
	447	30	05:30–23:00	Vrilissia	176	2,095
	451	30	05:30–23:30	Vrilissia-Penteli	371	4,417
Koropi (KR)	309	30	05:00–23:30	Koropi	321	3,821
	330	45	06:00–21:30	Koropi	319	3,798

Both stations are equipped with P&R facilities which could encourage carpooling for multimodal travellers. Table 4 shows their main features. Note that in DP's P&R station, due to parking charges, there is a low to middle utilization rate.

At DP hub, the P&R operator leases the land from the Metro's owner (ATTIKO METRO). Average parking duration is in the range of 6–8 h. There is no strict parking enforcement in the area, thus resulting to intense parking spillover and lower parking demand at the facility. Parking availability is typically quite good. At KR station, the

Table 4. P&R facilities features in the selected intermodal hubs

Metro/suburban rail station	Area (m²)	Capacity	Fees per hour
Doukissis Plakentias (DP)	15,200- paved	630 spaces	0.5€ (up to 12 h per day, 7 days a week)
Koropi (KR)	6,100- unpaved	300 spaces	Free

parking lot is saturated every workday during morning peak period. Furthermore, spillover parking of about 300 additional cars is noticed on a regular basis.

3.2   Survey Method and Instruments

The method adopted for data collection is the controlled experimentation based on the choice between alternative hypothetical scenarios (travel options). This is because carpooling is a rather infrequent modal choice in practice. The Stated Preference (SP) technique is particularly effective in this respect (Louvière et al. 2000). This technique forces the respondents to trade off among conditions regarding specific attributes.

The chosen survey instrument is combined with revealed preference (RP) queries about the actual behaviour (i.e. the actual journey) to contextualize the hypothetical scenarios. The use of mobile devices for conducting SP interviews enables the interactive generation of realistic alternative scenarios. SP experiments explicitly acknowledge user preferences for carpooling.

The computer-assisted questionnaire to be used for the combined RP/SP survey consists of three main parts. The first one pertains to the travel behaviour of the respondent, capturing in this way the current preferences of the trip makers and the characteristics of the on-going journey. The second part includes questions about the socioeconomic features of the respondent and his/her household. The third part pertains to the SP of the respondents. Specific questions in the survey form aim at capturing the interviewees' potential attitudinal and behavioural changes under different circumstances. This part also includes the SP cards to be presented to the interviewees. Combinations of presented options with different attribute values/levels in the form of game cards are chosen in a semi-dynamic way by the survey software to reflect the real trip and person characteristics corresponding to each person.

3.3   Sampling Method and Sample Size

The population to be sampled comprises intermodal hub users at the two stations who make the first/last part of their journey by one of the following modes:

- Public Transport Feeder bus, falling in one of the bus lines of Table 3
- Driving Alone (SOV) and parking at or outside the designated P&R facility
- Driving with one passenger and parking at or outside the designated P&R facility
- Riding a car as passenger; car is parked at or outside the designated P&R facility

Trip makers who are dropped off/picked up by a family member or friend are not included in the targeted sample, since the alternative travel options are deemed inferior to the current ones. In other words, these trip makers will be most likely non traders. A point to be explored is whether current car drivers and riders from different households who share a car but do not share the travel costs, will consider formal carpooling as a potential travel option either as drivers or as riders and under which conditions.

Target respondents are people above the age of 18, i.e. persons eligible to drive. Furthermore, the respondents' population is categorised into two main groups according to their main trip purpose, namely commuting and other purpose. Business trips are not considered. The sampling procedure does not include by design car drivers being in need of their car during the day. Users of company cars are excluded from the survey. It is assumed that car trips shorter than 2 kms (i.e. about 5 min) are not worth of the carpool coordination effort, case that will be checked through the survey instrument.

According to the ATTIKO METRO transportation model developed in the Metro Development Study, approximately 39% of the road-side travellers' access/egress the two intermodal hubs of DP and KR by bus feeder and 61% by car/taxi. However, it is expected that the population of respondents will access or egress to a higher percentage by car; at least one third of the retrieved P&R users will be drawn from cars with an occupancy of 2 or more, also including non-household members, thus enriching the carpool share. Pertaining to the existing users of bus feeder lines, the intention is to promote the carpool alternative when the bus service is either not available (night) or very thin (weekend). Especially for aged persons (being at risk of social isolation) or persons without driver's license in low density areas, carpooling is a value alternative.

The travel options considered in the SP survey are four: PT Bus (PTB), Drive Alone (SOV), Drive with other passengers (HOV) or carpool driver (CPD) and riding a car as passenger (PAS) or carpool rider (CPR). The travel options will appear as triplets or pairs on the game cards, meaning that the respondent will have to choose one option among the current one and the alternative options, each time a game card is presented to him. The following travel choice sets shown in Table 5 will be investigated.

Table 5. Travel choice sets to be examined

	Travel option 1 (actual)	Travel option 2	Travel option 3
Choice set 1	PT feeder bus	Carpool driver	Carpool rider
Choice set 2	Car driver (SOV)	Carpool driver	Carpool rider
Choice set 3	Car driver (HOV)	–	Carpool rider
Choice set 4	Car passenger*	Carpool driver	–

* Conditions to be met: licence holder & car available and work purpose

The sampling method chosen is the one used for choice-based surveys (similar to quota sampling). A minimum sample size should be reached for each group in the population to ensure reliable findings. By combining the current travel modes for the first/last part of the inward or outward trip and the trip purpose we end up with 8 groups.

A minimum number of 60 valid questionnaires per group are deemed adequate for the research purposes. This threshold strongly depends on the number of game cards to be presented to each interviewee. Considering that 8 choice games with alternative travel options will be shown to each interviewee, 480 observations per group will be reached. The proportion between inward and outward trips will be locked up after the completion of a pilot survey. Table 6 shows the groups to be surveyed and the indicative sample size for each hub location and trip purpose. The targeted sample for other purposes is slightly higher than the one for commuting, to account for wider variation.

Table 6. Sample size per population group, intermodal hub location and trip purpose

Intermodal hub	Doukissis Plakentias				Koropi				Total
Trip purpose	Travel mode								
	PT bus	Car			PT bus	Car			
		SOV driver	HOV driver	Rider		SOV driver	HOV driver	Rider	
Commuting	35	35	30	35	35	35	35	35	**280**
Other	40	40	40	40	40	40	40	40	**320**
Total questionnaires	**75**	**75**	**75**	**75**	**75**	**75**	**75**	**75**	**600**
Expected valid questionnaires	**60**	**60**	**60**	**60**	**60**	**60**	**60**	**60**	**480**

3.4 SP Design

The RP part of the questionnaire reports values on current trip characteristics to the intermodal hubs, as well as socioeconomic features of travellers (e.g. car ownership level, number of driver licenses, PT travelcard holding, distance home - bus stop, employment status, work time flexibility). A research hypothesis is that people in households with fewer cars than drivers are more prone for carpooling. Current values are used as seeds to calculate attribute values for the SP part of the questionnaire. Attitudinal responses rule out carpooling as alternative filter for non-traders.

The attributes presented in the PT (bus feeder) and SOV alternatives are constant among alternatives, i.e. variable attributes are presented only for the carpooling alternatives (driver, rider). Note that driving alone a car or using bus feeder is conditioned by car availability or PT service availability respectively. Carpooling depends not only on car availability but also on the willingness to share a car.

Based on existing knowledge from the international bibliography, issues of interest in this research refer to the:

- Value of Guarantee Ride Home (GRH) utility
- Value of Detour Time disutility; max. excess time (5-10 min. in the given setting), driver-relevant
- Value of utility for carpooling household members (vs friends vs unknown persons)
- Value of Wait Time (for GRH) disutility
- Value of Walk Time disutility; riders are more prone to carpool when picked up at home; max. threshold of walk time to meeting point (5 min. in the given setting), rider-relevant
- Parking Cost share with non-household members and resulting parking cost savings
- Value of additional riders' disutility (for non-household members)
- Value of different vs same gender of ridemates (dis)utility
- Value of Dynamic Ridesharing Platform (in)convenience (dis)utility

The attributes selected to form the utility functions for the discrete choice models to be constructed along with the levels that will form the different values for the game cards are presented in Table 7. In total 6 attributes will be studied in the SP survey and the resulting discrete choice models. Three of them (travel cost, travel time and flexible carpool schedule) will receive three value levels (L, M, H), whereas the other three (i.e. preferential parking, meeting point and GRH) will receive two levels. The first four alternatives refer to the current existing travel options as recorded by the RP survey. The other two refer to the travel options under investigation through the SP survey.

Travel time is specified as an alternative-specific attribute and the travel cost as a generic variable. Depending on transport mode, travel time consists of different components such as in-vehicle time, parking search time, walking time, etc. (see notation after Table 7). Separate specifications are considered, referring to riders being household members or non-household members respectively. In the former case it is expected that carpooling with household members is a utility for the driver, in the latter case a disutility. The GRH insurance for carpool riders unsuccessfully requesting a carpool driver pertains either to a PT ticket voucher once a week or to a taxi ride 6 times a year (for a ride up to 15 kms when a bus feeder is not available within 40 min. or more).

The reference value for each attribute per travel option is as follows:

- For the current option is the one obtained from the RP survey or from the AM transportation model (e.g. travel time between a location and the intermodal hubs, travel distance, travel cost based on distance, parking cost, etc.)
- For carpool travel options it is calculated by taking into account the initial reference values as previously described and then by properly adjusting for the new conditions. For instance, for the 'carpooling driver' option, the travel cost obtained from the survey is increased to account for any detour required to pick up the carpool rider and then is divided by two, since the total travel cost is equally split among the travellers. An assumption is made that most carpools will include two ridemates only. Similarly, the reference travel time for this option is increased by the detour extra time for the driver and the walk plus the wait time for the rider.

Table 7. Trip attributes and attribute levels for current and carpooling travel options

Alternative (Travel Option)	Attribute	Reference Source/Value	Variations		
			L	M	H
PT Bus (PTB)	Travel Cost (ticket)	0 €	n.a.	#	n.a.
	Travel Time (WLT + IVT + WLK + WAT[a])	TM[c]		#	
Drive Alone (SOV)	Car Travel cost (fuel + parking)	TM[c]	n.a.	#	n.a.
	Travel Time (IVT + PST)	TM + RP[b]		#	
Drive not alone (HOV)	Travel Cost (fuel + parking)	RP	n.a.	#	n.a.
	Travel Time (WAT + IVT + WLK + WAT[a])	TM[c]		#	
Car Rider (PAS)	Travel Cost	0 €	n.a.	#	n.a.
	Travel Time (IVT + WLK + WAT[a])	TM[c]		#	
Carpool Driver (CPD)	Travel cost (fuel + parking)	½ Car Cost	-25%	#	+25%
	Travel Time (IVT + DTT +PST)	TTT + 5 m	#	+20%	+40%
	Preferential Parking	-		Yes	No
	Flexible Schedule (1h, 3h, 12h)	-		12 h	3h	1h
Carpool Rider (CPR)	Travel cost (fuel + parking)	½ Car Cost	-25%	#	+25%
	Travel Time (WAT + IVT + WLK+PST)	TTT + 10 m	-30%	#	+30%
	Meeting Point (home, Out of home)	-		HM	-	OHM
	Flexible Schedule (1h, 3h, 12h)	-		12h	3h	1h
	GRH (1 PT ticket/week, 6 taxi rides/year)	-		PT	-	Taxi

# denotes reference value. For current travel options it is obtained either from available data or from RP survey; for carpool options it is calculated as shown in the respective cells
[a] Different for each Intermodal hub   [b] Respondent specific
[c] TM: ATTIKO METRO (AM) Transportation Model

WLT: Walking Time   PST: Parking Search Time   TTT: (Total) Travel Time
IVT: In Vehicle Time   DTT: Detour Travel Time   WAT: Wait Time

Emphasis is posed on non-household members and unknowns who are the main focus group of the RIDE2RAIL app. Equal sharing of parking cost as well as of fuel and toll cost is the typical case, especially with unknowns.

Based on the number of attributes to be examined and the number of attribute levels, the total, the number of possible combinations in the SP game sets will be $3^3*2^1*3^3*2^2 = 5,832$. This figure represents the full factorial SP design. A fractional factorial, facing satisfactorily the main effects, would result to 24 combinations, which are far too many to be negotiated by the interviewees. For this reason, it has been decided to split these 24 combinations into 3 blocks. Each block should be treated by 15 to 20 respondents (FSGV 1996). A random selection special routine, developed in R software language (R Core Team 2013), returned the 3 * 8 combinations.

The Tables 8, 9 and 10 below present the 8 combinations per block for the carpool driver and carpool rider travel options.

A pilot survey which is part of the overall survey planning will help standardizing the survey instrument and test the complexity of choice situations. It will also indicate whether the survey can be completed on site. An alternative scheme of intercepting potential respondents will be tested, asking for contact details and cooperation and continuing with a same day online SP experiment for the given journey.

Table 8. SC game cards - block 1

CPD attributes				CPR attributes				
a1	a2	a3	a4	a1	a2	a3	a4	a5
H	L	L	M	H	H	L	L	L
H	M	H	H	M	H	M	M	L
H	M	H	H	H	L	L	H	L
H	H	H	M	M	H	M	H	L
H	M	L	H	M	H	M	H	L
L	M	L	H	H	L	L	M	H
L	L	L	L	M	L	M	M	H
L	L	H	M	M	H	M	M	H

Table 9. SC game cards - block 2

CCPD attributes				CPR attributes				
a1	a2	a3	a4	a1	a2	a3	a4	a5
H	M	H	L	H	L	L	L	L
M	M	H	H	M	H	L	M	L
L	M	L	M	M	L	M	M	L
L	L	H	M	H	L	M	M	L
M	M	H	L	H	L	H	M	L
M	L	H	M	H	H	L	H	L
H	M	H	L	H	L	H	L	H
M	L	H	M	H	L	M	M	H

Table 10. SC game cards - block 3

CPD attributes				CPR attributes				
a1	a2	a3	a4	a1	a2	a3	a4	a5
M	L	H	L	H	H	L	L	L
H	L	H	L	M	L	M	L	L
M	M	H	H	M	H	H	L	L
L	H	H	L	M	L	H	H	L
H	M	L	H	M	L	H	L	H
H	M	H	M	H	L	H	M	H
H	M	L	H	M	L	L	H	H
H	M	H	H	M	L	L	H	H

4   Further Steps and Outlook

Further steps in this research include pilot survey, full survey execution, data analysis, model specification, model estimation and algorithmic use in the RIDE2RAIL transit-rideshare app to be developed. The generalized costs of carpool drivers and riders for the given setting will be compared.

Carpool infrastructure (e.g. preferential parking) is an essential means to promote ridesharing. The RIDE2RAIL consortium makes arrangements to undersign collaboration agreements with locally affected municipalities and P&R providers aiming at the promotion of ridesharing during the pilot phase of the project. Pure tangible incentive mechanisms are foreseen in this respect. P&R managers providing dedicated carpool lots should benefit from a municipal tax exemption. Thus, municipalities are incentive providers for P+R operators and the latter are sponsors for carpoolers respectively. Carpool lots will be branded by an effective signage and marking and will be used as meeting points for outward carpool trips.

The Athens pilot, which shall test the RIDE2RAIL platform, will recruit control and experiment groups among SP respondents with enroute meeting points or relatively close home locations.

The discrete choice models which will be developed will be used for testing specific policies regarding the travellers who can combine carpooling access/egress to the Metro/Suburban rail intermodal hubs. The policies to be tested will pertain mainly to:

- Value of providing preferential parking at a discounted fee and close to the rail platform. The value depends on the magnitude of parking cost and walk time coefficients
- Value of providing a GRH for carpool riders
- Value of providing a carpool matching service for drivers and riders

Acknowledgments. This work is funded by the EU SHIFT2RAIL programme under grant agreement no. 881825 'RIDE2RAIL – Travel Companion enhancements and RIDE-sharing services synchronized to RAIL and Public Transport' (duration December 2019–May 2022).

References

Amey, A., Attanucci, J., Mishalani, R.: Real-time ridesharing, opportunities and challenges in using mobile phone technology to improve rideshare services. Transp. Res. Rec. **2217**, 103–110 (2011)

Buliung, R., Soltys, K., Habel, C., Lanyon, R.: The "driving" factors behind successful carpool formation and use. Transp. Res. Rec. **2118**, 31–38 (2009)

Ciari, F., Axhausen, K.W.: Choosing carpooling or car sharing as a mode - Swiss stated choice experiments. In: 91st Annual Meeting of the Transportation Research Board, Washington, D. C. (2012)

Correia, G., Viegas, J.M.: Carpooling and carpool clubs: clarifying concepts and assessing value enhancement possibilities through a stated preference web survey in Lisbon, Portugal. Transp. Res. Part A: Policy Pract. **45**(2), 81–90 (2011)

FSGV: Hinweise zur Messung von Praeferenzstrukturen mit Stated Preference Methoden, vol. 129 (1996)

Furuhata, M., Dessouky, M., Ordóñez, F., Brunet, M.E., Wang, X., Koenig, S.: Ridesharing: the state-of-the-art and future directions. Transp. Res. Part B: Methodol. **57**, 28–46 (2013)

Hunt, J.D., McMillan, J.D.P.: Stated-preference examination of attitudes toward carpooling to work in Calgary. Transp. Res. Rec. **1598**, 9–17 (1997)

ICARO: Increase of CAR occupancy through innovative measures and technical instruments. Project Final Report, European Commission, 4th Framework Programme, Vienna (1999)

Li, J., Mattingly, S., Rasmidatta, I., Sadabadi, K.F., Burris, M.: Who chooses to carpool and why? examination of Texas carpoolers. Transp. Res. Rec. **2021**, 110–117 (2007)

Lee, B., Aultman-Hall, L., Coogan, M., Adler, T.: Rideshare mode potential in non-metropolitan areas of the northeastern United States. J. Transp. Land Use **9**(3), 111–126 (2016)

Louvière, J.J., Hensher, D.A., Swait, J.D.: Stated Choice Methods, Analysis and Applications, 1st edn. Cambridge University Press, Cambridge (2000)

Menczer, W.: Guaranteed ride home programs. J. Public Transp. **10**(4), 131–150 (2007)

Merriman, D.: How many parking spaces does it take to create one additional transit passenger. Reg. Sci. Urban Econ. **28**(5), 565–584 (1998)

Morrall, J., Bolger, D.: The relationship between downtown parking supply and transit use. ITE J. **66**(2), 32–36 (1996)

Olsson, L.E., Maier, R., Friman, M.: Why do they ride with others? Meta-analysis of factors influencing travelers to carpool. Sustainability **11**(8), 1–16 (2019)

Polydoropoulou, A., Deloukas, A., Anastassaki, A.: Modal policies in Attika region: an impact assessment study. In: European Transport Conference Proceedings, Loughborough University (1998)

Papaioannou, P., Georgiou, G.: The implementation of an HOV lane in Thessaloniki: impacts on traffic and the environment. Techika Chronika Sci. J. TCG **I**(3), 57–69 (2001)

R Core Team: R: A language and environment for statistical computing (version 3.0.2). R Foundation for Statistical Computing, Vienna, Austria (2013). http://www.R-project.org/

Spanos, I., Deloukas, A., Anastassaki, A.: A stated choice experiment: value of travel characteristics in the context of Attica. IFAC Proc. Vol. **30**(8), 427–433 (1997)

Stiglic, M., Agatz, M., Savelsbergh, M., Gradisar, M.: Enhancing urban mobility: integrating ride-sharing and public transit. Comput. Oper. Res. **90**, 12–21 (2018)

Tahmasseby, S., Kattan, L., Barbour, B.: Propensity to participate in a peer-to-peer social-network-based carpooling system. J. Adv. Transp. **50**(2), 240–254 (2016)

The Transit Cooperative Research Program (TCRP): Synthesis Report 98: Ridesharing as a Complement to Transit: a Synthesis of Transit Practice, Transportation Research Board of the National Academies, Washington, D.C. (2012)

Van der Waerden, P., Lem, A., Wim Schaefer, W.: Investigation of factors that stimulate car drivers to change from car to carpooling in city center oriented work trips. Transp. Res. Procedia **10**, 335–344 (2015)

The Benefit of Engage the "Crowd" Encouraging a Bottom-up Approach for Shared Mobility Rating

Giovanni Tesoriere and Tiziana Campisi

University of Enna Kore, Cittadella Universitaria, 94100 Enna, Italy
tiziana.campisi@unikore.it

Abstract. Today transport systems have become multimodal and the evolution of shared mobility has made it possible to define forms of shared and green mobility such as e-bikes or PMVs (Personal Mobility Vehicles) while the supply of cars or van sharing reduces the use of private vehicles, often providing the possibility of renting electric vehicles with low environmental impact. When designing the shared mobility service it is useful to have a global vision that takes into account not only the business and future scenarios of the infrastructure, but also a data support linked to the needs of the users who will have to use it.

Democratic and participatory planning makes it possible to directly involve the crowd and encourage a bottom-up approach to mobility. This provides the basis for different planning and design assessments. This work has focused on a statistical evaluation before and after and the results have been elaborated through a longitudinal approach, comparing the judgement before and after (2018–2020) the advent of car sharing in the city examined. The study highlights the weaknesses generated by the creation of the present car-sharing service implemented in a small town in Sicily (Italy). The results highlight the lack of a preventive analysis of transport demand and this criticality lays the basis for future research aimed at improving the supply of shared mobility by involving the majority of the population in the planning of the service and allowing the combined implementation of the car and bike sharing service.

Keywords: Shared mobility · Crowdsourcing · Participatory planning

1 Introduction

Generally speaking, urban mobility planning and rules (at various scales) need to consider the development of new forms of shared mobility [1].

Several approaches and analyses can help to improve the overall vision of transport. Integrated design through the approach of the Building Information Model for Infrastructures (I-BIM) can improve the transport offer as it considers not only the geometric aspect but also the cost and safety aspects [2].

The use of data that comes not only from inspections but also from the population can make the work at various levels more comprehensive, such as

© Springer Nature Switzerland AG 2020
O. Gervasi et al. (Eds.): ICCSA 2020, LNCS 12250, pp. 836–850, 2020.
https://doi.org/10.1007/978-3-030-58802-1_60

- political research (evaluation of tenders and financial resources)
- operations (optimisation of traffic management events and emergencies)
- monitoring action and application (selecting the bottom-up or top-down approach)

In this way crowdsourcing information is useful for the best direct management of shared mobility and indirectly for sustainable mobility.

According to [3] the well-being of each user that is also defined as eudaimonia contains those factors (e.g. comfort, safety, autonomy, self-confidence, physical and mental health) that can influence the choice of the trip and consequently the optimization of the service.

There are several works in literature that show that the development of shared mobility has not been homogeneous in Italy and other European countries. In accordance with [4], between 2010 and 2015 significant progress has been made in sustainable mobility linked to state and international financial support that has facilitated the implementation of smart mobility projects.

Several innovative approaches in the literature show how it is possible to plan traffic scenarios according to vehicular and non vehicular flows, evaluating the service level of the infrastructure [5–7].

This assessment can provide the user with a strict assessment of safety, driving comfort and possible effects of vehicle congestion.

Considering infrastructures with numerous crossings or routes dedicated only to pedestrians, it is necessary to evaluate the possibility of using innovative technology that can make the crossing safer, especially if traffic lights are used [8]; moreover, for pedestrian infrastructures it is useful to calculate the PLOS, thus allowing an evaluation of the areas where cars are excluded and micromobility attached [9].

An optimal urban planning must be linked to a solid technical-scientific basis (top-down approach), but it must also consider a bottom-up approach to mitigate critical issues, monitoring the state of the art through the implementation of survey campaigns such as questionnaires or interviews in accordance with [10, 11]. Local mobility projects are often characterised by strict administrative procedures and are thus often blocked. According to [12], it is therefore considered appropriate to adopt new dynamic strategies so that a bottom-up or external approach can be considered as the key to real change.

Many studies in the literature examine walking accessibility, availability and travel conditions and this is of fundamental importance to understand whether other forms of sustainable mobility can be spread in an urban context considering the able and disabled [13–16].

The development of shared mobility must therefore be based on this dynamic vision. In general, car or van sharing is based on the innovative concept that allows companies, but also private users, to take a means of transport for people in the first case and to transport furniture, bulky objects, household appliances or work materials through a platform [17]. Through a dedicated website, it is possible to book the service guaranteeing flexibility and convenient rates for the user.

This research is based on the evaluation of the development of mobility sharing in a small Italian city. It focuses on the acquisition and processing of data through longitudinal analysis, i.e. before and after the implementation of a car sharing service by a private company, which manages the service in almost the entire regional territory for car, van and bicycle sharing. The analysis of the period before use, in most cases, is carried out on the basis of the experience described by the respondents and, when possible, by integrating the data with some cross-references (e.g. fuel costs to check the mileage of cars over a given period). The qualifying aspect of this survey method is to accurately assess how the behaviour of the respondent changed after they started using a shared mobility service.

On the other hand, one of the critical points of this survey method is the self-perception accuracy of the interviewees on some mobility habits such as the actual duration of the trips, the time dedicated to them, the frequency of use especially when referring to past experiences, maybe referring to the previous year.

Other weak points are that the evaluation is only about the period of short-term impact and attributing the changes to a single factor, e.g. the availability and use of a given shared mobility service, rather than to a set of factors that are difficult to decipher the individual contribution. This work shows the judgements made by the same sample of users after about 1 year.

2 Sharing Mobility Development

Shared mobility is often a socio-economic phenomenon influenced by the users of the service. In particular, it is clear that sharing mobility consists of a general transformation in the behaviour of people who tend to progressively favour temporary access mobility services rather than the use of their own means of transport and, on this basis, join new lifestyles that promote efficiency, sustainability and sharing. Sharing or renting are among the strategies that are most being implemented in the transport sector to avoid the use of private vehicles.

Proper management of the service makes it possible to:

- facilitate shared mobility and travel;
- create flexible, scalable and original services;
- allow interactivity between users/operators and/or peer collaboration;
- maximise the use of latent resources.

Over the last twenty years, various types of media sharing have evolved, understood as grouping or sharing [18, 19].

The vehicle fleet has evolved with the implementation of vans and small buses and a variation in vehicle fuel systems from classic petrol or diesel to hybrid or current electric vehicles. These services have become almost complementary to the emergence of electric charging stations and car parks dedicated to sharing. The development of micro-mobility is affecting this sector, although legislation is not yet comprehensive in many European countries.

In agreement with [20] it is necessary to examine users' needs to improve services related to shared mobility systems, in order to define the right balance between transport supply and demand in view of the development of Mobility as a Service, understood as an optimal and integrated service.

In accordance with [21] not only the instrumental attributes of the car, but also the psychological disposition, in particular the psychological property, of potential customers must be taken into account when developing measures to stimulate car sharing services in society. Table 1 summarises the characteristics of the various services mentioned above

Table 1. Sharing mobility development and classification

| | Sharing mobility | | | | |
	Ridesourcing/TNC, Ridesplitting/Taxi, Ehail)	Ride/Car Pooling	Car	Bike	Micromoblity
Vehicle type	Fuel/ diesel cars Hybrid cars Electric cars VAN e-VAN			Classic bike e-bike	Classic Scooter e-scooter Segway Hoverboard Monowheel
Sharing type	Fuel/ diesel cars Hybrid cars Electric cars VAN e-VAN	Urban Extra-urban Dedicated Carpooling VAN	B2C RT OW Free Floating Station based -P2P	Dock based Hub based Pure dockless Electric assist	Low-tech GPS system
Distance	>3miles			* <0,5miles = walking 0,5–3miles	

3 Methodology

The study was conducted by implementing a survey on the evaluation of the service provided with reference to the users' vision before and after implementation and limited only to the local use of car sharing.

The work was then carried out considering a request for ideas, suggestions, opinions, addressed to users pursuing the phenomenon of crowdsourcing, widely used in transport planning, for example to map options for urban and non-urban routes and to consider different transport modes [22, 23].

The evaluation was carried out on a sample of 370 users and the survey campaign was conducted for the first evaluation in the period February-March 2018 and then repeated in the period October-December 2019.

The analysis was conducted in a context where a car sharing service was set up by a private company that manages shared mobility in 12 other cities (in the south-west of the island of Sicily) and was implemented in Enna from April 2019.

The variables taken into consideration and examined concern respectively: socio-demographic attributes, transport habits and judgements on shared mobility.

As far as the socio-demographic variables are concerned, the following Table 2 shows the studied attributes.

Table 2. Socio-economic variable implemented by survey

	Variable	Possible reply	Variable	Possible reply
Socio-economic	Gender	Male Female	Driver licence ownership	Yes only for moped Yes for car and moped No
	Age	30–45 46–65 >65	Driver licence experience	<5 year 6–10 year 11–20year >21year
	Job	Employee Freelance Unemployed Retiree	Car ownership	Yes No
	Residence in Enna	Yes No	Bike ownership	Yes No

The second section of the survey focused on the main reason of travel and previous experience with sharing mobility services as shown in the table below (Table 3):

Table 3. Investigated variable related to transport attitude

	Variable	Possible reply	Variable	Possible reply
Transport attitude	Main reason of travel by car on daily time	H-W (home-work) H-L (home-leisure) other	Main reason of travel by car on holiday- time	H-W (home-work) H-L (home-leisure) other
	Italian car sharing experience	Yes No	Outside car sharing experience	Yes No
	Italian VAN sharing experience	Yes No	Outside VAN sharing experience	Yes No
	Italian bike sharing experience	Yes No	Outside bike sharing experience	Yes No

Through the Likert type judgment scales [24], it was possible to describe the data for the third section.

This approach makes it possible to express a judgment defined by a predetermined interval.

The third section has been divided into two parts, both described by a series of statements and criteria for a one-dimensional scale.

Table 4 below shows the evaluation criteria and the ranges adopted.

Table 4. Investigated opinions and criteria about sharing development in Enna

	Vehicle type	Criteria	Likert scale value
Implementation of a simple car sharing service	Car	1. Advantageous rates	0 = no
	VAN	2. Presence of city cars in the fleet	1 = partially agree
		3. Easy booking system	2 = yes
		4. Easy search of parking area in each town area	
		5. Accessible vehicle for all	
		6. High technology applied	
Possible use of car sharing in Enna	Car	Judgment expressed on a Likert scale before and after the advent of the service in the city	0 = impossible
	VAN		1 = partially possible
			2 = medium possible
			3 = high possible

3.1 Before and After Analysis

By comparing the opinions expressed in the two periods of time before and after the advent of shared mobility in Enna, it was possible to apply a transversal analysis to the data and to highlight its evolutions and differences.

The data were collected through online questionnaires and partially through paper questionnaires.

The transversal analysis was based on a reference framework for the study of the implementation components and citizens' attitudes usually found in these transport policies. The cross-sectional (or prevalence) studies are based on the observation of the sample to compare user reviews before and after the use of some transport services.

Prevalence surveys are similar to descriptive studies, but differ from them in that they do not use existing data, but provide the direct survey defined in time. This type of analysis allows to have a general picture in two different time periods but of the same group of subjects under examination (called population or sample), in relation to the studied phenomenon, i.e. the diffusion of shared mobility. The phases of a transversal study can be identified by:

- identification of the problem to be monitored (shared urban mobility with specific reference to car sharing)
- choice of population (i.e. sampling of citizens with preference in this study of people >30 with economic independence living in Enna);
- data collection (through the use of panel-survey)
- data analysis and interpretation (through statistical evaluation and the implementation of appropriate result comparison tables)

3.2 Study Area

The city of Enna is located in a mountain area and consists of 3 large districts, namely Enna Alta which includes the old town on top of the mountain, Enna Bassa on the slopes of the plateau which is home to the university and many shopping centers and finally the district of Pergusa characterized by the presence of the natural lake and green areas and countryside that is a tourist vocation.

The high slope and the climatic and meteorological conditions strongly limit the use of mobility on two wheels for about 5–6 months a year.

The city is inhabited by almost 27 thousand inhabitants and almost 10 thousand students who reside and have their residence 70% in the part of Lower Enna.

The city of Enna has a barycentric position compared to other Sicilian cities, it is characterized from the point of view of transport from a railway station located about 10 km in the outskirts and about 1 h there is the airport of Catania.

Connections with other cities are mainly by private transport or regional buses.

The local public transport is characterized by 5 public urban lines that connect the three districts and the areas most frequented by workers, students and inhabitants. Each bus route is described in Fig. 1.

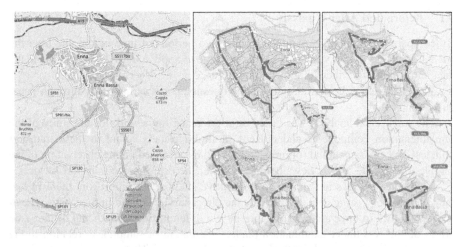

Fig. 1. Local bus service and itineraries (Source: Map data copyrighted OpenStreetMap contributors and available from https://www.openstreetmap.org)

Referring to the terminuses located in the different parts of the city it is possible to observe that generally the Enna Alta/Enna Bassa movement takes place in 30 min (about 6 km) instead the one from Enna Alta/ Pergusa (about 10 km) in 45 min. The urban public transport service ensures only in 50% of the territory one stop every 500 m.

The areas less connected by this type of transport are those of Pergusa and part of Enna Bassa near the railway station. This deficit does not guarantee intermodal transport. The local company offers a discounted season ticket for people over 65 and for high school and university students.

The taxi service with and without driver is rarely used by the local population for travel.

The car and other vehicle rental service is operated by local private companies and is generally preferred by 3% of the population only for occasional activities such as weddings or daily round trips.

Since April 2019 there is a car sharing service with 6 vehicles and a van available for the transfer of people and small goods.

This service managed by a private company (AMIGO-AMAT spa) will also be combined with the bike sharing service that will use pedal assisted bicycles and station based service (Fig. 2).

Fig. 2. Enna with its sub areas and the sharing mobility service

3.3   Data Collection

The survey conducted is therefore configured as a longitudinal survey of panel type on line on google platform and partly of paper type with face to face interview considering the same questions.

The sample was chosen by limiting only the age group or the over-30 s to better assess citizens who tend to have an income and therefore a likely possibility to pay for sharing services.

The interviewed population is resident and therefore excludes commuting workers and university students. The answers were given to a closed questionnaire with single answer to be selected or single answer on Likert scale

- socio-demographic data,
- travel habits
- consideration of the car/van sharing service considering before and after the period.

Through a statistical survey it was possible to compare the judgments as described below.

4 Survey Results

4.1 Descriptive Statistics

Through a descriptive statistical analysis it was possible to obtain results for the different sections of the questionnaire and to prepare an evaluation of the differences in the answers given by the same people before and after the advent of car sharing and van sharing. The data show a homogeneity of data both in terms of gender and age.

4.2 Results

The sample was identified in a causal way and through the compilation of an online survey with the identification of users it was possible to compare the opinions expressed before and after the advent of the sharing service.

The urban context of Enna has been characterized for several decades by the exclusive use of private vehicles.

This phenomenon is linked to the fact that until a few years ago there was no high-frequency urban transport service and its stops were not able to reach certain neighbourhoods.

Moreover, before 2017 the service was marked by long waiting times and delays of more than 15 min per journey. From the point of view of soft mobility, there are several problems related to the absence of sidewalks, high gradients and weather conditions.

The pedestrian area is more widespread in the historic city centre. The socio-demographic data were highlighted in the first section of the survey.

The results show that the totality of the sample lives in Enna (50% Enna high, 40% Enna low and 10% Pergusa). From the working point of view 60% are employees and collaborators.

Gender is defined by 46% of women and 54% of men.

The age group studied covers the range between 30 and over 65 years of age. The first range from 30 to 45 corresponds to 26% of the total sample, the second range from 46 to 65 corresponds to 40% and the third to over 65 with a value of 34%.

Considering the work activities, 59% of the sample works with freelance activities for 36% and employees for 23%.

It has been recorded that over 68% of the sample has a driving licence with over 38% with driving experience between 11 and 20 years and about 25% with 20 years pf experience.

Considering the Italian shared mobility experience, the sample responded positively for 45% as regards car use, 49% as regards bicycle use and about 20% as regards van use. In the foreign sector, on the other hand, there was a reduced value for both the car and the van, respectively 31% and 10% instead of an increase of 55% for the use of bike sharing compared to the national one.

As regards car ownership, it was obtained that 80% of the sample owns a vehicle, while only 25% owns a bicycle.

These data allow us to assume that the ownership of the bike is lower than that of the car is due not only to the travel habits but also to the geographic and geomorphological conditions of the place of residence, which with steep gradients does not facilitate cycling.

Another critical point found in the area is the absence of dedicated lanes. The analysis investigated the travel habits in weekdays and holidays considering the following reasons of home-work (H-W), home-school (H-S) and leisure-time-home (H-L).

During working days about 60% of the population travels by car, 20% by bus and 20% on foot.

On weekdays, the percentage of journeys on foot has risen to 55%.

Among the main reasons for leisure time on weekdays is shopping or going to a hospital/ doctor's surgery, while on public holidays the main reason for leisure is to take a walk in open spaces such as squares and go to church.

The third section analysed the answers of the sample before and after the establishment of the car sharing service in Enna by a private company in collaboration with the Municipality.

The users were asked to express a judgement through Likert scales from 0 to 2 (0 = no, 1 = partially agree and 2 = yes) to see how easy it is to move to Enna with the car sharing service and to evaluate different reasons, a judgement scale from 0 to 3 (0 = impossible; 1 = partially possible; 2 = half possible; 3 = high possible) was evaluated the propensity to use this service.

Table 5 below shows the comparison before and after the judgements in the above section.

As regards the service with a van type vehicle, the results show that the presence of more vans could improve the service as there is higher demand than the current supply. Some criteria marked by (*) have recorded the same values before and after the advent of car sharing in Enna, however, with regard to the tariff, again after the establishment of the service and its use, users agree on the choice of a more advantageous tariff. In the same way, the sample showed a greater need to equip vans with a more innovative technology as described in Table 6.

The judgment of each user regarding the propensity to use the service was assessed as shown below in Table 7.

The shared mobility service is currently used by 15–20% of the population.

The opinion of the sample shows that the sharing mode is not easily used by the inhabitants at the moment.

Table 5. Sample opinion (before and after) about car sharing service

Implementation of a simple car sharing service (enter 0 = no 1 = partially agree or 2 = yes)

Criteria	Before			After			Comparison
	0	1	2	0	1	2	
Advantageous rates	9 (2%)	79 (61%)	282 (76%)	193 (52%)	177 (48%)	0 (0%)	Increase in negative or partial judgment
Presence of city cars in the fleet	19 (5%)	290 (78%)	61 (16%)	86 (23%)	248 (67%)	36 (10%)	
Easy booking system	14 (4%)	225 (61%)	131 (35%)	9 (2%)	169 (46%)	192 (52%)	Increase in positive judgment
Easy park in each town area	16 (4%)	110 (30%)	244 (66%)	142 (38%)	165 (45%)	63 (17%)	Increase in negative or partial judgment
Accessible vehicle for all	23 (6%)	164 (44%)	183 (49%)	211 (57%)	159 (43%)	0 (0%)	
High technology applied	17 (5%)	245 (66%)	108 (29%)	141 (38%)	210 (57%)	19 (0%)	

Table 6. Sample opinion (before and after) about van sharing service

Implementation of a simple van sharing service (enter 0 = no 1 = partially agree or 2 = yes)

Criteria	Before			After			Comparison
	0	1	2	0	1	2	
Advantageous rates	69 (19%)	101 (27%)	200 (54%)	110 (30%)	221 (60%)	39 (11%)	Increase in negative or partial judgment
Presence of van in the fleet (more than one)	38 (10%)	160 (43%)	172 (16%)	37 (10%)	103 (28%)	230 (62%)	Increase in positive judgment
Easy booking system*	14 (4%)	225 (61%)	131 (35%)	9 (2%)	169 (46%)	192 (52%)	
Easy park in each town area *	16 (4%)	110 (30%)	244 (66%)	142 (38%)	165 (45%)	63 (17%)	Increase in negative or partial judgment
Accessible vehicle for all*	23 (6%)	164 (44%)	183 (49%)	211 (57%)	159 (43%)	0 (0%)	
High technology applied	39 (11%)	200 (54%)	131 (35%)	51 (38%)	290 (57%)	29 (5%)	

Table 7. Overall opinion on the possible choice of car sharing service

Possible use of car sharing in Enna (0 = impossible −1 = partially possible −2 = medium possible −3 = high possible)			
User rating	Before	After	Before/after
0	14 (4%)	146 (39%)	D < 0 (−132)
1	98 (26%)	191 (52%)	D < 0 (−93)
2	178 (48%)	33 (9%)	D < 0 (145)
3	80 (22%)	0 (0%)	D < 0 (80)

An improvement of the service could be focused on preventive survey campaigns aimed at mitigating the current problems of the service and to enhance its value as a result of the likely demand for local transport.

In contrast to the choice of van sharing as described in Table 8.

Table 8. overall opinion on the possible choice of van sharing service

Possible use of van sharing in Enna (0 = impossible 1 = partially possible 2 = medium possible 3 = high possible)			
User rating	Before	After	Before/after
0	21 (6%)	18 (5%)	D < 0 (3)
1	75 (20%)	105 (28%)	D < 0 (−30)
2	168 (45%)	189 (51%)	D < 0 (−21)
3	106 (29%)	58 (16%)	D < 0 (48)

5 Discussion

This work shows a description of the spread of shared mobility by considering the opinions of the population through a longitudinal before-and-after analysis.

The bottom-up approach in the field of mobility, which involves citizens in judging a service, has shown that it can contribute to the planning phase of a city's transport systems, highlighting some critical issues related to the place of application and providing benefits applicable to future political strategies of the city. The implementation of a car sharing system must include an upstream analysis of users in order to calibrate the service offer and thus increase its attractiveness.

Although the service applied in the Enna context is a mixed station-based and free floating service, there is a serious problem regarding costs and availability of parking in some areas.

The design hypothesis of defining an integrated car and bike sharing service is not easy to implement due to the high gradient of the roads and the lack of dedicated lanes.

The bike sharing service could be implemented only in the lower part of Enna Bassa and Pergusa assuming alternative cycling routes, not related to vehicular mobility (use of secondary roads instead of state and municipal roads). A reduction in the cost of the subscription and a reshaping of the fare were requested by the sample of users, as well as the desire to have a service with a small engine and manual gearbox.

A positive opinion was expressed about the van service that should be characterized by an increase in the number of vehicles in the fleet managed by the company. This cross-cutting analysis confirms the need to attach great importance to the implementation of participatory planning through the collaboration of citizens, in order to optimize and mitigate the critical issues related to transport decisions taken or to be taken. The inclusion of electric bikes and micro-mobility within the service will ensure short distance journeys where there is no great variation in gradient, reducing the use of private cars. It also highlights some practices that suggest ways of future research, expanding the sample and the time to be analyzed.

Acknowledgments. This study was supported by the MIUR (Ministry of Education, Universities and Research [Italy]) through a project entitled WEAKI TRANSIT: WEAK-demand areas Innovative TRANsport Shared services for Italian Towns (Project code: 20174ARRHT/CUP Code: J74I19000320008), financed with the PRIN 2017 (Research Projects of National Relevance) programme. We authorize the MIUR to reproduce and distribute reprints for Governmental purposes, notwithstanding any copyright notations thereon. Any opinions, findings and conclusions or recommendations expressed in this material are those of the authors, and do not necessarily reflect the views of the MIUR.

References

This paper is the result of the joint work of the authors. 'Abstract' 'Introduction' 'Methodology' and 'Results' were written jointly by the authors. TC focused on the state of the art. GT designed the methodological approach and discussion. Supervision and research funding TC and GT.

1. Papa, R., Gargiulo, C., Russo, L.: The evolution of smart mobility strategies and behaviors to build the smart city. In: 2017 5th IEEE International Conference on Models and Technologies for Intelligent Transportation Systems (MT-ITS), pp. 409–414. IEEE, June 2017. https://doi.org/10.1109/MTITS.2017.8005707
2. Campisi, T., Acampa, G., Marino, G., Tesoriere, G.: Cycling master plans in Italy: the I-BIM feasibility tool for cost and safety assessments. Sustainability **12**(11), 4723 (2020)
3. Vaitsis, P., Basbas, S., Nikiforiadis, A.: How eudaimonic aspect of subjective well-being affect transport mode choice? The case of Thessaloniki, Greece. Soc. Sci. **8**(1), 9 (2019). https://doi.org/10.3390/socsci8010009
4. Ignaccolo, M., Inturri, G., Giuffrida, N., Le Pira, M., Torrisi, V.: Public engagement for designing new transport services: investigating citizen preferences from a multiple criteria perspective. Transp. Res. Procedia **37**, 91–98 (2019). https://doi.org/10.1016/j.trpro.2018.12.170
5. Tesoriere, G., Campisi, T., Canale, A., Zgrablić, T.: The surrogate safety appraisal of the unconventional elliptical and turbo roundabouts. J. Adv. Transp. (2018). https://doi.org/10.1155/2018/2952074

6. Campisi, T., Deluka-Tibljaš, A., Tesoriere, G., Canale, A., Rencelj, M., Šurdonja, S.: Cycling traffic at turbo roundabouts: some considerations related to cyclist mobility and safety. Transp. Res. Procedia **45**, 627–634 (2020). https://doi.org/10.1016/j.trpro.2020.03.048

7. Tesoriere, G., Canale, A., Severino, A., Mrak, I., Campisi, T.: The management of pedestrian emergency through dynamic assignment: some consideration about the "Refugee Hellenism" Square of Kalamaria (Greece). In: AIP Conference Proceedings, vol. 2186, no. 1, p. 160004. AIP Publishing LLC, December 2019. https://doi.org/10.1063/1.5138072

8. Campisi, T., Canale, A., Tesoriere, G., Lovric, I., Čutura, B.: The importance of assessing the level of service in confined infrastructures: some considerations of the Old Ottoman Pedestrian Bridge of Mostar. Appl. Sci. **9**(8), 1630 (2019). https://doi.org/10.3390/app9081630

9. Pau, G., Campisi, T., Canale, A., Severino, A., Collotta, M., Tesoriere, G.: Smart pedestrian crossing management at traffic light junctions through a fuzzy-based approach. Fut. Internet **10**(2), 15 (2018). https://doi.org/10.3390/fi10020015

10. Pinna, F., Masala, F., Garau, C.: Urban policies and mobility trends in Italian smart cities. Sustainability **9**(4), 494 (2017). https://doi.org/10.3390/su9040494

11. Breuer, J., Walravens, N., Ballon, P.: Beyond defining the smart city. Meeting top-down and bottom-up approaches in the middle. Tema. J. Land Use Mob. Environ. (2014)

12. Van Brussel, S., Boelens, L., Lauwers, D.: Evolution of mobility governance in Flanders: opening up for bottom-up initiatives or suffering from lock-in? In: Real Corp 2015. CORP (2015)

13. Rahman, M.T., Nahiduzzaman, K.: Examining the walking accessibility, willingness, and travel conditions of residents in Saudi cities. Int. J. Environ. Res. Public Health **16**(4), 545 (2019). https://doi.org/10.3390/ijerph16040545

14. Garau, C., Annunziata, A., Coni, M.: A methodological framework for assessing practicability of the urban space: the survey on conditions of practicable environments (SCOPE) procedure applied in the case study of Cagliari (Italy). Sustainability **10**(11), 4189 (2018). https://doi.org/10.3390/su10114189

15. Mrak, I., Campisi, T., Tesoriere, G., Canale, A., Cindrić, M.: The role of urban and social factors in the accessibility of urban areas for people with motor and visual disabilities. In: AIP Conference Proceedings, vol. 2186, no. 1, p. 160008. AIP Publishing LLC, December 2019. https://doi.org/10.1063/1.5138076

16. Ghorbanzadeh, O., Moslem, S., Blaschke, T., Duleba, S.: Sustainable urban transport planning considering different stakeholder groups by an interval-AHP decision support model. Sustainability **11**(1), 9 (2019). https://doi.org/10.3390/su11010009

17. Alfian, G., Rhee, J., Kang, Y.S., Yoon, B.: Performance comparison of reservation based and instant access one-way car sharing service through discrete event simulation. Sustainability **7**(9), 12465–12489 (2015). https://doi.org/10.3390/su70912465

18. Roscia, M., Lazaroiu, G.C., Mingrone, L., Pignataro, G.: Innovative approach of the sharing e-mobility. In: 2016 International Symposium on Power Electronics, Electrical Drives, Automation and Motion (SPEEDAM), pp. 1120–1126. IEEE, June 2016 https://doi.org/10.1109/SPEEDAM.2016.7526011

19. Campisi, T., Torrisi, V., Ignaccolo, M., Inturri, G., Tesoriere, G.: University propensity assessment to car sharing services using mixed survey data: the Italian case study of Enna city. Transp. Res. Procedia **47**, 433–444 (2020). https://doi.org/10.1016/j.trpro.2020.03.155

20. Canale, A., Tesoriere, G., Campisi, T.: The MAAS development as a mobility solution based on the individual needs of transport users. In: AIP Conference Proceedings, vol. 2186, no. 1, p. 160005. AIP Publishing LLC, December 2019. https://doi.org/10.1063/1.5138073

21. Paundra, J., Rook, L., van Dalen, J., Ketter, W.: Preferences for car sharing services: effects of instrumental attributes and psychological ownership. J. Environ. Psychol. **53**, 121–130 (2017). https://doi.org/10.1016/j.jenvp.2017.07.003
22. Jestico, B., Nelson, T., Winters, M.: Mapping ridership using crowdsourced cycling data. J. Transp. Geogr. **52**, 90–97 (2016). https://doi.org/10.1016/j.jtrangeo.2016.03.006
23. Nash, A.: How Crowdsourcing Can Help Public Transport Innovate Success-fully in an Era of Rapid Change (No. 17-00453) (2017)
24. Bertram, D.: Likert scales (2007). Accessed 2 Nov 2013

i-CHANGE: A Platform for Managing Dockless Bike Sharing Systems

Lazaros Apostolidis[1]([✉]), Symeon Papadopoulos[1]([✉]), Maria Liatsikou[1]([✉]),
Ioannis Fyrogenis[2]([✉]), Efthymis Papadopoulos[2]([✉]), George Keikoglou[3]([✉]),
Konstantinos Alexiou[3]([✉]), Nasos Chondros[3]([✉]), Ioannis Kompatsiaris[1]([✉]),
and Ioannis Politis[2]([✉])

[1] Centre for Research and Technology Hellas, Thessaloniki, Greece
{laaposto,papadop,maria_liatsikou,ikom}@iti.gr
[2] Aristotle University of Thessaloniki, Thessaloniki, Greece
{fyrogeni,efthympg,pol}@civil.auth.gr
[3] Brainbox Technology, Kalamaria, Greece
{gkeikoglou,kostas,nasos}@brainbox.gr

Abstract. The new generation of bike-sharing services without docking stations is spreading around large cities of the world. The paper provides a technical specification of a platform, for managing a dockless bike sharing system. The bicycles of the platform are equipped with GPS devices and GPRS cards that can transmit, over the Internet, their exact location at any time. We collect and store all events derived from a user's interaction with the system and in addition the trajectory points of a route during a rent order. The platform aims to fulfill the requirements of bikers, administrators and the research community through the collection, analysis and exploitation of bike sharing data.

In the context of the platform, an app for smart devices is implemented for citizens to access the system. A dashboard is offered to the administrator as a valuable tool to inspect, promote the system and evaluate its usage. Last, all stored anonymised data can be accessible for further analysis by the research community through a REST API. The i-CHANGE platform is currently pilot tested in the city of Thessaloniki, Greece.

Keywords: Micromobility · Bike sharing · Dockless systems · API · IT system

1 Introduction

The rapid population growth combined with the increase of urbanization makes the need for mobility in existing transportation networks increasingly challenging. Residents of large cities are facing the problem of traffic congestion in daily commuting. Thus, micromobility is gradually becoming popular worldwide due to a series of benefits that it offers for everyday commuting compared to the

© Springer Nature Switzerland AG 2020
O. Gervasi et al. (Eds.): ICCSA 2020, LNCS 12250, pp. 851–867, 2020.
https://doi.org/10.1007/978-3-030-58802-1_61

traditional transportation modes, like cars, buses and trains. Micromobility is a term which refers to light-weight means of transportation, such as bicycles and scooters, designed for individual use. It is a cost effective alternative, especially for last-mile trips. Besides cost, citizens save time, avoid traffic congestion and emissions are reduced. Bike-sharing has been gaining ground lately as a sustainable and environmentally friendly urban transportation mode. Bicycles available for hiring are distributed within cities by companies which offer micromobility sharing services.

Recently, technological platforms have been developed to enhance urban mobility. The authors in [10] propose a methodological approach with respect to a real-time traffic monitoring and supervising system, which also offers *"info-mobility"* services. The tools which are incorporated include traffic and environmental monitoring and management, vehicle routing, real-time minimum path calculation, etc. Several smart mobility sharing platforms have also been developed since the emergence of micromobility services. In this paper we present i-CHANGE, an integrated platform for managing a dockless bike sharing system, which attempts to serve both the users' and administrator needs in a large variety of aspects, but also to fulfill research needs by offering valuable insights with respect to transportation patterns.

Bicycles of the system have a lock integrated in their frame for securing the bicycle anywhere (inside a defined geo-fenced area) without the need of a docking station. The platform is designed for better system inspection (e.g. information around completed orders) and for providing critical information (e.g. possibly damaged or stolen bicycles) to the administrator. It is built to promote sustainable transportation by replacing the main traditional option of private car with bicycle and change the ownership approach and philosophy with the approach of sharing.

The study of established relevant platforms for good practices was the first step in the design process of the platform. The next step was the analysis of user requirements, both for riders and the administrator of the system, as well as the consideration of hardware and software needs and limitations. The platform also serves the research community by making its data available, always in compliance with the GDPR regulation[1] for protecting personal information.

2   Related Work

Micromobility is a rapidly growing field of urban transportation research. There has been a plethora of work related to various bike-sharing research problems. Early work refers to the generations of bike-sharing and its growth, bike-share usage and user preferences in various cities, barriers with respect to safety concerns and helmet legislation. Other works evaluate the impacts of bike-sharing on car use reduction and health and investigate the rebalancing problem [2]. Recently, dockless bike-sharing services have emerged as the last generation of

---

[1] https://gdpr.eu/.

these services. The lack of stations provides more flexibility to users and overcomes other barriers like limited budget and space for infrastructure. A considerable body of literature has studied various aspects of such services [1,3,5,6,9,11].

Numerous studies have examined the implications of dockless bike-sharing services. Mobike, which is one of the largest dockless bike-sharing companies, has written a white paper [3] with the support of the China New Urbanization Research Institute and Tsinghua University, based on analysis conducted on the trip data and user questionnaires in 36 cities in China. It presents the effects of bike-sharing on people's travel behavior, urban environment, pollution decrease and energy saving. This report provides statistics about user profiles and their trip purposes, bike and car usage as a result of bike-sharing expansion, integration of a dockless system with public transportation and its effect on carbon footprint reduction and energy saving.

As datasets are becoming available, studies started investigating the spatial and temporal patterns of bike usage. A study conducted on real time data from a major dockless bike operator in Singapore analyzed the spatiotemporal patterns on the system usage [9]. The impacts of built environment, access to public transportation and weather conditions on the spatiotemporal distribution of trip demand have been examined. The results reveal that diverse land use, easy access to public transport and supportive cycling facilities positively affect bike usage. A recent work [6] focused on identifying spatiotemporal similarities and differences in the activity patterns of six micromobility sharing services, including five operators of dockless electric scooters and one of dockless electric bikes, operating within Washington D.C. The bicycle service offers a far smaller vehicle fleet than the scooter services (the proportion is less than 35%) but it is used for longer trips, as its average trip distance and duration are much longer. The bike-sharing service presents generally different spatiotemporal patterns from the scooter-sharing services, explained by the operating difference between the two modes. Moreover, the difference in travel time between micromobility and ride-hailing services was examined, revealing that the former are faster on average during weekday rush hours for conducting short trips in the city center.

A large body of studies has focused on the prediction of the travel demand of the dockless bike-sharing systems leveraging the existence of relevant datasets. This is a spatiotemporal data mining task, offering valuable information for the development of efficient rebalancing strategies. Statistical techniques have been applied [9], but they have recently been replaced by more advanced machine learning approaches due to their powerful feature learning capabilities, especially in the case of large amounts of available data [11]. Hybrid deep learning models have been applied on GPS data of bike sharing operators in cities of China to address both temporal and spatial dependencies of the bike-sharing systems. Two recent works leveraged GPS data of bike sharing operators in cities of China to predict the spatiotemporal distribution of dockless bike-sharing [1,5].

A number of relevant software platforms for bike-sharing management have also been studied. These platforms are BLOOM[2], Joyride[3], HOPR[4] and LINKA[5]. Table 1 summarizes the features included in these platforms. It is evident from the table that none of the platforms has managed to support all of them.

Table 1. Features of bike-sharing management platforms.

Features/platform	BLOOM	Joyride	HOPR	LINKA
Real-time tracking	✓	✓	✓	✓
Statistics for admin/rider	✓	✓	✓	✓
Live alerts from users	✓	✓	✓	✓
Geo-fencing	✓	✓	✓	✓
Bike reservations	✓		✓	
Location-based ads	✓	✓		
Incentives for good etiquette			✓	
Maintenance and technician App				✓

The established practices along with user requirements and the research community needs were taken into consideration in the design of the i-CHANGE platform. As a result, i-CHANGE is a complete smart mobility sharing platform, which incorporates most of the features mentioned in Table 1 and more than that, such as an interactive map with various useful features for the application users and a social media monitoring service for the system administrator. In addition, it includes features derived from traffic analysis on the area where the system operates and data mining techniques applied on the collected data of the system. In the following sections the architecture of i-CHANGE platform along with the system components and their services are thoroughly described.

3   i-CHANGE System Architecture

The i-CHANGE platform is designed to support the operation of a dockless bike sharing system. Bicycles are strategically placed at different locations, covering a large geo-fenced area. Riders can start and terminate a rent at any point inside that area. Each bicycle has a GPS device, a GPRS card and a controller for handling events (e.g. unlock the bicycle on demand) integrated in their frame. Figure 1 depicts a high-level view of the system architecture.

---

[2] http://bloom.bike/.
[3] https://joyride.city/.
[4] https://gohopr.com/.
[5] https://www.linkafleets.com/.

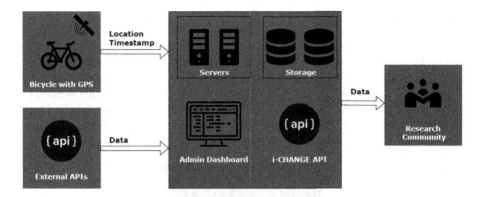

Fig. 1. System architecture of i-CHANGE.

Every time a user interacts with a bicycle (e.g. unlock), the exact location (in terms of latitude and longitude) is calculated from the GPS device, the timestamp of the event is attached and the data are transmitted with the help of the GPRS card to the system servers where they are stored. While a bicycle is rented, its location is periodically recorded to get the trajectory points.

The stored data derived from the users' rents are enriched with data from external APIs (e.g. weather data). The combined data could lead to useful information through additional analysis. The system implements an API for publishing the stored data for research exploitation and a dashboard to serve the needs of the admin user for system monitoring.

From the analysis of stored data, personal information about the users of the system could be potentially extracted. Working hours or home location could for instance be revealed in a relatively straightforward way. In order to prevent private information leaks and protect users, the data is anonymised before being exposed through the API. A unique identifier is assigned to each user of the system. All the identifiers are replaced with new ones on a daily basis. As a result, recurring routes cannot be attributed to specific users. Moreover, explicit personal information (e.g. email) is not accessible outside the system.

4   i-CHANGE Platform

The i-CHANGE platform integrates all the components of the system. It provides an app for smart devices to users. Through this app bikers have access to a set of useful geospatial information and traffic insights. Furthermore, through the i-CHANGE dashboard, the admin users can evaluate the system status, check statistics, manage promotional campaigns (e.g. free vouchers), evaluate the effect of actions taken, get meaningful insights, understand user needs and reach social media content referring to relevant topics (e.g. bike sharing platforms). The research community may have access to bike mobility data through an API.

4.1   Application

To successfully interact with the bike sharing system, users have to install an app on their device. The data that a user has to fill in order to create an account, include the full name, the email, a selected password and a confirmation of it and a telephone number. Moreover, users have to explicitly declare that they accept the terms of use of the app. The app is named EazymovGR and can be found on the App Store[6] for iOS devices and on Google Play[7] for Android devices.

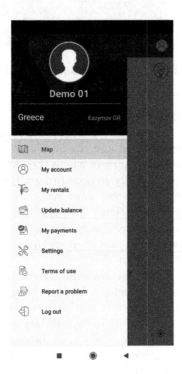

Fig. 2. Menu from app for smart devices.

The app implements a menu (see Fig. 2) through which a user can:

– Create an account. The mandatory fields are a name, a valid email address[8], a password and a contact number. The user has to accept the terms of use, before registering into the system.
– Log in to account. With the email and password used in the registration, users can access their accounts. The app offers password reset functionality.

---

[6] https://apps.apple.com/us/app/eazymovgr/id1492459234?ls=1.

[7] https://play.google.com/store/apps/details?id=gr.brainbox.eazymovandroid.

[8] App checks for valid email formats name@domain and if no other registered user exists with the same address.

- See the exact locations of the bicycles in the map and the level of battery for each one. Moreover, users can get the unique identifier of each bicycle (it is also printed on the bicycle frame), to locate it among others when there are many stacked in a very short distance.
- Unlock a bicycle. By scanning a QR code that is located in the bicycle frame a user can initiate a rent. For reading the QR code, the camera of the smart device is used. In low light conditions the app can open the device flashlight.
- Terminate an order. By locking the bicycle manually, the app notifies the biker that the bicycle is locked and the order has successfully ended. Upon termination of an order, time and cost are displayed.
- See history of rentals. Information accompanying each rental includes the bicycle unique identifier, the timestamp that has started and ended, the duration and the cost.
- Update their balance. Users can top up their accounts by selecting one of the predefined amounts[9]. Through a secure payment system users fill their credit card details and if the charge is successful the corresponding amount is added to the user's balance.
- See history of payments. For every payment, the app displays the timestamp and the amount charged.
- Modify account information. A user can change the information that has been provided in the step of registration, like setting a new password.
- Report problems in bicycles. Each bicycle is divided into 14 control points[10]. A user can select the number of the bicycle part that has failed, include a small description of the problem and submit the report. The app then notifies the administrator to take action and repair the bicycle, if necessary.
- Read the Terms of Use they have agreed to.
- Log out. Users can log out from their accounts at any time.

4.2   Traffic Macro-based Data

A novel part of the i-CHANGE approach is the combination of micro-based mobility data (e.g. trajectories of rides) with macro-based strategic traffic data. Within the context of the i-CHANGE platform, a strategic macroscopic traffic simulation model was developed for the city of Thessaloniki with the use of the software PTV Visum[11]. Based on the traditional four-step travel demand model and the study of human behavior, the area where the system is established was divided in 370 different traffic zones (see Fig. 3). Based on the software and the analysis made, information about trips between each zone (and in-zone) was extracted. The implemented traffic model includes three transportation modes: private car, public transportation and walking. For each one of them, transportation time and cost are calculated from/to each traffic zone.

---

[9] Choice among 2, 5, 10, 20 and 50 Euro.

[10] Mudguard, Large Basket, Exposure Area, Bicycle Frame, Electrical Assistance, Brakes, Lights, Seat Height Adjustment Lever, Saddle, Kickstand, Front Wheel, Rear Wheel, Lock.

[11] https://www.ptvgroup.com/en/solutions/products/ptv-visum/.

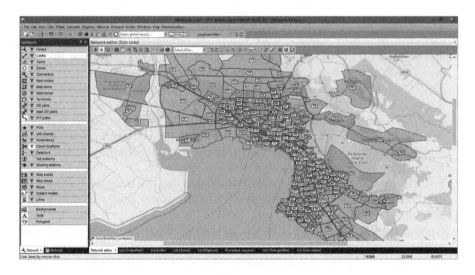

Fig. 3. Calculated traffic zones extracted from VISUM software.

Table 2. The components of traffic simulation matrices.

Component	Comments
Driving time in minutes	–
Driving cost in Euros	The cost is calculated based on an equation that models distance and fuel consumption
Bus riding duration	The diagonal of this array is always zero because in-zone trips are not conducted by bus due to the small coverage of the calculated traffic zones. Negative cell value (-1) indicates no bus connection between the two zones
Bus riding cost in Euros	Costs are summed if more than one bus is required to complete the trip. The diagonal of this array is always zero. Negative value (-1) in a cell means that a bus connection between the zones does not exist
Walking duration in minutes	–
Walking cost in Euros	All values of this table have zero values, as walking does not have any measured cost

Six skim matrices were constructed with dimensions 370×370 (all the pairs of traffic zones). For example, the value in cell $<200, 302>$ in the matrix of transportation cost with private car declares the cost in Euro needed for moving from zone 200 to zone 302. Values in the diagonal represent metrics for intrazonal trips. Table 2 contains the components of the six matrices.

The i-CHANGE platform uses these arrays for comparing time and cost metrics of renting one of the system bicycles, with the corresponding values of other transportation mode choices. When an order is completed, a visualization (Fig. 4) is presented that summarizes how much time and money is saved or lost compared to the case the user had conducted the same trip from one zone to another making a different choice (private car, bus, walking). Users can inspect the exact deviation in minutes and Euros.

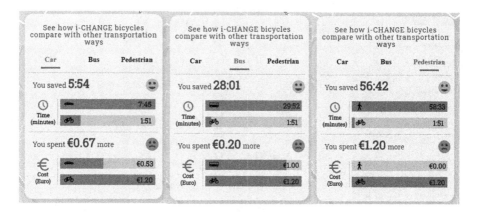

Fig. 4. Time and cost comparison of i-CHANGE bikes with other modes of transport.

4.3 Interactive Map

Through an interactive map that is integrated in the app for smart devices, users can access a series of helpful information that are relative to their exact location (extracted from the device GPS). Figure 5 depicts an instance of the map that contains all the information. For easier interpretation, different icons and colors have been assigned to each type of information. The users can select to show only specific information on the map, by ticking the corresponding entry from the menu on the left. Moreover, they can close the menu to view the map in full screen. Zoom and pan functionalities are implemented for easier map navigation.

The i-CHANGE platform communicates with various external APIs in order to collect the information that is included in the map. This consists of the following:

- The exact locations of the i-CHANGE bicycles that are closest to the user's location. For each one of them, the distance from his/her location, the level of battery and the serial number are displayed.
- Alternative transportation. The closest to the user's location bus stations and bus lines are shown on the map. For each station the corresponding distance and its name are shown, and for each bus line the name, number, route length and direction are displayed. In the area where i-CHANGE is established, another bike sharing system (with docking stations) is in operation. For this system the map shows the location of the closest to the user's location stations and for each one of them it shows the corresponding distance, the available bikes and the name.
- Weather forecast. Temperature and weather description (e.g. partly cloudy) for the user's current location and for a time window of 3 h ahead, are displayed.

Fig. 5. Interactive map with geographical information.

- Infrastructure. The established bike lane network is projected on the map.
- Points of interest. Exploiting public data offered by Foursquare[12], users get the locations of the closest points of interest (e.g. restaurants). For each one of them, the distance from the user's location, the name and the address are displayed.

4.4 Data Processing and Mining

The i-CHANGE platform collects and stores a large amount of data that derives from users' interaction with the system. With the use of data mining algorithms, useful insights can be extracted like transportation patterns. Two visualizations are implemented into the admin dashboard, with the first one analyzing the timestamps of orders and the second one their locations.

Figure 6 depicts the visualization for the time analysis. Orders are aggregated by hour of the day (00:00–23:00) and day of week (Monday - Sunday). Admin users can easily understand rush hours, prepare the system for periods with high demands or schedule the maintenance and rebalancing of the bicycles when the system needs are low. Selecting a time window is also possible, for monitoring specific periods of time (e.g. weekends) and seeing how rush hours are changing.

Figure 7 depicts the spatial analysis of the rents' starting points locations. The area, in which the bike sharing system is established is divided into a set of clusters, so that the distance between points in the same cluster is minimized and the distance between points in different clusters is maximized [4, 12]. Cluster coloring is based on the number of starting points inside it. The administrator can inspect which areas need a larger volume of bicycles and which less, to plan a more efficient placement of bicycles according to users' needs. The administrator can also select a specific time window to see how clusters are modified.

---

[12] https://foursquare.com/.

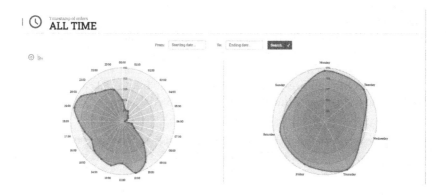

Fig. 6. Time analysis of orders.

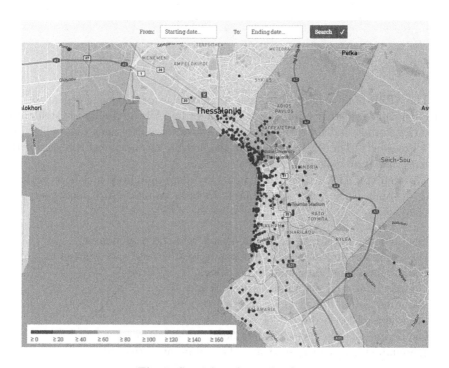

Fig. 7. Spatial analysis of orders.

4.5   API

The i-CHANGE platform provides controlled access to all the stored (anonymised) data that comes from users' rents. To this end, an API has been defined and implemented. To obtain access to the API and its data, it is mandatory to register an account with the system. The permission is given only to accredited personnel. The API only accepts requests that originate from users with verified accounts and respecting the defined rate limit (180 calls per 15 min). Figure 8 depicts a user account with access to the API.

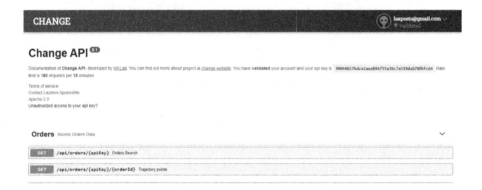

Fig. 8. User account with API access to orders data

The API is built to handle two specific calls. One for retrieving orders and one for retrieving trajectory points for a specific order. All the results are structured in JSON format and have the necessary informative messages (e.g. when rate limit exceeded). The API implements pagination to customize the size of the response based on caller needs.

Through the API a user can search for orders matching specific criteria. A series of input parameters are available to filter results. More specifically, the user can set:

- The number of returned orders in a page and the page number.
- The minimum and maximum timestamp of start and end event of an order.
- The minimum and maximum order time.
- The minimum and maximum order distance
- The minimum and maximum order cost.
- The status of the order.
- The unique bicycle and user identifiers.
- A bounding box for the start and the end point of the order.

The response consists of an array of orders that matches the input parameters. For each one of them, the API returns the distance, time and cost, the bicycle, user[13] and order unique identifier and the exact location and timestamp of start and end point.

The second call provides information for a specific order. More specifically, it returns all the trajectory points of the route of an order. The only input parameter that is required is the unique identifier of the order the user is interested in. The response consists of an array with all the trajectory points. For each one of them the exact location (latitude and longitude) and the corresponding timestamp are returned.

Both calls include in the response informative messages for the (developer) user: Messages that describe the status of the call (e.g. successful), all the input parameters, the remaining calls before hitting the rate limit and the time left to refresh the number of calls back to zero.

4.6   Admin Dashboard

For the administrator of the system, the i-CHANGE platform provides a dashboard that summarizes and presents via various visualizations all the stored data. The dashboard includes notifications, aggregate statistics, maps, information for registered users, completed rents, bicycles and users of the i-CHANGE API. Figure 9 depicts an instance of the dashboard and menu.

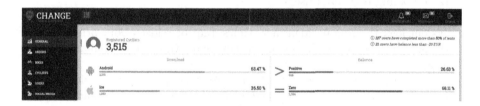

Fig. 9. Admin dashboard of i-CHANGE and its menu.

From the menu the administrator is able to access data for:

– General statistics. The number of registered users, the percentage of them that has positive, negative and zero balance in their accounts and the percentage of the platform they are using (iOS, Android, Web) are displayed. The number of orders and how many of them were completed or cancelled is presented along with the average ride time, distance and cost. The location of the available bicycles is shown in a map and for each one of them the status of their battery.
– Completed orders. Two maps with zoom and pan functionalities are offered. The first one is a heatmap that shows all the intermediate points of the routes during rents and the second one all the start and end points of rents. Orders can be filtered by time so that the two maps include data from a specific time

---

[13] It refers to the identifier after the process of anonymisation.

window only. Moreover, a timeline shows the number of completed rents and data can be aggregated for 6 h, one day and one week. The admin user can focus on a specific time window and zoom the timeline at convenience.

– Bicycles. A table is presented containing one record for every bicycle of the system. The table columns include bicycle unique identifier, serial number, status, level of battery, total distance covered, total time used, number of orders completed, if any action needs to be taken (e.g. maintenance) and its exact location in the map. By selecting a bicycle, all orders that have been completed with this bike are shown in another table. For each order the administrator gets its unique identifier, serial number, status, the unique identifier of user that made the order, the start and end timestamp, the distance covered, the total time and cost. In addition, a map showing the exact route followed is revealed by clicking a specific order. The table implements searching and sorting functionalities.

– Registered users. For each user that has created an account in the system, the administrator can inspect the unique identifier, the platform used for registration, the timestamp of registration, the balance and the numbers of orders completed. Like bicycles, by selecting one user's record the system returns all the orders that are completed by the specific user combined with a heatmap showing the areas that he/she is mostly active in when renting a bicycle. Searching and sorting functionalities are also implemented for the table holding registered users.

– API users. For each user using the API of the i-CHANGE platform, the system logs the unique identifier, timestamp of registration, private key, if the account is verified, the email and how many times the rate limit has been exceed.

– Social media content. The i-CHANGE platform implements a service for monitoring and searching over the social media platforms of Twitter and YouTube. The administrator can set a list of keywords around a topic (e.g. bike sharing systems) and relevant content posted on Twitter and YouTube will be gathered and indexed minutes after it is published. The administrator can modify the list at any time, by adding or removing keywords. Based on the active list of keywords, all relevant posts related are presented, including metadata (time of publication, author, etc.).

Through the dashboard, the administrator can also receive notifications and messages. Notifications include actions that need immediate attention, like when an unusually long order is noticed and probably the user forgot to lock the bicycle and terminate the rent. Messages include information for the system, like when a new user creates an account for using the API.

4.7 Social Media Monitoring

The i-CHANGE platform integrates an open source solution [8] for monitoring relevant content from popular social media networks (e.g. Twitter). The collection of posts takes place in real time. With the formation of appropriate API calls, the framework continuously tracks the social media platforms, while at the same time it respects the set API usage rate limits. As soon as a relevant post is uploaded, it is collected (seconds to minutes after its publication). In addition to the text of the publication, the framework collects information about the users that published them, the embedded media items and the linked URLs.

The i-CHANGE administrator provides as input a list of keywords/hashtags to track, and the social media monitoring framework fetches relevant content from social media platforms by querying the respective platform API. The list can be edited at any time, by adding or removing keywords. All gathered posts are stored inside a common pool of content that is indexed and is then easy to query using the open-source Solr library[14]. A simple "feed" interface enables the administrator to browse through the collected posts and filter based on keyword/phrase, as well as on other criteria.

Using the social media monitoring framework, the administrator can track online conversations about the system of bicycles in order to gain insights from influencers, identify bikers' and citizens' concerns and more. Users of the bike sharing system that had a bad experience and report it in social media can be identified, so that the administrator can contact them to get feedback on their experience and, if appropriate, try to compensate them (e.g. provide a free ride). The feedback can also be used to avoid having disappointed users in the future. Besides posts with negative experiences, the administrator can learn about the operation of the system and even discover new ways of promoting it to new users. Another use of the framework is market research and intelligence. For instance, the administrator could monitor competitors' social media campaigns and take appropriate actions (e.g. promotional vouchers).

5 Future Work

In the future, we plan to examine a wider variety of algorithms for data mining and apply them to the collected data of the system. The algorithms will be rated based on outcomes and how they can help the administrator make the operation of the system optimal, fulfil users' needs and maximize gains. New visualizations will be added to the dashboard, providing new ways of exploring the stored data. Bike-sharing demand will be spatially and temporally modeled in order to make short-term predictions. Outlier detection will be applied for identifying rare data deviating significantly from the "average" behaviour [7].

Future steps also include activities to promote the system to new users and engage even more the already registered ones. The tasks cover the following:

- Bicycle pre-booking. Users will be able to reserve a bicycle for a short time. In this period the bicycle cannot be rented by anyone else. Pre-booking ensures that the bicycle will remain available while this user is directed to it.
- Gamification. Integrate game mechanics into the platform to motivate participation, engagement, and loyalty of users.

---

[14] https://lucene.apache.org/solr/.

- Increase use for commuting trips. Provide motivation for citizens to use bicycle for their daily commutes to and from work.
- Recreational transportation. Attract citizens to use bicycles for recreation.
- Approaching high altitude inaccessible areas with the supply of electric bicycles.
- Provide access to disabled citizens with the supply of bicycles produced for people with disabilities or limitations.
- Rebalancing of bicycles. As the platform is based on a dockless system, the problem of bicycle imbalance is critical and results to significant impact on service quality and company revenue. A model for bicycle rebalancing that reduces cost and maximizes administrator gain will be developed.
- Maintenance plan. Based on historic data, a model that predicts when a bicycle might need maintenance will be developed.

Acknowledgements. This research was co-financed by the European Regional Development Fund of the European Union and Greek national funds through the Operational Program Competitiveness, Entrepreneurship and Innovation, under the call RESEARCH – CREATE – INNOVATE (project code:T1EDK-04582)

References

1. Ai, Y., et al.: A deep learning approach on short-term spatiotemporal distribution forecasting of dockless bike-sharing system. Neural Comput. Appl. **31**(5), 1665–1677 (2018). https://doi.org/10.1007/s00521-018-3470-9
2. Fishman, E.: Bikeshare: a review of recent literature. Transp. Rev. **36**(1), 92–113 (2016)
3. Global, M.: Beijing Tsinghua Tongheng Planning and Design Institute, & China New Urbanization Research Institute, 19 May 2017. The mobike white paper: Bikeshare in the city
4. Han, J., Kamber, M., Tung, A.K.: Spatial clustering methods in data mining. In: Geographic Data Mining and Knowledge Discovery, pp. 188–217 (2001)
5. Li, Y., Shuai, B.: Origin and destination forecasting on dockless shared bicycle in a hybrid deep-learning algorithms. Multimed. Tools Appl. **79**, 5269–5280 (2018)
6. McKenzie, G.: Urban mobility in the sharing economy: a spatiotemporal comparison of shared mobility services. Comput. Environ. Urban Syst. **79**, 101418 (2020)
7. Roy, P.R., Bilodeau, G.-A.: Road user abnormal trajectory detection using a deep autoencoder. In: Bebis, G., et al. (eds.) ISVC 2018. LNCS, vol. 11241, pp. 748–757. Springer, Cham (2018). https://doi.org/10.1007/978-3-030-03801-4_65
8. Schinas, M., Papadopoulos, S., Apostolidis, L., Kompatsiaris, Y., Mitkas, P.A.: Open-source monitoring, search and analytics over social media. In: Kompatsiaris, I., et al. (eds.) INSCI 2017. LNCS, vol. 10673, pp. 361–369. Springer, Cham (2017). https://doi.org/10.1007/978-3-319-70284-1_28
9. Shen, Y., Zhang, X., Zhao, J.: Understanding the usage of dockless bike sharing in Singapore. Int. J. Sustain. Transp. **12**(9), 686–700 (2018)
10. Torrisi, V., Ignaccolo, M., Inturri, G.: Innovative transport systems to promote sustainable mobility: developing the model architecture of a traffic control and supervisor system. In: Gervasi, O., et al. (eds.) ICCSA 2018. LNCS, vol. 10962, pp. 622–638. Springer, Cham (2018). https://doi.org/10.1007/978-3-319-95168-3_42

11. Xu, C., Ji, J., Liu, P.: The station-free sharing bike demand forecasting with a deep learning approach and large-scale datasets. Transp. Res. Part C: Emerg. Technol. **95**, 47–60 (2018)
12. Xu, R., Wunsch, D.: Survey of clustering algorithms. IEEE Trans. Neural Netw. **16**(3), 645–678 (2005)

Bivariate Analysis of the Influencing Factors of the Upcoming Personal Mobility Vehicles (PMVs) in Palermo

Tiziana Campisi[1](✉)🆔, Kh Md Nahiduzzaman[2]🆔, Dario Ticali[1]🆔, and Giovanni Tesoriere[1]🆔

[1] University of Enna Kore, Cittadella Universitaria, 94100 Enna, Italy
tiziana.campisi@unikore.it
[2] The University of British Columbia, Okanagan, Canada

Abstract. The micro-mobility sector is spreading in the Italian and European urban context. The use of micro-mobility vehicles is often adopted to reach areas with particular transit restrictions or to avoid the problem of parking and congestion on the roads. Although personal mobility vehicles (PMV) are characterized by a growing technology, they still have problems related to driving safety in shared road spaces, not only for the inadequacy of infrastructure but also for some regulatory deficiencies and user behaviour. The Italian legislation is very recent and regulates the operational characteristics of the various vehicles and limits their use to certain age groups and in some areas of the cities. The present work focuses on the analysis of the attitudes and perceptions of a sample of users using micro-mobility in the centre of Palermo, one of the metropolises of Southern Italy. The results were obtained by administering questionnaires to a sample of specific users and the data were studied through a bivariate statistical analysis that highlights the significance of the comparison between two variables. The sample was chosen in collaboration with an association of citizens that promotes group activities by moving with means of micro-mobility in Palermo. Several correlations between the variables were addressed and among these some socio-economic ones were related to the propensity to rent and the perception of safety during the use of PMVs in Palermo. From this comparison, conclusions and notes useful for further research steps emerge.

Keywords: Micro mobility · PMV · Bivariate analysis · New mobility users

1 Introduction

Three factors that characterize the success of mobility in an urban context are related to

- the regulation of the society promoting standards for sustainable and resilient mobility.
- industry and its innovative, low-impact processes.
- citizens defined as users of goods and services who have to implement policies and strategies to protect the environment and the city.

© Springer Nature Switzerland AG 2020
O. Gervasi et al. (Eds.): ICCSA 2020, LNCS 12250, pp. 868–881, 2020.
https://doi.org/10.1007/978-3-030-58802-1_62

The development of mobility is part of this approach, adopting various forms of transport that may not favor motor vehicles, in order to reduce noise and environmental impact and thus traffic congestion.

Micro-mobility is one of the types of means of transport that provide a potential reduction in congestion. It is often believed that this transport system can replace or complement walking. Unfortunately, it is not yet clear how these electrically powered devices can contribute to the reduction of greenhouse gas emissions [1].

At present, the macro-category of PMVs generally includes electric bicycles, scooters and mopeds to which other vehicles used mainly for recreational purposes (e.g. segways, hoverboards and monowheels) have also been attached for less than a decade, the latter being governed by regulations are still under development for many countries. Among the problems that characterize the PMVs there are the safe parking areas, especially for shared vehicles. In fact, shared micromobility vehicles parked in public have spaces spread in some states of America and Europe and allow users who do not want to buy these vehicles to use them and park them in well-defined areas [2]. Unfortunately, there are now numerous acts of vandalism that cause these vehicles to be thrown into rivers and oceans.

Another negative aspect of sharing is linked to the location of the areas for the acquisition and return of the vehicles, which are only available in certain designated areas, usually central areas and therefore exclude suburban areas or often even areas with multimodal exchange areas. Among the countries where regulation is still difficult to implement is China, where there has been a high increase in sales and use of PMV [3].

The available literature suggests that performance, effort expectations, social influence, perceived risk and policy measures have a positive impact on users' intentions to drive PMV on the road. However, there are some after-effects due to accidents that users have on board these vehicles and that generate health problems caused by the posture and mechanics of the vehicle make the user more exposed to direct impact with the infrastructure, other people or vehicles. For instance, Yarmohammadi et al. [4] describe patients with facial injuries after the use of standing electric scooters and in this case the severity of the injuries highlights this important emerging health risk and policy implications. Users are satisfied to use PMV but the problem of accident risk makes them desist from using them [5]. In addition, there are four adjustment variables: gender, age, level of education and experience while observing others driving PMV on the road. Segways offer older users the opportunity to increase their range of mobility and can also be useful as a training tool. In terms of the physical discomfort caused by these means of transport, no statistically significant differences have been found between the average lower body muscle effort caused by walking and the use of a Segway. The systematic use of a segway can be an interesting option for developing physical training programmes to prevent falls [6].

With the increasing popularity of hoverboards in recent years, several centres have noted orthopedic injuries associated with cyclists. The use of appropriate protective devices, such as wrist protectors, as well as adult supervision, can help mitigate injuries associated with the use of this device [7].

Often the correlation between micromobility sharing and APPs means that they can only be used with a smartphone, connected to a credit card. The literature also finds that, in terms of safety, casual users sharing vehicles are less likely to wear helmets than owners who use them regularly [8]. An analysis and improvement in infrastructure planning design phases that also consider costs and safety in an integrated manner can mitigate the possible impacts, especially for cyclists and users of PMVs. In particular, the use of IBIM (building information model for Infrastructures) models can help the integrated vision of these aspects and the choice of the best design scheme to be adopted both in the design phase and in the redevelopment of an infrastructure [9].

In addition, the use of technology such as GPS or ITS systems can improve the knowledge of the transport habits of users and control the real time conditions of the transport system. In fact, for a greater control of the sharing service or for the control of the flows from own vehicles or the interaction of the flows of PMV with the other modes of transport, it is useful to develop systems that take into account the interaction and implementation of the dedicated technical platforms [10–12]. Moreover, the perception of the transport service from the perspective of Mobility as a service can facilitate the transport choices of users [13, 14].

Municipal administrators therefore play a key role in the authorisation or prohibition of operators and in defining the conditions under which the service can be provided. The spread of sharing mobility (especially cars and bikes) in different European cities and did not allow different population groups to move easily, considering the need to travel and the motivation to move [15, 16].

Shared micromobility vehicles, starting from the definition of a comprehensive national regulation, will have to circulate according to regulatory standards that define where they can be used (e.g. roads, cycle paths, sidewalks, pedestrian areas,), at what speed (e.g. 30 km/h), after what training, at what age and according to what safety standards (e.g. helmet, lights, direction indicators, etc.). Often devices, such as a helmet, to improve safety when using these vehicles have caused stronger pain and more adequate problems than those used in road cycling [17].

For example, electric scooters have become very popular but with regulatory defects compared to those with "classic" power supply and this poses additional safety problems that require special attention. Looking at possible future developments, micromobility is not necessarily limited to personal mobility, but could also become the way to manage personal deliveries and includes a shared fleet of delivery shuttles or autonomous delivery shuttles for drones that could be made available for occasional (short-term) rental via a smartphone to send or receive small packages within designated areas. Cities have reacted strongly to the advent of shared micro-mobility in different ways, ranging from total prohibition to total openness, with many nuances in between. Some have adapted their policy over time to developments in the sector, although this also includes public reaction. The following paragraphs show how Italy has only recently enacted legislation on the use of micromobility, which in some respects is not yet exhaustive as described in paragraph 2. Moreover, the methodology applied for the acquisition of data related to this research has been considered in a metropolitan context of Southern Italy as reported in paragraph 3. The data were statistically analyzed through a bivariate analysis in order to understand the correlation between the variables and their significance. These results were discussed in the last part of the work, providing ideas for the next stages of research.

2 PMV and Italian Rules

The use of PMV in Italy has recently grown both because of a wide range of choices at lower prices and because they are means that allow unlicensed people to move. Users choose this mode of transfer both to avoid using the private vehicle that tends to congestion on most roads during rush hour, being often only one person on board, and to move in a restricted traffic zone (ZTL in Italy).

After the first road accidents, the Italian government stopped using some electric means of transport, such as segways, hoverboards and so on. Until mid-2019, in fact, Italian law was unable to identify these types of transport. Therefore, the Italian national government decided to make a provisional and experimental decree to observe the behaviour of users after a proposed regulation. In July 2019, a decree (No 162, dated 12 July 2019) was issued by the Italian Ministry of Transport to define electric vehicles, including segways, hoverboards, etc., and how they can be used in urban areas. It states that for the following two years (2020–2021) all electric vehicles can legally circulate in urban areas, but with certain restrictions as follows:

- bicycles and hoverboard seat and gear wheels are excluded;
- hoverboard, monowheel, segway and similar can circulate only on pedestrian area, with a specific limit of speed (6 km/h).
- the users have to put helmet and specific high visibility clothing
- all municipalities have to adopt a specific regulatory to allow electric vehicle circulation.

This decree also authorized the owners of segways, hoverboards and monowheels in Italy, which are self-balanced devices, as well as scooters which are non-self-balanced vehicles and for which energy is supplied. Moreover, municipalities are required to authorise the circulation of these devices on an experimental basis, as well as to provide parking spaces, exclusively in urban areas and only on certain stretches of road. In addition, the rule stipulates that the devices may only be operated by adults or minors with a driving license, which is required in Italy when mopeds and microcars are to be driven. Since 1st March 2020, the new rules on the circulation of electric scooters have come into force, establishing new restrictions and new penalties, for example on the use of PMV by minors who must not be accompanied by more than two, on the devices to be adopted (night lighting, high visibility reflective vests or braces) and the transport of other people, objects or animals is prohibited. For rental services, a specific request will be made to the Municipality where, in addition to the number of licenses that can be activated and the maximum number of devices put into circulation, the obligation of insurance coverage for the performance of the service must be provided. Table 1 below shows the changes made in terms of characterization and use of the vehicles.

Table 1. Main characteristics of the principal PMV in Italy.

From 30th December 2019	e-scooter	Segway	Monowheel	Hoverboard
	Equivalent to electric scooters		Recognized as "self-balanced" devices	Equivalent to electric mopeds
Max Power (MP) and speed (MSp)	MP = 0.5 kW MSp = 20 km/h			
Transport	No transport of passengers No transport of things No trailer			No transport of passengers No transport of things No trailer
Action area	City area Cycle paths on the road, MSp = 30 km/h		Pedestrian and cycle paths; own cycle paths and on a reserved lane; "Zone 30"	Areas defined by Municipality; Pedestrian and cycle paths
Protection device	High-visibility retro-reflective vest. Braces in the evening and at night on the road or on the cycle path			
After 1st March 2020				
Novelties	Road MSp = 25 km/h; Pedestrian MSp = 6 km/h. Without lights ban on use in dark hours and bad weather conditions		Play areas the private road of one's own home, as well as on the dock	

3 Methodology

The analysis was conducted by defining an interview format, inviting an industry association to respond. The non-profit association "micro electric mobility Palermo" is composed of about 380 units, today is the only one present in the city.

A total of 133 interviews were collected that is more than 30% of the members of the association. The analysis has been carried out in a context in which many limited traffic areas have recently been established that drastically reduce the presence of vehicles, especially in the historical centre. Several areas in the common area allow an easy use of this mode of transport, amplified by the fact that in the historic centre there are no steep slopes or roads with impervious geometry. The variables taken into consideration and examined through the dissemination of the questionnaire in question are respectively

- socio-demographic attributes
- suitability for the micromobility transport system
- perception of use and environment

With regard to the socio-demographic variables, the following table shows the attributes investigated (Table 2).

Table 2. Socio-economic variable implemented by interview format

	Variable	Possible reply	Variable	Possible reply
Socio-economic	Gender	Male Female	Driver license ownership	Yes only for moped Yes for car and moped No
	Age	<18 18–27 28–45 46–65 >65	Car ownership	Yes No
	Job	Employee Freelance University student Undergraduate- high school student Unemployed	Residence in Palermo	Yes No
	PMV ownership	Yes No	Transport mode ownership (multiple reply)	Car Classic bike/ electric bicycle Scooter/ moped Hoverboard Segway Monowheel

The above variables have been statistically analyzed by evaluating their values in percentage form. In regards to transport attitude, the Table 3 below shows the attributes investigated.

Through Likert's scales, an assessment was made in the second and third sections of the interview.

The values used in the above scale were between 1 and 5 and they relate to the maximum disagreement or agreement respectively. The Likert scale allows for simple data processing and is obtained by measuring opinions and attitudes [18]. It is widely used because it is easy to construct.

The following Table 4 summarizes the attributes under investigation.

A bi-dimensional or bivariate analysis is in general useful to study the influence of different variables as for example in our work considering micro-mobility.

Table 3. Investigated variable related to transport attitude

	Variable	Possible reply	Variable	Possible reply
Transport attitude	Main reason of travel	H-S (home-school) H-W (home-work) H-L (home-leisure)	Average distances daily traveled (km)	<1 1–3 4–6 >6
	Accident experience	Yes No	Micro-mobility APP confidence	Yes No
	Use frequency	Daily basis Several times a week Several times a month Less than once a month	Ownership period	<1month 2–7 months 8–12 months >1 year

Table 4. Investigated variable related to user mode and road perception

	Variable	Possible reply
Mode and Infrastructure Perception	Safety on board	Likert Scale
	Economic savings	1 = completely
	Time savings	2 = disagree partially disagree
	Willingness to join in groups with the same means of transport	3 = I can't evaluate
	Infrastructures safety view	4 = partially in agreement
	Propensity to micro-mobility sharing/rent	5 = totally agree
	Propensity to recommend the use of micro mobility	

For the analysis it is necessary to consider a contingency table with columns r rows c.

The $\chi 2$ test procedure may be

- generalized to verify the independence between two
- categorical variables X and Y

In this context the null and void hypotheses are

- H0: the two categorical variables are independent (there is no relationship between the two variables)
- H1: the two categorical variables are dependent (there is a relationship between the two variables)

The test is based the equation below

$$x^2 = \sum\nolimits_{allcells} \left(f_{ob} - f_{aw}\right)^2 / f_{aw} \qquad (1)$$

The $\chi 2$ statistic is obtained by calculating for each cell of the contingency table the difference squared between the observed frequency (f_{ob}) and expected frequency (f_{aw}), divided by f_{aw}, and then adding the result obtained for each cell. The decision rule is to reject H0 if the value observed of the statistic χ^2 is greater than the critical value χ^2 of the distribution $\chi 2$ with $(r - 1) \times (c - 1)$ as the degree of freedom

4 Study Area of the Research

The analysis focuses on a sample of resident and non-resident users of the metropolis of Palermo located in southern Italy. The users interviewed share the membership of a non-profit association focused on micro-mobility issues. This association as of today is the only one based in Palermo (Fig. 1).

Fig. 1. Source(s) ``Micromobilità Palermo - Monopattini elettrici' no profit association

For PMV users, after the fines and the chaos over the rules, the city council approved a resolution that was then transformed into an ordinance of the traffic office to authorize the testing of new means of the so-called electric micro-mobility. This measure is similar to the one issued for tests already started in cities such as Milan, Turin and Pesaro.

This municipal ordinance allowed PMV users to circulate in pedestrian areas, without exceeding 6 kilometres per hour, on cycle paths, while scooters and hover-boards can only be used in pedestrian areas. Vehicles authorized for experimental circulation can be parked in the spaces reserved for bicycles and motor vehicles, ensuring reduced interference with cars and pedestrians. From an infrastructural point of view, since 2010 many cycle paths have been designed in Palermo to connect the historic centre and the Mondello seaside area with other peripheral areas. From the point of view of transport offer, in the city of Palermo there is the possibility to buy a single ticket for public transport and tram.

In Palermo there is not yet a shared PMV service but only a bike sharing service. The bike sharing service is integrated with the bike sharing service and has been managed by a private company (AMIGO spa) for a few years.

From the point of view of context, the city of Palermo, which has over 600,000 inhabitants and a large percentage of tourists, has undergone a transformation in mobility during the last decade with the growth of numerous day and night limited traffic areas and the presence of many common areas. In particular, the infrastructures of the historical centre such as Via Maqueda, Via Ruggero Settimo and a part of the area called "Cassaro" are located in limited traffic areas, with a low slope and wide surrounding spaces are suitable for the use of these vehicles as described in Fig. 2.

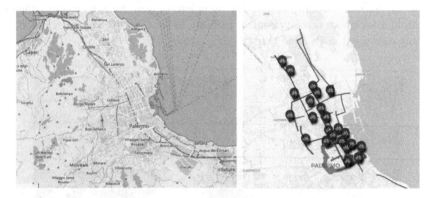

Fig. 2. Palermo maps and Palermo cycle routes (red lines) and restricted traffic area (purple line). (Color figure online) Source: Map data copyrighted OpenStreetMap contributors and available from https://www.openstreetmap.org

This research was focused on an interview format administered during the period between 16th of January and 28th of February 2020, with the method of face-to-face interviews. The main purpose of the questionnaire is to acquire information on users with particular reference to socio-demographic data, travel habits and sensations perceived during travel with PMV means. The data were then statistically processed and through a bivariate analysis they were compared in pairs in order to understand the dependency or independence between them.

5   Interview Results and Discussion

The acquired data show that there is gender heterogeneity and in the age group, in fact, there was a higher percentage of male users (68%) than women (32%). As far as the first section is concerned, it was recorded that the sample interviewed is almost entirely resident in Palermo (97%). More than 20% of the sample is between 18 and 27 years of age, while the highest percentage was recorded as 62% of the sample between 28 and 45 years of age, while the <18 and >65 bands recorded a value equal to and equal to 5%. As far as employment is concerned, a good percentage of respondents are employees and freelancers (32 and 40% of the sample respectively)The motivations for the daily commute by PMV were evaluated in terms of home-work, home-study and home-leisure reasons. It was recorded that the displacement with means of micro-mobility occurs mainly for work (60%) and to follow free time (37%) and school (3%).

As far as the possession of the driving license is concerned, 75% replied that they have one for driving a car, while 15% did not have one. The remaining percentage, on the other hand, concerned only the user of the motorbike with this driving license. About 65% of the sample had a car. Some of the interviewees stated that they rent PMVs in shops for short periods, as there is not yet a shared micromobility service in Palermo. As regards the main mode of transport used daily, the private vehicle (40%) is in first place followed by the assisted bicycle (25%), the scooter (20%) and single wheel (10%). Only 5% use the hoverboard in Palermo.

The second part of the interview investigated the interviewees' experience with PMV means and found that more than 40% of the sample has a small micromobility means that is between 2 and 7 months. In addition, more than 60% of the sample uses micromobility for travel over 6 km (medium distance) and a total of 35% for journeys under 3 km (short distance). As far as the accident aspect is concerned, 18% have already had an accident with the vehicle since they bought it, mostly caused by wet road conditions or poor maintenance. For better mobility, over 90% use dedicated apps, especially with scooters. With regard to the sensations experienced while driving micromobility vehicles in Palermo, the following Likert scale judgements were given in the table below (Table 5).

Table 5. Perception distribution considering Likert scale

	Variable	Distribution of the answers given by the sample according to the Likert scale				
		1	2	3	4	5
Mode and Infrastructure Perception	Safety on board	10%	15%	45%	15%	15%
	Economic savings	5%	12%	63%	12%	8%
	Time savings	2%	1%	7%	55%	35%
	Willingness to join in groups with the same means of transport	12%	3%	55%	25%	5%
	Infrastructures characteristic	1%	0%	29%	58%	12%
	Propensity to micro-mobility sharing/rent	1%	1%	6%	43%	49%
	Propensity to recommend the use of micro mobility	0%	5%	5%	35%	55%

After the statistical analysis, the chi square was evaluated by comparing the following pairs of values in the first section:

- socio-demographic variable (age)
- socio-demographic variable (work)
- rationale for the move

with the variables of the third section

- safety on board
- economic savings
- propensity to micro-mobility sharing/rent

These combinations have been taken into account to understand how much the driving of the micro-mobility vehicle, the petrol saving or wear and tear of a motorized vehicle and the propensity to use non-engineered vehicles varies according to the type of user and the motivation for the journey. These assessments have shown that the following Table 6 shows that.

Table 6. Results of chi square analysis

		p < .05	p < .01	p < .10	Degree of freedom	Result
Age	Propensity to micro-mobility sharing/rent	$\chi2 = 38.022$			16	Significant
	Economic savings	$\chi2 = 52.665$				
	Safety on board	$\chi2 = 48.4678$				
Job	Propensity to micro-mobility sharing/rent	$\chi2 = 33.6527$			16	Significant
	Economic savings	$\chi2 = 47.6266$				
	Safety on board	$\chi2 = 36.1799$				
Moving reason	Propensity to micro-mobility sharing/rent	$\chi2 = 10.3307$			8	Not significant
	Economic savings	$\chi2 = 27.4644$				Significant
	Safety on board	$\chi2 = 42.6707$				Significant

The degrees of freedom, calculated considering (number of rows-1)*(number of columns-1) show a value of 16 and 8 respectively. A contingency table with a maximum number of rows and columns of 5 was used for the chi-square evaluation.

The calculation was carried out through 3 steps, the first of which consists in evaluating the variables and the relative ranges to be considered; the second step focuses on the distribution of the values according to the rows and columns whose total value is equal to 100% of the interviewed sample (i.e. 133) and finally it was possible to evaluate the significance of the results obtained through a calculation function on excel sheet. The correlations analyzed allow us to understand how, as the degrees of freedom vary, for the variables acquired there can be dependence or independence between them.

The calculation of the $\chi2$ statistics allows us to identify how much the observed data deviate from those we have estimated in the independence hypothesis. If the value is low, the real and theoretical values are very similar; if the value is high, they deviate from each other. And if reality is very close to theory ($\chi2$ low), since the theoretical hypothesis is that the two variables are independent from each other, we will conclude that the two variables do not influence each other. Whereas if the $\chi2$ is high, it is not possible to say that the variables are independent, but they influence each other. The data obtained from these correlations with multi degrees of freedom reflect what is described in the literature in terms of the relationship between degrees of freedom and p-value [19].

6 Discussion and Conclusions

This work shows a description of the diffusion of micro mobility in Palermo with some references to the typical users. From a survey it was possible to define the typical user using micro mobility in Palermo in 2020. The common users is mostly a man, employee or freelance worker and aged between 28 and 45 years and who has had a PMV for less than a year. The bivariate analysis has shown that some of the variables investigated are closely connected

In particular, the age of the user and the type of work influence the perception of safe driving while on board the PMV, the economy of using this vehicle instead of others and the propensity to use shared or rented vehicles. The survey, however, did not reveal any significant between motivation to travel and propensity to rent or share the vehicle.

On the other hand, the motivation of the displacement has registered a significant correlation with both the security and the economy aspects. The sample is PMV users and for a more in-depth investigation it could be useful to investigate other sub-categories such as rejecters or those who have not yet used these means for the first time but tend to do so.

The limitations of this analysis lie in the smallness of the sample but this in turn depends on the recent legislation that protects the use of these means of transport. However, this work is a first step of analysis for all to understand at the present time the propensity to use micromobility in Palermo to obtain results that may be useful to calibrate a service of micromobility rental obtain results useful for local authorities in order to limit and/or guarantee the use of micromobility in the historical centre of the city of Palermo characterized by a growing expansion of the ZTL areas.

These results is going to provide, for example, a basis for companies to optimize their rental services. This work foresees an increase in the interviewed population and the application of multi-variable Logit models to study the probability of modal choice in the urban context of Palermo.

References

This paper is the result of the joint work of the authors. 'Abstract' 'Introduction' 'Methodology' and 'Results' were written jointly by the authors. TC and DT focused on the state of the art. TC designed the methodological approach and discussion. Supervision and research funding KN and GT

1. Zagorskas, J., Burinskienė, M.: Challenges caused by increased use of e-powered personal mobility vehicles in European cities. Sustainability **12**(1), 273 (2020). https://doi.org/10.3390/su12010273
2. https://www.forbes.com/sites/adeyemiajao/2019/02/01/everything-you-want-to-know-about-scooters-and-micro-mobility/#6bd93ae45de6
3. Yu, Z., Feng, Z., Jiang, K., Huang, Z., Yang, Z.: Riding personal mobility vehicles on the road: an analysis of the intentions of Chinese users. Cogn. Technol. Work 1–14 (2019). https://doi.org/10.1007/s10111-019-00617-9
4. Yarmohammadi, A., et al.: Characterization of facial trauma associated with standing e-scooter injuries. Ophthalmology (2020). https://doi.org/10.1016/j.ophtha.2020.02.007
5. Yang, H., Ma, Q., Wang, Z., Cai, Q., Xie, K., Yang, D.: Safety of micro-mobility: analysis of E-Scooter crashes by mining news reports. Accident Anal. Prevent. **143** (2020). https://doi.org/10.1016/j.aap.2020.105608
6. Berti, Z., et al.: Driving segway: a musculoskeletal investigation. In: Stanton, N. (ed.) AHFE 2019. AISC, vol. 964, pp. 585–595. Springer, Cham (2020). https://doi.org/10.1007/978-3-030-20503-4_53
7. Hosseinzadeh, P., et al.: Hoverboard injuries in children and adolescents: results of a multicenter study. J. Pediatric Orthopaed. B **28**(6), 555–558 (2019). https://doi.org/10.1097/BPB.0000000000000653
8. Shaheen, S., Cohen, A., Chan, N., Bansal, A.: Sharing strategies: carsharing, shared micromobility (bikesharing and scooter sharing), transportation network companies, microtransit, and other innovative mobility modes. In: Transportation, Land Use, and Environmental Planning, pp. 237–262. Elsevier (2020). https://doi.org/10.1016/B978-0-12-815167-9.00013-X
9. Campisi, T., Acampa, G., Marino, G.: Tesoriere, G.: Cycling master plans in Italy: the I-BIM feasibility tool for cost and safety assessments. Sustainability **12**(11), 4723 (2020). https://doi.org/10.3390/su12114723
10. Torrisi, V., Ignaccolo, M., Inturri, G.: Toward a sustainable mobility through a dynamic real-time traffic monitoring, estimation and forecasting system: the RE.S.E.T. project. In: Town and Infrastructure Planning for Safety and Urban Quality - Proceedings of the 23rd International Conference on Living and Walking in Cities, LWC 2017, pp. 241–250 (2018). https://doi.org/10.1201/9781351173360-32
11. Ignaccolo, M., Inturri, G., Giuffrida, N., Le Pira, M., Torrisi, V.: Public engagement for designing new transport services: investigating citizen preferences from a multiple criteria perspective. Transp. Res. Procedia **37**, 91–98 (2019). https://doi.org/10.1016/j.trpro.2018.12.170
12. Torrisi, V., Ignaccolo, M., Inturri, G.: Innovative transport systems to promote sustainable mobility: developing the model architecture of a traffic control and supervisor system. In: Gervasi, O., et al. (eds.) ICCSA 2018. LNCS, vol. 10962, pp. 622–638. Springer, Cham (2018). https://doi.org/10.1007/978-3-319-95168-3_42

13. Canale, A., Tesoriere, G., Campisi, T.: The MAAS development as a mobility solution based on the individual needs of transport users. In: AIP Conference Proceedings, vol. 2186, no. 1, p. 160005. AIP Publishing LLC, December 2019. https://doi.org/10.1063/1.5138073

14. Karlsson, I.C.M., et al.: Development and implementation of mobility-as-a-service-a qualitative study of barriers and enabling factors. Transp. Res. Part A Pol. Pract. **131**, 283–295 (2020). https://doi.org/10.1016/j.tra.2019.09.028

15. Campisi, T., Torrisi, V., Ignaccolo, M., Inturri, G., Tesoriere, G.: University propensity assessment to car sharing services using mixed survey data: the Italian case study of Enna city. Transp. Res. Procedia **47**, 433–440 (2020). https://doi.org/10.1016/j.trpro.2020.03.155

16. Kim, D., Park, Y., Ko, J.: Factors underlying vehicle ownership reduction among carsharing users: a repeated cross-sectional analysis. Transportation Research Part D: Transport and Environment **76**, 123–137 (2019). https://doi.org/10.1016/j.trd.2019.09.01817

17. Kim, I.H., Choi, K.M., Jun, J.I.: A survey on riding characteristics and helmet wearing conditions of bicycle and PMV (Personal Mobility Vehicle) riders. Fash. Text. Res. J. **20**(1), 63–74 (2018). https://doi.org/10.5805/SFTI.2018.20.1.63

18. Likert, R.: A technique for the measurement of attitudes. In: Archives of Psychology (1932)

19. Miller, R., Siegmund, D.: Maximally selected chi square statistics. Biometrics 1011–1016 (1982). https://doi.org/10.2307/2529881

Understanding the Key Factors of Shared Mobility Services: Palermo as a Case Study

Alessandro Emilio Capodici, Gabriele D'Orso[(✉)],
and Marco Migliore

Department of Engineering, University of Palermo, Viale delle Scienze Building
8, 90128 Palermo, Italy
{alessandro.capodici,gabriele.dorso,
marco.migliore}@unipa.it

Abstract. The potential success of shared mobility services in the urban area strongly depends on careful tariff planning, adequate sizing of the fleet and efficient integrated public transport system, as well as on the application of policies in favor of sustainable modes of transport. The balance between earnings and expenses is not always an easy target for the companies in those cities where these services are not well-rooted in the citizens' mobility habits. Often only large operators in the sector can continue to offer a service generating profit. However, several factors can determine the success or the failure of shared mobility services. The objective of this study is to identify, thanks to the help of a case study, success and failure factors, developing an approach that is supportive for companies in managing the services and optimizing fares and fleet to increase the number of members and maximize profits. The city of Palermo has been chosen as a case study: the "Amigo" carsharing service - partly station-based, partly free-floating - is a service managed by the municipal company AMAT S.p.A., which operates also the public transport service.

Keywords: Shared mobility · Fleet-size optimization · GIS · Bike sharing · Carsharing

1 Introduction

Shared mobility services have become in recent years increasingly present and used modes of transport in urban areas. In the past years, only a few carsharing companies competed for the slices of a rapidly growing market; now, many private and publicly-owned companies have entered in the shared mobility market and succeeded, creating a wide variety of shared mobility services. The success of these services can be found in its flexibility: members can use the car or the bike when they need it, booking the closest of those of the large fleet offered by the companies. Flexibility also means to be able to use different categories of vehicles according to own needs, such as city-cars, vans, or low-emission vehicles that often allow the user to move more freely, freeing himself from the restrictions on vehicular traffic adopted by municipal administrations. In this perspective, carsharing is an effective mode of transport especially for non-commuting trips and for those citizens who use both public transport and carsharing to satisfy their mobility needs in urban areas, not having a car always available.

© Springer Nature Switzerland AG 2020
O. Gervasi et al. (Eds.): ICCSA 2020, LNCS 12250, pp. 882–895, 2020.
https://doi.org/10.1007/978-3-030-58802-1_63

Bikesharing, on the other hand, is suitable for those who have to make trips - even commuting trips - characterized by an intermediate distance between acceptable walking distances and distances that must be traveled by public transport, or for those who use this service as a feeder system to reach the main public transport hubs.

These mobility services are now incentivized not only to counteract the excessive use of the private car and what it entails, i.e. air and noise pollution, and soil consumption, alongside restrictive policies (road pricing, the introduction of restricted traffic areas and parking pricing) but also to give concrete form to the concept of Mobility as a Service, i.e. the offer of a transport system that includes various mobility services, integrating them physically and in fares.

However, some factors largely affect the efficiency of these services, the level of service, and, consequently, demand satisfaction.

For this reason, the success of such services is built only with careful planning. This planning consists in finding the optimal location of the stations (in station-based services) or the width of the rental area (in free-floating services), in the optimization of the number of stations and the number of stalls, in the optimization of the vehicle relocation operations, and finally in the fares and fleet-size optimization. It may happen that citizens don't use carsharing because the companies adopt fares perceived as too high or operate the service with such a small fleet that does not guarantee users the availability of a car nearby at the time of booking. The same thing happens for bikesharing services that don't have an adequate number of bicycles. The attractiveness of the shared mobility services is determined by the level of service offered and by the costs. The level of service mainly depends on accessibility, i.e. the distance of the user's origin and destination from the pick-up and drop-off locations. However, accessibility depends also on the availability of vehicles at the stations, which is influenced by the fleet size and affects the operating and management costs of the system.

The paper aims to investigate the possible criticalities of shared mobility services, such as the size of the fleet and the lack of optimization of the fares to be adopted. The aim is also to propose an approach that allows solving the problems that the companies operating in the shared mobility sector must face, in order to increase the number of citizens who use these modes of transport as alternatives to private cars. The "Amigo" car-sharing service was chosen as a case study, active in the city of Palermo and managed by Amat S.p.A, a publicly-owned company that deals with city public transport. Section 2 will illustrate the existing literature on the sizing of shared mobility services' fleets and the design of fares. Section 3 will describe the methodology implemented and the factors assessed. Section 4 will introduce the case study; in particular, the shared mobility services in Palermo will be described; an analysis of the pedestrian access to the stations and the relationship between shared services and public transport will be carried out. In Sect. 5 other potential critical issues of the services will be analyzed, through the comparison with other Italian cases. Conclusions and suggestions for future research are given in Sect. 6.

2 Background

Many researchers have investigated the factors influencing the success of shared mobility services [2, 5, 12, 17]. Much of the scientific literature is aimed at methodologies for determining the optimal number, size, and position of bikesharing and carsharing stations or for optimizing fleet rebalancing operations to increase efficiency, members and, hence, the profit for companies. On the other hand, few researchers have been interested in adapting fares and sizing the fleet to achieve an adequate balance between profits and customer needs; research in this field has mainly concerned the case of carsharing systems with electric vehicles.

Boyaci et al. [4] developed, for example, a multi-objective model for the planning of one-way carsharing systems with electric vehicles and the determination of the optimal fleet size, taking into account the dynamic processes of relocation and rebalancing, as well as the costs and the benefits for users and the company.

Li et al. [10] proposed a Continuum Approximation model to determine the optimal location of the stations of an electric one-way car-sharing and the size of the fleet; this model is based on the criterion of minimizing the operating costs of the system (investments for the construction of the stations, vehicle charging, fleet rebalancing): in particular, the authors considered how the charging times between one rental and the next affect the actual availability of cars at the stations.

The adequate size of the fleet of electric car-sharing service in Beijing [17] was estimated with a Monte Carlo simulation, considering the potential demand, arrival times, distance and travel time, as well as the charging times. Another proposed methodology for sizing the fleet of electric carsharing systems is the branch-and-price approach, which has the aim of minimizing the costs of the EV trip chain [15].

The rebalancing of the fleet and the assignment of personnel assigned to this operation were among the main factors considered by Xu et al. [16] in solving the problem of fleet sizing and trip pricing. The determination of the fares to be adopted to maximize profits in one-way car-sharing was also studied for Jorge et al. [9]: the researchers proposed an iterated local search (ILS) metaheuristic, taking into account how the possible variations to the travel rates by zone and by time slot can ensure that the rebalancing of the fleet can be done unknowingly by users, reducing company staff responsible for relocating shared cars. Perboli et al. [14] instead, simulated the introduction of new tariffs taking into account the different user-profiles and their needs.

The optimization of the location and size of the fleet can be the result of multi-agent simulations, in which supply and demand are modeled and the effects of the strategies proposed to increase the use of the available fleet are observed [1]. Barrios and Doig Godier [3] also used an agent-based model to optimize the fleet to maximize the number of trips for each vehicle.

Queue theory has also been used for station-based systems to optimize the fleet and optimally design the capacity of the stations [7, 8].

Finally, Nourinejad and Roorda [13] used an integrated dynamic simulation-optimization model to evaluate the performance of one-way systems, finding that increasing the booking time from 0 to 30 min can reduce the size of the fleet by 86% and that the latter is linked to the times of relocation of the vehicles and the dispersion of requests over time.

3 Methodology

The factors that lead to success or failure by operators can be manifold. These factors are reported in Table 1, making the appropriate distinction between those related to bikesharing (dockless D and dock-based DB) and those related to carsharing (free-floating FF and station-based SB).

Table 1. Key success and failure factors of shared mobility services.

		Carsharing		Bike-sharing	
		FF	SB	D	DB
Key success factors	Fare integration	X	X	X	X
	Modal integration with public transport	X	X	X	X
	Fares that facilitate the rebalancing of the fleet	X	X	X	X
	Fleet optimization	X	X	X	X
	Optimization of the location of the stations in relation to the main attractor poles	–	X	–	X
	Traffic restrictions and pricing policies applied	X	X	X	X
	Presence of different types of vehicles in the fleet	X	X	–	–
	Presence of changing rooms and showers in the workplace	–	–	X	X
Failure factors	Fleet undersizing	X	X	X	X
	Fleet oversizing	X	X	X	X
	Absence of cycle paths	–	–	X	X
	Absence of charging stations for electric vehicles	X	X	–	–
	Absence of bicycle racks	–	–	X	–
	Lack of integration with public transport	X	X	X	X
	Poor pedestrian accessibility of the stations	–	X	–	X
	Bad fares	X	X	X	X
	Inefficient public transport system	X	X	X	X
	Adverse weather conditions, air pollution or adverse topography	–	–	X	X
	Occupation of stalls by unauthorized vehicles	–	X	–	–
	Long on-street parking search time	X	–	–	–
	Non-user-friendly booking systems	X	X	X	X

Many of the factors are, as already stated, related to the level of service offered by shared mobility systems: a number of vehicles in the fleet that does not guarantee the availability of the car to users at the time of booking strongly affects the success of these services in the urban area, as well as an inaccurate location of parking stalls in relation to the distance from the main attractor poles and their pedestrian accessibility [6]. Even fares perceived as too high by users or designed without an appropriate graduality, as well as complex booking systems, which require time and numerous steps, can influence the choice to make use of these services. Even too low tariffs and a high number of vehicles available to users are the cause of failure of these services: in these cases, the revenues would not cover the expenses made by the company for system management, even if the number of users attracted by the system could be higher. On the other hand, fares that are modulated based on requests and that facilitate the spontaneous rebalancing of the fleet, and a varied offer regarding the type of vehicles are strengths for companies. Integration with public transport - including fare integration - is also a strong incentive for the use of shared mobility services, as the two systems are complementary: it is possible to implement an integration between shared mobility services and public transport through mobility packages. Modal integration with public transport and the efficiency of the latter play an important role in the choice of shared mobility services since the users to whom these services are addressed are generally those who renounce the purchase of a car in favor of public transport for commuting trips and in favor of carpooling and bikesharing for non-commuting trips.

Other factors are, however, external to shared mobility companies. The weather (e.g., sunny, rain or snow), temperature, and air-pollution are factors that strongly affects the success of a bikesharing system. Usually, adverse weather conditions and colder temperature would significantly discourage travelers from cycling. The topography also affects the choice of bikesharing. Steeper roads, in particular, would significantly discourage the use of a bicycle. Air pollution can also decrease the number of cycling commuters on the road.

With regards to environmental and land use impacts, cycling-related infrastructure is an important factor that can impact bikesharing systems. An increase in the number of cycle lanes and bikesharing docks can promote the use of this non-motorized mode of transportation, reducing travel time and increasing safety and convenience.

Companies operating in the shared mobility sector should take these factors into consideration, evaluating them in advance.

Having identified the key success and failure factors for shared mobility services, this paper, therefore, aims to illustrate how these factors actually influence the success of shared mobility services in relation to a case study. The city of Palermo was chosen as a case study, in which both bikesharing and carsharing services are active. In particular, pedestrian access to the stations of both services and modal integration with public transport were assessed; the fare integration, the booking systems, and the city public transport system were subsequently discussed. Finally, the fairness of fleet size and fares was assessed, making a comparison with successful existing systems in other Italian cities.

4   The Case Study

The bikesharing and carsharing services in the city of Palermo are managed by the municipal company AMAT S.p.A, which also manages urban public transport. The "Car Sharing Palermo" service was developed in 2009, while the implementation of the bike-sharing system, called "BiciPA", took place in 2016: both services were cofinanced by the Italian Ministry of the Environment. The bikesharing service has a fleet of 400 bicycles and 39 cycle docks (Fig. 1).

AMAT offers a station-based carsharing service (one-way and round trip) with 82 parking spaces located throughout the city and a fleet of 126 cars of various types (city cars, station wagons, vans). Moreover, AMAT has introduced in 2018 24 electric cars in the central area of Palermo for the free-floating service, identifying a rental area of 4.88 km^2 (Fig. 2).

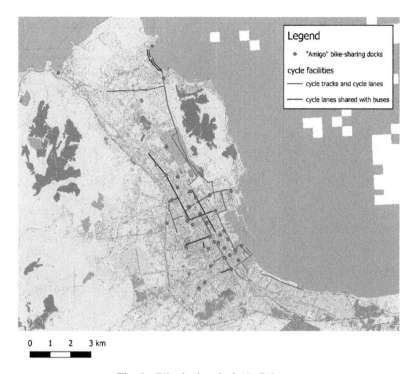

0   1   2   3 km

Fig. 1. Bikesharing docks in Palermo.

The company has recently created a single platform, called "Amigo", which gives the possibility to use both shared mobility services. Booking is via app or web. The registration for the two services is unique and costs € 25.

The analysis of the financial statements of the AMAT S.p.A. company highlights an alarming fact: the sector is largely at a loss and the usage by the customers does not balance the costs that the company has to face. It is, therefore, necessary to analyze which reasons these losses have. First of all, the potential demand of the carsharing service that has been assessed as 10,000 daily users in Palermo in Migliore et al. [11] results in a lower number of members, equal to 4195 in 2020.

Pedestrian access to the bike-sharing and carsharing stations was first determined. This was done using the GIS software QGIS, carrying out buffering operations and processing the ISTAT data of the population census of 2011. The catchment areas and the number of citizens who reside or work at a walkable distance from the stations was assessed. The maximum distance considered walkable has been set at 500 m. For bikesharing, the autonomous and active population was considered, i.e. those aged between 14 and 70 years. For the calculation of potential users for carsharing, reference was made to citizens over the age of 18.

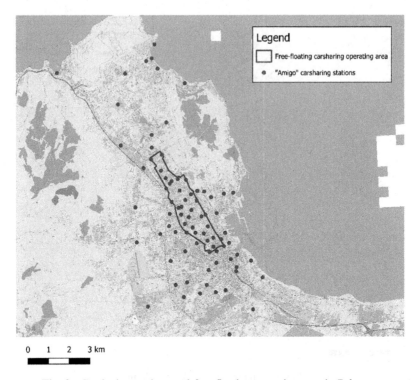

Fig. 2. Carsharing stations and free-floating operating area in Palermo.

The results of the accessibility analysis in cartographic terms, i.e. the catchment areas considering the maximum walking distance along the road network, are shown in Figs. 3 and 4.

The number of residents and employees who live or work at a distance of 500 m from the bikesharing and carsharing stations is shown in Table 2 for both systems. In addition, the total number of residents and employees potentially served by considering both services is also reported.

Considering the distribution of citizens' residences in the territory, it is noted that bikesharing covers only 20% of potential users, while the carsharing service has greater accessibility (38%). Considering the accessibility of both services overall, in any case, they remain inaccessible for most of the potential users (61%). The accessibility of shared mobility services is greater if we consider the workplaces present in the area: 64% of the workplaces are located less than 500 m from a carsharing station or a bikesharing dock.

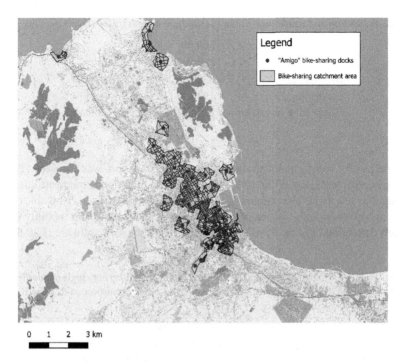

Fig. 3. Bikesharing catchment area (500 m).

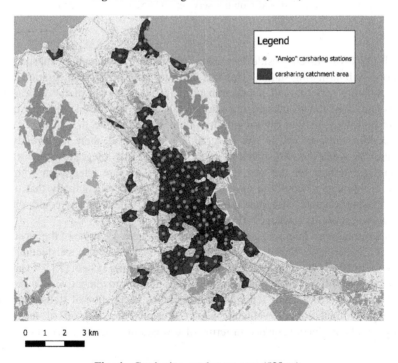

Fig. 4. Carsharing catchment area (500 m).

Table 2. Population and employees within the catchment areas of the shared mobility services.

	500 m	
	Population	Employees
Bikesharing	93,710 (20%)	78,783 (42%)
Carsharing	199,835 (38%)	118,498 (63%)
Bikesharing or carsharing	216,612 (39%)	120,918 (64%)

Subsequently, physical integration with public transport was assessed. Figure 5 shows the catchment areas of the high-frequency or regular public transport lines (tram, train, and bus line 101). The number of citizens who live or work at a walkable distance both from regular or high-frequency public transport and from shared mobility services has been determined (Table 3). It was assessed using the GIS software (Fig. 6).

Table 3. Population and employees within the high-frequency or high-regularity public transport catchement area and within the areas with public transport and shared mobility services within a walkable distance.

	500 m	
	Population	Employees
Public transport	176,274 (32%)	86,929 (46%)
Public transport & shared mobility services	97,452 (17%)	70,254 (37%)

Only 17% of citizens reside less than 500 m from both public transport and a carsharing or bikesharing station. This fact indicates poor physical integration between shared mobility services and public transport. In fact, only 39 of the 82 carsharing stations and 22 of the 43 bikesharing stations fall within a walkable distance from the stops of high-frequency or high-regularity public transport line.

Therefore, the presence of fare integration was assessed: there is currently a fare integration between the two shared mobility systems. This integration consists of the common registration for the two services. There is no fare integration with public transport, although it would be easy to implement since the company that manages public transport operates also shared mobility services. The company could, therefore, create several mobility packages for different types of users.

Not advantageous fares and a complex booking system are some of the most critical issues of the services. This fact was highlighted by a customer satisfaction survey carried out in 2017 [11]. The users indicate an easier booking system (22.7%) and more promotions and offers (14.3%) as possible areas for improvement of the carsharing service. Another critical issue reported by users is the occupation of stalls reserved for carsharing by unauthorized vehicles, which prevents the drop-off of the vehicle, causing significant inconvenience in terms of a waste of time to search for a parking space.

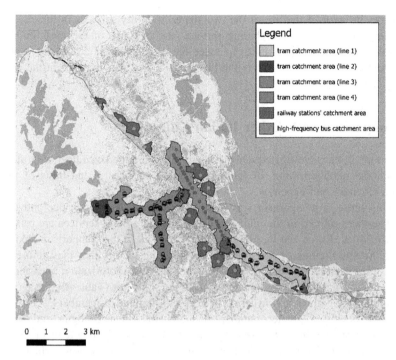

Fig. 5. High-frequency or high-regularity public transport catchment area (500 m).

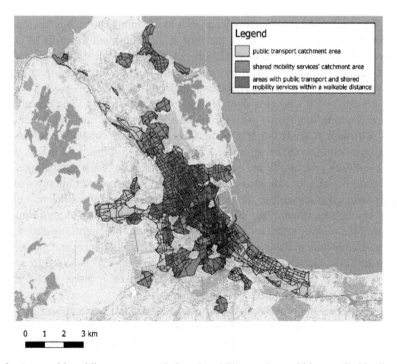

Fig. 6. Areas with public transport and shared mobility services within a walkable distance.

Factors in favor of the use of the two shared mobility services in the city are the convenient fares of the bike sharing service (the free use of bicycles for the first 30 min) as well as the possibility to enter the restricted traffic area for carsharing vehicles, the possibility to drive in the bus lanes and to park for free in the on-street parking spaces.

5   Comparison with Other Italian Cities

Furthermore, it was investigated whether there were an undersized fleet or tariffs not in line with the main operators of Italian carsharing services at the basis of the gap between revenues and expenses.

In this sense, a comparison was made between the Amigo service and the carsharing services offered in the main Italian cities where these services are established and used: Milan, Rome, Turin, Florence, and Bologna. In the comparison, taking into account the specificities of the different cities, some factors that may influence the success of the service were discussed: population density, motorization rates and age of the vehicles in circulation, the efficiency of public transport (Table 4). Table 5 shows the results of the comparison in terms of fleet and number of members.

Despite having a greater number of inhabitants than Bologna and Florence, Palermo has a smaller fleet of carsharing vehicles. It is possible to note that in these two cities, as well as in Turin, Milan, and Rome, there are several operators, which increase the supply. Furthermore, if you compare the number of free-floating vehicles available, the Amat service has only 24 electric vehicles available: a much lower number than the services of the other cities.

The fleet under-sizing inevitably leads to a lower number of members, due to the unavailability of close shared cars at the time of booking, and therefore to an unsatisfactory level of service. The unavailability of shared vehicles was indicated as the most urgent area for improvement by users of the service during the customer satisfaction survey (28.4% of the interviewees indicated it).

The citizens of Palermo also show a deep-rooted use of the private car: after Turin and Rome, Palermo is the city with the highest motorization rate and the circulating vehicles are older than in the other cities: about 43% of circulating vehicles have emission standards equal to or lower than the Euro 3. This is the sign that the inhabitants do not give up private cars in favor of the more recent carsharing vehicles. The affection for private cars also derives from a public transport supply that is significantly reduced compared to the other cities. Furthermore, the efficiency of public transport is much less than in the other cities: from the data of the Moovit Report, it is evident that the waiting time at the public transport stop in Palermo is about 25 min, more than double than in the cities of Milan, Bologna, and Florence, and greater than in the cities of Turin and Rome. Besides, the public transport user is forced to walk long distances to reach his destination, an irrefutable sign of reduced public transport accessibility in Palermo compared to other cities.

This means that the typical carsharing user - the one who uses public transport for commuting trips and the shared mobility service for non-commuting trips - does not manifest itself, mainly due to the lack of reliability that is attributed to public transport.

Table 4. Specificities of the analysed cities.

	Population [inhabitants]	Population density [people per km²]	Motorization rate [cars per 1000 people][a]	Percentage of cars with Euro 3 standard or lower[a] [%]	Public transport[b]: available seat-kilometres [km]	Public transport[c]: average waiting time [min]	Public transport[c]: average walking distance during a single commute by transit [m]
Torino	874,935	6,729.75	666	27.4	6016	13.17	726.25
Milano	1,387,171	7,635.66	512	29.2	16218	9.1	715
Bologna	392,027	2,783.1	540	23.1	3742	10.04	762.5
Firenze	379,563	3,709.57	530	24.3	5541	10.51	753.75
Roma	2,879,728	2,236.93	623	30.9	6823	16	663.75
Palermo	659,894	4,109.18	596	42.5	2034	24.19	811.25

[a] ACI, 2018
[b] ISTAT, 2015
[c] Moovit Global Public Transport Report, 2019

Table 5. Comparison between the carsharing operators in the Italian cities.

	Operators		Fares	Fares (1 h and 10 km)	Vehicles per city	Vehicles	Subscribers
Torino	SB	Bluetorino	0.195 €/min	11.7 €	908	187	–
	FF	car2go	0.19 − 0.29 €/min	11.4 − 17.4 €		721	181,215
		Enjoy	0.25 €/min	15 €			
Milano	SB	Ubeeqo	5 €/h	5 €	3201	150	–
	FF	car2go	0.19 − 0.29 €/min	11.4 − 17.4 €		3051	815,868
		Drivenow	0.31 €/min	18.6 €			
		Enjoy	0.25 €/min	15 €			
		Share'ngo	0.28 €/min	16.8 €			
Bologna	FF	Corrente	0.25 €/min	12€ (sale)	220	120	13,976
		Enjoy	0.25 €/min	15 €		100	
Firenze	FF	Adduma car	0.18 €/min	10.8 €	522	100	125,493
		car2go	0.19 − 0.29 €/min	11.4 − 17.4 €		422	
		Enjoy	0.25 €/min	15 €			
		Share'ngo	0.28 €/min	16.8 €			
Roma	SB	Carsharing Roma	3 €/h + 0.59 €/km	8.9 €	2303	192	–
	FF	car2go	0.19 − 0.29 €/min	11.4 − 17.4 €		2111	584,966
		Enjoy	0.25 €/min	15 €			
		Share'ngo	0.28 €/min	16.8 €			
Palermo	SB/FF	amigo	SB: 2.40 €/h + 0.54 €/km FF: 0.24 €/min	SB: 7.8 € FF: 14.4 €	150	150	4,195

From the comparison of the number of carsharing members in Table 5, it can be seen that the number of members in Palermo is very low than in the other cities, although in these cities there are different operators. The station-based service fares are lower than those on the market (except for the Ubeeqo service in Milan), while the free-floating service fares are in line with the other Italian carsharing services.

6 Discussion and Conclusion

The paper highlighted how to evaluate certain factors such as the number of vehicles in the fleet, pedestrian accessibility, fare designing and integration with local public transport before the launch of the service is fundamental for a company that operates shared mobility services, such as carsharing and bikesharing. These factors affect the success of the shared mobility service in the urban area, in terms of citizens who will be members of the service. The unavailability of vehicles, the distance of the stations from the attractor poles, too expensive or too low fares, and the inefficiency of local public transport lead to a service not rooted in the citizens' mobility habits.

To highlight how these factors affect the success of the services and propose an approach to their evaluation, the "Amigo" shared mobility services platform of the city of Palermo was chosen as a case study. In particular, through GIS processing, data analysis and comparison with the services present in other Italian cities, it has been shown that there is a very small fleet compared to that of other cities and public transport is less efficient in Palermo. The location of bikesharing docks and carsharing stations means that the access to shared mobility services is limited: 61% of potential users live more than 500 m from a carsharing station or a bikesharing dock. It has also been found that physical integration with high-frequency or regular public transport lines is also poor: only 17% of potential users reside at a distance less than 500 m from a carsharing station or a bikesharing dock and from a public transport stop to take a regular, high-frequency public transport line. Other failure factors are the lack of fare integration with public transport, a complex booking system and the propensity for the use of the private car by the inhabitants of Palermo. The costs of using the services and the advantages offered by the operator (entry into the restricted traffic area, the possibility of free parking, use of bicycles for free for the first 30 min) were found in line with the services offered in other Italian cities.

The approach used is generalizable and applicable to identify critical issues and potentialities of shared mobility services in other cities and other contexts.

References

1. Balac, M., Ciari, F.: Enhancement of the carsharing fleet utilization. In: 15th Swiss Transport Research Conference (2015)
2. Balac, M., Ciari, F., Axhausen, K.W.: Modeling the impact of parking price policy on free-floating carsharing: case study for Zurich, Switzerland. Transp. Res. Part C Emerg. Technol. **77**, 207–225 (2017). https://doi.org/10.1016/J.TRC.2017.01.022

3. Barrios, J.A., Godier, J.D.: Fleet sizing for flexible carsharing systems: simulation-based approach. Transp. Res. Rec. **2416**(1), 1–9 (2014). https://doi.org/10.3141/2416-01

4. Boyacı, B., Zografos, K.G., Geroliminis, N.: An optimization framework for the development of efficient one-way car-sharing systems. Eur. J. Oper. Res. **240**, 718–733 (2015). https://doi.org/10.1016/J.EJOR.2014.07.020

5. Celsor, C., Millard-Ball, A.: Where does carsharing work? Using geographic information systems to assess market potential. Transp. Res. Rec. (2007). https://doi.org/10.3141/1992-08

6. D'Orso, G., Migliore, M.: A GIS-based method for evaluating the walkability of a pedestrian environment and prioritized investments. J. Transp. Geogr. **82**, 102555 (2020). https://doi.org/10.1016/j.jtrangeo.2019.102555

7. George, D.K., Xia, C.H.: Fleet-sizing and service availability for a vehicle rental system via closed queueing networks. Eur. J. Oper. Res. **211**, 198–207 (2011). https://doi.org/10.1016/J.EJOR.2010.12.015

8. Hu, L., Liu, Y.: Joint design of parking capacities and fleet size for one-way station-based carsharing systems with road congestion constraints. Transp. Res. Part B Methodol. **93**, 268–299 (2016). https://doi.org/10.1016/J.TRB.2016.07.021

9. Jorge, D., Molnar, G., de Almeida Correia, G.H.: Trip pricing of one-way station-based carsharing networks with zone and time of day price variations. Transp. Res. Part B Methodol. **81**, 461–482 (2015). https://doi.org/10.1016/J.TRB.2015.06.003

10. Li, X., Ma, J., Cui, J., Ghiasi, A., Zhou, F.: Design framework of large-scale one-way electric vehicle sharing systems: A continuum approximation model. Transp. Res. Part B Methodol. **88**, 21–45 (2016). https://doi.org/10.1016/J.TRB.2016.01.014

11. Migliore, M., D'Orso, G., Caminiti, D.: The current and future role of carsharing in palermo: analysis of collected data and results of a customer satisfaction survey. In: 2018 IEEE International Conference on Environment and Electrical Engineering and 2018 IEEE Industrial and Commercial Power Systems Europe (EEEIC/I&CPS Europe), Palermo, pp. 1–6 (2018). https://doi.org/10.1109/eeeic.2018.8494010

12. Nobis, C.: Carsharing as key contribution to multimodal and sustainable mobility behavior: carsharing in Germany. Transp. Res. Rec. **1986**(1), 89–97 (2006). https://doi.org/10.1177/0361198106198600112

13. Nourinejad, M., Roorda, M.J.: A dynamic carsharing decision support system. Transp. Res. Part E Logist. Transp. Rev. **66**, 36–50 (2014). https://doi.org/10.1016/j.tre.2014.03.003

14. Perboli, G., Ferrero, F., Musso, S., Vesco, A.: Business models and tariff simulation in car-sharing services. Transp. Res. Part A Policy Pract. **115**, 32–48 (2018). https://doi.org/10.1016/j.tra.2017.09.011

15. Xu, M., Meng, Q.: Fleet sizing for one-way electric carsharing services considering dynamic vehicle relocation and nonlinear charging profile. Transp. Res. Part B Methodol. **128**, 23–49 (2019). https://doi.org/10.1016/J.TRB.2019.07.016

16. Xu, M., Meng, Q., Liu, Z.: Electric vehicle fleet size and trip pricing for one-way carsharing services considering vehicle relocation and personnel assignment. Transp. Res. Part B Methodol. **111**, 60–82 (2018). https://doi.org/10.1016/J.TRB.2018.03.001

17. Yoon, T., Cherry, C.R., Jones, L.R.: One-way and round-trip carsharing: a stated preference experiment in Beijing. Transp. Res. Part D Transp. Environ. **53**, 102–114 (2017). https://doi.org/10.1016/J.TRD.2017.04.009

18. Yoon, T., Cherry, C.R., Ryerson, M.S., Bell, J.E.: Carsharing demand estimation and fleet simulation with EV adoption. J. Clean. Prod. **206**, 1051–1058 (2019). https://doi.org/10.1016/J.JCLEPRO.2018.09.124

International Workshop on Advances in Information Systems and Technologies for Emergency Management, Risk Assessment and Mitigation Based on the Resilience Concepts (ASTER 2020)

Typological Inventory of Residential Reinforced Concrete Buildings for the City of Potenza

Amedeo Flora[✉], Chiara Iacovino, Donatello Cardone,
and Marco Vona

School of Engineering, University of Basilicata,
Viale dell'Ateneo Lucano 10, 85100 Potenza, Italy
{amedeo.flora, chiara.iacovino, donatello.cardone,
marco.vona}@unibas.it

Abstract. The seismic vulnerability assessment of the built heritage located on a specific area represents an important starting point for both the evaluation of the consequences in the aftermath of significant seismic events and a proper management of the post-seismic reconstruction phase. In other words, the vulnerability assessment represents one of the main input elements for resilience analysis at urban scale. However, facing with a large-scale study, a building-specific assessment approach appears extremely difficult and time-consuming. In this optic, the definition of territorial-specific structural typologies and corresponding vulnerability classes represent a powerful tool for a rapid estimation of the "global vulnerability" of an examined area. As a matter of fact, the classification of the built heritage in a limited number of structural typologies (featuring similar characteristics) could sensibly reduce the complexity of the vulnerability assessment, hence resilience analysis, at urban scale.

In this paper, an investigation on the built heritage of the city centre of Potenza (south of Italy) is proposed. In particular, the main typological and structural features of the residential Reinforced Concrete (RC) constructions, detected in the investigated territory, have been identified through an integrated approach involving: Census data, documentary analyses, site and virtual inspections (i.e. GIS-based analysis). The typological-structural characterization represents the first step of a comprehensive study, carried out within the PON-AIM 2014–2020 project, aimed at the evaluation of the seismic resilience of the examined area.

Keywords: Built heritage · Reinforced concrete buildings · Seismic resilience · Census · Documental analysis · GIS technology

1 Introduction

The definition of potential seismic scenarios and possible resiliency objectives on a territorial scale can be performed at different levels of detail, depending on the territorial unit size, the robustness of seismic hazard data and the accuracy of the vulnerability model. From a practical point of view, the adoption of a building-specific

© Springer Nature Switzerland AG 2020
O. Gervasi et al. (Eds.): ICCSA 2020, LNCS 12250, pp. 899–913, 2020.
https://doi.org/10.1007/978-3-030-58802-1_64

vulnerability model appears a feasible option only for territorial units characterized by a limited size. Moreover, it is worth noting that, in many cases, the built heritage of most of the cities is characterized by homogeneous areas (defined as "compartment"), featuring the same historical, urbanistic and constructive peculiarities. All that considered, the identification of a certain number of territorial-specific structural typologies represents a pragmatic choice for the simplified estimation of the "global vulnerability" of a given area. As a matter of fact, such an approach sensibly reduces the time required for a building-specific approach while maintaining a sufficient accuracy for the preliminary assessment, screening and prioritization of a large building stock.

Different criteria can be adopted for the identification of the structural typologies associated with a given territory. The simpler is the adopted criterion the lower is the accuracy level of the consequent vulnerability assessment. The more elementary typologies inventories classify buildings based on the material of the structural resisting system [1, 2]. However, the inventory accuracy can be significantly improved considering additional information on buildings' peculiarities (e.g. age of construction, number of storeys, non-structural elements dimensions and materials, vertical and horizontal system, etc.).

Several sources of information are available for the inventory compiling. For what concerns the Italian background, the reference database on the built heritage is provided by the Italian National Statistics Institute (ISTAT). Contrary to the data provided by other European countries, the ISTAT database on built heritage is sufficiently stocked. Indeed, data on age of construction, structural material, number of storeys and building area/volume are available. Unfortunately, such data are aggregated at Census Tract (CT) level due to the Italian privacy policy, thus limiting the robustness of the information.

The present paper describes the preliminary activities of a comprehensive research project, funded by the Operative National Program (PON) of Research and Innovation (2014–2010), aimed at the seismic vulnerability assessment, and consequent resilience capacity analysis, of the city centre of Potenza (southern Italy). In particular, an inventory of the main structural typologies of residential Reinforced Concrete constructions is presented herein. Different sources of information have been employed for the inventory compiling: Census data, documentary analyses, site and virtual inspections (i.e. GIS-based analysis). In the first part, aggregated and disaggregated data are presented. In the second part, a number of structural typologies are tentatively identified for the following seismic performance assessment.

2 Previous Approaches for Typologies Inventory Compiling

Building typologies identification is a fundamental preliminary step for any vulnerability or loss assessment process. Indeed, the computational effort associated with a building-specific approach appears unfeasible for areas or regions with a building population of hundreds or thousands elements. As mentioned before, grouping buildings in a limited number of structural typologies increases the manageability of the examined case-studies maintaining a sufficient accuracy for vulnerability analysis. Obviously, the level of accuracy depends on the completeness and consistency of the assumed classification approach. In the last decades, several international building classification schemes have been proposed. Most of them have been also integrated in comprehensive methodologies for the evaluation of the building vulnerability and implemented within international seismic codes [3, 4]. The building classification schemes are characterized by different levels of detail. The classification with respect to the construction material represents the most basic approach. The latter has been adopted within MSK–64 and later in the European Macroseismic Scale EMS [1, 2]. The second generation of building classifications [5] introduced new and more specific parameters. In particular, age of construction/design code level, primary load bearing structure (only vertical or vertical and horizontal) and total height/number of storeys have been taken into account. Recently, very accurate building classification schemes have been proposed [6]. Specific characteristics (such as orientation of the lateral load-resisting systems, building shape in plan, structural irregularities, exterior wall materials and dimensions, etc.) affecting the seismic performances of the building are considered.

However, it is worth noting that the prevalence of a construction typology on a certain territory depends on many different factors such as: (i) geological and topographical conditions (influencing the local availability of building construction materials), (ii) traditional building technologies, (iii) socio-economic conditions, (iv) meteorological conditions (influencing the selection of materials and non-structural elements dimensions), (v) hazard history, etc. This leads to the existence of several territorial-specific typologies that are not included in the major international building' classifications. As a consequence, many customized classifications have been developed at regional scale. The most common approach for the definition of a customized classification consists in the employment of a Census database as primary source of information. The heterogeneous data provided by Census on buildings are then integrated using other territorial-specific sources of information (documental analysis, virtual and in situ inspections, etc.) [7, 8].

3   Case-Study

Potenza municipality is the chief-town of the Basilicata region (southern Italy) counting a population of about 70.000 people (ISTAT 2011) [15], located on a hill in the axial-active seismic belt (30 to 50 km wide) of southern Apennines. During his history, Potenza was hit by several strong earthquakes (intensity higher than or equal to VIII MCS). In particular, the 1826 and 1857 events caused severe damage in the entire town [9] imposing a massive demolition and reconstruction activity [9] in the historical city centre. During the 30s and 40s the demographic increment produced the migration of the population to new urban areas located in the north of the city territory. In this context, an important public housing plan was pursued by the local organization of Social Housing (Azienda Territoriale per l'Edilizia Residenziale, ATER) creating two new residential neighborhoods (i.e. Santa Maria and Verderuolo districts). In the aftermath of the Irpinia and Basilicata earthquake (November 1980), a massive reconstruction plan, funded by the Italian Government (law 219/81), involved several existing buildings in the Potenza municipality.

An investigation on the built heritage of the city of Potenza is proposed in this paper. In particular, two main sample areas are chosen for this study: the hilltop town ("old town centre", shown in yellow in Fig. 2 and labeled as C1) and the "residential public housing neighborhood" (shown in blue in Fig. 2 and labeled as C2). Those areas can be considered as homogeneous zones (compartments) featuring specific historical, urbanistic and constructive peculiarities. Moreover, such compartments include most of the historical built heritage of the city, developed in two main periods: 1850–1950 and 1945–1990, respectively. Due to the small amount and specific peculiarities of public buildings, only private residential buildings will be considered herein (Fig. 1).

Fig. 1. Geographical location and urban area of Potenza (Basilicata Region, Southern Italy)

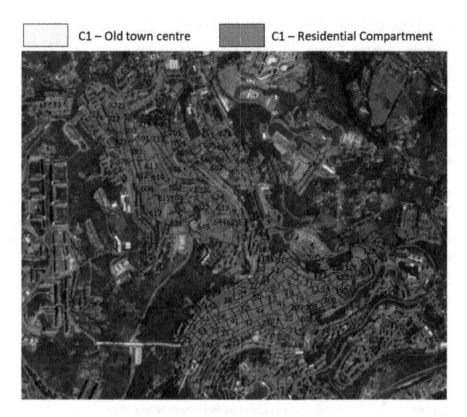

Fig. 2. Census tracts of the old town centre (yellow) and residential (blue) compartments (Color figure online)

4   Building Typologies Inventory Assembling Approach

As mentioned in Sect. 2, in some cases, customized schemes are needed to properly classify the built heritage at territorial scale. In the present paper, a specific building typologies inventory referred to the examined compartments (C1 and C2) is proposed. The assembling approach is based on the combination of two different informative levels. The preliminary source of information is represented by the Census data provided by the Italian Institute of Statistics (ISTAT). Due to the privacy policy, such data are available only in an aggregated form. In other words, while it is possible to know, for example, the number of RC buildings in a certain CT, the user cannot directly derive the number of those buildings featuring 2, 3 or more than 3 storeys or, similarly, the number of RC buildings realized in a specific period of time. As a consequence, a specific de-aggregation procedure is needed in order to use such data for a suitable classification. For this reason, the primary Census data are successively integrated through secondary sources of information represented by extensive documental and virtual analysis and specific building surveys.

4.1   Analyzing Census Data in Aggregated Form

Generally speaking, Census data represent a fundamental source for a building typologies classification. Differently from other European countries, the data provided by the Italian Institute of Statistics (ISTAT) are extremely populated (repeated every 10 years) and homogeneously distributed on the entire national territory. Table 1 summarizes the Census Variables (CVs) provided for each CT within the ISTAT "building database". Figures 3, 4 and 5 show the aggregated restitutions for buildings located in the two examined compartments. For the sake of completeness, some synthetic data are also summarized in Table 2.

Based on the aggregated Census data, some preliminary important considerations can be made. First of all, the data provided in Fig. 3 outline that, in both compartments, the percentage of masonry buildings is prevalent. As expected, this percentage is extremely high in the old town centre (C1), being equal to approximately the 80% (see Fig. 3(a)). However a significant percentage of RC buildings is also observed (approximately equal to 20%).

Table 1. Relevant Census Variables (CV) for buildings (ISTAT 2011)

Census variable	Description
E3	Total number of residential buildings
E5	Number of Masonry residential buildings
E6	Number of Reinforced Concrete (RC) residential buildings
E7	Number of residential buildings realized with other materials
E8	Number of residential buildings built before 1919
E9	Number of residential buildings built in the period 1919–45
E10	Number of residential buildings built in the period 1946–60
E11	Number of residential buildings built in the period 1961–70
E12	Number of residential buildings built in the period 1971–80
E13	Number of residential buildings built in the period 1981–90
E14	Number of residential buildings built in the period 1991–2000
E15	Number of residential buildings built in the period 2001–2005
E16	Number of residential buildings built after 2005
E17	Number of residential buildings with 1 Storey
E18	Number of residential buildings with 2 Storeys
E19	Number of residential buildings with 3 Storeys
E20	Number of residential buildings with 4 or more than 4 Storeys

This is probably due to some political decisions on the old town planning taken between 1945 and 1970 [9, 10]. As a matter of fact, in the mentioned period, many old masonry buildings in the historical centre (namely, C1 compartment) were demolished and replaced by new RC buildings. Similar interventions were carried in the aftermath of the Irpinia and Basilicata earthquake (30th November 1980) that strongly hit the city centre of Potenza. This lead to a not negligible percentage (around 10%) of RC buildings realized in the period 1981–1990. For what concerns the residential compartment (C2), a percentage of RC buildings lower than 30% is observed (see Fig. 3b)). This is quite unexpected since most of the buildings located in C2 (more than 70%) have been realized during the period 1960–1990 (see Fig. 4(b)), considered as the "golden age" for RC buildings. However, the previous consideration is completely overturned reanalyzing the same data in terms of building volume. Actually, RC buildings located in the residential compartment typically feature a number of stories greater than masonry buildings, so that their average volume is sensibly larger (approximately 3,800 m^3 against approximately 540 m^3) [11]. All that considered, the construction volume occupied in C2 by RC buildings represent approximately the 77% of the total.

Another interesting consideration is that the percentage of buildings realized in the period 1971–1980 and after 1981 is not negligible for both compartments. As a matter of fact, 1971 and 1981 represent turning points from a technical point of view. In the early 1971, new regulations concerning the administrative management of the design process for new buildings were enforced by the Italian Government [12]. Such regulations determined a stronger control on bureaucratic procedures and (structural and non-structural) material' acceptance criteria, while only slight differences in terms of seismic capacity. Actually, the gravity load design philosophy continued to represent the general design practice, leading to RC buildings featuring the same structural peculiarities of those realized in the pre-1971 period. On the contrary, the Irpinia and Basilicata earthquake (1980) forced the Italian Government to introduce some specific regulations for the damaged territories [13], classifying Campania, Puglia and Basilicata regions as seismic zones. As a consequence, buildings realized in the aftermath of the mentioned regulations feature an enhanced seismic behavior taking into account the effect of lateral seismic loads. All that considered, two major classes of buildings can be identified with respect to the age of construction (a_c), or level of code design, namely: pre- and post-1981. The percentages of buildings afferent to the aforementioned classes are reported in columns 5 and 6 of Table 2, respectively.

Finally, considering that the seismic behavior is strongly affected by the structure height, important considerations can be derived analyzing the aggregated data with respect to the number of storeys (n_s).

As showed in Fig. 5, buildings featuring more than 3 storeys (labeled as "4+") are prevalent in both compartments (51% in the old town centre and 78% in the residential compartment). Unfortunately, as mentioned before, based on the Census aggregated data no specific information are available to effectively separate the percentages of medium-rise ($4 \leq n_s \leq 6$) and high rise ($n_s > 6$) buildings. On the other hand, the percentage of low-rise building (namely, 1- to 3-storeys) can be directly estimated appearing not negligible, in particular in the old city centre compartment (being equal to approximately 30%).

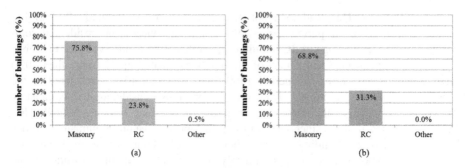

Fig. 3. Percentage distribution of residential buildings in terms of construction materials for (a) old town centre and (b) residential compartments (ISTAT 2011).

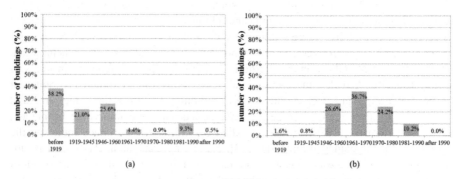

Fig. 4. Percentage distribution of residential buildings in terms of age of construction for (a) old town centre and (b) residential compartments (ISTAT 2011).

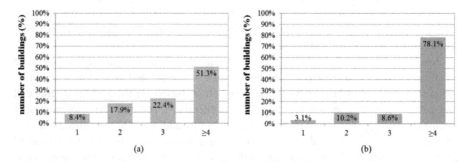

Fig. 5. Percentage distribution of residential buildings in terms of number of storeys for (a) old town centre and (b) residential compartments (ISTAT 2011).

Table 2. Synthetic relevant data referred to the examined compartments (ISTAT 2011)

Compartment	No. of buildings	Masonry	RC	Pre-81	Post-81	$n_s \leq 3$	$n_s > 3$
C1	429	76%	24%	90%	10%	49%	51%
C2	128	69%	31%	90%	10%	22%	78%

4.2 Secondary Sources of Information

Based on the Census data described in the previous section, two main variables emerged as significant classification parameters, namely, the number of storeys (n_s) and the age of construction (a_c). Innovative techniques such as GIS-technology and High Resolution optical satellite imagery have been used to rapidly collect geo-referenced information on the number of storeys of the building stocks located in the examined compartments [14], thus allowing a proper de-aggregation of the mentioned Census data. In order to limit the number of typologies for a suitable management of the building inventory, three macro-classes of buildings have been defined with respect to the parameter n_s. As a matter of fact, several studies confirmed that, all other variables being equal, RC buildings characterized by 1 to 3 storeys (low-rise buildings) exhibit approximately the same seismic response [7, 8]. Similar considerations can be drawn for buildings featuring 4 to 6 storeys (medium-rise buildings) and for buildings with 7 to 10 storeys (high-rise buildings). As a consequence, the following classes have been defined herein: "Lr" (1–3 storeys), "Mr" (4 to 6 storeys) and "Hr" (7 to 10 storeys).

With reference to the second parameter (namely, a_c), two major classes of buildings have been identified: Pre- and Post-1981. Clearly, the identification of these two groups of buildings is not merely temporal but is more properly related to the reference design code. As a matter of fact, the introduction of new seismic regulations [13] led to specific peculiarities for buildings designed after 1981. In order to identify the main characteristics of the two mentioned classes of buildings (pre- and post-1981), a comprehensive documental analysis has been carried out. In particular, a large database provided by the local organization of Social Housing (Azienda Territoriale per l'Edilizia Residenziale, ATER), strongly involved in the residential compartment construction and in the post-seismic reconstruction, has been analyzed. Moreover, some building-by-building surveys, providing detailed data for both dimensional and structural peculiarities for a single building in an investigated area, have been performed. Finally, several information have been gathered interviewing local technicians with deep knowledge of the construction characteristics.

Table 3 summarizes the main peculiarities of pre- and post-1981 buildings derived from the aforesaid investigation. As can be seen, the typical lateral resisting system of pre-1981 buildings is characterized by perimeter and internal mono-directional resisting frames (RC frame buildings). External deep beams (characterized by a size reduction at higher floors) and internal shallow beams were typically adopted. On the contrary, resisting frames in both principal directions with a wide use of shallow beams has been generally observed for post-1981 buildings. Important information regarding non-structural elements have been also collected. In particular, pre-1981 buildings feature heavy masonry infills (generally constituted by solid bricks) in the most of

Table 3. Main peculiarities of pre- and post-1981 buildings.

	Design code level	Resisting system	Structural elements	Non-structural elements	Horizontal system
Pre-1981	Gravity load design	– Perimeter resisting frames – Internal resisting frames in only one direction	– External deep beams internal shallow beams – Staircase: knee beams and cantilever steps	– Heavy masonry infills (solid bricks) – Light double layer masonry infills in some cases (buildings realized between 1960 and 1980)	– Unidirectional reinforced concrete T-beams and hollow tiles mixed floor
Post-1981	Earthquake resistant design	Resisting frames in both principal directions	– External deep beams (size reduction at higher floors); Wide use of internal shallow beams. – Staircase: knee beams and cantilever steps; Waist-slab staircases in a few cases realized in the 90 s	– Light masonry infills – Hollow clay bricks arranged in two layers (12 + 8 cm) separated by a 10 cm interspace	– Unidirectional reinforced concrete T-beams and hollow tiles mixed floor

Table 4. Preliminary macro-typologies inventory for the examined compartments

Macro typology ID	Description
L	Bidirectional resisting system Light masonry infills Earthquake resistant design
M	One direction resisting system Light masonry infills Gravity load design
H	One direction resisting system Heavy masonry infills Gravity load design

Fig. 6. Example of Pilotis-storey building (Via Roma, Potenza – C2 compartment).

cases. Light masonry infills (realized using a double layer of hallow bricks 10 + 10 cm or 12 + 8 cm) have been observed in a limited number of cases, in particular for buildings realized in the period 1960–1980. External masonry infills constituted by hollow clay bricks arranged in two layers (12 + 8 cm) and separated by a 10 cm cavity were typically adopted for post-1981 buildings. Clearly, the combination of the mentioned characteristics for each class of buildings produces a different seismic behavior and, as a consequence, a different seismic vulnerability.

Table 5. Building typologies inventory for the examined compartments

Macro typology ID			Number of storeys			Staircase typology		Vertical irregularities		ID
L	M	H	Lr	Mr	Hr	K	s	PF	IF	
×			×			×		×		L,Lr,k,PF
×			×			×			×	L,Lr,k,IF
×			×				×	×		L,Lr,s,PF
×			×				×		×	L,Lr,s,IF
×				×		×		×		L,Mr,k,PF
×				×		×			×	L,Mr,k,IF
×				×			×	×		L,Mr,s,PF
×				×			×		×	L,Mr,s,IF
×					×	×		×		L,Hr,k,PF
×					×	×			×	L,Hr,k,IF
×					×		×	×		L,Hr,s,PF
×					×		×		×	L,Hr,s,IF
	×		×			×		×		M,Lr,k,PF
	×		×			×			×	M,Lr,k,IF
	×		×				×	×		M,Lr,s,PF
	×		×				×		×	M,Lr,s,IF
	×			×		×		×		M,Mr,k,PF
	×			×		×			×	M,Mr,k,IF
	×			×			×	×		M,Mr,s,PF
	×			×			×		×	M,Mr,s,IF
	×				×	×		×		M,Hr,k,PF
	×				×	×			×	M,Hr,k,IF
	×				×		×	×		M,Hr,s,PF

(continued)

Typological Inventory of Residential Reinforced Concrete Buildings   911

Table 5. (continued)

Macro typology ID			Number of storeys			Staircase typology		Vertical irregularities		ID
L	M	H	Lr	Mr	Hr	K	s	PF	IF	
	x				x		x		x	M,Hr,s,IF
		x	x			x		x		H,Lr,k,PF
		x	x			x			x	H,Lr,k,IF
		x	x				x	x		H,Lr,s,PF
		x	x				x		x	H,Lr,s,IF
		x		x		x		x		H,Mr,k,PF
		x		x		x			x	H,Mr,k,IF
		x		x			x	x		H,Mr,s,PF
		x		x			x		x	H,Mr,s,IF
		x			x	x		x		H,Hr,k,PF
		x			x	x			x	H,Hr,k,IF
		x			x		x	x		H,Hr,s,PF
		x			x		x		x	H,Hr,s,IF

Based on the aforementioned considerations, a preliminary typologies inventory, in terms of seismic vulnerability, can be defined. In particular, three different macro-typologies can be considered, featuring Low [L], Medium [M] and High [H] vulnerability (see Table 4). The preliminary inventory proposed in Table 4 can be further refined considering other specific building characteristics (namely, "attributes") that effectively affect the seismic behavior. Besides the aforementioned number of storeys (n_s), significant attributes emerged from the described documental and in situ investigation (see Table 5). Among those, irregularities in elevation and staircase typology cannot be ignored for a comprehensive evaluation of the building typologies. Vertical irregularities are frequent for both pre-1981 (generally for those built in the 70s) and post-1981 (namely, 80s and 90s) buildings. In particular, such irregularities are mainly represented by an open ground storey (pilotis-storey, PF) as shown in Fig. 6. Similarly, two main staircase typologies have been observed, although knee beams with cantilever steps represented the typical solution for pre-1981 buildings and for most of post-1981 buildings. Waist-slab staircases have been observed in a few cases for post-1981 buildings (generally for those realized in the 90s).

It is worth noting that slightly differences have been observed in terms of other attributes, such as roof type, horizontal floor types (always constituted by composite RC beams and clay blocks), state of preservation, etc. As a consequence, such attributes have been neglected in the final inventory. Finally, it is also worth noting that the (in plan) structural configuration and the structural element dimensions (derived from the described investigation) will be opportunely taken into account at a later stage of the analysis and, in particular, during the numerical modeling of the selected archetype buildings. The final building inventory, obtained adopting the classification approach described in the previous sections is shown in Table 5. As can be seen, a total of 36 classes have been identified.

5   Conclusions

In this paper, a simplified approach aimed at the assembling of a building typologies inventory is presented and applied to the urban residential area of Potenza (southern Italy). In particular, the proposed approach combines the primary-level information collected by a Census-based database with a complementary informative database based on specific documental/virtual analysis, building-by-building surveys and expert judgment. A preliminary inventory composed by three macro-typologies has been defined based on heuristic criteria. Such preliminary inventory has been then refined considering specific building structural peculiarities affecting the seismic behavior. Thereby, 36 typologies have been identified.

The research activity described in this paper represents the primary step of a comprehensive study for the evaluation of the seismic resilience of the investigated area. A complementary study, regarding the masonry residential buildings located in the same compartments, has been carried out in parallel by the same authors of this paper.

Acknowledgments. This research was funded by the PON-AIM 2014–2020 project supported by the Italian Ministry of University and Public Instruction.

References

1. Grunthal, G.: European Macroseismic Scale (EMS-92), Chaiers du Centre Européen de Géodynamique et de Séismologie, 15 (1992)
2. Grunthal, G.: European Macroseismic Scale (EMS-98), Cahiers du Centre Européen de Géodynamique et de Séismologie, Luxembourg (1998)
3. ATC (Applied Technology Council): Earthquake Damage Evaluation Data for California, Applied Technology Council Report ATC-13, Redwood City, CA (1985)
4. Federal Emergency Management Agency: FEMA 154 – Rapid Visual Screening of Buildings for Potential Seismic Hazards: A Handbook. Earthquake Hazards Reduction Series 41, 2nd edn. (2002)
5. Federal Emergency Management Agency: HAZUS-MH MR4 Technical Manual, Washington, D.C. (2003)
6. Brzev, S., Scawthorn, C., Charleson, A.W., Jaiswal, K.: Interim overview of GEM building taxonomy V2.0. Report produced in the context of the GEM Building Taxonomy Global Component, Version 1.0 (2012)
7. Polese, M., Gaetani d'Aragona, M., Prota, A.: Simplified approach for building inventory and seismic damage assessment at the territorial scale: an application for a town in southern Italy. Soil Dyn. Earthq. Eng. **121**, 405–420 (2019)
8. Corlito, V., De Matteis, G.: Typological-structural characterization and seismic vulnerability assessment of reinforced concrete buildings in the Caserta district through the parameters of the CARTIS form. In: XV Convegno Nazionale ANIDIS, L'ingegneria Sismica in Italia, Ascoli Piceno (2019)
9. Gizzi, F.T., Masini, N.: Historical earthquakes and damage patterns in Potenza (Basilicata, Southern Italy). Ann. Geophys. **50**(5) (2007)
10. Dolce, D., Masi, A., Marino, M., Vona, M.: Earthquake damage scenarios of the building stock of Potenza (Southern Italy) including site effects. Bull. Earthq. Eng. **1**, 115–140 (2003). https://doi.org/10.1023/A:1024809511362
11. Chiauzzi, L., Masi, A., Mucciarelli, M., Vona, M., et al.: Building damage scenarios based on exploitation of Housner intensity derived from finite faults ground motion simulations. Bull. Earthq. Eng. **10**, 517–545 (2012). https://doi.org/10.1007/s10518-011-9309-8
12. Norme per la disciplina delle opere di conglomerato cementizio armato, normale e precompresso ed a struttura metallica (GU n.321) (1971). (in Italian)
13. Decreto Ministeriale: Dichiarazione in zone sismiche nelle regioni Basilicata, Campania e Puglia, 7 March 1981. (in Italian)
14. Comber, A., et al.: Using shadows in high-resolution imagery to determine building height. Remote Sens. Lett. **3**(7), 551–556 (2012)
15. (ISTAT 2011) 15° Censimento della popolazione e delle abitazioni, Istituto Nazionale di Statistica (ISTAT), 9 October 2011 (in Italian)

Defining a Masonry Building Inventory for the City of Potenza

Chiara Iacovino[✉], Amedeo Flora, Donatello Cardone, and Marco Vona

School of Engineering, University of Basilicata, Viale dell'Ateneo Lucano 10, 85100 Potenza, Italy
{chiara.iacovino,amedeo.flora,donatello.cardone, marco.vona}@unibas.it

Abstract. The seismic vulnerability assessment of masonry built heritage is an importance issue in Italy, due to the high seismic hazard of the territory and the huge amount of masonry buildings located in the exposed areas. The evaluation of the seismic performance of buildings can be useful to assess possible damages occurred after an earthquake, the direct costs which would result from it, the "pre" and "post" loss distribution in an urban area and the most vulnerable buildings. At urban scale, a building-specific assessment approach appears extremely difficult and time-consuming because of the large number of constructions. Therefore, being able to classify the built heritage in a limited number of territorial-specific structural typologies with similar characteristics would significantly simplify the vulnerability assessment.

This paper shows a typological and structural classification of existing masonry buildings of the historic center of Potenza (south of Italy) aimed at designing a virtual city consisting of different buildings categories. The main typological and structural features of the masonry constructions (MUR) have been identified through documentary analyses, Census data, site investigation and GIS-based analysis by considering the frequency of significant structural parameters. This represents the starting point of a comprehensive research study, carried out within the PON-AIM 2014–2020 project, aimed at the evaluation of the seismic resilience of the investigated area.

Keywords: Existing masonry buildings · Built heritage · Resilience

1 Introduction

The historic and recent earthquakes showed the problem of the seismic vulnerability of existing masonry constructions, most of which were generally designed without proper seismic resistance features. Therefore, the assessment of existing residential and historic masonry structures in highly seismic zones remains an important issue and a considerable challenge due to the nature and characteristics of these structures. The vulnerability assessment of these constructions has been investigated in the literature through different methods and focusing on different modeling issues [1–3].

Masonry structures are a much diffused type of construction which can be built rapidly, cheaply and often without any plan or particular technical competence.

© Springer Nature Switzerland AG 2020
O. Gervasi et al. (Eds.): ICCSA 2020, LNCS 12250, pp. 914–927, 2020.
https://doi.org/10.1007/978-3-030-58802-1_65

Masonry also represents the structural type of a large architectural heritage that needs to be preserved. Moreover, old unreinforced masonry buildings constitute the large majority of most urban aggregates in several seismic prone countries. The main characteristics of masonry buildings are high rigidity, low tensile and shear strength, low ductility and low capacity of bearing reverse loading. These are the main reasons for the frequent collapse of masonry buildings during earthquakes, often responsible for a considerable number of casualties.

A wide multiplicity of typologies can be found depending on available materials, climatic and functional requirements, technical knowledge and traditional practice specific to different countries [4]. Indeed, a wide variety of materials, both natural and artificial, and different structural typologies have been adopted in the past centuries for the construction of traditional masonry buildings. Therefore, the analysis of masonry constructions could be rather complex both for the variability of the materials used and for the lack of knowledge of some parameters (e.g. the construction systems adopted, the mechanical properties of the materials and the structural details, the changes occurred over time).

Detailed seismic vulnerability evaluation is a complex and expensive approach and can only be performed on a limited number of buildings. It is therefore very important to use simpler procedures that can help to rapidly evaluate the vulnerability profile of different types of buildings. In Europe and Italy, the built heritage of most of the cities is characterized by homogeneous areas, named compartment, featuring the same historical, urbanistic and constructive peculiarities. The identification of a limited number of territorial-specific structural typologies sensibly reduces the time-consuming with respect to a building-specific approach while maintaining a sufficient accuracy of the vulnerability assessment.

This paper presents the preliminary results of an ongoing research project, funded by the Operative National Program (PON) of Research and Innovation (2014–2010), finalized at assessing the seismic vulnerability of the city center of Potenza (southern Italy) and defining better resilience-building strategies in order to minimize losses and recovery time after an earthquake. This first step of the project consists of a critical survey of typological and structural characteristics of the investigated sample of buildings, such as building typology, construction period, adopted design standards, construction materials and structural configuration. In particular, an inventory of the main structural typologies of the residential masonry (MUR) constructions is presented herein. The characterization of the most frequent MUR typologies in the investigated area has been achieved through Census data, documentary analyses, site and virtual inspections (i.e. GIS-based analysis). In the first part, aggregated and disaggregated data are presented. In the second part, the structural typologies inventory is proposed.

2 Previous Approaches for Typologies Inventory Compiling

Building typologies identification is a fundamental preliminary step for any vulnerability or loss assessment process. Based on construction techniques, local and regional traditions, hazard history, climate conditions, and available materials, buildings can vary widely from one region to another. In order to manage these issues when characterizing the building stock at a city wide scale, a common approach is the identification of a set of building types. The definition of building types depends on data availability and resources.

In the last decades, several international building classification schemes have been proposed. Most of them have been also integrated in comprehensive methodologies for the evaluation of the building vulnerability and implemented within international seismic codes [5, 6]. The building classification schemes are characterized by different levels of detail. The classification with respect to the construction material represents the most basic approach. The latter has been adopted within MSK–64 and later in the European Macroseismic Scale EMS [7, 8]. The second generation of building classifications introduced new and more specific parameters, such as age of construction/design code level, primary load bearing structure (only vertical or vertical and horizontal) and total height/number of stories [9]. Recently, very accurate building classification schemes have been proposed considering building shape in plan, structural irregularities, exterior wall materials and dimensions, that can affect the seismic performances [10].

The most common approach for the definition of a customized classification at regional scale consists in the employment of a Census database as primary source of information. The heterogeneous data provided by Census on buildings are then integrated using other territorial-specific sources of information (documental analysis, virtual and in situ inspections, etc.) [11, 12].

3 Description of the Case-Study

This work is carried out on the city of Potenza, located in Basilicata on a hill in the axial-active seismic belt (30 to 50 km wide) of southern Apennines (Fig. 1). The city was hit by several strong earthquakes (intensity higher than or equal to VIII MCS). In particular, the 1826 and 1857 events caused severe damage in the entire town imposing a massive demolition and reconstruction activity in the historical city center [13]. In the aftermath of the Irpinia and Basilicata earthquake (November 1980), a massive reconstruction plan, funded by the Italian Government (law 219/81), involved several existing buildings in the Potenza municipality.

An investigation on the built heritage of the city of Potenza is proposed in this paper. In particular, two main sample areas have been chosen for this study: the "old town center" and the "residential public housing neighborhood". Those areas can be considered as homogeneous zones (compartments) featuring specific historical, urbanistic and constructive peculiarities. Moreover, such compartments include most of the historical built heritage of the city, developed in two main periods: 1850–1950 and 1945–1990, respectively. Due to the small amount and to the specific peculiarities of the public buildings, only the private residential building stocks will be considered herein.

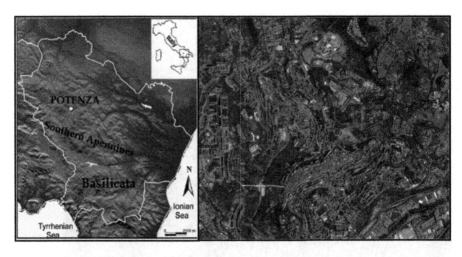

Fig. 1. Geographical location and urban area of Potenza (Basilicata Region, Southern Italy).

4   Building Typologies Definition

This work presents a specific building typologies inventory referred to the examined areas, issued by the combination of two different informative levels. Official national census databases provided by the Italian Institute of Statistics (ISTAT) were used as the primary source for the classification of the building stock, because they constitute the most reliable data source about buildings. Due to the privacy policy, such data are available only in the aggregated form: the number of masonry buildings in a certain census tract (CT) is known, but the number of masonry buildings realized in a specific period of construction or the number of masonry buildings featuring 2, 3 or more than 3 stories is unknown. For this reason, the primary Census data are successively integrated through secondary sources of information represented by extensive documental and virtual analysis and specific building surveys.

4.1   Census Data in Aggregated Form

Census data represent a fundamental source for a building typologies classification. In Italy, as in other countries, census data collection process provides a unique opportunity to build a complete small area mapping. The data provided by ISTAT are extremely populated (repeated every 10 years) and homogeneously distributed on the entire national territory.

Figure 2 shows the census areas of the city of Potenza and Table 1 reports the values of resident population and residential buildings in each Census Area. The old town center is included in area number 1 while the residential public housing neighborhood falls in census area number 3.

Figure 3 shows the selected census tracts of the old town center (in yellow and labeled as C1) and of the residential public housing neighborhood (in blue and labeled as C2).

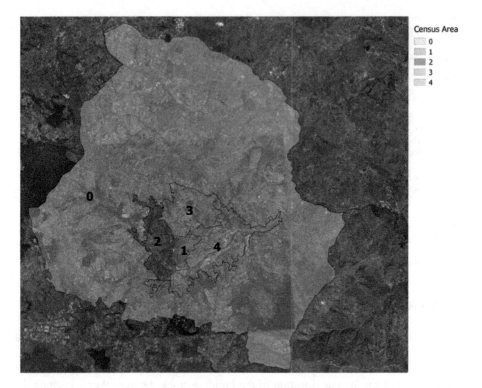

Census Area
- 0
- 1
- 2
- 3
- 4

Fig. 2. Census areas of Potenza (ISTAT, 2011).

Table 1. Resident population and number of buildings in each Census Area (ISTAT, 2011).

Census area	Resident population	Residential buildings
0	10344	3132
1	12876	765
2	13343	915
3	14952	973
4	15262	2257

A list of available census variables useful for impact assessment referring to residential buildings is provided for each CT within the ISTAT "building database" referring to the 2001 census campaign [14]. Table 2, Table 3, Table 4 show the aggregated restitutions for buildings located in the two examined compartments.

Analyzing ISTAT data, the percentage of masonry buildings is prevalent in both compartments. This percentage is extremely high in the old town center (C1), being equal to approximately the 80%. Reinforced concrete buildings represent around 20% of the total, probably due to the demolition and reconstruction of old masonry buildings occurred between 1945 and 1970 [13, 15]. The percentage of masonry buildings is also

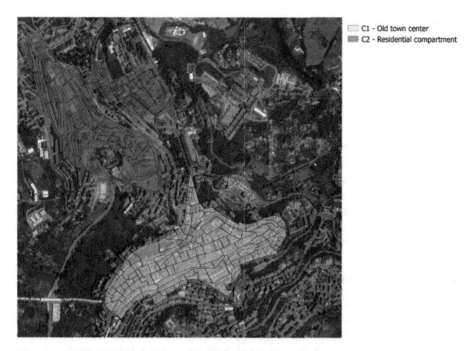

C1 - Old town center
C2 - Residential compartment

Fig. 3. Census tracts of the old town center (yellow) and residential (blue) compartments. (Color figure online)

Table 2. Percentage distribution of residential buildings in terms of construction materials for old town center (C1) and residential (C2) compartments.

	Masonry	RC	Other
C1	75.8%	23.8%	0.4%
C2	68.8%	31.2%	0.0%

Table 3. Percentage distribution of residential buildings in terms of age of construction for old town center (C1) and residential (C2) compartments.

	<1919	1919–1945	1946–1960	1961–1970	1971–1980	1981–1990	≥ 1991
C1	38.2%	21.0%	25.6%	4.4%	0.9%	9.3%	0.5%
C2	1.6%	0.8%	26.6%	36.7%	24.2%	10.1%	0.0%

high in the residential compartment (C2), where most of the buildings were built with load-bearing masonry structure during the period 1940–1960.

The percentage of buildings realized in the period 1971–1980 and after 1981 is not negligible. The whole historical center was subjected to significant seismic improvement interventions in the aftermath of the Irpinia and Basilicata earthquake (30th November 1980) that strongly hit the city center of Potenza.

Table 4. Percentage distribution of residential buildings in terms of number of stories for old town center (C1) and residential (C2) compartments (ISTAT, 2011).

	1	2	3	≥ 4
C1	8.4%	17.9%	22.4%	51.3%
C2	3.1%	10.2%	8.6%	78.1%

Finally, Table 4 shows that buildings featuring more than 4 stories are prevalent in both compartments (around 51% in the old town center and 78% in the residential compartment). Unfortunately, as mentioned before, based on the Census aggregated data no specific information is available to effectively separate the percentages of medium-rise and high rise buildings. On the other hand, the percentage of low-rise building (1–3 stories) can be directly estimated appearing not negligible, in particular in the old city center compartment (being equal to approximately 30%).

4.2   Secondary Sources of Information

Based on the Census data described in the previous section, two main variables emerged as significant classification parameters, namely the number of stories and the age of construction. Several studies showed that there is a close correlation between the period of construction and the structural behavior, almost independently of other construction characteristics, such as the state of conservation, which could improve or worsen the basic structural behavior [16].

The characterization of the masonry typologies in the investigated areas has been performed identifying the most significant parameters in addition to the number of stories and the construction period. The types of vertical structures (regular or irregular masonry), the horizontal structure (deformable or semi-rigid or rigid slab), the presence of mixed structures, the roof types, the presence of vaults, the presence of seismic structural intervention have been considered.

A comprehensive documental analysis has been carried out to identify the main characteristics of masonry buildings. In particular, a large database provided by the local organization of Social Housing (Azienda Territoriale per l'Edilizia Residenziale, ATER), strongly involved in the residential compartment construction and in the post-seismic reconstruction, has been analyzed. Moreover, a number of building-by-building surveys, providing detailed data for both dimensional and structural peculiarities for a single building in an investigated area, have been performed. Finally, other information has been gathered interviewing local technicians with deep knowledge of the construction characteristics.

Table 5 summarizes the main peculiarities of masonry constructions (MUR) derived by the described investigation with an example of building for each typology. Figure 4 shows the macro-classes in a GIS map.

The MUR1 typology concerns the first urban village built outside the historical center of the city in the 1920s. The buildings are made of square local stone or solid brick masonry with floors with hollow bricks and steel beams. Connections or devices for absorbing forces (e.g. steel roads) were not provided. The seismic behavior of this

Table 5. Preliminary macro-typologies inventory for the examined compartments.

PARAMETER	CHARACTERISTIC
MUR1	Regular masonry (solid brick masonry) Semi-rigid slab (floor with hollow bricks and steel beams) Absence of vaults Absence of mixed structures Pitched roof with wood structure and planking Absence of seismic interventions
MUR2	Regular masonry (cut stone with good bonding) Semi-rigid (vault floor with bricks and steel beams) Absence of vaults Absence of mixed structures Pitched roof with brick-concrete slab Localized interventions
MUR3	Regular masonry (solid brick masonry) Rigid slab (floor with reinforced brick-concrete slab) Absence of vaults Absence of mixed structures Pitched roof with brick-concrete slab Absence of seismic interventions

MUR4 	Regular masonry (solid brick masonry) Rigid slab (floor with reinforced brick-concrete slab) Absence of vaults External masonry with internal RC frames Pitched roof with brick-concrete slab Absence of interventions
MUR5 	Regular masonry (solid brick masonry) Rigid slab (floor with reinforced brick-concrete slab) Absence of vaults Absence of mixed structures Pitched roof with brick-concrete slab Seismic improvement interventions

typology of construction is almost always ruled by the out of the plane mechanisms, because of the lack of effective connections between vertical and horizontal elements, giving rise to very high vulnerability to horizontal loads.

Between 1920 and 1940, the expansion of the city continued with the construction of the first buildings belonging to the National Institute for Housing of State Employees (INCIS) building program. The features of the MUR2 typology are external walls made of cut stone with good bonding and lime mortar, and vault floor with bricks and steel beams. Over the years, some of these buildings have been subjected to strengthening interventions, consisting mainly of widespread connections (insertion of metal bars or RC beams).

During the 1940s, the demographic increment produced the migration of the population to new urban areas located in the north of the city territory. In this context, an important public housing plan was pursued by the local organization of Social Housing (Azienda Territoriale per l'Edilizia Residenziale, ATER) creating two new residential neighborhoods. The third typology, named MUR3, groups masonry

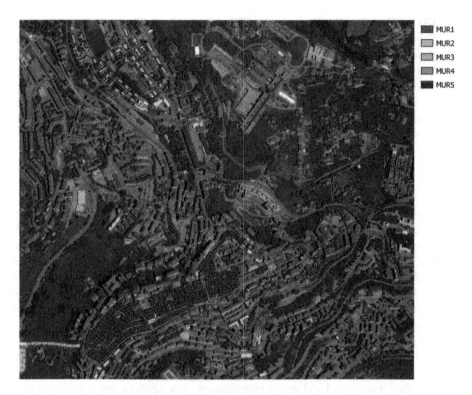

MUR1
MUR2
MUR3
MUR4
MUR5

Fig. 4. Macro-classes of masonry buildings located in the old town center and in the residential compartments.

constructions made by solid brick masonry and lime mortar with rigid slab (reinforced brick-concrete) and connections between vertical walls and the horizontal elements. This type of buildings is quite always characterized by a box-like seismic behavior, so being able to develop the more effective in plane mechanisms of the walls.

During the reconstruction after the Second World War, within a decade, in the 1950s, the urban landscape was remodeled with the presence of RC buildings, where the use of load-bearing masonry progressively gave way to the use of lightweight infills. An evolution, characterized by a higher heterogeneity in the building solutions was noticed: from structures in masonry to mixed structures where horizontal and vertical RC elements are in contact with masonry. The MUR4 typology is characterized by external masonry walls and internal RC beam-column systems with reinforced brick-concrete floor.

The 1980 Irpinia-Basilicata earthquake devastated a wide area of the Southern Apennines, especially Campania and Basilicata where about thirty towns were completely destroyed. In Potenza 10000 people became homeless and public buildings suffered heavy damage. For this reason, the old town was subjected to a massive repair and reconstruction plan. The MUR5 typology characterizes the reconstructed buildings of the historical center. The "ancient" masonry, characterized by disordered rubble stone with friable mortar and textures made of irregular and sub-horizontal courses, was replaced by regular masonry of solid brick stones. The deformable timber floors without steel chains and RC tie-beams were replaced by rigid floors with reinforced brick-concrete slab. Widespread seismic improvement interventions (application of diffused tie-roads, filling the voids and/or cracks inside the wall by injecting of new mortar, substitution of damaged elements along cracking lines with new ones, etc.) were performed. It is worth nothing that the historical center of Potenza, like most of the historical centers in Italy, consists of several masonry aggregates, interconnected, multilevel, masonry cells, which share common structural elements (walls, roofs, staircases, etc.) This affects not only the individual behavior of each construction but also their combined behavior. For this reason, besides analyzing the seismic response of each individual structural unit, its role within the aggregate will be analyzed with the aim to highlight the different behavior of the unit when considered as isolated or part of an aggregate.

The preliminary inventory proposed in Table 5 has been further refined considering other specific building characteristics that effectively affect the seismic behavior. In addition to the aforementioned number of stories, significant attributes emerged from the described documental and in situ investigation. Among those, irregularities in plan and the presence of connections between slabs and walls cannot be ignored for a comprehensive evaluation of the building typologies. With regard to the number of stories, the analyzed data showed that masonry constructions in the investigated areas can be grouped into three classes: low-rise buildings "Lr" (1–2 stories), medium-rise buildings "Mr" (3–4 stories) and high-rise buildings "Hr" (5–6 stories). With reference to the second parameter, two major classes of buildings have been identified: regular "Reg." and irregular "Irreg." building shape in plan. Finally, the presence of slab-wall connections has been considered. As described above, after the 1940s there was the transition from deformable or semi-rigid floors to rigid reinforced concrete floors. In fact, the analyzed documents showed that the masonry buildings built in the 1950s and 1960s, representative of the residential compartment, have rigid floors with RC beam. So, other two classes have been considered taking into account the presence or not of slab-wall connections, named "C" and "Nc" respectively.

The final building inventory, obtained adopting the classification approach described in the previous sections, is proposed in Table 6.

Table 6. Building typologies inventory for the examined compartments.

MACRO-CLASS	Number of stories			Shape in plan		Slab-wall connections		ID
	Lr	Mr	Hr	Reg.	Irreg.	C	Nc	
MUR1	x			x		x		MUR1, Lr, Reg, C
	x			x			x	MUR1, Lr, Reg, Nc
	x				x	x		MUR1, Lr, Irreg, C
	x				x		x	MUR1, Lr, Irreg, Nc
		x		x		x		MUR1, Mr, Reg, C
		x		x			x	MUR1, Mr, Reg, Nc
		x			x	x		MUR1, Mr, Irreg, C
		x			x		x	MUR1, Mr, Irreg, Nc
			x	x		x		MUR1, Hr, Reg, C
			x	x			x	MUR1, Hr, Reg, Nc
			x		x	x		MUR1, Hr, Irreg, C
			x		x		x	MUR1, Hr, Irreg, Nc
MUR2	x			x		x		MUR2, Lr, Reg, C
	x			x			x	MUR2, Lr, Reg, Nc
	x				x	x		MUR2, Lr, Irreg, C
	x				x		x	MUR2, Lr, Irreg, Nc
		x		x		x		MUR2, Mr, Reg, C
		x		x			x	MUR2, Mr, Reg, Nc
		x			x	x		MUR2, Mr, Irreg, C
		x			x		x	MUR2, Mr, Irreg, Nc
			x	x		x		MUR2, Hr, Reg, C
			x	x			x	MUR2, Hr, Reg, Nc
			x		x	x		MUR2, Hr, Irreg, C
			x		x		x	MUR2, Hr, Irreg, Nc
MUR3	x			x		x		MUR3, Lr, Reg, C
	x			x			x	MUR3, Lr, Reg, Nc
	x				x	x		MUR3, Lr, Irreg, C
	x				x		x	MUR3, Lr, Irreg, Nc
		x		x		x		MUR3, Mr, Reg, C
		x		x			x	MUR3, Mr, Reg, Nc
		x			x	x		MUR3, Mr, Irreg, C
		x			x		x	MUR3, Mr, Irreg, Nc
			x	x		x		MUR3, Hr, Reg, C
			x	x			x	MUR3, Hr, Reg, Nc
			x		x	x		MUR3, Hr, Irreg, C
			x		x		x	MUR3, Hr, Irreg, Nc
MUR4	x			x		x		MUR4, Lr, Reg, C
	x			x			x	MUR4, Lr, Reg, Nc
	x				x	x		MUR4, Lr, Irreg, C
	x				x		x	MUR4, Lr, Irreg, Nc
		x		x		x		MUR4, Mr, Reg, C
		x		x			x	MUR4, Mr, Reg, Nc
		x			x	x		MUR4, Mr, Irreg, C
		x			x		x	MUR4, Mr, Irreg, Nc
			x	x		x		MUR4, Hr, Reg, C
			x	x			x	MUR4, Hr, Reg, Nc
			x		x	x		MUR4, Hr, Irreg, C
			x		x		x	MUR4, Hr, Irreg, Nc

(continued)

Table 6. (*continued*)

MACRO-CLASS	Number of stories			Shape in plan		Slab-wall connections		ID
	Lr	Mr	Hr	Reg.	Irreg.	C	Nc	
MUR5	x			x		x		MUR5, Lr, Reg, C
	x			x			x	MUR5, Lr, Reg, Nc
	x				x	x		MUR5, Lr, Irreg, C
	x				x		x	MUR5, Lr, Irreg, Nc
		x		x		x		MUR5, Mr, Reg, C
		x		x			x	MUR5, Mr, Reg, Nc
		x			x	x		MUR5, Mr, Irreg, C
		x			x		x	MUR5, Mr, Irreg, Nc
			x	x		x		MUR5, Hr, Reg, C
			x	x			x	MUR5, Hr, Reg, Nc
			x		x	x		MUR5, Hr, Irreg, C
			x		x		x	MUR5, Hr, Irreg, Nc

5 Conclusions

In this paper, a simplified approach aimed at assembling a building typologies inventory is presented and applied for the urban residential area of Potenza (southern Italy). In particular, the proposed approach combines the primary informative level represented by Census-based database with a second complementary informative level based on specific documental/virtual analysis, building-by-building surveys and expert judgment. A preliminary inventory composed by five macro-typologies has been defined. Such preliminary inventory has been then refined considering specific building structural peculiarities affecting the seismic behavior. Sixty typologies have been finally identified. It is worth noting that the structural element dimensions (derived from the described investigation), the building position in a block aggregate (isolated, corner, end or central) and the percentage and arrangement of openings in walls will be opportunely taken into account at a later stage of the PON AIM research project and, in particular, during the numerical modeling of the selected archetype buildings.

The research activity described in this paper represents the primary step of a comprehensive study for the evaluation of the seismic resilience of the investigated area. A complementary study regarding the reinforced concrete residential buildings located in the examined compartments has been carried out in parallel by the same Authors of this paper.

Acknowledgements. This research was funded by the PON-AIM 2014–2020 project supported by the Italian Ministry of University and Public Instruction.

References

1. Miano, A., De Silva, D., Chiumiento, G., Capasso, M.L.: Seismic and fire assessment and upgrading process for historical buildings: the case study of Palazzo Colonna in Caggiano. Front. Built Environ. **6**(22) (2020). https://doi.org/10.3389/fbuil.2020.00022

2. Chieffo, N., Clementi, F., Formisano, A., Lenci, S.: Comparative fragility methods for seismic assessment of masonry buildings located in Muccia (Italy). J. Build Eng. **25**, 100813 (2019). https://doi.org/10.1016/j.jobe.2019.100813
3. Ferrante, A., Clementi, F., Milani, G.: Dynamic behavior of an inclined existing Masonry tower in Italy. Front. Built Environ. **5**(33) (2019). https://doi.org/10.3389/fbuil.2019.00033
4. Tomaževič, M.: Earthquake-Resistant Design of Masonry Buildings. Series on Innovation in Structures and Construction, vol. 1, Imperial College Press, London (1999)
5. ATC (Applied Technology Council), Earthquake Damage Evaluation Data for California, Applied Technology Council Report ATC-13, Redwood City, CA (1985)
6. Federal Emergency Management Agency, FEMA 154 – Rapid Visual Screening of Buildings for Potential Seismic Hazards: A Handbook. Second Edition, Earthquake Hazards Reduction Series, vol. 41 (2002)
7. Grunthal, G.: European Macroseismic Scale (EMS-92), Chaiers du Centre Européen de Géodynamique et de Séismologie, vol. 15 (1992)
8. Grunthal, G.: European Macroseismic Scale (EMS–98), 15 Cahiers du Centre Européen de Géodynamique et de Séismologie, Luxembourg (1998)
9. Federal Emergency Management Agency, HAZUS-MH MR4 Technical Manual, Washington, D.C. (2003)
10. Brzev, S., Scawthorn, C., Charleson, A.W., Jaiswal, K.: Interim Overview of GEM Building Taxonomy V2.0, Report produced in the context of the GEM Building Taxonomy Global Component, Version 1.0 (2012)
11. Polese, M., Gaetani d'Aragona, M., Prota, A.: Simplified approach for building inventory and seismic damage assessment at the territorial scale: an application for a town in southern Italy. Soil Dyn. Earthq. Eng. **121**, 405–420 (2019)
12. Corlito, V., De Matteis, G.: Typological-structural characterization and seismic vulnerability assessment of masonry buildings in the Caserta district through the parameters of the CARTIS form. In: XV Convegno Nazionale ANIDIS, L'ingegneria Sismica in Italia, Ascoli Piceno (2019)
13. Gizzi, F.T., Masini, N.: Historical earthquakes and damage patterns in Potenza (Basilicata, Southern Italy). Ann. Geophys. **50**(5), 676–687 (2007)
14. Edifici ed abitazioni Censimento 2001. Dati definitivi. (in Italian), 2004, released by ISTAT on 9 December 2004
15. Dolce, D., Masi, A., Marino, M., Vona, M.: Earthquake damage scenarios of the building stock of Potenza (Southern Italy) including site effects. Bull. Earthq. Eng. **1**, 115–140 (2003)
16. Calderoni, B., Sandoli, A., Cordasco, E.A.: Valutazione speditiva della vulnerabilità sismica dei centri urbani italiani: classificazione tipologica strutturale degli edifici esistenti in muratura ed in c.a. Structural Magazine (2017). https://doi.org/10.12917/stru210.09

A Model to Mitigate the Peripheralization Risk at Urban Scale

Gerundo Roberto[⊠], Nesticò Antonio[iD], Marra Alessandra[iD], and Carotenuto Maria

DICIV – Department of Civil Engineering, University of Salerno, Via Giovanni Paolo II, 132, 84084 Fisciano, Italy
{r.gerundo,anestico,almarra}@unisa.it,
carotenutomaria91@gmail.com

Abstract. The uncontrolled expansion of built-up areas and of multiple forms of poverty, on a global level, determines a new geography of degradation, extended both to suburbs and to central zones, thus exposing cities, in their entirety, at risk of peripheralization. In this framework, counteracting actions at the urban scale, such as regeneration programmes, need to be targeted primarily at areas of significant risk, occurring with a combination of vulnerability factors, in three dimensions: social, building and urban. Furthermore, in order to be effective, such programmes must be geared to maximizing risk mitigation. This is possible when the planning of interventions takes into account the evaluation results of the better design alternative in order to reduce pre-existing vulnerability. Such an approach constitutes the novelty of the study. So, the aim of the work is to provide an innovative model for the mitigation of peripheralization risk at urban scale. For this purpose, the contribution defines a set of mitigation indicators and a protocol for evaluating the most effective design alternative based on the Analytic Hierarchy Process (AHP).

Keywords: Peripheralization risk · Urban regeneration · Mitigation indicators · Analytic Hierarchy Process (AHP)

1 Introduction

Due to global urbanization trends, at different observation scales, complex peripheralization processes have produced new and diversified peripherality conditions. On an urban scale, in particular, such conditions are no longer recognizable in peripheries, i.e. neighborhoods born on the edge of historic cities since the post-war period [1–5].

Rather, peripheral condition is understood both in spatial sense, with reference to suburban areas, where the identified risk is mainly related to the phenomenon of sprawl and land consumption, both in aspatial sense. In this case, reference is made to degraded areas, while the identified risk is connected to poor quality of buildings, lack

G. Roberto and N. Antonio designed the research. All authors contributed to the definition of the methodology. M. Alessandra prepared a draft manuscript. G. Roberto and N. Antonio enriched and revised the manuscript.

© Springer Nature Switzerland AG 2020
O. Gervasi et al. (Eds.): ICCSA 2020, LNCS 12250, pp. 928–939, 2020.
https://doi.org/10.1007/978-3-030-58802-1_66

of services and reduced quality of life for the population. More generally, it refers to the multidimensional concept of urban poverty [6–10], or to the European one of deprivation [11, 12].

Issues such as reducing land consumption and urban poverty through the regeneration of deprived areas are central to the recent recommendations of the European Union [13, 14] and to the New Urban Agenda, in which urban planning is recognised as playing a key role in the definition of enforcement actions [15].

Since the 1990 s in developed countries, including Italy, tools to combat the degradation of urban areas have been tried. Such instruments, supported by public funding, are known as complex programmes. On an urban scale, they refer to planning tools implementing the general development plan, with the aim of lowering physical and functional degradation of neighborhoods, also including social animation initiatives. To this end, 'complex' programmes provide a plurality of project actions and involve multiple subjects [16].

Over the years, the European Commission has financed several actions to reduce degradation, from complex programs to more recent urban regeneration projects[1].

Urban areas targeted for funding have often been peripheries, which in Europe and in Italy are traditionally associated with degraded neighbourhoods [17–20].

In Italy, where there is still no national legislation for urban regeneration, scientific criteria are generally not used for the identification of degraded areas subject to intervention, but their recognition is usually delegated to the municipal authorities on the occasion of sporadic calls for funding. As a result, urban regeneration interventions translate into operations often independent of urban planning, mainly driven by economic convenience in real estate transformations.

In contrast to this, some scholars propose multi-criteria evaluations of project proposals, in order to maximize public benefits. Among the different techniques, the use of the Analytical Hierarchy Process (AHP) is frequent. Compared to other models, the AHP allows to consider a greater number of criteria, an important feature for the technical-economic evaluation of complex urban programmes [24–29].

However, the continued expansion of cities, which is accompanied by the increasing spread of degradation and multiple forms of poverty even in traditionally central areas [30–34], requires a change of approach, especially in the light of the multiplication of natural and man-made hazards [35], which end up accentuating peripheralization processes.

Thus, in the light of the new urban and socio-economic geography, regeneration interventions must be directed primarily to areas with a significant co-presence of potential degradation factors. Consequently, the choice by decision makers of the best design alternative must be informed by the knowledge of vulnerability levels that characterize areas subject to intervention, and oriented towards the solution that maximizes their reduction.

---

[1] In chronological order (with date of first appearance): Urban Pilot Projects (1989–1993); Community Initiatives POVERTY III (1989–1993); URBAN I (1994–1999); URBAN II (2000–2006); URBACT II (2007–2013); URBACT III (2014–2020).

To this end, it is necessary to integrate the phase of interventions planning in highly vulnerable areas with that of the multi-criteria evaluation of the most effective project. This integration constitutes novelty element of this work.

The contribution is part of a wider research project, which proposes a methodology for the localization of the areas subject to urban regeneration with reference to the general theory of territorial risk. According to this approach, priority areas are those in which the greatest risk of peripheralization occurs, determined by high levels of aggregated vulnerability. The latter, in turn, is given by the combination of social, building and urban vulnerability, and it is measured with reference to quantitative indicators, describing the potential degradation factors of the goods exposed in the social, building and urban domains of the city. With regard to these dimensions, the elements at risk are, respectively, population, buildings and urban fabric [36–39].

The objective of this paper is to characterize a model for the mitigation of peripheralization risk at urban scale. Specifically, the proposed methodology aims to provide a decision support system useful for assessing the effectiveness of urban regeneration programmes in high-risk areas, therefore priority of intervention. Following a brief description of the approach and of AHP technique on which the model is based (Sect. 2), the contribution proposes a set of indicators for the mitigation of the social, building and urban vulnerability of priority areas (Sect. 3). The hierarchical structure that conforms the study protocol, as well as the calculation algorithms that govern the system, are in Sect. 4. Section 5 reports the conclusions of the research, notes the effectiveness of the model for selecting the investment best able to pursue the objectives, and finally outlines research perspectives.

2 Methodological Approach

The proposed methodology requires the previous identification of urban areas most at risk, where regeneration interventions should be prioritized. Given that a high risk level depends on a significant aggregated vulnerability, the method for estimating that vulnerability is crucial. This is especially true because in the international scientific community there is no agreement on both the most appropriate set of vulnerability indicators and how to combine them. In the broader research project to which the work belongs, a set of indicators has already been designed with reference to the social, building and urban domains. In addition, a method of combining vulnerability indicators based on fuzzy logic was proposed, allowing to manage the uncertainty related to their aggregation [36].

Following the above-mentioned work, the method here proposed identifies a set of mitigation indicators, which allow to estimate the effects of project initiatives on social, building and urban domains, with the aim of reducing vulnerability and, therefore, risk.

Subsequently the procedure is articulated in the own phases of the Analytic Hierarchy Process (AHP). Specifically, the AHP provides for three basic steps: structuring the problem hierarchically; comparing judgments; synthesizing priorities [40, 41]. The first phase consists in defining the hierarchy, explaining: the objective of the evaluation; the criteria, which coincide to the domains examined; the sub-criteria, to which the mitigation indicators correspond. The second phase allows the relative importance of the criteria and sub-criteria to be measured in respect to the general objective. This phase is divided into further sub-phases:

- pairwise comparison of the design alternatives with respect to each sub-criterion;
- pairwise comparison of sub-criteria;
- pairwise comparison of the criteria.

The last step allows the choice of the best design alternative on the basis of the assessments carried out (Fig. 1).

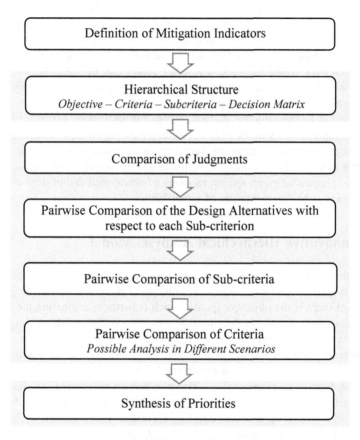

Fig. 1. Workflow of the proposed methodology.

3   Definition of Mitigation Indicators

This phase is carried out with specific reference to vulnerability indicators used for the localization of priority urban areas of intervention.

The indicators of social vulnerability are: unemployment rate; failure to reach minimum levels of education; incidence of the elderly.

Building vulnerability indicators, on the other hand, refer to the quality of building-housing stock. In particular, they measure the state of conservation and technological obsolescence of buildings.

Finally, the indicators for urban domain measure the fragmentation of urban fabric and the composition of the latter, with reference to non-permeable areas.

Other indicators of urban vulnerability are the lack of services and the presence of urban criticalities, such as disused or abandoned areas and solid waste accumulation zones [36].

So, mitigation indicators proposed in this contribution (Table 1) are able to measure the impact of urban transformation interventions on the vulnerability factors described above. With reference to the social domain, they measure actions aimed at improving employment, education and demographic structure, in terms of number of new employees, graduates in secondary school, ability of the city physical-functional structure to attract young families. The latter action can be measured by qualitative judgment, which is associated with a scalar value from 1 to 7. It is the only qualitative indicator out of the total of those proposed.

With regard to the building domain, mitigation indicators measure interventions that lead to improvements in the state of building-housing stock, in terms of number of buildings recovered and/or adequate from a hygienic-sanitary point of view.

For the urban domain, indicators estimate actions aimed at increasing supply of services and permeable green spaces, recovery of abandoned and/or degraded areas, as well as reducing the fragmentation of urban fabric.

4   An Innovative Hierarchical Analysis Model

The definition of the hierarchy is fundamental for the modeling of the complex problem [42]. The proposed dominance hierarchy consists of three levels, as in Fig. 2. At the highest level there is the objective (goal), which consists in evaluating the best design alternative in terms of peripheralization risk mitigation in the social, building and urban domains. At the second level there are the criteria (C_i), which, in this case, correspond to the vulnerability domains analyzed: the social criterion (C_s); the building criterion (C_b); the urban criterion (C_u). At the third level there are the subcriteria (C_{ij}), to which mitigation indicators correspond (I_{Mij}). Those indicators are: three (I_{Ms1}, I_{Ms2}, I_{Ms3}) for the subcriteria of the social domain (C_{s1}, C_{s2}, C_{s3}); three more (I_{Mb1}, I_{Mb2}, I_{Mb3}) for the subcriteria of the building domain (C_{b1}, C_{b2}, C_{b3}); four (I_{Mu1}, I_{Mu2}, I_{Mu3}, I_{Mu4}) for the subcriteria of the urban domain (C_{u1}, C_{u2}, C_{u3}, C_{u4}).

All ten sub-criteria are measurable for each of the k design alternatives among which the decision maker is called to choose. This is in order to mitigate the vulnerability components of the risk for the area under consideration.

For each design alternative, the values of mitigation indicators constitute the lines of the decision matrix, while the columns relate to the values of the specific sub-criterion for all the project proposals. The decision matrix, therefore, is of the type in Table 2.

Starting from the decision matrix, we proceed to the pairwise comparison of the design alternatives P_k with respect to each sub-criterion. Thus, for the ten defined

Table 1. Mitigations indicators, unit of measurement and definition.

Mitigation indicator		U.M.	Definition
SOCIAL DOMAIN			
I_{Ms1}	New employees	n.	Number of new employees in the age group corresponding to the workforce
I_{Ms2}	New graduates at secondary school cycle (middle school)	n.	Population of 15 years and over who will obtain a middle school diploma per year
I_{Ms3}	Ability to attract young families	value	Ability to attract young families of city physical-functional structure: 1. very shoddy; 2. shoddy; 3. very low; 4. low; 5. medium; 6. medium-high; 7. high
BUILDING DOMAIN			
I_{Mb1}	Recovered buildings of historical, architectural or artistic value	n.	Number of buildings with historical, architectural or artistic value subject to restoration
I_{Mb2}	Recovered residential buildings in bad and mediocre conservation state	n.	Number of residential buildings subject to extraordinary maintenance or renovation
I_{Mb3}	Improper housing recovered	n.	Number of improper housing subject to health and hygiene improvements
URBAN DOMAIN			
I_{Mu1}	Edge density	m/ha	Ratio between total sum of perimeters of the polygons of built areas and the total surface of investigated area
I_{Mu2}	Increment of permeable areas	m^2	Surface for additional permeable areas
I_{Mu3}	Increase in urban planning standards	m^2	Surface provided for additional urban planning standards
I_{Mu4}	Urban critical areas retrieved	m^2	Surface of enclosed recovered spaces: abandoned production areas; areas with newly built artifacts that have not been used; undeveloped areas devoid of specific use or abandoned; areas with waste accumulation

sub-criteria, there are ten comparison matrices, in which the elements a_{ij} represent the dominance coefficients, obtained using the Saaty semantic scale (Table 3).

By placing on this scale the values from time to time to be compared, if they fall into the same band, the dominance coefficient a_{ij} of each value with respect to the other is 1; if a band separates them, the coefficient a_{ij} is 3 for the highest value and the reciprocal 1/3 for the lowest value; if there are two bands between them, a_{ij} is 5 for the highest value and it is 1/5 for the lowest one, and so on. Intermediate coefficients may also be used.

The subsequent pairwise comparison between sub-criteria, belonging to the same domain, aims to establish their reciprocal importance.

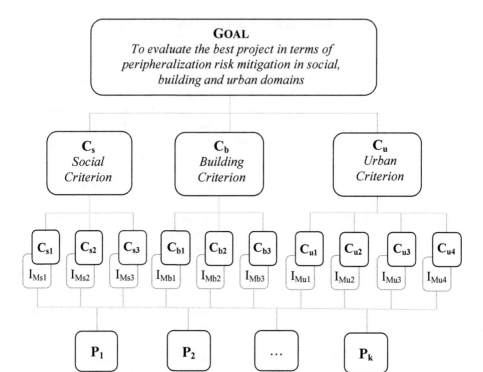

Fig. 2. Hierarchical structure of the proposed model.

Table 2. Decision matrix scheme.

	C_{s1} [n.]	C_{s2} [n.]	C_{s3} [value]	C_{b1} [n.]	C_{b2} [n.]	C_{b3} [n.]	C_{u1} [m/ha]	C_{u2} [m^2]	C_{u3} [m^2]	C_{u4} [m^2]
P_1										
P_2										
...										
P_k										

Table 3. Semantic scale of Saaty.

Intensity	1	3	5	7	9	2-4-6-8
Judgement of Importance	Equal	Moderate	High	Very high	Extreme	Intermediate levels

Finally, the comparison in pairs between criteria aims to establish the importance of one domain with respect to the other. In this regard, in relation to different possible objectives of Economic Policy, the analysis can be developed with reference to several scenarios. For example, the study may consider the following two scenarios:

- *scenario 0*, whereby all criteria have the same importance;
- *scenario 1*, where the weight of the criteria depends on the vulnerability levels obtained from the peripheralization risk analysis.

In scenario 1, the more vulnerable a domain is, the more important are the actions aimed at that specific dimension. For each domain, vulnerability mapping returns different vulnerability classes: *low; medium; high; very high*. The linguistic values *low, medium, high and very high*, can be converted into proportional scalars. In particular, the low value will correspond to the scalar 1, the medium value 2, the high value 3, while the very high value 4.

At this point we proceed with the pairwise comparison, in order to establish the relative importance of the elements according to the scale in Fig. 3. This figure allows to divide the four ranges 1(low) - 2(medium) - 3(high) - 4(very high) into the 5 typical Saaty value ranges 0–0, 8–1, 6–2, 4–3, 2–4, 0 returned in the lower part of Fig. 3. Thus, the matrix of Table 4 is derived.

In order to evaluate the priority of one project proposal over the other, we refer to the principle of hierarchical composition, determining the importance of each element of the hierarchy in relation to the objective. More precisely, in the calculation of the orders, each proposal has a priority equal to:

$$PP_k : \sum wP_{kij} \, wC_{ij} \, WC_i$$

Where:
PP_k = priority of the k-th project proposal;
wP_{kij} = normalized vector of subcriteria for each project proposal;
wC_{ij} = normalized vector of subcriteria for each domain;
WC_i = normalized vector of criteria;
with $k = 1, \ldots, n$; $i = s, b, u$; $j = 1, \ldots, 4$.

Ultimately, with reference to each of the proposed scenarios, a summary matrix is obtained. Such matrices allow to identify the priorities of the different design alternatives in order to guide the decision maker's choice.

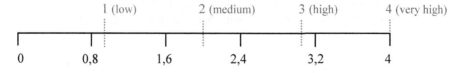

Fig. 3. Positioning on the graduated scale of values corresponding to vulnerability levels.

Table 4. Matrix for assigning weights to the criteria.

	Low	Medium	High	Very high
Low	1,000	0,333	0,167	0,111
Medium	3,000	1,000	0,333	0,167
High	6,000	3,000	1,000	0,333
Very high	9,000	6,000	3,000	1,000

5 Conclusions

The uncontrolled growth of urban areas and of multiple forms of poverty, accentuated by natural and man-made hazards which must be faced with increasing urgency, determines a new geography of degradation. This decay extends to both suburbs and central areas, exposing cities, in their entirety, to a peripheralization risk.

In order to optimize the use of scarce resources available, planning tools to combat urban scale degradation – among others, mention can be made of regeneration pro-grammes – must be directed primarily to areas most at risk and aimed at maximizing its mitigation.

In this context, our research highlights the need to integrate the planning of urban regeneration interventions with the technical-economic evaluation of the most effective design alternative in terms of vulnerability mitigation, in the various dimensions examined: social, building and urban. For this purpose, an innovative multi-criteria model is proposed that can take into account the different factors and levels of vulnerability in the domains investigated. The algorithms of the analysis model are based on the logical schemes that characterize the Analytical Hierarchy Process (AHP).

For the model implementation, a set of mitigation indicators is defined, with reference to the vulnerability factors considered to locate priority areas of intervention. Mitigation indicators are defined so as to analytically estimate the benefits brought by project actions, such as to determine the reduction of vulnerability indicators values.

It should be noted that the selection of mitigation indicators is carried out in order to build a complete, non-redundant and coherent set, generalized for urban-scale interventions. In addition, as well as for the AHP model implementation, the same indicators can also be used for temporal monitoring of the improvement effects produced by the projects on the specific vulnerability components.

Once the values of the proposed mitigation indicators have been clarified, the model allows to select the design solution that maximizes the reduction of pre-existing vulnerability levels.

The structure of the model, the indicators on which it is based and the aims that the model tends to pursue, constitute novelty of the work.

Research prospects concern the application of the proposed model to case studies, which is, moreover, already in progress with fully satisfactory indications.

References

1. Copus, A.K.: From core-periphery to polycentric development. Concepts of spatial and aspatial peripherality. Eur. Plann. Stud. **9**(4), 539–552 (2001). https://doi.org/10.1080/713666491
2. Taylor, P.J., Lang, R.E.: The shock of the new: 100 concepts describing recent urban change. Environ. Plann. **36**, 951–958 (2004). https://doi.org/10.1068/a375
3. Kühn, M., Bernt, M.: Peripheralization and power – theoretical debates. In: Fischer-Tahir, A., Naumann, M. (eds.) Peripheralization. Springer, Wiesbaden (2013). https://doi.org/10.1007/978-3-531-19018-1_15
4. Kühn, M.: Peripheralization. Theoretical concepts explaining socio-spatial inequalities. Eur. Plann. Stud. **23**(2), 367–378 (2015). https://doi.org/10.1080/09654313.2013.862518
5. United Nations Human Settlements Programme: The fundamentals of urbanization. Evidence base for policy making, UN-Habitat (2016). ISBN 978-92-1-132730-4. https://unhabitat.org/the-fundamentals-of-urbanization-evidence-base-for-policy-making. Accessed 30 Apr 2020
6. Conway, M., Konvitz, J.: Meeting the challenge of distressed urban areas. Urban Stud. **37**(4), 749–774 (2000)
7. Baharaoglu, D., Kessides, C.: Urban poverty. In: A Sourcebook for Poverty Reduction Strategies, Chapter 16. World Bank, Washington D.C. (2002)
8. Bernt, M., Colini, L.: Exclusion, marginalization and peripheralization. Conceptual concerns in the study of urban inequalities, Working Paper. Leibniz Institute for Regional Development and Structural Planning, Erkner, Germany (2013)
9. Geneletti, D., La Rosa, D., Spyra, M., Cortinovis, C.: A review of approaches and challenges for sustainable planning in urban peripheries. Landscape Urban Plann. **165**, 231–243 (2017). https://doi.org/10.1016/j.landurbplan.2017.01.013
10. Gerundo, R., Marra, A.: Il rischio nei fenomeni di periferizzazione delle aree urbane e metropolitane. Urbanistica Informazioni **278 s.i.**, 338–342 (2018)
11. Townsend, P.: Deprivation. J. Soc. Policy **16**(2), 125–146 (1987). 10.1017/S0047279400020341
12. Ministry of Housing, Communities and Local Government: The English Indices of Deprivation 2019, Statistical Release. (2019). https://assets.publishing.service.gov.uk/government/uploads/system/uploads/attachment_data/file/835115/IoD2019_Statistical_Release.pdf. Accessed 30 Apr 2020
13. European Commission-EU: Guidelines on best practice to limit, mitigate or compensate soil sealing, Luxembourg (2012)
14. European Commission-EU: Integrated regeneration of deprived areas and the new cohesion policy approach, Luxembourg (2015)
15. United Nations-UN: New Urban Agenda. A/RES/71/256 (2017)
16. Gerundo, R.: I programmi urbani complessi. Graffiti, Napoli (2000)
17. Guiducci, R.: Periferie tra degrado e riqualificazione, Laterza, Bari (1993)
18. Oliva, F.: Il sistema insediativo. In: Selicato, F., Rotondo, F.: Progettazione Urbanistica. Teorie e Tecniche. McGrawHill, Milano (2010)
19. Decree of the Italian Prime Minister n. 249, October 15th 2015. Interventi per la riqualificazione sociale e culturale delle aree urbane degradate. http://www.mit.gov.it/sites/default/files/media/notizia/201601/dpcm_15_ottobre_2015.pdf. Accessed 30 Apr 2020

20. Decree of the Italian Prime Minister, May 25th 2016. Bando per la presentazione di progetti per la predisposizione del Programma straordinario di intervento per la riqualificazione urbana e la sicurezza delle periferie delle città metropolitane e dei comuni capoluogo di provincia. http://www.governo.it/sites/governo.it/files/Bando_periferie_urbane.pdf. Accessed 30 Apr 2020

21. Nijkamp, P., Rietveld, P., Voogd, H.: Multicriteria Evaluation in Physical Planning. North Holland Publications, Amsterdam (1990)

22. Vincke, P.: Multicriteria Decision-Aid. Wiley, New York (1992)

23. Tzeng, G.H., Huang, J.J.: Multiple Attribute Decision Making Methods and Applications. CRC Press, Taylor & Francis Group, Boca Raton (2011)

24. Stanghellini, S., Mambelli, T.: La valutazione dei programmi di riqualificazione urbana proposti dai soggetti privati. Scienze Regionali 2(1) (2003)

25. De Mare, G., Nesticò, A., Tajani, F.: Building investments for the revitalization of the territory: a multisectoral model of economic analysis. In: Murgante, B., et al. (eds.) ICCSA 2013. LNCS, vol. 7973, pp. 493–508. Springer, Heidelberg (2013). https://doi.org/10.1007/978-3-642-39646-5_36

26. Nesticò, N., Sica, F.: The sustainability of urban renewal projects: a model for economic multi-criteria analysis. J. Prop. Invest. Finance 35(4), 397–409 (2017). https://doi.org/10.1108/JPIF-01-2017-0003

27. Nesticò, N., Somma, P.: Comparative analysis of multi-criteria methods for the enhancement of historical buildings. Sustainability 11(17), 4526 (2019). https://doi.org/10.3390/su11174526

28. Guarini, M.R., Nesticò, A., Morano, P., Sica, F.: A multicriteria economic analysis model for urban forestry projects. In: Calabrò, F., Della Spina, L., Bevilacqua, C. (eds.) ISHT 2018. SIST, vol. 100, pp. 564–571. Springer, Cham (2019). https://doi.org/10.1007/978-3-319-92099-3_63

29. Nesticò, A., Maselli, G.: Sustainability indicators for the economic evaluation of tourism investments on islands. J. Cleaner Prod. 248, Article no. 119217 (2020). https://doi.org/10.1016/j.jclepro.2019.119217

30. Gerundo, R., Fasolino, I., Grimaldi, M.: ISUT model. a composite index to measure the sustainability of the urban transformation. In: Papa, R., Fistola, R. (eds.) Smart Energy in the Smart City. GET, pp. 117–130. Springer, Cham (2016). https://doi.org/10.1007/978-3-319-31157-9_7

31. Sebillo, M., Vitiello, G., Grimaldi, M., Buono, D.D.: SAFE (safety for families in emergency). In: Misra, S., et al. (eds.) ICCSA 2019. LNCS, vol. 11620, pp. 424–437. Springer, Cham (2019). https://doi.org/10.1007/978-3-030-24296-1_34

32. Fasolino, I., Naddeo, V., Grimaldi, M., Zarra, T.: Odour control strategies for a sustainable nuisances action plan. Glob. Nest J. 4, 734–741 (2016). https://doi.org/10.30955/gnj.002109

33. Naddeo, V., Fasolino, I., Grimaldi, M., Zarra, T.: Implementation of integrated nuisances action plan. Chem. Eng. Trans. 54, 19–24 (2016). https://doi.org/10.3303/cet1654004

34. Grimaldi, M., Sebillo, M., Vitiello, G., Pellecchia, V.: An ontology based approach for data model construction supporting the management and planning of the integrated water service. In: Misra, S., et al. (eds.) ICCSA 2019. LNCS, vol. 11624, pp. 243–252. Springer, Cham (2019). https://doi.org/10.1007/978-3-030-24311-1_17

35. Sebillo, M., Vitiello, G., Grimaldi, M., De Piano, A.: A citizen-centric approach for the improvement of territorial services management. ISPRS Int. J. Geo-Inf. 9(4), 223 (2020). https://doi.org/10.3390/ijgi9040223

36. Gerundo, R., Marra, A., De Salvatore, V.: Construction of a composite vulnerability index to map peripheralization risk in urban and metropolitan areas. Sustainability 12(11), 4641 (2020). https://doi.org/10.3390/su12114641

37. Gerundo, R., Grimaldi, M., Marra, A.: A methodology hazard-based for the mitigation of the radon risk in the urban planning. UPLanD J. Urban Plann. Landscape Environ. Des. **1**(1), 27–38 (2016). https://doi.org/10.6092/2531-9906/5031

38. Gerundo, R., Fasolino, I: Sicurezza territoriale ed efficienza urbanistica. Edizioni Scientifiche Italiane, Napoli (2010)

39. Office of the United Nations Disaster Relief Coordinator: Natural disasters and vulnerability analysis. Report of Expert Group Meeting, 9–12 July 1979. United Nations, Geneva, Switzerland (1980). https://digitallibrary.un.org/record/95986. Accessed 30 Apr 2020

40. Saaty, T.L.: A scaling method for priorities in hierarchy structures. J. Math. Psychol. **15**(3), 234–281 (1977)

41. Saaty, T.L.: The Analytic Hierarchy Process. McGraw-Hill, New York (1980). Reprinted by RWS Publications, 4922 Ellsworth Avenue, Pittsburgh, PA, 15213 (2000)

42. Saaty, T.L.: Decision Making for Leaders: The Analytic Hierarchy Process for Decision in a Complex Word. RWS Publications, Pittsburg (1999)

Changing from the Emergency Plan to the Resilience Plan: A Novel Approach to Civil Protection and Urban Planning

Marco Vona[(✉)]

School of Engineering, University of Basilicata, 85100 Potenza, Italy
marco.vona@unibas.it

Abstract. Seismic risk study and consequent mitigation strategies have become always more important. In modern communities are complex communities; therefore, there are complex processes based on strongly different topics: urban planning, socio-economic dynamics, the need to preserve cultural heritage, safety, and natural hazard effects. In last years, a significant change in point of view seems necessary. In particular, the seismic risk mitigation (and more generally, the natural risks mitigation) must become one of the main topic in urban planning and governance of communities. it is to be highlighted that in past earthquekas higher consequences and losses have been generally caused in the medium and long term by the low or lack of resilience of the communities. However, in recent years, the concrete application of the concept of the resilience have taken on a key role in seismic risk studies. In particular, the resilience assessment of the housing stock, both qualitatively and quantitatively can be considered the core of the problem. In this study, based on the concept of resilience a change in urban planning and emergency management tools is defined. A case study is considered to show a first application. The improvement of the resilience of the investigated town is defined on several strategies and then it is quantified.

Keywords: Seismic risk mitigation · Residential building stock · Seismic losses · Resilient quantitative approach · Civil protection · Resilience plan

1 Introduction

Currently, the unique way to reduce the natural disasters' effects are the mitigation and prevention strategies. They are based on the resilience's concept and it is expected to be the most common approach for future developments. The decision makers' activities should be based on the operational tools and the population should be encouraged to apply these tools. The development of resilient communities must be considered the main goal of risk prevention and mitigation programs.

In several studies, the concept of resilience has been integrated with classic risk analysis statements [1–4]. The recovery process must be defined in quantitative ways, as a convolution of several functions. In the recovery process, social, economic, and public support are essential to guarantee an immediate response and acceptable levels of service in a reasonable time.

© Springer Nature Switzerland AG 2020
O. Gervasi et al. (Eds.): ICCSA 2020, LNCS 12250, pp. 940–949, 2020.
https://doi.org/10.1007/978-3-030-58802-1_67

Four fundamental properties are generally considered in the resilience analysis.

1. Robustness: reduced loss of functionality.
2. Redundancy: the ability of a system to create alternatives.
3. Rapidity: the ability achieve goals in a timely manner.
4. Resourcefulness: the ability to use resources to achieve the selected goals.

Based on these principles, several methods have been developed in recent years to quantify the resilience to disastrous phenomena. Community resilience must include normal mitigation procedures and emergency management activities. More specifically, a community is considered resilient if it has:

- low probability of damage;
- low consequences due to damage;
- low recovery times.

Conceptually, resilience should be considered as the global effects of mitigation measures in "peace time" and quality of management in emergency times. Nevertheless, the real improvement of the community resilience must be based on mitigation measures in peace time. Quality, quantity, and effects of management in emergency times must be considered as the consequence of the mitigation measures. Emergency procedures, tools, and materials are defined (or should be defined) based on mitigation measures.

In this study, a proposal is reported for new urban planning and civil protection tools based on resilience. The resilience of the community is clearly quantified. The proposal is based on a de-aggregation process of the resilience of the community and its sub-sections. Emergency management are not considered but they should be defined in subsequent step.

2   Resilience Tools

Currently, the relationship between civil protection goals and resilience concepts is increasingly used. An example of real application is implementation in the state of California, in particular in the cities of Los Angeles and San Francisco. Resilience has been considered as the core of the mitigation strategies [5]. Several actions and some provision are defined for existing buildings, structures and infrastructures [6, 7].

Unfortunately, these cases can be considered as virtuous exceptions. Nevertheless a significant number of studies and consequent applications be found in the literature, a few applications have been performed, often related to single objects, such as critical facilities and service networks (hospitals, lifelines).

Actually, in Italy and other Mediterranean earthquake-prone countries, the resilience is strongly related to their socioeconomic, structural, and infrastructural conditions, and further need to protect and preserve the cultural heritage.

The recent earthquakes have highlighted the high level of economic and social losses. The community showed a strong decline, reaching an unacceptable standard of life or leading the community to extinction [8]. For this reason, proactive strategies must be considered for modifying and improving the resilience performance of communities.

In past earthquake, the Italian buildings stock (both public and private) exhibited a considerable fragility due to the structural types and their interaction. On the other side, public and private resources are often few and not sufficient to retrofit of these buildings. However, the government strategies can play a key role based on specific subsidies and incentives, insurance and retrofit obligation, declassification for building use, and so on [9].

In this way, the beneficial effects of the real application of the concepts of resilience should be clearly highlighted. Consequently, the resilience concepts must be the guide line in the activities of mitigation of seismic risk. These concepts should be clearly included in the current civil protection procedures. Thus, the emergency plan should become the resilience plan of community.

The civil protection activities resilience-based approach should be a strategy based on the planning of public and private seismic vulnerability reduction according to urban planning, following:

- reduction of the seismic damage, losses.
- Reduction of the recovery time.
- Reduction of the downtime.
- Use of less financial resources.

The core of the proposal is the resilience index [10], based on a combination of resilience for building types in specific areas (at the urban scale):

$$R_{index}(I) = \sum_{area=1}^{n} \left\{ W_{area} \cdot \left(1 - \sum_{type=1}^{m} \frac{E[T_{RB}|C_{r,r|I}]}{T_{LC}} E[C_{r,r}|d_{l,type|I}] P[d_l = d_{l,type}|I] \right) \right\}$$

(1)

where the weight factor W_{area} is considered to define the relative importance of a single area of the community rather than the others. The evaluation is based on a seismic scenario; thus, the expected ratio is defined. The considered resilience model links the functionality losses directly to the seismic vulnerability of buildings. Finally, the building recovery time T_{RB} and the control time T_{LC} are needed, and they are defined based on the level of damage, difficulty in work activities, and available economic resources.

Based on available data, it is possible define the optimal way to analyses and evaluation. In a wide territorial scale and historical centre, damage probability matrix (DPM [11]) can be used to vulnerability characterization. The repair cost (RC) and repair time functions are derived from the damage level. The building recovery time are derived by the level of damage to a building, difficulty in work activities, available economic resource. Operatively, the seismic resilience is based on the following steps:

- Selection of the seismic scenario event.
- Evaluation of seismic vulnerability (based on a well-validated model).
- Analysis of the damage scenario.
- Evaluation of losses, restoration time, and resilience index.

Based on this approach, emergency plans become the community resilience plans containing prevision, tools to forecast losses, and strategies for prevention in a practical way.

The community's resilience function is defined as reported in Fig. 1. It is based on three different parts:

1. partial and rapid return to partial functionality in the short term (a few days)
2. pseudo-horizontal phase (planning and implantation of preliminary activities for the reconstruction process)
3. increase in functionality due to the progressive repair works.

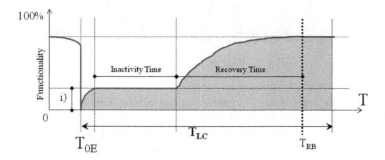

Fig. 1. Resilience-based flowchart of the adopted methodology [9].

3   The Case Study

A first practical application of the proposal is reported in this study. As a case study, the town of Miglionico (a little town in the south of Italy) is considered. It can be considered a typical mountain historical centre in Italy. The mitigation needs must coexist and overlap with the conservation requirements of historic buildings. It is located in a medium to low seismicity zone where a significantly high vulnerability (due to the lack of mitigation strategies). The investigated town has been divided into two main residential zones: the historical centre and the new zone. An earthquake scenario event is considered (Fig. 2).

The vulnerability of the buildings is investigated and their seismic damage is evaluated. In this study, damage probability matrices (DPMs) are used [11]. This approach can be considered as an optimal solution to study the seismic performances of the considered existing masonry buildings. Consequently, some typical retrofit strategies are considered regarding the retrofit goals and repair costs.

EMS-98 intensity is used as seismic input in the DPMs to obtain the damage scenario of the residential buildings under study. This approach is based on four vulnerability classes, ranging from high (class A) to low vulnerability (class D). The building stock is defined by an in-situ survey and after the typological survey [12], the seismic vulnerability evaluation carried [11].

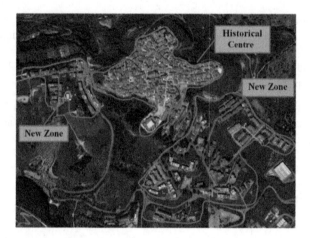

Fig. 2. View of the Miglionico village.

The buildings are generally organised in aggregates. This is a typical urban configuration of the historical centres. The most widespread materials and structural configuration are investigated based on detailed information and interior inspections. Their structural characteristics are considered as: thickness of the masonry walls, connections between orthogonal masonry walls, and connections between masonry walls and slabs. The in-situ survey is coherent to the most commonly used survey form, based on the typological part of the survey form for usability and damage (AeDES). Structural characteristics are reported in GIS (Geograpical Information System). In Fig. 3, the results of the in-situ survey is reported. Based on the survey, six homogenous zones have been defined: four homogenous zones in the historical centre and other two zones outside the historical centre.

The high, medium, medium-low, and low vulnerabilities (vulnerability classes A, B, C, and D, respectively) are considered. The low vulnerability (class D) is assigned for the structures built or retrofitted according to the seismic classification after 1980 with modern seismic code. In Fig. 4, the vulnerability distributions are reported.

To achieve the goal of this study, one damage scenario for the entire building stock is defined. About the selected seismic intensity, the historical data show a clear lack of information until '800. Consequently, another event (I_{EMS98} = VIII) is selected with higher intensity. It is represent the higher return period event. Obviously, more accurate hazard analyses can be performed but they are outside the scope of this study.

Based on the building vulnerability and selected earthquake event, the estimation of the building damage is obtained. As a consequence, the losses can be estimated based on the resilience concepts. The resilience is evaluated for the building stock. In particular, the resilience's curve has been defined for each of the six areas.

The robustness is evaluated as the residual functionality (non-damaged buildings). The recovery time is the main issue for decision-making in the retrofitting strategies. It is clearly dependent on the building types and their expected damage, socioeconomic and political conditions, and financial resources. The recovery time is assessed based on the data available from the L'Aquila earthquake (2009) and the subsequent

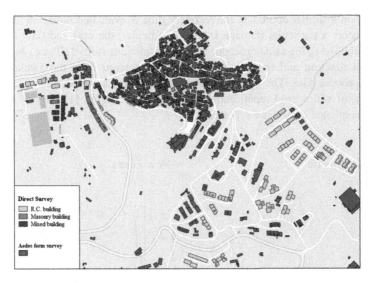

Fig. 3. In situ direct survey.

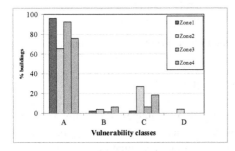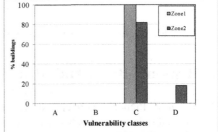

Fig. 4. Statistical distributions of the vulnerability Classes in Miglionico town.

reconstruction process [13, 14]. The available data on the progress of the reconstruction process are used to define the step functions in the current state. Rapidity is based on repair operations and their costs.

For the considered case study, the repair costs (using the price list for the Basilicata Region) have been defined considered the repair costs related to evaluated damage levels. A global repair cost has assigned and then normalized to a rebuilding cost of 1100 €/m². Based on the evaluated damage levels, the cost ratio $C_{r,r}$ is evaluated, which ranges between 0 and 1.

Based on the past post-earthquake data, time intervals are estimated. The inactivity time is evaluated as 21 months for the four areas of the historic centre and 9 months for the two expansion zones. The trend of the functionality curve first considers the recovery of buildings with a low damage level and then considers the recovery of buildings with higher damage levels. The considered control time is $T_{LC} = 18$ years.

Based on a similar approach, the recovery time is evaluated based on the required time to restore a particular damage level. In particular, the cost and time models are validated following the same procedure used in a previous study [10], i.e., based on the repair cost function and there pair time function derived from the available reconstruction process data. The set of repair work activities are evaluated in accordance with the most widespread repair and strengthening techniques [13, 14]. In Fig. 5, the obtained resilience curves are reported.

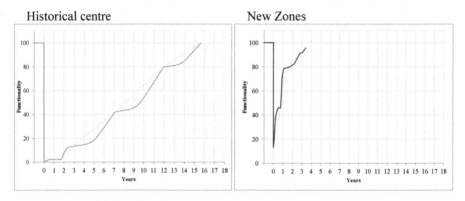

Fig. 5. Resilience performances for the historical centre and new zones.

4   Resilience-Based Mitigation Strategies

Based on resilience's concept, different mitigation strategies are defined for the investigated case study. Each strategy is able to increase resilience to varying degrees. Consequently, the key to optimal selection is a quantitative evaluation of the resilience. The basic principle to define an effective strategy to enhance the resilience is derived from the target performances for buildings after the retrofit program. To define an operative resilience plan, the resilience-based strategy is developed considering the retrofit goal (performance target).

Three different goals for seismic retrofit are considered, based on the Italian law, which is based on tax deductions for interventions. The tax deduction is linked to the seismic upgrade, based on the following improvement of the class of risk:

- 70–75% for 1 class of risk;
- 80–85% for 2 or more classes.

Independently on the type of seismic retrofit, a shift to a lower vulnerability class from the current one is considered. The class of risk is directly linked to the vulnerability class and the functionality curve is defined following the previous showed procedure. In this case a direct proportionality relationship is considered between the functionality reduction and inactivity time.

In the first strategy, one shift of vulnerability class (1-V) is considered; two shifts of the vulnerability class (2-V) and on total upgrade (TU) are considered respectively for the second and third strategy. From new vulnerability classes, news seismic scenarios are derived (I_{EMS98} = VIII). Consequently, new resilience curves are obtained (Fig. 6).

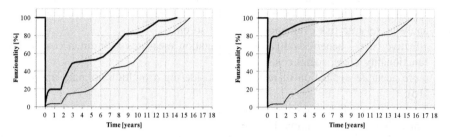

Fig. 6. One shift of vulnerability class (1-V) on the left and total upgrade (TU) on the right: resilience curves for Historical center.

Moreover, after 18 years, a community cannot be considered resilient. Consequently, different control time value (5 years) is considered and significant different RI values are obtained. In Fig. 7, the results and comparison of the current state (CS) and the considered mitigation strategies are reported.

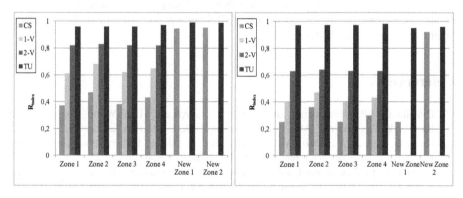

Fig. 7. IEMS98 = VIII: Effects of different seismic mitigation strategies: resilience index for T_{LC} = 18 years (left) and T_{LC} = 5 years (right).

5   Conclusion

In this study, a novel approach to civil protection and urban planning is defined. The proposal is a resilience-based approach which the concepts of resilience and their quantification are considered to direct impact on urban regulations and planning. Several interesting seismic risk reduction strategies are defined and the operational tools are determined. Although the study is based on simple data and not very accurate information, the results highlighted a significant enhanced of the resilience of the community.

The study can be considered a work in progress and the next steps can be summarized as:

- more accurate approaches for each step of the proposed methodology as new and specific, accurate, or simplified procedures for fragility curves, seismic hazard analysis, seismic risk evaluation [15], and so on;
- effective cost – benefit evaluation of mitigation measures as indirect cost, loss of functionality costs, social costs, etc.;
- more accurate evaluation of resilience considering a multidisciplinary approaches [16];
- increase the resilience based several mitigation activities and measure to be taken in peace time (see for example [17, 18]).

The proposal should be considered as an improvement of the new Civil Italian Protection code [19], which currently neglects operational approaches based on the resilience concepts. This study proposes a new approach, which replaces the existing civil protection plan with a resilience community plan. The concept of changing from emergency plan to resilience plan should be considered as a natural evolution of emergency plan.

Several development and improvement can be defined considering more accurate tools. For example, fragility and vulnerability function can be considered for buildings, based on analytical models and accurate methodologies [20, 21]. These methodologies should be defined in uniform way for each building types, particularly in a wide territorial scale and on historical centres.

References

1. Cimellaro, G.P.: New trends on resiliency research. In: 16th World Conference on Earthquake Engineering, 16WCEE 2017 Santiago Chile, 9th–13th January 2017
2. Ceré, G., Rezgui, Y., Zhao, W.: Critical review of existing built environment resilience frameworks: directions for future research. Int. J. Disaster Risk Reduct. 25, 173–189 (2017)
3. McAllister, T.: Developing Guidelines and Standards for Disaster Resilience of the Built Environment: A Research Needs Assessment, NIST Technical Note 1795 (2013)
4. Tilio, L., Murgante, B., Di Trani, F., Vona, M., Masi, A.: Mitigation of urban vulnerability through a spatial multicriteria approach. Disaster Adv. 5(3), 138–143 (2012)
5. Jones, L.M., et al.: The Shake Out Scenario: U.S. Geological Survey Open-File Report 2008 1150 and California Geological Survey Preliminary Report 25 (2008). http://pubs.usgs.gov/of/2008/1150/
6. Jones, L.M.: Resilience by design: bringing science to policy makers, resilience by design: bringing science to policy makers. Seismolog. Res. Lett. 86(2A), 294–301 (2015). https://doi.org/10.1785/0220150010
7. ATC. Here Today—Here Tomorrow, The Road to Earthquake Resilience in San Francisco, Com-munity Action Plan for Seismic Safety, ATC-52-2 Report, Applied Technology Council, Redwood City, California (2010)

8. Vona, M., Harabaglia, P., Murgante, B.: Thinking about resilience cities studying Italian earthquake. Urban Des. Plan. **169**, 185–199 (2016)
9. Ministerial Decree 58/2017. "Sisma Bonus—Linee Guida per la Classificazione del Rischio Sismico delle Costruzioni Nonché le Modalità per L'attestazione, da Parte di Professionisti Abilitati, Dell'efficacia Degli Interventi Effettuati"; Ministero delle Infrastrutture e dei Trasporti:Rome, Italy, 28 February 2017. (In Italian)
10. Vona, M., Mastroberti, M., Mitidieri, L., Tataranna, S.: New resilience model of communities based on numerical evaluation and observed post seismic reconstruction process. Int. J. Disaster Risk Reduct. **28**, 602–609 (2018)
11. Chiauzzi, L., et al.: Building damage scenarios based on exploitation of Housner intensity derived from finite faults ground motion simulations. Bull. Earthq. Eng. **10**, 517–545 (2012)
12. Vona, M., Manganelli, B., Tataranna, S.: Conservation, enhancement and resilience of historical and cultural heritage exposed to natural risks and social dynamics. Smart Innov. Syst. Technol. **101**, 426–433 (2019)
13. Di Ludovico, M., Prota, A., Moroni, C., Manfredi, G., Dolce, M.: Reconstruction process of damaged residential buildings outside historical centres after the L'Aquila earthquake: part I—"light damage" reconstruction. Bull. Earthq. Eng. **15**(2), 667–692 (2016). https://doi.org/10.1007/s10518-016-9877-8
14. Di Ludovico, M., Prota, A., Moroni, C., Manfredi, G., Dolce, M.: Reconstruction process of damaged residential buildings outside historical centres after the L'Aquila earthquake: part II—"heavy damage" reconstruction. Bull. Earthq. Eng. **15**(2), 693–729 (2016). https://doi.org/10.1007/s10518-016-9979-3
15. Vona, M.: A novel approach to improve the code provision based on a seismic risk index for existing buildings. J. Build. Eng. **28**(101037), 2020 (2020)
16. Vona, M., Anelli, A., Mastroberti, M., Murgante, B., Santa-Cruz, S.: Prioritization Strategies to reduce the seismic risk of the public and strategic buildings. Disaster Adv. **10**(4), 1–15 (2017)
17. Anelli, A., Santa-Cruz, S., Vona, M., Tarque, N., Laterza, M.: A proactive and resilient seismic risk mitigation strategy for existing school buildings. Struct. Infrastruct. Eng. **15**(2), 137–151 (2019)
18. Manganelli, B., Vona, M., De Paola, P.: Evaluating the cost and benefits of earthquake protection of buildings. J. Eur. Real Estate Res. **11**(2), 263–278 (2018). https://doi.org/10.1108/JERER-09-2017-0029
19. Decreto Legislativo Legislative Decree n. 224, 2 gennaio 2018, n. 1, Codice della protezione civile. GU n.17 del 22 January 2018
20. Vona, M., Manganelli, B., Tataranna, S., Anelli, A.: An optimized procedure to estimate the economic seismic losses of existing reinforced concrete buildings due to seismic damage. Buildings **8**, 144 (2018)
21. Anelli, A., Mori, F., Vona, M.: Fragility curves of the urban road network based on the debris distributions of interfering buildings. Appl. Sci. **10**, 1289 (2020)

Local Geology and Seismic-Induced Damages: The Case of Amatrice (Central Italy)

Sergio Cappucci[1] ⓘ, Giacomo Buffarini[1] ⓘ, Ludovica Giordano[1,2] ⓘ,
Salomon Hailemikael[1] ⓘ, Guido Martini[1] ⓘ,
and Maurizio Pollino[1,2(✉)] ⓘ

[1] ENEA - Italian National Agency for New Technologies, Energy and
Sustainable Economic Development, Rome, Italy
{sergio.cappucci, giacomo.buffarini, ludovica.giordano,
salomon.hailemikael, guido.martini,
maurizio.pollino}@enea.it
[2] EISAC.it - Italian Node of the European Infrastructure Simulation
and Analysis Centre, Rome, Italy

Abstract. On 24th August 2016 the first earthquake (Mw 6.2) of a long-lasting sequence struck Central Italy. The 24th August mainshock was in the surroundings of Amatrice, Central Italy, where about 300 people died. Most of the buildings were damaged and immediately after the earthquake Italian National Civil Protection (DPC) started coordinating the emergency and post-emergency activities. The latter included geological and geotechnical investigations for seismic microzonation carried out by the Centre for Seismic Microzonation (CMS) and the creation of a dedicated task force for rubbles management in the town of Amatrice. The present study presents preliminary results of the spatial correlation between the distribution of building damages generated by the 24th August earthquake, obtained by means of the Copernicus Emergency Management System (EMS) services, and the results of the seismic microzonation study of the village. We observed a spatial correlation between damages of buildings and seismic ground motion amplification, quantitatively estimated through an amplification factor (FHa). In particular, we observed an increasing trend of higher damaged buildings when FHa grows.

Keywords: Earthquake · Urban geology · Seismic microzonation ·
COPERNICUS Emergency Management System · Rubbles · Geomatics ·
LIDAR · Post-emergency management

1 Introduction

In 2016-17, Central Italy was affected by a complex seismic sequence on an area of Apennines covering large part of Lazio, Marche, Umbria and Abruzzo Regional administrative territories.

On 24th August 2016 at 01:36 (UTC) a 6.2 MW earthquake struck the Central Italy area between the municipalities of Amatrice and Arquata del Tronto (Fig. 1-b) causing about 300 victims and more than 35,000 homeless [1, 2]. Referring to the Italian Strong

© Springer Nature Switzerland AG 2020
O. Gervasi et al. (Eds.): ICCSA 2020, LNCS 12250, pp. 950–962, 2020.
https://doi.org/10.1007/978-3-030-58802-1_68

Motion Network [3] the nearest accelerometric station AMT, located about 400 m northward the Amatrice historic centre with an epicentral distance (R_{epi}) of about 8.5 km, recorded a Peak Ground Acceleration (PGA) of 0.868 g [4].

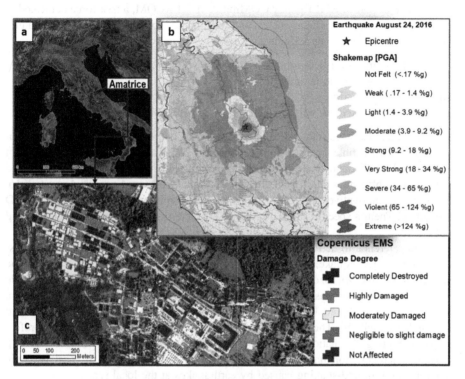

Fig. 1. a) Amatrice location (Central Italy); b) Shakemap of the earthquake occurred on August 24, 2016 (source: INGV, The Italian National Institute of Geophysics and Volcanology); c) Copernicus EMS damage grading map produced after the August 24, 2016 event (source: [5]).

Then, the sequence developed in the surrounding of Norcia, situated about 30 km northward Amatrice, with two events on 26th October (at 19:18 UTC; 6.1 MW) close Castelsantangelo sul Nera and on 30th October (at 06:40 UTC; 6.6 MW) nearby Norcia. The accelerometric recordings obtained in Amatrice station (AMT) showed for the 26th October shock ($R_{epi} \cong 33.3$ km) a PGA of 0.093 g and for the 30th October one ($R_{epi} \cong 26.4$ km) a PGA of 0.532 g.

The last phase of the sequence, was located south of Amatrice in the Montereale area and included two mainshocks occurred on 18th January 2017 at 10:14 (MW 5.7) and 10:25 (MW 5.6) recorded in AMT respectively with PGA of 0.326 g ($R_{epi} \cong$ 11.3 km) and 0.159 g ($R_{epi} \cong 14.4$ km).

The cumulative damage effect observed in Amatrice directly reflects the strong ground shaking caused by the sequence of earthquakes [1]. The 24th August Mainshock damage distribution in Amatrice was analysed by Copernicus Emergency Management

System, EMS [5] (Fig. 1-c). The *"Completely Destroyed"* and *"Highly Damaged"* buildings are constrained in the north-western part of Amatrice historic centre.

Immediately after the 24th August mainshock, Italian National Civil Protection (DPC) was in charge of emergency and post-emergency activities coordination. ENEA participated as part of EMERgency COMmittee (EMERCOM, a task force dedicated to overcome and manage Emergencies and Elimination of Consequences of Natural Disasters) to the following activities:

  i)   working group for determination of rubble volumes,
  ii) seismic microzonation activities,
  iii) macroseismic survey for the determination of earthquake intensities (QUEST),
  iv) survey of co-seismic earthquake ruptures (EMERGEO).

With reference to activity i) in a previous work a method for the rapid estimation of the volumes of rubble heaps within the area of Amatrice was implemented [6]. In particular, LiDAR data were exploited to provide the geometric features (location and volume) of rubble piles distributed after the earthquake occurred on 24th August, 2016, by using an innovative procedure, based on photo-interpretation and volumes 3-D modelling. Then, a specific study on rubbles characterisation has been recently carried out [7].

With reference to activity ii), following the Ordinance n. 24 of Special Commissioner for the Earthquake, the Seismic Microzonation Center (CMS) coordinated the studies of Seismic Microzonation of Level 3 (SM3) in 138 municipalities. The Seismic Microzonation Center was founded in 2015 by the agreement between several Italian research institutions and University departments under the aegis of Italian National Research Council [8]. The seismic microzonation studies were conducted by professionals adopting the national guidelines implemented by SM Working Group [9]. Seismic microzonation has the objective of evaluating the effect of local geologic conditions on ground-shaking caused by earthquakes at the local scale.

In particular, the definition of seismic microzones focuses on ground-motion amplification factors together with areas susceptible to seismically induced instabilities like landslides, soil liquefactions or ground failures. Based on a detailed geological model of the area, the SM3 analysis required the collection of geological, geophysical, and geotechnical data and provide a detailed classification of the territory in microzones characterized by the same level of ground motion amplification expressed through an amplification factor. The ground motion amplification was evaluated by numerical simulations [10].

The amplification factors (FHa) were calculated as the ratio between the integral of acceleration elastic response spectra (5% damping) of seismic inputs (made available by CMS [8]) and the integral of simulated acceleration elastic response spectra (5% damping) of output at ground surface. Integration were performed considering three period-intervals, namely 0.1–0.5 s, 0.4–0.8 s and 0.7–1.1 s, in order to evaluate the amplification level variation as a function of structural period. The seismic input was provided for a seismic hazard level with probability of exceedance of 10% in 50 years.

In the present work, the results of SM3 study of Amatrice Municipality has been jointly analysed with the observed damage after the 24th August mainshock. In particular, the amplification factor maps of Amatrice downtown have been spatially correlated to the building damage level distribution, focusing on the 0.1–0.5 s interval of periods that is considered representative of the fundamental period of the building stock in Amatrice.

2 Study Area

Amatrice is placed in the Central Italy section of the Apennines chain (Fig. 1-a). This area is interested, since upper Pliocene, by extensional tectonics with active seismogenic faults affecting the entire NW-SE oriented ridge [11–17].

The study of the seismic events occurred in the past as well as recent seismicity and seismotectonic studies, have revealed that Amatrice area has high seismic hazard at national level (PGA 0.25–0.275 g with probability of exceedance of 10% in 50 years).

The Amatrice basin is a morpho-structural depression filled by the Miocene siliciclastic deposits of the Laga Formation and overlaid by quaternary continental units [18]. The Laga Formation is made of alternation of sandstone and siltstone layers and represents the geologic bedrock of the area. The town lies on a fluvial terrace within the Tronto river valley. This terrace is mainly made of gravels and sands directly overlying the bedrock [18]. Like many other villages in Central Italy, urban development was directed towards the top of the hill and in the proximity of the edges of the terrace; it is the part of the mountain that allowed a better protection against attacks and control of surrounding areas as well as protection from floods in the river valley below. But these areas are also prone to ground-motion amplification effects generated by earthquakes. An example of geological cross-section elaborated through the ridge of Amatrice is reported in Fig. 2.

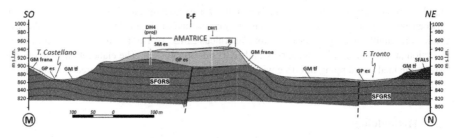

Fig. 2. SO-NE geological profile of the Amatrice Ridge. (source: [18] modified). The engineering geological units are classified according to SM Working Group [8]. Cover terrains: RI - Anthropic deposits; GPes - mixed gravels and sands in alluvial fan; GMtf - mixed gravels, sands and silts in terraced alluvial deposits; SMes - silty sands in alluvial deposits. Geological bedrock: SFALS - alternation of contrasting lithotypes, stratified and altered or fractured; SFGRS - stratified, grainy cemented lithotypes, altered or fractured.

3 Data and Materials

3.1 Dataset

The core dataset is made up of:

1. Damage Grading Map (Damaged/collapsed buildings): delimitation and classification provided by Copernicus EMS [5] (Fig. 1-c and Fig. 3-a).
2. Datasets exploited within previous studies [6, 7] on the same area (LiDAR and RGB Orthophotos) and related outputs produced (Fig. 3-b).
3. 1:5,000 Digital Cartography [19] (Fig. 3-c).
4. Seismic Microzonation - Level 3 (SM3) Map for Amatrice [18] (Fig. 3-d).

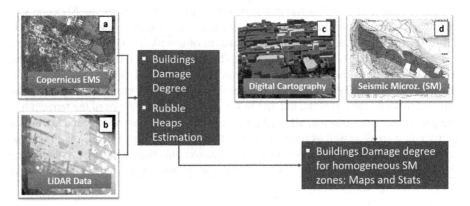

Fig. 3. Flow diagram of the procedure exploited for evaluating and mapping the relationship between building damage degree and seismic microzonation. Input data for building damage grading and rubble heaps geometries from: Copernicus EMS (a); 1 m resolution DTM from Light Detection and Ranging (LiDAR) survey and RGB orthophotos (b). The elaboration of maps and stats is obtained overlapping in GIS environment digital cartography (c) and areal distribution of SM3 amplification factors (d).

3.2 Methodology

A flow diagram of the adopted methodology, including the rubbles estimation performed in the abovementioned previous works [6, 7], is reported in Fig. 3.

In the present paper the grading map provided by Copernicus EMS in the immediate post-event phase [5] was exploited to take into account the level of damage for buildings. According to Copernicus EMS categories, buildings were classified into five levels of damage: *"Not Affected", "Negligible to slight damage", Moderately damaged", Highly damaged", "Completely Destroyed"*. These data were opportunely combined in GIS environment together with 1:5,000 digital cartography [19] and Seismic Microzonation Map (SM3) [18]. For each building, the following attributes were available in an enriched GIS layer: area, perimeter, volume, level of damage (EMS grading), SM3 amplification factor (FHa).

Detailed data about buildings vulnerability are not available. Due to the lack of knowledge, in the present study a uniform class B, according to EMS-98 European Macroseismic Scale [20], has been hypothesized for the building stock even though the masonry building quality in the area is often very poor. As most of the buildings had a height between 6 and 12 meters, their first modal shape period has been evaluated with the following formula:

$$T_1 = C_1 H^{3/4}$$

where T is the fundamental resonance period in seconds, H is the building height in meters and $C_1 = 0.050$ for masonry building. The first modal shape period is therefore approximated between 0.2 and 0.3 s (Italian Building Code NTC 2018) [21]. More data about building vulnerability could refine the results, but the saturation effect due to the strong shaking makes sense of the assumption made.

4   Results

The overlay of the SM3 and Copernicus EMS allowed to obtain statistical (Table 1) and visual (Fig. 4, Fig. 5 and Fig. 6) results.

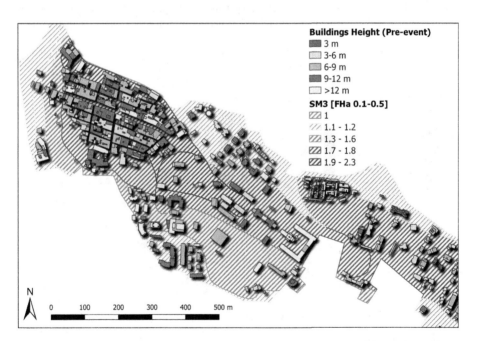

Fig. 4. Buildings' heights in the town of Amatrice (source: [19]: spatial overlay with the amplification factor values (FHa) distribution from Level 3 Seismic Microzonation (SM3) related to period interval of 0.1–0.5 s (source: [18])

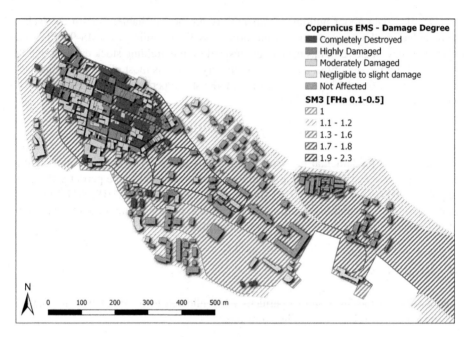

Fig. 5. Building damage degree (source: [5]) spatially overlapped to the Seismic Microzonation of Level 3 (SM3) map. FHa values are related to period interval of 0.1–0.5 s (source: [18])

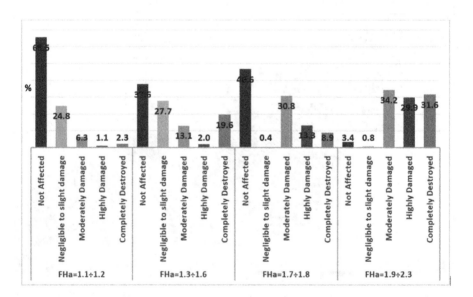

Fig. 6. Percentages of buildings stock surface, subdivided according to the five damage degree levels [5], within each different homogeneous FHa zone [18]

Table 1. Number of buildings and related areas in m^2: subdivision according to their respective damage degree levels (source: [5]) and area percentage distribution for homogeneous FHa values (period interval 0.1–0.5 s) (source: [18])

Homogeneous Amplification Factor (FHa) Zones	FHa-A Homogeneous FHa zones Area (m^2)	Damage degree	N. of buildings	BA - Building Area (m2)	% BA/BA_{tot} in relative FHa zone	% $(BA/FHa\text{-}A)$
1.1-1.2		Completely Destroyed	2	321.971	2.30	0.3%
		Highly Damaged	1	155.24	1.11	0.1%
		Moderately Damaged	4	886.21	6.32	0.8%
		Negligible to slight damage	11	3481.7503	24.82	3.3%
		Not Affected	43	9182.6762	65.46	8.7%
	153601.01		61	14027.85	100.00	13.2%
1.3-1.6		Completely Destroyed	9	2193.39	19.64	2.5%
		Highly Damaged	4	223.12	2.00	0.3%
		Moderately Damaged	8	1457.40	13.05	1.7%
		Negligible to slight damage	9	3097.47	27.74	3.5%
		Not Affected	12	4195.59	37.57	4.8%
	89845.49		42	11167	100.00	12.8%
1.7-1.8		Completely Destroyed	18	3113	8.93	1.3%
		Highly Damaged	17	4633.76	13.29	2.0%
		Moderately Damaged	64	10740.99	30.81	4.7%
		Negligible to slight damage	1	123.98	0.36	0.1%
		Not Affected	62	16255.45	46.62	7.0%
	230971.53		162	34867.64	100.00	15.1%
1.9-2.3		Completely Destroyed	68	10943.30	31.61	13.5%
		Highly Damaged	47	10363.59	29.94	12.8%
		Moderately Damaged	60	11854.09	34.24	14.6%
		Negligible to slight damage	2	292.15	0.84	0.4%
		Not Affected	7	1163.48	3.36	1.4%
	8109980		184	34617	100.00	42.7%
Total	555517.84		449			

In Fig. 4 are depicted the buildings heights, which are considered as proxy for estimating the building fundamental resonance period. The city centre shows a dense agglomeration of structures with an elevation between 6 and 12 m. The minority of buildings have an elevation below 6 m or above 12 m.

Figure 5 clearly shows how areas classified with higher FHa values are more densely urbanized. The spatial correlation between damages of buildings and seismic amplification, as expected, is evident. Buildings affected by higher damage levels are concentrated within the areas with higher FHa values (Table 1; Fig. 5 and Fig. 6) that, unfortunately, correspond to the densely urbanised city centre.

The present analysis highlighted a general positive correlation between the increasing trend of higher damaged buildings and growing FHa (Fig. 6). Actually, as shown in Fig. 6, this trend is straightforward for the *"Moderately damaged"* and *"Highly damaged"* classes, but not for the other two classes. The numbers for *"Negligible to slight damage"* and *"Completely Destroyed"* classes do not regularly increase with increasing FHa interval (from 1.1–1.2 to 1.9–2.3). However, if we consider the *"Completely destroyed"* class, its decreasing value within the 1.7–1.8 FHa interval is associated to a significant increase in the *"Highly damaged"* (contiguous) class, suggesting possible misclassification error among these two classes. As well, within the same 1.7–1.8 FHa interval the *"Not affected"* class is characterised by an increasing value (with respect to that of the lower 1.3–1.6 FHa interval) again associated to a very small amount of the buildings in the *"Negligible to slight damage"* class and so on. This result might be likely attributed to possible misclassification of damage level between contiguous damage classes.

5 Discussion

In some spot we have verified that Copernicus EMS attributed a *"slightly/moderately damage"* to a single construction; but the building was actually formed by two contiguous parts: one "not affected" or "slightly damaged" and the other one "completely destroyed" or "highly damaged". Some apparently anomalous results of Fig. 6 could be explained according to the hypothesis that an irregular trend can be related to the influence of factors not included in the present analysis, e.g., different vulnerability of contiguous buildings. With regards to this latter issue, further investigations are under development. More coherent results might possibly be obtained by stratifying buildings according to their vulnerability, estimated following EMS-98 classes, and performing a separate analysis for each vulnerability class. Of course, it would be worth following such an approach as long as the number of buildings within each class is statistically significant.

Moreover, some of the buildings in the South-East part of Amatrice (where FHa values are high; Fig. 5) were "not affected" or "slightly damaged". The reason is probably due to their more recent construction (seismic vulnerability of more recent buildings is still under investigation). Obviously, less damaged buildings within seismic microzones characterised by high values of FHa demonstrates that construction techniques can reduce vulnerability to seismic hazard. This should be carefully considered in the framework of urban development planning. Buildings located in seismic zones, especially the older ones, should be carefully checked in order to assess their vulnerability.

It is worth highlighting that their seismic retrofit can benefit, even totally, of financial support from the Italian Government ("Sisma Bonus", D.L. N. 63/2013 and D.L. N. 34/2019).

Geomatics, geomorphology and applied geology are increasingly interlinked as they represent the basis for innovative design/reconstruction models and adoption for modern, more efficient and smart new infrastructure in a variety of environmental contexts [6, 9, 22–25].

The advantages for central and local administrations from the exploitation of Geomatics techniques are clear, not only during the emergency management or in the recovery phases [26], but also in the framework of planning activities [27]. A number of new applications can derive from the results of the research described in the present paper, such as the advanced mapping of soil and subsoil characteristics. The classification of the territory in seismic microzones, among others, allows to identify a range of services to citizens and stakeholders. Such approach can represents the geospatial basis [28] for an effective territorial planning (urban development, exploitation of natural resources, agricultural, industrial and commercial purposes, etc.), by properly taking into account natural constraints and hazards.

The drama of catastrophic events could also represent an opportunity not only from the technical point to have new safer buildings (not necessarily preserving the original urban layout) after the reconstruction phase, but also for social and economic development. In this sense, a detailed knowledge and mapping of seismic microzones is fundamental to support the local urban planning, especially in the reconstruction phases. This is a very complex task, but the approach developed in the present study can be exploited for a proper allocation of residential and industrial areas in safer zones (even different from the original locations), whereas areas falling in more hazardous microzones could be reconverted to other uses (green infrastructures, parks, urban gardens, parking and stocking areas).

6   Conclusions

The present study exploited the levels of building damage from Copernicus EMS data [5], readily available after the 24th August 2016 earthquake, and the Seismic Microzonation study [18] within Amatrice Municipality. This has allowed to investigate the role of seismic ground-motion amplification on the observed buildings damages.

Even if very simplified assumption has been made on the seismic vulnerability of the building stock within the town, which mainly influenced the damage levels, our analysis pointed out that a significant impact was also exerted by the local geological conditions. In fact, ground-motion amplifications due to local geological conditions are well known effects and the quantitative analysis of such ground motion characteristics is fundamental for damage evaluation as well as future urban planning and reconstruction. This information can be summarized in seismic microzonation maps, where each microzone area is associated to an amplification factor (FHa). In addition, more advanced methods, including 3D numerical simulations of the Amatrice hill seismic response (like in [29]) and detailed models of the building stock vulnerability, provide quantitative insight on the specific role exerted by vulnerability and local geology on the observed damage.

Geological and geomorphological studies of urban systems and the reliable modelling of the subsoil on which they arise are continuously evolving. It is a branch of geology still under development, especially from a methodological point of view. In addition, GIS processing allows to effectively support spatial analysis opening many research and technological challenges [21–25, 30–32]. The present paper highlight that the capability to correlate seismic ground-motion amplification and the buildings damage through GIS applications, can be the driver for an efficient intervention in order to reduce building's vulnerability of existing construction, as well as new urban development models during the reconstruction phase.

In addition, an interdisciplinary and multidisciplinary approach that considers historical, geo-archaeological, geo-environmental, and seismological data can be effectively used to implement the methods of surface and subsoil geology characterisation. The use of multi-source dataset allows to perform detailed reconstructions of anthropic interventions in urban areas, as well as interactions between natural events and the human being.

Acknowledgments. Thanks to the Center for Seismic Microzonation and to the National Civil Protection for the fruitful discussion and support. Thanks to Eng. F. Campopiano, G. Farrace, P. Pagliara and I. Postiglione of National Civil Protection for the fruitful discussion and suggestions and to all staff involved during the emergency action. The work presented in the paper has been conducted also in the framework of ARCH Project (European Union's Horizon 2020 research and innovation programme under grant agreement N°820999) and of EISAC.it (www. eisac.it), a joint ENEA and INGV collaboration agreement, aiming at supporting Operators and Public Authorities in better protecting assets and in enhancing their resilience with respect to all hazards.

References

1. Rossi, A.: The 2016–2017 earthquake sequence in Central Italy: macroseismic survey and damage scenario through the EMS-98 intensity assessment. Bull. Earthq. Eng. **17**(5), 2407–2431 (2019). https://doi.org/10.1007/s10518-019-00556-w
2. Amatrice, Norcia, Visso Seismic Sequence, INGV. http://terremoti.ingv.it/it/ultimi-eventi/1023-sequenza-sismica-in-italia-centrale-aggiornamenti.html. Accessed 28 Mar 2020
3. Italian Strong Motion Network (Rete Accelerometrica Nazionale - RAN). http://www.protezionecivile.gov.it/en/risk-activities/seismic-risk/activities/italian-strong-motion-network. Accessed 04 May 2020
4. Luzi, L, Puglia, R., Russo, E.: ORFEUS WG5: engineering strong motion database, version 1.0. Istituto Nazionale di Geofisica e Vulcanologia, Observatories & Research Facilities for European Seismology (2016). https://doi.org/10.13127/esm
5. Copernicus EMS activation, 24 August 2016. http://emergency.copernicus.eu/mapping/list-of-components/EMSR177. Accessed 28 Mar 2020
6. Cappucci, S., et al.: Earthquake's rubble heaps volume evaluation: expeditious approach through earth observation and geomatics techniques. In: Gervasi, O., et al. (eds.) ICCSA 2017. LNCS, vol. 10405, pp. 261–277. Springer, Cham (2017). https://doi.org/10.1007/978-3-319-62395-5_19
7. Pollino, M., et al.: Assessing earthquake-induced urban rubble by means of multiplatform remotely sensed data. ISPRS Int. J. Geo-Inf. **9**, 262 (2020)

8. The Center for Seismic Microzonation (CentroMS). https://www.centromicrozonazionesis mica.it/en/. Accessed 04 May 2020

9. SM Working Group: Seismic microzonation addresses and criteria. Civil Protection Department and Conference of Regions and Autonomous Provinces (2008). http://www. protezionecivile.gov.it/httpdocs/cms/attach_extra/GuidelinesForSeismicMicrozonation.pdf. Accessed 04 May 2020

10. Amanti, M., et al.: Geological and geotechnical models definition for 3rd level seismic microzonation studies in Central Italy. Bull. Earthquake Eng., 33 p. (2020). https://doi.org/ 10.1007/s10518-020-00843-x

11. Pizzi, A., Galadini, F.: Pre-existing cross-structures and active fault segmentation in the northern-centralk Apennines (Italy). Tectonophysics **476**, 304–319 (2009)

12. Coltorti, M., Farabollini, P.: Quaternary evolution of the Castelluccio di Norcia Basin (Umbria-Marchean Apennines, Italy). Il Quaternario **8**, 149–166 (1995)

13. King, G.C.P.: Speculations on the geometry of the initiation and termination processes of earthquake rupture and its relation to morphology and geological structure. Pure Appl. Geophys. **124**(3), 567–585 (1986)

14. Hernandez, B., et al.: Rupture history of the 1997 Umbria-Marche (Central Italy) main shocks from the inversion of GPS, DInSAR and near field strong motion data. Ann. Geophys. **47**, 1355–1376 (2004)

15. Valensise, G., Pantosti, D.: The investigation of potential earthquake sources in peninsular Italy: a review. J. Seismol. **5**, 5287–306 (2001)

16. Calamita, F., Pizzi, A.: Tettonica quaternaria nella dorsal appenniniica umbro-marchigiana e bacini intrappenninici associate. Studi Geologici Camerti, SI, 17–25 (1992)

17. Cacciuni, A., Centamore, E., Di Stefano, R., Dramis, F.: Evoluzione morfotettonica della conca di Amatrice. Studi Geologici Camerti **2**, 95–100 (1995)

18. Regione Lazio, Microzonazione Sismica Livello 3 - Ordinanza n. 24/2017. http://www. regione.lazio.it/prl_ambiente/?vw=contenutidettaglio&id=238

19. Regione Lazio, Carta Tecnica Regionale Numerica (CTRN). http://dati.lazio.it/catalog/it/ dataset?tags=CTR. Accessed 23 Apr 2020

20. Grünthal, G., Musson, R., Schwarz, J., Stucchi, M.: European Macroseismic Scale 1998 (EMS-98). Cahiers du Centre Europèen de Géodynamique et de Séismologie, vol. 15, Luxembourg (1998)

21. Norme tecniche per le costruzioni - NTC 2018. Gazzetta Ufficiale Serie Generale n.42 del 20-02-2018, n. 8) and Ministero delle Infrastrutture e dei Trasporti - Circolare 21 gennaio 2019, n. 7 C.S.LL.PP. https://www.gazzettaufficiale.it/eli/id/2018/2/20/18A00716/sg

22. Pascucci, V., Cappucci, S., Andreucci, S., Donda, F.: Sedimentary features of the offshore part of the la Pelosa Beach (Sardinia, Italy). Rendiconti Online Soc. Geol. Ital. **2**, 1–3 (2008)

23. Taramelli, A., Valentini, E., Innocenti, C., Cappucci, S.: FHyL: field spectral libraries, airborne hyperspectral images and topographic and bathymetric LiDAR data for complex coastal mapping. In: 2013 IEEE International Geoscience and Remote Sensing Symposium (IGARSS), Melbourne, Australia, 21–26 July 2013, pp. 2270–2273 (2013)

24. Ausili, A., et al.: New approaches for multi-source data sediment characterisation, thickness assessment and clean up strategies. Chem. Eng. Trans. **28**, 6 (2012)

25. Cappucci, S., Valentini, E., Del Monte, M., Paci, M., Filipponi, F., Taramelli, A.: Detection of natural and anthropic features on small Islands. J. Coastal Res. **77**, 74–88 (2017)

26. Giovinazzi, S., et al.: Towards a decision support tool for assessing, managing and mitigating seismic risk of electric power networks. In: Gervasi, O., et al. (eds.) ICCSA 2017. LNCS, vol. 10406, pp. 399–414. Springer, Cham (2017). https://doi.org/10.1007/978-3-319-62398-6_28

27. Matassoni, L., Giovinazzi, S., Pollino, M., Fiaschi, A., La Porta, L., Rosato, V.: A geospatial decision support tool for seismic risk management: florence (Italy) case study. In: Gervasi, O., Murgante, B., et al. (eds.) ICCSA 2017. LNCS, vol. 10405, pp. 278–293. Springer, Cham (2017). https://doi.org/10.1007/978-3-319-62395-5_20
28. Di Pietro, A., Lavalle, L., La Porta, L., Pollino, M., Tofani, A., Rosato, V.: Design of DSS for supporting preparedness to and management of anomalous situations in complex scenarios. In: Setola, R., Rosato, V., Kyriakides, E., Rome, E. (eds.) Managing the Complexity of Critical Infrastructures. SSDC, vol. 90, pp. 195–232. Springer, Cham (2016). https://doi.org/10.1007/978-3-319-51043-9_9
29. Razzano, R., et al.: Modelling the three-dimensional site response in the village of Amatrice, Central Italy. EGU General Assembly 2020, Online, 4–8 May 2020, EGU2020-22483 (2020). https://doi.org/10.5194/egusphere-egu2020-22483
30. Conti, M., Cappucci, S., La Monica, G.B.: Sediment dynamic of nourished sandy beaches. Rendiconti Online Soc. Geol. Ital. **8**, 31–38 (2009)
31. Pallottini, E., Cappucci, S.: Beach-dune system interaction and evolution. Rendiconti Online Soc. Geol. Ital. **8**, 87–97 (2009)
32. Cappucci, S., De Cassan, M., Grillini, M., Proposito, M., Screpanti, A.: Multisource water characterisation for water supply and management strategies on a small Mediterranean Island. Hydrogeol. J. **1**, 1–17 (2020)

Optimization of Low-Cost Monitoring Systems for On-Site Earthquake Early-Warning of Critical Infrastructures

Antonino D'Alessandro[1], Salvatore Scudero[1(✉)], Giovanni Vitale[1,2],
Andrea Di Benedetto[1,3], and Giosuè Lo Bosco[3,4]

[1] Istituto Nazionale di Geofisica e Vulcanologia,
Osservatorio Nazionale Terremoti, 00143 Rome, Italy
{antonino.dalessandro,salvatore.scudero}@ingv.it
[2] Dipartimento Scienze della Terra e del Mare DiSTeM,
Università degli Studi di Palermo, 90123 Palermo, Italy
[3] Dipartimento di Matematica e Informatica,
Università degli Studi di Palermo, 90123 Palermo, Italy
[4] Dipartimento di Scienze per l'innovazione tecnologica,
Istituto Euro Mediterraneo di Scienza e Tecnologia, 90139 Palermo, Italy

Abstract. In the last years, monitoring systems based on low-cost and miniaturized sensors (MEMS) revealed as a very successful compromise between the availability of data and their quality. Also applications in the field of seismic and structural monitoring have been constantly increasing in term of number and variety of functions. Among these applications, the implementation of systems for earthquake early warning is a cutting-edge topic, mainly for its relevance for the society as millions of peoples in various regions of the world are exposed to high seismic hazard. This paper introduces the optimization of an already established seismic (and structural) monitoring system, that would make it suitable for the implementation of the earthquake early warning. In particular, the sampling code has been improved and a new triggering algorithm able to automatically detect the ground shaking due to the propagation of the seismic waves has been developed. The preliminary results indicate that the system is very flexible and easy to implement, and encourage to perform further developing steps.

Keywords: Seismic monitoring · Structural monitoring · MEMS · Earthquake early warning · Trigger algorithm

1 Introduction

In the last decade, the technological development resulted in the increasing interest in the monitoring of the urban centers and their built heritage exposed to seismic risk. As an example, the recent seismic history of Italy proves that the effects of large earthquakes are often destructive in the high vulnerable urban

© Springer Nature Switzerland AG 2020
O. Gervasi et al. (Eds.): ICCSA 2020, LNCS 12250, pp. 963–975, 2020.
https://doi.org/10.1007/978-3-030-58802-1_69

areas. Specifically designed monitoring networks are essential to cope with the seismic risk in the urban areas, to assess the damage scenarios which are useful for the preservation of the strategic functions and services, and to improve the community resilience to earthquakes [12].

The possibility to establish local-scale networks has been favored by the technological development of the sensors, data transmission, computational power, and data storage capability. Local-scale networks can be established in relatively short times and with limited costs, usually resorting to micro electro-mechanical systems (MEMS) sensors which enable high-density of nodes, easy installation and low-costs (Fig. 1). A large number of institutions (either scientific and for civil protection) around the world have gained interest in this promising technology over the past decade by designing and implementing urban or regional seismic networks based on the MEMS technology (see [18] and [31] for a complete review).

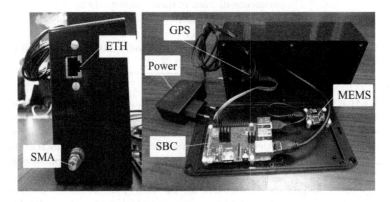

Fig. 1. Example of an operational MEMS station in an urban seismic network; from [14]

The application and reliability of these devices have been evaluated [16,17] and they are able to record strong regional earthquakes or even moderate local earthquakes (M~3) [7,13,15,24,26,38]. The main tasks of an urban seismic network can be summarized with a continuous chain of actions, before, during, and after that the strong ground motion reach the nodes of the network. These tasks include the rapid evaluation of earthquake damage through the automatic production of shakemaps, the procedures for search and rescue, the seismic microzonation. However, the most crucial action would be a system for a rapid alert. The seismic monitoring station at each site detects the P-wave arrivals using an automatic earthquake recognition procedure and estimates the intensity of the impending strong shakings in a few fractions of second. The warning can be issued before S-wave arrivals, taking advantage of the difference between the P and S waves velocities (Fig. 2).

Earthquake early warning systems can be implemented in existing urban scale network, especially when they are already operating into strategic buildings, which should be the priority structures for warning systems. Strategic buildings are identified owing to their function in case of emergency or their value in term of exposed peoples. The most vulnerable buildings are hospitals, schools, and all the facilities devoted to public security.

This paper presents the optimization of the computation performance of a monitoring device already operating in urban seismic networks located in Italy. Moreover, an automatic procedure for earthquake recognition is proposed. The algorithm is flexible to provide reliable results both for local, moderate earthquakes and for large, regional earthquakes. The developed codes can be easily implemented in the monitoring devices and, upon further tests, would allow to upgrade the monitoring system into an early warning system.

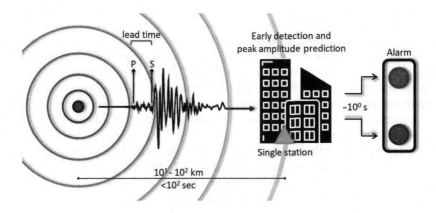

Fig. 2. Scheme of the on-site earthquake early warning system.

2   Earthquake Early Warning Systems

Systems for rapid warning in case of potential damaging earthquakes are rapid developing in many regions of the world. From experimental systems, they are becoming more and more reliable so that, in some case, they have been adopted as institutional systems. The objective of such systems is to provide an alarm with sufficiently in advance to take some pre-arranged actions.

The first example of a country-scale earthquake early warning (EEW) is the "ShakeAlert" which is mainly based in California and operates also in others countries in the western United States. It has been developed, improved, and tested and in about 10 years [10,20,21,25] and in October, 2019 it became fully operating [34]. ShakeAlerts gives a real-time alert for moderate to large earthquakes directly to the smartphones of the users within tens of seconds before the arrival of the ground shaking. Two different approaches are usually adopted for EEW, which mainly depend on the distance from the potentially damaging seismic sources, but also on the specific aims of the warning system [2,3,30,33]. The regional (or network based) approach includes a monitoring network in the vicinity of a known earthquake source. The signals are elaborated as soon as they are received in the various nodes and when the size of the event exceed a given threshold, a warning is sent to the target area (usually tens to one hundred km away).

The on-site approach (Fig. 2) include a single station in the target site which is usually in the proximity of a known earthquake source. The signal is elaborated in order to estimate the peak ground motion at the site. A real-time alarm, which valid only for the site of the station, is sent for a given expected amplitude.

Both the approaches have pros and cons. The warning time of an EEW system is constrained by the arrivals of the seismic waves taking into account that P-waves are the faster but with a lower energy content, while S-waves are slower but more energetic. For the regional system, the warning time is the temporal difference between the P-wave arrival at the network and S-wave arrival at the site; for the on-site system the warning time is the difference between the P- and S-waves arrivals at the site. Within a certain distance ($\sim$35 km) the on-site systems is the one that provide the most rapid alarm, but at longer distance the regional one ensure an increasing warning time. The regional approach provide a more robust evaluation of the earthquake parameters and of the expected peak ground shaking, while the on-site systems have a rougher estimation on the earthquake parameters.

The prediction of the peak ground shaking from the first onset of the signal is the most critical issue in the on-site EEW [27]. Several algorithms have been proposed to accomplish this task. The algorithms are based on empirical relationships between early P-wave arrivals and peak ground motion associated to the S-waves calibrated on catalogues of past earthquakes in the target region. In the last 15 years have been proposed many of these algorithms for several regions in the world [4–6, 8, 9, 11, 19, 22, 23, 32, 36, 37, 39].

It is at short distance from the epicenter of severe earthquakes, that the EEW system are potentially more useful, even though the warning time is extremely reduced. The warning time depends on the time required for the earthquake to evolve and the time for the seismic waves to arrive at the target location; additional time is due to the time required for elaboration of the signal and the alarm sending [28]. For this reason, the data processing system of the EEW should be realized in order to reduce the computation time and the latency as much is possible.

3   MEMS-Based Monitoring Station

The cheap MEMS technology allows the creation of low-cost monitoring stations and entire networks for seismic observation and structural health monitoring. Multiple MEMS stations can be purchased with the same resources as a single traditional system. For some purposes, these devices can be as efficient as the one used in the traditional seismic networks. The monitoring stations considered in this work is the one developed by [14] (Fig. 1) and it is here briefly described in its hardware and software components.

3.1 Hardware

The monitoring stations are based on the MEMS Phidgets 1043_0 sensor, triaxial accelerometer with digital output, suitable, in term of bandwidth and selfnoise, for the detection of strong seismic events and for structural monitoring [16]. In particular, the Phidget 1043_0 accelerometer integrates a three-axis capacitive accelerometer. The analog-to-digital converter (ADC) is internal to the device, for which the outputs are already in digital format. By setting the full scale in the range of ± 2 g, the resolution stands at $76.3\,\mu$g and the white noise at $280\,\mu$g. By integrating 24-bit ADCs and 4.5 Hz bandwidth velocimeters, it will be possible to merge the information of both systems and reconstruct the complete shape of all the components of the agitation and explore a wider frequency band [35].

The brain of the seismic station is a single board computer (SBC; Raspberry Pi3), equipped with a 1.2 GHz 64-bit quad-core ARM processor and which runs a dedicated code. The ADC samples the signals when the analog sensor is incorporated. The ADC provides digital output that can be managed and processed by the SBC. The scheme of operation of the station is shown in Fig. 3.

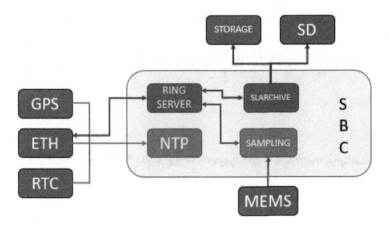

Fig. 3. Scheme for an earthquake monitoring station based on MEMS.

3.2 Software

The code is automatically executed when SBC starts. After checking if the various hardware components are connected correctly and functioning, the software runs the sampling thread from the digital sensor (or from the ADC). The sampling frequency is by 100 Hz (can be varied from 1 500 Hz); synchronization with UTC time is ensured by the NTP (Network Time Protocol) service which retrieves the time from the GPS integrated in the system if there is a fix of at least 4 satellites, otherwise it relies on the servers used by the network. The synchronization of the signals between the various stations is fundamental for determining the relative position of the earthquake epicentre. In fact, the location of earthquakes is essentially based on the readings of the travel time of the seismic phases. In the absence of connectivity, the system initially synchronizes via an RTC (Real Time Clock) waiting for the GPS fix.

The waveform file contains all the components sampled by the station, it is written in miniSEED format in the form of BigStreang (multi-track format). The miniSEED (or mSEED) is a short version of the SEED (Standard for the Exchange of Earthquake Data) format, primarily intended for the storage and exchange of seismological time series data [1]. Reading the input data from the sensor and writing mSEED data files require appropriate libraries (both in C and Python). The local transmission and storage of data takes advantage of the ring-server and slarchive, conceived by the Incorporated Research Institutions for Seismology (IRIS) for the transmission and storage of mSEED data; they are widely tested and used in the scientific community. The role of the *ring-server* is to connect the sample loop with the software that manages the seismic recording tracks. The role of the *slarchive* is to query the ring-server and store the data into a local archive 3.

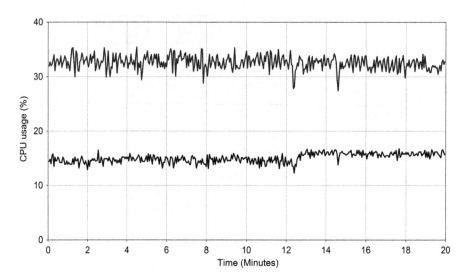

Fig. 4. Percentage of CPU usage for the C (blue line) and the Python (red line) processes. (Color figure online)

4   Code Optimization and Implementation

The optimization of the performance of the code of the monitoring system includes both the part devoted reading and writing tasks (sampling code), and the part devoted to the continuous inspection of the signal with the task to discriminate the onset of the ground shaking from the background noise (trigger algorithm).

4.1 Sampling Code

The earlier version on the sampling code was implemented with Python [13,14]. As upgrade step, a new sampling software has been developed in C. The choice of C language is motivated by the large availability of compilers and high efficiency of the developed code.

Data from the MEMS sensor can be easily acquired by the C implementation through the use of the *phidget22* library [29]. In particular, the accelerometer class *PhidgetAccelerometer* is used to get samples from the MEMS. Through the *functionPhidgetAccelerometer_create(ch)* an instance of a Phidget channel *ch* is created, and a *PhidgetReturnCode* is returned. All the features of the accelerometer are accessed through the channel *ch*. The function *Phidget_openWaitForAttachment* is used to open the channel and to set also a timeout value in milliseconds (in this case is set it to 5,000). This function blocks the access to the device until the channel is opened or a timeout occurs. The function *PhidgetAccelerometer_setDataInterval* is be used to set the rate in seconds at which the device channel will deliver data to channel *ch*; in our case this value is set to 1.

To measure in real-time the change in *accelerationPhidgetAccelerometer_setOnAccelerationChangeHandler()* event is used. This event is caught continuously in run time and it uses a callback function to constantly detect the changes in acceleration values. In this callback function the code reads the samples from MEMS using the function *PhidgetAccelerometer_getAcceleration* and the time component from the system, writing them in pipe system call. The *pipe* system call manages simultaneously the sampling and the packaging. Instead, in an infinite loop the samples are read, and the time component from the pipe and save them to file using microsecond info. To avoid signal loss, the microsecond is the time unit associated to the samples. In summary, the samples and the associated time component are read at a sampling rate 100 Hz; files are then saved in files in ASCII format. ASCII format is then converted into mSEED standard format using the ascii2mseed library [https://github.com/iris-edu/ascii2mseed].

C is faster than Python because is compiled vs interpreted programming language. The performance of the C and Python processes have been tested simultaneously on the same seismic station. It emerged that, for 20 min of parallel execution, the percentage use of the RAM is fixed at 0.4% for the C process and 7.2% for the Python process; therefore, C uses around 70% less RAM than Python. The percentage use of CPU is 15.06 ± 0.84 and 32.58 ± 1.24 for C and Python processes respectively (Fig. 4); therefore, C uses around 50% less CPU than Python. These CPU load times show that the C implementation is preferable. The efficiency of the sampling process reflects on the rapidity of the earthquake detection, and consequently the promptness of the alert message. The sampling code is the base for the triggering algorithm described in the following paragraph.

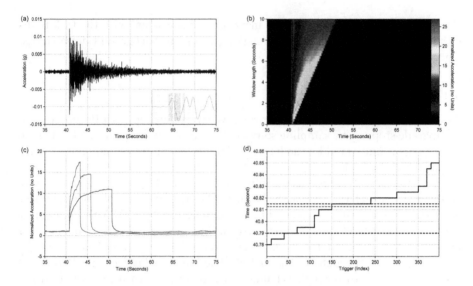

Fig. 5. Synthetic seismogram for M = 3 earthquake, with hypocentral depth of 2 km and observed at epicentral distance of 5 km; (a) the original seismogram with the triggers highlighted in red; (b) the SD value (normalized acceleration) determined for the sliding windows of different width; (c) the SD value for windows of 2.5 s (red), 5 s (green), and 10 s (blue); (d) trigger time (continuous black line) obtained for different sliding windows and different trigger threshold (dashed blue line = theoretical value; dashed green line = mean value; dashed red line = median value); the trigger times are also shown in the inset of (a). (Color figure online)

4.2   Trigger Algorithm

In literature there are many algorithms for the real-time triggering of seismic events. Most of these are based on complex algorithms, necessary for correct application in standard velocimeters or accelerometers. A monitoring network based on homogeneous MEMS sensors, such as those described in this paper, certainly has some advantages. Although MEMS accelerometers have a low sensitivity, which makes them unusable for recording small earthquakes, they have a high temporal stability of self-noise which makes the implementation of trigger algorithms quite simple. For this reason, a simple algorithm that determines the Standard Deviation (SD) of the signal in variable-width moving windows has been implemented. For zero average signals, such as in the case of seismograms, the standard deviation is equal to the Root Mean Square (RMS) of the signal. SD is therefore a quantity linked to the variations in signal energy and so the SD determined in variable-width moving windows, can measure the energy variations present in the signal and which is related to the arrival of a new seismic phases. At each time unit, the quantity SD is calculated for a time window w with the following formula:

$$SD_{w_t} = \sqrt{\frac{\sum_{i=1}^{N}(a_i)^2}{N}} \qquad (1)$$

where a is the measured acceleration and $N = W * f$, for each window w of duration W sampled at frequency f.

The ability to detect changes in energy is linked to the correct choice of the window width (W). Narrow windows will be able to measure sudden changes in energy, like the ones linked to high frequency seismic events; wide windows will better measure slow changes in energy, like the ones related to low frequency events. Since it is not possible to know in advance the frequency content of an earthquake, an effective triggering algorithm will implement multiple sliding windows of variable width W. Small magnitude events recorded at small epicentral distances are generally rich in high frequencies (up to 100 Hz), while moderate to strong magnitude events recorded at greater distances are typically rich in low frequencies (1 Hz). For this reason, after several optimization tests, the triggering algorithm is based on 40 simultaneous moving windows, with a temporal width of 0.25 to 10 s, geometrically spaced (geometric factor of 2). Each value of SD relative to a window (calculated with Eq. 1) is normalized for the SD value of the previous window. This allows to measure relative energy variations in the signal, rather than absolute variations. Multiple value strategy has been used also in the choice of the trigger threshold because a threshold too low can generate false alarms, but a threshold too high may fail to trigger some events, or trigger them with considerable delay. After several optimization test, 10 trigger levels have been used, from 3 to 30, geometrically spaced (geometric factor of 2).

Figures 5 and 6 show the application of triggering algorithm on two synthetic seismograms: the first one refers to a M = 3 earthquake, with hypocentral depth of 2 km and observed at epicentral distance of 5 km, while the second one refers to a M = 5 earthquake, with hypocentral depth of 10 km and observed at epicentral distance of 50 km. The two synthetic cases aims at simulate two representative situations: a shallow little earthquake recorded in epicentral area and rich in high frequencies, and a moderate earthquake recorded at regional distance and rich in lower frequencies. In both Figs. 5 and 6 four panels are shown: (a) the original seismogram with the triggers highlighted as vertical red line; please note that the temporal scale is not the same because of the different duration of the events; (b) the SD value (normalized acceleration) determined for the sliding windows of different width; (c) the SD value for three specific windows (red line = 2.5 s, green line = 5 s, blue line = 10 s); (d) trigger time (continuous black line) obtained for different sliding windows and different trigger threshold (dashed blue line = theoretical value; dashed green line = mean value; dashed red line = median value).

In both the cases the implemented algorithm is able to early detect the arrival of the seismic shaking just from the first instants of the P-wave. Regardless of the window and the threshold used, the first P-wave arrival, i.e. the beginning of the earthquake, is detected in a few tenths of a second. The simultaneous use of windows of different widths and different detection thresholds guarantee the possibility for the specific case of setting robust validation algorithms able to avoid false alarms.

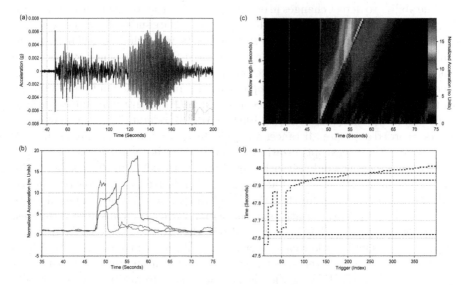

Fig. 6. Synthetic seismogram for M = 5 earthquake, with hypocentral depth of 10 km and observed at epicentral distance of 50 km; (a) the original seismogram with the triggers highlighted in red; (b) the SD value (normalized acceleration) determined for the sliding windows of different width; (c) the SD value for windows of 2.5 s (red), 5 s (green), and 10 s (blue); (d) trigger time (dashed black line) obtained for different sliding windows and different trigger threshold (dashed blue line = theoretical value; dashed green line = mean value; dashed red line = median value); the trigger times are also shown in the inset of (a). (Color figure online)

5   Discussion and Conclusion

For an effective EEW system, each step of the system must be optimized to be performed in the shortest time possible and to be the most reliable possible. The ability to promptly and properly target the arrival of an earthquake are the first and fundamental steps for the implementation of a protection system for critical infrastructure. However, as results clearly from the two cases shown in this paper, the quick detection of a seismic event is not enough for the implementation of an onsite early alarm. A further indispensable condition is necessary, namely that the site to be protected is sufficiently far from the seismic source in order to have enough time to send the alarm (Fig. 2). In the first case (Fig. 5) the lead time is extremely short and after the detection of the event, there would be only a few seconds to implement any form of protection; in the second case (Fig. 6), the lead time is more than one minute, therefore sufficiently in advance before the arrival of the most energetic part of the seismic waves which is carried by the surface waves.

The approach proposed in this paper is flexible and easy to implement, also in already established seismic (or structural) monitoring systems. The next steps in the pursuit of the optimization of the proposed system will be:

i) bypass the conversion from ASCII to mSEED in C process to further reduce the latency and increase the effective time to give an alarm;
ii) define standard and robust tests to assess the performance of the trigger algorithm and define appropriate confidence thresholds in the evaluation of false alarms and missed detections;
iii) validate the system through dedicated simulations and detailed statistical analyses;
iv) tune the whole system for some representative applications within the wide range of potential real-cases (distance from source, expected magnitude, type of building, etc.).

References

1. Ahern, T., Casey, R., Barnes, D., Benson, R., Knight, T.: Seed standard for the exchange of earthquake data reference manual format version 2.4. Incorporated Research Institutions for Seismology (IRIS), Seattle (2007)
2. Allen, R.M., Gasparini, P., Kamigaichi, O., Bose, M.: The status of earthquake early warning around the world: an introductory overview. Seismol. Res. Lett. **80**(5), 682–693 (2009)
3. Allen, R.M., Melgar, D.: Earthquake early warning: advances, scientific challenges, and societal needs. Annu. Rev. Earth Planet. Sci. **47**, 361–388 (2019)
4. Bindi, D., Iervolino, I., Parolai, S.: On-site structure-specific real-time risk assessment: perspectives from the REAKT project. Bull. Earthq. Eng. **14**(9), 2471–2493 (2016). https://doi.org/10.1007/s10518-016-9889-4
5. Böse, M., Hauksson, E., Solanki, K., Kanamori, H., Wu, Y.M., Heaton, T.: A new trigger criterion for improved real-time performance of onsite earthquake early warning in Southern California. Bull. Seismol. Soc. Am. **99**(2A), 897–905 (2009)
6. Böse, M., Heaton, T., Hauksson, E.: Rapid estimation of earthquake source and ground-motion parameters for earthquake early warning using data from a single three-component broadband or strong-motion sensor. Bull. Seismol. Soc. Am. **102**(2), 738–750 (2012)
7. Chung, A.I., Cochran, E.S., Kaiser, A.E., Christensen, C.M., Yildirim, B., Lawrence, J.F.: Improved rapid magnitude estimation for a community-based, low-cost MEMS accelerometer network. Bull. Seismol. Soc. Am. **105**(3), 1314–1323 (2015)
8. Chung, A.I., Henson, I., Allen, R.M.: Optimizing earthquake early warning performance: ElarmS-3. Seismol. Res. Lett. **90**(2A), 727–743 (2019)
9. Cochran, E.S., et al.: Event detection performance of the plum earthquake early warning algorithm in Southern California. Bull. Seismol. Soc. Am. **109**(4), 1524–1541 (2019)

10. Cochran, E.S., et al.: Earthquake early warning ShakeAlert system: testing and certification platform. Seismol. Res. Lett. **89**(1), 108–117 (2018)
11. Colombelli, S., Caruso, A., Zollo, A., Festa, G., Kanamori, H.: A P wave-based, on-site method for earthquake early warning. Geophys. Res. Lett. **42**(5), 1390–1398 (2015)
12. D'Alessandro, A., et al.: Urban seismic networks, structural health and cultural heritage monitoring: the national earthquakes observatory (INGV, Italy) experience. Front. Built Environ. **5**, 127 (2019)
13. D'Alessandro, A., et al.: Monitoring earthquake through MEMS sensors (MEMS project) in the town of Acireale (Italy). In: IEEE International Symposium on Inertial Sensors and Systems (INERTIAL), pp. 1–4. IEEE (2018)
14. D'Alessandro, A., et al.: Sviluppo di una stazione sismica low-cost basata su tecnologia mems. Quaderni di Geofisica (2019)
15. D'Alessandro, A., Luzio, D., D'Anna, G.: Urban mems based seismic network forpost-earthquakes rapid disaster assessment. Advances in Geosciences (2014)
16. D'Alessandro, A., et al.: Characterization of mems accelerometer self-noise by means of PSD and Allan variance analysis. In: 7th IEEE International Workshop on Advances in Sensors and Interfaces (IWASI), pp. 159–164. IEEE (2017)
17. D'Alessandro, A., D'Anna, G.: Suitability of low-cost three-axis mems accelerometers in strong-motion seismology: tests on the LIS331DLH (iPhone) accelerometer. Bull. Seismol. Soc. Am. **103**(5), 2906–2913 (2013)
18. D'Alessandro, A., Scudero, S., Vitale, G.: A review of the capacitive MEMS for seismology. Sensors **19**(14), 3093 (2019)
19. Festa, G., Zollo, A., Lancieri, M.: Earthquake magnitude estimation from early radiated energy. Geophys. Res. Lett. **35**, L22307 (2008)
20. Given, D.D., et al.: Revised technical implementation plan for the ShakeAlert system–an earthquake early warning system for the West Coast of the United States. Technical report, US Geological Survey (2018)
21. Given, D.D., et al.: Technical implementation plan for the ShakeAlert production system: an earthquake early warning system for the West Coast of the United States. Technical report, US Geological Survey (2014)
22. Huang, T.C., Wu, Y.M.: A robust algorithm for automatic P-wave arrival-time picking based on the local extrema Scalogram. Bull. Seismol. Soc. Am. **109**(1), 413–423 (2019)
23. Kanamori, H.: Real-time seismology and earthquake damage mitigation. Ann. Rev. Earth Planet. Sci. **33**, 195–214 (2005)
24. Kim, Y., Kang, T.S., Rhie, J.: Development and application of a real-time warning system based on a MEMS seismic network and response procedure for the day of the national college entrance examination in South Korea. Seismol. Res. Lett. **88**(5), 1322–1326 (2017)
25. Kohler, M.D., et al.: Earthquake early warning ShakeAlert system: west coast wide production prototype. Seismol. Res. Lett. **89**(1), 99–107 (2018)
26. Lawrence, J.F., et al.: Rapid earthquake characterization using mems accelerometers and volunteer hosts following the m 7.2 Darfield, New Zealand, earthquake. Bull. Seismol. Soc. Am. **104**(1), 184–192 (2014)
27. Minson, S.E., et al.: The limits of earthquake early warning accuracy and best alerting strategy. Sci. Rep. **9**(1), 1–13 (2019)
28. Minson, S.E., Meier, M.A., Baltay, A.S., Hanks, T.C., Cochran, E.S.: The limits of earthquake early warning: timeliness of ground motion estimates. Sci. Adv. **4**(3), eaaq0504 (2018)

29. Phidgets, I.: Phidget22 software libraries (2020). www.phidgets.com/docs/ Phidget22. Accessed March 2020
30. Satriano, C., Wu, Y.M., Zollo, A., Kanamori, H.: Earthquake early warning: concepts, methods and physical grounds. Soil Dyn. Earthquake Eng. **31**(2), 106–118 (2011)
31. Scudero, S., D'Alessandro, A., Greco, L., Vitale, G.: Mems technology in seismology: a short review. In: IEEE International Conference on Environmental Engineering (EE), pp. 1–5. IEEE (2018)
32. Spallarossa, D., Ferretti, G., Scafidi, D., Turino, C., Pasta, M.: Performance of the RSNI-picker. Seismol. Res. Lett. **85**(6), 1243–1254 (2014)
33. Tajima, F., Hayashida, T.: Earthquake early warning: what does "seconds before a strong hit" mean? Progress Earth Planet. Sci. **5**(1), 63 (2018). https://doi.org/ 10.1186/s40645-018-0221-6
34. USGS, the State of California: ShakeAlert: An Earthquake Early Warning System for the West Coast of the United States (2020). www.shakealert.org. Accessed March 2020
35. Vitale, G., Greco, L., D'Alessandro, A., Scudero, S.: Bandwidth extension of a 4.5 Hz geophone for seismic monitoring purpose. In: IEEE International Conference on Environmental Engineering (EE), pp. 1–5. IEEE (2018)
36. Wu, Y.M., Kanamori, H.: Development of an earthquake early warning system using real-time strong motion signals. Sensors **8**(1), 1–9 (2008)
37. Wu, Y.M., Mittal, H., Huang, T.C., Yang, B.M., Jan, J.C., Chen, S.K.: Performance of a low-cost earthquake early warning system (P-Alert) and shake map production during the 2018 Mw 6.4 Hualien, Taiwan, earthquake. Seismol. Res. Lett. **90**(1), 19–29 (2019)
38. Yildirim, B., Cochran, E.S., Chung, A., Christensen, C.M., Lawrence, J.F.: On the reliability of quake-catcher network earthquake detections. Seismol. Res. Lett. **86**(3), 856–869 (2015)
39. Zollo, A., Lancieri, M., Nielsen, S.: Earthquake magnitude estimation from peak amplitudes of very early seismic signals on strong motion records. Geophys. Res. Lett. **33**, L23312 (2006)

International Workshop on Advances in Web Based Learning (AWBL 2020)

Industry 4.0 Briefcase: An Innovative Engineering Outreach Project for Professions of the Future

Mustafa M. Inceoglu[1]([✉]) [iD] and Birol Ciloglugil[2] [iD]

[1] Faculty of Education, Department of Computer Education and Instructional Technology, Ege University, Bornova, 35100 Izmir, Turkey
mustafa.inceoglu@ege.edu.tr
[2] Faculty of Engineering, Department of Computer Engineering, Ege University, Bornova, 35100 Izmir, Turkey
birol.ciloglugil@ege.edu.tr

Abstract. This paper presents an engineering outreach project titled "Industry 4.0 Briefcase" that has been developed to introduce the concept of Industry 4.0 to undergraduate students. The project aims to support participants to become aware of Industry 4.0 related topics such as machine learning, data mining, industrial automation, human-machine interface, and product life cycle, and to stimulate the curiosity of them towards these topics. The scope of the project consists of presentations, experimental applications, observations, individual and collaborative studies, assessment and evaluation practices, e-learning applications, and a social program. The project was conducted as a one- week program at a public university in Turkey with the participation of 18 under-graduate 3rd-year students. Participants consist of students from computer engineering and software engineering departments of the engineering faculties and the business department of the faculty of economics and administrative sciences. Thus, participants of the project had the opportunity to exchange information with students and faculty members from different academic back-grounds. The study utilized the mixed methods approach by performing both quantitative and qualitative measurements. To collect data, mini projects and project evaluation forms were used for quantitative measurements and daily virtual classroom sessions and a general evaluation session (focus group inter-view) were used for qualitative measurements. The success rates of the partic-ipants based on the evaluation of the reports they presented were obtained as 91% in data mining, 95% in industrial automation and human-machine inter-face, and 89% in machine learning course, respectively. It was observed that the overall satisfaction level of the participants from the project activities was over 95%. These findings were also supported by the qualitative findings as the students indicated their overall satisfaction from the organization of the project and stated that working in teams and attending the social program contributed to developing positive relationships with each other and increasing their success.

Keywords: Engineering education · Engineering outreach · Industry 4.0 concepts · Industrial automation

© Springer Nature Switzerland AG 2020
O. Gervasi et al. (Eds.): ICCSA 2020, LNCS 12250, pp. 979–988, 2020.
https://doi.org/10.1007/978-3-030-58802-1_70

1   Introduction

Nowadays, Industry 4.0 is one of the most studied concepts in all engineering fields. This concept has its roots in the industrial revolution. According to the Cambridge dictionary, the industrial revolution is defined as "the period of time during which work began to be done more by machines in factories than by hand at home" [1]. The topic of Industry 4.0 was first defined by the German Government and adds a new layer of automation to the foundation provided by the industrial revolution. Industry 4.0 includes nine main topics: autonomous robots, simulation, system integration, internet of things, cybersecurity, cloud computing, additive manufacturing, augmented reality, and big data [2]. In recent years, the interest of academia, industry, governments, and non-governmental organizations on the topic of Industry 4.0 has been increasing. According to [3], the number of academic conferences and academic articles on Industry 4.0 has doubled in 2015 compared to 2013.

In [4], the focus was on facilitating mobile learning processes in vocational, technical, and engineering education, and also integrating business scenarios of Industry 4.0 into learning environments. The learning environments include distribution of classical learning materials such as pictures, videos, or simulations, where workplace-related learning environments are considered particularly important.

By utilizing web-based technologies, [5] discusses how a remote and distributed control system can be used to create an efficient laboratory learning model and enable remote access to physical processes. Besides, how to diagnose faults by using online, remote technologies and SCADA is also demonstrated.

On the other hand, there are also studies approaching robotics and other technologies covered by Industry 4.0 from educational perspectives. These studies are commonly organized around the world as educational robot camps. Carnegie-Mellon University [6] and the University of Minnesota [7] robot camps can be given as examples of these activities. In [8], it is emphasized that the main objectives of these camps are to direct secondary and high school students to a career in technology, computer, and engineering. In [9], it was pointed out that in educational robot camps, students were given the opportunity to apply the information they learned in their schools with appropriate group sizes. Similar studies can also be organized as engineering outreach projects [10]. When these types of studies are examined, it can be observed that robot camps are mostly organized with the participants consisting of middle and high school students and their objectives are limited.

In addition to these resources, widely used massive open online learning environments such as Coursera [11], and EdX [12] include the topics covered by Industry 4.0 as separate courses.

Advancements in computer technologies and the Internet do not only effect industrial areas, but also change higher education processes. Recently, in higher education, solving real-world problems, interdisciplinary work, and teamwork skills have attracted more attention [13]. Therefore, especially engineering students are required to experience these skills during their undergraduate studies [14, 15]. For this purpose, an engineering outreach project titled "Industry 4.0 Briefcase" was planned and carried out to both increase the motivation of undergraduate students of engineering and business school for topics covered by Industry 4.0 and to reinforce their individual and teamwork skills.

The project was titled "Industry 4.0 Briefcase" because it combines different components of Industry 4.0 as a briefcase. The main aim of the project is to stimulate the curiosity of the participants towards Industry 4.0 related topics such as machine learning, data mining, industrial automation, human-machine interface, and product life cycle to increase their awareness. In addition to the academic content of the project, learning experiences such as learning by doing/living, and individual and teamwork activities were included in the project. As these experiences are among the essential learning experiences of the Industry 4.0 era [16], the project was specifically designed to have these experiences as much as possible throughout the project.

The rest of the paper is organized as follows; Sect. 2 introduces the method followed in the study. Section 3 presents the application process, Sect. 4 provides the findings, and finally, Sect. 5 concludes the paper.

2 Method

In this section, the research model, study group, data collection tools, and the application process will be examined.

Research Model
In this project, a mixed-methods approach which is based on qualitative and quantitative measurements was used. During the study, as the data collection tools, mini projects, and project evaluation form were used for quantitative measurements and daily virtual classroom sessions and a general evaluation session (focus group interview) were used for qualitative measurements. The triangulation method was used for evaluation purposes. In the triangulation method, quantitative and qualitative data are collected and analyzed together at the same time. The priority is equal for both data types. Data analysis is usually done separately, and integration takes place during the interpretation of the findings [17].

Study Group
The study group of the project consists of 18 engineering and business school undergraduate students. Application requirements for the project were to be at least a third grade (junior) student and to have a grade point average of at least 2 out of 4. The participants were selected from the applicants after the announcements were made to the computer engineering, software engineering, and management information system (MIS) departments. The distribution of the participants according to their departments is presented in Table 1. In addition, four project staff were assigned as guides to quickly solve the problems that participants may encounter during the course of the project.

Data Collection Tools
In this study, two separate groups of data collection tools were used to collect quantitative and qualitative data. Mini project evaluation form and general project evaluation form were used as data collection tools for quantitative measurements.

Table 1. Distribution of the participants (according to their departments)

Name of dept.	Num. of participants	Percentage
Computer eng.	12	66.7%
Software eng.	1	5.6%
Man. Inf. systems	5	27.7%
Total	18	100.0%

Video recordings of the daily virtual classroom sessions and the general evaluation session (focus group interview) were used for qualitative measurements.

3 Application Process

The project was conducted in five days between July 01-05, 2019. Academic activities were organized on various topics throughout the project and carried out with the order of introduction to Industry 4.0, product life cycle, data mining, industrial automation, human-machine interface, techno-park introduction, entrepreneurship presentation, and machine learning. In addition to the academic activities, an opening ceremony session, a technical trip, coffee & meal breaks, and a closing ceremony session were held respectively. All of the theoretical and practical activities (except the social activities) carried out during the project and types of these activities are summarized in Table 2, which presents the daily program of the project. The numbers in parentheses of the type of activities indicate the number of lessons the activity took in the program.

As listed in Table 2, a total of 27 h of academic activities were organized during the Industry4.0 Briefcase project. 33.3% of these activities were organized as presentations, 37.0% were practical activities involving applied laboratory work, 14.8% were distance learning activities as virtual classroom sessions, and 14.8% took place as the technical trip.

The first day of the program (July 1, 2019) started with the opening ceremony, an ice-breaking event, and the introduction of the project staff and the participants. Then, a presentation on the main concepts of Industry 4.0 was made and the content of the project was explained. As the main activity of the first day, the session on "Product Lifecycle Management" was held for 3 h in total. The first two hours of this session were theoretical and the last hour was laboratory work where the participants were divided into groups and the product life cycles of different products were discussed.

The Data Mining course, which was conducted on the second day of the project (July 2, 2019), started with 2-h of theoretical narration and continued with 3-h of laboratory work. Basic concepts of data mining and a basket analysis application software were introduced at the theoretical lectures. Then, at the practical hours, the participants were provided with a database containing sample products and sales records of an imaginary company and were asked to examine this database, prepare the inputs for data analysis, and analyze the sales data with the basket analysis software presented in the theoretical lectures. Finally, the findings obtained with the analysis were reported and presented by the participants.

Table 2. Daily activity program of the project

Date	Activity	Type of Activity
1.7.2019	Opening ceremony	
	Introduction to industry 4.0	Theoretical (1)
	Product lifecycle management presentation	Theoretical (2) Laboratory work (1)
	Evaluation	Virtual class (1)
2.7.2019	Data mining	Theoretical (2) Laboratory work (3)
	Evaluation	Virtual class (1)
3.7.2019	Industrial automation and human-machine interface	Theoretical (1) Laboratory work (4)
	Evaluation	Virtual class (1)
4.7.2019	Techno-park presentation	Theoretical (1)
	Entrepreneurship company presentation	Theoretical (1)
	Machine learning	Theoretical (1) Laboratory work (2)
	Evaluation	Virtual class (1)
5.7.2019	Technical tour	Technical tour (4)
	Focus group interview meeting closing ceremony	

On the third day, the project continued with 3 h of Industrial Automation and 2 h of Human Machine Interface courses, all of which were practical studies. For evaluation purposes, students formed groups of two members, and each group was asked to carry out two projects for each topic. The first project involved counting the number of products on a conveyor carrying the products, and the second project was to write a program to control a lamp with SCADA [18]. At the end of the day, the groups presented their project reports for each project.

The fourth day of the project started with the description of topics such as technopark, intellectual property rights, and patents. Then, the technopark established at the university campus was introduced and the representative of a technopark entrepreneurship company working on Industry 4.0 presented their work. In the afternoon session, the machine learning course was held in the form of 1 h of theoretical presentation and 2 h of practice. As part of the practical study, the participants were divided into groups, and the groups were provided supplier selection records of an imaginary company and were asked to prepare the inputs for data analysis and find out the regression model. The results of the study were reported by the groups and the reports were presented at the end of the day.

On the last day of the project, the factory of a German textile company was visited and the real-world applications of the topics covered within the first four days of the project were examined in a factory environment. The German textile company is selected for the technical trip because it is one of the few companies that successfully apply Industry 4.0 processes. During the technical trip, the participants had the opportunity to observe the applications of big data, industrial automation systems, and machine learning. Finally, at the end of the day, as the final activity of the project, a focus group interview was conducted with all of the participants. During the focus group interview, the previously prepared questions of a semi-structured interview form were answered by the participants. This interview was recorded on video and then, transcribed and analyzed.

Among the academic activities, theoretical courses such as introduction to Industry 4.0, product life cycle, technopark introduction, and entrepreneurship presentation were organized as presentations and included question-answer sessions by applying narrative/lecture and question-answer teaching methods. The other academic activities were carried out in two parts in a laboratory environment. In the first part, the topics were explained by using narrative/lecture and demonstration methods. In the second half of the courses, the participants were divided into groups and each group was assigned a mini project on the related topic and was asked to carry out the group project collaboratively. When the group projects were completed, the group members prepared and submitted reports both individually and as a group. After completion of each course, these reports were evaluated and the participants were given scores. Mini group projects were used three times during the project, on the second, third, and fourth days of the project. Mini projects are very useful to evaluate students' level of knowledge and to determine misconceptions and the concepts that are not fully learned after theoretical lessons [19].

At the end of each day, except for the last day, a virtual classroom session was also held to gather feedback from the participants about their experiences and impressions during that day. Adobe Connect Pro [20] virtual classroom interface was used for virtual classroom sessions between 8:00 pm and 8:30 pm. During this evaluation activity, the participants were asked to evaluate the activities performed that day verbally. In the virtual classroom sessions, the content of the activities and the approaches of the instructors who carried out these activities were also discussed. Besides, the participants were asked if they were satisfied with the social activities of that day. All virtual classroom sessions were recorded for evaluation purposes.

4 Results and Discussion

The quantitative and qualitative results of the project are presented below.

Quantitative Results

After the data mining, industrial automation & human-machine interface, and machine learning activities carried out during the project, the participants were divided into groups of two and carried out mini projects. The results of these mini projects are presented as both individual and group reports. The evaluation results of these mini project reports presented at the end of each activity are presented in Table 3.

At the end of the project, a general evaluation form was applied to the participants. In this form, the participants were asked to evaluate all activities carried out during the project on a 3-point Likert scale (Dissatisfied, Undecided/Neither Satisfied nor Dissatisfied, Satisfied). The evaluation results of the general evaluation form regarding the activities of the project are presented in Table 4.

Table 3. Average scores of mini-projects

Activity name	Num. of participants	Average scores of mini-projects
Data Mining	18	91%
Industrial automation and human-machine interface	18	95%
Machine learning	17	89%

Table 4. Average scores of the general evaluation form

Activity Name	Not Satisfied	Undecided	Satisfied
Industry 4.0 presentation	0.00%	11.10%	88.90%
Product lifecycle management presentation	0.00%	5.60%	94.40%
Data mining	0.00%	5.60%	94.40%
Industrial automation and human-machine interface	0.00%	0.00%	100.00%
Technopark presentation	0.00%	5.60%	94.40%
Machine learning	5.60%	5.60%	88.90%
Technical tour	0.00%	0.00%	100.00%
Social events (meal, coffee break)	0.00%	0.00%	100.00%
Average	**0.70%**	**4.19%**	**95.11%**

As can be seen from Table 4, the average satisfaction level of the participants is over 95%. The highest satisfaction levels are obtained in the activities where the participants are actively involved in the education process. It was observed that the participants were more passive in activities that they evaluated with lower satisfaction levels.

Qualitative Results

Daily virtual classroom sessions were organized with the participation of the students for the evaluation of the activities carried out during each day except for the last day. The data obtained from the virtual classroom sessions were evaluated and categorized as negative and positive. The findings are reported together with the data obtained from the focus group interview.

The focus group interview was held as a 60-min session on the last day of the project. In the focus group interview, the participants were asked to evaluate the project in all aspects. The negative aspects students declared are presented in Table 5, and the positive feedback gathered from the participants are presented in Table 6, together with the findings of the daily virtual classroom sessions, with their frequencies, respectively.

As stated in Table 5, the main negative aspects expressed by the participants are mostly related to the project duration being too short and some activities being only in the form of presentations.

Table 5. Negative qualitative feedback on the project

Category	Frequency
It would be nice if the project was conducted longer than a week	6
It was boring that some of the activities were instructed only through presentations	4
Some of the activities continued until late hours, as a result, we were very tired	2
It would be more fun if the project had more participants	2
The early start of the activities in the morning caused me to feel sleepless	2

Table 6. Positive qualitative feedback on the project

Category	Frequency
The technical trip was useful to reinforce the topics covered in the activities	15
The fact that many activities were practical increased my motivation	14
Social events were very well organized and sufficient	11
The lecturers teaching the courses were competent in their fields	11
The teamwork at some activities helped us to reinforce the topics	11
Having a mini project at the end of some activities helped us better understand the topics	7
Topics discussed at the activities were important for our career development	4

As given in Table 6, most of the participants stated that it was useful to reinforce the topics covered in the activities with a technical trip, their motivation levels increased due to many activities being practical, the social activities were well designed and applied, the lecturers teaching the courses are competent in their fields, and performing teamwork oriented activities contributed positively to their understanding of the topics.

The negative and the positive feedback of the participants regarding the project were categorized into four and seven main groups in Table 5 and Table 6, respectively. Therefore, the number of positive aspects reported by the students was higher than the number of negative aspects. Also, the number of students expressing positive feedback (frequency values at the tables) was much higher than the number of students mentioning negative feedback.

When the quantitative and qualitative findings were analyzed together, it can be observed that the quantitative and qualitative findings of the study complement each other. Overall, the participants were successful at the mini projects and stated higher satisfaction levels at the survey and the focus group interview for the activities they were more actively involved in the education process. Thus, it can be interpreted that practical activities such as applied laboratory works and mini projects contributed to the success of the project.

5   Conclusion

This paper presents an innovative engineering outreach project titled "Industry 4.0 Briefcase" that introduces Industry 4.0 related topics such as machine learning, data mining, industrial automation, human-machine interface, and product life cycle to undergraduate students. Thus, the main aim of the project is to increase awareness of the participants about these topics by organizing activities that stimulate their curiosity. After getting theoretical knowledge and performing practical laboratory work during the first four days of the outreach program, at the last day of the project, the participants had the opportunity to observe the topics they learned during the project in a real-world setting by attending the technical trip to a factory employing Industry 4.0 technologies.

It was observed that the students participated in the activities with a high level of motivation throughout the project. Thus, the overall participation rate during the project was over 90%. It is noteworthy that the participation of students in both individual and group activities is very high. As a result of the evaluation of the reports submitted by the participants after conducting mini projects, the success rates were obtained as 91% in data mining, 95% in industrial automation and human-machine interface, and 89% in machine learning courses, respectively. The results of the general evaluation form applied at the end of the project revealed that the participants were over 95% satisfied with the theoretical and practical activities, social program, and technical trip. The findings of the general evaluation form were also supported by the qualitative findings of the daily virtual classroom sessions and the focus group interview. The factors that may have been effective on obtaining positive findings can be interpreted as the subject of the project being a novel and interesting topic as Industry 4.0 is gathering more and more attention recently, and students developing positive relationships with their teammates as a result of working as teams and attending the social program.

The main contribution of this study is its novelty as one of the first outreach projects on Industry 4.0 concepts since this type of outreach studies are not very common in the literature. On the other hand, the duration and the size of the study group are the main limitations of this study, as the project was carried out in a limited time with a relatively low number of participants due to budget constraints and other restrictions. Thus, the generalization of the findings of this study are limited; however, the study is a good step for further research studies. For future work, organizing an outreach project with more participants that will be spread over a longer period will increase the contribution to the field.

Acknowledgment. This material is partially based upon work supported by the Scientific and Technological Research Council of Turkey (TUBITAK) under Grant No. 218B148.

References

1. The industrial revolution. https://dictionary.cambridge.org/dictionary/english/industrial-revolution. Accessed 04 Jan 2020
2. Industry 4.0: the fourth industrial revolution. https://www.i-scoop.eu/industry-4-0/. Accessed 04 Jan 2020

3. Liao, Y., Deschamps, F., Loures, E.F.R., Ramos, L.F.P.: Past, present and future of industry 4.0: a systematic literature review and research agenda proposal. Int. J. Prod. Res. **55**(12), 3609–3629 (2016)
4. Jaschke, S.: Mobile learning applications for technical vocational and engineering education: the use of competence snippets in laboratory courses and industry 4.0. In: 2014 International Conference on Interactive Collaborative Learning (ICL) Proceedings, Dubai, pp. 605–608. IEEE (2014)
5. Golob, M., Britana, B.: Web-based control and process automation education and industry 4.0. Int. J. Eng. Educ. **34**(4), 1199–1211 (2018)
6. Nourbakhsh I.R., Hamner, E., Crowley, K., Wilkonson K.: Formal measures of learning in a secondary school mobile robotics course. In: IEEE International Conference on Robotics and Automation Proceedings, New Orleans USA, vol. 2, pp. 1831–1836, IEEE (2004)
7. Cannon, K.R., Panciera, K.A., Papanikolopoulos, N.P.: Second annual robotics summer camp for underrepresented students. In: Proceeding of the 12th SIGCSE Conference on Innovation and Technology in Computer Science Education, Norway, pp. 14–18, ACM (2007)
8. Teaching with lego mindstorm robots: effects on learning environment and attitudes toward science. https://www.researchgate.net/publication/252616085_Teaching_with_LEGO_ mindstorms_robots_Effects_on_learning_environment_and_attitudes_toward_science. Accessed 01 May 2020
9. Ucgul, M., Cagiltay, K.: Design and development issues for educational robotics training camps. Int. J. Technol. Des. Educ. **24**(2), 203–222 (2014). https://doi.org/10.1007/s10798-013-9253-9
10. Ciloglugil, B., Aslan, B.G., Inceoglu, M.M.: Lise Öğrencilerine Bilgisayar Donanımı Öğretimi: Devremi Kuruyorum. Ege Egitim Dergisi **18**(1), 266–287 (2017). https://doi.org/ 10.12984/egeefd.282481
11. Coursera. https://www.coursera.org. Accessed 04 Jan 2020
12. EdX. http://www.edx.org. Accessed 04 Jan 2020
13. Ciloglugil, B., Balci, B., Uslu, N.A.: Acquisition of teamwork competence in a hardware course: perceptions and co-regulation of computer engineering students. Int. J. Eng. Educ. **36**(1), 388–398 (2020)
14. Erol, S., Jager, A., Hold, P., Ott, K., Sihn, W.: Tangible Industry 4.0: a scenario-based approach to learning for the future of production. In: 6th CIRP Conference on Learning Factories proceedings, pp. 13–18. Elsevier (2016)
15. Balci, B., Ciloglugil, B.: Öğrencilerin Takım Çalışması Yeteneklerinin Bireysel ve Akran Değerlendirmeleri ile İncelenmesi. Ege Eğitim Teknolojileri Dergisi **3**(1), 1–10 (2019). https://dergipark.org.tr/en/pub/eetd/issue/47459/571981
16. Moncada, C.B., Buhangin, J.F., Angalan, N.Q.: Review of industry 4.0 competencies and virtual learning environment in engineering education. Int. J. Eng. Educ. **36**(1), 40–47 (2020)
17. Baskale, H.: Determination of validity, reliability and sample size in qualitative studies. Dokuz Eylül Üniversitesi Hemşirelik Fakültesi Dergisi **9**(1), 23–28 (2016)
18. SCADA System (Supervisory Control and Data Acquisition): What is SCADA? https:// www.plcacademy.com/scada-system/. Accessed 02 Jan 2020
19. Roediger, H.L., Putnam, A.L., Smith, M.A.: Ten benefits of testing and their applications to educational practice. In: Medin, D.L (ed.) Psychology of Learning and Motivation-Advances in Research and Theory, vol. 55, no. 1, pp. 1–36. Academic Press, Cambridge (2011)
20. Adobe web conferencing software. https://www.adobe.com/products/adobeconnect.html. Accessed 04 Jul 2020

Investigating the Effect of a Mobile Learning Application for Graph Theory Education on Academic Performance

Birol Ciloglugil[1]([envelope]) [iD] and Mustafa Murat Inceoglu[2] [iD]

[1] Department of Computer Engineering, Ege University,
Bornova, 35100 Izmir, Turkey
birol.ciloglugil@ege.edu.tr
[2] Department of Computer Education and Instructional Technology, Ege University,
Bornova, 35100 Izmir, Turkey
mustafa.inceoglu@ege.edu.tr

Abstract. In this study, the effectiveness of using a mobile learning application developed for graph theory education is investigated by evaluating its impact on the academic performance of students for three academic years. The mobile application supports graph operations such as creating/editing graphs, running basic graph algorithms on graphs, and observing their step-by-step execution. Students can also test their knowledge level by using the quiz section of the mobile learning application. The study is conducted at a public university in Turkey with the participation of voluntary freshman students that take the Discrete Structures course. Graph theory is lectured for three weeks as the final subject of the course. Various features of the mobile application were introduced to the students by the lab assistant at laboratory sessions of 45 min that were conducted for a period of three weeks after the theoretical lectures in which the graph theory topics were covered. After these introduction sessions, students were able to use the mobile application as a supplementary tool any time they want. In order to investigate the effect of using the mobile learning application on the academic performance of students, a quasi-experimental research design with experimental and control groups was utilized. Quantitative data were collected by using the grades students achieved from the questions related to graph theory in the final exams of the course. The data for each year was analyzed by performing independent groups t-tests. The results of the statistical analyzes indicated that the usage of the mobile learning application contributed statistically significantly to the grades of the students in the experimental group for each year it was applied.

Keywords: Mobile learning · Graph theory · Engineering education

1 Introduction

Graph theory is part of the curriculum in many engineering departments as it is one of the main topics in discrete mathematics that serves an important

O. Gervasi et al. (Eds.): ICCSA 2020, LNCS 12250, pp. 989–1000, 2020.
https://doi.org/10.1007/978-3-030-58802-1_71

foundation for many topics in related courses in the following semesters [1]. Therefore, it can be stated that effective teaching of graph theory is an essential part of engineering education. Graph theory is generally lectured as part of the Discrete Structures course in various engineering disciplines [1]. Since it is important for many engineering disciplines and can be used in multidisciplinary areas, supporting graph theory education with supplementary e-learning tools can increase the comprehension level and academic performance of students.

In this regard, there are various studies on developing e-learning tools that target graph theory. Some of them focus on using graph theory on e-learning systems [2], while some of them try to provide tools that enable users to perform graph operations. In this paper, we focused on the latter group and provided a brief overview of the related work in this category. Table 1 presents a summary of these studies in chronological order.

- Cabri-Graph is an application that enables users to create their own graphs or use the graphs already available in the library of the application. Cabri-Graph is developed in accordance with the interface of Apple Macintosh computers and it can display properties of the graphs and can generate random graphs [3].
- Visualizations and algorithms of several graph algorithms such as Dijkstra's shortest path algorithm and graph coloring algorithm are presented in [4]. This study, called DIDAGRAPH, is designed to give information about how the related graph algorithms work. Opinions of the students were not taken into consideration and the effectiveness of the application on academic achievement was not evaluated.
- IAPPGA application is an online Java package that creates graphs online or works by loading the graph from the existing neighborhood matrices of them into the graphical user interface [5]. It allows students to create directed or undirected graphs interactively.
- A library of mobile graph algorithms for engineering students, called MOGRAPH, that works on mobile devices using the Windows Mobile operating system, was developed in [6]. Basic graph algorithms such as DFS, BFS, Dijkstra, Euler, Hamilton, and graph coloring were covered in [6], and opinions of students about the application were obtained through a questionnaire.
- In [7], students between the ages of 5–17 are lectured about two of the basic computer science topics; introduction to graph theory, and the shortest path problem. The developed software works only on the computers where it is installed and there is no web version. The usage of the application by the students was observed and the results of the study revealed that students in the age group 5–11 had higher motivation than students in the other age group.
- Graphtea is developed with the aim of teaching graphs and it is possible to work on predefined graphs in the software or use graphs created by the user [8]. Besides, the use of basic graph algorithms is examined in this study. Graphtea can be downloaded, installed, and used as an application.

– A mobile learning application developed to support teaching graph theory topics taught in the discrete structures course is presented in [9]. The application was evaluated with experimental and control groups with the participation of voluntary students taking the course. As a result of the study, it was observed that mobile application usage increased the academic achievements of the students in a significant way.

Table 1. E-learning tools developed for graph theory education.

Reference	Year	Main contribution of the study
[3]	1995	Enables creation of the user's own graphs and usage of graphs available at the application library
[4]	1998	Supports visualization of Dijkstra shortest path algorithm and graph coloring algorithm
[5]	2005	An online Java package that supports working with directed or undirected graphs that can be created online or loaded from existing neighborhood matrices
[6]	2007	A library of mobile graph algorithms such as DFS, BFS, Dijkstra, Euler, Hamilton, and graph coloring developed for engineering students
[7]	2012	Examines motivation levels of students between the ages of 5–17 based on graph theory topics (i.e. shortest path problem)
[8]	2014	Developed as an educational tool that supports working with predefined graphs in the software or graphs created by the users, and the users can examine how basic graph algorithms operate
[9]	2017	A mobile learning application developed to support the teaching of graph theory topics and the evaluation of its effectiveness on the academic achievements of students

Mobile learning can be indicated as an important educational technology component, especially in higher education [10]. With their widespread usage in daily life, mobile devices provide various opportunities to enhance and reinforce teaching and learning activities [11,12]. The main aim of using mobile devices in the educational context is to extend and enhance student learning [13]. The mobile learning technology is also utilized to support collaborative learning [14].

The systematic review on the use of mobile learning in higher education by [13] indicated that the majority of the studies focused on the impact of mobile learning on student achievement. Relatively fewer studies that introduce and evaluate specific mobile learning systems were also reported. In this regard, there are also some studies on developing mobile learning tools that target graph theory [1,6,8,9]. In this paper, the effect of the mobile learning application developed for graph theory education and presented in [9] on the academic performance of students is examined. Thus, the research question of this study can be summarized as:

Is there any statistically significant difference on academic achievement of computer engineering students in the experiment group that use the mobile learning application for graph theory education as a supplementary tool and the control group that followed regular instruction, based on scores of graph theory related questions of the final exams for three academic years?

The rest of the paper is organized as follows; Section 2 briefly introduces the mobile learning application developed for graph theory education. Section 3 presents the method followed in this study. Section 4 provides the results and a discussion of the findings. Finally, Sect. 5 concludes the paper.

2   The Mobile Learning Application

Graph theory is covered by the discrete structures course and it lays the foundation especially for the data structures course in the following semester. Therefore, a mobile learning application for graph theory education has been developed and used as a supplementary tool towards the end of the semester at the discrete structures course [9].

Students can create special graph types automatically, form new graphs on their own, edit previously created graphs, view adjacency and incidence matrices of the graphs, execute six types of graph algorithms on the graphs they formed, and take quizzes to test their knowledge levels anytime they want. The graph algorithms supported by the mobile learning application are DFS (Depth First Search) Algorithm [15–17], BFS (Breadth First Search) Algorithm [15–17], Dijkstra's Shortest Path Algorithm [15,16,18], Euler Path/Circuit Algorithm [15,16], Hamilton Path/Circuit Algorithm [15,16], and Graph Coloring Algorithm [15,16]. Quizzes contain three questions where each question has to be answered in five minutes.

The basic functionalities of the mobile learning application can be summarized as the categories listed below:

- "Creating, editing, and viewing graphs":
    - "Creating special graph types automatically":
        * "Complete graphs"
        * "Cycles"
        * "Wheels"
    - "Editing new or previously created graphs":
        * "Adding a new vertex"
        * "Deleting a vertex"
        * "Renaming a vertex"
        * "Moving a vertex"
        * "Adding a new edge"
        * "Deleting an edge"

        * "Assigning/updating edge weight values"
        * "Changing the graph type to work with (directed/undirected graph)"
- "Viewing different representations of graphs":
  * "Viewing adjacency matrices of graphs"
  * "Viewing incidence matrices of graphs"
- "Executing graph algorithms":
  - "DFS (Depth First Search) Algorithm"
  - "BFS (Breadth First Search) Algorithm"
  - "Dijkstra's Shortest Path Algorithm"
  - "Euler Path/Circuit Algorithm"
  - "Hamilton Path/Circuit Algorithm"
  - "Graph Coloring Algorithm"
- "Taking quizzes"

For more information about the mobile learning application, readers can refer to [9].

3 Method

The method followed in this study is examined under four subsections; research model, study group, data collection instruments, and research process.

3.1 Research Model

This study utilizes a quasi-experimental research design with experimental and control groups [19]. The research model is applied for three consecutive years and students in both groups were determined on a voluntary basis each year. To examine the effects of the usage of the mobile learning application, the academic performance of the students in experimental and control groups were evaluated.

3.2 Study Group

The study is conducted with freshman students taking the Discrete Structures course at a public university in Turkey for a period of three academic years. The distribution of the participants at each academic year is presented in Table 2 in chronological order. The number of students in the experimental groups has increased at each academic year and the number of students in the control groups has decreased accordingly. The total number of students who participated in the study at each year is relatively stable around 120–140 students. Students in both groups were determined on a voluntary basis each year. Hence, students volunteered to be in the experimental groups. Therefore, the increase in the number of participants at the experimental groups each year can be explained with the satisfaction levels of students from the previous years who recommend them to participate in the study.

Table 2. Distribution of students in the study group according to academic years.

Academic year	Number of participants		
	Experimental group	Control group	Total
1st year	34	107	141
2nd year	52	72	124
3rd year	75	46	121

3.3   Research Process

Graph theory is lectured for three weeks as the final subject of the Discrete Structures course. The mobile learning application is used as a supplementary tool to reinforce the teaching of the graph theory related topics. Laboratory sessions were organized for three weeks after the theoretical lectures where the graph theory related topics of the Discrete Structures course were covered. Laboratory studies were conducted under the supervision of the lab assistant as sessions of 45 min. In laboratory studies, practical examples of the graph theory related topics lectured at the course that week were applied by using the mobile learning application. The participants were able to perform various graph operations in an applied manner. Students were also given the opportunity to use the mobile application anytime they want after lab sessions.

3.4   Data Collection Instruments and Data Analysis

The effect of the mobile learning application usage on the academic performance of the students was examined by using quantitative data analyzes. The grades students achieved from the questions related to graph theory in the final exams of the course were used as quantitative data. The distribution of points in the final exams according to academic years is given in Table 3. The data for each year was analyzed by performing descriptive statistical analyzes, Levene's test, and independent groups t-tests. SPSS v22 was used for quantitative data analyzes.

Table 3. Distribution of points in the final exams according to academic years.

Academic year	Points available in the final exam		
	Graph questions	Other questions	Total
1st year	45	55	100
2nd year	67	33	100
3rd year	60	40	100

The number of students in the experimental and control groups was not close to each other for both academic years the study has been conducted. This can be explained by the way the groups were constituted, as the experimental groups consisted of voluntary students, and the control groups were automatically formed with the rest of the students taking the course. Levene's test is a statistical test used to determine whether the groups that are compared have equal population variances [19]. Hence, in this study, Levene's tests have been carried out for the data of each year to assess if the assumption of the equality of variances has been met.

4   Results and Discussion

In order to address our research question, the final exams of three academic years were used as data sources. The distribution of points in the final exams at each academic year was presented in Table 3. Thus, the maximum score that can be taken by students is different at each academic year. The descriptive data including N (number of participants), mean, and standard deviation of the related questions in the final exams for experimental and control groups are presented as tables for the 1st, 2nd, and 3rd year of the study at Table 4, Table 5, and Table 6, respectively.

Table 4. Descriptive statistics for the 1st year.

Group	Question type	N	Mean	Std. dev.
Experimental	Graph questions (45p)	34	31.65	7.555
	Other questions (55p)	34	41.79	13.323
Control	Graph questions (45p)	107	23.02	11.063
	Other questions (55p)	107	31.88	14.822

Table 5. Descriptive statistics for the 2nd year.

Group	Question type	N	Mean	Std. dev.
Experimental	Graph questions (67p)	52	52.28	11.748
	Other questions (33p)	52	13.68	8.297
Control	Graph questions (67p)	72	42.86	14.523
	Other questions (33p)	72	9.99	7.389

The Levene test results for the graph questions were determined as $F(1,139) = 7.700, p > 0.05$ for the first academic year, $F(1,122) = 3.288, p > 0.05$ for the second academic year, $F(1,119) = 2.385, p > 0.05$ for the third academic year, respectively. Hence, variances of the experimental and control groups that were compared each year were equal and the assumption of the equality of variances has been met.

Table 6. Descriptive statistics for the 3rd year.

Group	Question type	N	Mean	Std. dev.
Experimental	Graph questions (60p)	75	40.52	7.858
	Other Questions (40p)	75	24.81	5.606
Control	Graph questions (60p)	46	35.28	9.568
	Other questions (40p)	46	21.48	7.272

Independent groups t-tests were used to determine whether there is a statistically significant difference in the academic performances of the students in experimental and control groups. The t-tests were conducted for each year and the results for the 1st, 2nd, and 3rd years of the study are presented in Table 7, Table 8, and Table 9, respectively.

As presented in Table 7, for the first year, the mean score of the experimental group for the graph questions is $M = 31.65$, while the mean score of the control group is $M = 23.02$. The t-test result indicates that there was a statistically significant difference in favor of the experimental group $(t(141) = 4.245; p < 0.05)$ on their academic performance on graph theory questions of the final exam. This finding remarks that the mobile learning application is effective in increasing the academic performance of students in the experimental group on graph theory questions of the final exam.

Besides, the academic performance of the participants on other questions of the final exam was also analyzed. The mean score of the experimental group is $M = 41.79$, whereas the mean score of the control group is $M = 31.88$ (Table 7). The t-test result reports that there was a significant difference in favor of the experimental group $(t(141) = 3.484; p < 0.05)$. This finding points out that the grades of students in the experimental group were also increased on other questions of the final exam.

Table 7. Result of the independent groups t-test for the 1st year.

Question type	Group	N	Mean	Std. dev.	df	t	p
Graph questions (45p)	Experimental	34	31.65	7.555	141	4.245	.000
	Control	107	23.02	11.063			
Other questions (55p)	Experimental	34	41.79	13.323	141	3.484	.001
	Control	107	31.88	14.822			

The results of the independent groups t-test for the second year are presented in Table 8. The mean score of the experimental group for the graph questions of the final exam is $M = 52.28$, while the mean score of the control group is $M = 42.86$. The t-test result indicates a statistically significant difference in favor of the experimental group $(t(124) = 3.887; p < 0.05)$. This finding notifies that the mobile learning application contributed to the academic performance of students in the experimental group.

When the academic performance of the students on other questions of the final exam was analyzed, it was observed that the mean score of the experimental group is M = 13.68, whereas the mean score of the control group is M = 9.99. The t-test result reports a significant difference in favor of the experimental group (t(124) = 2.629; p < 0.05). This finding is parallel with the finding of graph questions; hence, it can be pointed out that the success level of students in the experimental group was increased on both graph theory questions and other questions of the final exam.

Table 8. Result of the independent groups t-test for the 2nd year.

Question type	Group	N	Mean	Std. dev.	df	t	p
Graph questions (67p)	Experimental	52	52.28	11.748	124	3.887	.000
	Control	72	42.86	14.523			
Other questions (33p)	Experimental	52	13.68	8.297	124	2.629	.01
	Control	72	9.99	7.389			

Table 9 presents the results of the independent groups t-test for the third year. The mean score of the experimental group for the graph questions is M = 40.52, while the mean score of the control group is M = 35.28. The t-test result indicates that there was a significant difference in favor of the experimental group (t(121) = 3.293; p < 0.05) on grades the students received from graph theory questions of the final exam. This finding remarks that, based on graph theory questions of the final exam, the mobile learning application positively affected the academic success of the experimental group more than the control group.

On the other hand, when grades of the other questions of the final exam were examined, the mean score of the experimental group is observed as M = 24.81, whereas the mean score of the control group is M = 21.48. The t-test result reports a statistically significant difference in favor of the experimental group (t(121) = 2.844; p < 0.05). This finding points out that students in the experimental group were more successful than the students in the control group when other questions of the final exam were evaluated, too.

When the findings of the t-tests for both years were examined together, it can be concluded that the mobile learning application was effective on the academic success of students at each year it was utilized as a supplementary tool. An interesting finding is observed when non-graph theory related questions of the final exams were analyzed, as there is a statistically significant difference between the academic performance of students in experimental and control groups in favor of the experimental group at each year. This can be explained with the experimental group being formed voluntarily. Thus, students with more self-regulation skills had chosen to participate in the study, and therefore their grades in both graph

Table 9. Result of the independent groups t-test for the 3rd year.

Question type	Group	N	Mean	Std. dev.	df	t	p
Graph questions (60p)	Experimental	75	40.52	7.858	121	3.293	.001
	Control	46	35.28	9.568			
Other questions (40p)	Experimental	75	24.81	5.606	121	2.844	.005
	Control	46	21.48	7.272			

theory questions and other questions had increased in a statistically meaningful way.

Another notable observation involves the change in the study group each year. It can be observed in Table 2 that the number of students in the experimental group had increased each year. This can be based on the suggestion of students who took the course in the previous academic year. It can also be interpreted as the adoption of the mobile application by the learners and the lecturers. However, more research on the attitudes of the participants towards the m-learning system needs to be conducted to provide a generalization [10].

Even though the mobile learning paradigm is based on using portable mobile devices and learning any time at anywhere, it is reported in [13] that most of the m-learning studies in the literature took place in traditional classroom settings. The mobile application utilized in this study can be used by the participants in a portable way; however, it is also used in a formal application setting during the lab sessions. Thus, this can be seen as a limitation of this study, and further research can be conducted in informal settings.

5   Conclusion

In this paper, the effect of using a mobile learning application developed as a supplementary tool for graph theory education on the academic performance of students is investigated. Different features of the mobile application were introduced at laboratory sessions that were organized for three weeks after the theoretical lectures of the course in which the graph theory topics were lectured. Students were able to use the mobile application any time they want after these introduction sessions. The evaluation was carried out for three editions of the Discrete Structures course. At each academic year, a quasi-experimental research design with experimental and control groups was utilized. The grades students achieved from both graph theory related questions and other questions in the final exams of the course were used as data sources. The data for each year was examined by independent groups t-tests. The results of the statistical analyzes indicated that the mobile learning application contributed in a statistically significant way to the grades of the students in the experimental group for each year it was utilized as a supplementary tool.

The study group can be interpreted as the main limitation of this study. Students of a particular university at three academic years constituted the study group. Thus, in order to generalize the results of this study, conducting experimental studies at the same course in different universities can be planned for future work. The adoption of the m-learning system can be investigated in future studies by focusing on the attitudes of the learners towards the use of the m-learning system utilized in this study. More emphasis can be put on how the participants learn with m-learning technology and develop higher-order skills. Thus, the effect of personal factors such as learning styles and cognitive styles can also be suggested as a future research direction.

It is planned to extend the functionalities of the mobile application with more graph algorithms for future work. Moreover, the interaction of the users with the mobile learning application can be tracked and personal recommendations can be provided to users based on the user histories. Thus, extending the m-learning application to provide an adaptive mobile application with recommender system support can be considered as future work.

References

1. Çiloğlugil, B.: Mobil Çizge Öğrenme Sistemi Gerçekleştirimi (Implementation Of A Mobile Graph Learning System - in Turkish). Yüksek Lisans Tezi (MSc Thesis - in Turkish), Ege Üniversitesi (2006)
2. Nabiyev, V.V., Cakiroglu, U., Karal, H., Erumit, A.K., Cebi, A.: Application of graph theory in an intelligent tutoring system for solving mathematical word problems. Eurasia J. Math. Sci. Technol. Educ. **12**, 687–701 (2016)
3. Carbonneaux, Y., Laborde, J.-M., Madani, R.M.: CABRI-graph: a tool for research and teaching in graph theory. In: Brandenburg, F.J. (ed.) GD 1995. LNCS, vol. 1027, pp. 123–126. Springer, Heidelberg (1996). https://doi.org/10.1007/BFb0021796
4. Dagdilelis, V., Satratzemi, M.: DIDAGRAPH: software for teaching graph theory algorithms. ACM SIGCSE Bull. **30**(3), 64–68 (1998)
5. Wu, M.: Teaching graph algorithms using online java package IAPPGA. ACM SIGCSE Bull. **37**(4), 64–68 (2005)
6. Inceoglu, M.M., Ciloglugil, B., Karabulut, K.: MOGRAPH: mobile graph algorithms library for engineering students. Int. J. Eng. Educ. **23**(3), 499–507 (2007)
7. Gibson, J.P.: Teaching graph algorithms to children of all ages. In: Proceedings of the 17th ACM Annual Conference on Innovation and Technology in Computer Science Education, pp. 34–39, July 2012
8. Rostami, M.A., Azadi, A., Seydi, M.: GraphTea: interactive graph self-teaching tool. In: Proceedings of 2014 International Conference Education & Educational Technology II, pp. 48–52 (2014)
9. Çiloğlugil, B., Inceoglu, M.M.: Çizge Teorisi Eğitimi için Bir Mobil Öğrenme Uygulaması (A Mobile Learning Application for Graph Theory Education - in Turkish). Ege Eğitim Teknolojileri Dergisi **1**(1), 28–41 (2017). https://dergipark.org.tr/en/pub/eetd/issue/29867/303101
10. Al-Emran, M., Elsherif, H.M., Shaalan, K.: Investigating attitudes towards the use of mobile learning in higher education. Comput. Hum. Behav. **56**, 93–102 (2016)
11. Jan, S. R., Ullah, F., Ali, H., Khan, F.: Enhanced and effective learning through mobile learning an insight into students perception of mobile learning at university level. Int. J. Sci. Res. Sci. Eng. Technol. (IJSRSET) (2016). Print ISSN, 2395–1990

12. Martin, F., Ertzberger, J.: Here and now mobile learning: an experimental study on the use of mobile technology. Comput. Educ. **68**, 76–85 (2013)
13. Crompton, H., Burke, D.: The use of mobile learning in higher education: a systematic review. Comput. Educ. **123**, 53–64 (2018)
14. Fu, Q.K., Hwang, G.J.: Trends in mobile technology-supported collaborative learning: a systematic review of journal publications from 2007 to 2016. Comput. Educ. **119**, 129–143 (2018)
15. Rosen, K.H.: Discrete Mathematics and its Applications. Higher Education. 4th edn. McGraw-Hill, New York (1995)
16. Johnsonbaugh, R.: Discrete Mathematics, 4th edn. Prentice-Hall, New York (1997)
17. Lafore, R., Waite, M.: Data Structures & Algorithms in Java, pp. 251–313. Sams (2003)
18. Kruse, R., Tondo, C.L.: Data Structures and Program Design in C. Pearson Education India, Boston (2007)
19. Creswell, J.W.: Educational Research Planning Conducting and Evaluating Quantitative and Qualitative Research. Pearson, Boston (2012)

Author Index

Printed in the United States
By Bookmasters